St. Luke Lutheran School, Itasca, Ill.

The Handbook

to the

Lutheran Hymnal

By W. G. POLACK
Concordia Seminary
SAINT LOUIS, MISSOURI

Second and Revised Edition

Concordia Publishing House
Saint Louis   Missouri

783.9
P
4464

Copyright 1942
by
CONCORDIA PUBLISHING HOUSE
St. Louis, Mo.
PRINTED IN THE UNITED STATES OF AMERICA

THIS VOLUME IS DEDICATED
TO MY WIFE, THE DEVOTED
MOTHER OF OUR CHILDREN

PREFACE

The *Lutheran Hymnal* has its antecedents in earlier English hymn collections used by the respective synods of the Synodical Conference.

The Norwegian Synod of the American Evangelical Lutheran Church has been using the *Lutheran Hymnary* of 1913, originally published by authority of the Norwegian Evangelical Lutheran Synod, the Hauge Evangelical Lutheran Synod, and the United Norwegian Lutheran Church of America.

The Slovak Evangelical Lutheran Synod of the United States of America has been using the *Evangelical Lutheran Hymn-book* of 1912, published by the Evangelical Lutheran Synod of Missouri, Ohio, and Other States.

The Joint Synod of Wisconsin, Minnesota, Michigan, and Other States published its first English hymn-book in 1910. It was a text edition, containing 115 hymns, and was entitled *Church Hymnal*. This was followed in 1920 by its *Book of Hymns*, with tunes, containing 320 hymns. The chief editors were the Revs. O. Hagedorn and H. K. Moussa. The collection was based largely on the *Evangelical Lutheran Hymn-book* of 1912.

The English hymnals used by individual congregations of the Evangelical Lutheran Synod of Missouri, Ohio, and Other States antedate any official hymnals published by that body. Some congregations used the *Hymn-book for Use of Ev. Luth. Schools and Congregations,* published by the Lutheran Publishing House, Decorah, Ia., 1879, containing translations by Prof. August Crull. Others used the hymnal published by Concordia Publishing House very likely in 1888. It was a small collection of hymns, entitled *Hymns of the Ev. Luth. Church for the Use of English Lutheran Missions.* It contained 33 hymns, with the music for the soprano voice only placed above the hymns. This collection also contained translations by Prof. August Crull. It passed through many printings until it was superseded either by the "Grey Hymnal" or by the "Baltimore Hymnal." Other congregations, for a time at least, used hymnals published by the Joint Synod of Ohio, the General Council, and the Tennessee Synod.

The English Lutheran Conference of Missouri, the forerunner of the English Evangelical Lutheran Synod of Missouri and Other States, now the English District of the Evangelical Lutheran Synod of Missouri, Ohio, and Other States, published its own hymnal. This hymnal had been prepared by Prof. August Crull of Concordia College, Fort Wayne, Ind., and was presented by him to the Conference at its meeting in 1888. It was published under the title *Evangelical Lutheran Hymn-book,* at Baltimore, 1889, by the Lutheran Publication Board, for the Conference. It was a text edition only and contained 400 hymns, the three ecumenical creeds of Christendom, the Augsburg Confession, and an order for morning service and evening service which had been prepared by a committee elected by the Conference for that purpose. This was commonly known as the "Baltimore Hymnal." A new edition of this hymnal was ordered by the Conference when it constituted itself as a synod in 1891. Fifty hymns were added, and the Common Service, Matins, and Vespers were included after permission had been received from the General Synod, the General Council, and the United Synod of the South, a joint committee of these bodies having prepared the orders. This new edition, also published at Baltimore, appeared in 1892. It also was a text edition only. Later this hymnal was published at Pittsburgh and was thereafter known as the "Pittsburgh Hymnal." An edition was also published at Chicago in 1895. It contained, besides the Common Service, Matins, and Vespers, other liturgical material and a selection of psalms. An edition of this hymnal, in which the liturgical section was abridged, appeared in 1905.

In the same year Concordia Publishing House published the so-called "Grey Hymnal," edited by Prof. F. Bente of Concordia Seminary, St. Louis. It was entitled *Hymnal for Evangelical Lutheran Missions* and contained the text of 199 hymns, without music, three doxologies, no order of service, except for Communion, and a list of antiphons or versicles.

In the meantime the English Evangelical Lutheran Synod of Missouri, Ohio, and Other States had appointed a Tune-book Committee, composed in 1891 of the Revs. W. Dallmann, Theo. Huegli, A. S. Bartholomew, and Oscar Kaiser, which was to prepare an edition of its *Evangelical Lutheran Hymn-book* with tunes. This committee in 1897 included the Revs. W. Dallmann, C. C. Morhart, H. B. Hemmeter, Oscar Kaiser, Adam Detzer, and W. P. Sachs.

The work proceeded slowly. Ultimately Teachers Herman Ilse and H. A. Polack were appointed as a special committee on the music of the *Hymn-book*. When in 1911, at St. Louis, the English Evangelical Lutheran Synod of Missouri became the English District of the Evangelical Lutheran Synod of Missouri, Ohio, and Other States, the *Evangelical Lutheran Hymn-book,* which was ready for publication, was presented to Synod. It appeared in the spring of 1912 and became the official English hymnal of Synod. It contained a liturgical section of 112 pages, 567 hymns, 8 chants, and 17 doxologies.

When the Delegate Convention of the Evangelical Lutheran Synod of Missouri, Ohio, and Other States, in triennial assembly at River Forest, Ill., in 1929, authorized the revision of the *Evangelical Lutheran Hymn-book* of 1912, it was stipulated that the sister synods of the Synodical Conference of North America be requested to cooperate in order that the final result might be a common English hymnal for that federation. Dr. F. Pfotenhauer, President of the Missouri Synod, appointed the Committee on English Hymnology and Liturgics for this group, consisting of the following members: The Rev. Prof. W. G. Polack, Chairman, the Rev. Prof. L. Fuerbringer, D. D., the Rev. O. Kaiser, the Rev. Prof. L. Blankenbuehler, and Mr. B. Schumacher. This committee held its organization meeting at St. Louis, Mo., Nov. 20, 1929, and tentatively outlined its program.

In the meantime the sister synods of the Synodical Conference, through their respective presidents, had reacted favorably to the suggested plan of cooperation and on Jan. 3, 1930, the Intersynodical Committee on Hymnology and Liturgics was organized in Milwaukee, Wis., with the Rev. Prof. W. G. Polack as Chairman and Mr. B. Schumacher as Secretary. In addition to the representatives of the Missouri Synod mentioned above, the committee included the following representatives: The Rev. Prof. J. Meyer and the Rev. O. Hagedorn (Joint Synod of Wisconsin); the Revs. N. A. Madson and C. Anderson

(Norwegian Synod); the Rev. J. Pelikan (Slovak Synod). The latter was present at the second meeting, April, 1930.

In 1931 Dr. L. Fuerbringer tendered his resignation, owing to his increased duties as President of Concordia Seminary, St. Louis, and was made honorary member of the committee. The Rev. Wm. Moll of Fort Wayne was later appointed by Pres. F. Pfotenhauer to take his place as member of the committee. The Rev. Prof. J. Meyer also resigned and was made honorary member, and the Rev. Prof. A. Zich was appointed in his place. The Rev. O. Hagedorn was removed from the committee by death, and the Rev. Arthur Voss was appointed in his place in 1932. In 1933 the Rev. A. Harstad was appointed to the committee as third representative of the Norwegian Synod. In 1934 the Rev. Wm. Moll resigned from the committee on account of failing health, and the Rev. O. H. Schmidt was appointed in his place. When the Rev. J. Pelikan resigned in 1938, the Revs. J. Bajus and J. Kucharik were appointed to represent the Slovak Synod. When death took the Rev. Prof. A. Zich from the committee, the Rev. W. J. Schaefer, who had been active for years as a subcommittee member, was appointed to succeed him.

The individuals who assisted in the work, as members of subcommittees, for longer or shorter periods, are the following: The Revs. W. M. Czamanske, W. Lochner, W. Burhop, K. Ehlers, J. H. Deckmann, C. M. Waller, C. Hoffmann, C. Bergen, G. W. Fischer; the Rev. Profs. W. Schaller, W. Buszin, R. W. Heintze, M. Lochner; Profs. K. Haase, E. Backer; the Rev. Drs. J. H. Ott, P. E. Kretzmann, A. W. Wismar, S. C. Ylvisaker.

In its plan of work the committee proceeded to study, through subcommittees, the hymns (a) of English and American origin (not by Lutheran authors); (b) of German origin; (c) of Scandinavian origin; (d) of American Lutheran origin; (e) of ancient and medieval origin; (f) the music of the hymns; and (g) the liturgy.

These following general guiding principles were accepted:

1. *Hymns:*
    a. They must be of intrinsic value as to content;
    b. They must be distinctively Christian.
2. *Translations:*
    a. They must be of good form;
    b. They must be in idiomatic English.
3. *Tunes:*
    a. They must be suited to the text;
    b. They must be good church music. (Exceptions may be made in such cases in which texts and tunes are so wedded as to be practically inseparable.)

As to the liturgical section of *The Lutheran Hymnal*, the committee held it to be within the scope of its work to make no changes in the liturgies as such but to simplify the rubrics as much as possible, to correct any discrepancies, to supply the most necessary general rubrics, to add the graduals for the Sundays, feasts, and festivals in the church-year, to provide the introits, graduals, collects, etc., for the minor festivals, etc. Additional psalms were added, and all tables of lessons, etc., were carefully checked. All musical settings for the responses and chants were likewise revised.

While the committee was engaged in its task, it received many suggestions from members in all parts of the Synodical Conference and made periodical reports in the *Lutheran Witness* as follows: Jan. 16, 1934; March 27, 1934; Nov. 5, 1935; Oct. 20, 1936, and Nov. 9, 1937; a report in pamphlet form in the spring of 1938, a report to the respective synods in 1938, and a final comprehensive report, in pamphlet form, May 1, 1939. After having carefully considered all criticisms and suggestions which were submitted to the committee on the basis of these reports, and after having then reviewed once more its entire work of over ten years, the committee finally turned over the manuscript to Concordia Publishing House, St. Louis, Mo., in April, 1940. This publication house had undertaken the work of producing the hymnal for the synods directly interested. The suggestions of the committee as to the style of type, the arrangement of the pages, the paper, the binding, etc., were painstakingly followed by Concordia Publishing House, which had also previously given its full cooperation to the committee in various ways.

The committee had planned to include among the indexes of *The Lutheran Hymnal* an index of Bible texts, of authors and composers, of original first lines, and of topics. However, in order not to bulk the hymnal too much, the committee requested its chairman to include these indexes in the *Handbook to the Lutheran Hymnal*.

INTRODUCTION

The Lutheran Hymnal contains 644 hymns, 16 spiritual songs, and, besides those included in the orders of matins and vespers, 8 canticles and chants. The term *hymn* in this connection is used in its special sense of church-hymn. St. Augustine defined a hymn as "praise to God with song." That is a very general definition. In the usage of the Church, in order to distinguish it from a carol, a spiritual song, an anthem, a gospel-song, or a canticle, the hymn has come to have a more specific meaning.

The term *carol*, originally a dance song, now signifies a popular, spiritual folk-song, usually of praise and joy. The carol originated in the later Middle Ages and was frequently addressed to the Virgin Mary. Carols are less formal than hymns, and sometimes are trivial and even nonsensical. They are ballad-like in character and include lullabies, shepherds' songs, songs of the Wise Men, and sometimes are based on ancient legends connected with the life of our Lord or the Holy Family. A *spiritual song* is more formal than a carol and designates a song of a spiritual, religious nature. An *anthem,* according to Webster, "formerly, a psalm or hymn sung antiphonally, or responsively, is now a sacred choral composition, usually sung by a church choir, with words usually from the Scriptures." A *canticle,* originally a little song, now refers to a non-metrical spiritual song or chant, sometimes a Scriptural song, sometimes a Scriptural paraphrase. Examples are the Gloria Patri, the Magnificat, the Te Deum, the Beatitudes. A *gospel-song,* in contrast to a hymn, has been defined as "a religious exhortation to fellow-men."

What then is a *hymn?* It has been rightly said that "it is much easier to say what is not a hymn than what is a hymn." Certainly, there is no agreement among authorities as to what really constitutes a hymn; and yet, when we consult the latest hymnals published by the leading denominations in Great Britain and America, we find that these hymnals are closer to being collections of *hymns* than they have ever been before. And while the committee which edited *The Lutheran Hymnal* had set for itself a rather high standard as to what constitutes a hymn, yet, for obvious reasons that standard could not always be adhered to rigidly, for, as Prof. L. Blankenbuehler states in *The Christian Hymn,* "the line between the hymn and the spiritual song, an individualized, subjective lyrical poem or prayer, is at times very tenuous."

If we were to venture a definition of a church-hymn, we could hardly improve on that by Harvey B. Marks, in his *The Rise and Growth of English Hymnody:* "A hymn is a sacred poem expressive of devotion, spiritual experience, or religious truth, fitted to be sung by an assembly of people." A church-hymn, then, must be a song, a popular poetical expression of that which the believers have in common. It must be true, Biblical, Christian, edifying, simple yet dignified in language, excellent in content and form, devotional in tone, churchly and congregational in viewpoint and sentiment.

It must contain nothing that is untrue, questionable, unclear, uncouth, offensive. It must not be unrythmical, humorous, sentimental, too imaginary, and too allegorical.

A true church-hymn is reverent in its language and by that token will inspire the singer with reverence. The reverent language of our best hymns is the result of their being thoroughly Scriptural and in perfect harmony with their lofty religious themes. True church hymns are objective in character. That does not mean that they are always "we" hymns. The use of the personal pronoun "I" and "my" in a hymn does not necessarily imply a lack of objectivity any more than does the use of "I" in the Apostles' Creed. Nor does the fact that a spiritual song is extremely subjective *eo ipso* mean that it must be condemned as altogether unfit for use by Christians. There are many such that are very properly loved and sung by God's children in their homes, in schools, and in social gatherings, but they are not churchly and congregational in character and for that reason are not true church hymns.

A true church-hymn is centered in God or in some great doctrine of our faith or is an expression of hope, faith, confidence, and reliance in Him or His Word. It must have spiritual warmth and power. High literary quality should be there, but that alone does not make a poem a hymn. The vigor and strength, as well as the fervor of faith, must definitely be present in a true church-hymn. F. J. Gillman in his *Evolution of the English Hymn* reminds us of St. Paul's definition of the purpose of song-worship in the Apostolic Church — "teaching and admonishing one another," and says: "a hymn has a teaching office and an office of mutual encouragement and edification, as well as an office of prayer and praise."

A few examples will be sufficient by way of illustration. "Beautiful Isle of Somewhere," still a favorite in many circles as a solo for funerals, whatever its merits may be as a lyric, lacks every element of a true hymn except that of language, and its vagueness alone should eliminate it from any service that is intended to be Christian. Nor is there any excuse for its use in a Christian burial service, as long as we have hymns expressive of the great Christian hope in death like "I Know That My Redeemer Lives"; "Jerusalem the Golden"; "Oh, How Blest are Ye Whose Toils are Ended"; "When My Last Hour is Close at Hand"; etc. Again, why should a fine Christian marriage ceremony be spoiled by the singing of a secular love-song such as "I Love You Truly"? A church wedding ceremony has as its chief aim the consecration of a marriage to the Triune God. We have excellent hymns that emphasize the Christian teachings concerning marriage. These, and songs of a similar high Scriptural character, alone have a proper place in a Christian wedding service. Furthermore, it has become quite customary in recent years to include Katharine Lee Bates's beautiful patriotic song "O Beautiful for Spacious Skies" in American hymnals. The fact that it is one of the most poetical patriotic songs ever produced in our country is undeniable; but it contains nothing distinctively Christian and at the same time has certain elements that are not true. Her statement regarding the Pilgrims in stanza two is not historically accurate. The New England theocracy was a far cry from our later constitutional separation of Church and State, with freedom of thought, expression, and religion. Her third and fourth stanzas reflect a chiliastic ideal for which the Scriptures give us no warrant. Again, it is so distinctively American that it can be sung only by Americans. A hymnal such as *The Lutheran Hymnal,* which will be used not only in our country but also in

[X]

Canada, England, Africa, China, India, New Zealand, and in South America, must contain national hymns that apply equally to all these countries and their Christian peoples.

A careful study of *The Lutheran Hymnal* will show that, including the carols and spiritual songs, it contains 313 original hymns and 347 translations. The translations are divided as follows: From the German, 248; from the Latin, 46; from the Scandinavian, 31; from the Greek, 9; from the Slovak, 6; from the French, 2; from the Italian, 2; from the Dutch, Welsh, and Finnish, each 1. The original hymns may be classified as follows: British (written in English by English, Welsh, Scotch, or Irish poets), 267; American, 45; Canadian, 1. The translators are as follows: American, 47; British, 42. These numbers are interesting. They indicate that the editorial committee covered a wide field in search of hymns suitable for inclusion in *The Lutheran Hymnal* without losing sight of the fact that the hymnal must be thoroughly *Lutheran* in content. For it goes without saying that purity of doctrine was the first and foremost concern, and a goodly number of the hymns which were altered in the process of editing were altered in the interest of doctrinal soundness.

When Dr. C. F. W. Walther and several of his associates in the forties of the last century prepared the *Kirchengesangbuch für Evangelisch-Lutherische Gemeinden*, which became the official German hymn-book of the Evangelical Lutheran Synod of Missouri, Ohio, and Other States (organized in 1847 at Chicago, Ill.), he gave the principles according to which the selection for that *Gesangbuch* was made, as follows:

In the selection of the adopted hymns the chief consideration was that they be pure in doctrine; that they had found almost general acceptance within the true German Lutheran Church and thereby had received the almost unanimous testimony that they had come forth out of the true spirit; that they express not so much the changing conditions of individual persons as rather the language of the whole Church, because the book was to be used primarily in public worship; and finally, that they, though bearing the imprint of Christian simplicity, be not merely rimed prose, but the products of a truly Christian poesy. The editors have been fully conscious of the difficulty of their task; they have altogether despaired of their own wisdom and pleaded earnestly with God for the illumination and direction of His Holy Spirit and especially for the gift of trying and discerning the spirits.

The editorial committee for *The Lutheran Hymnal* followed the same principles. As a matter of course, the great body of Lutheran hymnody (German, Scandinavian, Slovak, and American) was the first source on which it drew; the fact that the figures for the Scandinavian and Slovak hymns seem low is explained by the circumstance that much of the bulk of the hymnody of these groups is drawn from German sources. Even as Walther and his associates also chose hymns of medieval Roman Catholic, Reformed, and Pietistic sources, so the editorial committee did likewise, centering its efforts naturally in the field of English and American Protestant hymnody, but drawing liberally also from the ancient Greek and Latin hymns. The results show that the children of God of all ages of our Christian era and of all Christian lands have by their sacred song given splendid evidence of the unity of the saints.

In selecting the music of *The Lutheran Hymnal,* the editorial committee also exercised extreme care so as to give the great musical heritage of our Church, the Lutheran *chorale,* its due place, and at the same time not to ignore the excellent tunes that have become the heritage of the English-speaking Christian world. To its knowledge the committee has not omitted a single *chorale* suitable for congregational singing, some being included that are not generally known in the German Lutheran churches of America and Canada, but which were resurrected from the dust of the centuries as a result of the diligent research carried on by the music editors of English and American hymnals. Less worthy tunes have been omitted, except in a few instances where text and tune are so intimately bound together that it was deemed advisable to let well enough alone. Sometimes the tune not preferred by the editorial committee is given as "second tune." In general, the committee has tried to give such tunes only as are by common consent considered the best from the musical heritage of the Church. Although each hymn has its tune setting, there are only 380 tunes in *The Lutheran Hymnal,* a number of tunes being repeated. In naming the tunes the best usage in English and American hymnals has been followed, but the German titles of the *chorales* have been consistently retained, although usually abbreviated for practical reasons. As in the case of the authors, the national origins of the composers are an evidence of the ecumenical character of *The Lutheran Hymnal.* The composers classify as follows: American, 18; British, 59; German, 58; Scandinavian, 4; French, 3; Italian, 2; and Dutch, Finnish, Hebrew, Polish, Russian, and Slovak, each 1.

Since the Lutheran Church is a liturgical Church, the hymns have been arranged according to the church-year, both for the sake of the pastor who must select the hymns for the service, as well as for the individual who wishes to use the hymnal for family or personal devotion. Since many of the hymns, however, are also suitable for other occasions, the reader is referred to the subject index at the end of this volume for aid in this respect. The index of Biblical references will also prove helpful in selecting hymns for specific occasions and purposes. The other indexes will likewise be of use in one way or other.

Finally, the compiler of this volume wishes to acknowledge the aid which he has received from the works of others who have labored in the field before him as indicated in the list of books given in the bibliography. A special word of thanks is due the Rev. John Bajus of Granite City, Ill., for his help in the preparation of the subject index and the Rev. Prof. L. Blankenbuehler for helpful suggestions.

Table of Contents

	PAGE
Preface	V
Introduction	IX

PART I
Notes on the Hymns and Tunes 1-468

Adoration
	HYMN
Opening of Service	1-6
Lord's Day	7-12
Worship and Praise	13-44
Close of Service	45-54

The Church-Year
Advent	55-75
Christmas	76-109
New Year's Eve	110-113
New Year	114-125
Epiphany	126-134
Transfiguration	135
Presentation	136-139
Lent	140-159
Palm Sunday	160-162
Maundy Thursday	163-164
Good Friday	165-186
Easter	187-211
Ascension	212-223
Pentecost	224-236
Trinity	237-253
St. Michael's and All Angels	254-257
Reformation	258-269
St. Andrew	270
St. John the Apostle	271
St. John the Baptist	272
Holy Innocents	273
Annunciation	274
Visitation	275

Invitation
276-281

The Word
Law and Gospel	282-297

The Sacraments
Baptism	298-303
Lord's Supper	304-316

Confession and Absolution
317-331

Confirmation
332-338

The Redeemer
339-368

Faith and Justification
369-392

Sanctification (The Christian Life)
Consecration	393-405
New Obedience	406-424
Trust	425-437
Stewardship	438-443
Christian Warfare	444-453

Prayer
454-459

The Church
Communion of Saints	460-481
Ministry	482-493
Missions	494-512

Cross and Comfort
513-535

Times and Seasons
Morning	536-550
Evening	551-565
Harvest and Thanksgiving	566-574
The Nation	575-584

The Last Things
Death and Burial	585-602
Resurrection	603
Judgment	604-612
Life Everlasting	613-619

The Christian Home
Marriage	620-623
The Family	624-626
Christian Education	627-631

Special Occasions
Corner-Stone Laying	632-633
Dedication	634-638
Church Anniversary	639-640
Theological Institutions	641
Foreign Missionaries	642
Absent Ones	643
The Long-Meter Doxology	644

Carols and Spiritual Songs
645-660

PART II
	PAGE
Biographical and Historical Notes on the Authors and Composers	469-605
Bibliography	606-608

PART III
INDEXES	609-681
Biblical References	611
Table of Hymns for Feasts, Festivals, and Sundays of the Church-Year	614
First Lines of Original Hymns	617
First Lines of Stanzas (Except of First Stanzas)	622
Alphabetical Index of Tunes	639
Metrical Index of Tunes	642
Index of Subjects (Topical Index)	646
Alphabetical Index of Authors	670
Alphabetical Index of Composers	673
Alphabetical Index of Translators	675
First Lines of Hymns	676

PART I
NOTES ON THE HYMNS AND TUNES

OPENING OF SERVICE

Adoration

Open Now Thy Gates of Beauty   1

1. Open now thy gates of beauty,
   Zion, let me enter there,
   Where my soul in joyful duty
   Waits for Him who answers prayer.
   Oh, how blessed is this place,
   Filled with solace, light, and grace!

   Tut mir auf die schöne Pforte,
   Führt in Gottes Haus mich ein!
   Ach, wie wird an diesem Orte
   Meine Seele fröhlich sein!
   Hier ist Gottes Angesicht,
   Hier ist lauter Trost und Licht.

2. Lord, my God, I come before Thee,
   Come Thou also unto me;
   Where we find Thee and adore Thee,
   There a heaven on earth must be.
   To my heart, oh, enter Thou,
   Let it be Thy temple now!

   Herr, ich bin zu dir gekommen;
   Komme du nun auch zu mir!
   Wo du Wohnung hast genommen,
   Ist der Himmel hell vor mir.
   Zeuch in meinem Herzen ein,
   Lass es deinen Himmel sein!

3. Here Thy praise is gladly chanted,
   Here Thy seed is duly sown;
   Let my soul, where it is planted,
   Bring forth precious sheaves alone,
   So that all I hear may be
   Fruitful unto life in me.

   Mache mich zum guten Lande,
   Wenn dein Saatkorn auf mich fällt;
   Gib mir Licht in dem Verstande,
   Und was mir wird vorgestellt,
   Präge du dem Herzen ein;
   Lass es mir zur Frucht gedeihn.

4. Thou my faith increase and quicken,
   Let me keep Thy gift divine,
   Howsoe'er temptations thicken;
   May Thy Word still o'er me shine
   As my guiding star through life,
   As my comfort in my strife.

   Stärk in mir den schwachen Glauben,
   Lass dein teures Kleinod mir
   Nimmer aus dem Herzen rauben,
   Halte mir dein Wort stets für;
   Ja, das sei mein Morgenstern,
   Der mich führet zu dem Herrn!

5. Speak, O God, and I will hear Thee,
   Let Thy will be done indeed;
   May I undisturbed draw near Thee
   While Thou dost Thy people feed.
   Here of life the fountain flows,
   Here is balm for all our woes.

   Rede, Herr, so will ich hören,
   Und dein Wille werd' erfüllt!
   Lass nichts meine Andacht stören,
   Wenn der Brunn' des Lebens quillt.
   Speise mich mit Himmelsbrot,
   Tröste mich in aller Not!

This hymn was written by Benjamin Schmolck and was first published in his *Kirchen-Gefährte,* 1732, in 7 stanzas and in his *Klage und Reigen,* 1734, entitled "The First Step into the Church" (Third Commandment). The translation by Catherine Winkworth appeared in her *Chorale Book for England,* 1863, No. 13; Stanzas 3 and 7 of the original were omitted, very likely because the figures of speech in these stanzas are difficult of reproduction in English. These stanzas are:

Lass in Furcht mich vor dich treten,
Heilige mir Leib und Geist,
Dass mein Singen und mein Beten
Dir ein lieblich Opfer heisst.
Heilige mir Mund und Ohr,
Zeuch das Herz zu dir empor!

Öffne mir die Lebensauen,
Dass mein Geist sich weiden kann;
Lass mir Heil vom Himmel tauen,
Zeige mir die rechte Bahn
Hier aus diesem Jammertal
Zu dem ew'gen Ehrensaal!

The Committee changed Line 6, Stanza 4, where Miss Winkworth used "polestar" for the German "Leitstern"; also Line 1, Stanza 2, where the translator had "Yes, my God," etc.

Catherine Winkworth is one of the outstanding English translators of German hymns. John Dahle, in his *Library of Christian Hymns,* rightly states: "Others have reached eminent heights in certain respects. But as to faithfulness toward the original, both in respect to contents and meter, clearness of thought, and euphony of language, no one has surpassed her." Miss Winkworth has also been the most prolific of all the translators of German hymns and has done more than any other translator to make the great gems of German hymnody known in the English-speaking world. *The Lutheran Hymnal* has 73 of her translations in whole or in part.

OPENING OF SERVICE

The tune "Neander" is by Joachim Neander. In the original edition of his works, published in Bremen in 1680, called A *und* Ω, *Bremen,* 19 melodies were by Neander. This tune was one, and was given with his hymns "Unser Herrscher, unser König" (Our Ruler, Our King), and is therefore also called "Unser Herrscher." In some hymnals the tune is called "Magdeburg," in others "Ephesus."

2   To Thy Temple I Repair

1. To Thy temple I repair;
Lord, I love to worship there
When within the veil I meet
Christ before the mercy-seat.

2. I through Him am reconciled,
I through Him become Thy child.
Abba, Father, give me grace
In Thy courts to seek Thy face.

3. While Thy glorious praise is sung,
Touch my lips, unloose my tongue,
That my joyful soul may bless
Christ the Lord, my Righteousness.

4. While the prayers of saints ascend,
God of Love, to mine attend.
Hear me, for Thy Spirit pleads;
Hear, for Jesus intercedes.

5. While I hearken to Thy Law,
Fill my soul with humble awe
Till Thy Gospel bring to me
Life and immortality.

6. While Thy ministers proclaim
Peace and pardon in Thy name,
Through their voice, by faith, may I
Hear Thee speaking from the sky.

7. From Thy house when I return,
May my heart within me burn
And at evening let me say,
"I have walked with God today."

This hymn, by James Montgomery, was first published in 1812, in *Collyer's Collection,* and entitled "A Sabbath Hymn." It is sometimes given as "In Thy presence we appear" and "To Thy presence I repair."

The tune "Gott sei Dank durch alle Welt," also called "Lübeck," "Berlin," and "Carinthia," is based on the setting found in Johann Anastasius Freylinghausen's *Neues Geistreiches Gesangbuch,* published at Halle, 1704. The composer is unknown.

3   Lord Jesus Christ, Be Present Now

1. Lord Jesus Christ, be present now,
Our hearts in true devotion bow,
Thy Spirit send with grace divine,
And let Thy truth within us shine.

2. Unseal our lips to sing Thy praise,
Our souls to Thee in worship raise,
Make strong our faith, increase our light
That we may know Thy name aright:

3. Until we join the hosts that cry,
"Holy art Thou, O Lord, most high!"
And in the light of that blest place
Fore'er behold Thee face to face.

4. Glory to God the Father, Son,
And Holy Spirit, Three in One!
To Thee, O blessed Trinity,
Be praise throughout eternity!

Herr Jesu Christ, dich zu uns wend,
Dein'n Heil'gen Geist du zu uns send!
Mit Lieb' und Gnad', Herr, uns regier
Und uns den Weg zur Wahrheit führ.

Tu auf den Mund zum Lobe dein,
Bereit das Herz zur Andacht fein,
Den Glauben mehr, stärk den Verstand,
Dass uns dein Nam' werd' wohl bekannt,

Bis wir singen mit Gottes Heer:
Heilig, heilig ist Gott der Herr!
Und schauen dich von Angesicht
In ew'ger Freud' und sel'gem Licht.

Ehr' sei dem Vater und dem Sohn,
Dem Heil'gen Geist in einem Thron;
Der Heiligen Dreieinigkeit
Sei Lob und Preis in Ewigkeit!

This hymn is often ascribed to Wm. II, Duke of Saxe-Weimar, but this is doubtful. According to Koch the hymn was included in Johannes Niedling's *Lutherisch Handbüchlein* (1st edition, Altenburg, 1638). However, this is uncertain. Niedling was instructor at the "gelehrten Schule" in Altenburg. The

OPENING OF SERVICE

hymn is entitled "A heartfelt petition of pious Christians for grace and the help of the Holy Spirit during divine service, before the sermon," in Niedling's fourth edition, 1655. In the *Cantionale Sacrum* (Gotha, 2d ed., 1651) the hymn was entitled "To be sung before the sermon." This is, as far as we know, the first time the hymn appeared in print. Duke William's name was not attached to the hymn until 1676.

The translation is by Catherine Winkworth, with some alterations by the Committee. It was first published in her *Chorale Book for England* in 1863.

The composer of the tune "Herr Jesu Christ, dich zu uns wend" is unknown, and the exact date of its first publication is not altogether definite. It appeared in the appendix of *Pensum Sacrum,* published at Görlitz in 1648. Koch, however, states positively that it was already printed in *Cantionale Germanicum,* published in Dresden, 1628, in the form as in *The Lutheran Hymnal,* except that it is written in G major.

God Himself Is Present 4

1. God Himself is present:
Let us now adore Him
And with awe appear before Him.
God is in His temple —
All within keep silence,
Prostrate lie with deepest reverence.
Him alone God we own,
Him, our God and Savior;
Praise His name forever.

2. God Himself is present:
Hear the harps resounding;
See the hosts the throne surrounding!
"Holy, holy, holy" —
Hear the hymn ascending,
Songs of saints and angels blending.
Bow Thine ear To us here:
Hear, O Christ, the praises
That Thy Church now raises.

3. O Thou Fount of blessing,
Purify my spirit,
Trusting only in Thy merit.
Like the holy angels,
Who behold Thy glory,
May I ceaselessly adore Thee.
Let Thy will Ever still
Rule Thy Church terrestrial
As the hosts celestial.

1. Gott ist gegenwärtig!
Lasset uns anbeten,
Und in Ehrfurcht vor ihn treten.
Gott ist in der Mitten;
Alles in uns schweige,
Und sich innigst vor ihm beuge.
Wer ihn kennt, wer ihn nennt,
Schlagt die Augen nieder;
Kommt, ergebt euch wieder!

2. Gott ist gegenwärtig,
Dem die Cherubinen
Tag und Nacht mit Ehrfurcht dienen;
Heilig, heilig singen
Alle Engelchören,
Wenn sie Gott mit Jauchzen ehren.
Herr, vernimm unsre Stimm',
Da auch wir Geringen
Unsre Opfer bringen.

4. Majestätisch Wesen!
Möcht' ich dich recht preisen,
Und im Geist dir Dienst erweisen
Möcht' ich wie die Engel
Immer vor dir stehen
Und dich gegenwärtig sehen!
Lass mich dir für und für
Trachten zu gefallen,
Liebster Gott, in allen.

The above three stanzas of this hymn are only a part of the original German text. The other stanzas are the following:

3. Wir entsagen willig
Allen Eitelkeiten,
Aller Erdenlust und Freuden.
Da liegt unser Wille,
Seele, Leib und Leben,
Dir zum Eigentum ergeben.
Du allein sollst es sein,
Unser Gott und Herre,
Dir gebühret die Ehre.

5. Luft, die alles füllet,
Drin wir immer schweben;
Aller Dinge Grund und Leben,
Meer ohn' Grund und Ende,
Wunder aller Wunder,
Ich senk' mich in dich hinunter;
Ich in dir, du in mir,
Lass mich ganz verschwinden,
Dich mir sehn und finden.

6. Du durchdringest alles,
Lass dein schönstes Lichte,
Herr, berühren mein Gesichte.
Wie die zarten Blumen
Willig sich entfalten
Und der Sonne stille halten,
Lass mich so still und froh
Deine Strahlen fassen
Und dich wirken lassen.

7. Mache mich recht kindlich,
Innig abgeschieden,
Sanfte und voll stillen Frieden!
Mach mich reines Herzens,
Dass ich deine Klarheit
Schauen mag in Geist und Wahrheit.
Lass mein Herz himmelwärts
Wie ein Adler schweben
Und in dir nur leben.

[5]

8. Herr, komm in mir wohnen,
   Lass mein Geist auf Erden
   Dir ein Heiligtum noch werden!
   Komm, du treuer Heiland,
   Dich in mir verkläre,
   Dass ich dich stets lieb' und ehre.
   Wo ich geh', sitz' und steh',
   Lass mich dich erblicken
   Und vor dir mich bücken.

The author of this hymn was Gerhard Tersteegen. It appeared in his *Geistliches Blumengärtlein* as No. 11 in Book III, entitled "Remembrance of the glorious and delightful presence of God," 1729.

The translation before us is based on that written by the English Moravian Frederick William Foster (1760—1835). He was a bishop in the Moravian Church and editor and compiler of the *Moravian Hymn-Book*. Julian also mentions the Rev. John Miller as cotranslator with Foster. He was a Moravian preacher in England and Ireland from 1768 to 1810. According to the same authority the translation first appeared in the *Moravian Hymn-Book* of 1789.

The tune "Wunderbarer König," also called "Arnsberg" and "Gott ist gegenwärtig," is very likely by Joachim Neander. It appeared in his collection *Glaub- und Liebes-Übung*, set to the hymn "Wunderbarer König" (see Hymn No. 41).

5   Lord, Open Thou My Heart to Hear

1. Lord, open Thou my heart to hear
   And through Thy Word to me draw near;
   Let me Thy Word e'er pure retain,
   Let me Thy child and heir remain.

   Herr, öffne mir die Herzenstür,
   Zeuch mein Herz durch dein Wort zu dir,
   Lass mich dein Wort bewahren rein.
   Lass mich dein Kind und Erbe sein!

2. Thy Word doth deeply move the heart,
   Thy Word doth perfect health impart,
   Thy Word my soul with joy doth bless,
   Thy Word brings peace and happiness.

   Dein Wort bewegt des Herzens Grund;
   Dein Wort macht Leib und Seel' gesund;
   Dein Wort ist, das mein Herz erfreut;
   Dein Wort gibt Trost und Seligkeit.

3. To God the Father, God the Son,
   And God the Spirit, Three in One,
   Shall glory, praise, and honor be
   Now and throughout eternity.

   Ehr' sei dem Vater und dem Sohn,
   Dem Heil'gen Geist in einem Thron;
   Der Heiligen Dreieinigkeit
   Sei Lob und Preis in Ewigkeit!

This hymn, written by Johannes Olearius, was included in the 1671 edition of his *Geistliche Singe-Kunst* and entitled *Holy Scripture. After the Sermon*. The German text is accordingly a prayer that the Word which has been heard may be received and applied by the Christian. The English translation has changed the sense of the opening lines so as to make it more a hymn for the beginning of worship or one to be sung just before the sermon.

The translation is by Dr. Matthias Loy and appeared in the *Evangelical Lutheran Hymnal* (Ohio Synod) in 1880.

The composer of the tune "Erhalt uns, Herr, bei deinem Wort" is unknown. It appeared in Joseph Klug's *Geistliche Lieder zu Wittenberg*, 1543. According to Winterfeld, the tune was written by Luther himself for his hymn "Erhalt uns, Herr, bei deinem Wort," a children's hymn against the two arch-enemies of Christ, the Pope and the Turk, hence often called the Pope-and-Turk Tune. (See Hymn No. 261.) The tune is found in many hymnals and is also called "Preserve us, Lord," "Reading," "Spires," "Wittenberg." It is based on a plainsong melody.

OPENING OF SERVICE. — LORD'S DAY

Kyrie, God Father in Heaven Above   6

Kyrie, God Father in heaven above,
Great art Thou in grace and love;
Of all things the Maker and Preserver.
Eleison, eleison!
Kyrie, O Christ, our King,
Salvation for sinners Thou didst bring.
O Lord Jesus, God's own Son,
Our Mediator at the heav'nly throne,
Hear our cry and grant our supplication.
Eleison, eleison!
Kyrie, O God the Holy Ghost,
Guard our faith, the gift we need the most;
Do Thou our last hour bless;
Let us leave this sinful world with
    gladness.
Eleison, eleison!   Amen.

Kyrie, Gott Vater in Ewigkeit,
Gross ist dein' Barmherzigkeit,
Aller Ding' ein Schöpfer und Regierer.
Eleison, eleison!
Christe, aller Welt Trost
Uns Sünder allein du hast erlöst.
O Jesu, Gottes Sohn,
Unser Mittler bist in dem höchsten
    Thron;
Zu dir schreien wir aus Herzensbegier:
Eleison, eleison!
Kyrie, Gott Heiliger Geist,
Tröst, stärk uns im Glauben allermeist,
Dass wir am letzten End'
Fröhlich abscheiden aus diesem Elend.
Eleison, eleison!

This hymn is, in its original text, a paraphrase of the Latin sequence *Kyrie summum: Kyrie, Fons bonitatis, Pater ingenite,* of 12th-century origin, if not earlier.

Wackernagel (III, No. 250) gives the date and place of origin "perhaps Wittenberg, 1541." It is sometimes ascribed to Johann Spangenberg (1484 to 1550), the first evangelical preacher at Nordhausen; later church superintendent at Eisleben, Martin Luther's birthplace. He published *Cantiones ecclesiasticae,* etc. *Kirchengesänge Deudtsch,* etc. at Magdeburg in 1545; but this hymn is not included. In the hymn-book of Caspar Löner, Nördlingen, 1545, the superscription of this hymn is: "On other festivals and on Sundays one sings as follows. The *Kyrie eleison* for Sundays." Another direction given in a later work was: "*Kyrie summum* is sung from Trinity until Christmas." This was in complete harmony with the use of the Latin original in the Middle Ages.

Our translation was prepared for *The Lutheran Hymnal* in 1939.

This custom was also transferred to the Lutheran Church in America, especially the congregations of German origin, in many of which it is still sung in the German-language services.

Zahn gives the setting of the tune "Kyrie, Gott Vater" as in *Teutsch Kirchenamt,* Erfurt, 1525, stating that the melody had only the text:

Herr, erbarm dich unser.   (Lord, have mercy on us)
Christ, erbarm dich unser. (Christ, have mercy on us)
Herr, erbarm dich unser.   (Lord, have mercy on us)

As We Begin Another Week   7

1. As we begin another week,
In Jesus' name this boon we seek:
God, grant that through these seven days
No evil may befall our ways.

2. Thy gentle blessings, Lord, outpour
On all our labor evermore;
Our hearts with Thy good Spirit fill
That we may gladly do Thy will.

3. In every season, every place,
May we regard Thy Word of grace
Until, when life's brief day is past,
We reach eternal joy at last

4. And keep with angels in Thy rest
The endless Sabbaths of the blest.
This grant to us through Christ, Thy Son,
Who reigns with Thee upon Thy throne.

Heut' fangen wir in Gottes Nam'n
Ein' neue Woch' zu leben an.
Hilf, Gott, dass uns die sieben Tag'
Kein Unglück überfallen mag!

Gib deinen Segen mildiglich
Zu unsrer Arbeit stetiglich,
Regier uns auch durch deinen Geist,
Dass wir gern tun, was du uns heisst.

Zu aller Zeit, an allem Ort
Vor Augen hab'n dein göttlich Wort,
Bis wir nach dieser kurzen Zeit
Erlang'n die ew'ge Seligkeit

Und feiern mit den Engelein
Ein'n Sabbat nach dem andern fein.
Das gib durch Christum, deinen Sohn,
Der mit dir herrscht in einem Thron!

LORD'S DAY

This hymn by Martin Wandersleben first appeared anonymously, in five stanzas, in *Neuvermehrtes und zu Übung Christl. Gottseligkeit eingerichtetes Meiningisches Gesangbuch,* Meiningen, 1697, almost thirty years after the author's death. There it was coupled with the tune "Herr Jesu Christ, mein's Lebens Licht," with which it is still associated. The translation is our own and was prepared especially for *The Lutheran Hymnal* in 1940.

The tune, "Herr Jesu Christ, mein's Lebens Licht," is of unknown authorship. It is found in *As Hymnodus Sacer,* Leipzig, 1625, a collection of twelve hymns with eight tunes, published by Christian Gall. It was set to the hymn of Martin Behm "Herr Jesu Christ, mein's Lebens Licht." (See Hymn No. 148.) The tune is called "Breslau" in some collections.

8   Father, Who the Light This Day

1. Father, who the light this day
   Out of darkness didst create,
   Shine upon us now, we pray,
     While within Thy courts we wait.
   Wean us from the works of night,
   Make us children of the light.

2. Savior, who this day didst break
     The dark prison of the tomb,
   Bid our slumbering souls awake,
     Shine through all their sin and gloom;
   Let us, from our bonds set free,
   Rise from sin and live to Thee.

3. Blessed Spirit, Comforter,
     Sent this day from Christ on high,
   Lord, on us Thy gifts confer,
     Cleanse, illumine, sanctify.
   All Thy fulness shed abroad;
   Lead us to the truth of God.

The author of this cento is Julia Anne Elliott. In 1835 her husband published *Psalms and Hymns for Public, Private, and Social Worship,* to which she contributed eleven hymns, at first anonymously; her initials were added in 1839. This hymn was among them. Originally it was published in seven stanzas. Our hymn is made up of Stanzas 3, 4, and 5. Mrs. Elliott strangely confused the seventh day on which the Creator rested and the first day of the week, the Christian Sunday. This error was altered by an unknown hand. We give the original version for the sake of comparison:

1. Hail, thou bright and sacred morn,
     Risen with gladness in thy beams!
   Light, which not of earth is born,
     From thy dawn in glory streams:
   Airs of heaven are breathed around,
   And each place is holy ground.

2. Sad and weary were our way,
     Fainting oft beneath our load,
   But for thee, thou blessed day,
     Resting-place on life's rough road!
   Here flow forth the streams of grace;
   Strengthened hence, we run our race.

3. Great Creator! who this day
     From Thy perfect work didst rest;
   By the souls that own Thy sway
     Hallowed be its hours and blest;
   Cares of earth aside be thrown,
   This day given to heaven alone!

4. Savior! who this day didst break
     The dark prison of the tomb,
   Bid my slumbering soul awake,
     Shine through all its sin and gloom;
   Let me, from my bonds set free,
   Rise from sin and live to thee!

5. Blessed Spirit! Comforter!
     Sent this day from Christ on high;
   Lord, on me Thy gifts confer,
     Cleanse, illumine, sanctify!
   All Thine influence shed abroad,
   Lead me to the truth of God!

6. Soon, too soon, the sweet repose
     Of this day of God will cease;
   Soon this glimpse of heaven will close,
     Vanish soon the hours of peace;
   Soon return the toil, the strife,
   All the weariness of life.

7. But the rest which yet remains
     For Thy people, Lord, above
   Knows nor change nor fears nor pains,
     Endless as their Savior's love.
   Oh, may every Sabbath here
   Bring us to that rest more near!

LORD'S DAY

The composer of the tune "Fred til Bod" is Ludvig Mathias Lindeman. In 1871 he published his *Koralbog for den Norska Kirke.* This tune was included in this work. Though some of his melodies are based on older *chorale* tunes, many are original. They breathe a spirit of deep piety and often partake of the character of the folk-song.

The full title of the tune "Fred til Bod for bittert Savn" (Peace to soothe our bitter woes) shows that it was composed by Lindeman as a setting for the hymn by N. F. S. Grundtvig, which begins with those words.

O Day of Rest and Gladness   9

1. O day of rest and gladness,
    O day of joy and light,
 O balm of care and sadness,
    Most beautiful, most bright,
 On thee the high and lowly
    Before th' eternal throne
 Sing, "Holy, holy, holy,"
    To the great Three in One.

2. On thee at the Creation
    The light first had its birth;
 On thee for our salvation
    Christ rose from depth of earth;
 On thee our Lord victorious
    The Spirit sent from heaven,
 And thus on thee, most glorious,
    A threefold light was given.

3. Thou art a cooling fountain
    In life's dry, dreary sand;
 From thee, like Nebo's mountain,
    We view our Promised Land;
 A day of sweet refection,
    A day of holy love,
 A day of resurrection
    From earth to things above.

4. Today on weary nations
    The heavenly manna falls;
 To holy convocations
    The silver trumpet calls,
 Where Gospel-light is glowing
    With pure and radiant beams
 And living water flowing
    With soul-refreshing streams.

5. New graces ever gaining
    From this our day of rest,
 We reach the rest remaining
    To spirits of the blest.
 To Holy Ghost be praises,
    To Father, and to Son;
 The Church her voice upraises
    To Thee, blest Three in One.

This hymn for Lord's Day is one that has achieved quite general usage in the English-speaking Church, although not all hymnals agree on the number of stanzas. Christopher Wordsworth originally, in 1862, published it in six stanzas of eight lines, but for very evident reasons Stanza 3, 1—4, and Stanza 4, 1—4, are generally omitted. We give the original Stanzas 3 and 4 for the sake of comparison. The reader will see that Stanza 3 above is made up of the last four lines of each:

Thou art a port protected
    From storms that round us rise;
A garden intersected
    With streams of Paradise.
Thou art a cooling fountain
    In life's dry, dreary sand;
From thee, like Pisgah's mountain
    We view the Promised Land.

Thou art a holy ladder,
    Where angels go and come;
Each Sunday finds us gladder,
    Nearer to heaven, our home.
A day of sweet refection
    Thou art, a day of love,
A day of resurrection
    From earth to things above.

In 1872, in the sixth edition of his *Holy Year,* the author changed Lines 6—8 of Stanza 1 to read:

    "Through ages joined in time,
    Sing Holy, Holy, Holy,
    To the great God Triune."

Not all hymnals, however, have followed him in this, and it is open to question whether he thereby improved the hymn.

The last line of Stanza 2 originally read:

    "A triple light was given."

LORD'S DAY

The tune "Ellacombe" is found in a collection known as *Gesang Buch der Herzogl. Württembergischen Catholischen Hofkapelle,* 1784. The tune found its way into English hymnody after its appearance in a collection entitled *Vollständige Sammlung der gewöhnlichen Melodien zum Mainzer Gesangbuche* by Xavier Ludwig Hartig in 1833, set to the hymn "Der du im heil'gen Sakrament."

10 This Is the Day the Lord hath Made

1. This is the day the Lord hath made;
   He calls the hours His own;
   Let heaven rejoice, let earth be glad
   And praise surround the throne.

2. Today He rose and left the dead,
   And Satan's empire fell;
   Today the saints His triumphs spread
   And all His wonders tell.

3. Hosanna to th' anointed King,
   To David's holy Son!
   Help us, O Lord; descend and bring
   Salvation from the throne.

4. Blest be the Lord, who comes to men
   With messages of grace;
   Who comes in God His Father's name
   To save our sinful race.

5. Hosanna in the highest strains
   The Church on earth can raise.
   The highest heavens, in which He reigns,
   Shall give Him nobler praise.

The text is from *Psalms of David Imitated,* 1719, by Isaac Watts, based on Ps. 118: 24-26.

The tune "Nun danket all' und bringet Ehr'," also called "St. Mary Magdalene" and "Gräfenberg," according to Zahn is by Johann Crüger and is traceable to the fifth edition of his *Praxis Pietatis Melica,* Berlin, 1653. In the twenty-seventh edition, 1693 of Crüger's work, which we have before us, this tune is No. 1154.

11 Safely through Another Week

1. Safely through another week
   God has brought us on our way;
   Let us now a blessing seek,
   Waiting in His courts today:
   Day of all the week the best,
   Emblem of eternal rest.

2. Mercies multiplied each hour
   Through the week our praise demand;
   Guarded by almighty power,
   Fed and guided by His hand,
   How ungrateful we have been
   In repaying love with sin!

3. While we pray for pard'ning grace
   Through the dear Redeemer's name,
   Show Thy reconcilèd face,
   Look not on our sin and shame.
   From our worldly cares set free,
   May we rest this day in Thee!

4. As we come Thy name to praise,
   May we feel Thy presence near;
   May Thy glory meet our eyes
   While we in Thy house appear!
   Here afford us, Lord, a taste
   Of our everlasting feast.

5. May Thy Gospel's joyful sound
   Conquer sinners, comfort saints;
   Make the fruits of grace abound,
   Bring relief for all complaints.
   Thus may all our Sabbaths prove
   Till we join the Church above.

This hymn, written by John Newton for "Saturday Evening," was first published in R. Conyer's *Psalms and Hymns* in 1774 and then in the *Olney Hymns* in 1779. It is included in a few modern hymnals, but in an altered form, so that it can be sung on Sunday morning. In the original version, Stanza 1 reads thus:

Safely through another week
   God has brought us on our way;
Let us now a blessing seek,
   On th' approaching Sabbath Day:
Day of all the week the best,
Emblem of eternal rest.

LORD'S DAY

Stanza 4 reads thus:

> When the morn shall bid us rise,
> May we feel Thy presence near!
> May Thy glory meet our eyes
> When we in Thy house appear!
> There afford us, Lord, a taste
> Of our everlasting feast.

In Stanza 3 Montgomery had as Line 4:

> Shine away our sin and shame.

The tune "Voller Wunder" is by Johann Georg Ebeling. Our tune first appeared in his *Pauli Gerhardi Geistliche Andachten, bestehend in 120 violinen und general-bass,* 1666, set to the words of Gerhardt's wedding-hymn, "Voller Wunder, voller Kunst, voller Weisheit, voller Kraft."

This Day at Thy Creating Word — 12

1. This day at Thy creating word
First o'er the earth the light was poured:
O Lord, this day upon us shine
And fill our souls with light divine.

2. This day the Lord for sinners slain
In might victorious rose again:
O Jesus, may we raisèd be
From death of sin to life in Thee!

3. This day the Holy Spirit came
With fiery tongues of cloven flame:
O Spirit, fill our hearts this day
With grace to hear and grace to pray.

4. O day of light and life and grace,
From earthly toil sweet resting-place,
Thy hallowed hours, blest gift of love,
Give we again to God above.

5. All praise to God the Father be,
All praise, eternal Son, to Thee,
Whom, with the Spirit, we adore
Forever and forevermore.

This hymn by William Walsham How was first published in Morrell and How's *Psalms and Hymns,* 1854, beginning with the line:

> "This day the light of heavenly birth
> First streamed upon the new-born earth."

No doubt, because of the inaccuracy of that statement, Bishop How changed these lines in the enlarged edition, 1864, and began the hymn thus:

> "This day by Thy creating word," etc.

In 1871 it was again published in *Church Hymns,* after revision by the author, and a doxology was added. This is the authorized text of the hymn, as above. In the earlier form the first two lines of the second stanza read:

> "This day the Savior left the grave,
> And rose omnipotent to save."

In the conclusion of a supplementary chapter of Bishop How's biography by his son, there is an interesting comment, written by Dr. Boyd Carpenter, on hymn-writing that is worthy of consideration:

> It is the fate of a hymn-writer to be forgotten. Of the millions who Sunday after Sunday sing hymns in our churches not more than a few hundred know or consider whose words they are singing. The hymn remains; the name of the writer passes away. Bishop Walsham How was prepared for this; his ambition was not to be remembered but to be helpful. He gave free liberty to any to make use of his hymns. It was enough for him if he could enlarge the thanksgivings of the Church or minister by

song to the souls of men. There will be few to doubt that his unselfish wish will be fulfilled. Some of his hymns . . . will continue to be sung for long years to come; they will cheer and console the hearts of millions; many who hear will take up their burden and their hope again. We are told that when Melanchthon and his comrades, shortly after Luther's death, fled to Weimar, they heard a child singing the stirring words of Luther's "Ein' feste Burg." "Sing, dear daughter, sing," said Melanchthon, "you know not what great people you are comforting." Even so the voice of the hymn-writer carries comfort to unknown hearts and to after-ages.

The writer dies; the hymn remains; the song goes on; tired men listen and find rest. Struggling men are encouraged to struggle once again; statesmen, philanthropists, the broken-hearted, and the despairing are helped. Sing on; you know not what great people you are comforting. Such a reward is better than fame. It is as if, even after life is ended, the power to give a cup of cold water to a fainting soul in the name of Christ was not denied to the singer of the Church.

The tune "Winchester New" is found in the *Musicalisch Hand-Buch*, published in Hamburg, 1690, where it was set to the hymn "Wer nur den lieben Gott lässt walten," by Georg Neumark. (See Hymn No. 518.) The composer is unknown. The tune is also called "Frankfort" or "Crasselius."

13   Before Jehovah's Awe-full Throne

1. Before Jehovah's awe-full throne,
Ye nations, bow with sacred joy.
Know that the Lord is God alone;
He can create and He destroy.

2. His sov'reign power, without our aid,
Made us of clay and formed us men;
And when like wandering sheep we strayed,
He brought us to His fold again.

3. We are His people, we His care,
Our souls and all our mortal frame.
What lasting honors shall we rear,
Almighty Maker, to Thy name?

4. We'll crowd Thy gates with thankful songs,
High as the heavens our voices raise;
And earth, with her ten thousand tongues,
Shall fill Thy courts with sounding praise.

5. Wide as the world is Thy command,
Vast as eternity Thy love;
Firm as a rock Thy truth must stand
When rolling years shall cease to move.

This hymn first appeared in Watts's *Psalms of David Imitated*, 1719. It is a metrical paraphrase of Ps. 100. Its original form was in six stanzas, beginning:

> Sing to the Lord with joyful voice;
> Let every land His name adore;
> The British isle shall send the noise
> Across the ocean to the shore.

The third line of this stanza, in the early American editions of Watts, was changed to read,

> America shall send the noise

John Wesley altered the first two lines of the second stanza from:

> Nations attend before His throne
> With solemn fear, with sacred joy,

to:

> Before Jehovah's awe-full throne,
> Ye nations, bow with sacred joy.

This version first appeared in Wesley's *Psalms and Hymns,* Charleston, **S. C.** (1736—37). Wesley dropped Watts's first stanza, altered his second stanza, and made it his first; retained Watts's third unaltered as his second, his fourth unaltered as his third, the fifth unaltered as his fourth, and Watts's sixth as his fifth. An unknown hand altered the line "Firm as a rock Thy truth must stand" to "shall stand" for the "Additional Hymns" added to the *Wesleyan Hymn-Book* of 1797.

We have adopted the spelling of the word "awful" as "awe-full," following *The Methodist Hymnal of 1935,* in order to convey more fully its original meaning, and have followed this spelling in all other hymns where the word occurs.

The tune "Old Hundredth" was set to Ps. 134 in the old *Genevan Psalter,* 1551. It was first published in England with a metrical version of Ps. 100 by Wm. Kethe. (See Hymn No. 14.) It has ever since been called "Old Hundredth" or "Old Hundred."

We give the following brief historical sketch of the French *Genevan Psalter:*

Texts. — Clement Marot, French poet (1497—1544), made at different times versions of several psalms, to the number of thirty, which were collected into a volume in 1542. Before this, however, they had circulated largely in MS. and had even found favor at the court of the King of France.

Two years before this, in 1539, when John Calvin was at Strassburg, he compiled a small collection of psalms with tunes, and there are found 12 of Marot's versions, which Calvin had got somewhere, but with a spurious text. This Strassburg book was the basis of the true *Genevan Psalter,* which Calvin prepared on his return to Geneva in 1542. In this the whole thirty psalms of Marot are included. Up to this time Calvin and Marot had no personal intercourse or acquaintance whatever with each other. But when Marot fled from Paris owing to the wrath of the Sorbonne and arrived at Geneva soon after Calvin, the latter got him to continue the translations. Marot then wrote 19 more, which, with the Song of Simeon, make up what is known as the "Fifty Psalms of Marot." Marot left Geneva a year afterwards and died in 1544 at Turin. So the *Genevan Psalter* stood till 1551, when Calvin asked his friend Theodore Beza, who had then settled at Geneva, to continue the work. Beza added thirty-four new versions, making eighty-three in all. About 1554 he added six more, another about 1555, and the remaining sixty in 1562.

Tunes. — The tunes of the Strassburg book of 1539 were mostly German, either borrowed from local sources or some perhaps written for the occasion. Those in the Genevan book of 1542 were taken from the Strassburg book or were new. Then came the edition of 1543, with Marot's new psalms and, of course, new tunes. To Beza's new psalms of 1551 and the complete edition of 1562 new tunes were also added. It should be remembered that from 1542 to 1562 alterations were made in each edition either by modification of the existing tune or by the substitution of a new one. After 1562 no change was ever made. It will thus be seen that the *Genevan Psalter* was a growth of twenty years and that the 150 psalms in it are of different dates, *viz:*

30	_____1542	34	_____1551	1	_____1555
19	_____1543	6	_____1554	60	_____1562

The tunes as they appear in the final edition of 1562 are likewise of various dates, but not necessarily those of the psalms to which they belong. For instance, one psalm of 1542 might retain its original tune to the end. Another psalm of the same date might have been set to three or four tunes in succession, till set finally in 1562. In other cases the final form of a tune was not quite the same as its first.

Composers. — In those days "composing" meant "compounding." A composer troubled himself little about originality. If his purpose was answered by piecing stock musical phrases together in a new arrangement, he did so; and very many of the older tunes were so constructed. The tune "Old Hundredth" is very likely one of these, although there is still much controversy as to its real origin.

To assign *any* tune in the Genevan book (1542—1562) to Guillaume Franc is utterly wrong. Franc was engaged as master of the children in St. Peter's Church at Geneva in 1542, but there is not a trace of evidence that he had anything to do with the editing of the Psalter. He left Geneva soon afterwards and settled at Lausanne, where he *did* edit a psalter which was indeed printed at Geneva but was confounded with the Genevan book by writers who did not know the facts.

The *Genevan Psalter* contained melodies only. After it was completed in 1562, Goudimel harmonized the tunes for private use (as singing in parts was never permitted in the "Reformed Church" till the present century). Goudimel had nothing to do with the compiling or musical editing of that work, and in fact was not even a Protestant till about 1555. On the other hand, there is positive evidence in existence that the editor from 1545 to 1557 was Louis Bourgeois; and there is every reason to believe he edited the book from the beginning in 1542.

The number of distinct tunes in the *Psalter* of 1562 is 125 (two of which are those to the Decalog and Song of Simeon), so that 27 psalms are sung to tunes of other psalms. (Cp. Cowan and Love, *The Music of the Church Hymnary*, 1901.)

"Old Hundredth" was sometimes named "Savoy" from its use by a Huguenot congregation established in the Savoy, London, during the reign of Elizabeth.

14 All People that on Earth do Dwell

1. All people that on earth do dwell,
   Sing to the Lord with cheerful voice.
   Him serve with fear, His praise forthtell;
   Come ye before Him and rejoice.

2. The Lord, ye know, is God indeed;
   Without our aid He did us make.
   We are His folk, He doth us feed,
   And for His sheep He doth us take.

3. Oh, enter, then, His gates with praise,
   Approach with joy His courts unto;
   Praise, laud, and bless His name always.
   For it is seemly so to do.

4. For why? The Lord, our God, is good;
   His mercy is forever sure.
   His truth at all times firmly stood
   And shall from age to age endure.

5. To Father, Son, and Holy Ghost,
   The God whom heaven and earth adore,
   From men and from the angel host
   Be praise and glory evermore.

The date and place of the birth of William Kethe, the author of this hymn, are unknown. He was an exile from Scotland for some time during the

Marian persecutions; at Frankfort in 1555 and at Geneva in 1557. During this exile he contributed twenty-four metrical psalms to the *Psalm Book* prepared by these English refugees and also helped in the translation of the Bible. In 1561 he was made rector of Childe Okeford, Dorset, and probably remained there until his death, about 1593.

The hymn is first found in the *Fourscore and Seven Psalms of David*, Geneva, 1561, and in the *Psalmes* issued by John Day in London the same year. The doxology was added.

The text is the original, unchanged, except for the ancient spellings, such as "yt" for "that," "ye" for "the," "shep" for "sheep," "indure" for "endure," "folck" for "folk." The last has been given, erroneously, as "flock" in many modern hymnals. Whether to retain the question-mark after "For why?" which means "because," is a matter of opinion. We retained it, as it is in keeping with the quaintness of the entire text.

For details on the tune "Old Hundredth" see Hymn No. 13.

From All that Dwell below the Skies   15

1. From all that dwell below the skies
Let the Creator's praise arise;
Alleluia! Alleluia!
Let the Redeemer's name be sung
Through every land, by every tongue.
Alleluia! Alleluia! Alleluia!
Alleluia! Alleluia!

2. Eternal are Thy mercies, Lord;
Eternal truth attends Thy Word:
Alleluia! Alleluia!
Thy praise shall sound from shore to shore
Till suns shall rise and set no more.
Alleluia! Alleluia! Alleluia!
Alleluia! Alleluia!

Isaac Watts published this paraphrase of Psalm 117 (the shortest chapter in the Bible) in his *Psalms of David Imitated,* 1719. Two stanzas were added by an unknown poet and first published, c. 1780, in *A Pocket Hymn-Book designed as a constant Companion for the pious collected from various authors.* (York, England, Robert Spence, Publisher.) John Wesley reprinted these two stanzas in his own *Pocket Hymn-Book,* 1786. It is possible that these stanzas are by John Wesley himself or by his brother, Charles Wesley. It may be, however, that Spence himself wrote them for his collection, published five or six years before John Wesley's. These are the added stanzas:

> Your lofty themes, ye mortals, bring;
> In songs of praise divinely sing;
> The great salvation loud proclaim
> And shout for joy the Savior's name.
>
> In every land begin the song;
> To every land the strains belong;
> In cheerful sounds all voices raise
> And fill the world with loudest praise.

Because of the majestic beauty and simplicity of the stanzas by Watts the hymn was retained in its original form, except that the "alleluias" were added for the sake of the tune.

The tune "Lasst uns erfreuen," long forgotten, has been restored in some of the best modern hymnals. It comes to us from the *Geistliche Kirchengesäng,* Cologne, 1623, where it is set to an Easter hymn, beginning with the line "Lasst uns erfreuen herzlich sehr." It is, as Percy Dearmer writes, a remarkable example, not only of economy of structure but of the accumulating force of repetition. The tune is also called "Easter Alleluja" and "St. Francis."

WORSHIP AND PRAISE

16   Blessed Jesus, at Thy Word

1. Blessed Jesus, at Thy word
   We are gathered all to hear Thee;
   Let our hearts and souls be stirred
   Now to seek and love and fear Thee,
   By Thy teachings, sweet and holy,
   Drawn from earth to love Thee solely.

2. All our knowledge, sense, and sight
   Lie in deepest darkness shrouded
   Till Thy Spirit breaks our night
   With the beams of truth unclouded.
   Thou alone to God canst win us;
   Thou must work all good within us.

3. Glorious Lord, Thyself impart,
   Light of Light, from God proceeding;
   Open Thou our ears and heart,
   Help us by Thy Spirit's pleading;
   Hear the cry Thy people raises,
   Hear and bless our prayers and praises.

4. Father, Son, and Holy Ghost,
   Praise to Thee and adoration!
   Grant that we Thy Word may trust
   And obtain true consolation
   While we here below must wander,
   Till we sing Thy praises yonder.

Liebster Jesu, wir sind hier,
  Dich und dein Wort anzuhören;
Lenke Sinnen und Begier
  Auf die süssen Himmelslehren,
Dass die Herzen von der Erden
Ganz zu dir gezogen werden.

Unser Wissen und Verstand
  Ist mit Finsternis umhüllet,
Wo nicht deines Geistes Hand
  Uns mit hellem Licht erfüllet.
Gutes denken, Gutes dichten
Musst du selbst in uns verrichten.

O du Glanz der Herrlichkeit,
  Licht vom Licht aus Gott geboren,
Mach uns allesamt bereit,
  Öffne Herzen, Mund und Ohren!
Unser Bitten, Flehn und Singen
Lass, Herr Jesu, wohl gelingen!

Vater, Sohn, Heiliger Geist,
  Dir sei ewig Preis und Ehre!
Tröst die Herzen allermeist
  Mit dem Wort der reinen Lehre
Hier in diesen Sterblichkeiten,
Bis wir dort dein Lob ausbreiten.

Magister Tobias Clausnitzer is the author of this widely used hymn. According to some authorities it was first published in 1663 in the *Altdorffisches Gesangbüchlein*, others give the original publication date as 1667. It was published in three stanzas as a Sunday hymn before the sermon, without the author's name. It appeared with Clausnitzer's name in the *Nürnberg Gesangbuch*, 1676. The doxology, by an unknown author, was added in the *Berliner Gesangbuch*, 1707. Our copy of Crüger's *Praxis Pietatis Melica* (ed. 1693) has the hymn in the appendix, in three stanzas only, and bearing the initials M. T. C. The translation of Stanzas 1—3 is by Catherine Winkworth and was first published in her *Lyra Germanica*, 2d series, 1858. The translator of Stanza 4 is unknown.

The tune "Liebster Jesu," also called "Dessau," was composed by Johann Rudolph Ahle, 1664, for Franz Joachim Burmeister's Advent hymn "Ja, er ist's, das Heil der Welt," and transferred to Clausnitzer's hymn in the *Altdorfer Gesangbuch*, 1671.

17   Oh, Worship the King

1. Oh, worship the King
     All glorious above;
   Oh, gratefully sing
     His power and His love,
   Our Shield and Defender,
     The Ancient of Days,
   Pavilioned in splendor
     And girded with praise!

2. Oh, tell of His might,
     Oh, sing of His grace,
   Whose robe is the light,
     Whose canopy space!
   His chariots of wrath
     The deep thunder-clouds form,
   And dark is His path
     On the wings of the storm.

3. This earth, with its store
     Of wonders untold,
   Almighty, Thy power
     Hath founded of old,
   Hath stablished it fast
     By a changeless decree,
   And round it hath cast,
     Like a mantle, the sea.

4. Thy bountiful care
     What tongues can recite?
   It breathes in the air,
     It shines in the light,
   It streams from the hills,
     It descends to the plain,
   And sweetly distils
     In the dew and the rain.

WORSHIP AND PRAISE

5. Frail children of dust
 And feeble as frail,
In Thee do we trust
 Nor find Thee to fail.
Thy mercies, how tender,
 How firm to the end,
Our Maker, Defender,
 Redeemer, and Friend!

6. O measureless Might,
 Ineffable Love,
While angels delight
 To hymn Thee above,
Thy humbler creation,
 Though feeble their lays,
With true adoration
 Shall sing to Thy praise.

The author, Sir Robert Grant, based this hymn on Kethe's 104th Psalm in the *Fourscore and Seven Psalms* of 1561. It was published in Bickensteth's *Christian Psalmody*, 1833. The text is altered in the last line of stanza six, which was "Shall lisp to Thy praise."

The tune "Hanover" is ascribed to William Croft. "Hanover" first appeared in *A Supplement to the New Version of Psalms by Dr. Brady and Mr. Tate*, etc., the sixth edition, corrected and much enlarged (1708), where it is set to the version of Ps. 67, beginning "Our God, bless us all with mercy and love," and headed "A New Tune to the 149th Psalm of the New Version, and the 104th Psalm of the Old." No composer's name is given, but William Croft is thought to have had a hand in the production of the book, and this tune has been attributed to him, mainly on this ground. It has also, since about the end of the 18th century, been frequently ascribed to Handel, but for this ascription the evidence is even more uncertain. Handel did not come to England until 1710, and it is, at least, unlikely that he should have contributed to an English collection of 1708, and the earliest name given to the tune seems to be "St. George's," and not "Hanover," so that this latter name cannot well be regarded as evidence in Handel's favor. In all collections contemporary with both Croft and Handel the tune seems to be anonymous, ascription to either being found only a considerable time after their respective deaths. Thus it is anonymous in Broome's *Choice Collection* (c. 1728), Gawthorn's *Harmonica Perfecta* (1730), *The Foundery Collection* (1742), Riley's *Parochial Music Corrected* (1762), Wesley's *Sacred Melody* (1765), and others. In Turle and Taylor's *The People's Music Book* (1844), it is attributed to Handel in the text, but to Croft in the Index, with a note: "This tune has been ascertained to be the composition of Dr. Croft, by satisfactory evidence, since the page in which it is contained was printed." What this "satisfactory evidence" was, however, is not revealed. On the whole, the attribution to Croft seems probable, but it cannot be regarded as certain. The famous tune has long been closely associated with the present words.

Lord, We Come Before Thee Now 18

1. Lord, we come before Thee now,
At Thy feet we humbly bow;
Oh, do not our suit disdain!
Shall we seek Thee, Lord, in vain?

2. Lord, on Thee our souls depend;
In compassion now descend,
Fill our hearts with Thy rich grace,
Tune our lips to sing Thy praise.

3. In Thine own appointed way
Now we seek Thee, here we stay.
Lord, we know not how to go
Till a blessing Thou bestow.

4. Send some message from Thy Word
That may joy and peace afford;
Let Thy Spirit now impart
Full salvation to each heart.

5. Comfort those who weep and mourn,
Let the time of joy return;
Those that are cast down lift up,
Make them strong in faith and hope.

6. Grant that all may seek and find
Thee a gracious God and kind.
Heal the sick, the captive free;
Let us all rejoice in Thee.

This hymn was written by William Hammond and first published in his *Psalms and Hymns*, 1745. Originally it was in eight stanzas of eight lines each.

WORSHIP AND PRAISE

In 1760 Martin Madan reduced it to six stanzas of four lines each. In this form the hymn is usually found in modern hymnals. Another of Hammond's hymns, which are marked by Scriptural fidelity and earnestness, though not included in our hymnal, is worthy of a place in this volume. It is his beautiful exhortation to Christian singing:

1. Awake and sing the song
    Of Moses and the Lamb;
  Tune every heart and every tongue
    To praise the Savior's name.

2. Sing of His dying love;
    Sing of His rising power;
  Sing how He intercedes above
    For those whose sins He bore.

3. If you have felt His grace,
    You'll not refuse to sing,
  But summon all your powers to praise
    Your Savior and your King.

4. Look back and see the state
    Wherein your nature lay;
  Then wonder at His love so great,
    Who did your ransom pay.

5. His faithfulness proclaim
    While life and health are given;
  Join hands and hearts to praise His name
    Till we all meet in heaven.

6. May Jesus' Word take place
    And wisdom in us dwell
  That we His miracles of grace
    In psalms and hymns may tell.

7. Tell in seraphic strains
    What Christ has done for you,
  How He has taken off your chains
    And formed your hearts anew.

8. Be careful to approve
    Yourselves His children dear;
  Admonish and provoke to love,
    To righteousness and fear.

9. Leave carnal joys below,
    To men of meaner taste;
  Think, speak, and sing of nothing now
    But Christ the first and last.

10. Are you in deep distress?
    Then sing to ease the smart.
  Are you rejoiced? Let psalms express
    The gladness of your heart.

11. When Paul and Silas sung,
    The earth began to quake;
  The prison-doors were open flung,
    Her firm foundations shake.

12. The prisoners' bands were loosed —
    Who can the Lord control?
  May equal powers be now diffused
    And free each captive soul.

13. Sing till you feel your hearts
    Ascending with your tongues;
  Sing till the love of sin departs
    And grace inspires your songs.

14. Sing till you hear Christ say,
    "Your sins are all forgiven";
  Go on, rejoicing all the way,
    And sing your souls to heaven.

The tune "Vienna," also called "St. Boniface," "Ravenna," and "Ohne Rast," is by Justin Heinrich Knecht and is found in *Vollständige Sammlung*, etc., Stuttgart, 1799, a collection edited by Knecht and J. F. Christmann, where it is set to Johann Adolf Schlegel's hymn "Ohne Rast und unverweilt." It was composed in 1797.

19   All Praise to God, Who Reigns Above

1. All praise to God, who reigns above,
    The God of all creation,
  The God of wonders, power, and love,
    The God of our salvation!
  With healing balm my soul He fills,
  The God who every sorrow stills, —
    To God all praise and glory!

2. What God's almighty power hath made
    His gracious mercy keepeth;
  By morning dawn or evening shade
    His watchful eye ne'er sleepeth;
  Within the kingdom of His might
  Lo, all is just and all is right, —
    To God all praise and glory!

3. I cried to Him in time of need:
    Lord God, oh, hear my calling!
  For death He gave me life indeed
    And kept my feet from falling.
  For this my thanks shall endless be;
  Oh, thank Him, thank our God,
    with me, —
    To God all praise and glory!

Sei Lob und Ehr' dem höchsten Gut,
  Dem Vater aller Güte,
Dem Gott, der alle Wunder tut,
  Dem Gott, der mein Gemüte
Mit seinem reichen Trost erfüllt,
Dem Gott, der allen Jammer stillt.
  Gebt unserm Gott die Ehre!

Was unser Gott geschaffen hat,
  Das will er auch erhalten,
Darüber will er früh und spat
  Mit seiner Gnade walten.
In seinem ganzen Königreich
Ist alles recht und alles gleich.
  Gebt unserm Gott die Ehre!

Ich rief dem Herrn in meiner Not:
  Ach Gott, vernimm mein Schreien!
Da half mein Helfer mir vom Tod
  Und liess mir Trost gedeihen.
Drum dank', ach Gott, drum dank' ich
  dir!
Ach danket, danket Gott mit mir!
  Gebt unserm Gott die Ehre!

4. The Lord forsaketh not His flock,
    His chosen generation;
   He is their Refuge and their Rock,
    Their Peace and their Salvation.
   As with a mother's tender hand
   He leads His own, His chosen band, —
    To God all praise and glory!

5. Ye who confess Christ's holy name,
    To God give praise and glory!
   Ye who the Father's power proclaim,
    To God give praise and glory!
   All idols under foot be trod,
   The Lord is God! The Lord is God!
    To God all praise and glory!

6. Then come before His presence now
    And banish fear and sadness;
   To your Redeemer pay your vow
    And sing with joy and gladness:
   Though great distress my soul befell,
   The Lord, my God, did all things well, —
    To God all praise and glory!

Der Herr ist noch und nimmer nicht
 Von seinem Volk geschieden,
Er bleibet ihre Zuversicht,
 Ihr Segen, Heil und Frieden.
Mit Mutterhänden leitet er
Die Seinen stetig hin und her.
 Gebt unserm Gott die Ehre!

Ihr, die ihr Christi Namen nennt,
 Gebt unserm Gott die Ehre!
Ihr, die ihr Gottes Macht bekennt,
 Gebt unserm Gott die Ehre!
Die falschen Götzen macht zu Spott.
Der Herr ist Gott, der Herr ist Gott!
 Gebt unserm Gott die Ehre!

So kommet vor sein Angesicht
 Mit jauchzenvollem Springen,
Bezahlet die gelobte Pflicht
 Und lasst uns fröhlich singen:
Gott hat es alles wohl bedacht
Und alles, alles recht gemacht.
 Gebt unserm Gott die Ehre!

This hymn of praise and thanksgiving, with its beautiful refrain, was written by Johann Jakob Schütz and first published in his *Christliches Gedenkbüchlein*, etc., Frankfurt am Main, 1675, in nine stanzas. The cento is made up of Stanzas 1, 3, 4, 5, 8, and 9 of the original. An English version of the omitted stanzas is the following:

2. The angel host, O King of kings,
    Thy praise forever telling,
   In earth and sky all living things
    Beneath Thy shadow dwelling,
   Adore and praise their Maker's might,
   Whose wisdom orders all things right;
    To God all praise and glory!

6. When earth can comfort us no more
    Nor human help availeth,
   The Maker comes Himself, whose store
    Of blessing never faileth,
   And bends on them a Father's eyes
   Whom earth all rest and hope denies;
    To God all praise and glory!

7. Thus all my pilgrim way along
    I'll sing aloud Thy praises
   That men may hear the grateful song
    My voice unwearied raises:
   Be joyful in the Lord, my heart!
   Both soul and body, bear your part!
    To God all praise and glory!

The great German hymnologist Eduard Emil Koch speaks of this hymn "as outweighing many hundred others; and a classical hymn, which from its first appearance attracted unusual attention." Therefore it was taken up into almost all German hymnals, even though the author was extremely pietistic and separatistic in his attitude otherwise. There is really no trace of his extreme Pietism in the hymn.

The composite translation is based on that by Catherine Winkworth in her *Lyra Germanica*, 1858, and *The Chorale Book for England*, 1863.

The tune "Lobet den Herrn, ihr Heiden all'" is by Melchior Vulpius and first appeared in his *Ein schön geistlich Gesangbuch*, etc., Jena, 1609, where it was set to an Epiphany hymn, based on Ps. 117, beginning with that line, by an anonymous author. Although the tune has never received general acceptance even in the hymnals of Germany, it has maintained itself in some down to the present time. Its widest usage has been as a choir piece. When sung by a congregation that has a command of the melody, the hymn has remarkable power.

WORSHIP AND PRAISE

20   God of Mercy, God of Grace

1. God of mercy, God of grace,
Show the brightness of Thy face;
Shine upon us, Savior, shine,
Fill Thy Church with light divine,
And Thy saving health extend
Unto earth's remotest end.

2. Let the people praise Thee, Lord!
Be by all that live adored;
Let the nations shout and sing
Glory to their Savior King,
At Thy feet their tribute pay,
And Thy holy will obey.

3. Let the people praise Thee, Lord!
Earth shall then her fruits afford,
God to man His blessing give,
Man to God devoted live;
All below and all above
One in joy and light and love.

Henry Francis Lyte published this hymn in his *Spirit of the Psalms*, 1834. It is a paraphrase of Ps. 67. As this joyous hymn emphasizes especially the gratitude that is due our heavenly Father for the fruits of the earth, it reflects the background of the author, who through all his ministry served a rural parish.

The tune "Ratisbon" is ascribed to Johann Gottlob Werner. It appeared in his *Choralbuch zu den neuen sächsischen Gesangbüchern*, Leipzig, 1815 (1813 according to Koch), set to the words "Jesu, meines Lebens Leben" (see Hymn No. 151), which seems to be based on an older tune by Joachim Neander, in his *Choralbuch* of 1680.

Johann Gottlob Werner was born near Leipzig in 1777 and died at Chemnitz, July 19, 1822. He was a well-known organist, composer, and teacher of music.

21   Jehovah, Let Me Now Adore Thee

1. Jehovah, let me now adore Thee,
For where is there a God such, Lord, as Thou?
With songs I fain would come before Thee;
Oh, let Thy Holy Spirit teach me now
To praise Thee in His name through whom alone
Our songs can please Thee, through Thy blessed Son!

2. O Father, draw me to my Savior
That Thy dear Son may draw me unto Thee;
Thy Spirit guide my whole behavior
And rule both sense and reason thus in me
That, Lord, Thy peace from me may ne'er depart,
But wake sweet melodies within my heart.

3. Grant that Thy Spirit prompt my praises,
Then shall my singing surely please Thine ear;
Sweet are the sounds my heart then raises,
My prayer in truth and spirit Thou wilt hear.
Then shall Thy Spirit raise my heart to Thee
To sing Thee psalms of praise in high degree.

4. For He can plead for me with sighings
That are unspeakable to lips like mine;
He bids me pray with earnest cryings,
Bears witness with my soul that I am Thine,
Joint heir with Christ, and thus may dare to say:
O heavenly Father, hear me when I pray!

Dir, dir Jehova, will ich singen,
Denn wo ist doch ein solcher Gott wie du?
Dir will ich meine Lieder bringen,
Ach gib mir deines Geistes Kraft dazu,
Dass ich es tu' im Namen Jesu Christ,
So wie es dir durch ihn gefällig ist.

Zeuch mich, o Vater, zu dem Sohne,
Damit dein Sohn mich wieder zieh' zu dir;
Dein Geist in meinem Herzen wohne
Und meine Sinne und Verstand regier',
Dass ich den Frieden Gottes schmeck' und fühl'
Und dir darob im Herzen sing' und spiel'.

Verleih mir, Höchster, solche Güte,
So wird gewiss mein Singen recht getan,
So klingt es schön in meinem Liede,
Und ich bet' dich im Geist und Wahrheit an,
So hebt dein Geist mein Herz zu dir empor,
Dass ich dir Psalmen sing' im höhern Chor.

Denn der kann mich bei dir vertreten
Mit Seufzern, die ganz unaussprechlich sind,
Der lehret mich recht gläubig beten,
Gibt Zeugnis meinem Geist, dass ich dein Kind
Und ein Miterbe Jesu Christi sei,
Daher ich Abba, lieber Vater! schrei'.

WORSHIP AND PRAISE

5. When thus my heart in prayer
    ascendeth,
Through Thine own Holy Spirit,
    unto Thee,
Thy heart, O Father, kindly bendeth
    Its fervent love and favor unto me,
Rejoicing my petition to fulfil
Which I have made according to Thy will.

6. And what Thy Spirit thus hath taught me
    To seek from Thee must needs be such
    a prayer
As Thou wilt grant through Him who bought
    me
And raised me up to be Thy child and heir.
In Jesus' name I boldly seek Thy face
And take from Thee, my Father, grace for
    grace.

Wenn dies aus meinem Herzen schallet
    Durch deines Heil'gen Geistes Kraft
    und Trieb,
So bricht dein Vaterherz und wallet
    Ganz brünstig gegen mich vor heisser
    Lieb',
Dass mir's die Bitte nicht versagen kann,
Die ich nach deinem Willen hab' getan.

Was mich dein Geist selbst bitten lehret,
    Das ist nach deinem Willen
    eingericht't
Und wird gewiss von dir erhöret,
    Weil es im Namen deines Sohns
    geschieht,
Durch welchen ich dein Kind und
    Erbe bin
Und nehme von dir Gnad' um Gnade hin.

This hymn by Bartholomäus Crasselius was first published in eight stanzas in *Geistreiches Gesangbuch,* Halle, 1697. It is a glorious hymn of praise that has long been a favorite in the evangelical churches of Germany. The translation is a somewhat altered form of Catherine Winkworth's as it appeared in her *Chorale Book for England,* 1863. The omitted stanzas, seven and eight, are the following, in translation:

7. O joy! my hope and trust are founded
    On His sure Word and witness in the
    heart;
I know Thy mercies are unbounded,
    And all good gifts Thou freely wilt impart;
Nay, more is lavished by Thy bounteous
    hand
Than I can ask or seek or understand.

8. O bliss! in Jesus' name I've tendered
    My prayer; He pleads at Thy right
    hand for me.
Yea and Amen in Him is rendered
    What I in faith and spirit ask of Thee.
O joy for me! and praise be ever Thine
Whose wondrous love has made such
    blessings mine!

The tune "Dir, dir, Jehovah," sometimes erroneously ascribed to Crasselius, has been coupled with this text since its first publication in 1704, in Freylinghausen's *Neues Geistreiches Gesangbuch.* It is an altered form of the melody "Wer nur den lieben Gott lässt walten," which is first found in *Musikalisch Hand-Buch,* etc., Hamburg, 1690. The composer is not known. In England the tune is called "Winchester New" and has been altered to fit the long meter. (See Hymn No. 12.)

Lord, When We Bend Before Thy Throne   22

1. Lord, when we bend before Thy throne
    And our confessions pour,
Teach us to feel the sins we own
    And hate what we deplore.

2. Our broken spirit pitying see,
    True penitence impart;
Then let a kindling glance from Thee
    Beam hope upon the heart.

3. When our responsive tongues essay
    Their grateful hymns to raise,
Grant that our souls may join the lay
    And mount to Thee in praise.

4. When we disclose our wants in prayer,
    May we our wills resign
And not a thought our bosom share
    That is not wholly Thine.

5. May faith each meek petition fill
    And waft it to the skies;
And teach our hearts 'tis goodness still
    That grants it or denies.

This hymn is the most popular production of Joseph Dacre Carlyle. It was first published in John Fawcett's *Psalms and Hymns,* Carlisle, 1802, as a hymn for Lent. In its original form it contained the following Stanza 4, now usually omitted:

    Then on Thy glories while we dwell,
        Thy mercies we'll review
    Till love divine transported tell
        Our God's our Father, too.

The tune "St. Flavian," also called "Prescot," is an abridgment of the tune found in John Day's *Psalter,* 1562, set to a metrical version of Ps. 132,

23   Hallelujah! Let Praises Ring

1. Hallelujah! Let praises ring!
To God the Father let us bring
Our songs of adoration.
To Him through everlasting days
Be worship, honor, power, and praise,
Whose hand sustains creation.
Singing, ringing:
Holy, holy, God is holy, —
Spread the story
Of our God, the Lord of Glory.

2. Hallelujah! Let praises ring!
Unto the Lamb of God we sing,
In whom we are elected.
He bought His Church with His own blood,
He cleansed her in that blessed flood,
And as His Bride selected.
Holy, holy
Is our union And communion.
His befriending
Gives us joy and peace unending.

3. Hallelujah! Let praises ring!
Unto the Holy Ghost we sing
For our regeneration.
The saving faith in us He wrought
And us unto the Bridegroom brought,
Made us His chosen nation.
Glory! Glory!
Joy eternal, Bliss supernal;
There is manna
And an endless, glad hosanna.

4. Hallelujah! Let praises ring!
Unto our Triune God we sing;
Blest be His name forever!
With angel hosts let us adore
And sing His praises more and more
For all His grace and favor!
Singing, ringing:
Holy, holy, God is holy, —
Spread the story
Of our God, the Lord of Glory!

Halleluja! Lob, Preis und Ehr'
Sei unserm Gott je mehr und mehr
Für alle seine Werke;
Von Ewigkeit zu Ewigkeit
Sei in uns allen ihm bereit
Dank, Weisheit, Kraft und Stärke!
Klinget, singet:
Heilig, heilig, freilich, freilich,
Heilig ist Gott,
Unser Gott, der Herr Zebaoth!

Halleluja! Preis, Ehr' und Macht
Sei auch dem Gotteslamm gebracht,
In dem wir sind erwählet,
Das uns mit seinem Blut erkauft,
Damit besprenget und getauft
Und sich mit uns vermählet!
Heilig, selig
Ist die Freundschaft und Gemeinschaft,
Die wir haben
Und darinnen uns erlaben.

Halleluja! Gott Heil'ger Geist
Sei ewiglich von uns gepreist,
Durch den wir neugeboren,
Der uns mit Glauben ausgeziert,
Dem Bräutigam uns zugeführt,
Den Hochzeitstag erkoren!
Eia, ei da,
Da ist Freude, da ist Weide,
Da ist Manna
Und ein ewig Hosianna!

Halleluja! Lob, Preis und Ehr'
Sei unserm Gott je mehr und mehr
Und seinem grossen Namen!
Stimmt an mit aller Himmelsschar
Und singet nun und immerdar
Mit Freuden: Amen, Amen!
Klinget, singet:
Heilig, heilig, freilich, freilich,
Heilig ist Gott,
Unser Gott, der Herr Zebaoth!

This hymn is an example of the strange changes through which some of our hymns have passed before receiving their final form. In 1642 Martin Rinckart, best known for his hymn "Now Thank We All Our God" (see Hymn No. 36), published a *Bridal Mass* (*Leibliche, Geistliche und Himmlische Braut Messe*) in which he included a wedding hymn, based on Rev. 21 and 22. In 1655 an unknown poet published a new version of this hymn, changing it into a burial hymn. Finally, in 1698, in the *Geistreiches Gesangbuch,* Darmstadt, four stanzas of this hymn appeared as a hymn of praise to the Holy Trinity. In this form the hymn was taken over into other collections and became very popular. It has sometimes been erroneously ascribed to Bartholomäus Crasselius.

The translation is composite.

The tune "Wie schön leuchtet der Morgenstern" is the "Queen of *Chorales,*" by Philipp Nicolai, and was originally published in 1599 with his hymn "How Lovely Shines the Morning Star." (See Hymn No. 343.)

24   Lord of My Life, Whose Tender Care

1. Lord of my life, whose tender care
Hath led me on till now,
Here lowly, at the hour of prayer,
Before Thy throne I bow.
I bless Thy gracious hand and pray
Forgiveness for another day.

2. Oh, may I daily, hourly, strive
In heavenly grace to grow,
To Thee and to Thy glory live,
Dead to all else below!
Tread in the path my Savior trod,
Though thorny, yet the path of God.

3. With prayer my humble praise I bring
   For mercies day by day.
Lord, teach my heart Thy love to sing;
   Lord, teach me how to pray.
All that I have and am, to Thee
I offer through eternity.

This hymn first appeared in the *Church of England Magazine,* February, 1838, and was signed "Ω (Omega), Chelsea." It became popular and was included in English and American hymnals. Sometimes it is found as "Lord of *our* life," etc.

The tune "O Jesu" appeared in *J. B. Reimann's Org. v. Hirschb., Sammlung alter und neuer Melodien Evang. Lieder,* etc. (1747). It was a collection of tunes for the *Hirschberger Gesangbuch* of 1741. This tune is very likely by Johann Balthasar Reimann himself. It was set to the hymn "O Jesu, warum legst du mir so viele Lasten auf."

I Will Sing My Maker's Praises — 25

1. I will sing my Maker's praises
   And in Him most joyful be,
For in all things I see traces
   Of His tender love to me.
Nothing else than love could move Him
   With such sweet and tender care
Evermore to raise and bear
   All who try to serve and love Him.
All things else have but their day,
God's great love abides for aye.

2. Yea, so dear did He esteem me
   That His Son He loved so well
He hath given to redeem me
   From the quenchless flames of hell.
O Thou Spring of boundless blessing,
   How could e'er my feeble mind
Of Thy depth the bottom find
   Though my efforts were unceasing?
All things else have but their day,
God's great love abides for aye.

3. All that for my soul is needful
   He with loving care provides,
Nor of that is He unheedful
   Which my body needs besides.
When my strength cannot avail me,
   When my powers can do no more,
Doth my God His strength outpour;
   In my need He doth not fail me.
All things else have but their day,
God's great love abides for aye.

4. When I sleep, He still is near me,
   O'er me rests His guardian eye;
And new gifts and blessings cheer me
   When the morning streaks the sky.
Were it not for God's protection,
   Had His countenance not been
Here my guide, I had not seen
   E'er the end of my affliction.
All things else have but their day,
God's great love abides for aye.

5. As a father never turneth
   Wholly from a wayward child,
For the prodigal still yearneth,
   Longing to be reconciled,
So my many sins and errors
   Find a tender, pardoning God,
Chastening frailty with His rod,
   Not in vengeance, with His terrors.
All things else have but their day,
God's great love abides for aye.

Sollt' ich meinem Gott nicht singen?
   Sollt' ich ihm nicht fröhlich sein?
Denn ich seh' in allen Dingen,
   Wie so gut er's mit mir mein'.
Ist doch nichts als lauter Lieben,
   Das sein treues Herze regt,
Das ohn' Ende hebt und trägt,
   Die in seinem Dienst sich üben.
Alles Ding währt seine Zeit,
Gottes Lieb' in Ewigkeit.

Sein Sohn ist ihm nicht zu teuer,
   Nein, er gibt ihn für mich hin,
Dass er mich vom ew'gen Feuer
   Durch sein teures Blut gewinn'.
O du unergründ'ter Brunnen,
   Wie will doch mein schwacher Geist,
Ob er sich gleich hoch befleisst,
   Deine Tief' ergründen können?
Alles Ding währt seine Zeit,
Gottes Lieb' in Ewigkeit.

Meiner Seele Wohlergehen
   Hat er ja recht wohl bedacht.
Will dem Leibe Not zustehen,
   Nimmt er's gleichfalls wohl in acht.
Wenn mein Können, mein Vermögen
   Nichts vermag, nichts helfen kann,
Kommt mein Gott und hebt mir an
   Sein Vermögen beizulegen.
Alles Ding währt seine Zeit,
Gottes Lieb' in Ewigkeit.

Wenn ich schlafe, wacht sein Sorgen
   Und ermuntert mein Gemüt,
Dass ich alle lieben Morgen
   Schaue neue Lieb' und Güt'.
Wäre mein Gott nicht gewesen,
   Hätte mich sein Angesicht
Nicht geleitet, wär' ich nicht
   Aus so mancher Angst genesen.
Alles Ding währt seine Zeit,
Gottes Lieb' in Ewigkeit.

Wie ein Vater seinem Kinde
   Sein Herz niemals ganz entzeucht,
Ob es gleich bisweilen Sünde
   Tut und aus der Bahne weicht:
Also hält auch mein Verbrechen
   Mir mein frommer Gott zugut,
Will mein Fehlen mit der Rut'
   Und nicht mit dem Schwerte rächen.
Alles Ding währt seine Zeit,
Gottes Lieb' in Ewigkeit.

WORSHIP AND PRAISE

6. Since, then, neither change nor coldness
In my Father's love can be,
Lo! I lift my hands with boldness,
As Thy child I come to Thee.
Grant me grace, O God, I pray Thee,
That I may with all my might,
All my lifetime, day and night,
Love and trust Thee and obey Thee
And, when this brief life is o'er,
Praise and love Thee evermore.

Weil denn weder Ziel noch Ende
Sich in Gottes Liebe find't,
Ei, so heb' ich meine Hände
Zu dir, Vater, als dein Kind,
Bitte, woll'st mir Gnade geben,
Dich aus aller meiner Macht
Zu umfangen Tag und Nacht
Hier in meinem ganzen Leben,
Bis ich dich nach dieser Zeit
Lob' und lieb' in Ewigkeit.

Paul Gerhardt, the "prince of German hymnists," first published this hymn in the fifth edition of Johann Crüger's *Praxis Pietatis Melica,* Berlin, 1653. It was in twelve stanzas. Its beautiful refrain, which no translation has reproduced exactly, fittingly summarizes the reasons for the Christian's praise and thanksgiving to his Maker. The hymn is numbered among Gerhardt's very best productions. The cento is composed of Stanzas 1, 3, 5, 7, 9, and 12 of the original.

The translation is composite.

The tune "Sollt' ich meinem Gott nicht singen" was composed by Johann Schop for Johann Rist's Easter hymn "Lasset uns den Herren preisen, o ihr Christen, überall," published with that text in Rist's *Himmlische Lieder,* Lüneburg, 1641. In the course of time, however, this tune became wedded to this hymn of Gerhardt's and is the most widely used in spite of the fact that at least twenty tunes have been composed for Gerhardt's text. The congregation that masters this tune possesses a treasure of which it will never grow weary.

26   Praise the Almighty, My Soul, Adore Him

1. Praise the Almighty, my soul, adore Him!
Yea, I will laud Him until death.
With songs and anthems I'll come before Him
As long as He doth give me breath.
From Him my life and all things came;
Bless, O my soul, His holy name.
Hallelujah! Hallelujah!

2. Trust not in princes, they are but mortal;
Earth-born they are and soon decay.
Naught are their counsels at life's last portal,
When the dark grave doth claim its prey.
Since, then, no man can help afford,
Trust ye in Christ, our God and Lord.
Hallelujah! Hallelujah!

3. Blessed, yea, blessed is he forever
Whose help is in the Lord most high,
Whom from the saving faith naught can sever
And who in hope to Christ draws nigh.
To all who trust in Him, our Lord,
Counsel and aid He doth afford.
Hallelujah! Hallelujah!

4. God the Almighty, the great Creator,
Ruler of sky and land and sea,
All things ordainèd, and sooner or later
They come to pass unfailingly.
His rule is over rich and poor,
His promise ever standeth sure.
Hallelujah! Hallelujah!

5. Penitent sinners, for mercy crying,
Pardon and peace from Him obtain;
Ever the wants of the poor supplying,
Their faithful God He doth remain.
He helps His children in distress,
The widows and the fatherless.
Hallelujah! Hallelujah!

Lobe den Herren, o meine Seele!
Ich will ihn loben bis in Tod;
Weil ich noch Stunden auf Erden zähle,
Will ich lobsingen meinem Gott.
Der Leib und Seel' gegeben hat,
Werde gepriesen früh und spat.
Halleluja! Halleluja!

Fürsten sind Menschen, vom Weib geboren,
Und kehren um zu ihrem Staub;
Ihre Anschläge sind auch verloren,
Wenn nun das Grab nimmt seinen Raub.
Weil denn kein Mensch uns helfen kann,
Rufe man Gott um Hilfe an!
Halleluja! Halleluja!

Selig, ja selig ist der zu nennen,
Des Hilfe der Gott Jakobs ist,
Welcher vom Glauben sich nichts lässt trennen
Und hofft getrost auf Jesum Christ.
Wer diesen Herrn zum Beistand hat,
Findet am besten Rat und Tat.
Halleluja! Halleluja!

Dieser hat Himmel, Meer und die Erden,
Und was darinnen ist, gemacht.
Alles muss pünktlich erfüllet werden,
Was er uns einmal zugedacht.
Er ist's, der Herrscher aller Welt,
Welcher uns ewig Glauben hält.
Halleluja! Halleluja!

Zeigen sich welche, die Unrecht leiden,
Er ist's, der ihnen Recht verschafft.
Hungrigen will er zu Speis' bescheiden,
Was ihnen dient zur Lebenskraft.
Die hart Gebundnen macht er frei,
Seine Genad' ist mancherlei.
Halleluja! Halleluja!

[24]

6. Praise, O mankind, now the name so holy
    Of Him who doth such wondrous things!
   All that hath being, to praise Him solely,
    With happy heart its "Amen" sings!
   Children of God, with angel host
   Praise Father, Son, and Holy Ghost!
    Hallelujah! Hallelujah!

Rühmet, ihr Menschen, den hohen Namen
 Des, der so grosse Wunder tut!
Alles, was Odem hat, rufe Amen!
 Und bringe Lob mit frohem Mut.
Ihr Kinder Gottes, lobt und preist
Vater und Sohn und Heil'gen Geist!
 Halleluja! Halleluja!

This hymn by Johann Daniel Herrnschmidt was first published in the second part of Freylinghausen's *Gesangbuch*, Halle, 1714, in eight stanzas. It is a highly poetical version of Ps. 146. The translation gives Stanzas 1, 2, 3, 4, a combination of Stanzas 5 and 6, and Stanza 8.

The translation by Alfred Brauer first appeared in the *Australian Lutheran Hymn Book*, 1925. It was slightly altered for *The Lutheran Hymnal*.

The striking tune "Lobe den Herren, o meine Seele," inseparably united with this hymn, has sometimes been erroneously ascribed to Herrnschmidt. It is by an unknown composer and first appeared in *Anhang der Seelen-Harpff, Onolzbach*, 1665, set to the hymn "Lobet den Herren aller Herren." The tune is one of the most brilliant gems in our *chorale* treasury.

Oh, Bless the Lord, My Soul 27

1. Oh, bless the Lord, my soul!
    Let all within me join
   And aid my tongue to bless His name
    Whose favors are divine.

2. Oh, bless the Lord, my soul,
    Nor let His mercies lie
   Forgotten in unthankfulness
    And without praises die!

3. 'Tis He forgives thy sins;
    'Tis He relieves thy pain;
   'Tis He that heals thy sicknesses
    And makes thee young again.

4. He crowns thy life with love
    When ransomed from the grave;
   He that redeemed my soul from hell
    Hath sovereign power to save.

5. He fills the poor with good;
    He gives the sufferers rest:
   The Lord hath judgments for the proud
    And justice for th' opprest.

6. His wondrous works and ways
    He made by Moses known,
   But sent the world His truth and grace
    By His beloved Son.

Isaac Watts first published this hymn in his *Psalms of David Imitated*, 1719, as a metrical paraphrase of Ps. 108:1-7.

The tune "St. Thomas," also called "William's," is found in Aaron William's *New Universal Psalmodist*, 1770, and is the first tune in Book III, *Psalmody in Miniature* of 1778, by the same composer. In the *Psalmodist* the tune is called "St. Thomas's" and is set to Ps. 48, "Great is the Lord, our God." The tune is a great favorite in England and America.

Now Let All Loudly Sing Praise 28

1. Now let all loudly
    Sing praise to God the Lord;
   Christendom, proudly
    Laud Him with one accord.
   Gently He bids thee come before Him;
   Haste, then, O Israel, now adore Him.

2. For the Lord reigneth
    Over the universe,
   All He sustaineth,
    All things His praise rehearse,
   The angel host His glory telling,
   Psalter and harp are the anthem swelling.

Nun preiset alle
 Gottes Barmherzigkeit!
Lob ihn mit Schalle,
 Werteste Christenheit!
Er lässt dich freundlich zu sich laden;
Freue dich, Israel, seiner Gnaden!

Der Herr regieret
 über die ganze Welt.
Was sich nur rühret,
 Ihm auch zu Füssen fällt.
Viel tausend Engel um ihn schweben,
Psalter und Harfen ihm Ehre geben.

[25]

3. Come, heathen races,
   Cast off all grief and care,
   For pleasant places
   Your Savior doth prepare
   Where His blest Word abroad is sounded,
   Pardon for sinners and grace unbounded.

4. Richly He feeds us
   Always and everywhere;
   Gently He leads us
   With a true father's care;
   The late and early rains He sends us,
   Daily His blessing, His love, attends us.

5. Sing we His praises
   Who is thus merciful;
   Christendom raises
   Songs to His glorious rule.
   Rejoice! No foe shall now alarm us;
   He will protect us, and who can harm us?

Wohlauf, ihr Heiden,
   Das Trauern lasset sein!
   Zu grünen Weiden
   Stellet euch willig ein!
   Da lässt er uns sein Wort verkünden,
   Machet uns ledig von allen Sünden.

Er gibet Speise
   Reichlich und überall,
   Nach Vaters Weise
   Sättigt er allzumal.
   Er schaffet früh- und späten Regen,
   Füllet uns alle mit seinem Segen.

Drum preis und ehre
   Seine Barmherzigkeit,
   Sein Lob vermehre,
   Werteste Christenheit!
   Uns soll hinfort kein Unfall schaden:
   Freue dich, Israel, seiner Gnaden!

Matthäus Appelles von Löwenstern published this hymn in *Geistliche Kirchen- und Haus-Musik* (Breslau, 1644), where it is No. 12 of his "Apellis-Lieder." It was entitled "Alcaic Ode" because of its metrical form. It was there coupled with the tune, also by von Löwenstern, to which it has since been wedded. The hymn has found a wide appeal and has been included in many hymnals outside of the English-speaking world.

The translation is by Catherine Winkworth, somewhat altered, published originally in her *Chorale Book for England*, 1863.

29   Through All the Changing Scenes of Life

1. Through all the changing scenes of life,
   In trouble and in joy,
   The praises of my God shall still
   My heart and tongue employ.

2. Of His deliverance I will boast
   Till all that are distrest
   From my example comfort take
   And charm their griefs to rest.

3. Oh, magnify the Lord with me,
   With me exalt His name!
   When in distress to Him I cried,
   He to my rescue came.

4. The hosts of God encamp around
   The dwellings of the just;
   Deliverance He affords to all
   Who on His succor trust.

5. Oh, make but trial of His love!
   Experience will decide
   How blest are they, and only they,
   Who in His truth confide.

6. Fear Him, ye saints, and you will then
   Have nothing else to fear;
   Make you His service your delight,
   He'll make your wants His care.

This is a cento from Tate and Brady's metrical version of Ps. 34, which appeared in 1696 in *A New Version of the Psalms fitted to the Tunes used in the Churches*, by Nahum Tate and Nicholas Brady. In its original form their Ps. 34 contained eighteen stanzas.

The *New Version* of Tate and Brady with its paraphrases did much to free English hymnody from the shackles of the metrical psalm as found in the *Old Version;* it forms a transition to the "hymn of human composure," in the interest of which Isaac Watts did his pioneer work.

The tune "Ich singe dir mit Herz und Mund" is first found in Balthasar König's *Harmonischer Liederschatz*, Frankfurt, 1738, set to Paul Gerhardt's beautiful hymn of praise beginning with that line. (See Hymn No. 569.) The composer is unknown.

Oh, that I Had a Thousand Voices 30

1. Oh, that I had a thousand voices
   To praise my God with thousand tongues!
   My heart, which in the Lord rejoices,
   Would then proclaim in grateful songs
   To all, wherever I might be,
   What great things God hath done for me.

2. O all ye powers that He implanted,
   Arise, and silence keep no more;
   Put forth the strength that He hath granted,
   Your noblest work is to adore.
   O soul and body, be ye meet
   With heartfelt praise your Lord to greet!

3. Ye forest leaves so green and tender,
   That dance for joy in summer air;
   Ye meadow grasses, bright and slender;
   Ye flowers so wondrous sweet and fair;
   Ye live to show His praise alone,
   With me now make His glory known.

4. All creatures that have breath and motion,
   That throng the earth, the sea, and sky,
   Now join me in my heart's devotion,
   Help me to raise His praises high.
   My utmost powers can ne'er aright
   Declare the wonders of His might.

5. Lord, I will tell, while I am living,
   Thy goodness forth with every breath
   And greet each morning with thanksgiving
   Until my heart is still in death;
   Yea, when at last my lips grow cold,
   Thy praise shall in my sighs be told.

6. O Father, deign Thou, I beseech Thee,
   To listen to my earthly lays;
   A nobler strain in heaven shall reach Thee,
   When I with angels hymn Thy praise
   And learn amid their choirs to sing
   Loud hallelujahs to my King.

O dass ich tausend Zungen hätte
Und einen tausendfachen Mund,
So stimmt' ich damit in die Wette
Vom allertiefsten Herzensgrund
Ein Loblied nach dem andern an
Von dem, was Gott an mir getan!

Was schweigt ihr denn, ihr meine Kräfte?
Auf, auf, braucht allen euren Fleiss
Und stehet munter im Geschäfte
Zu Gottes, meines Herren, Preis!
Mein Leib und Seele, schicke dich
Und lobe Gott herzinniglich!

Ihr grünen Blätter in den Wäldern,
Bewegt und regt euch doch mit mir!
Ihr schwanken Gräschen in den Feldern,
Ihr Blumen, lasst doch eure Zier
Zu Gottes Ruhm belebet sein
Und stimmet lieblich mit mir ein!

Ach alles, alles, was ein Leben
Und einen Odem in sich hat,
Soll sich mir zum Gehilfen geben,
Denn mein Vermögen ist zu matt
Die grossen Wunder zu erhöhn,
Die allenthalben um mich stehn.

Ich will von deiner Güte singen,
Solange sich die Zunge regt,
Ich will dir Freudenopfer bringen,
Solange sich mein Herz bewegt.
Ja, wenn der Mund wird kraftlos sein,
So stimm' ich doch mit Seufzen ein.

Ach nimm das arme Lob auf Erden,
Mein Gott, in allen Gnaden hin!
Im Himmel soll es besser werden,
Wenn ich bei deinen Engeln bin.
Da sing' ich dir im höhern Chor
Viel tausend Halleluja vor.

This cento from Johann Mentzer's hymn "O dass ich tausend Zungen hätte" is composed of Stanzas 1, 3, 4, 5, 14, and 15 of the original, which first appeared in Freylinghausen's *Neues Geistreiches Gesangbuch,* Halle, 1704. Another cento of this hymn is the Trinity hymn No. 243, composed of Stanzas 1, 6, 7, 8, and 12.

Mentzer's hymn is one of the finest and most popular hymns of praise that have come to us from the German.

We know nothing definite about the circumstances under which this hymn was written. Lauxmann says this hymn was written in 1704, after Mentzer's house had burned down. But a Pastor Richter at Kemnitz, where Mentzer was pastor from 1696 on, claimed that the parsonage there had been built in the years 1696—97 and had never been destroyed by fire. However, in 1697 a farmhouse near by was demolished by lightning, and this may have given Mentzer the incentive to write the hymn, to impress the truth that the Christian has many reasons for praise and thanksgiving even in the midst of calamities that may befall him.

The composite translation is based on those by Dr. H. Mills (*Horae Germanicae,* 1845) and Catherine Winkworth (*Lyra Germanica,* 1st series, 1855).

The tune "O dass ich tausend Zungen hätte" is very likely by Johann Balthasar König, published in his *Harmonischer Liederschatz,* Frankfurt, 1738, where it was set to Angelus Silesius's hymn "Ach sagt mir nichts von Gold und Schätzen." It has practically become wedded to Mentzer's hymn.

31   When All Thy Mercies, O My God

1. When all Thy mercies, O my God,
   My rising soul surveys,
   Transported with the view, I'm lost
   In wonder, love, and praise.

2. Ten thousand thousand precious gifts
   My daily thanks employ;
   Nor is the least a cheerful heart
   That tastes those gifts with joy.

3. Through every period of my life
   Thy goodness I'll pursue
   And after death, in distant worlds,
   The glorious theme renew.

4. When nature fails, and day and night
   Divide Thy works no more,
   My ever grateful heart, O Lord,
   Thy mercies shall adore.

5. Through all eternity to Thee
   A joyful song I'll raise;
   But, oh! eternity's too short
   To utter all Thy praise.

This cento by Joseph Addison is composed of Stanzas 1, 10, 11, 12, and 13 of the poem as it appeared in thirteen stanzas in his *Spectator*, Saturday, August 9, 1712, where it formed the conclusion of an essay on "Gratitude." He had written:

> There is not a more pleasing exercise of the mind than gratitude. It is accompanied with such an inward satisfaction that the duty is sufficiently rewarded by the performance. If gratitude is due from man to man, how much more from man to his Maker! Every blessing we enjoy, by what means soever it may be derived upon us, is the gift of Him who is the great Author of good and Father of mercies.

The omitted Stanzas 2 to 9 are as follows:

2. Oh, how shall words with equal warmth
   The gratitude declare
   That glows within my ravished heart?
   But Thou canst read it there.

3. Thy providence my life sustained
   And all my wants redrest
   When in the silent womb I lay
   And hung upon the breast.

4. To all my weak complaints and cries
   Thy mercy lent an ear
   Ere yet my feeble thoughts had learned
   To form themselves in prayer.

5. Unnumbered comforts to my soul
   Thy tender care bestowed
   Before my infant heart conceived
   From whom those comforts flowed.

6. When in the slippery paths of youth
   With heedless steps I ran,
   Thine arm unseen conveyed me safe
   And led me up to man.

7. Through hidden dangers, toils, and death
   It gently cleared my way,
   And through the pleasing snares of vice,
   More to be feared than they.

8. When worn with sickness, oft hast Thou
   With health renewed my face;
   And when in sins and sorrows sunk,
   Revived my soul with grace.

9. Thy bounteous hand with worldly bliss
   Has made my cup run o'er
   And in a kind and faithful friend
   Has doubled all my store.

The tune "Winchester Old" first appeared in *The Whole Book of Psalms*, Thomas Este, 1592, set to a metrical version of Ps. 84 and ascribed to G. Kirby.

32   Redeemed, Restored, Forgiven

1. Redeemed, restored, forgiven,
   Through Jesus' precious blood,
   Heirs of His home in heaven,
   Oh, praise our pardoning God!
   Praise Him in tuneful measures
   Who gave His Son to die;
   Praise Him whose sevenfold treasures
   Enrich and sanctify.

2. Once on the dreary mountain
   We wandered far and wide,
   Far from the cleansing fountain,
   Far from the pierced side;
   But Jesus sought and found us
   And washed our guilt away;
   With cords of love He bound us
   To be His own for aye.

WORSHIP AND PRAISE

3. Dear Master, Thine the glory
   Of each recovered soul.
   Ah! who can tell the story
   Of love that made us whole?
   Not ours, not ours, the merit;
   Be Thine alone the praise
   And ours a thankful spirit
   To serve Thee all our days.

4. Now keep us, holy Savior,
   In Thy true love and fear
   And grant us of Thy favor
   The grace to persevere
   Till, in Thy new creation,
   Earth's time-long travail o'er,
   We find our full salvation
   And praise Thee evermore.

Sir Henry William Baker wrote this hymn during a holiday in Ireland. It is dated "Killarney, Sept. 1876." It was published in the following November in the *Monkland Parish Magazine*. The compilers of *Hymns Ancient and Modern* included it in *Hymns for Mission Churches* and, in 1889, in the Supplement to the Revised Edition of *Hymns Ancient and Modern*.

The tune "Ich dank' dir, lieber Herre" was originally combined with the secular folk-song "Entlaubt ist uns der Walde gen disem Winter Kalt," popular as early as the fifteenth century. The oldest printed source is Hans Gerle's *Musika Teutsch*, etc., Nürnberg, 1532. The melody was taken over, in altered forms, into the hymnals of the Church soon afterwards.

The Lord hath Helped Me Hitherto   33

1. The Lord hath helped me hitherto
   By His surpassing favor;
   His mercies every morn were new,
   His kindness did not waver.
   God hitherto hath been my Guide,
   Hath pleasures hitherto supplied,
   And hitherto hath helped me.

   Bis hieher hat mich Gott gebracht
   Durch seine grosse Güte;
   Bis hieher hat er Tag und Nacht
   Bewahrt Herz und Gemüte;
   Bis hieher hat er mich geleit't,
   Bis hieher hat er mich erfreut,
   Bis hieher mir geholfen.

2. I praise and thank Thee, Lord, my God,
   For Thine abundant blessing
   Which heretofore Thou hast bestowed
   And I am still possessing.
   Inscribe this on my memory:
   The Lord hath done great things for me
   And graciously hath helped me.

   Hab Lob und Ehre, Preis und Dank
   Für die bisher'ge Treue,
   Die du, o Gott, mir lebenslang
   Bewiesen täglich neue!
   In mein Gedächtnis schreib' ich an:
   Der Herr hat grosse Ding' getan
   An mir und mir geholfen.

3. Help me henceforth, O God of grace,
   Help me on each occasion,
   Help me in each and every place,
   Help me through Jesus' Passion;
   Help me in life and death, O God,
   Help me through Jesus' dying blood;
   Help me as Thou hast helped me!

   Hilf ferner auch, mein treuer Hort,
   Hilf mir zu allen Stunden!
   Hilf mir an all und jedem Ort,
   Hilf mir durch Jesu Wunden;
   Hilf mir im Leben, Tod und Not
   Durch Christi Schmerzen, Blut und Tod:
   Hilf mir, wie du geholfen!

This is one of our most popular hymns of praise from the German. The author, Ämilie Juliane, countess of Schwarzburg-Rudolstadt, published it, in 1699, in her devotional book *Tägliches Morgen-, Mittags- und Abend-Opffer*, Rudolstadt, to be sung on "Wednesdays after the meal."

The translation is by Prof. August Crull, 1882.

The tune "Allein Gott in der Höh' sei Ehr'" first appeared in Valentin Schumann's *Geistliche Lieder*, Leipzig, 1539, coupled with Nikolaus Decius's hymn beginning with the same line. (See Hymn No. 237.) It is generally ascribed to Nikolaus Decius. It is evidently an adaptation from an old liturgical tone to the words "et in terra pax hominibus bonae voluntatis" in the "Gloria ad Kyrie magnum dominicale." (S. Kümmerle.) Johann Sebastian Bach uses this *chorale* in several of his cantatas, and Felix Mendelssohn uses it in his *St. Paul*.

34   My Soul, Now Bless Thy Maker

1. My soul, now bless thy Maker!
    Let all within me bless His name
 Who maketh thee partaker
    Of mercies more than thou dar'st claim.
 Forget Him not whose meekness
    Still bears with all thy sin,
 Who healeth all thy weakness,
    Renews thy life within;
 Whose grace and care are endless
    And saved thee through the past;
 Who leaves no sufferer friendless,
    But rights the wronged at last.

2. He shows to man His treasure
    Of judgment, truth, and righteousness,
 His love beyond all measure,
    His yearning pity o'er distress,
 Nor treats us as we merit,
    But lays His anger by.
 The humble, contrite spirit
    Finds His compassion nigh;
 And high as heaven above us,
    As break from close of day,
 So far, since He doth love us,
    He puts our sins away.

3. For as a tender father
    Hath pity on his children here,
 He in His arms will gather
    All who are His in childlike fear.
 He knows how frail our powers
    Who but from dust are made;
 We flourish like the flowers,
    And even so we fade;
 The wind but o'er them passes,
    And all their bloom is o'er, —
 We wither like the grasses,
    Our place knows us no more.

4. God's grace alone endureth,
    And children's children yet shall prove
 How He with strength assureth
    The hearts of all that seek His love.
 In heaven is fixed His dwelling,
    His rule is over all;
 Angels, in might excelling,
    Bright hosts, before Him fall.
 Praise Him, who ever reigneth,
    All ye who hear His Word,
 Nor our poor hymns disdaineth —
    My soul, oh, bless the Lord!

Nun lob, mein' Seel', den Herren,
    Was in mir ist, den Namen sein!
Sein' Wohltat tut er mehren,
    Vergiss es nicht, o Herze mein!
Hat dir dein' Sünd' vergeben
    Und heilt dein' Schwachheit gross,
Errett't dein armes Leben,
    Nimmt dich in seinen Schoss,
Mit rechtem Trost beschüttet,
    Verjüngt dem Adler gleich.
Der Kön'g schafft Recht, behütet,
    Die leiden in sein'm Reich.

Er hat uns wissen lassen
    Sein herrlich Recht und sein Gericht,
Dazu sein' Güt' ohn' Massen,
    Es mangelt an Erbarmung nicht.
Sein'n Zorn lässt er wohl fahren,
    Straft nicht nach unsrer Schuld,
Die Gnad' tut er nicht sparen,
    Den Blöden ist er hold.
Sein' Güt' ist hoch erhaben
    Ob den'n, die fürchten ihn.
So fern der Ost vom Abend,
    Ist unsre Sünd' dahin.

Wie sich ein Mann erbarmet
    Über sein' junge Kinderlein,
So tut der Herr uns Armen,
    So wir ihn kindlich fürchten rein.
Er kennt das arm' Gemächte
    Und weiss, wir sind nur Staub,
Gleichwie das Gras, von Rechte,
    Ein' Blum' und fallend Laub,
Der Wind nur drüber wehet,
    So ist es nimmer da:
Also der Mensch vergehet,
    Sein End', das ist ihm nah.

Die Gottesgnad' alleine
    Bleibt stet und fest in Ewigkeit
Bei seiner lieben G'meine,
    Die steht in seiner Furcht bereit,
Die seinen Bund behalten.
    Er herrscht im Himmelreich.
Ihr starken Engel, waltet
    Sein's Lobs und dient zugleich
Dem grossen Herrn zu Ehren
    Und treibt sein heil'ges Wort,
Mein' Seel' soll auch vermehren
    Sein Lob an allem Ort.

Martin Chemnitz, the great Lutheran theologian and one of the authors of the *Formula of Concord,* is given as authority for the statement that Johann Gramann (Graumann; Poliander) wrote this hymn in 1525, based on Ps. 103, at the request of his friend the Margrave Albrecht of Brandenburg-Ansbach, a follower of Luther's and supporter of the Reformation. It is without question one of our most majestic and most fervent hymns of praise, one that should be in the reportory of every Lutheran congregation. A fifth stanza, evidently not by Gramann, appeared in 1555 and was added to the hymn in a number of German hymnals. It reads:

5. Sei Lob und Preis mit Ehren
    Gott Vater, Sohn und Heil'gem Geist!
 Der woll' in uns vermehren,
    Was er uns aus Genad' verheisst,
 Dass wir ihm fest vertrauen,
    Gänzlich uns lass'n auf ihn,
 Von Herzen auf ihn bauen,
    Dass uns'r Herz, Mut und Sinn
 Ihm festiglich anhangen.
    Drauf singen wir zur Stund':
 Amen, wir werd'n's erlangen,
    Glaub'n wir aus Herzensgrund.

WORSHIP AND PRAISE

The hymn was used by Gustavus Adolphus on April 24, 1632, at the first restored Protestant service in Augsburg and also by the inhabitants of Osnabrück, in Westphalia, as a thanksgiving at the close of the Thirty Years' War on October 25, 1648.

The translation is by Catherine Winkworth, slightly altered, in her *Chorale Book for England,* 1863.

The composer of the tune "Nun lob', mein' Seel'" is unknown, although it may have been written by Dr. Gramann or by Johann Kugelmann, in whose *Concentus Novi,* etc., it first appeared in 1540.

Songs of Praise the Angels Sang — 35

1. Songs of praise the angels sang,
Heaven with alleluias rang,
When creation was begun,
When God spake and it was done.

2. Songs of praise awoke the morn
When the Prince of Peace was born;
Songs of praise arose when He
Captive led captivity.

3. Heaven and earth must pass away;
Songs of praise shall crown that day.
God will make new heavens and earth;
Songs of praise shall hail their birth.

4. And shall man alone be dumb
Till that glorious kingdom come?
No; the Church delights to raise
Psalms and hymns and songs of praise.

5. Saints below, with heart and voice,
Still in songs of praise rejoice;
Learning here, by faith and love,
Songs of praise to sing above.

6. Borne upon their latest breath,
Songs of praise shall conquer death;
Then, amidst eternal joy,
Songs of praise their powers employ.

James Montgomery first published this hymn in 1819. It bore the title "God Worthy of All Praise." It is a typical Montgomery hymn, showing a wide knowledge of the Scriptures. In this hymn he calls on man to praise God and to follow the example of the angels, who sang in praise of the creation (Job 38:7) and at the birth of Christ (Luke 2:14) and who will sing at the final consummation of all things.

The third line of Stanza 1 was originally "When Jehovah's work begun." Most modern hymnals agree in using the line as altered in our text.

The tune "Innocents," also called "All Saints," has been difficult to trace to its original source. It is thought to be an old French melody of the thirteenth century. Lightwood tells us that the tune occurs at the end of Vol. III of the *Parish Choir,* published by the Society for Promoting Church Music, middle of the last century, where it appears among a number of old psalm-tunes and where it is appointed to be sung to a hymn for *Holy Innocents' Day,* hence the name "Innocents." The composer is unknown. Hymn-book editors seem generally agreed that it is of French, thirteenth-century origin.

Now Thank We All Our God — 36

1. Now thank we all our God
With heart and hands and voices,
Who wondrous things hath done,
In whom His world rejoices;
Who from our mother's arms
Hath blessed us on our way
With countless gifts of love,
And still is ours today.

2. Oh, may this bounteous God
Through all our life be near us,
With ever joyful hearts
And blessed peace to cheer us;
And keep us in His grace
And guide us when perplexed
And free us from all ills
In this world and the next.

Nun danket alle Gott
Mit Herzen, Mund und Händen,
Der grosse Dinge tut
An uns und allen Enden,
Der uns von Mutterleib
Und Kindesbeinen an
Unzählig viel zugut
Und noch jetzund getan!

Der ewig reiche Gott
Woll' uns bei unserm Leben
Ein immer fröhlich Herz
Und edlen Frieden geben
Und uns in seiner Gnad'
Erhalten fort und fort
Und uns aus aller Not
Erlösen hier und dort!

3. All praise and thanks to God
   The Father now be given,
The Son, and Him who reigns
   With them in highest heaven:
The one eternal God,
   Whom earth and heaven adore!
For thus it was, is now,
   And shall be evermore.

Lob, Ehr' und Preis sei Gott
   Dem Vater und dem Sohne
Und dem, der beiden gleich
   Im höchsten Himmelsthrone,
Dem dreieinigen Gott,
   Als es im Anfang war
Und ist und bleiben wird
   Jetzund und immerdar!

This German "Te Deum" was, according to James Mearns, published in Martin Rinckart's *Jesu Hertz-Büchlein*, 1663. He adds: "There does not seem any good reason for supposing that it did not appear in the first edition, 1636." In this book the hymn was entitled "Grace" ("Tisch-Gebetlein," *i. e.*, a short table-prayer). The various stories told about the origin of this hymn seem to be legendary; nor was it written in thanksgiving for the Peace of Westphalia, 1648, which put an end to the Thirty Years' War.

The first two stanzas of the hymn are evidently based on Ecclus. 50: 22-24: "Now, therefore, bless ye the God of all, which only doeth wondrous things everywhere, which exalteth our days from the womb and dealeth with us according to His mercy. He grant us joyfulness of heart and that peace may be in our days in Israel forever; that He would confirm His mercy with us and deliver us at His time." The last stanza is a metrical form of the "Gloria Patri." See also Ecclus. 39, last verse.

The translation is by Catherine Winkworth, *Lyra Germanica*, second series, 1858.

The tune "Nun danket alle Gott," also called "Wittenberg," is found in the third edition of Johann Crüger's *Praxis Pietatis Melica*, 1648, and is very likely by Crüger himself. The hymn was sung to this tune to celebrate the Peace of Westphalia, December 10, 1648, and has since been widely used for all celebrations of praise and thanksgiving.

37   Lord, 'Tis Not that I did Choose Thee

1. Lord, 'tis not that I did choose Thee;
   That, I know, could never be;
For this heart would still refuse Thee
   Had Thy grace not chosen me.
Thou hast from the sin that stained me
   Washed and cleansed and set me free
And unto this end ordained me,
   That I ever live to Thee.

2. 'Twas Thy grace in Christ that called me,
   Taught my darkened heart and mind;
Else the world had yet enthralled me,
   To Thy heavenly glories blind.
Now my heart owns none above Thee;
   For Thy grace alone I thirst,
Knowing well that, if I love Thee,
   Thou, O Lord, didst love me first.

3. Praise the God of all creation;
   Praise the Father's boundless love.
Praise the Lamb, our Expiation,
   Priest and King enthroned above.
Praise the Spirit of salvation,
   Him by whom our spirits live.
Undivided adoration
   To the great Jehovah give.

This hymn by Josiah Conder was first published in Dr. John Leifchild's *Original Hymns*, 1843, in this form under the title *Chosen of God:*

1. 'Tis not that I did choose Thee,
   For, Lord, that could not be;
This heart would still refuse Thee;
   But thou hast chosen me; —
Hast, from the sin that stained me
   Washed me and set me free
And to this end ordained me,
   That I should live to Thee.

2. 'Twas sovereign mercy called me
   And taught my opening mind;
The world had else enthralled me,
   To heavenly glories blind.
My heart owns none above Thee;
   For Thy rich grace I thirst;
This knowing, — if I love Thee,
   Thou must have loved me first.

WORSHIP AND PRAISE

In the *Church Praise Book*, New York, 1882, it was altered and the 7, 6 meter changed by an unknown hand to 8, 5, thus:

1. Lord, 'tis not that I did choose Thee,
    That could never be;
  For this heart would still refuse Thee,
    Thou hast chosen me:
  Hast from all the sin that stained me
    Washed and set me free
  And unto this end ordained me,
    That I live to Thee.

2. 'Twas Thy sovereign mercy called me,
    Taught my opening mind;
  Else the world had yet enthralled me,
    To Thy glories blind.
  Now my heart owns none above Thee;
    For Thy grace I thirst,
  Knowing well that, if I love Thee,
    Thou didst love me first.

This Doxology was added later:

    Praise the God of all creation
      For His boundless love;
    Praise the Lamb, our Expiation,
      Priest enthroned above;
    Praise the Spirit of salvation,
      Him by whom we live;
    Undivided adoration
      To the Godhead give.

The present version is from the *Australian Lutheran Hymn-Book*, 1925. The editors of that book altered the text to eliminate the Calvinistic theology in Stanza 2 and to give the hymn a metrical form to which a familiar tune might be used.

The tune "O du Liebe meiner Liebe," also called "Cassel" and "Lucerne," is from Johann Thommen's *Erbaulicher Musikalischer Christenschatz*, Basel, 1745, set to a German hymn of unknown authorship, beginning with the same line. It was already in use among the Moravian Brethren at Herrnhut before that date. Thommen calls it a "Herrnhut tune." Among them it was called "O gesegnetes Regieren." It is supposed to have been a folk-tune originally, used with a popular song, beginning "Sollen nun die grünen Jahre."

The Lord, My God, be Praised   38

1. The Lord, my God, be praised,
    My Light, my Life from heaven;
  My Maker, who to me
    Hath soul and body given;
  My Father, who doth shield
    And keep me day by day,
  Doth make each moment yield
    New blessings on my way.

2. The Lord, my God, be praised,
    My Trust, my Life from heaven,
  The Father's own dear Son,
    Whose life for me was given;
  Who for my sin atoned
    With His most precious blood,
  Who giveth me by faith
    The highest heavenly good.

3. The Lord, my God, be praised,
    My Hope, my Life from heaven,
  The Spirit, whom the Son
    In love to me hath given.
  'Tis He revives my heart,
    'Tis He that gives me power,
  Help, comfort, and support
    In sorrow's gloomy hour.

4. The Lord, my God, be praised,
    My God, who ever liveth,
  To whom the heavenly host
    All praise and honor giveth.
  The Lord, my God, be praised,
    In whose great name I boast,
  God Father, God the Son,
    And God the Holy Ghost.

Gelobet sei der Herr,
  Mein Gott, mein Licht, mein Leben,
Mein Schöpfer, der mir hat
  Mein Leib und Seel' gegeben,
Mein Vater, der mich schützt
  Von Mutterleibe an,
Der alle Augenblick'
  Viel Gut's an mir getan!

Gelobet sei der Herr,
  Mein Gott, mein Heil, mein Leben,
Des Vaters liebster Sohn,
  Der sich für mich gegeben,
Der mich erlöset hat
  Mit seinem teuren Blut,
Der mir im Glauben schenkt
  Das allerhöchste Gut!

Gelobet sei der Herr,
  Mein Gott, mein Trost, mein Leben,
Des Vaters werter Geist,
  Den mir der Sohn gegeben,
Der mir mein Herz erquickt,
  Der mir gibt neue Kraft,
Der mir in aller Not
  Rat, Trost und Hilfe schafft!

Gelobet sei der Herr,
  Mein Gott, der ewig lebet,
Den alles lobt, was
  In allen Lüften schwebet!
Gelobet sei der Herr,
  Des Name heilig heisst:
Gott Vater, Gott der Sohn
  Und Gott der werte Geist,

5. To Him with joyful song
   Our praises we are bringing
  And with the angel throng
   Thrice "Holy" we are singing.
  With one united voice
   The Church doth Him adore,
  The Lord, my God, be praised
   Now and forevermore.

Dem wir das Heilig jetzt
 Mit Freuden lassen klingen
Und mit der Engel Schar
 Das Heilig! Heilig! singen,
Den herzlich lobt und preist
 Die ganze Christenheit.
Gelobet sei mein Gott
 In alle Ewigkeit!

This is one of the best hymns of Johann Olearius. Originally written for Trinity Sunday and based on the Gospel for that feast, it was first published in his monumental hymnal *Geistliche Singekunst*, 1671. It was entitled "Encouragement from the Gospel to thankful meditation on this great mystery."

The translation is by Prof. August Crull, altered.

For the tune "Nun danket alle Gott" see Hymn No. 36.

39   Praise to the Lord, the Almighty

1. Praise to the Lord, the Almighty,
    the King of creation!
  O my soul, praise Him,
    for He is thy Health and Salvation!
  Join the full throng;
  Wake, harp and psalter and song;
  Sound forth in glad adoration!

Lobe den Herren, den mächtigen König
 der Ehren!
Meine geliebete Seele, das ist mein
 Begehren.
Kommet zuhauf!
Psalter und Harfe, wacht auf!
Lasset die Musikam hören!

2. Praise to the Lord, who o'er all things
    so wondrously reigneth,
  Who, as on wings of an eagle, uplifteth,
    sustaineth.
  Hast thou not seen
  How thy desires all have been
  Granted in what He ordaineth?

Lobe den Herren, der alles so herrlich
 regieret,
Der dich auf Adelers Fittichen sicher
 geführet,
Der dich erhält,
Wie es dir selber gefällt.
Hast du nicht dieses verspüret?

3. Praise to the Lord, who hath fearfully,
    wondrously, made thee;
  Health hath vouchsafed and, when heedlessly
    falling, hath stayed thee.
  What need or grief
  Ever hath failed of relief? —
  Wings of His mercy did shade thee.

Lobe den Herren, der künstlich und
 fein dich bereitet,
Der dir Gesundheit verliehen, dich
 freundlich geleitet!
In wieviel Not
Hat nicht der gnädige Gott
Über dir Flügel gebreitet!

4. Praise to the Lord, who doth prosper
    thy work and defend thee,
  Who from the heavens the streams of His
    mercy doth send thee.
  Ponder anew
  What the Almighty can do,
  Who with His love doth befriend thee.

Lobe den Herren, der deinen Stand
 sichtbar gesegnet,
Der aus dem Himmel mit Strömen
 der Liebe geregnet!
Denke daran,
Was der Allmächtige kann,
Der dir mit Liebe begegnet!

5. Praise to the Lord! Oh, let all that
    is in me adore Him!
  All that hath life and breath, come now
    with praises before Him!
  Let the Amen
  Sound from His people again;
  Gladly for aye we adore Him.

Lobe den Herren, was in mir ist lobe
 den Namen!
Alles, was Odem hat, lobe mit Abrahams
 Samen!
Er ist dein Licht,
Seele, vergiss es ja nicht!
Lobende, schliesse mit Amen!

This is one of the most widely sung praise-hymns of the Christian Church. The author is Joachim Neander. The hymn was first published in Neander's *Glaub- und Liebesübung: aufgemuntert durch einfältige Bundes Lieder und Danck-Psalmen*, Bremen, 1679.

The translation is by Catherine Winkworth, slightly altered. It appeared in her *Chorale Book for England* in 1863.

The tune "Lobe den Herren, den mächtigen König der Ehren" first appeared in *Ander Theil des Erneuerten Gesangbuch*, 2d edition, Stralsund, 1665, where it was set to the hymn "Hast du denn, Liebster, dein Angesicht gänzlich verborgen." Neander adapted this tune to his text in 1679, a union that has continued to this day.

The God of Abraham Praise   40

1. The God of Abraham praise;
All praisèd be His name
Who was and is and is to be
And still the same!
The one eternal God,
Ere aught that now appears;
The First, the Last: beyond all thought
His timeless years!

2. The God of Abraham praise,
At whose supreme command
From earth I rise and seek the joys
At His right hand.
I all on earth forsake,
Its wisdom, fame, and power,
And Him my only Portion make,
My Shield and Tower.

3. He by Himself hath sworn, —
I on His oath depend, —
I shall, on eagles' wings upborne,
To heaven ascend;
I shall behold His face,
I shall His power adore
And sing the wonders of His grace
Forevermore.

4. The whole triumphant host
Give thanks to God on high;
"Hail, Father, Son, and Holy Ghost!"
They ever cry.
Hail, Abraham's God and mine! —
I join the heavenly lays, —
All might and majesty are Thine,
And endless praise.

Tradition has it that the author, Thomas Olivers, wrote this hymn at the home of his friend John Bakewell, at Westminster, in 1770. In Josiah Miller's *Singers and Songs of the Church,* 1869, we are told:

> The son of a Wesleyan minister said a few years ago: "I remember my father telling me that he was once standing in the aisle of the City Road Chapel during a conference in Wesley's time. Thomas Olivers, one of the preachers, came down to him and said, 'Look at this; I have rendered it from the Hebrew, giving it, as far as I could, a Christian character, and I have called on Leon, the Jew, who has given me a synagog melody to suit it; here is the tune, and it is to be called Leoni.'"

The hymn is a free Christian rendering of the Hebrew *Yigdal,* or Doxology, which summarizes in metrical form the thirteen articles of the Hebrew Creed. The cento before us is made up of Stanzas 1 (as altered in the Presbyterian *Hymnal*), 2, 4, and 12 of the hymn, of which the other stanzas and Olivers's original first stanza read as follows:

1. The God of Abrah'm praise,
Who reigns enthroned above;
Ancient of everlasting days
And God of Love:
JEHOVAH GREAT I AM!
By earth and heaven confest;
I bow and bless the sacred Name,
Forever blessed.

3. The God of Abrah'm praise,
Whose all-sufficient grace
Shall guide me all my happy days
In all my ways:
He calls a worm his friend!
He calls himself my God!
And he shall save me to the end
Through Jesus' blood.

5. Though nature's strength decay,
And earth and hell withstand,
To Canaan's bounds I urge my way
At His command:
The watery deep I pass,
With Jesus in my view;
And through the howling wilderness
My way pursue.

6. The goodly land I see,
With peace and plenty blessed;
A land of sacred liberty
And endless rest.
There milk and honey flow;
And oil and wine abound,
And trees of life forever grow,
With mercy crowned.

7. There dwells the Lord, our King,
THE LORD OUR RIGHTEOUSNESS
(Triumphant o'er the world and sin),
The Prince of Peace;
On Sion's sacred height,
His kingdom still maintains;
And glorious with His saints in light
Forever reigns.

8. He keeps His own secure,
He guards them by His side,
Arrays in garments, white and pure,
His spotless bride:
With streams of sacred bliss,
With groves of living joys —
With all the fruits of Paradise
He still supplies.

9. Before the great THREE-ONE
They all exulting stand;
And tell the wonders he hath done
Through all their land;
The listening spheres attend
And swell the growing fame
And sing the songs which never end,
The wondrous NAME.

10. The God who reigns on high,
The great archangels sing,
And "Holy, holy, holy," cry,
"ALMIGHTY KING!
"Who Was and Is the same
"And evermore shall be.
"JEHOVAH — FATHER — GREAT I AM!
"We worship Thee."

WORSHIP AND PRAISE

11. Before the SAVIOR'S face
The ransomed nations bow;
O'erwhelmed at His almighty grace,
Forever new:
He shows His prints of love —
They kindle — to a flame!
And sound through all the worlds above
The slaughtered LAMB.

The hymn was published as a tract, *A Hymn to the God of Abraham*, undated, by Olivers, and passed through at least eight editions within a very short time.

The tune "Yigdal" or "Leoni" was obtained by Olivers from Meyer Leon, as stated above. It is probably of seventeenth-century origin. It is said that Meyer Leon, a cantor in the Duke's Place Synagog in London, who had a wide reputation as a singer, was dismissed from the synagog for taking part in a performance of the *Messiah*.

41   Wondrous King, All-Glorious

1. Wondrous King, all-glorious,
Sovereign Lord victorious,
Oh, receive our praise with favor!
From Thee welled God's kindness
Though we in our blindness
Strayed from Thee, our blessed Savior.
Strengthen Thou, Help us now;
Let our tongues be singing,
Thee our praises bringing.

2. Heavens, spread the story
Of our Maker's glory,
All the pomp of earth obscuring.
Sun, thy rays be sending,
Thy bright beams expending,
Light to all the earth assuring.
Moon and star, Praise afar
Him who glorious made you;
The vast heavens aid you.

3. O my soul, rejoicing,
Sing, thy praises voicing,
Sing, with hymns of faith adore Him!
All who here have being,
Shout, your voices freeing,
Bow down in the dust before Him.
He is God Sabaoth;
Praise alone the Savior
Here and there forever!

4. Hallelujahs render
To the Lord most tender,
Ye who know and love the Savior.
Hallelujahs sing ye,
Ye redeemed, oh, bring ye
Hearts that yield Him glad behavior.
Blest are ye Endlessly;
Sinless there forever,
Ye shall laud Him ever.

Wunderbarer König,
Herrscher von uns allen,
Lass dir unser Lob gefallen!
Deines Vaters Güte
Hast du lassen triefen,
Ob wir schon von dir wegliefen.
Hilf uns noch, stärk uns doch,
Lass die Zunge singen,
Lass die Stimme klingen!

Himmel, lobe prächtig
Deines Schöpfers Taten
Mehr als aller Menschen Staaten.
Grosses Licht der Sonne,
Schiesse deine Strahlen,
Die das grosse Rund bemalen.
Lobet gern, Mond und Stern',
Seid bereit, zu ehren
Einen solchen Herren!

O du, meine Seele,
Singe fröhlich, singe!
Singe deine Glaubenslieder!
Was den Odem holet,
Jauchze, preise, klinge;
Wirf dich in den Staub danieder!
Er ist Gott Zebaoth.
Er sei zu loben
Hier und ewig droben.

Halleluja bringe,
Wer den Herren kennet,
Wer den Herren Jesum liebet.
Hallelujah singe,
Welcher Christum nennet,
Sich von Herzen ihm ergibet.
O wohl dir, glaube mir,
Endlich wirst du droben
Ohne Sünd' ihn loben!

This hymn by Joachim Neander appeared in 1680 in "A und Ω." *Joachimi Neandri Glaub- und Liebesübung: — aufgemuntert durch einfältige Bundes Lieder und Dank-Psalmen.* Bremen, Hermann Brauer, 1680. It was entitled "Thanksgiving, Inciting Oneself to the Praise of God." It is based on Ps. 50:6. Neander had written in Stanza 1: "Deine Vaters Güte" (Thy fatherly goodness), referring to the First Person of the Holy Trinity; but by 1698 the line was altered by an unknown editor to "Deines Vaters Güte" (Thy Father's goodness), thus changing the address of the hymn to Jesus Christ as the

WORSHIP AND PRAISE

"wondrous King, all-glorious." Other hymnals followed this reading. The translation prepared in 1938 by the Rev. William J. Schaefer has done likewise. The hymn has enjoyed a wide usage in German churches.

The melody "Wunderbarer König" appeared with the text at its publication and is generally ascribed to Joachim Neander himself. (See Hymn No. 4.)

O Thou Love Unbounded 42

1. O Thou Love unbounded,
   Grant to eyes enshrouded,
   E'en for earthly sight beclouded,
 Grace to see Thy patience,
   All the world enfolding,
   Thy long-suffering thus beholding.
 Lo, its rays,
 To Thy praise,
   Joy to men bestowing,
   Like the sun are glowing.

2. All Thy vast dominion —
   Earth and air and ocean —
   Is the field of Thy devotion;
 And Thy great long-suffering,
   Ever newly tested,
   With more beauty is invested.
 Oh, how far
 Its wings are
   As they stretch forth daily
   Over hill and valley!

3. All our words are feeble
   As the heart upraises
   For Thy patience, Lord, its praises.
 With untold transgressions
   Day by day Thou bearest,
   Many million sinners sparest!
 Daily new
 Lovest, too,
   All who here offend Thee. —
   Who can comprehend Thee?

4. Sinners Thou forgivest,
   Hear'st when they implore Thee,
   When they, weeping, come before Thee;
 Thy right hand may threaten,
   Yet Thy mercy yearneth
   And Thine anger from us turneth,
 Though we may
 Yet delay
   Truly to espouse Thee,
   To new wrath arouse Thee.

5. Lord, no one has ever,
   Who on Thee believed,
   Justice here for grace received.
 All guilt Thou removest
   When we bow before Thee
   And in penitence implore
     Thee;
 For our smart
 Moves Thy heart;
   Thou wouldst mercy show us
   And with grace endow us.

6. O Most High, we praise Thee
   That Thou us regardest
   Nor our evil deeds rewardest!
 Zion's Hope, continue
   Thy dominion o'er us,
   Wielding well Thy scepter for us
 Lovingly,
 Patient be,
   Lord, we now implore Thee:
   Thine shall be the glory!

Unumschränkte Liebe,
   Gönne blöden Augen,
   Die sonst kaum auf Erden taugen,
 Dass sie in die Strahlen
   Deiner Langmut blicken,
   Die den Erdkreis wärmend schmücken
 Und zugleich
 Freudenreich
   Bösen und den Deinen
   Mit der Sonne scheinen.

Wasser, Luft und Erde,
   Ja, dein ganz Gebiete
   Ist ein Schauplatz deiner Güte;
 Deiner Langmut Ehre
   Wird durch neue Proben
   Immer herrlicher erhoben.
 O wie weit,
 O wie breit
   Über Berg' und Hügel
   Streckt sich ihre Flügel!

Was wir davon denken,
   Was wir sagen können,
   Ist ein Schatten nur zu nennen.
 Tag für Tag zu leiden,
   Tag für Tag zu dulden
   So viel' Millionen Schulden
 Und dazu
 Ohne Ruh'
   Lieben für das Hassen:
   Herr, wer kann das fassen?

Du vergibest Sünde,
   Hörst der Sünder Flehen,
   Wenn sie weinend vor dir stehen;
 Deine Rechte drohet
   Und erbarmt sich wieder,
   Legt die Pfeile gerne nieder.
 Tiefen Schmerz
 Fühlt dein Herz,
   Wenn durch ernste Strafen
   Du musst Bess'rung schaffen.

Herr, es hat noch keiner,
   Der zu dir gegangen,
   Für Genade Recht empfangen.
 Wer zu deinen Füssen
   Sich mit Tränen senket,
   Dem wird Straf' und Schuld
     geschenket;
 Unser Schmerz
 Rührt dein Herz,
   Und du willst der Armen
   Gnädig dich erbarmen.

König, sei gepriesen,
   Dass du so verschonest
   Und uns nicht nach Werken lohnest.
 Deiner Hand sei Ehre,
   Die so wohl regieret
   Und mit Ruhm den Zepter führet.
 Fahre fort
 Zions Hort,
   Langmut auszuüben
   Und die Welt zu lieben!

WORSHIP AND PRAISE

This unusual hymn of praise has been called "the pearl of all of Rambach's poetry" by none other than Wilhelm Nelle in his book *Geschichte des deutschen evangelischen Kirchenliedes*, one of the important works of its kind published in the present century. He adds further that because of its cumbersome first lines, in the original German, the hymn has been largely overlooked and neglected. The author, Johann Jakob Rambach, was one of the outstanding leaders among the German Pietists. The hymn before us, his best hymn and undoubtedly one of the best ever written in praise of the long-suffering of God, was first published in Rambach's *Geistreiches Haus-Gesangbuch*, Frankfurt and Leipzig, 1735. The translation is our own and was written for *The Lutheran Hymnal* in 1940.

For comments on the tune "Wunderbarer König" see Hymn No. 4.

43   We Sing the Almighty Power of God

1. We sing the almighty power of God,
Who bade the mountains rise,
Who spread the flowing seas abroad
And built the lofty skies.

2. We sing the wisdom that ordained
The sun to rule the day;
The moon shines, too, at His command,
And all the stars obey.

3. We sing the goodness of the Lord,
Who fills the earth with food,
Who formed His creatures by a word
And then pronounced them good.

4. Lord, how Thy wonders are displayed
Where'er we turn our eyes,
Whene'er we view the ground we tread
Or gaze upon the skies!

5. There's not a plant nor flower below
But makes Thy glories known;
And clouds arise and tempests blow
By order from Thy throne.

6. On Thee each moment we depend;
If Thou withdraw, we die.
Oh, may we ne'er that God offend
Who is forever nigh!

Isaac Watts first published this hymn in his *Divine and Moral Songs*, 1715, entitled "Praise for Creation and Providence."

For comments on the tune "Ich singe dir" see Hymn No. 29.

44   Ye Lands, to the Lord Make a Jubilant Noise

1. Ye lands, to the Lord make a jubilant noise;
Glory be to God!
Oh, serve Him with joy, in His presence now rejoice;
Sing praise unto God out of Zion!

2. Not we, but the Lord is our Maker, our God;
Glory be to God!
His people we are, and the sheep led by His rod;
Sing praise unto God out of Zion!

3. Oh, enter His gates with thanksgiving and praise;
Glory be to God!
To bless Him and thank Him our voices we will raise;
Sing praise unto God out of Zion!

4. For good is the Lord, and His mercy is sure;
Glory be to God!
To all generations His truth shall still endure;
Sing praise unto God out of Zion!

Al verden nu raabe for Herren med Fryd,
Lovet väre Gud!
Träd frem for hans ansigt med sang og jubellyd,
Guds menighed love nu Herren!

Kom, kjend Gud, din herre, du intet selv formaar,
Lovet väre Gud!
Han, han har dig gjort til sit folk og födes faar,
Guds menighed love nu Herren!

Gaar ind ad hans porte med lov og takkesang,
Lovet väre Gud!
Velsigner, höilover evindelig hans navn,
Guds menighed love nu Herren!

Guds godhed og miskundhed er ny i evighed,
Lovet väre Gud!
Fra slegt og til slegt skal hans sandhed vare ved,
Guds menighed love nu Herren!

[38]

CLOSE OF SERVICE

This Norwegian hymn by Ulrik V. Koren was first published in 1874 as a metrical version of Ps. 100. The translation is that by Mrs. Harriet Reynolds Spaeth, written in 1898, published in *The Lutheran Hymnary*, 1913, in an altered form.

The tune "Guds Menighed, syng" is by Erik Christian Hoff and was composed originally c. 1860 for a Norwegian text beginning with those words.

Now, the Hour of Worship O'er   45

1. Now, the hour of worship o'er,
   Teaching, hearing, praying, singing,
Let us gladly God adore,
   For His Word our praises bringing;
For the rich repast He gave us
Bless the Lord, who deigned to save us.

2. Now the Blessing cheers our heart,
   By His grace to us extended.
Let us joyfully depart;
   Be our souls to God commended.
May His Spirit ever guide us
And with all good gifts provide us!

3. Bless our going out, we pray,
   Bless our entrance in like measure;
Bless our bread, O Lord, each day,
   Bless our toil, our rest, our pleasure;
Bless us when we reach death's portal,
Bless us then with life immortal.

Nun Gott Lob, es ist vollbracht
   Singen, Beten, Lehren, Hören.
Gott hat alles wohl gemacht,
   Drum lasst uns sein Lob vermehren.
Unser Gott sei hoch gepreiset,
Dass er uns so wohl gespeiset.

Weil der Gottesdienst ist aus
   Und uns mitgeteilt der Segen,
So gehn wir mit Freud' nach Haus,
   Wandeln fein auf Gottes Wegen.
Gottes Geist uns ferner leite
Und uns alle vollbereite!

Unsern Ausgang segne Gott,
   Unsern Eingang gleichermassen,
Segne unser täglich Brot,
   Segne unser Tun und Lassen,
Segne uns mit sel'gem Sterben
Und mach uns zu Himmelserben!

According to *Koch,* this popular hymn for the close of worship was first published by Hartmann Schenk in his devotional book *Güldene Betkunst,* etc., Nürnberg, 1680. However, *Fischer* claims that this is an error, but nevertheless acknowledges Schenk's authorship on the authority of Schenk's sons, who possessed the original manuscript, and beginning with the *Schleusinger Gesangbuch,* 1692, his authorship seems to have been generally accepted by hymnbook editors.

The translation is a composite one, except the last stanza, which was prepared for *The Lutheran Hymnal* by Oscar Kaiser in 1938.

The tune "Liebster Jesu" is discussed under Hymn No. 16.

On What has Now been Sown   46

1. On what has now been sown
   Thy blessing, Lord, bestow;
The power is Thine alone
   To make it spring and grow.
Do Thou in grace the harvest raise,
And Thou alone shalt have the praise.

2. To Thee our wants are known,
   From Thee are all our powers;
Accept what is Thine own
   And pardon what is ours.
Our praises, Lord, and prayers receive
And to Thy Word a blessing give.

3. Oh, grant that each of us
   Now met before Thee here
May meet together thus
   When Thou and Thine appear
And follow Thee to heaven, our home.
E'en so, Amen, Lord Jesus, come!

This cento is another interesting example of the manner in which some of our favorite hymns received their final form. Stanza 1 is the last stanza of John Newton's interesting hymn entitled "Travailing in Birth for Souls. Gal. 4:19," first published in 1779, *Olney Hymns*, Book II, reading:

1. What contradictions meet
    In ministers' employ!
It is a bitter sweet,
    A sorrow full of joy:
No other post affords a place
    For equal honor or disgrace!

2. Who can describe the pain
    Which faithful preachers feel,
Constrained to speak in vain
    To hearts as hard as steel?
Or who can tell the pleasures felt
    When stubborn hearts begin to melt?

3. The Savior's dying love,
    The soul's amazing worth,
Their utmost efforts move
    And draw their bowels forth:
They pray and strive, their rest departs,
    Till Christ be formed in sinners' hearts.

4. If some small hope appear,
    They still are not content,
But with a jealous fear,
    They watch for the event:
Too oft they find their hopes deceived,
    Then how their inmost souls are grieved!

5. But when their pains succeed
    And from the tender blade
The ripening ears proceed,
    Their toils are overpaid:
No harvest joy can equal theirs
    To find the fruit of all their cares.

6. On what has now been sown,
    Thy blessing, Lord, bestow;
The power is Thine alone,
    To make it spring and grow:
Do Thou the gracious harvest raise,
    And Thou alone shalt have the praise.

Stanzas 2 and 3 are Newton's "Short Hymn for Close of Divine Service," *Olney Hymns*, Book III, 1779.

The tune "Darwall's 148th," also called "Darwall," by John Darwall, appeared in Aaron Williams's *New Universal Psalmodist*, 1770, where it was set to a new version of Ps. 148.

47 Savior, Again to Thy Dear Name We Raise

1. Savior, again to Thy dear name we raise
    With one accord our parting hymn of praise.
Once more we bless Thee ere our worship cease,
Then, lowly bending, wait Thy word of peace.

2. Grant us Thy peace upon our homeward way;
With Thee began, with Thee shall end, the day;
Guard Thou the lips from sin, the hearts from shame,
That in this house have called upon Thy name.

3. Grant us Thy peace, Lord, through the coming night;
Turn Thou for us its darkness into light.
From harm and danger keep Thy children free,
For dark and light are both alike to Thee.

4. Grant us Thy peace throughout our earthly life,
Our balm in sorrow and our stay in strife;
Then, when Thy voice shall bid our conflict cease,
Call us, O Lord, to Thine eternal peace.

This hymn ranks with the best evening hymns of the Church and is the most popular of the author's hymns. It was originally written by John Ellerton in five stanzas for the Festival of the Malpas, Middlewich, and the Nantwich Choral Association in 1866, and then revised and shortened to four stanzas by the author for the appendix to the original edition of *Hymns Ancient and Modern*, 1868. The text agrees with this version, except Line 3 of Stanza 1, which reads:

"We stand to bless Thee ere our worship cease."

The omitted stanza is:

"Grant us Thy peace — the peace Thou didst bestow
On Thine apostles in Thine hour of woe;
The peace Thou broughtest when at eventide
They saw Thy piercèd hands, Thy wounded side."

The tune "Ellers" is by Edward John Hopkins and was composed for this hymn in 1869.

CLOSE OF SERVICE

How Blest Are They Who Hear God's Word 48

1. How blest are they who hear God's Word
 And keep and heed what they have heard!
    They wisdom daily gather;
 Their light shines brighter day by day,
 And while they tread life's weary way,
 They have the oil of gladness
    To soothe their pain and sadness.

2. God's Word a treasure is to me,
 Through sorrow's night my sun shall be,
    The shield of faith in battle.
 The Father's hand hath written there
 My title as His child and heir,
 "The kingdom's thine forever."
    That promise faileth never.

3. Today I was my Savior's guest,
 My soul was here so richly blest,
    The Bread of Life receiving.
 Oh, may thereby my faith prevail,
 So that its fruits shall never fail
 Till my account is given
    Before the throne in heaven!

O salig den, Guds Ord har hört,
Bevaret og til Nytte fört!
   Han daglig Visdom lärte;
Fra Lys til Lys han vandre kan,
Og har i Livets Prövestand
En Salve for sit Hjerte
   Mod al sin Nöd og Smerte.

Guds Ord det er min rige Skat,
Min Sol i Sorgens mörke Nat,
   Mit Sverd i Troens Krige.
Guds Finger selv i Ordet skrev
Min Barne-Ret, mit Arve-Brev;
Den Skrift skal aldrig svige:
   Kom, arv et evigt Rige!

Jeg gik som til et däkket Bord
Idag og hörte Herrens Ord
   Og Själen sanked Föde.
Gid Troen derved vokse saa,
At Troens Frugt ei savnes maa,
Naar jeg for ham skal möde,
   Som for os alle döde!

This hymn was published by the Norwegian bishop Johan Nordahl Brun in his *Evangeliske Sange* (*Evangelical Hymns*) in 1786. Of his hymns the pious bishop stated: "Our divine worship is that garden from which I have gathered my flowers." This is one of his better hymns and bears witness "to a life of faith, which has its fountain in God Himself and which is nourished by His Word."

The translation is by Oluf H. Smeby and was published in *The Lutheran Hymnary*, 1913.

The tune "Min Själ og Aand" first appeared in Hans Thomissön's *Psalmebog*, 1569, as a setting for the hymn "Om himmeriges rige, saa ville vi tale." According to John Dahle it was written in the Phrygian mode, but has undergone many changes in the course of time.

Almighty God, Thy Word is Cast 49

1. Almighty God, Thy Word is cast
    Like seed into the ground;
 Now let the dew of heaven descend
    And righteous fruits abound.

2. Let not the foe of Christ and man
    This holy seed remove,
 But give it root in every heart
    To bring forth fruits of love.

3. Let not the world's deceitful cares
    The rising plant destroy,
 But let it yield a hundredfold
    The fruits of peace and joy.

4. Oft as the precious seed is sown,
    Thy quickening grace bestow
 That all whose souls the truth receive
    Its saving power may know.

John Cawood published this hymn in five stanzas in 1819. It is said to have been written in 1815. It was to be used "after the sermon." The omitted stanza is:

> Nor let Thy Word, so kindly sent
> To raise us to Thy throne,
> Return to Thee and sadly tell
> That we reject Thy Son.

The tune "Dundee" first appeared in the *Scottish Psalter,* 1615, and is there called "French Tune." It must not be confused with the tune "Windsor" (see Hymn No. 176), which is also called "Dundee" in some collections. Our tune came to England in 1621, appearing in Ravencroft's *Psalmes,* set to Ps. 36 and given the name "Dundy Tune."

CLOSE OF SERVICE

50   Lord, Dismiss Us with Thy Blessing

1. Lord, dismiss us with Thy blessing,
   Fill our hearts with joy and peace.
   Let us each, Thy love possessing,
   Triumph in redeeming grace.
   Oh, refresh us, Oh, refresh us,
   Traveling through this wilderness!

2. Thanks we give and adoration
   For Thy Gospel's joyful sound.
   May the fruits of Thy salvation
   In our hearts and lives abound;
   Ever faithful, Ever faithful,
   To the Truth may we be found!

3. So whene'er the signal's given
   Us from earth to call away,
   Borne on angels' wings to heaven,
   Glad the summons to obey,
   May we ever, May we ever,
   Reign with Christ in endless day!

There has been much dispute over the authorship of this popular hymn. Julian, in his *Dictionary of Hymnology*, devotes almost two pages to a detailed discussion of the hymns, four in all, that have been published with the same opening line. His conclusion is that John Fawcett is the author of our hymn, which was first published anonymously in 1773 in the *Supplement to the Shawbury Hymn Book*.

The first tune, "Regent Square," is by Henry Smart, written for *Psalms and Hymns for Divine Worship* (English Presbyterian), 1867. It was set to Horatius Bonar's hymn "Glory Be to God the Father." (See Hymn No. 244.)

The second tune, "New Ulm," is by Fritz Reuter and was written in 1910 for this hymn.

51   Now May He Who from the Dead

1. Now may He who from the dead
   Brought the Shepherd of the sheep,
   Jesus Christ, our King and Head,
   All our souls in safety keep!

2. May He teach us to fulfil
   What is pleasing in His sight,
   Perfect us in all His will,
   And preserve us day and night!

3. To that dear Redeemer's praise,
   Who the covenant sealed with blood,
   Let our hearts and voices raise
   Loud thanksgivings to our God.

John Newton published this hymn in the *Olney Hymns*, 1779, to be sung "after the sermon." It is based on Heb. 13:20-22.

The tune "Buckland" is by Leighton George Hayne, from *The Merton Tune Book*, 1863, which he edited together with H. W. Sergeant.

52   Almighty Father, Bless the Word

1. Almighty Father, bless the Word
   Which through Thy grace we now have heard,
   Oh, may the precious seed take root,
   Spring up, and bear abundant fruit!

2. We praise Thee for the means of grace
   As homeward now our steps we trace.
   Grant, Lord, that we who worshiped here
   May all at last in heaven appear.

This hymn is of unknown authorship and date. It was taken from *The Lutheran Hymnary*, 1913, where it is No. 56, set to the tune "Wenn wir in höchsten." (See Hymn No. 141.) Originally it seems to have appeared in Dr. W. A. Muhlenberg's *Church Poetry*, Philadelphia, 1823, as a hymn for "after the sermon."

For comments on the tune "Old Hundredth" see Hymn No. 13.

CLOSE OF SERVICE

Abide, O Dearest Jesus 53

1. Abide, O dearest Jesus,
Among us with Thy grace
That Satan may not harm us
Nor we to sin give place.

2. Abide, O dear Redeemer,
Among us with Thy Word
And thus now and hereafter
True peace and joy afford.

3. Abide with heavenly brightness
Among us, precious Light;
Thy truth direct and keep us
From error's gloomy night.

4. Abide with richest blessings
Among us, bounteous Lord;
Let us in grace and wisdom
Grow daily through Thy Word.

5. Abide with Thy protection
Among us, Lord, our Strength,
Lest world and Satan fell us
And overcome at length.

6. Abide, O faithful Savior,
Among us with Thy love;
Grant steadfastness and help us
To reach our home above.

Ach bleib mit deiner Gnade
Bei uns, Herr Jesu Christ,
Dass uns hinfort nicht schade
Des bösen Feindes List!

Ach bleib mit deinem Worte
Bei uns, Erlöser wert,
Dass uns beid' hier und dorte
Sei Güt' und Heil beschert!

Ach bleib mit deinem Glanze
Bei uns, du wertes Licht;
Dein' Wahrheit uns umschanze,
Damit wir irren nicht!

Ach bleib mit deinem Segen
Bei uns, du reicher Herr!
Dein' Gnad' und all's Vermögen
In uns reichlich vermehr!

Ach bleib mit deinem Schutze
Bei uns, du starker Held,
Dass uns der Feind nicht trutze,
Noch fäll' die böse Welt!

Ach bleib mit deiner Treue
Bei uns, mein Herr und Gott!
Beständigkeit verleihe,
Hilf uns aus aller Not!

This is one of our most popular hymns from the German. Josua Stegmann, according to James Mearnes, included this hymn in his *Suspiria Temporum*, Rinteln, 1628. A. F. W. Fischer, however, claims that it did not appear until 1630 in Stegmann's *Ernewerter Hertzen Seufftzer*, etc. Lüneburg. It has as its key-note the prayer of the two disciples at Emmaus, Luke 24:29.

It has often been translated into English and other languages. The translation is by Prof. Aug. Crull. A French translation begins with the line

"Demeure dans ta grace."

The tune "Christus, der ist mein Leben" is by Melchior Vulpius, first published in *Ein schön geistlich Gesangbuch*, etc., Jena, 1609. Johann Sebastian Bach uses this melody in his *chorale* cantata *Christus, der ist mein Leben*.

Guide Me, O Thou Great Jehovah 54

1. Guide me, O Thou great Jehovah,
   Pilgrim through this barren land.
I am weak but Thou art mighty;
   Hold me with Thy powerful hand.
      Bread of heaven,
Feed me till I want no more.

2. Open now the crystal fountain
   Whence the healing stream doth flow;
Let the fiery, cloudy pillar
   Lead me all my journey through.
      Strong Deliverer,
Be Thou still my Strength and Shield.

3. When I tread the verge of Jordan,
   Bid my anxious fears subside;
Death of death and hell's Destruction,
   Land me safe on Canaan's side.
      Songs of praises
I will ever give to Thee.

Arglwydd, arwain trwy'r anialwch
   Fi bererin gwael ei wedd,
Nad oes ynof nerth na bywyd,
   Fel yn gorwedd yn y bedd:
      Hollalluog
Ydyw'r un a'm cwyd i'r lan.

Agor y ffynnonau melus
   Sydd yn tarddu o'r Graig i maes;
'Rhyd yr anial mawr canlyned
   Afon iachawdwriaeth grâs;
      Rho imi hyny;
Dim i mi ond dy fwynhau.

Ymddiriedaf yn dy allu,
   Mawr yw'r gwaith a wnest erioed:
Ti gest angau, ti gest uffern,
   Ti gest Satan dan dy droed:
      Pen Calfaria,
Nac aed hwnw byth o'm cof.

CLOSE OF SERVICE

This hymn was originally published in Welsh in five stanzas, 1745, by William Williams, in his *Alleluia*, Bristol. Its title was "Strength to Pass through the Wilderness." Three stanzas were translated into English by Peter Williams and published in his *Hymns on Various Subjects*, 1771. Stanza 1 as in our text, Stanzas 2 and 3 as follows:

Open Thou the pleasant fountains,
  Where the living waters flow:
Let the river of salvation
  Follow all the desert through.
    May Thy presence
Alway lead and comfort me.

Lord, I trust Thy mighty power,
  Wondrous are Thy works of old;
Thou deliverest Thine from thraldom
  Who for naught themselves have sold;
    Thou didst conquer
Sin and Satan and the grave.

These stanzas are a translation of Stanzas 1, 3, 5, of the original.

William Williams, c. 1772, translated the hymn, retaining Peter Williams's Stanza 1 and then altering the other two and adding the following Stanza 4:

> Musing on my habitation,
>   Musing on my heavenly home,
> Fills my soul with heavenly longings:
>   Come, my Jesus, quickly come.
>   Vanity is all I see;
> Lord, I long to be with Thee.

He published this version in a tract entitled:

> "A Favorite Hymn,
>   sung by
> Lady Huntingdon's Young Collegians.
> Printed by the desire of many Christian friends."
>
> *Lord, give to it Thy blessing!*

Dr. Elvet Lewis wrote: "What Paul Gerhardt has been to Germany, what Isaac Watts has been to England, that and more has William Williams of Pantecelyn been to Wales."

The tune "Guide Me" is by George William Warren and was written in 1884.

ADVENT

The Church Year

Come, Thou Precious Ransom, Come   55

1. Come, Thou precious Ransom, come,
   Only Hope for sinful mortals!
   Come, O Savior of the world!
   Open are to Thee all portals.
   Come, Thy beauty let us see;
   Anxiously we wait for Thee.

2. Enter now my waiting heart,
   Glorious King and Lord most holy.
   Dwell in me and ne'er depart,
   Though I am but poor and lowly.
   Ah, what riches will be mine
   When Thou art my Guest Divine!

3. My hosannas and my palms
   Graciously receive, I pray Thee;
   Evermore, as best I can,
   Savior, I will homage pay Thee,
   And in faith I will embrace,
   Lord, Thy merit through Thy grace.

4. Hail, hosanna, David's Son!
   Help, Lord, hear our supplication!
   Let Thy kingdom, scepter, crown,
   Bring us blessing and salvation,
   That forever we may sing:
   Hail, hosanna! to our King.

Komm, du wertes Lösegeld,
Dessen alle Heiden hoffen;
Komm, o Heiland aller Welt,
Tor' und Türen stehen offen;
Komm in ungewohnter Zier,
Komm, wir warten mit Begier!

Zeuch auch in mein Herz hinein,
O du grosser Ehrenkönig,
Lass mich deine Wohnung sein!
Bin ich armer Mensch zu wenig,
Ei, so soll mein Reichtum sein,
Dass du bei mir ziehest ein.

Nimm mein Hosianna an
Mit den Siegespalmenzweigen!
Soviel ich nur immer kann,
Will ich Ehre dir erzeigen
Und im Glauben dein Verdienst
Mir zueignen zum Gewinst.

Hosianna, Davids Sohn!
Ach Herr, hilf, lass wohl gelingen!
Lass dein Zepter, Reich und Kron'
Uns viel Heil und Segen bringen,
Dass in Ewigkeit besteh':
Hosianna in der Höh'!

Johann Gottfried Olearius first published this hymn in his book *Jesus! Poetische Erstlinge an geistlichen Deutschen Liedern und Madrigalen*, Halle, 1664. It is based on Matt. 21:5-9. It was entitled "On Advent." The hymn has long been a favorite Advent hymn in the Lutheran Church.

The translation is by Prof. August Crull, somewhat altered.

The tune "Meinen Jesum lass' ich nicht" is found in the Darmstadt hymnal, *Neuverfertigtes Gesangbuch*, 1699, set to the text of the hymn beginning with that line. (See Hymn No. 365.) The composer is unknown. It has long been a popular melody.

Jesus Came, The Heavens Adoring   56

1. Jesus came, the heavens adoring,
   Came with peace from realms on high;
   Jesus came for man's redemption,
   Lowly came on earth to die;
   Alleluia! Alleluia!
   Came in deep humility.

2. Jesus comes again in mercy
   When our hearts are bowed with care;
   Jesus comes again in answer
   To an earnest, heartfelt prayer;
   Alleluia! Alleluia!
   Comes to save us from despair.

3. Jesus comes to hearts rejoicing,
   Bringing news of sins forgiven;
   Jesus comes in sounds of gladness,
   Leading souls redeemed to heaven.
   Alleluia! Alleluia!
   Now the gate of death is riven.

4. Jesus comes in joy and sorrow,
   Shares alike our hopes and fears;
   Jesus comes, whate'er befalls us,
   Glads our hearts, and dries our tears;
   Alleluia! Alleluia!
   Cheering e'en our failing years.

5. Jesus comes on clouds triumphant
   When the heavens shall pass away;
   Jesus comes again in glory.
   Let us, then, our homage pay,
   Alleluia! ever singing
   Till the dawn of endless day.

This hymn by Godfrey Thring appeared in Chope's *Hymnal*, 1864. It beautifully emphasizes the advents of the Lord: in humility for redemption; in mercy to the sinner; and in glory.

The tune "Sieh, hier bin ich" is from the Darmstadt hymnal *Geistreiches Gesangbuch*, 1698, set to Joachim Neander's hymn "Sieh, hier bin ich, Ehrenkönig."

[45]

ADVENT

57   O Bride of Christ, Rejoice

1. O bride of Christ, rejoice;
   Exultant raise thy voice
   To hail the day of glory
   Foretold in sacred story.
   Hosanna, praise, and glory!
   Our King, we bow before Thee.

2. Let shouts of gladness rise
   Triumphant to the skies.
   Now comes the King most glorious
   To reign o'er all victorious:
   Hosanna, etc.

3. He wears no kingly crown,
   Yet as a King is known;
   Though not arrayed in splendor,
   He still makes death surrender.
   Hosanna, etc.

4. The weak and timid find
   How meek He is and kind;
   To them He gives a treasure
   Of bliss beyond all measure.
   Hosanna, etc.

5. Thy heart now open wide,
   Bid Christ with thee abide.
   He graciously will hear thee
   And be forever near thee.
   Hosanna, etc.

6. Then go thy Lord to meet;
   Strew palm-leaves at His feet;
   Thy garments spread before Him
   And honor and adore Him.
   Hosanna, etc.

7. E'en babes with one accord
   With thee shall praise the Lord
   And every Gentile nation
   Respond with exultation:
   Hosanna, etc.

Fryd dig, du Kristi Brud,
Imod din Herre Gud!
For Haanden er hans Naade,
Som dig Profeten spaade.
Hosianna, Häder og Äre
Skal denne vor Konning väre!

Gak ud af dit Paulun,
Og se et glädligt Syn:
Her rider Ärens Konning,
Gläd dig, du Zions Dronning!
Hosianna o. s. v.

Et Asen hannem bär,
Som dog en Herre er,
Hans Pral er saare ringe,
Dog kan han Döden tvinge.
Hosianna o. s. v.

Sagtmodelig og god
I Sind og saa i Mod
Han Naade har at före,
Den skal hans Brud tilhöre.
Hosianna o. s. v.

Lad op dine Porte vid',
Kristus ind til dig rid!
Han agter dig at gjeste,
Din Salighed til Bedste.
Hosianna o. s. v.

Strö Grene paa hans Vei,
Spar dine Kläder ei,
Alt Folket bäre Palmer,
Og synge aandelige Salmer!
Hosianna o. s. v.

Umyndig' Börn og smaa
Skal gjöre ligesaa,
Den ganske hele Skare
Skal synge uden Fare:
Hosianna o. s. v.

    This hymn from the Danish is of unknown origin. It may be as early as the year 1600 A. D.

    The translation is by Victor O. Petersen, 1899, and is taken from *The Lutheran Hymnary*, 1913.

    The tune "Wo soll ich fliehen hin" is from Kaspar Stieler's *Der bussfertige Sünder oder geistliches Handbüchlein,* etc., Nürnberg, 1679. It may be a composition of Stieler's. It was set to Johann Heermann's repentance hymn, beginning with that line.

58   O Lord, How Shall I Meet Thee

1. O Lord, how shall I meet Thee,
   How welcome Thee aright?
   Thy people long to greet Thee,
   My Hope, my heart's Delight!
   O kindle, Lord, most holy,
   Thy lamp within my breast
   To do in spirit lowly
   All that may please Thee best.

2. Thy Zion strews before Thee
   Green boughs and fairest palms,
   And I, too, will adore Thee
   With joyous songs and psalms.
   My heart shall bloom forever
   For Thee with praises new
   And from Thy name shall never
   Withhold the honor due.

Wie soll ich dich empfangen,
Und wie begegn' ich dir,
O aller Welt Verlangen,
O meiner Seele Zier?
O Jesu, Jesu, setze
Mir selbst die Fackel bei,
Damit, was dich ergötze
Mir kund und wissend sei.

Dein Zion streut dir Palmen
Und grüne Zweige hin,
Und ich will dir in Psalmen
Ermuntern meinen Sinn.
Mein Herze soll dir grünen
In stetem Lob und Preis
Und deinem Namen dienen,
So gut es kann und weiss.

[46]

ADVENT

  3. I lay in fetters, groaning,
     Thou com'st to set me free;
   I stood, my shame bemoaning,
     Thou com'st to honor me;
   A glory Thou dost give me,
     A treasure safe on high,
   That will not fail or leave me
     As earthly riches fly.

  4. Love caused Thy incarnation,
     Love brought Thee down to me;
   Thy thirst for my salvation
     Procured my liberty.
   O love beyond all telling,
     That led Thee to embrace,
   In love all love excelling,
     Our lost and fallen race!

  5. Rejoice, then, ye sad-hearted,
     Who sit in deepest gloom,
   Who mourn o'er joys departed
     And tremble at your doom.
   Despair not, He is near you,
     Yea, standing at the door,
   Who best can help and cheer you
     And bids you weep no more.

  6. Ye need not toil nor languish
     Nor ponder day and night
   How in the midst of anguish
     Ye draw Him by your might.
   He comes, He comes all willing,
     Moved by His love alone,
   Your woes and troubles stilling;
     For all to Him are known.

  7. Sin's debt, that fearful burden,
     Let not your souls distress;
   Your guilt the Lord will pardon
     And cover by His grace.
   He comes, for men procuring
     The peace of sin forgiven,
   For all God's sons securing
     Their heritage in heaven.

  8. What though the foes be raging,
     Heed not their craft and spite;
   Your Lord, the battle waging,
     Will scatter all their might.
   He comes, a King most glorious,
     And all His earthly foes
   In vain His course victorious
     Endeavor to oppose.

  9. He comes to judge the nations,
     A terror to His foes,
   A Light of consolations
     And blessed Hope to those
   Who love the Lord's appearing.
     O glorious Sun, now come,
   Send forth Thy beams so cheering,
     And guide us safely home.

    Ich lag in schweren Banden,
      Du kommst und machst mich los;
    Ich stund in Spott und Schanden,
      Du kommst und machst mich gross
    Und hebst mich hoch zu Ehren
      Und schenkst mir grosses Gut,
    Das sich nicht lässt verzehren,
      Wie irdisch Reichtum tut.

    Nichts, nichts hat dich getrieben
      Zu mir vom Himmelszelt
    Als das geliebte Lieben,
      Damit du alle Welt
    In ihren tausend Plagen
      Und grossen Jammerlast,
    Die kein Mund aus kann sagen,
      So fest umfangen hast.

    Das schreib dir in dein Herze,
      Du hochbetrübtes Heer,
    Bei denen Gram und Schmerze
      Sich häuft je mehr und mehr.
    Seid unverzagt! Ihr habet
      Die Hilfe vor der Tür;
    Der eure Herzen labet
      Und tröstet, steht allhier.

    Ihr dürft euch nicht bemühen
      Noch sorgen Tag und Nacht,
    Wie ihr ihn wollet ziehen
      Mit eures Armes Macht;
    Er kommt, er kommt mit Willen,
      Ist voller Lieb' und Lust,
    All' Angst und Not zu stillen
      Die ihm an euch bewusst.

    Auch dürft ihr nicht erschrecken
      Vor eurer Sündenschuld.
    Nein, Jesus will sie decken
      Mit seiner Lieb' und Huld.
    Er kommt, er kommt den Sündern
      Zu Trost und wahrem Heil,
    Schafft, dass bei Gottes Kindern
      Verbleib' ihr Erb' und Teil.

    Was fragt ihr nach dem Schreien
      Der Feind' und ihrer Tück'?
    Ihr Herr wird sie zerstreuen
      In einem Augenblick.
    Er kommt, er kommt ein König,
      Dem wahrlich alle Feind'
    Auf Erden viel zu wenig
      Zum Widerstande seind.

    Er kommt zum Weltgerichte,
      Zum Fluch dem, der ihm flucht;
    Mit Gnad' und suessem Lichte
      Dem, der ihn liebt und sucht.
    Ach komm, ach komm, o Sonne,
      Und hol uns allzumal
    Zum ew'gen Licht und Wonne
      In deinen Freudensaal!

This great Advent hymn by Paul Gerhardt was first published in the *Crüger-Runge Gesangbuch*, Berlin, 1653, in ten stanzas. The composite translation, based on Catherine Winkworth's (*Chorale Book for England*, 1863), omits Stanza 3:

        What hast Thou left ungranted
          To give me glad relief?
        When soul and body panted
          In utmost depth of grief,
        In deepest degradation,
          Devoid of joy and peace,
        Then, Thou, my soul's Salvation,
          Didst come to bring release.

The hymn, one of Gerhardt's finest productions, may have been written long before its first publication, perhaps during the terrors of the Thirty Years' War. Based on Matt. 21:1-9, the Gospel for the first Sunday in Advent, it is undoubtedly one of our best Advent hymns.

The first tune, "Valet will ich dir geben," is the one most commonly used with this hymn. It is also called "St. Theodulph" and, especially when used with that author's "All Glory, Laud, and Honor" (see Hymn No. 160), is an excellent *chorale* tune. It is by Melchior Teschner. It appeared in 1615, in a twelve-page tract, published in Leipzig, containing Valerius Herberger's hymn "Valet will ich dir geben" and two melodies by Teschner. This is the second one, and it is supposed to have been written in 1613, the same year in which Herberger wrote his hymn. Bach uses this tune in his *St. John's Passion*.

The second tune, "Wie soll ich dich," was written for this hymn of Gerhardt's by Johann Crüger and appeared with the hymn's first publication in 1653.

59   Hail to the Lord's Anointed

1. Hail to the Lord's Anointed,
   Great David's greater Son!
   Hail, in the time appointed,
   His reign on earth begun!
   He comes to break oppression,
   To set the captive free,
   To take away transgression,
   And rule in equity.

2. He comes with succor speedy
   To those who suffer wrong;
   To help the poor and needy
   And bid the weak be strong;
   To give them songs for sighing,
   Their darkness turn to light,
   Whose souls, condemned and dying,
   Were precious in His sight.

3. He shall come down like showers
   Upon the fruitful earth,
   And joy and hope, like flowers,
   Spring in His path to birth.
   Before Him on the mountains
   Shall peace, the herald, go
   And righteousness, in fountains,
   From hill to valley flow.

4. Arabia's desert ranger
   To Him shall bow the knee,
   The Ethiopian stranger
   His glory come to see;
   With offerings of devotion
   Ships from the isles shall meet
   To pour the wealth of ocean
   In tribute at His feet.

5. Kings shall bow down before Him
   And gold and incense bring;
   All nations shall adore Him,
   His praise all peoples sing;
   To Him shall prayer unceasing
   And daily vows ascend,
   His kingdom still increasing,
   A kingdom without end.

6. O'er every foe victorious,
   He on His throne shall rest,
   From age to age more glorious,
   All blessing and all-blest.
   The tide of time shall never
   His covenant remove;
   His name shall stand forever, —
   That name to us is Love.

This is James Montgomery's best psalm rendering. It is based on Ps. 72 and was written in eight stanzas for, and included in, a Christmas Ode which was sung at one of the Moravian settlements, perhaps Fulneck, in the United Kingdom, Christmas, 1821. It was published in the following year in the *Evangelical Magazine* and entitled "Imitation of the 72d Psalm (Tune: Culmstock)."

The text includes Stanzas 1, 2, 4, 5, 6, Lines 1—4, and 7, Lines 1—4, and 8 of the original.

In the original version Stanza 3, after our Stanzas 1 and 2, reads:

    By such shall He be feared
      While sun and moon endure,
    Beloved, obeyed, revered;
      For He shall judge the poor,
    Through changing generations,
      With justice, mercy, truth,
    While stars maintain their stations
      Or moons renew their youth.

ADVENT

The original Stanzas 6 and 7 read:

Kings shall fall down before Him
 And gold and incense bring;
All nations shall adore Him,
 His praise all people sing;
For He shall have dominion
 O'er river, sea, and shore,
Far as the eagle's pinion
 Or dove's light wing can soar.

For Him shall prayer unceasing
 And daily vows ascend,
His kingdom still increasing,
 A kingdom without end.
The mountain dews shall nourish
 A seed in weakness sown,
Whose fruit shall spread and flourish
 And shake like Lebanon.

Doctor Julian says:

Of all Montgomery's renderings and imitations of the psalms this is the finest. It forms a rich and splendid Messianic hymn. Its success has been great, partly due at the first to the publicity given to it by Dr. Adam Clarke in his *Commentary on the Bible,* in which it appeared in 1822 with a special note at the end of his exposition of Ps. 72:

I need not tell the intelligent reader that he has seized the spirit, and exhibited some of the principal beauties, of the Hebrew bard; though (to use his own words in a letter to me) his "hand trembled to touch the harp of Zion." I take the liberty here to register a wish, which I have strongly expressed to himself, that he would favor the Church of God with a metrical version of the whole book.

It is interesting to compare Montgomery's rendering of this psalm with that of Isaac Watts, "Jesus Shall Reign Where'er the Sun." (See Hymn No. 511.)

The tune "Freut euch, ihr lieben" is by Leonhart Schröter and was published in his *Neuwe Weyhnachtliedlein,* 1537, set to the Christmas hymn "Freut euch, ihr lieben Christen, freut euch von Herzen sehr!" by an unknown author of the early sixteenth century.

Hark, a Thrilling Voice is Sounding   60

1. Hark, a thrilling voice is sounding!
 "Christ is nigh!" we hear it say;
"Cast away the works of darkness,
 O ye children of the day!"

2. Startled at the solemn warning,
 Let the earth-bound soul arise;
Christ, her Sun, all sloth dispelling,
 Shines upon the morning skies.

3. Lo, the Lamb, so long expected,
 Comes with pardon down from heaven.
Let us haste, with tears of sorrow,
 One and all, to be forgiven.

4. That, when next He comes with glory
 And the world is wrapped in fear,
He may shield us with His mercy
 And with words of love draw near.

5. Honor, glory, might, dominion,
 To the Father and the Son,
With the everlasting Spirit,
 While eternal ages run!

Vox clara ecce intonat,
 Obscura quaeque increpat;
Bellantur eminus somnia,
 Ab aether Christus promicat.

Mens iam resurgat torpida,
 Quae sorde exstat saucia:
Sidus refulget iam novum,
 Ut tollat omne noxium.

E sursum Agnus mittitur
 Laxare gratis debitum;
Omnes pro indulgentia
 Vocem demus cum lacrimis:

Secundo ut cum fulserit
 Mundumque horror cinxerit,
Non pro reatu puniat,
 Sed pius nos tunc protegat.

Laus, honor, virtus, gloria
 Deo Patri cum Filio,
Sancto simul Paraclito
 In sempiterna saecula.

The Latin original of this hymn is of unknown authorship, early tenth century. The translation by Edward Caswall appeared in his *Lyra Catholica,* 1849, the first line reading:

"Hark, an awe-full voice is sounding."

The tune "O der alles" appeared in the second edition of Freylinghausen's *Neues Geistreiches Gesangbuch,* Halle, 1705, set to the hymn "O der alles hätt' verloren," ascribed to Gottfried Arnold. The composer is unknown.

ADVENT

61   Comfort, Comfort, Ye My People

1. Comfort, comfort, ye My people,
   Speak ye peace, thus saith our God;
   Comfort those who sit in darkness,
   Mourning 'neath their sorrows' load.
   Speak ye to Jerusalem
   Of the peace that waits for them;
   Tell her that her sins I cover
   And her warfare now is over.

2. Yea, her sins our God will pardon,
   Blotting out each dark misdeed;
   All that well-deserved His anger
   He no more will see or heed.
   She hath suffered many a day,
   Now her griefs have passed away;
   God will change her pining sadness
   Into ever-springing gladness.

3. Hark, the Herald's voice is crying
   In the desert far and near,
   Bidding all men to repentance
   Since the Kingdom now is here.
   Oh, that warning cry obey!
   Now prepare for God a way;
   Let the valleys rise to meet Him
   And the hills bow down to greet Him.

4. Make ye straight what long was crooked,
   Make the rougher places plain;
   Let your hearts be true and humble,
   As befits His holy reign.
   For the glory of the Lord
   Now o'er earth is shed abroad,
   And all flesh shall see the token
   That His Word is never broken.

Tröstet, tröstet meine Lieben,
   Tröstet mein Volk, spricht mein Gott;
Tröstet, die sich jetzt betrüben
   Über Feindes Hohn und Spott.
Weil Jerusalem wohl dran,
Redet sie gar freundlich an;
Denn ihr Leiden hat ein Ende,
Ihre Ritterschaft ich wende.

Ich vergeb' all ihre Sünden,
   Ich tilg' ihre Missetat.
Ich will nicht mehr sehn noch finden,
   Was die Straf' erwecket hat;
Sie hat ja zweifältig Leid
Schon empfangen; ihre Freud'
Soll sich täglich neu vermehren
Und ihr Leid in Freud' verkehren.

Eine Stimme lässt sich hören
   In der Wüste weit und breit,
Alle Menschen zu bekehren:
   Macht dem Herrn den Weg bereit,
Machet Gott ein' ebne Bahn;
Alle Welt soll heben an,
Alle Tale zu erhöhen,
Dass die Berge niedrig stehen.

Ungleich soll nun eben werden
   Und, was höckricht, gleich und schlecht;
Alle Menschen hier auf Erden
   Sollen leben schlecht und recht;
Denn des Herren Herrlichkeit,
Offenbar zu dieser Zeit,
Macht, dass alles Fleisch kann sehen,
Wie, was Gott spricht, muss geschehen.

This hymn by Johann Olearius was originally written for the festival of St. John the Baptist and is based on Is. 40:1-8, the Epistle for that day. It appeared in the author's *Geistliche Singe-Kunst,* Leipzig, 1671.

The translation is an altered form of Catherine Winkworth's *Chorale Book for England,* 1863.

The tune "Freu dich sehr," also called "Psalm 42," is from the Genevan Psalter" of 1551, either composed or arranged by Louis Bourgeois, set to the metrical version of Psalm 42. The melody appeared set to the text of the anonymous burial hymn "Freu dich sehr, o meine Seele" in the *Threnodiae* of Christopher Demantius, Freiberg, 1620. The tune has had its widest use in the German evangelical churches.

62   Oh, Come, Oh, Come, Emmanuel

1. Oh, come, oh, come, Emmanuel,
   And ransom captive Israel
   That mourns in lonely exile here
   Until the Son of God appear.
   Rejoice! Rejoice! Emmanuel
   Shall come to thee, O Israel.

2. Oh, come, Thou Rod of Jesse, free
   Thine own from Satan's tyranny;
   From depths of hell Thy people save
   And give them victory o'er the grave.
   Rejoice! Rejoice! Emmanuel
   Shall come to thee, O Israel.

3. Oh, come, Thou Dayspring from on high,
   And cheer us by Thy drawing nigh;
   Disperse the gloomy clouds of night
   And death's dark shadows put to flight.
   Rejoice! Rejoice! Emmanuel
   Shall come to thee, O Israel.

Veni, veni, Emmanuel;
Captivum solve Israel,
Qui gemit in exilio,
Privatus Dei Filio.
Gaude, gaude; Emmanuel
Nascetur pro te, Israel.

Veni, o Iesse Virgula;
Ex hostis tuos ungula,
De specu tuos tartari
Educ et antro barathri.
Gaude, gaude; Emmanuel
Nascetur pro te, Israel.

Veni, veni, o Oriens;
Solare nos adveniens;
Noctis depelle nebulas
Dirasque noctis tenebras.
Gaude, gaude; Emmanuel
Nascetur pro te, Israel.

ADVENT

    4. Oh, come, Thou Key of David, come
    And open wide our heavenly home;
    Make safe the way that leads on high
    And close the path to misery.
    Rejoice! Rejoice! Emmanuel
    Shall come to thee, O Israel.

    Veni, Clavis Davidica;
    Regna reclude caelica;
    Fac iter tutum superum,
    Et claude vias inferum.
    Gaude, gaude; Emmanuel
    Nascetur pro te, Israel.

In the Medieval Church it was customary to chant the great antiphons at evensong during Advent, from December 17 to 24. Their address was to our Savior, and they reflect a joyful anticipation of His advent. They are therefore probably not of Roman origin, although they were introduced in Rome already before the 9th century. Some unknown Latin writer of the twelfth century later versified five of the great antiphons, of which four compose the Latin text above.

This hymn was put into English dress by Dr. John Mason Neale and published in his *Medieval Hymns,* 1851, beginning "Draw nigh, draw nigh, Emmanuel."

Dr. Neale afterwards revised his translation for the trial copy of *Hymns Ancient and Modern,* 1859, and the text above is his unaltered, but with the fifth stanza omitted. This stanza, without the refrain, reads:

    Oh, come, oh, come, Thou Lord of might,
    Who to Thy tribes on Sinai's height
    In ancient times didst give the Law
    In cloud and majesty and awe.

Modern hymn-books do not agree as to the merits of Dr. Neale's translation. Some use a translation by Dr. Henry Sloane Coffin, president of Union Theological Seminary, New York, others that of Dr. T. A. Lacy, an Anglican theologian, who was a member of the editorial committee of the *English Hymnal,* 1906.

The tune is commonly called "Veni, Emmanuel" and has usually been given as of 13th-century origin; but all efforts to trace it have been in vain. Authorities now seem to be agreed that it is an adaptation of a plain-song *Kyrie.*

On Jordan's Bank the Baptist's Cry   63

    1. On Jordan's bank the Baptist's cry
    Announces that the Lord is nigh;
    Come, then, and hearken, for he brings
    Glad tidings from the King of kings.

    2. Then cleansed be every Christian breast
    And furnished for so great a Guest.
    Yea, let us each our hearts prepare
    For Christ to come and enter there.

    3. For Thou art our Salvation, Lord,
    Our Refuge, and our great Reward.
    Without Thy grace our souls must fade
    And wither like a flower decayed.

    4. Lay on the sick Thy healing hand
    And make the fallen strong to stand;
    Show us the glory of Thy face
    Till beauty springs in every place.

    5. All praise, eternal Son, to Thee
    Whose advent sets Thy people free,
    Whom, with the Father, we adore
    And Holy Ghost forevermore.

    Iordanis oras praevia
    Vox ecce Baptistae quatit:
    Praeconis ad grandes sonos
    Ignavus abscedat sopor.

    (Auctoris adventum sui
    Tellus et aether et mare
    Praegestiente sentiunt
    Et iam salutant gaudio.)

    Mundemus et nos pectora:
    Deo propinquanti viam
    Sternamus, et dignam domum
    Tanto paremus hospiti.

    Tu nostra, tu, Iesu, salus;
    Tu robur et solatium:
    Arens ut herba, te sine
    Mortale tabescit genus.

    Aegris salutarem manum
    Extende; prostratos leva;
    Ostende vultum; iam suus
    Mundo reflorescet decor.

    Qui liberator advenis,
    Fili, tibi laus maxima
    Cum Patre et almo Spiritu
    In sempiterna saecula.

ADVENT

This great Advent hymn was written by Charles Coffin and included in the *Paris Breviary*, 1736. The omitted Stanza 2 reads in Chandler's translation:

> E'en now the air, the sea, the land,
> Feel that their Maker is at hand;
> The very elements rejoice
> And welcome Him with cheerful voice.

The translation is John Chandler's, 1837, only in Stanzas 1 to 3, the last two stanzas are by an unknown translator. Chandler's read:

> Stretch forth Thy hand to heal our sore
> And make us rise to fall no more;
> Once more upon Thy people shine
> And fill the world with love divine.
>
> To Him who left the throne of heaven
> To save mankind all praise be given!
> Like praise be to the Father done,
> And Holy Spirit, Three in One!

The tune "Puer nobis nascitur," also called "Splendor," is from Michael Prätorius's *Musae Sioniae*, Vol. VI, 1609, where it was set to a German translation of the old Latin carol "Geborn ist Gottes Söhnelein," evidently based on the fifteenth-century tune used with the carol, found in *Christliches Gesangbüchlein*, Cyriak Spangenberg, Eisleben, 1568.

64   Jesus, Thy Church with Longing Eyes

1. Jesus, Thy Church with longing eyes
   For Thine expected coming waits.
   When will the promised light arise
   And glory beam from Zion's gates?

2. E'en now, when tempests round us fall
   And wintry clouds o'ercast the sky,
   Thy words with pleasure we recall
   And deem that our redemption's nigh.

3. Come, gracious Lord, our hearts renew,
   Our foes repel, our wrongs redress,
   Man's rooted enmity subdue,
   And crown Thy Gospel with success.

4. Oh, come and reign o'er every land;
   Let Satan from his throne be hurled,
   All nations bow to Thy command.
   And grace revive a dying world.

5. Teach us in watchfulness and prayer
   To wait for the appointed hour
   And fit us by Thy grace to share
   The triumphs of Thy conquering power.

William Hiley Bathhurst published this hymn in his *Psalms and Hymns*, 1831, in six four-line stanzas, under the heading "Second Advent." It is one of the best of Bathhurst's hymns. The stanza omitted in our text, No. 5 of the original, reads:

> Yes, Thou wilt speedily appear!
> The smitten earth already reels;
> And not far off we seem to hear
> The thunder of Thy chariot-wheels.

The tune "O Jesu Christ, mein's" is not to be confused with "Herr Jesu Christ, mein's." (See Hymn No. 7.) This tune is by an unknown composer and first appeared in the Nürnberg hymnal *Nürnbergisches Gesangbuch*, 1676.

65   When Sinners See Their Lost Condition

1. When sinners see their lost condition
   And feel the pressing load of sin
   And Jesus cometh on His mission
   To heal the sin-sick heart within,
   All grief must flee before His grace,
   And joy divine will take its place.

   Naar Synderen ret ser sin Vaade,
    I Själen dybt besväret gaar,
   Og Jesus kommer med sin Naade
    Og lägger den paa Hjertets Saar,
   Da slukkes Sorgen salig ud,
   Da blir der Gläde stor i Gud.

ADVENT

2. When Jesus enters meek and lowly
   To fill the home with sweetest peace;
  When hearts have felt His blessing holy
   And found from sin complete release,
  Then light and calm within shall reign
  And hearts divided love again.

3. When Jesus enters land and nation
   And moves the people with His love;
  When, yielding to His kind persuasion,
   Our hearts His truth and blessing prove,
  Then shall our life on earth be blest,
  The peace of God on us shall rest.

4. When Jesus comes, — O blessed story! —
   He works a change in heart and life;
  God's kingdom comes with power and glory
   To young and old, to man and wife;
  Through Sacrament and living Word
  Faith, love, and hope are now conferred.

5. Then stilled are cries and lamentation,
   Then loosed is Satan's every band,
  In death is hope and consolation,
   The soul is safe in Jesus' hand.
  When we shall walk through death's dark vale,
  His rod and staff shall never fail.

6. Oh, may He soon to every nation
   Find entrance where He is unknown,
  With life and light and full salvation,
   That heathendom may be o'erthrown
  And healing to the hearts may come
  In heathen land and Christian home!

Naar Jesus kommer ind i Huset
 Og hans den söde Hilsens Fred
Har alle Hjerter gjennemsuset,
 Og sänket sig i Själen ned,
Da blir der stille, lyst og mildt,
Da enes atter, hvad er skilt.

Naar Jesus kommer ind i Landet
 Og fanger Folket med sin Magt,
Og alle Hjerter have sandet
 Hans Ord, og gjort med ham sin Pagt,
Da blir der lysteligt at bo
I Herrens Fred og stille Ro.

Naar Jesus kommer — kjärt at sigen,
 Der blir et ganske andet Liv,
Et sandt og elskeligt Guds Rige
 Hos Smaa og Store, Mand og Viv,
Og Kjärlighed og Himlens Haab
Alt ved Guds Aand og Ord og Daab.

Da stilles Jammeren og Nöden,
 Da brydes alle Satans Baand,
Da blir der trostefuldt i Döden,
 Thi Själen er i Jesu Haand;
Naar vi skal vandre Dödens Dal,
Hans Kjäp og Stav os troste skal.

O maatte han nu snart faa träde
 Derind, hvor han er ubekjendt,
Og bringe Liv og Lys og Gläde,
 At Hedenskab kan vorde endt,
Og läget alle Hjertesaar
I Kristnes Hus og Hednings Gaard!

This is an abridged form of the hymn by Magnus B. Landstad, first published in nine stanzas, in his *Salmer og Sange til Brug ved Missions-möder og Missionsfeste*, 1863. John Dahle writes: "The religious fervor and depth of feeling characterizing this hymn make it one of the best Landstad hymns." The omitted stanzas, seven to nine, read in translation:

7. Behold, He at the door is knocking!
   Hark how He pleads our souls to win!
  Who hears His voice — the door unlocking —
   To sup with him He enters in!
  How blest the day, my soul, how blest,
  When Jesus comes to be thy Guest!

8. Behold, He at the door is calling;
   Oh, heed, my soul, what He doth say!
  Deny Him not — O thought appalling —
   And turn Him not from thee away.
  My soul gives answer deep within:
  Thou Blessed of the Lord, come in.

9. Come Thou who spreadest joy and gladness,
    Forever bide with me and mine
   And bring to those who sit in sadness
    And gloom of death Thy light divine.
   A voice comes from my soul within:
   Thou Blessed of the Lord, come in!

Like Montgomery's hymn "Hail to the Lord's Anointed," this hymn is also suitable for mission services.

The translation is by Oluf H. Smeby, 1909, as altered in *The Lutheran Hymnary*, 1913.

The tune "Wer weiss, wie nahe" is by Christian Möck and was published in the Bavarian *Choral-Buch*, 1820, where it was set to G. Neumark's hymn "Wer nur den lieben Gott lässt walten." (See Hymn No. 518.)

Hark the Glad Sound! The Savior Comes 66

1. Hark the glad sound! The Savior comes,
    The Savior promised long;
   Let every heart prepare a throne
    And every voice a song.

2. He comes the prisoners to release,
    In Satan's bondage held.
   The gates of brass before Him burst,
    The iron fetters yield.

[53]

ADVENT

3. He comes from thickest films of vice
   To clear the mental ray
   And on the eyeballs of the blind
   To pour celestial day.

4. He comes the broken heart to bind,
   The bleeding soul to cure,
   And with the treasures of His grace
   To enrich the humble poor.

5. Our glad hosannas, Prince of Peace,
   Thy welcome shall proclaim
   And heaven's eternal arches ring
   With Thy beloved name.

Philip Doddridge wrote this masterpiece on December 28, 1735, in seven stanzas. He preached his Christmas sermon on Luke 4:18, 19 on that day and had written this hymn to be sung after the sermon by the congregation. Our cento omits Stanzas 2 and 6 of the original, which read:

2. On Him the Spirit, largely poured,
   Exerts its sacred fire;
   Wisdom and might and zeal and love
   His holy breast inspire.

6. His silver trumpets publish loud
   The Jub'lee of the Lord;
   Our debts are all remitted now,
   Our heritage restored.

Lord Selborne says of this hymn: "A more sweet, vigorous, and perfect composition is not to be found even in the whole body of ancient hymns."

Stanza 3 of our hymn is based on Lines 39 and 40 of Alexander Pope's *Messiah:*

He from thick films shall purge the visual ray,
And on the sightless eyeballs pour the day.

A number of translations have been made of this hymn in various languages, including Latin.

The tune "Chesterfield," also called "Richmond," but which must not be confused with the tune "Richmond" by Asa Brooks Everett, is by Thomas Haweis and was first published in his *Carmina Christi,* 1792, adapted to the text of his hymn "O Thou from Whom All Goodness Flows." (See Hymn No. 515.)

67   The Bridegroom Soon Will Call Us

1. The Bridegroom soon will call us:
   Come, all ye wedding-guests!
   May not His voice appal us
   While slumber binds our breasts!
   May all our lamps be burning
   And oil be found in store
   That we, with Him returning,
   May open find the door!

   Der Bräut'gam wird bald rufen:
   Kommt all', ihr Hochzeitsgäst'!
   Hilf, Gott, dass wir nicht schlafen,
   In Sünden schlummern fest,
   Bald hab'n in unsern Händen
   Die Lampen, Öl und Licht
   Und dürfen uns nicht wenden
   Von deinem Angesicht.

2. There shall we see delighted
   Our dear Redeemer's face,
   Who leads our souls benighted
   To glory by His grace.
   The patriarchs shall meet us,
   The prophets' holy band,
   Apostles, martyrs, greet us
   In that celestial land.

   Da werden wir mit Freuden
   Den Heiland schauen an,
   Der durch sein Blut und Leiden
   Den Himmel aufgetan,
   Die lieben Patriarchen,
   Propheten allzumal,
   Die Märt'rer und Apostel
   Bei ihm, ein' grosse Zahl.

3. They will not blush to own us
   As brothers, sisters dear;
   Love ever will be shown us
   When we with them appear.
   We all shall come before Him
   Who for us man became,
   As Lord and God adore Him,
   And ever bless His name.

   Die werden uns annehmen
   Als ihre Brüderlein,
   Sich unser gar nicht schämen,
   Uns mengen mitten ein.
   Wir werden alle treten
   Zur Rechten Jesu Christ,
   Als unsern Gott anbeten,
   Der unsers Fleisches ist.

4. Our Father, rich in blessing,
   Will give us crowns of gold
   And, to His bosom pressing,
   Impart a bliss untold,
   Will welcome with embraces
   Of never-ending love,
   And deck us with His graces
   In blissful realms above.

   Gott wird sich zu uns kehren,
   Ein'm jeden setzen auf
   Die güldne Kron' der Ehren
   Und herzen freundlich drauf,
   Wird uns an sein' Brust drücken
   Aus Lieb' ganz väterlich,
   An Leib und Seel' uns schmücken
   Mit Gaben mildiglich.

[54]

ADVENT

 5. In yonder home shall never
  Be silent music's voice;
 With hearts and lips forever
  We shall in God rejoice.
 The angels shall adore Him,
  All saints shall sing His praise
 And bring with joy before Him
  Their sweetest heavenly lays.

 6. In mansions fair and spacious
  Will God the feast prepare
 And, ever kind and gracious,
  Bid us its riches share.
 There bliss that knows no measure
  From springs of love shall flow,
 And never-changing pleasure
  His bounty will bestow.

 7. Thus God shall from all evil
  Forever make us free,
 From sin and from the devil,
  From all adversity,
 From sickness, pain, and sadness,
  From troubles, cares, and fears,
 And grant us heavenly gladness
  And wipe away our tears.

 Da wird man hören klingen
  Die rechten Saitenspiel';
 Die Musikkunst wird bringen
  In Gott der Freuden viel.
 Die Engel werden singen,
  All' Heil'gen Gottes gleich,
 Mit himmelischen Zungen
  Ewig in Gottes Reich.

 Er wird uns fröhlich leiten
  Ins ew'ge Paradeis,
 Die Hochzeit zu bereiten
  Zu seinem Lob und Preis.
 Da wird sein Freud' und Wonne
  In rechter Lieb' und Treu'
 Aus Gottes Schatz und Bronne
  Und täglich werden neu.

 Also wird Gott erlösen
  Uns gar aus aller Not,
 Vom Teufel, allem Bösen,
  Von Trübsal, Angst und Spott,
 Von Trauern, Weh und Klagen,
  Von Krankheit, Schmerz und Leid,
 Von Schwermut, Sorg' und Zagen,
  Von aller bösen Zeit.

This cento is only a small portion of Johann Walther's original hymn "Herzlich tut mich erfreuen," first published at Wittenberg in 1552, in 33 (34?) stanzas, with the title "A Beautiful Spiritual and Christian New Miner's Song of the Last Day and Eternal Life." The most popular form of the hymn is that from which the translation was made, including in order Stanzas 31, 8, 9, 16, 18, 17, 13, and was first used thus in Melchior Franck's *Rosetulum musicum*, 1628.

 The translation is by Matthias Loy, although we are not certain that Stanzas 5 and 7 are by him. If so, they were not included in the Ohio Synod's *Hymnal* of 1880, from which the translation of the other stanzas is taken.

 The tune "Ach Gott vom Himmelreiche" is from Michael Prätorius's *Musae Sioniae*, VII, 1609.

The Advent of Our King   68

 1. The advent of our King
  Our prayers must now employ,
 And we must hymns of welcome sing
  In strains of holy joy.

 2. The everlasting Son
  Incarnate deigns to be;
 Himself a servant's form puts on
  To set His servants free.

 3. O Zion's Daughter, rise
  To meet thy lowly King,
 Nor let thy faithless heart despise
  The peace He comes to bring.

 4. As Judge, on clouds of light,
  He soon will come again
 And His true members all unite
  With Him in heaven to reign.

 5. Before the dawning day
  Let sin's dark deeds be gone,
 The old man all be put away,
  The new man all put on.

 6. All glory to the Son,
  Who comes to set us free,
 With Father, Spirit, ever One,
  Through all eternity.

 Instantis adventum Dei
 Poscamus ardenti prece,
 Festique munus inclytum
 Praeoccupemus canticis.

 Aeterna proles feminae
 Non horret includi sinu;
 Fit ipse servus, ut iugo
 Nos servitutis eximat.

 Mansuetus et clemens venit;
 Occurre, festina, Sion:
 Ultro tibi quam porrigit,
 Ne dura pacem respuas.

 Mox nube clara fulgurans
 Mundi redibit arbiter,
 Suique membra corporis
 Caelo triumphator vehet.

 Fetus tenebrarum, die
 Cedant propinquo crimina;
 Adam reformetur vetus,
 Imago succedat novi.

 Qui liberator advenis,
 Fili, tibi laus maxima
 Cum Patre et almo Spiritu
 In sempiterna saecula.

ADVENT

This hymn is by Charles Coffin and was included in the *Paris Breviary*, 1736, as a hymn for "Sundays and Ferialdays in Advent." Our translation is an altered form of John Chandler's, which first appeared in his *Hymns of the Primitive Church*, 1837.

For comments on the tune "St. Thomas" see Hymn No. 27.

69   Arise, Sons of the Kingdom

1. Arise, sons of the Kingdom!
    The King is drawing nigh;
Arise and hail with gladness
    The Ruler from on high.
Ye Christians, hasten forth!
    Your praise and homage bring Him
    And glad hosannas sing Him;
Naught else your love is worth.

2. Arise, ye drooping mourners!
    The King is very near;
Away with grief and sorrow!
    For, lo, your Help is here.
Behold, in many a place —
    Oh, blessed consolation! —
    You find Him, your Salvation,
Within His means of grace.

3. Arise, ye much afflicted!
    The King is not afar.
Rejoice, ye long dejected,
    Behold the Morning Star!
The Lord will give you joy;
    Though troubles now distress you,
    With comfort He will bless you,
E'en death will He destroy.

4. Arise, ye poor and needy!
    The King provides for you;
He comes with succor speedy,
    With mercy ever new.
Receive your gracious King,
    The Giver of all blessing,
    Hail Him, His name confessing,
And glad hosannas sing.

5. Be righteous, ye His subjects,
    The King is just and true;
Prepare for Him a highway,
    Make all things straight and new.
For, lo, He means it well;
    Then willing bear the crosses
    That He Himself imposes,
Nor let your courage fail.

6. Oh, rich the gifts Thou bringest,
    Thyself made poor and weak!
O Love beyond expression,
    That thus can sinners seek!
For this, O Lord, will we
    Our joyous tribute bring Thee
    And glad hosannas sing Thee
And ever grateful be.

Auf, auf, ihr Reichsgenossen,
    Der König kommt heran!
Empfahet unverdrossen
    Den grossen Wundermann.
Ihr Christen, geht herfür,
    Lasst uns vor allen Dingen
    Ihm Hosianna singen
Mit heiliger Begier.

Auf, ihr betrübten Herzen,
    Der König ist gar nah!
Hinweg, all' Angst und Schmerzen,
    Der Helfer ist schon da!
Seht, wie so mancher Ort
    Hochtröstlich ist zu nennen,
    Da wir ihn finden können
Im Nachtmahl, Tauf' und Wort.

Auf, auf, ihr Vielgeplagten,
    Der König ist nicht fern!
Seid fröhlich, ihr Verzagten!
    Dort kommt der Morgenstern.
Der Herr will in der Not
    Mit reichem Trost euch speisen;
    Er will euch Hilf' erweisen,
Ja dämpfen gar den Tod.

Frischauf in Gott, ihr Armen,
    Der König sorgt für euch!
Er will durch sein Erbarmen
    Euch machen gross und reich.
Der an ein Tier gedacht,
    Der wird auch euch ernähren;
    Was Menschen nur begehren,
Das steht in seiner Macht.

Seid fromm, ihr Untertanen,
    Der König ist gerecht,
Lasst uns den Weg ihm bahnen
    Und machen alles schlecht.
Fürwahr, er meint es gut;
    Drum lasset uns die Plagen,
    Die er uns schickt, ertragen
Mit unerschrocknem Mut.

Nun, Herr, du gibst uns reichlich,
    Wirst selbst doch arm und schwach;
Du liebest unvergleichlich,
    Du jagst den Sündern nach.
Drum woll'n wir insgemein
    Die Stimmen hoch erschwingen,
    Dir Hosianna singen
Und ewig dankbar sein.

This cento by Johann Rist is composed of Stanzas 1, 2, 3, 7, 5, and 12 of the original. The hymn first appeared in the author's *Sabbatische Seelenlust*, Lüneburg, 1651, entitled "On the Gospel of the First Sunday in Advent, which is written by the Holy Evangelist Matthew at the 21st chapter."

The translation is based on Catherine Winkworth's *Lyra Germanica*, Second Series, 1858.

The tune "Aus meines Herzens Grunde" was published in *New Katechismus-Gesangbüchlein*, Hamburg, 1598, edited by David Wolder, who used it, however, with the text of Johann Walther's hymn "Herzlich tut mich erfreuen." (See Hymn No. 67.)

ADVENT

Hosanna to the Living Lord   70

1. Hosanna to the living Lord!
Hosanna to the Incarnate Word!
To Christ, Creator, Savior, King,
Let earth, let heaven, hosanna sing.

2. O Savior, with protecting care
Abide in this Thy house of prayer,
Where we Thy parting promise claim,
Assembled in Thy sacred name.

3. But, chiefest, in our cleansèd breast,
Eternal, bid Thy Spirit rest
And make our secret soul to be
A temple pure and worthy Thee.

4. So in the last and dreadful Day,
When earth and heaven shall melt away,
Thy flock, redeemed from sinful stain,
Shall swell the sound of praise again.

Reginald Heber first published this hymn in the *Christian Observer*, 1811. Then it appeared, in a much improved form, in Heber's posthumous *Hymns*, in 1827, as the first hymn for Advent Sunday. The omitted Stanza 2 reads:

> Hosanna, Lord, Thine angels cry;
> Hosanna, Lord, Thy saints reply:
> Above, beneath us, and around,
> The dead and living swell the sound.

For comments on the tune "Vom Himmel hoch" see Hymn No. 85.

Watchman, Tell Us of the Night   71

1. Watchman, tell us of the night,
What its signs of promise are.
Traveler, o'er yon mountain's height,
See that glory-beaming star.
Watchman, doth its beauteous ray
Aught of joy or hope foretell?
Traveler, yes; it brings the day,
Promised day of Israel.

2. Watchman, tell us of the night;
Higher yet that star ascends.
Traveler, blessedness and light,
Peace and truth, its course portends.
Watchman, will its beams alone
Gild the spot that gave them birth?
Traveler, ages are its own;
See, it bursts o'er all the earth.

3. Watchman, tell us of the night,
For the morning seems to dawn.
Traveler, darkness takes its flight;
Doubt and terror are withdrawn.
Watchman, let thy wanderings cease;
Hie thee to thy quiet home.
Traveler, lo, the Prince of Peace,
Lo, the Son of God, is come!

This hymn was first published by John Bowring in his *Hymns*, 1825. It is based on Is. 21:11. He is said to have first heard it sung, years after he had written it, in Asiatic Turkey by a group of American missionaries in a prayer-meeting.

Dr. C. S. Robinson writes:

Perhaps no piece can be found which is more familiar to the American churches than this hymn. The brief prediction in Isaiah 21:11, 12, however, on which it is based, is one of the most obscure in the Bible. The entire prophecy is contained in two verses of the chapter and appears to bear no relation to what goes before it or what follows. But the image it presents is singularly dramatic and picturesque. The scene is laid in the midst of the Babylonian Captivity. A lonely watchman is represented as standing on the ramparts of some tower along the defenses of the citadel. He seems to be anxiously looking for the issues of the siege leveled against it. The time is midnight. Calamity is over the land. The people are afflicted. Their enemies are pressing them hard. That solitary sentinel sadly remains at his post, peering into the unlit gloom, trying to discern signs of deliverance. But the heavens are starless, and the impenetrable clouds keep rolling on. Suddenly an unknown voice pierces the air.

Whether in wailing sorrow or in bitter taunt, is not evident; but out of the stillness already grown oppressive breaks the question with repetitious pertinacity: "Watchman, what of the night? Watchman, what of the night?" The sentinel waits through a moment of surprised meditation and then tranquilly answers: "The morning cometh and also the night; if ye will inquire, inquire ye: return, come." Then the dialog lapses into silence again, and the night gathers its unbroken shadows deeper than ever.

It seems to us that the hymn is not only a fitting Advent hymn, but that it has special significance in our day as a missionary hymn. With skepticism, agnosticism, atheism, and liberalism making inroads on the churches at home and abroad, we need to be aroused to renewed interest and zeal in the cause of sending and bringing the Gospel of the Prince of Peace to those who have it not or who once had it and lost it.

The tune "St. George," which is not to be confused with other tunes by the same name, was composed by George J. Elvey and was written for Thorne's musical counterpart of *Selection of Psalm and Hymn Tunes*, 1858, by Morrell and How. It was there set to James Montgomery's mission hymn "Hark, the Song of Jubilee." In the original edition of *Hymns Ancient and Modern* this tune was set to Henry Alford's hymn "Come, Ye Thankful People, Come" and is virtually wedded to that hymn. However, the tune seems to fit the spirit of Bowring's hymn very nicely.

72 Rejoice, Rejoice, Believers

1. Rejoice, rejoice, believers,
   And let your lights appear!
   The evening is advancing,
   And darker night is near.
   The Bridegroom is arising,
   And soon He draweth nigh;
   Up, pray and watch and wrestle!
   At midnight comes the cry.

2. The watchers on the mountain
   Proclaim the Bridegroom near;
   Go meet Him as He cometh,
   With hallelujahs clear.
   The marriage-feast is waiting,
   The gates wide open stand;
   Up, up, ye heirs of glory;
   The Bridegroom is at hand!

3. Ye saints, who here in patience
   Your cross and sufferings bore,
   Shall live and reign forever,
   When sorrow is no more.
   Around the throne of glory
   The Lamb ye shall behold;
   In triumph cast before Him
   Your diadems of gold!

4. Our Hope and Expectation,
   O Jesus, now appear;
   Arise, Desire of nations,
   O'er this benighted sphere.
   With hearts and hands uplifted,
   We plead, O Lord, to see
   The day of earth's redemption,
   That brings us unto Thee!

Ermuntert euch, ihr Frommen
   Zeigt eurer Lampen Schein!
Der Abend ist gekommen,
   Die finstre Nacht bricht ein.
Es hat sich aufgemachet
   Der Bräutigam mit Pracht:
Auf, betet, kämpft und wachet!
   Bald ist es Mitternacht.

Die Wächter Zions schreien:
   Der Bräutigam ist nah;
Begegnet ihm in Reihen
   Und singt Halleluja!
Die Tür ist aufgeschlossen,
   Die Hochzeit ist bereit:
Auf, auf, ihr Reichsgenossen!
   Der Bräut'gam ist nicht weit.

Die ihr Geduld getragen
   Und mit gestorben seid,
Sollt nun nach Kreuz und Klagen
   In Freuden sonder Leid
Mitleben und -regieren
   Und vor des Lammes Thron
Mit Jauchzen triumphieren
   In einer Siegeskron'.

O Jesu, meine Wonne,
   Komm bald und mach dich auf!
Geh auf, verlangte Sonne,
   Und fördre deinen Lauf!
O Jesu, mach ein Ende
   Und führ uns aus dem Streit!
Wir heben Haupt und Hände
   Nach der Erlösungszeit.

This cento is from a hymn of ten stanzas by Laurentius Laurenti. It is his finest hymn and emphasizes our Lord's Second Advent. The hymn was published in the author's *Evangelica Melodica*, 1700, entitled "for the 27th Sunday

ADVENT

after Trinity." The complete hymn — our cento contains only Stanzas 1, parts of 2 and 3, 7, and 10 — unites the imagery of the parable of the Ten Virgins, Matt. 25:1-13 with that of Rev. 20—21.

The translation is an altered form of Sarah Findlater's, which appeared in *Hymns from the Land of Luther* (by her and her sister, Jane Borthwick), 1854, first series.

Another stanza from the original (Stanza 8) translated by Mrs. Findlater, beautiful for its imagery, reads:

> Palms of victory are there;
> There radiant garments are;
> There stands the peaceful harvest,
> Beyond the reach of war.
> There, after stormy winter,
> The flowers of earth arise
> And from the grave's long slumber
> Shall meet again our eyes.

For comments on the tune "Valet will ich dir geben" see Hymn No. 58.

Lift Up Your Heads, Ye Mighty Gates   73

1. Lift up your heads, ye mighty gates!
Behold, the King of Glory waits;
The King of kings is drawing near,
The Savior of the world is here.
Life and salvation He doth bring,
Wherefore rejoice and gladly sing:
   We praise Thee, Father, now,
   Creator, wise art Thou!

2. A Helper just He comes to thee,
His chariot is humility,
His kingly crown is holiness,
His scepter, pity in distress,
The end of all our woe He brings;
Wherefore the earth is glad and sings:
   We praise Thee, Savior, now,
   Mighty in deed art Thou!

3. O blest the land, the city blest,
Where Christ the Ruler is confessed!
O happy hearts and happy homes
To whom this King in triumph comes!
The cloudless Sun of joy He is,
Who bringeth pure delight and bliss.
   We praise Thee, Spirit, now,
   Our Comforter art Thou!

4. Fling wide the portals of your heart;
Make it a temple set apart
From earthly use for Heaven's employ,
Adorned with prayer and love and joy.
So shall your Sovereign enter in
And new and nobler life begin.
   To Thee, O God, be praise
   For word and deed and grace!

5. Redeemer, come! I open wide
My heart to Thee; here, Lord, abide!
Let me Thy inner presence feel,
Thy grace and love in me reveal;
Thy Holy Spirit guide us on
Until our glorious goal is won.
   Eternal praise and fame
   We offer to Thy name.

Macht hoch die Tür, die Tor' macht weit,
Es kommt der Herr der Herrlichkeit,
Ein König aller Königreich',
Ein Heiland aller Welt zugleich,
Der Heil und Leben mit sich bringt;
Derhalben jauchzt, mit Freuden singt:
   Gelobet sei mein Gott,
   Mein Schöpfer, reich von Rat!

Er ist gerecht, ein Helfer wert,
Sanftmütigkeit ist sein Gefährt,
Sein Königskron' ist Heiligkeit,
Sein Zepter ist Barmherzigkeit.
All unsre Not zum End' er bringt.
Derhalben jauchzt, mit Freuden singt:
   Gelobet sei mein Gott,
   Mein Heiland, gross von Tat!

O wohl dem Land, o wohl der Stadt,
So diesen König bei sich hat!
Wohl allen Herzen insgemein,
Da dieser König ziehet ein!
Er ist die rechte Freudensonn',
Bringt mit sich lauter Freud' und Wonn'.
   Gelobet sei mein Gott,
   Mein Tröster, früh und spat!

Macht hoch die Tür, die Tor' macht weit,
Eu'r Herz zum Tempel zubereit't,
Die Zweiglein der Gottseligkeit
Steckt auf mit Andacht, Lust und Freud'!
So kommt der König auch zu euch,
Ja Heil und Leben mit zugleich.
   Gelobet sei mein Gott,
   Voll Rat, voll Tat, voll Gnad'!

Komm, o mein Heiland Jesu Christ,
Mein's Herzens Tür dir offen ist!
Ach zeuch mit deiner Gnade ein,
Dein' Freundlichkeit auch uns erschein',
Dein Heil'ger Geist uns führ' und leit'
Den Weg zur ew'gen Seligkeit!
   Dem Namen dein, o Herr,
   Sei ewig Preis und Ehr'!

This is one of our finest Advent hymns from the German. Georg Weissel based it on Ps. 24 and wrote it for use on the first Sunday in Advent. It was first published in Part One of the *Preussische Fest-Lieder*, Elbing, 1642.

The translation is by Catherine Winkworth, from her *Lyra Germanica*, First Series, 1855, altered for *The Lutheran Hymnal*.

ADVENT

The first tune "Macht hoch die Tür" is from Johann Crüger's *Praxis Pietatis Melica,* Berlin, 1661. It is more than likely by Crüger himself. It is undoubtedly the best of our three tunes. The most popular tune, however, is our second, by Johann A. Freylinghausen, which appeared in his *Neues Geistreiches Gesangbuch,* Halle, 1704. Some musicians think it is a recast of Crüger's tune "in the Freylinghausen manner"; others consider it an original melody. Our third tune, known in our circles as "the Milwaukee tune," is by August Lemke, 1849.

74   Once He Came in Blessing

1. Once He came in blessing,
All our ills redressing;
Came in likeness lowly,
Son of God most holy;
Bore the cross to save us,
Hope and freedom gave us.

Gottes Sohn ist kommen
Uns allen zu Frommen
Hier auf diese Erden
In armen Gebärden,
Dass er uns von Sünde
Freiet' und entbünde.

2. Still He comes within us,
Still His voice would win us
From the sins that hurt us;
Would to Truth convert us
From our foolish errors
Ere He comes in terrors.

Er kommt auch noch heute
Und lehret die Leute,
Wie sie sich von Sünden
Zur Buss' sollen wenden,
Von Irrtum und Torheit
Treten zu der Wahrheit.

3. Thus, if thou hast known Him,
Not ashamed to own Him,
But wilt trust Him boldly
Nor dost love Him coldly,
He will then receive thee,
Heal thee, and forgive thee.

Die sich sein nicht schämen
Und sein'n Dienst annehmen
Durch ein'n rechten Glauben
Mit ganzem Vertrauen,
Denen wird er eben
Ihre Sünd' vergeben.

4. He who thus endureth
Bright reward secureth.
Come, then, O Lord Jesus,
From our sins release us;
Let us here confess Thee
Till in heaven we bless Thee.

Ei nun, Herre Jesu,
Schicke unser Herz zu,
Dass wir alle Stunden
Rechtgläubig erfunden,
Darinnen verscheiden
Zur ewigen Freuden.

This hymn by Johann Roh was first published in *Ein Gesangbuch der Brüder inn Behemen und Merherrn,* Nürnberg, 1544. There were nine stanzas. Our cento is composed of Stanzas 1, 2, 3, and 9.

Miss Catherine Winkworth's translation in *Chorale Book for England,* 1863, is used unaltered. She included an additional stanza before the last one in our text (Stanza 5 of the original), which reads:

> But through many a trial,
> Deepest self-denial,
> Long and brave endurance,
> Must thou win assurance
> That His own He makes thee,
> And no more forsakes thee.

The tune "Gottes Sohn ist kommen" is ascribed to Michael Weisse and was originally set to Weisse's hymn for Advent "Menschenkind, merk eben," 1531. It was set to Roh's hymn when it appeared in 1544.

75   Ye Sons of Men, Oh, Hearken

1. Ye sons of men, oh, hearken:
Your heart and mind prepare,
To hail the almighty Savior,
O sinners, be your care.
He who of grace alone
Our Life and Light was given,
The promised Lord from heaven,
Unto our world is shown.

Mit Ernst, o Menschenkinder,
Das Herz in euch bestellt,
Damit das Heil der Sünder,
Der grosse Wunderheld,
Den Gott aus Gnad' allein
Der Welt zum Licht und Leben
Versprochen hat zu geben,
Bei allen kehre ein.

CHRISTMAS

2. Prepare the way before Him;
   Prepare for Him the best.
Cast out whate'er offendeth
   This great, this heavenly Guest.
Make straight, make plain, the way:
   The lowly valleys raising,
The heights of pride abasing,
   His path all even lay.
	Bereitet doch fein tüchtig
	   Den Weg dem grossen Gast,
	Macht seine Steige richtig,
	   Lasst alles, was er hasst;
	Macht alle Bahnen recht,
	   Das Tal lasst sein erhöhet;
	Macht niedrig, was hoch stehet,
	   Was krumm ist, gleich und schlecht.

3. The humble heart and lowly
   God lifteth up on high:
Beneath His feet in anguish
   The haughty soul shall lie.
The heart, sincere and right,
   That heeds God's invitation
And makes true preparation,
   It is the Lord's delight.
	Ein Herz, das Demut übet,
	   Bei Gott am höchsten steht;
	Ein Herz, das Hochmut liebet,
	   Mit Angst zugrunde geht;
	Ein Herz, das richtig ist
	   Und folget Gottes Leiten,
	Das kann sich recht bereiten,
	   Zu dem kommt Jesus Christ.

4. Prepare my heart, Lord Jesus,
   Turn not from me aside,
And grant that I receive Thee
   This blessed Advent-tide.
From stall and manger low
   Come Thou to dwell within me;
Loud praises will I sing Thee
   And forth Thy glory show.
	Ach, mache du mich Armen
	   In dieser Gnadenzeit,
	Aus Güte und Erbarmen,
	   Herr Jesu, selbst bereit!
	Zieh in mein Herz hinein
	   Vom Stall und von der Krippen,
	So werden Herz und Lippen
	   Dir ewig dankbar sein.

There is some uncertainty as to the authorship of this hymn, whether it was written by Valentin Thilo, Jr., or by his father of the same name. However, Stanzas 1 to 3 of the German text upon which our translation is based seem to be those written by the younger Thilo and were first published, 1642, in Part One of *Preussische Fest-Lieder,* Elbing. The fourth stanza, an alteration of Thilo's fourth, by an unknown writer, is from the Hanoverian hymnal *Das Hannoverische etc. Gesangbuch,* 1659. Koch considers Stanza 3 the best stanza and thinks that Thilo there pictured the character of his beloved sister. She was the wife of a Königsberg pastor and died of the pestilence August 16, 1639.

The translation is based on that by Arthur Tozer Russell, *Psalms and Hymns,* 1851.

For comments on the tune, "Aus meines Herzens Grunde," see Hymn No. 69.

A Great and Mighty Wonder   76

1. A great and mighty wonder,
   A full and holy cure:
The Virgin bears the Infant
   With virgin honor pure!
Repeat the hymn again:
   "To God on high be glory
And peace on earth to men!"

2. The Word becomes incarnate
   And yet remains on high,
And cherubim sing anthems
   To shepherds from the sky.
Repeat the hymn again:
   "To God on high be glory
And peace on earth to men!"

3. While thus they sing your Monarch,
   Those bright angelic bands,
Rejoice, ye vales and mountains,
   Ye oceans, clap your hands.
Repeat the hymn again:
   "To God on high be glory
And peace on earth to men!"

4. Since all He comes to ransom,
   By all be He adored,
The Infant born in Bethl'em,
   The Savior and the Lord.
Repeat the hymn again:
   "To God on high be glory
And peace on earth to men!"

5. And idol forms shall perish,
   And error shall decay,
And Christ shall wield His scepter,
   Our Lord and God for aye.
Repeat the hymn again:
   "To God on high be glory
And peace on earth to men!"

This hymn is a translation from the Greek, Μέγα καὶ παράδοξον Θαῦμα, of St. Germanus, 634—734. The translation by John Mason Neale first appeared in his *Hymns of the Eastern Church* (1862), where the hymn was erroneously ascribed to St. Anatolius. Neale's first stanza has been altered; it read:

> A great and mighty wonder,
> A full and blessed cure!
> The Virgin bears the Infant
> In holiness secure.

The other alterations are only slight, changing Neale's four-line stanzas to six-line stanzas. The editors of the *English Hymnal*, 1906, first coupled this hymn with the tune "Es ist ein' Ros'," also called "Rosa Mystica," a traditional carol melody of Germany (*Alte Catholische Geistliche Kirchengesäng*, Cologne, 1599, published by A. Quental). This union was made possible by using Neale's third stanza (omitting its first line, "And we with them triumphant") as a refrain. The result is very effective. The present setting of the tune is from Michael Prätorius's *Musae Sioniae*, 1609.

77   All My Heart This Night Rejoices

1. All my heart this night rejoices
   As I hear Far and near
   Sweetest angel voices.
   "Christ is born," their choirs are singing
   Till the air Everywhere
   Now with joy is ringing.

2. Forth today the Conqueror goeth,
   Who the foe, Sin and woe,
   Death and hell, o'erthroweth.
   God is man, man to deliver;
   His dear Son Now is one
   With our blood forever.

3. Shall we still dread God's displeasure,
   Who, to save, Freely gave
   His most cherished Treasure?
   To redeem us, He hath given
   His own Son From the throne
   Of His might in heaven.

4. Should He who Himself imparted
   Aught withhold From the fold,
   Leave us broken-hearted?
   Should the Son of God not love us,
   Who, to cheer Sufferers here,
   Left His throne above us?

5. If our blessed Lord and Maker
   Hated men, Would He then
   Be of flesh partaker?
   If He in our woe delighted,
   Would He bear All the care
   Of our race benighted?

6. He becomes the Lamb that taketh
   Sin away And for aye
   Full atonement maketh.
   For our life His own He tenders
   And our race, By His grace,
   Meet for glory renders.

7. Hark! a voice from yonder manger,
   Soft and sweet, Doth entreat:
   "Flee from woe and danger.
   Brethren, from all ills that grieve you
   You are freed; All you need
   I will surely give you."

Fröhlich soll mein Herze springen
Dieser Zeit, Da vor Freud'
Alle Engel singen.
Hört, hört, wie mit vollen Chören
Alle Luft Laute ruft:
Christus ist geboren!

Heute geht aus seiner Kammer
Gottes Held, Der die Welt
Reisst aus allem Jammer.
Gott wird Mensch dir, Mensch, zugute.
Gottes Kind, Das verbind't
Sich mit unserm Blute.

Sollt' uns Gott nun können hassen,
Der uns gibt, Was er liebt
Über alle Massen?
Gott gibt, unserm Leid zu wehren,
Seinen Sohn Aus dem Thron
Seiner Macht und Ehren.

Sollte von uns sein gekehret,
Der sein Reich Und zugleich
Sich uns selbst verehret?
Sollt' uns Gottes Sohn nicht lieben,
Der jetzt kömmt, Von uns nimmt,
Was uns will betrüben?

Hätte vor der Menschen Orden
Unser Heil Einen Greu'l,
Wär' er nicht Mensch worden.
Hätt' er Lust zu unserm Schaden,
Ei, so würd' Unsre Bürd'
Er nicht auf sich laden.

Er nimmt auf sich, was auf Erden
Wir getan, Gibt sich an,
Unser Lamm zu werden,
Unser Lamm, das für uns stirbet
Und bei Gott Für den Tod
Gnad' und Fried' erwirbet.

Nun, er liegt in seiner Krippen,
Ruft zu sich Mich und dich,
Spricht mit süssen Lippen:
Lasset fahr'n, o liebe Brüder,
Was euch quält, Was euch fehlt,
Ich bring' alles wieder.

CHRISTMAS

8. Come, then, banish all your sadness,
   One and all, Great and small;
   Come with songs of gladness.
   Love Him who with love is glowing;
   Hail the Star, Near and far
   Light and joy bestowing.

9. Ye whose anguish knew no measure,
   Weep no more; See the door
   To celestial pleasure.
   Cling to Him, for He will guide you
   Where no cross, Pain, or loss
   Can again betide you.

10. Hither come, ye heavy-hearted,
    Who for sin, Deep within,
    Long and sore have smarted;
    For the poisoned wounds you're feeling
    Help is near, One is here
    Mighty for their healing.

11. Hither come, ye poor and wretched;
    Know His will Is to fill
    Every hand outstretchèd.
    Here are riches without measure;
    Here forget All regret,
    Fill your hearts with treasure.

12. Let me in my arms receive Thee;
    On Thy breast Let me rest,
    Savior, ne'er to leave Thee.
    Since Thou hast Thyself presented
    Now to me, I shall be
    Evermore contented.

13. Guilt no longer can distress me;
    Son of God, Thou my load
    Bearest to release me.
    Stain in me Thou findest never;
    I am clean, All my sin
    Is removed forever.

14. I am pure, in Thee believing,
    From Thy store Evermore
    Righteous robes receiving.
    In my heart I will enfold Thee,
    Treasure rare, Let me there,
    Loving, ever hold Thee.

15. Dearest Lord, Thee will I cherish.
    Though my breath Fail in death,
    Yet I shall not perish.
    But with Thee abide forever
    There on high, In that joy
    Which can vanish never.

Ei, so kommt und lasst uns laufen!
Stellt euch ein, Gross und klein,
Eilt mit grossem Haufen!
Liebt den, der vor Liebe brennet;
Schaut den Stern, Der uns gern
Licht und Labsal gönnet.

Die ihr schwebt in grossen Leiden,
Sehet, hier Ist die Tür
Zu den wahren Freuden.
Fasst ihn wohl, er wird euch führen
An den Ort, Da hinfort
Euch kein Kreuz wird rühren.

Wer sich fühlt beschwert im Herzen,
Wer empfind't Seine Sünd'
Und Gewissensschmerzen,
Sei getrost, hier wird gefunden,
Der in Eil' Machet heil
Die vergift'ten Wunden.

Die ihr arm seid und elende,
Kommt herbei, Füllet frei
Eures Glaubens Hände!
Hier sind alle guten Gaben
Und das Gold, Da ihr sollt
Euer Herz mit laben.

Süsses Heil, lass dich umfangen,
Lass mich dir, Meine Zier,
Unverrückt anhangen!
Du bist meines Lebens Leben;
Nun kann ich Mich durch dich
Wohl zufrieden geben.

Meine Schuld kann mich nicht drücken,
Denn du hast Meine Last
All' auf deinem Rücken.
Kein Fleck ist an mir zu finden,
Ich bin gar Rein und klar
Aller meiner Sünden.

Ich bin rein um deinetwillen;
Du gibst g'nug Ehr' und Schmuck,
Mich darein zu hüllen.
Ich will dich ins Herze schliessen;
O mein Ruhm, Edle Blum',
Lass dich recht geniessen!

Ich will dich mit Fleiss bewahren,
Ich will dir Leben hier,
Dir will ich abfahren;
Mit dir will ich endlich schweben
Voller Freud' Ohne Zeit
Dort im andern Leben.

According to Zahn (6481) this beautiful hymn of Paul Gerhardt's appeared in Johann Crüger's *Praxis Pietatis Melica*, Berlin, in 1653, together with the tune, "Fröhlich soll mein Herze," composed for it by Crüger. The beauty of this *chorale* is evident on the first reading. Widely used for many years in German Lutheran circles, it deserves to be introduced into the Christmas heritage of our people, especially for its clear and simple presentation of the purpose of our Lord's birth. Its use may lead some lost or straying soul to the true faith in Christ in the future as it has in the past. A classical instance is that of Carl H. von Bogatzky, author of the hymn "Awake, Thou Spirit, Who Didst Fire" (Hymn No. 494). For we are told that at the second day of the Christmas celebration in Glaucha, near Halle, in 1715, he was brought to a clear understanding of the doctrine of justification by faith by the singing of Stanzas 13 and 14.

Although, on account of its length, many hymnals use it in an abridged form, we hesitated to shorten it because its structure would then have been spoiled. How well planned the hymn is may be seen from the following analysis:

First a trumpet-blast: Christ is born; God's Champion has appeared as a bridegroom from his chamber (1, 2). In the following 4 stanzas the poet seeks to set forth the mighty value of the Incarnation: Is it not love when God gives us the Son of His Love (3), the Kingdom of Joy (4), and His fellowship (5)? Yes, it is indeed the Lamb of God who bears the sin of the world (6). Now he places himself as herald by the cradle of the divine Child (7). He bids, as in Matt. 11:28, all men (8), all they that labor (9), all the heavy laden (10), and all the poor (11), to draw near. Then, in conclusion, he approaches in supplication, as the shepherds and the Wise Men (12—15). He adores the Child as his Source of life (12), his Lamb of God (13), his Glory (14), and promises to be ever true to Him (15). It is a glorious series of Christmas thoughts, laid as a garland on the manger at Bethlehem. (*Koch,* VIII, 26.)

The translation is an altered form of Catherine Winkworth's, in *Lyra Germanica,* second series, 1858.

78   Hail the Day So Rich in Cheer

1. Hail the day so rich in cheer
   For each earth-born creature!
God's own Son from heaven draws near,
   Takes our human nature;
Of a virgin born is He;
Mary, by the Lord's decree,
   Is become a mother.
See the miracle of love:
God Himself, from heaven above,
   Came to be our Brother!

2. Child of wonder, virgin-born,
   King of all creation,
On this happy Christmas morn
   Come for our salvation!
Were this Child for us not born,
We should all be lost, forlorn,
   No true hope possessing.
Dear Lord Jesus, thanks to Thee
Now and through eternity
   For this grace and blessing!

Der Tag, der ist so freudenreich
   Aller Kreature,
Denn Gottes Sohn vom Himmelreich
   Über die Nature
Von einer Jungfrau ist gebor'n,
Maria, du bist auserkor'n,
   Dass du Mutter wärest.
Was geschah so wunderlich?
Gottes Sohn vom Himmelreich,
   Der ist Mensch geboren.

Ein Kindelein so löbelich
   Ist uns geboren heute
Von einer Jungfrau säuberlich
   Zu Trost uns armen Leuten.
Wär' uns das Kindlein nicht gebor'n,
So wär'n wir allzumal verlor'n;
   Das Heil ist unser aller.
Ei, du süsser Jesu Christ,
Dass du Mensch geboren bist,
   Behüt't uns vor der Hölle!

This hymn comes to us from the Latin "Dies est laetitia" through the German. James Mearns thinks it is of German origin. He further states that Luther spoke of this hymn as a work of the Holy Spirit. It is found in Latin and German versions, but the author and the original text cannot be determined. The German version is given by *Wackernagel* as a fifteenth-century translation from the Latin. Some of the various German versions have as many as thirteen stanzas.

Our translation was prepared especially for *The Lutheran Hymnal* in 1940.

The tune "Der Tag, der ist" is also at least of fifteenth-century origin. It is found in M. Vehe's *Ein neues Gesangbüchlein, Geistliche Lieder,* Strassburg, 1537. It had previously appeared in the hymnbook of the Bohemian Brethren by Michael Weisse, 1531. The tune has also been set to a harvest hymn by Eleanor Farjeon, in *Songs of Praise,* and is called "Cornfields."

CHRISTMAS

Rejoice, Rejoice, This Happy Morn 79

Rejoice, rejoice, this happy morn,
A Savior unto us is born,
The Christ, the Lord of Glory.
His lowly birth in Bethlehem
The angels from on high proclaim
And sing redemption's story.
My soul, extol God's great favor,
Bless Him ever For salvation,
Give Him praise and adoration.

Os er idag en Frelser föd,
Guds Salvede i vores Kjöd,
En Herre til Guds Ære.
Nu er han föd i Davids Stad,
Den Sön, som Englene tilbad,
Velsignet evig være!
Min Själ, kjend vel Denne Naade,
Fri fra Vaade, Mät dit Öie ved
Opgangen af det Höie!

In Scandinavian Lutheran circles, we are informed, it is customary in the service on Christmas Day, after the pastor has delivered the introduction to his sermon, for the congregation to rise and sing this hymn of one stanza. After which it is seated, and the pastor proceeds with the preaching of the sermon.

This hymn is from the pen of Birgitte Boye and was published in *Guldberg's Hymn Book*, 1778. The translation is by Carl Döving, made in 1911 and published in *The Lutheran Hymnary*, 1913.

For comments on the tune "Wie schön leuchtet" see Hymn No. 23.

All Praise to Thee, Eternal God 80

1. All praise to Thee, eternal God,
Who, clothed in garb of flesh and blood,
Dost take a manger for Thy throne,
While worlds on worlds are Thine alone.
   Hallelujah!

2. Once did the skies before Thee bow;
A virgin's arms contain Thee now,
While angels, who in Thee rejoice,
Now listen for Thine infant voice.
   Hallelujah!

3. A little Child, Thou art our Guest
That weary ones in Thee may rest;
Forlorn and lowly is Thy birth
That we may rise to heaven from earth.
   Hallelujah!

4. Thou comest in the darksome night
To make us children of the light,
To make us in the realms divine,
Like Thine own angels, round Thee shine.
   Hallelujah!

5. All this for us Thy love hath done;
By This to Thee our love is won;
For this our joyful songs we raise
And shout our thanks in ceaseless praise.
   Hallelujah!

Gelobet seist du, Jesu Christ,
Dass du Mensch geboren bist
Von einer Jungfrau, das ist wahr;
Des freuet sich der Engel Schar.
   Kyrieleis!

Den aller Welt Kreis nie beschloss,
Der liegt in Marien Schoss;
Er ist ein Kindlein worden klein,
Der alle Ding' erhält allein.
   Kyrieleis!

Der Sohn des Vaters, Gott von Art,
Ein Gast in der Welt hier ward
Und führt uns aus dem Jammertal,
Er macht uns Erben in sein'm Saal.
   Kyrieleis!

Das ew'ge Licht geht da herein,
Gibt der Welt ein'n neuen Schein;
Es leucht't wohl mitten in der Nacht
Und uns des Lichtes Kinder macht.
   Kyrieleis!

Das hat er alles uns getan,
Sein' gross' Lieb' zu zeigen an,
Des freu' sich alle Christenheit
Und dank' ihm des in Ewigkeit.
   Kyrieleis!

This hymn may be a translation of the eleventh-century Latin sequence:

"Grates nunc omnes reddamus Domino Deo, qui sua nativitate nos liberavit de diabolica potestate.

"Huic oportet, ut canamus cum angelis semper: Gloria in excelsis."

A German first stanza, probably written in the district of Celle, is dated 1370. This stanza and "Christ is Arisen" (Hymn No. 187) and "Now Do We Pray God the Holy Ghost" (Hymn No. 231) were the three hymns which the German people were permitted to sing in German at Christmas, Easter, and Pentecost as sequence hymns during the late Middle Ages. To this stanza Martin Luther added six more of his own, ending each stanza with a *Kyrieleis*, and published the hymn on a broadsheet in Wittenberg with the title "Ain Deütsch hymnus oder lobsang auff Weyhenacht." This broadsheet very likely was distributed for Christmas of 1523. The hymn was then also included in *Eyn Enchiridion,* Erfurt, 1524. We believe we are justified in saying that this hymn is the first Christmas hymn of the Reformation and thus the first of the many Christmas hymns and carols of Protestantism that have enriched our treasury of Christian song during the past four hundred years. Bach used this hymn and its tune in his *Choralkantate* for Christmas Day. In his *Christmas Oratorio* he also used one of the stanzas, the sixth of the German text. The translation appeared in the *American Sabbath Hymn Book,* 1854, by an unknown writer.

The cento contains Stanzas 1, 3, 5, 4, and 7 of the original German.

The tune "Gelobet seist du, Jesu" is apparently much older than the German text. It was published with the text on the broadsheet mentioned above, and is probably of early 15th-century origin.

81   O Jesus Christ, Thy Manger Is

1. O Jesus Christ,
Thy manger is
My paradise at which my soul reclineth.
For there, O Lord,
Doth lie the Word
Made flesh for us; herein Thy grace
   forthshineth.

2. He whom the sea
And wind obey
Doth come to serve the sinner in great
   meekness.
Thou, God's own Son,
With us art one,
Dost join us and our children in our
   weakness.

3. Thy light and grace
Our guilt efface,
Thy heavenly riches all our loss
   retrieving.
Immanuel,
Thy birth doth quell
The power of hell and Satan's bold
   deceiving.

4. Thou Christian heart,
Whoe'er thou art,
Be of good cheer and let no sorrow move
   thee!
For God's own Child,
In mercy mild,
Joins thee to Him; — how greatly God must
   love thee!

5. Remember thou
What glory now
The Lord prepared thee for all earthly
   sadness.
The angel host
Can never boast
Of greater glory, greater bliss or gladness.

6. The world may hold
Her wealth and gold;
But thou, my heart, keep Christ as thy true
   Treasure.
To Him hold fast
Until at last
A crown be thine and honor in full
   measure.

O Jesu Christ,
Dein Kripplein ist
Mein Paradies, da meine Seele weidet!
Hier ist der Ort,
Hier liegt das Wort
Mit unserm Fleisch persönlich
   angekleidet.

Dem Meer und Wind
Gehorsam sind,
Gibt sich zum Dienst und wird ein
   Knecht der Sünder.
Du, Gottes Sohn,
Wirst Erd' und Ton,
Gering und schwach wie wir und unsre
   Kinder.

Sein Licht und Heil
Macht alles heil;
Der Himmelsschatz bringt allen Schaden
   wieder.
Der Freudenquell
Immanuel
Schlägt Teufel, Höll' und all ihr Reich
   danieder.

Drum, frommer Christ,
Wer du auch bist,
Sei gutes Muts und lass dich nicht
   betrüben!
Weil Gottes Kind
Dich ihm verbind't,
So kann's nicht anders sein, Gott muss
   dich lieben.

Gedenke doch,
Wie herrlich hoch
Er über allen Jammer dich
   geführet!
Der Engel Heer
Ist selbst nicht mehr
Als eben du mit Seligkeit gezieret.

Lass aller Welt
Ihr Gut und Geld
Und siehe nur, dass dieser Schatz dir
   bleibe!
Wer den hier fest
Hält und nicht lässt,
Den ehrt und krönt er dort an Seel'
   und Leibe.

CHRISTMAS

This hymn by Paul Gerhardt and its tune by Johann Crüger first appeared in *Praxis Pietatis Melica,* 1653, under the title "At the Manger in Bethlehem." There were fifteen stanzas, of which our cento includes Stanzas 1, 2, 6, 7, 8, and 15. These stanzas emphasize the incarnation; the mystery of godliness — God manifest in the flesh; the redemption through Christ; our comfort in His grace; the glory that is ours; the resolution to abide in the true faith to the end.

The translation is composite and was prepared for *The Lutheran Hymnal.*

The tune "O Jesu Christ, dein Kripplein" is by Johann Crüger and appeared with the text in 1653.

Come Rejoicing, Praises Voicing 82

1. Come rejoicing, Praises voicing,
    Christmas Day is breaking;
Now th' Eternal, Lord supernal,
    Human form is taking.
On the hay — lo, behold
Virgin's Son, as foretold —
Lies the precious Infant in the wintry cold.

2. Unabated, For Him waited
    Many generations;
Him now proudly Angels loudly
    Praise the Hope of nations.
Let us, then, gladly sing,
Let our songs gaily ring,
As we to this holy Child our praises bring.

3. Tender Flower, Mighty Tower,
    Jesus Christ, our Savior;
Heavenly Treasure, Without measure
    Thee we love forever.
Lord and King without end,
Our poor hearts now befriend,
All Thy gifts of grace and goodness to us send.

Čas radosti, veselosti
    světu nastal nyní;
Neb Bůh věčný, nekonečný
    narodil se z panny;
V městečku Betlémě,
V jesličkách na slámě
Leží malé pacholátko na zimě.

Co jsme všickni lidé hříšní
    radostně čekali,
To anjelé dnes vesele
    nám jsou zvěstovali:
A protož plesejme,
Všickni se radujme,
Pacholátku, nemluvňátku zpívejme.

Spasiteli, kvítku milý,
    Pane náš Ježíši,
Z čisté panny narozený,
    poklade nejdražší,
Králi náš, Pane náš,
Skloň se k nám jako Pán,
Dej milosti, své radosti dojít nám.

This hymn comes to us through the Bohemian and Slovak from the Latin. It is based on the medieval Latin Christmas hymn,

> Omnis mundus iucundetur nato Salvatore,
> Casta mater, quae concepit Gabrielis ore.
> Sinceris mentibus,
> Sonoris vocibus
> Exultemus et laetemur hodie.
> Christus natus ex Maria virgine.

The Slovak version is by Juraj Tranovsky. It appeared in his *Hymnal* in 1674.

The translation is composite and was prepared for *The Lutheran Hymnal.*

The tune "Gladness" seems to be based on the melody used with the Latin original, perhaps an ancient Bohemian folk-tune that dates from the 12th century.

Hark! What Mean Those Holy Voices 83

1. Hark! what mean those holy voices
    Sweetly sounding through the skies?
Lo, the angelic host rejoices,
    Heavenly hallelujahs rise.

2. Listen to the wondrous story
    Which they chant in hymns of joy,
Glory in the highest, glory!
    Glory be to God most high!

3. Peace on earth, good will from heaven,
    Reaching far as man is found;
Souls redeemed and sins forgiven!
    Loud our golden harps shall sound.

4. Christ is born, the great Anointed;
    Heaven and earth, His praises sing!
Oh, receive whom God appointed
    For your Prophet, Priest, and King.

5. Hasten, mortals, to adore Him,
    Learn His name and taste His joy,
Till in heaven ye sing before Him,
    "Glory be to God most high!"

6. Let us learn the wondrous story
    Of our great Redeemer's birth;
Spread the brightness of His glory
    Till it cover all the earth.

John Cawood's fine Christmas hymn first appeared in Thomas Cotterill's *Selection of Psalms and Hymns,* 1819 (8th ed.). It may have been written as early as 1816. There are a few alterations in our text. Cawood had written, for example, the first stanza thus:

> Hark! what mean those holy voices,
> Sweetly *warbling* in the skies?
> *Sure* the angelic host rejoices;
> *Loudest* hallelujahs rise.

The tune "Stuttgart," also called "Sollt' es gleich bisweilen scheinen," appeared in Christian Friedrich Witt's *Psalmodia Sacra,* Gotha, 1715, where it was set to Christoph Tietze's (Titius) hymn beginning with that line. The tune is very much like Witt's own composition.

84 Christians, Awake, Salute the Happy Morn

1. Christians, awake, salute the happy morn
Whereon the Savior of the world was born.
Rise to adore the mystery of love
Which hosts of angels chanted from above;
With them the joyful tidings first begun
Of God Incarnate and the Virgin's Son.

2. Then to the watchful shepherds it was told,
Who heard the angelic herald's voice, "Behold,
I bring good tidings of a Savior's birth
To you and all the nations upon earth;
This day hath God fulfilled His promised word;
This day is born a Savior, Christ the Lord."

3. He spake; and straightway the celestial choir
In hymns of joy, unknown before, conspire;
The praises of redeeming love they sang,
And heaven's whole orb with alleluias rang.
God's highest glory was their anthem still,
Peace upon earth, and unto men good will.

4. To Bethlehem straight th' enlightened shepherds ran
To see the wonder God had wrought for man
And found, with Joseph and the blessed maid,
Her Son, the Savior, in a manger laid;
Then to their flocks, still praising God, return.
And their glad hearts with holy rapture burn.

5. Oh, may we keep and ponder in our mind
God's wondrous love in saving lost mankind!
Trace we the Babe, who hath retrieved our loss,
From His poor manger to His bitter cross,
Tread in His steps, assisted by His grace,
Till man's first heavenly state again takes place.

6. Then may we hope, th' angelic hosts among,
To sing, redeemed, a glad triumphal song.
He that was born upon this joyful day
Around us all His glory shall display.
Saved by His love, incessant we shall sing
Eternal praise to heaven's almighty King.

It is said that the Church is indebted to John Byrom's daughter Dolly for this hymn based on the Christmas story in Luke 2. She had asked her father in 1749 to write her a poem for a Christmas present. On that Christmas morning at breakfast she found on her plate a sheet, still preserved in Manchester, containing this poem, headed, "Christmas Day. For Dolly." Not long afterwards John Wainwright composed the tune "Yorkshire," also called "Stockport," for it, and on the following Christmas, Byrom wrote in his notebook: "Christmas, 1750. The singing men and boys (the choir of Manchester Parish Church) with Mr. Wainwright came here and sang 'Christians, Awake.'"

Originally the poem contained forty-eight lines. Our cento has thirty-six lines. The omitted lines can well be dispensed with, but some of them are of no mean merit. Byrom had written, for instance, after Line 4, Stanza 4:

> Amazed the wondrous story they proclaim,
> The first apostles of His infant fame,
> While Mary keeps and ponders in her heart
> The heavenly vision which the swains impart.

CHRISTMAS

Byrom had a flair for apt phrases. He is the author of the proverbial phrase "tweedledum and tweedledee." It is part of his epigram written when the friends of Händel and Buoncini were squabbling over their relative merits as musicians and composers:

> Some say, compared to Buoncini,
> That mynheer Handel is a ninny;
> Others aver that he to Handel
> Is scarcely fit to hold a candle.
> Strange all this difference should be
> 'Twixt tweedledum and tweedledee.

From Heaven Above to Earth I Come — 85

1. "From heaven above to earth I come
To bear good news to every home;
Glad tidings of great joy I bring,
Whereof I now will say and sing:

2. "To you this night is born a child
Of Mary, chosen virgin mild;
This little child, of lowly birth,
Shall be the joy of all the earth.

3. "This is the Christ, our God and Lord,
Who in all need shall aid afford;
He will Himself your Savior be
From all your sins to set you free.

4. "He will on you the gifts bestow
Prepared by God for all below,
That in His kingdom, bright and fair,
You may with us His glory share.

5. "These are the tokens ye shall mark:
The swaddling-clothes and manger dark;
There ye shall find the Infant laid
By whom the heavens and earth were made."

6. Now let us all with gladsome cheer
Go with the shepherds and draw near
To see the precious gift of God,
Who hath His own dear Son bestowed.

7. Give heed, my heart, lift up thine eyes!
What is it in yon manger lies?
Who is this child, so young and fair?
The blessed Christ-child lieth there.

8. Welcome to earth, Thou noble Guest,
Through whom the sinful world is blest!
Thou com'st to share my misery;
What thanks shall I return to Thee?

9. Ah, Lord, who hast created all,
How weak art Thou, how poor and small,
That Thou dost choose Thine infant bed
Where humble cattle lately fed!

10. Were earth a thousand times as fair,
Beset with gold and jewels rare,
It yet were far too poor to be
A narrow cradle, Lord, for Thee.

11. For velvets soft and silken stuff
Thou hast but hay and straw so rough,
Whereon Thou, King, so rich and great,
As 'twere Thy heaven, art throned in state.

12. And thus, dear Lord, it pleaseth Thee
To make this truth quite plain to me,
That all the world's wealth, honor, might,
Are naught and worthless in Thy sight.

Vom Himmel hoch, da komm' ich her,
Ich bring' euch gute neue Mär,
Der guten Mär bring' ich so viel,
Davon ich sing'n und sagen will.

Euch ist ein Kindlein heut' gebor'n
Von einer Jungfrau auserkor'n,
Ein Kindelein, so zart und fein,
Das soll eur' Freud' und Wonne sein.

Es ist der Herr Christ, unser Gott,
Der will euch führ'n aus aller Not,
Er will eu'r Heiland selber sein,
Von allen Sünden machen rein.

Er bringt euch alle Seligkeit,
Die Gott der Vater hat bereit,
Dass ihr mit uns im Himmelreich
Sollt leben nun und ewiglich.

So merket nun das Zeichen recht,
Die Krippe, Windelein so schlecht,
Da findet ihr das Kind gelegt,
Das alle Welt erhält und trägt.

Des lasst uns alle fröhlich sein
Und mit den Hirten gehn hinein,
Zu sehn, was Gott uns hat beschert,
Mit seinem lieben Sohn verehrt.

Merk auf, mein Herz, und sieh dorthin!
Was liegt dort in dem Krippelein?
Wer ist das schöne Kindelein?
Es ist das liebe Jesulein.

Bis willekomm, du edler Gast!
Den Sünder nicht verschmähet hast
Und kommst ins Elend her zu mir,
Wie soll ich immer danken dir?

Ach Herr, du Schöpfer aller Ding',
Wie bist du worden so gering,
Dass du da liegst auf dürrem Gras,
Davon ein Rind und Esel asz!

Und wär' die Welt vielmal so weit,
Von Edelstein und Gold bereit't,
So wär' sie doch dir viel zu klein,
Zu sein ein enges Wiegelein.

Der Sammet und die Seide dein,
Das ist grob Heu und Windelein,
Darauf du König gross und reich
Herprangst, als wär's dein Himmelreich.

Das hat also gefallen dir,
Die Wahrheit anzuzeigen mir:
Wie aller Welt Macht, Ehr' und Gut
Vor dir nichts gilt, nichts hilft noch tut.

[69]

13. Ah, dearest Jesus, holy Child, Make Thee a bed, soft, undefiled, Within my heart, that it may be A quiet chamber kept for Thee.	Ach mein herzliebes Jesulein, Mach dir ein rein, sanft Bettelein, Zu ruhen in mein's Herzens Schrein, Dass ich nimmer vergesse dein!
14. My heart for very joy doth leap, My lips no more can silence keep; I, too, must sing with joyful tongue That sweetest ancient cradle-song:	Davon ich allzeit fröhlich sei, Zu springen, singen immer frei Das rechte Susaninne schon, Mit Herzenslust den süssen Ton.
15. Glory to God in highest heaven, Who unto us His Son hath given! While angels sing with pious mirth A glad new year to all the earth.	Lob, Ehr' sei Gott im höchsten Thron, Der uns schenkt seinen ein'gen Sohn! Des freuen sich der Engel Schar Und singen uns solch neues Jahr.

Martin Luther wrote this Christmas hymn for his children for the Christmas of 1534. Lauxmann, in *Koch,* writes of its origin:

> Luther was accustomed every year to prepare for his family a happy Christmas Eve's entertainment, . . . and for this festival of his children he wrote this Christmas hymn. Its opening lines are modeled on the song "Aus fremden Landen komm' ich her"; and throughout he successfully catches the ring of the popular sacred song. It is said that Luther celebrated the festival in his own house in this original fashion: By his orders the first seven verses of this hymn were sung by a man dressed as an angel, whom the children greeted with the eighth and following verses.

The hymn was first published in *Geistliche Lieder D. Mart. Luther* (Wittenberg, Joseph Klug), where it was coupled with the folk tune "Ich kumm' aus frembden Landen her." The tune, "Vom Himmel hoch," perhaps by Luther himself, with which this hymn is now universally sung, first appeared with the text in *Geistliche Lieder, auffs new gebessert und gemehrt, zu Wittenberg, Gedruckt zu Leyptzik durch Valten Schumann,* 1539.

J. S. Bach has several settings of the tune, one of them in his great *Christmas Oratorio.*

The translation is an altered form of Catherine Winkworth's version, *Lyra Germanica, first series,* 1855. There are many other English translations in use, to say nothing of the versions in other languages. A Scottish version that may have had its origin during Luther's lifetime is found in the *Gude and Godlic Ballatis* of John Wedderburn, a Dundee merchant, who entered the priesthood and, coming under the suspicion of heresy, fled to Wittenberg in 1539, where he and other Scottish refugees associated with Luther and his friends. The tenth stanza of this translation is a good example of Wedderburn's vigorous style:

> And war the warld ten tymes sa wyde,
> Cled ouir with golde and stanis of pryde,
> Unworthie were it zit to Thee,
> Under Thy feit ane stule to be!

86   Christ the Lord to Us is Born

1. Christ the Lord to us is born, Hallelujah!
On this joyous Christmas morn, Hallelujah!
Of a virgin lowly,
He, the King most holy,
  Born this day to save us.
	Narodil se Kristus Pán, Veselme se;
	Z růže květ vykvetl nám, Radujme se!
	Z života čistého,
	Z rodu královského
	  Již nám narodil se.

2. Prophesied in days of old, Hallelujah!
God has sent Him as foretold,
  Hallelujah!
Of a virgin lowly,
He, the King most holy,
  Born this day to save us.
	Který prorokován jest, Veselme se;
	Ten na svět k nám poslán jest, Radujme se!
	Z života čistého,
	Z rodu královského
	  Již nám narodil se.

CHRISTMAS

3. Our poor human form He took, Hallelujah!
Realms of heaven He forsook, Hallelujah!
Of a virgin lowly,
He, the King most holy,
  Born this day to save us.

4. Prostrate lies the Evil One, Hallelujah!
God has saved us through His Son, Hallelujah!
Of a virgin lowly,
He, the King most holy,
  Born this day to save us.

5. Grace divine, be with us still, Hallelujah!
Keep us from all harm and ill, Hallelujah!
For the sake of Jesus,
Who from sin now saves us,
  Grant to us Thy mercy.

6. Grant us, Lord, a blessed end, Hallelujah!
To our souls Thy comfort send, Hallelujah!
Come to us, dear Jesus,
Born this day to save us,
  Bless us all forever.

Aj, člověčenství naše, Veselme se,
Ráčil jest vzíti na se, Radujme se!
Z života čistého,
Z rodu královského
  Již nám narodil se.

Goliáš již obloupen, Veselme se,
Člověk hříšný vykoupen, Radujme se!
Z života čistého,
Z rodu královského
  Již nám narodil se.

Ó ty milosti Božská, Budiž s námi!
Dejž, ať zloba dábelská Nás nemámi;
Pro Syna milého,
Nám narozeného,
  Smiluj se nad námi!

Dejž nám dobré skončení, Ó Ježíši!
Ty věčné utěšení Věrných duší.
Přijď nám k spomožení,
Zbav od zatracení,
  Pro své narození!

This jubilant Christmas hymn comes to us from the Bohemian. Juraj Tranovsky, who was for Slovak hymnody what Luther was for German hymnody, included this hymn in the first edition of his *Tranoscius*, 1636. The author is unknown. The hymn is probably of early 15th-century origin. Tobias Závorka included this hymn in his collection of 1602. The translator of Stanzas 1—4 was Vincent Pizek; of Stanzas 5 and 6, John Bajus.

The tune, a Bohemian melody, is of 15th-century origin. The composer is unknown. It was named "Salvator natus" for *The Lutheran Hymnal*.

Joy to the World, the Lord is Come 87

1. Joy to the world, the Lord is come!
Let earth receive her King;
Let every heart prepare Him room
And heaven and nature sing.

2. Joy to the earth, the Savior reigns!
Let men their songs employ,
While fields and floods, rocks, hills, and plains
Repeat the sounding joy.

3. No more let sins and sorrows grow
Nor thorns infest the ground;
He comes to make His blessings flow
Far as the curse is found.

4. He rules the world with truth and grace
And makes the nations prove
The glories of His righteousness
And wonders of His love.

Isaac Watts, *Psalms of David Imitated*, 1719, based this hymn on the second part of Ps. 98. It was entitled "The Messiah's Second Coming and Kingdom."

There is some uncertainty about the origin of the tune "Antioch," also called "Messiah." It is given as an arrangement from Händel's *Messiah*, taken from the opening phrase of the chorus "Lift up your heads" and from the tenor recitative, "Comfort ye My people." James T. Lightwood holds that the tune is of American origin, and it has been ascribed to Lowell Mason. However, the *Handbook to the Hymnal* casts doubt upon this theory, and we think rightly, since the arrangement "is too much after the pattern of the fugue tunes which he [Mason] so much abhorred and so much wished to replace with tunes more dignified in form." We suggest that the congregation and choir sing the hymn antiphonally: the congregation Lines 1 and 2, the choir Lines 3 and 4, and both the refrain. In this way the most difficult parts, which few congregations ever sing well, are left to the choir.

CHRISTMAS

88 This Night a Wondrous Revelation

1. This night a wondrous revelation
   Makes known to me God's love and grace;
   The Child that merits adoration
   Brings light to our benighted race;
   And though a thousand suns did shine,
   Still brighter were that Light divine.

2. The Sun of Grace for thee is beaming;
   Rejoice, my soul, in Jesus' birth!
   The light from yonder manger streaming
   Sends forth its rays o'er all the earth.
   It drives the night of sin away
   And turns our darkness into day.

3. This light, which all thy gloom can banish,
   The bliss of heaven glorifies;
   When sun and moon and stars shall vanish,
   Its rays shall still illume the skies.
   This light through all eternity
   Thy heaven and all to thee shall be.

4. O Jesus, precious Sun of Gladness,
   Fill Thou my soul with light, I pray.
   Dispel the gloomy night of sadness
   And teach Thou me this Christmas Day
   How I a child of light may be,
   Aglow with light that comes from Thee.

Dies ist die Nacht, da mir erschienen
Des grossen Gottes Freundlichkeit!
Das Kind, dem alle Engel dienen,
Bringt Licht in meine Dunkelheit,
Und dieses Welt- und Himmelslicht
Weicht hunderttausend Sonnen nicht.

Lass dich erleuchten, meine Seele,
Versäume nicht den Gnadenschein!
Der Glanz in dieser kleinen Höhle
Streckt sich in alle Welt hinein,
Er treibet weg der Hölle Macht,
Der Sünden und des Kreuzes Nacht.

In diesem Lichte kannst du sehen
Das Licht der klaren Seligkeit.
Wenn Sonne, Mond und Stern' vergehen,
Vielleicht schon in ganz kurzer Zeit,
Wird dieses Licht mit seinem Schein
Dein Himmel und dein alles sein.

Drum, Jesu, schöne Weihnachtssonne,
Bestrahle mich mit deiner Gunst!
Dein Licht sei meine Weihnachtswonne
Und lehre mich die Weihnachtskunst,
Wie ich im Lichte wandeln soll
Und sei des Weihnachtsglaubens voll!

This hymn, by Caspar Friedrich Nachtenhöfer, was first published in the Coburg *Gesangbuch*, 1683, in five stanzas. Our text includes Stanzas 1, 2, 3, and 5 of the original. Arthur Tozer Russell, in his *Psalms and Hymns*, 1851, translated the omitted fourth stanza thus:

> Meanwhile, with faith and love's clear shining,
> Let all within be full of light,
> Thy heart in truth to God inclining —
> Else will his Sun retire from sight.
> Oh, wouldst thou live beneath His ray,
> Pursue no more sin's darksome way.

The translation is by Anna Hoppe, 1922.

For comments on the tune "O dass ich tausend" see Hymn No. 30.

89 To Thee My Heart I Offer

1. To Thee my heart I offer,
   O Christ-child sweet and dear;
   Upon Thy love relying,
   Oh, be Thou ever near!
   Take Thou my heart and give me Thine
   And let it be forever mine,
   O Jesus, holy, undefiled,
   My Savior meek and mild.

2. My heart within is glowing,
   O Christ-child sweet and dear.
   I love Thee, Lord and Savior;
   Oh, be Thou ever near!
   I see Thee in a manger laid,
   Near cattle resting unafraid;
   I see Thy deep humility
   And lowly bow to Thee.

3. What brought Thee to the manger,
   O Christ-child sweet and dear?
   Thy love for me, a stranger, —
   Oh, be Thou ever near!
   O Lord, how great is this Thy love
   That reaches down from heaven above,
   Thy love for us, by sin defiled,
   That made Thee, God, a child!

4. With all my heart and being,
   O Christ-child sweet and dear,
   I love Thee, and Thee only;
   Oh, be Thou ever near!
   My heart I in Thy manger lay,
   Let it remain there and for aye
   Draw it to Thee that it may be
   Secure eternally.

5. Let me be Thine forever,
   O Christ-child sweet and dear;
   Uphold me with Thy mercy
   And be Thou ever near.
   From Thee I gladly all receive,
   And what is mine to Thee I give.
   My heart, my soul, and all I own:
   Let these be Thine alone.

CHRISTMAS

This delightful manger song was brought to the attention of our Committee through the Slovak version. Both as to text and melody very little can be said about its origin. We have traced it back to 1653. The author is unknown. It was translated into Slovak by an unknown writer and included in the Slovak hymnal of *Tranoscius* in 1818, and perhaps earlier. It has since become a favorite in the Slovak churches. We have been able to find only three stanzas of the German original, which contains six. The Slovak text omits Stanza 4. The three German stanzas, 1, 3, and 5 of the original, are:

1. Mein Herz will ich dir schenken,
   Herzliebes Jesulein,
In deine Lieb' versenken,
   Liebreiches Kindelein.
Nimm hin mein Herz, gib mir das dein,
Lass beide Herzen *ein* Herz sein,
O du herzliebes Jesulein,
   Liebreiches Kindelein!

3. Wie liegst du da so gar veracht't,
   Herzliebes Jesulein!
Hat dich dein' Lieb' so arm gemacht,
   Liebreiches Kindelein?
O grosse Lieb', stark ist dein' Kraft,
Die uns hat Gott vom Himmel bracht,
O du herzliebes Jesulein,
   Liebreiches Kindelein!

5. Von ganzem Herzen lieb' ich dich,
   Herzliebes Jesulein;
Ich lieb' dich ganz inbrünstiglich,
   Liebreiches Kindelein.
All's, was du hast, das gibst du mir;
All's, was ich hab', das schenk' ich dir.
Herz, Lieb' und Blut, Ehr', Seel' und Gut,
   Dein soll es eigen sein.

The translation is composite and was written for *The Lutheran Hymnal*. The tune, which has been named "Cordis donum" *for the Lutheran Hymnal*, was coupled with the German text at its publication, in 1653, in the *Clausener Gesangbuch*. It is most likely also of German origin.

Come, Your Hearts and Voices Raising 90

1. Come, your hearts and voices raising,
Christ the Lord with gladness praising;
Loudly sing His love amazing,
   Worthy folk of Christendom.

Kommt und lasst uns Christum ehren,
Herz und Sinnen zu ihm kehren!
Singet fröhlich, lasst euch hören,
   Wertes Volk der Christenheit!

2. Sin and death may well be groaning,
Satan now may well be moaning;
We, our full salvation owning,
   Cast our every care away.

Sünd' und Hölle mag sich grämen,
Tod und Teufel mag sich schämen.
Wir, die unser Heil annehmen,
   Werfen allen Kummer hin.

3. See how God, for us providing,
Gave His Son and life abiding;
He our weary steps is guiding
   From earth's woe to heavenly joy.

Sehet, was hat Gott gegeben!
Seinen Sohn zum ew'gen Leben!
Dieser kann und will uns heben
   Aus dem Leid in's Himmels Freud'.

4. Christ, from heaven to us descending
And in love our race befriending,
In our need His help extending,
   Saved us from the wily Foe.

Seine Seel' ist uns gewogen,
Lieb' und Gunst hat ihn gezogen,
Uns, die Satanas betrogen,
   Zu besuchen aus der Höh'.

5. Jacob's Star in all its splendor
Beams with comfort sweet and tender,
Forcing Satan to surrender,
   Breaking all the powers of hell.

Jakobs Stern ist aufgegangen,
Stillt das sehnliche Verlangen,
Bricht den Kopf der alten Schlange
   Und zerstört der Hölle Reich.

6. From the bondage that oppressed us,
From sin's fetters that possessed us,
From the grief that sore distressed us,
   We, the captives, now are free.

Unser Kerker, da wir sassen
Und mit Sorgen ohne Massen
Uns das Herze selbst abfrassen,
   Ist entzwei, und wir sind frei.

7. Oh, the joy beyond expressing
When by faith we grasp this blessing
And to Thee we come confessing,
   That our freedom Thou hast wrought!

O du hochgesegn'te Stunde,
Da wir das von Herzensgrunde
Glauben und mit unserm Munde
   Danken dir, o Jesulein!

8. Gracious Child, we pray Thee, hear us,
From Thy lowly manger cheer us,
Gently lead us and be near us
   Till we join the angelic choir.

Schönstes Kindlein in dem Stalle,
Sei uns freundlich, bring uns alle
Dahin, wo mit süssem Schalle
   Dich der Engel Heer erhöht!

This hymn by Paul Gerhardt was first published in Johann Ebeling's *Geistliche Andachten,* Berlin, 1667. It is based on Luke 2:15.

The composite translation was prepared for *The Lutheran Hymnal.*

The tune "Quem Pastores" has long been associated with this hymn. It is the melody of a German Christmas matin carol of 14th-century origin. One of the old texts of this carol begins: "Den die Hirten lobeten ser." The tune was first published in Valentin Triller's *Ein Christlich Singebuch fur Layen und Gelerten,* Breslau, 1555, set to the Latin text of "Quem Pastores" and a German text, beginning "Preis sei Gott im höchsten Throne."

91   Let the Earth Now Praise the Lord

1. Let the earth now praise the Lord,
Who hath truly kept His word
And the sinners' Help and Friend
Now at last to us doth send.

2. What the fathers most desired,
What the prophets' heart inspired,
What they longed for many a year,
Stands fulfilled in glory here.

3. Abram's promised great Reward,
Zion's Helper, Jacob's Lord, —
Him of twofold race behold, —
Truly came, as long foretold.

4. Welcome, O my Savior, now!
Hail! My Portion, Lord, art Thou.
Here, too, in my heart, I pray,
Oh, prepare Thyself a way!

5. King of Glory, enter in;
Cleanse it from the filth of sin,
As Thou hast so often done;
It belongs to Thee alone.

6. As Thy coming was in peace,
Quiet, full of gentleness,
Let the same mind dwell in me
That was ever found in Thee.

7. Comfort my desponding heart;
Thou my Strength and Refuge art.
I am weak, and cunningly
Satan lays his snares for me.

8. Bruise for me the Serpent's head,
That, set free from doubt and dread,
I may cleave to Thee in faith,
Safely kept through life and death,

9. And when Thou dost come again
As a glorious King to reign,
I with joy may see Thy face,
Freely ransomed by Thy grace.

Gott sei Dank durch alle Welt,
Der sein Wort beständig hält
Und der Sünder Trost und Rat
Zu uns hergesendet hat.

Was der alten Väter Schar
Höchster Wunsch und Sehnen war,
Und was sie geprophezeit,
Ist erfüllt nach Herrlichkeit.

Zions Hilf' und Abrams Lohn,
Jakobs Heil, der Jungfrau'n Sohn,
Der wohl zweigestammte Held,
Hat sich treulich eingestellt.

Sei willkommen, o mein Heil!
Hosianna, o mein Teil!
Richte du auch eine Bahn
Dir in meinem Herzen an.

Zeuch, du Ehrenkönig, ein,
Es gehöret dir allein;
Mach es, wie du gerne tust,
Rein von allem Sündenwust.

Und gleichwie dein' Ankunft war
Voller Sanftmut, ohn' Gefahr,
Also sei auch jederzeit
Deine Sanftmut mir bereit.

Tröste, tröste meinen Sinn,
Weil ich schwach und blöde bin
Und des Satans schlaue List
Sich zu hoch an mir vermisst.

Tritt der Schlange Kopf entzwei,
Dass ich, aller Ängste frei,
Dir im Glauben um und an
Selig bleibe zugetan.

Dass, wenn du, o Lebensfürst,
Prächtig wiederkommen wirst,
Ich dir mög' entgegengehn
Und vor Gott gerecht bestehn.

This hymn by Heinrich Held first appeared in Johann Crüger's *Praxis Pietatis Melica,* 1659. Since then it has become a general favorite in many lands, and deservedly so, as it is one of our best Advent and Christmas hymns.

The translation is by Catherine Winkworth (except Stanza 7), *Chorale Book for England,* 1863. The seventh stanza is by an unknown translator.

For comments on the tune "Nun komm, der Heiden Heiland" see Hymn No 95.

[74]

Now Sing We, Now Rejoice 92

1. Now sing we, now rejoice,
Now raise to heaven our voice;
He from whom joy streameth
   Poor in a manger lies;
Not so brightly beameth
   The sun in yonder skies.
Thou my Savior art!
Thou my Savior art!

2. Come from on high to me;
I cannot rise to Thee
Cheer my wearied spirit,
   O pure and holy Child;
Through Thy grace and merit,
   Blest Jesus, Lord most mild,
Draw me unto Thee!
Draw me unto Thee!

3. Now through His Son doth shine
The Father's grace divine.
Death o'er us had reignèd
   Through sin and vanity;
He for us obtainèd
   Eternal joy on high.
May we praise Him there!
May we praise Him there!

4. Oh, where shall joy be found?
Where but on heavenly ground?
Where the angels singing
   With all His saints unite,
Sweetest praises bringing
   In heavenly joy and light.
Oh, that we were there!
Oh, that we were there!

Nun singet und seid froh,
Jauchzt all' und saget so:
Unsers Herzens Wonne
   Liegt in der Krippe bloss,
Leuchtet als die Sonne
   In seiner Mutter Schoss.
Du bist A und O.
Du bist A und O.

Sohn Gottes in der Höh',
Nach dir ist mir so weh!
Tröste mein Gemüte,
   O Kindlein zart und rein,
Und durch deine Güte,
   O liebstes Jesulein,
Zeuch mich hin nach dir!
Zeuch mich hin nach dir!

Gross ist des Vaters Huld,
Der Sohn tilgt unsre Schuld;
Da wir ganz verdorben
   Durch Sünd' und Eitelkeit,
Hat er uns erworben
   Die ew'ge Himmelsfreud'.
Eia, wär'n wir da!
Eia, wär'n wir da!

Wo ist der Freudenort?
Sonst nirgend mehr denn dort,
Da die Engel singen
   Dem lieben Jesulein
Und die Psalmen klingen
   Im Himmel hell und rein.
Eia, wär'n wir da!
Eia, wär'n wir da!

This hymn is an altered form of the translation, by Arthur Tozer Russell (*Psalms and Hymns,* 1851), of the pure German version (*Hannoversches Gesang-Buch,* 1646, author unknown) of one of our oldest Christmas songs. The original form of the text was a macaronic, a mixture of Latin and German. It is by an unknown author and at least of 14th-century origin. It is found in a number of variant texts. The following is one of the best:

1. In dulci iubilo,
Nu singet und seyt fro!
Unsers herzen wonne
   Leyt in praesepio
Und leuchtet als die sonne
   Matris in gremio
Alpha es et O!
Alpha es et O!

2. O Iesu, parvule,
Nach dir ist mir so we;
Tröst mir myn gemüte,
   O puer optime,
Durch aller juncfrawen güte,
   O princeps gloriae.
Trahe me post te!
Trahe me post te!

3. O Patris caritas!
O Nati lenitas!
Wir weren all verloren
   Per nostra crimina;
So hat er uns erworben
   Coelorum gaudia.
Eya, wär wir da!
Eya, wär wir da!

4. Ubi sunt gaudia?
Nirgend mer denn da,
Da die engel singen
   Nova cantica,
Und die schellen klingen
   In Regis curia.
Eya, wär wir da!
Eya, wär wir da!

It has been claimed that this mixed-language form of a hymn marks the beginning of the German spiritual song, showing German hymning "stretching forth its head like the chick through the breaking egg-shell." This, however, is not the case because we have many German spiritual songs that originated before and during the time of the "mixed" hymns. The macaronic was rather, as *Nelle* says, the result of the delight which many people took in this type. Luther is credited, by Albert F. W. Fischer, with having changed the third stanza of the macaronic to its present form. Prior to that time this stanza overemphasized the place of the Virgin in the plan of salvation.

The tune "In dulci iubilo" is of 14th-century German origin.

CHRISTMAS

93   O Lord, We Welcome Thee

1. O Lord, we welcome Thee,
   Our hearts for joy are leaping.
Thou, Jesus, dearest Child,
   Thy precious promise keeping,
Art come from heaven to earth
   To be our Brother dear;
Thou gracious Son of God,
   Wilt banish all our fear.

2. The mighty Son of God,
   His majesty concealing,
Dwells with our fallen race
   To give us balm and healing.
The everlasting God
   Descends from realms above,
Becomes a winsome Child,
   Reveals His Father's love.

3. Ah, sweet and gentle name!
   Its echoes far are sounding,
It pierces hearts of stone
   And tells of love abounding.
O Jesus, dearest Child,
   On Thee will we rely,
And, calling on Thy name,
   We die not when we die.

4. To Thee alone we cling,
   For Thee all else forsaking;
On Thee alone we build
   Though heaven and earth be quaking.
To Thee alone we live,
   In Thee alone we die;
O Jesus, dearest Lord,
   With Thee we reign on high.

Ich freue mich in dir
   Und heisse dich willkommen,
Mein liebstes Jesulein;
   Du hast dir vorgenommen,
Mein Brüderlein zu sein.
   Ach, wie ein süsser Ton!
Wie freundlich sieht er aus,
   Der grosse Gottessohn!

Gott senkt die Majestät,
   Sein unbegreiflich Wesen,
In eines Menschen Leib;
   Nun muss die Welt genesen.
Der allerhöchste Gott
   Spricht freundlich bei mir ein,
Wird gar ein kleines Kind
   Und heisst mein Jesulein!

Wie lieblich klingt es mir,
   Wie schallt es in die Ohren!
Es kann durch Stahl und Erz
   Und harte Felsen bohren,
Das liebste Jesulein.
   Wer Jesum recht erkennt,
Der stirbt nicht, wenn er stirbt,
   Sobald er Jesum nennt.

Wohlan, so will ich mich
   An dich, o Jesu, halten,
Und sollte gleich die Welt
   In tausend Stücke spalten.
O Jesu, dir, nur dir,
   Dir leb' ich ganz allein,
Auf dich, allein auf dich,
   Mein Jesu, schlaf' ich ein.

Caspar Ziegler published this hymn in his *Jesus oder XX Elegien über die Geburt*, etc., Leipzig, 1648.

The translation is composite.

Bach has a *chorale* cantata on this hymn in which he uses a tune which Layriz dates c. 1714. This tune König, *Harmonischer Liederschatz*, 1738, has set to the hymn "O stilles Gotteslamm."

For comments on the tune "Nun danket alle Gott" see Hymn No. 36.

94   Hark! the Herald Angels Sing

1. Hark! the herald angels sing,
"Glory to the new-born King;
Peace on earth and mercy mild,
God and sinners reconciled!"
Joyful, all ye nations, rise,
Join the triumph of the skies;
With the angelic host proclaim,
"Christ is born in Bethlehem!"
   Hark! the herald angels sing,
   "Glory to the new-born King!"

2. Christ, by highest heaven adored,
Christ, the everlasting Lord,
Late in time behold Him come,
Offspring of a virgin's womb.
Veiled in flesh the Godhead see,
Hail the incarnate Deity!
Pleased as Man with man to dwell,
Jesus, our Immanuel!
   Hark! the herald angels sing,
   "Glory to the new-born King!"

3. Hail, the heavenly Prince of Peace!
Hail, the Sun of Righteousness!
Light and life to all He brings,
Risen with healing in His wings.
Mild He leaves His throne on high,
Born that man no more may die;
Born to raise the sons of earth;
Born to give them second birth.
   Hark! the herald angels sing,
   "Glory to the new-born King!"

4. Come, Desire of nations, come,
Fix in us Thy humble home;
Oh, to all Thyself impart,
Formed in each believing heart!
Hark! the herald angels sing,
"Glory to the new-born King;
Peace on earth and mercy mild,
God and sinners reconciled!"
   Hark! the herald angels sing,
   "Glory to the new-born King!"

This is one of the most popular Christmas hymns in our language. It is much altered from the original form in which Charles Wesley first published it in his *Hymns and Sacred Poems,* 1739, which was as follows:

1. Hark! how all the welkin rings!
Glory to the King of kings!
Peace on earth and mercy mild,
God and sinners reconciled!
Joyful, all ye nations, rise,
Join the triumph of the skies;
Universal nature say,
"Christ the Lord is born today!"

2. Christ, by highest heaven adored;
Christ, the everlasting Lord:
Late in time behold Him come,
Offspring of a virgin's womb:
Veiled in flesh the Godhead see;
Hail the Incarnate Deity,
Pleased as man with men to appear,
Jesus, our Immanuel here!

3. Hail! the heavenly Prince of Peace!
Hail! the Son of righteousness!
Light and life to all He brings,
Risen with healing in His wings.
Mild He lays His glory by,
Born that man no more may die,
Born to raise the sons of earth,
Born to give them second birth.

4. Come, Desire of nations, come,
Fix in us Thy humble home!
Rise, the woman's conquering Seed,
Bruise in us the Serpent's head!
Now display Thy saving power,
Ruined nature now restore,
Now in mystic union join
Thine to ours and ours to Thine!

5. Adam's likeness, Lord, efface;
Stamp Thy image in its place;
Second Adam from above,
Reinstate us in Thy love!
Let us Thee, though lost, regain,
Thee, the Life, the Inner Man.
Oh, to all Thyself impart,
Formed in each believing heart!

In a later edition, 1743, Wesley gave it in a revised form and omitted the last stanza. Some hymnals still use this form, which is usually sung to a traditional English melody, arranged by R. Vaughn Williams, and called *Dent Dale.*

Our version is that now commonly used, which is the result of revisions made by George Whitefield in his *Collection,* 1753, who gave it the familiar first line, and by Martin Madan, in his *Psalms and Hymns,* 1760, who also altered it. Additional alterations were made by others. The refrain was not added until 1782.

This is the only one of Charles Wesley's hymns to be included in the Church of England's *Book of Common Prayer.*

The tune *Mendelssohn* is from the *Festgesang for Male Chorus and Orchestra,* composed for, and first sung at, the festival held in Leipzig, June, 1840, to celebrate the invention of printing. Dr. W. H. Cummings, organist at Waltham Abbey, adapted the tune for this hymn, 1856. In some books the tune is called *St. Vincent;* in others, *Bethlehem.*

Songs of Praise Discussed, adds this interesting comment on the tune:

"It is curious that some years previous to the publication of Dr. Cummings's adaptation, Mendelssohn, in writing to his English publishers on the subject of an English translation of the *Festgesang,* said: "I must repeat the wish I already expressed in my letter to Mr. Bartholomew. I think there ought to be other words to No. 2. If the right ones are hit at, I am sure that piece will be liked very much by the singers and hearers, but it will never do to sacred words. There must be a national and merry subject found out, something to which the soldierlike and buxom motion of the piece has some relation, and the words must express something gay and popular, as the music tries to do it."

CHRISTMAS

95   Savior of the Nations, Come

1. Savior of the nations, come,
Virgin's Son, make here Thy home!
Marvel now, O heaven and earth,
That the Lord chose such a birth.

2. Not by human flesh and blood,
By the Spirit of our God,
Was the Word of God made flesh —
Woman's Offspring, pure and fresh.

3. Wondrous birth! O wondrous Child
Of the Virgin undefiled!
Though by all the world disowned,
Still to be in heaven enthroned.

4. From the Father forth He came
And returneth to the same,
Captive leading death and hell —
High the song of triumph swell!

5. Thou, the Father's only Son,
Hast o'er sin the victory won.
Boundless shall Thy kingdom be;
When shall we its glories see?

6. Brightly doth Thy manger shine,
Glorious is its light divine.
Let not sin o'ercloud this light;
Ever be our faith thus bright.

7. Praise to God the Father sing,
Praise to God the Son, our King,
Praise to God the Spirit be
Ever and eternally.

Nun komm, der Heiden Heiland,
Der Jungfrauen Kind erkannt!
Dass sich wundre alle Welt,
Gott solch' Geburt ihm bestellt.

Nicht von Mann's Blut noch von Fleisch,
Allein von dem Heil'gen Geist
Ist Gott's Wort worden ein Mensch
Und blüht ein' Frucht Weibesfleisch.

Der Jungfrau Leib schwanger ward,
Doch blieb Keuschheit rein bewahrt,
Leucht't hervor manch' Tugend schön,
Gott da war in seinem Thron.

Er ging aus der Kammer sein,
Dem kön'glichen Saal so rein,
Gott von Art und Mensch ein Held,
Sein'n Weg er zu laufen eilt.

Sein Lauf kam vom Vater her
Und kehrt' wieder zum Vater,
Fuhr hinunter zu der Höll'
Und wieder zu Gottes Stuhl.

Der du bist dem Vater gleich,
Führ' hinaus den Sieg im Fleisch,
Dass dein' ew'ge Gott'sgewalt
In uns das krank' Fleisch erhalt'.

Dein' Krippe glänzt hell und klar,
Die Nacht gibt ein neu Licht dar,
Dunkel muss nicht kommen drein,
Der Glaub' bleibt immer im Schein.

Lob sei Gott dem Vater g'tan,
Lob sei Gott sein'm ein'gen Sohn,
Lob sei Gott dem Heil'gen Geist
Immer und in Ewigkeit!

This hymn comes to us, through the German, from the Latin of St. Ambrose:

1. Veni, Redemptor gentium;
Ostende partum virginis;
Miretur omne saeculum.
Talis decet partus Deo.

2. Non ex virili semine,
Sed mystico spiramine
Verbum Dei factum est caro,
Fructusque ventris floruit.

3. Alvus tumescit virginis,
Claustrum pudoris permanet;
Vexilla virtutum micant,
Versatur in templo Deus.

4. Procedit e thalamo suo,
Pudoris aulo regia,
Geminae gigans substantiae,
Alacris ut currat viam.

5. Egressus eius a Patre,
Regressus eius ad Patrem;
Excursus usque ad inferos,
Recursus ad sedem Dei.

6. Aequalis aeterno Patri,
Carnis tropaeo accingere,
Infirma nostri corporis
Virtute firmans perpeti.

7. Praesepe iam fulget tuum,
Lumenque nox spirat novum,
Quod nulla nox interpolet
Fideque iugi luceat.

8. Gloria tibi, Domine,
Qui natus es de virgine,
Cum Patre et sancto Spiritu,
In sempiterna saecula.

It will be noted that the fourth stanza of the Latin text has been omitted in our version. *Julian* informs us that the Latin hymn, though included in older breviaries, is not in the *Roman Breviary* "and can hardly be said to be in use at the present day, a somewhat unfortunate ecclesiastical prudery having set aside this noble composition." The same authority, however, adds: "It must be confessed that a strictly literal English version is hardly desirable for modern congregational use."

Luther's German version appeared with the tune in both editions of *Eyn Enchiridion,* Erfurt, 1524, and in Johann Walther's *Geystliche gesangk Buchleyn,* Wittenberg, 1524.

The translation is a slightly altered form of the version by William M. Reynolds and first appeared in 1860.

The tune "Nun komm, der Heiden Heiland," also called "Veni Redemptor gentium," one of the heritages of the Middle Ages, is adapted from the arrangement found in *Geistliches Gesangbüchlein,* Wittenberg, 1524.

Oh, Rejoice, Ye Christians, Loudly 96

1. Oh, rejoice, ye Christians, loudly,
   For our joy hath now begun;
   Wondrous things our God hath done.
   Tell abroad His goodness proudly
   Who our race hath honored thus
   That He deigns to dwell with us.
   Joy, O joy, beyond all gladness,
   Christ hath done away with sadness!
   Hence, all sorrow and repining,
   For the Sun of Grace is shining!

2. See, my soul, thy Savior chooses
   Weakness here and poverty;
   In such love He comes to thee
   Nor the hardest couch refuses;
   All He suffers for thy good,
   To redeem thee by His blood.
   Joy, O joy, beyond all gladness,
   Christ hath done away with sadness!
   Hence, all sorrow and repining,
   For the Sun of Grace is shining!

3. Lord, how shall I thank Thee rightly?
   I acknowledge that by Thee
   I am saved eternally.
   Let me not forget it lightly,
   But to Thee at all times cleave
   And my heart true peace receive.
   Joy, O joy, beyond all gladness,
   Christ hath done away with sadness!
   Hence, all sorrow and repining,
   For the Sun of Grace is shining!

4. Jesus, guard and guide Thy members,
   Fill Thy brethren with Thy grace,
   Hear their prayers in every place.
   Quicken now life's faintest embers;
   Grant all Christians, far and near,
   Holy peace, a glad New Year!
   Joy, O joy, beyond all gladness,
   Christ hath done away with sadness!
   Hence, all sorrow and repining,
   For the Sun of Grace is shining!

Freuet euch, ihr Christen alle!
Freue sich, wer immer kann,
Gott hat viel an uns getan.
Freuet euch mit grossem Schalle,
Dass er uns so hoch geacht't,
Sich mit uns befreund't gemacht.
Freude, Freude über Freude!
Christus wehret allem Leide.
Wonne, Wonne über Wonne!
Er ist die Genadensonne.

Siehe, siehe, meine Seele,
Wie dein Heiland kommt zu dir,
Brennt in Liebe für und für,
Dass er in der Krippe Höhle
Harte lieget dir zugut,
Dich zu lösen durch sein Blut.
Freude, Freude über Freude!
Christus wehret allem Leide.
Wonne, Wonne über Wonne!
Er ist die Genadensonne.

Jesu, wie soll ich dir danken?
Ich bekenne, dass von dir
Meine Seligkeit herrühr'.
O lass mich von dir nicht wanken,
Nimm mich dir zu eigen hin,
So empfindet Herz und Sinn
Freude, Freude über Freude!
Christus wehret allem Leide.
Wonne, Wonne über Wonne!
Er ist die Genadensonne.

Jesu, nimm dich deiner Glieder
Ferner in Genaden an!
Schenke, was man bitten kann,
Zu erquicken deine Brüder;
Gib der ganzen Christenschar
Frieden und ein sel'ges Jahr.
Freude, Freude über Freude!
Christus wehret allem Leide.
Wonne, Wonne über Wonne!
Er ist die Genadensonne.

This beautiful Christmas hymn by Christian Keimann (Keymann) was published in A. Hammerschmidt's *Musikalische Andachten* (Freiberg, Saxony) in 1646 and set to this tune, "Freuet euch, ihr Christen," by Andreas Hammerschmidt. According to *Koch* it was written by Keimann for his scholars to be used at a Christmas celebration in 1645 and published at Görlitz, 1646, with the heading *Der neugeborne Jesus.*

Catherine Winkworth published it in her *Chorale Book for England* in 1863, set to Hammerschmidt's tune. Her translation is followed throughout in the text, save in Stanza 3, Lines 2 to 6, where she departed from the definiteness of the original and wrote:

I acknowledge that from Thee
Every blessing flows for me.
Let me not forget it lightly,
But to Thee through all things cleave;
So shall heart and mind receive.

Hammerschmidt's tune was introduced by Hallelujah, repeated twelve times, which was to be sung at the beginning and the end of the hymn.

CHRISTMAS

97   Let Us All with Gladsome Voice

1. Let us all with gladsome voice
    Praise the God of heaven,
Who, to bid our hearts rejoice,
    His own Son hath given.

2. To this vale of tears He comes,
    Here to serve in sadness,
That with Him in heaven's fair homes
    We may reign in gladness.

3. We are rich, for He was poor;
    Is not this a wonder?
Therefore praise God evermore
    Here on earth and yonder.

4. O Lord Christ, our Savior dear,
    Be Thou ever near us.
Grant us now a glad new year.
    Amen, Jesus, hear us!

Lasst uns alle fröhlich sein,
    Preisen Gott den Herren,
Der sein liebes Söhnelein
    Uns selbst tut verehren!

Er kommt in das Jammertal,
    Wird ein Knecht auf Erden,
Damit wir im Himmelssaal
    Grosse Herren werden.

Er wird arm, wir werden reich,
    Ist das nicht ein Wunder?
Drum lobt Gott im Himmelreich
    Allzeit wie jetzunder!

O Herr Christ, nimm unser wahr
    Durch dein'n heil'gen Namen!
Gib uns ein gut neues Jahr!
    Wer's begehrt, sprech': Amen.

    This hymn and its tune have been ascribed to Urban Langhans, a Saxon choirmaster and "diaconus" who lived in the middle of the sixteenth century; but his authorship is doubtful. According to Mearns, in *Julian,* the first stanza was quoted in a printed sermon of Martin Hammer's, Leipzig, 1620. The full text, with the tune, "Lasst uns alle," first appeared in *Dresdenisch Gesangbuch Christlicher Psalmen und Kirchenlieder, Ander Theil,* Dresden, 1632.

    The translation is an altered form of Catherine Winkworth's *Chorale-Book for England,* 1863. Her translation of the second and fourth stanzas reads:

Down to this sad earth He comes,
    Here to serve us deigning,
That with Him in yon fair homes
    We may once be reigning.

Look on all who sorrow here,
    Lord, in pity bending,
Grant us now a glad New Year
    And a blessed ending.

98   Of the Father's Love Begotten

1. Of the Father's love begotten
    Ere the worlds began to be,
He is Alpha and Omega,
    He the Source, the Ending He,
Of the things that are, that have been,
    And that future years shall see
        Evermore and evermore.

2. Oh, that birth forever blessèd
    When the Virgin, full of grace,
By the Holy Ghost conceiving,
    Bare the Savior of our race,
And the Babe, the world's Redeemer,
    First revealed His sacred face
        Evermore and evermore.

3. O ye heights of heaven, adore Him;
    Angel hosts, His praises sing;
Powers, dominions, bow before Him
    And extol our God and King.
Let no tongue on earth be silent,
    Every voice in concert ring
        Evermore and evermore.

4. This is He whom Heaven-taught singers
    Sang of old with one accord;
Whom the Scriptures of the prophets
    Promised in their faithful word.
Now He shines, the Long-expected;
    Let creation praise its Lord
        Evermore and evermore.

Corde natus ex Parentis
    Ante mundi exordium,
Alpha et a cognominatus,
    Ipse fons et clausula
Omnium quae sunt, fuerunt,
    Quaeque post futura sunt,
        Saeculorum saeculis.

O beatus ortus ille,
    Virgo cum puerpera
Edidit nostram salutem,
    Feta sancto Spiritu,
Et puer, redemptor orbis,
    Os sacratum protulit,
        Saeculorum saeculis.

Psallat altitudo caeli,
    Psallant omnes angeli;
Quidquid est virtutis usquam
    Psallat in laudem Dei:
Nulla linguarum silescat,
    Vox et omnis consonet,
        Saeculorum saeculis.

Ecce, quem vates vetusti
    Concinebant saeculis,
Quem prophetarum fideles
    Paginae spoponderant,
Emicat promissus olim;
    Cuncta conlaudent eum,
        Saeculorum saeculis.

CHRISTMAS

5. Christ, to Thee, with God the Father, And, O Holy Ghost, to Thee Hymn and chant and high thanksgiving And unending praises be, Honor, glory, and dominion, And eternal victory Evermore and evermore.	Tibi, Christe, sit cum Patre Hagioque Pneumate Hymnus, decus, laus perennis Gratiarum actio, Honor, virtus, victoria, Regnum aeternaliter, Saeculorum saeculis.

This cento by the Spanish poet Aurelius Prudentius is taken from the *Hymna omnis horae* in his *Liber Cathemerinon IX*. The translation is by John M. Neale, *Hymnal Noted*, 1854, and Henry W. Baker, *Hymns Ancient and Modern*, 1861. Other stanzas in their translation are the following.

After our Stanza 1:

2. At His word they were created; He commanded; it was done: Heaven and earth and depths of ocean In their threefold order one; All that grows beneath the shining Of the moon and orbèd sun, Evermore and evermore.	3. He is found in human fashion Death and sorrow here to know That the race of Adam's children, Doomed by Law to endless woe, May not henceforth die and perish In the dreadful gulf below, Evermore and evermore.

After our Stanza 4:

7. Righteous Judge of souls departed, Righteous King of them that live, On the Father's throne exalted, None in might with Thee may strive; Who at last in vengeance coming Sinners from Thy face shalt drive Evermore and evermore.	8. Thee let old men, Thee let young men, Thee let boys in chorus sing; Matrons, virgins, little maidens, With glad voices answering; Let their guileless songs reecho And the heart its music bring Evermore and evermore.

The plainsong tune "Divinum mysterium," also called "Corde natus," found in manuscripts of the 12th century, has reached us by an interesting route. In 1580 Didrick Pedersen (Petri), a young Finlander, attended college at Rostock. In 1582 he published a collection of school and sacred songs gathered there, among them this tune. A rare copy of this old book, *Piae Cantiones* (Greifswald), came in 1853 into the hands of Thomas Helmore, master of the Children of the Chapels Royal in England and editor of the *Hymnal Noted*. He edited the tune with the present words. The earlier rhythm has been restored in the present form of the tune. The melody was in use during the 13th century, set to the hymn "Divinum mysterium."

Now are the Days Fulfilled 99

1. Now are the days fulfilled, God's Son is manifested, Now His great majesty In human flesh is vested. Behold the mighty God, By whom all wrath is stilled, The woman's promised Seed — Now are the days fulfilled.	Nun ist die Zeit erfüllt, Des Höchsten Sohn ist kommen Und hat das arme Fleisch Der Menschen angenommen. Hier ist der Mann, der Herr, Der Furcht und Strafe stillt, Des Weibes Same kommt: Nun ist die Zeit erfüllt.
2. Now are the days fulfilled, Lo, Jacob's Star is shining; The gloomy night has fled Wherein the world lay pining. Now, Israel, look on Him Who long thy heart hath thrilled; Hear Zion's watchmen cry: Now are the days fulfilled.	Nun ist die Zeit erfüllt, Der Stern aus Jakob funkelt, Die trübe Nacht ist hin, Die alle Welt verdunkelt. Hier ist es, Israel, Was du erwarten willt; Der Zionshüter schreit: Nun ist die Zeit erfüllt.

3. Now are the days fulfilled,
   The child of God rejoices;
   No bondage of the Law,
   No curses that it voices,
   Can fill our hearts with fear;
   On Christ our hope we build.
   Behold the Prince of Peace —
   Now are the days fulfilled.

Nun ist die Zeit erfüllt,
Der Stab von Aaron blühet,
Worauf das alte Bild
Der heil'gen Lade siehet.
Es hat sich Rat, Kraft, Held
In armen Staub verhüllt
Und wird ein schwaches Kind:
Nun ist die Zeit erfüllt.

Nun ist die Zeit erfüllt,
Die Kindschaft ist erworben.
Was unter dem Gesetz
Und dessen Fluch verdorben,
Das hört nun weiter nicht,
Wie Zorn und Eifer brüllt.
Gott ruft den Frieden aus;
Nun ist die Zeit erfüllt.

We have been unable to trace the authorship of this hymn. It is not found in many hymnals. The *Rochlitzer Gesangbuch* of 1746 is one of the few that have it.

The translation is an altered form of that by Frederick W. Herzberger, published in the *Selah Song-Book*.

For comments on the tune "Was frag' ich nach der Welt" see Hymn No. 430.

100   Christians, Sing Out with Exultation

1. Christians, sing out with exultation
   And praise your Benefactor's name!
   Today the Author of salvation,
   The Father's Well-belovèd, came.
   Of undefilèd virgin mother
   An Infant, all divine, was born,
   And God Himself became your Brother
   Upon this happy Christmas morn.

2. In Him eternal might and power
   To human weakness hath inclined;
   And this poor Child brings richest dower
   Of gifts and graces to mankind.
   While here His majesty disguising,
   A servant's form the Master wears,
   Behold the beams of glory rising
   E'en from His poverty and tears.

3. A stable serves Him for a dwelling
   And for a bed a manger mean;
   Yet o'er His head, His advent telling,
   A new and wondrous star is seen.
   Angels rehearse to men the story,
   The joyful story, of His birth;
   To Him they raise the anthem — "Glory
   To God on high and peace on earth!"

4. For through this holy incarnation
   The primal curse is done away;
   And blessèd peace o'er all creation
   Hath shed its pure and gentle ray.
   Then, in that heavenly concert joining,
   O Christian men, with one accord,
   Your voices tunefully combining,
   Salute the birthday of your Lord.

Faisons éclater notre joie,
Et louons notre Bienfaiteur;
Le Père éternel nous envoie
Son Bien-aimé pour Rédempteur.
D'une vierge chaste et féconde
Un enfant divin nous est né,
Aujourd'hui le Sauveur du monde,
Le Fils de Dieu, nous est donné.

En Lui la suprême puissance
Se trouve avec l'infirmité;
Une éternelle et pure essence
S'unit à notre humanité;
Dans la bassesse on Le voit naitre,
Sous la forme de serviteur,
Mais c'est alors qu'il fait paraitre
Plusieurs rayons de Sa grandeur.

Il n'a pour palais qu'une étable,
Et qu'une crèche pour berceau;
Mais cet enfant incomparable
Fait briller un astre nouveau.
A Sa naissance les saints Anges
Font ouïr leur voix dans ces lieux;
Ils disent, chantant Ses louanges,
"Gloire soit à Dieu dans les cieux!"

Mortels! le Maître du tonnerre
Contre vous n'est plus irrité;
La paix va régner sur la terre,
Dieu pour vous est plein de bonté.
Joignons notre sainte harmonie
A leurs concerts mélodieux;
Louons le Prince de la vie,
Qui vient Se montrer à nos yeux.

This hymn was written by Benedict Pictet, a pastor of the French Reformed Church in the latter half of the 17th century. He was a member of a committee of three appointed to review the new version of the Psalms in French verse by Conrart, published in 1677. The committee did its task and after the example of the Lutheran Church added some Gospel hymns. In 1705 Pictet

[82]

published anonymously *Cinquante-Quatre Cantiques Sacrez pour les Principales Solemnitez*, which was intended to be a supplement to the authorized Genevan Psalter. This hymn was one of this collection.

There are five stanzas in the original. The omitted stanza reads:

> Approchons-nous, avec les Mages,
> Du berceau de notre Sauveur;
> Rendons-Lui nos justes hommages,
> Et présentons-Lui notre coeur.
> L'or et l'encens de l'Arabie
> Plaisent bien moins à notre Roi,
> Que la sainteté de la vie,
> Qu'un coeur plein d'amour et de foi.

The translation is by Henry Lascelles Jenner (1820—1898), bishop of Dunedin, England. He was both hymn-writer and musician.

The tune *Navarre* is that used for Ps. 118 in the *Genevan Psalter* and is one of the best compositions of Louis Bourgeois. It first appeared in the edition of 1544.

O Gladsome Light, O Grace   101

1. O gladsome Light, O Grace
Of God the Father's Face,
   The eternal splendor wearing;
Celestial, holy, blest,
Our Savior Jesus Christ,
   Joyful in Thine appearing.

2. Now, ere day fadeth quite,
We see the evening light,
   Our wonted hymn outpouring,
Father of might unknown,
Thee, His incarnate Son,
   And Holy Ghost adoring.

3. To Thee of right belongs
All praise of holy songs,
   O Son of God, Life-giver;
Thee, therefore, O Most High,
The world doth glorify
   And shall exalt forever.

Φῶς ἱλαρὸν ἁγίας δόξης,
'Αθανάτου Πατρὸς οὐρανίου,
'Αγίου, μάκαρος,
'Ιησοῦ Χριστέ,
'Ελθόντες ἐπὶ τὴν ἡλίου δύσιν,
'Ιδόντες φῶς ἑσπερινόν,
'Υμνοῦμεν Πατέρα καὶ Υἱόν
Καὶ ῞Αγιον Πνεῦμα Θεόν.
῎Αξιόν σε ἐν πᾶσι καίροις
'Υμνεῖσθαι φωναῖς ὁσίαις,
Υἱὲ Θεοῦ,
Ζωὴν ὁ διδούς,
Διὸ ὁ κόσμος σε δοξάζει.

This is one of our oldest Christian hymns and is dated c. 200. "Shepherd of Tender Youth" (see Hymn No. 628), a paraphrase of a hymn ascribed to St. Clement of Alexandria, is perhaps older. St. Basil of Caesarea quotes this hymn in the fourth century and states that it is of ancient tradition. In the Eastern churches this "Candlelight Hymn" is still used as an evening hymn. Its text, however, is very appropriate also for Christmas. We may, in fact, call it the oldest Christmas hymn of the Church, excluding, of course, the *Gloria in excelsis* of the angels.

The English text, published in the *Yattenden Hymnal* in 1895, is by Robert Bridges, poet laureate of England. He had written it for his congregation at Yattenden, where he lived and worked as superintendent of music.

The tune is called "Nunc Dimittis." It was composed by Louis Bourgeois for the *Genevan Psalter*, 1549. It may have been an adaptation of an existing tune, as some of its phrases are reminiscent of the old German Christmas carol "Es ist ein' Ros' entsprungen." (See Hymn No. 76.) In the *Genevan Psalter* it was set to the "Nunc Dimittis."

102   Oh, Come, All Ye Faithful

1. Oh, come, all ye faithful, triumphantly sing;
Come, see in the manger our Savior and King!
To Bethlehem hasten with joyful accord;
Oh, come, let us adore Him, Christ the Lord!

2. True Son of the Father, He comes from the skies;
To be born of a virgin He doth not despise.
To Bethlehem hasten with joyful accord;
Oh, come, let us adore Him, Christ the Lord!

3. Hark, hark, to the angels all singing in heaven,
"To God in the highest all glory be given!"
To Bethlehem hasten with joyful accord;
Oh, come, let us adore Him, Christ the Lord!

4. To Thee, then, O Jesus, this day of Thy birth
Be glory and honor through heaven and earth,
True Godhead incarnate, omnipotent Word!
Oh, come, let us adore Him, Christ the Lord!

Adeste, fideles,
Laeti triumphantes;
Venite, venite in Bethlehem;
Natum videte
Regem Angelorum:
Venite, adoremus Dominum.

Deum de Deo;
Lumen de Lumine,
Gestant puellae viscera
Deum Verum,
Genitum, non factum:
Venite, adoremus Dominum.

Cantet nunc hymnos,
Chorus Angelorum:
Cantet nunc aula celestium,
Gloria
In excelsis Deo!
Venite, adoremus Dominum.

Ergo Qui natus
Die hodierna,
Iesu, Tibi sit gloria:
Patris Aeterni
Verbum Caro factum!
Venite, adoremus Dominum.

Most authorities place the origin of this hymn into the 17th or 18th century. There are no manuscript copies earlier than the middle of the 18th century. Though written in Latin by an unknown author, it may be of English origin, as it made its first appearance in English Roman Catholic books. It is possible, because of its great popularity in France, that it originated there and was brought thence to England. The hymn has been ascribed to St. Bonaventura, prominent scholastic teacher of the 13th century, but without historical foundation.

The hymn seems to have been composed in eight stanzas originally. The cento above contains Stanzas 1, 2, 7, and 8.

The tune "Adeste fideles" was evidently composed for the hymn. The oldest manuscript yet discovered containing hymn and tune is in a volume preserved at Stonyhurst College, Lancashire, dated 1751, by John Francis Wade, called *Cantus Diversi*. Wade seems to have occupied himself in writing out music for use in Roman Catholic circles. The hymn is given by him in four stanzas, with the music repeated to each stanza. It is entitled "In Nativitate Domini Hymnus."

In view of the fact that this hymn has been translated into at least 125 languages, it may be called the most popular of all Christmas hymns.

The translation is by Edward Caswall, in his *Lyra Catholica*, 1849, and altered by Philip Schaff for his *Christ in Song*, 1870.

Another widely used English translation is by Frederick Oakeley, Murray's *Hymnal*, 1852, which reads:

1. Oh, come, all ye faithful, joyful and triumphant;
Oh, come ye, oh, come ye to Bethlehem;
Come and behold Him born the King of angels.
Oh, come, let us adore Him, oh, come, let us adore Him,
Oh, come, let us adore Him, Christ the Lord.

2. God of God, Light of Light,
Lo, He abhors not the Virgin's womb;
Very God, begotten, not created.
Oh, come, let us adore Him, etc.

3. Sing, choirs of angels, sing in exultation,
Sing, all ye citizens of heaven above,
Glory to God in the highest.
Oh, come, let us adore Him, etc.

4. Yea, Lord, we greet Thee, born this happy morning;
Jesus, to Thee be glory given;
Word of the Father, now in flesh appearing.
Oh, come, let us adore Him, etc.

CHRISTMAS

To Shepherds as They Watched by Night   103

1. To shepherds as they watched by night
Appeared a host of angels bright;
Behold the tender Babe, they said,
In yonder lowly manger laid.

2. At Bethlehem, in David's town,
As Micah did of old make known;
'Tis Jesus Christ, your Lord and King,
Who doth to all salvation bring.

3. Oh, then rejoice that through His Son
God is with sinners now at one;
Made like yourselves of flesh and blood,
Your brother is the eternal God.

4. What harm can sin and death then do?
The true God now abides with you.
Let hell and Satan rage and chafe,
Christ is your Brother — ye are safe.

5. Not one He will or can forsake
Who Him his confidence doth make.
Let all his wiles the Tempter try,
You may his utmost powers defy.

6. Ye shall and must at last prevail;
God's own ye are, ye cannot fail.
To God forever sing your praise
With joy and patience all your days.

Vom Himmel kam der Engel Schar,
Erschien den Hirten offenbar;
Sie sagten ihn'n: Ein Kindlein zart,
Das liegt dort in der Krippe hart

Zu Bethlehem in Davids Stadt,
Wie Micha das verkündet hat.
Es ist der Herre Jesus Christ,
Der euer aller Heiland ist.

Des sollt ihr billig fröhlich sein,
Dass Gott mit euch ist worden ein.
Er ist gebor'n eu'r Fleisch und Blut,
Eu'r Bruder ist das ew'ge Gut.

Was kann euch tun die Sünd' und Tod?
Ihr habt mit euch den wahren Gott.
Lasst zürnen Teufel und die Höll',
Gott's Sohn ist worden eu'r Gesell.

Er will und kann euch lassen nicht,
Setzt ihr auf ihn eur' Zuversicht.
Es mögen euch viel fechten an:
Dem sei Trotz, der's nicht lassen kann!

Zuletzt müsst ihr doch haben recht,
Ihr seid nun worden Gott's Geschlecht.
Des danket Gott in Ewigkeit,
Geduldig, fröhlich allezeit!

According to *Julian*, Martin Luther wrote this hymn in 1543, basing it on Luke 2:10, 11. It was to be used when his Christmas hymn "From Heaven Above" (see Hymn No. 85) was thought to be too long. It was first published in Joseph Klug's *Geistliche Lieder*, Wittenberg, 1543.

The translation is by Richard Massie, slightly altered, which first appeared in his *Martin Luther's Spiritual Songs*, 1854.

For comments on the tune "Puer nobis nascitur" see Hymn No. 63.

Now Praise We Christ, the Holy One   104

1. Now praise we Christ, the Holy One,
The blessed Virgin Mary's Son,
Far as the glorious sun doth shine,
E'en to the world's remote confine.

2. He who Himself all things did make
A servant's form vouchsafed to take
That He as man mankind might win
And save His creatures from their sin.

3. The grace and power of God the Lord
Upon the mother was outpoured;
A virgin pure and undefiled
In wondrous wise conceived a child.

4. The noble mother bore a Son, —
For so did Gabriel's promise run, —
Whom John confessed and leaped with joy
Ere yet the mother knew her boy.

5. Upon a manger filled with hay
In poverty content He lay;
With milk was fed the Lord of all,
Who feeds the ravens when they call.

6. The heavenly choirs rejoice and raise
Their voice to God in songs of praise.
To humble shepherds is proclaimed
The Shepherd who the world hath framed.

A solis ortus cardine
Ad usque terrae limitem,
Christum canamus principem
Natum Maria virgine.

Beatus auctor saeculi
Servile corpus induit,
Ut carne carnem liberans,
Ne perderet, quod condidit.

Clausa puellae viscera
Caelestis intrat gratia;
Venter puellae baiulat
Secreta, quae non noverat.

Enixa est puerpera,
Quem Gabriel praedixerat,
Quem matris alvo gestiens
Clausus Iohannes senserat.

Faeno iacere pertulit,
Praesepe non abhorruit,
Parvoque lacte pastus est,
Per quem nec ales esurit.

Gaudet chorus caelestium,
Et angeli canunt Deum,
Palamque fit pastoribus
Pastor, creator omnium.

7. All honor unto Christ be paid, Pure Offspring of the favored maid, With Father and with Holy Ghost, Till time in endless time be lost.	Gloria tibi, Domine, Qui natus es de virgine, Cum Patre et Sancto Spiritu, In sempiterna saecula. Amen.

This hymn is part of a longer poem by Coelius Sedulius, written in the first half of the fifth century, in twenty-three stanzas, entitled "Paean Alphabeticus de Christo," a song of praise to Christ written according to the letters of the alphabet. It presents a devout picture of the life of our Lord in verse.

Martin Luther published a German translation of this hymn in *Eyn Enchiridion,* Erfurt, 1524, as follows:

1. Christum wir sollen loben schon,
Der reinen Magd Marien Sohn,
Soweit die liebe Sonne leucht't
Und an aller Welt Ende reicht.

2. Der selig' Schöpfer aller Ding'
Zog an ein's Knechtes Leib gering,
Dass er das Fleisch durchs Fleisch erwürb'
Und sein Geschöpf nicht all's verdürb'.

3. Die göttlich' Gnad' vom Himmel gross
Sich in die keusche Mutter goss;
Ein Mägdlein trug ein heimlich Pfand,
Das der Natur war unbekannt.

4. Das züchtig' Haus des Herzens zart
Gar bald ein Tempel Gottes ward;
Die kein Mann rührte noch erkannt,
Von Gottes Wort man schwanger fand.

5. Die edle Mutter hat gebor'n
Den Gabriel verhiess zuvorn,
Den Sankt Johann's mit Springen zeigt',
Da er noch lag im Mutterleib.

6. Er lag im Heu mit Armut gross,
Die Krippe hart ihn nicht verdross;
Es ward ein' kleine Milch sein' Speis',
Der nie kein Vöglein hungern liess.

7. Des Himmels Chör' sich freuen drob,
Und die Engel singen Gott Lob;
Den armen Hirten wird vermeld't
Der Hirt und Schöpfer aller Welt.

8. Lob, Ehr' und Dank sei dir gesagt,
Christ, gebor'n von der reinen Magd,
Mit Vater und dem Heil'gen Geist
Von nun an bis in Ewigkeit!

The translation is an altered form of that by Richard Massie in *Martin Luther's Spiritual Songs,* 1854. Massie's translation of the omitted fourth stanza reads:

The holy maid became the abode
And temple of the living God,
And she, who knew not man, was blest
With God's own Word made manifest.

The tune "Christum wir sollen loben schon" is based on the ancient plainsong melody used with the text. Its first appearance in a hymn-book was in the Erfurt *Enchiridion* of 1524 with the text. It has been called "a most elegant example of the Phrygian tone." It has been associated with this hymn in England since Anglo-Saxon times.

105   Praise God the Lord, Ye Sons of Men

1. Praise God the Lord, ye sons of men,
Before His highest throne;
Today He opens heaven again
And gives us His own Son.

2. He leaves His heavenly Father's throne,
Is born an infant small,
And in a manger, poor and lone,
Lies in a humble stall.

3. He veils in flesh His power divine
A servant's form to take;
In want and lowliness must pine
Who heaven and earth did make.

4. He nestles at His mother's breast,
Receives her tender care,
Whom angels hail with joy most blest,
King David's royal heir.

Lobt Gott, ihr Christen allzugleich,
In seinem höchsten Thron,
Der heut' aufschleusst sein Himmelreich
Und schenkt uns seinen Sohn!

Er kommt aus seines Vaters Schoss
Und wird ein Kindlein klein,
Er liegt dort elend, nackt und bloss
In einem Krippelein.

Er äussert sich all seiner G'walt,
Wird niedrig und gering
Und nimmt an sich ein's Knechts Gestalt,
Der Schöpfer aller Ding'.

Er liegt an seiner Mutter Brust,
Ihr' Milch ist seine Speis',
An dem die Engel sehn ihr' Lust,
Denn er ist Davids Reis,

5. 'Tis He who in these latter days
   From Judah's tribe should come,
   By whom the Father would upraise
   The Church, His Christendom.

Das aus sei'm Stamm entspriessen sollt'
In dieser letzten Zeit,
Durch welchen Gott aufrichten wollt'
Sein Reich, die Christenheit.

6. A wondrous change which He doth make!
   He takes our flesh and blood,
   And He conceals for sinners' sake
   His majesty of God.

Er wechselt mit uns wunderlich:
Fleisch und Blut nimmt er an
Und gibt uns in sein's Vaters Reich
Die klare Gottheit dran.

7. He serves that I a lord may be;
   A great exchange indeed!
   Could Jesus' love do more for me
   To help me in my need?

Er wird ein Knecht und ich ein Herr,
Das mag ein Wechsel sein!
Wie könnt' es doch sein freundlicher,
Das herz'ge Jesulein?

8. He opens us again the door
   Of Paradise today;
   The angel guards the gate no more,
   To God our thanks we pay.

Heut' schleusst er wieder auf die Tür
Zum schönen Paradeis;
Der Cherub steht nicht mehr dafür.
Gott sei Lob, Ehr' und Preis!

Nikolaus Herman first published this hymn in his collection *Die Sonntags Euangelia vber das gantze Jar* etc., Wittenberg, 1560. In these songs on the Gospels of the church year he had three for Christmas, of which this was the first. It became one of the most popular German Christmas hymns.

It has been frequently translated into English. The translation in *The Lutheran Hymnal* was written by August Crull.

The tune "Lobt Gott, ihr Christen" is also by Nikolaus Herman. It first appeared in his *Ein Christlicher Abentreien*, etc., Leipzig, 1554, set to his children's song on the life and office of John the Baptist, beginning: "Kommt her, ihr liebste Schwesterlein," and then he coupled the tune with this Christmas hymn at its publication in 1560.

The People That in Darkness Sat — 106

1. The people that in darkness sat
   A glorious light have seen;
   The light has shined on them who long
   In shades of death have been.

2. To hail Thee, Sun of Righteousness,
   The gathering nations come;
   They joy as when the reapers bear
   Their harvest treasures home.

3. For Thou their burden dost remove
   And break the tyrant's rod
   As in the day when Midian fell
   Before the sword of God.

4. To us a Child of hope is born,
   To us a Son is given,
   And on His shoulder ever rests
   All power in earth and heaven.

5. His name shall be the Prince of Peace,
   The Everlasting Lord,
   The Wonderful, the Counselor,
   The God by all adored.

6. His righteous government and power
   Shall over all extend;
   On judgment and on justice based,
   His reign shall have no end.

7. Lord Jesus, reign in us, we pray,
   And make us Thine alone,
   Who with the Father ever art
   And Holy Spirit, one.

This hymn is by John Morison, dated 1770. It was first published in the Draft Scottish *Translations and Paraphrases*, 1781, where the opening line reads: "The race that long in darkness pined." In the *Evangelical Lutheran Hymn-Book* a portion of this hymn was used (No. 155), beginning with Stanza 4 above. Our text is as altered for *Hymns Ancient and Modern*, 1861, by the editors of that volume.

For comments on the tune "Lobt Gott, ihr Christen" see Hymn No. 105.

CHRISTMAS

107   We Christians May Rejoice Today

1. We Christians may Rejoice today,
   When Christ was born to comfort and to save us.
   Who thus believes No longer grieves,
   For none are lost who grasp the hope He gave us.

2. Oh, wondrous joy That God most high
   Should take our flesh and thus our race should honor!
   A virgin mild Hath borne this Child;
   Such grace and glory God hath put upon her.

3. Sin brought us grief, But Christ relief,
   When down to earth He came for our salvation.
   Since God with us Is dwelling thus,
   Who dares to speak the Christian's condemnation?

4. Then hither throng With happy song
   To Him whose birth and death are our assurance;
   Through whom are we At last set free
   From sins and burdens that surpassed endurance.

5. Yea, let us praise Our God and raise
   Loud hallelujahs to the skies above us.
   The bliss bestowed Today by God
   To ceaseless thankfulness and joy should move us.

1. Wir Christenleut' Hab'n jetzund Freud,
   Weil uns zu Trost ist Christus Mensch geboren,
   Hat uns erlöst; Wer sich des tröst't
   Und glaubet's fest, soll nicht werden verloren.

2. Ein Wunderfreud': Gott selbst wird heut'
   Ein wahrer Mensch von Maria geboren;
   Ein' Jungfrau zart Sein' Mutter ward,
   Von Gott dem Herren selbst dazu erkoren.

3. Die Sünd' macht Leid, Christus bringt Freud',
   Weil er zu uns in diese Welt gekommen.
   Mit uns ist Gott Nun in der Not;
   Wer ist, der jetzt uns Christen kann verdammen?

4. Drum sag' ich Dank Mit dem Gesang
   Christo, dem Herrn, der uns zugut Mensch worden,
   Dass wir durch ihn Nun all' los sind
   Der Sündenlast und unträglicher Bürden.

5. Halleluja, Gelobt sei Gott!
   Singen wir all' aus unsers Herzens Grunde;
   Denn Gott hat heut' Gemacht solch' Freud',
   Der wir vergessen soll'n zu keiner Stunde.

This hymn by Caspar Füger (Fugger) was first published in *Drey schöne Newe Geistliche Gesenge*, 1592, entitled "Another Christmas hymn" ("Ein ander Weihnachtslied"). Whether it was written by father or son, both of whom bore the same name, is uncertain.

The translation, by Catherine Winkworth, appeared in her *Chorale-Book for England*, 1863.

For comments on the tune "O Jesu Christ, dein Kripplein" see Hymn No. 81.

108   We Sing, Immanuel, Thy Praise

1. We sing, Immanuel, Thy praise,
   Thou Prince of Life and Fount of grace,
   Thou Flower of heaven and Star of morn,
   Thou Lord of lords, Thou Virgin-born.
   Hallelujah!

2. For Thee, since first the world was made,
   So many hearts have watched and prayed;
   The patriarchs' and prophets' throng
   For Thee have hoped and waited long.
   Hallelujah!

3. Now art Thou here, Thou Ever-blest!
   In lowly manger dost Thou rest.
   Thou, making all things great, art small;
   So poor art Thou, yet clothest all.
   Hallelujah!

1. Wir singen dir, Immanuel,
   Du Lebensfürst und Gnadenquell,
   Du Himmelsblum' und Morgenstern,
   Du Jungfrauensohn, Herr aller Herr'n.
   Halleluja!

2. Von Anfang, da die Welt gemacht,
   Hat so manch Herz nach dir gewacht,
   Dich hat gehofft so lange Jahr'
   Der Väter und Propheten Schar.
   Halleluja!

3. Nun, du bist hier. Da liegest du,
   Hältst in dem Kripplein deine Ruh',
   Bist klein und machst doch alles gross,
   Bekleid'st die Welt und kommst doch bloss.
   Halleluja!

CHRISTMAS

4. From Thee above all gladness flows,
Yet Thou must bear such bitter woes;
The Gentiles' Light and Hope Thou art,
Yet findest none to soothe Thine heart.
    Hallelujah!

5. But I, Thy servant, Lord, today
Confess my love and freely say,
I love Thee truly, but I would
That I might love Thee as I should.
    Hallelujah!

6. I have the will, the power is weak;
Yet, Lord, my humble offering take
And graciously the love receive
Which my poor heart to Thee can give.
    Hallelujah!

7. Had I no load of sin to bear,
Thy grace, O Lord, I could not share;
In vain hadst Thou been born for me
If from God's wrath I had been free.
    Hallelujah!

8. Thus will I sing Thy praises here
With joyful spirit year by year;
And when we reckon years no more,
May I in heaven Thy name adore!
    Hallelujah!

Du bist der Ursprung aller Freud'
Und duldest so viel Herzeleid;
Bist aller Heiden Trost und Licht,
Suchst selber Trost und find'st ihn nicht.
    Halleluja!

Ich aber, dein geringster Knecht,
Ich sag' es frei und mein' es recht:
Ich liebe dich, doch nicht so viel,
Als ich dich gerne lieben will.
    Halleluja!

Der Will' ist da, die Kraft ist klein;
Doch wird dir nicht zuwider sein
Mein armes Herz, und was es kann,
Wirst du in Gnaden nehmen an.
    Halleluja!

Hätt' ich nicht auf mir Sündenschuld,
Hätt' ich kein Teil an deiner Huld;
Vergeblich wär'st du mir gebor'n,
Wenn ich nicht wär' in Gottes Zorn.
    Halleluja!

Ich will dein Halleluja hier
Mit Freuden singen für und für,
Und dort in deinem Ehrensaal
Soll's schallen ohne Zeit und Zahl.
    Halleluja!

This cento includes Stanzas 1, 3, 6, 9, 11, 12, 17, and 20 of Paul Gerhardt's hymn, originally published in sixteen stanzas in Crüger's *Praxis Pietatis Melica*, Berlin, 1653, and then in twenty stanzas in Ebeling's *Geistliche Andachten*, 1667. Although it is now seldom sung in its entirety on account of its length, it is a beautiful hymn to Immanuel, the Longed-for by the patriarchs and prophets.

The translation is a composite based on the versions by Catherine Winkworth, *Lyra Germanica*, first series, 1855, and Frances Elizabeth Cox, *Lyra Messianica*, 1864.

The tune "Erschienen ist" is by Nikolaus Herman. It was composed in 1559 and published in the following year in his collection *Sonntags Euangelia*, etc., Wittenberg, where it was set to his Easter hymn "Erschienen ist der herrlich' Tag."

While Shepherds Watched Their Flocks by Night   109

1. While shepherds watched their flocks
        by night,
All seated on the ground,
The angel of the Lord came down,
    And glory shone around.
"Fear not," said he, for mighty dread
    Had seized their troubled minds;
"Glad tidings of great joy I bring
    To you and all mankind.

2. "To you, in David's town, this day,
    Is born of David's line
A Savior, who is Christ the Lord;
    And this shall be the sign:
The heavenly Babe you there shall find
    To human view displayed,
All meanly wrapped in swaddling-clothes
    And in a manger laid."

3. Thus spake the seraph, — and forthwith
    Appeared a shining throng
Of angels, praising God, and thus
    Addressed their joyful song:
"All glory be to God on high,
    And to the earth be peace;
Good will henceforth from Heaven to men
    Begin and never cease."

The author, Nahum Tate, first published this hymn in the *Supplement* to the *New Version of the Psalms*, 1700, in six stanzas of four lines. It is offered unaltered in our text. This hymn has the distinction of being one of the few hymns which were allowed to be sung in English churches side by side with the metrical psalms. The title of the hymn when first published was "Song of the Angels at the Nativity of Our Blessed Savior." It has been translated into most of the living languages and into classical Latin.

The tune "Bethlehem" or "Evangel" is founded on a setting by Gottfried Wilhelm Fink, 1842, for the German song of Matthias Claudius "War einst ein Riese Goliath."

110   Across the Sky the Shades of Night

1. Across the sky the shades of night
   This New Year's Eve are fleeting.
   We deck Thine altar, Lord, with light,
   In solemn worship meeting;
   And as the year's last hours go by,
   We raise to Thee our earnest cry,
   Once more Thy love entreating.

2. Before the cross subdued we bow,
   To Thee our prayers addressing,
   Recounting all Thy mercies now,
   And all our sins confessing;
   Beseeching Thee this coming year
   To keep us in Thy faith and fear
   And crown us with Thy blessing.

3. And while we pray, we lift our eyes
   To dear ones gone before us,
   Safe home with Thee in Paradise,
   Whose peace descendeth o'er us;
   And beg of Thee, when life is past,
   To reunite us all at last
   With those who've gone before us.

4. We gather up in this brief hour
   The memory of Thy mercies:
   Thy wondrous goodness, love, and power
   Our grateful song rehearses;
   For Thou hast been our Strength and Stay
   In many a dark and dreary day
   Of sorrow and reverses.

5. In many an hour when fear and dread,
   Like evil spells, have bound us
   And clouds were gathering overhead,
   Thy providence hath found us.
   In many a night when seas ran high,
   Thy gracious presence, drawing nigh,
   Hath made all calm around us.

6. Then, O great God, in years to come,
   Whatever may betide us,
   Right onward through our journey home
   Be Thou at hand to guide us;
   Nor leave us till at close of life
   Safe from all perils, toil, and strife,
   Heaven shall enfold and hide us.

This solid hymn for New Year's Eve was written by James Hamilton to be sung to the *chorale* tune ascribed to Nikolaus Decius "Allein Gott in der Höh'." The hymn appeared in Thring's *Collection*, 1882.

For comments on the tune "Allein Gott in der Höh' " see Hymn No. 33.

111   Thou Who Roll'st the Year Around

1. Thou who roll'st the year around,
   Crowned with mercies large and free,
   Rich Thy gifts to us abound;
   Warm our praise shall rise to Thee.

2. Kindly to our worship bow
   While our grateful thanks we tell,
   That, sustained by Thee, we now
   Bid the parting year farewell.

3. All its numbered days are sped,
   All its busy scenes are o'er,
   All its joys forever fled,
   All its sorrows felt no more.

4. Mingled with the eternal past,
   Its remembrance shall decay,
   Yet to be revived at last
   At the solemn Judgment Day.

5. All our follies, Lord, forgive;
   Cleanse us from each guilty stain.
   Let Thy grace within us live
   That we spend not years in vain.

6. Then when life's last eve shall come,
   Happy spirits, may we fly
   To our everlasting home,
   To our Father's house on high!

Ray Palmer wrote this hymn for the close of the year in 1832.

The tune "Aus der Tiefe," also called "Heinlein," first appeared in the *Nürnbergisches Gesang-Buch*, 1676, set to the hymn "Aus der Tiefe rufe ich," a hymn, based on Ps. 130, by Christoph Schwämlein. It is one of three tunes marked by the initial M. H. *Zahn* ascribes them to Martin Herbst, while F. Layriz attributes them to M. Heinlein, an unknown individual. Others credit the composer Paul Heinlein (1626—1686) with the composition.

NEW YEAR'S EVE

To God the Anthem Raising 112

1. To God the anthem raising,
Sing, Christians, great and small;
Sing out, His goodness praising,
Oh, thank Him one and all!
Behold how God this year,
Which now is safely ended,
Hath in His love befriended
His children far and near.

2. Let us consider rightly
His mercies manifold
And let us not think lightly
Of all His gifts untold.
Let thankfulness recall
How God this year hath led us,
How He hath clothed and fed us,
The great ones and the small.

3. To Church and State He granted
His peace in every place,
His vineyard He hath planted
Among us by His grace.
His ever bounteous hand
Prosperity hath given
And want and famine driven
From this our native land.

4. His Father heart is yearning
To take us for His own
When, our transgressions mourning,
We trust in Christ alone;
When in His name we pray
And humbly make confession,
He pardons our transgression
And is our faithful Stay.

5. Our God hath well defended,
Hath kept us through His grace;
But if He had contended
With us our sins to trace
And given us our meed,
We all would then be lying
In sin and sorrow dying,
Each one for his misdeed.

6. O Father dear in heaven,
For all Thy gifts of love
Which Thou to us hast given
We lift our thanks above.
In Jesus' name we here,
To Thee our prayers addressing,
Still ask Thee for Thy blessing:
Grant us a joyful year.

Helft mir Gott's Güte preisen,
Ihr lieben Kinderlein,
Mit G'sang und andrer Weisen
Ihm allzeit dankbar sein,
Vornehmlich zu der Zeit,
Da sich das Jahr tut enden,
Die Sonn' sich zu uns wenden,
Das Neujahr ist nicht weit.

Ernstlich lasst uns betrachten
Des Herren reiche Gnad'
Und so gering nicht achten
Sein' unzählig' Wohltat,
Stets führen zu Gemüt,
Wie er dies Jahr hat geben
All' Notdurft diesem Leben
Und uns vor Leid behüt't,

Lehramt, Schul', Kirch' erhalten
In gutem Fried' und Ruh',
Nahrung für Jung' und Alte
Bescheret auch dazu
Und gar mit milder Hand
Sein' Güter ausgespendet,
Verwüstung abgewendet
Von dieser Stadt und Land.

Er hat unser verschonet
Aus väterlicher Gnad';
Wenn er sonst hätt' belohnet
All unsre Missetat
Mit gleicher Straf' und Pein,
Wir wären längst gestorben,
In mancher Not verdorben,
Hie wir voll Sünden sein.

Nach Vaters Art und Treuen
Er uns so gnädig ist;
Wenn wir die Sünd' bereuen,
Glauben an Jesum Christ
Herzlich, ohn' Heuchelei,
Tut er all' Sünd' vergeben,
Lindert die Straf' daneben,
Steht uns in Nöten bei.

All solch dein' Güt' wir preisen,
Vater im Himmelsthron,
Die du uns tust beweisen
Durch Christum, deinen Sohn,
Und bitten ferner dich:
Gib uns ein fröhlich Jahre,
Vor allem Leid bewahre
Und nähr uns mildiglich!

Paul Eber wrote this acrostic hymn on the name "Helena," as the first letters in the German stanzas indicate. The name was borne both by his wife and his daughter. The oldest text is found in *Gesangbuch*, Kopfenhagen 1571. A better text appeared in the *Gesangbuch* of Johann Eichorn, Frankfurt an der Oder, c. 1580. The hymn was entitled "A Thanksgiving and Prayer for the New Year, in Remembrance of God's Goodness, for the Children." In German hymnals a doxology is often appended as Stanza 7. This was added in 1649.

The translation is by Carl Döving, 1907, and appeared in *The Lutheran Hymnary*, 1913.

The tune "Helft mir Gott's Güte" is by Wolfgang Figulus and appeared in his *Cantionum sacrarum*, Frankfurt, 1575.

NEW YEAR'S EVE. — NEW YEAR

113   While with Ceaseless Course the Sun

1. While with ceaseless course the sun
Hasted through the former year,
Many souls their race have run,
Nevermore to meet us here;
Fixed in an eternal state,
They have done with all below.
We a little longer wait,
But how little, none can know.

2. As the wingèd arrow flies
Speedily the mark to find;
As the lightning from the skies
Darts and leaves no trace behind,
Swiftly thus our fleeting days
Bear us down life's rapid stream.
Upward, Lord, our spirits raise;
All below is but a dream.

3. Thanks for mercies past receive,
Pardon of our sins renew;
Teach us henceforth how to live
With eternity in view.
Bless Thy Word to young and old,
Fill us with a Savior's love;
And when life's short tale is told,
May we dwell with Thee above.

John Newton first published this hymn in his *Twenty-six Letters on Religious Subjects, etc., by Omikron,* 1774. It was entitled "For the New Year" and is suitable both for New Year's Eve and New Year's Day.

The tune "Christe, wahres Seelenlicht" appeared in Freylinghausen's *Neues Geistreiches Gesangbuch,* Halle, 1704, set to the morning hymn by Christoph Prätorius, beginning with that line.

114   Jesus! Name of Wondrous Love

1. Jesus! Name of wondrous love,
Name all other names above,
Unto which must every knee
Bow in deep humility.

2. Jesus! Name decreed of old,
To the maiden mother told —
Kneeling in her lowly cell —
By the angel Gabriel.

3. Jesus! Name of priceless worth
To the fallen sons of earth,
For the promise that it gave,
"Jesus shall His people save."

4. Jesus! Name of mercy mild,
Given to the holy Child
When the cup of human woe
First He tasted here below.

5. Jesus! Only name that's given
Under all the mighty heaven
Whereby man, to sin enslaved,
Bursts his fetters and is saved.

6. Jesus! Name of wondrous love,
Human name of God above;
Pleading only this, we flee,
Helpless, O our God, to Thee.

The author is William Walsham How. The hymn was first published in Morrell and How's *Psalms and Hymns,* 1854. It is particularly appropriate for New Year's Day or the festival of the Circumcision. Biblical references are Phil. 2:10; Rom. 14:11; Luke 1:31; Matt. 1:21; Luke 2:21; and Acts 4:12.

The Church has a number of hymns and poems on the name of our Lord, but none is more a hymn than this one by Bishop How, with the possible exception of Hymn No. 116. Among the others an interesting one is that by William Augustus Mühlenberg in 1842 and revised in 1868 for Dr. Schaff's collection, *Christ in Song,* which was intended to offset the Roman Catholic use of the name of Mary, especially in connection with the rosary. It reads:

1. Jesus' name shall ever be
For my heart its Rosary.
I will tell it o'er and o'er,
Always dearer than before.

2. Ave Mary may not be
For my heart its Rosary;
Jesus, Savior, all in all, —
Other name why should I call?

3. Morning hymns and evening lays,
Noontide prayer and midnight praise,
Heart and voice, and tune and time,
Jesus' name they all shall chime.

4. Ever new and fresh the strain;
Of all themes the sweet refrain:
Time bring what it may along,
Jesus still the unchanging song.

NEW YEAR

5. Redolent with healing balm,
Pleasure's charm and trouble's calm;
All of Heaven my hope and claim,
Grace on grace in Jesus' name.

6. In my soul each deepest chord
Ring it out, One Savior Lord;
Jesus, the eternal hymn
Forth from saint and seraphim.

7. Breathe it, then, my every breath;
Linger on my last in death;
Jesus — Rest in paradise;
Jesus — Glory in the skies!

For comments on the tune "Gott sei Dank" see Hymn No. 2.

O Blessed Day When First was Poured — 115

1. O blessed day when first was poured
The blood of our redeeming Lord!
O blessed day when Christ began
His saving work for sinful man!

Felix dies, quam proprio
Iesus cruore consecrat:
Felix dies, qua gestiit
Opus salutis aggredi.

2. While from His mother's bosom fed,
His precious blood He wills to shed;
A foretaste of His death He feels,
An earnest of His love reveals.

Vix natus, ecce lacteum
Profundit infans sanguinem:
Libamen es hoc funeris,
Amoris hoc praeludium.

3. Scarce come to earth, His Father's will
With prompt obedience to fulfil,
A victim even now He lies
Before the day of sacrifice.

Intrans in orbem, iam Patris
Mandata promptus exequi,
Statum praeoccupat diem;
Ex qua potest, fit victima.

4. In love our guilt He undertakes;
Sinless, for sin atonement makes.
The great Lawgiver for our aid
Obedient to the Law is made.

Amore se facit reum,
Poenasque solvit innocens;
Sub lege factus legifer,
A lege nos ut eximat.

5. Lord, circumcise our heart, we pray,
And take what is not Thine away.
Write Thine own name upon our hearts,
Thy Law within our inward parts.

Tu, Christe, quod non est tuum
Nostro recide pectore:
Inscribe nomen, intimis
Inscribe legem cordibus.

6. O Lord, the Virgin-born, to Thee
Eternal praise and glory be,
Whom with the Father we adore
And Holy Ghost forevermore.

Qui natus es de virgine,
Iesu, tibi sit gloria
Cum Patre cumque Spiritu
In sempiterna saecula. Amen.

This hymn was written by Abbé Sebastian Besnault, a priest of St. Maurice at Sens. It was published in the *Sens Breviary*, 1726, in seven stanzas. The omitted Stanza 5 reads:

The wound He through the Law endures
Our freedom from that Law secures;
Henceforth a holier law prevails,
That law of love, which never fails.

The translation is an altered form of the version by John Chandler, first published in his *Hymns of the Primitive Church*, 1837.

The tune "Angelus" or "Whitsun Hymn" is from a melody set by Georg Joseph to the hymn "Du meiner Seelen güldne Zier" by Johann Scheffler (Angelus Silesius) in *Heilige Seelenlust*, Breslau, 1657.

To the Name of Our Salvation — 116

1. To the name of our salvation
Laud and honor let us pay,
Which for many a generation
Hid in God's foreknowledge lay;
But with holy exultation
We may sing aloud today.

Gloriosi salvatoris
Nominis praeconia,
Quae in corde Genitoris
Latent ante saecula,
Mater caeli plena roris
Pandit nunc ecclesia.

2. Jesus is the name we treasure,
   Name beyond what words can tell;
Name of gladness, name of pleasure,
   Ear and heart delighting well;
Name of sweetness, passing measure,
   Saving us from sin and hell.

3. 'Tis the name for adoration;
   'Tis the name of victory;
'Tis the name for meditation
   In this vale of misery;
'Tis the name for veneration
   By the citizens on high.

4. 'Tis the name that whoso preacheth
   Speaks like music to the ear;
Who in prayer this name beseecheth
   Sweetest comfort findeth near;
Who its perfect wisdom reacheth
   Heavenly joy possesseth here.

5. Jesus is the name prevailing
   Over every name by right;
At this name, in terror quailing,
   Powers of hell are put to flight;
God, in mercy never failing,
   Saves us by this name of might.

6. Therefore we in love adoring
   This most blessed name revere,
Holy Jesus, Thee imploring
   So to write it in us here
That hereafter, heavenward soaring,
   We may sing with angels there.

Nomen dulce, nomen gratum,
   Nomen ineffabile,
Dulce 'Iesus' appellatum,
   Nomen delectabile,
Laxat poenas et reatum;
   Nomen est amabile.

Hoc est nomen adorandum,
   Nomen summae gloriae,
Nomen semper meditandum
   In valle miseriae,
Nomen digne venerandum
   Supernorum curiae.

Nomen istud praedicatum
   Melos est auditui;
Nomen istud invocatum
   Dulce mel est gustui:
Iubilus est cogitatum
   Spiritali visui.

Hoc est nomen exaltatum
   Iure super omnia,
Nomen mire formidatum,
   Effugans daemonia,
Ad salutem nobis datum
   Divina clementia.

Nomen ergo tam beatum
   Veneremur cernui;
Sit in corde sic firmatum,
   Quod non possit erui,
Ut in coelis potestatum
   Copulemur coetui. Amen.

This hymn is by an unknown author. It is found in late medieval breviaries, beginning with that of Antwerp, 1496.

The translation is an altered form of that by John M. Neale, in his *Medieval Hymns*, 1851.

For comments on the tune "Sieh hier bin ich" see Hymn No. 56.

117   The Ancient Law Departs

1. The ancient Law departs,
      And all its fears remove,
   For Jesus makes with faithful hearts
      A covenant of love.

2. The Light of Light Divine,
      True brightness undefiled,
   He bears for us the pain of sin
      A holy, spotless Child.

3. His infant body now
      Begins the cross to feel;
   Those precious drops of blood that flow
      For death the Victim seal.

4. Today the name is Thine
      At which we bend the knee.
   They call Thee Jesus, Child Divine;
      Our Jesus deign to be.

5. All praise, eternal Son,
      For Thy redeeming love,
   With Father, Spirit, ever One
      In glorious might above. Amen.

Debilis cessent elementa legis;
   Sat diu mentes timor occupavit;
Foedus aeterni stabilire Iesus
   Coepit amoris.

Sole de vero radius, paterni
   Luminis purus sine nube splendor,
Probra peccati puer ecce tinctus
   Sanguine praefert.

Stillat excisos pueri per artus
   Efficax noxas abolere sanguis:
Obligat morti pretiosa totum
   Stilla cruorem.

Haec dies nomen tibi comparavit,
   O puer, pronus quod adoret orbis,
Et simul dici, simul ipse Iesus
   Incipis esse.

Summa laus Patri, simul aequa Nato,
   Qui suo mundum redimit cruore;
Par sit amborum tibi laus per omne,
   Spiritus, aevum. Amen.

Abbé Sebastian Besnault first published this hymn in the *Sens Breviary*, 1726, with this as the first line,

   Iam satis mentes timor occupavit.

The version above is from the *Paris Breviary*, 1736.

NEW YEAR

The translation is an altered form of that which was made by the compilers of *Hymns Ancient and Modern,* 1861.

The tune "Potsdam" first appeared in Mercer's *Church Psalter and Hymnbook,* 1854. It is an adaptation from the subject of Johann Sebastian Bach's second fugue in E major of his *Forty-eight Preludes and Fugues.*

Father, Let Me Dedicate   118

1. Father, let me dedicate
   All this year to Thee,
   In whatever earthly state
   Thou wilt have me be.
   Not from sorrow, pain, or care
   Freedom dare I claim;
   This alone shall be my prayer:
   Glorify Thy name.

2. Can a child presume to choose
   Where or how to live?
   Can a father's love refuse
   All the best to give?
   More Thou givest every day
   Than the best can claim
   Nor withholdest aught that may
   Glorify Thy name.

3. If in mercy Thou wilt spare
   Joys that yet are mine;
   If on life, serene and fair,
   Brighter rays may shine,
   Let my glad heart while it sings
   Thee in all proclaim
   And, whate'er the future brings,
   Glorify Thy name.

4. If Thou callest to the cross
   And its shadow come,
   Turning all my gain to loss,
   Shrouding heart and home,
   Let me think how Thy dear Son
   To His glory came
   And in deepest woe pray on:
   "Glorify Thy name."

Lawrence Tuttiett first published this, his best-known hymn, in his *Gems of Thought on the Sunday Special Services,* 1864.

The tune "Glorification" is an adaptation by Herman Ilse, 1910, from Johann H. Tscherlitzky's "Gottes Lamm ruft: Gnade" in Gossner's *Choralbuch,* Leipzig, 1832. It was prepared for the *Evangelical Lutheran Hymn-Book,* 1912.

Great God, We Sing That Mighty Hand   119

1. Great God, we sing that mighty hand
   By which supported still we stand.
   The opening year Thy mercy shows;
   Let mercy crown it till it close.

2. By day, by night, at home, abroad,
   Still we are guarded by our God,
   By His incessant bounty fed,
   By His unerring counsel led.

3. With grateful hearts the past we own;
   The future, all to us unknown,
   We to Thy guardian care commit
   And, peaceful, leave before Thy feet.

4. In scenes exalted or depressed
   Be Thou our Joy and Thou our Rest.
   Thy goodness all our hopes shall raise,
   Adored through all our changing days.

5. When death shall interrupt our songs,
   And seal in silence mortal tongues,
   Our Helper, God, in whom we trust,
   In better worlds our soul shall boast.

This is a slightly altered form of Philip Doddridge's hymn, which first appeared in a posthumous edition of his *Hymns,* etc., 1755. It was headed "Help obtained of God. Acts 26:22. For the New Year."

The tune "Mendon" was introduced to American tune books by Samuel Dyer in the *Supplement of Samuel Dyer's Third Edition of Sacred Music,* 1828, where the tune, called "German Air," had one more note in each line and a different last line than the form now familiar. The omission of the additional note in the fourth edition of the book was accompanied with this comment: "It is believed that the present arrangement is the original form." It is thought Lowell Mason altered the last line when he began using it in his publications and that he gave it its present name.

NEW YEAR

120   Help Us, O Lord! Behold, We Enter

1. Help us, O Lord! Behold, we enter
Upon another year today;
In Thee our hopes and thoughts now center,
Renew our courage for the way.
New life, new strength, new happiness,
We ask of Thee, — oh, hear and bless!

2. May every plan and undertaking
This year be all begun with Thee;
When I am sleeping or am waking,
Still let me know Thou art with me.
Abroad do Thou my footsteps guide,
At home be ever at my side.

3. Be this a time of grace and pardon,
Thy rod I take with willing mind.
But suffer naught my heart to harden;
Oh, let me then Thy mercy find!
In Thee alone, my God, I live;
Thou only canst my sins forgive.

4. And may this year to me be holy;
Thy grace so fill my every thought
That all my life be pure and lowly
And truthful, as a Christian's ought.
So make me while yet dwelling here
Pious and blest from year to year.

5. Jesus, be with me and direct me;
Jesus, my plans and hopes inspire;
Jesus, from tempting thoughts protect me;
Jesus, be all my heart's Desire;
Jesus, be in my thoughts all day
Nor suffer me to fall away.

6. And grant, Lord, when the year is over,
That it for me in peace may close;
In all things care for me and cover
My head in time of fear and woes.
So may I when my years are gone
Appear with joy before Thy throne.

Hilf, Herr Jesu, lass gelingen,
Hilf, das neue Jahr geht an!
Lass es neue Kräfte bringen,
Dass aufs neu' ich wandeln kann!
Neues Heil und neues Leben
Wollest du aus Gnaden geben.

Meine Worte, meine Taten,
Was ich treibe fort und fort,
Müsse seliglich geraten,
Herr, durch dein lebendig Wort!
Lass mich deinen Geist erfüllen,
Zu vollbringen deinen Willen!

Lass dies sein ein Jahr der Gnaden;
Herr, vergib mir meine Schuld;
Was der Seele möchte schaden,
Wende ab nach deiner Huld!
Lass mich wachen, beten, ringen
Und durch dich die Welt bezwingen.

Herr, du wollest Gnade geben,
Dass dies Jahr mir heilig sei,
Dass ich christlich könne leben
Ohne Trug und Heuchelei;
Dass dein Pilger noch auf Erden
Möge dir geheiligt werden.

Jesu, lenke mein Beginnen
Immerdar nach deinem Sinn!
Jesu, führe all mein Sinnen
Auf die Ewigkeiten hin;
Lass Begierden und Gedanken
Nie von dir ins Ferne wanken!

Jesu, lass mich fröhlich enden
Dieses angefangne Jahr;
Trage mich auf deinen Händen,
Halte bei mir in Gefahr.
Freudig will ich dich umfassen,
Wenn ich soll die Welt verlassen!

Johann Rist first published this hymn, in sixteen stanzas, in the *Drittes Zehn* of his *Himmlische Lieder,* Lüneburg, 1642. The cento is composed of Stanzas 1, 4, 8, 13, 15, and 16. It has long been one of the favorite German New Year hymns. It was entitled "Godly beginning of the New Year in and with the most sweet name of Jesus."

The translation is by Catherine Winkworth in her *Chorale Book for England,* 1863.

The tune "Ich sterbe täglich" is from a manuscript in the Municipal Library, Leipzig, 1756. "Ich sterbe täglich, und mein Leben eilt immerfort zum Grabe hin" is a burial hymn written by Benjamin Schmolck and published in 1720.

121   For Thy Mercy and Thy Grace

1. For Thy mercy and Thy grace,
Faithful through another year,
Hear our song of thankfulness;
Savior and Redeemer, hear!

2. Lo, our sins on Thee we cast,
Thee, our perfect Sacrifice,
And, forgetting all the past,
Press unto our glorious prize.

3. Dark the future; let Thy light
Guide us, bright and Morning Star.
Fierce our foes and hard the fight;
Arm us, Savior, for the war.

4. In our weakness and distress,
Rock of strength, be Thou our Stay;
In the pathless wilderness
Be our true and living Way.

5. Who of us death's awful road
In the coming year shall tread,
With Thy rod and staff, O God,
Comfort Thou his dying bed.

6. Keep us faithful, keep us pure,
Keep us evermore Thine own.
Help, oh, help us to endure;
Fit us for the promised crown.

NEW YEAR

Henry Downton wrote this hymn in 1841 and first published it in the *Church of England Magazine,* 1843, in seven stanzas, entitled "A Hymn for the Commencement of the Year." Arthur Tozer Russell republished it in his *Psalms and Hymns,* 1851, slightly altered, omitting two stanzas. Since then it has been received into numerous hymnals, usually in an altered and abridged form. The version above omits Stanza 7, which reads:

> So within Thy palace gate
> We shall praise on golden strings
> Thee the only Potentate,
> Lord of lords and King of kings.

The tune "Culbach" is an adaptation of an old German melody and is from *Heilige Seelenlust,* etc., by Johann Scheffler (Angelus Silesius) and Georg Joseph, Breslau, 1657, where it is set to the hymn "Ach, wann kommt die Zeit heran," by Scheffler.

Now Let Us Come Before Him 122

1. Now let us come before Him,
With song and prayer adore Him,
Who to our life hath given
All needed strength from heaven.

Nun lasst uns gehn und treten
Mit Singen und mit Beten
Zum Herrn, der unserm Leben
Bis hierher Kraft gegeben.

2. The stream of years is flowing,
And we are onward going,
From old to new surviving
And by His mercy thriving.

Wir gehn dahin und wandern
Von einem Jahr zum andern,
Wir leben und gedeihen
Vom alten zu dem neuen.

3. In woe we often languish
And pass through times of anguish,
Of wars and trepidation
Alarming every nation.

Durch so viel Angst und Plagen,
Durch Zittern und durch Zagen,
Durch Krieg und grosse Schrecken,
Die alle Welt bedecken.

4. As mothers watch are keeping
O'er children who are sleeping,
Their fear and grief assuaging
When angry storms are raging,

Denn wie von treuen Müttern
In schweren Ungewittern
Die Kindlein hier auf Erden
Mit Fleiss bewahret werden:

5. So God His own is shielding
And help to them is yielding.
When need and woe distress them,
His loving arms caress them.

Also auch und nicht minder
Lässt Gott sich seine Kinder,
Wenn Not und Trübsal blitzen,
In seinem Schosse sitzen.

6. O Thou who dost not slumber,
Remove what would encumber
Our work, which prospers never
Unless Thou bless it ever.

Ach Hüter unsers Lebens,
Fürwahr, es ist vergebens
Mit unserm Tun und Machen,
Wo nicht dein' Augen wachen.

7. O God of Mercy, hear us;
Our Father, be Thou near us;
Mid crosses and in sadness
Be Thou our Fount of gladness.

Lass ferner dich erbitten,
O Vater, und bleib mitten
In unserm Kreuz und Leiden
Ein Brunnen unsrer Freuden.

8. To all who bow before Thee
And for Thy grace implore Thee,
Oh, grant Thy benediction
And patience in affliction.

Gib mir und allen denen,
Die sich von Herzen sehnen
Nach dir und deiner Hulde,
Ein Herz, das sich gedulde!

9. Be Thou a Helper speedy
To all the poor and needy,
To all forlorn a Father;
Thy erring children gather.

Sei der Verlassnen Vater,
Der Irrenden Berater,
Der Unversorgten Gabe,
Der Armen Gut und Habe!

10. Be with the sick and ailing,
Their Comforter unfailing;
Dispelling grief and sadness,
Oh, give them joy and gladness!

Hilf gnädig allen Kranken,
Gib fröhliche Gedanken
Den hochbetrübten Seelen,
Die sich mit Schwermut quälen!

11. Above all else, Lord, send us
Thy Spirit to attend us,
Within our hearts abiding,
To heaven our footsteps guiding.

Und endlich, was das meiste,
Füll uns mit deinem Geiste,
Der uns hier herrlich ziere
Und dort zum Himmel führe!

12. All this Thy hand bestoweth,
Thou Life, whence our life floweth.
To all Thy name confessing
Grant, Lord, Thy New Year's blessing.

Das alles woll'st du geben,
O meines Lebens Leben,
Mir und der Christenschare
Zum sel'gen neuen Jahre!

Paul Gerhardt first published this hymn in the Crüger-Runge *Gesang-Buch,* 1653, in fifteen stanzas. This cento omits Stanzas 7, 10, and 11. That the hymn was written during the Thirty Years' War is evident from the omitted stanzas, which read:

7. Our song to Thee ascendeth,
Who every day defendeth
Us, and whose arm averteth
The pain our hearts that hurteth.

10. Oh, close the gates of sorrow,
And by a glorious morrow
Of peace may places saddened
By bloodshed dire be gladdened.

11. With richest blessings crown us,
In all our days, Lord, own us;
Give grace, who grace bestowest,
To all, e'en to the lowest.

The translation is by John Kelly, altered. It first appeared in his *Paul Gerhardt's Spiritual Songs,* London, 1867. The English version of the omitted stanzas is by Kelly.

The tune "Nun lasst uns Gott dem Herren" has long been wedded to this text. It first appeared in Nikolaus Selneccer's *Christliche Psalmen, Lieder und Kirchengesenge,* etc., Leipzig, 1587. It may be by Antonio Scandelli. An improved form of the tune was published by Johann Crüger in the Berlin *Gesang-Buch,* 1653.

123   Our God, Our Help in Ages Past

1. Our God, our Help in ages past,
Our Hope for years to come,
Our Shelter from the stormy blast,
And our eternal Home!

2. Under the shadow of Thy throne
Thy saints have dwelt secure;
Sufficient is Thine arm alone,
And our defense is sure.

3. Before the hills in order stood
Or earth received her frame,
From everlasting Thou art God,
To endless years the same.

4. A thousand ages in Thy sight
Are like an evening gone,
Short as the watch that ends the night
Before the rising sun.

5. Thy word commands our flesh to dust:
"Return, ye sons of men!"
All nations rose from earth at first
And turn to earth again.

6. Time, like an ever-rolling stream,
Bears all its sons away;
They fly forgotten as a dream
Dies at the opening day.

7. Like flowery fields the nations stand,
Pleased with the morning light;
The flowers beneath the mower's hand
Lie withering ere 'tis night.

8. Our God, our Help in ages past,
Our Hope for years to come,
Be Thou our Guard while troubles last
And our eternal Home!

Isaac Watts first published this famous hymn, perhaps the greatest in the English language, in his *Psalms of David Imitated,* 1719, in nine stanzas, basing it on Ps. 90:1-5. It was headed "Man Frail and God Eternal." The omitted Stanza 6 reads:

The busy tribes of flesh and blood,
With all their lives and cares,
Are carried downwards by the flood
And lost in following years.

The alteration of the first line to "O God, our Help in ages past," found in some hymnals, was made by John Wesley in 1737.

The hymn is undoubtedly one of Watts's best compositions. It was written about 1714, according to Thomas Wright, in his *Life of Isaac Watts,* not long before Queen Anne's death, when all England was anxious about her probable successor. There are references to this hymn in Thackeray's *Henry Esmond* and in Charlotte Brontë's *Shirley*. F. J. Gillman declares: "If nothing else had come from his pen, it justifies its author's memorial in Westminster Abbey." He calls attention to this hymn's "simple strength, its transparency, its hold upon the common mind, its straightforwardness, its accentual and punctuative perfection, and its faithfulness to Scripture"; which is only another way of saying that it bears all the marks that we look for in a true church hymn.

The tune "St. Anne," now inseparably associated with this hymn, first appeared in Brady and Tate's *Supplement to the New Version of Psalms*, sixth edition, 1708, where it was set to the new version of Ps. 42. It is generally ascribed to William Croft. Within the last few years Croft's authorship of "St. Anne" has been called in question, that tune being found in the *seventh* edition of Abraham Barber's *Book of Psalms*, 1715, where it is called "Leeds Tune" and ascribed to a Mr. Denby. An earlier copy of the above work has been discovered, published probably in 1696 or 1697, but it does not contain "Leeds Tune." Whether it was added to Barber's collection before the appearance of "St. Anne" in the *Supplement* of 1708 is still uncertain. (J. Love, *Scottish Church Music*.)

O Lord, Our Father, Thanks to Thee 124

1. O Lord, our Father, thanks to Thee
 In this new year we render,
 For every evil had to flee
 Before Thee, our Defender.
 Our life was nourished, we were fed
 With rich supplies of daily bread,
 And peace reigned in our borders.

2. Lord Jesus Christ, our thanks to Thee
 In this new year we render;
 Thy reign hath kept Thy people free,
 Hath shown Thy mercies tender.
 Thou hast redeemed us with Thy blood,
 Thou art our Joy, our only Good,
 In life and death our Savior.

3. Lord Holy Ghost, our thanks to Thee
 In this new year we render,
 For Thou hast led our eyes to see
 Thy truth in all its splendor
 And thus enkindled from above
 Within our hearts true faith and love
 And other Christian virtues.

4. Our faithful God, we cry to Thee:
 Still bless us with Thy favor,
 Blot out all our iniquity,
 And hide our sins forever.
 Grant us a happy, good new year
 And, when the hour of death draws near,
 A peaceful, blest departure. Amen.

Herr Gott Vater, wir preisen dich
 Im lieben neuen Jahre,
 Denn du hast uns gar väterlich
 Behüt't vor aller G'fahre;
 Du hast dies Leben uns vermehrt,
 Das täglich' Brot reichlich beschert
 Und Fried' im Lande geben.

Herr Jesu Christ, wir preisen dich
 Im lieben neuen Jahre,
 Denn du regierst gar fleissiglich
 Dein' liebe Christenschare,
 Die du mit deinem Blut erlöst,
 Du bist ihr' einig' Freud' und Trost
 Im Leben und im Sterben.

Herr Heil'ger Geist, wir preisen dich
 Im lieben neuen Jahre,
 Denn du hast uns gar mildiglich
 Begnad't mit reiner Lehre,
 Dadurch den Glauben angezünd't,
 Die Lieb' gepflanzt im Herzensgrund
 Und andre schöne Tugend.

Du treuer Gott, wir bitten dich,
 Zeig uns auch fort dein' Hulde,
 Tilg unsre Sünde gnädiglich,
 Gedenk nicht alter Schulde,
 Bescher ein fröhlich's neues Jahr
 Und, wenn das Stündlein kommet dar,
 Ein selig Ende! Amen.

Cyriacus Schneegass published this hymn in his *Geistliche Lieder vnd Psalmen*, etc., Erfurt, 1597. It was headed "A New Year's Hymn." It may have appeared two years earlier in the author's *Weihenacht und New Jahrs-Gesäng*, also published at Erfurt, but this has not been verified.

The translation by August Crull appeared in the Ohio *Lutheran Hymnal*, 1880. It has been slightly altered.

For comments on the tune "Nun freut euch" see Hymn No. 387.

NEW YEAR. — EPIPHANY

125   The Old Year Now hath Passed Away

1. The old year now hath passed away;
We thank Thee, O our God, today
That Thou hast kept us through the year
When danger and distress were near.

2. We pray Thee, O eternal Son,
Who with the Father reign'st as One,
To guard and rule Thy Christendom
Through all the ages yet to come.

3. Take not Thy saving Word away,
Our souls' true comfort, staff, and stay.
Abide with us and keep us free
From errors, following only Thee.

4. Oh, help us to forsake all sin,
A new and holier course begin!
Mark not what once was done amiss;
A happier, better year be this,

5. Wherein as Christians we may live
Or die in peace that Thou canst give,
To rise again when Thou shalt come
And enter Thine eternal home.

6. There shall we thank Thee and adore
With all the angels evermore.
Lord Jesus Christ, increase our faith
To praise Thy name through life and death.

Das alte Jahr vergangen ist,
Wir danken dir, Herr Jesu Christ,
Dass du uns hast in aller G'fahr
So gnädiglich behüt't dies Jahr.

Wir bitten dich, ewigen Sohn
Des Vaters in dem höchsten Thron,
Du woll'st dein' arme Christenheit
Ferner bewahren allezeit.

Entzeuch uns nicht dein heilsam Wort,
Welch's ist der Seelen Trost und Hort,
Vor's Papsts Lehr' und Abgötterei
Bewahr uns, Herr, und steh uns bei!

Hilf, dass wir von der Sünd' ablan
Und fromm zu werden fahen an.
Kein'r Sünd' im alten Jahr gedenk,
Ein gnadenreich neu Jahr uns schenk,

Christlich zu leben, seliglich
Zu sterben und hernach fröhlich
Am Jüngsten Tag wied'r aufzustehn,
Mit dir in Himmel einzugehn,

Zu danken und zu loben dich
Mit allen Engeln ewiglich.
O Jesu, unsern Glauben mehr
Zu deines Namens Lob und Ehr'!

Johann Steuerlein, in 1588, published a collection of hymns entitled *"Sieben und Zwantzigk newe geistliche Gesenge,* etc., Erfurt. This hymn for New Year was among them, but it was not marked as by him, nor did he ever claim authorship. In this collection the hymn appeared in its full six stanzas for the first time. The first two stanzas had previously been published in a collection by Clement Stephani, in 1568. It is possible that Steuerlein composed Stanzas 3 to 6 and added them in 1588.

The translation is by Catherine Winkworth in her *Chorale Book for England,* 1863.

For comments on the tune "Herr Jesu Christ, dich" see Hymn No. 3.

126   Arise and Shine in Splendor

1. Arise and shine in splendor,
Let night to day surrender;
   Thy Light is drawing near.
Above thee day is beaming,
In matchless beauty gleaming;
   The glory of the Lord is here.

2. See earth in darkness lying,
The heathen nations dying
   In hopeless gloom and night.
To thee the Lord of heaven —
Thy Life, thy Hope — hath given
   Great glory, honor, and delight.

3. The world's remotest races,
Upon whose weary faces
   The sun looks from the sky,
Shall run with zeal untiring,
With joy thy Light desiring
   That breaks upon them from on high.

4. Lift up thine eyes in wonder;
See, nations gather yonder,
   They all come unto thee.
The world has heard thy story,
Thy sons come to thy glory,
   And daughters haste thy Light to see.

Brich auf und werde lichte,
Lass gehn die Nacht zunichte,
   Dein Licht kommt her zu dir;
Die Herrlichkeit des Herren
Glänzt prächtig weit und ferren
   Und zeigt sich um und über dir.

Zwar finster ist die Erde,
Der armen Heiden Herde
   Liegt dunkel weit und breit;
Dich hat der Herr, dein Leben,
Dein Heil und Trost, umgeben
   Mit grosser Ehr' und Herrlichkeit.

Die Völker auf der Erden,
So je beschienen werden
   Durchs klare Sonnenlicht,
Die sollen dein Licht kennen,
Zum Glanze fröhlich rennen,
   Der aus der Höh' des Himmels bricht.

Heb auf, heb dein Gesichte:
Das Volk folgt deinem Lichte,
   Die Welt kommt ganz zu dir;
Sie hat von dir vernommen,
Die Söhn' und Töchter kommen
   Und suchen deinen Ruhm und Zier.

EPIPHANY

5. Thy heart will leap for gladness When from the realms of sadness They come o'er land and sea. Thine eyes will wake from slumber When people without number Come thronging from afar to thee.	Dein Herze wird dir wallen, Wenn dir kommt zu Gefallen Die Anzahl um das Meer; Du wirst die Augen weiden Am Volke vieler Heiden, So dringt mit Haufen zu dir her.

Martin Opitz published this Epiphany hymn in his *Episteln,* 1628, in six stanzas. It was headed "On the Holy Three Kings' Day, Isaiah 60."

The translation is by Gerhard Gieschen, 1937, and was revised by him for *The Lutheran Hymnal* after it had previously appeared in the church publication called *Faith-Life.* The omitted Stanza 6 reads, as translated by Emmanuel Cronenwett for the Ohio *Lutheran Hymnal,* 1880:

> There are glad delegations
> From Ephah and far nations
>   And clouds from Midian;
> With gold shall Sheba cheer thee
> And incense; all that near thee
>   Shall sing thy praise, O chosen one!

The tune "O Welt, ich muss dich lassen" is ascribed to Heinrich Isaak. It is most commonly associated with Paul Gerhardt's great evening hymn "Nun ruhen alle Wälder" (see Hymn No. 554). It first appeared about 1490, set to a popular folk-song, "Innsbruck, ich muss dich lassen."

As with Gladness Men of Old   127

1. As with gladness men of old
Did the guiding star behold;
As with joy they hailed its light,
Leading onward, beaming bright,
So, most gracious Lord, may we
Evermore be led by Thee!

2. As with joyful steps they sped,
Savior, to Thy lowly bed,
There to bend the knee before
Thee whom heaven and earth adore,
So may we with willing feet
Ever seek Thy mercy-seat!

3. As they offered gifts most rare
At Thy cradle, rude and bare,
So may we with holy joy,
Pure and free from sin's alloy,
All our costliest treasures bring,
Christ, to Thee, our heavenly King!

4. Holy Jesus, every day
Keep us in the narrow way;
And when earthly things are past,
Bring our ransomed souls at last
Where they need no star to guide,
Where no clouds Thy glory hide.

5. In the heavenly country bright
Need they no created light;
Thou its Light, its Joy, its Crown,
Thou its Sun which goes not down.
There forever may we sing
Alleluias to our King!

During an illness, in 1860, William C. Dix wrote this hymn after reading the Gospel for Epiphany. It was first published in *Hymns of Love and Joy,* 1861. It was included in the first edition of *Hymns Ancient and Modern,* 1861. The version above is as revised, with the approval of the author, for the *Revised Version* of *Hymns Ancient and Modern,* 1875. The author originally had written in Stanza 2:

> To that lowly manger-bed

and

> Him whom heaven and earth adore,

and in Stanza 3:

> At that manger rude and bare.

According to Matt. 2:11 the Wise Men came to a house, not to a stable.

The tune "Dix," so called because of its association with this hymn, is also named "Treuer Heiland, wir sind hier." It is based on a melody by Konrad Kocher, set to a German hymn, beginning with that line in Kocher's *Stimmen aus dem Reiche Gottes,* Stuttgart, 1838. It was abridged and altered, and then coupled with Dix's hymn for *Hymns Ancient and Modern,* 1861. Mr. Dix did not like Kocher's tune, but the union of text and tune has nevertheless proved effective and popular.

128 Brightest and Best of the Sons of the Morning

1. Brightest and best of the sons of the morning,
   Dawn on our darkness and lend us thine aid;
   Star of the East, the horizon adorning,
   Guide where our infant Redeemer is laid.

2. Cold on His cradle the dewdrops are shining;
   Low lies His head with the beasts of the stall.
   Angels adore Him in slumber reclining,
   Maker and Monarch and Savior of all.

3. Shall we not yield Him, in costly devotion,
   Odors of Edom and offerings divine,
   Gems of the mountain and pearls of the ocean,
   Myrrh from the forest and gold from the mine?

4. Vainly we offer each ample oblation,
   Vainly with gifts would His favor secure.
   Richer by far is the heart's adoration;
   Dearer to God are the prayers of the poor.

5. Brightest and best of the sons of the morning,
   Dawn on our darkness and lend us thine aid;
   Star of the East, the horizon adorning,
   Guide where our infant Redeemer is laid.

Reginald Heber first published this classical hymn in *The Christian Observer,* November, 1811. Lord Macaulay's father was editor of this journal. Dr. Julian writes: "Few hymns of merit have troubled compilers more than this. Some have held that its use involved the worshiping of a star, while others have been offended with its meter as being too suggestive of a solemn dance." Be that as it may, the hymn is still very popular, as its inclusion in the best American hymnals shows.

The tune "Morning Star" for this hymn also seems to be growing in popularity in our country. It was part of an anthem composed by James P. Harding, in 1892, for use at Gifford Hall Mission in London. According to Robert Guy McCutchan the tune was first used in an American hymnal when it was included in *The New Psalms and Hymns,* Richmond, Va., 1901, by the Presbyterian Committee of Publication. It was set to Heber's hymn in *The Methodist Hymnal,* 1905, and also in the *Evangelical Lutheran Hymn-Book,* 1912.

129 Hail, Thou Source of Every Blessing

1. Hail, Thou Source of every blessing,
   Sovereign Father of mankind!
   Gentiles now, Thy grace possessing,
   In Thy courts admission find.
   Grateful now we fall before Thee,
   In Thy Church obtain a place,
   Now by faith behold Thy glory,
   Praise Thy truth, adore Thy grace.

2. Once far off, but now invited,
   We approach Thy sacred throne;
   In Thy covenant united,
   Reconciled, redeemed, made one.
   Now revealed to Eastern sages,
   See the Star of Mercy shine;
   Mystery hid in former ages,
   Mystery great of love divine.

3. Hail, Thou all-inviting Savior!
   Gentiles now their offerings bring;
   In Thy temples seek Thy favor,
   Jesus Christ, our Lord and King.
   May we, body, soul, and spirit,
   Live devoted to Thy praise,
   Glorious realms of bliss inherit,
   Grateful anthems ever raise!

This is the finest of Basil Woodd's hymns. It first appeared in his *The Psalms of David,* etc., c. 1810—20. Some hymnals have the text slightly altered.

EPIPHANY

As far as we have been able to determine, the text above is the original throughout.

The tune "O Durchbrecher" is from Johann Freylinghausen's *Neues geistreiches Gesangbuch*, Halle, 1704, where it was set to Gottfried Arnold's hymn "O Durchbrecher aller Bande."

O Jesus, King of Glory   130

1. O Jesus, King of Glory,
   Both David's Lord and Son!
Thy realm endures forever,
   In heaven is fixed Thy throne.
Help that in earth's dominions,
   Throughout from pole to pole,
Thy reign may spread salvation
   To each benighted soul.

2. The Eastern sages, bringing
   Their tribute-gifts to Thee,
Bear witness to Thy kingdom
   And humbly bow the knee.
To Thee the star is pointing
   And the prophetic Word;
Hence joyously we hail Thee:
   Our Savior and our Lord!

3. Thou art a mighty Monarch,
   As by Thy Word is told,
Yet carest Thou but little
   For earthly goods or gold;
On no proud steed Thou ridest,
   Thou wear'st no jeweled crown
Nor dwell'st in lordly castle,
   But bearest scoff and frown.

4. Yet art Thou decked with beauty,
   With rays of glorious light;
Thy works proclaim Thy goodness,
   And all Thy ways are right.
Vouchsafe to shield Thy people
   With Thine almighty arm
That they may dwell in safety
   From those who mean them harm.

5. Ah, look on me with pity
   Though I am weak and poor;
Admit me to Thy kingdom
   To dwell there, blest and sure.
I pray Thee, guide and keep me
   Safe from my bitter foes,
From sin and death and Satan;
   Free me from all my woes.

6. And bid Thy Word within me
   Shine as the fairest star;
Keep sin and all false doctrine
   Forever from me far.
Help me confess Thee truly
   And with Thy Christendom
Here own Thee King and Savior
   And in the world to come.

O König aller Ehren,
   Herr Jesu, Davids Sohn,
Dein Reich soll ewig währen,
   Im Himmel ist dein Thron.
Hilf, dass allhier auf Erden
   Den Menschen weit und breit
Dein Reich bekannt mög' werden
   Zur ew'gen Seligkeit!

Von deinem Reich auch zeugen
   Die Leut' aus Morgenland;
Die Knie sie vor dir beugen,
   Weil ihnen bist bekannt;
Der neu' Stern auf dich weiset,
   Dazu das göttlich' Wort,
Drum man dich billig preiset,
   Dass du bist unser Hort.

Du bist ein grosser König,
   Wie uns die Schrift vermeld't;
Doch achtest du gar wenig
   Vergänglich Gut und Geld,
Prangst nicht auf einem Rosse,
   Trägst keine güldne Kron',
Sitzt nicht im festen Schlosse,
   Hier hast du Spott und Hohn.

Doch bist du schön gezieret,
   Dein Glanz erstreckt sich weit,
Dein' Güt' allzeit floriret
   Und dein' Gerechtigkeit.
Du woll'st die Frommen schützen
   Durch dein' Macht und Gewalt,
Dass sie im Frieden sitzen,
   Die Bösen stürzen bald.

Du woll'st dich mein erbarmen,
   In dein Reich nimm mich auf,
Dein Güte schenk mir Armen
   Und segne meinen Lauf.
Mein'n Feinden woll'st du wehren,
   Dem Teufel, Sünd' und Tod,
Dass sie mich nicht versehren;
   Rett mich aus aller Not!

Du woll'st in mir entzünden
   Dein Wort, den schönsten Stern,
Dass falsche Lehr' und Sünden
   Sei'n von mein'm Herzen fern;
Hilf, dass ich dich erkenne
   Und mit der Christenheit
Dich meinen König nenne
   Jetzt und in Ewigkeit!

Martin Behm's great Epiphany hymn was first published in his *Centuria precationum rhythmicarum*, Wittenberg, 1606, based on the Epiphany Gospel, Matt. 2:1-12.

The translation is an altered form of Catherine Winkworth's in her *Chorale Book for England*, 1863. She had published an earlier version of Stanzas 1, 2, 5, and 6, in which she departed from the original meter, in her second series of *Lyra Germanica*, 1858.

For comments on the tune "Valet will ich dir geben" see Hymn No. 58.

EPIPHANY

131   The Star Proclaims the King Is Here

1. The star proclaims the King is here;
But, Herod, why this senseless fear?
He takes no realms of earth away
Who gives the realms of heavenly day.

Hostis Herodes impie,
Christum venire quid times?
Non eripit mortalia,
Qui regna dat caelestia.

2. The wiser Magi see from far
And follow on His guiding star;
And led by light, to light they press
And by their gifts their God confess.

Ibant magi, quam viderant,
Stellam sequentes praeviam:
Lumen requirunt lumine,
Deum fatentur munere.

3. Within the Jordan's crystal flood
In meekness stands the Lamb of God
And, sinless, sanctifies the wave,
Mankind from sin to cleanse and save.

Lavacra puri gurgitis
Caelestis Agnus attigit;
Peccata, quae non detulit,
Nos abluendo sustulit.

4. At Cana first His power is shown;
His might the blushing waters own
And, changing as He speaks the word,
Flow wine, obedient to their Lord.

Novum genus potentiae,
Aquae rubescunt hydriae,
Vinumque iussa fundere
Mutavit unda originem.

5. All glory, Jesus, be to Thee
For this Thy glad epiphany;
Whom with the Father we adore
And Holy Ghost forevermore.

Gloria tibi, Domine,
Qui apparuisti hodie,
Cum Patre et Sancto Spiritu
In sempiterna saecula. Amen.

This hymn is part of Coelius Sedulius's "Paean Alphabeticus de Christo." The beginning initials of the Latin stanzas show that we have a continuation of Hymn No. 104.

The translation is an altered form of that by John M. Neale, in his *Hymnal Noted*, 1852.

The tune "Wo Gott zum Haus" is from Klug's *Geistliche Lieder*, Wittenberg, 1535, where it was set to the hymn on Ps. 127, "Wo Gott zum Haus nicht gibt sein' Gunst," ascribed to Johann Kohlross.

132   O God of God, O Light of Light

1. O God of God, O Light of Light,
   Thou Prince of Peace, Thou King of kings!
To Thee where angels know no night
   The song of praise forever rings.
To Him who sits upon the throne,
   The Lamb once slain for sinful men,
Be honor, might, all by Him won,
   Glory and praise! Amen, Amen.

2. Deep in the prophets' sacred page,
   Grand in the poets' wingèd word,
Slowly in type, from age to age,
   Nations beheld their coming Lord,
Till through the deep Judean night
   Rang out the song "Good will to men!"
Hymned by the first-born sons of light,
   Reechoed now, "Good will!" Amen.

3. That life of truth, those deeds of love,
   That death of pain, mid hate and scorn,
These all are past, and now above
   He reigns our King, once crowned with thorn.
Lift up your heads, ye heavenly gates;
   So sang His hosts, unheard by men;
Lift up your heads, for you He waits.
   We lift them up. Amen, Amen.

4. Nations afar, in ignorance deep,
   Isles of the sea, where darkness lay,
These hear His voice, they wake from sleep,
   And throng with joy the upward way.
They cry with us, "Send forth Thy light,
   O Lamb, once slain for sinful men;
Burst Satan's bonds, O God of might;
   Set all men free!" Amen, Amen.

5. Sing to the Lord a glorious song,
   Sing to His name, His love forthtell;
Sing on, heaven's host, His praise prolong;
   Sing, ye who now on earth do dwell:
Worthy the Lamb for sinners slain;
   From angels praise and thanks from men;
Worthy the Lamb, enthroned to reign,
   Glory and power! Amen, Amen.

EPIPHANY

This hymn was written by Dr. John Julian for the Sheffield Church Choir's Union Festival, April 16, 1883, and first printed in the festival book. In 1884 it was included in Horder's *Congregational Hymns*. Since then it has been included in other hymn collections.

The tune "O grosser Gott" is from *Gesang- und Notenbuch*, Stuttgart, 1744.

Within the Father's House   133

1. Within the Father's house
 The Son hath found His home,
 And to His Temple suddenly
 The Lord of Life hath come.

2. The doctors of the Law
 Gaze on the wondrous Child
 And marvel at His gracious words
 Of wisdom undefiled.

3. Yet not to them is given
 The mighty truth to know,
 To lift the earthly veil which hides
 Incarnate God below.

4. The secret of the Lord
 Escapes each human eye,
 And faithful pondering hearts await
 The full epiphany.

5. Lord, visit Thou our souls
 And teach us by Thy grace
 Each dim revealing of Thyself
 With loving awe to trace,

6. Till from our darkened sight
 The cloud shall pass away
 And on the cleansèd soul shall burst
 The everlasting day;

7. Till we behold Thy face
 And know as we are known
 Thee, Father, Son, and Holy Ghost,
 Coequal Three in One.

This fine hymn on the Gospel for the First Sunday after Epiphany was first published by James R. Woodford in the *Parish Hymn Book*, 1863, of which he was one of the editors.

The tune "Franconia" was adapted by William H. Havergal, 1847, from the melody in Johann B. König's *Harmonischer Liederschatz*, Frankfurt a. M., 1738, where it was set to Georg W. Wedel's hymn "Was ist, das mich betrübt." König himself may be the composer.

Songs of Thankfulness and Praise   134

1. Songs of thankfulness and praise,
 Jesus, Lord, to Thee we raise,
 Manifested by the star
 To the sages from afar,
 Branch of royal David's stem,
 In Thy birth at Bethlehem.
 Anthems be to Thee addressed
 God in man made manifest.

2. Manifest at Jordan's stream,
 Prophet, Priest, and King supreme,
 And at Cana, Wedding-guest,
 In Thy Godhead manifest;
 Manifest in power divine,
 Changing water into wine.
 Anthems be to Thee addressed
 God in man made manifest.

3. Manifest in making whole
 Palsied limbs and fainting soul;
 Manifest in valiant fight,
 Quelling all the devil's might;
 Manifest in gracious will,
 Ever bringing good from ill.
 Anthems be to Thee addressed,
 God in man made manifest.

4. Sun and moon shall darkened be,
 Stars shall fall, the heavens shall flee;
 Christ will then like lightning shine,
 All will see His glorious sign;
 All will then the trumpet hear,
 All will see the Judge appear;
 Thou by all wilt be confessed,
 God in man made manifest.

5. Grant us grace to see Thee, Lord,
 Mirrored in Thy holy Word;
 May we imitate Thee now
 And be pure as pure art Thou
 That we like to Thee may be
 At Thy great Epiphany
 And may praise Thee, ever blest,
 God in man made manifest.

EPIPHANY. — PRESENTATION

Christopher Wordsworth published this hymn in his *Holy Year*, 1862, with the heading:

"Sixth Sunday after the Epiphany. — Recapitulation of the Subjects presented in the Services of former weeks throughout the season of Epiphany; and Anticipation of the future great and glorious Epiphany, at which Christ will appear again to judge the World."

For comments on the tune "St. George" see Hymn No. 71.

135   'Tis Good, Lord, to Be Here

1. 'Tis good, Lord, to be here,
   Thy glory fills the night;
   Thy face and garments, like the sun,
   Shine with unborrowed light.

2. 'Tis good, Lord, to be here,
   Thy beauty to behold
   Where Moses and Elijah stand,
   Thy messengers of old.

3. Fulfiller of the past,
   Promise of things to be,
   We hail Thy body glorified
   And our redemption see.

4. Before we taste of death,
   We see Thy kingdom come;
   We fain would hold the vision bright
   And make this hill our home.

5. 'Tis good, Lord, to be here.
   Yet we may not remain;
   But since Thou bidst us leave the mount,
   Come with us to the plain.

The Gospel for the Sixth Sunday after Epiphany brings the account of our Lord's transfiguration. This hymn specifically commemorates this important manifestation of our Savior's glory during the days of His humiliation on earth. The author, Joseph Armitage Robinson, was Vicar of All Saints' Church, Cambridge, England, when he wrote this hymn, in 1888. It received recognition by its inclusion in *Hymns Ancient and Modern,* edition of 1904.

For comments on the tune "Potsdam" see Hymn No. 117.

136   Angels from the Realms of Glory

1. Angels from the realms of glory,
   Wing your flight o'er all the earth;
   Ye who sang creation's story,
   Now proclaim Messiah's birth:
   Come and worship,
   Come and worship;
   Worship Christ, the new-born King.

2. Shepherds in the fields abiding,
   Watching o'er your flocks by night,
   God with man is now residing,
   Yonder shines the Infant Light:
   Come and worship,
   Come and worship;
   Worship Christ, the new-born King.

3. Sages, leave your contemplations;
   Brighter visions beam afar;
   Seek the great Desire of nations,
   Ye have seen His natal star:
   Come and worship,
   Come and worship;
   Worship Christ, the new-born King.

4. Saints, before the altar bending,
   Watching long in hope and fear,
   Suddenly the Lord, descending,
   In His Temple shall appear:
   Come and worship,
   Come and worship;
   Worship Christ, the new-born King.

James Montgomery first published this hymn in his newspaper *Iris,* Sheffield, December 24, 1816, in five stanzas, entitled "Nativity." He republished it in 1825, in his *Christian Psalmist,* with the title "Good Tidings of Great Joy to All People," making certain minor changes in the text. The omitted fifth stanza reads:

    Sinners, wrung with true repentance,
      Doomed for guilt to endless pains,
    Justice now revokes the sentence;
      Mercy calls you, Break your chains;
        Come and worship,
        Come and worship;
    Worship Christ, the new-born King.

PRESENTATION

While the hymn is widely used as a Christmas hymn, it is much more appropriate for the Festival of Presentation, as it recapitulates the facts of Christmas and Epiphany and then concludes with the presentation of our Lord in the Temple.

For comments on the tune "Regent Square" see Hymn No. 50 (first tune).

In Peace and Joy I Now Depart 137

1. In peace and joy I now depart
   At God's disposing;
   For full of comfort is my heart,
   Soft reposing.
   So the Lord hath promised me,
   And death is but a slumber.

2. 'Tis Christ that wrought this work for me,
   My faithful Savior,
   Whom Thou hast made mine eyes to see
   By Thy favor.
   Now I know He is my Life,
   My Help in need and dying.

3. Him Thou hast unto all set forth
   Their great Salvation
   And to His kingdom called the earth,
   Every nation,
   By Thy dear and wholesome Word,
   In every place resounding.

4. He is the Hope and saving Light
   Of lands benighted;
   By Him are they who dwelt in night
   Fed and lighted.
   He is Israel's Praise and Bliss,
   Their Joy, Reward, and Glory.

Mit Fried' und Freud' ich fahr' dahin
   In Gottes Willen;
Getrost ist mir mein Herz und Sinn,
   Sanft und stille,
Wie Gott mir verheissen hat:
   Der Tod ist mein Schlaf worden.

Das macht Christus, wahr'r Gottessohn,
   Der treue Heiland,
Den du mich, Herr, hast sehen lan
   Und g'macht bekannt,
Dass er sei das Leben mein
   Und Heil in Not und Sterben.

Den hast du allen vorgestellt
   Mit grossen Gnaden,
Zu seinem Reich die ganze Welt
   Heissen laden
Durch dein teuer, heilsam Wort,
   An allem Ort erschollen.

Er ist das Heil und selig Licht
   Für all die Heiden,
Zu 'rleuchten, die dich kennen nicht,
   Und zu weiden.
Er ist dein's Volks Israel
   Der Preis, Ehr', Freud' und Wonne.

This hymn by Martin Luther first appeared in *Geystliches Gesangk Buchleyn,* Wittenberg, 1524, with the heading "Simeon's Song of Praise" and with the reference to Luke 2:29-32.

The translation is an altered form of that by Leonard W. Bacon, published after his death, in 1884. Although Dr. Bacon based his translation on that by Catherine Winkworth in her *Chorale Book for England,* 1863, in which she departed from the original meter, there is so little of Miss Winkworth's text in his version that it may well be considered his own.

The tune "Mit Fried' und Freud'" appeared with the text at its first publication in 1524. The composer is unknown.

Thou Light of Gentile Nations 138

1. Thou Light of Gentile nations,
   Thou Savior from above,
   Drawn by Thy Spirit's leading,
   We come with joy and love
   Into Thy holy temple
   And wait with earnest mind
   As Simeon had waited
   His God and Lord to find.

2. Yea, Lord, Thy servants meet Thee,
   In every holy place
   Where Thy true Word has promised
   That we should see Thy face.
   Today Thou still dost grant us
   Who gather round Thee here
   In arms of faith to bear Thee
   As did that aged seer.

Herr Jesu, Licht der Heiden,
   Der Frommen Schatz und Lieb',
Wir kommen jetzt mit Freuden
   Durch deines Geistes Trieb
In diesen deinen Tempel
   Und suchen mit Begier
Nach Simeons Exempel
   Dich, grossen Gott, allhier.

Du wirst von uns gefunden,
   O Herr, an jedem Ort,
Dahin du dich verbunden
   Durch dein Verheissungswort;
Vergönnst noch heutzutage,
   Dass man dich gleicherweis'
Auf Glaubensarmen trage
   Wie dort der alte Greis.

3. Be Thou our Joy and Brightness,
   Our Cheer in pain and loss,
   Our Sun in darkest terror,
   The Glory round our cross,
   A Star for sinking spirits,
   A Beacon in distress,
   Physician, Friend, in sickness,
   In death our Happiness.

Sei unser Glanz in Wonne,
   Ein helles Licht in Pein,
   Im Schrecken unsre Sonne,
   Im Kreuz ein Gnadenschein,
   In Zagheit Glut und Flamme,
   In Not ein Freudenstrahl,
   In Krankheit Arzt und Amme,
   Ein Stern in Todesqual!

4. Let us, O Lord, be faithful
   Like Simeon to the end,
   So that his prayer exultant
   May from our hearts ascend:
   "O Lord, now let Thy servant
   Depart in peace, I pray,
   Since I have seen my Savior
   And here beheld His day."

Herr, lass uns auch gelingen,
   Dass letzt wie Simeon
   Ein jeder Christ kann singen
   Den schönen Schwanenton:
   Mir werden nun in Frieden
   Mein' Augen zugedrückt,
   Nachdem ich schon hienieden
   Den Heiland hab' erblickt.

5. My Savior, I behold Thee
   With faith's enlightened eye;
   Of Thee no foe can rob me,
   His threats I can defy.
   Within Thy heart abiding,
   As Thou, O Lord, in me,
   Death can no longer frighten
   Nor part my soul from Thee.

Ja, ja, ich hab' im Glauben,
   Mein Jesu, dich geschaut;
   Kein Feind kann dich mir rauben,
   Wie heftig er auch dräut.
   Ich wohn' in deinem Herzen
   Und in dem meinen du;
   Uns scheiden keine Schmerzen,
   Kein' Angst, kein Tod dazu.

6. Lord, here on earth Thou seemest
   At times to frown on me,
   And through my tears I often
   Can scarce distinguish Thee;
   But in the heavenly mansions
   Shall nothing dim my sight;
   There shall I see Thy glory
   In never-changing light.

Hier blickst du zwar zuweilen
   So scheel und schwül mich an,
   Dass oft vor Angst und Heulen
   Ich dich kaum kennen kann;
   Dort aber wird's geschehen,
   Dass ich von Angesicht
   Zu Angesicht soll sehen
   Dein immer klares Licht.

This is probably the finest hymn on the subject of our Lord's Presentation. Johann Franck published it in his *Geistliches Sion*, Guben, 1674, entitled "On the Festival of the Purification of Mary." It may have been written as early as 1646.

The translation of Stanzas 1 to 5 is an altered form of that by Catherine Winkworth in her *Chorale Book for England*, 1863. The translator of Stanza 6 is unknown.

For comments on the tune "Valet will ich dir geben" see Hymn No. 58.

139   In His Temple Now Behold Him

1. In His Temple now behold Him,
   See the long-expected Lord;
   Ancient prophets had foretold Him,—
   God has now fulfilled His word.
   Now, to praise Him, His redeemèd
   Shall break forth with one accord.

2. In the arms of her who bore Him,
   Virgin pure, behold Him lie,
   While His aged saints adore Him
   Ere in faith and hope they die.
   Hallelujah! Hallelujah!
   Lo! the incarnate God most high.

3. Jesus, by Thy presentation,
   Thou, who didst for us endure,
   Make us see our great salvation,
   Seal us with Thy promise sure,
   And present us in Thy glory
   To Thy Father, cleansed and pure.

4. Prince and Author of salvation,
   Be Thy boundless love our theme!
   Jesus, praise to Thee be given
   By the world Thou didst redeem,
   With the Father and the Spirit,
   Lord of majesty supreme!

Henry J. Pye, while rector of Clifton-Campville in Staffordshire, compiled a book of *Hymns*, 1851, in which this hymn was included. It was then included, in 1853, in the Cooke and Denton *Hymnal*, slightly altered, and with the addition of a fourth stanza by William Cooke.

For comments on the tune "Sieh, hier bin ich" see Hymn No. 56.

Jesus, I Will Ponder Now 140

1. Jesus, I will ponder now
On Thy holy Passion;
With Thy Spirit me endow
For such meditation.
Grant that I in love and faith
May the image cherish
Of Thy suffering, pain, and death,
That I may not perish.

2. Make me see Thy great distress,
Anguish, and affliction,
Bonds and stripes and wretchedness
And Thy crucifixion;
Make me see how scourge and rod,
Spear and nails, did wound Thee,
How for man Thou diedst, O God,
Who with thorns had crowned Thee.

3. Yet, O Lord, not thus alone
Make me see Thy Passion,
But its cause to me make known
And its termination.
Ah! I also and my sin
Wrought Thy deep affliction;
This indeed the cause hath been
Of Thy crucifixion.

4. Grant that I Thy Passion view
With repentant grieving
Nor Thee crucify anew
By unholy living.
How could I refuse to shun
Every sinful pleasure
Since for me God's only Son
Suffered without measure?

5. If my sins give me alarm
And my conscience grieve me,
Let Thy cross my fear disarm,
Peace of conscience give me.
Grant that I may trust in Thee
And Thy holy Passion.
If His Son so loveth me,
God must have compassion.

6. Grant that I may willingly
Bear with Thee my crosses,
Learning humbleness of Thee,
Peace mid pain and losses.
May I give Thee love for love!
Hear me, O my Savior,
That I may in heaven above
Sing Thy praise forever.

Jesu, deine Passion
Will ich jetzt bedenken;
Wollest mir vom Himmelsthron
Geist und Andacht schenken.
In dem Bild jetzund erschein,
Jesu, meinem Herzen,
Wie du, unser Heil zu sein,
Littest alle Schmerzen!

Meine Seele sehen mach
Deine Angst und Bande,
Deine Speichel, Schläg' und Schmach,
Deine Kreuzesschande,
Deine Geissel, Dornenkron',
Speer- und Nägelwunden,
Deinen Tod, o Gottessohn,
Und den Leib voll Schrunden!

Doch so lass mich nicht allein
Deine Marter sehen,
Lass mich auch die Ursach' fein
Und die Frucht verstehen!
Ach, die Ursach' war auch ich,
Ich und meine Sünde;
Diese hat gemartet dich,
Nicht das Heideng'sinde.

Jesu, lehr bedenken mich
Dies mit Buss' und Reue;
Hilf, dass ich mit Sünden dich
Martre nicht aufs neue!
Sollt' ich dazu haben Lust
Und nicht wollen meiden,
Was Gott selber büssen musst'
Mit so grossem Leiden?

Wenn mir meine Sünde will
Machen heiss die Hölle,
Jesu, mein Gewissen still,
Dich ins Mittel stelle!
Dich und deine Passion
Lass mich gläubig fassen;
Liebet mich sein lieber Sohn,
Wie kann Gott mich hassen?

Gib auch, Jesu, dass ich gern
Dir das Kreuz nachtrage,
Dass ich Demut von dir lern'
Und Geduld in Plage,
Dass ich dir geb' Lieb' um Lieb'!
Indes lass dies Lallen
(Bessern Dank ich dorten geb'),
Jesu, dir gefallen!

This hymn by Sigismund von Birken, like his hymn "Let Us Ever Walk with Jesus" (see Hymn No. 409), first appeared in *Heilige Karwochen,* Nürnberg, 1653. It is his finest hymn and a great favorite Lenten hymn in the Lutheran Church.

The translation is an altered form of that by August Crull.

The tune "Jesu Kreuz, Leiden und Pein" is by Melchior Vulpius and first appeared in his *Ein schön geistlich Gesang Buch,* etc., Jena, 1609, set to a hymn beginning with that line.

Enslaved by Sin and Bound in Chains 141

1. Enslaved by sin and bound in chains,
Beneath its dreadful tyrant sway,
And doomed to everlasting pains,
We wretched, guilty captives lay.

2. Nor gold nor gems could buy our peace,
Nor all the world's collected store
Suffice to purchase our release;
A thousand worlds were all too poor.

LENT

3. Jesus, the Lord, the mighty God,
An all-sufficient ransom paid.
O matchless price! His precious blood
For vile, rebellious traitors shed.

4. Jesus the Sacrifice became
To rescue guilty souls from hell;
The spotless, bleeding, dying Lamb
Beneath avenging Justice fell.

5. Amazing goodness! Love divine!
Oh, may our grateful hearts adore
The matchless grace nor yield to sin
Nor wear its cruel fetters more!

Anne Steele published this hymn in her *Poems on Subjects Chiefly Devotional*, 1760.
For comments on the tune "Wenn wir in höchsten Nöten" see Hymn No. 522.

142 A Lamb Goes Uncomplaining Forth

1. A Lamb goes uncomplaining forth,
    The guilt of all men bearing;
And laden with the sins of earth,
    None else the burden sharing!
Goes patient on, grows weak and faint,
To slaughter led without complaint,
    That spotless life to offer;
Bears shame and stripes, and wounds and death,
Anguish and mockery, and saith,
    "Willing all this I suffer."

2. This Lamb is Christ, the soul's great Friend,
    The Lamb of God, our Savior;
Him God the Father chose to send
    To gain for us His favor.
"Go forth, My Son," the Father saith,
"And free men from the fear of death,
    From guilt and condemnation.
The wrath and stripes are hard to bear,
But by Thy Passion men shall share
    The fruit of Thy salvation."

3. "Yea, Father, yea, most willingly
    I'll bear what Thou commandest;
My will conforms to Thy decree,
    I do what Thou demandest."
O wondrous Love, what hast Thou done!
The Father offers up His Son!
    The Son, content, descendeth!
O Love, how strong Thou art to save!
Thou beddest Him within the grave
    Whose word the mountains rendeth.

4. From morn till eve my theme shall be
    Thy mercy's wondrous measure;
To sacrifice myself for Thee
    Shall be my aim and pleasure.
My stream of life shall ever be
A current flowing ceaselessly,
    Thy constant praise outpouring.
I'll treasure in my memory,
O Lord, all Thou hast done for me,
    Thy gracious love adoring.

5. Of death I am no more afraid,
    New life from Thee is flowing;
Thy cross affords me cooling shade
    When noonday's sun is glowing.
When by my grief I am opprest,
On Thee my weary soul shall rest
    Serenely as on pillows.
Thou art my Anchor when by woe
My bark is driven to and fro
    On trouble's surging billows.

Ein Lämmlein geht und trägt die Schuld
    Der Welt und ihrer Kinder;
Es geht und träget in Geduld
    Die Sünden aller Sünder;
Es geht dahin, wird matt und krank,
Ergibt sich auf die Würgebank,
    Verzeiht sich aller Freuden;
Es nimmet an Schmach, Hohn und Spott,
Angst, Wunden, Striemen, Kreuz und Tod
    Und spricht: Ich will's gern leiden.

Das Lämmlein ist der grosse Freund
    Und Heiland meiner Seelen;
Den, den hat Gott zum Sündenfeind
    Und Sühner wollen wählen.
Geh hin, mein Kind, und nimm dich an
Der Kinder, die ich ausgetan
    Zur Straf' und Zornesruten.
Die Straf' ist schwer, der Zorn ist gross,
Du kannst und sollst sie machen los
    Durch Sterben und durch Bluten.

Ja, Vater, ja, von Herzensgrund,
    Leg' auf, ich will dir's tragen;
Mein Wollen hängt an deinem Mund,
    Mein Wirken ist dein Sagen.
O Wunderlieb', o Liebesmacht,
Du kannst, was nie kein Mensch gedacht,
    Gott seinen Sohn abzwingen!
O Liebe, Liebe, du bist stark,
Du streckest den ins Grab und Sarg,
    Vor dem die Felsen springen!

Ich will von deiner Lieblichkeit
    Bei Nacht und Tage singen,
Mich selbst auch dir zu aller Zeit
    Zum Freudenopfer bringen.
Mein Bach des Lebens soll sich dir
Und deinem Namen für und für
    In Dankbarkeit ergiessen,
Und was du mir zugut getan,
Das will ich stets, so tief ich kann,
    In mein Gedächtnis schliessen.

Was schadet mir des Todes Gift?
    Dein Blut, das ist mein Leben;
Wenn mich der Sonne Hitze trifft,
    So kann mir's Schatten geben.
Setzt mir der Wehmut Schmerzen zu
So find' ich bei dir meine Ruh'
    Als auf dem Bett ein Kranker;
Und wenn des Kreuzes Ungestüm
Mein Schifflein treibet um und um,
    So bist du dann mein Anker.

6. And when Thy glory I shall see
   And taste Thy kingdom's pleasure,
   Thy blood my royal robe shall be,
   My joy beyond all measure.
   When I appear before Thy throne,
   Thy righteousness shall be my crown, —
   With these I need not hide me.
   And there, in garments richly wrought
   As Thine own bride, I shall be brought
   To stand in joy beside Thee.

Wenn endlich ich soll treten ein
In deines Reiches Freuden,
So soll dies Blut mein Purpur sein,
Ich will mich darein kleiden.
Es soll sein meines Hauptes Kron',
In welcher ich will vor dem Thron
Des höchsten Vaters gehen
Und dir, dem er mich anvertraut,
Als eine wohlgeschmückte Braut
An deiner Seite stehen.

This hymn by Paul Gerhardt, founded on John 1:29, Is. 53:4-7, first appeared in the third edition of Johann Crüger's *Praxis Pietatis Melica*, 1648, in ten stanzas. *Lauxmann* calls it "the masterpiece of all Passion hymns." The cento includes Stanzas 1, 2, 3, 6, 9, and 10.

The translation is a composite prepared for *The Lutheran Hymnal.*

The omitted stanzas read:

4. Thou lay'st Him, Love, upon the cross,
   With nails and spear Him bruising;
   Thou slay'st Him as a lamb, His loss
   From soul and body oozing;
   From body 'tis the crimson flood
   Of precious sacrificial blood,
   From soul, the strength of anguish.
   My gain it is; sweet Lamb, to Thee
   What can I give whose love it can
   For me doth make Thee languish?

5. Lord, all my life I'll cleave to Thee,
   Thy love fore'er beholding,
   Thee ever, as Thou ever me,
   With loving arms enfolding.
   Yea, Thou shalt be my Beacon-light,
   To guide me safe through death's dark night,
   And cheer my heart in sorrow;
   Henceforth myself and all that's mine
   To Thee, my Savior, I consign,
   From whom all things I borrow.

7. Enlarge, my heart's own shrine, and swell,
   To thee shall now be given
   A treasure that doth far excel
   The worth of earth and heaven.
   Away with the Arabian gold,
   With treasures of an earthly mold!
   I've found a better jewel.
   My priceless treasure, Lord, my God,
   Is Thy most holy, precious blood,
   Which flowed from wounds so cruel.

8. This treasure ever I'll employ,
   This every aid shall yield me;
   In sorrow it shall be my joy,
   In conflict it shall shield me;
   In joy, the music of my feast,
   And when all else has lost its zest,
   This manna still shall feed me;
   In thirst my drink; in want my food;
   My company in solitude,
   To comfort and to lead me.

The tune "An Wasserflüssen Babylon" is first found in the third part of the Strassburg *Teutsch Kirchen ampt,* 1525, where it is set to Wolfgang Dachstein's hymn on Ps. 137, beginning:

An Wasserflüssen Babylon,
   Da sassen wir mit Schmerzen;
Als wir gedachten an Zion,
   Da weinten wir von Herzen.
Wir hingen auf mit schwerem Mut
Die Orgeln und die Harfen gut
   An ihren Bäum' und Weiden,
Die drinnen sind in ihrem Land,
Da mussten wir viel Schmach und Schand'
   Täglich von ihnen leiden.

The tune is ascribed to Dachstein, although without any definite proof.

O Dearest Jesus, What Law Hast Thou Broken   143

1. O dearest Jesus, what law hast Thou broken
   That such sharp sentence should on Thee be spoken?
   Of what great crime hast Thou to make confession, —
   What dark transgression?

Herzliebster Jesu, was hast du verbrochen,
Dass man ein solch scharf Urteil hat gesprochen?
Was ist die Schuld? In was für Missetaten
Bist du geraten?

LENT

2. They crown Thy head with thorns, they smite, they scourge Thee;
With cruel mockings to the cross they urge Thee;
They give Thee gall to drink, they still decry Thee;
They crucify Thee.

3. Whence come these sorrows, whence this mortal anguish?
It is my sins for which Thou, Lord, must languish;
Yea, all the wrath, the woe, Thou dost inherit,
This I do merit.

4. What punishment so strange is suffered yonder!
The Shepherd dies for sheep that loved to wander;
The Master pays the debt His servants owe Him,
Who would not know Him.

5. The sinless Son of God must die in sadness;
The sinful child of man may live in gladness;
Man forfeited his life and is acquitted, —
God is committed.

6. There was no spot in me by sin untainted;
Sick with sin's poison, all my heart had fainted;
My heavy guilt to hell had well-nigh brought me,
Such woe it wrought me.

7. O wondrous love, whose depth no heart hath sounded,
That brought Thee here, by foes and thieves surrounded!
All worldly pleasures, heedless, I was trying
While Thou wert dying.

8. O mighty King, no time can dim Thy glory!
How shall I spread abroad Thy wondrous story?
How shall I find some worthy gifts to proffer?
What dare I offer?

9. For vainly doth our human wisdom ponder, —
Thy woes, Thy mercy, still transcend our wonder.
Oh, how should I do aught that could delight Thee!
Can I requite Thee?

10. Yet unrequited, Lord, I would not leave Thee;
I will renounce whate'er doth vex or grieve Thee
And quench with thoughts of Thee and prayers most lowly
All fires unholy.

11. But since my strength will nevermore suffice me
To crucify desires that still entice me,
To all good deeds, oh, let Thy Spirit win me
And reign within me!

Du wirst verspeit, geschlagen und verhöhnet,
Gegeisselt und mit Dornen scharf gekrönet,
Mit Essig, als man dich ans Kreuz gehenket,
Wirst du getränket.

Was ist die Ursach' aller solcher Plagen?
Ach, meine Sünden haben dich geschlagen!
Ich, ach Herr Jesu, habe dies verschuldet,
Was du erduldet.

Wie wunderbarlich ist doch diese Strafe!
Der gute Hirte leidet für die Schafe,
Die Schuld bezahlt der Herre, der Gerechte,
Für seine Knechte.

Der Fromme stirbt, so recht und richtig wandelt;
Der Böse lebt, so wider Gott misshandelt;
Der Mensch verwirkt den Tod und ist entgangen,
Gott wird gefangen.

Ich war von Fuss auf voller Schand' und Sünden,
Bis zu dem Scheitel war nichts Gut's zu finden;
Dafür hätt' ich dort in der Hölle müssen
Ewiglich büssen.

O grosse Lieb', o Lieb' ohn' alle Masse,
Die dich gebracht auf diese Marterstrasse!
Ich lebte mit der Welt in Lust und Freuden,
Und du musst leiden.

Ach, grosser König, gross zu allen Zeiten,
Wie kann ich g'nugsam solche Treu' ausbreiten?
Kein menschlich Herze mag sich dies ausdenken,
Was dir zu schenken.

Ich kann's mit meinen Sinnen nicht erreichen,
Mit was doch dein Erbarmen zu vergleichen;
Wie kann ich dir denn deine Liebestaten
Im Werk erstatten?

Doch ist noch etwas, das dir angenehme:
Wenn ich des Fleisches Lüste dämpf' und zähme,
Dass sie aufs neu' mein Herze nicht entzünden
Mit alten Sünden.

Weil aber dies nicht steht in eignen Kräften,
Dem Kreuze die Begierden anzuheften,
So gib mir deinen Geist, der mich regiere,
Zum Guten führe!

LENT

12. I'll think upon Thy mercy without ceasing,
That earth's vain joys to me no more be pleasing;
To do Thy will shall be my sole endeavor
Henceforth forever.

13. Whate'er of earthly good this life may grant me,
I'll risk for Thee; no shame, no cross, shall daunt me;
I shall not fear what man can do to harm me
Nor death alarm me.

14. But worthless is my sacrifice, I own it;
Yet, Lord, for love's sake Thou wilt not disown it;
Thou wilt accept my gift in Thy great meekness
Nor shame my weakness.

15. And when, dear Lord, before Thy throne in heaven
To me the crown of joy at last is given,
Where sweetest hymns Thy saints forever raise Thee,
I, too, shall praise Thee.

Alsdann so werd' ich deine Huld betrachten,
Aus Lieb' zu dir die Welt für nichts erachten.
Ich werde mich bemühen, deinen Willen
Stets zu erfüllen.

Ich werde dir zu Ehren alles wagen,
Kein Kreuz nicht achten, keine Schmach noch Plagen,
Nichts von Verfolgung, nichts von Todesschmerzen
Nehmen zu Herzen.

Dies alles, ob's für schlecht zwar ist zu schätzen,
Wirst du es doch nicht gar beiseitesetzen.
In Gnaden wirst du dies von mir annehmen,
Mich nicht beschämen.

Wenn dort, Herr Jesu, wird vor deinem Throne
Auf meinem Haupte stehn die Ehrenkrone,
Da will ich dir, wenn alles wird wohl klingen,
Lob und Dank singen.

This beautiful and thoughtful hymn by Johann Heermann first appeared in his *Devoti Musica Cordis,* Breslau, 1630. It is entitled "The Cause of the bitter sufferings of Jesus Christ and consolation from His love and grace. From Augustine." It is based on the so-called *Meditations of St. Augustine,* chapter VII. This, however, is not an original work of Augustine, but rather a medieval compilation from various Church Fathers, including Augustine, Gregory the Great and Anselm of Canterbury. Chapter VII is by Anselm. The hymn is written in the Sapphic meter. However, the English translation does not always conform as well as it might.

The translation is an altered form of that by Catherine Winkworth in her *Chorale Book for England,* 1863.

The tune "Herzliebster Jesu" is by Johann *Crüger,* composed for this hymn and first published in his *Newes vollkömliches Gesangbuch,* etc., Berlin, 1640. The tune is based upon an older tune found in Johann Schein's *Cantional,* Leipzig, 1627, where it was set to Nikolaus Herman's burial hymn "Geliebter Freund, was tut ihr so verzagen."

Jesus, Grant that Balm and Healing 144

1. Jesus, grant that balm and healing
In Thy holy wounds I find,
Every hour that I am feeling
Pains of body and of mind.
Should some evil thought within
Tempt my treacherous heart to sin,
Show the peril, and from sinning
Keep me ere its first beginning.

2. Should some lust or sharp temptation
Prove too strong for flesh and blood,
Let me think upon Thy Passion,
And the breach is soon made good.
Or should Satan press me hard,
Let me then be on my guard,
Saying, "Christ for me was wounded,"
That the Tempter flee confounded.

Jesu, deine tiefen Wunden,
Deine Qual und bittern Tod
Lass mir geben alle Stunden
Trost in Leib's- und Seelennot!
Wenn mir fällt was Arges ein,
Lass mich denken deiner Pein,
Dass ich deine Angst und Schmerzen
Wohl erwäg' in meinem Herzen!

Will sich gern in Wollust weiden
Mein verderbtes Fleisch und Blut,
Lass mich denken, dass dein Leiden
Löschen muss der Hölle Glut!
Dringt der Satan ein zu mir,
Hilf, dass ich ihm halte für
Deiner Wunden Mal' und Zeichen,
Dass er von mir müsse weichen!

LENT

3. If the world my heart entices
   On the broad and easy road
   With its mirth and luring vices,
   Let me think upon the load
   Thou didst carry and endure
   That I flee all thoughts impure,
   Banishing each wild emotion,
   Calm and blest in my devotion.

4. Every wound that pains or grieves me,
   By Thy stripes, Lord, is made whole;
   When I'm faint, Thy Cross revives me,
   Granting new life to my soul.
   Yea, Thy comfort renders sweet
   Every bitter cup I meet;
   For Thy all-atoning Passion
   Has procured my soul's salvation.

5. O my God, my Rock and Tower,
   Grant that in Thy death I trust,
   Knowing Death has lost his power
   Since Thou trod'st him in the dust.
   Savior, let Thine agony
   Ever help and comfort me;
   When I die, be my Protection,
   Light and Life and Resurrection.

Wenn die Welt mich will verführen
Auf die breite Sündenbahn,
Woll'st du mich also regieren,
Dass ich alsdann schaue an
Deiner Marter Zentnerlast,
Die du ausgestanden hast,
Dass ich kann in Andacht bleiben,
Alle böse Lust vertreiben!

Gib für alles, was mich kränket,
Mir aus deinen Wunden Saft;
Wenn mein Herz hinein sich senket,
So gib neue Lebenskraft,
Dass mich stärk' in allem Leid
Deines Trostes Süssigkeit,
Weil du mir das Heil erworben,
Da du bist für mich gestorben.

Lass auf deinen Tod mich trauen,
O Mein Gott und Zuversicht!
Lass mich feste darauf bauen,
Dass den Tod ich schmecke nicht!
Deine Todesangst lass mich
Stets erquicken mächtiglich;
Herr, lass deinen Tod mir geben
Auferstehung, Heil und Leben!

This hymn by Johann Heermann first appeared in six stanzas, in the fourth edition of his *Devoti Musica Cordis*, etc., Leipzig and Breslau, 1644. It is entitled "Consolation from the wounds of Jesus in all manner of temptation. From the *Manual* of St. Augustine." The *Manuale* is a medieval compilation from various church fathers. Chapter XXII, on which this hymn is based, is by Bernard of Clairvaux. The hymn has long been a favorite in the Lutheran Church. Count Ludwig von Zinzendorf called it "the crown of all our old hymns."

The translation is composite.

The tune "Der am Kreuz" is a composition of Johann B. König. It first appeared in his *Harmonischer Liederschatz*, Frankfurt, 1738. It has its name from the Lenten hymn, ascribed to Johann Mentzer, "Der am Kreuz ist meine Liebe."

145   Jesus, Refuge of the Weary

1. Jesus, Refuge of the weary,
   Blest Redeemer, whom we love,
   Fountain in life's desert dreary,
   Savior from the world above,
   Oh, how oft Thine eyes, offended,
   Gaze upon the sinner's fall!
   Yet, upon the cross extended,
   Thou didst bear the pain of all.

2. Do we pass that cross unheeding,
   Breathing no repentant vow,
   Though we see Thee wounded, bleeding,
   See Thy thorn-encircled brow?
   Yet Thy sinless death hath brought us
   Life eternal, peace, and rest;
   Only what Thy grace hath taught us
   Calms the sinner's stormy breast.

3. Jesus, may our hearts be burning
   With more fervent love for Thee!
   May our eyes be ever turning
   To Thy cross of agony
   Till in glory, parted never
   From the blessed Savior's side,
   Graven in our hearts forever
   Dwell the cross, the Crucified!

"Giesù sommo conforto" is the title of the Italian original of this hymn by Girolamo Savonarola, the Italian Reformer, published in *Laudi Spirituali*, Venice, 1563, by Fra Serafino Razzi.

The translation is by Jane Francesca Wilde and was contributed by her to R. R. Madden's *Life and Martyrdom of Savonarola*, 1853.

For comments on the tune "O du Liebe" see Hymn No. 37.

LENT

Lamb of God, Pure and Holy   146

1. Lamb of God, pure and holy,
Who on the cross didst suffer,
Ever patient and lowly,
Thyself to scorn didst offer.
All sins Thou borest for us,
Else had despair reigned o'er us:
Have mercy on us, O Jesus!

    O Lamm Gottes, unschuldig
Am Stamm des Kreuzes geschlachtet,
Allzeit funden geduldig,
Wiewohl du warest verachtet:
All' Sünd' hast du getragen,
Sonst müssten wir verzagen.
Erbarm dich unser, O Jesu!

2. Lamb of God, pure and holy,
Who on the cross didst suffer,
Ever patient and lowly,
Thyself to scorn didst offer.
All sins Thou borest for us,
Else had despair reigned o'er us:
Have mercy on us, O Jesus!

    O Lamm Gottes, unschuldig
Am Stamm des Kreuzes geschlachtet,
Allzeit funden geduldig,
Wiewohl du warest verachtet:
All' Sünd' hast du getragen,
Sonst müssten wir verzagen.
Erbarm dich unser, O Jesu!

3. Lamb of God, pure and holy,
Who on the cross didst suffer,
Ever patient and lowly,
Thyself to scorn didst offer.
All sins Thou borest for us,
Else had despair reigned o'er us:
Thy peace be with us, O Jesus!

    O Lamm Gottes, unschuldig
Am Stamm des Kreuzes geschlachtet,
Allzeit funden geduldig,
Wiewohl du warest verachtet:
All' Sünd' hast du getragen,
Sonst müssten wir verzagen.
Gib uns dein'n Frieden, o Jesu!

This *Agnus Dei* is by Nikolaus Decius and first appeared in *Geystlyke leder*, etc., Rostock, 1531, in Low German, entitled "Dat Agnus Dei," and then in High German, in Valentin Schumann's *Gesang Buch*, Leipzig, 1539. It is a general favorite in the Lutheran Church and is commonly sung in the midweek Lenten services and on Good Friday just before the sermon.

The translation is composite.

The tune "O Lamm Gottes, unschuldig" is based on an ancient Gregorian setting for the *Agnus Dei* and may have been arranged for this hymn by Nikolaus Decius. It is first found in *Christliche Kirchen Ordnung. Fur arme ungeschickte Pfarrherrn gestelt*, etc., Erfurt, 1542.

O Christ, Thou Lamb of God   147

1. O Christ, Thou Lamb of God, that takest away the sin of the world, have mercy upon us!

    Christe, du Lamm Gottes, der du trägst die Sünd' der Welt, erbarm dich unser!

2. O Christ, Thou Lamb of God, that takest away the sin of the world, have mercy upon us!

    Christe, du Lamm Gottes, der du trägst die Sünd' der Welt, erbarm dich unser!

3. O Christ, Thou Lamb of God, that takest away the sin of the world, grant us Thy peace! Amen.

    Christe, du Lamm Gottes, der du trägst die Sünd' der Welt, gib uns dein'n Frieden! Amen.

This *Agnus Dei* for Lent and Holy Communion is a translation of the ancient chant "Agnus Dei, qui tollis peccata mundi, miserere nobis," based on John 1:29. At the third repetition the "miserere nobis" is replaced with "dona nobis pacem." It seems to have first appeared in its German form together with the tune "Christe, du Lamm Gottes" in Johann Bugenhagens *Kirchenordnung*, Braunschweig, 1528.

The English translator is unknown.

Lord Jesus Christ, My Life, My Light   148

1. Lord Jesus Christ, my Life, my Light,
My Strength by day, my Trust by night,
On earth I'm but a passing guest
And sorely with my sins opprest.

    O Jesu Christ, mein's Lebens Licht,
Mein Hort, mein Trost, mein' Zuversicht,
Auf Erden bin ich nur ein Gast,
Und drückt mich sehr der Sünden Last.

[115]

LENT

2. Far off I see my fatherland,
Where through Thy blood I hope to stand.
But ere I reach that Paradise,
A weary way before me lies.

3. My heart sinks at the journey's length,
My wasted flesh has little strength;
My soul alone still cries in me:
"Lord, take me home, take me to Thee!"

4. Oh, let Thy sufferings give me power
To meet the last and darkest hour!
Thy blood refresh and comfort me;
Thy bonds and fetters make me free.

5. Oh, let Thy holy wounds for me
Clefts in the rock forever be
Where as a dove my soul can hide
And safe from Satan's rage abide.

6. And when my spirit flies away,
Thy dying words shall be my stay.
Thy cross shall be my staff in life,
Thy holy grave my rest from strife.

7. Lord, in Thy nail-prints let me read
That Thou to save me hast decreed
And grant that in Thine opened side
My troubled soul may ever hide.

8. Since Thou hast died, the Pure, the Just,
I take my homeward way in trust.
The gates of heaven, Lord, open wide
When here I may no more abide.

9. And when the last Great Day shall come
And Thou, our Judge, shalt speak the doom,
Let me with joy behold the light
And set me then upon Thy right.

10. Renew this wasted flesh of mine
That like the sun it there may shine
Among the angels pure and bright,
Yea, like Thyself in glorious light.

11. Ah, then I'll have my heart's desire,
When, singing with the angels' choir,
Among the ransomed of Thy grace,
Forever I'll behold Thy face!

Ich hab' vor mir ein' schwere Reis'
Zu dir in's Himmels Paradeis;
Das ist mein rechtes Vaterland,
Darauf du hast dein Blut gewandt.

Zur Reis' ist mir mein Herz sehr matt,
Der Leib gar wenig Kräfte hat;
Allein mein' Seele schreit in mir:
Herr, hol mich heim, nimm mich zu dir!

Drum stärk mich durch das Leiden dein
In meiner letzten Todespein;
Dein Blutschweiss mich tröst' und equick',
Mach' mich frei durch dein' Band' und Strick'!

Die heiligen fünf Wunden dein
Lass mir rechte Felslöcher sein,
Darein ich flieh' als eine Taub',
Dass mich der höllisch' Weih nicht raub'.

Dein letztes Wort lass sein mein Licht,
Wenn mir der Tod das Herz zerbricht;
Behüte mich vor Ungebärd',
Wenn ich mein Haupt nun neigen werd'!

Lass mich durch deine Nägelmal'
Erblicken die Genadenwahl;
Durch deine aufgespaltne Seit'
Mein' arme Seele heimgeleit!

Auf deinen Abschied, Herr, ich trau',
Darauf mein' letzte Heimfahrt bau';
Tu mir die Himmelstür weit auf,
Wenn ich beschliess' mein's Lebens Lauf.

Am Jüngsten Tag erweck mein'n Leib,
Hilf, dass ich dir zur Rechten bleib',
Dass mich nicht treffe dein Gericht,
Welch's das erschrecklich' Urteil spricht.

Alsdann mein'n Leib erneure ganz,
Dass er leucht' wie der Sonne Glanz
Und ähnlich sei dein'm klaren Leib,
Auch gleich den lieben Engeln bleib'.

Wie werd' ich dann so fröhlich sein,
Werd' singen mit den Engelein
Und mit der Auserwählten Schar
Ewig schauen dein Antlitz klar.

Martin Behm first published this hymn, in fourteen stanzas, in a collection entitled *Christliche Gebet,* 1610, and then in his *Zehen Sterbegebet,* etc., appended to his *Centuria secunda,* Wittenberg, 1611. It was headed "Prayer for a blessed journey home, based upon Christ's Sufferings." It is his best hymn. The cento omits Stanzas 5, 6, 8, and 10. Some German hymnals have inserted a stanza, the fifth above, which is not by Behm. It is of unknown origin and first appeared in the hymn in the collection, *Kirchen- und Hausmusik,* Breslau, 1644. The omitted stanzas read in translation:

5. The blows and stripes that fell on Thee
Heal up the wounds of sin in me;
Thy crown of thorns, Thy foes' mad spite,
Let be my glory and delight.

6. That thirst and bitter draught of Thine
Cause me to bear with patience mine;
Thy piercing cry uphold my soul
When floods of anguish o'er me roll!

8. And when my lips grow white and chill,
Thy Spirit cry within me still
And help my soul Thy heaven to find
When these poor eyes grow dark and blind!

10. Thy cross shall be my staff in life,
Thy holy grave my rest from strife;
The winding-sheet that covered Thee,
Oh, let it be a shroud for me.

The translation is based on Catherine Winkworth's versions in her *Lyra Germanica,* second series, 1858, and in her *Chorale Book for England,* 1863. For comments on the tune "O Jesu Christ, mein's" see Hymn No. 64.

LENT

Come to Calvary's Holy Mountain   149

1. Come to Calvary's holy mountain,
    Sinners, ruined by the Fall;
  Here a pure and healing fountain
    Flows to you, to me, to all,
  In a full, perpetual tide,
  Opened when our Savior died.

2. Come in poverty and meanness,
    Come defiled, without, within;
  From infection and uncleanness,
    From the leprosy of sin,
  Wash your robes and make them white;
  Ye shall walk with God in light.

3. Come in sorrow and contrition,
    Wounded, impotent, and blind;
  Here the guilty free remission,
    Here the troubled peace, may find.
  Health this fountain will restore;
  He that drinks shall thirst no more.

4. He that drinks shall live forever;
    'Tis a soul-renewing flood.
  God is faithful; God will never
    Break His covenant of blood,
  Signed when our Redeemer died,
  Sealed when He was glorified.

This hymn by James Montgomery first appeared in Cotterill's *Selection,* 1819, entitled "The Open Fountain." It is based on Zech. 13:1, "In that day there shall be a fountain opened."

The tune "Consolation," also called "Naar mit Öie," is by Ludwig M. Lindeman and appeared in 1871 in his *Koralbog for den Norska Kirke,* set to H. A. Brorson's hymn "Naar mit Öie, trät af Möie."

Lord Jesus, Thou art Going Forth   150

(The Soul:)
1. Lord Jesus, Thou art going forth
    For me Thy life to offer;
  For me, a sinner from my birth,
    Who caused all Thou must suffer.
      So be it, then,
      Thou Hope of men;
  Thee I shall follow weeping,
      Tears flowing free
      Thy pain to see,
  Watch o'er Thy sorrows keeping.

(Jesus:)
2. O Soul, attend thou and behold
    The fruit of thy transgression!
  My portion is the curse of old
    And for man's sin My Passion.
      Now comes the night
      Of sin's dread might,
  Man's guilt I here am bearing.
      Oh, weigh it, Soul;
      I make thee whole,
  No need now of despairing.

(The Soul:)
3. 'Tis I, Lord Jesus, I confess,
    Who should have borne sin's wages
  And lost the peace of heavenly bliss
    Through everlasting ages.
      Instead 'tis Thou
      Who goest now
  My punishment to carry.
      Thy death and blood
      Lead me to God,
  By grace I there may tarry.

(Jesus:)
4. O Soul, I take upon Me now
    The pain thou shouldst have suffered.
  Behold, with grace I thee endow,
    Grace freely to thee offered.
      The curse I choose
      That thou might'st lose
  Sin's curse and guilt forever.
      My gift of love
      From heaven above
  Will give thee blessing ever.

So gehst du nun mein Jesu, hin,
  Für mich den Tod zu leiden,
Für mich, der ich ein Sünder bin,
  Der dich betrübt mit Freuden.
    Wohlan, fahr fort,
    Du edler Hort!
Mein' Augen sollen fliessen,
    Ein Tränensee
    Mit Ach und Weh,
Dein Leiden zu begiessen.

Ach Sünd', du schädlich Schlangengift,
  Wie weit kannst du es bringen!
Dein Lohn, der Fluch, mich jetzt betrifft,
  In Tod tut er mich zwingen.
    Jetzt kommt die Nacht
    Der Sündenmacht,
Fremd' Schuld muss ich abtragen.
    Betracht es recht,
    Du Sündenknecht,
Nun darfst du nicht verzagen!

Ich, ich, Herr Jesu, sollte zwar
  Der Sünden Strafe leiden
An Leib und Seel', an Haut und Haar,
  Auch ewig aller Freuden
    Beraubet sein
    Und leiden Pein,
So nimmst du hin die Schulde,
    Dein Blut und Tod
    Bringt mich vor Gott,
Ich bleib' in deiner Hulde.

Ja, liebe Seel', ich büss' die Schuld,
  Die du hätt'st sollen büssen;
Erkenne daraus meine Huld,
  Die ich dich lass' geniessen!
    Ich wähl' den Fluch,
    Dieweil ich such'
Vom Fluch dich zu befreien.
    Denk meiner Lieb',
    Durch deren Trieb
Die Segen dir gedeihen!

(The Soul:)
5. What can I for such love divine
   To Thee, Lord Jesus, render?
   No merit has this heart of mine;
   Yet while I live, I'll tender
     Myself alone,
     And all I own,
   In love to serve before Thee;
     Then when time's past,
     Take me at last
   To Thy blest home in glory.

Was kann für solche Liebe dir,
Herr Jesu, ich wohl geben?
Ich weiss und finde nichts an mir;
Doch will, weil ich werd' leben,
  Mich eigen dir,
  Herr, nach Gebühr
Zu dienen ganz verschreiben,
  Auch nach der Zeit
  In Ewigkeit
Dein Diener sein und bleiben.

This hymn, entitled "A Beautiful Hymn for Lent," is ascribed to Caspar Friedrich Nachtenhöfer, by *Wetzel*, who says it was written c. 1651 while Nachtenhöfer was tutor at Coburg. It is a hymn on Christ's way to the cross and in the form of a dialog between the soul and Christ. It first appeared in the *Neu-Vollständigers Brandenburgisches Gesang-Buch*, Culmbach and Bayreuth, 1668. In order to complete the sense, an additional stanza was inserted between the original third and fourth. This new stanza, according to Wetzel, is by Magnus Daniel Omeis (1646—1708), professor at Altdorf, and was included in the Altdorf *Gesang Buch*, 1699.

The translation is our own and was originally published in the *Lutheran Witness*, 1927, and revised for *The Lutheran Hymnal*.

The tune "So gehst du nun" is first found in the *Geistreiches Gesangbuch*, Darmstadt, 1698.

151   Christ, the Life of All the Living

1. Christ, the Life of all the living,
   Christ, the Death of death, our foe,
   Who, Thyself for me once giving
   To the darkest depths of woe, —
   Through Thy sufferings, death, and merit
   I eternal life inherit:
     Thousand, thousand thanks shall be,
     Dearest Jesus, unto Thee.

2. Thou, ah! Thou, hast taken on Thee
   Bonds and stripes, a cruel rod;
   Pain and scorn were heaped upon Thee,
   O Thou sinless Son of God!
   Thus didst Thou my soul deliver
   From the bonds of sin forever.
     Thousand, thousand thanks shall be,
     Dearest Jesus, unto Thee.

3. Thou hast borne the smiting only
   That my wounds might all be whole;
   Thou hast suffered, sad and lonely,
   Rest to give my weary soul;
   Yea, the curse of God enduring,
   Blessing unto me securing.
     Thousand, thousand thanks shall be,
     Dearest Jesus, unto Thee.

4. Heartless scoffers did surround Thee,
   Treating Thee with shameful scorn,
   And with piercing thorns they crowned Thee.
   All disgrace Thou, Lord, hast borne
   That as Thine Thou mightest own me
   And with heavenly glory crown me.
     Thousand, thousand thanks shall be,
     Dearest Jesus, unto Thee.

5. Thou hast suffered men to bruise Thee
   That from pain I might be free;
   Falsely did Thy foes accuse Thee, —
   Thence I gain security;
   Comfortless Thy soul did languish
   Me to comfort in my anguish.
     Thousand, thousand thanks shall be,
     Dearest Jesus, unto Thee.

Jesu, meines Lebens Leben,
Jesu, meines Todes Tod,
Der du dich für mich gegeben
In die tiefste Seelennot,
In das äusserste Verderben,
Nur dass ich nicht möchte sterben:
  Tausend-, tausendmal sei dir,
  Liebster Jesu, Dank dafür!

Du, ach, du hast ausgestanden
Lästerreden, Spott und Hohn,
Speichel, Schläge, Strick' und Bande,
Du gerechter Gottessohn,
Mich Elenden zu erretten
Von des Teufels Sündenketten!
  Tausend-, tausendmal sei dir,
  Liebster Jesu, Dank dafür!

Du hast lassen Wunden schlagen,
Dich erbärmlich richten zu,
Um zu heilen meine Plagen
Und zu setzen mich in Ruh'!
Ach, du hast zu meinem Segen
Lassen dich mit Fluch belegen!
  Tausend-, tausendmal sei dir,
  Liebster Jesu, Dank dafür!

Man hat dich sehr hart verhöhnet,
Dich mit grossem Schimpf belegt
Und mit Dornen gar gekrönet:
Was hat dich dazu bewegt?
Dass du möchtest mich ergötzen,
Mir die Ehrenkron' aufsetzen.
  Tausend-, tausendmal sei dir,
  Liebster Jesu, Dank dafür!

Du hast dich hart lassen schlagen
Zur Befreiung meiner Pein,
Fälschlich lassen dich anklagen.
Dass ich könnte sicher sein;
Dass ich möchte trostreich prangen,
Hast du sonder Trost gehangen.
  Tausend-, tausendmal sei dir,
  Liebster Jesu, Dank dafür!

LENT

6. Thou hast suffered great affliction
   And hast borne it patiently,
   Even death by crucifixion,
   Fully to atone for me;
   Thou didst choose to be tormented
   That my doom should be prevented.
   Thousand, thousand thanks shall be,
   Dearest Jesus, unto Thee.

7. Then, for all that wrought my pardon,
   For Thy sorrows deep and sore,
   For Thine anguish in the Garden,
   I will thank Thee evermore,
   Thank Thee for Thy groaning, sighing,
   For Thy bleeding and Thy dying,
   For that last triumphant cry,
   And shall praise Thee, Lord, on high.

Du hast dich in Not gestecket,
Hast gelitten mit Geduld,
Gar den herben Tod geschmecket,
Um zu büssen meine Schuld;
Dass ich würde losgezählet,
Hast du wollen sein gequälet.
Tausend-, tausendmal sei dir,
Liebster Jesu, Dank dafür!

Nun, ich danke dir von Herzen,
Jesu, für gesamte Not:
Für die Wunden, für die Schmerzen,
Für den herben, bittern Tod,
Für dein Zittern, für dein Zagen,
Für dein tausendfaches Plagen,
Für dein' Angst und tiefe Pein
Will ich ewig dankbar sein.

Ernst Homburg published this hymn for Passiontide with its striking refrain in his collection *Geistliche Lieder,* which was published in two parts, at Jena and Naumburg, 1659. This hymn was in Part I (according to *Koch* this part has the engraved title, Naumburg, 1658). It was headed "Hymn of Thanksgiving to His Redeemer and Savior for His Bitter Sufferings." In the preface to his *Geistliche Lieder* Homburg states: "I was specially induced and compelled [to the writing of hymns] by the anxious and sore domestic afflictions by which God . . . has for some time laid me aside."

The omitted Stanza 7 reads in translation, without the refrain:

That Thou wast so meek and stainless
Doth atone for my proud mood;
And Thy death makes dying painless,
All Thy ills have wrought our good;
Yea, the shame Thou didst endure
Is my honor and my cure.

Catherine Winkworth's translation of this hymn in her *Chorale Book for England,* 1863, omits Stanzas 3, 4, and 6 and also departs slightly from the original meter. The translation above is based on her text for Stanzas 1, 2, 5, and 7. Stanzas 3, 4, and 6 are a composite translation from the *Evangelical Lutheran Hymn-Book,* 1912.

The tune "Jesu, meines Lebens Leben" is from *Kirchengesangbuch,* Darmstadt, 1687.

When o'er My Sins I Sorrow 152

1. When o'er my sins I sorrow,
   Lord, I will look to Thee
   And hence my comfort borrow
   That Thou wast slain for me;
   Yea, Lord, Thy precious blood was spilt
   For me, O most unworthy,
   To take away my guilt.

2. Oh, what a marvelous offering!
   Behold, the Master spares
   His servants, and their suffering
   And grief for them He bears.
   God stoopeth from His throne on high;
   For me, His guilty creature,
   He deigns as man to die.

3. My manifold transgression
   Henceforth can harm me none
   Since Jesus' bloody Passion
   For me God's grace hath won.
   His precious blood my debts hath paid;
   Of hell and all its torments
   I am no more afraid.

Wenn meine Sünd' mich kränken,
O mein Herr Jesu Christ,
So lass mich wohl bedenken,
Wie du gestorben bist
Und alle meine Schuldenlast
Am Stamm des heil'gen Kreuzes
Auf dich genommen hast!

O Wunder ohne Massen,
Wenn man's betrachtet recht:
Es hat sich martern lassen
Der Herr für seinen Knecht;
Es hat sich selbst der wahre Gott
Für mich verlornen Menschen
Gegeben in den Tod.

Was kann mir denn nun schaden
Der Sünden grosse Zahl?
Ich bin bei Gott in Gnaden,
Die Schuld ist allzumal
Bezahlt durch Christi teures Blut,
Dass ich nicht mehr darf fürchten
Der Hölle Qual und Glut.

LENT

4. Therefore I will forever
   Give glory unto Thee,
   O Jesus, loving Savior,
   For what Thou didst for me.
   I'll spend my breath in songs of thanks
   For Thy sad cry, Thy sufferings,
   Thy wrongs, Thy guiltless death.

Drum sag' ich dir von Herzen
Jetzt und mein Leben lang
Für deine Pein und Schmerzen,
O Jesu, Lob und Dank,
Für deine Not und Angstgeschrei,
Für dein unschuldig Sterben,
Für deine Lieb' und Treu'.

Justus Gesenius first published this warm and deeply moving hymn for Lent in the *Hannover Gesang Buch*, 1646, in eight stanzas.

The translation of Stanza 1 is by Catherine Winkworth in her *Chorale Book for England*, 1863; of Stanzas 2 to 4, composite from the *Evangelical Lutheran Hymn-Book*, 1912. The omitted stanzas, 5 to 8, read in translation:

5. Then let Thy woes, Thy patience,
   My heart with strength inspire
   To vanquish all temptations,
   And spurn all low desire;
   This thought I fain would cherish most —
   What pain my soul's redemption
   To Thee, O Savior, cost!

6. Whate'er may be the burden,
   The cross here on me laid;
   Be shame or want my guerdon,
   I'll bear it with Thine aid;
   Give patience, give me strength to take
   Thee for my bright example,
   And all the world forsake.

7. And let me do to others
   As Thou hast done to me,
   Love all men as my brothers,
   And serve them willingly,
   With ready heart, nor seek my own,
   But as Thou, Lord, hast helped us,
   From purest love alone.

8. And let Thy cross upbear me
   With strength when I depart;
   Tell me that naught can tear me
   From my Redeemer's heart,
   But since my trust is in Thy grace
   Thou wilt accept me yonder,
   Where I shall see Thy face.

The tune "Wenn meine Sünd'" is by Michael Prätorius. It was published in *Musae Sioniae*, 1609.

153   Stricken, Smitten, and Afflicted

1. Stricken, smitten, and afflicted,
   See Him dying on the tree!
   'Tis the Christ by man rejected;
   Yes, my soul, 'tis He! 'tis He!
   'Tis the long-expected Prophet,
   David's Son, yet David's Lord;
   Proofs I see sufficient of it:
   'Tis the true and faithful Word.

2. Tell me, ye who hear Him groaning,
   Was there ever grief like His?
   Friends through fear His cause disowning,
   Foes insulting His distress;
   Many hands were raised to wound Him,
   None would interpose to save;
   But the deepest stroke that pierced Him
   Was the stroke that Justice gave.

3. Ye who think of sin but lightly
   Nor suppose the evil great
   Here may view its nature rightly,
   Here its guilt may estimate.
   Mark the Sacrifice appointed,
   See who bears the awful load;
   'Tis the WORD, the LORD'S ANOINTED,
   Son of Man and Son of God.

4. Here we have a firm foundation;
   Here the refuge of the lost;
   Christ's the Rock of our salvation,
   His the name of which we boast.
   Lamb of God, for sinners wounded,
   Sacrifice to cancel guilt!
   None shall ever be confounded
   Who on Him their hope have built.

Thomas Kelly first published this hymn in his *Hymns on Various Passages of Scripture*, Dublin, 1804. It is a very popular Lenten hymn in Lutheran circles.

The tune "O mein Jesu, ich muss sterben" is from *Geistliche Volkslieder*, Paderborn, 1850.

154   Alas! and Did My Savior Bleed

1. Alas! and did my Savior bleed,
   And did my Sovereign die?
   Would He devote that sacred head
   For such a worm as I?

2. Was it for crimes that I had done
   He groaned upon the tree?
   Amazing pity, grace unknown,
   And love beyond degree!

3. Well might the sun in darkness hide
   And shut his glories in
   When God, the mighty Maker, died
   For man the creature's sin.

4. Thus might I hide my blushing face
   While His dear cross appears,
   Dissolve my heart in thankfulness,
   And melt mine eyes to tears.

5. But drops of grief can ne'er repay
   The debt of love I owe;
   Here, Lord, I give myself away,
   'Tis all that I can do.

[120]

Isaac Watts first published this famous hymn in six stanzas in his *Hymns and Spiritual Songs,* 1707, entitled "Godly Sorrow Arising from the Sufferings of Christ." The second stanza, marked in the original text to be left out if desired, reads:

> Thy body slain, sweet Jesus, Thine,
> And bathed in its own blood,
> While all exposed to wrath divine,
> The glorious Sufferer stood!

In some quarters there has been objection to the last line of Stanza 1, and some hymnals have the line as altered thus:

> For sinners such as I

and at least one hymnal has the line changed to:

> For such an one as I.

The editorial committee for *The Lutheran Hymnal* felt justified in retaining the line as Watts had written it originally, as unobjectionable in the context, while generally sharing the negative attitude toward the so-called "vermicular hymns" or "worm hymns." It is true that the Bible calls a man a worm in order to show his utter abasement before God, as in Job 25:6, "Man, that is a worm," and in Ps. 22:6, the expression is placed into the mouth of the suffering Redeemer: "But I am a worm and no man." Nevertheless, the fact that a matter may be true does not always justify its use in poetry, and "worm hymns" such as the following have been rightly objected to:

> Oh, may Thy powerful Word
> Inspire this feeble worm
> To rush into Thy kingdom, Lord,
> And take it as by storm,

and:

> Worms, strike your harps, your voices tune,
> And warble forth your lays;
> Leap from the earth with pious mirth
> To trumpet forth your praise.

This hymn is still a very general favorite in the English-speaking Christian world, even though a number of modern hymnals omit it altogether. It is said to have been the means of conversion of former Governor A. H. Colquitt of Georgia. The following incident is related of this conversion by the Methodist Bishop Warren A. Candler:

> Just before he arose to address the meeting, the choir sang one of the sweetest hymns of Watts. It seemed to fill him with holy rapture. When he rose to speak, his handsome face shone with supernatural brightness, his lustrous eyes were filled with tears, and his utterance was choked with emotion as he said impulsively: "Oh, how I love that song! It was my mother's song. And today, if I could hear her sing it again, I should have greater joy than if I had heard all the choirs of heaven."

"Alas! and did my Savior bleed!" — that was the song they sang. Because his Savior bled and died that men might live, this noble man has found at last the eternal home and the "vanished hand" for which he sighed.

The tune "Martyrdom," also called "Fenwick" and "Drumclog," is by Hugh Wilson. It is supposed to have been composed before 1800. When it appeared in *"The Seraph, a Selection of Psalms and Hymns,* Glasgow, 1827, a footnote stated that it was a composition by Hugh Wilson, a native of Fenwick. The tune had previously been published in *Sacred Music,* etc., Edinburgh, 1825, the year after the composer's death.

155 Sweet the Moments, Rich in Blessing

1. Sweet the moments, rich in blessing,
   Which before the cross we spend,
   Life and health and peace possessing
   From the sinner's dying Friend.

2. Here we rest in wonder, viewing
   All our sins on Jesus laid;
   Here we see redemption flowing
   From the sacrifice He made.

3. Here we find the dawn of heaven
   While upon the cross we gaze,
   See our trespasses forgiven,
   And our songs of triumph raise.

4. Oh, that, near the cross abiding,
   We may to the Savior cleave,
   Naught with Him our hearts dividing,
   All for Him content to leave!

5. Lord, in loving contemplation
   Fix our hearts and eyes on Thee
   Till we taste Thy full salvation
   And Thine unveiled glory see.

This hymn is first of all a recast by Walter Shirley of James Allen's hymn "While My Jesus I'm Possessing," which appeared in *The Kendall Hymn Book*, 1757, in six eight-line stanzas. This recast, which has little of Allen's hymn in it save some of the thoughts, was published by Shirley in Lady Huntingdon's *Collection of Hymns*, 1770, in the following form:

1. Sweet the moments, rich in blessing,
   Which before the cross I spend;
   Life and health and peace possessing
   From the sinner's dying Friend.
   Here I'll sit, forever viewing
   Mercy's streams in streams of blood;
   Precious drops my soul bedewing,
   Plead and claim my peace with God.

2. Truly blessed is this station
   Low before the cross to lie
   While I see divine compassion
   Floating in His languid eye.
   Here it is I find my heaven
   While upon the Lamb I gaze;
   Love I much? I've much forgiven,
   I'm a miracle of grace.

3. Love and grief my heart dividing,
   With my tears His feet I'll bathe;
   Constant still in faith abiding,
   Life deriving from His death.
   May I still enjoy this feeling,
   In all need to Jesus go;
   Prove His wounds each day more healing
   And Himself more deeply know.

Then, in Cooke and Denton's *Church Hymnal*, 1853, an altered version of Shirley's Stanza 1 and the first half of Stanza 2 appeared, to which were added the following lines to make three eight-line stanzas:

Lord, in ceaseless contemplation
Fix our hearts and eyes on Thee
Till we taste Thy whole salvation
And unveiled Thy glories see.

For Thy sorrows we adore Thee,
For the griefs that wrought our peace;
Gracious Savior, we implore Thee
In our hearts Thy love increase.
Unto Thee, the world's Salvation,
Father, Spirit, unto Thee,
Low we bow in adoration,
Ever-blessed One and Three.

Other hymn-book editors made changes and divided the hymn into four-line stanzas. The text above is an altered form of Shirley's first two stanzas, and the last stanza is from the Cooke and Denton addition.

The tune "Ringe recht," also called "Batty," "Turnan," and "Invitation," is from Johann Thommen's *Musikalischer Christenschatz*, Basel, 1745, where it was set to the beautiful hymn of Johann Joseph Winckler "Ringe recht, wenn Gottes Gnade dich nun ziehet und bekehrt."

LENT

Not All the Blood of Beasts 156

1. Not all the blood of beasts
   On Jewish altars slain
   Could give the guilty conscience peace
   Or wash away the stain.

2. But Christ, the heavenly Lamb,
   Takes all our sins away;
   A sacrifice of nobler name
   And richer blood than they.

3. My faith would lay her hand
   On that dear head of Thine
   While like a penitent I stand
   And there confess my sin.

4. My soul looks back to see
   The burden Thou didst bear
   When hanging on the cursed tree
   And knows her guilt was there.

5. Believing, we rejoice
   To see the curse remove;
   We bless the Lamb with cheerful voice
   And sing His bleeding love.

Isaac Watts published this hymn in the enlarged edition of his *Hymns and Spiritual Songs*, 1709. The text is slightly altered, chiefly in Stanza 4, Line 4, where Watts had

And *hopes* her guilt was there.

This change was made, with others not so happy, in the *Wesleyan Hymn Book*, 1875.

The tune "Southwell" is from William Daman's *Psalmes of David*, 1579, where it is set to a metrical version of Ps. 45.

There Is a Fountain Filled with Blood 157

1. There is a fountain filled with blood
   Drawn from Immanuel's veins,
   And sinners plunged beneath that flood
   Lose all their guilty stains.

2. The dying thief rejoiced to see
   That fountain in his day;
   And there have I, as vile as he,
   Washed all my sins away.

3. Dear dying Lamb, Thy precious blood
   Shall never lose its power
   Till all the ransomed Church of God
   Be saved to sin no more.

4. E'er since by faith I saw the stream
   Thy flowing wounds supply,
   Redeeming love has been my theme
   And shall be till I die.

5. When this poor lisping, stammering tongue
   Lies silent in the grave,
   Then in a nobler, sweeter song
   I'll sing Thy power to save.

This hymn of William Cowper's was probably written in 1771. It first appeared in Conyer's *Collection of Psalms and Hymns*, 1772, in seven stanzas. The omitted Stanzas 6 and 7 read:

6. Lord, I believe Thou hast prepared
   (Unworthy though I be)
   For me a blood-bought free reward,
   A golden harp for me.

7. 'Tis strung and tuned for endless years
   And formed by power divine
   To sound in God the Father's ears
   No other name but Thine.

Many alterations of Cowper's text have been made by hymn-book editors. Exception has been taken to the first stanza. James Montgomery, for instance, wrote: "I entirely rewrote the first verse. ... The words are objectionable as representing a fountain being *filled,* instead of *springing up.* I think my version is unobjectionable."

This is Montgomery's:

From Calvary's cross a fountain flows
Of water and of blood,
More healing than Bethesda's pool
Or famed Siloam's flood.

[123]

Others have taken exception to Stanza 2, Lines 3 and 4, and various changes have been made, none of which, however, are an improvement of the positive, Scriptural truth expressed by Cowper.

Aside from dropping Stanzas 6 and 7, which are admittedly of inferior quality, no change in Cowper's text has been made for *The Lutheran Hymnal*, except that the lines of the last stanza have been inverted so as not to end the hymn "in the grave."

The first tune, "Horsley," is from *Twenty-four Psalm Tunes and Eight Chants*, 1844, by William Horsley. It is often used with the hymn "There Is a Green Hill Far Away."

The second tune, "Cowper," also called "Fountain," "Cleansing Fountain," inferior musically, is by Lowell Mason. It was composed in 1830 for this hymn and was first published in Hastings's *Spiritual Songs*, 1832.

158   Glory Be to Jesus

1. Glory be to Jesus,
   Who in bitter pains
   Poured for me the life-blood
   From His sacred veins!

2. Grace and life eternal
   In that blood I find;
   Blest be His compassion,
   Infinitely kind!

3. Blest through endless ages
   Be the precious stream
   Which from endless torments
   Did the world redeem!

4. Abel's blood for vengeance
   Pleaded to the skies;
   But the blood of Jesus
   For our pardon cries.

5. Oft as earth exulting
   Wafts its praise on high,
   Angel hosts rejoicing
   Make their glad reply.

6. Lift we, then, our voices,
   Swell the mighty flood,
   Louder still and louder
   Praise the precious blood!

Viva! Viva! Gesù! che per mio bene
Tutto il sangue verso dalle sue vene.

Il sangue di Gesù fu la mia vita;
Benedetta la Sua bontà infinita.

Questo sangue in eterno sia lodato,
Che dall' inferno il mondo ha riscattato.

D'Abele il sangue gridava venedetta,
Quel di Gesù per noi perdono aspetta.

Se di Gesù si esalta il divin sangue,
Tripudia il ciel, trema l'abisso e langue.

Diciamo dunque insiem con energia
Al sangue di Gesù gloria si dia. Amen.

The Italian author of this hymn is unknown, though it has been ascribed to St. Alfonso Liguori. It is first found in an Italian collection, *Raccolta di Orazioni*, etc., attributed to an Italian priest called Galli, who died in 1845; but as Pope Pius VII (1800—1823) already granted indulgences of 100 days "to all the faithful who say or sing" this hymn, its origin is commonly placed into the 18th century.

The translation is by Edward Caswall. It was published in his *Hymns for the Use of the Birmingham Oratory*, 1857, in nine stanzas. The stanzas omitted above are four, five, and seven.

The tune "Wem in Leidenstagen" or "Caswall" or "Filitz," commonly associated with this hymn, is by Friedrich Filitz and is found in his *Vierstimmiges Choralbuch*, Berlin, 1847, set to the Siegmund H. Oswald's hymn beginning with that line.

LENT. — PALM SUNDAY

Go to Dark Gethsemane 159

1. Go to dark Gethsemane,
    Ye that feel the Tempter's power;
  Your Redeemer's conflict see,
    Watch with Him one bitter hour;
  Turn not from His griefs away,
  Learn of Jesus Christ to pray.

2. Follow to the judgment-hall,
    View the Lord of life arraigned;
  Oh, the wormwood and the gall!
    Oh, the pangs His soul sustained!
  Shun not suffering, shame, or loss;
  Learn of Him to bear the cross.

3. Calvary's mournful mountain climb;
    There, adoring at His feet,
  Mark that miracle of time,
    God's own sacrifice complete.
  "It is finished!" hear Him cry;
  Learn of Jesus Christ to die.

4. Early hasten to the tomb
    Where they laid His breathless clay;
  All is solitude and gloom, —
    Who hath taken Him away?
  Christ is risen! He meets our eyes.
  Savior, teach us so to rise.

This favorite Lenten hymn was first published by James Montgomery, in 1820, in Cotterill's *Collection* and then revised and republished, in 1825, in Montgomery's *Christian Psalmist*. There is little similarity, save in Stanza 1, between these versions. The text above is the revised form. The hymn was entitled by the author "Christ our Example in Suffering."

The tune "Gethsemane," also called "Petra" or "Redhead No. 76," wedded to this hymn, is by Richard Redhead from his *Church Hymn Tunes*, 1853. It is frequently used with Toplady's hymn "Rock of Ages." (See Hymn No. 376.)

All Glory, Laud, and Honor 160

1. All glory, laud, and honor
    To Thee, Redeemer, King,
  To whom the lips of children
    Made sweet hosannas ring.
  Thou art the King of Israel,
    Thou David's royal Son,
  Who in the Lord's name comest,
    The King and Blessed One.

2. All glory, laud, and honor
    To Thee, Redeemer, King,
  To whom the lips of children
    Made sweet hosannas ring.
  The company of angels
    Are praising Thee on high,
  And mortal men and all things
    Created make reply.

3. All glory, laud, and honor
    To Thee, Redeemer, King,
  To whom the lips of children
    Made sweet hosannas ring.
  The people of the Hebrews
    With psalms before Thee went;
  Our praise and prayer and anthems
    Before Thee we present.

4. All glory, laud, and honor
    To Thee, Redeemer, King,
  To whom the lips of children
    Made sweet hosannas ring.
  To Thee, before Thy Passion,
    They sang their hymns of praise;
  To Thee, now high exalted,
    Our melody we raise.

5. All glory, laud, and honor
    To Thee, Redeemer, King,
  To whom the lips of children
    Made sweet hosannas ring.
  Thou didst accept their praises;
    Accept the prayers we bring,
  Who in all good delightest,
    Thou good and gracious King.

Gloria, laus et honor tibi sit, rex,
    Christe, redemptor,
  cui puerile decus prompsit hosanna
    pium.

Israel tu rex, Davidis et inclyta proles,
  nomine qui in Domini, rex benedicte,
    venis.

Coetus in excelsis te laudat caelicus
    omnis
  et mortalis homo, cuncta creata simul.

Plebs Hebraea tibi cum palmis obvia
    venit;
  cum prece, voto, hymnis adsumus ecce
    tibi.

Hi tibi passuro solvebant munia laudis;
  nos tibi regnanti pangimus ecce melos.

Hi placuere tibi; placeat devotio nostra,
  rex pie, rex clemens, cui bona cuncta
    placent. Amen.

This hymn of praise is frequently called the hymn of St. Theodulph, who was born in Italy about the year 770. He entered a monastery, and because of his outstanding scholarship he eventually became an abbot. During the stormy days of the turbulent times in which he lived he was frequently sought as a mediator by opposing factions. He attracted the attention of the great Charlemagne, who took Theodulph with him on his return to France and made him Bishop of Orleans. After the death of Charlemagne enemies conspired against the bishop, and he was finally arrested and imprisoned in a monastery at Angers, where he languished in close confinement for three long years until he died, September 18, 821.

The following story regarding the origin of the hymn is told by Clichtoveus, A. D. 1516. In his prison-cell Bishop Theodulph composed a long poem for the procession of the people on Palm Sunday. It so happened that on Palm Sunday of the year 821 Emperor Louis the Pious and his retinue passed by the prison on their way to church and heard St. Theodulph singing joyfully the hymn which he had composed for that day. When the emperor asked for the name of the singer and was told that it was Bishop Theodulph, he declared, "The bishop is no traitor," and ordered his release at once and his restoration to office.

It seems to be fairly well established that the hymn was composed while St. Theodulph was in confinement, even though we cannot be so sure about the veracity of the rest of the account and his liberation from prison on account of it.

The translation is an altered form of that by John M. Neale in his *Hymnal Noted*, 1854.

For comments on the tune "Valet will ich dir geben," also called "St. Theodulph," see Hymn No. 58.

161   Hosanna, Loud Hosanna

1. Hosanna, loud hosanna,
   The little children sang;
   Through pillared court and Temple
   The lovely anthem rang.
   To Jesus, who had blessed them,
   Close folded to His breast,
   The children sang their praises,
   The simplest and the best.

2. From Olivet they followed
   Mid an exultant crowd,
   The victor palm-branch waving
   And chanting clear and loud.
   The Lord of men and angels
   Rode on in lowly state
   Nor scorned that little children
   Should on His bidding wait.

3. "Hosanna in the highest!"
   That ancient song we sing,
   For Christ is our Redeemer,
   The Lord of heaven our King.
   Oh, may we ever praise Him
   With heart and life and voice
   And in His blissful presence
   Eternally rejoice.

This hymn by Jeannette Threlfall first appeared in 1873 in her volume of poems *Sunshine and Shadow*. It has become very popular as a hymn for Palm Sunday or the First Sunday in Advent.

For comments on the tune "Ellacombe" see Hymn No. 9.

PALM SUNDAY

Ride On, Ride On, in Majesty 162

1. Ride on, ride on, in majesty!
Hark! all the tribes hosanna cry.
O Savior meek, pursue Thy road,
With palms and scattered garments strowed.

2. Ride on, ride on, in majesty!
In lowly pomp ride on to die.
O Christ, Thy triumphs now begin
O'er captive death and conquered sin.

3. Ride on, ride on, in majesty!
The angel armies of the sky
Look down with sad and wondering eyes
To see the approaching Sacrifice.

4. Ride on, ride on, in majesty!
Thy last and fiercest strife is nigh;
The Father on His sapphire throne
Expects His own anointed Son.

5. Ride on, ride on, in majesty!
In lowly pomp ride on to die.
Bow Thy meek head to mortal pain,
Then take, O Christ, Thy power and reign.

Henry H. Milman first published this hymn with twelve others in Heber's posthumous *Hymns,* etc., 1827, and again in his *Selection of Psalms and Hymns,* 1837. The alteration in the text is one now quite generally accepted, in Stanza 1, Line 3, where Milman had

Thine humble beast pursues his road.

Heber, author of "From Greenland's Icy Mountains" and other well-known hymns, had written, in late 1820, asking Milman's cooperation by contributing to a collection of hymns which he was preparing. "I know with what facility you write poetry, and all the world knows with what success you write religious poetry." In appreciation of the thirteen contributions made by Milman, Heber wrote: "You have indeed sent me a most powerful reinforcement to my projected hymn-book. A few more such hymns and I shall not need, nor wait for, the aid of Scott and Southey."

Milman's "Ride On, Ride On, in Majesty" is considered by many one of the finest hymns ever written in English, and it is the only hymn of his that is still widely used. Another hymn, less well known, is said by H. Leigh Bennett to have no peer in its presentation of Christ's sympathy with human suffering. It was written for the Second Sunday in Lent and reads:

1. When our heads are bowed with woe,
When our bitter tears o'erflow,
When we mourn the lost, the dear,
Gracious Son of Mary, hear.

2. Thou our throbbing flesh hast worn,
Thou our mortal griefs hast borne,
Thou hast shed the human tear;
Gracious Son of Mary, hear.

3. When the sullen death-bell tolls
For our own departing souls,
When our final doom is near,
Gracious Son of Mary, hear.

4. Thou hast bowed the dying head,
Thou the blood of life hast shed,
Thou hast filled a mortal bier;
Gracious Son of Mary, hear.

5. When the heart is sad within
With the thought of all its sin,
When the spirit shrinks with fear,
Gracious Son of Mary, hear.

6. Thou the shame, the grief, hast known;
Though the sins were not Thine own,
Thou hast deigned their load to bear;
Gracious Son of Mary, hear.

Of Milman's poetry a critic once said: "Every page exhibits some beautiful expression, some pathetic turn, some original thought, or some striking image." His hymn for the Second Sunday in Advent is a good example of this:

1. The chariot! the chariot! its wheels roll on fire
As the Lord cometh down in the pomp of His ire;
Self-moving, it drives on its pathway of cloud,
And the heavens with the burden of Godhead are bowed.

2. The glory! the glory! by myriads are poured
The hosts of the angels to wait on their Lord,
And the glorified saints and the martyrs are there,
And all who the palm-wreath of victory wear.

> 3. The trumpet! the trumpet! the dead have all heard;
> Lo! the depths of the stone-covered charnel are stirred;
> From the sea, from the land, from the south and the north,
> The vast generations of men are come forth.
>
> 4. The judgment! the judgment! the thrones are all set,
> Where the Lamb and the white-vested elders are met;
> All flesh is at once in the sight of the Lord,
> And the doom of eternity hangs on His word.

For comments on the tune "Winchester New" see Hymn No. 12.

163   The Death of Jesus Christ, Our Lord

1. The death of Jesus Christ, our Lord,
We celebrate with one accord;
It is our comfort in distress,
Our heart's sweet joy and happiness.

2. He blotted out with His own blood
The judgment that against us stood;
He full atonement for us made,
And all our debt He fully paid.

3. That this is now and ever true
He gives an earnest ever new:
In this His holy Supper here
We taste His love so sweet, so near.

4. His Word proclaims, and we believe,
That in this Supper we receive
His very body, as He said,
His very blood for sinners shed.

5. A precious food is this indeed, —
It never fails us in our need, —
A heavenly manna for our soul,
Until we safely reach our goal.

6. Oh, blest is each believing guest
Who in this promise finds His rest;
For Jesus will in love abide
With those who do in Him confide.

7. The guest that comes with true intent
To turn to God and to repent,
To live for Christ, to die to sin,
Will thus a holy life begin.

8. They who His Word do not believe,
This food unworthily receive,
Salvation here will never find, —
May we this warning keep in mind!

9. Help us sincerely to believe
That we may worthily receive
Thy Supper and in Thee find rest.
Amen, he who believes is blest.

1. Wår Herres Jesu Kristi död
Hugswalar oss i all wår nöd,
Och när wi tänke deruppå,
En hjertans glädje wi då få.

2. Afplanat har han med sitt blod
Den handskrift, som emot oss stod;
Ty han war oss så god och huld,
Att han betalte all wår skuld.

3. Att detta trofast är och sant,
Han gifwer oss en säker pant
Uti sin helga nattward, der
Wi smake huru ljuf han är.

4. Hans heliga lekamen sann,
Hans dyra blod, som för oss rann,
Wi undfå wid hans helga bord,
Som han har lofwat i sitt ord.

5. En harlig spis är detta wisst,
På hwilken aldrig blifwer brist,
Ett himmelskt manna, som war själ
Till ewigt lif bewarar wäl.

6. Säll är då hwarje wärdig gäst,
Som lit till Jesu ord har fäst;
Ty Jesus will med kärlek bo
Hos den, som har en stadig tro;

7. Och som will helgad bli i Gud,
Ej wika från hans ord och bud,
Men Kristo lefwer, synden dör
Och så Guds helga wilja gör.

8. Men den owärdig gar härtill,
Ej tror, ej sig omwända will,
Han äter döden uti sig
Och blir fördömd ewinnerlig.

9. Gif oss att tro af hjertans grund,
Att wi få frälsning och miskund
Utaf din nådes fullhet stor.
Amen, wälsignad den det tror!

This great Communion hymn by Haquin Spegel was written in 1686 and included in Jesper Swedberg's *Psalm-Book*, 1696, in the preparation of which Spegel had collaborated with Swedberg. This hymn has been called "a classic example of how Spegel could set forth in song the objective truths of the Christian faith." The omitted ninth stanza reads:

> O Jesus Christ, our Brother dear,
> Unto Thy cross we now draw near;
> Thy sacred wounds indeed make whole
> A wounded and benighted soul.

The translation is an altered form of that by Olof Olsson. It appeared in the *Evangelical Lutheran Hymn-Book*, 1912, and in *The Hymnal* (Augustana Synod), 1925.

MAUNDY THURSDAY. — GOOD FRIDAY

The tune "Gottlob, es geht nunmehr zu Ende" is an old German melody found in various forms in German collections. Its source is unknown. It has its name from its association with Christian Weise's burial hymn beginning with that line. It first appeared in print in *Sammlung alter und neuer . . . Melodien*, by Johann G. Wagner, 1742. The present form of the tune is based upon Johann S. Bach's *Vierstimmige Choralgesänge*, 1769.

'Twas on That Dark, That Doleful Night   164

1. 'Twas on that dark, that doleful night
When powers of earth and hell arose
Against the Son of God's delight
And friends betrayed Him to His foes.

2. Before the mournful scene began,
He took the bread and blessed and brake.
What love through all His actions ran!
What wondrous words of grace He spake!

3. "This is My body, broke for sin;
Receive and eat the living food";
Then took the cup and blessed the wine:
" 'Tis the new covenant in My blood."

4. "Do this," He said, "till time shall end,
In memory of your dying Friend.
Meet at My table and record
The love of your departed Lord."

5. Jesus, Thy feast we celebrate;
We show Thy death, we sing Thy name,
Till Thou return and we shall eat
The marriage supper of the Lamb.

This cento is composed of Stanzas 1, 2, 3, 6, and 7 of Isaac Watts's Communion hymn, based on 1 Cor. 11:23 ff., which first appeared in his *Hymns and Spiritual Songs*, 1709. The omitted Stanzas 4 and 5 read:

4. For us His flesh with nails was torn,
He bore the scourge, He felt the thorn;
And justice poured upon His head
Its heavy vengeance in our stead.

5. For us His vital blood was spilt
To buy the pardon of our guilt
When for black crimes of biggest size
He gave His soul a sacrifice.

The tune "St. Cross" is by John B. Dykes and was written by him for F. W. Faber's hymn "Oh, Come and Mourn with Me Awhile," in *Hymns Ancient and Modern*, 1861.

Behold the Lamb of God!   165

1. Behold the Lamb of God!
O Thou for sinners slain,
Let it not be in vain
  That Thou hast died!
Thee for my Savior let me take,
My only refuge let me make
  Thy piercèd side.

2. Behold the Lamb of God!
Into the sacred flood
Of Thy most precious blood
  My soul I cast.
Wash me and make me pure and clean,
Uphold me through life's changeful scene,
  Till all be past.

3. Behold the Lamb of God!
All hail, incarnate Word!
Thou everlasting Lord,
  Purge out our leaven;
Clothe us with godliness and good,
Feed us with Thy celestial food,
  Manna from heaven.

4. Behold the Lamb of God!
Worthy is He alone
To sit upon the throne
  Of God above,
One with the Ancient of all days,
One with the Paraclete in praise,
  All Light, all Love!

This cento is an altered form of the hymn written by Matthew Bridges, which was first published in his *Hymns of the Heart*, etc., 1848, entitled "Ecce Agnus Dei."

The original text is given by *Julian* as follows:

1. Behold the Lamb!
Oh! Thou for sinners slain,
Let it not be in vain
  That Thou hast died;
Thee for my Savior let me
  take, —
Thee, Thee alone, my Refuge make, —
  Thy piercèd side!

2. Behold the Lamb!
Into the sacred flood
Of Thy most precious blood
  My soul I cast.
Wash me and make me pure and clean,
Uphold me through life's changeful
  scene
Till all be past!

GOOD FRIDAY

3. Behold the Lamb!
Archangels, — fold your wings, —
Seraphs, — hush all the strings
  Of million lyres:
The Victim, veil'd on earth, in love, —
Unveil'd, — enthron'd, — ador'd above,
  All heaven admires!

4. Behold the Lamb!
Drop down, ye glorious skies, —
He dies, — He dies, — He dies, —
  For man once lost!
Yet, lo, He lives, — He lives, — He lives, —
And to His Church Himself He gives, —
  Incarnate Host!

5. Behold the Lamb!
All hail, Eternal Word!
Thou Universal Lord,
  Purge out our leaven;
Clothe us with godliness and good,
Feed us with Thy celestial food,
  Manna from heaven!

6. Behold the Lamb!
Saints, wrapt in blissful rest,
Souls, waiting to be blest,
  Oh! Lord, how long!
Thou Church on earth, o'erwhelm'd with fears,
Still in this vale of woe and tears
  Swell the full song.

7. Behold the Lamb!
Worthy is He alone,
Upon the iris throne
  Of God above!
One with the Ancient of all days,
One with the Paraclete in praise,
  All light, all love!"

The tune "Ecce Agnus," or "Munich," is an adaptation of the melody "Wir Christenleut'" from the Dresden *Neues Gesangbuch,* 1593, where it was set to the famous Christmas hymn by Caspar Füger. (See Hymn No. 107.)

166   Savior, When in Dust to Thee

1. Savior, when in dust to Thee
Low we bow the adoring knee,
When, repentant, to the skies
Scarce we lift our weeping eyes,
Oh, by all Thy pains and woe
Suffered once for man below,
Bending from Thy throne on high,
Hear our solemn litany!

2. By Thy helpless infant years,
By Thy life of want and tears,
By Thy days of sore distress
In the savage wilderness,
By the dread, mysterious hour
Of the insulting Tempter's power,
Turn, O turn, a favoring eye,
Hear our solemn litany!

3. By Thine hour of dire despair,
By Thine agony of prayer,
By the cross, the nail, the thorn,
Piercing spear, and torturing scorn,
By the gloom that veiled the skies
O'er the dreadful sacrifice,
Listen to our humble cry,
Hear our solemn litany!

4. By Thy deep expiring groan,
By the sad sepulchral stone,
By the vault whose dark abode
Held in vain the rising God,
Oh, from earth to heaven restored,
Mighty, reascended Lord,
Listen, listen, to the cry
Of our solemn litany!

Robert Grant first published his famous Lenten *Litany* in the *Christian Observer,* 1815, in five stanzas. The omitted Stanza 3 reads:

By the sacred griefs that wept
O'er the grave where Lazarus slept;
By the boding tears that flowed
Over Salem's loved abode;
By the anguished sigh that told
Treachery lurked within Thy fold;
From Thy seat above the sky
Hear our solemn litany.

The tune "Spanish Chant" is from an old seventeenth-century melody, arranged by Benjamin Carr, 1824.

167   O Darkest Woe

1. O darkest woe!
Ye tears, forth flow!
  Has earth so sad a wonder?
  God the Father's only Son
  Now is buried yonder.

O Traurigkeit,
O Herzeleid!
  Ist das nicht zu beklagen?
  Gott des Vaters einig Kind
  Wird ins Grab getragen.

GOOD FRIDAY

2. O sorrow dread!
God's Son is dead!
 But by His expiation
Of our guilt upon the cross
 Gained for us salvation.

3. O sinful man!
It was the ban
 Of death on thee that brought Him
Down to suffer for thy sins
 And such woe hath wrought Him.

4. Lo, stained with blood,
The Lamb of God,
 The Bridegroom, lies before thee,
Pouring out His life that He
 May to life restore thee.

5. O Ground of faith,
Laid low in death,
 Sweet lips, now silent sleeping!
Surely all that live must mourn
 Here with bitter weeping.

6. Oh, blest shall be
Eternally
 Who oft in faith will ponder
Why the glorious Prince of Life
 Should be buried yonder.

7. O Jesus blest,
My Help and Rest
 With tears I now entreat Thee:
Make me love Thee to the last,
 Till in heaven I greet Thee!

O grosse Not!
Gott selbst ist tot,
 Am Kreuz ist er gestorben,
Hat dadurch das Himmelreich
 Uns aus Lieb' erworben.

O Menschenkind,
Nur deine Sünd'
 Hat dieses angerichtet,
Da du durch die Missetat
 Warest ganz vernichtet.

Dein Bräutigam,
Das Gotteslamm,
 Liegt hier mit Blut beflossen,
Welches er ganz mildiglich
 Hat für dich vergossen.

O süsser Mund,
O Glaubensgrund,
 Wie bist du doch zerschlagen!
Alles, was auf Erden lebt,
 Muss dich ja beklagen.

O selig ist
Zu aller Frist,
 Der dieses recht bedenket,
Wie der Herr der Herrlichkeit
 Wird ins Grab gesenket!

O Jesu, du
Mein' Hilf' und Ruh',
 Ich bitte dich mit Tränen:
Hilf, dass ich mich bis ins Grab
 Nach dir möge sehnen!

The first stanza of this hymn for the burial of our Lord is anonymous and is first found in the *Würzburger Gesangbuch* (Roman Catholic), 1628. Johann Rist added seven stanzas and published the hymn in the *Erste Zehen* of his *Himmlische Lieder,* Lüneburg, 1641. He wrote: "The first stanza of this funeral hymn, along with its devotional melody, came accidentally into my hands. As I was greatly pleased with it, I added the other seven as they stand here." The omitted Stanza 6 reads:

O lieblich Bild,
Schön zart und mild,
Du Söhnlein der Jungfrauen,
Niemand kann dein heisses Blut
Sonder Reu' anschauen.

The translation is an altered form of that by Catherine Winkworth, in her *Chorale Book for England,* 1863, except Stanza 2, which is a composite.

The tune "O Traurigkeit" is also from the Würzburg *Gesangbuch,* 1628. The composer is unknown. *Fischer* and also *Kümmerle* give as the source of the tune the *Himmlische Harmoney,* etc., Meyntz (Mainz), 1628.

The Royal Banners Forward Go 168

1. The royal banners forward go;
The cross shines forth in mystic glow
Where He in flesh, our flesh who made,
Our sentence bore, our ransom paid;

2. Where deep for us the spear was dyed,
Life's torrent rushing from His side,
To wash us in that precious flood
Where mingled water flowed and blood.

3. Fulfilled is all that David told
In true prophetic song of old;
Amidst the nations, God, saith he,
Hath reigned and triumphed from the tree.

Vexilla regis prodeunt,
Fulget crucis mysterium,
Quo carne carnis conditor
Suspensus est patibulo:

Quo vulneratus insuper
Mucrone diro lanceae,
Ut nos lavaret crimine,
Manavit unda et sanguine.

Impleta sunt, quae cecinit
David fideli carmine,
Dicendo nationibus:
Regnabit a ligno Deus.

GOOD FRIDAY

4. O Tree of beauty, Tree of light,
O Tree with royal purple dight;
Elect, on whose triumphal breast
Those holy limbs should find their rest;

5. On whose dear arms, so widely flung,
The weight of this world's ransom hung
The price of humankind to pay
And spoil the spoiler of his prey.

6. O Cross, our one reliance, hail!
So may thy power with us avail
To give new virtue to the saint
And pardon to the penitent.

7. To Thee, eternal Three in One,
Let homage meet by all be done
Whom by the cross Thou dost restore,
Preserve, and govern evermore.

Arbor decora et fulgida,
Ornata regis purpura,
Electa digno stipite,
Tam sancta membra tangere.

Beata, cuius brachiis
Pretium pependit seculi,
Statera facta est corporis
Praedam tulitque tartari.

O crux ave, spes unica,
Hoc passionis tempore:
Auge piis iustitiam
Reisque dona veniam.

Te summa Deus Trinitas
Collaudat omnis spiritus:
Quos per crucis mysterium
Salvas, rege per secula.

This cento comes to us from the sixth century. Its author, Bishop Venantius Fortunatus (530—609), was one of the popular Latin hymn-writers of the early Middle Ages. Archbishop Trench describes Fortunatus as a "clever, frivolous, self-indulgent, and vain character." His contributions to the hymnology of his day seem to have been very considerable, but the general quality of his poetry is not very high. He represents the "last expiring effort of the Latin muse in Gaul" to retain something of the "old classical culture amid the advancing tide of barbarism." However, in some of his efforts, as in this hymn, he rises above his level to lofty heights of true poetry.

The account usually given about the origin of this hymn is very likely legendary. Mearns gives this summary of the story in Julian's *Dictionary of Hymnology:*

> Fortunatus was then living at Poitiers, where his friend Queen Rhadegunda founded a nunnery. Before the consecration of the nunnery church she desired to present certain relics to it, and among these she obtained from the Emperor Justin II a fragment of the so-called True Cross, from which circumstance the nunnery received its name of the Holy Cross. This relic was sent in the first instance to Tours and was left in charge of the Bishop in order that he might convey it to Poitiers. In the Abbé E. Briand's *Sainte Radegonde,* its journey to Poitiers is thus described: "Escorted by a numerous body of clergy and of the faithful holding lighted torches, the Bishop started in the midst of liturgical chants, which ceased not to resound in honor of the hallowed wood of the Redemption. A league from Poitiers the pious cortège found the delegates of Rhadegunda, Fortunatus at their head, rejoicing in the honor which had fallen to them; some carrying censers with perfumed incense, others torches of white wax. The meeting took place at Migné, at the place where, twelve centuries and a half later, the cross appeared in the air. It was on this occasion that the hymn "Vexilla Regis" was heard for the first time, the chant of triumph composed by Fortunatus to salute the arrival of the True Cross. . . . It was the 19th of November, 569."

The popularity of this hymn is attested by the fact that many have essayed to put it into English. Julian lists 37 English translations. The third stanza has been the crux of the translators. Percy Dearmer rightly says: "The reference is to Ps. 96:10; but neither in the Hebrew, the authentic Septuagint, the present Vulgate, nor of course in the English versions is there anything answering to this." Perhaps Fortunatus referred to an interpolated text. It is generally

GOOD FRIDAY

conceded that John Mason Neale's translation of this stanza is the finest rendering of these lines. The translation otherwise is only partly based on Neale, *Medieval Hymns,* 1851, his excellent first stanza being retained.

The tune "Vexilla Regis" or "St. Cecilia" was written for this hymn by John Hampton and included in the *Revised Edition* of *Hymns Ancient and Modern,* 1875.

Jesus Christ, Our Lord Most Holy   169

1. Jesus Christ, our Lord most holy,
Lamb of God so pure and lowly,
Blameless, blameless, on the cross art offered,
Sinless, sinless, for our sins hast suffered.

2. Weep now, all ye wretched creatures,
As ye view His gracious features.
Jesus, Jesus, on the cross is dying,
Nature, nature, in dark gloom is sighing.

3. Christ, His last word having spoken,
Bows His head as life is broken.
Mournful, mournful, stands His mother weeping,
Loved ones, loved ones, silent watch are keeping.

4. The great veil was torn asunder,
Earth did quake mid roars of thunder,
Boulders, boulders, into bits were breaking;
Sainted, sainted, dead from death were waking.

5. As His side with spear was riven,
Blood and water forth were given.
Jesus, Jesus, sinners' only Savior,
Mercy, mercy, grant to us forever.

Jezu Kriste, Pane milý,
Beránku Boží nevinný,
Vznesls, vznesls na kříž ruce svoje,
Pro ne-, pro nespraved'nosti moje.

Plač Ho, člověče mizerný,
Pohleď, jak jest milosrdný;
Ježíš, Ježíš na kříži umírá,
Slunce, slunce svou jasnost zakrývá.

Pán řekl ostatní slova,
Sklonila se jeho hlava;
Matka, matka pod Ním žalostivá
Stojí, stojí, sotva že jest živa.

Opona se jest roztrhla,
Země se ukrutně třásla,
Skály, skály tvrdé se pukaly,
Mrtví, mrtví z hrobů ven vstávali.

Naskrze mu bok probili,
Krev i vodu vycedili;
Smyj se, smyj se našimi slzami,
Jezu, Jezu smiluj se nad námi.

This excellent Good Friday hymn appeared about the middle of the 16th century and is attributed to Michal Grodzki. We have been unable to ascertain any particulars of the author's life.

The translation by John Bajus was prepared in 1939 for *The Lutheran Hymnal.*

The tune "Teshiniens" is from a 16th-century Polish melody. It was given this name in *The Lutheran Hymnal* in order to commemorate the birthplace (*Tesin*) of Juraj Tranovsky, who included both hymn and tune in his *Tranoscius.*

O Perfect Life of Love   170

1. O perfect life of love!
All, all, is finished now,
All that He left His throne above
To do for us below.

2. No work is left undone
Of all the Father willed;
His toil, His sorrows, one by one,
The Scriptures have fulfilled.

3. No pain that we can share
But He has felt its smart;
All forms of human grief and care
Have pierced that tender heart.

4. And on His thorn-crowned head
And on His sinless soul
Our sins in all that guilt were laid
That He might make us whole.

5. In perfect love He dies;
For me He dies, for me.
O all-atoning Sacrifice,
I cling by faith to Thee.

6. In every time of need,
Before the judgment-throne,
Thy works, O Lamb of God, I'll plead,
Thy merits, not mine own.

7. Yet work, O Lord, in me
As Thou for me hast wrought;
And let my love the answer be
To grace Thy love has brought.

GOOD FRIDAY

This hymn, on the Savior's sixth word, John 19:30: "It is finished!" is a classic in its concise presentation of the doctrine of the atonement. It was written by Henry W. Baker and published in the revised edition of *Hymns Ancient and Modern*, 1875.

For comments on the tune "Southwell" see Hymn No. 156.

171   Upon the Cross Extended

1. Upon the cross extended,
See, world, thy Lord suspended,
  Thy Savior yields His breath.
The Prince of Life from heaven
Himself hath freely given
  To shame and blows and bitter death.

O Welt, sieh hier dein Leben
Am Stamm des Kreuzes schweben,
  Dein Heil sinkt in den Tod!
Der grosse Fürst der Ehren
Lässt willig sich beschweren
  Mit Schlägen, Hohn und grossem Spott.

2. Come hither now and ponder,
'Twill fill thy soul with wonder,
  Blood streams from every pore.
Through grief whose depth none knoweth,
From His great heart there floweth
  Sigh after sigh of anguish o'er.

Tritt her und schau mit Fleisse:
Sein Leib ist ganz mit Schweisse
  Des Blutes überfüllt;
Aus seinem edlen Herzen
Vor unerschöpften Schmerzen
  Ein Seufzer nach dem andern quillt.

3. Who is it that hath bruised Thee?
Who hath so sore abused Thee
  And caused Thee all Thy woe?
While we must make confession
Of sin and dire transgression,
  Thou deeds of evil dost not know.

Wer hat dich so geschlagen,
Mein Heil, und dich mit Plagen
  So übel zugericht't?
Du bist ja nicht ein Sünder
Wie wir und unsre Kinder,
  Von Übeltaten weisst du nicht.

4. I caused Thy grief and sighing
By evils multiplying
  As countless as the sands.
I caused the woes unnumbered
With which Thy soul is cumbered,
  Thy sorrows raised by wicked hands.

Ich, ich und meine Sünden,
Die sich wie Körnlein finden
  Des Sandes an dem Meer,
Die haben dir erreget
Das Elend, das dich schläget,
  Und das betrübte Marterheer.

5. 'Tis I who should be smitten
My doom should here be written:
  Bound hand and foot in hell.
The fetters and the scourging,
The floods around Thee surging,
  'Tis I who have deserved them well.

Ich bin's, ich sollte büssen,
An Händen und an Füssen
  Gebunden in der Höll';
Die Geisseln und die Banden
Und was du ausgestanden,
  Das hat verdienet meine Seel'.

6. The load Thou takest on Thee,
That pressed so sorely on me,
  It crushed me to the ground.
The cross for me enduring,
The crown for me securing,
  My healing in Thy wounds is found.

Du nimmst auf deinen Rücken
Die Lasten, die mich drücken
  Viel schwerer als ein Stein.
Du wirst ein Fluch, dagegen
Verehrst du mir den Segen,
  Dein Schmerzen muss mein Labsal sein.

7. A crown of thorns Thou wearest,
My shame and scorn Thou bearest,
  That I might ransomed be.
My Bondsman, ever willing,
My place with patience filling,
  From sin and guilt hast made me free.

Du setzest dich zum Bürgen,
Ja lässest dich gar würgen
  Für mich und meine Schuld.
Mir lässest du dich krönen
Mit Dornen, die dich höhnen,
  Und leidest alles mit Geduld.

8. Thy cords of love, my Savior,
Bind me to Thee forever,
  I am no longer mine.
To Thee I gladly render
All that my life can render
  And all I have to Thee resign.

Ich bin, mein Heil, verbunden
All' Augenblick' und Stunden
  Dir überhoch und sehr.
Was Leib und Seel' vermögen,
Das soll ich billig legen
  Allzeit an deinen Dienst und Ehr'.

9. Thy cross I'll place before me,
Its saving power be o'er me,
  Wherever I may be;
Thine innocence revealing,
Thy love and mercy sealing,
  The pledge of truth and constancy.

Ich will's vor Augen setzen,
Mich stets daran ergötzen,
  Ich sei auch, wo ich sei.
Es soll mir sein ein Spiegel
Der Unschuld und ein Siegel
  Der Lieb' und unverfälschten Treu'.

GOOD FRIDAY

10. How God at our transgression
  To anger gives expression,
  How loud His thunder rolls,
  How fearfully He smiteth,
  How sorely He requiteth, —
  All this Thy sufferings teach my soul.

11. When evil men revile me,
  With wicked tongues defile me,
  I'll curb my vengeful heart.
  The unjust wrong I'll suffer,
  Unto my neighbor offer
  Forgiveness for each bitter smart.

12. Thy groaning and Thy sighing,
  Thy bitter tears and dying,
  With which Thou wast opprest, —
  They shall, when life is ending,
  Be guiding and attending
  My way to Thine eternal rest.

Wie heftig unsre Sünden
  Den frommen Gott entzünden,
  Wie Rach' und Eifer gehn,
  Wie grausam seine Ruten,
  Wie zornig seine Fluten,
  Will ich aus deinem Leiden sehn.

Wenn böse Zungen stechen,
  Mir Glimpf und Namen brechen,
  So will ich zähmen mich;
  Das Unrecht will ich dulden,
  Dem Nächsten seine Schulden
  Verzeihen gern und williglich.

Dein Seufzen und dein Stöhnen
  Und die viel tausend Tränen,
  Die dir geflossen zu,
  Die sollen mich am Ende
  In deinen Schoss und Hände
  Begleiten zu der ew'gen Ruh'.

This cento includes Stanzas 1 to 7, 9, 11, 12, 14, and 16 of Paul Gerhardt's great hymn, first published in the third edition of Johann Crüger's *Praxis Pietatis Melica,* 1648. It is a profound meditation on the Lord's Passion. Stanzas 3 to 5 were favorites of Johann Sebastian Bach, who used them in his *St. Matthew Passion* and *St. John Passion.*

The translation is an altered form of that by John Kelly in his *Paul Gerhardt's Spiritual Songs,* London, 1867. The omitted stanzas read:

8. Into death's jaws Thou springest,
  Deliverance to me bringest
  From such a monster dire.
  My death away Thou takest,
  Thy grave its grave Thou makest;
  Of love, O unexampled fire!

10. Not much can I be giving
  In this poor life I'm living,
  But one thing do I say:
  Thy death and sorrows ever,
  Till soul from body sever,
  My heart remember shall for aye.

13. From them shall I be learning
  How I may be adorning
  My heart with quietness
  And how I still should love them
  Whose malice aye doth move them
  To grieve me by their wickedness.

15. I'll on the cross unite me
  To Thee, what doth delight me
  I'll there renounce for aye.
  Whate'er Thy Spirit's grieving,
  There I'll for aye be leaving
  As much as in my strength doth lay.

The tune "O Welt, sieh hier" is by Heinrich Friese, 1703.

For comments on the tune "O Welt, ich muss dich lassen" see Hymn No. 126.

O Sacred Head, Now Wounded   172

1. O sacred Head, now wounded,
  With grief and shame weighed down,
  Now scornfully surrounded
  With thorns, Thine only crown.
  O sacred Head, what glory,
  What bliss, till now was Thine!
  Yet, though despised and gory,
  I joy to call Thee mine.

2. Men mock and taunt and jeer Thee,
  Thou noble countenance,
  Though mighty worlds shall fear Thee
  And flee before Thy glance.
  How art Thou pale with anguish,
  With sore abuse and scorn!
  How doth Thy visage languish
  That once was bright as morn!

3. Now from Thy cheeks has vanished
  Their color, once so fair;
  From Thy red lips is banished
  The splendor that was there.
  Grim Death, with cruel rigor,
  Hath robbed Thee of Thy life;
  Thus Thou hast lost Thy vigor,
  Thy strength, in this sad strife.

O Haupt voll Blut und Wunden,
  Voll Schmerz und voller Hohn,
  O Haupt, zum Spott gebunden
  Mit einer Dornenkron',
  O Haupt, sonst schön gezieret
  Mit höchster Ehr' und Zier,
  Jetzt aber höchst schimpfieret:
  Gegrüsset sei'st du mir!

Du edles Angesichte,
  Davor sonst schrickt und scheut
  Das grosse Weltgewichte,
  Wie bist du so bespeit!
  Wie bist du so erbleichet!
  Wer hat dein Augenlicht,
  Dem sonst kein Licht nicht gleichet,
  So schändlich zugericht't?

Die Farbe deiner Wangen,
  Der roten Lippen Pracht
  Ist hin und ganz vergangen;
  Des blassen Todes Macht
  Hat alles hingenommen,
  Hat alles hingerafft,
  Und daher bist du kommen
  Von deines Leibes Kraft.

4. My burden in Thy Passion,
    Lord, Thou hast borne for me,
  For it was my transgression
    Which brought this woe on Thee.
  I cast me down before Thee,
    Wrath were my rightful lot;
  Have mercy, I implore Thee;
    Redeemer, spurn me not!

5. My Shepherd, now receive me;
    My Guardian, own me Thine.
  Great blessings Thou didst give me,
    O Source of gifts divine!
  Thy lips have often fed me
    With words of truth and love,
  Thy Spirit oft hath led me
    To heavenly joys above.

6. Here I will stand beside Thee,
    From Thee I will not part;
  O Savior, do not chide me!
    When breaks Thy loving heart,
  When soul and body languish
    In death's cold, cruel grasp,
  Then, in Thy deepest anguish,
    Thee in mine arms I'll clasp.

7. The joy can ne'er be spoken,
    Above all joys beside,
  When in Thy body broken
    I thus with safety hide.
  O Lord of life, desiring
    Thy glory now to see,
  Beside Thy cross expiring,
    I'd breathe my soul to Thee.

8. What language shall I borrow
    To thank Thee, dearest Friend,
  For this, Thy dying sorrow,
    Thy pity without end?
  Oh, make me Thine forever!
    And should I fainting be,
  Lord, let me never, never,
    Outlive my love for Thee.

9. My Savior, be Thou near me
    When death is at my door;
  Then let Thy presence cheer me,
    Forsake me nevermore!
  When soul and body languish,
    Oh, leave me not alone,
  But take away mine anguish
    By virtue of Thine own!

10. Be Thou my Consolation,
    My Shield when I must die;
  Remind me of Thy Passion
    When my last hour draws nigh.
  Mine eyes shall then behold Thee,
    Upon Thy cross shall dwell,
  My heart by faith enfold Thee.
    Who dieth thus dies well!

Nun, was du, Herr, erduldet,
  Ist alles meine Last;
Ich hab' es selbst verschuldet,
  Was du getragen hast.
Schau her, hier steh' ich Armer,
  Der Zorn verdienet hat;
Gib mir, o mein Erbarmer,
  Den Anblick deiner Gnad'!

Erkenne mich, mein Hüter,
  Mein Hirte, nimm mich an!
Von dir, Quell aller Güter,
  Ist mir viel Gut's getan.
Dein Mund hat mich gelabet
  Mit Milch und süsser Kost;
Dein Geist hat mich begabet
  Mit mancher Himmelslust.

Ich will hier bei dir stehen,
  Verachte mich doch nicht!
Von dir will ich nicht gehen,
  Wenn dir dein Herze bricht;
Wenn dein Haupt wird erblassen
  Im letzten Todesstoss,
Alsdann will ich dich fassen
  In meinen Arm und Schoss.

Es dient zu meinen Freuden
  Und kommt mir herzlich wohl,
Wenn ich in deinem Leiden,
  Mein Heil, mich finden soll.
Ach, möcht' ich, o mein Leben,
  An deinem Kreuze hier
Mein Leben von mir geben,
  Wie wohl geschähe mir!

Ich danke dir von Herzen,
  O Jesu, liebster Freund,
Für deines Todes Schmerzen,
  Da du's so gut gemeint.
Ach gib, dass ich mich halte
  Zu dir und deiner Treu'
Und, wenn ich nun erkalte,
  In dir mein Ende sei!

Wenn ich einmal soll scheiden,
  So scheide nicht von mir;
Wenn ich den Tod soll leiden,
  So tritt du dann herfür;
Wenn mir am allerbängsten
  Wird um das Herze sein,
So reiss mich aus den Ängsten
  Kraft deiner Angst und Pein!

Erscheine mir zum Schilde,
  Zum Trost in meinem Tod,
Und lass mich sehn dein Bilde
  In deiner Kreuzesnot!
Da will ich nach dir blicken,
  Da will ich glaubensvoll
Dich fest an mein Herz drücken.
  Wer so stirbt, der stirbt wohl.

This classic hymn of Paul Gerhardt's is based on the Latin "Salve caput cruentatum," the seventh and last of a series of poems (*Rhythmica Oratio*) addressed to Christ on the cross, each poem addressing itself to a separate member of the Lord's body: the feet, the knees, the hands, the side, the breast, the heart, and the head. This series of poems is attributed to Bernard of Clairvaux. Paul Gerhardt's hymn is a very free paraphrase of Bernard's Latin text. It first appeared in Crüger's *Praxis Pietatis Melica*, Frankfurt, 1656. The hymn has long been a favorite in Evangelical Christendom. Lauxmann, in *Koch*, writes:

"Bernard's original is powerful and searching, but Gerhardt's hymn is

GOOD FRIDAY

still more powerful and more profound, as redrawn from the deeper spring of Evangelical Lutheran Scriptural knowledge and fervency of faith."

Recent research shows that Bernard's authorship cannot well be maintained.

Stanza 10 is widely used as a prayer for the dying. When the great Lutheran missionary C. F. W. Schwartz, in 1798, lay dying in India, where he had labored for half a century, his native pupils gathered around him, and sang in their own tongue the last stanzas of this hymn, Schwartz himself joining in until his breath failed in death.

The translation is a composite prepared for *The Lutheran Hymnal.*

The tune "Herzlich tut mich" was composed by Hans Leonhard Hassler for the secular song "Mein G'müt ist mir verwirret" and first appeared in *Lustgarten Neuer Teutschen Gesäng,* etc., Nürnberg, 1601. It was coupled by J. Schein, in his *Cantional,* etc., 1627, with the hymn of Christoph Knoll "Herzlich tut mich verlangen"; by J. Crüger in his *Praxis Pietatis Melica,* 1648, with the hymn of J. Schein "Ach, Herr, mich armen Sünder"; in the *Praxis* of 1656 the tune is used with this text. Johann Sebastian Bach, in his *St. Matthew Passion,* has this tune, where it produces a most profound effect when sung immediately upon the account of the Savior's death.

The following quotation from C. J. Philipp Spitta's *Life of Bach* is interesting in this connection:

Bach has distinguished one of the *chorales* introduced from the rest by repetition, thus making it the center of the church sentiment of the whole work. Among the fourteen simply set *chorales* included in the work in its original form the melody "O Thou whose Head was Wounded" occurs five times; it was a favorite melody with Bach, and there is no other that, throughout his long life, he used so frequently or more thoroughly exhausted as to its harmonic possibilities for every variety of purpose. It comes in three times in the second part: first when Jesus silently bows to His fate at Pilate's decision. . . . It was a beautiful idea to associate the pious submissiveness of Jesus with a congregational meditation on it. . . . Apparently Bach felt chiefly the need for bringing in the melody. . . . The second time the *chorale* is sung is in the second section, immediately before the progress to the cross, when the soldiers have crowned the Savior with thorns and mocked Him and smitten Him; and we here have the first two verses of the hymn addressed to the head of Christ.

Nothing more suitable could be found for this place, and the effect is consequently deeply touching. The third time it is the last *chorale* of the work, and it comes in after the words "But Jesus cried with a loud voice and departed." . . . This climax has always been justly regarded as one of the most thrilling of the whole work.

Lord Jesus, We Give Thanks to Thee 173

1. Lord Jesus, we give thanks to Thee
That Thou hast died to set us free;
Made righteous through Thy precious blood,
We now are reconciled to God.

Wir danken dir, Herr Jesu Christ,
Dass du für uns gestorben bist
Und hast uns durch dein teures Blut
Gemacht vor Gott gerecht und gut,

GOOD FRIDAY

2. By virtue of Thy wounds we pray,
True God and Man, be Thou our Stay,
Our Comfort when we yield our breath,
Our Rescue from eternal death.

Und bitten dich, wahr'r Mensch und Gott,
Durch dein' heilig' fünf Wunden rot,
Erlös' uns von dem ew'gen Tod
Und tröst uns in der letzten Not!

3. Defend us, Lord, from sin and shame;
Help us by Thine almighty name
To bear our crosses patiently,
Consoled by Thy great agony,

Behüt uns auch vor Sünd' und Schand',
Reich uns dein' allmächtige Hand,
Dass wir im Kreuz geduldig sei'n,
Uns trösten deiner schweren Pein

4. And thus the full assurance gain
That Thou to us wilt true remain
And not forsake us in our strife
Until we enter into life.

Und draus schöpfen die Zuversicht,
Dass du uns werd'st verlassen nicht,
Sondern ganz treulich bei uns stehn,
Bis wir durchs Kreuz ins Leben gehn.

This hymn by Christoph Fischer (Vischer) is included in the second part of the *Dresden Gesangbuch,* 1597. According to *Mützell* it bore the title "A children's hymn, composed by M. [Magister] Christoph Vischer for the Christian community at Schmalkalden upon the strengthening use of the bitter sufferings and death of Christ Jesus, our Savior."

The translation is by August Crull.

The tune "Wir danken dir" is from the Collection *Bergkreyen* Wittenberg, 1562.

174   Throned upon the Awe-full Tree

1. Throned upon the awe-full tree,
King of grief, I watch with Thee.
Darkness veils Thine anguished face;
None its lines of woe can trace,
None can tell what pangs unknown
Hold Thee silent and alone.

2. Silent through those three dread hours,
Wrestling with the evil powers,
Left alone with human sin,
Gloom around Thee and within,
Till the appointed time is nigh,
Till the Lamb of God may die.

3. Hark the cry that peals aloud
Upward through the whelming cloud!
Thou, the Father's only Son,
Thou, His own Anointed One,
Thou dost ask Him, Can it be?
"Why hast Thou forsaken Me?"

4. Lord, should fear and anguish roll
Darkly o'er my sinful soul,
Thou, who once wast thus bereft,
That Thine own might ne'er be left,
Teach me by that bitter cry
In the gloom to know Thee nigh.

John Ellerton wrote this hymn in 1875, and it was published in the same year in the revised edition of *Hymns Ancient and Modern.* It is one of his finest hymns.

For comments on the tune "Gethsemane" see Hymn No. 159.

175   When I Survey the Wondrous Cross

1. When I survey the wondrous cross
On which the Prince of glory died,
My richest gain I count but loss
And pour contempt on all my pride.

2. Forbid it, Lord, that I should boast
Save in the death of Christ, my God;
All the vain things that charm me most,
I sacrifice them to His blood.

3. See, from His head, His hands, His feet,
Sorrow and love flow mingled down.
Did e'er such love and sorrow meet
Or thorns compose so rich a crown?

4. Were the whole realm of nature mine
That were a tribute far too small;
Love so amazing, so divine,
Demands my soul, my life, my all.

Isaac Watts first published this, the best of all his hymns, in 1707, in his *Hymns and Spiritual Songs* in five stanzas. It was entitled "Crucifixion to the World by the Cross of Christ. Gal. 6:14." The omitted Stanza 4 reads:

His dying crimson, like a robe,
Spreads o'er His body on the tree;
Then I am dead to all the globe,
And all the globe is dead to me.

GOOD FRIDAY

In the second edition of *Hymns and Spiritual Songs,* 1709, this stanza appears in brackets to indicate that it might be omitted without distorting the sense. In Stanza 1 Watts has "Where the young Prince of Glory dy'd"; in Stanza 5, "That were a present far too small."

Matthew Arnold holds this to be the finest hymn in the English language. A few years ago an Oriental asserted that this was one of the favorite hymns of Mahatma Gandhi.

The tune "Hamburg" is based on the First Gregorian Tone. It was arranged by Lowell Mason, 1824, and set to the hymn "Sing to the Lord with Joyful Voice," Watts's Ps. 100. D. R. Breed, in his *History and Use of Hymns and Hymn Tunes,* writes: "The dignity, solemnity, and breadth of the old Gregorian Music is well reproduced in 'Hamburg,' most appropriately set to that greatest of all hymns, 'When I Survey the Wondrous Cross.'"

The tune "Rockingham Old," also called "Rockingham" and "Communion," first appeared in Edward Miller's *The Psalms of David,* etc., 1790. It was based on a tune called "Tunbridge," found in Aaron Williams's *Supplement to Psalmody in Miniature,* 1780. The tune received its name from the marquis of Rockingham, a friend and patron of Miller's. It is called "Old" to distinguish it from another tune, "Rockingham New," by Lowell Mason, 1830.

Behold the Savior of Mankind   176

1. Behold the Savior of mankind
   Nailed to the shameful tree!
   How vast the love that Him inclined
   To bleed and die for thee!

2. Hark how He groans while nature shakes
   And earth's strong pillars bend!
   The Temple's veil in sunder breaks,
   The solid marbles rend.

3. 'Tis done; the precious ransom's paid;
   "Receive my soul!" He cries.
   See where He bows His sacred head;
   He bows His head and dies.

4. But soon He'll break death's envious chain
   And in full glory shine.
   O Lamb of God, was ever pain,
   Was ever love, like Thine?

Samuel Wesley, Sr., the father of John and Charles Wesley, wrote this hymn prior to the fire which destroyed his rectory at Epworth in 1709. Wesley was saved from death by being rescued through the window by some of his parishioners. During the fire the manuscript of this hymn was blown from the house into the garden and subsequently found there. It was first published here in America, included by John Wesley in his *Psalms and Hymns,* Charleston, S. C., 1736—7.

The original contained six stanzas. The omitted stanzas, also omitted at the original publication by John Wesley, read:

2. Though far unequal our low praise
   To Thy vast sufferings prove,
   O Lamb of God, thus all our days,
   Thus will we grieve and love.

6. Thy loss our ruins did repair;
   Death by Thy death is slain;
   Thou wilt at length exalt us where
   Thou dost in glory reign.

The tune "Windsor" is by Christopher Tye and appeared in his *Acts of the Apostles,* 1553.

Our Blessed Savior Spoke Seven Times   177

1. Our blessed Savior seven times spoke
   When on the cross our sins He took
   And died lest man should perish.
   Let us His last and dying words
   In our remembrance cherish.

Da Jesus an des Kreuzes Stamm
Der ganzen Welt Sünd' auf sich nahm,
Sprach er in seinen Schmerzen
Noch sieben Wort', die lasset uns
Erwägen wohl im Herzen.

GOOD FRIDAY

2. "Father, forgive these men, for, lo,
They truly know not what they do."
So far His love extended.
Forgive us, Lord, for we, too, have
Through ignorance offended.

3. Now to the contrite thief He cries:
"Thou, verily, in Paradise
Shalt meet Me ere tomorrow."
Lord, take us to Thy kingdom soon
Who linger here in sorrow.

4. To weeping Mary, standing by,
"Behold thy son!" now hear Him cry;
To John, "Behold thy mother!"
Provide, O Lord, for those we leave;
Let each befriend the other.

5. The Savior's fourth word was "I thirst!"
O mighty Prince of Life, Thy thirst
For us and our salvation
Is truly great; do help us, then,
That we escape damnation.

6. The fifth, "My God, My God, oh, why
Forsake Me?" Hark, the awe-full cry!
Lord, Thou wast here forsaken
That we might be received on high;
Let this hope not be shaken.

7. The sixth, when victory was won,
"'Tis finished!" for Thy work was done.
Grant, Lord, that, onward pressing,
We may the Work Thou dost impose
Fulfil with Thine own blessing.

8. The last, as woe and sufferings end,
"O God, My Father, I commend
Into Thy hands My spirit."
Be this, dear Lord, my dying wish;
O heavenly Father, hear it.

9. Whoe'er, by sense of sin opprest,
Upon these words his thoughts will rest,
He joy and hope obtaineth
And, through God's love and boundless grace
A peaceful conscience gaineth.

10. O Jesus Christ, Thou Crucified,
Who hast for our offenses died,
Grant that we e'er may ponder
Thy wounds, Thy cross, Thy bitter death,
Both here below and yonder.

Zum ersten: Vater, strafe nicht
An ihnen, was mir jetzt geschicht.
Weil sie es nicht verstehen.
Vergib uns, Gott, wenn wir auch noch
Aus Irrtum was begehen!

Zum andern er des Schächers dacht':
Fürwahr, du wirst noch vor der Nacht
In meinem Reich heut' leben.
O Herr, nimm uns auch bald zu dir,
Die wir im Elend schweben.

Zum dritten: Deinen Sohn sieh, Weib!
Johannes, ihr zu Dienste bleib
Und sie als Mutter liebe!
Versorg, Herr, die wir lassen hier,
Dass niemand sie betrübe!

Zum vierten sagte er: Mich dürst't!
O Jesu, grosser Lebensfürst,
Du hast Durst und Verlangen
Nach unsrer Seligkeit; drum hilf,
Dass wir sie auch empfangen.

Zum fünften: O mein Gott, mein Gott,
Wie lässt du mich so in der Not?
Hier wirst du, Herr, verlassen,
Dass uns Gott wieder dort aufnehm'.
Den Trost lass uns wohl fassen.

Zum sechsten: Hiermit ist. vollbracht
Und alles nunmehr gutgemacht.
Gib, dass wir auch durchdringen,
Und was du, Herr, uns auferlegt,
Hilf seliglich vollbringen.

Zum siebenten: Ich meine Seel',
O Gott, mein Vater, dir befehl'
Zu deinen treuen Händen.
Dies Wort sei unser letzter Wunsch,
Wenn wir das Leben enden.

Wer oft an diese Wort' gedenkt,
Wenn seine Missetat ihn kränkt,
Der wird es wohl geniessen;
Denn er durch Gottes Gnad' erlangt
Ein ruhiges Gewissen.

Verleih uns dies, Herr Jesu Christ,
Der du für uns gestorben bist!
Gib, dass wir deine Wunden,
Dein Leiden, Marter, Kreuz und Tod
Betrachten alle Stunden!

This hymn of pre-Reformation origin is credited to Johann Böschenstain. According to Wackernagel it first appeared in a leaflet, c. 1515, in nine stanzas, beginning "Da Jesus an dem Kreutze stund." It has erroneously been called a translation from the Latin hymn of Peter Bolandus "Stabat ad lignum crucis." The hymn appeared in a new form in the Hanover *Gesangbuch,* 1646, in ten stanzas, beginning "Da Jesus an des Kreuzes Stamm."

The translation is based on that by Frances E. Cox in her *Sacred Hymns from the German,* 1841. The translation of the last stanza was composed by W. Dallmann, B. H. Hemmeter, and Oscar Kaiser, in 1906, for the *Evangelical Lutheran Hymn-Book,* 1912.

The tune "Da Jesus an des Kreuzes" is from an old German melody, very likely not of secular origin. It first appeared in the Babst *Gesangbuch,* 1545, set to the hymn "In dich hab' ich gehoffet, Herr," by Adam Reusner. (See Hymn No. 524.)

GOOD FRIDAY

We Sing the Praise of Him Who Died 178

1. We sing the praise of Him who died,
   Of Him who died upon the cross;
   The sinners' Hope let men deride,
   For this we count the world but loss.

2. Inscribed upon that cross we see
   In shining letters "God is Love."
   He bears our sins upon the tree,
   He brings us mercy from above.

3. The cross! — it takes our guilt away,
   It holds the fainting spirit up,
   It cheers with hope the gloomy day,
   And sweetens every bitter cup.

4. It makes the coward spirit brave
   And nerves the feeble arm for fight;
   It takes all terror from the grave
   And gilds the bed of death with light.

5. The balm of life, the cure of woe,
   The measure and the pledge of love,
   The sinners' refuge here below,
   The angels' theme in heaven above.

Thomas Kelly first published this hymn in his *Hymns*, etc., 1815, headed "God forbid that I should glory save in the Cross: Gal. 6:14." In this work he gave the last two lines of Stanza 5 thus:

'Tis all that sinners want below;
'Tis all the angels know above.

In later editions these lines were altered to the form given in the text above. Lord Selborne said, in 1866, that this hymn "is distinguished by a calm, subdued power, rising gradually from a very low to a very high key."

For comments on the tune "O Jesu Christ, mein's" see Hymn No. 64.

On My Heart Imprint Thine Image 179

On my heart imprint Thine image,
  Blessed Jesus, King of Grace,
That life's riches, cares, and pleasures
  Have no power Thee to efface.
This the superscription be:
Jesus, crucified for me,
Is my life, my hope's Foundation,
And my Glory and Salvation.

Skriv dig, Jesu, paa mit Hjerte,
  O min Konge og min Gud,
At ei Vellyst eller Smerte
  Dig formaar at slette ud.
Denne Opskrift paa mig set:
Jesus udaf Nazaret,
Den korsgästede, min Äre
Og min salighed skal väre!

This stanza is the fifteenth of Thomas Kingo's Passion hymn "Bryder frem, I hule Sukke", which contains twenty-nine stanzas, dated 1689. Landstad, in his *Salmebog*, has made three hymns from twelve of Kingo's hymns. The stanza is based on Matt. 27:37 and Luke 23:38.

The translated is an altered form of that by Peer O. Strömme, 1898.

For comments on the tune "Der am Kreuz" see Hymn No. 144.

The Seven Words on the Cross 180-186

I. Luke 23:34

1. Jesus, in Thy dying woes,
   Even while Thy life-blood flows,
   Craving pardon for Thy foes:
   Hear us, holy Jesus.

2. Savior, for our pardon sue
   When our sins Thy pangs renew,
   For we know not what we do:
   Hear us, holy Jesus.

3. Oh, may we who mercy need
   Be like Thee in heart and deed
   When with wrong our spirits bleed:
   Hear us, holy Jesus.

II. Luke 23:43

1. Jesus, pitying the sighs
   Of the thief who near Thee dies,
   Promising him Paradise:
   Hear us, holy Jesus.

2. May we in our guilt and shame
   Still Thy love and mercy claim,
   Calling humbly on Thy name:
   Hear us, holy Jesus.

3. May our hearts to Thee incline,
   Looking from our cross to Thine;
   Cheer our souls with hope divine:
   Hear us, holy Jesus.

III. John 19:26, 27

1. Jesus, loving to the end
Her whose heart Thy sorrows rend,
And Thy dearest human friend:
   Hear us, holy Jesus.

2. May we in Thy sorrows share,
For Thy sake all peril dare,
And enjoy Thy tender care:
   Hear us, holy Jesus.

3. May we all Thy loved ones be,
All one holy family,
Loving for the love of Thee:
   Hear us, holy Jesus.

IV. Matt. 27:46

1. Jesus, whelmed in fears unknown,
With our evil left alone,
While no light from heaven is shown:
   Hear us, holy Jesus.

2. When we vainly seem to pray
And our hope seems far away,
In the darkness be our Stay:
   Hear us, holy Jesus.

3. Though no Father seem to hear,
Though no light our spirits cheer,
May we know that God is near:
   Hear us, holy Jesus.

V. John 19:28

1. Jesus, in Thy thirst and pain,
While Thy wounds Thy life-blood drain,
Thirsting more our love to gain:
   Hear us, holy Jesus.

2. Thirst for us in mercy still,
Satisfy Thy loving will:
All Thy holy work fulfil,
   Hear us, holy Jesus.

3. May we thirst Thy love to know;
Lead us in our sin and woe
Where the healing waters flow:
   Hear us, holy Jesus.

VI. John 19:30

1. Jesus, all our ransom paid,
All Thy Father's will obeyed,
By Thy sufferings perfect made:
   Hear us, holy Jesus.

2. Save us in our soul's distress,
Be our Help to cheer and bless
While we grow in holiness:
   Hear us, holy Jesus.

3. Brighten all our heavenward way
With an ever holier ray
Till we pass to perfect day:
   Hear us, holy Jesus.

VII. Luke 23:46

1. Jesus, all Thy labor vast,
All Thy woe and conflict past,
Yielding up Thy soul at last:
   Hear us, holy Jesus.

2. When the death shades round us lower,
Guard us from the Tempter's power,
Keep us in that trial hour:
   Hear us, holy Jesus.

3. May Thy life and death supply
Grace to live and grace to die,
Grace to reach the home on high:
   Hear us, holy Jesus.

This series of hymns on the Seven Words first appeared in Thomas B. Pollock's *Metrical Litanies,* etc., Oxford, 1870. They are outstanding for their devotional tone and their succinct application.

The tune "Septem Verba" was composed in 1939 by Bernhard Schumacher for *The Lutheran Hymnal.*

187   Christ is Arisen

1. Christ is arisen
From the grave's dark prison.
We now rejoice with gladness;
Christ will end all sadness.
   Lord, have mercy.

2. All our hopes were ended
Had Jesus not ascended
From the grave triumphantly.
For this, Lord Christ, we worship Thee.
   Lord, have mercy.

3. Hallelujah!
Hallelujah!
Hallelujah!
We now rejoice with gladness.
Christ will end all sadness.
   Lord, have mercy.

Christ ist erstanden
Von der Marter alle;
Des soll'n wir alle froh sein,
Christ will unser Trost sein.
   Kyrieleis!

Wär' er nicht erstanden,
So wär' die Welt vergangen;
Seit dass er erstanden ist,
So lob'n wir den Herrn Jesum Christ.
   Kyrieleis!

Halleluja!
Halleluja!
Halleluja!
Des soll'n wir alle froh sein,
Christ will unser Trost sein.
   Kyrieleis!

EASTER

This is the oldest German Easter hymn and one of the earliest German hymns of any kind. According to *Wackernagel* it is found in four versions in the twelfth century. The same authority gives seventeen fifteenth-century versions that vary from five lines to eleven stanzas.

The three-stanza version is from *Geistliche Lieder,* Erfurt, 1531, and Klug's *Gesangbuch,* Wittenberg, 1529. Luther's estimate of it is this: "After a time one tires of singing all other hymns, but the 'Christ ist erstanden' one can always sing again."

The translation is our own and was prepared in 1939 for *The Lutheran Hymnal.*

The tune "Christ ist erstanden" is as old as the hymn and is based on the Gregorian Chant for the Latin Easter sequence, "Victimae paschali." (See Hymn No. 191.)

Hallelujah! Jesus Lives! 188

1. Hallelujah! Jesus lives!
 He is now the Living One;
From the gloomy house of death
 Forth the Conqueror has gone,
Bright Forerunner to the skies
Of His people, yet to rise.

2. Jesus lives! Let all rejoice;
 Praise Him, ransomed ones of earth.
Praise Him in a nobler song,
 Cherubim of heavenly birth.
Praise the Victor-King, whose sway
Sin and death and hell obey.

3. Jesus lives! Why weepest thou?
 Why that sad and frequent sigh?
He who died our Brother here
 Lives our Brother still on high,
Lives forever to bestow
Blessings on His Church below.

4. Jesus lives! And thus, my soul,
 Life eternal waits for thee;
Joined to Him, thy living Head,
 Where He is, thou, too, shalt be;
With Himself, at His right hand,
Victor over death shalt stand.

5. Jesus lives! To Him my heart
 Draws with ever new delight.
Earthly vanities, depart,
 Hinder not my heavenward flight.
Let this spirit ever rise
To its magnet in the skies.

6. Hallelujah, angels, sing!
 Join us in our hymn of praise,
Let your chorus swell the strain
 Which our feebler voices raise:
Glory to our God above
And on earth His peace and love!

Halleluja, Christus lebt!
 Er war tot und lebet wieder.
Aus der Nacht des Grabes schwebt
 Schon der Erstling seiner Brüder,
Sprengt für sie des Todes Tor,
Und tritt im Triumph hervor.

Christus lebt! O jauchzet ihm!
 Dankt, ihr gottversöhnten Sünder!
Jauchzet mit, ihr Seraphim!
 Dankt dem grossen Überwinder,
Dem an seinem Siegestag
Sünd' und Tod' und Höll' erlag!

Christus lebt! Wer ist betrübt,
 Schlägt die Augen mutlos nieder?
Der uns bis in Tod geliebt,
 Unser Bruder, lebet wieder.
Endlos ist sein Leben nun,
Uns ohn' Ende wohlzutun.

Christus lebt! Wer an ihn glaubt,
 Stirbt nicht, ob der Leib auch sterbe.
Christi Glied, du folgst dem Haupt,
 Erbst mit ihm sein Lebenserbe,
Stehst mit ihm — Halleluja! —
Siegreich überm Grabe da.

Christus lebt; und zu ihm zieht
 Mich sein Geist mit sanftem Zuge.
Flieht, ihr Weltgefühle, flieht;
 Hemmt nicht meine Seel' im Fluge!
Denn mein Herz fliegt ohne Ruh'
Seinem Urmagnete zu.

Auf! in eurem Jubelklang
 Singt mit uns, ihr Himmelschöre!
Singt den frohen Lobgesang:
 Gott sei in den Höhen Ehre,
Friede jedem Erdenteil,
Und der Menschheit Gottes Heil!

Carl B. Garve first published this hymn in *Christliche Gesänge,* Görlitz, 1825, in eight stanzas. The translation is by Jane Borthwick in her *Hymns from the Land of Luther,* fourth series, 1862. The omitted Stanzas 4 and 6 read:

4. Christus lebt; euch grüsst sein Mund:
 "Seht, ich leb', und ihr sollt leben!
Tut es meinen Brüdern kund,
 Dass sie sich vom Staub' erheben!
Bei mir sollen im Verein
Alle meine Brüder sein."

6. Christus lebt! Sein Lebenspfand,
 Christi Geist, lebt mir im Herzen;
Furcht und Unruh' sind verbannt,
 Leer die Quelle meiner Schmerzen,
Und auf meinem Angesicht
Glänzt des ew'gen Lebens Licht.

For comments on the tune "Fred til Bod" see Hymn No. 8.

[143]

EASTER

189   He is Arisen! Glorious Word!

He is arisen! Glorious word!
Now reconciled is God, my Lord;
The gates of heaven are open.
My Jesus did triumphant die,
And Satan's arrows broken lie,
  Destroyed hell's direst weapon.
    Oh, hear
    What cheer!
    Christ victorious
    Riseth glorious,
    Life He giveth —
He was dead, but see, He liveth!

Han er opstanden! Store Bud!
Min Gud er en forsonet Gud,
Min Himmel er nu aaben!
Min Jesu seierrige Död
Fordömmelsernes Pile bröd,
  Og knuste Mörkets Vaaben.
    O Röst,
    Min Tröst!
    Ved hans Seier,
    Som jeg eier,
    Helved bäver;
Han var död, men se, han lever!

This hymn of one stanza by Birgitte K. Boye first appeared in *Guldberg's Hymn Book*, 1778. "It is to be sung before the reading of the Gospel from the pulpit, from Easter to Ascension." (Dahle.) The translation is by George T. Rygh, 1909, and appeared in *The Lutheran Hymnary*, 1913.

For comments on the tune "Wie schön leuchtet" see Hymn No. 23.

190   Christ the Lord is Risen Again

1. Christ the Lord is risen again!
Christ has broken death's strong chain!
Hark, the angels shout for joy
Singing evermore on high:
  Hallelujah!

2. He who gave for us His life,
Who for us endured the strife,
Is our Paschal Lamb today.
We, too, sing for joy and say:
  Hallelujah!

3. He who bore all pain and loss
Comfortless upon the cross
Lives in glory now on high,
Pleads for us and hears our cry:
  Hallelujah!

4. He whose path no records tell
Hath descended into hell;
He the strong man armed hath bound
And in highest heaven is crowned.
  Hallelujah!

5. He who slumbered in the grave
Is exalted now to save;
Now through Christendom it rings
That the Lamb is King of kings.
  Hallelujah!

6. Now He bids us tell abroad
How the lost may be restored,
How the penitent forgiven,
How we, too, may enter heaven.
  Hallelujah!

7. Thou our Paschal Lamb indeed,
Christ, today Thy people feed;
Take our sins and guilt away
That we all may sing for aye:
  Hallelujah!

Christus ist erstanden
Von des Todes Banden;
Des freuet sich der Engel Schar,
Singend im Himmel immerdar:
  Halleluja!

Der für uns sein Leben
In Tod hat gegeben,
Der ist nun unser Osterlamm,
Des wir uns freuen allesamt.
  Halleluja!

Der, ans Kreuz gehangen,
Kein'n Trost konnt' erlangen,
Der lebet nun in Herrlichkeit,
Uns zu vertreten stets bereit.
  Halleluja!

Der so ganz verschwiegen
Zur Hölle gestiegen,
Den wohlgerüst'ten Starken band,
Der wird nun in der Höh' erkannt.
  Halleluja!

Der da lag begraben,
Der ist nun erhaben,
Und sein Tun wird kräftig erweist
Und in der Christenheit gepreist.
  Halleluja!

Er lässt nun verkünden
Vergebung der Sünden,
Und wie man die durch rechte Buss'
Nach seiner Ordnung suchen muss.
  Halleluja!

O Christe, Osterlamm,
Speis uns heut' allesamt,
Nimm weg all unsre Missetat,
Dass wir dir singen früh und spat:
  Halleluja!

Michael Weisse first published this hymn in *Ein New Gesengbuchlen*, Jung Bunzlau, Bohemia, 1531. It is based on the ancient hymn "Christ ist erstanden." (See Hymn No. 187.)

The translation is by Catherine Winkworth in her *Lyra Germanica*, second series, 1858, and in *Chorale Book for England*, 1863.

The tune "Christus ist erstanden" is based on "Christ ist erstanden." (See Hymn No. 187.)

EASTER

Christ the Lord is Risen Today; Alleluia! 191

1. Christ the Lord is risen today; Alleluia!
Christians, haste your vows to pay; Alleluia!
Offer ye your praises meet Alleluia!
At the Paschal Victim's feet. Alleluia!

2. For the sheep the Lamb hath bled, Alleluia!
Sinless in the sinners' stead. Alleluia!
"Christ is risen," today we cry; Alleluia!
Now He lives no more to die. Alleluia!

3. Christ, the Victim undefiled, Alleluia!
God and man hath reconciled Alleluia!
While in strange and awe-full strife Alleluia!
Met together Death and Life: Alleluia!

4. Christians, on this happy day Alleluia!
Haste with joy your vows to pay. Alleluia!
"Christ is risen," today we cry; Alleluia!
Now He lives no more to die. Alleluia!

5. Christ, who once for sinners bled, Alleluia!
Now the First-born from the dead, Alleluia!
Throned in endless might and power, Alleluia!
Lives and reigns forevermore. Alleluia!

6. Hail, eternal Hope on high! Alleluia!
Hail, Thou King of victory! Alleluia!
Hail, Thou Prince of Life adored! Alleluia!
Help and save us, gracious Lord. Alleluia!

Victimae Paschali
Laudes immolent Christiani.

Agnus redemit oves;
Christus innocens Patri
Reconciliavit
Peccatores.

Mors et vita duello
Conflixere mirando;
Dux vitae mortuus
Regnat vivus.

"Dic nobis, Maria,
Quid vidisti in via?"
"Sepulchrum Christi viventis,
Et gloriam vidi resurgentis;
Angelicos testes,
Sudarium et vestes.
Surrexit Christus, spes mea,
Praecedet suos in Galilea."

Credendum est magis soli
Mariae veraci
Quam Iudaeorum turbae fallaci.
Scimus Christum resurrexisse
Ex mortuis vere.
Tu nobis, Victor Rex, miserere.

This ancient Easter sequence is of 11th- or 12th-century origin and of unknown authorship. It has been attributed to a number of medieval writers, but without any certainty. Luther estimated it highly and practically incorporated Stanza 3 in his hymn "Christ lag in Todesbanden." (See Hymn No. 195, 2.)

The translation is by Jane E. Leeson and first appeared in H. Formby's *Hymns,* 1851, where it is in four eight-line stanzas. Here the third stanza is omitted.

The tune "Llanfair" (thlahn-viar), also called "Bether," is by Robert Williams, 1817. Robert Guy McCutchan, in *Our Hymnody,* directs attention to the fact that Williams's authorship of the tune is not undisputed. It may be a traditional Welsh air.

Awake, My Heart, with Gladness 192

1. Awake, my heart, with gladness,
See what today is done,
Now after gloom and sadness
Comes forth the glorious Sun!
My Savior there was laid
Where our bed must be made
When to the realms of light
Our spirit wings its flight.

2. The Foe in triumph shouted
When Christ lay in the tomb,
But, lo, he now is routed,
His boast is turned to gloom.
For Christ again is free;
In glorious victory
He who is strong to save
Has triumphed o'er the grave.

Auf, auf, mein Herz, mit Freuden,
Nimm wahr, was heut' geschieht!
Wie kommt nach grossem Leiden
Nun ein so grosses Licht!
Mein Heiland war gelegt
Da, wo man uns hinträgt,
Wenn von uns unser Geist
Gen Himmel ist gereist.

Er war ins Grab gesenket,
Der Feind trieb gross Geschrei.
Eh' er's vermeint und denket
Ist Christus wieder frei
Und ruft: Viktoria!
Schwingt fröhlich hier und da
Sein Fähnlein als ein Held,
Der Feld und Mut behält.

3. This is a sight that gladdens;
   What peace it doth impart!
   Now nothing ever saddens
   The joy within my heart;
   No gloom shall ever shake,
   No foe shall ever take,
   The hope which God's own Son
   In love for me hath won.

4. Now hell, its prince, the devil,
   Of all their power are shorn;
   Now I am safe from evil,
   And sin I laugh to scorn.
   Grim death with all his might
   Cannot my soul affright;
   He is a powerless form,
   Howe'er he rave and storm.

5. The world against me rageth,
   Its fury I disdain;
   Though bitter war it wageth,
   Its work is all in vain.
   My heart from care is free,
   No trouble troubles me.
   Misfortune now is play,
   And night is bright as day.

6. Now I will cling forever
   To Christ, my Savior true;
   My Lord will leave me never,
   Whate'er He passes through.
   He rends Death's iron chain,
   He breaks through sin and pain,
   He shatters hell's dark thrall, —
   I follow through it all.

7. To halls of heavenly splendor
   With Him I penetrate;
   And trouble ne'er may hinder
   Nor make me hesitate.
   Let tempests rage at will,
   My Savior shields me still;
   He grants abiding peace
   And bids all tumult cease.

8. He brings me to the portal
   That leads to bliss untold
   Whereon this rime immortal
   Is found in script of gold:
   "Who there My cross hath shared
   Finds here a crown prepared;
   Who there with Me has died
   Shall here be glorified."

Das ist mir anzuschauen
   Ein rechtes Freudenspiel;
   Nun soll mir nicht mehr grauen
   Vor allem, was mir will
   Entnehmen meinen Mut
   Zusamt dem edlen Gut,
   So mir durch Jesum Christ
   Aus Lieb' erworben ist.

Die Höll' und ihre Rotten,
   Die krümmen mir kein Haar;
   Der Sünden kann ich spotten,
   Bleib' allzeit ohn' Gefahr;
   Der Tod mit seiner Macht
   Wird schlecht bei mir geacht't;
   Er bleibt ein totes Bild,
   Und wär' er noch so wild.

Die Welt ist mir ein Lachen
   Mit ihrem grossen Zorn;
   Sie zürnt und kann nichts machen,
   All' Arbeit ist verlor'n.
   Die Trübsal trübt mir nicht
   Mein Herz und Angesicht;
   Das Unglück ist mein Glück,
   Die Nacht mein Sonnenblick.

Ich hang' und bleib' auch hangen
   An Christo als ein Glied;
   Wo mein Haupt durch ist gangen,
   Da nimmt er mich auch mit.
   Er reisset durch den Tod,
   Durch Welt, durch Sünd' und Not,
   Er reisset durch die Höll',
   Ich bin stets sein Gesell.

Er dringt zum Saal der Ehren,
   Ich folg' ihm immer nach
   Und darf mich gar nicht kehren
   An einzig Ungemach.
   Es tobe, was da kann,
   Mein Haupt nimmt sich mein an;
   Mein Heiland ist mein Schild,
   Der alles Toben stillt.

Er bringt mich an die Pforten,
   Die in den Himmel führt,
   Daran mit güldnen Worten
   Der Reim gelesen wird:
   Wer dort wird mit verhöhnt,
   Wird hier auch mit gekrönt;
   Wer dort mit sterben geht,
   Wird hier auch mit erhöht.

Paul Gerhardt's most excellent Easter hymn first appeared in Johann Crüger's *Praxis Pietatis Melica*, 1648, in nine stanzas. The translation is an altered form of that by John Kelly in his *Paul Gerhardt's Spiritual Songs*, 1867. The omitted Stanza 3 reads:
   Upon the grave is standing
   The Hero, looking round;
   The Foe, no more withstanding,
   His weapons on the ground
   Throws down, his hellish power
   To Christ he must give o'er
   And to the Victor's bands
   Must yield his feet and hands.

The tune "Auf, auf, mein Herz" is by Johann Crüger, 1648.

193   Christ the Lord is Risen Today

1. Christ the Lord is risen today,
   Sons of men and angels say.
   Raise your joys and triumphs high;
   Sing, ye heavens, and, earth, reply.

2. Love's redeeming work is done,
   Fought the fight, the battle won.
   Lo, our Sun's eclipse is o'er;
   Lo, He sets in blood no more.

EASTER

3. Vain the stone, the watch, the seal;
Christ has burst the gates of hell.
Death in vain forbids His rise;
Christ has opened Paradise.

4. Lives again our glorious King;
Where, O Death, is now thy sting?
Once He died our souls to save;
Where thy victory, O Grave?

5. Soar we now where Christ has led,
Following our exalted Head.
Made like Him, like Him we rise;
Ours the cross, the grave, the skies.

6. Hail the Lord of earth and heaven!
Praise to Thee by both be given!
Thee we greet triumphant now:
Hail, the Resurrection Thou!

This cento is composed of Stanzas 1 to 5 and 10 of Charles Wesley's famous Easter hymn, in eleven stanzas, first published in *Hymns and Sacred Poems*, 1739. In Stanza 4, Line 4, Wesley has:

Where's thy victory, boasting Grave?

The omitted stanzas read:

6. What though once we perished all,
Partners in our parents' fall?
Second life we all receive,
In our heavenly Adam live.

7. Risen with Him, we upward move,
Still we seek the things above,
Still pursue and kiss the Son
Seated on his Father's throne.

8. Scarce on earth a thought bestow,
Dead to all we leave below;
Heaven our aim and loved abode,
Hid our life with Christ in God;

9. Hid till Christ, our Life, appear
Glorious in His members here;
Joined to Him, we then shall shine
All immortal, all divine.

11. King of Glory, Soul of bliss,
Everlasting life is this:
Thee to know, Thy power to prove,
Thus to sing, and thus to love.

The tune "Orientis partibus" is based on a medieval French melody. It is found in a French manuscript, *Office de la Circoncision*, etc., Sens, by Pierre de Corbeil, archbishop of Sens (d. 1222), and in a similar manuscript from Beauvais.

Abide with Us, the Day is Waning   194

1. "Abide with us, the day is waning,"
Thus prayed the two while on the way;
We read that Thou, O Lord, remaining,
Didst all their doubts and fears allay.
Incline Thine ear, Thou King of Grace,
When, praying thus, we seek Thy face.

Bliv hos os, Mester, Dagen helder!
Saa bad i Emmaus de To.
O Tröst, som Skriften mig fortäller,
Du blev, du gav dem Hjertero!
Hör ogsaa os, o du Guds Sön!
Vi bede just den samme Bön.

2. At eventide, Thy Spirit sending,
Help us, O Lord, our watch to keep,
In prayer devout before Thee bending
Ere we our eyelids close in sleep,
Confessing sin in deed and word
With hope of mercy from the Lord.

Bliv hos os, Mester, Dagen helder!
O Mester, hver en Aftenstund!
At vi den rette Bön maa bede,
För öiet lukker sig til Blund,
Med ydmygt Suk for Hjertets Bröst,
Med haab om Naadens Himmeltröst.

3. Abide with us; with heavenly gladness
Illumine, Lord, our darkest day;
And when we weep in pain and sadness,
Be Thou our Solace, Strength, and Stay.
Tell of Thy woe, Thy victory won,
When Thou didst pray: "Thy will be done."

Bliv hos os, Mester, med din Gläde,
Naar Lykkens Aftensol gaar ned,
Naar Smertens Dugg vil Kinden väde,
Da styrk os i Taalmodighed!
Fortäl os om den egen Ve,
At du lod Herrens Vilje ste!

4. Abide with us, O Savior tender,
That bitter day when life shall end,
When to the grave we must surrender,
And fear and pain our hearts shall rend.
The shield of faith do Thou bestow
When trembling we must meet the foe.

Bliv hos os du, naar Dagen helder,
Den sidste Livets tunge Dag,
Naar dödens Nat med Magt udvälder,
Og Frygt og Sorg gjör fälles Sag,
Med Troens Skjold udruste du
Den bange Själ mod Dodens Gru!

5. When earthly help no more availeth,
To sup with us Thou wilt be nigh;
Thou givest strength that never faileth,
In Thee we grave and death defy.
While earth is fading from our sight,
Our eyes behold the realms of light.

Mens Verdens Tröst da intet kräger,
Du holder Nadverd her med os,
Vi drikke Kraft af Naadens Böger,
Og byde Morkets Magter Traads.
Med brustet Blik, med freidigt Sind,
Vi skue klart i Himlen ind.

[147]

EASTER

Caspar J. Boye first published this hymn in his collection *Aandelige Digte og Sange*, Copenhagen, 1834, basing it on the Gospel for Easter Monday, Luke 24:13-35. The translation by Oluf H. Smeby, 1909, appeared in *The Lutheran Hymnary*, 1913.

For comments on the tune "Wer nur den lieben Gott" see Hymn No. 518.

195 Christ Jesus Lay in Death's Strong Bands

1. Christ Jesus lay in death's strong bands,
   For our offenses given;
   But now at God's right hand He stands
   And brings us life from heaven;
   Therefore let us joyful be
   And sing to God right thankfully
   Loud songs of hallelujah!
   Hallelujah!

Christ lag in Todesbanden,
Für unsre Sünd' gegeben,
Der ist wieder erstanden
Und hat uns bracht das Leben.
Des wir sollen fröhlich sein,
Gott loben und dankbar sein
Und singen: Halleluja!
Halleluja!

2. It was a strange and dreadful strife
   When Life and Death contended;
   The victory remained with Life,
   The reign of Death was ended;
   Holy Scripture plainly saith
   That Death is swallowed up by Death,
   His sting is lost forever.
   Hallelujah!

Es war ein wunderlicher Krieg,
Da Tod und Leben rungen;
Das Leben, das behielt den Sieg,
Es hat den Tod verschlungen.
Die Schrift hat verkündet das,
Wie ein Tod den andern frass,
Ein Spott der Tod ist worden.
Halleluja!

3. Here the true Paschal Lamb we see,
   Whom God so freely gave us;
   He died on the accursed tree —
   So strong His love! — to save us.
   See, His blood doth mark our door;
   Faith points to it, Death passes o'er,
   And Satan cannot harm us.
   Hallelujah!

Hier ist das rechte Osterlamm,
Davon Gott hat geboten,
Das ist dort an des Kreuzes Stamm
In heisser Lieb' gebraten;
Des Blut zeichnet unsre Tür,
Das hält der Glaub' dem Tod für,
Der Würger kann nicht würgen.
Halleluja!

4. So let us keep the festival
   Whereto the Lord invites us;
   Christ is Himself the Joy of all,
   The Sun that warms and lights us.
   By His grace He doth impart
   Eternal sunshine to the heart;
   The night of sin is ended.
   Hallelujah!

So feiern wir dies hohe Fest
Mit Herzensfreud' und Wonne,
Das uns der Herre scheinen lässt;
Er ist selber die Sonne,
Der durch seiner Gnaden Glanz
Erleucht't unsre Herzen ganz,
Der Sünd' Nacht ist vergangen.
Halleluja!

5. Then let us feast this Easter Day
   On Christ, the Bread of heaven;
   The Word of Grace hath purged away
   The old and evil leaven.
   Christ alone our souls will feed,
   He is our meat and drink indeed;
   Faith lives upon no other.
   Hallelujah!

Wir essen nun und leben wohl
In rechten Osterfladen;
Der alte Sauerteig nicht soll
Sein bei dem Wort der Gnaden.
Christus will die Koste sein
Und speisen die Seel' allein;
Der Glaub' kein's andern lebet.
Halleluja!

This cento is composed of Stanzas 1 and 4 to 7 of Martin Luther's Easter hymn, first published in *Eyn Enchiridion*, Erfurt, 1524, entitled "The hymn 'Christ ist erstanden' (see Hymn No. 187) improved." However, the traces of this ancient hymn are very slight. *Julian* estimates this hymn as "second only to his unequaled 'Ein' feste Burg.'" The omitted Stanzas 2 and 3 read:

2. No son of man could conquer Death,
   Such mischief sin had wrought us,
   For innocence dwelt not on earth,
   And therefore Death had brought us
   Into thraldom from of old
   And ever grew more strong and bold
   And kept us in his bondage.
   Hallelujah!

3. But Jesus Christ, God's only Son,
   To our low state descended,
   The cause of Death He has undone,
   His power forever ended,
   Ruined all his right and claim
   And left him nothing but the name, —
   His sting is lost forever.
   Hallelujah!

The translation is an altered form of that by Richard Massie in his *Martin Luther's Spiritual Songs*, 1854.

The tune "Christ lag in Todesbanden" is based on the medieval melody for "Christ ist erstanden." (See Hymn No. 187.)

EASTER

I Am Content! My Jesus Liveth Still 196

1. I am content! My Jesus liveth still,
  In whom my heart is pleased.
He hath fulfilled the Law of God for me,
  God's wrath He hath appeased.
Since He in death could perish never,
I also shall not die forever.
  I am content!

2. I am content! My Jesus is my Head;
  His member I will be.
He bowed His head when on the cross He died
  With cries of agony.
Now death is brought into subjection
For me, too, by His resurrection.
  I am content!

3. I am content! My Jesus is my Lord,
  My Prince of Life and Peace;
His heart is yearning for my future bliss
  And for my soul's release.
The home where He, my Master, liveth
He also to His servant giveth.
  I am content!

4. I am content! My Jesus is my Light,
  My radiant Sun of Grace.
His cheering rays beam blessings forth for all,
  Sweet comfort, hope, and peace.
This Easter sun doth bring salvation
And everlasting exultation.
  I am content!

5. I am content! Lord, draw me unto Thee
  And wake me from the dead
That I may rise forevermore to be
  With Thee, my living Head.
The fetters of my body sever,
Then shall my soul rejoice forever.
  I am content!

Ich habe g'nug: mein Jesus lebet noch,
  Der mich vergnügen kann;
Er hat den Zorn des Vaters ausgesöhnt
  Und für mich g'nuggetan.
Kann er im Tode nicht verderben,
So werd' ich auch nicht ewig sterben.
  Ich habe g'nug.

Ich habe g'nug: mein Jesus ist mein Haupt,
  Ich bin sein teures Glied.
Das neigte sich mit grossem Angstgeschrei,
  Als er am Kreuz verschied;
Nun hat er's wieder aufgerichtet
Und meinen Tod zugleich vernichtet.
  Ich habe g'nug.

Ich habe g'nug: mein Jesus ist mein Herr
  Und teurer Lebensfürst;
Der hat ein Herz, das nach der Menschen Heil
  Und Wohlergehen dürst't.
Wo sich der Herr hat hinbegeben,
Da soll der Diener gleichfalls leben.
  Ich habe g'nug.

Ich habe g'nug: mein Jesus ist mein Glanz
  Und heller Gnadenschein.
Dies Freudenlicht lässt keinen ohne Trost
  Und unvergnüget sein;
Denn von derselben Ostersonne
Kommt Leben, Seligkeit und Wonne.
  Ich habe g'nug.

Ich habe g'nug, nur zeuch mich, Herr, nach dir,
  Damit ich aufersteh',
Wenn du aufstehst, und endlich wohlvergnügt
  Zu deiner Freud' eingeh'.
Zeuch mich aus dieses Leibes Höhle,
So rufet die erfreute Seele:
  Ich habe g'nug!

Johann J. Möller, according to the *Kirchengesangbuch für Ev.-Lutherische Gemeinden*, St. Louis, is the author of this hymn. We have been unable to verify this.

The translation is an altered form of that by August Crull in the *Evangelical Lutheran Hymn-Book*, St. Louis, 1912.

The tune "Es ist genug" is from Johann R. Ahle's collection, *Drittes Zehn neuer geistlicher Arien*, Mühlhausen, 1672, where it is set to the hymn "Es ist genug, so nimm, Herr, meinen Geist" by Franz J. Burmeister.

Where Wilt Thou Go Since Night Draws Near 197

1. Where wilt Thou go since night draws near,
  O Jesus Christ, Thou Pilgrim dear?
Lord, make me happy, be my Guest,
And in my heart, oh, deign to rest.

2. Grant my request, O dearest Friend,
For truly I the best intend;
Thou knowest that Thou ever art
A welcome Guest unto my heart.

Wo willst du hin, weil's Abend ist,
  O liebster Pilgrim Jesu Christ?
Komm, lass mich so glückselig sein
Und kehr' in meinem Herzen ein!

Lass dich erbitten, liebster Freund,
Dieweil es ist so gut gemeint!
Du weisst, dass du zu aller Frist
Ein herzenslieber Gast mir bist.

[149]

EASTER

3. The day is now far spent and gone,
The shades of night come quickly on;
Abide with me, Thou heavenly Light,
And do not leave me in this night.

4. Enlighten me that from the way
That leads to heaven I may not stray,
That I may never be misled,
Though night of sin is round me spread.

5. And when I on my death-bed lie,
Help me that I in peace may die.
Abide! I will not let Thee go.
Thou wilt not leave me, Lord, I know.

Es hat der Tag sich sehr geneigt,
Die Nacht sich schon von ferne zeigt;
Drum wollest du, o wahres Licht,
Mich Armen ja verlassen nicht!

Erleuchte mich, dass ich die Bahn
Zum Himmel sicher finden kann,
Damit die dunkle Sündenmacht
Mich nicht verführt noch irremacht!

Vor allem aus der letzten Not
Hilf mir durch einen sanften Tod!
Herr Jesu, bleib, ich halt' dich fest;
Ich weiss, dass du mich nicht verlässt.

This hymn by an unknown author is from the *Plönisches Gesangbuch*, 1674. It is a recast of Johann Scheffler's (Angelus Silesius's) hymn beginning with the same line, published in his *Heilige Seelen-Lust*, etc., Breslau, 1657.

The translation is an altered form of that by August Crull in the *Evangelical Lutheran Hymn-Book*, St. Louis, 1912.

The tune "Ach bleib bei uns" is from *Geistliche Lieder*, Leipzig, 1589.

198 He's Risen, He's Risen, Christ Jesus, the Lord

1. He's risen, He's risen, Christ Jesus, the Lord;
He opened death's prison, the Incarnate Word.
Break forth, hosts of heaven, in jubilant song,
And, earth, sea, and mountain, the paean prolong.

2. The Foe was triumphant when on Calvary
The Lord of creation was nailed to the tree.
In Satan's domain did the hosts shout and jeer,
For Jesus was slain, whom the evil ones fear.

3. But short was their triumph, the Savior arose,
And Death, hell, and Satan He vanquished, His foes;
The conquering Lord lifts His banner on high.
He lives, yea, He lives, and will nevermore die.

4. Oh, where is thy sting, Death? We fear thee no more;
Christ rose, and now open is fair Eden's door.
For all our transgressions His blood doth atone;
Redeemed and forgiven, we now are His own.

5. Then sing your hosannas and raise your glad voice;
Proclaim the blest tidings that all may rejoice.
Laud, honor, and praise to the Lamb that was slain,
Who sitteth in glory and ever shall reign.

Erstanden, erstanden ist Jesus Christ,
Es freue sich, was auf Erden ist,
Es jauchze der Himmel mit seinem Heer;
O hüpfet, ihr Berge, und brause, du Meer!
Kyrieleis.

Der Feind triumphierte auf Golgatha,
Die Hölle durchtönte Viktoria,
Denn endlich hatte der Finsternis Macht
Den Fürsten des Lebens ans Kreuz gebracht.
Kyrieleis.

Doch Trotz dir, du Hölle, und Trotz dir, o Welt,
Der Herzog des Heiles behält das Feld.
Kaum waren vergangen der Tage drei,
So war dein Gefangener los und frei.
Kyrieleis.

Wo ist nun dein Stachel, o Todesgestalt?
Wo ist nun dein Sieg, o Höllengewalt?
Wo ist nun, o Sünde, deine Kraft?
Wo sind nun, Gesetz, deine Flüche und Haft?
Kyrieleis.

Der Herr ist erstanden, das Grab ist leer,
Entschlafen ist nun unsrer Sünden Heer;
Nun jauchze alles, was Sünder heisst,
Und preise den Vater, Sohn und Geist.
Kyrieleis.

This cento is from the Easter hymn, in eleven stanzas, by Carl Ferdinand Wilhelm Walther. It is found in the biography of *C. F. W. Walther* by Martin Günther, 1890, where it is given with the tune, which Walther also composed, and the heading "On the First Easter Day, April 8, 1860, on the Ocean." It was therefore composed on the journey Walther took that year to Germany for recuperation. Stanzas 5 to 9 of the original are omitted.

The rather free translation is by Anna M. Meyer and was first published in the *Lutheran Witness*, 1937.

Jesus Christ is Risen Today, Alleluia!   199

1. Jesus Christ is risen today,
   Alleluia!
   Our triumphant holy day,
   Alleluia!
   Who did once upon the cross
   Alleluia!
   Suffer to redeem our loss.
   Alleluia!

2. Hymns of praise, then, let us sing
   Alleluia!
   Unto Christ, our heavenly King,
   Alleluia!
   Who endured the cross and grave
   Alleluia!
   Sinners to redeem and save.
   Alleluia!

3. But the pains which He endured
   Alleluia!
   Our salvation have procured.
   Alleluia!
   Now above the sky He's King,
   Alleluia!
   Where the angels ever sing.
   Alleluia!

4. Sing we to our God above,
   Alleluia!
   Praise eternal as His love:
   Alleluia!
   Praise Him, all ye heavenly host,
   Alleluia!
   Father, Son, and Holy Ghost.
   Alleluia!

This triumphant Easter hymn is based upon a Latin original, at least as to the theme and the first stanza. The Latin original, of which there are a number of texts dating from the fourteenth century upward, begins:

1. Surrexit Christus hodie
   Humano pro solamine,

2. Mortem qui passus pridie
   Miserrimo pro homine.

3. Mulieres, o tremulae,
   In Galilaeam pergite, etc.

Some texts have four, some six, and some eleven stanzas. The Latin author is unknown.

The English version of the hymn became popular in English circles by its appearance in the *Supplement* to the *New Version* of Brady and Tate, edition c. 1816. The first English translation appeared in 1708 in *Lyra Davidica*, etc., London (J. Walsh). It was in three stanzas, of which the first was substantially our first above. In Arnold's *Compleat Psalmodist*, 2d edition, 1749, the modern English version appeared. The first stanza of the first translation was slightly changed, and new Stanzas 2 and 3 were added. These are substantially as above. Then in Lord Selborne's *Book of Praise*, 1862, and Thring's *Collection*, 1882, the doxology, as above, was added.

The tune "Easter Hymn" is based on the melody in J. Walsh's *Lyra Davidica*, etc., 1708.

I Know that My Redeemer Lives   200

1. I know that my Redeemer lives;
   What comfort this sweet sentence gives!
   He lives, He lives, who once was dead;
   He lives, my ever-living Head.

2. He lives triumphant from the grave,
   He lives eternally to save,
   He lives all-glorious in the sky,
   He lives exalted there on high.

3. He lives to bless me with His love,
   He lives to plead for me above,
   He lives my hungry soul to feed,
   He lives to help in time of need.

4. He lives to grant me rich supply,
   He lives to guide me with His eye,
   He lives to comfort me when faint,
   He lives to hear my soul's complaint.

5. He lives to silence all my fears,
   He lives to wipe away my tears,
   He lives to calm my troubled heart,
   He lives all blessings to impart.

6. He lives, my kind, wise, heavenly Friend,
   He lives and loves me to the end;
   He lives, and while He lives, I'll sing;
   He lives, my Prophet, Priest, and King.

7. He lives and grants me daily breath;
   He lives, and I shall conquer death;
   He lives my mansion to prepare;
   He lives to bring me safely there.

8. He lives, all glory to His name!
   He lives, my Jesus, still the same.
   Oh, the sweet joy this sentence gives,
   "I know that my Redeemer lives!"

EASTER

This Easter hymn by Samuel Medley first appeared in G. Whitefield's *Psalms and Hymns,* 21st edition, 1775, in nine stanzas.

The tune "Duke Street" first appeared in *A Select Collection of Psalm and Hymn Tunes,* Glasgow, 1793. It was composed by John Hatton.

201   Jesus Lives! The Victory's Won

1. Jesus lives! The victory's won!
   Death no longer can appal me;
   Jesus lives! Death's reign is done!
   From the grave Christ will recall me.
   Brighter scenes will then commence;
   This shall be my confidence.

2. Jesus lives! To Him the throne
   High o'er heaven and earth is given.
   I shall go where He is gone,
   Live and reign with Him in heaven.
   God is faithful. Doubtings, hence!
   This shall be my confidence.

3. Jesus lives! For me He died,
   Hence will I, to Jesus living,
   Pure in heart and act abide,
   Praise to Him and glory giving.
   Freely God doth aid dispense;
   This shall be my confidence.

4. Jesus lives! I know full well
   Naught from me His love shall sever;
   Life nor death nor powers of hell
   Part me now from Christ forever.
   God will be a sure Defense;
   This shall be my confidence.

5. Jesus lives! and now is death
   But the gate of life immortal;
   This shall calm my trembling breath
   When I pass its gloomy portal.
   Faith shall cry, as fails each sense,
   Jesus is my confidence!

Jesus lebt, mit ihm auch ich;
Tod, wo sind nun deine Schrecken?
Jesus lebt und wird auch mich
Von den Toten auferwecken.
Er verklärt mich in sein Licht:
Dies ist meine Zuversicht.

Jesus lebt. Ihm ist das Reich
Über alle Welt gegeben.
Mit ihm werd' ich auch zugleich
Ewig herrschen, ewig leben.
Gott erfüllt, was er verspricht:
Dies ist meine Zuversicht.

Jesus lebt. Sein Heil ist mein:
Sein sei auch mein ganzes Leben;
Reines Herzens will ich sein
Und den Lüsten widerstreben.
Er verlässt den Schwachen nicht:
Dies ist meine Zuversicht.

Jesus lebt. Ich bin gewiss;
Nichts soll mich von Jesu scheiden,
Keine Macht der Finsternis,
Keine Herrlichkeit, kein Leiden.
Er gibt Kraft zu jeder Pflicht:
Dies ist meine Zuversicht.

Jesus lebt. Nun ist der Tod
Mir der Eingang in das Leben.
Welchen Trost in Todesnot
Wird er meiner Seele geben,
Wenn sie gläubig zu ihm spricht:
Herr, Herr, meine Zuversicht!

Christian Fuerchtegott Gellert first published this, one of his best hymns, in his *Geistliche Oden und Lieder,* Leipzig, 1757, in six stanzas. It is often used as a funeral hymn and as a hymn for the consecration of a graveyard.

The translation is by Frances E. Cox in her *Sacred Hymns from the German,* 1841, altered. The omitted Stanza 3 reads:

    Jesus lives! Who now despairs
      Spurns the word which God hath spoken;
    Grace to all that word declares,
      Grace whereby sin's yoke is broken.
    Christ rejects not penitence;
    This shall be my confidence.

For comments on the tune "Jesus, meine Zuversicht" see Hymn No. 206.

202   Welcome, Happy Morning!

1. "Welcome, happy morning!" Age to age shall say;
   "Hell today is vanquished, heaven is won today!"
   Lo, the Dead is living, God forevermore!
   Him, their true Creator, all His works adore.
   "Welcome, happy morning!" age to age shall say;
   "Hell today is vanquished, heaven is won today!"

2. Maker and Redeemer, Life and Health of all,
Thou from heaven beholding human nature's fall,
Of the Father's Godhead, true and only Son,
Manhood to deliver manhood didst put on.
"Welcome, happy morning!" age to age shall say;
"Hell today is vanquished, heaven is won today!"

3. Thou, of life the Author, death didst undergo,
Tread the path of darkness, saving strength to show.
Come, then, True and Faithful, now fulfil Thy word;
'Tis Thine own third morning — rise, O buried Lord!
"Welcome, happy morning!" age to age shall say;
"Hell today is vanquished, heaven is won today!"

4. Loose the souls long prisoned, bound with Satan's chain;
All that now is fallen raise to life again.
Show Thy face in brightness, bid the nations see;
Bring again our daylight; day returns with Thee.
"Welcome, happy morning!" age to age shall say;
"Hell today is vanquished, heaven is won today!"

This cento is composed of Stanzas 1 and 4 to 6 of John Ellerton's free translation in six stanzas of the Latin Easter hymn of Venantius Fortunatus. The original is a poem of 110 lines on our Lord's resurrection, beginning:

Tempora florigero rutilant distincta sereno.

The poem was addressed to Bishop Felix of Nantes in Brittany († 582). Ellerton's translation, dated 1868, was first published in Borthwick's *Supplementary Hymn and Tune Book*, 1869. The omitted Stanzas 2 and 3 read:

2. Earth with joy confesses, clothing her for spring,
All good gifts returned with her returning King.
Bloom in every meadow, leaves on every bough,
Speak His sorrows ended, hail His triumph now.

3. Months in due succession, days of lengthening light,
Hours and passing moments, praise Thee in their flight;
Brightness of the morning, sky and fields and sea,
Vanquisher of darkness, bring their praise to Thee.

The tune "Sei du mir gegrüsset" is from the *Enchiridion*, Lübeck, 1545.

Morning Breaks upon the Tomb 203

1. Morning breaks upon the tomb;
Jesus scatters all its gloom.
Day of triumph through the skies;
See the glorious Savior rise.

2. Ye who are of death afraid
Triumph in the scattered shade.
Drive your anxious cares away;
See the place where Jesus lay.

3. Christian, dry your flowing tears
Chase your unbelieving fears;
Look on His deserted grave,
Doubt no more His power to save.

This hymn by William B. Collyer was first published in his *Hymns, Partly Collected*, etc., 1812, in four stanzas, entitled "Jesus Rising — An Easter Hymn." In our version Stanzas 2 and 3 are inverted.

The omitted stanza reads:

So the rising sun appears,
Shedding radiance o'er the spheres;
So returning beams of light
Chase the terrors of the night.

For comments on the tune "Innocents" see Hymn No. 35.

EASTER

204   Come, Ye Faithful, Raise the Strain

1. Come, ye faithful, raise the strain
   Of triumphant gladness;
   God hath brought His Israel
   Into joy from sadness.
   'Tis the spring of souls today:
   Christ hath burst His prison
   And from three days' sleep in death
   As a sun hath risen.

2. All the winter of our sins,
   Long and dark, is flying
   From His light, to whom we give
   Laud and praise undying.
   Neither could the gates of death
   Nor the tomb's dark portal
   Nor the watchers nor the seal
   Hold Thee as a mortal.

3. But today amidst Thine own
   Thou didst stand, bestowing
   That Thy peace which evermore
   Passeth human knowing.
   Come, ye faithful, raise the strain
   Of triumphant gladness;
   God hath brought His Israel
   Into joy from sadness.

Αἴσωμεν, πάντες λαοί,
τῷ ἐκ πικρᾶς δουλείας
Φαραὼ τὸν Ἰσραὴλ ἀπαλλάξαντι
καὶ ἐν βυθῷ θαλάσσης
ποδὶ ἀβρόχως ὁδηγήσαντι
ᾠδὴν ἐπινίκιον,
ὅτι δεδόξασται.

Σήμερον ἔαρ ψυχῶν,
ὅτι Χριστὸς ἐκ τάφου,
ὥσπερ ἥλιος, ἐκλάμψας τριήμερος
τὸν ζοφερὸν χειμῶνα
ἀπήλασε τῆς ἁμαρτίας ἡμῶν,
αὐτὸν ἀνυμνήσωμεν,
ὅτι δεδόξασται.

Ἡ βασιλὶς τῶν ὡρῶν
τῇ λαμπροφόρῳ ἡμέρᾳ
ἡμερῶν τε βασιλίδι φανότατα
δωροφοροῦσα, τέρπει
τὸν ἔγκριτον τῆς ἐκκλησίας λαόν,
ἀπαύστως ἀνυμνοῦσα
τὸν ἀναστάτα Χριστόν.

Πύλαι θανάτου, Χριστέ,
οὐδὲ τοῦ τάφου σφραγῖδες,
οὐδὲ κλεῖθρα τῶν θυρῶν Σοι ἀντέστησαν,
ἀλλ' ἀναστὰς ἐπέστης
τοῖς φίλοις σου εἰρήνην, Δέσποτα,
δωρούμενος τὴν πάντα
νοῦν ὑπερέχουσαν.

This hymn by John of Damascus was written about the middle of the eighth century. It is based on the Song of Moses, Ex. 15. The translation is an altered form of that by John M. Neale in the *Christian Remembrances*, 1859. Neale's original is as follows:

1. Come, ye faithful, raise the strain
   Of triumphant gladness!
   God hath brought His Israel
   Into joy from sadness:
   Loosed from Pharaoh's bitter yoke
   Jacob's sons and daughters,
   Led them with unmoistened foot
   Through the Red Sea waters.

2. 'Tis the spring of souls today:
   Christ hath burst His prison
   And from three days' sleep in death
   As a sun hath risen.
   All the winter of our sins,
   Long and dark, is flying
   From His light, to whom we give
   Laud and praise undying.

3. Now the queen of seasons, bright
   With the day of splendor,
   With the royal feast of feasts,
   Comes its joy to render;
   Comes to glad Jerusalem,
   Who with true affection
   Welcomes in unwearied strains
   Jesus' resurrection.

4. Neither might the gates of death
   Nor the tomb's dark portal
   Nor the watchers nor the seal
   Hold Thee as a mortal;
   But today amidst the Twelve
   Thou didst stand, bestowing
   That Thy peace which evermore
   Passeth human knowing.

The tune "Schwing dich auf" is from *Geistliche Andachten*, Berlin, 1666, by Johann Georg Ebeling, where it was set to Paul Gerhardt's hymn of comfort "Schwing dich auf zu deinem Gott."

205   The Day of Resurrection

1. The day of resurrection,
   Earth, tell it out abroad,
   The Passover of gladness,
   The Passover of God.
   From death to life eternal,
   From this world to the sky,
   Our Christ hath brought us over
   With hymns of victory.

Ἀναστάσεως ἡμέρα,
λαμπρυνθῶμεν λαοί.
Πάσχα Κυρίου, πάσχα.
Ἐκ γὰρ θανάτου πρὸς ζωήν,
καὶ ἐκ γῆς πρὸς οὐρανόν,
Χριστὸς ὁ θεὸς
ἡμᾶς διεβίβασεν,
ἐπινίκιον ᾄδοντας.

[154]

EASTER

2. Our hearts be pure from evil
   That we may see aright
The Lord in rays eternal
   Of resurrection light
And, listening to His accents,
   May hear, so calm and plain,
His own "All hail!" and, hearing,
   May raise the victor strain.

3. Now let the heavens be joyful,
   Let earth her song begin,
Let all the world keep triumph
   And all that is therein.
Let all things, seen and unseen,
   Their notes of gladness blend;
For Christ the Lord hath risen, —
   Our joy, that hath no end.

Καθαρθῶμεν τὰς αἰσθήσεις,
καὶ ὀψόμεθα
τῷ ἀπροσίτῳ θωτὶ
τῆς ἀναστάσεως Χριστὸν
ἐξαστράπτοντα, καὶ
»Χαίρετε« φάσκοντος
τρανῶς ἀκουσόμεθα,
ἐπινίκιον ᾄδοντες.

Οὐρανοὶ μὲν ἐπαξίως
εὐφραινέσθωσαν,
γῆ δὲ ἀγαλλιάσθω·
ἑορταζέτω δὲ κόσμος
ὁρατός τε ἅπας
καὶ ἀόρατος,
Χριστὸς γὰρ ἐγήγερται,
εὐφροσύνη αἰώνιος.

This hymn by John of Damascus is part of the Golden Canon for Easter Day. It forms the first of the eight odes that make up this canon. It has been called "the grandest piece in Greek sacred poetry." It was written about the middle of the eighth century. The translation is an altered form of that by John M. Neale in his *Hymns of the Eastern Church*, 1862, beginning " 'Tis the day of resurrection." It was first published as a hymn for congregational use in the *Parish Hymn Book*, 1863, beginning "The Day of Resurrection."

The tune "Lancashire" (one of a number of tunes by that name) is by Henry Smart and was composed in 1836 for Heber's hymn "From Greenland's Icy Mountains." It first appeared in *Psalms and Hymns for Divine Worship*, 1867.

Jesus Christ, My Sure Defense   206

1. Jesus Christ, my sure Defense
   And my Savior, ever liveth;
Knowing this, my confidence
   Rests upon the hope it giveth
Though the night of death be fraught
Still with many an anxious thought.

2. Jesus, my Redeemer, lives;
   I, too, unto life shall waken.
Endless joy my Savior gives;
   Shall my courage, then, be shaken?
Shall I fear, or could the Head
Rise and leave His members dead?

3. Nay, too closely am I bound
   Unto Him by hope forever;
Faith's strong hand the Rock hath found,
   Grasped it, and will leave it never;
Even death now cannot part
From its Lord the trusting heart.

4. I am flesh and must return
   Unto dust, whence I am taken;
But by faith I now discern
   That from death I shall awaken
With my Savior to abide
In His glory, at His side.

5. Glorified, I shall anew
   With this flesh then be enshrouded;
In this body I shall view
   God, my Lord, with eyes unclouded;
In this flesh I then shall see
Jesus Christ eternally.

Jesus, meine Zuversicht
   Und mein Heiland, ist im Leben;
Dieses weiss ich, sollt' ich nicht
   Darum mich zufrieden geben,
Was die lange Todesnacht
Mir auch für Gedanken macht?

Jesus, er, mein Heiland, lebt;
   Ich werd' auch das Leben schauen,
Sein, wo mein Erlöser schwebt;
   Warum sollte mir denn grauen?
Lässet auch ein Haupt sein Glied,
Welches es nicht nach sich zieht?

Ich bin durch der Hoffnung Band
   Zu genau mit ihm verbunden;
Meine starke Glaubenshand
   Wird in ihn gelegt befunden,
Dass mich auch kein Todesbann
Ewig von ihm trennen kann.

Ich bin Fleisch und muss daher
   Auch einmal zu Asche werden;
Das gesteh' ich, doch wird er
   Mich erwecken aus der Erden,
Dass ich in der Herrlichkeit
Um ihn sein mög' allezeit.

Dann wird eben diese Haut
   Mich umgeben, wie ich gläube,
Gott wird werden angeschaut
   Dann von mir in diesem Leibe,
Und in diesem Fleisch werd' ich
Jesum sehen **ewiglich**.

EASTER

6. Then these eyes my Lord shall know,
   My Redeemer and my Brother;
   In His love my soul shall glow, —
   I myself, and not another!
   Then the weakness I feel here
   Shall forever disappear.

Dieser meiner Augen Licht
   Wird ihn, meinen Heiland, kennen;
   Ich, ich selbst, kein Fremder nicht,
   Werd' in seiner Liebe brennen;
   Nur die Schwachheit um und an
   Wird von mir sein abgetan.

7. They who sorrow here and moan
   There in gladness shall be reigning;
   Earthly here the seed is sown,
   There immortal life attaining.
   Here our sinful bodies die,
   Glorified to dwell on high.

Was hier kranket, seufzt und fleht,
   Wird dort frisch und herrlich gehen;
   Irdisch werd' ich ausgesät,
   Himmlisch werd' ich auferstehen;
   Hier geh' ich natürlich ein,
   Nachmals werd' ich geistlich sein.

8. Then take comfort and rejoice,
   For His members Christ will cherish.
   Fear not, they will hear His voice;
   Dying, they shall never perish;
   For the very grave is stirred
   When the trumpet's blast is heard.

Seid getrost und hocherfreut,
   Jesus trägt euch, meine Glieder!
   Gebt nicht Raum der Traurigkeit!
   Sterbt ihr, Christus ruft euch wider,
   Wenn die letzt' Drommet' erklingt,
   Die auch durch die Gräber dringt.

9. Laugh to scorn the gloomy grave
   And at death no longer tremble;
   He, the Lord, who came to save
   Will at last His own assemble.
   They will go their Lord to meet,
   Treading death beneath their feet.

Lacht der finstern Erdenkluft,
   Lacht des Todes und der Höllen;
   Denn ihr sollt euch durch die Luft
   Eurem Heiland zugesellen!
   Dann wird Schwachheit und Verdruss
   Liegen unter eurem Fuss.

10. Oh, then, draw away your hearts
    Now from pleasures base and hollow.
    There to share what He imparts,
    Here His footsteps ye must follow.
    Fix your hearts beyond the skies,
    Whither ye yourselves would rise.

Nur dass ihr den Geist erhebt
   Von den Lüsten dieser Erden
   Und euch dem schon jetzt ergebt,
   Dem ihr beigefügt wollt werden
   Schick das Herze da hinein,
   Wo ihr ewig wünscht zu sein!

This splendid Easter hymn, based on 1 Cor. 15:35 ff. and Job 19:25-27, is attributed to Louise Henrietta, Electress of Brandenburg; but there is no certain proof that she wrote any hymns. The hymn first appeared anonymously in the Crüger-Runge *Gesangbuch,* Berlin, 1653, together with the tune. Rambach calls the hymn "an acknowledged masterpiece of Christian poetry," and C. von Winterfeld states, "it will ever remain a treasure."

The translation is based on that of Catherine Winkworth in her *Chorale Book for England,* 1863.

The tune "Jesus, meine Zuversicht" is also by an unknown composer. It may be based on an older melody, which Johann Crüger recast to be used with this text, and it may be an original composition, perhaps by Crüger himself. At any rate, it stands as a pearl among our *chorale* tunes. The tune appeared for the first time in *Geistliche Lieder und Psalmen* (Runge), Berlin, 1653.

207 Like the Golden Sun Ascending

1. Like the golden sun ascending,
   Breaking through the gloom of night,
   On the earth his glory spending
   So that darkness takes to flight,
   Thus my Jesus from the grave
   And Death's dismal, dreadful cave
   Rose triumphant Easter morning
   At the early purple dawning.

Som den gyldne Sol frembryder
   Gjennem den kulsorte Sky,
   Og sin Straaleglans udstyder,
   Saa at Mörk og Mulm maa fly,
   Saa min Jesus af sin Grav
   Og der dybe Dödsens Hav
   Opstod ärefuld af Döde
   Imod Paaske Morgenröde.

2. Thanks to Thee, O Christ victorious!
   Thanks to Thee, O Lord of Life!
   Death hath now no power o'er us,
   Thou hast conquered in the strife.
   Thanks because Thou didst arise
   And hast opened Paradise!
   None can fully sing the glory
   Of the resurrection story.

Tak, o store Seierherre,
   Tak, o Livsens Himmel-Helt,
   Som ei Döden kunde sperre
   I det helvedmörke Telt!
   Tak, fordi at du opstod,
   Og sik Döden under Fod!
   Ingen Tunge kan den Gäde
   Med tilhörlig Lov udkvöde.

3. Though I be by sin o'ertaken,
   Though I lie in helplessness,
   Though I be by friends forsaken
   And must suffer sore distress,
   Though I be despised, contemned,
   And by all the world condemned,
   Though the dark grave yawn before me,
   Yet the light of hope shines o'er me.

4. Thou hast died for my transgression,
   All my sins on Thee were laid;
   Thou hast won for me salvation,
   On the cross my debt was paid.
   From the grave I shall arise
   And shall meet Thee in the skies.
   Death itself is transitory;
   I shall lift my head in glory.

5. Grant me grace, O blessed Savior,
   And Thy Holy Spirit send
   That my walk and my behavior
   May be pleasing to the end;
   That I may not fall again
   Into death's grim pit and pain,
   Whence by grace Thou hast retrieved me
   And from which Thou hast relieved me.

6. For the joy Thy advent gave me,
   For Thy holy, precious Word;
   For Thy Baptism, which doth save me,
   For Thy blest Communion board;
   For Thy death, the bitter scorn,
   For Thy resurrection morn,
   Lord, I thank Thee and extol Thee,
   And in heaven I shall behold Thee.

Ligger jeg i Syndens Veie,
   Ligger jeg i Armod ned,
Ligger jeg i Sygdoms Leie,
   Ligger jeg i Uselhed,
Ligger jeg forträngt, forhadt
Og af Verden slet forladt,
Skal jeg Hus i Graven tage,
O, her er dog Haab tilbage!

Du for Synden een Gang döde,
   Dermed er min Synd betalt,
Armod, Uselhed og Möde,
   Ja min Sygdom bar du alt.
Jeg ved dig opreises skal,
Og af Dödsens dybe Dal
Skal jeg Hovedet oprette,
Al min Nöd kan det forlette.

Söde Jesu, giv mig Naade
   Ved din gode Helligaand,
At jeg saa min Gang kan raade,
   Og veiledes ved din Haand,
At jeg ei skal falde hen
Udi Dödsens Svelg igjen,
Hvoraf du mig engang rykte,
Der du Döden undertrykte!

Tak for al din Födsels Gläde,
   Tak for dit det Guddoms Ord,
Tak for Daabens hellig' Väde,
   Tak for Naaden paa dit Bord,
Tak for Dödsens bitre Ve,
Tak for din Opstandelse,
Tak for Himlen, du har inde,
Der skal jeg dig se og finde!

This cento is composed of Stanzas 1, 2, 4, 5, 9, and 10 of Thomas Kingo's classic hymn for Easter. The hymn was first published in *En Ny Kirke-Psalmebog* (Vinterparten), 1689. It was later included in Kingo's *Salmebog*, with slight alterations. The omitted stanzas read:

3. For my heart finds consolation,
   And my fainting soul grows brave,
   When I stand in contemplation
   At Thy dark and dismal grave;
   When I see where Thou didst sleep
   In death's dungeon dark and deep,
   Yet didst break all bands asunder,
   Must I not rejoice and wonder?

6. Satan's arrows all lie broken,
   Death and hell have met their doom;
   Christ, Thy rising is the token:
   Thou hast triumphed o'er the tomb;
   Thou hast buried all my woe,
   And my cup doth overflow;
   By Thy resurrection glorious
   I shall wave my palms victorious.

7. As the Son of God I know Thee,
   For I see Thy sovereign power;
   Sin and death shall not o'erthrow me
   Even in my dying hour;
   For Thy resurrection is
   Surety for my heavenly bliss,
   And my baptism a reflection
   Of Thy death and resurrection.

8. Unto life Thou shalt arouse me
   By Thy resurrection's power;
   Though the hideous grave shall house me
   And my flesh the worms devour;
   Fire and water may destroy
   My frail body, yet with joy
   I shall rise as Thou hast risen
   From the deep sepulchral prison.

The translation is by George T. Rygh, 1908, and was included in *The Lutheran Hymnary*, 1913.

The tune "Werde munter" is by Johann Schop and appeared in *Das Dritte Zehn*, Lüneburg, 1642, set to Johann Rist's evening hymn "Werde munter, mein Gemüte."

Ye Sons and Daughters of the King — 208

1. Ye sons and daughters of the King,
   Whom heavenly hosts in glory sing;
   Today the grave hath lost its sting:
      Alleluia!

2. On that first morning of the week,
   Before the day began to break,
   The Marys went their Lord to seek:
      Alleluia!

O filii et filiae,
Rex caelestis, Rex gloriae,
Morte revixit hodie.
   Alleluia!

Et Maria Magdalene
Et Iacobi et Salome
Venerunt corpus ungere.
   Alleluia!

EASTER

3. An angel bade their sorrow flee,
For thus he spake unto the three:
"Your Lord is gone to Galilee":
Alleluia!

In albis sedens angelus
Praedixit mulieribus,
"In Galilaea est Dominus."
Alleluia!

4. That night the Apostles met in fear,
Amidst them came their Lord most dear
And said: "Peace be unto you here":
Alleluia!

Discipulis adstantibus
In medio stetit Christus,
Dicens, "Pax vobis omnibus."
Alleluia!

5. When Thomas afterwards had heard
That Jesus had fulfilled His word,
He doubted if it were the Lord:
Alleluia!

Postquam audivit Didymus
Quia surrexerat Iesus,
Remansit fide dubius.
Alleluia!

6. "Thomas, behold My side," saith He,
"My hands, My feet, My body, see;
"And doubt not, but believe in Me":
Alleluia!

"Vide, Thoma, vide latus,
Vide pedes, vide manus;
Noli esse incredulus."
Alleluia!

7. No longer Thomas then denied;
He saw the feet, the hands, the side;
"Thou art my Lord and God," he cried:
Alleluia!

Quando Thomas vidit Christum,
Pedes, latus suum, manus,
Dixit, "Tu es Deus meus."
Alleluia!

8. Blessed are they that have not seen
And yet whose faith hath constant been,
In life eternal they shall reign:
Alleluia!

Beati, qui non viderunt
Et firmiter crediderunt;
Vitam aeternam habebunt.
Alleluia!

9. On this most holy day of days
To God your hearts and voices raise
In laud and jubilee and praise:
Alleluia!

In hoc festo sanctissimo
Sit laus et iubilatio:
Benedicamus Domino.
Alleluia!

10. And we with holy Church unite,
As evermore is just and right,
In glory to the King of light:
Alleluia!

Ex quibus nos humillimas,
Devotas atque debitas
Deo dicamus gratias.
Alleluia!

There is still some uncertainty as to the authorship of this hymn. *Julian* dates it not earlier than the 17th century. The earliest known text is in the *Office de la Semaine Sainte,* Paris, 1674. The historical edition of *Hymns Ancient and Modern* attributes some of the stanzas to Jean Tisserand, a Franciscan friar, who died in Paris 1494 and whose verses were published in a booklet between 1518 and 1536.

The translation is by John M. Neale in his *Medieval Hymns,* 1851.

The tune "Gelobt sei Gott," also called "Vulpius," is by Melchior Vulpius and appeared in his *Ein schön geistlich Gesangbuch,* etc., Jena, 1609, where it was set to Michael Weisse's hymn "Gelobt sei Gott im höchsten Thron."

209 Who Is This that Comes from Edom

1. Who is this that comes from Edom,
All His raiment stained with blood;
To the captive speaking freedom,
Bringing and bestowing good;
Glorious in the garb He wears,
Glorious in the spoil He bears?

2. 'Tis the Savior, now victorious,
Traveling onward in His might;
'Tis the Savior; oh, how glorious
To His people is the sight!
Satan conquered and the grave,
Jesus now is strong to save.

3. Why that blood His raiment staining?
'Tis the blood of many slain;
Of His foes there's none remaining,
None the contest to maintain.
Fall'n they are, no more to rise;
All their glory prostrate lies.

4. Mighty Victor, reign forever,
Wear the crown so dearly won;
Never shall Thy people, never,
Cease to sing what Thou hast done.
Thou hast fought Thy people's foes;
Thou hast healed Thy people's woes.

This hymn by Thomas Kelly first appeared in his *Hymns,* etc., third edition, 1809. It was intended for use on Ascension Day.

For comments on the tune "Neander" see Hymn No. 1.

EASTER

The Strife Is O'er, the Battle Done 210

1. Alleluia! Alleluia! Alleluia!
   The strife is o'er, the battle done;
   Now is the Victor's triumph won;
   Now be the song of praise begun.
   Alleluia!

2. Death's mightiest powers have done their worst,
   And Jesus hath His foes dispersed;
   Let shouts of praise and joy outburst.
   Alleluia!

3. On the third morn He rose again
   Glorious in majesty to reign;
   Oh, let us swell the joyful strain!
   Alleluia!

4. He closed the yawning gates of hell;
   The bars from heaven's high portals fell.
   Let songs of praise His triumph tell.
   Alleluia!

5. Lord, by the stripes which wounded Thee,
   From death's dread sting Thy servants free
   That we may live and sing to Thee.
   Alleluia!

Alleluia, Alleluia, Alleluia.
Finita iam sunt praelia,
Est parta iam victoria;
Gaudeamus et canamus:
Alleluia!

Post fata mortis barbara
Devicit Iesus tartara;
Applaudamus et psallamus:
Alleluia!

Surrexit die tertia
Caelesti clarus gratia
Insonemus et cantemus:
Alleluia!

Sunt clausa stygis ostia,
Et caeli patent atria;
Gaudeamus et canamus:
Alleluia!

Per tua, Iesu, vulnera
Nos mala morte libera,
Ut vivamus et canamus:
Alleluia! Amen.

This hymn has not been traced back farther than the Jesuit *Symphonia Sirenum, Cologne,* 1695. The translation is an altered form of that by Francis Pott, c. 1859, and was included in his *Hymns Fitted to the Order of Common Prayer,* 1861.

The tune "Palestrina," also called "Victory," is an adaptation by William H. Monk from the "Gloria" of Palestrina's *Magnificat Tertii Toni,* 1591.

Lo! Judah's Lion Wins the Strife 211

1. Lo, Judah's Lion wins the strife
   And reigns o'er death to give us life.
   Hallelujah!
   Oh, let us sing His praises!

2. 'Tis He whom David did portray
   When he did strong Goliath slay.
   Hallelujah!
   Oh, sing with gladsome voices!

3. Like Samson, Christ great strength employed
   And conquered hell, its gates destroyed.
   Hallelujah!
   Oh, let us sing His praises!

4. The power of death He brake in twain
   When He to life arose again.
   Hallelujah!
   To Him all praise be given!

5. He led to freedom all oppressed
   And pardon won for sin-distressed.
   Hallelujah!
   Oh, praise Him for His mercy!

6. In festal spirit, song, and word
   To Jesus, our victorious Lord,
   Hallelujah!
   All praise and thanks be rendered.

7. All honor, glory, praise, be given
   Our Triune God, who reigns in heaven.
   Hallelujah!
   Now gladly sing we: Amen.

Aj, ten silný lev udatný
Kristus vstal z mrtvých, Pán milý:
Hallelujah, vesele sezpívejme!

Kteréhožto ruku silnou
David znamenal udatnou.
Hallelujah, rcemež všickni vesele!

On obra toho silného
Přemoh', vzav loupeže jeho:
Hallelujah, buď Jemu z toho chvála!

Sprostil nás jeho trápení,
Odňal od nás pohanění;
Hallelujah, smiloval se nad námi.

Tot jest Samson přeudatný,
Jenž pobral pekelné brány;
Hallelujah, všickni spolu spívejme!

V těchto hodech převeselých,
Slavného Vítězitele;
Hallelujah, písně Jemu zpívejme!

Pochvalmež Svatou Trojici,
Boha nerozdílné moci:
Hallelujah, rcemež: Amen! vesele.

ASCENSION

This hymn is a cento from the Bohemian. It is of unknown authorship. It appeared in a publication printed at Trencin by Nykodem Czjzka, 1660. It was received into the *Tranoscius*, edition 1727. The cento omits Stanzas 6 to 8 of the original.

The translation was prepared for *The Lutheran Hymnal* by John Bajus in 1940. It inverts the order of the stanzas as they are in the original thus: Stanzas 2, 3, and 4 are Stanzas 3, 4, and 5 in English; Stanza 5 is Stanza 2 in English.

The tune "Judah's Lion" is from a Bohemian melody, c. 1600. It appeared in Skultely's *Tune Book*, 1798. It was given its name "Judah's Lion" for *The Lutheran Hymnal*.

212   A Hymn of Glory Let Us Sing

1. A hymn of glory let us sing;
New songs throughout the world shall ring:
Christ, by a road before untrod,
Ascendeth to the throne of God.

2. The holy apostolic band
Upon the Mount of Olives stand;
And with His followers they see
Jesus' resplendent majesty.

3. To whom the angels, drawing nigh,
"Why stand and gaze upon the sky?
This is the Savior!" thus they say;
"This is His noble triumph-day."

4. "Again shall ye behold Him so
As ye today have seen Him go,
In glorious pomp ascending high,
Up to the portals of the sky."

5. Oh, grant us thitherward to tend
And with unwearied hearts ascend
Unto Thy kingdom's throne, where Thou,
As is our faith, art seated now.

6. Be Thou our Joy and strong Defense
Who art our future Recompense:
So shall the light that springs from Thee
Be ours through all eternity.

7. O risen Christ, ascended Lord,
All praise to Thee let earth accord,
Who art, while endless ages run,
With Father and with Spirit One.

This Latin hymn is attributed to the Venerable Bede. It is found in no MSS. earlier than the eleventh century. The original is in eleven four-line stanzas, and its opening line is "Hymnum canamus Domino." One manuscript has "Hymnum canamus gloriae." It is the latter text upon which the translation is based.

The translation is by Benjamin Webb and first appeared in the *Hymnal Noted*, 1854.

For comments on the tune "Lasst uns erfreuen" see Hymn No. 15.

213   Hail the Day that Sees Him Rise

1. Hail the day that sees Him rise
To His throne above the skies!
Christ, the Lamb for sinners given,
Reascends His native heaven.

2. There the glorious triumph waits:
Lift your heads, eternal gates.
He hath conquered death and sin;
Take the King of Glory in!

3. See, the heaven its Lord receives,
Yet He loves the earth He leaves;
Though returning to His throne,
Still He calls mankind His own.

4. See, He lifts His hands above;
See, He shows the prints of love.
Hark! His gracious lips bestow
Blessings on His Church below.

5. Still for us He intercedes;
His prevailing death He pleads,
Near Himself prepares our place,
Harbinger of human race.

6. There we shall with Thee remain
Partners of Thy endless reign,
There Thy face unclouded see,
Find our heaven of heavens in Thee.

Charles Wesley first published this hymn in *Hymns and Sacred Poems*, 1739, in ten stanzas. The cento includes Stanzas 1, 2, 4, 5, 6, and 10. The omitted stanzas read:

[160]

ASCENSION

3. Circles round with angel powers,
Their triumphant Lord and ours,
Conqueror over death and sin;
Take the King of Glory in!

7. Master (will we ever say),
Taken from our head today,
See Thy faithful servants, see,
Ever gazing up to Thee.

8. Grant, though parted from our sight
High above yon azure height,
Grant our hearts may thither rise,
Following Thee beyond the skies.

9. Ever upward let us move,
Wafted on the wings of love;
Looking when our Lord shall come,
Longing, gasping, after home.

For comments on the tune "Orientis partibus" see Hymn No. 193.

Lo, God to Heaven Ascendeth   214

1. Lo, God to heaven ascendeth!
   Throughout its regions vast
With shouts triumphant blendeth
   The trumpet's thrilling blast:
Sing praise to Christ the Lord;
   Sing praise with exultation,
   King of each heathen nation,
The God of hosts adored!

2. With joy is heaven resounding
   Christ's glad return to see;
Behold the saints surrounding
   The Lord who set them free.
Bright myriads, thronging, come;
   The cherub band rejoices,
   And loud seraphic voices
All welcome Jesus home.

3. From cross to throne ascending,
   We follow Christ on high
And know the pathway wending
   To mansions in the sky.
Our Lord is gone before;
   Yet here He will not leave us,
   But soon in heaven receive us
And open wide the door.

4. Our place He is preparing;
   To heaven we, too, shall rise,
With Him His glory sharing,
   Be where our Treasure lies.
Bestir thyself, my soul!
   Where Jesus Christ has entered,
   There let thy hope be centered;
Press onward toward the goal.

5. Let all our thoughts be winging
   To where Thou didst ascend,
And let our hearts be singing:
   "We seek Thee, Christ, our Friend,
Thee, God's exalted Son,
   Our Life, and Way to heaven,
   To whom all power is given,
Our Joy and Hope and Crown."

Gott fähret auf gen Himmel
   Mit frohem Jubelschall,
Mit prächtigem Getümmel
   Und mit Posaunenhall.
Lobsingt, lobsinget Gott!
   Lobsingt, lobsingt mit Freuden
   Dem Könige der Heiden,
Dem Herren Zebaoth!

Der Herr wird aufgenommen,
   Der ganze Himmel lacht;
Um ihn gehn alle Frommen,
   Die er hat freigemacht.
Es holen Jesum ein
   Die lautern Cherubinen,
   Den hellen Seraphinen,
Muss er willkommen sein.

Wir wissen nun die Stiege,
   Die unser Haupt erhöht;
Wir wissen zur Genüge,
   Wie man zum Himmel geht.
Der Heiland geht voran,
   Will uns nicht nach sich lassen,
   Er zeiget uns die Strassen,
Er bricht uns sichre Bahn.

Wir sollen himmlisch werden,
   Der Herre macht uns Platz.
Wir gehen von der Erden
   Dorthin, wo unser Schatz.
Ihr Herzen, macht euch auf!
   Wo Jesus hingegangen,
   Dahin sei das Verlangen,
Dahin sei euer Lauf!

Lasst uns gen Himmel springen
   Mit herzlicher Begier,
Lasst uns zugleich auch singen:
   Dich, Jesu, suchen wir,
Dich, o du Gottessohn,
   Dich Weg, dich wahres Leben,
   Dem alle Macht gegeben,
Dich, unsers Hauptes Kron'!

This hymn, by Gottfried W. Sacer, founded on Ps. 47:5-7, appeared in seven stanzas in *Ander Theil des erneuerten Gesang-Buchs*, Stralsund, 1665. It had been included, in 1661, in an anonymous collection of poems, which he had written between 1659 and 1660 during his stay at Greifswald.

The translation is an altered form of that by Frances E. Cox in her *Sacred Hymns from the German*, 1841. The omitted stanzas are:

6. Farewell with all thy treasures,
   O world, to falsehood given!
Thy dross gives no true pleasures;
   We seek the joys of heaven.
The Savior is our Prize;
   He comforts us in sadness
   And fills our hearts with gladness;
To Him we lift our eyes.

7. When, on our vision dawning,
   Will break the wished-for hour
Of that all-glorious morning
   When Christ shall come with power?
Oh, come, thou welcome day,
   When we, our Savior meeting,
   His second advent greeting,
Shall hail the Heaven-sent ray.

For comments on the tune "Aus meines Herzens Grunde" see Hymn No. 69.

ASCENSION

215   Draw Us to Thee

1. Draw us to Thee,
For then shall we
   Walk in Thy steps forever
And hasten on
Where Thou art gone
   To be with Thee, dear Savior.

2. Draw us to Thee,
Lord, lovingly;
   Let us depart with gladness
That we may be
Forever free
   From sorrow, grief, and sadness.

3. Draw us to Thee;
Oh, grant that we
   May walk the road to heaven!
Direct our way
Lest we should stray
   And from Thy paths be driven.

4. Draw us to Thee
That also we
   Thy heavenly bliss inherit
And ever dwell
Where sin and hell
   No more can vex our spirit.

5. Draw us to Thee
Unceasingly,
   Into Thy kingdom take us;
Let us fore'er
Thy glory share,
   Thy saints and joint heirs make us.

Zeuch uns nach dir,
So laufen wir
   Mit herzlichem Verlangen
Hin, da du bist,
O Jesu Christ,
   Aus dieser Welt gegangen.

Zeuch uns nach dir
In Liebsbegier,
   Ach reiss uns doch von hinnen,
So dürfen wir
Nicht länger hier
   Den Kummerfaden spinnen.

Zeuch uns nach dir,
Herr Christ, ach führ
   Uns deine Himmelsstege!
Wir irr'n sonst leicht
Und sind verscheucht
   Vom rechten Lebenswege.

Zeuch uns nach dir,
So folgen wir
   Dir nach in deinen Himmel,
Dass uns nicht mehr
Allhier beschwer'
   Das böse Weltgetümmel.

Zeuch uns nach dir
Nur für und für
   Und gib, dass wir nachfahren
Dir in dein Reich,
Und mach uns gleich
   Den auserwählten Scharen!

Friedrich Funcke first published this hymn in the *Lüneburg Stadt Gesang Buch*, 1686. It is based on Solomon's Song 1:4.

The translation is by August Crull.

The tune "Ach Gott und Herr" is from Christoph Peter's *Andachts-Zymbeln*, Freyberg, 1655, where it was set to Martin Rutilius's hymn "Ach Gott und Herr." (See Hymn No. 317.)

216   On Christ's Ascension I Now Build

1. On Christ's ascension I now build
The hope of my ascension;
   This hope alone has ever stilled
   All doubt and apprehension;
For where the Head is, there full well
I know His members are to dwell
   When Christ shall come and call them.

2. Since He returned to claim His throne,
Great gifts for men obtaining,
   My heart shall rest in Him alone,
   No other rest remaining;
For where my Treasure went before,
There all my thoughts shall ever soar
   To still their deepest yearning.

3. Oh, grant, dear Lord, this grace to me,
Recalling Thine ascension,
   That I may ever walk with Thee,
   Adorning Thy redemption;
And then, when all my days shall cease,
Let me depart in joy and peace
   In answer to my pleading.

Auf Christi Himmelfahrt allein
Ich meine Nachfahrt gründe
   Und allen Zweifel, Angst und Pein
   Hiermit stets überwinde;
Denn weil das Haupt im Himmel ist,
Wird seine Glieder Jesus Christ
   Zur rechten Zeit nachholen.

Weil er gezogen himmelan
Und grosse Gab' empfangen,
   Mein Herz auch nur im Himmel kann,
   Sonst nirgend Ruh' erlangen;
Denn wo mein Schatz ist kommen hin,
Da ist auch stets mein Herz und Sinn,
   Nach ihm mich sehr verlanget.

Ach Herr, lass diese Gnade mich
Von deiner Auffahrt spüren,
   Dass mit dem wahren Glauben ich
   Mög' meine Nachfahrt zieren
Und dann einmal, wenn dir's gefällt,
Mit Freuden scheiden aus der Welt.
   Herr, höre doch mein Flehen!

ASCENSION

Josua Wegelin first published this hymn in his *Augspurger Bet Büchlein*, Nürnberg, 1636. Its original German form differed from that in common use since it was recast for the Lüneburg *Gesang Buch*, 1661, probably by its compiler, Ernst Sonnemann. Wegelin's first line read: "Allein auf Christi Himmelfahrt."

The translation by William M. Czamanske was prepared for *The Lutheran Hymnal* in 1938.

For comments on the tune "Nun freut euch" see Hymn No. 387.

Oh, Sing with Exultation — 217

1. Oh, sing with exultation,
   Sing to the Lord, rejoice,
   And in His congregation
   Shout with triumphant voice.
   For, lo, at God's right hand
   Is Christ in glory seated;
   With death and hell defeated,
   As Victor doth command.

2. Since Christ, our Lord, is living,
   We nevermore shall die;
   To God the glory giving,
   We rise to Him on high.
   Though chastened we may be
   And to our graves be taken,
   We unto life shall waken
   And live eternally.

3. Christ is the sure Foundation
   The builders did reject,
   But He for our salvation
   Is precious and elect
   And made the Corner-stone
   On which the Church is founded;
   This marvel now is sounded,
   The work of God alone.

4. To Thee, O Christ, be glory,
   Who camest in His name!
   Thy people sing the story
   Thy praises to proclaim.
   We thank Thee and adore,
   O Christ, our Lord and Savior;
   Thy grace and boundless favor
   Stand fast forevermore.

Om Salighed og Gläde
  Der nu skal synges fridt
I de forlöstes Säde
  Og guds Paulaner vidt,
Thi ved Guds höire Haand
  Er Kristus höit ophöiet,
  Ham Seier stor tilföiet,
Han Döden overvandt.

Mens han er saa i Live,
  Da dö vi ingenlund,
Men skulle frelste blive,
  Fortälle Guds Miskund;
Om vi end refses saa,
  Vi lägges lukt i Grave,
  Dog skal vi Livet have,
Udödelig opstaa.

Den Kirkesteen grundfaste,
  Den Herre Jesus Krist,
De Bygningsmänd forkaste,
  Men han er bleven vist
Til Hoved-Hjörnesteen
  For Kirken Guds paa Jorde,
  Den Gjerning Herren gjorde,
Des undres hver og een!

Dig, Jesu Krist, ske Äre,
  Som kom i Herrens Navn!
Guds Folk velsignet väre
  Af Herrens Hus og Stavn!
Vi takke hver for sig
  Den Herre overmaade,
  Thi hans Miskund og Naade
Staar fast evindelig!

This hymn by Anders C. Arrebo first appeared in his *Kong David's Psalter*, 1623, in seven stanzas. It was revised and shortened by M. B. Landstad for his *Salmebog*.

The translation is by Carl Döving, 1907, and was included in *The Lutheran Hymnary*, 1913.

For comments on the tune "Aus meines Herzens Grunde" see Hymn No. 69.

See, the Conqueror Mounts in Triumph — 218

1. See, the Conqueror mounts in triumph;
   See the King in royal state,
   Riding on the clouds, His chariot,
   To His heavenly palace gate!
   Hark, the choirs of angel voices
   Joyful alleluias sing,
   And the portals high are lifted
   To receive their heavenly King.

2. Who is this that comes in glory
   With the trump of jubilee?
   Lord of battles, God of armies, —
   He hath gained the victory.
   He who on the cross did suffer,
   He who from the grave arose,
   He hath vanquished sin and Satan;
   He by death hath spoiled His foes.

[163]

ASCENSION

3. While He lifts His hands in blessing,
   He is parted from His friends;
   While their eager eyes behold Him,
   He upon the clouds ascends.
   He who walked with God and pleased Him,
   Preaching truth and doom to come,
   He, our Enoch, is translated
   To His everlasting home.

4. Now our heavenly Aaron enters
   With His blood within the veil;
   Joshua now is come to Canaan,
   And the kings before Him quail.
   Now He plants the tribes of Israel
   In their promised resting-place;
   Now our great Elijah offers
   Double portion of His grace.

5. Thou hast raised our human nature
   On the clouds to God's right hand;
   There we sit in heavenly places,
   There with Thee in glory stand.
   Jesus reigns, adored by angels;
   Man with God is on the throne.
   Mighty Lord, in Thine ascension
   We by faith behold our own.

6. Glory be to God the Father;
   Glory be to God the Son,
   Dying, risen, ascending for us,
   Who the heavenly realm hath won;
   Glory to the Holy Spirit!
   To One God in Persons Three
   Glory both in earth and heaven,
   Glory, endless glory, be.

This hymn was first published in Christopher Wordsworth's *Holy Year*, 1862. It is perhaps Wordsworth's finest composition. Dr. Julian says that it is the nearest approach in style and treatment to a Greek ode known to us in the English language. The same writer adds: "The amount of Holy Scripture compressed into these forty lines (he does not include the doxology) is wonderful. Prophecy, types, historical facts, doctrinal teaching, ecstatic praise, all are here; and the result is one grand rush of holy song."

In its original form the hymn had four additional stanzas, which follow our fifth, and in some hymnals are included as Part II:

6. Holy Ghost, Illuminator,
   Shed Thy beams upon our eyes,
   Help us to look up with Stephen
   And to see beyond the skies,
   Where the Son of Man in glory
   Standing is at God's right hand,
   Beckoning on His martyr army,
   Succoring His faithful band.

7. See Him who is gone before us
   Heavenly mansions to prepare;
   See Him who is ever pleading
   For us with prevailing prayer;
   See Him who with sound of trumpet
   And with His angelic train,
   Summoning the world to Judgment,
   On the clouds will come again.

8. Raise us up from earth to heaven,
   Give us wings of faith and love,
   Gales of holy aspirations
   Wafting us to realms above,
   That, with hearts and minds uplifted,
   We with Christ, our Lord, may dwell
   Where He sits enthroned in glory
   In His heavenly citadel.

9. So at last, when He appeareth,
   We from our own graves may spring,
   With our youth renewed like eagles',
   Flocking round our heavenly King,
   Caught up on the clouds of heaven,
   And may meet Him in the air,
   Rise to realms where He is reigning
   And may reign forever there.

The tune "Rex Gloriae" is by Henry Smart. It was written for the *Appendix* to the original edition of *Hymns Ancient and Modern*, 1868.

219 The Head That Once was Crowned with Thorns

1. The Head that once was crowned with thorns
   Is crowned with glory now;
   A royal diadem adorns
   The mighty Victor's brow.

2. The highest place that heaven affords
   Is His, is His by right,
   The King of kings and Lord of lords,
   And heaven's eternal Light;

3. The Joy of all who dwell above,
   The Joy of all below
   To whom He manifests His love
   And grants His name to know.

4. To them the cross, with all its shame,
   With all its grace, is given;
   Their name an everlasting name,
   Their joy the joy of heaven.

5. They suffer with their Lord below,
   They reign with Him above,
   Their profit and their joy to know
   The mystery of His love.

6. The cross He bore is life and health,
   Though shame and death to Him:
   His people's hope, His people's wealth,
   Their everlasting theme.

Thomas Kelly published this hymn in his *Hymns*, etc., edition of 1820. It is based on Heb. 2:10, entitled "Christ Perfect through Sufferings."

The tune "St. Magnus," also called "Nottingham," is by Jeremiah Clark. It first appeared in *The Divine Companion*, etc., second edition, 1709.

ASCENSION

Jesus, My Great High Priest 220

1. Jesus, my great High Priest,
    Offered His blood and died;
My guilty conscience seeks
    No sacrifice beside.
His powerful blood did once atone,
And now it pleads before the throne.

2. To this dear Surety's hand
    Will I commit my cause;
He answers and fulfils
    His Father's broken laws.
Behold my soul at freedom set;
My Surety paid the dreadful debt.

3. My Advocate appears
    For my defense on high;
The Father bows His ears
    And lays His thunder by.
Not all that hell or sin can say
Shall turn His heart, His love, away.

4. Should all the hosts of death
    And powers of hell unknown
Put their most dreadful forms
    Of rage and mischief on,
I shall be safe, for Christ displays
Superior power and guardian grace.

This cento is taken from Isaac Watts's hymn "on the names and titles of Jesus Christ" beginning "Join all the glorious names," which was first published in his *Hymns and Sacred Songs*, 1709, in twelve stanzas. The cento includes 8, 7, 9, and 12 of the original. The omitted stanzas, 1 to 6, 10 and 11, read:

1. Join all the glorious names
    Of wisdom, love, and power
That ever mortals knew,
    That angels ever bore;
All are too mean to speak His worth,
Too mean to set my Savior forth.

2. But, oh, what gentle terms,
    What condescending ways,
Doth our Redeemer use
    To teach His heavenly grace!
Mine eyes with joy and wonder see
What forms of love He bears for me.

3. Arrayed in mortal flesh,
    He like an angel stands
And holds the promises
    And pardons in His hands.
Commissioned from His Father's throne
To make His grace to mortals known.

4. Great Prophet of my God
    My tongue would bless Thy name;
By Thee the joyful news
    Of our salvation came,
The joyful news of sins forgiven,
Of hell subdued, and peace with Heaven.

5. Be Thou my Counselor,
    My Pattern, and my Guide,
And through this desert land
    Still keep me near Thy side.
Oh, let my feet ne'er run astray
Nor rove nor seek the crooked way!

6. I love my Shepherd's voice;
    His watchful eyes shall keep
My wand'ring soul among
    The thousands of His sheep;
He feeds His flock, He calls their names,
His bosom bears the tender lambs.

10. My dear almighty Lord,
    My Conqueror and my King,
Thy scepter and Thy sword,
    Thy reigning grace, I sing.
Thine is the power! Behold, I sit
In willing bonds beneath Thy feet.

11. Now let my soul arise
    And tread the Tempter down;
My Captain leads me forth
    To conquest and a crown.
A feeble saint shall win the day
Though death and hell obstruct the way.

The tune "Bevan" is by John Goss. Composed in 1853, it appeared in Peter Maurice's collection *Choral Harmony*, etc., 1854.

Hark! Ten Thousand Harps and Voices 221

1. Hark! ten thousand harps and voices
    Sound the note of praise above;
Jesus reigns, and heaven rejoices, —
    Jesus reigns, the God of Love.
See, He sits on yonder throne;
Jesus rules the world alone.

2. Come, ye saints, unite your
        praises
    With the angels round His throne;
Soon, we hope, our God will raise us
    To the place where He is gone.
Meet it is that we should sing,
"Glory, glory, to our King!"

3. Sing how Jesus came from heaven,
    How He bore the cross below,
How all power to Him is given,
    How He reigns in glory now;
'Tis a great and endless theme,
Oh, 'tis sweet to sing of Him!

4. Jesus, hail! Thy glory brightens
    All above and gives it worth;
Lord of Life, Thy smile enlightens,
    Cheers, and charms Thy saints on earth.
When we think of love like Thine,
Lord, we own it love divine.

5. King of Glory, reign forever;
    Thine an everlasting crown.
Nothing from Thy love shall sever
    Those whom Thou hast made Thine
        own,
Happy objects of Thy grace,
Destined to behold Thy face.

6. Savior, hasten Thine appearing;
    Bring, oh, bring, the glorious day
When, the awe-full summons hearing,
    Heaven and earth shall pass away;
Then with golden harps we'll sing,
"Glory, glory, to our King!"

ASCENSION

Thomas Kelly first published this hymn in his *Hymns*, etc., second edition, 1806, in seven stanzas, headed, "Let all the angels of God worship Him." Heb. 1:6. The omitted second stanza reads:

> Well may angels bright and glorious
> Sing the praises of the Lamb;
> While on earth He proved victorious,
> Now He bears a matchless name.
> Well may angels sing of Him;
> Heaven supplies no richer theme.

For comments on the tune "Neander" see Hymn No. 1.

222   Look, Ye Saints, the Sight Is Glorious

1. Look, ye saints, the sight is glorious;
See the Man of Sorrows now!
From the fight returned victorious,
Every knee to Him shall bow.
Crown Him! Crown Him!
Crowns become the Victor's brow.

2. Crown the Savior! Angels, crown Him!
Rich the trophies Jesus brings;
On the seat of power enthrone Him
While the vault of heaven rings.
Crown Him! Crown Him!
Crown the Savior King of kings.

3. Sinners in derision crowned Him,
Mocking thus the Savior's claim;
Saints and angels crowd around Him,
Own His title, praise His name.
Crown Him! Crown Him!
Spread abroad the Victor's fame!

4. Hark, those bursts of acclamation!
Hark, those loud triumphant chords!
Jesus takes the highest station;
Oh, what joy the sight affords!
Crown Him! Crown Him
King of kings and Lord of lords!

This hymn by Thomas Kelly first appeared in his *Hymns on Various Passages*, third edition, 1809, headed "He shall reign forever and ever." Rev. 11:15. It ranks with many of the best English hymns and enjoys a deservedly wide popularity.

The tune "Coronae" was written by William H. Monk in 1871.

223   We Thank Thee, Jesus, Dearest Friend

1. We thank Thee, Jesus, dearest Friend,
That Thou didst into heaven ascend.
O blessed Savior, bid us live
And strength to soul and body give.
Hallelujah!

2. Ascended to His throne on high,
Hid from our sight, yet always nigh;
He rules and reigns at God's right hand
And has all power at His command.
Hallelujah!

3. The man who trusts in Him is blest
And finds in Him eternal rest;
This world's allurements we despise
And fix on Christ alone our eyes.
Hallelujah!

4. We therefore heartily rejoice
And sing His praise with cheerful voice;
He captive led captivity,
From bitter death He set us free.
Hallelujah!

5. Through Him we heirs of heaven are made;
O Brother, Christ, extend Thine aid
That we may firmly trust in Thee
And through Thee live eternally.
Hallelujah!

1. Wir danken dir, Herr Jesu Christ,
Dass du gen Himmel g'fahren bist.
O starker Gott, Immanuel,
Stärk uns an Leib, stärk uns an Seel'!
Halleluja!

2. Gen Himmel ist er g'fahren hoch
Und ist doch allzeit bei uns noch;
Sein' Macht und G'walt unendlich ist,
Wahr'r Gott und Mensch zu aller Frist.
Halleluja!

3. Wohl dem, der ihm vertrauen tut
Und hat zu ihm ein'n frischen Mut.
Welt, wie du willst, wer fragt nach dir?
Nach Christo steht unsre Begier.
Halleluja!

4. Wir freuen uns aus Herzensgrund
Und singen fröhlich mit dem Mund:
Unser Bruder, Fleisch, Bein und Blut
Ist unser allerhöchstes Gut.
Halleluja!

5. Durch ihn der Himmel unser ist;
Hilf uns, o Bruder Jesu Christ,
Dass wir nur fest vertraun auf dich
Und durch dich leben ewiglich!
Halleluja!

The original is ascribed to Nikolaus Selnecker because a hymn of four stanzas with this beginning is found in Selnecker's *Der Psalter*, at the end of

PENTECOST

Ps. 68, published in 1572. Later a form in thirteen stanzas appeared in Praetorius's *Musae Sioniae,* 1607, author unknown. Our hymn has Stanzas 1, 3, 7, 8, and 10 of this version. The omitted stanzas read:

2. Now His disciples all rejoice
And sing His praise with cheerful voice:
Come, let us grateful offerings bring;
Our Brother is our God and King.

4. Above the heavens in glory raised,
By angel hosts forever praised,
All creatures His dominion own,
He holds an everlasting throne.

5. He rules and reigns at God's right hand
And has all power at His command;
All things are subject to His rod —
The Son of Man and Son of God.

6. The world and sin and Satan fell
He overthrew, with death and hell;
Dispute who will His mighty reign,
He still the Victor must remain.

9. With deepest joy our voice we raise
And sing our grateful song of praise;
Our Brother, our own flesh and bone,
Is God and King, our Joy alone.

11. Amen, Amen, O Lord, we cry;
Do Thou, who art exalted high,
In Thy pure faith preserve our hearts
And shield us from all Satan's darts.

12. Come, blessed Lord, to Judgment come
And take us to our glorious home
That all our woes on earth may cease
And we may dwell in heavenly peace.

13. A glad Amen shall close our song;
Our souls for rest in glory long,
Where we with angel hosts again
Shall sing in nobler strains Amen.

The translation, slightly altered, is by Matthias Loy and was included in the Ohio *Lutheran Hymnal* of 1880.

For comments on the tune "Erschienen ist der herrlich' Tag" see Hymn No. 108.

Come, Holy Ghost, God and Lord! 224

1. Come, Holy Ghost, God and Lord!
Be all Thy graces now outpoured
On each believer's mind and heart;
Thy fervent love to them impart.
Lord, by the brightness of Thy light,
Thou in the faith dost men unite
Of every land and every tongue;
This to Thy praise, O Lord, our God, be sung.
Hallelujah! Hallelujah!

2. Thou holy Light, Guide Divine,
Oh, cause the Word of Life to shine!
Teach us to know our God aright
And call Him Father with delight.
From every error keep us free;
Let none but Christ our Master be
That we in living faith abide,
In Him, our Lord, with all our might confide.
Hallelujah! Hallelujah!

3. Thou holy Fire, Comfort true,
Grant us the will Thy work to do
And in Thy service to abide;
Let trials turn us not aside.
Lord, by Thy power prepare each heart
And to our weakness strength impart
That bravely here we may contend,
Through life and death to Thee, our Lord, ascend.
Hallelujah! Hallelujah!

Komm, Heiliger Geist, Herre Gott,
Erfüll mit deiner Gnaden Gut
Deiner Gläubigen Herz, Mut und Sinn,
Dein' brünstig Lieb' entzünd' in ihn'n!
O Herr, durch deines Lichtes Glast
Zu dem Glauben versammelt hast
Das Volk aus aller Welt Zungen;
Das sei dir, Herr, zu Lob gesungen!
Halleluja! Halleluja!

Du heiliges Licht, edler Hort,
Lass uns leuchten des Lebens Wort
Und lehr uns Gott recht erkennen,
Von Herzen Vater ihn nennen!
O Herr, behüt vor fremder Lehr',
Dass wir nicht Meister suchen mehr
Denn Jesum mit rechtem Glauben
Und ihm aus ganzer Macht vertrauen!
Halleluja! Halleluja!

Du heilige Brunst, süsser Trost,
Nun hilf uns fröhlich und getrost
In dein'm Dienst beständig bleiben,
Die Trübsal uns nicht abtreiben!
O Herr, durch dein' Kraft uns bereit
Und stärk des Fleisches Blödigkeit,
Dass wir hier ritterlich ringen,
Durch Tod und Leben zu dir dringen!
Halleluja! Halleluja!

This hymn of Martin Luther's first appeared in *Eyn Enchiridion,* etc., Erfurt, 1524, entitled "Der Gesang Veni Sancte Spiritus." In the Wittenberg *Gesangbuch,* 1531, was added: "Improved by Dr. Mart. Luther."

The basis for the hymn is the medieval Latin antiphon "Veni Sancte Spiritus: reple tuorum corda fidelium, et tui amoris in eius ignem ascende: Qui per diversitatem linguarum cunctarum gentes in unitate fidei congregasti. Alleluia. Alleluia." An old German stanza, probably of fifteenth-century

PENTECOST

origin, a very free metrical version of this antiphon, was in use in Luther's day. Luther improved this stanza and added two original stanzas, which he then published in the Erfurt *Enchiridion* in 1524.

The translation is composite and was prepared for *The Lutheran Hymnal.* It is based on Catherine Winkworth's, *Lyra Germanica,* first series, 1855.

The tune "Komm, Heiliger Geist, Herre Gott" is found in two fifteenth-century manuscripts, now in the Munich library. The tune was set to Luther's hymn in the Erfurt *Enchiridion,* 1524.

225   Come, Holy Spirit, Come

1. Come, Holy Spirit, come!
   Let Thy bright beams arise;
   Dispel the sorrow from our minds,
   The darkness from our eyes.

2. Revive our drooping faith,
   Our doubts and fears remove,
   And kindle in our breasts the flame
   Of never-dying love.

3. Convince us of our sin,
   Then lead to Jesus' blood,
   And to our wondering view reveal
   The mercies of our God.

4. 'Tis Thine to cleanse the heart,
   To sanctify the soul,
   To pour fresh life into each part,
   And new-create the whole.

5. Dwell, therefore, in our hearts;
   Our minds from bondage free;
   Then shall we know and praise and love
   The Father, Son, and Thee.

Joseph Hart published this hymn for Whitsuntide in his *Hymns on Various Subjects,* 1759, in nine stanzas. The cento is composed of Stanzas 1, 3, 4, 6, and 9. The omitted stanzas read:

2. Cheer our desponding hearts,
   Thou heavenly Paraclete;
   Give us to lie with humble hope
   At our Redeemer's feet.

5. Show us that loving Man
   That rules the courts of bliss,
   The Lord of hosts, the mighty God,
   The eternal Prince of Peace.

7. If Thou, Celestial Dove,
   Thine influence withdraw,
   What easy victims soon we fall
   To conscience, wrath, and Law!

8. No longer burns our love,
   Our faith and patience fail,
   Our sin revives, and death and hell
   Our feeble souls assail.

For comments on the tune "Boylston" see Hymn No. 464.

226   Come, Oh, Come, Thou Quickening Spirit

1. Come, oh, come, Thou quickening Spirit,
   God from all eternity!
   May Thy power never fail us;
   Dwell within us constantly.
   Then shall truth and life and light
   Banish all the gloom of night.

2. Grant our hearts in fullest measure
   Wisdom, counsel, purity,
   That they ever may be seeking
   Only that which pleaseth Thee.
   Let Thy knowledge spread and grow,
   Working error's overthrow.

3. Show us, Lord, the path of blessing;
   When we trespass on our way,
   Cast, O Lord, our sins behind Thee
   And be with us day by day.
   Should we stray, O Lord, recall;
   Work repentance when we fall.

Komm, o komm, du Geist des Lebens,
Wahrer Gott von Ewigkeit!
Deine Kraft sei nicht vergebens,
Sie erfüll' uns jederzeit;
So wird Geist und Licht und Schein
In dem dunkeln Herzen sein.

Gib in unser Herz und Sinnen
Weisheit, Rat, Verstand und Zucht,
Dass wir andres nichts beginnen,
Denn was nur dein Wille sucht!
Dein' Erkenntnis werde gross
Und mach uns von Irrtum los!

Zeige, Herr, die Wohlfahrtsstege!
Das, was wider dich getan,
Räume ferner aus dem Wege;
Schlecht und recht sei um und an!
Wirke Reu' an Sünden Statt,
Wenn der Fuss gestrauchelt hat!

[168]

4. With our spirit bear Thou witness
That we are the sons of God
Who rely upon Him solely
When we pass beneath the rod;
For we know, as children should,
That the cross is for our good.

5. Prompt us, Lord, to come before Him
With a childlike heart to pray;
Sigh in us, O Holy Spirit,
When we know not what to say.
Then our prayer is not in vain,
And our faith new strength shall gain.

6. If our soul can find no comfort
And despondency grows strong
That the heart cries out in anguish:
"O my God, how long, how long?"
Comfort then the aching breast,
Grant us courage, patience, rest.

7. Holy Spirit, strong and mighty,
Thou who makest all things new,
Make Thy work within us perfect
And the evil Foe subdue.
Grant us weapons for the strife
And with victory crown our life.

8. Guard, O God, our faith forever;
Let not Satan, death, or shame
Ever part us from our Savior;
Lord our Refuge is Thy name.
Though our flesh cry ever: Nay!
Be Thy Word to us still Yea!

9. And when life's frail thread is breaking,
Then assure us more and more,
As the heirs of life unending,
Of the glory there in store,
Glory never yet exprest,
Glory of the saints at rest.

Lass uns stets dein Zeugnis fühlen,
Dass wir Gottes Kinder sind,
Die auf ihn alleine zielen,
Wenn sich Not und Drangsal find't;
Denn des Vaters liebe Rut'
Ist uns allewege gut.

Reiz uns, dass wir zu ihm treten
Frei mit aller Freudigkeit;
Seufz auch in uns, wenn wir beten,
Und vertritt uns allezeit!
So wird unsre Bitt' erhört
Und die Zuversicht gemehrt.

Wird auch uns nach Troste bange,
Dass das Herz oft rufen muss:
Ach, mein Gott, mein Gott, wie lange?
Ei, so mache den Beschluss;
Sprich der Seele tröstlich zu
Und gib Mut, Geduld und Ruh'!

O du Geist der Kraft und Stärke,
Du gewisser, neuer Geist,
Fördre in uns deine Werke,
Wenn der Satan Macht beweist;
Schenk uns Waffen in dem Krieg
Und erhalt in uns den Sieg!

Herr, bewahr auch unsern Glauben,
Dass kein Teufel, Tod noch Spott
Uns denselben möge rauben!
Du bist unser Schutz und Gott.
Sagt das Fleisch gleich immer nein,
Lass dein Wort gewisser sein.

Wenn wir endlich sollen sterben,
So versichre uns je mehr,
Als des Himmelreiches Erben,
Jener Herrlichkeit und Ehr',
Die uns unser Gott erkiest
Und nicht auszusprechen ist.

This fine hymn of invocation to the Holy Spirit by Heinrich Held is found in an edition of Johann Crüger's *Praxis Pietatis Melica,* published at Stettin around 1664.

The translation is an altered form of that by Charles W. Schaeffer, 1866.

The tune "Komm, o komm, du Geist" is attributed to Johann Christoph Bach, Eisenach, said to have been composed in 1680. It first appeared in print in 1693 in the *Gesang-Buch,* Meiningen, set to the hymn "Ich begehr' nicht mehr zu leben," a burial hymn by Georg Neumark.

Come, Holy Ghost, in Love 227

1. Come, Holy Ghost, in love
Shed on us from above
Thine own bright ray.
Divinely good Thou art;
Thy sacred gifts impart
To gladden each sad heart.
Oh, come today!

2. Come, tenderest Friend and best,
Our most delightful Guest,
With soothing power.
Rest which the weary know,
Shade mid the noontide glow,
Peace when deep griefs o'erflow,
Cheer us this hour.

Veni, Sancte Spiritus,
Et emitte caelitus
Lucis tuae radium:
Veni, Pater pauperum;
Veni, Dator munerum;
Veni, Lumen cordium,

Consolator optime,
Dulcis Hospes animae,
Dulce Refrigerium,
In labore Requies,
In aestu Temperies,
In fletu Solacium.

3. Come, Light serene and still,
Our inmost bosoms fill,
    Dwell in each breast.
We know no dawn but Thine;
Send forth Thy beams divine
On our dark souls to shine
    And make us blest.

4. Exalt our low desires,
Extinguish passion's fires,
    Heal every wound.
Our stubborn spirits bend,
Our icy coldness end,
Our devious steps attend
    While heavenward bound.

5. Come, all the faithful bless;
Let all who Christ confess
    His praise employ.
Give virtue's rich reward,
Victorious death accord
And, with our glorious Lord,
    Eternal joy.

O Lux beatissima,
Reple cordis intima
    Tuorum fidelium.
Sine tuo numine
Nihil est in homine,
    Nihil est innoxium.

Lava, quod est sordidum,
Riga, quod est aridum,
    Rege, quod est devium,
Fove, quod est languidum,
Flecte, quod est rigidum,
    Sana, quod est saucium.

Da tuis fidelibus
In te confidentibus
    Sacrum septenarium;
Da virtutis meritum,
Da salutis exitum,
    Da perenne gaudium. Amen.

This is the Golden Sequence, one of the "loveliest of all the hymns in the whole circle of Latin poetry" (Archbishop Trent). It is of early thirteenth-century origin, although of uncertain authorship. It has been attributed to Robert II of France, Stephen Langton, Innocent III, and others. The authorship of the last-named is considered the most plausible by competent authorities.

The translation is by Ray Palmer and first appeared in the *Sabbath Hymn Book*, Andover, 1858.

For comments on the tune "Italian Hymn" see Hymn No. 239.

228   Oh, Enter, Lord, Thy Temple

1. Oh, enter, Lord, Thy temple,
    Be Thou my spirit's Guest,
Who gavest me, the earth-born,
    A second birth more blest.
Thou in the Godhead, Lord,
    Though here to dwell Thou deignest,
    Forever equal reignest,
Art equally adored.

2. Oh, enter, let me know Thee
    And feel Thy power within,
The power that breaks our fetters
    And rescues us from sin;
Oh, wash and cleanse Thou me
    That I may serve Thee truly
    And render honor duly
With perfect heart to Thee.

3. Thou art, O Holy Spirit,
    The true anointing Oil,
Through which are consecrated
    Soul, body, rest, and toil
To Christ, whose guardian wings,
    Where'er their lot appointed,
    Protect His own anointed,
His prophets, priests, and kings.

4. Thou, Holy Spirit, teachest
    The soul to pray aright;
Thy songs have sweetest music,
    Thy prayers have wondrous might.
Unheard they cannot fail,
    They pierce the highest heaven
    Till He His help hath given
Who surely helpeth all.

Zeuch ein zu meinen Toren,
    Sei meines Herzens Gast,
Der du, da ich geboren,
    Mich neugeboren hast,
O hochgeliebter Geist
    Des Vater und des Sohnes,
    Mit beiden gleichen Thrones,
Mit beiden gleich gepreist!

Zeuch ein, lass mich empfinden
    Und schmecken deine Kraft,
Die Kraft, die uns von Sünden
    Hilf' und Errettung schafft!
Entsünd'ge meinen Sinn,
    Dass ich mit reinem Geiste
    Dir Ehr' und Dienste leiste,
Die ich dir schuldig bin!

Du bist das heil'ge Öle,
    Dadurch gesalbet ist
Mein Leib und meine Seele
    Dem Herren Jesu Christ
Zum wahren Eigentum,
    Zum Priester und Propheten,
    Zum König, den in Nöten
Gott schützt im Heiligtum.

Du bist ein Geist, der lehret,
    Wie man recht beten soll;
Dein Beten wird erhöret,
    Dein Singen klinget wohl;
Es steigt zum Himmel an,
    Es steigt und lässt nicht abe,
    Bis der geholfen habe,
Der allen helfen kann.

5. Thy gift is joy, O Spirit,
   Thou wouldst not have us pine;
   In darkest hours Thy comfort
   Doth ever brightly shine.
   And, oh, how oft Thy voice
   Hath shed its sweetness o'er me
   And opened heaven before me
   And bid my heart rejoice!

Du bist ein Geist der Freuden,
Vom Trauern hältst du nichts,
Erleuchtest uns im Leiden
Mit deines Trostes Licht.
Ach ja, wie manches Mal
Hast du mit süssen Worten
Mir aufgetan die Pforten
Zum güldnen Freudensaal!

6. All love is Thine, O Spirit;
   Thou hatest enmity;
   Thou lovest peace and friendship,
   All strife wouldst have us flee;
   Where wrath and discord reign,
   Thy whisper kindly pleadeth
   And to the heart that heedeth
   Brings love and light again.

Du bist ein Geist der Liebe,
Ein Freund der Freundlichkeit,
Willst nicht, dass uns betrübe
Zorn, Zank, Hass, Neid und Streit.
Der Feindschaft bist du feind,
Willst, dass durch Liebesflammen
Sich wieder tun zusammen,
Die voller Zwietracht seind.

7. Our path in all things order
   According to Thy mind,
   And when this life is over
   And all must be resigned,
   Oh, grant us then to die
   With calm and fearless spirit
   And after death inherit
   Eternal life on high.

Richt unser ganzes Leben
Allzeit nach deinem Sinn,
Und wenn wir's sollen geben
In's Todes Hände hin,
Wenn's mit uns hier wird aus,
So hilf uns fröhlich sterben
Und nach dem Tod ererben
Des ew'gen Lebens Haus!

Paul Gerhardt first published this Pentecost hymn of sixteen stanzas in the *Crüger-Runge Gesang Buch,* 1653, in a selection of twelve stanzas. Few German hymns carried the complete text, as some of the stanzas were no longer applicable to the times. We have it before us, at this writing, in *Geistlicher Liederschatz,* Berlin, second edition, 1840, Samuel Elsner, publisher. From this complete form it is very evident that Gerhardt wrote the hymn during the Thirty Years' War. Stanzas 9, 10, and 12 of the complete version are a fervent prayer for peace and for repentance.

9. Thou art the true, the only Source
   Whence concord comes to men;
   Oh, that Thy power may have free course
   And bring us peace again!
   Oh, hear and stem this mighty flood
   That o'er us death and sorrow spreads!
   Alas! each day afresh it sheds
   Like water human blood.

10. And let our nation learn to know
    What and how deep our sin;
    Nay, let God's judgments come if so
    A fire be lit within
    The hearts that loved themselves to please.
    In bitter shame now let them burn
    And, loving Thee, repentant spurn
    Their selfish worldly ease.

12. Arise and make an end to all
    Our heartache and our pain;
    The wandering flock and lost recall
    And grant them joy again.
    To peace and wealth the lands restore,
    Wasted with fire or plague or sword;
    Come to Thy ruined churches, Lord,
    And bid them bloom once more.

What an eloquent plea, certainly very timely for our day!

The cento above includes Stanzas 1, 2, 4, 5, 6, 7, and 16.

The translation is an altered form of that by Catherine Winkworth in her *Chorale Book for England,* 1863. Her version in that collection was a recast of her translation in *Lyra Germanica,* first series, 1855, from which the three stanzas quoted above are taken.

The tune "Zeuch ein" is by Johann Crüger, written for this hymn. It appeared with the text in the *Crüger-Runge Gesang Buch,* Berlin, 1653, and also in Crüger's *Praxis,* etc., fifth edition, 1653.

229   Holy Spirit, Hear Us

1. Holy Spirit, hear us
   On this sacred day;
   Come to us with blessing,
   Come with us to stay.

2. Come as once Thou camest
   To the faithful few
   Patiently awaiting
   Jesus' promise true.

3. Up to heaven ascending,
   Our dear Lord has gone;
   Yet His little children
   Leaves He not alone.

4. To His blessed promise
   Now in faith we cling.
   Comforter, most holy,
   Spread o'er us Thy wing.

5. Lighten Thou our darkness,
   Be Thyself our Light;
   Strengthen Thou our weakness,
   Spirit of all might.

6. Spirit of Adoption,
   Make us overflow
   With Thy sevenfold blessing
   And in grace to grow.

7. Into Christ baptizèd
   Grant that we may be
   Day and night, dear Spirit,
   Perfected by Thee!

This hymn is not to be confused with that by W. H. Parker, beginning

> Holy Spirit, hear us;
> Help us while we sing,
> Breathe into the music
> Of the praise we bring.

Joseph Mohr is credited with the authorship of this hymn, which is dated 1816. We have not been able to verify this nor to locate the original text. The translation, which, we suspect, is very free, is by Claudia F. Hernaman.

For comments on the tune "Wem in Leidenstagen" see Hymn No. 158.

230   Holy Spirit, God of Love

1. Holy Spirit, God of love,
   Who our night dost brighten,
   Shed on us from heaven above,
   Now our faith enlighten.
   In Thy light we gather here;
   Show us that Christ's promise clear
   Is Amen forever.
   Jesus, our ascended Lord,
   Oh, fulfil Thy gracious Word:
   Bless us with Thy favor!

O Lue fra Guds Kjärlighed,
O Visdom fra det Höie,
Som faldt paa dine Vidner ned,
Oplys vor Troes Öie!
Om Ordets Lys vi samles her,
Viis os, at Kristi Lofte er
Et evigt Ja og Amen!
O himmelfarne Frelsere,
Vi vente din Forjättelse,
Velsign os allesammen!

This hymn of one stanza by Birgitte K. Boye was first published in *Guldberg's Hymn Book,* 1778. It is to be sung "on Pentecost Day before the reading of the Gospel from the pulpit." The direction has in mind the ancient custom, that, according to Luther's own suggestion, the text for the day would be the Gospel. After the pastor has delivered the introduction of the sermon and read the text, the congregation rises and sings this stanza.

The translation is by George T. Rygh, 1908, slightly altered. It appeared in *The Lutheran Hymnary,* 1913.

For comments on the tune "Der Tag, der ist" see Hymn No. 78.

231   We Now Implore God the Holy Ghost

1. We now implore God the Holy Ghost
   For the true faith, which we need the most,
   That in our last moments He may befriend us
   And, as homeward we journey, attend us.
   Lord, have mercy!

Nun bitten wir den Heiligen Geist
Um den rechten Glauben allermeist,
Dass er uns behüte an unserm Ende,
Wenn wir heimfahr'n aus diesem Elende
Kyrieleis!

2. Shine in our hearts, O most precious Light,
That we Jesus Christ may know aright,
Clinging to our Savior, whose blood hath bought us,
Who again to our homeland hath brought us.
Lord, have mercy!

3. Thou sacred Love, grace on us bestow,
Set our hearts with heavenly fire aglow
That with hearts united we love each other,
Of one mind, in peace with every brother.
Lord, have mercy!

4. Thou highest Comfort in every need,
Grant that neither shame nor death we heed,
That e'en then our courage may never fail us
When the Foe shall accuse and assail us.
Lord, have mercy!

Du wertes Licht, gib uns deinen Schein,
Lehr uns Jesum Christ kennen allein,
Dass wir an ihm bleiben, dem treuen Heiland,
Der uns bracht hat zum rechten Vaterland.
Kyrieleis!

Du süsse Lieb', schenk uns deine Gunst,
Lass uns empfinden der Liebe Brunst,
Dass wir uns von Herzen einander lieben
Und im Frieden auf einem Sinn bleiben.
Kyrieleis!

Du höchster Tröster in aller Not,
Hilf, dass wir nicht fürchten Schand' noch Tod,
Dass in uns die Sinne doch nicht verzagen,
Wenn der Feind wird das Leben verklagen!
Kyrieleis!

Nû biten wir den heiligen geist
umbe den rechten glouben allermeist,
daz er uns behüete an unsrem ende,
sô wir heim suln varn ûz disem ellende.
Kyrieleis.

This stanza, quoted in a sermon by the Franciscan brother and famous medieval preacher, Berthold of Regensburg († 1272), gave the impetus for this hymn. The stanza no doubt was suggested by the sequence "Veni, Sancte Spiritus." According to *Koch* it was sung by the people in the Pentecost service "during the ceremony in which a wooden dove was lowered by a cord from the roof of the chancel or a living dove was thence let fly down."

Martin Luther recognized the value of the stanza, calling it "einen feinen, schönen Gesang," and added three stanzas of his own, invoking the Holy Spirit as the true Light, as the sacred Love, and as the highest Comfort. His version first appeared in Johann Walther's *Geystlich gesangk Buchleyn*, Wittenberg, 1524. The hymn is generally appointed for Whitsuntide, but has also been used for Holy Communion, for the ordination of ministers, as a hymn before the sermon, and for the beginning of worship.

The translation is composite and was prepared for *The Lutheran Hymnal*.

The tune "Nun bitten wir" is evidently as old as the text of the first stanza and was used with Luther's version in Walther's hymn-book, 1524.

Let Songs of Praises Fill the Sky 232

1. Let songs of praises fill the sky:
Christ, our ascended Lord,
Sends down His Spirit from on high
According to His word.
All hail the day of Pentecost,
The coming of the Holy Ghost!

2. The Spirit by His heavenly breath
Creates new life within;
He quickens sinners from the death
Of trespasses and sin.
All hail the day of Pentecost,
The coming of the Holy Ghost!

3. The things of Christ the Spirit takes
And shows them unto men;
The fallen soul His temple makes,
God's image stamps again.
All hail the day of Pentecost,
The coming of the Holy Ghost!

4. Come, Holy Spirit, from above
With Thy celestial fire;
Come and with flames of zeal and love
Our hearts and tongues inspire.
Be this our day of Pentecost,
The coming of the Holy Ghost!

Thomas Cotterill first published this hymn anonymously in his *Selection*, 1819; then, with his name, in Montgomery's *Christian Psalmist*, 1825.

The tune "Erfurt" is by Herman Ilse, one of the music editors of the *Evangelical Lutheran Hymn-Book*, 1912, and was included in that volume, where it was also set to this hymn.

PENTECOST

233   Come, Holy Ghost, Creator Blest

1. Come, Holy Ghost, Creator blest,
Vouchsafe within our souls to rest;
Come with Thy grace and heavenly aid
And fill the hearts which Thou hast made.

2. To Thee, the Comforter, we cry,
To Thee, the Gift of God Most High,
The Fount of life, the Fire of love,
The soul's Anointing from above.

3. The sevenfold gifts of grace are Thine,
O Finger of the Hand Divine;
True promise of the Father Thou,
Who dost the tongue with speech endow.

4. Thy light to every thought impart
And shed Thy love in every heart;
The weakness of our mortal state
With deathless might invigorate.

5. Drive far away our wily Foe
And Thine abiding peace bestow;
If Thou be our protecting Guide,
No evil can our steps betide.

6. Make Thou to us the Father known,
Teach us the eternal Son to own
And Thee, whose name we ever bless,
Of both the Spirit, to confess.

7. Praise we the Father and the Son
And Holy Spirit, with them One;
And may the Son on us bestow
The gifts that from the Spirit flow! Amen.

Veni, Creator Spiritus,
Mentes tuorum visita,
Imple superna gratia
Quae Tu creasti pectora.

Qui Paracletus diceris,
Donum Dei altissimi,
Fons vivus, Ignis, Charitas,
Et spiritalis Unctio.

Tu septiformis munere,
Dextrae Dei Tu digitus,
Tu rite promisso Patris,
Sermone ditas guttura.

Accende lumen sensibus,
Infunde amorem cordibus,
Infirma nostri corporis
Virtute firmans perpeti.

Hostem repellas longius,
Pacemque dones protinus,
Ductore sic Te praevio
Vitemus omne noxium.

Per Te sciamus, da, Patrem,
Noscamus atque Filium,
Te utriusque Spiritum
Credamus omni tempore.

Sit laus Patri cum Filio,
Sancto simul Paracleto,
Nobisque mittat Filius
Charisma Sancti Spiritus.

    This hymn has taken a deeper hold on Western Christendom than any other medieval hymn except the *Te Deum,* and yet very little is known definitely about its authorship. It has been attributed to Charlemagne, Gregory the Great, Ambrose of Milan, and Rhabanus Maurus.

    The translation is an altered form of that by Edward Caswall in his *Lyra Catholica,* 1849.

    The tune "Komm, Gott Schöpfer" is the ancient melody for the Latin text. It was coupled with Martin Luther's German version of the Latin hymn in the Erfurt *Enchiridion,* 1524, and in Johann Walther's *Chorgesang-Buch,* 1525.

234   Holy Ghost, with Light Divine

1. Holy Ghost, with light divine
Shine upon this heart of mine;
Chase the shades of night away,
Turn the darkness into day.

2. Let me see my Savior's face,
Let me all His beauties trace;
Show those glorious truths to me
Which are only known to Thee.

3. Holy Ghost, with power divine
Cleanse this guilty heart of mine;
In Thy mercy pity me,
From sin's bondage set me free.

4. Holy Ghost, with joy divine
Cheer this saddened heart of mine;
Yield a sacred, settled peace,
Let it grow and still increase.

5. Holy Spirit, all divine,
Dwell within this heart of mine;
Cast down every idol-throne,
Reign supreme, and reign alone.

6. See, to Thee I yield my heart,
Shed Thy life through every part;
A pure temple I would be,
Wholly dedicate to Thee.

    Andrew Reed entitled this hymn "Prayer to the Spirit" and first published it in his *Collection,* 1817, in four eight-line stanzas. We have not found any modern hymn-book that has the complete hymn. Most of them use the four-

PENTECOST

line stanza form, and the stanzas range from four to six. One of the omitted parts, belonging after Stanza 5, reads:

> Bid my sin and sorrow cease,
> Fill me with Thy heavenly peace;
> Joy divine I then shall prove,
> Light of Truth — and Fire of Love.

The tune "Light Divine" by Orlando Gibbons is also called "Song 13." It appeared in *The Hymns and Songs of the Church* by George Wither, in 1623, where it was set to a metrical paraphrase of a part of the Song of Solomon.

O Holy Spirit, Enter In — 235

1. O Holy Spirit, enter in
And in our hearts Thy work begin,
  Thy temple deign to make us;
Sun of the soul, Thou Light Divine,
Around and in us brightly shine,
  To joy and gladness wake us.
    That we, In Thee
    Truly living, To Thee giving
      Prayer unceasing,
    May in love be still increasing.

2. Give to Thy Word impressive power
That in our hearts, from this good hour,
  As fire it may be glowing;
That we confess the Father, Son,
And Thee, the Spirit, Three in One,
  Thy glory ever showing.
    Stay Thou, Sway now
    Our souls ever That they never
      May forsake Thee,
    But by faith their Refuge make Thee.

3. Thou Fountain whence all wisdom flows
Which God on pious hearts bestows,
  Grant us Thy consolation
That in our pure faith's unity
We faithful witnesses may be
  Of grace that brings salvation.
    Hear us, Cheer us
    By Thy teaching; Let our preaching
      And our labor
    Praise Thee, Lord, and serve our neighbor.

4. Left to ourselves, we shall but stray;
Oh, lead us on the narrow way,
  With wisest counsel guide us
And give us steadfastness that we
May ever faithful prove to Thee
  Whatever woes betide us.
    Come, Friend, And mend
    Hearts now broken, Give a token
      Thou art near us,
    Whom we trust to light and cheer us.

5. Thy heavenly strength sustain our heart
That we may act the valiant part
  With Thee as our Reliance,
Be Thou our Refuge and our Shield
That we may never quit the field,
  But bid all foes defiance.
    Descend, Defend
    From all errors And earth's terrors;
      Thy salvation
    Be our constant consolation.

6. O mighty Rock, O Source of Life,
Let Thy dear Word, mid doubt and strife,
  Be strong within us burning
That we be faithful unto death,
In Thy pure love and holy faith,
  From Thee true wisdom learning.
    Thy grace And peace
    On us shower; By Thy power
      Christ confessing,
    Let us win our Savior's blessing.

O Heil'ger Geist, kehr bei uns ein
Und lass uns deine Wohnung sein,
  O komm, du Herzenssonne!
Du Himmelslicht, lass deinen Schein
Bei uns und in uns kräftig sein
  Zu steter Freud' und Wonne,
    Dass wir in dir
    Recht zu leben uns ergeben
      Und mit Beten
    Oft deshalben vor dich treten.

Gib Kraft und Nachdruck deinem Wort,
Lass es wie Feuer immerfort
  In unsern Herzen brennen,
Dass wir Gott Vater, seinen Sohn,
Dich, beider Geist, in einem Thron
  Für wahren Gott bekennen.
    Bleibe, treibe
    Und behüte das Gemüte,
      Dass wir glauben
    Und im Glauben standhaft bleiben!

Du Quell, draus alle Weisheit fleusst,
Die sich in fromme Seelen geusst,
  Lass deinen Trost uns hören,
Dass wir in Glaubenseinigkeit
Auch können alle Christenheit
  Dein wahres Zeugnis lehren!
    Höre, lehre,
    Herz und Sinnen zu gewinnen,
      Dich zu preisen,
    Gut's dem Nächsten zu erweisen!

Steh uns stets bei mit deinem Rat
Und führ uns selbst den rechten Pfad,
  Die wir den Weg nicht wissen!
Gib uns Beständigkeit, dass wir
Getreu dir bleiben für und für,
  Wenn wir nun leiden müssen!
    Schaue, baue,
    Was zerrissen und geflissen,
      Dir zu trauen
    Und auf dich allein zu bauen!

Lass uns dein' edle Balsamkraft
Empfinden und zur Ritterschaft
  Dadurch gestärket werden,
Auf dass wir unter deinem Schutz
Begegnen aller Feinde Trutz,
  Solang wir sind auf Erden!
    Lass dich reichlich
    Auf uns nieder, dass wir wieder
      Trost empfinden,
    Alles Unglück überwinden!

Du starker Fels und Lebenshort,
Lass uns dein himmelsüsses Wort
  In unsern Herzen brennen,
Dass wir uns mögen nimmermehr
Von deiner weisheitreichen Lehr'
  Und reinen Liebe trennen!
    Fliesse, giesse
    Deine Güte ins Gemüte,
      Dass wir können
    Christum unsern Heiland nennen!

[175]

PENTECOST

7. O gentle Dew, from heaven now fall
With power upon the hearts of all,
Thy tender love instilling,
That heart to heart more closely bound,
In kindly deeds be fruitful found,
The law of love fulfilling;
Dwell thus In us.
Envy banish; Strife will vanish
Where Thou livest.
Peace and love and joy Thou givest.

Du süsser Himmelstau, lass dich
In unsre Herzen kräftiglich
Und schenk uns deine Liebe,
Dass unser Sinn verbunden sei
Dem Nächsten stets mit Liebestreu'
Und sich darinnen übe!
Kein Neid, kein Streit
Dich betrübe, Fried' und Liebe
Müssen schweben;
Fried' und Freude wirst du geben!

8. Grant that our days, while life shall last,
In purest holiness be passed,
Be Thou our Strength and Tower.
From sinful lust and vanity
And from dead works set Thou us free
In every evil hour.
Keep Thou Pure now
From offenses Heart and senses;
Blessed Spirit!
Let us heavenly life inherit.

Gib, dass in reiner Heiligkeit
Wir führen unsre Lebenszeit,
Sei unsres Geistes Stärke,
Dass uns forthin sei unbewusst
Die Eitelkeit, des Fleisches Lust
Und seine toten Werke!
Rühre, führe
Unser Sinnen und Beginnen
Von der Erden,
Dass wir Himmelserben werden!

Michael Schirmer first published this hymn, in 1640, in Johann Crüger's *Newes vollkömmliches Gesangbuch,* Berlin, 1640, in seven stanzas, the third stanza being a recast of Stanza 7 of Johann Heermann's "Wir wissen nicht, Herr Zebaoth." In the Hanoverian *Gesangbuch,* Lüneburg, 1659, the hymn appeared much altered, the fifth stanza, in a recast, becoming Stanza 2. To this version later hymn-books added Schirmer's original fifth stanza and thus formed a hymn of eight stanzas, as above.

The translation is an altered form of that by Catherine Winkworth, in her *Chorale Book for England,* 1863.

For comments on the tune "Wie schön leuchtet" see Hymn No. 23.

236   Creator Spirit, by Whose Aid

1. Creator Spirit, by whose aid
The world's foundations first were laid,
Come, visit every humble mind;
Come, pour Thy joys on humankind;
From sin and sorrow set us free
And make Thy temples worthy Thee.

2. O Source of uncreated light,
The Father's promised Paraclete,
Thrice holy Fount, thrice holy Fire,
Our hearts with heavenly love inspire;
Come and Thy sacred unction bring
To sanctify us while we sing.

3. Plenteous of grace, descend from high
Rich in Thy sevenfold energy;
Make us eternal truths receive
And practice all that we believe;
Give us Thyself that we may see
The Father and the Son by Thee.

4. Immortal honor, endless fame,
Attend the almighty Father's name;
The Savior Son be glorified,
Who for lost man's redemption died;
And equal adoration be,
Eternal Paraclete, to Thee.

This is another translation of the "Veni Creator Spiritus, Mentes" (see Hymn No. 233), which appeared in John Dryden's *Miscellaneous Poems* (Part III), 1693, in seven stanzas of unequal length, 39 lines in all. The text was altered and abbreviated for use in the hymnals. The omitted portions of Dryden's poem, to be inserted between Stanzas 2 and 4 above, read:

Plenteous of grace, descend from high,
Rich in Thy sevenfold energy.
Thou Strength of His almighty hand
Whose power does heaven and earth command;
Proceeding Spirit, our Defense,
Who dost the gift of tongues dispense
And crown'st Thy gift with eloquence.

Refine and purge our earthly parts;
But, oh, inflame and fire our hearts:
Our frailties help, our vice control,
Submit the senses to the soul;
And when rebellious they are grown,
Then lay Thy hand and hold them down.

    Chase from our minds the infernal Foe
    And peace, the fruit of love, bestow;
    And lest our feet should step astray,
    Protect and guide us in the way.
    Make us eternal truths receive
    And practice all that we believe.
    Give us Thyself that we may see
    The Father and the Son by Thee.

For comments on the tune "All' Ehr' und Lob" see Hymn No. 238.

All Glory Be to God on High 237

1. All glory be to God on high,
Who hath our race befriended!
To us no harm shall now come nigh,
The strife at last is ended;
God showeth His good will to men,
And peace shall reign on earth again;
Oh, thank Him for His goodness!

2. We praise, we worship Thee, we trust,
And give Thee thanks forever,
O Father, that Thy rule is just
And wise and changes never.
Thy boundless power o'er all things reigns,
'Tis done whate'er Thy will ordains:
Well for us that Thou rulest!

3. O Jesus Christ, Thou only Son
Of God, Thy heavenly Father,
Who didst for all our sins atone
And Thy lost sheep dost gather:
Thou Lamb of God, to Thee on high,
From out our depths, we sinners cry,
Have mercy on us, Jesus!

4. O Holy Ghost, Thou precious Gift,
Thou Comforter unfailing,
O'er Satan's snares our souls uplift
And let Thy power availing
Avert our woes and calm our dread.
For us the Savior's blood was shed;
We trust in Thee to save us.

Allein Gott in der Höh' sei Ehr'
Und Dank für seine Gnade,
Darum dass nun und nimmermehr
Uns rühren kann kein Schade.
Ein Wohlgefall'n Gott an uns hat,
Nun ist gross' Fried' ohn' Unterlass,
All' Fehd' hat nun ein Ende.

Wir loben, preis'n, anbeten dich
Für deine Ehr'; wir danken,
Dass du, Gott Vater, ewiglich
Regierst ohn' alles Wanken.
Ganz ungemess'n ist deine Macht,
Fort g'schieht, was dein Will' hat bedacht;
Wohl uns des feinen Herren!

O Jesu Christ, Sohn eingebor'n
Deines himmlischen Vaters,
Versöhner der'r, die war'n verlor'n,
Du Stiller unsers Haders,
Lamm Gottes, heil'ger Herr und Gott,
Nimm an die Bitt' von unsrer Not,
Erbarm' dich unser aller!

O Heil'ger Geist, du höchstes Gut,
Du allerheilsamst' Tröster,
Vor's Teufels G'walt fortan behüt',
Die Jesus Christ erlöset
Durch grosse Mart'r und bittern Tod,
Abwend all unsern Jamm'r und Not!
Darauf wir uns verlassen.

This version of the "Gloria in excelsis," very likely by Nikolaus Decius, first appeared, in Low German, in the Rostock *Gesang Buch*, 1525. In High German, together with the tune, it first appeared in Valten Schumann's *Gesangbuch*, Leipzig, 1539. It became very popular, although *Fischer* calls attention to the fact that Martin Luther received neither this nor any other hymns by Decius into his collections.

The translation is an altered form of that by Catherine Winkworth in her *Chorale Book for England*, 1863.

The tune "Allein Gott in der Höh'" is also attributed to Decius and first appeared in 1539, as above. It is derived from the ancient *Gloria* tune used in the "Kyrie maius dominicale."

All Glory Be to God Alone 238

1. All glory be to God alone,
Forevermore the Highest One,
Who doth our sinful race befriend
And grace and peace to us extend.
Among mankind may His good will
All hearts with deep thanksgiving fill.

2. We praise Thee, God, and Thee we bless;
We worship Thee in humbleness;
From day to day we glorify
Thee, everlasting God on high.
Of Thy great glory do we sing,
And e'er to Thee our thanks we bring.

3. Lord God, our King on heaven's throne,
Our Father, the Almighty One;
O Lord, the Sole-begotten One,
Lord Jesus Christ, the Father's Son,
True God from all eternity,
O Lamb of God, to Thee we flee:

All' Ehr' und Lob soll Gottes sein,
Er ist und heisst der Höchst' allein.
Sein Zorn auf Erden hab' ein End',
Sein' Fried' und Gnad' sich zu uns wend'.
Den Menschen das gefalle wohl,
Dafür man herzlich danken soll.

Ach lieber Gott, dich loben wir
Und preisen dich mit ganzer B'gier,
Auch kniend wir anbeten dich,
Dein' Ehr' wir rühmen stetiglich;
Wir danken dir zu aller Zeit
Um deine grosse Herrlichkeit.

Herr Gott, im Himmel Kön'g du bist,
Ein Vater, der allmächtig ist.
Du Gottes Sohn vom Vater bist
Einig gebor'n, Herr Jesu Christ.
Herr Gott, du zartes Gotteslamm,
Ein Sohn aus Gott des Vaters Stamm,

4. Thou dost the world's sin take away;
Have mercy on us, Lord, we pray.
Thou dost the world's sin take away;
Give ear unto the prayer we say.
Thou sitt'st at God's right hand for aye;
Have mercy on us, Lord, we pray.

5. Thou only art the Holy One,
Thou art o'er all things Lord alone;
O Jesus Christ, we glorify
Thee only as the Lord Most High;
Thou art, the Holy Ghost with Thee,
One in the Father's majesty.

6. Amen, this ever true shall be,
As angels sing adoringly.
By all creation, far and wide,
Thou, Lord, art ever glorified;
And Thee all Christendom doth praise
Now and through everlasting days.

Der du der Welt Sünd' trägst allein,
Woll'st uns gnädig, barmherzig sein!
Der du der Welt Sünd' trägst allein,
Lass dir unsre Bitt' g'fällig sein!
Der du gleich sitzt dem Vater dein,
Woll'st uns gnädig, barmherzig sein!

Du bist und bleibst heilig allein,
Über alles der Herr allein.
Der Allerhöchst' allein du bist,
Du lieber Heiland, Jesu Christ,
Samt dem Vater und Heil'gen Geist
In göttlicher Majestät gleich.

Amen, das ist gewisslich wahr,
Das bekennt aller Engel Schar
Und alle Welt, so weit und breit,
Dich lobt und ehret allezeit.
Dich rühmt die ganze Christenheit
Von Anfang bis in Ewigkeit.

This seems to have been Martin Luther's favorite metrical version of the "Gloria in Excelsis." It follows the Latin text much more closely than does Decius' "Allein Gott in der Höh' sei Ehr'." (See Hymn No. 237.) It first appeared in Joseph Klug's *Gesangbuch*, Wittenberg, 1543. The author is unknown, although some authorities ascribe both text and tune to Martin Luther, as, for example, Dr. Konrad Ameln, one of the editors of the second edition of Schöberlein's *Schatz des liturgischen Chor- und Gemeindegesangs*, which appeared under the title *Handbuch der deutschen evangelischen Kirchenmusik*.

Our translation was prepared for *The Lutheran Hymnal* in 1940.

The tune "All' Ehr' und Lob" is by an unknown composer and first appeared in the *Kirchengesangbuch*, Strassburg, 1541.

239   Come, Thou Almighty King

1. Come, Thou almighty King,
Help us Thy name to sing,
   Help us to praise!
Father all-glorious,
O'er all victorious,
Come and reign over us,
   Ancient of Days.

2. Come, Thou Incarnate Word,
Gird on Thy mighty sword,
   Our prayer attend;
Come and Thy people bless
And give Thy Word success;
Stablish Thy righteousness,
   Savior and Friend!

3. Come, holy Comforter,
Thy sacred witness bear
   In this glad hour.
Thou, who almighty art,
Now rule in every heart
And ne'er from us depart,
   Spirit of Power!

4. To the great One in Three
Eternal praises be
   Hence evermore!
His sovereign majesty
May we in glory see
And to eternity
   Love and adore!

Though widely used and frequently translated, yet this hymn, like a goodly number of our best hymns, is of unknown authorship. It has been attributed to Charles Wesley, probably because it was published, in 1757, together with one of his hymns, in a little pamphlet containing only these two hymns; but there is no vestige of proof that this hymn came from the pen of the great "Bard of Methodism."

The omitted Stanza 2 reads:

> Jesus, our Lord, arise;
> Scatter our enemies,
>   And make them fall;
> Let Thine almighty aid
> Our sure defense be made;
> Our souls on Thee be stayed.
>   Lord, hear our call!

The tune "Italian Hymn," also called "Trinity," "Florence," "Moscow," etc., is one of several hymns by Felice de Giardini in *The Collection of Psalm and Hymn Tunes*, etc., London, 1769, published by Martin Madan, where it was set, in three-part harmony, to this hymn.

TRINITY

Father Most Holy, Merciful, and Tender 240

1. Father most holy, merciful, and tender;
   Jesus, our Savior, with the Father reigning;
   Spirit all-kindly, Advocate, Defender,
   Light never waning.

2. Trinity sacred, Unity unshaken;
   Deity perfect, giving and forgiving,
   Light of the angels, Life of the forsaken,
   Hope of all living.

3. Maker of all things, all Thy creatures praise Thee;
   Lo, all things serve Thee through Thy whole creation.
   Hear us, Almighty, hear us as we raise Thee
   Our adoration.

4. To the all-ruling Triune God be glory!
   Highest and Greatest, help Thou our endeavor;
   We, too, would praise Thee, giving honor worthy
   Now and forever.

O Pater sancte, mitis atque pie,
O Iesu Christe, Fili venerande,
Paracliteque Spiritus o alme,
Deus aeterne,

Trinitas sancta unitasque firma,
Deitas vera, bonitas immensa,
Lux angelorum, salus orphanorum,
Spesque cunctorum,

Serviunt tibi cuncta, quae creasti;
Te tuae cunctae laudant creaturae;
Nos quoque tibi psallimus devoti;
Tu nos exaudi.

Gloria tibi, omnipotens Deus,
Trinus et unus, magnus et excelsus;
Te decet hymnus, honor, laus, et decus
Nunc et in aevum. Amen.

This Trinity hymn of unknown authorship is dated c. 900. It was an office hymn for that feast in the Sarum, York, Aberdeen, Old Roman (Venice, 1478), and other breviaries. In its external form it is a sapphic, but its rhythm is not the classical one.

The translation is by Percy Dearmer and was made for the *English Hymnal*, 1906.

For comments on the tune "Herzliebster Jesu" see Hymn No. 143.

Father, in Whom We Live 241

1. Father, in whom we live,
   In whom we are and move,
   All glory, power, and praise receive
   For Thy creating love.

2. O Thou Incarnate Word,
   Let all Thy ransomed race
   Unite in thanks with one accord
   For Thy redeeming grace.

3. Spirit of Holiness,
   Let all Thy saints adore
   Thy sacred gifts and join to bless
   Thy heart-renewing power.

4. Eternal Triune Lord,
   Let all the hosts above,
   Let all the sons of men record,
   And dwell upon, Thy love.

Charles Wesley first published the hymn from which this cento is taken in four eight-line stanzas, in his *Hymns for Those that Seek,*" etc., 1747.

The tune "Dover," also called "Hampton" and "Durham," is by Aaron Williams and appeared c. 1770 in his *Psalmody in Miniature.*

Father of Heaven, Whose Love Profound 242

1. Father of heaven, whose love profound
   A ransom for our souls hath found,
   Before Thy throne we sinners bend;
   To us Thy pardoning love extend.

2. Almighty Son, Incarnate Word,
   Our Prophet, Priest, Redeemer, Lord,
   Before Thy throne we sinners bend;
   To us Thy saving grace extend.

3. Eternal Spirit, by whose breath
   The soul is raised from sin and death,
   Before Thy throne we sinners bend;
   To us Thy quickening power extend.

4. Thrice holy! Father, Spirit, Son,
   Mysterious Godhead, Three in One,
   Before Thy throne we sinners bend;
   Grace, pardon, life, to us extend.

Edward Cooper, according to his son Henry G. Cooper, contributed this hymn to the *Uttoxeter Selection*, 1805. It is based on the Litany.

For comments on the tune "Angelus" see Hymn No. 115.

TRINITY

243   Oh, that I Had a Thousand Voices

1. Oh, that I had a thousand voices
To praise my God with thousand tongues!
My heart, which in the Lord rejoices,
Would then proclaim in grateful songs
To all, wherever I might be,
What great things God hath done for me.

2. Dear Father, endless praise I render
For soul and body, strangely joined;
I praise Thee, Guardian kind and tender,
For all the noble joys I find
So richly spread on every side
And freely for my use supplied.

3. I praise Thee, Savior, whose compassion
Hath brought Thee down to ransom me;
Thy pitying heart sought my salvation,
Though keenest woes were heaped on Thee,
Brought me from bondage full release,
Made me Thine own and gave me peace.

4. Glory and praise, still onward reaching,
Be Thine, O Spirit of all grace,
Whose holy power and faithful teaching
Give me among Thy saints a place!
Whate'er of good by me is done
Is of Thy grace and light alone.

5. Shall I not, then, be filled with gladness?
Shall I not praise Thee evermore
And triumph over fear and sadness,
E'en when my cup of woe runs o'er?
Though heaven and earth shall pass away,
Thy loving-kindness stands for aye.

O dass ich tausend Zungen hätte
Und einen tausendfachen Mund,
So stimmt' ich damit in die Wette
Vom allertiefsten Herzensgrund
Ein Loblied nach dem andern an
Von dem, was Gott an mir getan!

Dir sei, o allerliebster Vater,
Unendlich Lob für Seel' und Leib!
Lob sei dir, mildester Berater,
Für allen edlen Zeitvertreib,
Den du mir in der ganzen Welt
Zu meinem Nutzen hast bestellt.

Mein treuster Jesu, sei gepriesen,
Dass dein erbarmungsvolles Herz
Sich mir so hilfreich hat erwiesen
Und mich durch Blut und Todesschmerz
Von aller Teufel Grausamkeit
Zu deinem Eigentum befreit.

Auch dir sei ewig Ruhm und Ehre,
O heilig werter Gottesgeist,
Für deines Trostes süsse Lehre,
Die mich ein Kind des Lebens heisst.
Ach, wo was Gut's von mir geschicht,
Das wirket nur dein göttlich Licht!

Wie sollt' ich nun nicht voller Freuden
In deinem steten Lobe stehn?
Wie sollt' ich auch im tiefsten Leiden
Nicht triumphierend einhergehn?
Und fiele auch der Himmel ein,
So will ich doch nicht traurig sein.

This cento is composed of Stanzas 1, 6, 7, 8, and 12 of Johann Mentzer's great hymn. For further comments see the other cento, Hymn No. 30.

The composite translation was prepared for *The Lutheran Hymnal.*

The tune "O dass ich tausend" is not to be confused with the tune of the same name by Johann B. König. (See Hymn No. 30.) This tune is by Kornelius Heinrich Dretzel, who edited *Des evangelischen Zions Musikalische Harmonie,* Nürnberg, 1731, in which this tune appeared.

244   Glory Be to God the Father

1. Glory be to God the Father,
Glory be to God the Son,
Glory be to God the Spirit:
Great Jehovah, Three in One!
Glory, glory,
While eternal ages run!

2. Glory be to Him who loved us,
Washed us from each spot and stain;
Glory be to Him who bought us,
Made us kings with Him to reign!
Glory, glory,
To the Lamb that once was slain!

3. Glory to the King of angels,
Glory to the Church's King,
Glory to the King of nations;
Heaven and earth, your praises bring!
Glory, glory,
To the King of Glory sing!

4. Glory, blessing, praise eternal!
Thus the choir of angels sings;
Honor, riches, power, dominion!
Thus its praise creation brings.
Glory, glory,
Glory to the King of kings!

Horatius Bonar first published this hymn of praise in his *Hymns of Faith and Hope,* third series, 1866. It calls to mind the joyful praise in Rev. 1:5, 6: "Unto Him that loved us and washed us from our sins in His own blood and hath made us kings and priests unto God and His Father: to Him be glory and dominion forever and ever. Amen."

The tune "Worcester" is by Walter Grenville Whinfield († 1919). We have not been able to discover the date of this composition.

God Loved the World So that He Gave 245

1. God loved the world so that He gave
His only Son the lost to save
That all who would in Him believe
Should everlasting life receive.

2. Christ Jesus is the Ground of faith,
Who was made flesh and suffered death;
All that confide in Him alone
Are built on this chief Corner-stone.

3. God would not have the sinner die,
His Son with saving grace is nigh,
His Spirit in the Word doth teach
How man the blessed goal may reach.

4. Be of good cheer, for God's own Son
Forgives all sins which thou hast done;
Thou'rt justified by Jesus' blood,
Thy Baptism grants the highest good.

5. If thou be sick, if death draw near,
This truth thy troubled heart can cheer:
Christ Jesus saves my soul from death,
That is the firmest ground of faith.

6. Glory to God the Father, Son,
And Holy Spirit, Three in One!
To Thee, O blessed Trinity,
Be praise now and eternally!

Also hat Gott die Welt geliebt,
Dass er uns seinen Sohn hergibt,
Dass, wer ihm traut und glaubt allein,
Kann und soll ewig selig sein.

Der Glaubensgrund ist Jesus Christ,
Der für uns selbst Mensch worden ist.
Wer seinem Mittler fest vertraut,
Der bleibt auf diesen Grund gebaut.

Dein Gott will nicht des Sünders Tod,
Sein Sohn hilft uns aus aller Not,
Der Heil'ge Geist lehrt dich durchs Wort,
Dass du wirst selig hier und dort.

Drum sei getrost, weil Gottes Sohn
Die Sünd' vergibt, der Gnadenthron;
Du bist gerecht durch Christi Blut,
Die Tauf' schenkt dir das höchste Gut.

Bist du krank, kommst du gar in Tod,
So merk dies wohl in aller Not;
Mein Jesus macht die Seel' gesund,
Das ist der rechte Glaubensgrund.

Ehr' sei dem Vater und dem Sohn
Samt Heil'gem Geist in *einem* Thron,
Welch's ihm auch also sei bereit't
Von nun an bis in Ewigkeit.

This hymn, by an unknown author, is from the *Kirchengesangbuch für Evangelisch-Lutherische Gemeinden*, St. Louis, where the source is given as *Bollhagen Gesangbuch*, 1791. We have been unable to trace it further.

The translation is by August Crull, slightly altered, in the *Evangelical Lutheran Hymn-Book*, 1912.

The tune "St. Crispin" was composed in 1862 by George J. Elvey. It appeared in *A Selection of Psalm and Hymn Tunes*, edited by E. H. Thorne, 1863. It was composed for the hymn "Just as I Am." (See Hymn No. 388.)

Holy, Holy, Holy, Lord God Almighty 246

1. Holy, holy, holy, Lord God Almighty!
Early in the morning our song shall rise to Thee;
Holy, holy, holy, merciful and mighty!
God in Three Persons, blessed Trinity!

2. Holy, holy, holy! All the saints adore Thee,
Casting down their golden crowns around the glassy sea;
Cherubim and seraphim falling down before Thee,
Which wert and art and evermore shalt be.

3. Holy, holy, holy! Though the darkness hide Thee,
Though the eye of sinful man Thy glory may not see,
Only Thou art holy; there is none beside Thee,
Perfect in power, in love, and purity.

4. Holy, holy, holy! Lord God Almighty!
All Thy works shall praise Thy name in earth and sky and sea.
Holy, holy, holy, merciful and mighty!
God in Three Persons, blessed Trinity!

This great Trinity hymn is a metrical paraphrase of Rev. 4:8-11, "And the four beasts had each of them six wings about him; and they were full of eyes within; and they rest not day and night, saying, Holy, holy, holy, Lord God Almighty, which was and is and is to come. And when those beasts give glory and honor and thanks to Him that sat on the throne, who liveth forever and ever, the four and twenty elders fall down before Him that sat on the throne and worship Him that liveth forever and ever and cast their crowns before the throne, saying, Thou art worthy, O Lord, to receive glory and honor and power;

for Thou hast created all things, and for Thy pleasure they are and were created."

The hymn was written by Reginald Heber. It was first published in *A Selection of Psalms and Hymns for the Parish Church of Banbury*, third edition, 1826, and then in the author's posthumous *Hymns*, etc., 1827. It was intended for use on Trinity Sunday.

The tune "Nicaea" was written for the hymn by John B. Dykes and appeared in *Hymns Ancient and Modern*, 1861. It was named "Nicaea" because the doctrine of the Trinity was definitely established as a dogma in the Church at the Council of Nicaea, 325 A. D., against the Arians.

247   God the Father, Be Our Stay

1. God the Father, be our Stay,
   Oh, let us perish never.
   Cleanse us from our sins, we pray,
   And grant us life forever.
      Keep us from the Evil One;
   Uphold our faith most holy,
   Grant us to trust Thee solely
   With humble hearts and lowly.
      Let us put God's armor on:
   With all true Christians running
   Our heavenly race and shunning
   The devil's wiles and cunning.
      Amen, Amen, this be done,
   So sing we, Hallelujah!

2. Jesus Christ, be Thou our Stay, etc.

3. Holy Ghost, be Thou our Stay, etc.

Gott der Vater wohn' uns bei
Und lass' uns nicht verderben,
Mach' uns aller Sünden frei
Und helf' uns selig sterben!
   Vor dem Teufel uns bewahr',
Halt uns bei festem Glauben
Und auf dich lass uns bauen,
Aus Herzensgrund vertrauen.
   Dir uns lassen ganz und gar,
Mit allen rechten Christen
Entfliehen Teufels Listen,
Mit Waffen Gott's uns fristen!
   Amen, Amen, das sei wahr,
So singen wir: Halleluja!

Jesus Christus wohn' uns bei usw.

Heilig Geist, der wohn' uns bei usw.

This is a medieval litany, revised by Martin Luther. Its origin is fifteenth century or earlier. *Wackernagel* gives a version of 1422, in 15 lines, beginning "Sanctus Petrus won uns bey." In some parts of Germany it was used "in time of Processions or St. Mark's Day and in Rogation Week." Luther recast portions of the earlier version, removed the invocations to Mary, the Angels, and the saints, and published his version in Johann Walther's *Geystliche gesangk Buchleyn*, Wittenberg, 1524.

The translation is an altered form of that by Richard Massie in his *Martin Luther's Spiritual Songs*, London, 1854.

The tune "Gott der Vater wohn'" is of 14th-century origin. It appeared with the revised hymn of Luther in 1524, as above.

248   Father of Glory, to Thy Name

1. Father of glory, to Thy name
   Immortal praise we give,
   Who dost an act of grace proclaim
   And bid us rebels live.

2. Immortal honor to the Son,
   Who makes Thine anger cease;
   Our lives He ransomed with His own
   And died to make our peace.

3. To Thine almighty Spirit be
   Immortal glory given,
   Whose teachings bring us near to Thee
   And train us up for heaven.

4. Let men with their united voice
   Adore the eternal God
   And spread His honors and their joys
   Through nations far abroad.

5. Let faith and love and duty join
   One grateful song to raise;
   Let saints in earth and heaven combine
   In harmony and praise.

TRINITY

This Trinity hymn by Isaac Watts is from his *Sermons*, c. 1721. For a concise presentation of the essentials of our holy faith and the resultant duty of praise by word and deed this hymn is almost in a class by itself.

For comments on the tune "Nun danket all'" see Hymn No. 10.

Isaiah, Mighty Seer, in Days of Old   249

1. Isaiah, mighty seer, in days of old
The Lord of all in spirit did behold
   High on a lofty throne, in splendor bright,
   With flowing train that filled the Temple quite.
Above the throne were stately seraphim,
Six wings had they, these messengers of Him.
   With twain they veiled their faces, as was meet,
   With twain in reverent awe they hid their feet,
And with the other twain aloft they soared.
One to the other called and praised the Lord:
   "Holy is God, the Lord of Sabaoth!
   Holy is God, the Lord of Sabaoth!
   Holy is God, the Lord of Sabaoth!
   Behold, His glory filleth all the earth!"
The beams and lintels trembled at the cry,
And clouds of smoke enwrapped the throne on high.

Jesaia, dem Propheten, das geschah,
Dass er im Geist den Herren sitzen sah
   Auf einem hohen Thron in hellem Glanz,
   Seines Kleides Saum den Chor füllet' ganz.
Es stunden zween Seraph bei ihm daran,
Sechs Flügel sah er einen jeden han:
   Mit zween verbargen sie ihr Antlitz klar,
   Mit zween bedeckten sie die Füsse gar,
Und mit den andern zween sie flogen frei,
Genander riefen sie mit grossem G'schrei:
   Heilig ist Gott, der Herre Zebaoth!
   Heilig ist Gott, der Herre Zebaoth!
   Heilig ist Gott, der Herre Zebaoth!
   Sein' Ehr' die ganze Welt erfüllet hat.
Von dem G'schrei zittert' Schwell' und Balken gar,
Das Haus auch ganz voll Rauchs und Nebels war.

This is Luther's famous German *Sanctus*, based on Is. 6:1-4. It was first published in his *Deutsche Messe*, etc., 1526, together with its traditional melody.

According to the rubrics of Luther's order of service for Holy Communion the bread was first consecrated and distributed, and then was sung either this *Sanctus* or Luther's "Gott sei gelobet" (see Hymn No. 313) or John Huss's "Iesus Christus, nostra salus" (see Hymn No. 311). The wine was then consecrated and received.

The translation, a composite, was prepared for *The Lutheran Hymnal*.

The tune "Jesaia, dem Propheten," inseparably connected with this hymn, is by Martin Luther himself.

Holy God, We Praise Thy Name   250

1. Holy God, we praise Thy name;
   Lord of all, we bow before Thee.
All on earth Thy scepter claim,
   All in heaven above adore Thee.
Infinite Thy vast domain,
Everlasting is Thy reign.

2. Hark! the glad celestial hymn
   Angel choirs above are raising;
Cherubim and seraphim,
   In unceasing chorus praising,
Fill the heavens with sweet accord:
Holy, holy, holy, Lord!

3. Lo, the apostles' holy train
   Join Thy sacred name to hallow;
Prophets swell the glad refrain,
   And the white-robed martyrs follow,
And from morn to set of sun
Through the Church the song goes on.

Grosser Gott, wir loben dich,
   Herr, wir preisen deine Stärke,
Vor dir beugt die Erde sich
   Und bewundert deine Werke.
Wie du warst vor aller Zeit,
So bleibst du in Ewigkeit.

Alles, was dich preisen kann,
   Cherubim und Seraphinen,
Stimmen dir ein Loblied an.
   Alle Engel, die dir dienen,
Rufen dir in sel'ger Ruh':
Heilig, heilig, heilig! zu.

Der Apostel heil'ger Chor,
   Der Propheten grosse Menge
Schickt zu deinem Thron empor
   Neue Lob- und Dankgesänge.
Der Blutzeugen grosse Schar
Lobt und preist dich immerdar.

TRINITY

4. Holy Father, holy Son,
   Holy Spirit, three we name Thee;
   Though in essence only one,
   Undivided God we claim Thee
   And, adoring, bend the knee
   While we own the mystery.

Sie verehrt den Heil'gen Geist,
   Welcher uns mit seinen Lehren
   Und mit Troste kräftig speist;
   Der, o König aller Ehren,
   Der mit dir, Herr Jesu Christ,
   Und dem Vater ewig ist.

This cento is a portion of the very popular German *Te Deum* "Grosser Gott, wir loben dich," which appeared in eight stanzas in the *Allgemeines Katholisches Gesangbuch,* Vienna (undated), c. 1775, together with the tune. Both author and composer are unknown, although some have credited Peter Ritter (1760—1846) with the tune. This is hardly probable, as he was only a boy when it was first published.

The translation is by Clarence A. Walworth, slightly altered. It is dated 1853 in the *Evangelical Hymnal,* New York, 1880, where it seems to have first appeared. The translation is rather free, and Walworth condensed the original eight stanzas into seven. The stanzas above are one to four of Walworth's version. The omitted Stanzas 5 to 7 read:

5. Thou art King of Glory, Christ;
   Son of God, yet born of Mary.
   For us sinners sacrificed,
   As to death a Tributary,
   First to break the bars of death,
   Thou hast opened heaven to faith.

6. From Thy high celestial home,
   Judge of all, again returning,
   We believe that Thou shalt come
   On the dreadful Doomsday morning,
   When Thy voice shall shake the earth
   And the startled dead come forth.

7. Spare Thy people, Lord, we pray,
   By a thousand snares surrounded;
   Keep us without sin today,
   Never let us be confounded.
   Lo, I put my trust in Thee;
   Never, Lord, abandon me. Amen.

The tune "Grosser Gott" has been widely used in English hymnals, in a slightly recast form, under such names as "Hursley," "Pascal," "Paris," "Stillorgan," "Frammingham." (See "Hursley," Hymn No. 551.)

251   We All Believe in One True God

1. We all believe in one true God,
   Who created earth and heaven,
   The Father, who to us in love
   Hath the right of children given.
   He both soul and body feedeth,
   All we need He doth provide us;
   He through snares and perils leadeth,
   Watching that no harm betide us.
   He careth for us day and night,
   All things are governed by His might.

Wir glauben all' an *einen* Gott,
   Schöpfer Himmels und der Erden,
   Der sich zum Vater geben hat,
   Dass wir seine Kinder werden.
   Er will uns allzeit ernähren,
   Leib und Seel' auch wohl bewahren,
   Allem Unfall will er wehren,
   Kein Leid soll uns widerfahren;
   Er sorget für uns, hüt't und wacht,
   Es steht alles in seiner Macht.

2. We all believe in Jesus Christ,
   His own Son, our Lord, possessing
   An equal Godhead, throne, and might,
   Source of every grace and blessing.
   Born of Mary, virgin mother,
   By the power of the Spirit,
   Made true man, our elder Brother,
   That the lost might life inherit;
   Was crucified for sinful men
   And raised by God to life again.

Wir glauben auch an Jesum Christ,
   Seinen Sohn und unsern Herren,
   Der ewig bei dem Vater ist,
   Gleicher Gott von Macht und Ehren;
   Von Maria, der Jungfrauen,
   Ist ein wahrer Mensch geboren
   Durch den Heil'gen Geist im Glauben,
   Für uns, die wir war'n verloren,
   Am Kreuz gestorben und vom Tod
   Wieder auferstanden durch Gott.

3. We all confess the Holy Ghost,
   Who sweet grace and comfort giveth
   And with the Father and the Son
   In eternal glory liveth;
   Who the Church, His own creation,
   Keeps in unity of spirit.
   Here forgiveness and salvation
   Daily come through Jesus' merit.
   All flesh shall rise, and we shall be
   In bliss with God eternally. Amen.

Wir glauben an den Heil'gen Geist,
   Gott mit Vater und dem Sohne,
   Der aller Blöden Tröster heisst
   Und mit Gaben zieret schöne,
   Die ganz' Christenheit auf Erden
   Hält in *einem* Sinn gar eben;
   Hier all' Sünd' vergeben werden,
   Das Fleisch soll auch wieder leben.
   Nach diesem Elend ist bereit
   Uns ein Leben in Ewigkeit. Amen.

TRINITY

This is Luther's metrical paraphrase of the Nicene Creed. It was first published in *Geistliche gesangk Buchleyn,* Wittenberg, 1524, and again in 1525, together with the second tune.

The translation is composite.

The first tune of "Wir glauben all' an einen Gott" is from the manuscript *Choral-Buch* of Cantor Wagner, Langenöls, 1742.

The second tune is based upon the old Latin *Credo* in use at least as early as 1300. It is not certain whether Luther or his friend Johann Walther recast the tune for this hymn.

We All Believe in One True God   252

1. We all believe in one true God,
Father, Son, and Holy Ghost,
Ever-present Help in need,
  Praised by all the heavenly host,
By whose mighty power alone
All is made and wrought and done.

2. We all believe in Jesus Christ,
  Son of God and Mary's Son,
Who descended from His throne
  And for us salvation won;
By whose cross and death are we
Rescued from all misery.

3. We all confess the Holy Ghost,
  Who from both fore'er proceeds;
Who upholds and comforts us
  In all trials, fears, and needs.
Blest and holy Trinity,
Praise forever be to Thee!

Wir glauben all' an *einen* Gott,
  Vater, Sohn und Heil'gen Geist,
Der uns hilft in aller Not,
  Den die Schar der Engel preist,
Der durch seine grosse Kraft
Alles wirket, tut und schafft.

Wir glauben auch an Jesum Christ,
  Gottes und Marien Sohn,
Der vom Himmel kommen ist
  Und uns führt in's Himmels Thron
Und uns durch sein Blut und Tod
Hat erlöst aus aller Not.

Wir glauben auch an Heil'gen Geist,
  Der von beiden gehet aus,
Der uns Trost und Beistand leist't
  Wider alle Furcht und Graus.
Heilige Dreifaltigkeit,
Sei gepreist zu aller Zeit!

This metrical paraphrase of the Apostles' Creed is by Tobias Clausnitzer. It first appeared in the Culmbach-Bayreuth *Gesang-Buch,* 1668.

The translation is an altered form of that by Catherine Winkworth in her *Chorale Book for England,* 1863.

The tune "Wir glauben all' an einen Gott" was originally set to this hymn in the *Kirchengesangbuch,* Darmstadt, 1699. It was recast, however, in Dretzel's *Choral-Buch,* 1731, and in this form it is most widely used.

In One True God We All Believe   253

1. In one true God we all believe
And to His name all glory give.
Creator of all things is He
In the heaven, the earth, the sea.

2. We all believe in God's own Son,
Our Lord, the Sole-begotten One;
And by the Holy Ghost the same
Of a virgin man became.

3. By Pontius Pilate crucified,
He suffered on the Tree and died;
To show of Satan's reign the end,
He did into hell descend.

4. The same Lord Christ of Nazareth
Who for all sinners tasted death
The third day after He had died
Rose with body glorified.

Věříme v všemohoucího
Otce, i vševědoucího,
Jenž stvořil nebe s hvězdami
A zemi s úrodami.

I v Ježíše, Syna jeho,
Jednoho Pána našeho,
Duchem Svatým počatého,
Z panny narozeného.

Pod Pilátem ukřižován,
Trpěl, umřel i pochován,
Po smrti sstoupil do pekla,
Aby svým pomoh' z pekla.

Týž Pán Ježíš Nazaretský,
Kterýžto umřel za všecky,
Vstal vítězně třetího dne,
Vzal tělo oslavené.

[185]

5. In full accord with God's own Word
This holy body of our Lord,
Although in death's grim grasp it be,
Never would corruption see.

Tak jest na Něj to slušelo,
Aby jeho svaté tělo
Nevidělo porušení,
Než věčné oslavení.

6. He then ascended into heaven,
Where endless power to Him was given;
And there for us in all our needs
Graciously He intercedes.

Potomně vstoupil na nebe,
Sedí Otce na pravici,
A přimlouvá se za tebe
I za všecky věřící.

7. From thence He'll come, as once He said,
To judge the living and the dead.
O righteous Judge, our Savior, come,
Take us to our heavenly home!

Odtud zase má přijíti
Živé i mrtvé souditi.
Přijď, Kriste, nejvyšší soudi!
Tebeť prosíme chudí.

8. We all confess the Holy Ghost,
Who guides the Church, a chosen host,
And binds the saints in purest love
Here on earth and there above.

Věříme v Ducha Svatého,
Církev svatou řídícího,
V níž jest svatých obcování
V pořádném milování.

9. And to this truth we also cleave,
That we forgiveness do receive,
True peace and joy and comfort sweet,
Daily from the Paraclete.

Věříme též, že z milosti
A zásluh Páně hodnosti
Dojdem hříchů odpuštění,
I těl našich vzkříšení.

10. From death our bodies shall arise
To endless life beyond the skies;
By grace through Jesus we shall rest
There in heaven, forever blest.

I život věčný věříme,
Kterýž v Kristu obdržíme,
Jenž zhasil pekelný plamen:
Rcemež spoločně: Amen.

This is Juraj Tranovsky's free metrical paraphrase of the Apostles' Creed. It appeared in the first edition of the *Tranoscius*, 1636.

The translation is composite and was prepared for *The Lutheran Hymnal*.

The tune "Resurgenti Nazareno," a Bohemian melody, is dated 1505.

254   Lord God, We All to Thee Give Praise

1. Lord God, we all to Thee give praise,
Thanksgivings meet to Thee we raise,
That angel hosts Thou didst create
Around Thy glorious throne to wait.

Herr Gott, dich loben alle wir
Und sollen billig danken dir
Für dein Geschöpf der Engel schön,
Die um dich schweb'n vor deinem Thron.

2. They shine with light and heavenly grace
And constantly behold Thy face;
They heed Thy voice, they know it well,
In godly wisdom they excel.

Sie glänzen hell und leuchten klar
Und sehen dich ganz offenbar,
Dein' Stimm' sie hören allezeit
Und sind voll göttlicher Weisheit.

3. They never rest nor sleep as we;
Their whole delight is but to be
With Thee, Lord Jesus, and to keep
Thy little flock, Thy lambs and sheep.

Sie feiern auch und schlafen nicht,
Ihr Fleiss ist gar dahin gericht't,
Dass sie, Herr Christe, um dich sei'n
Und um dein armes Häufelein.

4. The ancient Dragon is their foe;
His envy and his wrath they know.
It always is his aim and pride
Thy Christian people to divide.

Der alte Drach' und böse Feind
Vor Neid, Hass und vor Zorne brennt;
Sein Dichten steht allein darauf,
Wie von ihm werd' zertrennt dein Hauf'.

5. As he of old deceived the world
And into sin and death has hurled,
So he now subtly lies in wait
To ruin school and Church and State.

Und wie er vormals bracht' in Not
Die Welt, führt er sie noch in Tod;
Kirch', Wort, Gesetz, all' Ehrbarkeit
Zu tilgen, ist er stets bereit.

6. A roaring lion, round he goes,
No halt nor rest he ever knows;
He seeks the Christians to devour
And slay them in his dreadful power.

Darum kein' Rast noch Ruh' er hat,
Brüllt wie ein Löw', tracht't früh und spat,
Legt Garn und Strick, braucht falsche List,
Dass er verderb', was christlich ist.

7. But watchful is the angel band
That follows Christ on every hand
To guard His people where they go
And break the counsel of the Foe.

Also schützt Gott noch heutzutag'
Vor Übel und gar mancher Plag'
Uns durch die lieben Engelein,
Die uns zu Wächtern geben sein.

8. For this, now and in days to be,
Our praise shall rise, O Lord, to Thee,
Whom all the angel hosts adore
With grateful songs forevermore.

Darum wir billig loben dich
Und danken dir, Gott, ewiglich,
Wie auch der lieben Engel Schar
Dich preiset heut' und immerdar.

Philip Melanchthon's hymn "Dicimus grates tibi" first appeared in ten stanzas in *De Angelis Duo Hymni*, Wittenberg, 1543. Later *Wackernagel* gives it in eleven stanzas as follows:

1. Dicimus grates tibi, summe rerum
Conditor, gnato tua quod ministros
flammeos finxit manus angelorum
agmina pura.

2. Qui tuae lucis radiis vibrantes
te vident laetis oculis, tuasque
hauriunt voces, sapientiaeque
fonte fruuntur.

3. Nos non ignavum finis esse vulgus,
nec per ingentes volitare frustra
aetheris tractus, temere nec inter
ludere ventos.

4. Sed iubes Christo comites adesse
et pios caetus hominum tueri,
qui tuas leges venerantur, atque
discere curant.

5. Impiis ardens odiis et ira
nam tuis castris draco semper infert
bella, qui primis scelus atque mortem
intulit orbi.

6. Hic domos, urbes, tua templa, gentes
et tuae legis monumenta tota
et bonos mores abolere tentat
funditus omnes,

7. Interim sed nos regit angelorum,
quae ducem Christum sequitur, caterva,
atque grassantis reprimit cruenta
arma draconis.

8. Angeli Lothon Sodomae tuentur,
inter infestos Clisaeus hostes,
angelis cinctus, nihil extimescit
bellica signa.

9. Tutus est inter medios leones,
angelis septus, Daniel propheta:
sic tegit semper Deus his ministris
omnia nostra.

10. Hoc tum munus celebramus una,
et tibi noster chorus angelique
gratias dicunt simul accinentes,
Conditor alme.

11. Et tuo templo vigiles ut addas
angelos semper, populoque, gnati,
qui tui verbum colit, obsecramus
pectore toto.

Paul Eber gave the hymn its German form. This version appeared in a separate print, c. 1554, at Nürnberg, in twelve stanzas. The cento, composed of Stanzas 1 to 6 and 11, is taken from the English translation by Emanuel Cronenwett. This translation appeared in the Ohio *Lutheran Hymnal*, 1880.

For comments on the tune "Old Hundredth" see Hymn No. 13.

Stars of the Morning, So Gloriously Bright 255

1. Stars of the morning, so gloriously bright,
Filled with celestial virtue and light,
These that, where night never followeth day,
Praise the Thrice Holy One ever and aye.

2. These are Thy ministers, these dost Thou own,
Lord God of Sabaoth, nearest Thy throne;
These are Thy messengers, these dost Thou send,
Help of the helpless ones, man to defend.

3. Then, when the earth was first poised in mid space,
Then, when the planets first sped on their race,
Then, when were ended the six days' employ,
Then all the sons of God shouted for joy.

4. Still let them succor us, still let them fight,
Lord of angelic hosts, battling for right,
Till, where their anthems they ceaselessly pour,
We with the angels may bow and adore. Amen.

Julian states that in John M. Neale's *Hymns of the Eastern Church*, 1862, this hymn appeared with the following title and note: "Stars of the Morning.

A cento from the Canon of the 'Bodiless Ones.' Tuesday in the Week of the Fourth Tone." The Greek original, by St. Joseph the Hymnographer, begins: Φωστῆρες τῆς ἀΰλου οὐσίας. Neale's translation is in five stanzas. It can hardly be called a translation, as Neale "followed the spirit rather than the letter of the original." The omitted Stanza 3 reads:

> These keep the guard amid Salem's dear bowers,
> Thrones, principalities, virtues, and powers,
> Where, with the living ones, mystical four,
> Cherubim, seraphim, bow and adore.

The tune "O quanta qualia" is found in *La Feillée's Methode du Plain-Chant*, 1808, but is probably of 17th-century origin. It has its name from its use with the hymn of Pierre Abélard, "O quanta qualia sunt illa sabbata," a hymn for Saturday evening worship. The famous scholar wrote it for the Abbey of the Paraclete at Nogent-sur-Seine, over which Héloïse presided. The original melody is not plain-song in the ancient sense.

256   Around the Throne of God a Band

1. Around the throne of God a band
Of glorious angels ever stand;
Bright things they see, sweet harps they hold,
And on their heads are crowns of gold.

2. Some wait around Him, ready still
To sing His praise and do His will;
And some, when He commands them, go
To guard His servants here below.

3. Lord, give Thy angels every day
Command to guide us on our way
And bid them every evening keep
Their watch around us while we sleep.

4. So shall no wicked thing draw near
To do us harm or cause us fear;
And we shall dwell, when life is past,
With angels round Thy throne at last.

John M. Neale first published this children's hymn in his *Hymns for Children*, first series, 1842, in nine stanzas (with the long-meter doxology of Thomas Ken). This cento contains Stanzas 1, 2, 8, and 9 of the original.

For comments on the tune "Winchester New" see Hymn No. 12.

257   Jesus, Brightness of the Father

1. Jesus, Brightness of the Father,
   Life and Strength of all who live,
For creating guardian angels
   Glory to Thy name we give
And Thy wondrous praise rehearse,
Singing in harmonious verse.

2. Blessed Lord, by their protection
   Shelter us from harm this day,
Keep us pure in flesh and spirit,
   Save us from the Foe, we pray,
And vouchsafe us by Thy grace
In Thy Paradise a place.

3. Glory to the almighty Father
   Sing we with the heavenly host;
Glory to the great Redeemer,
   Glory to the Holy Ghost;
Three in One and One in Three,
Throughout all eternity!

Tibi, Christe, splendor Patris,
   Vita, virtus cordium,
In conspectu angelorum
   Votis, voce psallimus;
Alternantes concrepando
Melos damus vocibus.

Quo custode procul pelle,
   Rex, Christe piissime,
Omne nefas inimici
   Mundo corde et corpore;
Paradiso redde tuo
Nos sola clementia.

Gloriam Patri melodis
   Personem vocibus,
Gloriam Christo canamus,
   Gloriam Paraclito,
Qui Deus trinus et unus
Extat ante saecula. Amen.

This hymn is ascribed to Rhabanus Maurus († 856), but his authorship is doubtful. The translation is an altered form of that by Edward Caswall in his *Lyra Catholica*, 1849.

For comments on the tune "Neander" see Hymn No. 1.

REFORMATION

Lord of Our Life and God of Our Salvation 258

1. Lord of our life and God of our
    salvation,
Star of our night and Hope of every
    nation,
Hear and receive Thy Church's
    supplication,
    Lord God Almighty.

2. See round Thine ark the hungry billows
    curling;
See how Thy foes their banners are un-
    furling.
Lord, while their darts envenomed they are
    hurling,
    Thou canst preserve us.

3. Lord, Thou canst help when earthly armor
    faileth;
Lord, Thou canst save when deadly sin
    assaileth;
Lord, o'er Thy Church nor death nor hell
    prevaileth;
    Grant us Thy peace, Lord:

4. Peace in our hearts, our evil thoughts
    assuaging;
Peace in Thy Church where brothers are
    engaging;
Peace when the world its busy war is
    waging,
    Calm Thy foes' raging.

5. Grant us Thy help till backward they are
    driven;
Grant them Thy truth that they may be
    forgiven;
Grant peace on earth or, after we have
    striven,
    Peace in Thy heaven.

Christe, du Beistand deiner Kreuz-
    gemeine,
Eile, mit Hilf' und Rettung uns
    erscheine;
Steure den Feinden, ihre Blut-
    gerichte
    Mache zunichte!

Streite doch selber für uns arme
    Kinder,
Wehre dem Teufel, seine Macht
    verhinder';
Alles, was kämpfet wider deine
    Glieder,
    Stürze danieder!

Frieden bei Kirch' und Schulen uns
    beschere,
Frieden zugleich der Obrigkeit
    gewähre,
Frieden dem Herzen, Frieden dem
    Gewissen
    Gib zu geniessen!

Also wird zeitlich deine Güt'
    erhoben,
Also wird ewig und ohn' Ende
    loben
Dich, o du Wächter deiner armen
    Herde,
    Himmel und Erde.

The earliest definite publication date of this hymn by Matthäus Apelles von Löwenstern is in *Kirchen- vnd Haus-Music*, Breslau, 1644, in four stanzas. It was entitled "Sapphic Ode. For spiritual and temporal peace." The English text is more a free paraphrase than a translation. It was contributed by Philip Pusey to A. R. Reinagle's *Psalms and Hymn Tunes*, Oxford, 1840.

For comments on the tune "Herzliebster Jesu" see Hymn No. 43.

Flung to the Heedless Winds 259

1. Flung to the heedless winds
    Or on the waters cast,
The martyrs' ashes, watched,
    Shall gathered be at last.
And from that scattered dust,
    Around us and abroad,
Shall spring a plenteous seed
    Of witnesses for God.

2. The Father hath received
    Their latest living breath,
And vain is Satan's boast
    Of victory in their death.
Still, still, though dead, they speak,
    And, trumpet-tongued, proclaim
To many a wakening land
    The one availing Name.

Die Asche will nicht lassen ab,
    Sie stäubt in allen Landen;
Hier hilft kein Bach, Loch, Grub'
    noch Grab;
Sie macht den Feind zuschanden.
Die er im Leben durch den Mord
Zu schweigen hat gedrungen,
Die muss er tot an allem Ort
Mit aller Stimm' und Zungen
Gar fröhlich lassen singen.

This hymn is from Martin Luther's first poetical production of which we have any record, his "Ein neues Lied wir heben an." It was a ballad written

REFORMATION

in 1523 to commemorate the martyrdom of two young Augustinian monks, Heinrich Voes and Johann Esch, who had been condemned to death and burned at the stake in Brussels on June 30, 1523, because of their Lutheran faith. It first appeared in part in *Eyn Enchiridion* Erfurt, 1524; Stanzas 9 and 10 were added in *Geystliche gesangk Buchleyn*, Wittenberg, 1524. Richard Massie, in his *Martin Luther's Spiritual Songs*, gives us this version of the ballad:

1. By help of God I fain would tell
   A new and wondrous story
   And sing a marvel that befell
   To His great praise and glory.
   At Brussels, in the Netherlands,
   He hath His banner lifted,
   To show His wonders by the hands
   Of two youths highly gifted
   With rich and heavenly graces.

2. One of these youths was called John,
   And Henry was the other,
   Rich in the grace of God was one,
   A Christian true his brother.
   For God's dear Word they shed their blood
   And from the world departed
   Like bold and pious sons of God;
   Faithful and lion-hearted,
   They won the crown of martyrs.

3. The old Arch-fiend did them immure,
   To terrify them seeking;
   They bade them God's dear Word abjure
   And fain would stop their speaking.
   From Louvain many Sophists came,
   Versed deeply in the schools,
   And met together at the game.
   The Spirit made them fools;
   They could not but be losers.

4. Now sweet, now harsher tones they tried,
   In artifice abounding;
   The youths did firm as rocks abide,
   The Sophists all confounding.
   The enemy waxed fierce in hate,
   And for their life-blood thirsted;
   He fumed and chafed that one so great
   Should by two babes be worsted
   And straightway sought to burn them.

5. Their monkish garb from them they take
   And gown of ordination;
   The youths a cheerful Amen spake
   And showed no hesitation.
   They thanked their God that by His aid
   They now had been denuded
   Of Satan's mock and masquerade,
   Whereby he had deluded
   The world with false pretenses.

6. Thus by the power of grace they were
   True priests of God's own making
   Who offered up themselves e'en there,
   Christ's holy orders taking.
   Dead to the world, they cast aside
   Hypocrisy's sour leaven,
   That, penitent and justified,
   They might go clean to heaven
   And leave all monkish follies.

7. They then were told that they must read
   A note which was dictated;
   They straightway wrote their faith and creed
   And not one jot abated.
   Now mark their heresy! "We must In God be firm believers,
   In mortal men not put our trust,
   For they are all deceivers";
   For this they must be burnèd.

8. Two fires were lit, the youths were brought,
   But all were seized with wonder
   To see them set the flames at naught
   And stood as struck with thunder.
   With joy they came in sight of all
   And sang aloud God's praises;
   The Sophists' courage waxèd small
   Before such wondrous traces
   Of God's almighty finger.

9. The scandal they repent and would Right gladly gloss it over,
   They dare not boast their deed of blood,
   But seek the stain to cover;
   They feel the shame within their breast
   And charge therewith each other;
   But now the Spirit cannot rest,
   For Abel 'gainst his brother
   Doth cry aloud for vengeance.

10. Their ashes never cease to cry,
    The fires are ever flaming,
    Their dust throughout the world doth fly,
    Their murderers' shame proclaiming.
    The voices, which with cruel hands
    They put to silence living,
    Are heard, though dead, throughout all lands
    Their testimony giving
    And loud hosannas singing.

11. From lies to lies they still proceed
    And feign forthwith a story
    To color o'er the murderous deed;
    Their conscience pricks them sorely.
    These saints of God e'en after death
    They slandered and asserted
    The youths had with their latest breath
    Confessed and been converted,
    Their heresy renouncing.

12. Then let them still go on and lie,
    They cannot win a blessing;
    And let us thank God heartily,
    His Word again possessing.
    Summer is even at our door,
    The winter now hath vanished,
    The tender flowerets spring once more,
    And He who winter banished
    Will send a happy summer.

This hymn is a paraphrase of Stanza 10. It appeared in D'Aubigne's *History of the Reformation*, Philadelphia, 1843, and is attributed to John Alexander

REFORMATION

Messenger. Schaff and Gilman, in *Library of Religious Poetry*, ascribe the translation to William Johnson Fox (1786—1864). We have not been able to verify this.

The tune "Denby" is by Charles J. Dale, 1904. It is in *The Lutheran Hymnary*, 1913, where it is set to "My Jesus, as Thou Wilt." (See Hymn No. 420.)

O Lord, Look Down from Heaven, Behold   260

1. O Lord, look down from heaven, behold
And let Thy pity waken;
How few are we within Thy fold,
Thy saints by men forsaken!
True faith seems quenched on every hand,
Men suffer not Thy Word to stand;
Dark times have us o'ertaken.

2. With fraud which they themselves invent
Thy truth they have confounded;
Their hearts are not with one consent
On Thy pure doctrine grounded.
While they parade with outward show,
They lead the people to and fro,
In error's maze astounded.

3. May God root out all heresy
And of false teachers rid us
Who proudly say: "Now, where is he
That shall our speech forbid us?
By right or might we shall prevail;
What we determine cannot fail;
We own no lord and master."

4. Therefore saith God, "I must arise,
The poor My help are needing;
To Me ascend My people's cries,
And I have heard their pleading.
For them My saving Word shall fight
And fearlessly and sharply smite,
The poor with might defending."

5. As silver tried by fire is pure
From all adulteration,
So through God's Word shall men endure
Each trial and temptation.
Its light beams brighter through the cross,
And, purified from human dross,
It shines through every nation.

6. Thy truth defend, O God, and stay
This evil generation;
And from the error of their way
Keep Thine own congregation.
The wicked everywhere abound
And would Thy little flock confound;
But Thou art our Salvation.

Ach Gott vom Himmel, sieh darein
Und lass dich des erbarmen;
Wie wenig sind der Heil'gen dein,
Verlassen sind wir Armen!
Dein Wort man nicht lässt haben wahr,
Der Glaub' ist auch verloschen gar
Bei allen Menschenkindern.

Sie lehren eitel falsche List,
Was eigner Witz erfindet;
Ihr Herz nicht eines Sinnes ist,
In Gottes Wort gegründet.
Der wählet dies, der andre das,
Sie trennen uns ohn' alle Mass'
Und gleissen schön von aussen.

Gott woll' ausrotten alle Lehr'r,
Die falschen Schein uns lehren,
Dazu ihr' Zung' stolz offenbar
Spricht: Trotz, wer will's uns wehren?
Wir haben Recht und Macht allein;
Was *wir* setzen, das gilt gemein;
Wer ist, der uns soll meistern?

Darum spricht Gott: Ich muss auf sein,
Die Armen sind verstöret,
Ihr Seufzen dringt zu mir herein,
Ich hab' ihr' Klag' erhöret.
Mein heilsam Wort soll auf den Plan,
Getrost und frisch sie greifen an
Und sein die Kraft der Armen.

Das Silber, durchs Feu'r siebenmal
Bewährt, wird lauter funden;
Am Gotteswort man warten soll
Desgleichen alle Stunden;
Es will durchs Kreuz bewähret sein,
Da wird sein' Kraft erkannt und Schein
Und leucht't stark in die Lande.

Das woll'st du, Gott, bewahren rein
Vor diesem argen G'schlechte,
Und lass uns dir befohlen sein,
Dass sich's in uns nicht flechte!
Der gottlos' Hauf' sich umher find't,
Wo diese losen Leute sind
In deinem Volk erhaben.

Martin Luther wrote this metrical paraphrase of Ps. 12 in 1523 and published it in the so-called *Achtliederbuch,* Wittenberg, 1524. It appeared in the same year in the Erfurt *Enchiridion* with the tune "Ach Gott vom Himmel," to which it has since been wedded.

The translation is a composite and was prepared for *The Lutheran Hymnal.* The composer is unknown.

Lord, Keep Us Steadfast in Thy Word   261

1. Lord, keep us steadfast in Thy Word;
Curb those who fain by craft and sword
Would wrest the Kingdom from Thy Son
And set at naught all He hath done.

Erhalt uns, Herr, bei deinem Wort
Und steur des Papsts und Türken Mord,
Die Jesum Christum, deinen Sohn,
Wollen stürzen von deinem Thron!

2. Lord Jesus Christ, Thy power make known,
For Thou art Lord of lords alone;
Defend Thy Christendom that we
May evermore sing praise to Thee.

Beweis dein' Macht, Herr Jesu Christ,
Der du Herr aller Herren bist;
Beschirm' dein' arme Christenheit,
Dass sie dich lob' in Ewigkeit!

3. O Comforter of priceless worth,
Send peace and unity on earth.
Support us in our final strife
And lead us out of death to life.

Gott Heil'ger Geist, du Tröster wert,
Gib dein'm Volk ein'rlei Sinn auf Erd',
Steh bei uns in der letzten Not,
G'leit uns ins Leben aus dem Tod!

This hymn, by Martin Luther, was first published in Joseph Klug's *Gesangbuch*, Wittenberg, 1543, entitled "A children's hymn, to be sung against the two arch-enemies of Christ and His holy Church, the Pope and the Turk." It is thought that Luther wrote the hymn in 1541 for a special service arranged in Wittenberg for prayer against the threatening Turkish army. As the singing in this service was to be done chiefly by the boys' choir, we have an explanation for the title of the hymn.

The translation is by Catherine Winkworth in her *Chorale Book for England*, 1863.

For comments on the tune "Erhalt uns, Herr" see Hymn No. 5.

262   A Mighty Fortress Is Our God

1. A mighty Fortress is our God,
A trusty Shield and Weapon;
He helps us free from every need
That hath us now o'ertaken.
The old evil Foe
Now means deadly woe;
Deep guile and great might
Are his dread arms in fight;
On earth is not his equal.

Ein' feste Burg ist unser Gott,
Ein' gute Wehr und Waffen;
Er hilft uns frei aus aller Not,
Die uns jetzt hat betroffen.
Der alt' böse Feind,
Mit Ernst er's jetzt meint,
Gross' Macht und viel List
Sein' grausam' Rüstung ist,
Auf Erd' ist nicht seinsgleichen.

2. With might of ours can naught be done,
Soon were our loss effected;
But for us fights the Valiant One,
Whom God Himself elected.
Ask ye, Who is this?
Jesus Christ it is,
Of Sabaoth Lord,
And there's none other God;
He holds the field forever.

Mit unsrer Macht ist nichts getan,
Wir sind gar bald verloren;
Es streit't für uns der rechte Mann,
Den Gott hat selbst erkoren.
Fragst du, wer der ist?
Er heisst Jesus Christ,
Der Herr Zebaoth,
Und ist kein andrer Gott,
Das Feld muss er behalten.

3. Though devils all the world should fill,
All eager to devour us,
We tremble not, we fear no ill,
They shall not overpower us.
This world's prince may still
Scowl fierce as he will,
He can harm us none,
He's judged; the deed is done;
One little word can fell him.

Und wenn die Welt voll Teufel wär'
Und wollt' uns gar verschlingen,
So fürchten wir uns nicht so sehr,
Es soll uns doch gelingen.
Der Fürst dieser Welt,
Wie sau'r er sich stellt,
Tut er uns doch nicht,
Das macht, er ist gericht't,
Ein' Wörtlein kann ihn fällen.

4. The Word they still shall let remain
Nor any thanks have for it;
He's by our side upon the plain
With His good gifts and Spirit.
And take they our life,
Goods, fame, child, and wife,
Let these all be gone,
They yet have nothing won;
The Kingdom ours remaineth.

Das Wort sie sollen lassen stahn
Und kein'n Dank dazu haben;
Er ist bei uns wohl auf dem Plan
Mit seinem Geist und Gaben.
Nehmen sie den Leib,
Gut, Ehr', Kind und Weib:
Lass fahren dahin,
Sie haben's kein'n Gewinn,
Das Reich muss uns doch bleiben.

It would lead us too far afield to discuss the various views as to the time and place of the origin of this great hymn by Martin Luther — the Battle Hymn of the Reformation. Suffice it to say that the weight of evidence points to 1529 as the year of its origin. The hymn was probably written for the Diet of Spires, which convened on April 20, 1529, when the German princes made their formal

REFORMATION

"protest" against the revocation of their liberties, and thus received the name "Protestants." Lauxmann, in *Koch,* writes: "Luther with this hymn entered a protest before all the German people against any endeavor to obstruct the Gospel."

"Ein' feste Burg" first appeared in Klug's *Gesangbuch,* Wittenberg, 1529, entitled "Der XXXXVI Psalm, *Deus noster refugium et virtus.*" The hymn is more than a metrical paraphrase of Ps. 46. It is really an original production on the theme of David's psalm, with some phrases reminiscent of the Biblical text.

The tune "Ein' feste Burg" is also Luther's composition. It appeared in Klug's *Geistliche Lieder,* Wittenberg, 1529, first edition (not extant), and in *Kirchen Gesenge,* Nürnberg, 1531.

This hymn of Luther's is not only used by Lutherans the world over. It is the Hymn of Protestantism. It would be hard to find a Protestant hymnal worthy of that name in which this hymn is not. It has been rightly called "the greatest hymn of the greatest man in the greatest period of German history." Its wide appeal is best illustrated by the fact that no Christian hymn has been translated into more languages than "Ein' feste Burg." Many great writers have essayed to put the hymn into English. There must be some seventy or eighty English versions at present. Thomas Carlyle, in his version "A safe stronghold our God is still" has given us one of the most excellent translations. It first appeared in *Fraser's Magazine,* 1831. Another outstanding version is that by F. H. Hedge, beginning, "A mighty fortress is our God, a bulwark," which appeared in *Gems of German Verse,* 1852. The translation above is composite and appeared in the Pennsylvania Lutheran *Church Book,* 1868. It was prepared by the editorial committee for that collection, which based its translation on Carlyle's version and the version, also based on Carlyle's, by W. M. Reynolds, which appeared in the General Synod's *Collection* of 1850.

The translation is the one that is most widely used by American Lutherans at the present time. Its value lies chiefly in its reproduction of the sturdy ruggedness of Luther's original.

This hymn is truly written out of the fulness of Luther's heart. There were moments in his life when even Luther felt something akin to despair. And in such hours he would say to Melanchthon, his faithful coworker, "Come, Philip, let us sing the 46th Psalm." And the two friends would sing lustily in Luther's own version — "Ein' feste Burg ist unser Gott." Uncounted wavering, doubting, fearful hearts have been strengthened by this hymn of faith, have been filled with new courage and power to battle for the right to remain true to the faith once delivered to the saints.

Dr. Benson therefore says rightly: "Such a hymn, with such a tune, spreads quickly, as may well be believed; quickly, as if the angels had been the carriers. But they were men who spread Luther's hymn of faith and courage from heart to heart and from lip to lip."

James Huneker, musical critic, wrote: "This hymn thunders at the very gate of heaven in its magnificent affirmation of belief."

We might go on recording the tributes of great men to this wonderful hymn, which Frederick the Great called "God Almighty's Grenadier March." We shall, however, confine ourselves to a quotation from Carlyle, who wrote:

"There is something in it like the sound of Alpine avalanches or the first murmur of earthquakes, in the very vastness of which dissonance a higher unison is revealed to us. . . . It is evident that to this man all Popes, cardinals, emperors, devils, all hosts and nations, were but weak, weak as the forest with all its strong trees might be to the smallest spark of electric fire."

The good this hymn has done, the faith it has inspired, the hearts it has comforted, the influence it has exerted, cannot be measured and will first be revealed to us in eternity, where the saints of God will praise their Lord and Redeemer for many blessings, not the least of which will be the privilege of having known and sung this hymn here on earth.

263   O Little Flock, Fear Not the Foe

1. O little flock, fear not the Foe
Who madly seeks your overthrow;
Dread not his rage and power.
What though your courage sometimes faints,
His seeming triumph o'er God's saints
Lasts but a little hour.

2. Be of good cheer; your cause belongs
To Him who can avenge your wrongs;
Leave it to Him, our Lord.
Though hidden yet from mortal eyes,
His Gideon shall for you arise,
Uphold you and His Word.

3. As true as God's own Word is true,
Not earth nor hell with all their crew
Against us shall prevail.
A jest and byword are they grown;
God is with us, we are His own;
Our victory cannot fail.

4. Amen, Lord Jesus, grant our prayer;
Great Captain, now Thine arm make bare,
Fight for us once again!
So shall Thy saints and martyrs raise
A mighty chorus to Thy praise,
World without end. Amen.

Verzage nicht, du Häuflein klein,
Obschon die Feinde willens sein,
Dich gänzlich zu verstören,
Und suchen deinen Untergang,
Davon dir wird recht angst und bang;
Es wird nicht lange währen.

Dich tröste nur, dass deine Sach'
Ist Gottes, dem befiehl die Rach'
Und lass allein ihn walten!
Er wird durch seinen Gideon,
Den er wohl weiss, dir helfen schon,
Dich und sein Wort erhalten.

So wahr Gott Gott ist und sein Wort,
Muss Teufel, Welt und Höllenpfort',
Und was dem will anhangen,
Endlich werden zu Hohn und Spott;
Gott ist mit uns und wir mit Gott,
Den Sieg woll'n wir erlangen!

Amen, das hilf, Herr Jesu Christ,
Dieweil du unser Schutzherr bist,
Hilf uns durch deinen Namen:
So wollen wir, deine Gemein',
Dich loben und dir dankbar sein
Und fröhlich singen Amen.

Although this hymn, specifically Stanzas 1 to 3, has been attributed to three men: King Gustavus Adolphus of Sweden, Jacob Fabricius, and Johann Michael Altenburg, it is now quite generally ascribed to the last-named.

The oldest record of the hymn is in two pamphlets, both published at Leipzig, one very likely in 1632, the other in 1633. In the form as above, except for an additional stanza, the hymn first appeared in the *Leipzig Gesang Buch*, 1638, where it is entitled "A Soul-rejoicing hymn of Consolation upon the watchword — God with us — used by the Evangelical army in the battle of Leipzig, 7th Sept., 1631, composed by M. Johann Altenburg, pastor at Gross Sömmern in Düringen." It is in five stanzas, the first three ascribed to Altenburg, the last two marked as "Additamentum Ignoti."

The use of this hymn in the famous battle of Lützen, where the great Swedish king lost his life, is thus described in *Julian:*

> It was on the morning of the 16 Nov., 1632, that the Catholic army under Wallenstein and the Evangelical under Gustavus Adolphus stood over against each other at Lützen ready to strike. As the morning dawned, Gustavus Adolphus summoned his court preacher Fabricius and commanded him, as also the army chaplains of all the other regiments, to hold a service

of prayer. During the service the whole host sang the pious king's battle hymn "Verzage nicht, du Häuflein klein." He himself was on his knees and prayed fervently. Meantime a thick mist had descended, which hid the fatal field, so that nothing could be distinguished. When the host had now been set in battle array, he gave them as watchword for the fight the saying, "God with us," mounted his horse, drew his sword, and rode along the lines of the army to encourage the soldiers for the battle. First, however, he commanded the tunes *Ein' feste Burg* and *Es woll' uns Gott genädig sein* to be played by the kettledrums and trumpets, and the soldiers joined as with one voice. The mist now began to disappear, and the sun shone through. Then, after a short prayer, he cried out: "Now will we set to, please God," and immediately after, very loud, "Jesu, Jesu, Jesu, help me today to fight for the honor of Thy holy name." Then he attacked the enemy at full speed, defended only by a leathern gorget. "God is my harness," he had said to the servant who wished to put on his armor. The conflict was hot and bloody. About 11 o'clock in the forenoon the fatal bullet struck him, and he sank, dying, from his horse, with the words "My God, my God!" Till twilight came on, the fight raged and was doubtful. But at length the Evangelical host obtained the victory, as it had prophetically sung at dawn.

The translation, slightly altered, is by Catherine Winkworth and first appeared in her *Lyra Germanica*, 1855.

The tune "Kommt her zu mir" is from an old German melody of the 15th century, which was used also for spiritual songs and then was introduced into the hymnody of the Church around 1530, when it was coupled with the hymn "Kommt her zu mir, spricht Gottes Sohn, all die ihr seid beschweret."

Preserve Thy Word, O Savior — 264

1. Preserve Thy Word, O Savior,
   To us this latter day
And let Thy kingdom flourish,
   Enlarge Thy Church, we pray.
Oh, keep our faith from failing,
   Keep hope's bright star aglow.
Let naught from Thy Word turn us
   While wandering here below.

2. Preserve, O Lord, Thine honor,
   The bold blasphemer smite;
Convince, convert, enlighten,
   The souls in error's night.
Reveal Thy will, dear Savior,
   To all who dwell below —
Thou Light of all the living —
   That men Thy name may know.

3. Preserve, O Lord, Thy Zion
   Bought dearly with Thy blood;
Protect what Thou hast chosen
   Against the foes' dread brood.
Be Thou her great Defender
   When dangers gather round;
E'en though the earth be crumbling,
   Safe will Thy Church be found.

4. Preserve, O Lord, Thy children,
   Thine own blest heritage;
Resist, disperse, and scatter
   Those who against Thee rage.
Let Thy commandments guide us,
   Grant us Thy heavenly food;
Clothe us in Thy rich garments,
   Bought with Thy precious blood.

Erhalt uns deine Lehre,
   Herr zu der letzten Zeit,
Erhalt dein Reich, vermehre
   Dein' edle Christenheit;
Erhalt standhaften Glauben,
   Der Hoffnung Leitsternstrahl;
Lass uns dein Wort nicht rauben
   In diesem Jammertal!

Erhalt dein' Ehr' und wehre
   Dem, der dir widerspricht;
Erleucht, Herr, und bekehre
   Allwissend ewig Licht,
Was dich bisher nicht kennet;
   Entdecke doch der Welt
(Der du dich Licht genennet),
   Was einzig dir gefällt!

Erhalt, was du gebauet
   Und durch dein Blut erkauft,
Was du dir hast vertrauet,
   Die Kirch', auf welch' anlauft
Der grimme Sturm des Drachen;
   Sei du ihr Schutz und Wall,
Dass, ob die Welt will krachen,
   Sie nimmermehr verfall'!

Erhalt, Herr, deine Schafe,
   Der grimme Wolf kommt an;
Erwach aus deinem Schlafe,
   Weil niemand retten kann
Als du, o grosser Hirte;
   Leit uns auf gute Weid',
Treib, nähr, erfreu, bewirte
   Uns in der wüsten Heid'!

REFORMATION

>   Erhalt uns, Herr, dein Erbe,
>   Dein wertes Heiligtum;
>   Zerreiss, zerschmeiss, verderbe,
>   Was wider deinen Ruhm!
>   Lass dein Gesetz uns führen,
>   Gönn uns dein Himmelsbrot,
>   Lass deinen Schmuck uns zieren,
>   Heil uns durch deinen Tod!

5. Preserve Thy Word and preaching,
The truth that makes us whole,
The mirror of Thy glory,
The power that saves the soul.
Oh, may this living water,
This dew of heavenly grace,
Sustain us while here living
Until we see Thy face!

>   Erhalt und lass uns hören
>   Dein Wort, das selig macht,
>   Den Spiegel deiner Ehren,
>   Das Licht in dieser Nacht,
>   Dass dieser Brunn uns tränke,
>   Der Himmelstau uns netz',
>   Dass diese Richtschnur lenke,
>   Der Honigseim ergötz'!

6. Preserve in wave and tempest
Thy storm-tossed little flock;
Assailed by wind and weather,
May it endure each shock.
Take Thou the helm, O Pilot,
And set the course aright;
Thus we shall reach the harbor
In Thine eternal light.

>   Erhalt in Sturm und Wellen
>   Dein Häuflein, lass doch nicht
>   Uns Wind und Wetter fällen,
>   Steur selbst dein Schiff und richt
>   Den Lauf, dass wir erreichen
>   Die Anfurt nach der Zeit
>   Und hilf uns Segel streichen
>   In sel'ger Ewigkeit!

This hymn by Andreas Gryphius first appeared in the Saubert *Gesangbuch,* Nürnberg, 1676, entitled "Of the Word of God and the Christian doctrine." The hymn is a recast of an earlier hymn by Josua Stegmann, published in his *Hertzen-Seufftzern,* Lüneburg, 1630. The hymn has not enjoyed a wide usage in the German churches, except here in America.

The translation is by William J. Schaefer and was prepared for *The Lutheran Hymnal* in 1938.

For comments on the tune "Herzlich tut mich" see Hymn No. 172.

265   Thine Honor Save, O Christ, Our Lord

1. Thine honor save, O Christ, our Lord!
Hear Zion's cries and help afford;
Destroy the wiles of mighty foes
Who now Thy Word and truth oppose.

> Rett, o Herr Jesu, rett dein' Ehr',
> Das Seufzen deiner Kirche hör,
> Der Feind' Anschläg' und Macht zerstör,
> Die jetzt verfolgen deine Lehr'!

2. Their craft and pomp indeed are great,
And of their power they boast and prate;
Our hope they scornfully deride
And deem us nothing in their pride.

> Gross ist ihr List, ihr Trutz und Macht,
> Sie fahren hoch daher mit Pracht,
> All unsre Hoffnung wird verlacht,
> Wir sind bei ihn'n wie nichts geacht't.

3. Forgive, O Lord, our sins forgive;
Grant us Thy grace and let us live.
Convince Thy foes throughout the land
That godless counsels shall not stand.

> Vergib uns unsre Missetat,
> Vertilg uns nicht, erzeige Gnad',
> Beweis den Feinden in der Tat,
> Es gelte wider dich kein Rat!

4. That Thou art with us, Lord, proclaim
And put our enemies to shame;
Confound them in their haughtiness
And help Thine own in their distress.

> Steh deinem kleinen Häuflein bei,
> Aus Gnaden Fried' und Ruh' verleih;
> Lass jedermann erkennen frei,
> Dass hier die rechte Kirche sei!

5. Preserve Thy little flock in peace,
Nor let Thy boundless mercy cease;
To all the world let it appear
That Thy true Church indeed is here.

> Lass sehn, dass du sei'st unser Gott,
> Der unsre Feinde setzt zu Spott,
> Wirft ihre Hoffart in den Kot
> Und hilft den Seinen aus der Not!

Johann Heermann first published this hymn in his *Devoti Musica Cordis,* Breslau, 1630. It was headed: "For times of persecution and distress of pious Christians."

The translation is by Matthias Loy in the Ohio *Lutheran Hymnal,* 1880, slightly altered.

For comments on the tune "Erhalt uns, Herr" see Hymn No. 5.

REFORMATION

O God, Our Lord, Thy Holy Word 266

1. O God, our Lord, Thy holy Word
Was long a hidden treasure
Till to its place It was by grace
Restored in fullest measure.
For this today Our thanks we say
And gladly glorify Thee.
Thy mercy show And grace bestow
On all who still deny Thee.

2. Salvation free By faith in Thee,
That is Thy Gospel's preaching,
The heart and core Of Bible-lore
In all its sacred teaching.
In Christ we must Put all our trust,
Not in our deeds or labor;
With conscience pure And heart secure
Love Thee, Lord, and our neighbor.

3. Thou, Lord, alone This work hast done
By Thy free grace and favor.
All who believe Will grace receive
Through Jesus Christ, our Savior.
And though the Foe Would overthrow
Thy Word with grim endeavor,
All he has wrought Must come to naught, —
Thy Word will stand forever.

4. My Lord art Thou, And for me now
Death holds no dreadful terrors;
Thy precious blood, My highest good,
Hath blotted out my errors.
My thanks to Thee! Thou wilt to me
Fulfil Thy promise ever
And mercy give While here I live
And heavenly bliss forever.

O Herre Gott, dein göttlich Wort
Ist lang verdunkelt blieben,
Bis durch dein' Gnad' uns ist gesagt,
Was Paulus hat geschrieben
Und andere Apostel mehr
Aus dein'm göttlichen Munde;
Des danken wir mit Fleiss, dass wir
Erlebet hab'n die Stunde.

Willst du nun fein gut Christe sein,
So musst du erstlich *glauben:*
Setz dein Vertraun — darauf fest bau
Hoffnung und Lieb' im Glauben! —
Allein auf Christ zu aller Frist,
Dein'n Nächsten lieb daneben;
Das G'wissen frei, rein Herz dabei
Kein' Kreatur kann geben.

Allein, Herr, du musst solches tun
Doch ganz aus lauter Gnaden;
Wer sich des tröst't, der ist erlöst,
Und kann ihm niemand schaden.
Ob wollten gleich Papst, Kaiser, Reich
Sie und dein Wort vertreiben,
Ist doch ihr' Macht geg'n dich nichts g'acht't,
Sie werden's lassen bleiben.

Gott ist mein Herr, so bin ich der,
Dem Sterben kommt zugute,
Weil du uns hast aus aller Last
Erlöst mit deinem Blute.
Das dank' ich dir, drum wirst du mir
Nach dein'r Verheissung geben,
Was ich dich bitt'; versag mir's nicht
Im Tod und auch im Leben!

This cento is from a hymn by an unknown author, which first appeared in the Erfurt *Enchiridion,* 1527. *Fischer* calls it one of the most esteemed hymns of the Reformation period. Martin Luther gave the hymn a place in his *Geistliche Lieder auffs new gebessert,* Wittenberg (J. Klug), 1529. For a time the hymn was attributed to the great Reformer; but it is not from his pen. The cento includes Stanzas 1, 3, 4, and 7 of the original eight stanzas. Our translation, a very free rendering of these stanzas, was prepared for *The Lutheran Hymnal* in 1939.

The tune "O Herre Gott," inseparably wedded to this hymn, appeared with the original text as above. The composer is unknown. It has all the characteristics of a folk-tune and is said to have been used with secular songs in the first decades of the 16th century.

Wilhelm Nelle writes: "Like Luther's 'Erhalt uns, Herr, bei deinem Wort' (see Hymn No. 261) this hymn was forbidden by the authorities, pastors were deposed from office for having it sung, in short, it has a history of battle and victory as the best hymn of Luther."

If God Had Not Been on Our Side 267

1. If God had not been on our side
And had not come to aid us,
The foes with all their power and pride
Would surely have dismayed us;
For we, His flock, would have to fear
The threat of men both far and near
Who rise in might against us.

Wär' Gott nicht mit uns diese Zeit,
So soll Israel sagen,
Wär' Gott nicht mit uns diese Zeit,
Wir hätten musst verzagen,
Die so ein armes Häuflein sind,
Veracht't von so viel Menschenkind,
Die an uns setzen alle.

2. Their furious wrath, did God permit,
   Would surely have consumed us
And as a deep and yawning pit
   With life and limb entombed us.
Like men o'er whom dark waters roll
Their wrath would have engulfed our soul
And, like a flood, o'erwhelmed us.

3. Blest be the Lord, who foiled their threat
   That they could not devour us;
Our souls, like birds, escaped their net,
   They could not overpower us.
The snare is broken — we are free!
Our help is ever, Lord, in Thee,
   Who madest earth and heaven.

Auf uns ist so zornig ihr Sinn,
   Wo Gott hätt' das zugeben,
Verschlungen hätten sie uns hin
   Mit ganzem Leib und Leben;
Wir wär'n, als die ein' Flut ersäuft,
Und über die gross Wasser läuft
   Und mit Gewalt verschwemmet.

Gott Lob und Dank, der nicht zugab,
   Dass ihr Schlund uns möcht' fangen!
Wie ein Vogel des Stricks kommt ab,
   Ist unsre Seel' entgangen;
Strick ist entzwei, und wir sind frei,
Des Herren Name steht uns bei,
   Des Gott's Himmels und Erden.

    Luther's metrical paraphrase of Ps. 124 first appeared in Johann Walther's *Geystliche Gesangk Buchleyn*, Wittenberg, 1524.

    The translation is composite and was prepared for *The Lutheran Hymnal*.

    The tune "Wär' Gott nicht mit uns" first appeared, set to this hymn, in Johann Walther's *Gesang Buch*, Wittenberg, 1537.

268   Zion Mourns in Fear and Anguish

1. Zion mourns in fear and anguish,
   Zion, city of our God.
"Ah," she says, "how sore I languish,
   Bowed beneath the chastening rod!
For my God forsook me quite
And forgot my sorry plight
Mid these troubles now distressing,
Countless woes my soul oppressing.

2. "Once," she mourns, "He promised plainly
   That His help should e'er be near;
Yet I now must seek Him vainly
   In my days of woe and fear.
Will His anger never cease?
Will He not renew His peace?
Will He not show forth compassion
And again forgive transgression?"

3. "Zion, surely I do love thee,"
   Thus to her the Savior saith,
"Though with many woes I prove thee
   And thy soul is sad to death.
For My troth is pledged to thee;
Zion, thou art dear to Me.
Deep within My heart I've set thee,
That I never can forget thee.

4. "Let not Satan make thee craven;
   He can threaten, but not harm.
On My hands thy name is graven,
   And thy shield is My strong arm.
How, then, could it ever be
I should not remember thee,
Fail to build thy walls, My city,
And look down on thee with pity?

5. "Ever shall Mine eyes behold thee;
   On My bosom thou art laid.
Ever shall My love enfold thee;
   Never shalt thou lack Mine aid.
Neither Satan, war, nor stress
Then shall mar thy happiness:
With this blessed consolation
Be thou firm in tribulation."

Zion klagt mit Angst und Schmerzen,
   Zion, Gottes werte Stadt,
Die er trägt in seinem Herzen,
   Die er sich erwählet hat.
Ach, spricht sie, wie hat mein Gott
Mich verlassen in der Not
Und lässt mich so harte pressen!
Meiner hat er ganz vergessen.

Der Gott, der mir hat versprochen
   Seinen Beistand jederzeit,
Der lässt sich vergebens suchen
   Jetzt in meiner Traurigkeit.
Ach, will er denn für und für
Grausam zürnen über mir?
Kann und will er sich der Armen
Jetzt nicht wie vorhin erbarmen?

Zion, o du Vielgeliebte!
   Sprach zu ihr des Herren Mund,
Zwar du bist jetzt die Betrübte,
   Seel' und Geist ist dir verwund't;
Doch stell alles Trauern ein!
Wo mag eine Mutter sein,
Die ihr eigen Kind kann hassen
Und aus ihrer Sorge lassen?

Lass dich nicht den Satan blenden,
   Der sonst nichts als schrecken kann!
Siehe, hier in meinen Händen
   Hab' ich dich geschrieben an.
Wie mag es denn anders sein?
Ich muss ja gedenken dein;
Deine Mauern will ich bauen
Und dich fort und fort anschauen.

Du bist mir stets vor den Augen,
   Du liegst mir in meinem Schoss
Wie die Kindlein, die noch saugen,
   Meine Treu' zu dir ist gross.
Mich und dich soll keine Zeit,
Keine Not, Gefahr noch Streit,
Ja der Satan selbst nicht scheiden!
Bleib getreu in allen Leiden!

    This hymn of Johann Heermann's, based on Is. 49:14-17, first appeared in his *Devoti Musica Cordis*, Breslau, 1636, in six stanzas.

[198]

REFORMATION. — ST. ANDREW

The translation is by Catherine Winkworth in her *Christian Singers of Germany*, 1869, altered. The omitted fourth stanza reads:

> And if thou couldst find a mother
> Who forgot her infant's claim
> Or whose wrath her love could smother,
> Yet would I be still the same;
> For My truth is pledged to thee,
> Zion, thou art dear to Me;
> I within My heart have set thee,
> And I never can forget thee.

The tune "Zion klagt" appeared with this hymn in Johann Crüger's *Newes vollkömmliches Gesangbuch*, etc., Berlin, 1640. It is a recast of a tune by Johann Herman Schein, composed, in 1623, for the hymn which he had written for the burial of his daughter:

> Seligkeit, Fried', Freud' und Ruh'
> Find' ich in meinem Gott.

O Lord, Our Father, Shall We be Confounded — 269

1. O Lord, our Father, shall we be confounded
Who, though by trials and by woes
   surrounded,
On Thee alone for help are still relying,
To Thee are crying?

2. Lord, put to shame Thy foes who breathe
   defiance
And vainly make their might their sole
   reliance;
In mercy turn to us, the poor and stricken,
Our hope to quicken.

3. Be Thou our Helper and our strong
   Defender;
Speak to our foes and cause them to
   surrender.
Yea, long before their plans have been
   completed,
They are defeated.

4. 'Tis vain to trust in man; for Thou,
   Lord, only
Art the Defense and Comfort of the lonely.
With Thee to lead, the battle shall be
   glorious
And we victorious.

5. Thou art our Hero, all our foes subduing;
Save Thou Thy little flock they are pursuing.
We seek Thy help; for Jesus' sake be
   near us.
Great Helper, hear us!

Herr, unser Gott, lass nicht zuschanden
   werden
Die, so in ihren Nöten und Beschwerden
Bei Tag und Nacht auf deine Güte hoffen
Und zu dir rufen!

Mache zuschanden alle, die dich hassen,
Die sich allein auf ihre Macht
   verlassen!
Ach kehre dich mit Gnaden zu uns
   Armen,
Lass dich's erbarmen

Und schaff uns Beistand wider unsre
   Feinde!
Wenn du ein Wort sprichst, werden sie
   bald Freunde,
Sie müssen Wehr und Waffen nieder-
   legen,
Kein Glied mehr regen.

Wir haben niemand, dem wir uns
   vertrauen;
Vergebens ist's auf Menschenhilfe bauen;
Mit dir wir wollen Taten tun und
   kämpfen,
Die Feinde dämpfen.

Du bist der Held, der sie kann untertreten
Und das bedrängte kleine Häuflein retten.
Wir suchen dich, wir schrein in Jesu
   Namen:
Hilf, Helfer! Amen.

Johann Heermann published this hymn in his *Devoti Musica Cordis*, Breslau, 1630.

The translation is by Catherine Winkworth in her *Christian Singers of Germany*, 1869, somewhat altered.

For comments on the tune "Herzliebster Jesu" see Hymn No. 143.

Jesus Calls Us; o'er the Tumult — 270

1. Jesus calls us; o'er the tumult
Of our life's wild, restless sea,
Day by day His sweet voice soundeth,
Saying, "Christian, follow Me."

2. As of old Saint Andrew heard it
By the Galilean lake,
Turned from home and toil and kindred,
Leaving all for His dear sake.

3. Jesus calls us from the worship
    Of the vain world's golden store,
   From each idol that would keep us,
    Saying, "Christian, love Me more."

4. In our joys and in our sorrows,
    Days of toil and hours of ease,
   Still He calls, in cares and pleasures,
    "Christian, love Me more than these."

5. Jesus calls us; by Thy mercies,
    Savior, make us hear Thy call,
   Give our hearts to Thine obedience,
    Serve and love Thee best of all. Amen.

The hymn, based on Matt. 4:18, 19, the beginning of the Gospel for St. Andrew's Day, by Mrs. Cecil F. Alexander, was first published in the collection *Hymns*, etc., by the Society for the Promotion of Christian Knowledge, 1852.

For comments on the tune "Stuttgart" see Hymn No. 83.

271   Word Supreme, Before Creation

1. Word Supreme, before creation
    Born of God eternally,
   Who didst will for our salvation
    To be born on earth and die,
   Well Thy saints have kept their station,
    Watching till Thine hour drew nigh.

2. Now 'tis come, and faith espies Thee;
    Like an eaglet in the morn
   One in steadfast worship eyes Thee,
    Thy beloved, Thy latest born.
   In Thy glory he descries Thee
    Reigning from the Tree of scorn.

3. Much he asked in loving wonder,
    On Thy bosom leaning, Lord.
   In the secret place of thunder
    Answer kind didst Thou accord,
   Wisdom for Thy Church to ponder
    Till the day of dread award.

4. Lo, heaven's doors lift up, revealing
    How Thy judgments earthward move;
   Scrolls unfolded, trumpets pealing,
    Wine-cups from the wrath above;
   Yet o'er all a soft voice stealing,
    "Little children, trust and love."

5. Thee, the almighty King eternal,
    Father of the eternal Word,
   Thee, the Father's Word supernal,
    Thee, of both the Breath adored,
   Heaven and earth and realms infernal
    Own one glorious God and Lord. Amen.

This hymn, in seven stanzas, by John Keble is dated "Hursley, April 19, 1856." It was first published in the *Salisbury Hymn Book*, 1857. It was probably suggested by the 11th-century sequence "Verbum Dei, Deo natum." The omitted Stanzas 3 and 4 read:

3. He upon Thy bosom lying
    Thy true tokens learned by heart;
   And Thy dearest pledge in dying,
    Lord, Thou didst to him impart;
   Showedst him how, all grace supplying,
    Blood and water from Thee start.

4. He first, hoping and believing,
    Did beside the grave adore;
   Latest he, the warfare leaving,
    Landed on the eternal shore;
   And his witness we receiving,
    Own Thee Lord forevermore.

For comments on the tune "Sieh hier bin ich" see Hymn No. 56.

272   When All the World was Cursed

1. When all the world was cursed
    By Moses' condemnation,
   Saint John the Baptist came
    With words of consolation.
   With true forerunner's zeal
    The Greater One he named,
   And Him, as yet unknown,
    As Savior he proclaimed.

2. Before he yet was born,
    He leaped in joyful meeting,
   Confessing Him as Lord
    Whose mother he was greeting.
   By Jordan's rolling stream,
    A new Elijah bold,
   He testified of Him
    Of whom the prophets told:

Es war die ganze Welt
 Von Mosis Fluch erschrecket,
Bis Sankt Johannes hat
 Den Finger ausgestrecket
Auf Jesum, welchen er
 Zum Heiland aller Welt
Als sein Vorläufer hat
 Gezeigt und vorgestellt,

Vor dem er ungebor'n
 Mit Freuden aufgesprungen,
Zu dem er sich bekannt
 Mit unberedter Zungen
In seiner Mutter Leib
 Und mit Elias' Geist
Bei Gross' und Kleinen ihn
 Gepredigt und geweist:

3. Behold the Lamb of God
   That bears the world's transgression,
   Whose sacrifice removes
   The Enemy's oppression.
   Behold the Lamb of God,
   Who beareth all our sin,
   Who for our peace and joy
   Will full atonement win.

   Sieh, das ist Gottes Lamm,
   Das unsre Sünde träget,
   Das sich der ganzen Welt
   Zum Opfer niederleget;
   Sieh, das ist Gottes Lamm,
   Bei dem man aller Sünd'
   Vergebung, Friede, Ruh'
   Und alle Gnade find't!

4. Thrice blessèd every one
   Who heeds the proclamation
   Which John the Baptist brought,
   Accepting Christ's salvation.
   He who believes this truth
   And comes with love unfeigned
   Has righteousness and peace
   In fullest measure gained.

   Wohl dem, der dieses Lamm,
   Das uns Johannes weiset,
   Im Glauben fest ergreift
   Und in dem Leben preiset!
   Wer dieser Tauf' gedenkt
   Und wahre Busse übt,
   Der wird von ihm auch sein
   Begnadet und geliebt.

5. Oh, grant, Thou Lord of Love,
   That we receive, rejoicing,
   The word proclaimed by John,
   Our true repentance voicing;
   That gladly we may walk
   Upon our Savior's way
   Until we live with Him
   In His eternal day.

   So gib, du grosser Gott,
   Dass wir Johannis Lehre
   Von Herzen nehmen an,
   Dass sich in uns bekehre,
   Was bös und sündlich ist,
   Bis wir nach dieser Zeit
   Mit Freuden gehen ein
   Zu deiner Herrlichkeit!

This hymn for St. John the Baptist's Day was written by Johann G. Olearius and first published in four stanzas, according to *Fischer,* in his *Geistliche Singe-Lust,* Arnstadt, 1697. *Julian,* however, states that it appeared in Olearius's *Jesus! Poetische Erstlinge,* etc., 1664, in five stanzas.

The translation by Paul E. Kretzmann was prepared for *The Lutheran Hymnal* in 1940.

For comments on the tune "Was frag' ich nach der Welt" see Hymn No. 430.

Sweet Flowerets of the Martyr Band 273

1. Sweet flowerets of the martyr band,
   Plucked by the tyrant's ruthless hand
   Upon the threshold of the morn,
   Like rosebuds by a tempest torn;

2. First victims for the incarnate Lord,
   A tender flock to feel the sword;
   Beside the very altar, gay,
   With palm and crown, ye seemed to play.

3. Ah, what availed King Herod's wrath?
   He could not stop the Savior's path.
   Alone, while others murdered lay,
   In safety Christ is borne away.

4. O Lord, the Virgin-born, to Thee
   Eternal praise and glory be,
   Whom with the Father we adore
   And Holy Ghost forevermore. Amen.

This cento is from Aurelius Prudentius's *Cathemerinon.* It is part of the twelfth poem, entitled "Hymnus Epiphaniae," which begins "Quicunque Christum quaeritis." It is one of this poet's best productions. In this cento, entitled "Salvete, flores martyrum," two stanzas are omitted.

The translation is by Henry W. Baker and first appeared in the *Revised Edition of Hymns Ancient and Modern,* 1875, but is here given in the altered form of the 1909 edition.

The tune "Das walt' Gott Vater" is from Daniel Vetter's *Musikalische Kirch- und Haus-Ergötzlichkeit,* Leipzig, 1713, where it was set to Martin Behm's hymn "Das walt' Gott Vater und Gott Sohn."

Praise We the Lord This Day 274

1. Praise we the Lord this day,
   This day so long foretold,
   Whose promise shone with cheering ray
   On waiting saints of old.

2. The Prophet gave the sign
   For faithful men to read:
   A virgin, born of David's line,
   Shall bear the promised Seed.

VISITATION

3. Ask not how this should be,
   But worship and adore
Like her whom God's own majesty
   Came down to shadow o'er.

4. Meekly she bowed her head
   To hear the gracious word,
Mary, the pure and lowly maid,
   The favored of the Lord.

5. Blessèd shall be her name
   In all the Church on earth,
Through whom that wondrous mercy came,
   The incarnate Savior's birth.

6. Jesus, the Virgin's Son,
   We praise Thee and adore,
Who art with God the Father One
   And Spirit evermore. Amen.

This hymn, by an unknown author, first appeared in *Hymns for the Festivals and Saints' Days*, etc., Oxford, 1846, beginning "Let us praise God this day." The altered form, as above, is from Fallow's *Selection*, 1847.

The tune "Swabia" is from *Davids Harpffenspiel*, etc., by Johann Martin Spiess, Heidelberg, 1745, where it is set to the hymn "Ach wachet! wachet auf!" by Joachim Neander.

275   My Soul doth Magnify the Lord

1. My soul doth magnify the Lord,
   My spirit shall in God rejoice;
My low estate He did regard,
   Exalting me by gracious choice.

2. Henceforth all men shall call me blest,
   For great things He hath done to me.
The mighty God is now my Guest;
   The Holy One hath set me free.

3. His mercy is on all who fear,
   Who trust in Him from age to age;
His arm of strength to all is near,
   The proud He scattereth though they rage.

4. The strong He casteth from their seat
   And raiseth men of low degree;
To hungry souls He giveth meat,
   The rich depart in poverty.

5. He helped His servant Israel;
   Remembering His eternal grace,
As from of old He did foretell
   To Abraham and all his race.

6. So praise with me the Holy One,
   Who cometh in humility.
Divine Redeemer, God's own Son,
   Eternal glory be to Thee! Amen.

This hymn is a free paraphrase by John Theodore Mueller of the German metrical *Magnificat*, "Mein' Seel', o Gott, muss loben dich," for the Visitation of the Virgin Mary (*Fünf auserlesene geistliche Lieder*, Marburg, 1535) of unknown authorship. The translation was prepared for *The Lutheran Hymnal* in 1940.

For comments on the tune "Wo Gott zum Haus" see Hymn No. 131.

Invitation

Come unto Me, Ye Weary 276

1. "Come unto Me, ye weary,
   And I will give you rest."
O blessed voice of Jesus,
   Which comes to hearts opprest!
It tells of benediction,
   Of pardon, grace, and peace,
Of joy that hath no ending,
   Of love which cannot cease.

2. "Come unto Me, ye wanderers;
   And I will give you light."
O loving voice of Jesus,
   Which comes to cheer the night!
Our hearts were filled with sadness,
   And we had lost our way;
But Thou hast brought us gladness
   And songs at break of day.

3. "Come unto Me, ye fainting,
   And I will give you life."
O cheering voice of Jesus,
   Which comes to aid our strife!
The Foe is stern and eager,
   The fight is fierce and long;
But Thou hast made us mighty
   And stronger than the strong.

4. "And whosoever cometh,
   I will not cast him out."
O patient love of Jesus,
   Which drives away our doubt,
Which, though we be unworthy
   Of love so great and free,
Invites us very sinners
   To come, dear Lord, to Thee!

William C. Dix first published this hymn in the *People's Hymnal*, 1867. It is one of his best productions.

The author related the circumstances under which this hymn was written in a letter to Mr. Jones, author of *Famous Hymns*, as follows:

> I was ill and depressed at the time, and it was almost to idle away the hours that I wrote the hymn. I had been ill for many weeks and felt weary and faint, and the hymn really expresses the languidness of body from which I was suffering at the time. Soon after its composition I recovered, and I always look back to that hymn as the turning-point in my illness.

The tune "Anthes" is by Friedrich K. Anthes, 1847.

I Heard the Voice of Jesus Say 277

1. I heard the voice of Jesus say,
   "Come unto Me and rest;
Lay down, thou weary one, lay down,
   Thy head upon My breast."
I came to Jesus as I was,
   Weary and worn and sad;
I found in Him a resting-place,
   And He has made me glad.

2. I heard the voice of Jesus say,
   "Behold, I freely give
The living water; thirsty one,
   Stoop down and drink and live."
I came to Jesus, and I drank
   Of that life-giving stream.
My thirst was quenched, my soul revived,
   And now I live in Him.

3. I heard the voice of Jesus say,
   "I am this dark world's Light.
Look unto Me; thy morn shall rise
   And all thy day be bright."
I looked to Jesus, and I found
   In Him my Star, my Sun;
And in that Light of Life I'll walk
   Till traveling days are done.

Horatius Bonar wrote this hymn during his ministry at Kelso and first published it in his *Hymns, Original and Selected*, 1846. It is often used in home mission services. It is based on John 1:16, but it blends into a perfect unity three other sayings of our Lord: Matt. 11:28; John 4:14; and John 8:12. The hymn is a good example of a hymn that is properly objective and congregational in character, even though the personal pronoun "I" is prominent. Dr. C. S. Robinson says of this hymn:

INVITATION

The two secrets of the wonderful popularity of this hymn are found in the fact that it introduces the words of our Lord in a picturesque way, as if one's ear had happened to catch them on the air and then his voice made an immediate response by "coming" toward the words of invitation and promise; and then, that it employs possessive pronouns for its phraseology, and so individualizes the believer. Christ says, "Come to Me," and the Christian says, "I came." Christ says, "I give the living water," and the listener answers, "*My* thirst was quenched." Christ says, "I am the Light," and the child of God replies, "I found in Him *my* Star, *my* Sun!"

The tune "Vox dilecti," wedded to this text, is by John B. Dykes. It first appeared, set to this hymn, in the *Appendix* to the *Original Edition of Hymns Ancient and Modern*, 1868. The tune was greatly admired by the late Peter C. Lutkin.

278   Delay Not, Delay Not, O Sinner, Draw Near

1. Delay not, delay not, O sinner, draw near,
The waters of life are now flowing for thee.
No price is demanded; the Savior is here;
Redemption is purchased, salvation is free.

2. Delay not, delay not, O sinner, to come,
For mercy still lingers and calls thee today.
Her voice is not heard in the vale of the tomb;
Her message, unheeded, will soon pass away.

3. Delay not, delay not! The Spirit of Grace,
Long grieved and resisted, may take His sad flight
And leave thee in darkness to finish thy race,
To sink in the gloom of eternity's night.

4. Delay not, delay not! The hour is at hand;
The earth shall dissolve, and the heavens shall fade.
The dead, small and great, in the Judgment shall stand;
What power, then, O sinner, shall lend thee its aid?

5. Delay not, delay not! Why longer abuse
The love and compassion of Jesus, thy God?
A fountain is opened; how canst thou refuse
To wash and be cleansed in His pardoning blood?

This hymn, an exhortation to repentance, was first published by Thomas Hastings in his *Spiritual Songs*, 1831. Duffield in his *English Hymns* writes regarding this hymn: "It is upon the same page with Knox's 'Acquaint thyself quickly, O sinner, with God,' is of the same meter, and perhaps was suggested by it, and written in order that the vacant space upon the page might be filled by a hymn of similar purport."

The tune "Maldwyn" is a 17th-century Welsh melody from David Evans's collection of tunes *Moliant Cenedl Dinbych*, 1920.

279   Today Thy Mercy Calls Us

1. Today Thy mercy calls us
To wash away our sin.
However great our trespass,
Whatever we have been,
However long from mercy
Our hearts have turned away,
Thy precious blood can cleanse us
And make us white today.

2. Today Thy gate is open,
And all who enter in
Shall find a Father's welcome
And pardon for their sin.
The past shall be forgotten,
A present joy be given,
A future grace be promised,
A glorious crown in heaven.

[204]

INVITATION

3. Today our Father calls us,
   His Holy Spirit waits;
   His blessed angels gather
   Around the heavenly gates.
   No question will be asked us
   How often we have come;
   Although we oft have wandered,
   It is our Father's home.

4. O all-embracing Mercy,
   O ever-open Door,
   What should we do without Thee
   When heart and eye run o'er?
   When all things seem against us,
   To drive us to despair,
   We know one gate is open,
   One ear will hear our prayer.

Oswald Allen published this hymn in his *Hymns of the Christian Life*, London, 1861. It was entitled "Today." The original had the singular pronoun "me" throughout.

For comments on the tune "Anthes" see Hymn No. 276.

Return, O Wanderer, Return   280

1. Return, O wanderer, return
   And seek an injured Father's face;
   Those warm desires that in thee burn
   Were kindled by reclaiming grace.

2. Return, O wanderer, return
   And seek a Father's melting heart;
   His pitying eyes thy grief discern,
   His hand shall heal thine inward smart.

3. Return, O wanderer, return;
   Thy Savior bids thy spirit live.
   Go to His bleeding feet and learn
   How freely Jesus can forgive.

4. Return, O wanderer, return
   And wipe away the falling tear;
   'Tis God who says, "No longer mourn";
   'Tis Mercy's voice invites thee near.

William B. Collyer first published this hymn in the *Evangelical Magazine*, 1806, in six stanzas, entitled "The Backslider." The cento omits Stanzas 3 and 6, which read:

3. Return, O wanderer, return;
   He hears thy deep repentant sigh;
   He saw thy softened spirit mourn
   When no intruding ear was nigh.

6. Return, O wanderer, return,
   Regain thy lost, lamented rest;
   Jehovah's melting bowels yearn
   To clasp His Ephraim to His breast.

The tune "Abends" by Herbert S. Oakeley was written in 1871 and appeared in the Irish *Church Hymnal*, Dublin, 1874. It was there set to John Keble's evening hymn "Sun of My Soul, Thou Savior Dear" (see Hymn No. 551), and thence the name "Abends."

The Savior Calls; Let Every Ear   281

1. The Savior calls; let every ear
   Attend the heavenly sound.
   Ye doubting souls, dismiss your fear;
   Hope smiles reviving round.

2. For every thirsty, longing heart
   Here streams of bounty flow
   And life and health and bliss impart
   To banish mortal woe.

3. Here springs of sacred pleasures rise
   To ease your every pain;
   Immortal fountain, full supplies!
   Nor shall you thirst in vain.

4. Ye sinners, come, 'tis Mercy's voice;
   The gracious call obey;
   Mercy invites to heavenly joys,
   And can you yet delay?

5. Dear Savior, draw reluctant hearts;
   To Thee let sinners fly
   And take the bliss Thy love imparts
   And drink and never die.

Anne Steele first published this hymn in her *Poems on Subjects Chiefly Doctrinal*, 1760. It was entitled "The Invitation."

The tune "Azmon," by Carl Gotthelf Gläser, also called "Denfield" and "Gaston," was introduced from German sources into this country by Lowell Mason. It appeared in his *Modern Psalmist*, Boston, 1839, where the source of this tune is given as follows: "Glaser, J. M., German, 1780." It has become a very popular tune in our country.

LAW AND GOSPEL

The Word

282   Christians, Come, in Sweetest Measures

1. Christians, come, in sweetest measures
Sing of those who spread the treasures
In the holy Gospels shrined;
Blessed tidings of salvation,
Peace on earth their proclamation,
Love from God to lost mankind.

2. See the rivers four that gladden
With their streams the better Eden,
Planted by our Savior dear.
Christ the Fountain, these the waters.
Drink, O Zion's sons and daughters;
Drink and find salvation here.

3. Here our souls, by Jesus sated,
More and more shall be translated
Earth's temptations far above;
Freed from sin's abhorred dominion,
Soaring on angelic pinion,
They shall reach the Source of love.

4. Then shall thanks and praise ascending
For Thy mercies without ending
Rise to Thee, O Savior blest.
With Thy gracious aid defend us,
Let Thy guiding light attend us,
Bring us to Thy place of rest.

This cento is from a Latin sequence, c. 1150, ascribed to Adam of St. Victor. The original poem is in ten stanzas, of which the cento includes Stanzas 1, and 8 to 10. The Latin text of Stanzas 1 and 8, reads:

Iucundare, plebs fidelis,
cuius Pater est in caelis,
recolens Ezechielis
   prophetae praeconia.
est Iohannes testis ipsi,
scribens in Apocalypsi,
'Vere vidi, vere scripsi
   vera testimonia.'

Paradisus his rigatur,
viret, floret, fecundatur;
his abundat, his rigatur
   quattuor fluminibus.
Fons est Christus, hi sunt rivi;
fons est altus, hi proclivi,
ut saporem fontis vivi
   ministrent fidelibus.

The translation is an altered form of that by Robert Campbell in his *Hymns and Anthems*, 1850.

For comments on the tune "Alles ist an Gottes Segen" see Hymn No. 425.

283   God's Word Is Our Great Heritage

1. God's Word is our great heritage
And shall be ours forever;
To spread its light from age to age
Shall be our chief endeavor.
Through life it guides our way,
In death it is our stay.
Lord, grant, while worlds endure,
We keep its teachings pure.
Throughout all generations.

Guds Ord det er vort Arvegods,
Det skal vort Afkoms være;
Gud giv os i vor Grav den Ros,
Vi holdt det höit in Ære!
Det er vor Hälp i Nöd,
Vor Tröst i Liv og Död;
O Gud, ihvor det gaar,
Lad dog, mens Verden staar,
Det i vor Ät nedarves!

This is the fifth stanza of Nikolai F. S. Grundtvig's Danish version of Martin Luther's "A Mighty Fortress." It was first published in *Salmer ved Jubelfesten*, 1817. Later it was given as a separate hymn in Danish and Norwegian hymnals. It is used on festival occasions and as a closing stanza.

The translation is by Ole G. Belsheim, 1909, and appeared in *The Lutheran Hymnary*, 1913.

The tune "Reuter" is a composition by Fritz Reuter and is dated 1916.

284   Father of Mercies, in Thy Word

1. Father of mercies, in Thy Word
What endless glory shines!
Forever be Thy name adored
For these celestial lines.

2. Here may the blind and hungry come
And light and food receive;
Here shall the lowliest guest have room
And taste and see and live.

3. Here springs of consolation rise
To cheer the fainting mind,
And thirsting souls receive supplies
And sweet refreshment find.

4. Here the Redeemer's welcome voice
Spreads heavenly peace around,
And life and everlasting joys
Attend the blissful sound.

LAW AND GOSPEL

5. Oh, may these heavenly pages be
My ever dear delight;
And still new beauties may I see
And still increasing light!

6. Divine Instructor, gracious Lord,
Be Thou forever near;
Teach me to love Thy sacred Word
And view my Savior here.

This hymn, entitled "Holy Scripture," first appeared in Anne Steele's *Poems on Subjects Chiefly Devotional*, 1760, in twelve stanzas. The hymn was shortened to six stanzas in the Bristol Baptist *Collection*, 1769. This cento has become widely used. The hymn is considered one of Miss Steele's best.

The tune "Bedford" by William Wheall cannot be exactly dated. It is called "Bedford" because the composer was organist of St. Paul's Church in that city. The earliest known book that contains it has no date. It is *The Divine Musick Scholars Guide*, etc., printed by Francis Timbrell, where it is set to Ps. 27 and Ps. 84. It is headed "Bedford tune. By Wm. Wheal." It is claimed to have appeared in *The Psalm-Singers' Magazine*, 1729; but as no copy of this periodical has been found, it cannot be verified. In the older and some modern collections the tune is in triple time. It appeared in common time in Wm. Gardiner's *Sacred Melodies*, 1812, set to Watts's "Our God, Our Help in Ages Past." (See Hymn No. 123.) Gardiner says regarding this tune: "This fine old tune was written by Wm. Wheall, organist of Bedford. Originally printed in the key of F and in triple time, I have changed the key to D and written it in common time, a measure that is more stately and better accords with that solemn grandeur in which it is disposed to move."

How Precious Is the Book Divine   285

1. How precious is the Book Divine,
By inspiration given!
Bright as a lamp its doctrines shine
To guide our souls to heaven.

2. Its light, descending from above
Our gloomy world to cheer,
Displays a Savior's boundless love
And brings His glories near.

3. It shows to man his wandering ways
And where his feet have trod,
And brings to view the matchless grace
Of a forgiving God.

4. O'er all the straight and narrow way
Its radiant beams are cast;
A light whose never weary ray
Grows brightest at the last.

5. It sweetly cheers our drooping hearts
In this dark vale of tears.
Life, light, and joy it still imparts
And quells our rising fears.

6. This lamp through all the tedious night
Of life shall guide our way
Till we behold the clearer light
Of an eternal day.

John Fawcett first published this hymn in his *Hymns*, etc., 1782. It was based on Ps. 119:105.

This is a hymn worth singing often in our day. The Bible, in spite of all the opposition of unbelief, is more widely distributed than ever. It is the perennial best seller. It is translated into more than a thousand tongues. Bible societies are busier than ever in their efforts to spread it still more widely. Let us sing this hymn and study our Bibles the more diligently!

The tune "Walder" is by Johann J. Walder and is dated 1788.

How Shall the Young Secure Their Hearts   286

1. How shall the young secure their hearts
And guard their lives from sin?
Thy Word the choicest rules imparts
To keep the conscience clean.

2. 'Tis like the sun, a heavenly light,
That guides us all the day,
And through the dangers of the night
A lamp to lead our way.

LAW AND GOSPEL

3. The starry heavens Thy rule obey,
The earth maintains her place;
And these Thy servants, night and day,
Thy skill and power express.

4. But still Thy Law and Gospel, Lord,
Have lessons more divine;
Not earth stands firmer than Thy Word,
Nor stars so nobly shine.

5. Thy Word is everlasting truth;
How pure is every page!
That holy Book shall guide our youth
And well support our age.

This hymn appeared in Isaac Watts's *Psalms of David Imitated,* 1719, in eight stanzas. This cento omits Stanzas 2, 4, and 5, which read:

When once it enters to the mind,
It spreads such light abroad
The meanest souls instruction find
And raise their thoughts to God.

The men that keep Thy Law with care
And meditate Thy Word
Grow wiser than their teachers are
And better know the Lord.

Thy precepts make me truly wise:
I hate the sinner's road;
I hate my own vain thoughts that rise,
But love Thy Law, my God.

The tune "St. Peter" is from Alexander R. Reinagle's *Psalm Tunes for the Voice and Pianoforte,* c. 1836, where it is set to Ps. 118. Reinagle was organist in St. Peter's-in-the-East at Oxford, and thence the name of the tune. The tune has also been called "St. Peter's, Oxford" and "Christchurch."

287   That Man a Godly Life Might Live

1. That man a godly life might live,
God did these Ten Commandments give
By His true servant Moses, high
Upon the Mount Sinai.
Have mercy, Lord!

2. I am thy God and Lord alone,
No other God beside Me own;
Put thy whole confidence in Me
And love Me e'er cordially.
Have mercy, Lord!

3. By idle word and speech profane
Take not My holy name in vain
And praise but that as good and true
Which I Myself say and do.
Have mercy, Lord!

4. Hallow the day which God hath blest
That thou and all thy house may rest;
Keep hand and heart from labor free
That God may so work in thee.
Have mercy, Lord!

5. Give to thy parents honor due,
Be dutiful, and loving, too,
And help them when their strength decays,
So shalt thou have length of days.
Have mercy, Lord!

6. In sinful wrath thou shalt not kill
Nor hate nor render ill for ill;
Be patient and of gentle mood,
And to thy foe do thou good.
Have mercy, Lord!

7. Be faithful to thy marriage vows,
Thy heart give only to thy spouse;
Thy life keep pure, and lest thou sin,
Use temperance and discipline.
Have mercy, Lord!

8. Steal not; all usury abhor
Nor wring their life-blood from the poor,
But open wide thy loving hand
To all the poor in the land.
Have mercy, Lord!

Dies sind die heil'gen Zehn Gebot',
Die uns gab unser Herre Gott
Durch Moses, seinen Diener treu,
Hoch auf dem Berg Sinai.
Kyrieleis!

Ich bin allein dein Gott, der Herr,
Kein' Götter sollst du haben mehr;
Du sollst mir ganz vertrauen dich,
Von Herzensgrund lieben mich.
Kyrieleis!

Du sollst nicht führen zu Unehr'n
Den Namen Gottes, deines Herrn;
Du sollst nicht preisen recht noch gut,
Ohn' was Gott selbst red't und tut.
Kyrieleis!

Du sollst heil'gen den Feiertag,
Dass du und dein Haus ruhen mag;
Du sollst von dein'm Tun lassen ab,
Dass Gott sein Werk in dir hab'.
Kyrieleis!

Du sollst ehr'n und gehorsam sein
Dem Vater und der Mutter dein,
Und wo dein' Hand ihn'n dienen kann,
So wirst du lang's Leben hab'n.
Kyrieleis!

Du sollst nicht töten zorniglich,
Nicht hassen noch selbst rächen dich,
Geduld haben und sanften Mut
Und auch dem Feind tun das Gut'.
Kyrieleis!

Dein Eh' sollst du bewahren rein,
Dass auch dein Herz kein' andre mein',
Und halten keusch das Leben dein
Mit Zucht und Mässigkeit fein.
Kyrieleis!

Du sollst nicht stehlen Geld noch Gut,
Nicht wuchern jemands Schweiss und Blut;
Du sollst auftun dein' milde Hand
Den Armen in deinem Land.
Kyrieleis!

LAW AND GOSPEL

9. Bear not false witness nor belie
Thy neighbor by foul calumny.
Defend his innocence from blame;
With charity hide his shame.
Have mercy, Lord!

Du sollst kein falscher Zeuge sein,
Nicht lügen auf den Nächsten dein;
Sein Unschuld sollst auch retten du
Und seine Schand' decken zu.
Kyrieleis!

10. Thy neighbor's house desire thou not,
His wife, nor aught that he hath got,
But wish that his such good may be
As thy heart doth wish for thee.
Have mercy, Lord!

Du sollst dein's Nächsten Weib und Haus
Begehren nicht noch etwas draus;
Du sollst ihm wünschen alles Gut',
Wie dir dein Herz selber tut.
Kyrieleis!

11. God these commandments gave therein
To show thee, child of man, thy sin
And make thee also well perceive
How man unto God should live.
Have mercy, Lord!

Die Gebot all' uns geben sind,
Dass du dein' Sünd', o Menschenkind,
Erkennen sollst und lernen wohl,
Wie man vor Gott leben soll.
Kyrieleis!

12. Help us, Lord Jesus Christ, for we
A Mediator have in Thee;
Our works cannot salvation gain;
They merit but endless pain.
Have mercy, Lord!

Das helf' uns der Herr Jesus Christ,
Der unser Mittler worden ist;
Es ist mit unserm Tun verlor'n,
Verdienen doch eitel Zorn.
Kyrieleis!

In the late Middle Ages the Ten Commandments were used for various purposes: on pilgrimages, as an introduction to the Litany during Lent, for examination in the confessional, and for the instruction of children. This metrical version by Martin Luther first appeared in *Eyn Enchiridion*, Erfurt, 1524.

The translation is an altered form of that by Richard Massie in his *Martin Luther's Spiritual Songs,* 1854.

The tune "Dies sind die heil'gen" is from an old German melody of the 13th century, which was used with a favorite pilgrim-song "In Gottes Namen fahren wir." It was apparently used with this hymn from the time of its first publication.

Lord, Help Us Ever to Retain   288

1. Lord, help us ever to retain
The Catechism's doctrine plain
As Luther taught the Word of Truth
In simple style to tender youth.

Herr Gott, erhalt uns für und für
Die reine Katechismuslehr',
Der jungen, einfältigen Welt
Durch deinen Luther vorgestellt:

2. Help us Thy holy Law to learn,
To mourn our sin, and from it turn
In faith to Thee and to Thy Son
And Holy Spirit, Three in One.

Dass wir lernen die Zehn Gebot',
Beweinen unsre Sünd' und Not
Und doch an dich und deinen Sohn
Glauben, im Geist erleuchtet schon;

3. Hear us, dear Father, when we pray
For needed help from day to day
That as Thy children we may live,
Whom Thou in Baptism didst receive.

Dich, unsern Vater, rufen an,
Der allen helfen will und kann,
Dass wir als Kinder nach der Tauf'
Christlich vollbringen unsern Lauf;

4. Lord, when we fall and sin doth stain,
Absolve and lift us up again;
And through the Sacrament increase
Our faith till we depart in peace.

So jemand fällt, nicht liegen bleib',
Sondern zur Beichte komm' und gläub',
Zur Stärkung nehm' das Sakrament.
Amen, Gott geb' ein selig End'!

Ludwig Helmbold first published this children's hymn in his *Dreyssig geistliche Lieder,* etc., Mühlhausen, 1594. It was intended to emphasize the value of the catechetical instruction by means of Luther's *Smaller Catechism.*

The translation is by Matthias Loy, somewhat altered. It appeared in the Ohio *Lutheran Hymnal,* 1880.

For comments on the tune "Herr Jesu Christ, mein's" see Hymn No. 7.

LAW AND GOSPEL

289   The Law Commands and Makes Us Know

1. The Law commands and makes us know
What duties to our God we owe;
But 'tis the Gospel must reveal
Where lies our strength to do His will.

2. The Law discovers guilt and sin
And shows how vile our hearts have been;
The Gospel only can express
Forgiving love and cleansing grace.

3. What curses doth the Law denounce
Against the man that fails but once!
But in the Gospel Christ appears,
Pardoning the guilt of numerous years.

4. My soul, no more attempt to draw
Thy life and comfort from the Law.
Fly to the hope the Gospel gives;
The man that trusts the promise lives.

This hymn appeared in Watt's *Hymns and Spiritual Songs*, 1709, headed "The Law and Gospel Distinguished."

For comments on the tune "Old Hundredth" see Hymn No. 13.

290   We Have a Sure Prophetic Word

1. We have a sure prophetic Word
By inspiration of the Lord;
And though assailed on every hand,
Jehovah's Word shall ever stand.

2. By powers of empire banned and burned,
By pagan pride rejected, spurned,
The Word still stands the Christian's trust
While haughty empires lie in dust.

3. Lo, what the Word in times of old
Of future days and deeds foretold
Is all fulfilled while ages roll,
As traced on the prophetic scroll.

4. Abiding, steadfast, firm, and sure,
The teachings of the Word endure.
Blest he who trusts this steadfast Word;
His anchor holds in Christ, the Lord.

Emanuel Cronenwett published this hymn, entitled "Holy Scripture," in the Ohio *Lutheran Hymnal*, 1880.

For comments on the tune "Wo Gott zum Haus" see Hymn No. 131.

291   Lamp of Our Feet Whereby We Trace

1. Lamp of our feet whereby we trace
Our path when wont to stray;
Stream from the fount of heavenly grace,
Brook by the traveler's way;

2. Bread of our souls whereon we feed,
True manna from on high;
Our guide and chart wherein we read
Of realms beyond the sky;

3. Pillar of fire, through watches dark,
Or radiant cloud by day;
When waves would break our tossing bark,
Our anchor and our stay:

4. Word of the ever-living God,
Will of His glorious Son;
Without thee, how could earth be trod
Or heaven itself be won?

5. Lord, grant us all aright to learn
The wisdom it imparts
And to its heavenly teaching turn
With simple, childlike hearts.

Bernard Barton published this hymn in his *Devotional Verses*, etc., 1826, in eleven stanzas. This cento includes Stanzas 1 to 3, and 9 and 11. The omitted stanzas, 4 to 8, and 10, read:

4. Pole-star on life's tempestuous deep,
Beacon, when doubts surround,
Compass by which our course we keep
Our deep sea-land to sound!

5. Riches in poverty, our aid
In every needful hour,
Unshaken rock, the pilgrim's shade,
The soldier's fortress tower!

6. Our shield and buckler in the fight,
Victory's triumphant palm,
Comfort in grief, in weakness, might,
In sickness, Gilead's balm!

7. Childhood's preceptor, manhood's trust
Old age's firm ally,
Our hope, when we go down to dust,
Of immortality!

8. Pure oracles of truth divine,
Unlike each fabled dream
Given forth from Delphos' mystic shrine
Or groves of Academe!

10. Unto unfold thy hidden worth,
Thy mysteries to reveal,
That Spirit which first gave thee forth
Thy volume must unseal.

For comments on the tune "St. Anne" see Hymn No. 123.

[210]

LAW AND GOSPEL

Lord Jesus Christ, with Us Abide 292

1. Lord Jesus Christ, with us abide,
For round us falls the eventide;
Nor let Thy Word, that heavenly light,
For us be ever veiled in night.

2. In these last days of sore distress
Grant us, dear Lord, true steadfastness
That pure we keep, till life is spent,
Thy holy Word and Sacrament.

3. Lord Jesus, help, Thy Church uphold,
For we are sluggish, thoughtless, cold.
Oh, prosper well Thy Word of grace
And spread its truth in every place!

4. Oh, keep us in Thy Word, we pray;
The guile and rage of Satan stay!
Oh, may Thy mercy never cease!
Give concord, patience, courage, peace.

5. O God, how sin's dread works abound!
Throughout the earth no rest is found,
And falsehood's spirit wide has spread,
And error boldly rears its head.

6. The haughty spirits, Lord, restrain
Who o'er Thy Church with might would reign
And always set forth something new,
Devised to change Thy doctrine true.

7. And since the cause and glory, Lord,
Are Thine, not ours, to us afford
Thy help and strength and constancy.
With all our heart we trust in Thee.

8. A trusty weapon is Thy Word,
Thy Church's buckler, shield, and sword.
Oh, let us in its power confide
That we may seek no other guide!

9. Oh, grant that in Thy holy Word
We here may live and die, dear Lord;
And when our journey endeth here,
Receive us into glory there.

Ach bleib bei uns, Herr Jesu Christ,
Weil es nun Abend worden ist;
Dein göttlich Wort, das helle Licht,
Lass ja bei uns auslöschen nicht!

In dieser, letzt'n, betrübten Zeit
Verleih uns, Herr, Beständigkeit,
Dass wir dein Wort und Sakrament
Rein b'halten bis an unser End'!

Herr Jesu, hilf, dein' Kirch' erhalt,
Wir sind gar sicher, faul und kalt!
Gib Glück und Heil zu deinem Wort,
Damit es schall' an allem Ort!

Erhalt uns nur bei deinem Wort
Und wehr des Teufels Trug und Mord!
Gib deiner Kirche Gnad' und Huld,
Fried', Einigkeit, Mut und Geduld!

Ach Gott, es geht gar übel zu,
Auf dieser Erd' ist keine Ruh',
Viel Sekten und viel Schwärmerei
Auf einen Haufen kommt herbei.

Den stolzen Geistern wehre doch,
Die sich mit G'walt erheben hoch
Und bringen stets was Neues her,
Zu fälschen deine rechte Lehr'.

Die Sach' und Ehr', Herr Jesu Christ,
Nicht unser, sondern dein ja ist;
Darum so steh du denen bei,
Die sich auf dich verlassen frei!

Dein Wort ist unsers Herzens Trutz
Und deiner Kirche wahrer Schutz;
Dabei erhalt uns, lieber Herr,
Dass wir nichts anders suchen mehr!

Gib, dass wir leb'n in deinem Wort
Und darauf ferner fahren fort
Von hinnen aus dem Jammertal
Zu dir in deinen Himmelssaal!

This hymn on the Word of God and the preservation of the Church appeared in the *Nürnberger Gesangbuch*, 1611, where it was attributed to Nikolaus Selnecker. It is based on Ps. 122. Selnecker is the author of Stanzas 3, 4, and 6 to 10. In this form the hymn appeared in Selnecker's *Psalmen*, Leipzig, 1578. The *Nürnberger Gesangbuch* text accordingly has two new stanzas at the beginning by an unknown author or authors. The fifth stanza is taken from another of Selnecker's hymns, beginning "Wir danken dir, Herr Jesu Christ."

The translation is composite.

For comments on the tune "Ach bleib bei uns" see Hymn No. 197.

O Holy Spirit, Grant Us Grace 293

1. O Holy Spirit, grant us grace
That we our Lord and Savior
In faith and fervent love embrace
And truly serve Him ever,
So that when death is drawing nigh,
We to His open wounds may fly
And find in them salvation.

2. Help us that we Thy saving Word
In faithful hearts may treasure;
Let e'er that Bread of Life afford
New grace in richest measure.
Yea, let us die to every sin,
For heaven create us new within
That fruits of faith may flourish.

Gott Heil'ger Geist, hilf uns mit Grund
Auf Jesum Christum schauen,
Damit wir in der letzten Stund'
Auf seine Wunden bauen,
Die er für uns nach Gottes Rat
Am heil'gen Kreuz empfangen hat
Zu Tilgung unsrer Sünden.

Durchs Wort in unsre Herzen schein
Und tu uns neu gebären,
Dass wir als Gottes Kinder rein
Vom bösen Wandel kehren
Und in dir bringen Früchte gut,
So viel, als unser blöder Mut
In diesem Fleisch kann tragen.

LAW AND GOSPEL

3. And when our earthly race is run,
   Death's bitter hour impending,
   Then may Thy work in us begun
   Continue till life's ending,
   Until we gladly may commend
   Our souls into our Savior's hand
   To rest in peace eternal.

In Sterbensnöten bei uns steh
Und hilf uns Wohl verscheiden,
Dass wir fein sanft aus allem Weh
Hinfahren zu den Freuden,
Die uns der fromme Vater wert
Aus lauter Gnade hat beschert
In Christo, seinem Sohne.

This hymn, by Bartholomäus Ringwaldt, appeared in his *Euangelia, auff alle Sontag*, etc., Frankfurt a. d. O., 1581.

The translation is by Oluf H. Smeby 1909. It appeared in *The Lutheran Hymnary* 1913.

For comments on the tune "Es ist gewisslich" see Hymn No. 604.

294   O Word of God Incarnate

1. O Word of God Incarnate,
   O Wisdom from on high,
   O Truth unchanged, unchanging,
   O Light of our dark sky, —
   We praise Thee for the radiance
   That from the hallowed page,
   A lantern to our footsteps,
   Shines on from age to age.

2. The Church from her dear Master
   Received the gift divine,
   And still that light she lifteth
   O'er all the earth to shine.
   It is the golden casket
   Where gems of truth are stored;
   It is the heaven-drawn picture
   Of Christ, the living Word.

3. It floateth like a banner
   Before God's host unfurled;
   It shineth like a beacon
   Above the darkling world;
   It is the chart and compass
   That o'er life's surging sea,
   Mid mists and rocks and quicksands,
   Still guides, O Christ, to Thee.

4. Oh, make Thy Church, dear Savior,
   A lamp of burnished gold
   To bear before the nations
   Thy true light as of old!
   Oh, teach Thy wandering pilgrims
   By this their path to trace
   Till, clouds and darkness ended,
   They see Thee face to face!

William Walsham How wrote this hymn in 1867 and published it the same year in the *Supplement* to Morrell and How's *Psalms and Hymns*.

The tune "Munich" is by an unknown composer. It appeared in the *Neuvermehrtes Gesangbuch*, Meiningen, 1693, where it was set to the hymn "O Gott, du frommer Gott" by Johann Heermann. (See Hymn No. 395.)

295   The Law of God Is Good and Wise

1. The Law of God is good and wise
   And sets His will before our eyes,
   Shows us the way of righteousness,
   And dooms to death when we transgress.

2. Its light of holiness imparts
   The knowledge of our sinful hearts
   That we may see our lost estate
   And seek deliverance ere too late.

3. To those who help in Christ have found
   And would in works of love abound
   It shows what deeds are His delight
   And should be done as good and right.

4. When men the offered help disdain
   And wilfully in sin remain,
   Its terror in their ear resounds
   And keeps their wickedness in bounds.

5. The Law is good; but since the Fall
   Its holiness condemns us all;
   It dooms us for our sin to die
   And has no power to justify.

6. To Jesus we for refuge flee,
   Who from the curse has set us free,
   And humbly worship at His throne,
   Saved by His grace through faith alone.

This hymn on the Law of God by Matthias Loy appeared in the Ohio *Lutheran Hymnal*, 1880. It had previously been published in the Ohio Synod's *Collection of Hymns*, fourth edition, 1863. It is a companion piece of his hymn on the Gospel. (See Hymn No. 297.)

For comments on the tune "Erhalt uns, Herr" see Hymn No. 5

Speak, O Lord, Thy Servant Heareth   296

1. Speak, O Lord, Thy servant heareth,
 To Thy Word I now give heed;
 Life and spirit Thy Word beareth,
 All Thy Word is true indeed.
 Death's dread power in me is rife;
 Jesus, may Thy Word of Life
 Fill my soul with love's strong fervor
 That I cling to Thee forever.

2. Oh, what blessing to be near Thee
 And to hearken to Thy voice!
 May I ever love and fear Thee
 That Thy Word may be my choice!
 Oft were hardened sinners, Lord,
 Struck with terror by Thy Word;
 But to him who for sin grieveth
 Comfort sweet and hope it giveth.

3. Lord, Thy words are waters living
 Where I quench my thirsty need;
 Lord, Thy words are bread life-giving,
 On Thy words my soul doth feed.
 Lord, Thy words shall be my light
 Through death's vale and dreary night;
 Yea, they are my sword prevailing
 And my cup of joy unfailing.

4. Precious Jesus, I beseech Thee,
 May Thy words take root in me;
 May this gift from heaven enrich me
 So that I bear fruit for Thee!
 Take them never from my heart
 Till I see Thee as Thou art,
 When in heavenly bliss and glory
 I shall greet Thee and adore Thee.

Rede, liebster Jesu, rede,
Denn dein Kind gibt acht darauf;
Stärke mich, denn ich bin blöde,
Dass ich meinen Lebenslauf
Dir zur Ehre setze fort.
Ach, lass stets dein heilig Wort
In mein Herz sein eingeschlossen,
Dir zu folgen unverdrossen!

Ach, wer wollte dich nicht hören,
Dich, du liebster Menschenfreund?
Sind doch deine Wort' und Lehren
Alle herzlich wohl gemeint.
Sie vertreiben alles Leid,
Selbst des Todes Bitterkeit
Muss vor deinen Worten weichen,
Nichts ist ihnen zu vergleichen.

Jesu, dein Wort soll mich laben;
Deine trosterfüllte Lehr'
Will ich in mein Herz eingraben.
Ach, nimm sie doch nimmermehr
Von mir weg in dieser Zeit,
Bis ich in der Ewigkeit
Werde kommen zu den Ehren,
Dich, o Jesu, selbst zu hören.

Unterdes vernimm mein Flehen;
Liebster Jesu, höre mich!
Lass bei dir mich feste stehen;
So will ich dich ewiglich
Preisen mit Herz, Sinn und Mund,
Ich will dir zu jeder Stund'
Ehr' und Dank in Demut bringen
Und dein hohes Lob besingen.

This hymn by Anna Sophia, countess of Hesse-Darmstadt, first appeared in her *Der treue Seelenfreund Christus Jesus,* etc., Jena, 1658, in five stanzas. The omitted Stanza 3 reads:

> Deine Worte sind der Stecken,
> Woran ich mich halten kann,
> Wenn der Teufel mich will schrecken
> Auf der schmalen Lebensbahn;
> Sie, sie führen ohne Qual
> Mich selbst durch des Todes Tal,
> Sind mein Schirm und meine Stütze
> Unter aller Kreuzeshitze.

The translation is by George T. Rygh, 1909. It appeared in *The Lutheran Hymnary,* 1913.

For comments on the tune "Werde munter" see Hymn No. 207.

The Gospel Shows the Father's Grace   297

1. The Gospel shows the Father's grace,
 Who sent His Son to save our race,
 Proclaims how Jesus lived and died
 That man might thus be justified.

2. It sets the Lamb before our eyes,
 Who made the atoning sacrifice,
 And calls the souls with guilt opprest
 To come and find eternal rest.

3. It brings the Savior's righteousness
 Our souls to robe in royal dress;
 From all our guilt it brings release
 And gives the troubled conscience peace.

4. It is the power of God to save
 From sin and Satan and the grave;
 It works the faith, which firmly clings
 To all the treasures which it brings.

5. It bears to all the tidings glad
 And bids their hearts no more be sad;
 The heavy-laden souls it cheers
 And banishes their guilty fears.

6. May we in faith its tidings learn
 Nor thanklessly its blessings spurn;
 May we in faith its truth confess
 And praise the Lord our Righteousness!

This hymn, a companion piece of Matthias Loy's hymn on the Law (see Hymn No. 295), first appeared in the Ohio Synod's *Collection of Hymns,* fourth edition, 1863, and then in the Ohio *Lutheran Hymnal,* 1880.

For comments on the tune "Herr Jesu Christ, dich" see Hymn No. 3.

The Sacraments

298   Baptized into Thy Name Most Holy

1. Baptized into Thy name most holy,
   O Father, Son, and Holy Ghost,
   I claim a place, though weak and lowly,
   Among Thy seed, Thy chosen host.
   Buried with Christ and dead to sin,
   Thy Spirit now shall live within.

2. My loving Father, Thou dost take me
   To be henceforth Thy child and heir;
   My faithful Savior, Thou dost make me
   The fruit of all Thy sorrows share;
   Thou, Holy Ghost, wilt comfort me
   When darkest clouds around I see.

3. And I have vowed to fear and love Thee
   And to obey Thee, Lord, alone;
   Because the Holy Ghost did move me,
   I dared to pledge myself Thine own,
   Renouncing sin to keep the faith
   And war with evil unto death.

4. My faithful God, Thou failest never,
   Thy covenant surely will abide;
   Oh, cast me not away forever
   Should I transgress it on my side!
   Though I have oft my soul defiled,
   Do Thou forgive, restore, Thy child.

5. Yea, all I am and love most dearly
   I offer now, O Lord, to Thee,
   Oh, let me make my vows sincerely
   And help me Thine own child to be!
   Let naught within me, naught I own,
   Serve any will but Thine alone.

6. And never let my purpose falter,
   O Father, Son, and Holy Ghost,
   But keep me faithful to Thine altar
   Till Thou shalt call me from my post.
   So unto Thee I live and die
   And praise Thee evermore on high.

Ich bin getauft auf deinen Namen,
Gott Vater, Sohn und Heil'ger Geist,
Ich bin gezählt zu deinem Samen,
Zum Volk, das dir geheiligt heisst,
Ich bin in Christum eingesenkt,
Ich bin mit seinem Geist beschenkt.

Du hast zu deinem Kind und Erben,
Mein lieber Vater, mich erklärt,
Du hast die Frucht von deinem Sterben,
Mein treuer Heiland, mir gewährt.
Du willst in aller Not und Pein,
O guter Geist, mein Tröster sein.

Doch habe ich dir Furcht und Liebe,
Treu' und Gehorsam zugesagt,
Ich hab' aus deines Geistes Triebe
Dein Eigentum zu sein gewagt,
Hingegen sagt' ich bis ins Grab
Des Satans schnöden Werken ab.

Mein treuer Gott, auf deiner Seite
Bleibt dieser Bund wohl feste stehn;
Wenn aber ich ihn überschreite,
So lass mich nicht verlorengehn!
Nimm mich, dein Kind, zu Gnaden an,
Wenn ich hab' einen Fall getan!

Ich gebe dir, mein Gott, aufs neue
Leib, Seel' und Herz zum Opfer hin.
Erwecke mich zu neuer Treue
Und nimm Besitz von meinem Sinn!
Es sei in mir kein Tropfen Blut,
Der nicht, Herr, deinen Willen tut.

Lass diesen Vorsatz nimmer wanken,
Gott Vater, Sohn und Heil'ger Geist!
Halt mich in deines Bundes Schranken,
Bis mich dein Wille sterben heisst!
So leb' ich dir, so sterb' ich dir,
So lob' ich dich dort für und für.

Johann J. Rambach first published this hymn in his *Erbauliches Handbüchlein für Kinder,* Giessen, 1734, in seven stanzas. It is headed "For Daily Renewal of the Baptismal Covenant." The omitted Stanza 6 reads in translation:

    Depart, depart, thou Prince of Darkness!
      No more by thee I'll be enticed.
    Mine is indeed a tarnished conscience,
      But sprinkled with the blood of Christ.
    Away, vain world! O sin, away!
    Lo, I renounce you all this day.

In many parts of the Church this hymn has long been a favorite hymn for confirmation.

The translation is an altered form of that by Catherine Winkworth in her *Chorale Book for England,* 1863.

For comments on the tune "O dass ich tausend" (Dretzel) see Hymn No. 243.

299   Dear Father, Who hast Made Us All

1. Dear Father, who hast made us all,
   To Thee Thy children humbly pray:
   Look on this babe, who at Thy call
   Now enters on life's narrow way.

O Vaterherz, das Erd' und Himmel schuf
  Nach seinem Liebesrat!
Dies Kindlein tritt nach deinem Gnadenruf
  Auf seinen Pilgerpfad.
Komm, neige dich zum Armen, Schwachen,
Ein Etwas aus dem Nichts zu machen,
  O Vaterherz!

BAPTISM

2. Dear Savior, for Thy love untold
   We bring this little child to Thee.
   Receive it, Shepherd, to Thy fold
   And keep it Thine eternally.

3. Dear Spirit, rest upon this child
   As Thou didst brood upon the sea,
   And make it pure and undefiled,
   A holy temple unto Thee.

4. O Triune God, we humbly pray
   That all Thy blessings be conferred
   Upon this child here cleansed today
   By means of water and the Word.

O Gottes Sohn, für uns am Kreuz
   erblasst,
Nimm es erbarmend ein
Zu deiner Schar, die du erkaufet hast,
   Dein Eigentum zu sein!
Leit es auf deinem Lebenswege,
Beschirmt von deiner Hirtenpflege,
   O Gottes Sohn!

O Heil'ger Geist, der überm Wasser
   schwebt,
Komm auch auf dieses Kind!
Gestalt es mit der Kraft, die ewig lebt,
   Wie Gottes Kinder sind,
Damit es früh schon auf der Erde
Dein Zögling und dein Tempel werde,
   O Heil'ger Geist!

Dreiein'ger Gott, was du gebeutst,
   geschieht;
Gib Kraft zu unserm Wort!
Dies Kindlein kaum die Erdensonne
   sieht;
Doch sieht es hier und dort
In Glauben, Hoffnung, Lieb' und Wonne
Dich selbst, du wahre Himmelssonne,
   Dreiein'ger Gott!

This beautiful hymn for Holy Baptism by Albert Knapp appeared in his *Christenlieder*, 1841. It calls upon God the Creator (st. 1), God the Redeemer (st. 2), God the Sanctifier (st. 3), on behalf of the child and closes with a petition to the Holy Trinity for lifelong blessing.

The translation, by Wm. Czamanske, was prepared for *The Lutheran Hymnal* in 1939.

For comments on the tune "Herr Jesu Christ, dich" see Hymn No. 3.

Dearest Jesus, We Are Here 300

1. Dearest Jesus, we are here,
   Gladly Thy command obeying;
   With this child we now draw near
   In accord with Thine own saying
   That to Thee it shall be given
   As a child and heir of heaven.

2. Yea, Thy word is clear and plain,
   And we would obey it duly:
   "He who is not born again,
   Heart and life renewing truly,
   Born of water and the Spirit,
   Can My kingdom not inherit."

3. Therefore hasten we to Thee,
   In our arms this infant bearing;
   Let us here Thy glory see,
   Let this child, Thy mercy sharing,
   In Thine arms be shielded ever,
   Thine on earth and Thine forever.

4. Gracious Head, Thy member own;
   Shepherd, take Thy lamb and feed it;
   Prince of Peace, make here Thy throne;
   Way of Life, to heaven lead it;
   Precious Vine, let nothing sever
   From Thy side this branch forever.

5. Now into Thy heart we pour
   Prayers that from our hearts proceeded.
   Our petitions heavenward soar;
   May our warm desires be heeded!
   Write the name we now have given,
   Write it in the book of heaven.

Liebster Jesu, wir sind hier,
   Deinem Worte nachzuleben.
Dieses Kindlein kommt zu dir,
   Weil du den Befehl gegeben,
Dass man sie zu Christo führe,
Denn das Himmelreich ist ihre.

Ja, es schallet allermeist
   Dieses Wort in unsern Ohren:
Wer durch Wasser und durch Geist
   Nicht zuvor ist neugeboren,
Wird von dir nicht aufgenommen
Und in Gottes Reich nicht kommen.

Darum eilen wir zu dir.
   Nimm das Pfand von unsern Armen,
Tritt mit deinem Glanz herfür
   Und erzeige dein Erbarmen,
Dass es dein Kind hier auf Erden
Und im Himmel möge werden!

Hirte, nimm dein Schäflein an;
   Haupt, mach es zu deinem Gliede;
Himmelsweg, zeig ihm die Bahn;
   Friedefürst, schenk ihm den Frieden;
Weinstock, hilf, dass diese Rebe
Auch im Glauben dich umgebe!

Nun, wir legen an dein Herz,
   Was vom Herzen ist gegangen;
Führ die Seufzer himmelwärts
   Und erfülle das Verlangen,
Ja, den Namen, den wir geben,
Schreib ins Lebensbuch zum Leben!

This hymn, by Benjamin Schmolck, first appeared, in seven stanzas, in his *Heilige Flammen*, etc., Striegau, 1704. It was headed "Good thoughts of the sponsors who journey with a child to Baptism." The omitted Stanzas 4 and 5 read in translation:

4. Wash it, Jesus, in Thy blood,
   From the sin-stain of its nature;
   Let it rise from out this flood
   Clothed in Thee, a new-born creature;
   May it, washed as Thou hast bidden,
   In Thine innocence be hidden.

5. Turn its darkness into light,
   To Thy grace receive and save it;
   Heal the Serpent's venomed bite
   In the font where now we lave it;
   Here let flow a Jordan river
   And from leprosy deliver.

The translation is an altered form of that by Catherine Winkworth in her *Chorale Book for England*, 1863.

For comments on the tune "Liebster Jesu" see Hymn No. 16.

301   He that Believes and is Baptized

1. He that believes and is baptized
   Shall see the Lord's salvation;
   Baptized into the death of Christ,
   He is a new creation.
   Through Christ's redemption he shall stand
   Among the glorious heavenly band
   Of every tribe and nation.

   Enhver som tror og bliver døbt,
   Han skal vist salig blive,
   Thi han ved Jesu Blod er kjøbt,
   Som vil sig ham indlive,
   Og blandt Guds Børns det hellig' Tal
   Til Himmeriges Æres Val
   Med Korsets Blod indskrive.

2. With one accord, O God, we pray:
   Grant us Thy Holy Spirit;
   Look Thou on our infirmity
   Through Jesus' blood and merit.
   Grant us to grow in grace each day
   That by this Sacrament we may
   Eternal life inherit.

   Vi sukke alle hjertelig,
   Og udi Troen sige
   Med Hjertens Bøn, enhver for sig:
   O Jesu, lad os stige
   Ved Daabens Kraft i Dyder frem,
   Og for os saa ved Troen hjem
   Til Ærens evig' Rige!

This hymn by Thomas Kingo first appeared in his *Hymnal Outline*, 1689, and then as a hymn for Holy Baptism in his official *Church Hymnal* of 1699.

The translation by George T. Rygh, 1909, was included in *The Lutheran Hymnary*, 1913.

For comments on the tune "Es ist das Heil" see Hymn No. 377.

302   The Savior Kindly Calls

1. The Savior kindly calls
   Our children to His breast;
   He folds them in His gracious arms,
   Himself declares them blest.

2. "Let them approach," He cries,
   "Nor scorn their humble claim;
   The heirs of heaven are such as these,
   For such as these I came."

3. With joy we bring them, Lord,
   Devoting them to Thee,
   Imploring that, as we are Thine,
   Thine may our offspring be.

Philip Doddridge's hymn "See Israel's Gentle Shepherd Stand" was first published in the posthumous edition of his *Hymns*, 1755, in five stanzas, according to *Julian*. It was headed "Christ's Condescending Regard to Little Children." In *A Collection of Hymns and a Liturgy for the Use of Evangelical Lutheran Churches*, New York, 1834, we find Doddridge's text given in six stanzas, as follows:

1. See Israel's gentle Shepherd stand
   With all-engaging charms.
   Hark how He calls the tender lambs
   And takes them in His arms!

2. "Permit them to approach," He cries,
   "Nor scorn their humble name;
   It was to save such souls as these
   With power and love I came."

BAPTSM. — THE LORD'S SUPPER

3. We bring them, Lord, with grateful hearts
  And yield them up to Thee;
  Rejoiced that we ourselves are Thine;
  Thine let our offspring be.
4. Thus Lydia's house was sanctified
  When she received the Word;
  Thus the believing jailer gave
  His family to the Lord.

5. Ye little flock, with pleasure hear;
  Ye children, seek His face
  And fly with transport to receive
  The Gospel of His grace.
6. If orphans they are left behind,
  Thy care, O God, we trust;
  And let Thy promise cheer our hearts
  If weeping o'er their dust.

Stanza 4 of this version is probably an insertion by an unknown hand. To this hymn Duffield remarks:

> Perhaps we forget the little phrases of the evangelists as to this incident. Matthew says that Christ was expected "to put His hands on them and pray"; Luke, that He should "touch" them; and Mark adds that He "took them up in His arms, put His hands upon them, and blessed them." And if it was a precious memory for such a child later in life to know that he had once been in the Savior's arms, how precious it must also be to one who knows — even in our days — that he has been committed to the Lord's love in his earliest moments!

Henry Ustic Onderdonk adapted the first three stanzas of Doddridge's hymn in his *Prayer Book Collection,* 1826, the first line reading: "The gentle Savior calls."

For comments on the tune "Franconia" see Hymn No. 133.

This Child We Dedicate to Thee 303

1. This child we dedicate to Thee,
  O God of grace and purity;
  Shield it from sin and threatening wrong,
  And let Thy love its life prolong.
2. Oh, may Thy Spirit gently draw
  Its willing soul to keep Thy Law!
  May virtue, piety, and truth
  Dawn even with its dawning youth!

3. We, too, before Thy gracious sight
  Once shared the blest baptismal rite
  And would renew its solemn vow
  With love and thanks and praises now.
4. Grant that with true and faithful heart
  We still may act the Christian's part,
  Cheered by each promise Thou hast given
  And laboring for the prize in heaven.

This hymn, by Samuel Gilman, dated 1823, is said to be a translation from the German. Putnam, in his *Singers and Songs of the Liberal Faith,* 1874, gives it in five stanzas as a translation from the German. We have been unable to confirm this claim. The German text that seems to be suggested, as Duffield, in his *English Hymns,* states, is the hymn by Christoph Friedrich Neander (1724—1802), beginning "Du wiesest, Jesu, [eh'mals] nicht die Kleinen," of which the *Württembergisches Gesangbuch,* Stuttgart, 1793, gives the following two stanzas:

1. Dir, Herr, sei dieses Kind empfohlen,
  Dir, dessen Treu' unwandelbar,
  Wir bringen's, wie du selbst befohlen,
  Dir in der heil'gen Taufe dar.
  Gib, Vater, gib an deinem Heil,
  An Jesu Christo gib ihm Teil.

2. Durch dieses Siegel deiner Gnade
  Wird jedes Recht der Christen sein;
  Du weihst es in dem Wasserbade
  Zu deinem Kind und Erben ein.
  Im Wasser, Vater, ströme du,
  Ström ihm des Geistes Gaben zu.

The tune "Uxbridge" by Lowell Mason appeared in 1830 in *The Boston Handel and Haydn Society Collection,* etc., 9th edition, where it was set to a cento from one of A. M. Toplady's hymns beginning "At anchor laid, remote from home."

An Awe-full Mystery Is Here 304

1. An awe-full mystery is here
  To challenge faith and waken fear:
  The Savior comes as food divine,
  Concealed in earthly bread and wine.

2. This world is loveless, — but above,
  What wondrous boundlessness of love!
  The King of Glory stoops to me
  My spirit's life and strength to be.

[217]

LORD'S SUPPER

3. In consecrated wine and bread
No eye perceives the mystery dread;
But Jesus' words are strong and clear:
"My body and My blood are here."

4. How dull are all the powers of sense
Employed on proofs of love immense!
The richest food remains unseen,
And highest gifts appear — how mean!

5. But here we have no boon on earth,
And faith alone discerns its worth:
The Word, not sense, must be our guide,
And faith assure, since sight's denied.

6. Lord, show us still that Thou art good
And grant us evermore this food.
Give faith to every wavering soul
And make each wounded spirit whole.

This hymn for Holy Communion is by Matthias Loy. It appeared in the Ohio *Lutheran Hymnal*, 1880. It emphasizes the Lutheran doctrine of the Real Presence in the Sacrament of the Altar.

For comments on the tune "St. Crispin" see Hymn No. 245.

305   Soul, Adorn Thyself with Gladness

1. Soul, adorn thyself with gladness,
Leave behind all gloom and sadness;
Come into the daylight's splendor,
There with joy thy praises render
Unto Him whose grace unbounded
Hath this wondrous supper founded.
High o'er all the heavens He reigneth,
Yet to dwell with thee He deigneth.

Schmücke dich, o liebe Seele,
Lass die dunkle Sündenhöhle,
Komm ans helle Licht gegangen,
Fange herrlich an zu prangen!
Denn der Herr, voll Heil und Gnaden,
Will dich jetzt zu Gaste laden;
Der den Himmel kann verwalten,
Will jetzt Herberg' in dir halten.

2. Hasten as a bride to meet Him
And with loving reverence greet Him;
For with words of life immortal
Now He knocketh at thy portal.
Haste to ope the gates before Him,
Saying, while thou dost adore Him,
Suffer, Lord, that I receive Thee,
And I nevermore will leave Thee.

Eile, wie Verlobte pflegen,
Deinem Bräutigam entgegen,
Der da mit dem Gnadenhammer
Klopft an deine Herzenskammer!
Öffn' ihm bald des Geistes Pforten,
Red ihn an mit schönen Worten:
Komm, mein Liebster, lass dich küssen,
Lass mich deiner nicht mehr missen!

3. He who craves a precious treasure
Neither cost nor pain will measure;
But the priceless gifts of heaven
God to us hath freely given.
Though the wealth of earth were proffered,
Naught would buy the gifts here offered:
Christ's true body, for thee riven,
And His blood, for thee once given.

Zwar in Kaufung teurer Waren
Pflegt man sonst kein Geld zu sparen;
Aber du willst für die Gaben
Deiner Huld kein Geld nicht haben,
Weil in allen Bergwerksgründen
Kein solch Kleinod ist zu finden,
Das die blutgefüllten Schalen
Und dies Manna kann bezahlen.

4. Ah, how hungers all my spirit
For the love I do not merit!
Oft have I, with sighs fast thronging,
Thought upon this food with longing,
In the battle well-nigh worsted,
For this cup of life have thirsted,
For the Friend who here invites us
And to God Himself unites us.

Ach, wie hungert mein Gemüte,
Menschenfreund, nach deiner Güte!
Ach, wie pfleg' ich oft mit Tränen
Mich nach dieser Kost zu sehnen!
Ach, wie pfleget mich zu dürsten
Nach dem Trank des Lebensfürsten!
Wünsche stets, dass mein Gebeine
Sich durch Gott mit Gott vereine.

5. In my heart I find ascending
Holy awe, with rapture blending,
As this mystery I ponder,
Filling all my soul with wonder,
Bearing witness at this hour
Of the greatness of Thy power;
Far beyond all human telling
Is the power within Him dwelling.

Beides Lachen und auch Zittern
Lässet sich in mir jetzt wittern;
Das Geheimnis dieser Speise
Und die unerforschte Weise
Machet, dass ich früh vermerke,
Herr, die Grösse deiner Werke.
Ist auch wohl ein Mensch zu finden,
Der dein' Allmacht sollt' ergründen?

6. Human reason, though it ponder,
Cannot fathom this great wonder
That Christ's body e'er remaineth
Though it countless souls sustaineth,
And that He His blood is giving
With the wine we are receiving.
These great mysteries unsounded
Are by God alone expounded.

Nein, Vernunft, die muss hier weichen,
Kann dies Wunder nicht erreichen,
Dass dies Brot nie wird verzehret,
Ob es gleich viel Tausend' nähret,
Und dass mit dem Saft der Reben
Uns wird Christi Blut gegeben.
O der grossen Heimlichkeiten,
Die nur Gottes Geist kann deuten!

LORD'S SUPPER

7. Jesus, Sun of Life, my Splendor,
Jesus, Thou my Friend most tender,
Jesus, Joy of my desiring,
Fount of life, my soul inspiring, —
At Thy feet I cry, my Maker,
Let me be a fit partaker
Of this blessed food from heaven,
For our good, Thy glory, given.

8. Lord, by love and mercy driven
Thou hast left Thy throne in heaven
On the cross for us to languish
And to die in bitter anguish,
To forego all joy and gladness
And to shed Thy blood in sadness.
By this blood, redeemed and living,
Lord, I praise Thee with thanksgiving.

9. Jesus, Bread of Life, I pray Thee,
Let me gladly here obey Thee.
By Thy love I am invited,
Be Thy love with love requited;
From this Supper let me measure,
Lord, how vast and deep love's treasure.
Through the gifts Thou here dost give me
As Thy guest in heaven receive me.

Jesu, meines Lebens Sonne,
Jesu, meine Freud' und Wonne,
Jesu, du mein ganz Beginnen,
Lebensquell und Licht der Sinnen,
Hier fall' ich zu deinen Füssen;
Lass mich würdiglich geniessen
Dieser deiner Himmelsspeise
Mir zum Heil und dir zum Preise!

Herr, es hat dein treues Lieben
Dich vom Himmel hergetrieben,
Dass du willig hast dein Leben
In den Tod für uns gegeben
Und dazu ganz unverdrossen,
Herr, dein Blut für uns vergossen,
Das uns jetzt kann kräftig tränken,
Deiner Liebe zu gedenken.

Jesu, wahres Brot des Lebens,
Hilf, dass ich doch nicht vergebens
Oder mir vielleicht zum Schaden
Sei zu deinem Tisch geladen!
Lass mich durch dies Seelenessen
Deine Liebe recht ermessen,
Dass ich auch, wie jetzt auf Erden,
Mög' dein Gast im Himmel werden!

The first stanza of this hymn by Johann Franck appeared in Johann Crüger's *Geistliche Kirchen Melodien,* 1649, set to the beautiful tune "Schmücke dich," which Crüger himself had composed for it. Whether the entire hymn was written in that year or earlier is not certain. Franck published it in his *Geistliches Sion,* etc., Guben, 1674, headed "Preparation for the Holy Communion." Both text and tune are truly great. *Julian* states:

> This hymn is perhaps the finest of all German hymns for the Holy Communion. It is an exhortation to the soul to arise and draw near to partake of the Heavenly Food and to meditate on the wonders of Heavenly Love, ending with a prayer for final reception at the Eternal Feast. It soon attained, and still retains, popularity in Germany (in many German churches it is still the unvarying hymn at the celebration), was one of the first hymns translated into Malabar, and passed into English in 1754.

The composite translation is an altered form of that by Catherine Winkworth in her *Lyra Germanica,* second series, 1858, and in her *Chorale Book for England,* 1863, with the addition of Stanzas 3, 6, and 8, which she omitted.

Lord Jesus Christ, Thou hast Prepared 306

1. Lord Jesus Christ, Thou hast prepared
A feast for our salvation,
It is Thy body and Thy blood;
And at Thy invitation
As weary souls, with sin opprest,
We come to Thee for needed rest,
For comfort and for pardon.

2. Although Thou didst to heaven ascend,
Where angel hosts are dwelling,
And in Thy presence they behold
Thy glory all excelling,
And though Thy people shall not see
Thy glory and Thy majesty
Till dawns the Judgment morning,

3. Yet, Savior, Thou art not confined
To any habitation,
But Thou art present everywhere
And with Thy congregation.
Firm as a rock this truth shall stand,
Unmoved by any daring hand
Or subtle craft and cunning.

Herr Jesu Christ, du hast bereit't
Für unsre matten Seelen
Dein Leib und Blut zu ein'r Mahlzeit,
Tust uns zu Gästen wählen.
Wir tragen unsre Sündenlast,
Drum kommen wir zu dir zu Gast
Und suchen Rat und Hilfe.

Ob du schon aufgefahren bist
Von dieser Erde sichtig
Und bleibst nunmehr zu dieser Frist
Von uns allhier unsichtig,
Bis dein Gericht dort wird angehn
Und wir vor dir all' werden stehn
Und dich fröhlich anschauen:

So bist du doch stets nach dein'm Wort
Bei uns und dein'r Gemeine
Und nicht gefang'n an einem Ort
Mit deinem Fleisch und Beine.
Dein Wort steht wie ein' Mauer fest,
Welch's sich niemand verkehren lässt,
Er sei so klug er wolle.

LORD'S SUPPER

4. We eat this bread and drink this cup,
   Thy precious Word believing
   That Thy true body and Thy blood
   Our lips are here receiving.
   This word remains forever true,
   And there is naught Thou canst not do;
   For Thou, Lord, art almighty.

5. Though reason cannot understand,
   Yet faith this truth embraces;
   Thy body, Lord, is everywhere
   At once in many places.
   How this can be I leave to Thee,
   Thy word alone sufficeth me,
   I trust its truth unfailing.

6. Lord, I believe what Thou hast said,
   Help me when doubts assail me;
   Remember that I am but dust
   And let my faith not fail me.
   Thy Supper in this vale of tears
   Refreshes me and stills my fears
   And is my priceless treasure.

7. Grant that we worthily receive
   Thy Supper, Lord, our Savior,
   And, truly grieving o'er our sins,
   May prove by our behavior
   That we are thankful for Thy grace
   And day by day may run our race,
   In holiness increasing.

8. For Thy consoling Supper, Lord,
   Be praised throughout all ages!
   Preserve it, for in every place
   The world against it rages.
   Grant that this Sacrament may be
   A blessed comfort unto me
   When living and when dying.

Du sprichst: Nehmt hin, das ist mein Leib,
Den sollt ihr mündlich essen;
Trinkt all' mein Blut, bei euch ich bleib',
Mein sollt ihr nicht vergessen.
Du hast's gered't, drum ist es wahr;
Du bist allmächtig, drum ist gar
Kein Ding bei dir unmöglich.

Und ob mein Herz hier nicht versteht,
Wie dein Leib an viel Orten
Zugleich sein kann, und wie's zugeht,
So trau' ich doch dein'n Worten;
Wie das sein kann, befehl' ich dir,
An deinem Worte g'nüget mir,
Dem stehet nur zu glauben.

Ich glaub', o lieber Herr, ich glaub',
Hilf meinem schwachen Glauben!
Ich bin doch nichts denn Asch' und Staub,
Dein's Worts mich nicht beraube!
Dein Wort, dein' Tauf' und dein Nachtmahl
Tröst't mich in diesem Jammertal;
Da liegt mein Schatz begraben.

Ach Herr, hilf, dass wir würdiglich
Gehen zu deinem Tische,
Beweinen unsre Sünd' herzlich,
Und uns wieder erfrische
Mit dein'm Verdienst und Wohltat gross,
Darauf wir traun ohn' Unterlass
Und unser Leben bessern.

Für solch dein tröstlich Abendmahl,
Herr Christ, sei hochgelobet!
Erhalt uns das, weil überall
Die Welt dawider tobet!
Hilf, dass dein Leib und Blut allein
Mein Trost und Labsal möge sein
Im letzten Stündlein! Amen.

Samuel Kinner published this hymn in Jeremiah Weber's *Gesang Buch*, Leipzig, 1638, entitled "A Beautiful Hymn on the Supper of Our Lord."

The translation is adapted from that by Emanuel Cronenwett in the Ohio *Lutheran Hymnal*, 1880.

The tune "Herr Jesu Christ, du hast bereit't" is by Peter Sohren, 1668. It first appeared in the *Praxis Pietatis Melica*, Frankfurt a. M., 1668, set to Johann Rist's hymn "Du Lebensbrot, Herr Jesu Christ." It is frequently given with that title.

307 Draw Nigh and Take the Body of the Lord

1. Draw nigh and take the body of the Lord
   And drink the holy blood for you outpoured.
   Offered was He for greatest and for least,
   Himself the Victim and Himself the Priest.

2. He that His saints in this world rules and shields
   To all believers life eternal yields,
   With heavenly bread makes them that hunger whole,
   Gives living waters to the thirsting soul.

3. Approach ye, then, with faithful hearts sincere
   And take the pledges of salvation here.
   O Judge of all, our only Savior Thou,
   In this Thy feast of love be with us now.

Sancti, venite, corpus Christi sumite,
Sanctum bibentes, quo redempti sanguine.

Pro universis immolatus Dominus,
Ipse sacerdos exstitit et hostia.

Sanctorum custos, rector quoque, Dominus,
Vitae perennis, largitur credentibus.

Caelestem panem dat esurientibus,
De fonte vivo praebet sitientibus.

Accedant omnes pura, mente creduli,
Sumant aeternam salutis custodiam.

Alpha et Omega, ipse Christus Dominus,
Venit venturus iudicare homines. Amen.

This cento is from the Latin hymn "Sancti, venite, corpus Christi sumite" of ancient Irish origin, dated c. 680, by an unknown author.

The translation is an altered form of that by John M. Neale in his *Medieval Hymns*, 1851. The omitted stanzas in Neale's translation read:

> By that pure body and that holy blood
> Saved and refreshed, we render thanks to God.
> Salvation's Giver, Christ, the only Son,
> By His dear cross and blood the world hath won.
>
> Victims were offered by the Law of old,
> Which in a type this heavenly mystery told.
> He, Lord of light and Savior of our race,
> Hath given to His saints a wondrous grace.

The tune "Old 124th" is from the *Genevan Psalter*, 1551. According to *Love* it has been a popular tune in Scotland and has remained fixed to the psalm to which it was first set. The following, by Calderwood the historian, relates how it was sung in 1582 on the return of John Durie after a temporary banishment:

> John Durie cometh to Leith at night, the 3rd September. Upon Tuesday the 4th of September, as he is coming to Edinburgh, there met him at the Gallowgreen 200, but ere he came to the Netherbow their number increased to 400; but they were no sooner entered but they increased to 600 or 700, and within short space the whole street was replenished even to Saint Geiles Kirk: the number was esteemed to 2,000. At the Netherbow they took up the 124th Psalme, "Now Israel may say," etc., and sung in such a pleasant tune in four parts, known to the most part of the people, that coming up the street all bareheaded till they entered in the Kirk, with such a great sound and majestie, that it moved both themselves and all the huge multitude of the beholders, looking out at the shots and over stairs, with admiration and astonishment; the Duke of Lennox himself beheld, and reave his beard for anger; he was more affrayed of this sight than anie thing that ever he had seene before in Scotland. When they came to the Kirk, Mr. James Lowsone made a short exhortation in the Reader's place, to move the multitude to thankfulness. Thereafter a psalm being sung, they departed with great joy.

Invited, Lord, by Boundless Grace   308

1. Invited, Lord, by boundless grace,
I stand a guest before Thy face;
As Host Thou spreadst no common food:
Here is Thy body and Thy blood.

2. How holy is this Sacrament
Where pardon, peace, and life are spent!
This bread and cup my lips have pressed;
Thou blessedst, and my soul is blessed.

3. Now lettest Thou Thy guest depart
With full assurance in his heart.
For such communion, Lord, with Thee
A new life may my offering be.

4. When Thou shalt in Thy glory come
To gather all Thy people home,
Then let me, as Thy heavenly guest,
In anthems praise Thee with the blest.

This hymn by Emanuel Cronenwett appeared in the Ohio *Lutheran Hymnal*, 1880.

For comments on the tune "Das walt' Gott Vater" see Hymn No. 273.

O Jesus, Blessed Lord, to Thee   309

1. O Jesus, blessed Lord, to Thee
My heartfelt thanks forever be,
Who hast so lovingly bestowed
On me Thy body and Thy blood.

O Jesu, söde Jesu, dig
Ske Hjertens Tak evindelig,
Som med dit eget Kjöd og Blod
Saa kjärlig mig bespise lod!

2. Break forth, my soul, for joy and say:
What wealth is come to me this day!
My Savior dwells within my heart:
How blest am I! How good Thou art!

Bryd ud, min Själ, med Tak, og sig
O hvor er jeg nu bleven rig!
Min Jesus imit Hjerte bor,
Tak, tak, hvad er min Gläde stor!

This hymn by Thomas Kingo was first published in *En Ny Kirke-Psalme-Bog*, Vinterparten, 1689, headed "Thanksgiving after the Lord's Supper." The translation by Arthur J. Mason is dated 1889. It was contributed by him to the *Supplement* to the revised edition of *Hymns Ancient and Modern*, 1889.

For comments on the tune "Old Hundredth" see Hymn No. 13.

310   Thy Table I Approach

1. Thy table I approach,
Dear Savior, hear my prayer;
Oh, let no unrepented sin
Prove hurtful to me there!

Ich trete frisch
Zu Gottes Tisch,
Hilf, Vater, hilf mit Gnaden,
Dass mir keine Missetat
Hierbei möge schaden!

2. Lo, I confess my sins
And mourn their wretched bands;
A contrite heart is sure to find
Forgiveness at Thy hands.

Ich leugne nicht,
Was mir gebricht,
Ich beichte meine Schulden;
Reu' für Sünden pflegst du ja,
Frommer Gott, zu dulden.

3. Thy body and Thy blood,
Once slain and shed for me,
Are taken here with mouth and soul,
In blest reality.

Dein Leib und Blut,
Das mir zugut
Gebrochen und vergossen,
Wird, o tiefe Wundertat!
Hier am Tisch genossen.

4. Search not how this takes place,
This wondrous mystery;
God can accomplish vastly more
Than seemeth plain to thee.

O grüble nicht,
Wie dies geschicht,
Noch ob es mag geschehen!
Gott kann überschwenglich tun,
Was wir nicht verstehen.

5. Vouchsafe, O blessed Lord,
That earth and hell combined
May ne'er about this Sacrament
Raise doubt within my mind.

Verleih, o Gott,
Durch Christi Tod,
Dass weder Welt noch Teufel
Mir an diesem Glaubenspunkt
Rege ein'gen Zweifel!

6. Oh, may I never fail
To thank Thee day and night
For Thy true body and true blood,
O God, my Peace and Light!

So will ich nie,
Nicht spät noch früh
Ermüden, sonder Wanken
Für dein teu'rvergossnes Blut
Dir, mein Gott, zu danken.

This cento is composed of Stanzas 1, 2, 5, 7, 10, and 11 of the hymn by Gerhard W. Molanus, which first appeared in the *Rinteln Gesang Buch*, 1673, in eleven stanzas.

The translation is by Matthias Loy, somewhat altered. It appeared in the Ohio *Lutheran Hymnal*, 1880.

The tune "St. Michael" is from the *Genevan Psalter*, 1551, where it was set to a metrical version of Ps. 101.

311   Jesus Christ, Our Blessed Savior

1. Jesus Christ, our blessed Savior,
Turned away God's wrath forever;
By His bitter grief and woe
He saved us from the evil Foe.

3. Whoso to this Board repaireth
May take heed how he prepareth;
For if he does not believe,
Then death for life he shall receive.

2. As His pledge of love undying
He, this precious food supplying,
Gives His body with the bread
And with the wine the blood He shed.

4. Praise the Father, who from heaven
Unto us such food hath given
And, to mend what we have done,
Gave into death His only Son.

LORD'S SUPPER

5. Thou shalt hold with faith unshaken
That this food is to be taken
By the sick who are distrest,
By hearts that long for peace and rest.

6. Christ says: "Come, all ye that labor,
And receive My grace and favor;
They who feel no want nor ill
Need no physician's help nor skill.

7. "Useless were for thee My Passion,
If thy works thy weal could fashion.
This feast is not spread for thee
If thine own Savior thou wilt be."

8. If thy heart this truth professes
And thy mouth thy sin confesses,
His dear guest thou here shalt be,
And Christ Himself shall banquet thee.

This hymn is from the Latin by John Huss, included in the *Monumentorum Joannis Hus, altera pars*, Nürnberg, 1558. His authorship is doubtful, however. Wackernagel gives the hymn in three forms, one of ten, a second of nine, and a third of seven stanzas. The last reads:

1. Iesus Christus, nostra salus,
Quod reclamat omnis malus,
Nobis in sui memoriam
Dedit hanc panis hostiam.

2. O quam sanctus panis iste!
Tu solus es, Iesu Christe,
Caro, cibus, sacramentum,
Quo non maius est inventum.

3. Hoc donum suavitatis
Charitasque deitatis,
Virtutis eucharistia,
Communionis gratia.

4. Ave deitatis forma,
Dei unionis norma:
In te quisque delectatur,
Qui te fide speculatur.

5. Non es panis, sed es Deus,
Homo, liberator meus,
Qui in cruce pependisti
Et in carne defecisti.

6. Esca, digna angelorum,
Pietatis lux sanctorum:
Lex moderna approbavit,
Quod antiqua figuravit.

7. Salutare medicamen,
Peccatorum relevamen,
Pasce nos, a malis leva,
Duc nos, ubi est lux tua.

Martin Luther gave the hymn a German form in ten stanzas, in *Eyn Enchiridion*, Erfurt, 1524, as follows:

1. Jesus Christus, unser Heiland,
Der von uns den Gotteszorn wandt',
Durch das bitter Leiden sein
Half er uns aus der Hölle Pein.

2. Dass wir nimmer des vergessen,
Gab er uns sein'n Leib zu essen,
Verborgen im Brot so klein,
Und zu trinken sein Blut im Wein.

3. Wer sich will zu dem Tisch machen,
Der hab' wohl acht auf sein' Sachen;
Wer unwürdig hinzugeht,
Für das Leben den Tod empfäht.

4. Du sollst Gott den Vater preisen,
Dass er dich so wohl wollt' speisen
Und für deine Missetat
In den Tod sein'n Sohn geben hat.

5. Du sollst glauben und nicht wanken,
Dass es Speise sei den Kranken,
Den'n ihr Herz von Sünden schwer
Und vor Angst ist betrübet sehr.

6. Solch' gross' Gnad' und Barmherzigkeit
Sucht ein Herz in grosser Arbeit.
Ist dir wohl, so bleib davon,
Dass du nicht kriegest bösen Lohn!

7. Er spricht selber: Kommt, ihr Armen,
Lasst mich über euch erbarmen!
Kein Arzt ist dem Starken not,
Sein' Kunst wird an ihm gar ein Spott.

8. Hätt'st du dir was konnt erwerben,
Was dürft' ich denn für dich sterben?
Dieser Tisch auch dir nicht gilt,
So du selber dir helfen willt.

9. Glaubst du das von Herzensgrunde
Und bekennest mit dem Munde,
So bist du recht wohl geschickt,
Und die Speise dein' Seel' erquickt.

10. Die Frucht soll auch nicht ausbleiben,
Deinen Nächsten sollst du lieben,
Dass er dein geniessen kann,
Wie dein Gott an dir hat getan.

The English text follows Luther, omitting Stanzas 6 and 10. The translator is unknown.

The tune "Jesus Christus, unser Heiland" is from Klug's *Geistliche Lieder*, Wittenberg, 1535. It is a recast of the medieval tune for the "Regina coeli."

LORD'S SUPPER

312   Lord Jesus Christ, Thou Living Bread

1. Lord Jesus Christ, Thou living Bread,
   May I for mine possess Thee.
   I would with heavenly food be fed;
   Descend, refresh, and bless me.
   Now make me meet for Thee, O Lord;
   Now, humbly by my heart implored,
   Grant me Thy grace and mercy.

2. Thou me to pastures green dost guide,
   To quiet waters lead me;
   Thy table Thou dost well provide
   And from Thy hand dost feed me.
   Sin, weakness, and infirmity
   Am I; O Savior, give to me
   The cup of Thy salvation.

3. O Bread of Heaven, my soul's Delight,
   For full and free remission
   With prayer I come before Thy sight,
   In sorrow and contrition.
   With faith adorn my soul that I
   May to Thy Table now draw nigh
   With Thine own preparation.

4. I merit not Thy favor, Lord,
   Sin now upon me lieth;
   Beneath my burden, self-abhorred,
   To Thee my spirit crieth.
   In all my grief this comforts me,
   That Thou on sinners graciously,
   Lord Jesus, hast compassion.

Du Lebensbrot, Herr Jesu Christ,
Mag dich ein Sünder haben,
Der nach dem Himmel hungrig ist
Und sich mit dir will laben,
So bitt' ich dich demütiglich,
Du wollest so bereiten mich,
Dass ich recht würdig werde.

Auf grüner Aue wollest du
Mich diesen Tag, Herr, leiten,
Den frischen Wassern führen zu,
Den Tisch für mich bereiten.
Ach, ich bin sündlich, matt und krank,
Lass, Herr, mich deinen Gnadentrank
Aus deinem Becher schmecken!

Du angenehmes Himmelsbrot,
Du wollest mir verzeihen,
Dass ich in meiner Seelennot
Zu dir muss kläglich schreien;
Dein Glaubensrock bedecke mich,
Auf dass ich möge würdiglich
An deiner Tafel sitzen!

Zwar ich bin deiner Gunst nicht wert,
Als der ich jetzt erscheine
Mit Sünden allzuviel beschwert,
Die schmerzlich ich beweine.
In solcher Trübsal tröstet mich,
Herr Jesu, dass du gnädiglich
Der Sünder dich erbarmest.

Johann Rist published this hymn in his *Hausmusik,* 1654, in eight stanzas. It was headed "a devotional hymn which may be sung when the people are about to take their place at the Holy Communion of the Lord." It is founded on Ps. 23. The cento includes Stanzas 1 to 3 and 5. The omitted stanzas read:

4. Tilg allen Hass und Bitterkeit,
   O Herr, aus meinem Herzen,
   Lass mich die Sünd' in dieser Zeit
   Bereuen ja mit Schmerzen;
   Du heissgebratnes Osterlamm,
   Du meiner Seele Bräutigam,
   Lass mich dich recht geniessen!

6. Ich bin ein Mensch, krank von der Sünd',
   Lass deine Hand mich heilen!
   Erleuchte mich, denn ich bin blind;
   Du kannst mir Gnad' erteilen.
   Ich bin verdammt, erbarme dich;
   Ich bin verloren, suche mich
   Und hilf aus lauter Gnaden!

7. Mein Bräutigam, komm her zu mir
   Und wohn in meiner Seelen;
   Lass mich dich küssen für und für
   Und mich mit dir vermählen!
   Ach, lass doch deine Süssigkeit
   Für meine Seele sein bereit
   Und stille ihren Jammer!

8. Du Lebensbrot, Herr Jesu Christ,
   Komm selbst, dich mir zu schenken!
   O Blut, das du vergossen bist,
   Komm eiligst, mich zu tränken!
   Ich bleib' in dir und du in mir,
   Drum wirst du, meiner Seele Zier,
   Auch mich dort auferwecken.

The translation is an altered form of that by Arthur T. Russell in his *Psalms and Hymns,* 1851.

For comments on the tune "Herr, wie du willst" see Hymn No. 406.

313   O Lord, We Praise Thee

1. O Lord, we praise Thee, bless Thee, and adore Thee,
   In thanksgiving bow before Thee.
   Thou with Thy body and Thy blood didst nourish
   Our weak souls that they may flourish:
       O Lord, have mercy!
   May Thy body, Lord, born of Mary,
   That our sins and sorrows did carry,
   And Thy blood for us plead
   In all trial, fear, and need:
       O Lord, have mercy!

Gott sei gelobet und gebenedeiet,
Der uns selber hat gespeiset
Mit seinem Fleische und mit seinem Blute,
Das gib uns, Herr Gott, zugute!
    Kyrieleison!
Herr, durch deinen heiligen Leichnam,
Der von deiner Mutter Maria kam,
Und das heilige Blut
Hilf uns, Herr, aus aller Not!
    Kyrieleison!

LORD'S SUPPER

2. Thy holy body into death was given,
Life to win for us in heaven.
No greater love than this to Thee could bind us;
May this feast thereof remind us!
    O Lord, have mercy!
Lord, Thy kindness did so constrain Thee
That Thy blood should bless and sustain me.
All our debt Thou hast paid;
Peace with God once more is made:
    O Lord, have mercy!

3. May God bestow on us His grace and favor
To please Him with our behavior
And live as brethren here in love and union
Nor repent this blest Communion!
    O Lord, have mercy!
Let not Thy good Spirit forsake us;
Grant that heavenly-minded He make us;
Give Thy Church, Lord, to see
Days of peace and unity:
    O Lord, have mercy!

Der heil'ge Leichnam ist für uns gegeben
Zum Tod, dass wir dadurch leben;
Nicht grössre Güte konnt' er uns geschenken,
Dabei wir sein soll'n gedenken.
    Kyrieleison!
Herr, dein' Lieb' so gross dich zwungen hat,
Dass dein Blut an uns gross' Wunder tat
Und bezahlt' unsre Schuld,
Dass uns Gott ist worden hold.
    Kyrieleison!

Gott geb' uns allen seiner Gnade Segen,
Dass wir gehn auf seinen Wegen
In rechter Lieb' und brüderlicher Treue,
Dass uns die Speis' nicht gereue.
    Kyrieleison!
Herr, dein Heil'ger Geist uns nimmer lass',
Der uns geb' zu halten rechte Mass,
Dass dein' arm' Christenheit
Leb' in Fried' und Einigkeit!
    Kyrieleison!

The first stanza of this hymn is of fifteenth-century origin and was sung by the people as a post-Communion hymn during the Mass and after the Epistle on Corpus Christi Day. Martin Luther added Stanzas 2 and 3 and published the hymn in *Eyn Enchiridion*, Erfurt, 1524. It has long been a favorite post-Communion hymn in the Lutheran Church.

The translation is composite and was prepared for *The Lutheran Hymnal*.

The tune "Gott sei gelobet" is an old German spiritual folk-tune. It was coupled with this hymn even in the pre-Reformation days. It appeared in Johann Walther's *Geistliche Gesangk Buchleyn*, 1524. German Roman Catholic hymnals of the Reformation age have both hymn and tune. It was a special favorite of Luther's, who speaks of it in his liturgical writings and refers to its popularity thus: "It is the laity that has sung and still sings it."

Lord Jesus Christ, We Humbly Pray 314

1. Lord Jesus Christ, we humbly pray
That we may feed on Thee today;
Beneath these forms of bread and wine
Enrich us with Thy grace divine.

2. The chastened peace of sin forgiven,
The filial joy of heirs of heaven,
Grant as we share this wondrous food,
Thy body broken and Thy blood.

3. Our trembling hearts cleave to Thy Word;
All Thou hast said Thou dost afford,
All that Thou art we here receive,
And all we are to Thee we give.

4. One bread, one cup, one body, we,
United by our life in Thee,
Thy love proclaim till Thou shalt come
To bring Thy scattered loved ones home.

5. Lord Jesus Christ, we humbly pray
To keep us steadfast to that day
That each may be Thy welcomed guest
When Thou shalt spread Thy heavenly feast.

This hymn by Henry Eyster Jacobs appeared in *The Common Service Book* (U. L. C. A,), Philadelphia, 1917, where it is dated 1910.

For comments on the tune "Herr Jesu Christ, dich" see Hymn No. 3.

I Come, O Savior, to Thy Table 315

1. I come, O Savior, to Thy Table,
    For weak and weary is my soul;
Thou, Bread of Life, alone art able
    To satisfy and make me whole:
Lord, may Thy body and Thy blood
Be for my soul the highest good!

Ich komm' zu deinem Abendmahle,
    Weil meine Seele hungrig ist,
Der du wohnst in dem Freudensaale
    Und meiner Seele Speise bist;
Mein Jesu, lass dein Fleisch und Blut
Sein meiner Seele höchstes Gut!

LORD'S SUPPER

2. Oh, grant that I in manner worthy
   May now approach Thy heavenly Board
   And, as I lowly bow before Thee,
   Look only unto Thee, O Lord!

3. Unworthy though I am, O Savior,
   Because I have a sinful heart,
   Yet Thou Thy lamb wilt banish never
   For Thou my faithful Shepherd art!

4. Oh, let me loathe all sin forever
   As death and poison to my soul
   That I through wilful sinning never
   May see Thy Judgment take its toll!

5. Thy heart is filled with fervent yearning
   That sinners may salvation see
   Who, Lord, to Thee in faith are turning;
   So I, a sinner, come to Thee.

6. Weary am I and heavy laden,
   With sin my soul is sore opprest;
   Receive me graciously, and gladden
   My heart, for I am now Thy guest.

7. Thou there wilt find a heart most lowly
   That humbly falls before Thy feet,
   That duly weeps o'er sin, yet solely
   Thy merit pleads, as it is meet.

8. By faith I call Thy holy Table
   The testament of Thy deep love;
   For, lo, thereby I now am able
   To see how love Thy heart doth move.

9. What higher gift can we inherit?
   It is faith's bond and solid base;
   It is the strength of heart and spirit,
   The covenant of hope and grace.

10. This feast is manna, wealth abounding
    Unto the poor, to weak ones power,
    To angels joy, to hell confounding,
    And life for us in death's dark hour.

11. Thy body, given for me, O Savior,
    Thy blood which Thou for me didst shed,
    These are my life and strength forever,
    By them my hungry soul is fed.

12. With Thee, Lord, I am now united;
    I live in Thee and Thou in me.
    No sorrow fills my soul, delighted
    It finds its only joy in Thee.

13. Who can condemn me now? For surely
    The Lord is nigh, who justifies.
    No hell I fear, and thus securely,
    With Jesus I to heaven rise.

14. Though death may threaten with disaster,
    It cannot rob me of my cheer;
    For He who is of death the Master
    With aid and comfort e'er is near.

15. My heart has now become Thy dwelling,
    O blessed Holy Trinity.
    With angels I, Thy praises telling,
    Shall live in joy eternally.

Gib, dass ich würdiglich erscheine
Bei deiner Himmelstafel hier,
Dass meine Seele nur alleine
Mit ihrer Andacht sei bei dir!

Unwürdig bin ich zwar zu nennen,
Weil ich in Sünden mich verirrt;
Doch wirst du noch dein Schäflein kennen,
Du bist ja mein getreuer Hirt.

Gib, dass die Sünde ich verfluche
Als meiner Seele Tod und Gift,
Dass ich mein Leben untersuche,
Dass mich nicht dein Gerichte trifft!

Dein Herz ist stets voll von Verlangen
Und brennt von sehnlicher Begier,
Die armen Sünder zu umfangen,
Drum komm' ich Sünder auch zu dir.

Mühselig bin ich und beladen
Mit einer schweren Sündenlast;
Doch nimm mich Sünder an zu Gnaden
Und speise mich als deinen Gast!

Du wirst ein solches Herze finden,
Das dir zu deinen Füssen fällt,
Das da beweinet seine Sünden,
Doch sich an dein Verdienst auch hält.

Ich kann dein Abendmahl wohl nennen
Nur deiner Liebe Testament;
Denn, ach, hier kann ich recht erkennen,
Wie sehr dein Herz vor Liebe brennt!

Es ist das Hauptgut aller Güter
Und unsers Glaubens Band und Grund,
Die grösste Stärke der Gemüter,
Die Hoffnung und der Gnadenbund.

Dies Mahl ist meiner Seele Weide,
Der Armen Schatz, der Schwachen Kraft,
Der Teufel Schreck, der Engel Freude,
Den Sterbenden ihr Lebenssaft.

Der Leib, den du für mich gegeben,
Das Blut, das du vergossen hast,
Gibt meiner Seele Kraft und Leben
Und meinem Herzen Ruh' und Rast.

Ich bin mit dir nun ganz vereinet,
Du lebst in mir und ich in dir,
Drum meine Seele nicht mehr weinet,
Es lacht nun lauter Lust bei ihr.

Wer ist, der mich nun will verdammen?
Der mich gerecht macht, der ist hie.
Ich fürchte nicht der Hölle Flammen,
Mit Jesu ich in Himmel zieh'.

Kommt gleich der Tod auf mich gedrungen,
So bin ich dennoch wohl vergnügt,
Weil der, so längst den Tod verschlungen,
Mir mitten in dem Herzen liegt.

Nun ist mein Herz ein Wohnhaus worden
Der Heiligen Dreifaltigkeit,
Nun steh' ich in der Engel Orden
Und lebe ewiglich erfreut.

This cento is composed of Stanzas 1 to 10, 14 to 17, and 21 of the hymn in twenty-one stanzas by Friedrich C. Heyder (1677—1754). The German text is in *Kirchengesangbuch fur Evangelisch-Lutherische Gemeinden*, St. Louis. Fischer states that *Wetzel* gives the hymn as originally in twenty-eight stanzas and that it first appeared in Blumberg's Zwickau *Gesangbuch*, 1710.

The translation is composite and was prepared for *The Lutheran Hymnal*. For comments on the tune "Ich sterbe täglich" see Hymn No. 120.

LORD'S SUPPER

O Living Bread from Heaven 316

1. O living Bread from heaven,
   How richly hast Thou fed Thy guest!
   The gifts Thou now hast given
   Have filled my heart with joy and rest.
   O wondrous food of blessing,
   O cup that heals our woes!
   My heart, this gift professing,
   In thankful songs o'erflows;
   For while the faith within me
   Was quickened by this food,
   My soul hath gazed upon Thee,
   My highest, only Good.

2. My God, Thou here hast led me
   Within Thy temple's holiest place
   And there Thyself hast fed me
   With all the treasures of Thy grace,
   Oh, boundless is Thy kindness,
   And righteous is Thy power,
   While I in sinful blindness
   Am erring hour by hour;
   And yet Thou com'st not spurning
   A sinner, Lord, like me!
   Thy grace and love returning,
   What gift have I for Thee?

3. A heart that hath repented
   And mourns for sin with bitter sighs, —
   Thou, Lord, art well contented
   With this my only sacrifice.
   I know that in my weakness
   Thou wilt despise me not,
   But grant me in Thy meekness
   The blessing I have sought;
   Yes, Thou wilt hear with favor
   The song that now I sing,
   For meet and right 'tis ever
   That I should sing Thy praise.

4. Grant what I have partaken
   May through Thy grace so work in me
   That sin be all forsaken
   And I may cleave alone to Thee
   And all my soul be heedful
   How I Thy love may know;
   For this alone is needful
   Thy love should in me glow.
   Then let no beauty ever,
   No joy, allure my heart,
   But what is Thine, my Savior,
   What Thou dost here impart.

5. Oh, well for me that, strengthened
   With heavenly food and comfort here,
   Howe'er my course be lengthened,
   I now may serve Thee free from fear!
   Away, then, earthly pleasure!
   All earthly gifts are vain;
   I seek a heavenly treasure,
   My home I long to gain,
   My God, where I shall praise Thee,
   Where none my peace destroy,
   And where my soul shall raise Thee
   Glad songs in endless joy.

Wie wohl hast du gelabet,
O liebster Jesu, deinen Gast,
Ja mich so reich begabet,
Da ich jetzt fühle Freud' und Rast!
O wundersame Speise,
O süsser Lebenstrank!
O Lieb'smahl, das ich preise
Mit einem Lobgesang,
Indem es hat erquicket
Mein Leben, Herz und Mut!
Mein Geist, der hat erblicket
Das allerhöchste Gut.

Du hast mich jetzt geführet,
O Herr, in deinen Gnadensaal,
Daselbst hab' ich berühret
Dein' edle Güter allzumal;
Da hast du mir gegeben,
Geschenket mildiglich
Das werte Brot zum Leben,
Das sehr ergötzet mich;
Du hast mir zugelassen,
Dass ich den Seelenwein
Im Glauben möchte fassen,
Und dir vermählet sein.

Ein Herz, durch Reu' zerschlagen,
Ein Herz, das ganz zerknirschet ist,
Das, weiss ich, wird behagen,
Mein Heiland, dir zu jeder Frist;
Du wirst es nicht verachten,
Demnach ich emsig bin,
Nach deiner Gunst zu trachten.
Nimm doch in Gnaden hin
Das Opfer meiner Zungen;
Denn billig wird jetzund
Dein teurer Ruhm besungen,
Herr Gott, durch meinen Mund.

Hilf ja, dass dies Geniessen
Des edlen Schatzes schaff' in mir
Ein heil'ges Tränenfliessen,
Dass ich mich wende stets zu dir.
Lass mich hinfüro spüren
Kein' andre Lieblichkeit,
Als welche pflegt zu rühren
Von dir zu dieser Zeit.
Lass mich ja nichts begehren
Als deine Lieb' und Gunst;
Denn niemand kann entbehren
Hier deiner Lieb' und Brunst.

Wohl mir, ich bin versehen
Mit Himmelsspeis' und Engeltrank;
Nun will ich rüstig stehen,
Zu singen dir Lob, Ehr' und Dank.
Ade, du Weltgetümmel,
Du bist ein eitler Tand!
Ich seufze nach dem Himmel,
Dem rechten Vaterland.
Ade, dort werd' ich leben
Ohn' Unglück und Verdruss;
Mein Gott, du wirst mir geben
Der Wollust Überfluss.

Johann Rist first published this hymn for Holy Communion in his collection *Neuer Himmlischer Lieder Sonderbares Buch*, Lüneburg, 1651, in nine stanzas. The cento omits Stanzas 3 to 6.

The translation is an altered form of that by Catherine Winkworth in her *Lyra Germanica*, second series. 1858.

For comments on the tune "Nun lob, mein' Seel'" see Hymn No. 34.

Confession and Absolution

317   Alas, My God, My Sins Are Great

1. Alas, my God, my sins are great,
   My conscience doth upbraid me;
   And now I find that in my strait
   No man hath power to aid me.

2. And fled I hence in my despair
   In some lone spot to hide me,
   My griefs would still be with me there
   And peace still be denied me.

3. Lord, Thee I seek. I merit naught;
   Yet pity and restore me.
   Just God, be not Thy wrath my lot;
   Thy Son hath suffered for me.

4. If pain and woe must follow sin,
   Then be my path still rougher.
   Here spare me not; if heaven I win,
   On earth I gladly suffer.

5. But curb my heart, forgive my guilt,
   Make Thou my patience firmer;
   For they must miss the good Thou wilt
   Who at Thy chastenings murmur.

6. Then deal with me as seems Thee best, —
   Thy grace will help me bear it, —
   If but at last I see Thy rest
   And with my Savior share it.

Ach Gott und Herr,
Wie gross und schwer
  Sind mein' begangne Sünden!
Da ist niemand,
Der helfen kann,
  In dieser Welt zu finden.

Lief' ich gleich weit
Zu dieser Zeit
  Bis an der Welt ihr' Enden
Und wollt' los sein
Des Kreuzes mein,
  Würd' ich doch solch's nicht wenden.

Zu dir flieh' ich,
Verstoss mich nicht,
  Wie ich's wohl hab' verdienet!
Ach Gott, zürn nicht,
Geh nicht ins G'richt,
  Dein Sohn hat mich versöhnet.

Soll's ja so sein,
Dass Straf' und Pein
  Auf Sünden folgen müssen,
So fahr hier fort
Und schone dort
  Und lass mich hier wohl büssen!

Gib, Herr, Geduld,
Vergiss der Schuld,
  Verleih ein g'horsam Herze;
Lass mich nur nicht,
Wie's oft geschicht,
  Mein Heil murrend verscherzen!

Handle mit mir,
Wie's dünket dir,
  Auf dein' Gnad' will ich's leiden;
Lass mich nur nicht
Dort ewiglich
  Von dir sein abgeschieden!

This hymn is found in several lengths, in six, in ten, and in thirteen stanzas. The form above, in six stanzas, seems to have been the original and was most likely written by Johann Major, although Martin Rutilius and Johann Göldel are sometimes given as authors. The first printed form of the hymn is in a sermon preached by Johann Major at Jena, July 2, 1613. This sermon made reference to a great storm at Weimar, May 29, 1613, which caused much devastation for miles around. The first edition of the sermon was printed at Jena, the second at Eisleben, also in 1613. In this edition there is printed at the end, by itself, a hymn in six stanzas. *Julian* gives the beginning of each stanza; they agree with this hymn. Whether Major added other stanzas to this hymn later is not known. That he is the author of the six-stanza form seems quite certain.

    The translation is an altered form of that by Catherine Winkworth in her *Chorale Book for England,* 1863.

    For comments on the tune "Ach Gott und Herr" see Hymn No. 215.

CONFESSION AND ABSOLUTION

Before Thee, God, Who Knowest All — 318

1. Before Thee, God, who knowest all,
   With grief and shame I prostrate fall.
   I see my sins against Thee, Lord,
   The sins of thought, of deed, and word.
   They press me sore; I cry to Thee:
   O God, be merciful to me!

2. O Lord, my God, to Thee I pray:
   Oh, cast me not in wrath away!
   Let Thy good Spirit ne'er depart,
   But let Him draw to Thee my heart
   That truly penitent I be:
   O God, be merciful to me!

3. O Jesus, let Thy precious blood
   Be to my soul a cleansing flood.
   Turn not, O Lord, Thy guest away,
   But grant that justified I may
   Go to my house at peace with Thee:
   O God, be merciful to me!

Jeg staar for Gud, som alting veed,
Og slaar mit Öie skamfuld ned,
Jeg ser min Synd, at den er stor
I Tanker, Gjerninger og Ord,
Det mig igjennem Hjertet skjär;
O Gud, mig Synder naadig vär!

O Herre Gud, hvad jeg har gjort,
Kast mig ei fra dir Aasyn bort,
Tag ei din Helligaand fra mig,
Men lad ham drage mig til dig,
Den rette Angers Vei mig lär;
O Gud, mig Synder naadig vär!

O Jesu, lad dit Blod, din Död
Mig redde ud af Syndens Nöd,
Forstod mig ei, hjölp, at jeg maa
Retfärdiggjort ved dig faa gaa
Ned til mit Hus, og glädes der;
O Gud, mig Synder naadig vär!

Magnus B. Landstad first published this hymn in his *Udkast til Kirkesalmebog*, 1861. The Scripture basis is as follows: Stanza 1, Ezra 9:6, 15; Stanza 2, Ps. 51:11; Stanza 3, Luke 18:14.

The translation is by Carl Döving, 1909. It appeared in *The Lutheran Hymnary*, 1913.

For comments on the tune "Vater unser" see Hymn No. 458.

In Thee Alone, O Christ, My Lord — 319

1. In Thee alone, O Christ, my Lord,
     My hope on earth remaineth;
   I know Thou wilt Thine aid afford,
     Naught else my soul sustaineth.
   No strength of man, no earthly stay
   Can help me in the evil day;
   Thou, only Thou, canst aid supply.
   To Thee I cry;
   On Thee I bid my heart rely.

2. My sins, O Lord, against me rise,
     I mourn them with contrition;
   Grant, through Thy death and sacrifice,
     To me a full remission.
   Lord, show before the Father's throne
   That Thou didst for my sins atone;
   So shall I from my load be freed.
   Thy Word I plead;
   Keep me, O Lord, each hour of need.

3. O Lord, in mercy stay my heart
     On faith's most sure foundation
   And to my inmost soul impart
     Thy perfect consolation.
   Fill all my life with love to Thee,
   Toward all men grant me charity;
   And at the last, when comes my end,
   Thy succor send.
   From Satan's wiles my soul defend.

Allein zu dir, Herr Jesu Christ,
  Mein' Hoffnung steht auf Erden;
Ich weiss, dass du mein Tröster bist,
  Kein Trost mag mir sonst werden.
Von Anbeginn ist nichts erkor'n,
Auf Erden ist kein Mensch gebor'n,
Der mir aus Nöten helfen kann;
Ich ruf' dich an,
Zu dem ich mein Vertrauen han.

Mein' Sünd' sind schwer und übergross
  Und reuen mich von Herzen,
Derselben mach mich quitt und loss
  Durch deinen Tod und Schmerzen
Und zeig mich deinem Vater an,
Dass du hast g'nug für mich getan,
So werd' ich quitt der Sündenlast.
Herr, halt mir fest,
Wes du dich mir versprochen hast!

Gib mir nach dein'r Barmherzigkeit
  Den wahren Christenglauben,
Auf dass ich deine Süssigkeit
  Möcht' inniglich anschauen,
Vor allen Dingen lieben dich
Und meinen Nächsten gleich als mich.
Am letzten End' dein' Hilf' mir send,
Dadurch behend
Des Teufels List sich von mir wend'.

Wilhelm Nelle calls this hymn "a presentation of the Christian life in a nutshell." The hymn first appeared in a hymn-book in the Low German Magdeburg *Gesangbuch*, 1542. An undated Nürnberg broadsheet, probably c. 1540, has it and ascribes it to Johann Schneesing. Mark Wagner, a pupil of Schneesing, definitely claims that Schneesing was the author. Konrad Hubert, to whom the hymn has also been attributed, probably had no more to do with it than to make a few changes in the text. Bunsen calls it "an

CONFESSION AND ABSOLUTION

immortal hymn of prayer of a confident faith." Martin Luther included it in the Valentin Babst *Gesang Buch*, 1545. The omitted Stanza 4 is a doxology.

The translation is an altered form of that by Arthur T. Russell in his *Psalms and Hymns*, 1851.

The tune "Allein zu dir" is from a separate print (broadsheet), undated, c. 1540, as above, on which the text is also given. The harmonization is by Johann Sebastian Bach.

320   Lord Jesus, Think on Me

1. Lord Jesus, think on me
And purge away my sin;
From earth-born passions set me free
And make me pure within.

2. Lord Jesus, think on me,
With many a care opprest;
Let me Thy loving servant be
And taste Thy promised rest.

3. Lord Jesus, think on me
Amid the battle's strife;
In all my pain and misery
Be Thou my Health and Life.

4. Lord Jesus, think on me
Nor let me go astray;
Through darkness and perplexity
Point Thou the heavenly way.

5. Lord Jesus, think on me
When floods the tempest high;
When on doth rush the enemy,
O Savior, be Thou nigh!

6. Lord Jesus, think on me,
That, when the flood is past,
I may the eternal brightness see
And share Thy joy at last.

7. Lord Jesus, think on me
That I may sing above
To Father, Spirit, and to Thee
The strains of praise and love.

Μνώεο, Χριστέ,
υἱὲ Θεοῖο
ὑψιμέδοντος,
οἰκέτω Σοῦ,
Κῆρ' ἀλιτροῖο
Τάδε γράψαντος·
Καί μοι ὄπασσον
λύσιν παθέων
κηριτρεφέων
τά μοι ἐμφυῆ
ψυχᾷ ῥυπαρᾷ·
δὸς δὲ ἰδέσθαι,
Σῶτερ 'Ιησοῦ,
ζαθέαν αἴγλαν
Σάν, ἔνθα φανεὶς
μέλψω ἀοιδάν
παίονι ψυχᾶν,
παίονι γυίων,
Πατρὶ σὺν μεγάλῳ
Πνεύματί Θ' 'Αγνῷ.

This Greek hymn is by Synesius, bishop of Cyrene († 430). The English paraphrase is by Allen W. Chatfield in his *Songs and Hymns*, etc., 1876, the complete form of which was in nine stanzas. Chatfield wrote: "In translating this ode, I gave my spirit more liberty. It may be considered as a paraphrase or amplification, rather than an exact translation, of the original."

For comments on the tune "Southwell" see Hymn No. 156.

321   O Faithful God, Thanks Be to Thee

1. O faithful God, thanks be to Thee
Who dost forgive iniquity.
Thou grantest help in sin's distress,
And soul and body dost Thou bless.

2. Thy servant now declares to me:
"Thy sins are all forgiven thee.
Depart in peace, but sin no more
And e'er My pardoning grace
adore."

3. O Lord, we bless Thy gracious heart,
For Thou Thyself dost heal our smart
Through Christ our Savior's precious blood,
Which for the sake of sinners flowed.

Wir danken dir, o treuer Gott,
Dass du uns hilfst aus Sündennot,
Vergibst uns alle Schuld und Fehl
Und hilfest uns an Leib und Seel'.

Durch's Beicht'gers Mund spricht du:
   Mein Kind,
Dir all Sünd' vergeben sind.
Geh in Fried hin, sünd'ge nicht mehr
Und allweg' dich zu mir bekehr!

Dir sei Dank für solch gnädig Herz,
Der du selbst heilest allen Schmerz
Durchs teure Blut des Herren Christ,
Welch's für all' Sünd' vergossen ist.

CONFESSION AND ABSOLUTION

4. Give us Thy Spirit, peace afford
Now and forever, gracious Lord.
Preserve to us till life is spent
Thy holy Word and Sacrament.

Gib uns dein'n Geist, gib Fried' und Freud'
Von nun an bis in Ewigkeit!
Dein Wort und heilig Sakrament
Erhalt bei uns bis an das End'.

This hymn by Nikolaus Selnecker appeared in *Drey Predigten*, etc., Heinrichstadt, 1572. The hymn was one of six in that volume on the Catechism. It was entitled "How one may find comfort in the blessed absolution."

The translation is composite.

For comments on the tune "Wenn wir in höchsten" see Hymn No. 522.

And Wilt Thou Pardon, Lord   322

1. And wilt Thou pardon, Lord,
A sinner such as I,
Although Thy book his crimes record
Of such a crimson dye?

2. So deep are they engraved,
So terrible their fear.
The righteous scarcely shall be saved,
And where shall I appear?

3. O Thou Physician blest,
Make clean my guilty soul
And me, by many a sin opprest,
Restore and keep me whole.

4. I know not how to praise
Thy mercy and Thy love;
But deign my soul from earth to raise
And learn from Thee above.

This hymn is based on the cento from a Greek canon by Joseph the Hymnographer, beginning with the line Τῶν Ἁμαρτιῶν μου τὴν πληθύν. The English version is virtually a new hymn by John M. Neale. It was published in Neale's *Hymns of the Eastern Church*, 1862, in five stanzas. The omitted Stanza 3 reads:

My soul, make all things known
To Him who all things sees
That so the Lamb may yet atone
For thine iniquities.

The tune "St. Bride," by Samuel Howard, is also called "Bridget," "All Saints," and "Kersall." It appeared as St. Bridget's Tune" in *Parochial Harmony*, 1762, set to Ps. 130. Mr. Howard was organist at St. Bride's Church, Fleet Street.

With Broken Heart and Contrite Sigh   323

1. With broken heart and contrite sigh,
A trembling sinner, Lord, I cry.
Thy pardoning grace is rich and free, —
O God, be merciful to me!

2. I smite upon my troubled breast,
With deep and conscious guilt opprest;
Christ and His Cross my only plea, —
O God, be merciful to me!

3. Far off I stand with tearful eyes
Nor dare uplift them to the skies;
But Thou dost all my anguish see, —
O God, be merciful to me!

4. Nor alms nor deeds that I have done
Can for a single sin atone.
To Calvary alone I flee, —
O God, be merciful to me!

5. And when, redeemed from sin and hell,
With all the ransomed throng I dwell,
My raptured song shall ever be,
God has been merciful to me.

Cornelius Elven wrote this as a Lenten hymn in January, 1852, for use by his own congregation at Bury St. Edmunds, Suffolk. It was published in the Baptist *Psalms and Hymns*, 1858.

The tune "St. Luke," by Jeremiah Clarke, was first published in Playford's *The Divine Companion*, 1701. It seems to have been written for Venantius Fortunatus's hymn "The Royal Banners Forward Go." (See Hymn No. 168.) It is one of Clarke's finest tunes, smooth, vocal, and expressive.

324   Jesus Sinners Doth Receive

1. Jesus sinners doth receive;
   Oh, may all this saying ponder
Who in sin's delusions live
   And from God and heaven wander!
Here is hope for all who grieve —
Jesus sinners doth receive.

2. We deserve but grief and shame,
   Yet His words, rich grace revealing,
Pardon, peace, and life proclaim.
   Here their ills have perfect healing
Who with humble hearts believe —
Jesus sinners doth receive.

3. Sheep that from the fold did stray
   No true shepherd e'er forsaketh;
Weary souls that lost their way
   Christ, the Shepherd, gently taketh
In His arms that they may live —
Jesus sinners doth receive.

4. Come, ye sinners, one and all,
   Come, accept His invitation;
Come, obey His gracious call,
   Come and take His free salvation!
Firmly in these words believe:
Jesus sinners doth receive.

5. I, a sinner, come to Thee
   With a penitent confession;
Savior, mercy show to me
   Grant for all my sins remission.
Let these words my soul relieve:
Jesus sinners doth receive.

6. Oh, how blest it is to know:
   Were as scarlet my transgression,
It shall be as white as snow
   By Thy blood and bitter Passion;
For these words I now believe:
Jesus sinners doth receive.

7. Now my conscience is at peace,
   From the Law I stand acquitted;
Christ hath purchased my release
   And my every sin remitted.
Naught remains my soul to grieve, —
Jesus sinners doth receive.

8. Jesus sinners doth receive.
   Also I have been forgiven;
And when I this earth must leave,
   I shall find an open heaven.
Dying, still to Him I cleave —
Jesus sinners doth receive.

Jesus nimmt die Sünder an;
   Saget doch dies Trostwort allen,
Welche von der rechten Bahn
   Auf verkehrten Weg verfallen!
Hier ist, was sie retten kann:
Jesus nimmt die Sünder an.

Keiner Gnade sind wir wert,
   Doch hat er in seinem Worte
Eidlich sich dazu erklärt.
   Sehet nur, die Gnadenpforte
Ist hier völlig aufgetan:
Jesus nimmt die Sünder an.

Wenn ein Schaf verloren ist,
   Suchet es ein treuer Hirte;
Jesus, der uns nie vergisst,
   Suchet treulich das Verirrte,
Dass es nicht verderben kann:
Jesus nimmt die Sünder an.

Kommet alle, kommet her,
   Kommet, ihr betrübten Sünder!
Jesus rufet euch, und er
   Macht aus Sündern Gottes Kinder.
Glaubet's doch und denket dran:
Jesus nimmt die Sünder an.

Ich Betrübter komme hier
   Und bekenne meine Sünden.
Lass, mein Heiland, mich bei dir
   Gnade zur Vergebung finden,
Dass dies Wort mich trösten kann:
Jesus nimmt die Sünder an.

Ich bin ganz getrostes Muts.
   Ob die Sünden blutrot wären,
Müssten sie kraft deines Bluts
   Dennoch sich in Schneeweiss kehren,
Da ich gläubig sprechen kann:
Jesus nimmt die Sünder an.

Mein Gewissen beisst mich nicht,
   Moses darf mich nicht verklagen;
Der mich frei und ledig spricht,
   Hat die Schulden abgetragen,
Dass mich nichts verdammen kann:
Jesus nimmt die Sünder an.

Jesus nimmt die Sünder an,
   Mich hat er auch angenommen
Und den Himmel aufgetan,
   Dass ich selig zu ihm kommen
Und auf den Trost sterben kann:
Jesus nimmt die Sünder an.

Erdmann Neumeister first published this hymn in his *Evangelischer Nachklang*, 1718. It is based on the Gospel for the Third Sunday after Trinity, Luke 15:1-10. It is also a fine hymn for missionary services.

The translation is composite.

For comments on the tune "Meinen Jesum lass' ich nicht" see Hymn No. 55.

325   O Thou that Hear'st when Sinners Cry

1. O Thou that hear'st when sinners cry
Though all my crimes before Thee lie,
Behold them not with angry look,
But blot their memory from Thy book.

2. Create my nature pure within
And form my soul averse to sin;
Let Thy good Spirit ne'er depart
Nor hide Thy presence from my heart.

3. I cannot live without Thy light,
Cast out and banished from Thy sight;
Thy holy joys, my God, restore
And guard me that I fall no more.

4. Though I have grieved Thy Spirit, Lord,
His help and comfort still afford
And let me now come near Thy throne
To plead the merits of Thy Son.

5. A broken heart, my God, my King,
Is all the sacrifice I bring.
Look down, O Lord, with pitying eye
And save the soul condemned to die.

6. Oh, may Thy love inspire my tongue
Salvation shall be all my song;
And all my powers shall join to bless
The Lord, my Strength and Righteousness.

Isaac Watts published this hymn in his *Psalms of David Imitated,* 1719, in eight stanzas. It is entitled "The Backslider Restored; or, Repentance and Faith in the Blood of Christ." The cento includes Stanzas 1 to 5 and 8. The omitted Stanzas 6 and 7 read:

6. My soul lies humbled in the dust
And owns Thy dreadful sentence just:
Look down, O Lord, with pitying eye
And save the soul condemned to die.

7. Then will I teach the world Thy ways,
Sinners shall learn thy sovereign grace;
I'll lead them to my Savior's blood,
And they shall praise a pard'ning God.

In Stanza 4 Watts has:

And let a wretch come near Thy throne;

and in Stanza 5, Lines 3 and 4:

The God of grace will ne'er despise
A broken heart for sacrifice.

For comments on the tune "Hamburg" see Hymn No. 175.

Lord, to Thee I Make Confession 326

1. Lord, to Thee I make confession;
I have sinned and gone astray,
I have multiplied transgression,
Chosen for myself my way.
Led by Thee to see my errors,
Lord, I tremble at Thy terrors.

2. Yet, though conscience' voice appal me,
Father, I will seek Thy face;
Though Thy child I dare not call me,
Yet receive me to Thy grace.
Do not for my sins forsake me;
Do not let Thy wrath o'ertake me.

3. For Thy Son did suffer for me,
Gave Himself to rescue me,
Died to heal me and restore me,
Reconciled me unto Thee.
'Tis alone His cross can vanquish
These dark fears and soothe this anguish.

4. Then on Him I cast my burden,
Sink it in the depths below.
Let me know Thy gracious pardon,
Wash me, make me white as snow.
Let Thy Spirit leave me never;
Make me only Thine forever.

Herr, ich habe missgehandelt,
Ja mich drückt der Sünden Last;
Ich bin nicht den Weg gewandelt,
Den du mir gezeiget hast,
Und jetzt wollt' ich gern aus Schrecken
Mich vor deinem Zorn verstecken.

Drum ich muss es nur bekennen:
Herr, ich habe missgetan,
Darf mich nicht dein Kind mehr nennen.
Ach, nimm mich zu Gnaden an;
Lass die Menge meiner Sünden
Deinen Zorn nicht gar entzünden!

Aber, Christe, deine Wunden,
Ja ein einzigs Tröpflein Blut,
Das kann meine Wunden heilen,
Löschen meiner Sünden Glut;
Drum will ich, mein' Angst zu stillen,
Mich in deine Wunden hüllen.

Dir will ich die Last aufbinden,
Wirf sie in die tiefe See;
Wasche mich von meinen Sünden,
Mache mich so weiss wie Schnee;
Lass dein'n guten Geist mich treiben,
Einzig stets bei dir zu bleiben!

This hymn by Johann Franck was written in 1649 or earlier. Its first stanza appeared in Johann Crüger's *Geistliche Kirchenmelodien,* Leipzig, 1649, with the tune by Crüger himself. The full text of eight stanzas was printed in the Berlin *Gesangbuch,* 1653. The cento includes Stanzas 1, 3, 7, and 8.

The translation is an altered form of that by Catherine Winkworth in her *Chorale Book for England,* 1863.

The tune "Herr, ich habe missgehandelt" is wedded to the text. We have here an excellent example of the harmony of words and music.

CONFESSION AND ABSOLUTION

327   Out of the Deep I Call

1. Out of the deep I call
   To Thee, O Lord, to Thee.
   Before Thy throne of grace I fall;
   Be merciful to me.

2. Out of the deep I cry,
   The woeful deep of sin,
   Of evil done in days gone by,
   Of evil now within;

3. Out of the deep of fear
   And dread of coming shame;
   All night till morning watch is near
   I plead the precious name.

4. Lord, there is mercy now,
   As ever was, with Thee.
   Before Thy throne of grace I bow;
   Be merciful to me.

Henry W. Baker published this hymn in the appendix to the original edition of *Hymns Ancient and Modern*, 1868.

For comments on the tune "Southwell" see Hymn No. 156.

328   O Jesus, Lamb of God, Thou Art

1. O Jesus, Lamb of God, Thou art
   The Life and Comfort of my heart.
   A sinner poor I come to Thee
   And bring my many sins with me.

2. O God, my sin indeed is great;
   I groan beneath the dreadful weight.
   Be merciful to me, I pray;
   Take guilt and punishment away.

3. Saint John the Baptist points to Thee
   And bids me cast my sin on Thee;
   For Thou hast left Thy throne on high
   To suffer for the world and die.

4. Help me to mend my ways, O Lord,
   And gladly to obey Thy Word.
   While here I live, abide with me;
   And when I die, take me to Thee.

O Lämmlein Gottes, Jesu Christ,
Der du mein Trost und Leben bist,
Ich armer Sünder komm' zu dir
Und bring' viel Missetat mit mir.

Ach Gott, ich hab' gesündigt sehr
Und mir gemacht ein' Bürde schwer;
Doch bitt' ich, woll'st mir gnädig sein
Und nehmen weg all' Schuld und Pein,

Wie Sankt Johann's der Täufer mich
Dies alles legen heisst auf dich,
Denn du sei'st da vom Himmelszelt,
Zu helfen mir und aller Welt.

Forthin will ich gern bessern mich,
Dein'm Wort gehorchen williglich.
Drum, o Herr, bleib allzeit bei mir
Und nimm mich endlich gar zu dir!

This hymn was written for St. John the Baptist's Day by Bartholomäus Helder. It appeared in the *Cantionale Sacrum*, Gotha, 1646. It is based on John 1:29.

The translation by August Crull appeared in the Ohio *Lutheran Hymnal*, 1880. The translation has been somewhat altered.

The tune "Weimar" is by Carl Philipp Emanuel Bach, from his *Gellert's geistliche Oden und Lieder mit Melodien*, fifth edition, 1784.

329   From Depths of Woe I Cry to Thee

1. From depths of woe I cry to Thee,
   Lord, hear me, I implore Thee.
   Bend down Thy gracious ear to me,
   My prayer let come before Thee.
   If Thou rememberest each misdeed,
   If each should have its rightful meed,
   Who may abide Thy presence?

2. Thy love and grace alone avail
   To blot out my transgression;
   The best and holiest deeds must fail
   To break sin's dread oppression.
   Before Thee none can boasting stand,
   But all must fear Thy strict demand
   And live alone by mercy.

Aus tiefer Not schrei' ich zu dir,
Herr Gott, erhör mein Rufen;
Dein' gnädig' Ohren kehr zu mir
Und meiner Bitt sie öffen!
Denn so du willst das sehen an,
Was Sünd' und Unrecht ist getan,
Wer kann, Herr, vor dir bleiben?

Bei dir gilt nichts denn Gnad' und Gunst,
Die Sünde zu vergeben:
Es ist doch unser Tun umsonst
Auch in dem besten Leben.
Vor dir niemand sich rühmen kann,
Des muss dich fürchten jedermann
Und deiner Gnade leben.

CONFESSION AND ABSOLUTION

3. Therefore my hope is in the Lord
   And not in mine own merit;
   It rests upon His faithful Word
   To them of contrite spirit
   That He is merciful and just;
   This is my comfort and my trust,
   His help I wait with patience.

4. And though it tarry till the night
   And till the morning waken,
   My heart shall never doubt His might
   Nor count itself forsaken.
   Do thus, O ye of Israel's seed,
   Ye of the Spirit born indeed;
   Wait for your God's appearing.

5. Though great our sins and sore our woes,
   His grace much more aboundeth;
   His helping love no limit knows,
   Our utmost need it soundeth.
   Our Shepherd good and true is He,
   Who will at last His Israel free
   From all their sin and sorrow.

Darum auf Gott will hoffen ich,
   Auf mein Verdienst nicht bauen;
Auf ihn mein Herz soll lassen sich
   Und seiner Güte trauen,
Die mir zusagt sein wertes Wort,
Das ist mein Trost und treuer Hort,
   Des will ich allzeit harren.

Und ob es währt bis in die Nacht
   Und wieder an den Morgen,
Doch soll mein Herz an Gottes Macht
   Verzweifeln nicht noch sorgen.
So tu' Israel rechter Art,
Der aus dem Geist erzeuget ward
   Und seines Gott' erharre.

Ob bei uns ist der Sünden viel,
   Bei Gott ist viel mehr Gnade,
Sein' Hand zu helfen hat kein Ziel,
   Wie gross auch sei der Schade.
Er ist allein der gute Hirt,
Der Israel erlösen wird
   Aus seinen Sünden allen.

Martin Luther wrote this metrical paraphrase of Ps. 130 in 1523, in four stanzas, and published it in *Etlich cristlich lider,* Wittenberg, 1524, and in *Eyn Enchiridion,* Erfurt, 1524. Stanza 2 of this version was then rewritten as Stanzas 2 and 3, and an improved five-stanza form was published in Johann Walther's *Geystliche gesangk Buchleyn,* Wittenberg, 1524. It was also included in Luther's *Christliche Geseng zum Begrebnis,* Wittenberg, 1542.

On May 9, 1525, this hymn was sung at the funeral of Luther's friend and patron Frederick the Wise in the Castle Church at Wittenberg. Like Watts's "Our God, our Help in ages past," this hymn is very appropriate at a Christian burial. This hymn was also sung at Halle, in 1546, when Luther's body was being brought from Eisleben to Wittenberg. When Luther, during the Diet of Augsburg, had to remain at Coburg, where he was constantly kept in touch with the trend of events, he frequently became very anxious about the fate of his cause. Then he would gather the servants of the castle about him and say: "Come, let us, despite the devil, sing 'Aus tiefer Not schrei' ich zu dir' and thereby praise and glorify God!"

The fine tune "Aus tiefer Not," also called "De profundis," "Luther's 130th," is possibly by Luther himself. It appeared with the five-stanza form in 1524. J. S. Bach built his cantata *Aus tiefer Not schrei' ich zu dir* for the Twenty-first Sunday after Trinity on this hymn.

This hymn is considered by many to be Luther's best production. It ranks with the finest German psalm versions, according to *Julian.*

The translation is an altered form of that by Catherine Winkworth in her *Chorale Book for England,* 1863.

I Come to Thee, O Blessed Lord   330

1. I come to Thee, O blessed Lord,
   Invited by Thy gracious Word
   To this Thy feast, to sup with Thee;
   Grant that a worthy guest I be.

2. I come to Thee with sin and grief,
   For Thou alone canst give relief.
   Thy death for me, dear Lord, I plead:
   O Jesus, help me in my need!

Jeg kommer her, o söde Gud,
Fordi at du har sendt mig Bud,
Til Höitid din og Nadverds Fest,
Hjälp, at jeg er en värdig Gjäst!

Jeg kommer her med Hjerte-Graad,
Fordi jeg veed mig ingen Raad
Og Redning i min Syndenöd;
Hjälp mig, o Jesu, for din Död!

CONFESSION AND ABSOLUTION

3. Shouldst Thou a strict account demand,
Who could, O Lord, before Thee stand?
Purge all my secret sins away:
Be Thou, O Christ, the sinner's Stay!

Dersom du Ondskab regne vil,
At staa for dig hvo tror sig til?
Rens mig af mine lönlig' Bröst,
Vär du den arme Synders Tröst!

4. O Jesus, Lamb of God, alone
Thou didst for all our sins atone;
Though I have sinned and gone astray,
Turn not, O Lord, Thy guest away.

O Jesu, du Guds Lam, som bar
Al Verdens Synd, og sonet har,
Hvor ilde jeg endog har gjort,
Kast mig ei fra dit Aasyn bort!

5. O Jesus, Lamb of God, alone
Thou didst for all our sins atone;
Be merciful, I Thee implore,
Be merciful forevermore.

O Jesu, du Guds Lam, som bar
Al Verdens Synd, og sonet har,
Miskunde dig nu over mig,
Miskunde dig evindelig!

Magnus B. Landstad's opening stanza of this hymn, dated 1863, is a translation of the following German stanza by an unknown author:

Ich stell' mich ein, o frommer Gott,
Zu deinem himmlischen Gastgebot,
Dazu du mich geladen hast;
Hilf, dass ich sei ein würdiger Gast.

The remaining stanzas Landstad added. The hymn was included in his *Salmebog*.

The translation is by Carl Döving, 1910. It was included in *The Lutheran Hymnary*, 1913.

For comments on the tune "Wenn wir in höchsten Nöten" see Hymn No. 522.

331   Yea, as I Live, Jehovah Saith

1. Yea, as I live, Jehovah saith,
I would not have the sinner's death,
But that he turn from error's ways,
Repent, and live through endless days.

So wahr ich leb', spricht Gott der Herr,
Des Sünders Tod ich nicht begehr',
Sondern dass er bekehre sich,
Tu' Buss' und lebe ewiglich.

2. To us therefore Christ gave command:
"Go forth and preach in every land;
Bestow on all My pardoning grace
Who will repent and mend their ways.

Drum Christ, der Herr, sein' Jünger sandt':
Geht hin, predigt in allem Land
Vergebung der Sünd' jedermann,
Dem's leid ist, glaubt und will ablan.

3. "All those whose sins ye thus remit
I truly pardon and acquit,
And those whose sins ye do retain
Condemned and guilty shall remain.

Wem ihr die Sünd' vergeben werd't,
Soll ihr'r los sein auf dieser Erd'.
Wem ihr sie b'hallt't im Namen mein,
Dem sollen sie behalten sein.

4. "What ye shall bind, that bound shall be;
What ye shall loose, that shall be free;
Unto My Church the keys are given
To ope and close the gates of heaven."

Was ihr bind't, soll gebunden sein;
Was ihr auflöst, das soll los sein.
Die Schlüssel zu dem Himmelreich
Hiermit ich euch geb' allen gleich.

5. The words which absolution give
Are His who died that we might live;
The minister whom Christ has sent
Is but His humble instrument.

Wenn uns der Beicht'ger absolviert,
Sein Amt der Herr Christ durch ihn führt
Und spricht uns selbst von Sünden rein;
Sein Werkzeug ist der Dien'r allein.

6. When ministers lay on their hands,
Absolved by Christ the sinner stands;
He who by grace the Word believes
The purchase of His blood receives.

Wem der Beicht'ger auflegt sein' Hand,
Dem löst Christ auf der Sünden Band
Und absolviert ihn durch sein Blut;
Wer's glaubt, aus Gnad' hat solches Gut.

7. All praise, eternal Son, to Thee
For absolution full and free,
In which Thou showest forth Thy grace;
From false indulgence guard our race.

Wen nun sein G'wissen beisst und nagt,
Die Sünd' quält, dass er schier verzagt,
Der halt' sich zu dem Gnadenthron,
Zum Wort der Absolution.

8. Praise God the Father and the Son
And Holy Spirit, Three in One,
As 'twas, is now, and so shall be
World without end, eternally!

Lob sei dir, wahrer Gottessohn,
Für die heil'g' Absolution,
Darin du zeigst dein' Gnad' und Güt';
Vor falschem Ablass uns behüt!

CONFESSION AND ABSOLUTION

Nikolaus Herman first published this hymn, in eleven stanzas, in his *Die Sontags Euangelia*, etc., Wittenberg, 1560. The title was "A hymn on the power of the keys and the virtue of holy absolution; for the children in Joachimsthal." It probably suggested the better-known hymn by Johann Heermann "So wahr ich lebe." The cento omits Stanzas 5, 7, 9, which read:

5. They who believe when ye proclaim
The joyful tidings in My name
That I for them My blood have shed,
Are free from guilt and Judgment dread.

7. However great our sin may be,
The absolution sets us free,
Appointed by God's own dear Son
To bring the pardon He has won.

9. This is the power of Holy Keys,
It binds and doth again release;
The Church retains them at her side,
Our mother and Christ's holy Bride.

The translation is an altered form of that by Matthias Loy in the Ohio *Lutheran Hymnal*, 1880.

For comments on the tune "St. Luke" see Hymn No. 323.

Confirmation

332   Arm These Thy Soldiers, Mighty Lord

1. Arm these Thy soldiers, mighty Lord,
With shield of faith and Spirit's sword.
Forth to the battle may they go
And boldly fight against the Foe.

2. With banner of the Cross unfurled,
They overcome the evil world
And so at last receive from Thee
The palm and crown of victory.

3. Come, ever-blessed Spirit, come
And make Thy servants' hearts Thy home.
May each a living temple be
Hallowed forever, Lord, to Thee.

4. Enrich that temple's holy shrine
With sevenfold gifts of grace divine;
With wisdom, light, and knowledge bless,
With counsel, strength, fear, godliness.

5. O Trinity in Unity,
One only God and Persons Three,
In whom, through whom, by whom, we live,
To Thee we praise and glory give.

6. Oh, grant us so to use Thy grace
That we may see Thy glorious face
And ever with the heavenly host
Praise Father, Son, and Holy Ghost!

This hymn is a slightly altered portion of Christopher Wordsworth's longer confirmation hymn "Father of All, in Whom We Live," published in his *Holy Year*, 1862. The original hymn is divided into three parts, as follows:

Part I: *Referring to the Whole Congregation,* in three eight-line stanzas, beginning: "Father of All, in Whom We Live."

Part II: *Referring to Those who Come to be Confirmed: to be used before the laying on of hands,* in five eight-line stanzas, beginning: "O God, in Whose All-searching Eye."

Part III: *After the Laying on of Hands: to be sung specifically by those who have been confirmed,* in three eight-line stanzas, beginning: "Our Hearts and Voices Let Us Raise."

Our hymn is from the second part, of which it is Stanzas 3 to 5. Stanzas 1 and 2 of this section read:

1. O God, in whose all-searching eye
Thy servants stand to ratify
The vow baptismal by them made
When first Thy hand was on them laid,
Bless them, O holy Father, bless,
Who Thee with heart and voice confess.
May they, acknowledged as Thine own,
Stand evermore before Thy throne.

2. O Christ, who didst at Pentecost
Send down from heaven the Holy Ghost
And at Samaria baptize
Those whom Thou didst evangelize,
And then on Thy baptized confer
Thy best of gifts, the Comforter,
By apostolic hands and prayer,
Be with us now as Thou wert there.

For comments on the tune "Erhalt uns, Herr" see Hymn No. 5.

333   Blessed Savior, Who hast Taught Me

1. Blessed Savior, who hast taught me
I should live to Thee alone,
All these years Thy hand hath brought me
Since I first was made Thine own.
At the font my vows were spoken
By my parents in the Lord;
That my vows shall be unbroken
At the altar I record.

2. I would trust in Thy protecting,
Wholly rest upon Thine arm,
Follow wholly Thy directing,
O my only Guard from harm.
Meet me now with Thy salvation
In Thy Church's ordered way;
Let me feel Thy confirmation
In Thy truth and fear today,

3. So that, might and firmness gaining,
Hope in danger, joy in grief,
Now and evermore remaining
In the one and true belief,
Resting in my Savior's merit,
Strengthened with the Spirit's strength,
With Thy saints I may inherit
All My Father's joy at length.

CONFIRMATION

John M. Neale first published this confirmation hymn in his *Hymns for the Young*, 1842, in six stanzas. It is seldom used in this form. The cento is composed of Stanzas 1, 5, and 6. In Stanza 6, Line 4, Neale has:

In the catholic belief.

Some centos also include Stanza 4 of the original:

In the world would foes assail me,
Craftier, stronger, far than I;
And the strife may never fail me,
Well I know, before I die.
Therefore, Lord, I come believing
Thou canst give the power I need,
Through the prayer of faith receiving
Strength, the Spirit's strength, indeed.

For comments on the tune "O du Liebe" see Hymn No. 37.

Let Me Be Thine Forever 334

1. Let me be Thine forever,
Thou faithful God and Lord;
Let me forsake Thee never
Nor wander from Thy Word.
Lord, do not let me waver,
But give me steadfastness,
And for such grace forever
Thy holy name I'll bless.

2. Lord Jesus, my Salvation,
My Light, my Life divine,
My only Consolation,
Oh, make me wholly Thine!
For Thou hast dearly bought me
With blood and bitter pain.
Let me, since Thou hast sought me,
Eternal life obtain.

3. And Thou, O Holy Spirit,
My Comforter and Guide,
Grant that in Jesus' merit
I always may confide,
Him to the end confessing
Whom I have known by faith.
Give me Thy constant blessing
And grant a Christian death.

Lass mich dein sein und bleiben,
Du treuer Gott und Herr;
Von dir lass mich nichts treiben,
Halt mich bei reiner Lehr';
Herr, lass mich nur nicht wanken,
Gib mir Beständigkeit!
Dafür will ich dir danken
In alle Ewigkeit.

Herr Jesu Christ, mein Leben,
Mein Heil und ein'ger Trost,
Dir tu' ich mich ergeben,
Du hast mich teu'r erlöst
Mit deinem Blutvergiessen,
Mit grossem Weh und Leid;
Lass mich des auch geniessen
Zu meiner Seligkeit!

O Heil'ger Geist, mein Tröster,
Mein Licht und teures Pfand,
Lass mich Christ, mein'n Erlöser,
Den ich im Glaub'n erkannt,
Bis an mein End' bekennen,
Stärk mich in letzter Not,
Von dir lass mich nichts trennen,
Gib einen sel'gen Tod!

In Nikolaus Selnecker's *Passio*, etc., Heinrichstadt, 1572, the author has the first stanza of this hymn as a "Prayer." In his *Psalter*, Leipzig, 1578, he brings it again at the end of Ps. 119, with the heading "Summary of Prayer." It seems that Selnecker used it as a daily prayer. In the *Rudolstädter Gesangbuch*, 1688, Stanzas 2 and 3 were added. The author of these is unknown. The hymn is a favorite hymn for confirmation in the Lutheran Church.

The translation is by Matthias Loy, somewhat altered. It appeared in the Ohio *Lutheran Hymnal*, 1880.

For comments on the tune "Ich dank' dir, lieber Herre" see Hymn No. 32.

My Maker, Be Thou Nigh 335

1. My Maker, be Thou nigh
The light of life to give
And guide me with Thine eye
While here on earth I live.
To Thee my heart I tender
And all my powers surrender;
Make it my one endeavor
To love and serve Thee ever.
Upon Thy promise I rely;
My Maker, be Thou nigh.

Mein Schöpfer, steh mir bei,
Sei meines Lebens Licht!
Dein Auge leite mich,
Bis mir mein Auge bricht!
Hier leg' ich Herz und Glieder
Vor dir zum Opfer nieder;
Bestimme meine Kräfte
Für dich und dein Geschäfte!
Du willst, dass ich der Deine sei:
Mein Schöpfer, steh mir bei!

[239]

2. My Savior, wash me clean
   With Thy most precious blood,
That takes away all sin
   And seals my peace with God.
My soul in peace abideth
   When in Thy wounds it hideth.
There I find full salvation
   And freedom from damnation.
Without Thee lost, defiled by sin,
   My Savior, wash me clean.

3. My Comforter, give power
   That I may stand secure
When in temptation's hour
   The world and sin allure.
The Son to me revealing,
   Inspire my thought and feeling,
His Word of grace to ponder,
   Nor let me from Him wander.
On me Thy gifts and graces shower:
   My Comforter, give power!

4. O Holy Trinity!
   To whom I all things owe,
Thine image graciously
   Within my heart bestow.
Choose me, though weak and lowly,
   To be Thy temple holy
Where praise shall rise unending
   For grace so condescending.
O heavenly bliss, Thine own to be,
   O Holy Trinity!

Mein Heiland, wasche mich
   Durch dein so teures Blut,
Das alle Flecken tilgt
   Und lauter Wunder tut!
Schliess die verirrte Seele
   In deine Wundenhöhle,
Dass sie von Zorn und Sünde
   Hier wahre Freiheit finde!
Ich bin verloren ohne dich:
   Mein Heiland, wasche mich!

Mein Tröster, gib mir Kraft,
   Wenn sich Versuchung zeigt!
Regiere meinen Geist,
   Wenn er zur Welt sich neigt!
Lehr mich den Sohn erkennen,
   Ihn meinen Herrn auch nennen,
Sein Gnadenwort verstehen,
   Auf seinen Wegen gehen!
Du bist, der alles Gute schafft:
   Mein Tröster, gib mir Kraft!

Gott Vater, Sohn und Geist,
   Dir bin ich, was ich bin.
Ach, drücke selbst dein Bild
   Recht tief in meinen Sinn!
Erwähle mein Gemüte
   Zum Tempel deiner Güte,
Verkläre an mir Armen
   Dein gnadenreich Erbarmen!
Wohl mir, wenn du der Meine heisst:
   Gott Vater, Sohn und Geist!

Johann J. Rambach published this hymn in his *Poetische Festgedanken,* 1729. It was accepted in the *Hannoverisches Gesang Buch,* 1740, together with the tune "Mein Schoepfer, steh mir bei" by Franz Heinrich Meyer, to which is has since been wedded.

The translation is by the Rev. E. Taylor of Melbourne, Australia, somewhat altered. It was prepared for the *Australian Lutheran Hymn-Book,* 1925.

336   My God, Accept My Heart This Day

1. My God, accept my heart this day
     And make it always Thine
   That I from Thee no more may stray,
     No more from Thee decline.

2. Before the cross of Him who died,
     Behold, I prostrate fall;
   Let every sin be crucified
     And Christ be All in all.

3. Anoint me with Thy Spirit's grace
     And seal me for Thine own
   That I may see Thy glorious face
     And worship near Thy throne.

4. May the dear blood once shed for me
     My blest atonement prove
   That I from first to last may be
     The purchase of Thy love!

5. Let every thought and work and word
     To Thee be ever given;
   Then life shall be Thy service, Lord,
     And death the gate of heaven.

Matthew Bridges wrote this hymn in connection with his entrance into the Roman Catholic Church. It appeared in his *Hymns of the Heart for the Use of Catholics,* 1848. Some collections have "My God, accept my heart, I pray"; others, "O God, accept," etc.; and some begin the hymn with Stanza 2.

For comments on the tune "Winchester Old" see Hymn No. 31.

337   Our Lord and God, Oh, Bless This Day

1. Our Lord and God, oh, bless this day
     And hear us, we implore Thee;
   None of Thy children turn away
     Who now appear before Thee.
   We come before Thy face
   And pray: Let Thy rich grace
   Descend from heaven above
   In all Thy wondrous love
     And keep us by Thy Spirit.

Lad denne Dag, o Herre Gud,
   For os velsignet være!
Fra Naadens Favn stöd ingen ud
   Af disse vore Kjære!
Vi for dit Aasyn staa,
Og bede, Store, Smaa:
Se, Fader, til os ned
I al din Miskundhed,
   Og lad din Aand os styrke!

CONFIRMATION

2. Oh, bless Thy Word to all the young;
Let them, Thy truth possessing,
Bear witness true with heart and tongue,
Their faith and ours confessing.
From mother's arms Thy grace
With love did them embrace;
Baptized into Thy name,
As Thine Thou didst them claim.
O Lord, as Thine now own them!

Sign Ordet i de Unges Mund,
Dets Kraft i Hjertet brände,
At de vor Tro og Troens Grund
Sandfärdig maa bekjende!
Engang de bares frem,
Og du velsigned dem;
Du tog de Smaa i Favn,
De döbtes i dit Navn,
O, kjendes ved dem, Herre!

3. When they their vows today renew,
Accept them with Thy favor;
And when they promise to be true,
May they forget it never!
But they are weak and frail
When Satan's hosts assail;
Oh, arm them with Thy might
And grant that in the fight
They unto death be faithful!

Lad dem, som fäste vil sin Pagt,
Dit Fader-Hjerte finde,
Og lad det Ja, her vorder sagt,
Dem aldrig gaa af Minde!
Men svag er dog enhver
Til Strid mod Helveds Här,
Styrk med din Kraftes Haand
Hver ärlig Själ og Aand
Til Enden tro at blive!

4. And when they leave their childhood home,
When Satan comes alluring,
May their baptismal grace become
A refuge reassuring!
Blest he who then can say:
"God's covenant stands for aye."
He ne'er shall be undone
Who trusts in God alone —
God is his mighty Father!

Engang de ud fra Fädrebo
Omkring i Verden vanker,
Da väre Daab og kristen Tro
Det arme Hjertes Anker!
Vel den, som sandt faar sagt:
Jeg staar med Gud i Pagt!
Den veed sig ei forladt,
Som Haab til Gud har sat,
De Faderlöses Fader.

Johan N. Brun's hymn "Gud Fader, Sön og Heligaand, vi vor din Throne knäle," in five stanzas, was published in *Evangeliske Sange,* Bergen, 1786. It was recast for the *Evangelical Christian Hymnal,* 1797, and then included by Landstad in his *Salmebog.*

The translation, by George T. Rygh (Stanzas 1 and 4) and Carl Döving (Stanzas 2 and 3), 1909, was included in *The Lutheran Hymnary,* 1913.

The tune "Reuter," dated 1916, is named for its composer, Fritz Reuter.

Thine Forever, God of Love 338

1. Thine forever, God of love!
Hear us from Thy throne above;
Thine forever may we be
Here and in eternity!

2. Thine forever! Oh, how blest
They who find in Thee their rest!
Savior, Guardian, heavenly Friend,
Oh, defend us to the end!

3. Thine forever, Lord of Life!
Shield us through our earthly strife.
Thou, the Life, the Truth, the Way,
Guide us to the realms of day.

4. Thine forever! Shepherd, keep
These Thy frail and trembling sheep
Safe alone beneath Thy care,
Let us all Thy goodness share.

5. Thine forever! Thou our Guide,
All our wants by Thee supplied,
All our sins by Thee forgiven;
Lead us, Lord, from earth to heaven.

Mary F. Maude wrote this hymn in 1847 for her Sunday-school class and published it the following year in a booklet, entitled *Twelve Letters on Confirmation.* The original is in seven stanzas. Two stanzas are omitted, and Stanzas 2 and 3 are transposed. The omitted stanzas read:

6. Thine forever in that day
When the world shall pass away,
When the trumpet note shall sound
And the nations underground

7. Shall the awful summons hear
Which proclaims the Judgment near.
Thine forever. 'Neath Thy wings
Hide and save us, King of kings.

For comments on the tune "Vienna" see Hymn No. 18.

The Redeemer

339   All Hail the Power of Jesus' Name

1. All hail the power of Jesus' name!
Let angels prostrate fall;
Bring forth the royal diadem
And crown Him Lord of all.

2. Crown Him, ye martyrs of our God,
Who from His altar call;
Extol the Stem of Jesse's rod
And crown Him Lord of all.

3. Ye seed of Israel's chosen race,
Ye ransomed from the Fall,
Hail Him who saves you by His grace
And crown Him Lord of all.

4. Hail Him, ye heirs of David's line,
Whom David Lord did call,
The God incarnate, Man divine,
And crown Him Lord of all.

5. Sinners, whose love can ne'er forget
The wormwood and the gall,
Go, spread your trophies at His feet
And crown Him Lord of all.

6. Let every kindred, every tribe,
On this terrestrial ball
To Him all majesty ascribe
And crown Him Lord of all.

7. Oh, that with yonder sacred throng
We at His feet may fall!
We'll join the everlasting song
And crown Him Lord of all.

Julian has an extensive discussion of this popular hymn in his *Dictionary of Hymnology* (p. 41 f.). It has been called "the most inspiring and triumphant hymn in the English language." It was written by Edward Perronet in 1779, and one stanza was published anonymously in the *Gospel Magazine* that year, with the tune by Wm. Shrubsole, afterwards called "Miles Lane." In 1780 the complete text by Perronet appeared in that magazine, in eight stanzas. It was entitled "On the Resurrection, the Lord Is King." By comparing the following original text, the reader can see how much later hymn-book compilers changed and improved the hymn:

1. All hail the power of Jesus' name!
Let angels prostrate fall;
Bring forth the royal diadem.
   To crown Him Lord of all!

2. Let high-born seraphs tune the lyre,
And, as they tune it, fall
Before His face who tunes their choir,
And crown Him Lord of all!

3. Crown Him, ye morning stars of light,
Who fixed this floating ball;
Now hail the Strength of Israel's might
And crown Him Lord of all!

4. Crown Him, ye martyrs of your God,
Who from His altar call;
Extol the Stem of Jesse's rod
And crown Him Lord of all!

5. Ye seed of Israel's chosen race,
Ye ransomed of the Fall,
Hail Him who saves you by His grace
And crown Him Lord of all!

6. Hail Him, ye heirs of David's line,
Whom David Lord did call,
The God incarnate, Man divine,
And crown him Lord of all!

7. Sinners, whose love can ne'er forget
The wormwood and the gall,
Go, spread your trophies at His feet
And crown Him Lord of all.

8. Let every tribe and every tongue
That bound creation's call
Now shout in universal song,
The crownèd Lord of all.

It has been rightly said:

> We have here another fine example of the splendid service rendered not only to an author and his hymn but to Christian hymnology by judicious editors who undertake to alter and improve the original. But for the changes and improvements made upon the original of this hymn, it could not possibly have gained the high place which it now holds among the foremost hymns of the Christian Church.

Many stories are told about the blessed use of this hymn. The following is an interesting example:

> An incident in the experience of Rev. E. P. Scott, a missionary in India, illustrates the power of this hymn and tune over even the worst and most

dangerous of heathen tribes. He had gone, against the remonstrances of his friends, to take the Gospel to one of the inland tribes noted for their murderous proclivities. He had no sooner arrived than he was met by a dozen pointed spears, and instant death seemed inevitable. While they paused a moment, he drew out his violin (with which he always accompanied his sacred songs) and, closing his eyes, began playing and singing this hymn. When he had finished, he opened his eyes to witness, as he thought, his own death at the point of their spears; but to his joy he found that the spears had fallen, and the murderers were all in tears. This song had saved him from death and opened an effectual door for preaching the Gospel to them. He remained with them many years, doing a great work for them and other surrounding tribes, and finally died among them, beloved and venerated of the whole tribe. He often related this incident.

The tune "Coronation," by Oliver Holden, appeared in the composer's *The Union Harmony*, 1793, set to this hymn. The organ upon which Holden composed this tune is preserved in the rooms of the Bostonian Society in the Old State House, Boston.

Awake, My Soul, to Joyful Lays   340

1. Awake, my soul, to joyful lays
And sing Thy great Redeemer's praise.
He justly claims a song from me, —
His loving-kindness, oh, how free!

2. He saw me ruined in the Fall,
Yet loved me notwithstanding all.
He saved me from my lost estate, —
His loving-kindness, oh, how great!

3. When I was Satan's easy prey
And deep in debt and bondage lay,
He paid His life for my discharge, —
His loving-kindness, oh, how large!

4. Through mighty hosts of cruel foes,
Where earth and hell my way oppose,
He safely leads my soul along, —
His loving-kindness, oh, how strong!

5. When trouble, like a gloomy cloud,
Has gathered thick and thundered loud,
He near my soul has always stood, —
His loving-kindness, oh, how good!

6. When earthly friends forsake me quite
And I have neither skill nor might,
He's sure my Helper to appear, —
His loving-kindness, oh, how near!

7. Too oft I feel my sinful heart
Prone from my Jesus to depart;
But though I have Him oft forgot,
His loving-kindness changes not.

8. When I shall pass death's gloomy vale
And all my mortal power must fail,
Oh, may my last, expiring breath
His loving-kindness sing in death!

9. Then shall I mount and soar away
To the bright world of endless day
And sing with rapture and surprise
His loving-kindness in the skies.

Samuel Medley published this hymn complete in his *Hymns*, etc., 1800. It had previously appeared in eight stanzas in *Collection of Hymns*, by J. H. Meyer, 1782. Though widely used in the hymnals of the Church, very few collections give the author's full text. Our text follows the alterations made by earlier compilers.

The tune "O Heilige Dreifaltigkeit" is by Nikolaus Herman, dated 1560. The melody was originally composed by Nikolaus Herman for the hymn "Wer hie für Gott will sein gerecht" and published in his *Sontags Euangelia uber das gantze Jar,* etc., Wittenberg, 1560. But since the hymn itself was little used, Herman transferred it to "Freut euch, ihr Christen alle gleich" in 1562. After that it was published in a number of other collections and there set to different texts, until Johann Stötzel set it to "O (Du) Heilige Dreifaltigkeit" in his *Harfen- und Psalterspiel,* Stuttgart, 1744. The last union of tune and text seems to have passed into common use.

341   Crown Him with Many Crowns

1. Crown Him with many crowns,
 The Lamb upon His throne;
 Hark how the heavenly anthem drowns
 All music but its own.
 Awake, my soul, and sing
 Of Him who died for thee
 And hail Him as thy matchless King
 Through all eternity.

2. Crown Him the Virgin's Son,
 The God incarnate born,
 Whose arm those crimson trophies won
 Which now His brow adorn;
 Fruit of the mystic rose,
 As of that rose the stem;
 The root whence mercy ever flows,
 The Babe of Bethlehem.

3. Crown Him the Lord of Love.
 Behold His hands and side,
 Rich wounds, yet visible above,
 In beauty glorified.

No angel in the sky
 Can fully bear that sight,
But downward bends his wondering eye
 At mysteries so bright.

4. Crown Him the Lord of Life
 Who triumphed o'er the grave
 And rose victorious in the strife
 For those He came to save.
 His glories now we sing
 Who died and rose on high,
 Who died eternal life to bring
 And lives that death may die.

5. Crown Him the Lord of Heaven,
 Enthroned in worlds above,
 Crown Him the King to whom is given
 The wondrous name of Love.
 Crown Him with many crowns
 As thrones before Him fall;
 Crown Him, ye kings, with many crowns
 For He is King of all.

Matthew Bridges published the original of this hymn in his *Hymns of the Heart*, etc., 2d edition, 1851. The text, as in the *Library of Religious Poetry*, Schaff and Gilman, 1881, is in 12 four-line stanzas, of which Stanzas 1 to 6, 11, and 12 form Stanzas 1 to 3 and 5 (somewhat altered), as above. The omitted stanzas read:

1. Crown Him the Lord of peace!
 Whose power a scepter sways
 From pole to pole that wars may cease,
 Absorbed in prayer and praise.

2. His reign shall know no end;
 And round his piercèd feet
 Fair flowers of paradise extend,
 Their fragrance ever sweet.

3. Crown Him the Lord of years,
 The Potentate of time,
 Creator of the rolling spheres,
 Ineffably sublime!

5. Glassed in a sea of light
 Whose everlasting waves
 Reflect His form — the Infinite!
 Who lives and loves and saves.

The fourth stanza of the hymn is an addition to the hymn by an unknown author.

The tune "Diademata" is by George J. Elvey and was written for the hymn. It appeared in the *Appendix* of the original edition of *Hymns Ancient and Modern*, 1868.

342   Chief of Sinners Though I Be

1. Chief of sinners though I be,
 Jesus shed His blood for me;
 Died that I might live on high,
 Lived that I might never die.
 As the branch is to the vine,
 I am His, and He is mine.

2. Oh, the height of Jesus' love!
 Higher than the heavens above,
 Deeper than the depths of sea,
 Lasting as eternity.
 Love that found me — wondrous thought! —
 Found me when I sought Him not.

3. Jesus only can impart
 Balm to heal the smitten heart;
 Peace that flows from sin forgiven,
 Joy that lifts the soul to heaven;
 Faith and hope to walk with God
 In the way that Enoch trod.

4. Chief of sinners though I be,
 Christ is All in all to me;
 All my wants to Him are known,
 All my sorrows are His own.
 Safe with Him from earthly strife,
 He sustains the hidden life.

5. O my Savior, help afford
 By Thy Spirit and Thy Word!
 When my wayward heart would stray,
 Keep me in the narrow way;
 Grace in time of need supply
 While I live and when I die.

William McComb published this hymn in his *Poetical Works*, 1864. It is entitled "Christ All in All."

For comments on the tune "Gethsemane" see Hymn No. 159.

How Lovely Shines the Morning Star 343

1. How lovely shines the Morning Star!
The nations see and hail afar
   The light in Judah shining.
Thou David's Son of Jacob's race,
My Bridegroom and my King of Grace,
   For Thee my heart is pining.
      Lowly, Holy,
Great and glorious, Thou victorious
   Prince of graces,
Filling all the heavenly places.

2. O highest joy by mortals won,
True Son of God and Mary's Son,
   Thou high-born King of ages!
Thou art my heart's most beauteous Flower,
And Thy blest Gospel's saving power
   My raptured soul engages.
      Thou mine, I Thine;
Sing hosanna! Heavenly manna
   Tasting, eating,
Whilst Thy love in songs repeating.

3. Now richly to my waiting heart,
O Thou, my God, deign to impart
   The grace of love undying.
In Thy blest body let me be,
E'en as the branch is in the tree,
   Thy life my life supplying.
      Sighing, Crying,
For the savor Of Thy favor;
   Resting never,
Till I rest in Thee forever.

4. A pledge of peace from God I see
When Thy pure eyes are turned to me
   To show me Thy good pleasure.
Jesus, Thy Spirit and Thy Word,
Thy body and Thy blood, afford
   My soul its dearest treasure.
      Keep me Kindly
In Thy favor, O my Savior!
   Thou wilt cheer me;
Thy Word calls me to draw near Thee.

5. Thou, mighty Father, in Thy Son
Didst love me ere Thou hadst begun
   This ancient world's foundation.
Thy Son hath made a friend of me,
And when in spirit Him I see,
   I joy in tribulation.
      What bliss Is this!
He that liveth To me giveth
   Life forever;
Nothing me from Him can sever.

6. Lift up the voice and strike the string,
Let all glad sounds of music ring
   In God's high praises blended.
Christ will be with me all the way,
Today, tomorrow, every day,
   Till traveling days be ended.
      Sing out, Ring out
Triumph glorious, O victorious,
   Chosen nation;
Praise the God of your salvation.

7. Oh, joy to know that Thou, my Friend,
Art Lord, Beginning without end,
   The First and Last, Eternal!
And Thou at length — O glorious grace! —
Wilt take me to that holy place,
   The home of joys supernal.
      Amen, Amen!
Come and meet me! Quickly greet me!
   With deep yearning,
Lord, I look for Thy returning.

Wie schön leuchtet der Morgenstern
Voll Gnad' und Wahrheit von dem Herrn,
   Die süsse Wurzel Jesse!
Du Sohn Davids aus Jakobs Stamm,
Mein König und mein Bräutigam,
   Hast mir mein Herz besessen,
      Lieblich, freundlich,
Schön und herrlich, gross und ehrlich,
   Reich von Gaben,
Hoch und sehr prächtig erhaben!

Ei meine Perl', du werte Kron',
Wahr'r Gottes- und Mariensohn,
   Ein hochgeborner König!
Mein Herz heisst dich ein Lilium,
Dein süsses Evangelium
   Ist lauter Milch und Honig.
      Ei mein Blümlein,
Hosianna, himmlisch Manna,
   Das wir essen,
Deiner kann ich nicht vergessen!

Geuss sehr tief in mein Herz hinein,
Du heller Jaspis und Rubin,
   Die Flamme deiner Liebe
Und erfreu' mich, dass ich doch bleib'
An deinem auserwählten Leib
   Ein' lebendige Rippe!
      Nach dir ist mir,
Gratiosa coeli rosa,
   Krank und glimmet
Mein Herz, durch Liebe verwundet.

Von Gott kommt mir ein Freudenschein,
Wenn du mit deinen Äugelein
   Mich freundlich tust anblicken.
O Herr Jesu, mein trautes Gut,
Dein Wort, dein Geist, dein Leib und Blut
   Mich innerlich erquicken!
      Nimm mich freundlich
In dein' Arme, dass ich warme
   Werd' von Gnaden!
Auf dein Wort komm' ich geladen.

Herr Gott Vater, mein starker Held,
Du hast mich ewig vor der Welt
   In deinem Sohn geliebet.
Dein Sohn hat mich ihm selbst vertraut,
Er ist mein Schatz, ich bin sein' Braut,
   Sehr hoch in ihm erfreuet.
      Eia, eia,
Himmlisch Leben wird er geben
   Mir dort oben!
Ewig soll mein Herz ihn loben.

Zwingt die Saiten in Zithara
Und lasst die süsse Musika
   Ganz freudenreich erschallen,
Dass ich möge ihn Jesulein,
Dem wunderschönen Bräut'gam mein,
   In steter Liebe wallen!
      Singet, springet,
Jubilieret, triumphieret,
   Dankt dem Herren!
Gross ist der König der Ehren!

Wie bin ich doch so herzlich froh,
Dass mein Schatz ist das A und O,
   Der Anfang und das Ende!
Er wird mich doch zu seinem Preis
Aufnehmen in das Paradeis,
   Des klopf' ich in die Hände.
      Amen! Amen!
Komm, du schöne Freudenkrone,
   Bleib nicht lange,
Deiner wart' ich mit Verlangen!

Philipp Nicolai published this "Queen of *Chorales*" in the *Appendix* of his *Frewden-Spiegel*, etc., Frankfurt a. M., 1599; but it was very likely written in 1597 or earlier. It will be noted that the first letters of the German stanzas are W, E, G, U, H, Z, W, which form an acrostic, referring to *Wilhelm Ernst, Graf und Herr zu Waldeck*, whose teacher Nicolai had been. The hymn is a great favorite and has a wide usage at festival occasions. The tune "Wie schön leuchtet" is also by Nicolai and appeared with the hymn in 1599.

The claim that this hymn is a spiritual recast of a somewhat popular love-song of the time has been exploded by such eminent hymnologists as Wackernagel, and by Curtz. The latter is the author of a monograph on Nicolai. The love-song in question is instead a parody of this hymn and did not appear until the middle of the 17th century.

The translation is composite and was prepared for *The Lutheran Hymnal*.

344   Come, Let Us Join Our Cheerful Songs

1. Come, let us join our cheerful songs
With angels round the throne.
Ten thousand thousand are their tongues,
But all their joys are one.

2. "Worthy the Lamb that died," they cry,
"To be exalted thus."
"Worthy the Lamb," our lips reply,
For He was slain for us.

3. Jesus is worthy to receive
Honor and power divine;
And blessings more than we can give
Be, Lord, forever Thine.

4. Let all creation join in one
To bless the sacred name
Of Him that sits upon the throne
And to adore the Lamb.

Isaac Watts published this hymn in his *Hymns and Spiritual Songs*, 1707, in five stanzas. The omitted Stanza 4 reads:

> Let all that dwell above the sky
> And air and earth and seas
> Conspire to lift Thy glories high
> And speak Thine endless praise.

For comments on the tune "Nun danket all'" see Hymn No. 10.

345   Jesus, Lover of My Soul

1. Jesus, Lover of my soul,
Let me to Thy bosom fly
While the nearer waters roll,
While the tempest still is high.
Hide me, O my Savior, hide,
Till the storm of life is past;
Safe into the haven guide.
Oh, receive my soul at last!

2. Other refuge have I none;
Hangs my helpless soul on Thee.
Leave, ah, leave me not alone,
Still support and comfort me!
All my trust on Thee is stayed,
All my help from Thee I bring;
Cover my defenseless head
With the shadow of Thy wing.

3. Wilt Thou not regard my call,
Wilt Thou not accept my prayer?
Lo, I sink, I faint, I fall;
Lo, on Thee I cast my care;
Reach me out Thy gracious hand!
While I of Thy strength receive,
Hoping against hope, I stand,
Dying, and, behold, I live!

4. Thou, O Christ, art all I want;
More than all in Thee I find.
Raise the fallen, cheer the faint,
Heal the sick, and lead the blind.
Just and holy is Thy name;
I am all unrighteousness,
False and full of sin I am;
Thou art full of truth and grace.

5. Plenteous grace with Thee is found,
Grace to cover all my sin.
Let the healing streams abound;
Make and keep me pure within.
Thou of life the Fountain art,
Freely let me take of Thee;
Spring Thou up within my heart,
Rise to all eternity.

Charles Wesley published this hymn in the *Wesley Hymns and Sacred Poems*, 1740, headed "In Temptation," the first line reading: "Jesu, Lover of my soul." In spite of the fact that the hymn is one of the most popular hymns in the English language, certain lines of the first stanza have been seriously objected to. To apply the intimate term "Lover" to our Lord has offended some, and they have changed the term to "Refuge" and "Savior." Yet Wesley's line has the sanction of the *Wisdom of Solomon* 11:26: "But Thou sparest all, for they are Thine, O Lord, Thou Lover of souls."

Others have objected to the line "While the nearer waters roll." Some have changed this line to "While the billows near me roll," others to "While the raging billows roll," still others to "While the threatening waters roll."

Some have changed the line: "Let me to Thy bosom fly" to "To Thy sheltering arms I fly," "We to Thee for safety fly," "To Thy sheltering cross we fly," and "To Thy sheltering wings I fly."

It seems that Charles Wesley was better informed about the storms at sea than his critics. *Julian* rightly says:

> The fact that in a wide expanse of waters a distant part may be lashed into fury by a passing storm whilst around a given ship there is perfect calm; and that these circumstances are often reversed, and the "nearer waters" are those affected and the distant waters are sleeping in the silent air — seems to have escaped the notice of the twoscore or more editors who have vainly striven to improve Wesley's text. In life as in nature storms are local. One ship may be dashed hither and thither by the fury of the "nearer waters," whilst another is sleeping in the far distance on a throbless sea. Men cry for help, not against dangers which are both distant and undefined, but out of the depths of their immediate troubles. Their life is amid "the *nearer* waters" of local surroundings and passions and temptations, and to them the *Lover* of souls is indispensable.

On the origin of the hymn *Julian* states:

> Many charming accounts of the origin of this hymn are extant, but unfortunately, some would add, they have no foundation in fact. The most that we can say is that it was written shortly after the great spiritual change which the author underwent in 1738 and that it was published within a few months of the official date (1739) which is given as the founding of Methodism. It had nothing whatever to do with the struggles and dangers with lawless men in after-years, nor with a dove driven to Wesley's bosom by a hawk nor with a sea-bird driven to the same shelter by a pitiless storm. These charming stories must be laid aside until substantiated by direct evidence from the Wesley books or from original manuscripts or printed papers as yet unknown.

The tune "Martyn," by Simeon B. Marsh, 1834, was written for the hymn "Mary at Her Savior's Tomb." Thomas Hastings seems to have been the first to use it with this hymn, a union of tune and text that time has not dissolved, even though many voices have been raised against it as an inferior tune.

THE REDEEMER

346   Jesus! and Shall It Ever Be

1. Jesus! and shall it ever be,
A mortal man ashamed of Thee?
Ashamed of Thee, whom angels praise,
Whose glories shine through endless days?

2. Ashamed of Jesus? Sooner far
Let evening blush to own a star.
He sheds the beams of light divine
O'er this benighted soul of mine.

3. Ashamed of Jesus? Just as soon
Let midnight be ashamed of noon.
'Tis midnight with my soul till He,
Bright Morning Star, bids darkness flee.

4. Ashamed of Jesus, that dear Friend
On whom my hopes of heaven depend?
No; when I blush, be this my shame,
That I no more revere His name.

5. Ashamed of Jesus? Yes, I may
When I've no guilt to wash away,
No tear to wipe, no good to crave,
No fear to quell, no soul to save.

6. Till then — nor is my boasting vain —
Till then I boast a Savior slain;
And oh, may this my glory be,
That Christ is not ashamed of me!

Joseph Grigg published this hymn in his *Four Hymns on Divine Subjects,* etc., 1765, as follows:

1. Jesus! and shall it ever be!
A mortal man ashamed of Thee?
Scorned be the thought by rich and poor;
Oh, may I scorn it more and more!

2. Ashamed of Jesus! Sooner far
Let evening blush to own a star.
Ashamed of Jesus! Just as soon
Let midnight blush to think of noon.

3. 'Tis evening with my soul till He,
That Morning Star, bids darkness flee;
He sheds the beam of noon divine
O'er all this midnight soul of mine.

4. Ashamed of Jesus! Shall yon field
Blush when it thinks who bids it yield?
Yet blush I must, while I adore,
I blush to think I yield no more.

5. Ashamed of Jesus, of that Friend
On whom for heaven my hopes depend!
It must not be! Be this my shame,
That I no more revere His name.

6. Ashamed of Jesus! Yes, I may
When I've no crimes to wash away,
No tear to wipe, no joy to crave,
No fears to quell, no soul to save.

7. Till then (nor is the boasting vain),
Till then I boast a Savior slain.
And oh, may this my portion be,
That Savior not ashamed of me.

At the publication of the hymn, omitting Stanzas 3 and 4, in the *Gospel Magazine,* 1774, it was stated that it was written "by a youth of ten years."

The form of the hymn as above is from Rippon's *Selection,* 1787, where it was given as "altered by B. Francis." A comparison of the two versions will readily show how decidedly improved the hymn thus became.

The tune "Federal Street" is by Henry K. Oliver. It was written in 1832 to a hymn by Anna Steele. It was first published by Lowell Mason in the *Boston Academy's Collection of Church Music,* 1836. The name "Federal Street" is from the street on which Oliver lived in Salem, Mass.

347   Jesus, Priceless Treasure

1. Jesus, priceless Treasure,
Fount of purest pleasure,
  Truest Friend to me.
Ah, how long in anguish
Shall my spirit languish,
  Yearning, Lord, for Thee?
Thou art mine, O Lamb divine!
I will suffer naught to hide Thee,
Naught I ask beside Thee.

2. In Thine arms I rest me;
Foes who would molest me
  Cannot reach me here.
Though the earth be shaking,
Every heart be quaking,
  Jesus calms my fear.
Lightnings flash And thunders crash;
Yet, though sin and hell assail me,
Jesus will not fail me.

Jesu, meine Freude,
Meines Herzens Weide,
  Jesu, meine Zier,
Ach, wie lang, ach lange
Ist dem Herzen bange
  Und verlangt nach dir!
Gotteslamm, mein Bräutigam,
Ausser dir soll mir auf Erden
Nichts sonst Liebers werden!

Unter deinem Schirmen
Bin ich vor den Stürmen
  Aller Feinde frei.
Lass den Satan wittern,
Lass die Welt erschüttern,
  Mir steht Jesus bei.
Ob es gleich kracht und blitzt,
Obgleich Sünd' und Hölle schrecken,
Jesus will mich decken.

3. Satan, I defy thee;
   Death, I now decry thee;
      Fear, I bid thee cease.
   World, thou shalt not harm me
   Nor thy threats alarm me
      While I sing of peace.
   God's great power Guards every hour;
   Earth and all its depths adore Him,
   Silent bow before Him.

   Trotz dem alten Drachen,
   Trotz dem Todesrachen,
      Trotz der Furcht dazu!
   Tobe, Welt, und springe,
   Ich steh' hier und singe
      In gar sichrer Ruh';
   Gottes Macht hält mich in acht;
   Erd' und Abgrund muss verstummen,
   Ob sie noch so brummen.

4. Hence, all earthly treasure!
   Jesus is my Pleasure,
      Jesus is my Choice.
   Hence, all empty glory!
   Naught to me thy story
      Told with tempting voice.
   Pain or loss, Or shame or cross,
   Shall not from my Savior move me
   Since He deigns to love me.

   Weg mit allen Schätzen,
   Du bist mein Ergötzen,
      Jesu, meine Lust!
   Weg, ihr eitlen Ehren,
   Ich mag euch nicht hören,
      Bleibt mir unbewusst!
   Elend, Not, Kreuz, Schmach und Tod
   Soll mich, ob ich viel muss leiden,
   Nicht von Jesu scheiden.

5. Evil world, I leave thee;
   Thou canst not deceive me,
      Thine appeal is vain.
   Sin that once did blind me,
   Get thee far behind me,
      Come not forth again.
   Past thy hour, O pride and power;
   Sinful life, thy bonds I sever,
   Leave thee now forever.

   Gute Nacht, o Wesen,
   Das die Welt erlesen,
      Mir gefällst du nicht!
   Gute Nacht, ihr Sünden,
   Bleibet weit dahinten,
      Kommt nicht mehr ans Licht!
   Gute Nacht, du Stolz und Pracht,
   Dir sei ganz, du Lasterleben,
   Gute Nacht gegeben!

6. Hence, all fear and sadness!
   For the Lord of gladness,
      Jesus, enters in.
   Those who love the Father,
   Though the storms may gather,
      Still have peace within.
   Yea, whate'er I here must bear,
   Thou art still my purest Pleasure,
   Jesus, priceless Treasure!

   Weicht, ihr Trauergeister,
   Denn mein Freudenmeister,
      Jesus, tritt herein!
   Denen, die Gott lieben,
   Muss auch ihr Betrüben
      Lauter Zucker sein.
   Duld' ich schon hier Spott und Hohn,
   Dennoch bleibst du auch im Leide,
   Jesu, meine Freude.

Johann Franck, according to Fischer, first published this hymn in *Andacht's Zymbeln*, Freyberg, 1655.

The composite translation is based on that by Catherine Winkworth in her *Chorale Book for England*, 1863.

The tune "Jesu, meine Freude" is by Johann Crüger and first appeared in his *Praxis Pietatis Melica*, Frankfurt, 1656, and not, as Winterfeld and others have it, in 1649. Zahn gives the date of the tune as *Praxis Pietatis Melica*, 1653. If this is correct, then that would also be the date of the first publication of the text.

Jesus, Jesus, Only Jesus 348

1. Jesus, Jesus, only Jesus,
      Can my heartfelt longing still.
   Lo, I pledge myself to Jesus
      What He wills alone to will.
   For my heart, which He hath filled,
   Ever cries, Lord, as Thou wilt.

   Jesus, Jesus, nichts als Jesus
      Soll mein Wunsch sein und mein Ziel.
   Jetzund mach' ich ein Verbündnis,
      Dass ich will, was Jesus will;
   Denn mein Herz, mit ihm erfüllt,
   Rufet nur: Herr, wie du willt!

2. One there is for whom I'm living,
      Whom I love most tenderly;
   Unto Jesus I am giving
      What in love He gave to me.
   Jesus' blood hides all my guilt;
   Lord, oh, lead me as Thou wilt.

   Einer ist es, dem ich lebe,
      Den ich liebe früh und spat.
   Jesus ist es, dem ich gebe,
      Was er mir gegeben hat.
   Ich bin in dein Blut verhüllt;
   Führe mich, Herr, wie du willt!

3. What to me may seem a treasure,
      But displeasing is to Thee,
   Oh, remove such harmful pleasure;
      Give instead what profits me.
   Let my heart by Thee be stilled;
   Make me Thine, Lord, as Thou wilt.

   Scheinet was, es sei mein Glücke,
      Und ist doch zuwider dir,
   Ach, so nimm es bald zurücke,
      Jesu, gib, was nützet mir!
   Gib dich mir, Herr Jesu, mild;
   Nimm mich dir, Herr, wie du willt.

4. Let me earnestly endeavor
  Thy good pleasure to fulfil;
In me, through me, with me ever,
  Lord, accomplish Thou Thy will.
In Thy holy image built,
Let me die, Lord, as Thou wilt.

5. Jesus, constant be my praises,
  For Thou unto me didst bring
Thine own self and all Thy graces
  That I joyfully may sing:
Be it unto me, my Shield,
As Thou wilt, Lord, as Thou wilt.

Und vollbringe deinen Willen
  In, durch und an mir, mein Gott.
Deinen Willen lass erfüllen
  Mich im Leben, Freud' und Not,
Sterben als dein Ebenbild,
Herr, wann, wo und wie du willt!

Sei auch, Jesu, stets gepriesen,
  Dass du dich und viel dazu
Hast geschenkt und mir erwiesen,
  Dass ich fröhlich singe nu:
Es geschehe mir, mein Schild,
Wie du willt, Herr, wie du willt!

This hymn is by Ludämilia Elisabeth and appeared in *Die Stimme der Freundin*, etc., Rudolstadt, 1687, entitled "Resignation to the Will of God." The first letter of each stanza in the original form the name JESUS.

The translation is by August Crull, altered. It appeared in the Ohio *Lutheran Hymnal*, 1880.

The tune "Jesus, Jesus, nichts als Jesus," according to *Zahn*, is found in the *Vollkommenes musikalisches Choral-Buch* of Bronner, Hamburg, 1715. Its ascription to Johann B. König by some authorities seems to be an error.

349   Jesus, Thy Boundless Love to Me

1. Jesus, Thy boundless love to me
  No thought can reach, no tongue declare;
Unite my thankful heart to Thee
  And reign without a rival there.
To Thee alone, dear Lord, I live;
Myself to Thee, dear Lord, I give.

2. Oh, grant that nothing in my soul
  May dwell but Thy pure love alone!
Oh, may Thy love possess me whole,
  My Joy, my Treasure, and my Crown!
All coldness from my heart remove;
My every act, word, thought, be love.

3. O Love, how cheering is Thy ray!
  All pain before Thy presence flies;
Care, anguish, sorrow, melt away
  Where'er Thy healing beams arise.
O Jesus, nothing may I see,
Nothing desire or seek, but Thee!

4. This love unwearied I pursue
  And dauntlessly to Thee aspire.
Oh, may Thy love my hope renew,
  Burn in my soul like heavenly fire!
And day and night be all my care
To guard this sacred treasure there.

5. Oh, draw me, Savior, e'er to Thee!
  So shall I run and never tire.
With gracious words still comfort me;
Be Thou my Hope, my sole Desire.
Free me from every guilt and fear;
No sin can harm if Thou art near.

O Jesu Christ, mein schönstes Licht,
  Der du in deiner Seelen
So hoch mich liebst, dass ich es nicht
  Aussprechen kann noch zählen:
Gib, dass mein Herz dich wiederum
  Mit Lieben und Verlangen
  Mög' umfangen
Und als dein Eigentum
  Nur einzig an dir hangen!

Gib, dass sonst nichts in meiner Seel'
  Als deine Liebe wohne;
Gib, dass ich deine Lieb' erwähl'
  Als meinen Schatz und Krone!
Stoss alles aus, nimm alles hin,
  Was dich und mich will trennen
  Und nicht gönnen,
Dass all mein Mut und Sinn
  In deiner Liebe brennen!

Wie freundlich, selig, süss und schön
  Ist, Jesu, deine Liebe!
Wo diese steht, kann nichts bestehn,
  Das meinen Geist betrübe;
Drum lass nichts andres denken mich,
  Nichts sehen, fühlen, hören,
  Lieben, ehren
Als deine Lieb' und dich,
  Der du sie kannst vermehren!

O dass ich wie ein kleines Kind
  Mit Weinen dir nachginge
So lange, bis dein Herz, entzünd't,
  Mit Armen mich umfinge
Und deine Seel' in mein Gemüt
  In voller, süsser Liebe
  Sich erhübe
Und also deiner Güt'
  Ich stets vereinigt bliebe!

Ach zeuch, mein Liebster, mich nach dir,
  So lauf' ich mit den Füssen,
Ich lauf' und will dich mit Begier
  In meinem Herzen küssen!
Ich will aus deines Mundes Zier
  Den süssen Trost empfinden,
  Der die Sünden
Und alles Unglück hier
  Kann leichtlich überwinden.

6. Still let Thy love point out my way;
   What wondrous things Thy love hath wrought!
Still lead me lest I go astray;
   Direct my work, inspire my thought;
And if I fall, soon may I hear
Thy voice and know that love is near!

Lass meinen Stand, darin ich steh',
   Herr, deine Liebe zieren
Und, wo ich etwa irregeh',
   Alsbald zurechteführen;
Lass sie mich allzeit guten Rat
   Und weise Werke lehren,
   Steuern, wehren
Der Sünd' und nach der Tat
   Bald wieder mich bekehren!

7. In suffering be Thy love my peace,
   In weakness be Thy love my power;
And when the storms of life shall cease,
   O Jesus, in that final hour,
Be Thou my Rod and Staff and Guide
And draw me safely to Thy side!

Lass sie sein meine Freud' in Leid,
   In Schwachheit mein Vermögen,
Und wenn ich nach vollbrachter Zeit
   Mich soll zur Ruhe legen,
Alsdann lass deine Liebestreu',
   Herr Jesu, bei mir stehen,
   Luft zuwehen,
Dass ich getrost und frei
   Mög' in dein Reich eingehen!

Paul Gerhardt's great hymn of love to Christ first appeared in Crüger's *Praxis Pietatis Melica*, Berlin, 1653, in sixteen stanzas. It is based on a prayer in Arndt's *Paradiesgärtlein*. John Wesley translated the entire hymn, changing the meter, and published it in *Hymns and Sacred Poems*, 1739, a very excellent production. The cento includes Stanzas 1, 2, 3, 8, 9, 15, and 16, with some alterations of Wesley's text.

For comments on the tune "Vater unser" see Hymn No. 458.

Jesus, the Very Thought of Thee   350

1. Jesus, the very thought of Thee
   With sweetness fills the breast;
But sweeter far Thy face to see
   And in Thy presence rest.

Iesu dulcis memoria,
Dans vera cordis gaudia;
Sed super mel et omnia
Dulcis eius praesentia.

2. Nor voice can sing, nor heart can frame,
   Nor can the memory find
A sweeter sound than Thy blest name,
   O Savior of mankind!

Nil canitur suavius,
Auditur nil iucundius,
Nil cogitatur dulcius,
Quam Iesus, Dei Filius.

3. O Hope of every contrite heart,
   O Joy of all the meek!
To those who fall, how kind Thou art,
   How good to those who seek!

Iesu, spes paenitentibus,
Quem pius es petentibus,
Quam bonus te quaerentibus!
Sed quid invenientibus

4. But what to those who find? Ah! this
   Nor tongue nor pen can show;
The love of Jesus, what it is,
   None but His loved ones know.

Nec lingua potest dicere,
Nec littera exprimere;
Experto potes credere,
Quid sit Iesum diligere.

5. Jesus, our only Joy be Thou
   As Thou our Prize wilt be!
Jesus, be Thou our Glory now
   And through eternity.

Tu esto nostrum gaudium,
Qui es futurus praemium;
Sit nostra in te gloria
Per cuncta semper saecula.

This cento is from the famous medieval hymn "Iesu dulcis memoria," usually attributed to Bernard of Clairvaux, whom Martin Luther called the most pious monk who ever lived. The hymn has been found in an eleventh-century manuscript, ascribed to a Benedictine abbess. The original is found in various forms, the fullest of which contains fifty stanzas.

The translation is by Edward Caswall, altered. It was published in his *Lyra Catholica*, 1849. The cento is Stanzas 1 to 5 of Caswall's translation. Hymn 361 is made up of Stanzas 6 to 10. In order to give the reader Caswall's full text, we add here Stanzas 11 to 15:

11. O Jesu! Thou the beauty art
    Of angel worlds above;
Thy name is music to the heart,
    Enchanting it with love.

12. Celestial sweetness unalloyed!
    Who eat Thee hunger still;
Who drink of Thee still feel a void,
    Which naught but Thou can fill.

THE REDEEMER

13. O my sweet Jesu! hear the sighs
    Which unto Thee I send;
    To Thee mine inmost spirit cries,
    My being's hope and end.

14. Stay with us, Lord, and with Thy light
    Illume the soul's abyss;
    Scatter the darkness of our night
    And fill the world with bliss.

15. O Jesu! spotless Virgin Flower,
    Our Life and Joy, to Thee
    Be praise, beatitude, and power,
    Through all eternity!

The tune "Clairvaux" was written for this hymn by Herman A. Polack in 1910 for inclusion in the *Evangelical Lutheran Hymn-Book*, 1912. It was sung to this hymn by the Cleveland Lutheran Teachers' Choir at the funeral of the composer in Pilgrim Lutheran Church, Lakewood, Ohio, in 1930.

351   Love Divine, All Love Excelling

1. Love Divine, all love excelling,
   Joy of heaven, to earth come down,
   Fix in us Thy humble dwelling,
   All Thy faithful mercies crown.
   Jesus, Thou art all compassion,
   Pure, unbounded love Thou art;
   Visit us with Thy salvation,
   Enter every trembling heart.

2. Breathe, oh, breathe Thy loving Spirit
   Into every troubled breast;
   Let us all in Thee inherit,
   Let us find the promised rest.
   Take away the love of sinning;
   Alpha and Omega be;
   End of faith as its beginning,
   Set our hearts at liberty.

3. Come, Almighty, to deliver;
   Let us all Thy life receive.
   Suddenly return and never,
   Nevermore, Thy temples leave.
   Thee we would be always blessing,
   Serve Thee as Thy hosts above,
   Pray and praise Thee without ceasing,
   Glory in Thy perfect love.

4. Finish, then, Thy new creation;
   Pure and spotless let us be.
   Let us see Thy great salvation
   Perfectly restored in Thee,
   Changed from glory into glory,
   Till in heaven we take our place,
   Till we cast our crowns before Thee,
   Lost in wonder, love, and praise.

Charles Wesley published this hymn in *Hymns for Those that Seek*, etc., 1747, the first line beginning "Love Divine, all loves excelling." There are several slight alterations. Wesley wrote: "Take way our *power* of sinning" and "Pure and *sinless* let us be."

For comments on the tune "O du Liebe" see Hymn No. 37.

352   O Savior, Precious Savior

1. O Savior, precious Savior,
   Whom, yet unseen, we love;
   O Name of might and favor,
   All other names above.
   We worship Thee, we bless Thee,
   To Thee, O Christ, we sing;
   We praise Thee and confess Thee,
   Our holy Lord and King.

2. O Bringer of salvation,
   Who wondrously hast wrought
   Thyself the revelation
   Of love beyond our thought,
   We worship Thee, we bless Thee,
   To Thee, O Christ, we sing;
   We praise Thee and confess Thee,
   Our gracious Lord and King.

3. In Thee all fulness dwelleth,
   All grace and power divine;
   The glory that excelleth,
   O Son of God, is Thine.
   We worship Thee, we bless Thee,
   To Thee, O Christ, we sing;
   We praise Thee and confess Thee,
   Our glorious Lord and King.

4. Oh, grant the consummation
   Of this our song above
   In endless adoration
   And everlasting love!
   Then shall we praise and bless Thee
   Where perfect praises ring
   And evermore confess Thee
   Our Savior and our King.

Frances R. Havergal wrote this hymn at Leanington in November, 1870. It first appeared in her *Under the Surface*, 1874. It was entitled "Christ Worshiped by the Church."

The tune "Angel's Story" was written by Arthur H. Mann for Mrs. E. H. Miller's hymn

      I love to hear the story
      Which angel voices tell,

and thence received its name. It first appeared in *The Methodist Sunday-school Hymnbook*, London, 1881.

Lord Jesus Christ, My Savior Blest 353

1. Lord Jesus Christ,
My Savior blest,
My Hope and my Salvation!
I trust in Thee;
Deliver me
From misery;
Thy Word's my consolation.

2. As Thou dost will,
Lead Thou me still
That I may truly serve Thee,
My God, I pray,
Teach me Thy way,
To my last day
In Thy true faith preserve me.

3. Most heartily
I trust in Thee;
Thy mercy fails me never.
Dear Lord, abide;
My Helper tried,
Thou Crucified,
From evil keep me ever.

4. Now henceforth must
I put my trust
In Thee, O dearest Savior.
Thy comfort choice,
Thy word and voice,
My heart rejoice
Despite my ill behavior.

5. When sorrows rise,
My refuge lies
In Thy compassion tender.
Within Thine arm
Can naught alarm;
Keep me from harm,
Be Thou my strong Defender.

6. I have Thy Word,
Christ Jesus, Lord;
Thou never wilt forsake me.
This will I plead
In time of need.
Oh, help me speed
When troubles overtake me!

7. Grant, Lord, I pray,
Thy grace each day
That I, Thy Law revering,
May live with Thee
And happy be
Eternally,
Before Thy throne appearing.

Herre Jesu Krist!
Min Frelser du est,
Til dig haaber jeg alene;
Jeg tror paa dig,
Forlad ikke mig
Saa elendelig,
Mig tröster dit Ord det rene.

Alt efter din Vilje,
O Herre, mig stille,
At jeg dig trolig kan dyrke;
Du est min Gud,
Lär mig dine Bud,
Al min Tid ud
Du mig i Troen styrke!

Nu vil jeg väre,
O Jesu kjäre,
Hvor du mig helst vil have,
Jeg lukker dig ind
I mit Hjerte og Sind,
O Herre min,
Med al din Naade og Gave!

Al min Tillid
Nu og al Tid
Har jeg til dig, o Herre!
Du est min Tröst,
Dit Ord og Röst
I al min Bröst
Min Hjertens Gläde mon väre.

Naar Sorgen mig tränger,
Efter dig mig forlänger,
Du kan mig bedst husvale;
Den du vil bevare,
Han er uden Fare,
Du mig forsvare,
Dig monne jeg mig befale!

Nu veed jeg vist,
Herre Jesu Krist,
Du vil mig aldrig forlade;
Du siger jo saa:
Kald du mig paa,
Hjälp skal du faa
I al din Sorg og Vaade.

O give det Gud,
Vi efter dine Bud
Kunde os saa stikke tilsammen,
At vi med dig
Evindelig
I Himmerig
Kunde leve i Salighed! Amen.

The hymn, very popular in Scandinavian circles, is by Hans C. Sthen. It was published in *Sthen's Vandrebog*, etc., c. 1578, in eight stanzas. It is an acrostic. The initial letters of the stanzas spell the words "Hans" and "Anno." Stanza 4 is omitted.

The translation is by Harriet R. Spaeth, 1898. It was included in *The Lutheran Hymnary*, 1913.

The tune "Herre Jesu Krist" is one of Ludvig M. Lindeman's finest compositions. It appeared in his *Koralbog*, 1871.

In the Cross of Christ I Glory 354

1. In the Cross of Christ I glory,
Towering o'er the wrecks of time.
All the light of sacred story
Gathers round its head sublime.

2. When the woes of life o'ertake me,
Hopes deceive, and fears annoy,
Never shall the Cross forsake me;
Lo, it glows with peace and joy.

3. When the sun of bliss is beaming
    Light and love upon my way,
   From the Cross the radiance streaming
    Adds more luster to the day.

4. Bane and blessing, pain and pleasure,
    By the Cross are sanctified;
   Peace is there that knows no measure,
    Joys that through all time abide.

This popular hymn, by John Bowring, appeared in his *Hymns*, 1825. It is based on Gal. 6:14. It is said that Bowring was inspired to write the hymn by the sight of an old Portuguese church at Macao, built three hundred years before and which time and the elements had turned into a crumbling ruin — all but the spire at the top of which an old bronze cross reflected the rays of the setting sun.

The tune "Rathbun" was written by Ithamar Conkey in 1849. Dr. McCutchan brings this interesting article on the tune from the Norwich *Bulletin:*

Doctor Hiscox was . . . pastor of the church. He had prepared a series of seven sermons from "The Words on the Cross."

One Sunday during the series it was a very rainy day. Mr. Conkey was sorely disappointed that the members of the choir did not appear, as only one soprano came. Mr. Conkey was so discouraged and disheartened that after the prelude he closed the organ and locked it and went to his home on Washington Street. The pastor and choir gallery were at opposite ends of the church, and he could leave without attracting the attention of the congregation.

That afternoon he sat down at the piano for practice; the thoughts suggested in the series of sermons Doctor Hiscox had prepared and the words of the hymn suggested to be sung, "In the Cross of Christ I glory," passing and repassing through his mind. He then and there composed the music which is now so universally familiar in churches of every denomination, known as "Rathbun." He admitted afterward the inspiration was a vivid contradiction of his feelings at the morning service.

He prepared the scores for his choir, and the following Saturday evening it was rehearsed, and Sunday at the morning service in the Central Baptist Church, Norwich, Connecticut, it was sung for the first time. . . . Mr. and Mrs. Beriah S. Rathbun were both members of the choir. Mrs. Rathbun was the leading soprano. Mr. Conkey named it "Rathbun" as a compliment to her. She was then twenty-four years old. She died when she was twenty-nine years old.

355   Thou Art the Way; to Thee Alone

1. Thou art the *Way;* to Thee alone
    From sin and death we flee;
   And he who would the Father seek
    Must seek Him, Lord, by Thee.

2. Thou art the *Truth;* Thy Word alone
    True wisdom can impart;
   Thou only canst inform the mind
    And purify the heart.

3. Thou art the *Life;* the rending tomb
    Proclaims Thy conquering arm;
   And those who put their trust in Thee
    Nor death nor hell shall harm.

4. Thou art the Way, the Truth, the Life;
    Grant us that Way to know,
   That Truth to keep, that Life to win,
    Whose joys eternal flow.

This is held by some to be the best of American hymns. It is one of the few hymns of American origin included in *Hymns Ancient and Modern*. It was written by George W. Doane and first published in his *Songs by the Way*, 1824.

The tune "Dundee" is from the *Scottish Psalter*, 1615. It appeared in *Psalms of David*, Edinburgh, 1615.

THE REDEEMER

Jesus, Savior, Come to Me 356

1. Jesus, Savior, come to me;
Let me ever be with Thee.
Come and nevermore depart,
Thou who reignest in my heart.

2. Lord, for Thee I ever sigh,
Nothing else can satisfy.
Ever do I cry to Thee:
Jesus, Jesus, come to me!

3. Earthly joys can give no peace,
Cannot bid my longing cease;
Still to have my Jesus near,
This is all my pleasure here.

4. All that makes the angels glad,
In their garb of glory clad,
Only fills me with distress
If Thy presence does not bless.

5. Thou alone, my God and Lord,
Art my Glory and Reward.
Thou hast bled for me and died;
In Thy wounds I safely hide.

6. Come, then, Lamb for sinners slain,
Come and ease me of my pain.
Evermore I cry to Thee:
Jesus, Jesus, come to me!

7. Patiently I wait Thy Day;
For this gift, O Lord, I pray,
That, when death shall come to me,
My dear Jesus Thou wilt be.

Jesu, komm doch selbst zu mir
Und verbleibe für und für;
Komm doch, werter Seelenfreund,
Liebster, den mein Herze meint!

Tausendmal begehr' ich dich,
Weil sonst nichts vergnüget mich;
Tausendmal schrei' ich zu dir:
Jesu, Jesu, komm zu mir!

Keine Lust ist auf der Welt,
Die mein Herz zufriedenstellt.
Dein, o Jesu, Beimirsein
Nenn ich meine Lust allein.

Aller Engel Glanz und Pracht
Und was ihnen Freude macht,
Ist mir, süsser Seelenkuss,
Ohne dich nichts als Verdruss.

Dich alleine, Gottes Sohn,
Heiss' ich meine Kron' und Lohn;
Du für mich verwund'tes Lamm
Bist allein mein Bräutigam.

O so komm doch, süsses Herz,
Und vermindre meinen Schmerz;
Denn ich schreie für und für:
Jesu, Jesu, komm zu mir!

Nun, ich warte mit Geduld,
Bitte noch um diese Huld,
Dass du woll'st in Todespein
Mir ein süsser Jesus sein.

Johann Scheffler (Angelus Silesius) published this popular hymn of longing for spiritual union with Christ in his *Heilige Seelenlust,* 1657, in nine stanzas. The omitted Stanzas 5 and 6 read:

5. Take Thou all away from me,
I shall still thus minded be,
Thou who madest me Thine own
Shalt be all my Joy alone.

6. None shall claim my heart beside,
None but Jesus crucified;
Savior, I am only Thine,
Other love shall ne'er be mine.

The translation is an altered form of that by Matthias Loy. It appeared in the *Evangelical Review,* Gettysburg, 1861, and was included in the Ohio *Lutheran Hymnal,* 1880.

For comments on the tune "Gott sei Dank" see Hymn No. 2.

Jesus, Thou Art Mine Forever 357

1. Jesus, Thou art mine forever,
Dearer far than earth to me;
Neither life nor death shall sever
Those sweet ties which bind to Thee.

2. All were drear to me and lonely
If Thy presence gladdened not;
While I sing to Thee, Thee only,
Mine's an ever blissful lot.

3. Thou alone art all my Treasure,
Who hast died that I may live;
Thou conferrest noblest pleasure,
Who dost all my sins forgive.

4. Brightest gems and fairest flowers
Lose their beauty in Thy frown;
Joy and peace, like balmy showers,
In Thy smile come gently down.

5. Jesus, Thou art mine forever;
Never suffer me to stray.
Let me in my weakness never
Cast my priceless pearl away.

6. Lamb of God, I do implore Thee,
Guard, support me, lest I fall.
Let me evermore adore Thee;
Be my everlasting All.

This hymn, by Matthias Loy, entitled "Jesus, All in All," first appeared in the Ohio Synod's *Collection of Hymns,* fourth edition, 1863.

For comments on the tune "Stuttgart" see Hymn No. 83.

[255]

358   Lamb of God, We Fall Before Thee

1. Lamb of God, we fall before Thee,
   Humbly trusting in Thy Cross.
   That alone be all our glory;
   All things else are only dross.

2. Thee we own a perfect Savior,
   Only Source of all that's good.
   Every grace and every favor
   Comes to us through Jesus' blood.

3. Jesus gives us true repentance
   By His Spirit sent from heaven;
   Whispers this transporting sentence,
   "Son, thy sins are all forgiven."

4. Faith He grants us to believe it,
   Grateful hearts His love to prize;
   Want we wisdom? He must give it,
   Hearing ears and seeing eyes.

5. Jesus gives us pure affections,
   Wills to do what He requires,
   Makes us follow His directions,
   And what He commands, inspires.

6. All our prayers and all our praises,
   Rightly offered in His name, —
   He that dictates them is Jesus;
   He that answers is the same.

Joseph Hart first published this hymn in his *Hymns*, etc., 1759, in four eight-line stanzas. The hymn was altered in *Hymnologia Christiana*, etc., B. H. Kennedy, 1863, and much improved. It is in this revised form that the hymn is now commonly used.

For comments on the tune "Ringe recht" see Hymn No. 155.

359   Christ, Whose Glory Fills the Skies

1. Christ, whose glory fills the skies,
   Thou, the true, the only Light,
   Sun of Righteousness, arise,
   Triumph o'er the shades of night.
   Dayspring from on high, be near;
   Day-star, in my heart appear.

2. Dark and cheerless is the morn
   Unaccompanied by Thee;
   Joyless is the day's return
   Till Thy mercy's beams I see,
   Till they inward light impart,
   Glad my eyes, and warm my heart.

3. Visit, then, this soul of mine,
   Pierce the gloom of sin and grief;
   Fill me, Radiancy Divine,
   Scatter all my unbelief.
   More and more Thyself display,
   Shining to the perfect day.

Charles Wesley published this hymn in *Hymns and Sacred Poems*, 1740. It was entitled "A Morning Hymn." It is one of Wesley's finest hymns.

For comments on the tune "Ratisbon" see Hymn No. 20.

360   Oh, for a Thousand Tongues to Sing

1. Oh, for a thousand tongues to sing
   My great Redeemer's praise,
   The glories of my God and King,
   The triumphs of His grace!

2. My gracious Master and my God,
   Assist me to proclaim,
   To spread through all the earth abroad,
   The honors of Thy name.

3. Jesus! — the name that charms our fears,
   That bids our sorrows cease;
   'Tis music in the sinner's ears,
   'Tis life and health and peace.

4. He breaks the power of canceled sin,
   He sets the prisoner free;
   His blood can make the foulest clean;
   His blood avails for me.

5. Look unto Him, ye nations; own
   Your God, ye fallen race.
   Look and be saved through faith alone,
   Be justified by grace.

6. See all your sins on Jesus laid;
   The Lamb of God was slain;
   His soul was once an offering made
   For every soul of man.

7. Glory to God and praise and love
   Be ever, ever given
   By saints below and saints above,
   The Church in earth and heaven.

Charles Wesley wrote this hymn in 1739 to celebrate the first anniversary of his spiritual rebirth. It was published in his *Hymns and Sacred Poems*,

THE REDEEMER

1740. The original, beginning "Glory to God and praise and love," has eighteen stanzas. The cento is composed of Stanzas 7 to 10, 13, 14, and 1. The complete hymn reads:

1. Glory to God, and praise and love,
Be ever, ever given;
By saints below and saints above,
The Church in earth and heaven.

2. On this glad day the glorious Sun
Of Righteousness arose;
On my benighted soul He shone
And filled it with repose.

3. Sudden expired the legal strife;
'Twas then I ceased to grieve.
My second, real, living life
I then began to live.

4. Then with my heart I first believed,
Believed with faith divine;
Power with the Holy Ghost received
To call the Savior mine.

5. I felt my Lord's atoning blood
Close to my soul applied;
Me, me, He loved, the Son of God;
For me, for me, He died!

6. I found, and owned His promise true,
Ascertained of my part;
My pardon passed in heaven, I knew,
When written on my heart.

7. Oh, for a thousand tongues to sing
My dear Redeemer's praise;
The glories of my God and King,
The triumphs of His grace!

8. My gracious Master and my God,
Assist me to proclaim,
To spread through all the earth abroad,
The honors of Thy name.

9. Jesus, the name that charms our fears,
That bids our sorrows cease;
'Tis music in the sinner's ears,
'Tis life and health and peace.

10. He breaks the power of canceled sin,
He sets the prisoner free;
His blood can make the foulest clean;
His blood availed for me.

11. He speaks; and listening to His voice,
New life the dead receive;
The mournful, broken hearts rejoice,
The humble poor believe.

12. Hear Him, ye deaf; His praise, ye dumb,
Your loosened tongues employ;
Ye blind, behold your Savior come;
And leap, ye lame, for joy.

13. Look unto Him, ye nations; own
Your God, ye fallen race;
Look and be saved through faith alone,
Be justified by grace.

14. See all your sins on Jesus laid:
The Lamb of God was slain;
His soul was once an offering made
For every soul of man.

15. Harlots and publicans and thieves
In holy triumph join.
Saved is the sinner that believes
From crimes as great as mine.

16. Murderers and all ye hellish crew,
Ye sons of lust and pride,
Believe the Savior died for you;
For me the Savior died.

17. Awake from guilty nature's sleep.
And Christ shall give you light:
Cast all your sins into the deep
And wash the Ethiop white.

18. With me, your chief, ye then shall know,
Shall feel, your sins forgiven,
Anticipate your heaven below,
And own that love is heaven.

In this connection it will be of interest to read what Charles Wesley has to say about his conversion in his *Journal:*

Sunday, May 21, 1738. I waked in expectation of His coming. At nine my brother and some friends came and sang a hymn to the Holy Ghost. My comfort and hope were hereby increased. In about half an hour they went. I betook myself to prayer, the substance as follows: "O Jesus, Thou hast said, 'I will come unto you;' Thou hast said, 'I will send the Comforter unto you.' Thou art God, who canst not lie. I wholly rely upon Thy most true promise; accomplish it in Thy time and manner." . . . Still I felt a violent opposition and reluctance to believe; yet still the Spirit of God strove with my own and the evil spirit till by degrees He chased away the darkness of my unbelief. I found myself convinced, I knew not how nor when, and immediately fell to intercession.

The tune "Beatitudo" was composed by John B. Dykes for the *Revised Edition of Hymns Ancient and Modern,* 1875, where it was set to the hymn "How Bright These Glorious Spirits Shine" by Isaac Watts and W. Cameron.

THE REDEEMER

361   O Jesus, King Most Wonderful

1. O Jesus, King most wonderful,
   Thou Conqueror renowned,
   Thou Sweetness most ineffable,
   In whom all joys are found!

2. When once Thou visitest the heart,
   Then truth begins to shine,
   Then earthly vanities depart,
   Then kindles love divine.

3. O Jesus, Light of all below,
   Thou Fount of life and fire,
   Surpassing all the joys we know,
   All that we can desire, —

4. May every heart confess Thy name
   And ever Thee adore
   And, seeking Thee, itself inflame
   To seek Thee more and more!

5. Thee may our tongues forever bless,
   Thee may we love alone,
   And ever in our lives express
   The image of Thine own!

---

1. Iesu, Rex admirabilis
   Et Triumphator nobilis,
   Dulcedo ineffabilis,
   Totus Desiderabilis,

2. Quando cor nostrum visitas,
   Tunc lucet ei veritas,
   Mundi vilescit vanitas,
   Et intus fervet caritas.

3. Iesu, Dulcedo cordium,
   Fons vitae, Lumen mentium,
   Excedis omne gaudium
   Et omne desiderium.

4. Iesum omnes agnoscite,
   Amorem eius poscite,
   Iesum ardenter quaerite,
   Quaerendo inardescite.

5. Te nostra, Iesu, vox sonet,
   Nostri te mores exprimant,
   Te corda nostra diligant
   Et nunc et in perpetuum.

This hymn is from the same poem as Hymn No. 350. The cento begins "Iesu, Rex admirabilis." For further comments on the origin and on the translation see under that hymn.

The tune "St. Agnes" is by John B. Dykes. It first appeared in the *Hymnal for Use in the English Church,* 1866, where it was set to this hymn.

362   My Soul's Best Friend, What Joy and Blessing

1. My soul's best Friend, what joy and blessing
   My spirit ever finds in Thee!
   From gloomy depths of doubt distressing
   Into Thine arms for rest I flee.
   There will the night of sorrow vanish
   When from my heart Thy love doth banish
   All anguish and all pain and fear.
   Yea, here on earth begins my heaven;
   Who would not joyful be when given
   A loving Savior always near!

2. For though the evil world revile me
   And prove herself my bitter foe
   Or by her smile seek to beguile me,
   I trust her not; her wiles I know.
   In Thee alone my soul rejoices,
   Thy praise alone it gladly voices,
   For Thou art true when friendships flee.
   The world may hate but cannot fell me;
   Would mighty waves of trial quell me,
   I anchor in Thy loyalty.

3. Through deserts of the cross Thou leadest;
   I follow, leaning on Thy hand.
   From out the cloud Thy child Thou feedest
   And givest water from the sand.
   I trust Thy ways, howe'er distressing;
   I know my path will end in blessing;
   Enough that Thou wilt be my Stay.
   For whom to honor Thou intendest
   Oft into sorrow's vale Thou sendest;
   The night must e'er precede the day.

4. My soul's best Friend, how well contented
   Am I, reposing on Thy breast;
   By sin no more am I tormented
   Since Thou dost grant me peace and rest.

---

1. Wie wohl ist mir, o Freund der Seelen,
   Wenn ich in deiner Liebe ruh'!
   Ich steige aus der Schwermut Höhlen
   Und eile deinen Armen zu;
   Da muss die Nacht des Trauerns scheiden,
   Wenn mit so angenehmen Freuden
   Die Liebe strahlt aus deiner Brust.
   Hier ist mein Himmel schon auf Erden;
   Wer wollte nicht vergnüget werden,
   Der in dir suchet Ruh' und Lust?

2. Die Welt mag meine Feindin heissen,
   Es sei also! Ich trau' ihr nicht,
   Wenn sie mir gleich will Lieb' erweisen
   Bei einem freundlichen Gesicht.
   In dir vergnügt sich meine Seele,
   Du bist mein Freund, den ich erwähle.
   Du bleibst mein Freund, wenn Freundschaft weicht.
   Der Welt Hass kann mich doch nicht fällen,
   Weil in den stärksten Unglückswellen
   Mir deine Treu' den Anker reicht.

3. Führst du mich in die Kreuzeswüsten,
   Ich folg' und lehne mich auf dich,
   Du nährest aus den Wolkenbrüsten
   Und labest aus dem Felsen mich.
   Ich traue deinen Wunderwegen,
   Sie enden sich in Lieb' und Segen.
   Genug, wenn ich dich bei mir hab'.
   Ich weiss, wen du willst herrlich zieren
   Und über Sonn' und Sterne führen,
   Den führest du zuvor hinab.

4. Wie ist mir denn, o Freund der Seelen,
   So wohl, wenn ich mich lehn' auf dich!
   Mich kann Welt, Not und Tod nicht quälen,
   Weil du, mein Gott, vergnügest mich.

Oh, may the grace that Thou hast given For me a foretaste be of heaven, Where I shall bask in joys divine! Away, vain world, with fleeting pleasures; In Christ I have abiding treasures. Oh, comfort sweet, my Friend is mine!	Lass solche Ruh' in dem Gemüte Nach deiner unumschränkten Güte Des Himmels süssen Vorschmack sein! Weg, Welt, mit allen Schmeicheleien! Nichts kann als Jesus mich erfreuen. O reicher Trost: mein Freund ist mein!

This hymn by Wolfgang C. Dessler, founded on Canticles 8:5, was first published in his *Gottgeheiligter Christen nützlich ergetzende Seelenlust,* etc., Nürnberg, 1692, in six stanzas. Lauxmann, in *Koch,* says of its origin:

> This hymn dates from the period when Dessler as a youth was residing in his native town of Nürnberg in ill health. He had given up the occupation of goldsmith and set himself to study at Altdorf, but lack of money and of health compelled him to abandon this also. He then maintained himself as a proof-reader in his native town and became the spiritual son and scholar in poesy of Erasmus Francisci, in whose powerful faith he found nourishment in his sorrows. Through his linguistic attainments as well as through his hymn he furthered the edification of the Christian populace; and what he here sang may have afforded stimulus to himself in the still greater troubles which he afterwards had to endure during his conrectorship and finally in his last thirty-five weeks' illness.

The cento omits Stanzas 3 and 5, which Catherine Winkworth translates thus:

3. The Law may threaten endless death
  From awful Sinai's burning hill,
Straightway from its consuming breath
  My soul through faith mounts higher still;
She throws herself at Jesus' feet
And finds with Him a safe retreat
  Where curse and death can never come.
Though all things threaten condemnation,
Yet, Jesus, Thou art my Salvation,
  For in Thy love I find my home.
	5. To others death seems dark and grim,
	  But not, Thou Life of life, to me.
	I know Thou ne'er forsakest him
	  Whose heart and spirit rest in Thee.
	Oh! who would fear his journey's close
	If from dark woods and lurking foes
	  He then find safety and release?
	Nay, rather, with a joyful heart
	From this dark region I depart
	  To Thy eternal light and peace.

The rather free translation is composite and was prepared for *The Lutheran Hymnal.*

The tune "Wie wohl ist mir" first appeared in Freylinghausen's *Geistreiches Gesang-Buch,* Halle, 1704. Tradition has it that it was composed by Dr. Christian F. Richter, the well-known physician at the Francke orphanage in Halle.

To Our Redeemer's Glorious Name — 363

1. To our Redeemer's glorious name
Awake the sacred song.
Oh, may His love, immortal flame,
Tune every heart and tongue!

2. His love, what human thought can reach,
What mortal tongue portray?
Imagination's utmost stretch
In wonder dies away.

3. He left His radiant throne on high,
Left realms of heavenly bliss,
And came to earth to bleed and die, —
Was ever love like this?

4. Dear Lord, while we adoring pay
Our humble thanks to Thee,
May every heart with rapture say,
"The Savior died for me!"

5. Oh, may the sweet, the blissful theme
Fill every heart and tongue
Till strangers love the charming name
And join the sacred song!

Anna Steele published this hymn in her *Poems on Subjects Chiefly Devotional,* 1760. It was headed "Praise to the Redeemer."

For comments on the tune "Bedford" see Hymn No. 284.

THE REDEEMER

364   How Sweet the Name of Jesus Sounds

1. How sweet the name of Jesus sounds
  In a believer's ear!
 It soothes his sorrows, heals his wounds,
  And drives away his fear.

2. It makes the wounded spirit whole
  And calms the troubled breast;
 'Tis manna to the hungry soul
  And to the weary, rest.

3. Dear name! The Rock on which I build,
  My Shield and Hiding-place;
 My never-failing Treasury, filled
  With boundless stores of grace.

4. By Thee my prayers acceptance gain
  Although with sin defiled.
 Satan accuses me in vain,
  And I am owned a child.

5. Jesus, my Shepherd, Guardian, Friend,
  My Prophet, Priest, and King,
 My Lord, my Life, my Way, my End,
  Accept the praise I bring.

6. Weak is the effort of my heart
  And cold my warmest thought;
 But when I see Thee as Thou art,
  I'll praise Thee as I ought.

7. Till then I would Thy love proclaim
  With every fleeting breath;
 And may the music of Thy name
  Refresh my soul in death!

"The name — JESUS" — under this title John Newton published this hymn in the *Olney Hymns*, 1779. Though most hymnals omit Stanza 4, this stanza has been retained because of the truth it stresses. In Stanza 5 Newton has "Jesus, my Shepherd, *Husband*, Friend." The Bride of the heavenly Bridegroom is not the individual Christian, but the Church as such.

For comments on the tune "St. Peter" see Hymn No. 286.

365   Jesus I Will Never Leave

1. Jesus I will never leave,
  Who for me Himself hath given;
 Firmly unto Him I'll cleave
  Nor from Him be ever driven.
 Life from Him doth light receive, —
 Jesus I will never leave.

2. Jesus I will never leave
  While on earth I am abiding;
 What I have to Him I give,
  In all cares in Him confiding.
 Naught shall me of Him bereave, —
 Jesus I will never leave.

3. Though my sight shall pass away,
  Hearing, taste, and feeling fail me;
 Though my life's last light of day
  Shall o'ertake and sore assail me;
 When His summons I receive,
 Jesus I will never leave.

4. Nor will I my Jesus leave
  When at last I shall come thither
 Where His saints He will receive,
  Where in bliss they live together.
 Endless joy to me He'll give, —
 Jesus I will never leave.

5. Not for earth's vain joys I crave
  Nor, without Him, heaven's pleasure;
 Jesus, who my soul did save,
  Evermore shall be my Treasure.
 He redemption did achieve, —
 Jesus I will never leave.

Meinen Jesum lass' ich nicht.
 Weil er sich für mich gegeben,
So erfordert meine Pflicht,
 Klettenweis' an ihm zu kleben;
Er ist meines Lebens Licht;
Meinen Jesum lass' ich nicht.

Jesum lass' ich nimmer nicht,
 Weil ich soll auf Erden leben;
Ihm hab' ich voll Zuversicht,
 Was ich bin und hab', ergeben,
Alles ist auf ihn gericht't;
Meinen Jesum lass' ich nicht.

Lass vergehen das Gesicht,
 Hören, Schmecken, Fühlen weichen,
Lass das letzte Tageslicht
 Mich auf dieser Welt erreichen,
Wenn der Lebensfaden bricht;
Meinen Jesum lass' ich nicht.

Ich werd' ihn auch lassen nicht,
 Wenn ich nun dahin gelanget,
Wo vor seinem Angesicht
 Frommer Christen Glaube pranget;
Mich erfreut sein Angesicht;
Meinen Jesum lass' ich nicht.

Nicht nach Welt, nach Himmel nicht
 Meine Seele wünscht und sehnet;
Jesum wünscht sie und sein Licht,
 Der mich hat mit Gott versöhnet,
Der mich freiet vom Gericht;
Meinen Jesum lass' ich nicht.

Jesum lass' ich nicht von mir,
 Geh' ihm ewig an der Seiten;
Christus wird mich für und für
 Zu dem Lebensbächlein leiten.
Selig, wer mit mir so spricht:
Meinen Jesum lass' ich nicht!

THE REDEEMER

Christian Keimann (Keymann) first published this hymn of love to Christ in A. Hammerschmidt's *Fest-, Buss- und Danklieder,* Zittau and Leipzig, 1658, in six stanzas. It is founded on the words of Jacob in Gen. 32:26. The hymn is an acrostic on the dying words of Johann Georg, Elector of Saxony, October 8, 1656. The first word in each of the first five stanzas forms the sentence "Meinen Jesum lass' ich nicht." In Stanza 6 the first letters in each line form the initials J. G. C. Z. S., *i. e.,* Johann Georg, Churfürst zu Sachsen, and in Line 6 the full motto is repeated as uttered by the Elector. Though Stanza 6 is omitted in the English text, it is given above for the purpose of showing the acrostic formation.

The translation is composite.

For comments on the tune "Meinen Jesus lass' ich nicht" see Hymn No. 55.

One Thing's Needful; Lord, This Treasure 366

1. One thing's needful; Lord, this treasure
   Teach me highly to regard;
   All else, though it first give pleasure,
   Is a yoke that presses hard.
   Beneath it the heart is still fretting and striving,
   No true, lasting happiness ever deriving.
   The gain of this one thing all loss can requite
   And teach me in all things to find true delight.

2. Wilt thou find this one thing needful,
   Turn from all created things
   Unto Jesus and be heedful
   Of the blessed joy He brings.
   For where God and Man both in one are united,
   With God's perfect fulness the heart is delighted;
   There, there, is the worthiest lot and the best,
   My One and my All, and my Joy and my Rest.

3. How were Mary's thoughts devoted
   Her eternal joy to find
   As intent each word she noted,
   At her Savior's feet reclined!
   How kindled her heart, how devout was its feeling,
   While hearing the lessons that Christ was revealing!
   For Jesus all earthly concerns she forgot,
   And all was repaid in that one happy lot.

4. Thus my longings, heavenward tending,
   Jesus, rest alone on Thee.
   Help me, thus on Thee depending;
   Savior, come and dwell in me.
   Although all the world should forsake and forget Thee,
   In love I will follow Thee, ne'er will I quit Thee.
   Lord Jesus, both spirit and life is Thy Word;
   And is there a joy which Thou dost not afford?

5. Wisdom's highest, noblest treasure,
   Jesus, lies concealed in Thee;
   Grant that this may still the measure
   Of my will and actions be,
   Humility there and simplicity reigning,
   In paths of true wisdom my steps ever training.
   Oh, if I of Christ have this knowledge divine,
   The fulness of heavenly wisdom is mine.

Eins ist not, ach Herr, dies eine
   Lehre mich erkennen doch!
Alles andre, wie's auch scheine,
   Ist ja nur ein schweres Joch,
Darunter das Herze sich naget und plaget
Und dennoch kein wahres Vergnügen erjaget.
Erlang' ich dies eine, das alles ersetzt,
So werd' ich mit einem in allem ergötzt.

Seele, willst du dieses finden,
   Such's bei keiner Kreatur;
Lass, was irdisch ist, dahinten,
   Schwing dich über die Natur.
Wo Gott und die Menschheit in einem vereinet,
Wo alle vollkommene Fülle erscheinet:
Da, da ist das beste, notwendigste Teil,
Mein ein und mein alles, mein seligstes Heil.

Wie Maria war beflissen
   Auf des einigen Geniess,
Da sie sich zu Jesu Füssen
   Voller Andacht niederliess —
Ihr Herze entbrannte, dies einzig zu hören,
Was Jesus, ihr Heiland, sie wollte belehren;
Ihr alles war gänzlich in Jesum versenkt,
Und wurde ihr alles in einem geschenkt —,

Also ist auch mein Verlangen,
   Liebster Jesu, nur nach dir;
Lass mich treulich an dir hangen,
   Schenke dich zu eigen mir!
Ob viel' auch umkehrten zum grössesten Haufen,
So will ich dir dennoch in Liebe nachlaufen,
Denn dein Wort, o Jesu, ist Leben und Geist;
Was ist wohl, das man nicht in Jesu geneusst?

Aller Weisheit höchste Fülle
   In dir ja verborgen liegt.
Gib nur, dass sich auch mein Wille
   Fein in solche Schranken fügt,
Worinnen die Demut und Einfalt regieret
Und mich zu der Weisheit, die himmlisch ist, führet.
Ach, wenn ich nur Jesum recht kenne und weiss,
So hab' ich der Weisheit vollkommenen Preis.

[261]

THE REDEEMER

6. Naught have I, O Christ, to offer
   Naught but Thee, my highest Good.
Naught have I, O Lord, to proffer
   But Thy crimson-colored blood.
Thy Death on the cross hath Death wholly
   defeated
And thereby my righteousness fully
   completed;
Salvation's white raiments I there did obtain,
And in them in glory with Thee I shall
   reign.

7. Therefore Thou alone, my Savior,
   Shalt be All in all to me;
Search my heart and my behavior,
   Root out all hypocrisy.
Restrain me from wandering on pathways
   unholy
And through all life's pilgrimage keep my
   heart lowly.
This one thing is needful, all others are vain;
I count all but loss that I Christ may obtain.

Nichts kann ich vor Gott ja bringen
   Als nur dich, mein höchstes Gut;
Jesu, es muss mir gelingen
   Durch dein rosinfarbnes Blut.
Die höchste Gerechtigkeit ist mir
   erworben,
Da du bist am Stamme des Kreuzes
   gestorben;
Die Kleider des Heils ich da habe erlangt,
Worinnen mein Glaube in Ewigkeit
   prangt.

Drum auch, Jesu, du alleine,
   Sollst mein ein und alles sein.
Prüf, erfahre, wie ich's meine,
   Tilge allen Heuchelschein!
Sieh, ob ich auf bösem, betrüglichem
   Stege,
Und leite mich, Höchster, auf ewigem
   Wege!
Gib, dass ich hier alles nur achte für Kot
Und Jesum gewinne! Dies eine ist not.

Johann H. Schröder published this hymn, in ten stanzas, in the *Geistreiches Gesangbuch,* Halle, 1697. It was entitled "One thing is needful. Luke 10:42. Jesus, who of God is made unto us Wisdom and Righteousness and Sanctification and Redemption. 1 Cor. 1:30." The cento omits Stanzas 7 to 9, which read:

7. Let my soul, in full exemption,
   Wake up in Thy likeness now;
Thou art made to me Redemption,
   My Sanctification Thou.
Whatever I need for my journey to heaven,
In Thee, O my Savior, is unto me given;
Oh, let me all perishing pleasure forego,
And Thy life, O Jesus, alone let me know.

8. Where should else my hopes be centered?
   Grace o'erwhelms me with its flood;
Thou, my Savior, once hast entered
   Holiest heaven through Thy blood.
Eternal redemption for sinners there finding,
From hell's dark dominion my spirit unbinding,
To me perfect freedom Thy entrance has bought,
And childlike to cry, "Abba, Father," I'm taught.

9. Christ Himself, my Shepherd, feeds me,
   Peace and joy my spirit fill;
In a pasture green He leads me
   Forth beside the waters still.
Oh, naught to my soul is so sweet and reviving
As thus unto Jesus alone to be living;
True happiness this, and this only, supplies,
Through faith on my Savior to fasten mine eyes.

The translation by Frances E. Cox appeared in her *Sacred Hymns from the German,* 1841. It has been altered for inclusion in *The Lutheran Hymnal.*

The tune "Eins ist not" is by Friedrich Layriz, dated 1849. It appeared in his *Geistliche Melodien,* II, 1850, set to this hymn. According to Zahn, Layriz discarded this tune and returned to Freylinghausen's in his *Kern des deutschen Kirchengesangs.*

367   Hail, Thou Once Despised Jesus

1. Hail, Thou once despisèd Jesus!
   Hail, Thou Galilean King!
Thou didst suffer to release us;
   Thou didst free salvation bring.
Hail, Thou universal Savior,
   Who hast borne our sin and shame,
By whose merits we find favor!
   Life is given through Thy name.

2. Paschal Lamb, by God appointed,
   All our sins on Thee were laid;
By almighty love anointed,
   Thou hast full atonement made.
Every sin may be forgiven
   Through the virtue of Thy blood;
Open is the gate of heaven,
   Peace is made 'twixt man and God.

3. Jesus, hail, enthroned in glory,
   There forever to abide!
   All the heavenly host adore Thee,
   Seated at Thy Father's side.
   There for sinners Thou art pleading,
   There Thou dost our place prepare,
   Ever for us interceding
   Till in glory we appear.

4. Worship, honor, power, and blessing
   Thou art worthy to receive;
   Loudest praises, without ceasing,
   Meet it is for us to give.
   Help, ye bright angelic spirits,
   Bring your sweetest, noblest lays;
   Help to sing our Savior's merits,
   Help to chant Immanuel's praise.

This hymn appeared in various forms in English and American hymnals. It was first published in a tract which is bound together in a volume of *Poetical Tracts,* 1757—74, in the Bodleian Library at Oxford. This pamphlet bears the title *A Collection of Hymns,* etc. On page 40 two stanzas of this hymn are given, Stanza 1 as above and Stanza 2 made up of Stanza 3, Lines 1 to 4, and Stanza 4, Lines 1 to 4 as above. In M. Madan's *Collection of Psalms and Hymns,* 1760, the hymn appeared in four stanzas, the first as above; the second (new) as above; the third, Lines 1 to 4, as above, and Lines 5 to 8 new; the fourth, Stanza 4, as above. In *Psalms and Hymns,* 1776, a revised text, by A. M. Toplady, appeared. The changes were made largely in the interest of his strict Calvinistic views. It is in this version that Lines 5 to 8 of Stanza 3, as above, are first found. Some hymn-books attribute the hymn to John Bakewell. This seems to be an error.

For comments on the tune "O Durchbrecher" see Hymn No. 129.

The Lord My Pasture Shall Prepare 368

1. The Lord my pasture shall prepare
   And feed me with a shepherd's care;
   His presence shall my wants supply
   And guard me with a watchful eye;
   My noonday walks He shall attend
   And all my midnight hours defend.

2. When in the sultry glebe I faint
   Or on the thirsty mountain pant,
   To fertile vales and dewy meads
   My weary, wanderng steps He leads,
   Where peaceful rivers, soft and slow,
   Amid the verdant landscape flow.

3. Though in the paths of death I tread,
   With gloomy horrors overspread,
   My steadfast heart shall fear no ill,
   For Thou, O Lord, art with me still;
   Thy friendly crook shall give me aid
   And guide me through the dreadful shade.

4. Though in a bare and rugged way,
   Through devious lonely wilds, I stray,
   Thy bounty shall my pains beguile;
   The barren wilderness shall smile,
   With sudden greens and herbage crowned,
   And streams shall murmur all around.

This seems to be the first of Joseph Addison's hymns. It was published in the *Spectator* on Saturday, July 26, 1712, in an article entitled "Divine Providence" and was introduced with these words: "David has very beautifully represented this steady reliance on God Almighty in his Twenty-third Psalm, which is a kind of pastoral hymn, and filled with those allusions which are usually found in that kind of writing. As the poetry is very exquisite, I shall present my readers with the following translation of it." It is signed "O."

The tune "Surrey" was composed for this hymn by Henry Carey. It is found in *Introduction to Psalmody,* c. 1723. It is also called "Yarmouth," "Addison's," etc.

Faith and Justification

369   All Mankind Fell in Adam's Fall

1. All mankind fell in Adam's fall,
One common sin infects them all;
From sire to son the bane descends,
And over all the curse impends.

2. Through all man's powers corruption creeps
And him in dreadful bondage keeps;
In guilt he draws his infant breath
And reaps its fruits of woe and death.

3. From hearts depraved, to evil prone,
Flow thoughts and deeds of sin alone;
God's image lost, the darkened soul
Nor seeks nor finds its heavenly goal.

4. But Christ, the second Adam, came
To bear our sin and woe and shame,
To be our Life, our Light, our Way,
Our only Hope, our only Stay.

5. As by one man all mankind fell
And, born in sin, was doomed to hell,
So by one Man, who took our place,
We all received the gift of grace.

6. We thank Thee, Christ; new life is ours,
New light, new hope, new strength, new powers;
May grace our every way attend
Until we reach our journey's end!

This hymn is a free translation, in long meter, of Lazarus Spengler's hymn "Durch Adams Fall ist ganz verderbt," which is in nine stanzas of eight lines. Spengler's hymn first appeared in the *Geystliche gesangk Buchleyn,* Wittenberg, 1524. *Julian* rightly states:

> During the Reformation period it attained a wide popularity as a didactic and confessional hymn of the Evangelical faith. It is one of the most characteristic hymns of the time, conceived in the spirit of deep and earnest piety, eminently Scriptural, and setting forth the Reformation teachings in concise and antithetical form, but is, however, too much like a system of theology in rime.

The English version is by Matthias Loy. It was included in the Ohio *Lutheran Hymnal,* 1880.

For comments on the tune "Wenn wir in höchsten Nöten" see Hymn No. 522.

370   My Hope is Built on Nothing Less

1. My hope is built on nothing less
Than Jesus' blood and righteousness;
I dare not trust the sweetest frame,
But wholly lean on Jesus' name.
On Christ, the solid Rock, I stand;
All other ground is sinking sand.

2. When darkness veils His lovely face,
I rest on His unchanging grace;
In every high and stormy gale
My anchor holds within the veil.
On Christ, the solid Rock, I stand;
All other ground is sinking sand.

3. His oath, His covenant, and blood
Support me in the whelming flood;
When every earthly prop gives way,
He then is all my Hope and Stay.
On Christ, the solid Rock, I stand;
All other ground is sinking sand.

4. When He shall come with trumpet sound,
Oh, may I then in Him be found,
Clothed in His righteousness alone,
Faultless to stand before the throne!
On Christ, the solid Rock, I stand;
All other ground is sinking sand.

Edward Mote first published this hymn in six stanzas in a separate print, beginning "Nor earth nor hell my soul can move," about the year 1834. He told the following story of its origin in the *Gospel Herald:*

> One morning it came into my mind, as I went to labor, to write an hymn on the "Gracious Experience of a Christian." As I went up Holborn, I had the chorus:
> On Christ, the solid Rock, I stand;
> All other ground is sinking sand.
>
> In the day I had four first verses complete and wrote them off. On the Sabbath following I met Brother King as I came out of Lisle Street Meet-

ing, . . . who informed me that his wife was very ill, and asked me to call and see her. I had an early tea and called afterwards. He said that it was his usual custom to sing a hymn, read a portion, and engage in prayer before he went to meeting. He looked for his hymn-book, but could find it nowhere. I said, "I have some verses in my pocket"; if he liked, we would sing them. We did; and his wife enjoyed them so much that after service he asked me, as a favor, to leave a copy of them for his wife. I went home and by the fireside composed the last two verses, wrote the whole off, and took them to Sister King. . . . As these verses so met the dying woman's case, my attention to them was the more arrested, and I had a thousand printed for distribution. I sent one to the *Spiritual Magazine*, without my initials, which appeared some time after this. Brother Rees of Crown Street, Soho, brought out an edition of hymns (1836), and this hymn was in it. David Denham introduced it (1837) with Rees's name and others after. . . . Your inserting this brief outline may in future shield me from the charge of stealth and be a vindication of truthfulness in my connection with the Church of God.

He published the hymn in his *Hymns of Praise*, 1836. The form in which the hymn is usually found is as above. In order to see the metamorphosis through which the hymn passed to reach that form, we give the complete original, without the refrain:

1. Nor earth nor hell my soul can move,
I rest upon unchanging love;
I dare not trust the sweetest frame,
But wholly lean on Jesus' name.

2. My hope is built on nothing less
Than Jesus' blood and righteousness;
Midst all the hell I feel within,
On His completed work I lean.

3. When darkness veils His lovely face,
I rest upon unchanging grace;
In every high and stormy gale
My anchor holds within the veil.

4. His oath, His covenant, and His blood
Support me in the sinking flood;
When all around my soul gives way,
He then is all my Hope and Stay.

5. I trust His righteous character,
His council, promise, and His power;
His honor and His name at stake
To save me from the burning lake.

6. When I shall launch in worlds unseen,
Oh, may I then be found in Him,
Dressed in His righteousness alone,
Faultless to stand before the throne!

The tune "Magdalen," also called "Rest," is by John Stainer. It was composed in 1873 for the London Church Choir Association. It was included in the *Revised Edition* of *Hymns Ancient and Modern*, 1875.

Jesus, Thy Blood and Righteousness 371

1. Jesus, Thy blood and righteousness
My beauty are, my glorious dress;
Midst flaming worlds, in these arrayed,
With joy shall I lift up my head.

2. Bold shall I stand in that great Day,
For who aught to my charge shall lay?
Fully through these absolved I am
From sin and fear, from guilt and shame.

3. The holy, meek, unspotted Lamb,
Who from the Father's bosom came,
Who died for me, e'en me t'atone,
Now for my Lord and God I own.

4. Lord, I believe Thy precious blood,
Which at the mercy-seat of God
Forever doth for sinners plead,
For me — e'en for my soul — was shed.

5. Lord, I believe were sinners more
Than sands upon the ocean shore,
Thou hast for all a ransom paid,
For all a full atonement made.

6. When from the dust of death I rise
To claim my mansion in the skies,
E'en then, this shall be all my plea:
Jesus hath lived and died for me.

7. Jesus, be endless praise to Thee,
Whose boundless mercy hath for me,
For me, and all Thy hands have made,
An everlasting ransom paid.

FAITH AND JUSTIFICATION

Nikolaus Ludwig von Zinzendorf wrote the original of this hymn in thirty-three stanzas, 1739, during his return journey from the island of St. Thomas, where the Moravians had a mission. It was published, in the same year, in *Appendix VIII* to the *Herrnhut Gesangbuch*. Stanza 1 is no doubt based on Paul Eber's hymn "In Christi Wunden schlaf' ich ein." (See Hymn No. 585.) John Wesley "freely reproduced and abridged the hymn" and published it in twenty-four stanzas in his *Hymns and Sacred Poems*, in 1740. Wesley's hymn, in abbreviated forms, is found in many modern hymnals. As we have not been able to find a complete version of Wesley's version, we are not able to say which stanzas comprise the cento above.

For comments on the tune "St. Crispin" see Hymn No. 245.

372   Through Jesus' Blood and Merit

1. Through Jesus' blood and merit
 I am at peace with God;
 What, then, can daunt my spirit,
 However dark my road?
 My courage shall not fail me,
 For God is on my side;
 Though hell itself assail me,
 Its rage I may deride.

2. There's naught that me can sever
 From the great love of God;
 No want, no pain whatever,
 No famine, peril, flood.
 Though thousand foes surround me,
 For slaughter mark Thy sheep,
 They never shall confound me,
 The victory I shall reap.

3. Yea, neither life's temptation
 Nor death's so trying hour,
 Nor angels of high station,
 Nor any other power,
 Nor things that now are present,
 Nor things that are to come,
 Nor height, however pleasant,
 Nor depth of deepest gloom,

4. Nor any creature ever
 Shall from the love of God
 This wretched sinner sever;
 For in my Savior's blood
 This love its fountain taketh;
 He hears my faithful prayer
 And nevermore forsaketh
 This child of His and heir.

Ich bin bei Gott in Gnaden
 Durch Christi Blut und Tod.
Was kann mir endlich schaden?
 Was acht' ich alle Not?
Ist er auf meiner Seiten,
 Gleichwie er wahrlich ist,
Lass immer mich bestreiten
 Auch alle Höllenlist.

Was wird mich können scheiden
 Von Gottes Lieb' und Treu'?
Verfolgung, Armut, Leiden
 Und Trübsal mancherlei?
Lass Schwert und Blösse walten,
 Man mag durch tausend Pein
Mich für ein Schlachtschaf halten,
 Der Sieg bleibt dennoch mein,

Dass weder Tod noch Leben
 Und keiner Engel Macht,
Wie hoch sie möchte schweben,
 Kein Fürstentum, kein' Pracht,
Nichts dessen, was zugegen,
 Nichts, was die Zukunft hegt,
Nichts, welches hoch gelegen,
 Nichts, was die Tiefe trägt,

Noch sonst, was je erschaffen,
 Von Gottes Liebe mich
Soll scheiden oder raffen;
 Denn diese gründet sich
Auf Christi, Tod und Sterben.
 Ihn fleh' ich gläubig an,
Der mich, sein Kind und Erben,
 Nicht lassen will noch kann.

According to *Fisher*, Simon Dach wrote this hymn on the death of Count Achatius of Dohna, February 16, 1651, in six stanzas. It is based on Rom. 8:31 ff. In German hymnals it is usually given in five stanzas. The cento includes Stanzas 1, 2, 4, and 5 of this version.

The omitted stanza reads in the original:

> Ich kann um dessentwillen,
> Der mich geliebet hat,
> G'nug meinen Unmut stillen
> Und fassen Trost und Rat;
> Denn das ist mein Vertrauen,
> Der Hoffnung bin ich voll,
> Die weder Drang noch Grauen
> Mir ewig rauben soll,

The translation is composite.

For comments on the tune "Ich dank' dir, lieber Herre" see Hymn No. 32.

FAITH AND JUSTIFICATION

By Grace I'm Saved, Grace Free and Boundless 373

1. By grace I'm saved, grace free and
     boundless;
   My soul, believe and doubt it not.
   Why stagger at this word of promise?
   Hath Scripture ever falsehood
     taught?
   Nay; then this word must true remain:
   By grace thou, too, shalt heaven obtain.

2. By grace! None dare lay claim to merit;
   Our works and conduct have no worth.
   God in His love sent our Redeemer,
     Christ Jesus, to this sinful earth;
   His death did for our sins atone,
   And we are saved by grace alone.

3. By grace! Oh, mark this word of promise
   When thou art by thy sins opprest,
   When Satan plagues thy troubled
     conscience,
   And when thy heart is seeking rest.
   What reason cannot comprehend
   God by His grace to thee doth send.

4. By grace God's Son, our only Savior,
   Came down to earth to bear our sin.
   Was it because of thine own merit
     That Jesus died thy soul to win?
   Nay, it was grace, and grace alone,
   That brought Him from His heavenly throne.

5. By grace! This ground of faith is
     certain;
   So long as God is true, it stands.
   What saints have penned by inspiration,
     What in His Word our God commands,
   What our whole faith must rest upon,
   Is grace alone, grace in His Son.

6. By grace to timid hearts that
     tremble,
   In tribulation's furnace tried, —
   By grace, despite all fear and
     trouble,
   The Father's heart is open wide.
   Where could I help and strength secure
   If grace were not my anchor sure?

7. By grace! On this I'll rest when dying;
   In Jesus' promise I rejoice;
   For though I know my heart's condition,
     I also know my Savior's voice.
   My heart is glad, all grief has flown,
   Since I am saved by grace alone.

Aus Gnaden soll ich selig werden!
   Herz, glaubst du's, oder glaubst du's
     nicht?
Was willst du dich so blöd' gebärden?
   Ist's Wahrheit, was die Schrift
     verspricht,
So muss auch dieses Wahrheit sein:
Aus Gnaden ist der Himmel dein.

Aus Gnaden! — Hier gilt kein Verdienen,
   Die eignen Werke fallen hin;
Gott, der aus Lieb' im Fleisch erschienen,
   Bringt uns den seligen Gewinn,
Dass uns sein Tod das Heil gebracht
Und uns aus Gnaden selig macht.

Aus Gnaden! — Merk dies Wort: Aus
     Gnaden,
Sooft dich deine Sünde plagt,
Sooft dir will der Satan schaden,
   Sooft dich dein Gewissen nagt.
Was die Vernunft nicht fassen kann,
Das beut dir Gott aus Gnaden an.

Aus Gnaden kam sein Sohn auf Erden
   Und übernahm die Sündenlast.
Was nötigt' ihn, dein Freund zu werden?
   Sag's, wo du was zu rühmen hast!
War's nicht, dass er dein Bestes wollt'
Und dir aus Gnaden helfen sollt'?

Aus Gnaden! — Dieser Grund wird
     bleiben,
Solange Gott wahrhaftig heisst.
Was alle Knechte Jesu schreiben,
   Was Gott in seinem Wort anpreist,
Worauf all unser Glaube ruht,
Ist Gnade durch des Lammes Blut.

Aus Gnaden bleibt dem blöden Herzen
   Das Herz des Vaters aufgetan,
Wenn's unter grösster Angst und
     Schmerzen
Nichts sieht und nichts mehr hoffen
     kann.
Wo nähm' ich oftmals Stärkung her,
Wenn Gnade nicht mein Anker wär'!

Aus Gnaden! — Hierauf will ich sterben.
   Ich fühle nichts, doch mir ist wohl;
Ich kenn' mein sündliches Verderben,
   Doch auch den, der mich heilen soll.
Mein Geist ist froh, die Seele lacht,
Weil mich die Gnade selig macht.

Christian L. Scheidt based this hymn on Eph. 2:8, 9. It was written in ten stanzas and appeared in the *Ebersdorfer Gesangbuch*, 1742. The cento omits Stanzas 6, 7, and 10, which read in the translation of M. Loy:

6. By grace! But think not, thou who livest
     Securely on in godless ways,
   That thou — though all are called —
     receivest
   The promised rest that wakes our praise;
   By grace none find in heaven a place
   Who live in sin in hope of grace.

7. By grace! They who have heard
     this sentence
   Must bid hypocrisy farewell;
   For only after deep repentance
   The soul what grace imports can tell:
   To sin while grace a trifle seems,
   To faith it bright with glory beams.

10. By grace! May sin and Satan hearken!
      I bear my flag of faith in hand
    And pass — for doubts my joy can't darken —
      The Red Sea to the Promised Land.
    I cling to what my Savior taught
    And trust it, whether felt or not.

The translation of the cento is composite.

For comments on the tune "O dass ich tausend" (Dretzel) see Hymn No. 243.

374   Grace! 'Tis a Charming Sound

1. Grace! 'Tis a charming sound,
   Harmonious to the ear;
   Heaven with the echo shall resound,
   And all the earth shall hear.

2. Grace first contrived the way
   To save rebellious man,
   And all the steps that grace display
   Which drew the wondrous plan.

3. Grace first inscribed my name
   In God's eternal book;
   'Twas grace that gave me to the Lamb,
   Who all my sorrows took.

4. Grace led my wandering feet
   To tread the heavenly road;
   And new supplies each hour I meet
   While pressing on to God.

5. Grace taught my soul to pray
   And made mine eyes o'erflow;
   'Twas grace that kept me to this day
   And will not let me go.

6. Grace all the work shall crown
   Through everlasting days;
   It lays in heaven the topmost stone
   And well deserves the praise.

This hymn is the combined work of two men. Philip Doddridge, in his posthumous *Hymns*, etc., 1755, has the hymn, headed "Salvation by Grace. Eph. 2:5," in four stanzas, Stanzas 1, 2, 4, and 6 above.

In his *Psalms and Hymns*, 1776, Augustus M. Toplady added Stanzas 3 and 5 above, and this seventh stanza:

       Oh, let Thy grace inspire
         My soul with strength divine!
       May all my powers to Thee aspire
         And all my days be Thine!

The tune "Energy," also called "St. Ethelwald," was composed by Wm. H. Monk. It appeared in the original edition of *Hymns Ancient and Modern*, 1861, where it was set to Charles Wesley's hymn "Soldiers of Christ, Arise." (See Hymn No. 450.)

375   If Thy Beloved Son, O God

1. If Thy beloved Son, O God,
   Had not to earth descended
   And in our mortal flesh and blood
   Had not sin's power ended,
   Then this poor, wretched soul of mine
   In hell eternally would pine
   Because of its transgression.

2. But now I find sweet peace and rest,
   Despair no more reigns o'er me;
   No more am I by sin opprest,
   For Christ has borne sin for me.
   Upon the cross for me He died
   That, reconciled, I might abide
   With Thee, my God, forever.

3. I trust in Him with all my heart;
   Now all my sorrow ceases;
   His words abiding peace impart,
   His blood from guilt releases.
   Free grace through Him I now obtain;
   He washes me from every stain,
   And pure I stand before Him.

4. All righteousness by works is vain,
   The Law brings condemnation;
   True righteousness by faith I gain,
   Christ's work is my salvation.
   His death, that perfect sacrifice,
   Has paid the all-sufficient price;
   In Him my hope is anchored.

5. My guilt, O Father, Thou hast laid
   On Christ, Thy Son, my Savior.
   Lord Jesus, Thou my debt hast paid
   And gained for me God's favor.
   O Holy Ghost, Thou Fount of grace,
   The good in me to Thee I trace;
   In faith do Thou preserve me.

   Wenn dein herzliebster Sohn, o Gott,
     Nicht wär' auf Erden kommen
   Und hätt', da ich in Sünden tot,
     Mein Fleisch nicht angenommen,
   So müsst' ich armes Würmelein
   Zur Hölle wandern in die Pein
     Um meiner Untat willen.

   Jetzt aber hab' ich Ruh' und Rast,
     Darf nimmermehr verzagen,
   Weil er die schwere Sündenlast
     Für mich hat selbst getragen.
   Er hat mit dir versöhnet mich,
   Da er am Kreuz liess töten sich,
     Auf dass ich selig würde.

   Drum ist getrost mein Herz und Mut
     Mit kindlichem Vertrauen.
   Auf dies sein rosinfarbnes Blut
     Will ich mein' Hoffnung bauen,
   Das er für mich vergossen hat,
   Gewaschen ab die Missetat,
     Dass ich schneeweiss bin worden.

   Nichts hilft mir die Gerechtigkeit,
     Die vom Gesetz herrühret;
   Wer sich in eignem Werk erfreut,
     Wird jämmerlich verführet.
   Des Herren Jesu Werk allein,
   Das macht's, dass ich kann selig sein,
     Weil ich fest an ihn glaube.

   Gott Vater, der du alle Schuld
     Auf deinen Sohn geleget;
   Herr Jesu, dessen Lieb' und Huld
     All meine Sünden träget;
   O Heil'ger Geist, des Gnad' und Kraft
   Allein das Gute in mir schafft:
     Lass mich ans End' beharren!

FAITH AND JUSTIFICATION

Johann Heermann first published this hymn in his *Devoti Musica Cordis*, etc., Breslau, 1630, in five stanzas, of which Stanzas 1 to 3 and 5 are the first four above. The last stanza, a doxology, is by an unknown hand and appeared in Braunschweig *Gesangbuch* 1661.

The translation is composite.

For comments on the tune "Nun freut euch" see Hymn No. 387.

Rock of Ages, Cleft for Me   376

1. Rock of Ages, cleft for me,
Let me hide myself in Thee;
Let the water and the blood
From Thy riven side which flowed
Be of sin the double cure,
Cleanse me from its guilt and power.

2. Not the labors of my hands
Can fulfil Thy Law's demands;
Could my zeal no respite know,
Could my tears forever flow,
All for sin could not atone;
Thou must save, and Thou alone.

3. Nothing in my hand I bring,
Simply to Thy cross I cling;
Naked, come to Thee for dress;
Helpless, look to Thee for grace;
Foul, I to the fountain fly, —
Wash me, Savior, or I die!

4. While I draw this fleeting breath,
When mine eyelids close in death,
When I soar to worlds unknown,
See Thee on Thy judgment-throne,
Rock of Ages, cleft for me,
Let me hide myself in Thee!

This hymn is held by many to be the greatest hymn in the English language. It was written by Augustus M. Toplady and appeared in full in the *Gospel Magazine*, March, 1776, of which Toplady was the editor. In October, 1775, in the same periodical, in an article by Toplady, entitled "Life a Journey," this paragraph had appeared:

Yet, if you fall, be humbled; but do not despair. Pray afresh to God, who is able to raise you up and to set you on your feet again. Look to the blood of the covenant and say to the Lord from the depth of your heart:

Rock of Ages, cleft for me,
Let me hide myself in thee!
Foul, I to the fountain fly:
Wash me, Savior, or I die.

Make those words of the apostle your motto: "Perplexed, but not in despair; cast down, but not destroyed."

It is likely that the hymn was written in 1775 and not published complete until March, 1776.

The hymn was headed "A Living and Dying Prayer for the Holiest Believer in the World."

In his *Psalms and Hymns*, 1776, Toplady published the hymn again, with some alterations in the last stanza. When the hymn was taken into hymnbooks, various editors made changes, some of which were not improvements, however.

The text above follows Toplady's text from his *Psalms and Hymns*, except in Line 2, Stanza 4, where the author had: "When my eye-strings break in death."

Julian states: "No other English hymn can be named which has laid so broad and firm a grasp upon the English-speaking world."

The tune "Toplady," composed for this hymn by Thomas Hastings in 1830, was first published in the collection, *Spiritual Songs for Social Worship*, 1831, edited by the composer and Lowell Mason.

377 Salvation unto Us has Come

1. Salvation unto us has come
By God's free grace and favor;
Good works cannot avert our doom,
They help and save us never.
Faith looks to Jesus Christ alone,
Who did for all the world atone;
He is our one Redeemer.

2. What God did in His Law demand
And none to Him could render
Caused wrath and woe on every hand
For man, the vile offender.
Our flesh has not those pure desires
The spirit of the Law requires,
And lost is our condition.

3. It was a false, misleading dream
That God His Law had given
That sinners should themselves redeem
And by their works gain heaven.
The Law is but a mirror bright
To bring the inbred sin to light
That lurks within our nature.

4. From sin our flesh could not abstain,
Sin held its sway unceasing;
The task was useless and in vain,
Our gilt was e'er increasing.
None can remove sin's poisoned dart
Or purify our guileful heart, —
So deep is our corruption.

5. Yet as the Law must be fulfilled
Or we must die despairing,
Christ came and hath God's anger stilled,
Our human nature sharing.
He hath for us the Law obeyed
And thus the Father's vengeance stayed
Which over us impended.

6. Since Christ hath full atonement made
And brought to us salvation,
Each Christian therefore may be glad
And build on this foundation.
Thy grace alone, dear Lord, I plead,
Thy death is now my life indeed,
For Thou hast paid my ransom.

7. Let me not doubt, but trust in Thee,
Thy Word cannot be broken;
Thy call rings out, "Come unto Me!"
No falsehood hast Thou spoken.
Baptized into Thy precious name,
My faith cannot be put to shame,
And I shall never perish.

8. The Law reveals the guilt of sin
And makes men conscience-stricken;
The Gospel then doth enter in
The sinful soul to quicken.
Come to the cross, trust Christ, and live;
The Law no peace can ever give,
No comfort and no blessing.

9. Faith clings to Jesus' cross alone
And rests in Him unceasing;
And by its fruits true faith is known,
With love and hope increasing.
Yet faith alone doth justify,
Works serve thy neighbor and supply
The proof that faith is living.

---

1. Es ist das Heil uns kommen her
Von Gnad' und lauter Güte,
Die Werke helfen nimmermehr,
Sie mögen nicht behüten,
Der Glaub' sieht Jesum Christum an
Der hat g'nug für uns all' getan,
Er ist der Mittler worden.

2. Was Gott im G'setz geboten hat,
Da man es nicht konnt' halten,
Erhub sich Zorn und grosse Not
Vor Gott so mannigfalten;
Vom Fleisch wollt' nicht heraus der Geist,
Vom G'setz erfordert allermeist,
Es war mit uns verloren.

3. Es war ein falscher Wahn dabei,
Gott hätt' sein G'setz drum geben,
Als ob wir möchten selber frei
Nach seinem Willen leben;
So ist es nur ein Spiegel zart,
Der uns zeigt an die sünd'ge Art,
In unserm Fleisch verborgen.

4. Nicht möglich war es, diese Art
Aus eignen Kräften lassen.
Wiewohl es oft versuchet ward,
Doch mehrt' sich Sünd' ohn Massen;
Denn Gleisnerswerk Gott hoch verdammt,
Und je dem Fleisch der Sünde Schand'
Allzeit war angeboren.

5. Doch musst' das G'setz erfüllet sein,
Sonst wär'n wir all' verdorben;
Darum schickt' Gott sein'n Sohn herein,
Der selber Mensch ist worden;
Das ganz' Gesetz hat er erfüllt,
Damit sein's Vaters Zorn gestillt,
Der über uns ging alle.

6. Und wenn es nun erfüllet ist
Durch den, der es konnt' halten,
So lerne jetzt ein frommer Christ
Des Glaubens recht' Gestalte.
Nicht mehr, denn: Lieber Herre mein,
Dein Tod wird mir das Leben sein,
Du hast für mich bezahlet!

7. Daran ich keinen Zweifel trag',
Dein Wort kann nicht betrügen.
Nun sagst du, dass kein Mensch verzag',
Das wirst du nimmer lügen:
Wer glaubt an mich und wird getauft,
Demselben ist der Himm'l erkauft,
Dass er nicht wird verloren.

8. Es wird die Sünd' durchs G'setz erkannt
Und schlägt das G'wissen nieder,
Das Evangelium kommt zuhand
Und stärkt den Sünder wieder
Und spricht: Nur kreuch zum Kreuz herzu,
Im G'setz ist weder Rast noch Ruh'
Mit allen seinen Werken!

9. Die Werk', die kommen g'wisslich her
Aus einem rechten Glauben;
Denn das nicht rechter Glaube wär',
Wollt'st ihn der Werk' berauben.
Doch macht allein der Glaub' gerecht,
Die Werke sind des Nächsten Knecht',
Dabei wir'n Glauben merken.

FAITH AND JUSTIFICATION

10. All blessing, honor, thanks, and praise
  To Father, Son, and Spirit,
 The God that saved us by His grace, —
  All glory to His merit!
 O Triune God in heaven above,
 Who hast revealed Thy saving love,
  Thy blessed name be hallowed.

Sei Lob und Ehr' mit hohem Preis
 Um dieser Gutheit willen
Gott Vater, Sohn, Heiligem Geist!
 Der woll' mit Gnad' erfüllen,
Was er in uns ang'fangen hat
Zu Ehren seiner Majestät,
 Dass heilig werd' sein Name.

This is the most famous hymn of Paul Speratus and also one of the oldest and best known of Lutheran hymns. It was probably written in the fall of 1523 and then included in the first Lutheran hymnal, the so-called *Achtliederbuch,* entitled *Etlich christlich lider,* 1524. It was headed "A Hymn of Law and Faith, Powerfully Furnished with God's Word," and was in fourteen stanzas. It has been called "the true confessional hymn of the Reformation" and the "poetical counterpart of Luther's preface to the Epistle to the Romans." Miles Coverdale translated it for his *Goostly Psalmes and Spiritualle Songes,* c. 1539. The cento omits Stanzas 8, 11, 12, and 14.

The translation is composite.

The tune "Es ist das Heil," wedded to this text, appeared in the *Etlich christlich lider,* 1524. While some authorities think the tune was originally used with a German folk-song, others, like *Erk,* maintain that it was a church-tune, because of the note attached to the tune in the Erfurt *Enchiridion,* 1524, which states that it was used with the Easter hymn "Frewt euch, yhr frawen und yhr man, das Christ ist auferstanden."

All that I Was, My Sin, My Guilt 378

1. All that I was, my sin, my guilt,
 My death, was all my own;
 All that I am I owe to Thee,
  My gracious God, alone.

2. The evil of my former state
 Was mine, and only mine;
 The good in which I now rejoice
  Is Thine, and only Thine.

3. The darkness of my former state,
 The bondage, all was mine;
 The light of life in which I walk,
  The liberty, is Thine.

4. Thy Word first made me feel my sin,
 It taught me to believe;
 Then, in believing, peace I found,
  And now I live, I live!

5. All that I am, e'en here on earth,
 All that I hope to be,
 When Jesus comes and glory dawns,
  I owe it, Lord, to Thee.

Horatius Bonar first published this hymn in his *Bible Hymn Book,* 1845, in five stanzas. It was based upon 1 Cor. 15:10: "By the grace of God I am what I am."

The tune "St. Bernard" was adapted from a melody in *Tochter Zion,* Köln, 1741, a publication by H. Lindenborn. The name "St. Bernard" was given this tune because, when John Richardson rearranged the melody and published it in *Easy Hymn Tunes . . . for Catholic Schools,* c. 1851, he set it to the hymn ascribed to St. Bernard "Jesus, the Very Thought of Thee." (See Hymn No. 350.)

I do Not Come Because My Soul 379

1. I do not come because my soul
 Is free from sin and pure and whole
  And worthy of Thy grace;
 I do not speak to Thee because
 I've ever justly kept Thy laws
  And dare to meet Thy face.

2. I know that sin and guilt combine
 To reign o'er every thought of mine
  And turn from good to ill;
 I know that, when I try to be
 Upright and just and true to Thee,
  I am a sinner still.

3. I know that often when I strive
   To keep a spark of love alive
   For Thee, the powers within
   Leap up in unsubmissive might
   And oft benumb my sense of right
   And pull me back to sin.

4. I know that, though in doing good
   I spend my life, I never could
   Atone for all I've done;
   But though my sins are black as night,
   I dare to come before Thy sight
   Because I trust Thy Son.

5. In Him alone my trust I place,
   Come boldly to Thy Throne of grace,
   And there commune with Thee.
   Salvation sure, O Lord, is mine,
   And, all unworthy, I am Thine,
   For Jesus died for me.

This fine and expressive hymn was first published in M. W. Stryker's *Church Song*, New York, 1889, with the note that it is by "Frank B. St. John, 1878." We have been unable to obtain further information about the author. The hymn is a classic on Rom. 7:19-25. Though we know only the author's name, we can be thankful that he gave to the Church a hymn that deserves to be sung by God's people until the end of time.

For comments on the tune "Kommt her zu mir" see Hymn No. 263.

380   Thy Works, Not Mine, O Christ

1. Thy works, not mine, O Christ,
   Speak gladness to this heart;
   They tell me all is done,
   They bid my fear depart.
   To whom save Thee, who canst alone
   For sin atone, Lord, shall I flee?

2. Thy wounds, not mine, O Christ,
   Can heal my bruisèd soul;
   Thy stripes, not mine, contain
   The balm that makes me whole.
   To whom save Thee, who canst alone
   For sin atone, Lord, shall I flee?

3. Thy cross, not mine, O Christ,
   Has borne the awe-full load
   Of sins that none could bear
   But the incarnate God.
   To whom save Thee, who canst alone
   For sin atone, Lord, shall I flee?

4. Thy death, not mine, O Christ,
   Has paid the ransom due;
   Ten thousand deaths like mine
   Would have been all too few.
   To whom save Thee, who canst alone
   For sin atone, Lord, shall I flee?

5. Thy righteousness, O Christ,
   Alone can cover me;
   No righteousness avails
   Save that which is of Thee.
   To whom save Thee, who canst alone
   For sin atone, Lord, shall I flee?

Horatius Bonar first published this hymn in his *Hymns of Faith and Hope*, first series, 1857, entitled "The Sinbearer."

The tune "St. John" is from *The Parish Choir*, Vol. 3, 1851. The composer is unknown.

381   I Know My Faith is Founded

1. I know my faith is founded
   On Jesus Christ, my God and Lord;
   And this my faith confessing,
   Unmoved I stand upon His Word.
   Man's reason cannot fathom
   The truth of God profound;
   Who trusts her subtle wisdom
   Relies on shifting ground.
   God's Word is all-sufficient,
   It makes divinely sure,
   And trusting in its wisdom,
   My faith shall rest secure.

Ich weiss, an wen ich gläube:
   Mein Jesus ist des Glaubens Grund;
   Bei dessen Wort ich bleibe,
   Und das bekennet Herz und Mund.
   Vernunft darf hier nichts sagen,
   Sie sei auch noch so klug;
   Wer Fleisch und Blut will fragen,
   Der fällt in Selbstbetrug.
   Ich folg' in Glaubenslehren
   Der Heil'gen Schrift allein;
   Was diese mich lässt hören,
   Muss unbeweglich sein.

FAITH AND JUSTIFICATION

 2. Increase my faith, dear Savior,
  For Satan seeks by night and day
  To rob me of this treasure
  And take my hope of bliss away.
  But, Lord, with Thee beside me,
   I shall be undismayed;
  And led by Thy good Spirit,
   I shall be unafraid.
  Abide with me, O Savior,
   A firmer faith bestow;
  Then I shall bid defiance
   To every evil foe.

 3. In faith, Lord, let me serve Thee;
  Though persecution, grief, and pain
  Should seek to overwhelm me,
   Let me a steadfast trust retain;
  And then at my departure
   Take Thou me home to Thee
  And let me there inherit
   All Thou hast promised me.
  In life and death, Lord, keep me
   Until Thy heaven I gain,
  Where I by Thy great mercy
   The end of faith attain.

 Herr, stärke mir den Glauben;
  Denn Satan trachtet Nacht und Tag,
  Wie er dies Kleinod rauben
  Und um mein Heil mich bringen mag.
  Wenn deine Hand mich führet,
   So werd' ich sicher gehn;
  Wenn mich dein Geist regieret,
   Wird's selig um mich stehn.
  Ach segne mein Vertrauen
   Und bleib mit mir vereint!
  So lass' ich nicht grauen
   Und fürchte keinen Feind.

 Lass mich im Glauben leben;
  Soll auch Verfolgung, Angst und Pein
  Mich auf der Welt umgeben,
   So lass mich treu im Glauben sein!
  Im Glauben lass mich sterben,
   Wenn sich mein Lauf beschliesst,
  Und mich das Leben erben,
   Das mir verheissen ist!
  Nimm mich in deine Hände
   Bei Leb- und Sterbenszeit,
  So ist des Glaubens Ende
   Der Seelen Seligkeit.

Erdmann Neumeister first published this hymn in his *Evangelischer Nachklang*, etc., first part, Hamburg, 1718.

The translation is composite.

For comments on the tune "Nun lob, mein' Seel' " see Hymn No. 34.

Lord, We Confess Our Numerous Faults   382

1. Lord, we confess our numerous faults;
 How great our guilt has been,
How vain and foolish all our thoughts,
 And all our lives were sin.

2. But, O my soul, forever praise,
 Forever love, His name
Who turns thy feet from dangerous ways
 Of folly, sin, and shame.

3. 'Tis not by works of righteousness
 Which our own hands have done,
But we are saved by God's free grace
 Abounding through His Son.

4. 'Tis from the mercy of our God
 That all our hopes begin;
'Tis by the Water and the Blood
 Our souls are washed from sin.

5. 'Tis through the purchase of His death
 Who hung upon the tree
The Spirit is sent down to breathe
 On such dry bones as we.

6. Raised from the dead, we live anew;
 And justified by grace,
We shall appear in glory, too,
 And see our Father's face.

Isaac Watts first published this hymn in his *Hymns and Spiritual Songs*, second edition, 1709. It was entitled "Salvation by Grace. Titus 3:3, 7."

For comments on the tune "St. Flavian" see Hymn No. 22.

Seek Where Ye May to Find a Way   383

1. Seek where ye may To find a way
 That leads to your salvation;
My heart is stilled, On Christ I build,
 He is the one Foundation.
His Word is sure, His works endure;
He doth o'erthrow My every foe;
Through Him I more than conquer.

2. Seek whom ye may To be your stay;
 None can redeem his brother.
All helpers failed, This Man prevailed,
 The God-man, and none other.
Our Servant-Lord Did help afford;
We're justified, For He hath died,
The Guiltless for the guilty.

Such', wer da will, Ein ander Ziel,
 Die Seligkeit zu finden;
Mein Herz allein Bedacht soll sein,
 Auf Christum sich zu gründen.
Sein Wort ist wahr, Sein Werk ist klar,
Sein heil'ger Mund Hat Kraft und Grund,
All' Feind' zu überwinden.

Such', wer da will, Nothelfer viel,
 Die uns doch nichts erworben;
Hier ist der Mann, Der helfen kann,
 Bei dem nie was verdorben!
Uns wird das Heil Durch ihn zuteil,
Uns macht gerecht Der treue Knecht,
Der für uns ist gestorben.

3. Seek Him alone, Who did atone,
   Who did your souls deliver;
   Yea, seek Him first, All ye who thirst
   For grace that faileth never.
   In every need Seek Him indeed;
   To every heart He will impart
   His blessings without measure.

4. My heart's Delight, My Crown most bright,
   Thou, Jesus, art forever.
   Nor wealth nor pride Nor aught beside
   Our bond of love shall sever.
   Thou art my Lord; Thy precious Word
   Shall be my guide, Whate'er betide.
   Oh, teach me, Lord, to trust Thee!

5. Hide not from me, I ask of Thee,
   Thy gracious face and favor.
   Though floods of woe Should o'er me flow,
   My faith shall never waver.
   From pain and grief Grant sweet relief;
   For tears I weep, Lord, let me reap
   Thy heavenly joy and glory.

Ach sucht doch den, Lasst alles stehn,
Die ihr das Heil begehret!
Er ist der Herr Und keiner mehr,
Der euch das Heil gewähret.
Sucht ihn all' Stund' Von Herzensgrund,
Sucht ihn allein, Denn wohl wird sein
Dem, der ihn herzlich ehret.

Mein's Herzens Kron', Mein' Freudensonn'
Sollst du, Herr Jesu, bleiben;
Lass mich doch nicht Von deinem Licht
Durch Eitelkeit vertreiben!
Bleib du mein Preis, Dein Wort mich speis;
Bleib du mein' Ehr', Dein Wort mich lehr',
An dich stets fest zu gläuben!

Wend von mir nicht Dein Angesicht,
Lass mich im Kreuz nicht zagen;
Weich nicht von mir, Mein' höchste Zier,
Hilf mir mein Leiden tragen;
Hilf mir zur Freud' Nach diesem Leid,
Hilf, dass ich mag Nach dieser Klag'
Dir ewig dort lobsagen!

Georg Weissel first published this hymn in *Preussische Fest Lieder durchs gantze Jahr*, Part I, Elbing, 1642. It had been written by him in 1623. When he became pastor in Königsberg in that year, in conjunction with his entrance into office there, he dedicated the newly built church (Alt-Rossgärtsche Kirche) on the Third Sunday in Advent. He had composed the hymn for this occasion.

The translation by Arthur Voss was prepared for *The Lutheran Hymnal* in 1938.

The tune "Such', wer da will" is by Johann Stobäus, adapted. Weissel intended this tune for his hymn. Stobäus, a good friend of Weissel's, had composed the tune for the wedding of a friend for the words "Wie's Gott bestellt, mir's wohl gefällt."

384   Oh, How Great Is Thy Compassion

1. Oh, how great is Thy compassion,
   Faithful Father, God of grace,
   That with all our fallen race
   And in our deep degradation
   Thou wast merciful that we
   Might be saved eternally!

2. Thy great love for this hath striven
   That we may from sin be free
   And forever live with Thee;
   Yea, Thy Son Himself hath given
   And extends an earnest call
   To His Supper unto all.

3. And for this our soul's salvation
   Voucheth Thy good Spirit, Lord,
   In Thy Sacraments and Word.
   He imparts true consolation,
   Granteth us the gift of faith
   That we fear nor hell nor death.

4. Lord, Thy mercy will not leave me, —
   Truth doth evermore abide, —
   Then in Thee I will confide.
   Since Thy Word cannot deceive me,
   My salvation is to me
   Well assured eternally.

5. I will praise Thy great compassion,
   Faithful Father, God of grace,
   That with all our fallen race
   And in our deep degradation
   Thou wast merciful that we
   Might bring endless praise to Thee.

Ach, wie gross ist deine Gnade,
Du getreues Vaterherz,
Dass dich unsre Not und Schmerz,
Dass dich aller Menschen Schade
Hat erbarmet väterlich,
Uns zu helfen ewiglich!

Du hast uns so hoch geliebet,
Dass der Mensch soll aller Pein
Frei und ewig selig sein,
Dass dein Sohn sich selbst hingibet
Und beruft uns allzumal
Zu dem grossen Abendmahl.

Ja, dein werter Geist bezeuget
Durch die Tauf' und Abendmahl
Unser Heil im Himmelssaal,
Der die Herzen zu dir neiget,
Weil er uns den Glauben schenkt,
Dass uns Höll' und Tod nicht kränkt.

Weil die Wahrheit nicht kann lügen,
Will ich dir vertrauen fest,
Weil du keinen nicht verlässt;
Weil dein Wort nicht kann betrügen,
Bleibt mir meine Seligkeit
Unverrückt in Ewigkeit.

Lob sei dir für deine Gnade,
Du getreues Vaterherz,
Dass dich meine Not und Schmerz,
Dass dich auch mein Seelenschade
Hat erbarmt so väterlich;
Drum lob' ich dich ewiglich.

FAITH AND JUSTIFICATION

Johann Olearius wrote this hymn for the Second Sunday after Trinity (Gospel: Luke 14:16-24). It appeared in his *Geistliche Singe-Kunst*, Leipzig, 1671. The translation is by August Crull, altered.

The tune "Ach, was soll ich Sünder machen" is by an unknown composer. It appeared in the secular collection *Schäffer-Belustigung, oder zur Lehr und Ergetzlichkeit angestimmter Hirthenlieder*, etc., Altdorf, 1653, set to the song "Sylvius ging durch die Matten." It came into church use in Angelus Silesius's *Heilige Seelenlust*, 1657, where it was set to a Roman Catholic text, and in Johann Flitner's *Himmlische Lustgärtlein*, 1661, where it was set to his hymn "Ach, was soll ich Sünder machen."

Now I have Found the Firm Foundation   385

1. Now I have found the firm foundation
   Which holds mine anchor ever sure;
   'Twas laid before the world's creation
   In Christ my Savior's wounds secure;
   Foundation which unmoved shall stay
   When heaven and earth will pass away.

2. It is that mercy never ending,
   Which human wisdom far transcends,
   Of Him who, loving arms extending,
   To wretched sinners condescends;
   Whose heart with pity still doth break
   Whether we seek Him or forsake.

3. Our ruin God hath not intended,
   For our salvation He hath yearned;
   For this His Son to earth descended
   And then to heaven again returned;
   For this so patient evermore
   He knocketh at our heart's closed door.

4. O depth of love, to me revealing
   The sea where my sins disappear!
   In Christ my wounds find perfect healing,
   There is no condemnation here;
   For Jesus' blood through earth and skies
   Forever "Mercy! Mercy!" cries.

5. I never will forget this crying;
   In faith I'll trust it all my days,
   And when o'er all my sins I'm sighing,
   Into the Father's heart I'll gaze;
   For there is always to be found
   Free mercy without end and bound.

6. Though I be robbed of every pleasure
   That makes my soul and body glad
   And be deprived of earthly treasure
   And be forsaken, lone, and sad,
   And my desire for help seem vain,
   His mercy shall with me remain.

7. Though earthly trials should oppress me
   And cares from day to day increase;
   Though earth's vain things should sore distress me
   And rob me of my Savior's peace;
   Though I be brought down to the dust,
   Still in His mercy I will trust.

8. When all my deeds I am reviewing,
   The deeds that I admire the most,
   I find in all my thought and doing
   That there is naught whereof to boast.
   Yet this sweet comfort shall abide —
   In mercy I can still confide.

Ich habe nun den Grund gefunden,
Der meinen Anker ewig hält.
Wo anders als in Jesu Wunden?
Da lag er vor der Zeit der Welt,
Der Grund, der unbeweglich steht,
Wenn Erd' und Himmel untergeht.

Es ist das ewige Erbarmen,
Das alles Denken übersteigt;
Es sind die offnen Liebesarme
Des, der sich zu dem Sünder neigt,
Dem allemal das Herze bricht,
Wir kommen oder kommen nicht.

Wir sollen nicht verloren werden,
Gott will, uns soll geholfen sein;
Deswegen kam der Sohn auf Erden
Und nahm hernach den Himmel ein;
Deswegen klopft er für und für
So stark an unsre Herzenstür.

O Abgrund, welcher alle Sünden
Durch Christi Tod verschlungen hat!
Das heisst die Wunde recht verbinden,
Da findet kein Verdammen statt,
Weil Christi Blut beständig schreit:
Barmherzigkeit! Barmherzigkeit!

Darein will ich mich gläubig senken,
Dem will ich mich getrost vertraun
Und, wenn mich meine Sünden kränken,
Nur bald nach Gottes Herzen schaun;
Da findet sich zu aller Zeit
Unendliche Barmherzigkeit.

Wird alles andre weggerissen,
Was Seel' und Leib erquicken kann,
Darf ich von keinem Troste wissen
Und scheine völlig ausgetan,
Ist die Errettung noch so weit:
Mir bleibet doch Barmherzigkeit.

Beginnt das Irdische zu drücken,
Ja häuft sich Kummer und Verdruss,
Dass ich mich noch in vielen Stücken
Mit eitlen Dingen mühen muss,
Darüber sich mein Geist zerstreut,
So hoff' ich auf Barmherzigkeit.

Muss ich an meinen besten Werken,
Darinnen ich gewandelt bin,
Viel Unvollkommenheit bemerken,
So fällt wohl alles Rühmen hin;
Doch ist auch dieser Trost bereit:
Ich hoffe auf Barmherzigkeit.

9. Let mercy cause me to be willing
   To bear my lot and not to fret.
   While He my restless heart is stilling,
   May I His mercy not forget!
   Come weal, come woe, my heart to test,
   His mercy is my only rest.

Es gehe mir nach dessen Willen,
   Bei dem so viel Erbarmen ist;
   Er wolle selbst mein Herze stillen,
   Damit es das nur nicht vergisst;
   So stehet es in Lieb' und Leid
   In, durch und auf Barmherzigkeit.

10. I'll stand upon this firm foundation
    As long as I on earth remain;
    This shall engage my meditation
    While I the breath of life retain;
    And then, when face to face with Thee,
    I'll sing of mercy, great and free.

Bei diesem Grunde will ich bleiben,
    Solange mich die Erde trägt;
    Das will ich denken, tun und treiben,
    Solange sich ein Glied bewegt.
    So sing' ich einstens höchst erfreut:
    O Abgrund der Barmherzigkeit!

Johann A. Rothe is the author of this fine hymn. It was first published in Zinzendorf's *Christ-Catholische Singe- und Bet-Büchlein,* 1727. The following paragraph from *Julian* shows that there is uncertainty as to its exact date:

In the *Historische Nachricht* (to the *Brüder Gesang Buch,* 1778), ed. 1835, p. 176, it is said to have been written for Zinzendorf's birthday, May 26, 1728. This is probably a misprint for 1725, and the hymn, as will be seen above, was in print in 1727. *Koch,* II, 241, suggests that it was written in return for the hymn "Christum über alles lieben" which Zinzendorf had sent to Rothe in 1722 (in the *Sammlung,* 1725, No. 652, and in the *Deutsche Gedichte,* 1735, p. 30, marked as "on a friend's birthday," and dated May 12, 1722). This, if correct, would rather suggest 1723 as the date of Rothe's hymn; only in that case Zinzendorf would almost certainly have included it in the *Sammlung* of 1725. Zinzendorf, it may be added, gives in his *Deutsche Gedichte* two other pieces written for Rothe's birthdays, one dated 1724, for his 36th birthday (beginning "Wer von der Erde ist"), the other dated 1728, for his 40th birthday (beginning "Der du der Herzen König bist").

It was suggested by Heb. 6:19.

The translation is composite.

For comments on the tune "O dass ich tausend" (König) see Hymn No. 30.

386 My Savior Sinners Doth Receive

1. My Savior sinners doth receive
   Who find no rest and no salvation,
   To whom no man can comfort give,
   So great their guilt and condemnation;
   For whom the world is all too small,
   Their sins themselves and God appal;
   With whom the Law itself hath broken,
   On whom its judgment hath been spoken, —
   To them the Gospel hope doth give:
   My Savior sinners doth receive.

Mein Heiland nimmt die Sünder an,
   Die unter ihrer Last der Sünden
   Kein Mensch, kein Engel trösten kann,
   Die nirgends Ruh' und Rettung finden;
   Den'n selbst die weite Welt zu klein,
   Die sich und Gott ein Greuel sein,
   Den'n Moses schon den Stab gebrochen
   Und sie der Hölle zugesprochen,
   Wird diese Freistatt aufgetan:
   Mein Heiland nimmt die Sünder an.

2. A love more deep than mother-love,
   With which His heart was overflowing,
   Drew Him to earth from heaven above,
   On sinners boundless grace bestowing.
   He in their stead a curse became,
   He bore the cross with all its shame;
   Brought full atonement by His suffering,
   Gave up His life for them an offering.
   This comfort doth the Gospel give:
   My Savior sinners doth receive.

Sein mehr als mütterliches Herz
   Trieb ihn von seinem Thron auf Erden.
   Ihn drang der Sünder Weh und Schmerz,
   An ihrer Statt ein Fluch zu werden.
   Er senkte sich in ihre Not
   Und schmeckte den verdienten Tod.
   Nun da er denn sein eigen Leben
   Zur teuren Zahlung hingegeben,
   Und seinem Vater g'nuggetan,
   So heisst's: Er nimmt die Sünder an.

3. His loving bosom still remains
   A haven for the heavy-laden;
   Christ frees them from their guilty stains,
   Their burdened heart doth ease and gladden.
   He casts into the unfathomed sea
   The load of their iniquity;
   He gives assurance by His Spirit
   That they are saved through His own merit.
   Yea, they shall live who this believe:
   My Savior sinners doth receive.

Nun ist sein aufgetaner Schoss
   Ein sichres Schloss gejagter Seelen,
   Er spricht sie von dem Urteil los
   Und tilget bald ihr ängstlich Quälen,
   Es wird ihr ganzes Sündenheer
   Ins unergründlich tiefe Meer
   Von seinem reinen Blut versenket.
   Der Geist, der ihnen wird geschenket,
   Schwingt über sie die Gnadenfahn'.
   Mein Heiland nimmt die Sünder an.

FAITH AND JUSTIFICATION

4. Say not: "My sins are far too great,
   His mercy I have scorned and slighted,
Now my repentance is too late;
   I came not when His love invited."
O trembling sinner, have no fear;
In penitence to Christ draw near.
Come now, though conscience still is chiding;
Accept His mercy, e'er abiding.
Come; blest are they who this believe:
My Savior sinners doth receive.

5. Oh, draw us ever unto Thee,
   Thou Friend of sinners, gracious Savior;
Help us that we may fervently
   Desire Thy pardon, peace, and favor.
When guilty conscience doth reprove,
Reveal to us Thy heart of love.
May we, our wretchedness beholding,
See then Thy pardoning grace unfolding
And say: "To God all glory be:
My Savior, Christ, receiveth me."

Sprich nicht: Ich hab's zu grob gemacht,
   Ich hab' die Güter seiner Gnaden
So lang und schändlich umgebracht;
   Er hat mich oft umsonst geladen.
Wofern du's nur jetzt redlich meinst
Und deinen Fall mit Ernst beweinst,
So soll ihm nichts die Hände binden
Und du sollst noch Genade finden;
Er hilft, wenn sonst nichts helfen kann.
Mein Heiland nimmt die Sünder an.

Ja, zeuch uns selber recht zu dir,
   Holdselig süsser Freund der Sünder;
Erfüll mit sehnender Begier
   Auch uns und alle Adamskinder!
Zeig uns bei unserm Seelenschmerz
Dein aufgespaltnes Liebesherz:
Und wenn wir unser Elend sehen,
So lass uns ja nicht stille stehen,
Bis dass ein jeder sagen kann:
Gott Lob, auch mich nimmt Jesus an!

Leopold F. Lehr wrote this hymn, based on Luke 15:2, between 1731 and 1732, in eleven stanzas. It is reminiscent of Erdmann Neumeister's hymn "Jesus sinners doth receive." (See Hymn No. 324.) It was first published in *Einige Geistliche Lieder*, Cöthen, 1733. The hymn has become a great favorite in many circles. Ernst G. Woltersdorf wrote a response to it in sixty-eight stanzas, beginning

   Yes, Jesus sinners doth receive,
   'Tis true, and true it will remain.

The cento includes Stanzas 1 to 3 and 9 and 11 of the original.

Lehr wrote the hymn at the time when he was tutor to the princesses of Anhalt-Cöthen. It was a period of severe spiritual conflicts for him, and this hymn on the grace of God in Christ was as cold water to his thirsty soul.

The translation is composite.

The tune "Mein Heiland" appeared in Johann Thommen's *Erbaulicher Musicalischer Christe-Schatz*, etc., Basel, 1745, set to this hymn. It is found in manuscript form as early as 1735. The composer is unknown.

Dear Christians, One and All, Rejoice   387

1. Dear Christians, one and all, rejoice,
   With exultation springing,
And, with united heart and voice
   And holy rapture singing,
Proclaim the wonders God hath done,
How His right arm the victory won;
   Right dearly it hath cost Him.

2. Fast bound in Satan's chains I lay,
   Death brooded darkly o'er me,
Sin was my torment night and day,
   In sin my mother bore me;
Yea, deep and deeper still I fell,
Life had become a living hell,
   So firmly sin possessed me.

3. My own good works availed me naught,
   No merit they attaining;
Free will against God's judgment fought,
   Dead to all good remaining.
My fears increased till sheer despair
Left naught but death to be my share;
   The pangs of hell I suffered.

4. But God beheld my wretched state
   Before the world's foundation,
And, mindful of His mercies great,
   He planned my soul's salvation.
A father's heart He turned to me,
Sought my redemption fervently:
   He gave His dearest Treasure.

Nun freut euch, liebe Christen g'mein,
   Und lasst uns fröhlich springen,
Dass wir getrost und all' in ein
   Mit Lust und Liebe singen,
Was Gott an uns gewendet hat,
Und seine süsse Wundertat;
   Gar teu'r hat er's erworben.

Dem Teufel ich gefangen lag,
   Im Tod war ich verloren,
Mein' Sünd' mich quälte Nacht und Tag,
   Darin ich war geboren.
Ich fiel auch immer tiefer drein,
Es war kein Gut's am Leben mein,
   Die Sünd' hatt' mich besessen.

Mein' gute Werk', die galten nicht,
   Es war mit ihn'n verdorben;
Der frei' Will' hasste Gott's Gericht,
   Er war zum Gut'n erstorben.
Die Angst mich zu verzweifeln trieb,
Dass nichts denn Sterben bei mir blieb,
   Zur Hölle musst' ich sinken.

Da jammert' Gott in Ewigkeit
   Mein Elend übermassen,
Er dacht' an sein' Barmherzigkeit,
   Er wollt' mir helfen lassen;
Er wandt' zu mir das Vaterherz,
Es war bei ihm fürwahr kein Scherz,
   Er liess's sein Bestes kosten.

5. He spoke to His beloved Son:
'Tis time to have compassion.
Then go, bright Jewel of My crown,
And bring to man salvation;
From sin and sorrow set him free,
Slay bitter death for him that he
  May live with Thee forever.

6. This Son obeyed His Father's will,
Was born of virgin mother,
And God's good pleasure to fulfil,
He came to be my Brother.
No garb of pomp or power He wore,
A servant's form, like mine, He bore,
  To lead the devil captive.

7. To me He spake: Hold fast to Me,
I am thy Rock and Castle;
Thy Ransom I Myself will be,
  For thee I strive and wrestle;
For I am with thee, I am thine,
And evermore thou shalt be Mine;
  The Foe shall not divide us.

8. The Foe shall shed My precious blood,
Me of My life bereaving.
All this I suffer for thy good;
Be steadfast and believing.
Life shall from death the victory win,
My innocence shall bear thy sin;
  So art thou blest forever.

9. Now to My Father I depart,
The Holy Spirit sending
And, heavenly wisdom to impart,
My help to thee extending.
He shall in trouble comfort thee,
Teach thee to know and follow Me,
  And in all truth shall guide thee.

10. What I have done and taught, teach thou,
My ways forsake thou never;
So shall My kingdom flourish now
And God be praised forever.
Take heed lest men with base alloy
The heavenly treasure should destroy;
  This counsel I bequeath thee.

Er sprach zu seinem lieben Sohn:
Die Zeit ist hier zu 'rbarmen;
Fahr hin, mein's Herzens werte Kron',
Und sei das Heil dem Armen
Und hilf ihm aus der Sündennot,
Erwürg' für ihn den bittern Tod
Und lass ihn mit dir leben!

Der Sohn dem Vater g'horsam ward,
Er kam zu mir auf Erden
Von einer Jungfrau rein und zart,
Er sollt' mein Bruder werden.
Gar heimlich führt' er sein' Gewalt,
Er ging in meiner armen G'stalt,
Den Teufel wollt' er fangen.

Er sprach zu mir: Halt dich an mich,
Es soll dir jetzt gelingen;
Ich geb' mich selber ganz für dich,
Da will ich für dich ringen;
Denn ich bin dein, und du bist mein,
Und wo ich bleib', da sollst du sein,
Uns soll der Feind nicht scheiden.

Vergiessen wird er mir mein Blut,
Dazu mein Leben rauben;
Das leid' ich alles dir zugut.
Das halt mit festem Glauben!
Den Tod verschlingt das Leben mein,
Mein' Unschuld trägt die Sünde dein:
Da bist du selig worden.

Gen Himmel zu dem Vater mein
Fahr' ich von diesem Leben,
Da will ich sein der Meister dein,
Den Geist will ich dir geben,
Der dich in Trübnis trösten soll
Und lehren mich erkennen wohl
Und in der Wahrheit leiten.

Was ich getan hab' und gelehrt,
Das sollst du tun und lehren,
Damit das Reich Gott's werd' gemehrt
Zu Lob und seinen Ehren,
Und hüt' dich vor der Menschen G'satz,
Davon verdirbt der edle Schatz!
Das lass' ich dir zur Letze.

This is Luther's first congregational hymn. It was written in 1523, soon after Luther had composed his famous ballad "Ein neues Lied wir heben an." (See Hymn No. 259.) It appeared in *Etlich cristlich lider,* Wittenberg, 1524, entitled "A Christian hymn of Dr. Martin Luther, setting forth the unspeakable grace of God and the true faith." The blessings wrought by this hymn are well summarized in this paragraph of Tileman Hesshusius:

> I do not doubt that through this one hymn of Luther many hundreds of Christians have been brought to the true faith who before could not endure the name of Luther; but the noble, precious words of the hymn have won their hearts, so that they are constrained to embrace the truth, so that in my opinion the hymns have helped the spread of the Gospel not a little.

The translation is an altered form of that by Richard Massie in his *Martin Luther's Spiritual Songs,* 1854.

The tune "Nun freut euch," also called "Luther" and "Altdorf," has been inseparably wedded to the hymn since its appearance with the text in 1524. It is said to have been written down by Luther from hearing it sung by a traveling artisan.

FAITH AND JUSTIFICATION

Just as I Am, without One Plea   388

1. Just as I am, without one plea
But that Thy blood was shed for me
And that Thou bidd'st me come to Thee,
O Lamb of God, I come, I come.

2. Just as I am and waiting not
To rid my soul of one dark blot,
To Thee, whose blood can cleanse each spot,
O Lamb of God, I come, I come.

3. Just as I am, though tossed about
With many a conflict, many a doubt,
Fightings and fears within, without,
O Lamb of God, I come, I come.

4. Just as I am, poor, wretched, blind;
Sight, riches, healing of the mind,
Yea, all I need, in Thee to find,
O Lamb of God, I come, I come.

5. Just as I am, Thou wilt receive,
Wilt welcome, pardon, cleanse, relieve;
Because Thy promise I believe,
O Lamb of God, I come, I come.

6. Just as I am; Thy love unknown
Has broken every barrier down.
Now to be Thine, yea, Thine alone,
O Lamb of God, I come, I come.

Charlotte Elliott wrote this hymn, which ranks with the finest in our language, in 1834, and published it two years later in *The Invalids' Hymn Book*. It was headed with the text John 6:37, "All that the Father giveth Me shall come to Me; and him that cometh to Me I will in no wise cast out." Many stories are told about the hymn's origin, which are apocryphal. Miss Elliott's niece tells us the facts: The author was living at Westfield Lodge, Brighton, in 1834. Her brother, the Rev. H. V. Elliott, was arranging a bazaar in order to raise funds to assist in the building of a college where the daughters of poor clergymen might be educated at low expense. Miss Elliott's illness prevented her attendance, but she spent the hours while the family attended the bazaar in writing this hymn.

Her brother's testimony to the hymn's usefulness follows: "In the course of a long ministry I hope I have been permitted to see some fruit of my labor, but I feel that far more has been done by a single hymn of my sister's."

"Just as I Am" has been translated into many European languages and into the languages of many distant lands.

For comments on the first tune, "St. Crispin," see Hymn No. 245.

The tune "Woodworth" is undoubtedly the most popular of William B. Bradbury's tunes. It first appeared in *Psalmistra*, 1849. H. Augustine Smith says that it is one of the tunes "that mark the transition from Lowell Mason's more churchly tunes to the livelier Gospel songs that followed." If sung in moderate time, with due regard to the phrasing, the overemphasis of its rhythmic character can be avoided.

Not What These Hands have Done   389

1. Not what these hands have done
Can save this guilty soul;
Not what this toiling flesh has borne
Can make my spirit whole.

2. Not what I feel or do
Can give me peace with God;
Not all my prayers and sighs and tears
Can bear my awe-full load.

3. Thy work alone, O Christ,
Can ease this weight of sin;
Thy blood alone, O Lamb of God,
Can give me peace within.

4. Thy love to me, O God,
Not mine, O Lord, to Thee,
Can rid me of this dark unrest
And set my spirit free.

5. Thy grace alone, O God,
To me can pardon speak;
Thy power alone, O Son of God,
Can this sore bondage break.

6. I bless the Christ of God,
I rest on love divine,
And with unfaltering lip and heart
I call this Savior mine.

Horatius Bonar first published this hymn, in twelve stanzas, in his *Hymns of Faith and Hope*, second series, 1861. It is usually found in an abridged form in English and American hymnals.

For comments on the tune "St. Bride" see Hymn No. 322.

390   Drawn to the Cross, which Thou hast Blest

1. Drawn to the Cross, which Thou hast blest
With healing gifts for souls distrest,
To find in Thee my life, my rest,
   Christ Crucified, I come.

2. Thou knowest all my griefs and fears,
Thy grace abused, my misspent years;
Yet now to Thee with contrite tears,
   Christ Crucified, I come.

3. Wash me and take away each stain;
Let nothing of my sin remain.
For cleansing, though it be through pain,
   Christ Crucified, I come.

4. And then for work to do for Thee,
Which shall so sweet a service be
That angels well might envy me,
   Christ Crucified, I come.

Genevieve M. Irons wrote this hymn in 1880. It was entitled "Consecration of Self to Christ." It was published in her *Corpus Christi*, 1884. This was a Roman Catholic manual for Holy Communion.

The tune "Dunstan," also called "Just as I Am," is by Joseph Barnby and is dated 1883. It appeared in *The Home and School Hymnal* of the Free Church of Scotland, 1893. It is often used with Charlotte Elliott's hymn "Just as I Am." (See Hymn No. 388.)

391   Blessed Are the Sons of God

1. Blessèd are the sons of God,
They are bought with Christ's own blood;
They are ransomed from the grave,
Life eternal they shall have:
With them numbered may we be
Here and in eternity!

2. They are justified by grace,
They enjoy the Savior's peace;
All their sins are washed away,
They shall stand in God's great Day:
With them numbered may we be
Here and in eternity!

3. They are lights upon the earth,
Children of a heavenly birth;
One with God, with Jesus one;
Glory is in them begun:
With them numbered may we be
Here and in eternity!

Joseph Humphreys wrote this hymn in eight stanzas. It was published in *Sacred Hymns for the Use of Religious Societies*, Bristol, 1743, headed "The Priviledges of God's Children." The original form of the hymn is as follows:

1. Blessèd are the sons of God.
They are bought with Christ's own blood,
They are ransomed from the grave,
Life eternal they shall have.

2. God did love them in His Son
Long before the world begun;
They the seal of this receive
When on Jesus they believe.

3. They are justified by grace,
They enjoy a solid peace;
All their sins are washed away,
They shall stand in God's great Day.

4. They produce the fruits of grace
In the works of righteousness.
They are harmless, meek, and mild,
Holy, humble, undefiled.

5. They are lights upon the earth,
Children of a heavenly birth;
Born of God, they hate all sin,
God's pure seed remains within.

6. They have fellowship with God,
Through the Mediator's blood;
One with God, with Jesus one,
Glory is in them begun.

7. Though they suffer much on earth,
Strangers quite to this world's mirth,
Yet they have an inward joy,
Pleasure which can never cloy.

8. They alone are truly blest,
Heirs of God, joint heirs with Christ;
With them numbered may I be
Here and in eternity!

R. Conyers, in his *Collection of Psalms and Hymns*, 1767, gave the hymn a new form by using the last two lines of Stanza 8 as a refrain and making a hymn of five eight-line stanzas. A. M. Toplady, in his *Psalms and Hymns*, 1776, gave the hymn its six-line-stanza form, ending each stanza with this refrain, making a hymn of six stanzas.

For comments on the tune "Voller Wunder" see Hymn No. 11.

FAITH AND JUSTIFICATION

Blest Is the Man, Forever Blest 392

1. Blest is the man, forever blest,
 Whose guilt is pardoned by his God,
 Whose sins with sorrow are confessed
  And covered with his Savior's blood.

2. Blest is the man to whom the Lord
 Imputes not his iniquities;
 He pleads no merit of reward
  And not on works but grace relies.

3. From guile his heart and lips are free;
 His humble joy, his holy fear,
 With deep repentance well agree
  And join to prove his faith sincere.

4. How glorious is that righteousness
 That hides and cancels all his sins,
 While bright the evidence of grace
  Through all his life appears and shines!

This is Isaac Watts's long-meter version of Ps. 32. It appeared in his *Psalms of David Imitated,* 1719, headed "Repentance and Free Pardon; or, Justification and Sanctification." Watts explains the liberty he has taken with the psalm thus:

These first two verses of this psalm being cited by the apostle in the 4th chapter of Romans to show the freedom of our pardon and justification by grace without works, I have, in this version of it, enlarged the sense, by mention of the blood of Christ and faith and repentance; and because the psalmist adds "A spirit in which is no guile," I have inserted that sincere obedience, which is Scriptural evidence of our faith and justification.

For comments on the tune "O Jesu Christ, mein's" see Hymn No. 64.

Sanctification

393   From God Shall Naught Divide Me

1. From God shall naught divide me,
    For He is true for aye
   And on my path will guide me,
    Who else should often stray.
   His right hand holdeth me;
    For me He truly careth,
    My burdens ever beareth
   Wherever I may be.

2. When man's help and affection
    Shall unavailing prove,
   God grants me His protection
    And shows His power and love.
   He helps in every need,
    From sin and shame redeems me,
    From chains and bonds reclaims me,
   Yea, e'en from death I'm freed.

3. God shall be my Reliance
    In sorrow's darkest night;
   Its dread I bid defiance
    When He is at my right.
   I unto Him commend
    My body, soul, and spirit, —
    They are His own by merit, —
   All's well then at the end.

4. Oh, praise Him, for He never
    Forgets our daily need;
   Oh, blest the hour whenever
    To Him our thoughts can speed;
   Yea, all the time we spend
    Without Him is but wasted,
    Till we His joy have tasted,
   The joy that hath no end.

5. Yea, when the world shall perish
    With all its pride and power,
   Whatever worldlings cherish
    Shall vanish in that hour.
   But though in death they make
    The deepest grave our cover,
    When there our sleep is over,
   Our God will us awake.

6. What though I here must suffer
    Distress and trials sore,
   I merit ways still rougher;
    And yet there is in store
   For me eternal bliss,
    Yea, pleasures without measure,
    Since Christ is now my Treasure
   And shall be evermore.

Von Gott will ich nicht lassen,
 Denn er lässt nicht von mir,
Führt mich auf rechter Strassen,
 Da ich sonst irrte sehr.
Reichet mir seine Hand.
 Den Abend wie den Morgen
 Tut er mich wohl versorgen,
Sei, wo ich woll', im Land.

Wenn sich der Menschen Hulde
 Und Wohltat all' verkehrt,
So find't sich Gott gar balde,
 Sein' Macht und Gnad' bewährt,
Hilfet aus aller Not,
 Errett't von Sünd' und Schanden,
 Von Ketten und von Banden,
Und wenn's auch wär' der Tod.

Auf ihn will ich vertrauen
 In meiner schweren Zeit;
Es kann mich nicht gereuen,
 Er wendet alles Leid.
Ihm sei es heimgestellt;
 Mein Leib, mein' Seel', mein Leben
 Sei Gott dem Herrn ergeben,
Er mach's, wie's ihm gefällt!

Lobt ihn mit Herz und Munde,
 Welch's er uns beides schenkt!
Das ist ein' sel'ge Stunde,
 Darin man sein gedenkt.
Sonst verdirbt alle Zeit,
 Die wir zubring'n auf Erden;
 Wir sollen selig werden
Und bleib'n in Ewigkeit.

Mag uns die Welt entgehen
 Mit ihrer stolzen Pracht,
Nicht Ruhm, nicht Gut bestehen,
 Die einst wir gross geacht't,
Mag man uns nach dem Tod
 Tief in die Erd' begraben:
 Wenn wir geschlafen haben,
Wird uns erwecken Gott.

Darum, ob ich schon dulde
 Hier Widerwärtigkeit,
Wie ich's auch wohl verschulde,
 Kommt doch die Ewigkeit,
Die aller Freuden voll;
 Dieselb' ohn' alles Ende,
 Dieweil ich Christum kenne,
Mir widerfahren soll.

Ludwig Helmbold wrote this hymn, c. 1563, in nine stanzas. *Koch* relates its origin thus:

  In 1563, while Helmbold was conrector of the *Gymnasium* at Erfurt, a pestilence broke out, during which about 4,000 of the inhabitants died. As all who could fled from the place, Dr. Pancratius Helbich, rector of the university (with whom Helmbold had formed a special friendship and whose wife was godmother of his eldest daughter), was about to do so, leaving behind him Helmbold and his family. Gloomy forebodings filled the hearts of the parting mothers. To console them and nerve them for parting, Helmbold composed this hymn on Ps. 73:23.

CONSECRATION

The hymn was first published as a broadsheet and dedicated to Dr. Helbich's wife. It is Helmbold's finest hymn. The cento omits Stanzas 4, 7, and 9.

The translation is an altered form of that by Catherine Winkworth in her *Chorale Book for England,* 1863.

The tune "Von Gott will ich nicht lassen" is from *Christliche vnd Tröstliche Tischgesenge,* Erfurt, 1572. It is supposed to be from a secular melody, a hunter's song, "Ich ging einmal spazieren."

My Faith Looks Up to Thee   394

1. My faith looks up to Thee,
 Thou Lamb of Calvary,
  Savior divine.
 Now hear me while I pray;
 Take all my guilt away;
 Oh, let me from this day
  Be wholly Thine!

2. May Thy rich grace impart
 Strength to my fainting heart,
  My zeal inspire!
 As Thou hast died for me,
 Oh, may my love to Thee
 Pure, warm, and changeless be,
  A living fire!

3. While life's dark maze I tread
 And griefs around me spread,
  Be Thou my Guide.
 Bid darkness turn to day,
 Wipe sorrow's tears away,
 Nor let me ever stray
  From Thee aside.

4. When ends life's transient dream,
 When death's cold, sullen stream
  Shall o'er me roll,
 Blest Savior, then, in love,
 Fear and distrust remove;
 Oh, bear me safe above,
  A ransomed soul!

Ray Palmer tells us that he wrote this hymn in 1830 shortly after graduating from Yale College, while serving as a teacher in New York. He was twenty-two years old at the time. Not long afterwards the text was given to Lowell Mason for use, if suitable, in *Spiritual Songs for Social Worship,* etc., a work which he and Thomas Hastings published in 1831. Lowell Mason composed the tune, there given as "My Faith Looks Up to Thee," but subsequently called "Olivet." Ray Palmer describes the circumstances thus:

> A year or two after the hymn was written, and when no one, so far as can be recollected, had ever seen it, Dr. Lowell Mason met the author in the street in Boston and requested him to furnish some hymns for a *Hymn and Tune Book* which, in connection with Doctor Hastings of New York, he was about to publish. The little book containing the hymn was shown him, and he asked for a copy. We stepped into a store together, and a copy was made and given to him, which, without much notice, he put into his pocket. On sitting down at home and looking it over, he became so much interested in it that he wrote for it the tune "Olivet," to which it has almost universally been sung. Two or three days afterward we met again in the street, when, scarcely waiting to salute the writer, he earnestly exclaimed: "Mr. Palmer, you may live many years and do many good things, but I think you will be best known to posterity as the author of 'My Faith Looks Up to Thee!'"

O God, Thou Faithful God   395

1. O God, Thou faithful God,
  Thou Fountain ever flowing,
 Who good and perfect gifts
  In mercy art bestowing,
 Give me a healthy frame,
  And may I have within
 A conscience free from blame,
  A soul unhurt by sin!

O Gott, du frommer Gott,
 Du Brunnquell guter Gaben,
Ohn' den nichts ist, was ist,
 Von dem wir alles haben:
Gesunden Leib gib mir,
 Und dass in solchem Leib
Ein' unverletzte Seel'
 Und rein Gewissen bleib'.

2. Grant Thou me strength to do
   With ready heart and willing
Whate'er Thou shalt command,
   My calling here fulfilling;
To do it when I ought,
   With all my might, and bless
The work I thus have wrought,
   For Thou must give success.

3. Oh, let me never speak
   What bounds of truth exceedeth;
Grant that no idle word
   From out my mouth proceedeth;
And then, when in my place
   I must and ought to speak,
My words grant power and grace
   Lest I offend the weak.

4. If dangers gather round,
   Still keep me calm and fearless;
Help me to bear the cross
   When life is dark and cheerless;
And let me win my foe
   With words and actions kind.
When counsel I would know,
   Good counsel let me find.

5. And let me with all men,
   As far as in me lieth,
In peace and friendship live.
   And if Thy gift supplieth
Great wealth and honor fair,
   Then this refuse me not,
That naught be mingled there
   Of goods unjustly got.

6. If Thou a longer life
   Hast here on earth decreed me;
If Thou through many ills
   To age at length wilt lead me,
Thy patience on me shed.
   Avert all sin and shame
And crown my hoary head
   With honor free from blame.

7. Let me depart this life
   Confiding in my Savior;
Do Thou my soul receive
   That it may live forever;
And let my body have
   A quiet resting-place
Within a Christian grave;
   And let it sleep in peace.

8. And on that solemn Day
   When all the dead are waking,
Stretch o'er my grave Thy hand,
   Thyself my slumbers breaking.
Then let me hear Thy voice,
   Change Thou this earthly frame,
And bid me aye rejoice
   With those who love Thy name.

Gib, dass ich tu' mit Fleiss,
   Was mir zu tun gebühret,
Wozu mich dein Befehl
   In meinem Stande führet!
Gib, dass ich's tue bald,
   Zu der Zeit, da ich soll,
Und wenn ich's tu', so gib,
   Dass es gerate wohl!

Hilf, dass ich rede stets,
   Womit ich kann bestehen,
Lass kein unnützes Wort
   Aus meinem Munde gehen;
Und wenn in meinem Amt
   Ich reden soll und muss,
So gib den Worten Kraft
   Und Nachdruck ohn' Verdruss!

Find't sich Gefährlichkeit,
   So lass mich nicht verzagen;
Gib einen Heldenmut,
   Das Kreuz hilf selber tragen!
Gib, dass ich meinen Feind
   Mit Sanftmut überwind'
Und, wenn ich Rats bedarf,
   Auch guten Rat erfind'!

Lass mich mit jedermann
   In Fried' und Freundschaft leben,
Soweit es christlich ist.
   Willst du mir etwas geben
An Reichtum, Gut und Geld,
   So gib auch dies dabei,
Dass von unrechtem Gut
   Nichts untermenget sei!

Soll ich auf dieser Welt
   Mein Leben höher bringen,
Durch manchen sauern Tritt
   Hindurch ins Alter dringen,
So gib Geduld. Vor Sünd'
   Und Schanden mich bewahr',
Auf dass ich tragen mag
   Mit Ehren graues Haar!

Lass mich an meinem End'
   Auf Christi Tod abscheiden,
Die Seele nimm zu dir
   Hinauf zu deinen Freuden,
Dem Leib ein Räumlein gönn
   Bei frommer Christen Grab,
Auf dass er seine Ruh'
   An ihrer Seite hab'.

Wenn du an jenem Tag
   Die Toten wirst aufwecken,
So tu auch deine Hand
   Zu meinem Grab ausstrecken;
Lass hören deine Stimm'
   Und meinen Leib weck auf
Und führ ihn schön verklärt
   Zum auserwählten Hauf'!

Johann Heermann first published this hymn in his *Devoti Musica Cordis*, Breslau, 1630, entitled "A Daily Prayer." *Fischer* says:

It is one of the poet's most widely used and signally blessed hymns and has been not unjustly called his Master Song. If it is somewhat "home-baked," yet it is excellent, nourishing bread. It gives a training in practical Christianity and specially strikes three notes — godly living, patient suffering, and happy dying.

The translation is an altered form of that by Catherine Winkworth in her *Lyra Germanica*, second series, 1858.

The tune "O Gott, Du Frommer Gott," also called "Munich," is by an unknown composer. It appeared in the *Neuvermehrtes Gesangbuch*, Meiningen, 1693.

CONSECRATION

Oh, for a Faith that Will Not Shrink 396

1. Oh, for a faith that will not
   shrink
   Though pressed by many a foe;
   That will not tremble on the brink
   Of poverty or woe;

2. That will not murmur nor complain
   Beneath the chastening rod,
   But in the hour of grief or pain
   Can lean upon its God;

3. A faith that shines more bright and clear
   When tempests rage without;
   That, when in danger, knows no fear,
   In darkness feels no doubt;

4. That bears unmoved the world's dread
   frown
   Nor heeds its scornful smile;
   That sin's wild ocean cannot drown
   Nor Satan's arts beguile;

5. A faith that keeps the narrow way
   Till life's last spark is fled
   And with a pure and heavenly ray
   Lights up the dying bed.

6. Lord, give us such a faith as this;
   And then, whate'er may come,
   We'll taste e'en now the hallowed bliss
   Of an eternal home.

William H. Bathurst first published this hymn in his *Psalms and Hymns*, etc., 1831, entitled "The Power of Faith." Most hymnals omit Stanza 4, which, it is thought, somewhat disturbs the tenderness and simplicity of the hymn.

For comments on the tune "St. Peter" see Hymn No. 286.

O Love, Who Madest Me to Wear 397

1. O Love, who madest me to wear
   The image of Thy Godhead here;
   Who soughtest me with tender care
   Through all my wanderings wild and
   drear, —
   O Love, I give myself to Thee,
   Thine ever, only Thine, to be.

2. O Love, who ere life's earliest dawn
   On me Thy choice hast gently laid;
   O Love, who here as man wast born
   And like to us in all things made, —
   O Love, I give myself to Thee,
   Thine ever, only Thine, to be.

3. O Love, who once in time wast slain,
   Pierced through and through with bitter
   woe;
   O Love, who, wrestling thus, didst gain
   That we eternal joy might know, —
   O Love, I give myself to Thee,
   Thine ever, only Thine, to be.

4. O Love, who thus hast bound me fast
   Beneath that easy yoke of Thine;
   Love, who hast conquered me at last,
   Enrapturing this heart of mine, —
   O Love, I give myself to Thee,
   Thine ever, only Thine, to be.

5. O Love, who lovest me for aye,
   Who for my soul dost ever plead;
   O Love, who didst my ransom pay,
   Whose power sufficeth in my stead, —
   O Love, I give myself to Thee,
   Thine ever, only Thine, to be.

6. O Love, who once shalt bid me rise
   From out this dying life of ours;
   O Love, who once above yon skies
   Shalt set me in the fadeless bowers, —
   O Love, I give myself to Thee,
   Thine ever, only Thine, to be.

Liebe, die du mich zum Bilde
   Deiner Gottheit hast gemacht;
Liebe, die du mich so milde
   Nach dem Fall hast wieder-
   bracht:
Liebe, dir ergeb' ich mich,
Dein zu bleiben ewiglich.

Liebe, die du mich erkoren,
   Eh' als ich erschaffen war;
Liebe, die du Mensch geboren
   Und mir gleich wardst ganz und gar:
Liebe, dir ergeb' ich mich,
Dein zu bleiben ewiglich.

Liebe, die für mich gelitten
   Und gestorben in der
   Zeit;
Liebe, die mir hat erstritten
   Ew'ge Lust und Seligkeit:
Liebe, dir ergeb' ich mich,
Dein zu bleiben ewiglich.

Liebe, die mich hat gebunden
   An ihr Joch mit Leib und Sinn;
Liebe, die mich überwunden
   Und mein Herze hat dahin:
Liebe, dir ergeb' ich mich,
Dein zu bleiben ewiglich.

Liebe, die mich ewig liebet,
   Die für meine Seele bitt't;
Liebe, die das Lösgeld gibet
   Und mich kräftiglich vertritt:
Liebe, dir ergeb' ich mich,
Dein zu bleiben ewiglich.

Liebe, die mich wird erwecken
   Aus dem Grab der Sterblichkeit;
Liebe, die mich wird umstecken
   Mit dem Laub der Herrlichkeit:
Liebe, dir ergeb' ich mich,
Dein zu bleiben ewiglich.

Johann Scheffler (Angelus Silesius) first published this hymn in his *Heilige Seelen-Lust*, etc., Breslau, 1657. It is one of his "most beautiful and profound

CONSECRATION

hymns of the spiritual love of the soul to her Savior." Some German hymnals have the following fourth stanza, which was inserted later. It is not by Scheffler:

> Liebe, die du Kraft und Leben,
> Licht und Wahrheit, Geist und Wort;
> Liebe, die sich bloss ergeben
> Mir zum Heil und Seelenhort:
> Liebe, dir ergeb' ich mich,
> Dein zu bleiben ewiglich.

The translation is by Catherine Winkworth in her *Lyra Germanica*, Second Series, 1858.

The tune "Heut' triumphieret Gottes Sohn" is from *Deutsche Geistliche Lieder, Frankfurt* a. O., 1601, where it is set to the Easter hymn of Basilius Förtsch, beginning with that line.

398 Renew Me, O Eternal Light

1. Renew me, O eternal Light,
And let my heart and soul be bright,
Illumined with the light of grace
That issues from Thy holy face.

2. Destroy in me the lust of sin,
From all impureness make me clean.
Oh, grant me power and strength, my God,
To strive against my flesh and blood!

3. Create in me a new heart, Lord,
That gladly I obey Thy Word
And naught but what Thou wilt, desire;
With such new life my soul inspire.

4. Grant that I only Thee may love
And seek those things which are above
Till I behold Thee face to face,
O Light eternal, through Thy grace.

Erneure mich, o ew'ges Licht,
Und lass von deinem Angesicht
Mein Herz und Seel' mit deinem Schein
Durchleuchtet und erfüllet sein!

Ertöt in mir die schnöde Lust,
Feg aus den alten Sündenwust;
Ach rüst mich aus mit Kraft und Mut,
Zu streiten wider Fleisch und Blut!

Schaff in mir, Herr, den neuen Geist,
Der dir mit Lust Gehorsam leist't
Und nichts sonst, als was du willst, will;
Ach Herr, mit ihm mein Herz erfüll!

Auf dich lass meine Sinnen gehn,
Lass sie nach dem, was droben, stehn,
Bis ich dich schau', o ew'ges Licht,
Von Angesicht zu Angesicht!

Johann F. Ruopp wrote this hymn in sixteen stanzas. His authorship is based on Freylinghausen's testimony. It appeared in Freylinghausen's *Gesangbuch*, 1714, in the cento above, Stanzas 1 to 3 and 8 of the original. Knapp, in his *Evangelischer Liederschatz*, gives the hymn in twelve stanzas.

The translation is by August Crull.

For comments on the tune "Herr Jesu Christ, mein's" see Hymn No. 7.

399 Thee Will I Love, My Strength, My Tower

1. Thee will I love, my Strength, my Tower;
Thee will I love, my Hope, my Joy;
Thee will I love with all my power,
With ardor time shall ne'er destroy.
Thee will I love, O Light Divine,
So long as life is mine.

2. Thee will I love, my Life, my Savior,
Who art my best and truest Friend;
Thee will I love and praise forever,
For never shall Thy kindness end;
Thee will I love with all my heart,
Thou my Redeemer art.

3. I thank Thee, Jesus, Sun from heaven,
Whose radiance hath brought light to me;
I thank Thee, who hast richly given
All that could make me glad and free;
I thank Thee that my soul is healed
By what Thy lips revealed.

Ich will dich lieben, meine Stärke,
Ich will dich lieben, meine Zier,
Ich will dich lieben mit dem Werke
Und immerwährender Begier;
Ich will dich lieben, schönstes Licht,
Bis mir (der Tod) das Herze bricht.

Ich will dich lieben, o mein Leben,
Als meinen allerbesten Freund;
Ich will dich lieben und erheben,
Solange mich dein Glanz bescheint;
Ich will dich lieben, Gotteslamm,
Als meinen (lieben) Bräutigam.

Ich danke dir, du wahre Sonne,
Dass mir dein Glanz hat Licht gebracht;
Ich danke dir, du Himmelswonne,
Dass du mich froh und frei gemacht;
Ich danke dir, du güldner Mund,
Dass du mich (ewig) machst gesund.

CONSECRATION

4. Oh, keep me watchful, then, and humble
   And suffer me no more to stray;
   Uphold me when my feet would stumble,
   Nor let me loiter by the way.
   Fill all my nature with Thy light,
   O Radiance strong and bright!

5. Oh, teach me, Lord, to love Thee truly
   With soul and body, head and heart,
   And grant me grace that I may duly
   Practice fore'er love's sacred art.
   Grant that my every thought may be
   Directed e'er to Thee.

6. Thee will I love, my Crown of gladness;
   Thee will I love, my God and Lord,
   Amid the darkest depths of sadness,
   Not for the hope of high reward, —
   For Thine own sake, O Light Divine,
   So long as life is mine.

Erhalte mich auf deinen Stegen
Und lass mich nicht mehr irregehn;
Lass meinen Fuss auf deinen Wegen
Nicht strauchein oder stille stehn;
Erleucht mir Leib und Seele ganz,
Du starker (schöner) Himmelsglanz.

Gib meinen Augen süsse Tränen,
Gib meinem Herzen keusche Brunst.
Lass meine Seele sich gewöhnen,
Zu üben in der Liebeskunst.
Lass meinen Sinn, Geist und Verstand
Stets sein zu dir, (o Gott,) gewandt.

Ich will dich lieben, meine Krone,
Ich will dich lieben, meinen Gott;
Ich will dich lieben ohne Lohne,
Auch in der allergrössten Not.
Ich will dich lieben, schönstes Licht,
Bis mir (der Tod) das Herze bricht.

Johann Scheffler (Angelus Silesius) published this hymn of "love to Christ," in his *Heilige Seelenlust*, etc., 1657, in eight stanzas. The cento omits Stanzas 3 and 4, in which he apparently refers to the time when he was a member of the Lutheran Church, before his conversion to Roman Catholicism. They read in translation thus:

3. Alas! that I so late have known Thee,
   Who art the Fairest and the Best;
   Nor sooner for my Lord could own Thee,
   Our highest Good, our only Rest!
   Now bitter shame and grief I prove
   O'er this my tardy love.

4. I wandered long in willing blindness,
   I sought Thee, but I found Thee not,
   For still I shunned Thy beams of kindness;
   The creature-light filled all my thought.
   And if at last I see Thee now,
   'Twas Thou to me didst bow!

The translation is an altered form of that by Catherine Winkworth in her *Chorale Book for England*, 1863.

The tune "Ich will dich lieben" is from the *Harmonischer Liederschatz*, Frankfurt, 1738, where it was set to this hymn.

Take My Life and Let It Be   400

1. Take my life and let it be
   Consecrated, Lord, to Thee;
   Take my moments and my days,
   Let them flow in ceaseless praise.

2. Take my hands and let them move
   At the impulse of Thy love;
   Take my feet and let them be
   Swift and beautiful for Thee.

3. Take my voice and let me sing
   Always, only, for my King;
   Take my lips and let them be
   Filled with messages from Thee.

4. Take my silver and my gold,
   Not a mite would I withhold;
   Take my intellect and use
   Every power as Thou shalt choose.

5. Take my will and make it Thine,
   It shall be no longer mine;
   Take my heart, it is Thine own,
   It shall be Thy royal throne.

6. Take my love, my Lord, I pour
   At Thy feet its treasure-store;
   Take myself, and I will be
   Ever, only, all, for Thee.

Frances R. Havergal wrote this hymn on February 4, 1874, in eleven two-line stanzas. She states:

> Perhaps you will be interested to know the origin of the consecration hymn "Take My Life." I went for a little visit of five days (to Areley House). There were ten persons in the house, some unconverted and long prayed for, some converted, but not rejoicing Christians. He gave me the prayer "Lord, give me *all* in this house!" And He just *did!* Before I left the house, every one had got a blessing. The last night of my visit after I had retired, the governess asked me to go to the two daughters. They were crying, etc.; then and there both of them trusted and rejoiced; it was

nearly midnight. I was too happy to sleep and passed most of the night in praise and renewal of my own consecration; and these little couplets formed themselves and chimed in my heart one after another till they finished with "Ever, only, all, for Thee!"

The hymn was first published in her *Royal Responses*, 1878. It has been translated into many languages.

The tune "Patmos," to which she intended the hymn to be sung, was composed by her father, William H. Havergal. It appeared in Havergal's *Psalmody*, 1871, from an unpublished manuscript dated 1869.

401   Praise to Thee and Adoration

1. Praise to Thee and adoration,
   Blessed Jesus, Son of God,
Who, to serve Thine own creation,
   Didst partake of flesh and blood.
Teach me that I never may
From Thy fold or pastures stray,
But with zeal and joy exceeding
Follow where Thy steps are leading.

   Lov og Tak og evig Ære
   Ske dig Guds enbaarne Søn,
   Som en Tjener vilde være,
   Kommen ud af Davids Kjøn!
   Søde Jesu, lär du mig,
   At jeg vandrer rettelig,
   Og i dine Fodspor träder,
   Ja udi din Vei mig gläder.

2. Let me never, Lord, forsake Thee,
   E'en though bitter pain and strife
On my way shall overtake me;
   But may I through all my life
Walk in fervent love to Thee,
In all woes for comfort flee
To Thy birth, Thy death, and Passion,
Till I see Thy full salvation.

   Lad mig aldrig dig forsage,
   Om end Kors og Kimmer mig
   Skal i denne Verden plage,
   Men at jeg dog hjärtelig
   Elsker dig indtil min Död,
   Og forlindrer al min Nöd
   Med din Födsel, Död og Smerte,
   Tag dem aldrig fra mit Hjerte!

This hymn by Thomas Kingo first appeared in his *En Ny Kirke-Psalmebog* (Vinterparten), 1689. It is based on John 21:19-24, the Gospel for Third Christmas Day. It is a closing hymn for that day. In Guldberg's *Hymn-Book* it is appointed to be sung after the sermon from Christmas until Candlemas.

The translation is based on that by Kristen Kvamme and others, 1904. It appeared in *The Lutheran Hymnary*, 1913.

For comments on the tune "Freu dich sehr" see Hymn No. 61.

402   O God, Forsake Me Not

1. O God, forsake me not!
   Thy gracious presence lend me;
Lead Thou Thy helpless child;
   Thy Holy Spirit send me
That I my course may run.
Be Thou my Light, my Lot,
My Staff, my Rock, my Shield, —
   O God, forsake me not!

   Ach Gott, verlass mich nicht,
   Gib mir die Gnadenhände!
   Ach führe mich, dein Kind,
   Dass ich den Lauf vollende
   Zu meiner Seligkeit;
   Sei du mein Lebenslicht,
   Mein Stab, mein Hort, mein Schutz:
   Ach Gott, verlass mich nicht!

2. O God, forsake me not!
   Take not Thy Spirit from me
And suffer not the might
   Of sin to overcome me.
Increase my feeble faith,
Which Thou Thyself hast wrought.
Be Thou my Strength and Power, —
   O God, forsake me not!

   Ach Gott, verlass mich nicht,
   Regiere du mein Wallen,
   Ach lass mich nimmermehr
   In Sünd' und Schande fallen!
   Gib mir den guten Geist,
   Gib Glaubenszuversicht,
   Sei meine Stärk' und Kraft;
   Ach Gott, verlass mich nicht!

3. O God, forsake me not!
   Lord, hear my supplication!
In every evil hour
   Help me o'ercome temptation;
And when the Prince of hell
   My conscience seeks to blot,
Be Thou not far from me, —
   O God, forsake me not!

   Ach Gott, verlass mich nicht,
   Ich ruf' aus Herzensgrunde.
   Ach Höchster, stärke mich
   In jeder bösen Stunde;
   Wenn mich Versuchung plagt
   Und meine Seel' anficht,
   So weiche nicht von mir:
   Ach Gott, verlass mich nicht!

CONSECRATION

4. O God, forsake me not!
    Thy mercy I'm addressing;
O Father, God of Love,
    Grant me Thy heavenly blessing
To do when duty calls
    Whate'er Thou didst allot,
To do what pleaseth Thee, —
    O God, forsake me not!

5. O God, forsake me not!
    Lord, I am Thine forever.
Grant me true faith in Thee;
    Grant that I leave Thee never.
Grant me a blessed end
    When my good fight is fought;
Help me in life and death, —
    O God, forsake me not!

Ach Gott, verlass mich nicht,
    Ach, lass dich doch bewegen,
Ach Vater, kröne doch
    Mit reichem Himmelssegen
Die Werke meines Amts,
    Die Werke meiner Pflicht,
Zu tun, was dir gefällt:
    Ach Gott, verlass mich nicht!

Ach Gott, verlass mich nicht,
    Ich bleibe dir ergeben.
Hilf mir, o grosser Gott,
    Recht glauben, christlich leben
Und selig scheiden ab,
    Zu sehn dein Angesicht!
Hilf mir in Not und Tod:
    Ach Gott, verlass mich nicht!

Salomo Franck is given credit for the authorship of this hymn, based on Ps. 38:22. It appeared in the *Appendix* to the *Anderer Teil des Naumburgischen Gesang Buchs*, 1714. In a later edition it was marked "Gottgelassen, Unverlassen, Salomon Francke."

The translation is by August Crull, altered.

For comments on the tune "O Gott, du frommer Gott" see Hymn No. 395.

Savior, Thy Dying Love   403

1. Savior, Thy dying love
    Thou gavest me;
Nor should I aught withhold,
    Dear Lord, from Thee.
In love my soul would bow,
My heart fulfil its vow,
Some offering bring Thee now,
    Something for Thee.

2. O'er the blest mercy-seat,
    Pleading for me,
My feeble faith looks up,
    Jesus, to Thee.
Help me the cross to bear,
Thy wondrous love declare,
Some song to raise or prayer,
    Something for Thee.

3. Give me a faithful heart,
    Likeness to Thee,
That each departing day
    Henceforth may see
Some work of love begun,
Some deed of kindness done,
Some wanderer sought and won,
    Something for Thee.

4. All that I am and have,
    Thy gifts so free,
In joy, in grief, through life,
    Dear Lord, for Thee!
And when Thy face I see,
My ransomed soul shall be
Through all eternity
    Something for Thee.

This hymn by Sylvanus D. Phelps was written in 1862 and published in the *Watchman and Reflecter*. Robert Lowry, who wrote the tune "Something for Jesus" to this hymn, says of it:

It is worth living seventy years even if nothing comes of it but one such hymn as
    Savior, Thy dying love
        Thou gavest me;
    Nor should I aught withhold,
        Dear Lord, from Thee.

Happy is the man who can produce one song which the world will keep on singing after its author shall have passed away. May the tuneful harp preserve its strings for many a long year yet and the last note reach us only when it is time for the singer to take his place in the heavenly choir.

The tune "Winterton" is by Joseph Barnby, 1892.

Soul, What Return Has God, Thy Savior   404

1. Soul, what return has God, thy Savior,
    For all He gives thee day by day?
Oh, hast thou in thy gift a favor
    That can delight and please Him? — Say!
The best of offerings He requires;
Thy heart it is that He desires.

Was gibst du denn, o meine Seele,
    Gott, der dir täglich alles gibt?
Was ist in deines Leibes Höhle,
    Das ihn vergnügt und ihm beliebt?
Es muss das Liebst' und Beste sein:
Gib ihm, gib ihm das Herz allein!

CONSECRATION

2. Give unto God thy heart's affection,
    Who else can claim thee as His own?
Should Satan hold thee in subjection?
    With him but pangs of hell are known.
To Thee alone, O Lord divine,
My heart and all I now resign.

3. Accept the gift which Thou requirest,
    My heart and soul, O gracious God,
The first-fruits Thou so much desirest,
    For which Thy Son paid with His blood.
To Thee I willingly assign
My heart, dear Lord, for it is Thine.

4. Whom should I give my heart's
        affection
    But Thee, who givest Thine to faith?
Thy fervent love is my protection;
    Lord, Thou hast loved me unto death.
My heart with Thine shall ever be
One heart throughout eternity.

Du musst, was Gottes ist, Gott geben.
    Sag, Seele, wem gebührt das Herz?
Dem Teufel nicht, er hasst das Leben,
    Wo dieser wohnt, ist Höllenschmerz.
Dir, dir, o Gott, dir soll allein
Mein Herz aufwärts gewidmet sein!

So nimm nun hin, was du verlangest,
    Die Erstgeburt ohn' alle List,
Das Herz, damit du, Schöpfer, prangest.
    Das dir so sauer worden ist;
Dir geb' ich's willig, du allein
Hast es bezahlt, es ist ja dein!

Wem sollt' ich mein Herz lieber gönnen
    Als dem, der mir das seine gibt?
Dich kann ich mein'n Herzliebsten
        nennen,
    Du hast mich in den Tod geliebt.
Mein Herz dein Herz ein Herz allein,
Soll dein und keines andern sein!

This hymn by Karl F. Lochner was published in *Der Geistlichen Erquick-Stunden*, etc., Nürnberg, 1673, in five stanzas, the second of which is rightly omitted in the hymnals. It reads in its original form:

>   Was sind die blosse ausen-Werke,
>   Wann sie dem Herzen unbekannt?
>   Nur Wolken, Spruer, Schalen, Quärke,
>   Weg mit dem öden heuchel-Tand!
>   Der Satan wehlet solchen Schein:
>   Gott aber will das Herz allein.

The translation is composite.

For comments on the tune "O dass ich tausend" (Dretzel) see Hymn No. 243.

405   I Gave My Life for Thee

1. I gave My life for thee,
    My precious blood I shed,
That thou might'st ransomed be
    And quickened from the dead.
I gave My life for thee;
What hast thou given for Me?

2. I spent long years for thee
    In weariness and woe
That an eternity
    Of joy thou mightest know.
I spent long years for thee;
Hast thou spent one for Me?

3. My Father's home of light,
    My rainbow-circled throne,
I left for earthly night,
    For wanderings sad and lone.
I left it all for thee;
Hast thou left aught for Me?

4. I suffered much for thee,
    More than My tongue may tell,
Of bitterest agony,
    To rescue thee from hell.
I suffered much for thee;
What canst thou bear for Me?

5. And I have brought to thee
    Down from My home above
Salvation full and free,
    My pardon and My love.
Great gifts I brought to thee;
What hast thou brought to Me?

6. Oh, let thy life be given,
    Thy years for Me be spent,
World's fetters all be riven,
    And joy with suffering blent!
I gave Myself for thee:
Give thou thyself to Me.

"Christ Desiring the Entire Devotion of His Servants" is the title of this hymn by Frances R. Havergal, written in 1858. In the S. P. C. K.'s *Church Hymns*, 1871, it was changed to "Thy life was given for me." Miss M. V. G. Havergal's account of its origin is as follows:

> In F. R. H.'s MS. copy she gives this title, "I did this for thee; what hast thou done for Me?" Motto placed under a picture of our Savior in the study of a German divine. On January 10, 1858, she had come in weary, and sitting down, she read the motto, and the lines of her hymn flashed upon

her. She wrote them in pencil on a scrap of paper. Reading them over, she thought them so poor that she tossed them on the fire, but they fell out untouched. Showing them some months after to her father, he encouraged her to preserve them and wrote the tune *Baca* specially for them. The hymn was printed on a leaflet, 1859, and in *Good Words*, February, 1860. Published also in *The Ministry of Song*, 1869. Though F. R. H. consented to the alterations in *Church Hymns*, she thought the original more strictly carried out the idea of the motto "I gave My life for thee; what hast thou done for Me?"

The tune "Old 120th" is from Thomas Este's *Psalmes*, 1592. It had appeared as early as 1570, set to the metrical version of Ps. 120 in Sternhold and Hopkins's *New Version*. It bears a close resemblance to the "Old 81st," from which it may have been derived.

Lord, as Thou Wilt, Deal Thou with Me   406

1. Lord, as Thou wilt, deal Thou with me;
No other wish I cherish.
In life and death I cling to Thee;
Oh, do not let me perish!
Let not Thy grace from me depart
And grant an ever patient heart
To bear what Thou dost send me.

2. Grant honor, truth, and purity,
And love Thy Word to ponder;
From all false doctrine keep me free.
Bestow, both here and yonder,
What serves my everlasting bliss;
Preserve me from unrighteousness
Throughout my earthly journey.

3. When, at Thy summons, I must leave
This vale of sin and sadness,
Give me Thy grace, Lord, not to grieve,
But to depart with gladness.
To Thee my spirit I commend;
O Lord, grant me a blessed end
Through Jesus Christ, my Savior.

Herr, wie du willst, so schick's mit mir
Im Leben und im Sterben!
Allein zu dir steht mein' Begier,
Lass mich, Herr, nicht verderben!
Erhalt mich nur in deiner Huld,
Sonst, wie du willst, gib mir Geduld,
Denn dein Will' ist der beste.

Zucht, Ehr' und Treu' verleih mir, Herr,
Und Lieb' zu deinem Worte!
Behüt mich, Herr, vor falscher Lehr'
Und gib mir hier und dorte,
Was dient zu meiner Seligkeit.
Wend ab all' Ungerechtigkeit
In meinem ganzen Leben!

Soll ich einmal nach deinem Rat
Von dieser Welt abscheiden,
Verleih, o Herr, mir deine Gnad',
Dass es gescheh' mit Freuden.
Mein Leib und Seel' befehl' ich dir.
O Herr, ein selig End' gib mir
Durch Jesum Christum! Amen.

Kaspar Bienemann wrote this hymn, according to *Julian*, under the following circumstances:

Written in 1574, while he was tutor to the children of Duke Johann Wilhelm of Sachsen-Weimar, in expectation of a coming pestilence. He taught it as a prayer to his pupil the Princess Maria, then three years old, the initial letters of the three stanzas (H. Z. S.) forming an acrostic on her title, *Hertzogin zu Sachsen*. The Princess afterwards adopted as her motto the words "Herr, wie du willt," and this motto forms the refrain of "Jesus, Jesus, nichts als Jesus," the best-known hymn of the Countess Ludämilia Elisabeth of Schwarzburg-Rudolstadt.

It was first published in the author's *Betbüchlein*, Leipzig, 1582.

The translation by Emanuel Cronenwett appeared in the Ohio *Lutheran Hymnal*, 1880. It has been somewhat altered.

The tune "Herr, wie du willst" is from the *Teutsch Kirchen ampt*, etc., Strassburg, 1525, where it is set to Martin Luther's "Aus tiefer Not schrei' ich zu dir."

NEW OBEDIENCE

407   Farewell I Gladly Bid Thee

1. Farewell I gladly bid thee,
 False, evil world, farewell.
 Thy life is vain and sinful,
 With thee I would not dwell.
 I long to be in heaven,
 In that untroubled sphere
 Where they will be rewarded
 Who served their God while here.

2. By Thy good counsel lead me,
 O Son of God, my Stay;
 In each perplexing trial
 Help me, O Lord, I pray.
 Mine hour of sorrow shorten,
 Support my fainting heart,
 From every cross deliver,
 The crown of life impart.

3. When darkness round me gathers,
 Thy name and cross, still bright,
 Deep in my heart are sparkling
 Like stars in blackest night.
 O heart, this image cherish:
 The Christ on Calvary,
 How patiently He suffered
 And shed His blood for me!

4. Lord, hide my soul securely
 Deep in Thy wounded side;
 From every danger shield me
 And to Thy glory guide.
 He has been truly blessèd
 Who reaches heaven above;
 He has found perfect healing
 Who rests upon Thy love.

5. Lord, write my name, I pray Thee,
 Now in the Book of Life
 And with all true believers
 Take me where joys are rife.
 There let me bloom and flourish,
 Thy perfect freedom prove,
 And tell, as I adore Thee,
 How faithful was Thy love.

Valet will ich dir geben,
 Du arge, falsche Welt,
Dein sündlich, böses Leben
 Durchaus mir nicht gefällt.
Im Himmel ist gut wohnen,
 Hinauf steht mein' Begier,
Da wird Gott ewig lohnen
 Dem, der ihm dient allhier.

Rat mir nach deinem Herzen,
 O Jesu, Gottes Sohn!
Soll ich hier dulden Schmerzen,
 Hilf mir, Herr Christ, davon!
Verkürz mir alles Leiden,
 Stärk meinen blöden Mut,
Lass mich selig abscheiden,
 Setz mich in dein Erbgut!

In meines Herzens Grunde
 Dein Nam' und Kreuz allein
Funkelt all' Zeit und Stunde,
 Drauf kann ich fröhlich sein.
Erschein mir in dem Bilde
 Zu Trost in meiner Not,
Wie du, Herr Christ, so milde
 Dich hast geblut't zu Tod!

Verbirg mein' Seel' aus Gnaden
 In deiner offnen Seit',
Rück sie aus allem Schaden
 Zu deiner Herrlichkeit!
Der ist wohl hier gewesen,
 Der kommt ins Himmelsschloss;
Der ist ewig genesen,
 Der bleibt in deinem Schoss.

Schreib meinen Nam'n aufs beste
 Ins Buch des Lebens ein
Und bind mein' Seel' fein feste
 Ins schöne Bündelein
Der'r, die im Himmel grünen
 Und vor dir leben frei,
So will ich ewig rühmen,
 Dass dein Herz treue sei.

Valerius Herberger first published this hymn on a broadsheet, entitled "A devout prayer with which the Evangelical citizens of Frawenstadt in the autumn of the year 1613 moved the heart of God the Lord so that He mercifully laid down His sharp rod of wrath under which nearly two thousand fell on sleep. And also a hymn of consolation in which a pious heart bids farewell (*Valet*) to this world. Both composed by Valerius Herberger, preacher at Kripplein Christi." Leipzig, 1614.

The title of the hymn itself is: "The Farewell (*Valet*) of Valerius Herberger that he gave to this world in the autumn of the year 1613, when he every hour saw death before his eyes, but mercifully and also as wonderfully as the three men in the furnace at Babylon was nevertheless spared."

The hymn in its original form is an acrostic on his name as follows: VALE (1) R (2) I (3) U (4) S (5). It is a favorite hymn in many circles.

The translation is an altered form of that by Catherine Winkworth in her *Chorale Book for England*, 1863.

For comments on the tune "Valet will ich dir geben" see Hymn No. 58.

NEW OBEDIENCE

Jesus Christ, My Pride and Glory 408

1. Jesus Christ, my Pride and Glory,
   He, the true and living Light,
   Strengthens me with glorious might.
   Christ, revealed in sacred story,
   Whom I now as Lord confess,
   Teaches me true holiness.

2. Let me live to praise Thee ever,
   Jesus, Thou my heart's Delight,
   Thou who leadest me aright.
   Let me cling to Thee forever,
   All the fleshly lusts deny,
   And the devil's hosts defy.

3. Grant me, Lord, Thy Holy Spirit
   That in all I follow Him
   Lest the light of faith grow dim.
   Let me ever trust Thy merit,
   Let Thy blessing me attend,
   From all evil me defend.

4. From all pain and imperfection,
   Gracious Lord, deliver me,
   Heaven's glory let me see.
   Keep me under Thy direction
   That the grace Thou gavest me
   I may praise eternally.

Jesus selbst, mein Licht, mein Leben,
Jesus, meiner Seele Zier,
Spricht: Kommt her, lernt all' von mir!
Jesus, dem ich mich ergeben,
Mein Heil und Gerechtigkeit,
Lehrt mich selbst die Frömmigkeit.

Lass mich dir zu Ehren leben,
Jesu, meines Herzens Licht,
Mein Trost, Heil und Zuversicht!
Lass mich dir allein ergeben,
Lass mich sterben dieser Welt,
Lass mich tun, was dir gefällt!

Führe mich auf deinen Wegen,
Gib mir deinen guten Geist,
Der mir Hilf' und Beistand leist'!
Lass mich deine Gnad' und Segen
Stets empfinden früh und spat,
Segne Denken, Wort und Tat,

Bis ich endlich werde kommen
Aus der Unvollkommenheit
Zu des Himmels Herrlichkeit,
Da ich denn mit allen Frommen
Deine grosse Gütigkeit
Preisen will in Ewigkeit.

Johann Olearius published this hymn, in seven stanzas, in his *Geistliche Singe-Kunst,* Leipzig, 1671, based on the Gospel for the First Sunday after Epiphany, Luke 2:41-52. The cento omits Stanzas 2 to 4, which read as follows:

2. Ach, wie ist mein Herz verderbet,
   Wie fest hält das Sündenband
   Leib und Seel', Sinn und Verstand!
   Was von Adam angeerbet,
   Sündlich Wesen, Fleisch und Blut,
   Bleibt Fleisch und tut nimmer gut.

3. Mein Gott, hilf du mir ausrotten
   Alles Unkraut, Hass und Neid,
   Hochmut, Ungerechtigkeit!
   Lass den Satan mich nicht spotten,
   Mach du mein Herz täglich neu,
   Mach mich aller Bosheit frei!

4. Pflanz in mein Herz und Gemüte
   Deine grosse Freundlichkeit,
   Dein' Geduld und Frömmigkeit,
   Deine Liebe, deine Güte,
   Andacht, Treu' und Heiligkeit,
   Wahrheit und Gerechtigkeit!

The translation is by Paul E. Kretzmann and was prepared for *The Lutheran Hymnal* in 1939.

For comments on the tune "Ach, was soll ich Sünder machen" see Hymn No. 384.

Let Us Ever Walk with Jesus 409

1. Let us ever walk with Jesus,
   Follow His example pure,
   Flee the world, which would deceive us
   And to sin our souls allure.
   Ever in His footsteps treading,
   Body here, yet soul above,
   Full of faith and hope and love,
   Let us do the Father's bidding.
   Faithful Lord, abide with me;
   Savior, lead, I follow Thee.

2. Let us suffer here with Jesus,
   To His image e'er conform;
   Heaven's glory soon will please us,
   Sunshine follow on the storm.
   Though we sow in tears of sorrow,
   We shall reap with heavenly joy;
   And the fears that now annoy
   Shall be laughter on the morrow.
   Christ, I suffer here with Thee
   There, oh, share Thy joy with me!

Lasset uns mit Jesu ziehen,
Seinem Vorbild folgen nach,
In der Welt der Welt entfliehen,
Auf der Bahn, die er uns brach,
Immer fort zum Himmel reisen,
Irdisch noch, schon himmlisch sein,
Glauben recht und leben fein,
In der Lieb' den Glauben weisen!
Treuer Jesu, bleib bei mir;
Gehe vor, ich folge dir!

Lasset uns mit Jesu leiden,
Seinem Vorbild werden gleich!
Nach dem Leiden folgen Freuden,
Armut hier macht dorten reich.
Tränensaat, die erntet Lachen,
Hoffnung tröstet mit Geduld.
Es kann leichtlich Gottes Huld
Aus dem Regen Sonne machen.
Jesu, hier leid' ich mit dir,
Dort teil deine Freud' mit mir!

NEW OBEDIENCE

3. Let us also die with Jesus.
   His death from the second death,
From our soul's destruction, frees us,
   Quickens us with life's glad breath.
Let us mortify, while living,
   Flesh and blood and die to sin;
   And the grave that shuts us in
Shall but prove the gate to heaven.
   Jesus, here I die to Thee
   There to live eternally.

4. Let us gladly live with Jesus;
   Since He's risen from the dead,
Death and grave must soon release us.
   Jesus, Thou art now our Head,
We are truly Thine own members;
   Where Thou livest, there live we.
   Take and own us constantly,
Faithful Friend, as Thy dear brethren.
   Jesus, here I live to Thee,
   Also there eternally.

Lasset uns mit Jesu sterben!
   Sein Tod uns vom andern Tod
Rettet und vom Seelverderben,
   Von der ewiglichen Not.
Lasst uns töten, weil wir leben,
   Unser Fleisch, ihm sterben ab,
   So wird er uns aus dem Grab
In das Himmelsleben heben.
   Jesu, sterb' ich, sterb' ich dir,
   Dass ich lebe für und für.

Lasset uns mit Jesu leben!
   Weil er auferstanden ist,
Muss das Grab uns wiedergeben.
   Jesu, unser Haupt du bist,
Wir sind deines Leibes Glieder;
   Wo du lebst, da leben wir.
   Ach, erkenn uns für und für,
Trauter Freund, für deine Brüder!
   Jesu, dir ich lebe hier,
   Dorten ewig auch bei dir.

Sigismund von Birken first published this hymn in *Heilige Karwochen,* Nürnberg, 1653. It was intended for the Passiontide and is based on the Gospel for Quinquagesima Sunday, Luke 18:31-43.

The translation is by J. Adam Rimbach, 1910, who relates the story of the translation as follows:

    The first hymn I ever translated was "Lasset uns mit Jesu ziehen." The inspiration to do it came as follows: At the convention of the Central District in La Porte, Ind., in 1900, Dr. F. Pieper preached the opening sermon and, after doing so, had that hymn sung. I had never heard it sung before, and I immediately fell in love with it. The next month I opened a school in my congregation in Ashland, Ky., and my wife taught that hymn to the children. They, too, were delighted with it and sang it lustily, and with their help we introduced it in the church, where it also met with great favor. But many of the people, including all the children, sang it much as a parrot will talk, without understanding what they were saying. For they did not understand German. So I thought to myself: "It is a pity we haven't that hymn in English," and one Sunday afternoon, having just finished memorizing my evening sermon, which was English, I tackled that hymn myself. And, lo! the heavenly Muse came to my assistance, and within an hour or two I had something like a translation completed. I sent a copy of it to Rev. F. W. Herzberger of St. Louis, who was the editor of a forerunner of the *Young Lutherans' Magazine,* and he graciously printed it. From there it found its way into our hymn-book; first into a small book of 200 hymns and then into the larger book (*The Evangelical Lutheran Hymn-Book,* 1912).

A few slight changes were made in the translation for *The Lutheran Hymnal* with the consent of the translator.

The tune "Lasset uns mit Jesu ziehen" is by Georg Gottfried Boltze. It was composed in 1788 for the hymn of Paul Gerhardt "Sollt' ich meinem Gott nicht singen" (see Hymn No. 25) and was published, set to that text, in Kühnau's *Choral-Buch,* 1790.

410   Jesus, Lead Thou On

1. Jesus, lead Thou on
Till our rest is won;
   And although the way be cheerless,
   We will follow calm and fearless.
Guide us by Thy hand
To our fatherland.

Jesu, geh voran
Auf der Lebensbahn,
   Und wir wollen nicht verweilen,
   Dir getreulich nachzueilen.
Führ uns an der Hand
Bis ins Vaterland!

2. If the way be drear,
If the Foe be near,
  Let not faithless fears o'ertake us;
  Let not faith and hope forsake us;
For through many a woe
To our home we go.

Soll's uns hart ergehn,
Lass uns feste stehn
  Und auch in den schwersten Tagen
  Niemals über Lasten klagen;
Denn durch Trübsal hier
Geht der Weg zu dir.

3. When we seek relief
From a long-felt grief;
  When temptations come alluring,
  Make us patient and enduring;
Show us that bright shore
Where we weep no more.

Rühret eigner Schmerz
Irgend unser Herz,
  Kümmert uns ein fremdes Leiden,
  O so gib Geduld zu beiden;
Richte unsern Sinn
Auf das Ende hin!

4. Jesus, lead Thou on
Till our rest is won.
  Heavenly Leader, still direct us,
  Still support, control, protect us,
Till we safely stand
In our fatherland.

Ordne unsern Gang,
Jesu, lebenslang!
  Führst du uns durch rauhe Wege,
  Gib uns auch die nöt'ge Pflege.
Tu uns nach dem Lauf
Deine Türe auf!

This cento has a peculiar history. Ludwig von Zinzendorf, in September, 1721, wrote the hymn "Seelenbräutigam, o du Gotteslamm" in eleven stanzas (not to be confused with the hymn by Adam Drese "Seelenbräutigam, Jesu, Gotteslamm") and in May of the same year the hymn "Glanz der Ewigkeit" in fifteen stanzas. Both hymns were published in his *Sammlung*, etc., Leipzig and Görlitz, 1725. This cento, probably by Christian Gregor, appeared in the Brüder *Gesang-Buch*, 1778. It is built up as follows:

Stanza 1 is Stanza 10 of "Seelenbräutigam."

Stanza 2 is Stanza 11 of "Glanz der Ewigkeit."

Stanza 3 is Stanza 4 of "Seelenbräutigam."

Stanza 4 is Stanza 11 of "Seelenbräutigam."

The cento has achieved a wide popularity.

The translation is an altered form of that by Jane Borthwick in her *Hymns from the Land of Luther*, 1854, which was an altered form of her version published in the *Free Church Magazine*, 1846. In Stanza 3, Lines 3 and 4, Miss Borthwick had

  When oppressed by new temptations,
  Lord, increase and perfect patience.

The tune "Seelenbräutigam" is by Adam Drese and was written for his own hymn "Seelenbräutigam, Jesu, Gotteslamm" and published in the Halle *Gesang-Buch* (Schütze), 1697.

From Eternity, O God   411

1. From eternity, O God,
  In Thy Son Thou didst elect me;
Therefore, Father, on life's road
  Graciously to heaven direct me;
Send to me Thy Holy Spirit
That His gifts I may inherit.

Gott, du hast in deinem Sohn
  Mich von Ewigkeit erwählet.
Sende nun von deinem Thron,
  Was noch meinem Heile fehlet,
Und gib mir des Geistes Gaben,
Sodann werd' ich alles haben.

2. Though alive, I'm dead in sin,
Lost to all good things by nature.
Holy Ghost, change me within,
  Make of me a new-born creature;
For the flesh works ruination
And can never gain salvation.

Ach, ich bin lebendig tot
  Und zum Guten ganz verloren!
Heil'ger Geist, mein Herr und Gott,
  Mache du mich neugeboren!
Denn das Fleisch ist mein Verderben
Und kann nicht den Himmel erben.

3. Drive away the gloomy night
  Of my heart's perverse reflection;
Quench all thoughts that are not right.
  Hold my reason in subjection;
Grant that I from Thee, with yearning,
Wisdom always may be learning.

Treibe weg die finstre Nacht
  Meiner irrigen Gedanken!
Dämpfe das, was Gott veracht't,
  Halte die Vernunft in Schranken,
Dass ich anders nicht als gerne
Selbst von dir die Weisheit lerne.

NEW OBEDIENCE

4. Oh, create a heart in me
   That in Thee, my God, believeth
   And o'er the iniquity
   Of my sins most truly grieveth.
   When dark hours of woe betide me,
   In the wounds of Jesus hide me.

5. As a branch upon a vine
   In my blessed Lord implant me;
   Ever of my Head divine
   To remain a member grant me.
   Oh, let Him, my Lord and Savior,
   Be my Life and Love forever!

6. Faith and hope and charity
   Graciously, O Father, give me;
   Be my Guardian constantly
   That the devil may not grieve me;
   Grant me humbleness and gladness,
   Peace and patience in my sadness.

7. Help me speak what's right and good
   And keep silence on occasion;
   Help me pray, Lord, as I should,
   Help me bear my tribulation;
   Help me die and let my spirit
   Everlasting life inherit.

Schaffe mir ein reines Herz,
   Dass ich stets an Gott gedenke
Und mich oft mit Reu' und Schmerz
   Über meine Sünden kränke;
Doch nach den betrübten Stunden
Führe mich in Jesu Wunden!

Pflanze mich daselbst in ihn
   Als ein Glied an seinem Leibe,
Und wenn ich sein eigen bin,
   Hilf mir, dass ich es auch bleibe!
Er sei Stock und ich die Rebe,
Dass ich ganz in Jesu lebe.

Hierzu bitt' ich diese drei:
   Glauben, Hoffnung und die Liebe.
Steh auch sonst mir also bei,
   Dass kein Teufel mich betrübe!
Gib mir Demut, Fried' und Freude
Und auch Sanftmut, wenn ich leide!

Hilf mir reden recht und wohl,
   Auch zuweilen gar nichts sagen;
Hilf mir beten, wie ich soll,
   Hilf mir auch mein Kreuze tragen!
Wenn es Zeit ist, hilf mir sterben
Und dabei den Himmel erben!

Caspar Neumann wrote this hymn for Whitsunday, in eight stanzas. It appeared in the Silesian *Vollkommen Kirchen Gesangbuch*, Breslau and Liegnitz, 1711.

The translation is an altered form of that by August Crull in the *Evangelical Lutheran Hymn-Book*, 1912. The omitted fourth stanza, in Crull's translation, reads:

4. All desire and thoughts of mine
   From my youth are only evil;
   Save me by Thy power divine
   From myself and from the devil;
   Give me strength in ample measure
   Both to will and do Thy pleasure.

For comments on the tune "Liebster Jesu" see Hymn No. 16.

412 May We Thy Precepts, Lord, Fulfil

1. May we Thy precepts, Lord, fulfil
   And do on earth our Father's will
   As angels do above;
   Still walk in Christ, the living Way,
   With all Thy children and obey
   The law of Christian love.

2. So may we join Thy name to bless,
   Thy grace adore, Thy power confess,
   From sin and strife to flee.
   One is our calling, one our name,
   The end of all our hopes the same,
   A crown of life with Thee.

3. Spirit of Life, of Love, and Peace,
   Unite our hearts, our joy increase,
   Thy gracious help supply.
   To each of us the blessing give
   In Christian fellowship to live,
   In joyful hope to die.

Edward Osler published this hymn in 1836, in *Psalms and Hymns*, etc., of which he and Prebendary W. J. Hall were the editors.

The tune "Meribah" is by Lowell Mason, 1839.

413 I Walk in Danger All the Way

1. I walk in danger all the way.
   The thought shall never leave me
   That Satan, who has marked his prey,
   Is plotting to deceive me.
   This Foe with hidden snares
   May seize me unawares
   If e'er I fail to watch and pray.
   I walk in danger all the way.

Jeg gaar i Fare, hvor jeg gaar,
   Min Själ skal altid tänke,
At Satan allevegne staar
   I Veien med sin Länke;
Hans skjulte Helved-Brand
Mig let forvilde kand,
Naar jeg ei paa min Skanse staar;
Jeg gaar i Fare, hvor jeg gaar.

NEW OBEDIENCE

2. I pass through trials all the way,
   With sin and ills contending;
In patience I must bear each day
   The cross of God's own sending.
Oft in adversity
I know not where to flee;
When storms of woe my soul dismay,
I pass through trials all the way.

3. Death doth pursue me all the way,
   Nowhere I rest securely;
He comes by night, he comes by day,
   And takes his prey most surely.
A failing breath, and I
In death's strong grasp may lie
To face eternity for aye.
Death doth pursue me all the way.

4. I walk with angels all the way,
   They shield me and befriend me;
All Satan's power is held at bay
   When heavenly hosts attend me;
They are my sure defense,
All fear and sorrow, hence!
Unharmed by foes, do what they may,
I walk with angels all the way.

5. I walk with Jesus all the way,
   His guidance never fails me;
Within His wounds I find a stay
   When Satan's power assails me;
And by His footsteps led,
My path I safely tread.
In spite of ills that threaten may,
I walk with Jesus all the way.

6. My walk is heavenward all the way;
   Await, my soul, the morrow,
When thou shalt find release for aye
   From all thy sin and sorrow.
All worldly pomp, begone!
To heaven I now press on.
For all the world I would not stay;
My walk is heavenward all the way.

Jeg gaar i Trängsel, hvor jeg gaar;
   Mod Synden skal jeg stride,
Om Gud med Korsets Ris mig slaar,
   Det skal jeg taalig lide,
Tidt ingen Vei jeg ser,
Hvor jeg kan vandre meer,
Naar modgangs Taage om mig staar;
Jeg gaar i Trängsel, hvor jeg gaar.

Jeg gaar til Döden, hvor jeg gaar,
   Og veed mig ikke sikker,
Ei nogen Dag og Time, naar
   Han har mig alt i Strikker.
Et lidet Aandefang
Kan ende al min Gang,
At jeg i Evigheden staar;
Jeg gaar til Döden, hvor jeg gaar.

Jeg gaar blandt Engle, hvor jeg gaar;
   De skal mig vel bevare,
Slet intet Satans Magt formaar
   I saadan Himmel-Skare.
Bort Verdens Suk og Sorg!
Jeg gaar i Engle-Borg,
Traads nogen rörer mig et Haar!
Jeg gaar blandt Engle, hvor jeg gaar.

Jeg gaar med Jesu, hvor jeg gaar,
   Han har mig ved sin Side,
Han skjuler mig med sine Saar,
   Og hjälper mig at stride,
Hvor han sit Fodspor lod,
Der setter jeg min Fod;
Traads al den Deel, mig ilde spaar,
Jeg gaar med Jesu, hvor jeg gaar.

Jeg gaar til Himlen, hvor jeg gaar;
   Frimodig da mit Hjerte!
Kun did, hvor du en Ende faar
   Paa al din Synd og Smerte!
Bort Verdens Lyst og Pragt,
Til Himlen staar min Agt!
Al Verdens Eie jeg forsmaar,
Jeg gaar till Himlen, hvor jeg gaar.

This hymn by Hans A. Brorson appeared in *Nogle Salmer om Troens Frugt*, 1734. The following Scripture-passages are the basis of the stanzas in their order: 1 Pet. 5:8; John 16:33; Ps. 90:5,6; Ps. 34:7; John 8:12; and Heb. 13:14; Phil. 3:20.

The translation is an altered form of that by Ditlef G. Ristad, 1908, and appeared in *The Lutheran Hymnary*, 1913.

The tune "Der lieben Sonne Licht und Pracht" is from Freylinghausen's *Geistreiches Gesangbuch*, Halle, 1704. It is said that Christian Scriver one night heard a frivolous folk-song sung to this melody, and, being shocked at hearing this fine tune used in dishonoring God's name, he wrote his evening hymn beginning with the line "Der lieben Sonne Licht und Pracht."

The Man Is Ever Blest   414

1. The man is ever blest
   Who shuns the sinners' ways,
Among their counsels never stands,
   Nor takes the scorners' place,

2. But makes the Law of God
   His study and delight
Amid the labors of the day
   And watches of the night.

3. He like a tree shall thrive,
   With waters near the root;
Fresh as the leaf his name shall live,
   His works are heavenly fruit.

4. Not so the ungodly race,
   They no such blessings find;
Their hopes shall flee like empty chaff
   Before the driving wind.

NEW OBEDIENCE

5. How will they bear to stand
   Before that judgment-seat
Where all the saints at Christ's right hand
   In full assembly meet?

6. He knows, and He approves,
   The way the righteous go;
But sinners and their works shall meet
   A dreadful overthrow.

This is Isaac Watts's short-meter metrical paraphrase of Ps. 1. It appeared as the second hymn in his *Psalms of David Imitated,* 1719.

For comments on the tune "St. Michael" see Hymn No. 310.

415 Lo, Many Shall Come from the East and the West

1. Lo, many shall come from the East and
      the West
   And sit at the feast of salvation
   With Abraham, Isaac, and Jacob, the blest,
   Obeying the Lord's invitation.
      Have mercy upon us, O Jesus!

2. But they who have always resisted His
      grace
   And on their own virtue depended
   Shall then be condemned and cast out from
      His face,
   Eternally lost and unfriended.
      Have mercy upon us, O Jesus!

3. Oh, may we all hear when our Shepherd
      doth call
   In accents persuasive and tender,
   That, while there is time, we make haste,
      one and all,
   And find Him, our mighty Defender!
      Have mercy upon us, O Jesus!

4. Oh, that we the throng of the ransomed
      may swell,
   To whom He hath granted remission!
   God graciously make us in heaven to dwell
   And save us from endless perdition.
      Have mercy upon us, O Jesus!

5. God grant that I may of His infinite love
      Remain in His merciful keeping
   And sit with the King at His table above
   When here in the grave I am sleeping.
      Have mercy upon us, O Jesus!

6. All trials are then like a dream that is past,
   Forgotten all trouble and sorrow;
   All questions and doubts have been answered
      at last;
   Then dawneth eternity's morrow.
      Have mercy upon us, O Jesus!

7. The heavens shall ring with an anthem
      more grand
   Than ever on earth was recorded;
   The blest of the Lord shall receive at His hand
   The crown to the victors awarded.
      Have mercy upon us, O Jesus!

Der mange skal komme fra Öst og fra
   Vest,
Og sidde tilbords i Guds Rige
Med Abraham, Isak og Jakob til Gjest
Hos ham, som böd ind os at stige.
   Miskunde dig over os, Jesu!

Men de, som modstode fra Morgen til
   Kveld,
Og stoled paa egen Dyds Styrke,
Fordömmes og kastes med Legem og
   Själ
Hen ud i det yderste Mörke.
   Miskunde dig over os, Jesu!

Gud lader os höre med Kjärligheds
   Brand
Vor Hyrdes hans Lokking saa blide,
At vi maatte skynde os, Kvinde og
   Mand,
Og sanke os til ham i Tide!
   Miskunde dig over os, Jesu!

Gid jeg maatte väre, og alle med mig,
   Blandt Guds den beseglede Skare,
Gud tage os naadig i Himlen til
   sig,
Og frelse fra Helvedes Fare!
   Miskunde dig over os, Jesu!

Gud giv mig at väre den salige Gjest,
   Som sidder hos Kongen for Borde,
At holde hos hannem den evige Fest,
Naar her de mig gjemme og jorde!
   Miskunde dig over os, Jesu!

Da glemmes der Kors, som paa Jorden
   jeg bar,
Da slukner saa mildelig Sorgen,
Da bliver opklaret, hvad gaadefuldt var,
Da rinder den lyse Dags Morgen.
   Miskunde dig over os, Jesu!

Da toner der gjennem den himmelske
   Hal
En Lovsang, som ikke har Mage.
For Stolen og Lammet de Salige skal
Sin Krone for Kampen modtage.
   Miskunde dig over os, Jesu!

Magnus B. Landstad based this hymn on the Gospel for the Third Sunday after Epiphany, Matt. 8:1-13. It appeared in his *Kirke-Salmebog, et Utkast,* 1861. The hymn is one of Landstad's best.

The translation is by Peer O. Strömme, 1909. It was included in *The Lutheran Hymnary,* 1913.

The tune "Der mange skal komme" is from Jesper Svedberg's *Then Swenska Psalmboken,* Stockholm, 1695, where it is set to the hymn "Himmelriket liknas widt tijo jungfruer."

[298]

NEW OBEDIENCE

Oh, that the Lord Would Guide My Ways 416

1. Oh, that the Lord would guide my ways
   To keep His statutes still!
   Oh, that my God would grant me grace
   To know and do His will!

2. Order my footsteps by Thy Word
   And make my heart sincere;
   Let sin have no dominion, Lord,
   But keep my conscience clear.

3. Assist my soul, too apt to stray,
   A stricter watch to keep;
   And should I e'er forget Thy way,
   Restore Thy wandering sheep.

4. Make me to walk in Thy commands, —
   'Tis a delightful road, —
   Nor let my head or heart or hands
   Offend against my God.

Isaac Watts first published this hymn in six stanzas in his *Psalms of David Imitated*, 1719. The cento omits Stanzas 2 and 3, which read:

2. Oh, send thy Spirit down to write
   Thy laws upon my heart,
   Nor let my tongue indulge deceit
   Nor act the liar's part.

3. From vanity turn off my eyes;
   Let no corrupt design
   Nor covetous desires arise
   Within this soul of mine.

The alterations are in the third stanza of the cento, which originally read:

My soul hath gone too far astray,
My feet too often slip;
Yet since I've not forgot Thy way,
Restore Thy wandering sheep.

The Scriptural basis of the stanzas in their order is: Ps. 119:5, 33; 119:133; 119:176; 119:35.

The tune "Evan" is by William H. Havergal, 1846, and was originally set to the poem of Robert Burns "O Thou dread power, who reign'st above."

How Can I Thank Thee, Lord 417

1. How can I thank Thee, Lord,
   For all Thy loving-kindness,
   That Thou hast patiently
   Borne with me in my blindness?
   When dead in many sins
   And trespasses I lay,
   I kindled, holy God,
   Thine anger every day.

2. It is Thy work alone
   That I am now converted;
   O'er Satan's work in me
   Thou hast Thy power asserted.
   Thy mercy and Thy grace
   That rise afresh each morn
   Have turned my stony heart
   Into a heart new-born.

3. I could but grieve Thee, Lord,
   And with my sins displease Thee;
   Yet to atone for sin
   My works could not appease Thee.
   Though I could fall from grace
   And choose the way of sin,
   I had no strength to rise,
   A new life to begin.

4. But Thou hast raised me up
   To joy and exultation
   And clearly shown the way
   That leads me to salvation.
   My sins are washed away,
   For this I thank Thee, Lord;
   And with my heart and soul
   All dead works are abhorred.

5. Grant that Thy Spirit's help
   To me be always given
   Lest I should fall again
   And lose the way to heaven;
   That He may give me strength
   In mine infirmity
   And e'er renew my heart
   To serve Thee willingly.

Was kann ich doch für Dank,
O Herr, dir dafür sagen,
Dass du mich mit Geduld
So lange Zeit getragen,
Da ich in mancher Sünd'
Und Übertretung lag
Und dich, du frommer Gott,
Erzürnte alle Tag'!

Dass ich nun bin bekehrt,
Hast du allein verrichtet;
Du hast des Satans Reich
Und Werk in mir vernichtet.
Herr, deine Güt' und Treu',
Die an die Wolken reicht,
Hat auch mein steinern Herz
Zerbrochen und erweicht.

Selbst könnt' ich dich zu viel
Beleidigen mit Sünden,
Ich konnte aber nicht
Selbst Gnade wieder finden;
Selbst fallen konnte ich
Und ins Verderben gehn,
Doch konnt' ich selber nicht
Von meinem Fall aufstehn.

Du hast mich aufgericht't
Und mir den Weg geweiset,
Den ich nun wandeln soll;
Dafür, Herr, sei gepreiset!
Gott sei gelobt, dass ich
Die alte Sünd' nun hass'
Und willig, ohne Furcht,
Die toten Werke lass'.

Damit ich aber nicht
Aufs neue wieder falle,
So gib mir deinen Geist,
Dieweil ich hier noch walle,
Der meine Schwachheit stärk'
Und in mir mächtig sei
Und mein Gemüte stets
Zu deinem Dienst erneu'.

6. Oh, guide and lead me, Lord,
   While here below I wander
   That I may follow Thee
   Till I shall see Thee yonder.
   For if I led myself,
   I soon would go astray;
   But if Thou leadest me,
   I keep the narrow way.

7. O Father, God of Love,
   Hear Thou my supplication;
   O Savior, Son of God,
   Grant me Thy full salvation;
   And Thou, O Holy Ghost,
   Be Thou my faithful Guide
   That I may serve Thee here
   And there with Thee abide.

Ach leit und führe mich,
Solang ich leb' auf Erden;
Lass mich nicht ohne dich
Durch mich geführet werden!
Führ' ich mich ohne dich,
So werd' ich bald verführt;
Wenn du mich führest selbst,
Tu' ich, was mir gebührt.

O Gott, du grosser Gott,
O Vater, hör mein Flehen!
O Jesu, Gottes Sohn,
Lass deine Kraft mich sehen!
O werter Heil'ger Geist,
Sei bei mir allezeit,
Dass ich dir diene hier
Und dort in Ewigkeit!

This hymn is attributed to David Denicke, although Justus Gesenius is also mentioned. It first appeared, in eight stanzas, in the Hanoverian *New Ordentlich Gesangbuch*, Braunschweig, 1648, entitled "Thanksgiving and Prayer of a Convert." Stanza 6 is an altered form of a stanza by Johann Heermann and first appeared as a short prayer in his *Devoti Musica Cordis*, 1630. The omitted second stanza reads in translation:

   2. Lord, Thou hast shown to me
      Divine commiseration:
      I persevered in sin,
      But Thou in great compassion;
      I did resist Thee, Lord,
      Deferring to repent;
      Thou didst defer Thy wrath
      And instant punishment.

The translation is an altered form of that by August Crull in the *Evangelical Lutheran Hymn-Book*, 1912.

For comments on the tune "O Gott, du frommer Gott" see Hymn No. 395.

418   My God, My Father, While I Stray

1. My God, my Father, while I stray
   Far from my home on life's rough way,
   Oh, teach me from my heart to say,
   "Thy will be done."

2. Though dark my path and sad my lot,
   Let me be still and murmur not
   Or breathe the prayer divinely taught,
   "Thy will be done."

3. What though in lonely grief I sigh
   For friends beloved, no longer nigh,
   Submissive still would I reply —
   "Thy will be done."

4. Though Thou hast called me to resign
   What most I prized, it ne'er was mine;
   I have but yielded what was Thine —
   "Thy will be done."

5. Should grief or sickness waste away
   My life in premature decay,
   My Father, still I strive to say,
   "Thy will be done."

6. Let but my fainting heart be blest
   With Thy sweet Spirit for its Guest;
   My God, to Thee I leave the rest —
   "Thy will be done."

7. Renew my will from day to day;
   Blend it with Thine and take away
   All that now makes it hard to say,
   "Thy will be done."

8. Then, when on earth I breathe no more,
   The prayer, oft mixed with tears before,
   I'll sing upon a happier shore,
   "Thy will be done."

This hymn by Charlotte Elliott, which ranks next to her hymn "Just as I am" in popularity, was published in four forms by the author between the years 1834 and 1839, sometimes in seven and again in eight stanzas; sometimes with the opening line "My God *and* Father, while I stray." Its first appearance was in the *Appendix* to the first edition of her *Invalid's Hymn Book*, 1834, entitled "Thy will be done."

The tune "Es ist kein Tag" is from Johann D. Meyer's *Geistliche Seelenfreud*, 1692.

NEW OBEDIENCE

O'er Jerusalem Thou Weepest 419

1. O'er Jerusalem Thou weepest
   In compassion, dearest Lord.
   Love divine, of love the deepest,
   O'er Thine erring Israel poured,
   Crieth out in bitter moan:
   "O loved city, hadst thou known
   This thy day of visitation,
   Thou wouldst not reject salvation."

2. By the love Thy tears are telling,
   O Thou Lamb for sinners slain,
   Make my heart Thy temple-dwelling,
   Purged from every guilty stain.
   Oh, forgive, forgive, my sin!
   Cleanse me, cleanse me, Lord, within!
   I am Thine since Thou hast sought me,
   Since Thy precious blood hath bought me.

3. O Thou Lord of my salvation,
   Grant my soul Thy blood-bought peace.
   By Thy tears of lamentation
   Bid my faith and love increase.
   Grant me grace to love Thy Word,
   Grace to keep the message heard,
   Grace to own Thee as my Treasure,
   Grace to love Thee without measure.

This hymn by Anna Hoppe is based on the Gospel for the Tenth Sunday after Trinity, Luke 19:41-48. It was written in 1919 and appeared in *The Hymnal* (Evangelical Lutheran Augustana Synod), Rock Island, 1925.

For comments on the tune "Freu dich sehr" see Hymn No. 61.

My Jesus, as Thou Wilt 420

1. My Jesus, as Thou wilt;
   Oh, may Thy will be mine!
   Into Thy hand of love
   I would my all resign.
   Through sorrow or through joy
   Conduct me as Thine own
   And help me still to say,
   My Lord, Thy will be done.

2. My Jesus, as Thou wilt.
   If needy here and poor,
   Give me Thy people's bread,
   Thy Word, so rich and sure.
   This manna from above
   Let my soul feed upon;
   And if all else should fail,
   My Lord, Thy will be done.

3. My Jesus, as Thou wilt.
   Though seen through many a tear,
   Let not my star of hope
   Grow dim or disappear.
   Since Thou on earth hast wept
   And sorrowed oft alone,
   If I must weep with Thee,
   My Lord, Thy will be done.

4. My Jesus, as Thou wilt.
   When death itself draws nigh,
   Unto Thy wounded side
   For refuge I would fly
   And, clinging to Thee, go
   Where Thou before hast gone.
   My times are in Thy hand:
   My Lord, Thy will be done.

5. My Jesus, as Thou wilt.
   All shall be well for me;
   Each changing future scene
   I gladly trust with Thee.
   Thus to my home above
   I travel calmly on
   And sing in life or death,
   My Lord, Thy will be done.

Mein Jesu, wie du willt,
So lass mich allzeit wollen;
Wenn Trübsal, Angst und Leid
Mich hier betreffen sollen,
So gib, dass allezeit
Dein Wille werd' erfüllt,
Ich leb' und sterbe dir;
Mein Jesu, wie du willt!

Mein Jesu, wie du willt!
Soll ich in Armut leben,
So mach hingegen du
Die Seele reich, daneben
Gib, dass dein Wort mir nur
Den Hunger allzeit stillt,
Und nimm sonst alles hin:
Mein Jesu, wie du willt!

Mein Jesu, wie du willt!
Soll ich in Tränen schwimmen,
So lass mein Fünklein Trost
Nicht ganz und gar verglimmen.
Hast du doch selbst geweint;
Drum, wenn's nicht anders gilt,
So wein' ich auch mit dir.
Mein Jesu, wie du willt!

Mein Jesu, wie du willt!
Soll ich denn endlich sterben,
Ich weiss, du lässt mich auch
Im Sterben nicht verderben,
Wenn meine Seele sich
In deine Wunden hüllt;
Drum soll's gestorben sein,
Mein Jesu, wie du willt!

Mein Jesu, wie du willt!
So bin ich auch zufrieden;
Hast du mir Lieb' und Leid,
Not oder Tod beschieden,
So nehm' ich's auf dein Wort,
Dein Wille werd' erfüllt.
Drum sag' ich noch einmal:
Mein Jesu, wie du willt!

Benjamin Schmolck published this hymn, in eleven stanzas, in his *Heilige Flammen*, etc., 1704. It is based on Mark 14:36. Each stanza begins and ends with "Mein Jesu, wie du willt." The cento omits Stanzas 2, 4, 6, 7, 8, and 9.

The translation, altered, is by Jane Borthwick in her *Hymns from the Land of Luther*, 1854. Miss Borthwick also translated Stanzas 4 and 8, thus:

4. My Jesus, as Thou wilt!
   If among thorns I go,
Still somewhere here and there
   Let a few roses blow.
But Thou on earth along
   Thy thorny path hast gone,
Then lead me after Thee.
   My Lord, Thy will be done.

8. My Jesus, as Thou wilt!
   If loved ones must depart,
Suffer not sorrow's flood
   To overwhelm my heart;
For they are blest with Thee,
   Their race and conflict won;
Let me but follow them.
   My Lord, Thy will be done.

For comments on the tune "Denby" see Hymn No. 259.

421   Come, Follow Me, the Savior Spake

1. Come, follow Me, the Savior spake,
   All in My way abiding;
Deny yourselves, the world forsake,
   Obey My call and guiding.
Oh, bear the cross, whate'er betide,
Take My example for your guide.

2. I am the Light, I light the way,
   A godly life displaying;
I bid you walk as in the day,
   I keep your feet from straying.
I am the Way, and well I show
How you must sojourn here below.

3. My heart abounds in lowliness,
   My soul with love is glowing,
And gracious words my lips express,
   With meekness overflowing.
My heart, My mind, My strength, My all,
To God I yield, on Him I call.

4. I teach you how to shun and flee
   What harms your soul's salvation,
Your heart from every guile to free,
   From sin and its temptation.
I am the Refuge of the soul
And lead you to your heavenly goal.

5. Then let us follow Christ, our
   Lord,
And take the cross appointed
And, firmly clinging to His Word,
   In suffering be undaunted.
For who bears not the battle's strain
The crown of life shall not obtain.

Mir nach! spricht Christus, unser Held,
   Mir nach, ihr Christen alle!
Verleugnet euch, verlasst die Welt,
   Folgt meinem Ruf und Schalle,
Nehmt euer Kreuz und Ungemach
Auf euch, folgt meinem Wandel nach!

Ich bin das Licht, ich leucht' euch für
   Mit heil'gem Tugendleben.
Wer zu mir kommt und folget mir,
   Darf nicht im Finstern schweben.
Ich bin der Weg, ich weise wohl,
Wie man wahrhaftig wandeln soll.

Mein Herz ist voll Demütigkeit,
   Voll Liebe meine Seele;
Mein Mund, der fleusst zu jeder Zeit
   Von süssem Sanftmutsöle;
Mein Geist, Gemüte, Kraft und Sinn
Ist Gott ergeben, schaut auf ihn.

Ich zeig' euch das, was schädlich ist,
   Zu fliehen und zu meiden
Und euer Herz von arger List
   Zu rein'gen und zu scheiden.
Ich bin der Seelen Fels und Hort
Und führ' euch zu der Himmelspfort'.

So lasst uns denn dem lieben Herrn
   Mit Leib und Seel' nachgehen
Und wohlgemut, getrost und gern
   Bei ihm im Leiden stehen!
Denn wer nicht kämpft, trägt auch die
   Kron'
Des ew'gen Lebens nicht davon.

Johann Scheffler (Angelus Silesius) based this hymn on Matt. 16:24. It appeared in his *Heilige Seelenlust*, 1668, in six stanzas, entitled "She [the Soul] Encourages to the Following of Christ." In the *Geistreiches Gesang-Buch*, Halle, 1704, Stanza 4 was added. Its author is unknown. The hymn has been called "a masterpiece of Scriptural didactic poetry." The cento omits Stanzas 5 and 6 of the seven-stanza form. They read in translation:

5. But if too hot you find the fray,
   I, at your side, stand ready;
I fight myself, I lead the way,
   At all times firm and steady.
A coward he who will not heed
When the chief Captain takes the lead.

6. Who seeks to find his soul's welfare
   Without Me, he shall lose it;
But who to lose it may appear,
   In God shall introduce it.
Who bears no cross nor follows hard
Deserves not Me nor My reward.

NEW OBEDIENCE

The translation, altered, is by Charles W. Schaeffer. It appeared in the *Evangelical Lutheran Hymn-Book*, 1912.

The tune "Mach's mit mir, Gott" is by Johann Hermann Schein, 1628. It is based on an older melody, set to the hymn "Ein wahrer Glaub' Gottes Zorn stillt" in Bartholomäus Gesius's *Geistliche Deutsche Lieder*, etc., Frankfurt a. d. O., 1607.

Savior, I Follow On   422

1. Savior, I follow on,
   Guided by Thee,
   Seeing not yet the hand
   That leadeth me.
   Hushed be my heart and still,
   Fear I no further ill,
   Only to meet Thy will
   My will shall be.

2. Riven the rock for me
   Thirst to relieve,
   Manna from heaven falls
   Fresh every eve.
   Never a want severe
   Causeth my eye a tear
   But Thou dost whisper near,
   "Only believe."

3. Often to Marah's brink
   Have I been brought;
   Shrinking the cup to drink,
   Help I have sought;
   And with the prayer's ascent
   Jesus the branch hath rent,
   Quickly relief hath sent,
   Sweetening the draught.

4. Savior, I long to walk
   Closer with Thee;
   Led by Thy guiding hand,
   Ever to be
   Constantly near Thy side,
   Quickened and purified,
   Living for Him who died
   Freely for me.

Charles S. Robinson published this hymn in his *Songs of the Church*, 1862. It was revised by him for *Songs for the Sanctuary*, 1865, and widely adopted in that form. However, the better hymnals of the present day do not contain this hymn.

For comments on the tune "Winterton" see Hymn No. 403.

Jesus, I My Cross have Taken   423

1. Jesus, I my cross have taken,
   All to leave and follow Thee;
   Destitute, despised, forsaken,
   Thou from hence my All shalt be.
   Perish every fond ambition,
   All I've sought or hoped or known;
   Yet how rich is my condition!
   God and heaven are still my own.

2. Let the world despise and leave me,
   They have left my Savior, too.
   Human hearts and looks deceive me;
   Thou art not, like them, untrue.
   And while Thou shalt smile upon me,
   God of wisdom, love, and might,
   Foes may hate and friends may shun me;
   Show Thy face, and all is bright.

3. Go, then, earthly fame and treasure!
   Come, disaster, scorn, and pain!
   In Thy service, pain is pleasure;
   With Thy favor, loss is gain.
   I have called Thee Abba, Father!
   I have stayed my heart on Thee.
   Storms may howl, and clouds may gather,
   All must work for good to me.

4. Man may trouble and distress me,
   'Twill but drive me to Thy breast;
   Life with trials hard may press me,
   Heaven will bring me sweeter rest.
   Oh, 'tis not in grief to harm me
   While Thy love is left to me;
   Oh, 'twere not in joy to charm me
   Were that joy unmixed with Thee.

5. Take, my soul, thy full salvation;
   Rise o'er sin and fear and care;
   Joy to find in every station,
   Something still to do or bear.
   Think what Spirit dwells within thee,
   What a Father's smile is thine,
   What a Savior died to win thee;
   Child of heaven, shouldst thou repine?

6. Haste, then, on from grace to glory,
   Armed by faith and winged by prayer;
   Heaven's eternal day's before thee,
   God's own hand shall guide thee there.
   Soon shall close the earthly mission,
   Swift shall pass thy pilgrim days,
   Hope soon change to glad fruition,
   Faith to sight, and prayer to praise.

Henry Francis Lyte based this hymn on Mark 10:28. It appeared in Lyte's *Sacred Poetry*, 1824, signed "G." The author acknowledged it as his own when it was published in an altered form in his *Poems Chiefly Religious*, 1833. It has found a place in many hymnals, though sometimes in an abbreviated form.

The tune "Hyfrydol" is by Rowland H. Pritchard, altered. It appeared in *Haleliwiah Drachefu*, Carmarthen, 1855.

NEW OBEDIENCE

424   My God, My Father, Make Me Strong

1. My God, my Father, make me strong,
When tasks of life seem hard and long,
To greet them with this triumph song:
 Thy will be done.

2. Draw from my timid eyes the veil
To show where earthly forces fail,
Thy power and love must still prevail —
 Thy will be done.

3. With confident and humble mind
Freedom in service I would find,
Praying through every toil assigned:
 Thy will be done.

4. Things deemed impossible I dare,
Thine is the call and Thine the care;
Thy wisdom shall the way prepare —
 Thy will be done.

5. All power is here and round me now;
Faithful I stand in rule and vow,
While 'tis not I, but ever Thou:
 Thy will be done.

6. Heaven's music chimes the glad days in;
Hope soars beyond death, pain, and sin;
Faith shouts in triumph, Love must win —
 Thy will be done!

    This hymn, by Frederick Mann, which appeared in *Songs of Praise*, 1931, is a companion hymn to Charlotte Elliott's "My God, My Father, while I Stray" (see Hymn No. 418). Percy Dearmer, in *Songs of Praise Discussed,* writes:

    There is a well-known hymn, "My God and Father, while I Stray," from Charlotte Elliott's *Invalid's Hymn Book* (1834), which marked the then common idea that the petition in the Lord's Prayer is a cry of resignation (instead of a prayer that the divine will may be carried out in the world), and therefore summed up the major sorrows of life as constituting God's will. To stop this, without depriving churchgoers of the shape of hymn they were used to, Mr. Mann wrote this, which has come speedily to the fore. Its cheerful optimism is the finer because he suffered under many disabilities, and few would have envied his apparently unsuccessful lot.

    We believe that both truths are to be found in the Third Petition, and therefore both hymns have a place in the hymnals of the Church.

    For comments on the tune "Es ist kein Tag" see Hymn No. 418.

425   All Depends on Our Possessing

1. All depends on our possessing
God's abundant grace and blessing,
 Though all earthly wealth depart.
He who trusts with faith unshaken
In His God is not forsaken
And e'er keeps a dauntless heart.

2. He who hitherto hath fed me
And to many joys hath led me,
 Is and ever shall be mine.
He who did so gently school me,
He who still doth guide and rule me,
Will remain my Help divine.

3. Many spend their lives in fretting
Over trifles and in getting
 Things that have no solid ground.
I shall strive to win a treasure
That will bring me lasting pleasure
And that now is seldom found.

4. When with sorrow I am stricken,
Hope my heart anew will quicken,
 All my longing shall be stilled.
To His loving-kindness tender
Soul and body I surrender;
 For on Him alone I build.

Alles ist an Gottes Segen
Und an seiner Gnad' gelegen,
 Über alles Geld und Gut.
Wer auf Gott sein' Hoffnung setzet,
Der behält ganz unverletzet
Einen freien Heldenmut.

Der mich hat bisher ernähret
Und mir manches Glück bescheret,
 Ist und bleibet ewig mein.
Der mich wunderlich geführet
Und noch leitet und regieret,
Wird forthin mein Helfer sein.

Viel' bemühen sich um Sachen,
Die nur Sorg' und Unruh' machen
 Und ganz unbeständig sind.
Ich begehr' nach dem zu ringen,
Was mir kann Vergnügen bringen
Und man jetzt gar selten find't.

Hoffnung kann das Herz erquicken;
Was ich wünsche, wird sich schicken,
 So es anders Gott gefällt.
Meine Seele, Leib und Leben
Hab' ich seiner Gnad' ergeben
Und ihm alles heimgestellt.

TRUST

5. Well He knows what best to grant me;
All the longing hopes that haunt me,
Joy and sorrow, have their day.
I shall doubt His wisdom never, —
As God wills, so be it ever, —
I to Him commit my way.

6. If on earth my days He lengthen,
He my weary soul will strengthen;
All my trust in Him I place.
Earthly wealth is not abiding,
Like a stream away is gliding;
Safe I anchor in His grace.

Er weiss schon nach seinem Willen
Mein Verlangen zu erfüllen,
Es hat alles seine Zeit.
Ich hab' ihm nichts vorzuschreiben;
Wie Gott will, so muss es bleiben,
Wenn Gott will, bin ich bereit.

6. Soll ich länger allhier leben,
Will ich ihm nicht widerstreben,
Ich verlasse mich auf ihn.
Ist doch nichts, das lang bestehet,
Alles Irdische vergehet
Und fährt wie ein Strom dahin.

This popular hymn of trust in God is by an unknown author and is dated c. 1673 by *Koch*. It was included in the Nürnberg *Gesang-Buch*, 1676.

The translation is an altered form of that by Catherine Winkworth in her *Lyra Germanica*, second series, 1858.

The tune "Alles ist an Gottes Segen" is from Johann B. König's *Harmonischer Liederschatz*, 1738. Perhaps it is by König himself.

The Lord My Shepherd Is   426

1. The Lord my Shepherd is,
I shall be well supplied.
Since He is mine and I am His,
What can I want beside?

2. He leads me to the place
Where heavenly pasture grows,
Where living waters gently pass
And full salvation flows.

3. If e'er I go astray,
He doth my soul reclaim
And guides me in His own right way
For His most holy name.

4. While He affords His aid,
I cannot yield to fear;
Though I should walk through death's dark shade,
My Shepherd's with me there.

5. Amid surrounding foes
Thou dost my table spread;
My cup with blessing overflows,
And joy exalts my head.

6. The bounties of Thy love
Shall crown my following days,
Nor from Thy house will I remove
Nor cease to speak Thy praise.

This is Isaac Watts's short-meter paraphrase of the 23d Psalm. It appeared in his *Psalms of David Imitated*, 1719.

For comments on the tune "Potsdam" see Hymn No. 117.

How Firm a Foundation, Ye Saints of the Lord   427

1. How firm a foundation, ye saints of the Lord,
Is laid for your faith in His excellent Word!
What more can He say than to you He hath said
Who unto the Savior for refuge have fled?

2. In every condition, — in sickness, in health,
In poverty's vale, or abounding in wealth,
At home and abroad, on the land, on the sea, —
The Lord, the Almighty, thy strength e'er shall be.

3. "Fear not, I am with thee, oh, be not dismayed,
For I am thy God and will still give thee aid;
I'll strengthen thee, help thee, and cause thee to stand,
Upheld by My righteous, omnipotent hand.

4. "When through the deep waters I call thee to go,
The rivers of sorrow shall not overflow;
For I will be with thee thy troubles to bless
And sanctify to thee thy deepest distress.

5. "When through fiery trials thy pathway shall lie,
My grace, all-sufficient, shall be thy supply.
The flames shall not hurt thee; I only design
Thy dross to consume and thy gold to refine.

6. "E'en down to old age all My people shall prove
My sovereign, eternal, unchangeable love;
And when hoary hairs shall their temples adorn,
Like lambs they shall still in My bosom be borne.

7. "The soul that on Jesus hath leaned for repose
I will not, I will not, desert to his foes;
That soul, though all hell should endeavor to shake,
I'll never, no never, no never, forsake!"

This hymn on the perseverance of the saints is of unknown authorship. It appeared in John Rippon's *Selection,* 1787, entitled "Exceeding Great and Precious Promises," and with the signature "K—." Later, in Fletcher's *Collection,* 1822, the "K—." is extended to "Kn," and in the edition of 1835 it is given as "Keen." Who this "Keen" was is not known. The hymn is another example of how an unknown author has contributed one of the truly great hymns to the hymn-treasury of Zion, and the number of those who have been comforted and strengthened by the words of this unknown author is inestimable.

That a hymn as fine as this has not had its own tune is well known. Usually it is sung to "Adeste Fideles" or "Portuguese Hymn" (see Hymn No. 102); but this is so thoroughly wedded to that Christmas hymn, and its joyful note does not harmonize with the spirit of this hymn. The tune "Firm Foundation" by Bernhard Schumacher, 1931, has therefore been selected for it in the hope that it will in time replace the use of the "Portuguese Hymn," which should be used exclusively for "Oh, Come, All Ye Faithful."

428   I Am Trusting Thee, Lord Jesus

1. I am trusting Thee, Lord Jesus,
Trusting only Thee;
Trusting Thee for full salvation,
Great and free.

2. I am trusting Thee for pardon;
At Thy feet I bow,
For Thy grace and tender mercy
Trusting now.

3. I am trusting Thee for cleansing
In the crimson flood;
Trusting Thee to make me holy
By Thy blood.

4. I am trusting Thee to guide me;
Thou alone shalt lead,
Every day and hour supplying
All my need.

5. I am trusting Thee for power;
Thine can never fail.
Words which Thou Thyself shalt give me
Must prevail.

6. I am trusting Thee, Lord Jesus;
Never let me fall.
I am trusting Thee forever
And for all.

Frances R. Havergal wrote this hymn of faith at Ormont Dessons, in September, 1874. It was first published in her *Loyal Responses,* 1878. The hymn was the author's own favorite and was found in her pocket Bible after her death.

For comments on the tune "Stephanos" see Hymn No. 513.

429   Lord, Thee I Love with All My Heart

1. Lord, Thee I love with all my heart;
I pray Thee, ne'er from me depart,
With tender mercy cheer me.
Earth has no pleasure I would share,
Yea, heaven itself were void and bare
If Thou, Lord, wert not near me.
And should my heart for sorrow break,
My trust in Thee no one could shake.
Thou art the Portion I have sought;
Thy precious blood my soul has bought.
Lord Jesus Christ,
My God and Lord, my God and Lord,
Forsake me not! I trust Thy Word.

Herzlich lieb hab' ich dich, o Herr,
Ich bitt', woll'st sein von mir nicht fern
Mit deiner Güt' und Gnaden.
Die ganze Welt nicht freuet mich,
Nach Himmel und Erd' nicht frag' ich,
Wenn ich *dich* nur kann haben;
Und wenn mir gleich mein Herz zerbricht,
So bist doch du mein' Zuversicht,
Mein Teil und meines Herzens Trost,
Der mich durch sein Blut hat erlöst.
Herr Jesu Christ,
Mein Gott und Herr, mein Gott und Herr,
In Schanden lass mich nimmermehr!

2. Yea, Lord, 'twas Thy rich bounty gave
My body, soul, and all I have
In this poor life of labor.
Lord, grant that I in every place
May glorify Thy lavish grace
And serve and help my neighbor.
Let no false doctrine me beguile
And Satan not my soul defile.
Give strength and patience unto me
To bear my cross and follow Thee.
   Lord Jesus Christ,
My God and Lord, my God and Lord,
In death Thy comfort still afford.

3. Lord, let at last Thine angels come,
To Abram's bosom bear me home,
That I may die unfearing;
And in its narrow chamber keep
My body safe in peaceful sleep
Until Thy reappearing.
And then from death awaken me
That these mine eyes with joy may see,
O Son of God, Thy glorious face,
My Savior and my Fount of grace.
   Lord Jesus Christ,
My prayer attend, my prayer attend,
And I will praise Thee without end.

Es ist ja, Herr, dein G'schenk und Gab'
Mein Leib und Seel' und was ich hab'
In diesem armen Leben.
Damit ich's brauch' zum Lobe dein,
Zu Nutz und Dienst des Nächsten mein,
Woll'st mir dein' Gnade geben!
Behüt mich, Herr, vor falscher Lehr',
Des Satans Mord und Lügen wehr,
In allem Kreuz erhalte mich,
Auf dass ich's trag' geduldiglich!
   Herr Jesu Christ,
Mein Herr und Gott, mein Herr und Gott,
Tröst mir mein' Seel' in Todesnot!

Ach, Herr, lass dein' lieb' Engelein
Am letzten End' die Seele mein
In Abrahams Schoss tragen!
Der Leib in sein'm Schlafkämmerlein
Gar sanft, ohn' ein'ge Qual und Pein,
Ruh' bis am Jüngsten Tage.
Alsdann vom Tod erwecke mich,
Dass meine Augen sehen dich
In aller Freud', o Gottes Sohn,
Mein Heiland und mein Gnadenthron!
   Herr Jesu Christ,
Erhöre mich, erhöre mich,
Ich will dich preisen ewiglich!

Martin Schalling wrote this hymn c. 1567. It first appeared in *Kurtze und sonderliche Newe Symbola*, etc., Nürnberg, 1571. This estimate of the hymn by *Koch* is fair: "This hymn, 'a prayer to Christ, the Consolation of the soul in life and in death,' after Pss. 18 and 73, is a treasure bequeathed to the Church from the heart of Schalling."

The translation is an altered form of that by Catherine Winkworth in her *Chorale Book for England*, 1863.

The tune "Herzlich lieb hab' ich dich, o Herr" belongs to the best of Lutheran *chorales*. Fortunate is the congregation that has learned to sing it and appreciate it. Its composer is not known. The tune first appeared in Bernhard Schmid's *Orgeltabulatur-Buch*, Strassburg, 1577, the full title of which is *Zwey Bücher einer neuen Künstlichen Tabulatur auf Orgel und Instrument*. Johann Sebastian Bach embodied this tune in his *Passion according to St. John*.

What Is the World to Me   430

1. What is the world to me
  With all its vaunted pleasure
When Thou, and Thou alone,
  Lord Jesus, art my Treasure!
Thou only, dearest Lord,
  My soul's Delight shalt be;
Thou art my Peace, my Rest, —
  What is the world to me!

2. The world is like a cloud
  And like a vapor fleeting,
A shadow that declines,
  Swift to its end retreating.
My Jesus doth abide,
  Though all things fade and flee;
My everlasting Rock, —
  What is the world to me!

3. The world seeks to be praised
  And honored by the mighty,
Yet never once reflects
  That they are frail and flighty.
But what I truly prize
  Above all things is He,
My Jesus, He alone, —
  What is the world to me!

Was frag' ich nach der Welt
  Und allen ihren Schätzen,
Wenn ich mich nur an dir,
  Herr Jesu, kann ergötzen!
Dich hab' ich einzig mir
  Zur Wollust vorgestellt,
Du, du bist meine Ruh';
  Was frag' ich nach der Welt!

Die Welt ist wie ein Rauch,
  Der in der Luft vergehet,
Und einem Schatten gleich,
  Der kurze Zeit bestehet;
Mein Jesus aber bleibt,
  Wenn alles bricht und fällt;
Er ist mein starker Fels,
  Was frag' ich nach der Welt!

Die Welt sucht Ehr' und Ruhm
  Bei hocherhabnen Leuten
Und denkt nicht einmal dran,
  Wie bald doch diese gleiten;
Das aber, was mein Herz
  Vor andern rühmlich hält,
Ist Jesus nur allein;
  Was frag' ich nach der Welt!

4. The world seeks after wealth
   And all that Mammon offers,
   Yet never is content
   Though gold should fill its coffers.
   I have a higher good,
   Content with it I'll be:
   My Jesus is my Wealth, —
   What is the world to me!

5. The world is sorely grieved
   Whenever it is slighted
   Or when its hollow fame
   And honor have been blighted.
   Christ, Thy reproach I bear
   Long as it pleaseth Thee;
   I'm honored by my Lord, —
   What is the world to me!

6. The world with wanton pride
   Exalts its sinful pleasures
   And for them foolishly
   Gives up the heavenly treasures.
   Let others love the world
   With all its vanity;
   I love the Lord, my God, —
   What is the world to me!

7. The world abideth not;
   Lo, like a flash 'twill vanish;
   With all its gorgeous pomp
   Pale death it cannot banish;
   Its riches pass away,
   And all its joys must flee;
   But Jesus doth abide, —
   What is the world to me!

8. What is the world to me!
   My Jesus is my Treasure,
   My Life, my Health, my Wealth,
   My Friend, my Love, my Pleasure,
   My Joy, my Crown, my All,
   My Bliss eternally.
   Once more, then, I declare:
   What is the world to me!

Die Welt sucht Geld und Gut
   Und kann nicht eher rasten,
   Sie habe denn zuvor
   Den Mammon in dem Kasten;
   Ich weiss ein besser Gut,
   Wonach mein Herze stellt:
   Ist Jesus nur mein Schatz,
   Was frag' ich nach der Welt!

Die Welt bekümmert sich,
   Im Fall sie wird verachtet,
   Und wenn man ihr mit List
   Nach ihren Ehren trachtet;
   Ich trage Christi Schmach,
   Solang es ihm gefällt;
   Wenn mich mein Heiland ehrt,
   Was frag' ich nach der Welt!

Die Welt kann ihre Lust
   Nicht hoch genug erheben,
   Sie darf noch wohl dazu
   Den Himmel dafür geben.
   Ein andrer halt's mit ihr,
   Der von sich selbst viel hält;
   Ich liebe meinen Gott,
   Was frag' ich nach der Welt!

Was frag' ich nach der Welt,
   Im Hui muss sie verschwinden;
   Ihr Ansehn kann durchaus
   Den blassen Tod nicht binden;
   Die Güter müssen fort,
   Und alle Lust verfällt.
   Bleibt Jesus nur bei mir,
   Was frag' ich nach der Welt!

Was frag' ich nach der Welt,
   Mein Jesus ist mein Leben,
   Mein Schatz, mein Eigentum,
   Dem ich mich ganz ergeben,
   Mein ganzes Himmelreich,
   Und was mir sonst gefällt.
   Drum sag' ich noch einmal:
   Was frag' ich nach der Welt!

Georg M. Pfefferkorn wrote this hymn in 1667, according to J. Avenarius in his *Liedercatechismus,* Leipzig, 1714. It was included in the *Stettinisches Vollständiges Gesang Buch,* Alten-Stettin, 1671, but without the author's name, and with his name in the Naumburg *Gesang Buch,* 1715. It is based on 1 John 2:15-17. Its theme is "Renunciation of the World."

The translation is by August Crull, altered.

Through the kindness of the Rev. Arthur W. Farlander, we are able to give the following on the tune "Was frag' ich nach der Welt":

"It is an anonymous melody first appearing in *Himmels-Lust und Welt-Unlust* compiled by A. Fritsch in Jena in 1679. It is sometimes called *Darmstadt* because it appeared subsequently in *Geistreiches Gesangbuch,* Darmstadt, 1698, set to the words of Dessler's hymn 'Was frag' ich nach der Welt.' In the Jena volume it was set to Jacob Schuetz's words: 'Die Wollust dieser Welt.' Bach uses the melody in several of his cantatas, chief among them being No. 45: 'Es ist dir gesagt, Mensch, was gut ist,' composed for the 8th Sunday after Trinity, c. 1740. In this work Bach uses the melody for the final chorale, the words being the second stanza of the hymn 'O Gott, du frommer Gott,' beginning: 'Gib, dass ich tu mit Fleiss.' Author of the hymn: J. Heermann."

TRUST

The King of Love My Shepherd Is 431

1. The King of Love my Shepherd is,
Whose goodness faileth never;
I nothing lack if I am His
And He is mine forever.

2. Where streams of living water flow,
My ransomed soul He leadeth,
And where the verdant pastures grow,
With food celestial feedeth.

3. Perverse and foolish oft I strayed,
But yet in love He sought me
And on His shoulder gently laid
And home, rejoicing, brought me.

4. In death's dark vale I fear no ill,
With Thee, dear Lord, beside me;
Thy rod and staff my comfort still,
Thy cross before to guide me.

5. Thou spreadst a table in my sight,
Thy unction grace bestoweth;
And, oh! the transport of delight
With which my cup o'erfloweth.

6. And so through all the length of days
Thy goodness faileth never.
Good Shepherd, may I sing Thy praise
Within Thy house forever!

This hymn by Henry W. Baker is undoubtedly one of the best English metrical paraphrases of Ps. 23. It was included in the *Appendix* to *Hymns Ancient and Modern*, 1868.

While many modern hymnals use the tune "Dominus Regit Me" by John B. Dykes for this hymn, we believe the tune "Ich dank' dir schon" is especially fitted for the spirit of the text. The tune is by Michael Prätorius and appeared in *Musae Sioniae* VIII, 1610, set to the morning hymn of unknown authorship beginning with that line.

In Hope My Soul, Redeemed to Bliss Unending 432

1. In hope my soul, redeemed to bliss unending,
To heaven's glorious height by faith ascending,
Is mindful ever
That Christ did sever
The bonds of death that I might live forever.

2. In Him I have salvation's way discovered,
The heritage for me He hath recovered.
Though death o'ertakes me,
Christ ne'er forsakes me,
To everlasting life He surely wakes me.

3. More radiant there than sun e'er shone in brightness,
My soul shall shine before God's throne in whiteness.
My God, who knows me,
In glory clothes me,
As He declared when for His own He chose me.

4. Oh, may I come where strife and grief are ended,
Where all Thy saints shall meet with peace attended!
Lord, grant Thy favor
And mercy ever
And turn my sorrow into joy forever.

5. Lord Jesus Christ, keep me prepared and waking
Till from the vale of tears Thy bride Thou'rt taking
To dwell in heaven,
Where joy is given
And clouds of darkness are forever riven.

This hymn is by Elle Andersdatter and is dated 1645. Its original first line reads: "I hoppet sig min frälsta själ förnöjir." We have been unable to obtain more data regarding the hymn. Further details about the author will be found in the biographical section of this book.

The translation is by George H. Trabert. It appeared in *The Hymnal* of the Evangelical Lutheran Augustana Synod, 1925.

The tune is also found in that collection, where it is simply given as "Northern Melody from 16th century." It has been named "Norrland" for *The Lutheran Hymnal*.

TRUST

433   Jesus, My Truth, My Way

1. Jesus, my Truth, my Way,
   My sure, unerring Light,
   On Thee my feeble soul I stay,
   Which Thou wilt lead aright.

2. My Wisdom and my Guide,
   My Counselor Thou art;
   Oh, let me never leave Thy side
   Nor from Thy paths depart!

3. Thou seest my feebleness;
   Jesus, be Thou my Power,
   My Help and Refuge in distress,
   My Fortress and my Tower.

4. Give me to trust in Thee;
   Be Thou my sure Abode;
   My Horn and Rock and Buckler be,
   My Savior and my God.

5. Myself I cannot save,
   Myself I cannot keep;
   But strength in Thee I surely have,
   Whose eyelids never sleep.

6. My soul to Thee alone
   Now, therefore, I commend.
   Thou, Jesus, having loved Thine own,
   Wilt love me to the end.

Charles Wesley published this hymn in *Hymns and Sacred Poems*, 1749, in seven eight-line stanzas. It is entitled "Leaning on Jesus." As we have not been able to locate a copy of the original text, it is not possible for us to explain the composition of the cento. The following two stanzas from the *Methodist Hymnal* follow the second stanza above:

1. I lift mine eyes to Thee,
   Thou gracious, bleeding Lamb,
   That I may now enlightened be
   And never put to shame.

2. I never will remove
   Out of Thy hands my cause,
   But rest in Thy redeeming love
   And hang upon the cross.

For comments on the tune "Swabia" see Hymn No. 274.

434   O God of Jacob, by Whose Hand

1. O God of Jacob, by whose hand
   Thy people still are fed;
   Who through this weary pilgrimage
   Hast all our fathers led,

2. Our vows, our prayers, we now present
   Before Thy throne of grace;
   God of our fathers, be the God
   Of their succeeding race.

3. Through each perplexing path of life
   Our wandering footsteps guide;
   Give us each day our daily bread
   And raiment fit provide.

4. Oh, spread Thy covering wings around
   Till all our wanderings cease
   And at our Father's loved abode
   Our souls arrive in peace.

5. Now with the humble voice of prayer
   Thy mercy we implore;
   Then with a grateful voice of praise
   Thy goodness we'll adore.

Philip Doddridge wrote this hymn on January 16, 1737, in the following form:

Jacob's Vow
From Gen. 28:20-22

1. O God of Bethel, by whose hand
   Thine Israel still is fed,
   Who through this weary pilgrimage
   Hast all our fathers led,

2. To Thee our humble vows we raise,
   To Thee address our prayer
   And in Thy kind and faithful breast
   Deposit all our care.

3. If Thou through each perplexing path
   Wilt be our constant Guide;
   If Thou wilt daily bread supply
   And raiment wilt provide;

4. If thou wilt spread Thy shield around
   Till these our wanderings cease
   And at our Father's loved abode
   Our souls arrive in peace,

5. To Thee as to our Covenant God
   We'll our whole selves resign
   And count that not our tenth alone
   But all we have is Thine.

In Job Orton's edition of Doddridge's *Hymns Founded on Various Texts in the Holy Scriptures*, etc., 1755, the hymn is given with the opening line:

O God of *Jacob*, by whose hand.

In John Logan's *Poems*, 1781, the hymn is given as recast by John Logan, omitting Doddridge's Stanza 5 and with a new fifth stanza. This is the text as above, save that Logan began the hymn:

O God of *Abraham*, by whose hand.

The tune "St. Savior," is by Frederick G. Baker, 1872. The name of the tune is from the St. Savior Church, Shanklin, Isle of Wight, where Baker served as organist.

My Spirit on Thy Care   435

1. My spirit on Thy care,
   Blest Savior, I recline;
   Thou wilt not leave me to despair,
   For Thou art Love divine.

2. In Thee I place my trust,
   On Thee I calmly rest;
   I know Thee good, I know Thee just,
   And count Thy choice the best.

3. Whate'er events betide,
   Thy will they all perform;
   Safe in Thy breast my head I hide
   Nor fear the coming storm.

4. Let good or ill befall,
   It must be good for me;
   Secure of having Thee in all,
   Of having all in Thee.

Henry F. Lyte published this hymn, dated 1834, in his *Spirit of the Psalms*. It is based on Ps. 31.

For comments on the tune "Potsdam" see Hymn No. 117.

The Lord's My Shepherd, I'll Not Want   436

1. The Lord's my Shepherd, I'll not want;
   He makes me down to lie
   In pastures green; He leadeth me
   The quiet waters by.

2. My soul He doth restore again
   And me to walk doth make
   Within the paths of righteousness,
   E'en for His own name's sake.

3. Yea, though I walk in death's dark vale,
   Yet will I fear no ill;
   For Thou art with me, and Thy rod
   And staff me comfort still.

4. My table Thou hast furnishèd
   In presence of my foes;
   My head Thou dost with oil anoint,
   And my cup overflows.

5. Goodness and mercy, all my life,
   Shall surely follow me;
   And in God's house forevermore
   My dwelling-place shall be.

This is the famous metrical version of the 23d Psalm as it appeared in the *Scottish Psalter*, 1650. It is based on the version of Francis Rous, which reads:

1. My Shepherd is the living Lord
   And He that doth me feed;
   How can I, then, lack anything
   Whereof I stand in need?

2. In pastures green and flourishing
   He makes me down to lye:
   And after drives me to the streames
   Which run most pleasantly.

3. And when I feele my selfe neere lost,
   Then home He me doth take,
   Conducting me in His right paths,
   Even for His owne Names sake.

4. And though I were even at death's doore,
   Yet would I feare none ill;
   Thy rod, Thy staff, do comfort me,
   And Thou art with me still.

5. Thou hast my table richly stor'd
   In presence of my foe;
   My head with oile Thou dost anoint,
   My cup doth overflow.

6. Thy grace and mercy all my daies
   Shall surely follow me;
   And ever in the house of God,
   My dwelling place shall be.

The tune "Belmont" is an adaptation from a tune by William Gardiner. The original is an eight-line tune and is from his *Sacred Melodies*, 1812.

STEWARDSHIP

437   Who Trusts in God, a Strong Abode

1. Who trusts in God a strong abode
   In heaven and earth possesses;
   Who looks in love to Christ above,
   No fear his heart oppresses.
   In Thee alone, dear Lord, we own
   Sweet hope and consolation,
   Our Shield from foes, our Balm for woes,
   Our great and sure Salvation.

2. Though Satan's wrath beset our path
   And worldly scorn assail us,
   While Thou art near, we will not fear;
   Thy strength shall never fail us.
   Thy rod and staff shall keep us safe
   And guide our steps forever;
   Nor shades of death nor hell beneath
   Our souls from Thee shall sever.

3. In all the strife of mortal life
   Our feet shall stand securely;
   Temptation's hour shall lose its power,
   For Thou shalt guard us surely.
   O God, renew with heavenly dew
   Our body, soul, and spirit
   Until we stand at Thy right hand
   Through Jesus' saving merit.

Wer Gott vertraut, hat wohl gebaut
Im Himmel und auf Erden.
Wer sich verlässt auf Jesum Christ,
Dem muss der Himmel werden.
Darum auf dich all' Hoffnung ich
Ganz fest und steif tu' setzen.
Herr Jesu Christ, mein Trost du bist
In Todesnot und Schmerzen.

Und wenn's gleich wär' dem Teufel sehr
Und aller Welt zuwider,
Dennoch so bist du, Jesu Christ,
Der sie all' schlägt danieder;
Und wenn ich dich nur hab' um mich
Mit deinem Geist und Gnaden,
So kann fürwahr mir ganz und gar
Wed'r Tod noch Teufel schaden.

Dein tröst' ich mich ganz sicherlich,
Denn du kannst mir wohl geben,
Was mir ist not, du treuer Gott,
In dies'm und jenem Leben.
Gib wahre Reu', mein Herz erneu',
Errette Leib und Seele!
Ach höre, Herr, dies mein Begehr,
Lass meine Bitt' nicht fehlen!

    This hymn was originally in one stanza. It is based on Ps. 73:25, 26. Joachim Magdeburg published it in his *Christliche und tröstliche Tischgesenge*, etc., Erfurt, 1572, where it is a hymn for Saturday evening. Stanzas 2 and 3 are first found in *Harmonia Cantionum Ecclesiasticarum*, Leipzig, 1597.

    The free translation is by Benjamin H. Kennedy in his *Hymnologia Christiana*, etc., 1863.

    The tune "Was mein Gott will" is from a French melody of 1529 to 1531, which appeared in *Trente et quatre chansons musicales*, etc., Paris, where it is set to the text of a French love-song, beginning "Il me suffit de tous mes maulx." Joachim Magdeburg took the tune from this hymn in 1572. The harmonization is by Johann Sebastian Bach. The great Lutheran musician had a particular liking for this melody, which he used more than any other single tune. He uses it in his *Passion according to St. Matthew;* again, in his *Choralkantate Was mein Gott will, das g'scheh' allzeit* for the Third Sunday after Epiphany; again, in his *Choralkantate Ich hab' in Gottes Herz und Sinn* for Septuagesima Sunday; and in four other cantatas.

438   Almighty Father, Heaven and Earth

1. Almighty Father, heaven and earth
   With lavish wealth before Thee bow;
   Those treasures owe to Thee their birth,
   Creator, Ruler, Giver, Thou.

2. The wealth of earth, of sky, of sea,
   The gold, the silver, sparkling gem,
   The waving corn, the bending tree,
   Are Thine; to us Thou lendest them.

3. To Thee, as early morning's dew,
   Our praises, alms, and prayer shall rise
   As rose, when joyous earth was new,
   Faith's patriarchial sacrifice.

4. We, Lord, would lay, at Thy behest
   The costliest offerings on Thy shrine;
   But when we give, and give our best,
   We give Thee only what is Thine.

5. O Father, whence all blessings come;
   O Son, Dispenser of God's store;
   O Spirit, bear our offerings home;
   Lord, make them Thine forevermore.

    Edward A. Dayman wrote this hymn in 1867. It first appeared in the *Sarum Hymnal*, 1868, as an offertory hymn. The text has been altered.

    For comments on the tune "O Heilige Dreifaltigkeit" see Hymn No. 340.

STEWARDSHIP

O God of Mercy, God of Might — 439

1. O God of mercy, God of might,
In love and pity infinite,
Teach us, as ever in Thy sight,
To live our life to Thee.

2. And Thou, who cam'st on earth to die
That fallen man might live thereby,
Oh, hear us; for to Thee we cry,
In hope, O Lord, to Thee.

3. Teach us the lesson Thou hast taught,
To feel for those Thy blood hath bought
That every word and deed and thought
May work a work for Thee.

4. All are redeemed, both far and wide,
Since Thou, O Lord, for all hast died.
Oh, teach us, whatsoe'er betide,
To love them all in Thee!

5. In sickness, sorrow, want, or care,
Whate'er it be, 'tis ours to share;
May we, where help is needed, there
Give help as unto Thee!

6. And may Thy Holy Spirit move
All those who live to live in love
Till Thou shalt greet in heaven above
All those who live to Thee.

Godfrey Thring wrote this hymn in 1877 as an offertory hymn. It appeared in his *Collection*, 1880. It was included in his *Church of England Hymn-Book*, 1882, headed Luke 10:36, 37: "Which, now, of these three was neighbor unto him that fell among the thieves?"

The tune "Isleworth" is by Samuel Howard and is taken from *Melodies of the Psalms of David*, etc., by Christopher Smart, 1765, where it is set to a metrical version of Ps. 6.

Lord, Lead the Way the Savior Went — 440

1. Lord, lead the way the Savior went,
By lane and cell obscure,
And let love's treasure still be spent,
Like His, upon the poor.

2. Like Him, through scenes of deep distress,
Who bore the world's sad weight,
We in their crowded loneliness
Would seek the desolate.

3. For Thou hast placed us side by side
In this wide world of ill;
And that Thy followers may be tried,
The poor are with us still.

4. Mean are all offerings we can make;
But Thou hast taught us, Lord,
If given for the Savior's sake,
They lose not their reward.

William Crosswell wrote this hymn in 1831 for the anniversary of the Howard Benevolent Society of Boston. It was intended for the work of mercy done by the deaconesses of the Church. It is generally used as a hymn for benevolent occasions.

The tune "Farrant" is attributed to Richard Farrant. It is adapted from the anthem "Lord, for Thy Tender Mercies' Sake," ascribed to him. Some writers ascribe the anthem to John Hilton, others to William Mundy.

We Give Thee But Thine Own — 441

1. We give Thee but Thine own,
Whate'er the gift may be;
All that we have is Thine alone,
A trust, O Lord, from Thee.

2. May we Thy bounties thus
As stewards true receive
And gladly, as Thou blessest us,
To Thee our first-fruits give!

3. Oh, hearts are bruised and dead,
And homes are bare and cold,
And lambs for whom the Shepherd bled
Are straying from the fold.

4. To comfort and to bless,
To find a balm for woe,
To tend the lone and fatherless,
Is angels' work below.

5. The captive to release,
To God the lost to bring,
To teach the way of life and peace,
It is a Christlike thing.

6. And we believe Thy Word,
Though dim our faith may be:
Whate'er for Thine we do, O Lord,
We do it unto Thee.

William W. How wrote this hymn in 1854. It was first published in Morrell and How, *Psalms and Hymns*, 1864.

For comments on the tune "Energy" see Hymn No. 374.

STEWARDSHIP. — CHRISTIAN WARFARE

442 Lord of Glory, Who hast Bought Us

1. Lord of Glory, who hast bought us
With Thy life-blood as the price,
Never grudging for the lost ones
That tremendous sacrifice;
And with that hast freely given
Blessings countless as the sand
To the unthankful and the evil
With Thine own unsparing hand;

2. Grant us hearts, dear Lord, to yield Thee
Gladly, freely, of Thine own;
With the sunshine of Thy goodness
Melt our thankless hearts of stone
Till our cold and selfish natures,
Warmed by Thee, at length believe
That more happy and more blessed
'Tis to give than to receive.

3. Wondrous honor hast Thou given
To our humblest charity
In Thine own mysterious sentence,
"Ye have done it unto Me."
Can it be, O gracious Master,
Thou dost deign for alms to sue,
Saying by Thy poor and needy,
"Give as I have given to you"?

4. Yes, the sorrow and the sufferings
Which on every hand we see
Channels are for tithes and offerings
Due by solemn right to Thee;
Right of which we may not rob Thee,
Debt we may not choose but pay,
Lest that face of love and pity
Turn from us another day.

5. Lord of Glory, who hast bought us
With Thy life-blood as the price,
Never grudging for the lost ones
That tremendous sacrifice,
Give us faith to trust Thee boldly,
Hope, to stay our souls on Thee;
But, oh! best of all Thy graces,
Give us Thine own charity.

Eliza Sibbald Alderson, sister of Henry W. Baker, wrote this hymn in 1864. It appeared in the *Appendix* to the original edition of *Hymns Ancient and Modern*, 1868. The hymn was submitted to the editorial committee of *Hymns Ancient and Modern* with the request that, if accepted, John B. Dykes be asked to write a tune for it. Dykes was not satisfied with the ending of the hymn, which originally closed, with Stanza 4, so he suggested the fifth stanza, a repetition of Stanza 1, Lines 1 to 4, and the four closing lines, which he wrote. The tune "Charitas" was composed by Dr. Dykes for this hymn.

For comments on the tune "Hyfrydol" see Hymn No. 423.

443 O Lord of Heaven and Earth and Sea

1. O Lord of heaven and earth and sea,
To Thee all praise and glory be.
How shall we show our love to Thee,
Who givest all?

2. The golden sunshine, vernal air,
Sweet flowers and fruit, Thy love declare.
When harvests ripen, Thou art there,
Who givest all.

3. For peaceful homes and healthful days,
For all the blessings earth displays,
We owe Thee thankfulness and praise,
Who givest all.

4. Thou didst not spare Thine only Son,
But gav'st Him for a world undone,
And freely with that Blessed One
Thou givest all.

5. Thou giv'st the Spirit's holy dower,
Spirit of Life and Love and Power,
And dost His sevenfold graces shower
Upon us all.

6. For souls redeemed, for sins forgiven,
For means of grace and hopes of heaven,
What can to Thee, O Lord, be given,
Who givest all?

7. We lose what on ourselves we spend;
We have as treasure without end
Whatever, Lord, to Thee we lend,
Who givest all;

8. To Thee, from whom we all derive
Our life, our gifts, our power to give.
Oh, may we ever with Thee live,
Who givest all!

Christopher Wordsworth first published this hymn in his *Holy Year*, third edition, 1863, in nine stanzas. Stanza 8, omitted, reads:

Whatever, Lord, we lend to Thee
Repaid a thousandfold will be;
Then gladly will we give to Thee,
Who givest all.

For comments on the tune "Es ist kein Tag" see Hymn No. 418.

CHRISTIAN WARFARE

Rise! To Arms! With Prayer Employ You   444

1. Rise! To arms! With prayer employ you,
O Christians, lest the Foe destroy you,
   For Satan has designed your fall.
Wield God's Word, a weapon glorious!
Against each foe you'll be victorious;
   Our God will set you o'er them all.
Is Satan strong and fell?
Here is Immanuel.
   Sing hosanna!
The strong ones yield,
With Christ our Shield,
And we as conquerors hold the field.

Rüstet euch, ihr Christenleute!
Die Feinde suchen euch zur Beute,
   Ja Satan selbst hat eu'r begehrt.
Wappnet euch mit Gottes Worte
Und kämpfet frisch an jedem Orte,
   Damit ihr bleibet unversehrt!
Ist euch der Feind zu schnell,
Hier ist Immanuel!
   Hosanna!
Der Starke fällt
Durch diesen Held,
Und wir behalten mit das Feld.

2. Cast afar this world's vain pleasures,
Aye, boldly fight for heavenly treasures,
   And steadfast be in Jesus' might.
He will help, whate'er betide you,
And naught will harm with Christ beside you;
   By faith you'll conquer in the fight.
Then shame, thou weary soul!
Look forward to the goal:
   There joy waits thee.
The race, then, run;
The combat done,
Thy crown of glory will be won.

Reinigt euch von euren Lüsten,
Besieget sie, die ihr seid Christen
   Und stehet in des Herren Kraft!
Stärket euch in Jesu Namen,
Dass ihr nicht strauchelt wie die Lahmen!
   Wo ist des Glaubens Eigenschaft?
Wer hier ermüden will,
Der schaue auf das Ziel,
   Da ist Freude.
Wohlan, so seid
Zum Kampf bereit,
So krönet euch die Ewigkeit!

3. Wisely fight, for time is fleeting,
The hours of grace are fast retreating;
   Short, short, is this our earthly way.
When the trump the dead is waking
And sinners all with fear are quaking,
   With joy the saints will greet that Day.
Bless God, our triumph's sure,
Though long we did endure
   Scorn and trial.
Thou, Son of God,
To Thine abode
Wilt lead the way Thyself hast trod.

Streitet recht die wenig Jahre,
Eh' ihr kommt auf die Totenbahre!
   Kurz, kurz ist unser Lebenslauf.
Wenn Gott wird die Toten wecken
Und Christus wird die Welt erschrecken,
   So stehen wir mit Freuden auf.
Gott Lob, wir sind versöhnt!
Dass uns die Welt noch höhnt,
   Währt nicht lange,
Und Gottes Sohn
Hat längstens schon
Uns beigelegt die Ehrenkron'.

4. Jesus, all Thy children cherish
And keep them that they never perish
   Whom Thou hast purchased with Thy blood.
Let new life to us be given
That we may look to Thee in heaven
   Whenever fearful is our mood.
Thy Spirit on us pour
That we may love Thee more —
   Hearts o'erflowing;
And then will we
Be true to Thee
In death and life eternally.

Jesu, stärke deine Kinder
Und mache die zu Überwindern,
   Die du erkauft mit deinem Blut.
Schaffe in uns neues Leben,
Dass wir uns stets zu dir erheben,
   Wenn uns entfallen will der Mut!
Geuss aus auf uns den Geist,
Dadurch die Liebe fleusst
   In die Herzen,
So halten wir
Getreu an dir
Im Tod und Leben für und für!

Wilhelm E. Arends is said to have contributed this and two other hymns to Freylinghausen's *Gesang-Buch*, 1714. Koch styles it "a call to arms for spiritual conflict and victory."

The translation is an altered form of that by John M. Sloan in Wilson's *Service of Praise*, 1865.

For comments on the tune "Wachet auf" see Hymn No. 609.

Am I a Soldier of the Cross   445

1. Am I a soldier of the Cross,
   A follower of the Lamb,
And shall I fear to own His cause
Or blush to speak His name?

2. Must I be carried to the skies
   On flowery beds of ease
While others fought to win the prize
And sailed through bloody seas?

3. Are there no foes for me to face?
   Must I not stem the flood?
Is this vile world a friend to grace
To help me on to God?

4. Sure I must fight if I would reign;
   Increase my courage, Lord!
I'll bear the toil, endure the pain,
Supported by Thy Word.

CHRISTIAN WARFARE

5. Thy saints in all this glorious war
Shall conquer though they die;
They see the triumph from afar
With faith's discerning eye.

6. When that illustrious Day shall rise
And all Thine armies shine
In robes of victory through the skies,
The glory shall be Thine.

Isaac Watts appended this hymn to a sermon on 1 Cor. 16:13, published in his *Sermons*, 1721—24. It was entitled "Holy Fortitude." In Stanza 5 Watts had

They see the triumph from afar
And seize it with their eye.

For comments on the tune "Winchester Old" see Hymn No. 31.

446   Rise, My Soul, to Watch and Pray

1. Rise, my soul, to watch and pray,
From thy sleep awaken;
Be not by the evil day
Unawares o'ertaken.
For the Foe, Well we know,
Oft his harvest reapeth
While the Christian sleepeth.

2. Watch against the devil's snares
Lest asleep he find thee;
For indeed no pains he spares
To deceive and blind thee.
Satan's prey Oft are they
Who secure are sleeping
And no watch are keeping.

3. Watch! Let not the wicked world
With its power defeat thee.
Watch lest with her pomp unfurled
She betray and cheat thee.
Watch and see Lest there be
Faithless friends to charm thee,
Who but seek to harm thee.

4. Watch against thyself, my soul,
Lest with grace thou trifle;
Let not self thy thoughts control
Nor God's mercy stifle.
Pride and sin Lurk within
All thy hopes to scatter;
Heed not when they flatter.

5. But while watching, also pray
To the Lord unceasing.
He will free thee, be thy Stay,
Strength and faith increasing.
O Lord, bless In distress
And let nothing swerve me
From the will to serve Thee.

6. Therefore let us watch and pray,
Knowing He will hear us
As we see from day to day
Dangers ever near us,
And the end Doth impend, —
Our redemption neareth
When the Lord appeareth.

Mache dich, mein Geist, bereit,
Wache, fleh und bete,
Dass dich nicht die böse Zeit
Unverhofft betrete;
Denn es ist Satans List
Über viele Frommen
Zur Versuchung kommen.

Wache, dass dich Satans List
Nicht im Schlaf antreffe,
Weil er sonst behende ist,
Dass er dich beäffe,
Und Gott gibt, die er liebt,
Oft in seine Strafen,
Wenn sie sicher schlafen.

Wache, dass dich nicht die Welt
Durch Gewalt bezwinge
Oder, wenn sie sich verstellt,
Wieder an sich bringe.
Wach und sieh, damit nie
Viel von falschen Brüdern
Unter deinen Gliedern!

Wache dazu auch für dich,
Für dein Fleisch und Herze,
Damit es nicht liederlich
Gottes Gnad' verscherze;
Denn es ist voller List
Und kann sich bald heucheln
Und in Hoffart schmeicheln.

Bete aber auch dabei
Mitten in dem Wachen;
Denn der Herre muss dich frei
Von dem allem machen,
Was dich drückt und bestrickt,
Dass du schläfrig bleibest
Und sein Werk nicht treibest.

Drum so lasst uns immerdar
Wachen, flehen, beten,
Weil die Angst, Not und Gefahr
Immer näher treten;
Denn die Zeit ist nicht weit,
Da uns Gott wird richten
Und die Welt vernichten.

Johann B. Freystein wrote this hymn in ten stanzas. It first appeared in *Geistreiches Gesang-Buch*, Halle, 1697. It is a stirring call to watchfulness against the world, the flesh, and Satan. It is based on Matt. 26:41. The cento omits Stanzas 2, 3, 8, and 9, which read in translation:

2. But first rouse thee and awake
From secure indifference;
Else will follow in its wake
Woe without deliverance.
O beware! Soul, take care!
Death in sins might find thee
Ere thou look behind thee.

3. Wake and watch, or else thy night
Christ can ne'er enlighten;
Far off still will seem the light
That thy path should brighten;
God demands Eyes and hands
Open for the offers
He so richly proffers.

[316]

CHRISTIAN WARFARE

8. Yea, indeed, He bids us pray,
   Promising to hear us,
E'er to be our Staff and Stay,
   Ever to be near us.
Ere we plead, Will He heed,
Strengthen, keep, defend us,
And deliverance send us.

9. Courage, then, for all things must
      Work for good and bless us
   If we but in prayerful trust
      To His Son address us;
   For He will Richly fill
   And His Spirit send us,
   Who to Him commend us.

The translation is an altered form of that by Catherine Winkworth in her *Chorale Book for England*, 1863.

The tune "Straf mich nicht" is from the *Hundert ahnmüthig- und sonderbahr geistlichen Arien*, published as an appendix to the Dresden *Gesang-Buch*, 1694, where it was set to the hymn by Johann G. Albinus "Straf mich nicht in deinem Zorn." According to Zahn the melody had appeared in a collection of dance music in 1681. The question whether the tune was first a dance tune or a church tune corrupted to dance use has not been answered.

Fight the Good Fight with All Thy Might   447

1. Fight the good fight With all thy might;
   Christ is thy Strength and Christ thy Right.
   Lay hold on life, and it shall be
   Thy joy and crown eternally.

2. Run the straight race Through God's good grace;
   Lift up thine eyes and seek His face.
   Life with its way before us lies;
   Christ is the Path and Christ the Prize.

3. Cast care aside; Upon thy Guide
   Lean, and His mercy will provide;
   Lean, and the trusting soul shall prove
   Christ is its Life and Christ its Love.

4. Faint not nor fear, His arms are near;
   He changeth not, and thou art dear.
   Only believe, and thou shalt see
   That Christ is All in all to thee.

This hymn by John S. B. Monsell was first published in his *Hymns of Love and Praise*, 1863.

For comments on the tune "Mendon" see Hymn No. 119.

Brief Life Is Here Our Portion   448

1. Brief life is here our portion;
      Brief sorrow, short-lived care.
   The life that knows no ending,
      The tearless life, is there.
   O happy retribution:
      Short toil, eternal rest;
   For mortals and for sinners
      A mansion with the blest!

2. And now we fight the battle,
      But then shall wear the crown
   Of full and everlasting
      And passionless renown;
   And now we watch and struggle,
      And now we live in hope,
   And Zion in her anguish
      With Babylon must cope.

3. But He whom now we trust in
      Shall then be seen and known;
   And they that know and see Him
      Shall have Him for their own.
   And there is David's fountain
      And life in fullest glow;
   And there the light is golden,
      And milk and honey flow.

4. The morning shall awaken,
      And shadows shall decay,
   And each true-hearted servant
      Shall shine as doth the day.
   There God, our King and Portion,
      In fulness of His grace
   Shall we behold forever
      And worship face to face.

Hic breve vivitur, hic breve plangitur,
   hic breve fletur;
Non breve vivere, non breve plaudere,
   retribuetur.

O retributio! stat brevis actio,
   vita perennis;
O retributio! caelica mansio
   stat lue plenis.

Sunt modo praelia, postmodo praemia,—
   qualia? plena:
Plena refectio, nullaque passio,
   nullaque poena.

Spe modo vivitur, et Sion angitur
   A Babylone;
Nunc tribulatio, tunc recreatio,
   sceptra, coronae.

Qui modo creditur, ipse videbitur
   atque scietur,
Ipse videntibus atque scientibus
   attribuetur.

Mane videbitur, umbra fugabitur,
   ordo patebit;
Mane nitens erit, et bona qui gerit,
   ille nitebit.

5. O sweet and blessed country,
   The home of God's elect!
O sweet and blessed country
   That eager hearts expect!
Jesus, in mercy bring us
   To that dear land of rest,
Who art, with God the Father
   And Spirit, ever blest.

Nunc tibi tristia, tunc tibi gaudia, —
   gaudia, quanta
Vox nequit edere, lumina cernere,
   tangere planta.

Pars mea, rex meus, in proprio Deus
   ipse decore
Visus amabitur, atque videbitur
   auctor in ore.

Hymns No. 605, 613, 614, and this hymn are portions of the great poem of three thousand lines, entitled *De Contemptu Mundi* (On Contempt of the World) written by Bernard of Morlas or Murles (not Morlaix, but the place is uncertain), while a monk at the famous monastery of Cluny, c. 1140, and dedicated to the abbot, Peter the Venerable. The opening lines of this poem are the Hymn No. 605.

The translations of all four hymns are by John M. Neale, which appeared in part in his *Sacred Latin Poetry*, 1849, and a larger portion, which he published in *The Rhythm of Bernard de Morlaix*, 1858.

The tune "Ewing" is dated 1853. The composer is Alexander Ewing. It was composed for Hymn No. 614. It is also called "Argyle," "St. Bride's," and "Bernard." It was originally written in triple time and published in Grey, *Manual of Psalms and Hymn Tunes*, 1857. The tune was included in the original edition of *Hymns Ancient and Modern*, 1861, and altered to common time. This was done without consulting the composer, who was away from England at the time. Mr. Ewing later stated: "In my opinion the alteration of the rhythm has very much vulgarized my little tune. It now seems to me a good deal like a polka. I hate to hear it."

449 My Soul, Be on Thy Guard

1. My soul, be on thy guard;
   Ten thousand foes arise,
And hosts of sin are pressing hard
   To draw thee from the skies.

2. Oh, watch and fight and pray,
   The battle ne'er give o'er;
Renew it boldly every day
   And help divine implore.

3. Ne'er think the victory won
   Nor lay thine armor down;
Thine arduous work will not be done
   Till thou obtain thy crown.

4. Fight on, my soul, till death
   Shall bring thee to thy God;
He'll take thee at thy parting breath
   To His divine abode.

George Heath published this hymn on steadfastness in his *Hymns and Poetic Essays*, etc., Bristol, 1781. In Stanza 4, Line 1, he had

Then persevere till death.

The tune "Schumann" is from Mason and Webb's *Cantica Laudis*, Boston, 1850. In that volume the tune is called "White." It is supposed to be an arrangement from Robert Schumann, but authorities have been unable to find anything among his writings from which it could have been derived.

450 Soldiers of Christ, Arise

1. Soldiers of Christ, arise
   And put your armor on,
Strong in the strength which God supplies
   Through His eternal Son;

2. Strong in the Lord of hosts
   And in His mighty power.
Who in the strength of Jesus trusts
   Is more than conqueror.

CHRISTIAN WARFARE

3. Stand, then, in His great might,
With all His strength endued;
But take, to arm you for the fight,
The panoply of God,

4. That, having all things done
And all your conflicts past,
Ye may o'ercome through Christ alone
And stand entire at last.

5. From strength to strength go on,
Wrestle and fight and pray;
Tread all the powers of darkness down
And win the well-fought day.

This short cento is taken from Charles Wesley's hymn of sixteen eight-line stanzas, which appeared in *Hymns and Sacred Poems*, 1749. The hymn has seldom been used in its entirety. *The Wesleyan Hymn Book*, 1780, had three hymns made up of twelve of its stanzas, namely, "Soldiers of Christ, Arise," "But Above All, Lay Hold," and "In Fellowship Alone." This cento is composed of Stanzas 1 and 2 of the original and the first four lines of Stanza 16.

The tune "Aynhoe" is adapted from the melody by James Nares. We have not been able to establish the date of this composition.

Stand Up! — Stand Up for Jesus 451

1. Stand up! — stand up for Jesus,
Ye soldiers of the Cross!
Lift high His royal banner,
It must not suffer loss.
From victory unto victory
His army shall He lead
Till every foe is vanquished
And Christ is Lord indeed.

2. Stand up! — stand up for Jesus!
The trumpet call obey;
Forth to the mighty conflict
In this His glorious day!
Ye that are men, now serve Him
Against unnumbered foes;
Let courage rise with danger
And strength to strength oppose.

3. Stand up! — stand up for Jesus!
Stand in His strength alone;
The arm of flesh will fail you,
Ye dare not trust your own.
Put on the Gospel armor,
Each piece put on with prayer;
Where duty calls or danger,
Be never wanting there.

4. Stand up! — stand up for Jesus!
The strife will not be long;
This day the noise of battle,
The next, the victor's song.
To him that overcometh
A crown of life shall be;
He with the King of Glory
Shall reign eternally.

This popular American hymn, by George Duffield, 1858, has an unusual origin, which the author himself gives in a letter dated May 29, 1883:

"Stand Up for Jesus" was the dying message of the Rev. Dudley A. Tyng to the Young Men's Christian Association and the ministers associated with them in the Noon-day Prayer Meeting during the great revival of 1858, usually known as "The Work of God in Philadelphia."

A very dear personal friend, I knew young Tyng as one of the noblest, bravest, *manliest* men I ever met. . . . The Sabbath before his death he preached in the immense edifice known as Jaynes's Hall, one of the most successful sermons of modern times. Of the five thousand men there assembled, at least one thousand, it was believed, were "the slain of the Lord." His text was Ex. 10:11, and hence the allusion in the third verse of the hymn.

The following Wednesday, leaving his study for a moment, he went to the barn floor, where a mule was at work on a horse-power shelling corn. Patting him on the neck, the sleeve of his silk study gown caught in the cogs of the wheel, and his arm was torn out by the roots! His death occurred in a few hours. . . .

The following Sunday the author of the hymn preached from Eph. 6:14, and the above verses were written simply as the concluding exhortation. The superintendent of the Sabbath-school had a fly-leaf printed for the children, — a stray copy found its way into a Baptist newspaper, — and from that paper it has gone in English and in German and Latin translations all over the world. The first time the author heard it sung outside of his own denomination was in 1864 as the favorite song of the Christian soldiers in the Army of the James. . . .

Notwithstanding the many mutilations and alterations and perversions to which this hymn has been subjected, it is but proper to say that since the night it was written, it has never been altered by the author in a single verse, a single line, or a single word, and it is his earnest wish that it shall continue unaltered until the Soldiers of the Cross shall replace it by something better.

The cento omits Stanzas 2 and 5 of the original, which read:

2. Stand up! — stand up for Jesus!
   The solemn watchword hear;
If, while ye sleep, He suffers,
   Away with shame and fear!
Where'er ye meet with evil,
   Within you or without,
Charge for the God of Battles
   And put the foe to rout.

5. Stand up! — stand up for Jesus!
   Each soldier to his post;
Close up the broken column
   And shout through all the host.
Make good the loss so heavy
   In those that still remain
And prove to all around you
   That death itself is gain.

The tune "Webb," also called "Goodwin" and "Franconia," is by George J. Webb. It was written on the ocean in 1830 to a secular song, beginning "'Tis dawn, the lark is singing," and published in *The Odeon,* in 1837. The tune is practically wedded to this hymn and to Hymn No. 497. "The morning light is breaking." Samuel W. Duffield, in his *English Hymns,* writes, "So nearly as can be ascertained, it was W. B. Bradbury who (in 1861) adapted" this tune to George Duffield's hymn.

452   The Son of God Goes Forth to War

1. The Son of God goes forth
   to war
   A kingly crown to gain.
His blood-red banner streams afar;
   Who follows in His train?
Who best can drink His cup of woe,
   Triumphant over pain,
Who patient bears his cross
   below, —
   He follows in His train.

2. The martyr first whose eagle eye
   Could pierce beyond the grave,
Who saw his Master in the sky
   And called on Him to save.
Like Him, with pardon on His tongue,
   In midst of mortal pain,
He prayed for them that did the wrong, —
   Who follows in his train?

3. A glorious band, the chosen few,
   On whom the Spirit came,
Twelve valiant saints; their hope they
   knew
And mocked the cross and flame.
They met the tyrant's brandished steel,
   The lion's gory mane;
They bowed their necks the death to
   feel, —
   Who follows in their train?

4. A noble army, men and boys,
   The matron and the maid,
Around the Savior's throne rejoice,
   In robes of light arrayed.
They climbed the steep ascent of heaven
   Through peril, toil, and pain.
O God, to us may grace be given
   To follow in their train!

This hymn, by Reginald Heber, appeared in his posthumous *Hymns Written and Adapted,* etc., 1827. The reference in Stanza 2 is to St. Stephen. It was written for St. Stephen's Day.

The tune "All Saints New," also called "Cutler," was written for this hymn by Henry S. Cutler. It appeared in *The Church Hymnal,* 1872.

CHRISTIAN WARFARE

We Are the Lord's; His All-Sufficient Merit 453

1. We are the Lord's; His all-sufficient merit,
Sealed on the cross, to us this grace accords.
We are the Lord's and all things shall inherit;
Whether we live or die, we are the Lord's.

2. We are the Lord's; then let us gladly tender
Our souls to Him in deeds, not empty words.
Let heart and tongue and life combine to render
No doubtful witness that we are the Lord's.

3. We are the Lord's; no darkness brooding o'er us
Can make us tremble while this star affords
A steady light along the path before us —
Faith's full assurance that we are the Lord's.

4. We are the Lord's; no evil can befall us
In the dread hour of life's fast-loosening cords;
No pangs of death shall even then appal us.
Death we shall vanquish, for we are the Lord's.

Wir sind des Herrn, wir leben oder sterben;
Wir sind des Herrn, der einst für alle starb;
Wir sind des Herrn und werden alles erben;
Wir sind des Herrn, der alles uns erwarb.

Wir sind des Herrn. So lasst uns ihm auch leben,
Sein eigen sein mit Leib und Seele gern
Und Herz und Mund und Wandel Zeugnis geben,
Es sei gewisslich wahr: Wir sind des Herrn.

Wir sind des Herrn. So kann im dunklen Tale
Uns nimmer graun, uns scheint ein heller Stern,
Der leuchtet uns mit ungetrübtem Strahle,
Es ist das teure Wort: Wir sind des Herrn!

Wir sind des Herrn. So wird er uns bewahren
Im letzten Kampf, wo andre Hilfe fern;
Kein Leid wird uns vom Tode widerfahren,
Das Wort bleibt ewig wahr: Wir sind des Herrn.

Karl J. P. Spitta founded this hymn on Rom. 14:8. It was first published in his *Psalter und Harfe,* second series, Leipzig, 1843.

The translation is by Charles T. Astley in his *Songs in the Night,* 1860.

The tune "Eirene" is by Frances R. Havergal, 1871. It is used also with Spitta's hymn "O Vaterhand, die mich so treu geführet," translated by Richard Massie as follows:

1. Father, whose hand hath led me so securely,
Father, whose ear hath listened to my prayer,
Father, whose eye hath watched o'er me so surely,
Whose heart hath loved me with a love so rare, —

2. Vouchsafe, O heavenly Father, to instruct me
In the straight way wherein I ought to go,
To life eternal and to heaven conduct me,
Through health and sickness, and through weal and woe.

3. O my Redeemer, who hast my redemption
Purchased and paid for by Thy precious blood,
Thereby procuring an entire exemption
From the dread wrath and punishment of God;

4. Thou who hast saved my soul from condemnation,
Redeem it also from the power of sin;
Be thou the Captain still of my salvation,
Through whom alone I can the victory win.

5. O Holy Ghost, who from the Father flowest
And from the Son, oh, teach me how to pray!
Thou, who the love and peace of God bestowest,
With faith and hope inspire and cheer my way.

6. Direct, control, and sanctify each motion
Within my soul and make it thus to be
Prayerful and still and full of deep devotion,
A holy temple, worthy, Lord, of Thee!

Prayer

454   Prayer Is the Soul's Sincere Desire

1. Prayer is the soul's sincere desire,
   Unuttered or exprest,
   The motion of a hidden fire
   That trembles in the breast.

2. Prayer is the burden of a sigh,
   The falling of a tear,
   The upward glancing of an eye,
   When none but God is near.

3. Prayer is the simplest form of speech
   That infant lips can try;
   Prayer the sublimest strains that reach
   The Majesty on high.

4. Prayer is the contrite sinner's voice
   Returning from his ways,
   While angels in their songs rejoice
   And cry, "Behold, he prays!"

5. Prayer is the Christian's vital breath,
   The Christian's native air,
   His watchword at the gates of death, —
   He enters heaven with prayer.

6. The saints in prayer appear as one
   In word and deed and mind,
   While with the Father and the Son
   Sweet fellowship they find.

7. Nor prayer is made by man alone, —
   The Holy Spirit pleads,
   And Jesus on the eternal throne
   For sinners intercedes.

8. O Thou by whom we come to God,
   The Life, the Truth, the Way,
   The path of prayer Thyself hast trod, —
   Lord, teach us how to pray.

James Montgomery wrote this hymn in 1818 at the request of the Rev. E. Bickersteth for his *Treatise on Prayer,* and in the same year it was printed in pamphlet form. In 1825 it was published in *The Christian Psalmist,* headed "What Is Prayer?" Dr. Percy Dearmer says that "it teaches the principles and practice of prayer with truth and power."

The tune "Burford," also called "Walton," "York," "Uxbridge," and "Norwich," is from John Chetham's *Psalms,* 1718, where it is set to the new version of Ps. 42, "As pants the hart for cooling streams." See Hymn No. 525.

455   Our Heavenly Father, Hear

1. Our heavenly Father, hear
   The prayer we offer now.
   Thy name be hallowed far and near;
   To Thee all nations bow.

2. Thy kingdom come; Thy will
   On earth be done in love
   As saints and seraphim fulfil
   Thy holy will above.

3. Our daily bread supply
   While by Thy word we live.
   The guilt of our iniquity
   Forgive as we forgive.

4. From dark temptation's power,
   From Satan's wiles, defend.
   Deliver in the evil hour
   And guide us to the end.

5. Thine shall forever be
   Glory and power divine;
   The scepter, throne, and majesty
   Of heaven and earth are Thine.

James Montgomery wrote this hymn, a metrical paraphrase of *The Lord's Prayer,* February 28, 1835, and published it the same year in *Hymns and Prayers.* It was repeated in his *Original Hymns,* 1853.

For comments on the tune "St. Bride" see Hymn No. 322.

456   Approach, My Soul, the Mercy-Seat

1. Approach, my soul, the mercy-seat
   Where Jesus answers prayer;
   There humbly fall before His feet,
   For none can perish there.

2. Thy promise is my only plea,
   With this I venture nigh;
   Thou callest burdened souls to Thee,
   And such, O Lord, am I.

PRAYER

3. Bowed down beneath a load of sin,
   By Satan sorely pressed,
   By wars without and fears within,
   I come to Thee for rest.

4. Be Thou my Shield and Hiding-place,
   That, sheltered near Thy side,
   I may my fierce Accuser face
   And tell him Thou hast died.

5. O wondrous Love, to bleed and die,
   To bear the cross and shame,
   That guilty sinners such as I
   Might plead Thy gracious name!

John Newton published this hymn in six stanzas in *Olney Hymns*, 1779. The omitted Stanza 6 reads:

"Poor tempest-tossed soul, be still,
   My promised grace receive":
'Tis Jesus speaks — I must, I will,
   I can, I do, believe.

It is one of the most popular of Newton's hymns.

The tune "Spohr" is an adaptation of a selection from Louis Spohr's oratorio *Calvary*, composed in 1835. It is often used with Tate and Brady's new version of Ps. 42, "As pants the hart for cooling streams." (See Hymn No. 525.)

What a Friend We Have in Jesus 457

1. What a Friend we have in Jesus,
   All our sins and griefs to bear!
   What a privilege to carry
     Everything to God in prayer!
   Oh, what peace we often forfeit,
   Oh, what needless pain we bear,
   All because we do not carry
     Everything to God in prayer!

2. Have we trials and temptations?
     Is there trouble anywhere?
   We should never be discouraged,
     Take it to the Lord in prayer.
   Can we find a Friend so faithful
     Who will all our sorrows share?
   Jesus knows our every weakness, —
     Take it to the Lord in prayer.

3. Are we weak and heavy laden,
     Cumbered with a load of care?
   Precious Savior, still our Refuge, —
     Take it to the Lord in prayer.
   Do Thy friends despise, forsake thee?
     Take it to the Lord in prayer;
   In His arms He'll take and shield thee,
     Thou wilt find a solace there.

Joseph Scriven wrote this hymn about 1855. It was first published in *Social Hymns*, etc., H. L. Hastings, Richmond, V., 1865. It was written to comfort the author's mother in a time of great sorrow.

The tune "Friend" or "Converse" is by Charles C. Converse, and is dated 1868. It was published in a small Sunday-school book called *Silver Wings*, in 1870. The arrangement in *The Lutheran Hymnal* is by Bernhard Schumacher.

In spite of the fact that the hymn, with its tune, has been criticized as being too much on the order of the sentimental gospel type, its popularity remains strong, and the hymn retains a place in modern hymnals.

Our Father, Thou in Heaven Above 458

1. Our Father, Thou in heaven above,
   Who biddest us to dwell in love,
   As brethren of one family,
   To cry in every need to Thee,
   Teach us no thoughtless words to say,
   But from our inmost heart to pray.

Vater unser im Himmelreich,
Der du uns alle heissest gleich
Brüder sein und dich rufen an
Und willst das Beten von uns hab'n,
Gib, dass nicht bet' allein der Mund,
Hilf, dass es geh' von Herzensgrund!

2. Thy name be hallowed. Help us, Lord,
   In purity to keep Thy Word,
   That to the glory of Thy name
   We walk before Thee free from blame.
   Let no false doctrine us pervert;
   All poor, deluded souls convert.

Geheiligt werd' der Name dein,
Dein Wort bei uns hilf halten rein,
Dass auch wir leben heiliglich,
Nach deinem Namen würdiglich.
Behüt uns, Herr, vor falscher Lehr',
Das arm' verführte Volk bekehr!

[323]

3. Thy kingdom come. Thine let it be
In time and in eternity.
Let Thy good Spirit e'er be nigh
Our hearts with graces to supply.
Break Satan's power, defeat his rage;
Preserve Thy Church from age to age.

4. Thy gracious will on earth be done
As 'tis in heaven before Thy throne;
Obedience in our weal and woe
And patience in all grief bestow.
Curb flesh and blood and every ill
That sets itself against Thy will.

5. Give us this day our daily bread
And let us all be clothed and fed.
From war and strife be our Defense,
From famine and from pestilence,
That we may live in godly peace,
Free from all care and avarice.

6. Forgive our sins, Lord, we implore,
Remove from us their burden sore,
As we their trespasses forgive
Who by offenses us do grieve.
Thus let us dwell in charity
And serve our brother willingly.

7. Into temptation lead us not.
When evil foes against us plot
And vex our souls on every hand,
Oh, give us strength that we may stand
Firm in the faith, a well-armed host,
Through comfort of the Holy Ghost!

8. From evil, Lord, deliver us;
The times and days are perilous.
Redeem us from eternal death,
And when we yield our dying breath,
Console us, grant us calm release,
And take our souls to Thee in peace.

9. Amen, that is, So shall it be.
Confirm our faith and hope in Thee
That we may doubt not, but believe
What here we ask we shall receive.
Thus in Thy name and at Thy word
We say: Amen. Oh, hear us, Lord! Amen.

Es komm' dein Reich zu dieser Zeit
Und dort hernach in Ewigkeit;
Der Heil'ge Geist uns wohne bei
Mit seinen Gaben mancherlei;
Des Satans Zorn und gross' Gewalt
Zerbrich, vor ihm dein' Kirch' erhalt!

Dein Will' gescheh, Herr Gott, zugleich
Auf Erden wie im Himmelreich;
Gib uns Geduld in Leidenszeit,
Gehorsam sein in Lieb' und Leid;
Wehr und steur allem Fleisch und Blut,
Das wider deinen Willen tut!

Gib uns heut' unser täglich Brot,
Und was man braucht zur Leibesnot;
B'hüt uns, Herr, vor Unfried' und Streit,
Vor Seuchen und vor teurer Zeit,
Dass wir in gutem Frieden stehn,
Der Sorg' und Geizes müssig gehn!

All unsre Schuld vergib uns, Herr,
Dass sie uns nicht betrübe mehr,
Wie wir auch unsern Schuldigern
Ihr' Schuld und Fehl' vergeben gern;
Zu dienen mach uns all' bereit
In rechter Lieb' und Einigkeit!

Führ uns, Herr, in Versuchung nicht;
Wenn uns der böse Geist anficht
Zur linken und zur rechten Hand,
Hilf uns tun starken Widerstand,
Im Glauben fest und wohlgerüst't
Und durch des Heil'gen Geistes Trost.

Von allem Übel uns erlös,
Es sind die Zeit und Tage bös;
Erlös uns von dem ew'gen Tod
Und tröst uns in der letzten Not;
Bescher uns auch ein selig End',
Nimm unsre Seel' in deine Händ'!

Amen, das ist, es werde wahr!
Stärk unsern Glauben immerdar,
Auf dass wir ja nicht zweifeln dran,
Was wir hiermit gebeten hab'n
Auf dein Wort in dem Namen dein;
So sprechen wir das Amen fein.

Martin Luther first published this hymn in 1539. It apparently appeared originally as a broadsheet and was also included in Valten Schumann's *Geistliche Lieder,* Leipzig, in the same year, together with the tune. Each stanza elaborates one of the petitions of the *Lord's Prayer,* the doxology excepted, and the last is on the Amen. We hold this to be Luther's finest hymn, placing it above his "Ein' feste Burg" and his "Aus tiefer Not." It is found in English as early as 1560 in *Psalmes of David,* by R. Cox, and in the 1568 edition of John Wedderburn's *Gude and Godlie Ballates.* It was added to the *Scottish Psalter* in 1595. This is the earliest English version (by Cox or Coxe) that we have been able to find and begins with this stanza:

> Our Father, which in heaven art,
> And mak'st us all one brotherhood,
> To call upon Thee with one heart
> Our heavenly Father and our God,
> Grant we pray not with lips alone,
> But with our heart's deep sigh and groan.

The translation is composite.

The tune "Vater unser," which appeared with the hymn in 1539, is of unknown authorship. Luther had written a tune for the text, which he, however, discarded and then allowed the hymn to be published with this tune, which he carefully revised.

Come, My Soul, Thy Suit Prepare

1. Come, my soul, thy suit prepare,
Jesus loves to answer prayer;
He Himself has bid thee pray,
Therefore will not say thee nay.

2. Thou art coming to a King,
Large petitions with thee bring;
For His grace and power are such
None can ever ask too much.

3. With my burden I begin:
Lord, remove this load of sin;
Let Thy blood, for sinners spilt,
Set my conscience free from guilt.

4. Lord, I come to Thee for rest,
Take possession of my breast;
There Thy blood-bought right maintain
And without a rival reign.

5. As the image in the glass
Answers the beholder's face,
Thus unto my heart appear;
Print Thine own resemblance there.

6. While I am a pilgrim here,
Let Thy love my spirit cheer;
As my Guide, my Guard, my Friend,
Lead me to my journey's end.

7. Show me what I have to do;
Every hour my strength renew.
Let me live a life of faith;
Let me die Thy people's death.

John Newton published this hymn in his *Olney Hymns*, 1779.

For comments on the tune "Vienna" see Hymn No. 18.

COMMUNION OF SAINTS

The Church

460   Behold the Sure Foundation-Stone

1. Behold the sure Foundation-stone
 Which God in Zion lays
 To build our heavenly hopes upon
 And His eternal praise.

2. Chosen of God, to sinners dear,
 Let saints adore the name;
 They trust their whole salvation here,
 Nor shall they suffer shame.

3. The foolish builders, scribe and priest,
 Reject it with disdain;
 Yet on this Rock the Church shall rest
 And envy rage in vain.

4. What though the gates of hell withstood,
 Yet must this building rise.
 'Tis Thine own work, Almighty God,
 And wondrous in our eyes.

Isaac Watts published this metrical paraphrase of Ps. 118:22, 23 in his *Psalms of David Imitated*, 1719, headed "Christ the Foundation of the Church."

For comments on the tune "St. Anne" see Hymn No. 123.

461   Hark! the Church Proclaims Her Honor

1. Hark! the Church proclaims her honor,
 And her strength is only this:
 God hath laid His choice upon her,
 And the work she doth is His.

2. He His Church hath firmly founded,
 He will guard what He began;
 We, by sin and foes surrounded,
 Build her bulwarks as we can.

3. Frail and fleeting are our powers,
 Short our days, our foresight dim,
 And we own the choice not ours,
 We were chosen first by Him.

4. Onward, then! For naught despairing,
 Calm we follow at His word,
 Thus through joy and sorrow bearing
 Faithful witness to our Lord.

5. Though we here must strive in weakness,
 Though in tears we often bend,
 What His might began in meekness
 Shall achieve a glorious end.

Das ist der Gemeinde Stärke —
 Sie bekennt es laut und frei —,
Dass zu ihrem grossen Werke
 Sie vom Herrn erkoren sei.

Er hat festgelegt die Gründe,
 Er ist seines Werkes Hort;
Wir, umgeben noch von Sünde,
 Bauen, wie wir können, fort.

Unsre Tage sind gezählet,
 Unsre Kräfte schwinden hin;
Wir nicht haben ihn erwählet,
 Sondern sind erwählt durch ihn.

Darum gehn wir ohne Zagen
 Ruhig unsern Pilgergang,
Wollen Jesu Zeugnis tragen
 Unter Schmerz und Lobgesang.

Ob wir auch mit Schwachheit rangen,
 Ob auch manche Träne fiel,
Er, der's mächtig angefangen,
 Führt es herrlich einst ans Ziel.

Samuel Preiswerk published this hymn in *Evangelischer Liederkranz*, Basel, 1844. It was written as a hymn for missions. It was included in Knapp's *Evangelischer Liederschatz*, 1850.

The translation is by Catherine Winkworth, *Lyra Germanica*, second series, 1858.

The tune "Lobt den Herrn, die Morgensonne" is from the *Evangelisches Choralbuch*, Halle, 1829, where it is set to J. S. Patzke's hymn beginning with that line.

462   I Love Thy Kingdom, Lord

1. I love Thy kingdom, Lord,
 The house of Thine abode,
The Church our blest Redeemer saved
 With His own precious blood.

2. I love Thy Church, O God,
 Her walls before Thee stand,
Dear as the apple of Thine eye
 And graven on Thy hand.

3. Should I with scoffers join
 Her altars to abuse?
No! Better far my tongue were dumb,
 My hand its skill should lose.

4. For her my tears shall fall,
 For her my prayers ascend,
To her my cares and toils be given
 Till toils and cares shall end.

5. Beyond my highest joy
    I prize her heavenly ways,
  Her sweet communion, solemn vows,
    Her hymns of love and praise.

6. Jesus, Thou Friend Divine,
    Our Savior and our King,
  Thy hand from every snare and foe
    Shall great deliverance bring.

7. Sure as Thy truth shall last,
    To Zion shall be given
  The brightest glories earth can yield
    And brighter bliss of heaven.

Timothy Dwight published this metrical paraphrase of Ps. 137, in eight stanzas, in his edition of Watts's *Psalms of David*, etc., 1800. The full title of this American edition of Watts is *The Psalms of David, etc. . . . By I. Watts, D. D. A New Edition in which the Psalms omitted by Dr. Watts are versified, local passages are altered, and a number of Psalms are versified anew in proper metres. By Timothy Dwight, D. D., etc. . . . To the Psalms is added a selection of Hymns, 1800.* This hymn is often given as "I Love Thy Zion, Lord." The omitted Stanza 3 reads:
  If e'er to bless thy sons
    My voice or hands deny,
  These hands let useful skill forsake,
    This voice in silence die.

For comments on the tune "St. Thomas" see Hymn No. 27.

For All the Saints Who from Their Labors Rest 463

1. For all the saints who from their labors rest,
  Who Thee by faith before the world confess,
  Thy name, O Jesus, be forever blest.
    Alleluia! Alleluia!

2. Thou wast their Rock, their Fortress, and their Might;
  Thou, Lord, their Captain in the well-fought fight;
  Thou, in the darkness drear, their one true Light.
    Alleluia! Alleluia!

3. Oh, may Thy soldiers, faithful, true, and bold,
  Fight as the saints who nobly fought of old
  And win with them the victor's crown of gold.
    Alleluia! Alleluia!

4. O blest communion, fellowship divine,
  We feebly struggle, they in glory shine;
  Yet all are one in Thee, for all are Thine.
    Alleluia! Alleluia!

5. And when the fight is fierce, the warfare long,
  Steals on the ear the distant triumph song,
  And hearts are brave again, and arms are strong.
    Alleluia! Alleluia!

6. But, lo, there breaks a yet more glorious day;
  The saints triumphant rise in bright array;
  The King of Glory passes on His way.
    Alleluia! Alleluia!

7. From earth's wide bounds, from ocean's farthest coast,
  Through gates of pearl streams in the countless host,
  Singing to Father, Son, and Holy Ghost.
    Alleluia! Alleluia!

8. The golden evening brightens in the west;
  Soon, soon, to faithful warriors cometh rest.
  Sweet is the calm of Paradise the blest.
    Alleluia! Alleluia!

William Walsham How first published this hymn in *Hymn for Saints' Day, and Other Hymns*, 1864, in eleven stanzas. Originally the author had written

"For all Thy saints," but altered the line later. The omitted stanzas are 3, 4, and 5, which read:

> 3. For the apostles' glorious company
> Who, bearing forth the cross o'er land and sea,
> Shook all the mighty world, we sing to Thee.
>
> 4. For the evangelists, by whose pure word
> Like fourfold stream, the garden of the Lord
> Is fair and fruitful, be Thy name adored.
>
> 5. For martyrs who with rapture-kindled eye
> Saw the bright crown descending from the sky
> And, dying, grasped it, Thee we glorify.

The author's sequence of stanzas has been changed in the text. The last stanza preceded Stanza 6. Thus the hymn originally closed with Stanza 7.

The tune "Sine nomine" was written for this hymn by R. Vaughan Williams. It appeared in the *English Hymnal,* 1906. It is a powerful tune, one of the finest hymn tunes by a modern composer, and the congregation that has mastered it will sing it with an ever-deepening appreciation.

464   Blest Be the Tie that Binds

1. Blest be the tie that binds
Our hearts in Christian love;
The fellowship of kindred minds
Is like to that above.

2. Before our Father's throne
We pour our ardent prayers;
Our fears, our hopes, our aims, are one,
Our comforts and our cares.

3. We share our mutual woes,
Our mutual burdens bear,
And often for each other flows
The sympathizing tear.

4. When here our pathways part,
We suffer bitter pain;
Yet, one in Christ and one in heart,
We hope to meet again.

5. This glorious hope revives
Our courage by the way,
While each in expectation lives
And longs to see the day.

6. From sorrow, toil, and pain,
And sin we shall be free
And perfect love and friendship reign
Through all eternity.

John Fawcett wrote this hymn in 1772. Miller, in his *Singers and Songs of the Church,* 1869, describes the circumstances of its origin thus: "This favorite hymn is said to have been written in 1772 to commemorate the determination of its author to remain with his attached people at Wainsgate. The farewell sermon was preached, the wagons were loaded, when love and tears prevailed, and Dr. Fawcett sacrificed the attractions of a London pulpit to the affection of his poor but devoted flock."

In Stanza 4, Line 1, Fawcett had:

> When we asunder part,
> It gives us inward pain.

The tune "Boylston," by Lowell Mason, was published in *The Choir,* in 1832. It was named for a town by that name in Massachusetts, his native State. In America it appears to be the indispensable tune for this hymn.

465   Christ Is Our Corner-Stone

1. Christ is our Corner-stone,
On Him alone we build;
With His true saints alone
The courts of heaven are filled.
On His great love
Our hopes we place
Of present grace
And joys above.

2. Oh, then, with hymns of praise
These hallowed courts shall ring;
Our voices we will raise
The Three in One to sing
And thus proclaim
In joyful song,
Both loud and long,
That glorious name.

COMMUNION OF SAINTS

<pre>
3. Here, gracious God, do Thou
     Forevermore draw nigh;
   Accept each faithful vow
     And mark each suppliant sigh.
   In copious shower
     On all who pray
     Each holy day,
   Thy blessing pour.

4. Here may we gain from heaven
     The grace which we implore,
   And may that grace, once given,
     Be with us evermore
   Until that day
     When all the blest
     To endless rest
   Are called away!
</pre>

This is John Chandler's version of the Latin hymn *Angularis fundamentum*. (See Hymn No. 466.) It appeared in his *Hymns of the Primitive Church*, 1837. The doxology is omitted.

For comments on the tune "Darwall's 148th" see Hymn No. 46.

Christ, Thou Art the Sure Foundation   466

<pre>
1. Christ, Thou art the sure Foundation,   Angularis fundamentum
     Thou the Head and Corner-stone;   lapis Christus missus est
   Chosen of the Lord and precious,   Qui conpage parietis
     Binding all the Church in one;   in utroque nectitur,
   Thou Thy Zion's Help forever   Quem Sion sancta suscepit,
     And her Confidence alone.   In quo credens permanet.

2. To this temple, where we call Thee,   Hoc in templo, summe Deus,
     Come, O Lord of hosts, today;   exoratus adveni,
   With Thy wonted loving-kindness   Et clementi bonitate
     Hear Thy servants as they pray   precum vota suscipe;
   And Thy fullest benediction   Largam benedictionem
     Shed within these walls alway.   hic infunde iugiter.

3. Here vouchsafe to all Thy servants   Hic promereantur omnes
     What they ask of Thee to gain,   petita adquirere,
   What they gain from Thee forever   Et adepta possidere
     With the blessed to retain,   cum sanctis perenniter,
   And hereafter in Thy glory   Paradisum introire,
     Evermore with Thee to reign.   translati in requiem.

4. Praise and honor to the Father,   Gloria et honor Deo
     Praise and honor to the Son,   usquequo altissimo,
   Praise and honor to the Spirit,   Una Patri Filioque
     Ever Three and ever One,   inclito Paraclito,
   One in might and one in glory,   Cui laus est et potestas
     While unending ages run.   per aeterna saecula.
</pre>

This hymn is the second part of the hymn *Urbs beata Ierusalem*, by an unknown Latin writer of probably the eighth century, one stanza being omitted.

John M. Neale's translation of the entire hymn appeared in his *Mediaeval Hymns*, 1851. It is as follows:

<pre>
1. Blessed City, heavenly Salem,   4. Many a blow and biting sculpture
     Vision dear of peace and love,   Polished well those stones elect,
   Who, of living stones upbuilded,   In their places now compacted
     Art the joy of heaven above: By the heavenly Architect;
   And, with angel hosts encircled,   Who therewith hath willed forever
     As a bride to earth dost move: That His palace should be decked.

2. From celestial realms descending   5. Christ is made the sure Foundation,
     Ready for the nuptial bed,   And the precious Corner-stone,
   Decked with jewels, to His presence   Who, the twofold walls surmounting,
     By her Lord shall she be led: Binds them closely into one;
   All her streets and all her bulwarks   Holy Sion's Help forever
     Of pure gold are fashionèd.   And her Confidence alone.

3. Bright with pearls her portal glitters,— 6. All that dedicated city,
     It is open evermore,—   Dearly loved by God on high,
   And by virtue of their merits   In exultant jubilation
     Thither faithful souls may soar   Pours perpetual melody:
   Who for Christ's dear name in this world   God the One and God the Trinal
     Pain and tribulation bore.   Lauding everlastingly.
</pre>

7. To this temple, where we call Thee,
   Come, O Lord of hosts, today,
   With Thy wonted loving-kindness
   Hear Thy servants as they pray
   And Thy fullest benediction
   Shed within these walls for aye.

8. Here vouchsafe to all Thy servants
   That they supplicate to gain,
   Here to have and hold forever
   Those good things their prayers obtain,
   And hereafter, in Thy glory,
   With Thy blessed ones to reign.

9. Laud and honor to the Father,
   Laud and honor to the Son,
   Laud and honor to the Spirit,
   Ever Three and ever One:
   Consubstantial, coeternal,
   While unending ages run.

For comments on the tune "Regent Square" see Hymn No. 50.

467   Built on the Rock the Church doth Stand

1. Built on the Rock the Church doth stand,
   Even when steeples are falling;
   Crumbled have spires in every land,
   Bells still are chiming and calling,
   Calling the young and old to rest,
   But above all the soul distrest,
   Longing for rest everlasting.

2. Surely in temples made with hands,
   God, the Most High, is not dwelling;
   High above earth His temple stands,
   All earthly temples excelling.
   Yet He whom heavens cannot contain
   Chose to abide on earth with men,
   Built in our bodies His temple.

3. We are God's house of living stones,
   Builded for His habitation;
   He through baptismal grace us owns
   Heirs of His wondrous salvation.
   Were we but two His name to tell,
   Yet He would deign with us to dwell,
   With all His grace and His favor.

4. Now we may gather with our King
   E'en in the lowliest dwelling;
   Praises to Him we there may bring,
   His wondrous mercy forthtelling.
   Jesus His grace to us accords;
   Spirit and life are all His words;
   His truth doth hallow the temple.

5. Still we our earthly temples rear
   That we may herald His praises;
   They are the homes where He draws near
   And little children embraces.
   Beautiful things in them are said;
   God there with us His covenant made,
   Making us heirs of His kingdom.

6. Here stands the font before our eyes
   Telling how God did receive us;
   The altar recalls Christ's sacrifice
   And what His table doth give us;
   Here sounds the Word that doth proclaim
   Christ yesterday, today, the same,
   Yea, and for aye our Redeemer.

7. Grant then, O God, where'er men roam,
   That, when the church-bells are ringing,
   Many in saving faith may come
   Where Christ His message is bringing:
   "I know Mine own, Mine own know Me;
   Ye, not the world, My face shall see.
   My peace I leave with you." Amen.

Kirken den er et gammelt Hus,
Staar, om end Taarnene falde;
Taarne fuld mange sank i Grus,
Klokker end kime og kalde,
Kalde paa Gammel og paa Ung,
Meest dog paa Själen trät og tung,
Syg for den evige Hvile.

Herren vor Gud vist ei bebor
Huse, som Händer mon bygge,
Arke-Paulunet var paa Jord
Kun af hans Tempel en Skygge,
Selv dog en Bolig underfuld
Bygde han sig i os af Muld,
Reiste af Gruset i Naade.

Vi er Guds Hus og Kirke nu,
Bygget af levende Stene,
Som under Kors med ärlig Hu
Troen og Daaben forene;
Var vi paa Jord ei meer end To,
Bygge dog vilde han og bo
Hos os med hele sin Naade.

Samles vi kan da med vor Drot
Selv i den laveste Hytte,
Finde med Peder, der er godt,
Tog ei al Verden i Bytte,
Aand er og Liv i allen Stund
Ordet til os af Jesu Mund;
Ordet kun helliger Huset.

Husene dog med Kirke-Navn,
Bygde til Frelserens Äre,
Hvor han de Smaa tog tidt i Favn,
Er os, som Hjemmet, saa kjäre,
Deilige Ting i dem er sagt,
Sluttet har der med os sin Pagt
Han, som os Himmerig skjänker.

Fonten os minder om vor Daab,
Altret om Nadverdens Naade,
Alt med Guds Ord om Tro og Haab
Og om Guds Kjärligheds Gaade,
Huset om ham, hvis Ord bestaar:
Kristus, idag alt som igaar,
Evig Guds Sön, vor Gjenlöser.

Give da Gud, at hvor vi bo,
Altid, naar Klokkerne ringe,
Folket forsamles i Jesu Tro
Der, hvor det pleied at klinge:
Verden vel ei, men I mig ser,
Alt hvad jeg siger, se, det sker!
Fred väre med eder alle!

This hymn first appeared in N. F. S. Grundtvig's *Sangvärk til den Danske Kirke*, 1837. Later the author revised and abbreviated it as above. It has become one of the most popular hymns in the Church among Scandinavian Christians.

The translation is by Carl Döving, 1909, altered. It appeared in *The Lutheran Hymnary*, 1913.

The tune "Kirken den er et" was composed by Ludvig M. Lindeman for this hymn. It was first published in W. A. Wexel's *Christelige Psalmer*, 1840. It was the composer's first church tune.

For All Thy Saints, O Lord — 468

1. For all Thy saints, O Lord,
    Who strove in Thee to live,
  Who followed Thee, obeyed, adored,
    Our grateful hymn receive.

2. For all Thy saints, O Lord,
    Who strove in Thee to die,
  Who counted Thee their great Reward,
    Accept our thankful cry.

3. They all in life and death,
    With Thee, their Lord, in view,
  Learned from Thy Holy Spirit's breath
    To suffer and to do.

4. For this Thy name we bless
    And humbly pray that we
  May follow them in holiness
    And live and die in Thee.

Richard R. Mant first published this hymn in six stanzas in his *Ancient Hymns*, etc., 1837. It usually appears in four stanzas. The omitted Stanzas 3 and 6 read:

3. Thy mystic members fit
    To join Thy saints above,
  In one unmixed communion knit
    And fellowship of love.

6. To God the Father, Son,
    And Spirit, ever blest,
  The One in Three, the Three in One,
    Be endless praise addressed.

The lines in Stanza 2 have been transposed. The stanza originally read:

2. For all Thy saints, O God,
    Accept our thankful cry,
  Who counted Christ their great Reward
    And yearned for Him to die.

For comments on the tune "Energy" see Hymn No. 374.

Glorious Things of Thee are Spoken — 469

1. Glorious things of thee are spoken,
    Zion, city of our God;
  He whose word cannot be broken
    Formed thee for His own abode.
  On the Rock of Ages founded,
    What can shake thy sure repose?
  With salvation's walls surrounded
    Thou may'st smile at all thy foes.

2. See, the streams of living waters
    Springing from eternal love
  Well supply thy sons and daughters
    And all fear of want remove.
  Who can faint while such a river
    Ever flows their thirst t'assuage —
  Grace, which, like the Lord, the Giver,
    Never fails from age to age?

3. Round each habitation hovering,
    See the cloud and fire appear,
  For a glory and a covering,
    Showing that the Lord is near.
  Thus they march, the pillar leading,
    Light by night and shade by day,
  Daily on the manna feeding
    Which He gives them when they pray.

4. Savior, since of Zion's city
    I through grace a member am,
  Let the world deride or pity,
    I will glory in Thy name.
  Fading is the worldling's pleasure,
    All his boasted pomp and show;
  Solid joys and lasting treasure
    None but Zion's children know.

John Newton first published this famous hymn on the Church in *Olney Hymns*, 1779, in five stanzas. The omitted Stanza 4 reads:

4. Blest inhabitants of Zion,
    Washed in the Redeemer's blood!
  Jesus, whom their souls rely on,
    Makes them kings and priests to God.
  'Tis His love His people raises
    Over self to reign as kings,
  And as priests, His solemn praises
    Each for a thank-offering brings.

The tune "Galilean" is by Joseph Barnby, 1883.

COMMUNION OF SAINTS

470   Rise Again, Ye Lion-Hearted

1. Rise again, ye lion-hearted
   Saints of early Christendom,
Whither is your strength departed,
   Whither gone your martyrdom?
Lo, love's light is on them,
Glory's flame upon them,
And their will to die doth quell
E'en the lord and prince of hell.

2. These the men by fear unshaken,
   Facing danger dauntlessly;
These no witching lust hath taken,
   Lust that lures to vanity.
Mid the roar and rattle
Of tumultuous battle
In desire they soar above
All that earth would have them love.

3. Great of heart, they know no turning,
   Honor, gold, they laugh to scorn,
Quench desires within them burning,
   By no earthly passion torn.
Mid the lion's roaring
Songs of praise outpouring,
Joyously they take their stand
On the arena's bloody sand.

4. Would to God that I might even
   As the martyred saints of old,
With the helping hand of Heaven,
   Steadfast stand, in battle bold!
O my God, I pray Thee,
In the combat stay me.
Grant that I may ever be
Loyal, staunch, and true to Thee.

Löwen, lasst euch wieder finden
   Wie im ersten Christentum,
Die nichts konnte überwinden!
   Seht nur an ihr Martertum,
Wie in Lieb' sie glühen,
Wie sie Feuer sprühen,
Dass sich vor der Sterbenslust
Selbst der Satan fürchten musst'!

In Gefahren unerschrocken
   Und von Lüsten unberührt,
Die aufs Eitle konnten locken,
   War man damals; die Begierd'
Ging nur nach dem Himmel,
Fern aus dem Getümmel
War erhoben das Gemüt,
Achtete, was zeitlich, nicht.

Ganz grossmütig sie verlachten,
   Was die Welt für Vorteil hält
Und wonach die meisten trachten,
   Es mocht' sein Ehr', Wollust, Geld.
Furcht war nicht in ihnen,
Auf die Kampfschaubühnen
Sprangen sie mit Freudigkeit,
Hielten mit den Tieren Streit.

O dass ich, wie diese waren,
   Mich befänd' auch in dem Stand!
Lass mich doch im Grund erfahren
   Dein' hilfreiche, starke Hand,
Mein Gott, recht lebendig!
Gib, dass ich beständig
Bis in Tod durch deine Kraft
Übe gute Ritterschaft!

  This hymn, by an unknown author, appeared in the hymnal *Anmütiger Blumenkranz,* etc., 1712, in thirteen stanzas. It is very likely based on a work by Gottfried Arnold, his *The First Love, i. e., a true Picture of the First Christians in their Living Faith and Holy Life,* 1696. The cento is composed of Stanzas 1, 2, 4, and 5 of the original.

  The translation is by Martin Franzmann in 1940.

  The tune "Löwen, lasst euch wiederfinden" was written for the hymn by Bernhard Klein in 1817. It first appeared in *Deutsche Lieder für Jung und Alt,* 1818.

471   Hark! the Sound of Holy Voices

1. Hark! the sound of holy voices
      Chanting at the crystal sea,
   Alleluia, Alleluia,
      Alleluia, Lord, to Thee.
   Multitudes which none can number
      Like the stars in glory stand,
   Clothed in white apparel, holding
      Palms of victory in their hand.

2. Patriarch and holy prophet,
      Who prepared the way of Christ,
   King, apostle, saint, confessor,
      Martyr, and evangelist,
   Saintly maiden, godly matron,
      Widows who have watched to prayer,
   Joined in holy concert, singing
      To the Lord of all, are there.

3. They have come from tribulation
      And have washed their robes in blood,
   Washed them in the blood of Jesus;
      Tried they were, and firm they stood.
   Mocked, imprisoned, stoned, tormented,
      Sawn asunder, slain with sword,
   They have conquered death and Satan
      By the might of Christ the Lord.

4. Marching with Thy cross, their banner,
      They have triumphed, following
   Thee, the Captain of salvation,
      Thee, their Savior and their King.
   Gladly, Lord, with Thee they suffered,
      Gladly, Lord, with Thee they died,
   And by death to life immortal
      They were born and glorified.

5. Now they reign in heavenly glory,
  Now they walk in golden light,
 Now they drink, as from a river,
  Holy bliss and infinite.
 Love and peace they taste forever
  And all truth and knowledge see
 In the beatific vision
  Of the blessed Trinity.

6. God of God, the One-begotten,
  Light of Light, Emmanuel,
 In whose body, joined together,
  All the saints forever dwell,
 Pour upon us of Thy fulness
  That we may forevermore
 God the Father, God the Spirit,
  One with Thee on high, adore.

Christopher Wordsworth first published this hymn in his *Holy Year*, 1862. It has become one of his most popular hymns. It was written for All Saints' Day and is in harmony with the Epistle for that festival, Rev. 7:2-7; like it, "it is the utterance in triumphant song of a vision of the final gathering of the saints."

For comments on the tune "O Durchbrecher" see Hymn No. 129.

Rise, Ye Children of Salvation 472

1. Rise, ye children of salvation,
  All who cleave to Christ, the Head.
 Wake, arise, O mighty nation,
  Ere the Foe on Zion tread.
 He draws nigh and would defy
 All the hosts of God Most High.

Auf, ihr Christen, Christi Glieder,
 Die ihr noch hängt an dem Haupt,
Auf, wacht auf, ermannt euch wieder,
 Eh' ihr werdet hingeraubt!
Satan beut an den Streit
Christo und der Christenheit.

2. Saints and heroes long before us
  Firmly on this ground have stood;
 See their banner waving o'er us,
  Conquerors through the Savior's blood.
 Ground we hold whereon of old
 Fought the faithful and the bold.

Diesen Sieg hat auch empfunden
 Vieler Heil'gen starker Mut,
Da sie haben überwunden
 Fröhlich durch des Lammes Blut.
Sollten wir denn allhier
Nicht auch streiten mit Begier?

3. Fighting, we shall be victorious
  By the blood of Christ, our Lord;
 On our foreheads, bright and glorious,
  Shines the witness of His Word;
 Spear and shield on battle-field,
 His great name we cannot yield.

Auf denn, lasst uns überwinden
 In dem Blute Jesu Christ
Und an unsre Stirne binden
 Sein Wort, so ein Zeugnis ist,
Das uns deckt und erweckt
Und nach Gottes Liebe schmeckt,

4. When His servants stand before Him,
  Each receiving his reward;
 When His saints in light adore Him,
  Giving glory to the Lord,
 "Victory!" our songs shall be
 Like the thunder of the sea.

Da Gott seinen treuen Knechten
 Geben wird den Gnadenlohn
Und die Hütten der Gerechten
 Stimmen an den Siegeston,
Da fürwahr Gottes Schar
Ihn wird loben immerdar.

This hymn, in eleven stanzas, written by Justus Falckner, first appeared in the *Geistreiches Gesang Buch*, Halle, 1697, entitled "Encouragement to Conflict in the Spiritual Warfare." As Falckner was the first Lutheran clergyman ordained in America, it is of special interest to American Lutherans. The cento includes Stanzas 1, 5, 9, and 11 of the original.

The translation is by Emma F. Bevan and was published in her *Songs of Eternal Life*, 1858.

For comments on the tune "Neander" see Hymn No. 1.

The Church's One Foundation 473

1. The Church's one foundation
  Is Jesus Christ, her Lord;
 She is His new creation
  By water and the Word.
 From heaven He came and sought her
  To be His holy bride;
 With His own blood He bought her,
  And for her life He died.

2. Elect from every nation,
  Yet one o'er all the earth,
 Her charter of salvation
  One Lord, one faith, one birth.
 One holy name she blesses,
  Partakes one holy food,
 And to one hope she presses,
  With every grace endued.

3. The Church shall never perish!
   Her dear Lord, to defend,
  To guide, sustain, and cherish,
   Is with her to the end.
  Though there be those that hate her,
   False sons within her pale,
  Against both foe and traitor
   She ever shall prevail.

4. Though with a scornful wonder
   Men see her sore oppressed,
  By schisms rent asunder,
   By heresies distressed,
  Yet saints their watch are keeping;
   Their cry goes up, "How long?"
  And soon the night of weeping
   Shall be the morn of song.

5. Mid toil and tribulation
   And tumult of her war
  She waits the consummation
   Of peace forevermore,
  Till with the vision glorious
   Her longing eyes are blest
  And the great Church victorious
   Shall be the Church at rest.

Samuel J. Stone wrote this hymn in 1866, revised and recast it in 1868, and added three stanzas in 1885 to make a total of ten. The cento is from the 1866 version.

The tune "Aurelia" was written by Samuel S. Wesley in 1864 as a setting for John Keble's wedding hymn "The Voice that Breathed o'er Eden." (See Hymn No. 622.)

474 Zion Stands by Hills Surrounded

1. Zion stands by hills surrounded,
   Zion, kept by power divine;
  All her foes shall be confounded
   Though the world in arms combine.
     Happy Zion,
  What a favored lot is thine!

2. Every human tie may perish,
   Friend to friend unfaithful prove,
  Mothers cease their own to cherish,
   Heaven and earth at last remove;
     But no changes
  Can attend Jehovah's love.

3. In the furnace God may prove thee,
   Thence to bring thee forth more bright,
  But can never cease to love thee;
   Thou art precious in His sight.
     God is with thee,
  God, thine everlasting Light.

Thomas Kelly published this hymn in five stanzas in his *Hymns on Various Passages of Scripture*, 1806. It is based on Ps. 125:2. The omitted Stanzas 3 and 4 read:

3. Zion's friend in nothing alters,
   Though all others may and do;
  His is love that never falters,
   Always to its object true.
     Happy Zion!
  Crowned with mercies ever new.

4. If thy God should show displeasure,
   'Tis to save and not destroy;
  If He punish, 'tis in measure;
   'Tis to rid thee of alloy.
     Be thou patient;
  Soon thy grief shall turn to joy.

The tune "Zion," also called "Holborn," is by Thomas Morely, organist at St. Alban's Church, Holborn, London, who contributed to the *St. Alban's Tune Book*.

475 Ye Watchers and Ye Holy Ones

1. Ye watchers and ye holy ones,
  Bright seraphs, cherubim, and thrones,
   Raise the glad strain, Alleluia!
  Cry out, dominions, princedoms, powers,
  Virtues, archangels, angels' choirs,
   Alleluia! Alleluia!

2. O higher than the cherubim,
  More glorious than the seraphim,
   Lead their praises, Alleluia!
  Thou Bearer of the eternal Word,
  Most gracious, magnify the Lord,
   Alleluia! Alleluia!

3. Respond, ye souls in endless rest,
  Ye patriarchs and prophets blest,
   Alleluia! Alleluia!
  Ye holy Twelve, ye martyrs strong,
  All saints triumphant, raise the song,
   Alleluia! Alleluia!

4. O friends, in gladness let us sing,
  Supernal anthems echoing,
   Alleluia! Alleluia!
  To God the Father, God the Son,
  And God the Spirit, Three in One,
   Alleluia! Alleluia!

John A. L. Riley contributed this hymn to *The English Hymnal*, 1906. The hymn has rapidly become a favorite in the English-speaking world. Perhaps this is due in part to its union with the fine old *chorale* tune "Lasst uns erfreuen." Like Luther's "Vater unser," see Hymn No. 458, this tune is especially fitted for men's voices.

For comments on the tune "Lasst uns erfreuen" see Hymn No. 15.

Ten Thousand Times Ten Thousand 476

1. Ten thousand times ten thousand,
   In sparkling raiment bright,
The armies of the ransomed saints
   Throng up the steeps of light.
'Tis finished, all is finished,
   Their fight with death and sin;
Fling open wide the golden gates
And let the victors in.

2. What rush of alleluias
   Fills all the earth and sky!
What ringing of a thousand harps
   Proclaims the triumph nigh!
O day, for which creation
   And all its tribes were made;
O joy, for all its former woes
   A thousandfold repaid!

3. Oh, then what raptured greetings
   On Canaan's happy shore;
What knitting severed friendships up
   Where partings are no more!
Then eyes with joy shall sparkle
   That brimmed with tears of late;
Orphans no longer fatherless
   Nor widows desolate.

4. Bring near Thy great salvation,
   Thou Lamb for sinners slain;
Fill up the roll of Thine elect,
   Then take Thy power and reign.
Appear, Desire of Nations;
   Thine exiles long for home.
Show in the heavens Thy promised sign;
   Thou Prince and Savior, come!

Henry Alford wrote this as "A Processional for Saints' Days." It first appeared in three stanzas in his *Year of Praise*, 1867. It was appropriately sung at the Dean's funeral, with the additional fourth stanza which he had written in 1870. The hymn is a favorite of many, among whom we may mention Dr. L. Fuerbringer, president of Concordia Seminary, St. Louis.

The tune "Alford" was composed by John B. Dykes for this hymn. It appeared in the *Revised Edition* of *Hymns Ancient and Modern*, 1875. At the composer's funeral in 1876 Henry W. Baker, in a letter to the widow, wrote: "We are going to sing [at Monkland] *only his tunes* to every hymn all next Sunday and the *Dies Irae* after evensong — for *him*; followed by "Ten Thousand Times Ten Thousand."

Lord Jesus, Thou the Church's Head 477

1. Lord Jesus, Thou the Church's Head,
   Thou art her one Foundation;
In Thee she trusts, before Thee bows,
   And waits for Thy salvation.
Built on this Rock secure,
Thy Church shall endure
E'en though the world decay
And all things pass away.
   Oh, hear, oh, hear us, Jesus!

2. O Lord, let this Thy little flock,
   Thy name alone confessing,
Continue in Thy loving care,
   True unity possessing.
Thy Sacraments, O Lord,
And Thy saving Word
To us e'er pure retain.
Grant that they may remain
   Our only strength and comfort.

O Jesu, einig wahres Haupt
   Der heiligen Gemeine,
Die an dich, ihren Heiland, glaubt,
   Und nur auf dir alleine
Als ihrem Felsen steht,
Der nie untergeht,
Wenngleich die ganze Welt
Zertrümmert und zerfällt:
   Erhör, erhör uns, Jesu!

Lass uns, dein kleines Häufelein,
   Das sich zu dir bekennet,
Dir ferner anbefohlen sein;
   Erhalt uns ungetrennet.
Wort, Tauf' und Abendmahl
Lass in seiner Zahl
Und ersten Reinigkeit
Bis an den Schluss der Zeit
   Zu unserm Troste bleiben

COMMUNION OF SAINTS

    3. Help us to serve Thee evermore
        With hearts both pure and lowly;
    And may Thy Word, that light divine,
        Shine on in splendor holy
    That we repentance show,
    In faith ever grow;
    The power of sin destroy
    And all that doth annoy.
        Oh, make us faithful Christians!

    4. And for Thy Gospel let us dare
        To sacrifice all treasure;
    Teach us to bear Thy blessed cross,
        To find in Thee all pleasure.
    Oh, grant us steadfastness
    In joy and distress,
    That we Thee ne'er forsake.
    Let us by grace partake
        Of endless joy and glory.

Hilf, dass wir dir zu aller Zeit
    Mit reinem Herzen dienen.
Lass uns das Licht der Seligkeit,
    Das uns bisher geschienen,
Zur Buss' kräftig sein
Und zum hellen Schein,
Der unsern Glauben mehrt,
Der Sünden Macht zerstört
    Und fromme Christen machet.

Lass uns beim Evangelio
    Gut, Blut und Leben wagen;
Mach uns dadurch getrost und froh,
    Das schwerste Kreuz zu tragen.
Gib Beständigkeit,
Dass uns Lust und Leid
Von dir nicht scheiden mag,
Bis wir den Jubeltag
    Bei dir im Himmel halten.

    Johann Mentzer wrote this hymn in seven stanzas. It appeared in the *Reibersdorfer Gesang Buch*, 1726. The cento includes Stanzas 1 to 4.

    The translation by William J. Schaefer was prepared for *The Lutheran Hymnal* in 1938.

    For comments on the tune "Reuter" see Hymn No. 283.

478   The Saints on Earth and Those Above

    1. The saints on earth and those above
        But one communion make;
    Joined to their Lord in bonds of love,
        All of His grace partake.

    2. One family, we dwell in Him,
        One Church above, beneath;
    Though now divided by the stream,
        The narrow stream, of death.

    3. One army of the living God,
        To His commands we bow;
    Part of the host have passed the flood,
        And part are crossing now.

    4. Lo, thousands to their endless home
        Are swiftly borne away;
    And we are to the margin come
        And soon must launch as they.

    5. Lord Jesus, be our constant Guide;
        Then, when the word is given,
    Bid death's cold flood its waves divide
        And land us safe in heaven.

    This cento is composed of Stanza 5 (altered) from Watts's hymn "Not to the Terrors of the Lord" (*Hymns and Spiritual Songs*, 1709) and Stanzas 2 to 5 from Charles Wesley's hymn (altered) "Come, Let Us Join Our Friends Above" (*Funeral Hymns*, 1759). The cento first appeared in Cotterill's *Selection*, 1815.

    For comments on the tune "St. Flavian" see Hymn No. 22.

479   Zion, Rise, Zion, Rise

    1. Zion, rise, Zion, rise,
        Zion, wake, arise, and shine!
    Let thy lamp be brightly burning,
        Never let thy love decline,
    Forward still with hopeful yearning.
    Zion, yonder waits the heavenly prize;
    Zion, rise! Zion, rise!

    2. Bear the cross, bear the cross.
        Zion, till Thy latest breath
    Bear the cross of scorn and jeering
        And be faithful unto death;
    See the crown of life appearing.
    Zion, count all other things as loss.
    Bear the cross, bear the cross!

Fahre fort, fahre fort,
    Zion, fahre fort im Licht!
Mache deinen Leuchter helle,
    Lass die erste Liebe nicht,
Suche stets die Lebensquelle!
Zion, dringe durch die enge Pfort'!
Fahre fort, fahre fort!

Leide dich, leide dich,
    Zion, leide ohne Scheu
Trübsal, Angst mit Spott und Hohne!
    Sei bis in den Tod getreu,
Siehe auf die Lebenskrone!
Zion, fühlest du der Schlange Stich,
Leide dich, leide dich!

COMMUNION OF SAINTS

3. Watch and pray, watch and pray!
   Zion, ever watch and pray
Lest the wicked world misguide thee
   From the narrow path to stray
And thy God reprove and chide thee.
Zion, work with zeal while it is day.
Watch and pray, watch and pray!

4. Run thy race, run thy race,
   Zion, swiftly run thy race!
Let no languor ever find thee
   Idle in the market-place.
Look not to the things behind thee.
Zion, daily strengthened by His grace,
Run thy race, run thy race!

Folge nicht, folge nicht,
   Zion, folge nicht der Welt,
Die dich suchet gross zu machen!
   Achte nichts ihr Gut und Geld,
Nimm nicht an den Stuhl des Drachen!
Zion, wenn sie dir viel Lust verspricht,
Folge nicht, folge nicht!

Halte aus, halte aus,
   Zion, halte deine Treu'!
Lass dich ja nicht laulich finden!
   Auf, das Kleinod rückt herbei!
Auf, verlasse, was dahinten!
Zion, in dem letzten Kampf und Strauss
Halte aus, halte aus!

    This hymn by Johann E. Schmidt was written in seven stanzas, based on the Letters to the Seven Churches in Asia. It first appeared in Freylinghausen's *Neues Geistreiches Gesang Buch,* Halle, 1704. The cento includes Stanzas 1, 2, 3, and 7 of the original.

    The composite translation is based on the translation in the *Australian Lutheran Hymn-Book,* 1925.

    The tune "Fahre fort" is by an unknown composer and appeared with the hymn, in 1704, to which it has since been wedded.

Lord of the Worlds Above   480

1. Lord of the worlds above,
   How pleasant and how fair
The dwellings of Thy love,
   Thine earthly temples are!
To Thine abode
   My heart aspires
   With warm desires
To see my God.

2. The sparrow, for her young,
   With pleasure seeks her nest,
And wandering swallows long
   To find their wonted rest.
My spirit faints
   With equal zeal
   To rise and dwell
Among Thy saints.

3. Oh, happy souls who pray
   Where God appoints to hear!
Oh, happy men who pay
   Their constant service there!
They praise Thee still;
   And happy they
   Who love the way
To Zion's hill.

4. They go from strength to strength
   Through this dark vale of tears
Till each arrives at length,
   Till each in heaven appears,
Oh, glorious seat
   When God, our King,
   Shall thither bring
Our willing feet!

    Isaac Watts first published the hymn from which this cento is derived in his *Psalms of David Imitated,* 1719, with the title "Longing for the House of God." It is his third metrical paraphrase of Ps. 84 and ranks among his best productions. As the metrical psalms in the English Church up to this time had been largely limited to a few simple meters, such as short meter, common meter, and long meter, the meter of this hymn was a somewhat daring departure from the traditional forms. It was an imitation of that used for the first time by John Pullain in his version of Ps. 148. For this reason Watts gave this hymn the heading "As the 148th Psalm."

    The omitted stanzas are the following:

5. To spend one sacred day
   Where God and saints abide
Affords diviner joy
   Than thousand days beside:
Where God resorts,
   I love it more
   To keep the door
Than shine in courts.

6. God is our Sun and Shield,
   Our Light and our Defense;
With gifts His hands are filled;
   We draw our blessings thence:
He shall bestow
   On Jacob's race
   Peculiar grace
And glory, too.

7. The Lord His people loves;
   His hand no good withholds
   From those His heart approves,
   From pure and pious souls.

   Thrice happy he,
   O God of hosts,
   Whose spirit trusts
   Alone in Thee.

For comments on the tune "Darwall's 148th" see Hymn No. 46.

481   Through the Night of Doubt and Sorrow

1. Through the night of doubt and sorrow
   Onward goes the pilgrim band,
   Singing songs of expectation,
   Marching to the Promised Land.
   Clear before us, through the darkness,
   Gleams and burns the guiding light.
   Brother clasps the hand of brother,
   Stepping fearless through the night.

   Igjennem Nat og Trängsel
   Gaar Själens Valfartsang
   Med stille Haab og Längsel,
   Med dyb Forventningssang.
   Det gjennem Natten luer,
   Det lysner gjennem Sky,
   Til Broder Broder skuer
   Og kjender ham paany.

2. One the light of God's own presence,
   O'er His ransomed people shed,
   Chasing far the gloom and terror,
   Brightening all the path we tread;
   One the object of our journey,
   One the faith which never tires,
   One the earnest looking forward,
   One the hope our God inspires.

   Vor Nat det Lys oplive,
   Som aldrig slukkes ud!
   Eet Sind os alle give
   I Trängsel Tröstens Gud!
   Eet Hjerte kjärligt lue
   I hver Korsdragers Bryst!
   Een Gud, til hvem vi skue!
   Een Tro, eet Haab, een Tröst!

3. One the strain the lips of thousands
   Lift as from the heart of one;
   One the conflict, one the peril,
   One the march in God begun;
   One the gladness of rejoicing
   On the far eternal shore,
   Where the one almighty Father
   Reigns in love forevermore.

   Een Röst fra tusind Munde!
   Een Aand i Tusinds Röst!
   Een Fred, hvortil vi stunde!
   Een Frelsens, Naadens Kyst!
   Een Sorg, eet Savn, een Längsel!
   Een Fader her og hist!
   Een Udgang af al Trängsel!
   Eet Liv i Jesu Christ!

4. Onward, therefore, pilgrim brothers!
   Onward, with the cross our aid!
   Bear its shame and fight its battle
   Till we rest beneath its shade.
   Soon shall come the great awaking,
   Soon the rending of the tomb,
   Then the scattering of all shadows,
   And the end of toil and gloom.

   Saa gaa vi med hverandre
   Den store Pilgrimsgang!
   Til Golgatha vi vandre
   I Aand med Bön og Sang.
   Fra Kors, fra Grav vi stige
   Med salig Lov og Pris
   Til den Opstandnes Rige,
   Til Frelsens Paradis!

This hymn is by the Danish poet Bernhardt Severin Ingemann. It was written in 1825, entitled "Unity and Progress," and was included in the Danish hymnal *Nyt Tilläg til Evangelisk-Christelig Psalmebog*, Copenhagen, 1859. The translation by Sabine Baring-Gould, published in *The People's Hymnal*, 1867, helped to make the hymn widely known in the English-speaking world. The translation is an altered form of Baring-Gould's as found in *Hymns Ancient and Modern*, 1875.

The tune "Baltimore" was written in 1910 by Bernhard Schumacher for "Glorious Things of Thee are Spoken." (See hymn No. 469.) It was selected for this hymn by the editorial committee and is published in *The Lutheran Hymnal* for the first time.

482   Dear Lord, to Thy True Servants Give

1. Dear Lord, to Thy true servants give
   The grace to Thee alone to live.
   Once bound by sin, but saved by Thee,
   They go to set the prisoners free,
   The Gospel-message to proclaim
   That men may call upon Thy name.

2. They gladly go at Thy command
   To spread Thy Word o'er sea and land.
   Be Thou with them and make them strong
   To heal sin's ills, to right the wrong.
   Thou rulest over wind and wave,
   And mighty is Thine arm to save.

3. When all their labor seems in vain,
   Revive their sinking hopes again;
   And when success crowns what they do,
   Oh, keep them humble, Lord, and true
   Until before Thy judgment-seat
   They lay their trophies at Thy feet.

This hymn is our own and was written in 1937 and dedicated to the graduating class of Concordia Seminary, St. Louis, of that year. In its original form the first line was "Dear Lord, to these Thy servants give."

For comments on the tune "Vater unser" see Hymn No. 458.

God of the Prophets, Bless the Prophets' Sons 483

1. God of the prophets, bless the prophets' sons;
   Elijah's mantle o'er Elisha cast.
   Each age its solemn task may claim but once;
   Make each one nobler, stronger, than the last.

2. Anoint them prophets. Make their ears attent
   To Thy divinest speech, their hearts awake
   To human need, their lips make eloquent
   To gird the right and every evil break.

3. Anoint them priests. Strong intercessors, they,
   For pardon and for charity and peace.
   Ah, if with them the world might, now astray,
   Find in our Lord from all its woes release!

4. Anoint them kings; aye, kingly kings, O Lord.
   Anoint them with the Spirit of Thy Son.
   Theirs not a jeweled crown, a blood-stained sword;
   Theirs, by sweet love, for Christ a kingdom won.

5. Make them apostles, heralds of Thy Cross;
   Forth may they go to tell all realms Thy grace.
   Inspired of Thee, may they count all but loss
   And stand at last with joy before Thy face.

This hymn was written by Denis Wortman in 1884, the year of the centennial of the New Brunswick Theological Seminary, of which he was a graduate (1860). It was entitled "Prayer for Young Ministers." According to Dr. W. C. Covert there were originally seven stanzas. We have been able to find only six. The omitted sixth stanza reads:

6. O mighty age of prophet-kings, return!
   O truth, O faith, enrich our urgent time!
   Lord Jesus Christ, again with us sojourn;
   A weary world awaits Thy reign sublime.

For comments on the tune "Old 124th" see Hymn No. 307.

We Bid Thee Welcome in the Name 484

1. We bid thee welcome in the name
   Of Jesus, our exalted Head.
   Come as a servant, — so He came, —
   And we receive thee in His stead.

2. Come as a shepherd; guard and keep
   This fold from hell and world and sin;
   Nourish the lambs and feed the sheep;
   The wounded heal, the lost bring in.

3. Come as a teacher sent from God,
   Charged His whole counsel to declare.
   Lift o'er our ranks the prophet's rod
   While we uphold thy hands with prayer.

4. Come as a messenger of peace,
   Filled with the Spirit, fired with love.
   Live to behold our large increase
   And die to meet us all above.

James Montgomery published this hymn in his *Christian Psalmist*, 1825, in six stanzas, under the title "On the Appointment of a Minister." The two omitted stanzas are:

3. Come as a watchman; take thy stand
   Upon the tower amidst the sky,
   And when the sword comes on the land,
   Call us to fight or warn to fly.

4. Come as an angel — hence to guide
   A band of pilgrims on their way,
   That softly walking at thy side,
   We fail not, faint not, turn nor stray.

It is a fitting hymn to be sung by a congregation at the installation of a pastor.

For comments on the tune "Herr Jesu Christ, mein's" see Hymn No. 7.

485   Lord Jesus, Who art Come

1. Lord Jesus, who art come
    A Teacher sent from heaven
 And by both word and deed
    God's truth to us hast given,
 Thou wisely hast ordained
    The holy ministry
 That we, Thy flock, may know
    The way to God through Thee.

2. Thou hast, O Lord, returned,
    To God's right hand ascending;
 Yet Thou art in the world,
    Thy kingdom here extending.
 Through preaching of Thy Word
    In every land and clime
 Thy people's faith is kept
    Until the end of time.

3. O blessed ministry
    Of reconciliation,
 That shows the way to God
    And brings to us salvation!
 By Thine evangel pure,
    Lord, Thou preserv'st Thy fold,
 Dost call, enlighten, keep,
    Dost comfort and uphold.

4. Preserve this ministry
    While harvest-days are keeping;
 And since the fields are white
    And hands are few for reaping,
 Send workers forth, O Lord,
    The sheaves to gather in
 That not a soul be lost
    Which Thou art come to win.

5. The servants Thou hast called
    And to Thy Church art giving
 Preserve in doctrine pure
    And holiness of living.
 Thy Spirit fill their hearts,
    Endue their tongues with power;
 What they should boldly speak,
    Oh, give them in that hour!

6. Yea, bless Thy Word alway,
    Our souls forever feeding;
 And may we never lack
    A faithful shepherd's leading!
 Seek Thou the wandering sheep,
    Bind up the sore opprest,
 Lift up the fallen ones,
    And grant the weary rest.

7. Bring those into Thy fold
    Who still to Thee are strangers;
 Guard those who are within
    Against offense and dangers.
 Press onward with Thy Word
    Till pastor and his fold
 Through faith in Thee, O Christ,
    Thy glory shall behold.

Herr Jesu, der du selbst
   Von Gott als Lehrer kommen
Und, was du aus dem Schoss
   Des Vaters hast genommen,
Den rechten Weg zu Gott
   Mit Wort und Werk gelehrt,
Sei für dein Predigtamt
   Gelobt von deiner Herd'!

Du bist zwar in die Höh'
   Zum Vater aufgefahren,
Doch gibst du noch der Welt
   Dein Wort mit grossen Scharen
Und baust durch diesen Dienst
   Die Kirche, deinen Leib,
Dass er im Glauben wachs'
   Und fest ans Ende bleib'.

Hab' Dank für dieses Amt,
   Durch das man dich selbst höret,
Das uns den Weg zu Gott
   Und die Versöhnung lehret,
Durchs Evangelium
   Ein Häuflein in der Welt
Berufet, sammelt, stärkt,
   Lehrt, tröstet und erhält!

Erhalt uns diesen Dienst
   Bis an das End' der Erden,
Und weil die Ernte gross,
   Gross' Arbeit und Beschwerden,
Send selbst Arbeiter aus
   Und mach sie klug und treu,
Dass Feld und Sä'mann gut,
   Die Ernte reichlich sei!

Die du durch deinen Ruf
   Der Kirche hast gegeben,
Erhalt bei reiner Lehr'
   Und einem heil'gen Leben!
Leg deinen Geist ins Herz,
   Das Wort in ihren Mund!
Was jeder reden soll,
   Das gib du ihm zur Stund'!

Ach segne all dein Wort
   Mit Kraft an unsern Seelen!
Lass deinen Schäflein nie
   An guter Weid' es fehlen;
Such das verirrte selbst,
   Bind das verwund'te zu,
Das schlafende weck auf,
   Das müde bring zur Ruh'!

Bring, was noch draussen ist,
   Zu deiner kleinen Herde!
Was drinnen ist, erhalt,
   Dass es gestärket werde!
Dring durch mit deinem Wort,
   Bis einstens Hirt und Herd'
Im Glauben, Herr, an dich
   Zusammen selig werd'!

Eberhard Ludwig Fischer published this hymn, originally in eight stanzas, in the *Württemberger Landes-Gesangbuch,* 1741, which Dr. Wilhelm Gottlieb Tafinger compiled with Fischer's assistance. The omitted Stanza 7 reads as follows:

    7. Bewahr vor Ketzerei,
       Vor Menschenlehr' und Dünkel!
    Lehr uns nach deiner Art
       Im Tempel, nicht im Winkel!
    Behüt vor Ärgernis,
       Vor Spaltung, die uns trennt;
    Erhalte rein und ganz
       Dein Wort und Sakrament!

The translation is composite.

For comments on the tune "O Gott, du frommer Gott" see Hymn No. 395.

O Thou Whose Feet have Climbed Life's Hill   486

1. O Thou whose feet have climbed life's hill
And trod the path of youth,
Our Savior and our Brother still,
Now lead us into truth.

2. The call is Thine; be Thou the Way,
And give us men, to guide.
Let wisdom broaden with the day;
Let human faith abide.

3. Who learn of Thee the truth shall find;
Who follow, gain the goal.
With reverence crown the earnest mind
And speak within the soul.

4. Awake the purpose high which strives
And, falling, stands again;
Conform the will of eager lives
To quit themselves like men.

5. Thy life the bond of fellowship,
Thy love the law that rules,
Thy name, proclaimed by every lip,
The Master of our schools.

This hymn was written by Louis FitzGerald Benson in February, 1891, at the request of the committee which was at work compiling the Presbyterian *Hymnal*, published in 1895. It was intended for use in the schools, colleges, and seminaries of the Church. It is suitable also for the service of installation of a teacher in church-schools.

For comments on the tune "Dundee" see Hymn No. 49.

How Beauteous Are Their Feet   487

1. How beauteous are their feet
Who stand on Zion's hill;
Who bring salvation on their tongues
And words of peace reveal!

2. How charming is their voice!
How sweet their tidings are!
"Zion, behold thy Savior-King;
He reigns and triumphs here."

3. How happy are the ears
That hear this joyful sound
Which kings and prophets waited for
And sought, but never found!

4. How blessed are the eyes
That see this heavenly light!
Prophets and kings desired it long,
But died without the sight.

5. The watchmen join their voice
And tuneful notes employ;
Jerusalem breaks forth in songs,
And deserts learn the joy.

6. The Lord makes bare His arm
Through all the earth abroad.
Let every nation now behold
Their Savior and their God.

Isaac Watts published this hymn in his *Hymns and Spiritual Songs*, 1707. It is based on Is. 52:7-10 and Matt. 13:16, 17. It was entitled "The Blessedness of the Gospel Times; or the Revelation of Christ to Jews and Gentiles." Though rightly placed under the *Ministry* in *The Lutheran Hymnal*, the hymn is also a hymn for *Missions*. It is one of the first missionary hymns ever published in the English language.

For comments on the tune "St. Michael" see Hymn No. 310.

Lord of the Harvest, Hear   488

1. Lord of the harvest, hear
Thy needy servants' cry;
Answer our faith's effectual prayer
And all our wants supply.

2. On Thee we humbly wait,
Our wants are in Thy view.
The harvest, truly, Lord, is great,
The laborers are few.

3. Anoint and send forth more
Into Thy Church abroad
And let them speak Thy Word of Power
As workers with their God.

4. Oh, let them spread Thy name,
Their mission fully prove,
Thy universal grace proclaim,
Thine all-redeeming love!

This hymn, by Charles Wesley, first appeared in *Hymns and Sacred Poems*, 1742, published by him and his famous brother, John. For obvious reasons it has been placed under the heading *Ministry,* although it is also suitable for *Missions.*

The tune "Aynhoe" is adapted from a melody by James Nares (1715—1783), an English organist and composer.

489   Lord of the Church, We Humbly Pray

1. Lord of the Church, we humbly pray
For those who guide us in Thy way
And speak Thy holy Word.
With love divine their hearts inspire
And touch their lips with hallowed fire
And needful strength afford.

2. Help them to preach the Truth of God,
Redemption through the Savior's blood,
Nor let the Spirit cease
On all the Church His gifts to shower —
To them a messenger of power;
To us, of life and peace.

3. So may they live to Thee alone,
Then hear the welcome word, "Well done,"
And take their crown above;
Enter into their Master's joy
And all eternity employ
In praise and bliss and love.

Edward Osler first published this hymn in Hall's *Mitre Hymn Book,* 1836, and again, slightly altered, in his *Church and King,* 1837. It is based on Charles Wesley's "Thou Jesu, Thou My Breast Inspire," published in the *Wesleyan Hymn Book,* 1780, which, in turn, is a cento from Charles Wesley's "O Thou Who at Thy Creature's Bar," a hymn of nine stanzas, twelve lines each, published in *Hymns and Sacred Poems,* 1749.

Of this hymn Dr. Jackson (*Memoirs of the Rev. Chas. Wesley,* abridged edition, 1848) writes:

> The first volume concludes with a hymn of unusual length and of almost unparalleled sublimity and force. Nothing could give so perfect a view of the spirit in which he had exercised his ministry, from the time at which he began his glorious career in Moorfields and Kennington-common, to this period of his life. In these noble verses he has strikingly depicted the mighty faith, the burning love to Christ, the yearning pity for the souls of men, the heavenly-mindedness, the animating hope of future glory, which characterized his public ministry and which not only enabled him to deliver his Lord's message before scoffing multitudes, but also carried him through his wasting labors and the riots of Bristol, of Cornwall, of Staffordshire, of Devizes, and of Ireland without a murmur. As a witness for Christ he freely sacrificed his reputation as a man of letters and of genius; and of life itself, comparatively speaking, he made no account.

For comments on the tune "Kommt her zu mir" see Hymn No. 263.

490   Pour Out Thy Spirit from on High

1. Pour out Thy Spirit from on high,
Lord, Thine assembled servants bless;
Graces and gifts to each supply
And clothe Thy priests with righteousness.

2. Before Thine altar when we stand
To teach the truth as taught by Thee,
Savior, like stars in Thy right hand,
The angels of Thy churches be.

3. Wisdom and zeal and faith impart,
Firmness with meekness, from above,
To bear Thy people on our heart
And love the souls whom Thou dost love;

4. To watch and pray and never faint
By day and night strict guard to keep,
To warn the sinner, cheer the saint,
Nourish Thy lambs, and feed Thy sheep.

5. Then, when our work is finished here,
We may in hope our charge resign.
When the Chief Shepherd shall appear,
O God, may they and we be Thine!

James Montgomery wrote this hymn on August 17, 1832, entitled "For a Meeting of Christian Ministers." It was first published in J. Birchell's *Selection of Hymns*, 1833. The hymn has been altered, and in its most popular form it begins with the line "Lord, Pour Thy Spirit from on High." This altered form made the hymn suitable for congregational singing at the ordination or installation of a minister. However, as it is our finest hymn for pastoral conferences in its original form, it has been included in *The Lutheran Hymnal* to serve that particular purpose.

For comments on the tune "O Jesu Christ, mein's" see Hymn No. 64.

Send, O Lord, Thy Holy Spirit   491

1. Send, O Lord, Thy Holy Spirit
   On Thy servant now, we pray;
Let him prove a faithful shepherd
   To Thy little lambs alway.
Thy pure teaching to proclaim,
To extol Thy holy name,
And to feed Thy lambs, dear Savior,
Make his aim and sole endeavor.

2. Thou, O Lord, Thyself hast called him
   For Thy precious lambs to care;
But to prosper in his calling,
   He the Spirit's gifts must share.
Grant him wisdom from above,
Fill his heart with holy love;
In all weakness be Thou near Him,
In his prayers, Good Shepherd, hear him.

3. Help, Lord Jesus, help him nourish
   Our dear children with Thy Word
That in constant love they serve Thee
   Till in heaven their song is heard.
Boundless blessings, Lord, bestow
On his faithful toil below
Till by grace to him is given
His reward, the crown of heaven.

Segne, Herr, mit deinem Geiste
   Deinen Diener immerdar,
Dass den rechten Dienst er leiste
   Dir an deiner Lämmerschar.
Deines Wortes reine Lehr',
Deines heil'gen Namens Ehr',
Deiner Lämmlein Seligkeit
Sei sein Ziel zu aller Zeit.

Du, o Herr hast ihn erwählet
   Zu dem Amt, so schön, doch schwer;
Ohne deinen Geist ihm fehlet
   Alle Hilfe, Kraft und Wehr.
Schenk ihm Weisheit und Verstand,
Stärk ihm Herz und Mund und Hand.
Hör uns, o Herr Jesu Christ,
Der du Hirt und Helfer bist!

Hilf, Herr Christ, ihm treulich weiden
   Unsre Kindlein auf den Au'n
Deines Worts, hilf ihm sie leiten,
   Dass sie selig einst dich schaun.
Hilf ihm tragen all' Beschwer,
Die sein Amt bringt mit sich her;
Krön ihn auch mit Herrlichkeit
Einst in sel'ger Ewigkeit.

We have been unable to determine the author of this 19th-century hymn. It became known in certain circles through the old German *Lieder-Perlen*, a Concordia Publishing House publication for use in our schools. It is to be used at the installation of a teacher. The translator is Frederick W. Herzberger.

For comments on the tune "Werde munter" see Hymn No. 207.

Lord of the Living Harvest   492

1. Lord of the living harvest
      That whitens o'er the plain,
   Where angels soon shall gather
      Their sheaves of golden grain,
   Accept these hands to labor,
      These hearts to trust and love,
   And deign with them to hasten
      Thy kingdom from above.

2. As laborers in Thy vineyard,
      Lord, send them out to be
   Content to bear the burden
      Of weary days for Thee,
   To ask no other wages
      When Thou shalt call them home
   Than to have shared the travail
      Which makes Thy kingdom come.

3. Be with them, God the Father;
      Be with them, God the Son;
   And God the Holy Spirit,
      Most blessed Three in One.
   Make them Thy faithful servants
      Thee rightly to adore
   And fill them with Thy fulness
      Both now and evermore.

This hymn by John Samuel Bewley Monsell was first published in 1866, in the second edition of his *Hymns of Love and Praise* in four stanzas. It is a

[343]

prayer for the ordained and is very suitable for use at the ordination or installation of a pastor or at services in connection with pastoral conferences. The omitted Stanza 3 reads:

>Come down, O Holy Spirit,
> And fill their souls with light,
>Clothe them in spotless raiment,
> In linen clean and white,
>Beside Thy sacred altar.
> Be with them where they stand
>To sanctify Thy people
> Through all this happy land.

In some hymnals this hymn is given in an altered form, with a change of the pronouns and the omission of Stanza 3, so that the hymn may be sung by the ordained themselves or by any group of church-workers.

For comments on the tune "Aurelia" see Hymn No. 473.

493   Thou Who the Night in Prayer Didst Spend

>1. Thou who the night in prayer didst spend
>And then didst Thine apostles send
>And bidd'st us pray the harvest's Lord
>To send forth sowers of Thy Word,
>Hear and Thy chosen servants bless
>With sevenfold gifts of holiness.
>
>2. Oh, may Thy pastors faithful be,
>Not laboring for themselves, but Thee!
>Give grace to feed with wholesome food
>Thy sheep and lambs bought by Thy blood,
>To tend Thy flock, and thus to prove
>How dearly they the Shepherd love.
>
>3. Oh, may Thy people faithful be
>And in Thy pastors honor Thee
>And with them work and for them pray
>And gladly Thee in them obey,
>Receive the prophet of the Lord
>And gain the prophet's own reward!
>
>4. So may we when our work is done
>Together stand before Thy throne
>And joyful hearts and voices raise
>In one united song of praise,
>With all the bright celestial host,
>To Father, Son, and Holy Ghost.

This cento is taken from Christopher Wordsworth's hymn "O Lord, Who in Thy Love Divine," *Holy Year*, 1862, where it appeared in ten stanzas. Our cento is composed of Stanzas 2, 5, 9, and 10, with slight alterations. As the original hymn is hardly known anywhere today, we give it complete, with its interesting first stanza, and the original capitalization, as found in the 1863 edition of the *Holy Year*:

>1. O Lord, Who in Thy love divine
>Didst leave in heaven the Ninety-nine,
>In pity for a World undone,
>And gav'st Thy life to save the one,
>And didst it on Thy shoulders bear
>In joy to heaven, receive our prayer.
>
>2. Thou who the night in prayer didst spend
>And then Thy Twelve Apostles send;
>And bidd'st us pray the Harvest's Lord
>To send forth sowers of the Word,
>Hear us and these Thy servants bless
>With sevenfold gifts of holiness.
>
>3. Look down, with gracious eye behold,
>With watchful care protect Thy Fold;
>Secure from hireling Shepherds keep,
>Which feed themselves, and not the sheep,
>And when the prowling wolf is nigh,
>Forsake the flock in fear and fly.
>
>4. O Thou, who didst at Pentecost
>Send down from heaven the Holy Ghost
>That He might with Thy Church abide
>Forever to defend and guide,
>Illuminate and strengthen, Lord,
>The Preachers of Thy Holy Word.
>
>5. May all Thy Pastors faithful be;
>Not laboring for themselves, but Thee;
>And may they feed with wholesome food
>The sheep and lambs bought by Thy Blood;
>Tending Thy flock, oh, may they prove
>How dearly they the Shepherd love!
>
>6. That which the Holy Scriptures teach,
>That, and that only, may they preach;
>May they the true Foundation lay,
>Build gold thereon, not wood or hay;
>And meekly preach in days of strife
>The sermon of a holy life.
>
>7. As ever in Thy holy Eyes,
>And Stewards of Thy Mysteries,
>May they the People teach to see
>Not, Lord, Thy Ministers, but Thee;
>To see a loving Savior's face
>Revealed in all the means of grace.
>
>8. May they Thy Word with boldness speak
>And bear with tenderness the weak;
>Not seeking their own things as best,
>But what may edify the rest;
>With wisdom and simplicity
>And, most of all, with charity.
>
>9. Oh, may Thy People loving be,
>And in Thy Pastors honor Thee,
>And working with them for them pray,
>And gladly Thee in them obey;
>Receive the prophet of the Lord
>And gain the prophet's own reward.
>
>10. So may we, when our work is done,
>Together stand before the Throne;
>And joyful hearts and voices raise,
>In one united song of praise,
>With all the bright celestial Host,
>To Father, Son, and Holy Ghost.

MISSIONS

The tune "St. Petersburg" is also known by such titles as "Wells," "Wellspring," and "Shangana." According to *Kümmerle* it is adapted from a portion of a mass by Dimitri S. Bortniansky, 1822. It was set to Gerhard Tersteegen's "Ich bete an die Macht der Liebe" in a number of German collections and has in recent years become very popular in our own country.

Awake, Thou Spirit, Who Didst Fire   494

1. Awake, Thou Spirit, who didst fire
   The watchmen of the Church's youth,
   Who faced the Foe's envenomed ire,
   Who witnessed day and night Thy truth,
   Whose voices loud are ringing still
   And bringing hosts to know Thy will.

2. Lord, let our earnest prayer be heard,
   The prayer Thy Son hath bid us pray;
   For, lo, Thy children's hearts are stirred
   In every land in this our day
   To cry with fervent soul to Thee,
   Oh, help us, Lord! So let it be!

3. Oh, haste to help ere we are lost!
   Send preachers forth, in spirit strong,
   Armed with Thy Word, a dauntless host,
   Bold to attack the rule of wrong;
   Let them the earth for Thee reclaim,
   Thy heritage, to know Thy name.

4. And let Thy Word have speedy course,
   Through every land be glorified,
   Till all the heathen know its force
   And fill Thy churches far and wide.
   Oh, spread the conquest of Thy Word
   And let Thy kingdom come, dear Lord!

Wach auf, du Geist der ersten Zeugen,
Die auf der Mau'r als treue Wächter stehn,
Die Tag' und Nächte nimmer schweigen
Und die getrost dem Feind entgegengehn;
Ja, deren Schall die ganze Welt durchdringt
Und aller Völker Scharen zu dir bringt.

Dein Sohn hat ja mit klaren Worten
Uns diese Bitte in den Mund gelegt.
O siehe, wie an allen Orten
Sich deiner Kinder Herz und Sinn bewegt,
Dich herzinbrünstig hierum anzuflehn;
Drum hör, o Herr, und sprich: Es soll geschehn!

So gib dein Wort mit grossen Scharen,
Die in der Kraft Evangelisten sein;
Lass eilend Hilf' uns widerfahren
Und brich in Satans Reich und Macht hinein.
O breite, Herr, auf weitem Erdenkreis
Dein Reich bald aus zu deines Namens Preis!

Ach, lass dein Wort recht schnelle laufen;
Es sei kein Ort ohn' dessen Glanz und Schein.
Ach, führe bald dadurch mit Haufen
Der Heiden Füll' in alle Tore ein!
Ja, wecke doch auch Israel bald auf
Und also segne deines Wortes Lauf!

This cento is from Carl H. v. Bogatzky's famous missionary hymn of fourteen stanzas, published in 1750 in his *Die Übung der Gottseligkeit in allerley Geistlichen Liedern,* Halle. It was entitled "For faithful laborers in the Harvest of the Lord, for the blessed spread of the Word to all the world." The cento is formed of Stanzas 1, 3, 5, and 7 of the original. The translation is a slightly altered form of Catherine Winkworth's *Lyra Germanica,* first series, 1855. In Stanza 4, Lines 5 and 6, Bogatzky's words, in translation, are:

> Wake Israel from his sleep, O Lord,
> And spread the conquest of Thy Word!

For comments on the tune "All' Ehr' und Lob" see Hymn No. 238.

From Greenland's Icy Mountains   495

1. From Greenland's icy mountains,
   From India's coral strand,
   Where Afric's sunny fountains
   Roll down their golden sand;
   From many an ancient river,
   From many a palmy plain,
   They call us to deliver
   Their land from error's chain.

2. What though the spicy breezes
   Blow soft o'er Ceylon's isle;
   Though every prospect pleases
   And only man is vile;
   In vain with lavish kindness
   The gifts of God are strown;
   The heathen in his blindness
   Bows down to wood and stone.

[345]

3. Can we whose souls are lighted
    With wisdom from on high,
Can we to men benighted
    The lamp of life deny?
Salvation, O salvation!
    The joyful sound proclaim
Till each remotest nation
    Has learned Messiah's name.

4. Waft, waft, ye winds, His story,
    And you, ye waters, roll,
Till like a sea of glory
    It spreads from pole to pole;
Till o'er our ransomed nature
    The Lamb for sinners slain,
Redeemer, King, Creator,
    In bliss returns to reign.

Reginald Heber, according to his wife, wrote this hymn in 1819. She describes the circumstances in *Memoirs*, Vol. 1. A more detailed account, however, of the hymn's origin is related by Thomas Edgeworth of Wrexham. The account, written on a fly-leaf of a facsimile of the original manuscript, reads:

"On Whitsunday, 1819, the late Dr. Shipley, Dean of St. Asaph, and Vicar of Wrexham, preached a sermon in Wrexham Church in aid of the Society for the Propagation of the Gospel in Foreign Parts. That day was also fixed upon for the commencement of the Sunday evening lectures intended to be established in the church, and the late Bishop of Calcutta (Heber), then rector of Hodnet, the Dean's son-in-law being together in the vicarage, the former requested Heber to write 'something for them to sing in the morning'; and he retired for that purpose from the table where the Dean and a few friends were sitting to a distant part of the room. In a short time the Dean enquired, 'What have you written?' Heber having then composed the three first verses, read them over. 'There, there, that will do very well,' said the Dean. 'No, no, the sense is not complete,' replied Heber. Accordingly he added the fourth verse, and the Dean being inexorable to his repeated request of 'Let me add another; oh, let me add another!' thus completed the hymn of which the annexed is a facsimile and which has since become so celebrated. It was sung the next morning in Wrexham Church the first time."

It is one of the most famous missionary hymns ever written and is an eloquent testimony to the missionary fervor which was sweeping over the Protestant churches at the time.

The tune "Missionary Hymn," also called "Heber" and "Gospel Banner," was written for this hymn by Lowell Mason and appeared in 1829 in *The Boston Handel and Haydn Society Collection,* 9th edition. J. T. Lightwood says this tune will not soon be forgotten if "modern editors will leave the simple, original, but effective harmonies alone."

496   Hark! the Voice of Jesus Crying

1. Hark! the voice of Jesus crying,
    "Who will go and work today?
Fields are white and harvests waiting,
    Who will bear the sheaves away?"
Loud and long the Master calleth,
    Rich reward He offers thee;
Who will answer, gladly saying,
    "Here am I, send me, send me"?

2. If you cannot speak like angels,
    If you cannot preach like Paul,
You can tell the love of Jesus,
    You can say He died for all.
If you cannot rouse the wicked
    With the Judgment's dread alarms,
You can lead the little children
    To the Savior's waiting arms.

3. If you cannot be a watchman,
    Standing high on Zion's wall,
Pointing out the path to heaven,
    Offering life and peace to all,
With your prayers and with your bounties
    You can do what God demands;
You can be like faithful Aaron,
    Holding up the prophet's hands.

4. Let none hear you idly saying,
    "There is nothing I can do,"
While the souls of men are dying
    And the Master calls for you.
Take the task He gives you gladly,
    Let His work your pleasure be;
Answer quickly when He calleth,
    "Here am I, send me, send me!"

Stanzas 1, 2, and 4 of this hymn are by Daniel March. The third stanza, by an unknown author, was put in place of March's second (March's third is our second), which reads:

> If you cannot cross the ocean,
>   And the heathen lands explore,
> You can find the heathen nearer,
>   You can help them at your door;
> If you cannot give your thousands,
>   You can give the widow's mite,
> And the least you give for Jesus
>   Will be precious in His sight.

The reason for omitting this stanza is because of the questions raised as to the correctness of the last four lines. No doubt March had the right thought in mind, but his words can be construed to mean just the opposite. The committee received dozens of requests from our people to alter these lines, and many suggestions were sent to us. However, none of these proved satisfactory, and therefore it was decided to drop the stanza altogether.

March was a Congregational pastor in Philadelphia when he wrote this hymn in 1868. He had been asked to preach a sermon to the Philadelphia Christian Association, on October 18, on the text Is. 6:8. At a late hour he learned that one of the hymns selected was not suitable. He wrote the hymn in "great haste," and it was sung from the manuscript. The hymn was first published in *The Hymnal of the Methodist Episcopal Church*, 1878.

For comments on the tune "Galilean" see Hymn No. 469.

The Morning Light is Breaking 497

1. The morning light is breaking,
    The darkness disappears;
  The sons of earth are waking
    To penitential tears.
  Each breeze that sweeps the ocean
    Brings tidings from afar
  Of nations in commotion,
    Prepared for Zion's war.

2. See heathen nations bending
    Before the God we love
  And thousand hearts ascending
    In gratitude above,
  While sinners, now confessing,
    The Gospel call obey
  And seek the Savior's blessing,
    A nation in a day.

3. Blest river of salvation,
    Pursue thine onward way;
  Flow thou to every nation
    Nor in thy richness stay;
  Stay not till all the lowly
    Triumphant reach their home;
  Stay not till all the holy
    Proclaim, "The Lord is come."

Samuel F. Smith, the author of "My Country, 'tis of Thee," wrote this hymn in 1832, under the title "Success of the Gospel," in four stanzas. It first appeared in *Spiritual Songs for Social Worship*, 1833. The omitted Stanza 2 reads:

> Rich dews of grace come o'er us,
>   In many a gentle shower,
> And brighter scenes before us
>   Are opening every hour.
> Each cry to heaven going,
>   Abundant answers brings,
> And heavenly gales are blowing
>   With peace upon their wings.

The hymn is very popular and has been translated into many languages. Smith wrote in 1883: "I have heard versions sung of it in Karen, Burman, Italian, Spanish, Portuguese, Swedish, German, and Telugu." Like the hymn "Stand Up! Stand Up for Jesus," it is wedded to the tune "Webb." For comments on the tune see Hymn No. 451.

498 Rise, Thou Light of Gentile Nations

1. Rise, Thou Light of Gentile nations,
    Jesus, bright and Morning Star;
   Let Thy Word, the gladsome tidings,
    Ring out loudly near and far,
   Bringing freedom to the captives,
    Peace and comfort to the slave,
   That the heathen, free from bondage,
    May proclaim Thy power to save.

2. See the blindness of the heathen,
    Strangers to Thy glorious light,
   Straying hopeless till they find Thee,
    Wandering aimless in the night.
   See their pitiful condition;
    Lo, gross darkness covers all,
   And no ray of hope refreshes
    Nor dispels the dreadful pall.

3. If Thou, merciful Redeemer,
    Hadst not saved us from this plight,
   In like darkness we should languish
    Hopeless, helpless, in sin's night.
   Lovingly Thou, Lord, didst seek us
    In the beauty of Thy grace;
   Now with joy we freely serve Thee,
    We, Thy blessed, chosen race.

4. Knowing Thee and Thy salvation,
    Grateful love dare never cease
   To proclaim Thy tender mercies,
    Gracious Lord, Thy heavenly peace.
   Sound we forth the Gospel-tidings
    To the earth's remotest bound
   That the sinner has been pardoned
    And forgiveness can be found.

5. May our zeal to help the heathen
    Be increased from day to day
   As we plead in true compassion
    And for their conversion pray.
   For the many faithful heralds,
    For the Gospel they proclaim,
   Let us all be cheerful givers
    To the glory of Thy name.

6. Savior, shine in all Thy glory
    On the nations near and far;
   From the highways and the byways
    Call them, O Thou Morning Star.
   Guide them whom Thy grace hath chosen
    Out of Satan's dreadful thrall
   To the mansions of Thy Father —
    There is room for sinners all.

Gehe auf, du Trost der Heiden,
 Jesu, heller Morgenstern!
Lass dein Wort, das Wort der Freuden,
 Laut erschallen nah und fern,
Dass es allen Frieden bringe,
 Die der Feind gefangen hält,
Und dir Lob und Preis erklinge
 Durch die ganze Heidenwelt!

Sieh die Not der geistlich Blinden,
 Welche deinen Glanz nicht sehn
Und, solang sie dich nicht finden,
 Trostlos in der Irre gehn!
Sieh den Jammer aller Heiden:
 Finsternis bedecket sie,
Und im Dunkel ihrer Leiden
 Labet sie die Hoffnung nie.

Ach, in diesen Finsternissen
 Lägen wir auch ganz und gar,
Wenn uns nicht herausgerissen
 Der Erbarmer wunderbar.
Freundlich ist er uns erschienen
 In der Gnade hehrer Pracht,
Dass wir nun mit Freuden dienen
 Dem, der uns so selig macht.

Da wir nun dein Heil erfahren,
 Darf die Liebe nimmer ruhn,
Es der Welt zu offenbaren,
 Wie du uns gebeutst zu tun:
Aller Kreatur zu künden
 Gottes Wort vom ew'gen Heil,
Dass Vergebung ihrer Sünden
 Allen Menschen werd' zuteil.

Mehr in uns dein Liebesfeuer,
 Herr, den Heiden beizustehn,
Dass wir betend immer treuer
 Um Erbarmung für sie flehn,
Dass wir gerne Gaben spenden
 Für dein Evangelium
Und viel fromme Boten senden,
 Zu verkünden deinen Ruhm!

Nun, so lass dein Licht erscheinen,
 Gott, den Heiden nah und fern!
Von den Strassen, von den Zäunen
 Rufe sie durch deinen Stern!
Führe, die du dir erkoren,
 Aus dem Reich des Teufels aus;
Denn für alle, die verloren,
 Ist noch Raum im Vaterhaus.

This hymn is by Herman Fick and was included in the 1917 edition of our German hymnal, *Kirchengesangbuch für Evangelisch-Lutherische Gemeinden*, etc., St. Louis. The translation is composite and was prepared for *The Lutheran Hymnal*.

For comments on the tune "O du Liebe" see Hymn No. 37.

499 Look from Thy Sphere of Endless Day

1. Look from Thy sphere of endless day,
    O God of mercy and of might!
   In pity look on those who stray
    Benighted in this land of light.

2. In peopled vale, in lonely glen,
    In crowded mart, by stream or sea,
   How many of the sons of men
    Hear not the message sent from Thee!

3. Send forth Thy heralds, Lord, to call
    The thoughtless young, the hardened old,
   A scattered, homeless flock, till all
    Be gathered to Thy peaceful fold.

4. Send them Thy mighty Word to speak
    Till faith shall dawn and doubt depart,
   To awe the bold, to stay the weak,
    And bind and heal the broken heart,

MISSIONS

> 5. Then all these wastes, a dreary scene,
> That makes us sadden as we gaze,
> Shall grow with living waters green
> And lift to heaven the voice of praise.

William Cullen Bryant wrote this hymn in 1840 for a missionary anniversary. Then in 1845 he printed privately, for circulation among his friends, a book of nineteen hymns. This hymn was one of them. It was published again in *Songs for the Sanctuary*, 1865, and has since been included in many hymnals.

For comments on the tune "St. Crispin" see Hymn No. 245.

May God Bestow on Us His Grace — 500

1. May God bestow on us His grace,
   With blessings rich provide us,
And may the brightness of His face
   To life eternal guide us
That we His saving health may know,
   His gracious will and pleasure,
And also to the heathen show
   Christ's riches without measure
And unto God convert them.

2. Thine over all shall be the praise
   And thanks of every nation,
And all the world with joy shall raise
   The voice of exultation;
For Thou shalt judge the earth, O Lord,
   Nor suffer sin to flourish;
Thy people's pasture is Thy Word
   Their souls to feed and nourish,
In righteous paths to keep them.

3. Oh, let the people praise Thy worth,
   In all good works increasing;
The land shall plenteous fruit bring forth,
   Thy Word is rich in blessing.
May God the Father, God the Son,
   And God the Spirit bless us!
Let all the world praise Him alone,
   Let solemn awe possess us.
Now let our hearts say, Amen.

Es woll' uns Gott genädig sein
   Und seinen Segen geben;
Sein Antlitz uns mit hellem Schein
   Erleucht' zum ew'gen Leben,
Dass wir erkennen seine Werk',
   Und was ihm liebt auf Erden,
Und Jesus Christus Heil und Stärk'
   Bekannt den Heiden werden
Und sie zu Gott bekehren.

So danken, Gott, und loben dich
   Die Heiden überalle,
Und alle Welt, die freue sich
   Und sing' mit grossem Schalle,
Dass du auf Erden Richter bist
   Und lässt die Sünd' nicht walten;
Dein Wort die Hut und Weide ist,
   Die alles Volk erhalten,
In rechter Bahn zu wallen.

Es danke, Gott, und lobe dich
   Das Volk in guten Taten;
Das Land bringt Frucht und bessert sich,
   Dein Wort ist wohl geraten.
Uns segne Vater und der Sohn,
   Uns segne Gott der Heil'ge Geist,
Dem alle Welt die Ehre tu',
   Vor ihm sich fürchte allermeist.
Nun sprecht von Herzen: Amen!

This is Martin Luther's Ps. 67, rewritten as a New Testament missionary hymn. It first appeared, without a tune, at the end of Luther's *Ein weise christlich Mess zuhalte*, Wittenberg, and in *Eyn Enchiridion*, Erfurt, 1524. The melody, "Es woll' uns Gott genädig sein" was first coupled with the text in *Teutsch Kirchenamt*, Strassburg, 1525. The composer is unknown. It is the first missionary hymn of Protestantism.

The translation is an altered form of that by Richard Massie, 1851.

This hymn was sung by Gustavus Adolphus's army before the battle of Lützen in 1632. Christian Frederick Schwartz, famous Lutheran missionary in India, one of the "forerunners" of William Carey, had the hymn sung at the opening service of the mission church in Trichinopoli, South India, July 11, 1792.

Soldiers of the Cross, Arise — 501

1. Soldiers of the Cross, arise,
   Gird you with your armor bright.
Mighty are your enemies,
   Hard the battle ye must fight.

2. O'er a faithless, fallen world
   Raise your banner in the sky;
Let it float there wide unfurled;
   Bear it onward, lift it high.

3. Mid the homes of want and woe,
   Strangers to the living Word,
Let the Savior's heralds go,
   Let the voice of hope be heard.

4. Where the shadows deepest lie,
   Carry truth's unsullied ray;
Where are crimes of blackest dye,
   There the saving sign display.

5. To the weary and the worn
    Tell of realms where sorrows cease;
   To the outcast and forlorn
    Speak of mercy and of peace.

6. Guard the helpless, seek the strayed,
    Comfort troubles, banish grief;
   In the might of God arrayed,
    Scatter sin and unbelief.

7. Be the banner still unfurled,
    Still unsheathed the Spirit's Sword;
   Spread Thy Word in all the world;
    Let Thy kingdom come, O Lord.

This home missions hymn by William Walsham How was first published in Morrel and How's *Psalms and Hymns,* 1854. When included in *Church Hymns,* 1871, published by the Society for the Promotion of Christian Knowledge, the author made changes in the last two stanzas. Our committee altered Lines 3 and 4 of Stanza 7. How's lines read:

> Till the kingdoms of the world
> Are the kingdoms of the Lord.

In the *Library of Religious Poetry,* edited by Philip Schaff and Arthur Gilman, this hymn is given in four eight-line stanzas, in which the eighth stanza closes with this doxology:

> Praise with songs of holy glee,
> Saints of earth and heavenly host,
> Godhead one in persons three,
> Father, Son, and Holy Ghost.

Bishop How's opening lines were evidently suggested by Charles Wesley's hymn

> Soldier of Christ, arise
> And put your armor on.

See Hymn No. 450.

For comments on the tune "Gott sei Dank" see Hymn No. 2.

502 Saints of God, the Dawn is Brightening

1. Saints of God, the dawn is brightening,
    Token of our coming Lord;
   O'er the earth the field is whitening;
    Louder rings the Master's word:
    Pray for reapers
   In the harvest of the Lord!

2. Now, O Lord, fulfil Thy pleasure,
    Breathe upon Thy chosen band,
   And with Pentecostal measure
    Send forth reapers o'er our land,
    Faithful reapers,
   Gathering sheaves for Thy right hand.

3. Soon shall end the time of weeping,
    Soon the reaping time will come,
   Heaven and earth together keeping
    God's eternal Harvest-home.
    Saints and angels
   Shout the world's great Harvest-home.

Duffield in his *English Hymns* tells us that this hymn was the result of a contest held in 1875 by the superintendent of home missions under the Presbyterian Board. To stimulate authors, a prize of $150 was offered for a suitable hymn on the subject of home missions in America. Of the 700 poems submitted, this hymn was the prize-winning selection. It was written by Mrs. Mary Maxwell. The award was made on September 28, 1875.

Originally the poem was in four stanzas. The omitted stanza, the author's third, was dropped because the second line is hardly true today, and the third line is not in agreement with facts. It reads:

> Broad the shadow of our nation,
> Eager millions hither roam;
> Lo, they wait for Thy salvation;
> Come, Lord Jesus, quickly come!
> By Thy Spirit
> Bring Thy ransomed people home.

For comments on "Regent Square" see Hymn No. 50.

MISSIONS

Rise, Crowned with Light, Imperial Salem, Rise 503

1. Rise, crowned with light, imperial Salem, rise!
Exalt thy towering head and lift thine eyes;
See heaven its sparkling portals wide display
And break upon thee in a flood of day.

2. See a long race thy spacious courts adorn;
See future sons and daughters, yet unborn,
In crowding ranks on every side arise
Demanding life, impatient for the skies.

3. See barbarous nations at thy gates attend,
Walk in the light, and in thy temple bend;
See thy bright altars thronged with prostrate kings,
While every land its joyful tribute brings.

4. The seas shall waste, the skies in smoke decay,
Rocks fall to dust, and mountains melt away;
But fixed this Word, this saving power, remains;
Thy realms shall last, thine own Messiah reigns.

This classical hymn is a part of Alexander Pope's *Messiah. A Sacred Eclogue in Imitation of Virgil's Pollio*. It appeared in Addison's *Spectator*, May 14, 1712, in 107 lines. The cento is taken from the last portion, which reads:

Rise, crowned with light, imperial Salem, rise!
Exalt thy towery head and lift thy eyes!
See a long race thy spacious courts adorn;
See future sons and daughters, yet unborn,
In crowding ranks on every side arise,
Demanding life, impatient for the skies!
See barbarous nations at thy gates attend,
Walk in thy light, and in thy temple bend;
See thy bright altars thronged with prostrate kings
And heaped with products of Sabean springs!
For thee Idume's spicy forests blow,
And seeds of gold in Ophir's mountains glow.
See heaven its sparkling portals wide display
And break upon thee in a flood of day.
No more the rising sun shall gild the morn
Nor evening Cynthia fill her silver horn;
But lost, dissolved in thy superior rays,
One tide of glory, one unclouded blaze
O'erflow thy courts: the light himself shall shine
Revealed, and God's eternal day be thine!
The seas shall waste, the skies in smoke decay,
Rocks fall to dust, and mountains melt away;
But fixed His Word, His saving power remains;
Thy realm forever lasts, thy own Messiah reigns!

This hymn is only one of a number of hymns that have been taken from Pope's *Messiah*.

For comments on the tune "Old 124th" see Hymn No. 307.

O Spirit of the Living God 504

1. O Spirit of the living God,
    In all Thy plenitude of grace,
Where'er the foot of man hath trod,
    Descend on our apostate race.

2. Give tongues of fire and hearts of love
    To preach the reconciling Word;
Give power and unction from above
    Where'er the joyful sound is heard.

3. Be darkness, at Thy coming, light;
    Confusion, order, in Thy path;
Souls without strength inspire with
        might;
    Bid mercy triumph over wrath.

4. O Spirit of the Lord, prepare
    A sinful world their God to meet;
Breathe Thou abroad like morning air
    Till hearts of stone begin to beat.

5. Baptize the nations; far and nigh
    The triumphs of the Cross record;
The name of Jesus glorify
    Till every kindred call Him Lord.

6. God from eternity hath willed
    All flesh shall His salvation see;
So be the Father's love fulfilled,
    The Savior's sufferings crowned
        through Thee.

This hymn by James Montgomery was written in 1823 and printed as a leaflet for use at the meeting of the Auxiliary Missionary Society in Salem Chapel, Leeds, England, to be sung by the assembly. It was published in the *Evangelical Magazine*, in August of the same year. When Montgomery published it in his *Christian Psalmist*, 1825, it bore the title "The Spirit Accompanying the Word of God." Because this hymn sets forth the relation of the Holy Spirit to the work of missions, it fills an important place among our missionary hymns.

The tune "Melcombe" is by Samuel Webbe. It appeared in 1782 in *An Essay on the Church Plain Chant,* without his name, but in 1792 his name was given as composer when the tune was included in *A Collection of Motetts,* etc.

505   O'er the Gloomy Hills of Darkness

1. O'er the gloomy hills of darkness,
   Cheered by no celestial ray,
   Sun of Righteousness, arising,
   Bring the bright, the glorious day.
   Let the morning
   Of Thy blessed Gospel dawn.

2. Kingdoms wide that sit in darkness,
   Grant them, Lord, the glorious light;
   And from eastern coast to western,
   May the morning chase the night
   And redemption,
   Freely purchased, win the day!

3. Fly abroad, eternal Gospel;
   Win and conquer, never cease.
   May Thy lasting, wide dominions
   Multiply and still increase!
   May Thy scepter
   Sway the enlightened world around!

This hymn by William Williams was first published in seven stanzas, in his *Gloria in Excelsis,* in 1772. Originally the first line read:

O'er those gloomy hills of darkness.

Mr. A. Morris writes: "The mountains known as the Black Mountain range in Carmanthenshire (Wales) may be seen from Pantecelyn, the poet's home. To any one who has been there and views the distant scene from the old home it calls forth in one's mind the 'gloomy hills of darkness,' and it is generally agreed that Williams derived his inspiration from that particular landscape."

This cento is the form in which the hymn is commonly used. The omitted stanzas have been dropped because they are of inferior merit. Two of these are sufficient to exemplify:

Let the Indian, let the Negro,
Let the rude barbarian see
That divine and glorious conquest,
Once obtained on Calvary;
Let the Gospel
Wide resound from pole to pole.

May the glorious day approaching,
Thine eternal love proclaim,
And the everlasting Gospel
Spread abroad Thy holy name
O'er the borders
Of the great Emmanuel's land.

Our poets are not always as effective in their efforts as they strive to be. Sometimes they are even unfortunate in their results, as the following stanza from another hymn of Williams exemplifies:

Hark, the voice of my Beloved!
Lo, He comes in greatest need,
Leaping on the lofty mountains,
Skipping o'er the hills with speed
To deliver
Me unworthy from all woe.

For comments on the tune "Guide Me" see Hymn No. 54.

MISSIONS

Send Thou, O Lord, to Every Place — 506

1. Send Thou, O Lord, to every place
Swift messengers before Thy face,
The heralds of Thy wondrous grace,
Where Thou Thyself wilt come.

2. Send men whose eyes have seen the King,
Men in whose ears His sweet words ring;
Send such Thy lost ones home to bring;
Send them where Thou wilt come, —

3. To bring good news to souls in sin,
The bruised and broken hearts to win;
In every place to bring them in
Where Thou Thyself wilt come.

4. Thou who hast died, Thy victory claim;
Assert, O Christ, Thy glory's name
And far to lands of pagan shame
Send men where Thou wilt come.

5. Gird each one with the Spirit's Sword,
The sword of Thine own deathless Word,
And make them conquerors, conquering Lord,
Where Thou Thyself wilt come.

6. Raise up, O Lord the Holy Ghost,
From this broad land a mighty host;
Their war-cry, "We will seek the lost
Where Thou, O Christ, wilt come!"

This beautiful hymn was written by Mary Cornelia Gates in 1888 and was first published in a hymnal when it was included in *Sursum Corda*, 1898.

For comments on the tune "Isleworth" see Hymn No. 439.

Spread, Oh, Spread, Thou Mighty Word — 507

1. Spread, oh, spread, thou mighty Word,
Spread the kingdom of the Lord,
Wheresoe'er His breath has given
Life to beings meant for heaven.

2. Tell them how the Father's will
Made the world and keeps it still,
How His only Son He gave
Man from sin and death to save.

3. Tell of our Redeemer's love,
Who forever doth remove
By His holy sacrifice
All the guilt that on us lies.

4. Tell them of the Spirit given
Now to guide us up to heaven,
Strong and holy, just and true,
Working both to will and do.

5. Up! the ripening fields ye see.
Mighty shall the harvest be;
But the reapers still are few,
Great the work they have to do.

6. Lord of Harvest, let there be
Joy and strength to work for Thee
Till the nations far and near
See Thy light and learn Thy fear.

Walte, walte nah und fern,
Allgewaltig Wort des Herrn,
Wo nur seiner Allmacht Ruf
Menschen für den Himmel schuf;

Wort vom Vater, der die Welt
Schuf und in den Armen hält
Und aus seinem Schoss herab
Seinen Sohn zum Heil ihr gab;

Wort von des Erlösers Huld,
Der der Erde schwere Schuld
Durch des heil'gen Todes Tat
Ewig weggenommen hat;

Kräftig Wort von Gottes Geist,
Der den Weg zum Himmel weist
Und durch seine heil'ge Kraft
Wollen und Vollbringen schafft.

Auf zur Ernt' in alle Welt!
Weithin wogt das weisse Feld;
Klein ist noch der Schnitter Zahl,
Viel der Garben überall.

Herr der Ernte, gross und gut,
Wirk zum Werke Lust und Mut;
Lass die Völker allzumal
Schauen deines Lichtes Strahl!

According to *Koch*, Jonathan Friedrich Bahnmeier first published this hymn in seven stanzas in 1827, with the first line reading, "Walte, fürder, nah und fern." This was later altered as we have it above.

The translation is by Catherine Winkworth, *Lyra Germanica*, second series, 1858, slightly altered.

The omitted stanza, Bahnmeier's fifth, reads in Miss Winkworth's translation:

Word of Life, most pure and strong,
Lo, for thee the nations long;
Spread till from its dreary night
All the world awakes to light.

The tune "Höchster Priester," also called "Jesu, komm doch selbst zu mir," is by an unknown composer, perhaps from among the Moravian Brethren. It appeared in Johann Thommen's *Erbaulicher musikalischer Christenschatz*, Basel, 1745, where it was set to Johann Scheffler's (Angelus Silesius's) hymn "Höchster Priester, der du dich selbst geopfert hast für mich."

508   Thou Whose Almighty Word

1. Thou whose almighty word
Chaos and darkness heard
   And took their flight,
Hear us, we humbly pray,
And where the Gospel day
Sheds not its glorious ray,
   Let there be light!

2. Thou who didst come to bring,
On Thy redeeming wing,
   Healing and sight,
Health to the sick in mind,
Sight to the inly blind,
Oh, now to all mankind
   Let there be light!

3. Spirit of Truth and Love,
Life-giving, holy Dove,
   Speed forth Thy flight;
Move on the water's face,
Bearing the lamp of grace,
And in earth's darkest place
   Let there be light!

4. Holy and blessed Three,
Glorious Trinity,
   Wisdom, Love, Might!
Boundless as ocean's tide,
Rolling in fullest pride,
Through the earth, far and wide,
   Let there be light!

According to the author's son, John Marriott wrote this widely used foreign-missions hymn about 1813. It was first printed in *The Evangelical Magazine*, June, 1825, and then in the *Friendly Visitor* in July. The hymn had been quoted at a meeting of the *London Missionary Society* on May 12, 1825. It had greatly impressed those present, and the interest aroused in the hymn caused it to be printed soon afterwards. Our text is as altered slightly by Dr. Thomas Raffles in his *Supplement to Dr. Watts's Psalms and Hymns*, 1853.

For comments on the tune "Italian Hymn" see Hymn No. 239.

509   There Still Is Room

1. There still is room!
His house is not yet filled,
Not all the guests are there.
Oh, bring them in!
Their hunger shall be stilled
With bread, yea, bread to spare.
Go, call them from the lanes and byways,
From winding roads and crowded highways.
   There still is room!

2. There still is time!
The Master's voice still rings,
And all His heralds plead:
"Oh, hide beneath
The covert of His wings
Against the time of need!"
The gracious call is still extended;
The day of grace is not yet ended.
   There still is time!

3. Now is the time!
How fast the moments fly!
How soon each hour is gone!
Ye virgins, hear
And heed the midnight cry;
Look for the break of dawn.
The Bridegroom comes; prepare to greet Him!
Rise! Trim your lamps! Go out to meet Him!
   Now is the time!

Es ist noch Raum!
Sein Haus ist noch nicht voll,
Sein Tisch ist noch zu leer.
Der Platz ist da,
Wo jeder sitzen soll,
Bringt seine Gäste her!
Geht, nötigt sie auf allen Strassen!
Der Herr hat viel bereiten lassen.
   Es ist noch Raum.

Es ist noch Zeit,
Die Liebe rufet noch,
Noch gehen Diener aus,
O Stadt, o Land,
O eilet heute noch
Ins grosse Rettungshaus!
Noch ist die Türe nicht verschlossen,
Die Gnadenzeit noch nicht verflossen.
   Es ist noch Zeit.

Doch ist es Zeit!
Die Stunden folgen schnell,
Es geht auf Mitternacht!
Bald schlägt es voll,
Und drüben schimmert's hell,
Ihr Jungfrauen, erwacht!
Der Bräutigam erscheint von weitem,
Auf, auf, die Lampen zu bereiten!
   Auf, es ist Zeit!

MISSIONS

This hymn, by an unknown author, was no doubt suggested by Ernest Gottlieb Woltersdorf's (1725—1761) longer hymn beginning with the same lines. It is based on the parable of the Great Supper, Luke 14.

The translation by William M. Czamanske was written in 1938.

For comments on the tune "Es ist genug" see Hymn No. 196.

Savior, Sprinkle Many Nations — 510

1. Savior, sprinkle many nations,
   Fruitful let Thy sorrows be;
   By Thy pains and consolations
   Draw the Gentiles unto Thee.
   Of Thy Cross the wondrous story,
   Be it to the nations told;
   Let them see Thee in Thy glory
   And Thy mercy manifold.

2. Let to mortals all be given
   Thee to know and life to gain,
   Thee, the very God of heaven,
   Thee, the Man for sinners slain.
   Speak Thou hope to every mortal
   Through the Gospel, sweet and blest;
   Lead them through Thy kingdom's portal
   To eternal peace and rest.

3. Great the need in every nation,
   Dense the darkness of sin's night;
   Let Thy Spirit bring salvation,
   Love's pure flame, and wisdom's light.
   Give the Word, Thy preachers strengthen
   With the prophets' power of old,
   Help them Zion's cords to lengthen,
   All Thy wandering sheep to fold.

Arthur Cleveland Coxe wrote a missionary hymn which began with the first stanza above. He says that it was "begun on Good Friday, 1850, and completed, 1851, in the grounds of Magdalen College, Oxford." The second and third stanzas of this hymn are as follows:

2. Far and wide, though all unknowing,
   Pants for Thee each mortal breast,
   Human tears for Thee are flowing,
   Human hearts in Thee would rest.
   Thirsting as for dews of even,
   As the new-mown grass for rain,
   Thee they seek as God of heaven,
   Thee as Man for sinners slain.

3. Savior, lo, the isles are waiting!
   Stretched the hand and strained the sight
   For Thy Spirit, new-creating
   Love's pure flame and wisdom's light.
   Give the Word and of the preacher
   Speed the foot and touch the tongue
   Till on earth by every creature
   Glory to the Lamb be sung.

As these two stanzas contain statements that have no Scripture basis, we were requested, in 1927, by the Revision Committee for the *Evangelical Lutheran Hymn-Book* to write other stanzas that might be substituted. The second and third stanzas above were the result. They were accepted for the 1927 revision of that *Hymn-Book* and also by our committee for *The Lutheran Hymnal*.

For comments on the tune "O du Liebe" see Hymn No. 37.

Jesus Shall Reign Where'er the Sun — 511

1. Jesus shall reign where'er the sun
   Does his successive journeys run,
   His kingdom stretch from shore to shore
   Till moons shall wax and wane no more.

2. For Him shall endless prayer be made
   And endless praises crown His head;
   His name, like sweet perfume, shall rise
   With every morning sacrifice.

3. People and realms of every tongue
   Dwell on His love with sweetest song;
   And infant voices shall proclaim
   Their early blessings on His name.

4. Blessings abound where'er He reigns;
   The prisoner leaps, unloosed his chains,
   The weary find eternal rest,
   And all the sons of want are blest.

5. Where He displays His healing power,
   Death and the curse are known no more;
   In Him the tribes of Adam boast
   More blessings than their father lost.

6. Let every creature rise and bring
   Peculiar honors to our King;
   Angels descend with songs again,
   And earth repeat the loud Amen.

This famous hymn of Isaac Watts, based on Ps. 72, shows how that great hymn-writer followed Luther's method of treating the Old Testament psalms for the New Testament Church. In the preface to his *Psalms of David Imitated,* Watts wrote:

"Where the original runs in the form of prophecy concerning Christ and His salvation, I have given an historical turn to the sense; there is no necessity that we should always sing in the obscure and doubtful style of prediction when the things foretold are brought into open light by a full accomplishment."

As first published, the hymn contained eight stanzas. Most modern English hymnals omit four of these. The two stanzas omitted above belong between our first and second and read:

Behold the islands with their kings,
And Europe her best tribute brings;
From north to south the princes meet
To pay their homage at His feet.

There Persia, glorious to behold,
There India shines in Eastern gold,
And barbarous nations at His word
Submit and bow and own their Lord.

Some hymnals have altered "For" into "To" in the first line of Stanza 2. The meaning is: "For Him, for the extension of His blessed kingdom in the world, and in the heart of him who offers the prayer." "Peculiar honors" means "honors appropriate to the various peoples who bring them."

G. J. Stevenson, in his *Methodist Hymn Book Notes,* relates the following example to show how the converted heathen have used Dr. Watts's great hymn:

"Perhaps one of the most interesting occasions on which this hymn was used was that on which King George the Sable of the South Sea Islands, but of blessed memory, gave a new constitution to his people, exchanging a heathen for a Christian form of government. Under the spreading branches of the banyan-trees sat some thousand natives from Tonga, Fiji, and Samoa on Whitsunday, 1862, assembled for divine worship. Foremost amongst them all sat King George himself. Around him were seated old chiefs and warriors who had shared with him the dangers and fortunes of many a battle; men whose eyes were dim, and whose powerful frames were bowed down with the weight of years. But old and young alike rejoiced together in the joys of that day, their faces, most of them, radiant with Christian joy, love, and hope. It would be impossible to describe the deep feeling manifested when the solemn service began by the entire audience singing Dr. Watts's hymn "Jesus Shall Reign Where'er the Sun." . . . Who so much as they could realize the full meaning of the poet's words? For they had been rescued from the darkness of heathenism and cannibalism, and they were that day met for the first time under a Christian constitution, under a Christian king, and with Christ Himself reigning in the hearts of most of those present. That was indeed Christ's kingdom set up in the earth."

For comments on the tune "Duke Street" see Hymn No. 200.

512 O Christ, Our True and Only Light

1. O Christ, our true and only Light,
Enlighten those who sit in night;
Let those afar now hear Thy voice
And in Thy fold with us rejoice.

O Jesu Christe, wahres Licht,
Erleuchte, die dich kennen nicht,
Und bringe sie zu deiner Herd',
Dass ihre Seel' auch selig werd'!

2. Fill with the radiance of Thy grace
The souls now lost in error's maze
And all whom in their secret minds
Some dark delusion haunts and blinds.

Erfüll mit deinem Gnadenschein,
Die in Irrtum verführet sein,
Auch die, so heimlich fichtet an
In ihrem Sinn ein falscher Wahn!

3. Oh, gently call those gone astray
That they may find the saving way!
Let every conscience sore opprest
In Thee find peace and heavenly rest.

Und was sich sonst verlaufen hat
Von dir, das suche du mit Gnad'
Und sein verwund't Gewissen heil,
Lass sie am Himmel haben teil!

4. Oh, make the deaf to hear Thy Word
And teach the dumb to speak, dear Lord,
Who dare not yet the faith avow,
Though secretly they hold it now.

Den Tauben öffne das Gehör,
Die Stummen richtig reden lehr',
Die nicht bekennen wollen frei,
Was ihres Herzens Glaube sei!

5. Shine on the darkened and the cold,
Recall the wanderers to Thy fold,
Unite all those who walk apart,
Confirm the weak and doubting heart,

Erleuchte, die da sind verblend't,
Bring her, die sich von uns getrennt,
Versammle, die zerstreuet gehn,
Mach feste, die im Zweifel stehn!

6. So they with us may evermore
Such grace with wondering thanks adore
And endless praise to Thee be given
By all Thy Church in earth and heaven.

So werden sie mit uns zugleich
Auf Erden und im Himmelreich,
Hier zeitlich und dort ewiglich
Für solche Gnade preisen dich.

This hymn by Johann Heermann, first published in his *Devoti Musica Cordis*, Breslau, 1630, was one of the "Songs of Tears" in the section entitled "In the Time of the Persecution and Distress of Pious Christians." We can understand what the author had in mind when we remember that he wrote during the dreadful years of the Thirty Years' War. That it is a splendid missionary hymn the contents show. It is perhaps Heermann's most widely used hymn in the English-speaking Church. Wackernagel writes: "When we consider the many kinds of trials, sufferings of body and soul, under which many would have lost courage and given up in despair, then Heermann's hymns will loom up before us as among the most exalted of spiritual poems. Here the cries of anguish of thousands, arising from the homes, from the streets, and from the fields of the beautiful country, have found an expression which is well-pleasing unto God; they have found the peace of prayer, through communion with the Lord. . . . How touchingly Heermann, in this hymn, prays for the enemies of the Church, for the weak, and for the faint-hearted! He does not desire the destruction of his enemies, but their repentance and, above all, their salvation."

The translation is an altered form of Catherine Winkworth's *Lyra Germanica*, second series, 1858.

For comments on the tune "O Jesu Christ, mein's" see Hymn No. 64.

Cross and Comfort

513   Art Thou Weary, Art Thou Troubled

1. Art thou weary, art thou troubled,
   Art thou sore distressed?
   "Come to Me," saith One, "and, coming,
   Be at rest."

2. Hath He marks to lead me to Him
   If He be my Guide?
   "In His feet and hands are wound-prints,
   And His side."

3. Hath He diadem, as Monarch,
   That His brow adorns?
   "Yea, a crown, in very surety,
   But of thorns."

4. If I find Him, if I follow,
   What His guerdon here?
   "Many a sorrow, many a labor,
   Many a tear."

5. If I still hold closely to Him,
   What hath He at last?
   "Sorrow vanquished, labor ended,
   Jordan passed."

6. If I ask Him to receive me,
   Will He say me nay?
   "Not till earth and not till heaven
   Pass away."

7. Finding, following, keeping, struggling,
   Is He sure to bless?
   "Saints, apostles, prophets, martyrs,
   Answer, Yes."

This great hymn by John Mason Neale was originally published in eleven stanzas. The following three stanzas belong after our Stanza 4:

    Is this all He hath to give me
      In my life below?
    "Joy unspeakable and glorious
      Thou shalt know."

    "All thy sins shall be forgiven,
      All things work for good;
    Thou shalt Bread of Life from heaven
      Have for food.

    "From the fountains of salvation
      Thou shalt water draw:
    Sweet shall be thy meditation
      In God's Law."

This stanza follows our Stanza 5:

    Festal palms and crown of glory,
      Robes in blood washed white,
    God in Christ His people's temple —
      There no night.

The text is but slightly altered. The original first line, "Art thou weary, art thou languid," in common with most modern hymnals, was changed as above. In Stanza 3, Line 1, Neale had: "Is there diadem" and in Line 3, Stanza 7, "Angels, martyrs, prophets, virgins."

Although Neale first published this hymn in *Hymns of the Eastern Church,* 1862, as a translation of a Greek hymn by Stephen the Sabaite (725—794), in the third edition of that work he explained that there was but little of the Greek original hymn in it.

The hymn may be sung antiphonally, the choir singing the questions and the congregation the answers.

The tune "Stephanos" was composed for this hymn by Henry W. Baker and was first published in the appendix to the original edition of *Hymns Ancient and Modern,* 1868.

514   God Moves in a Mysterious Way

1. God moves in a mysterious way
   His wonders to perform;
   He plants His footsteps in the sea
   And rides upon the storm.

2. Deep in unfathomable mines
   Of never-failing skill
   He treasures up His bright designs
   And works His sovereign will.

3. Ye fearful saints, fresh courage take;
　The clouds ye so much dread
Are big with mercy and shall break
　In blessings on your head.

4. Judge not the Lord by feeble sense,
　But trust Him for His grace;
Behind a frowning providence
　He hides a smiling face.

5. His purposes will ripen fast,
　Unfolding every hour;
The bud may have a bitter taste,
　But sweet will be the flower.

6. Blind unbelief is sure to err
　And scan His work in vain;
God is His own Interpreter,
　And He will make it plain.

John Newton first published this hymn of William Cowper's in the *Omicron Letters*, 1774. It was entitled "Light out of Darkness." The title evidently had reference to Cowper's mental affliction, under which he suffered periodically and during a lighter attack of which he wrote this hymn for his own spiritual strengthening. James Montgomery says it was written "in the twilight of departing reason." It has become one of the most widely used hymns in the English-speaking Church.

For comments on the tune "Dundee" see Hymn No. 49.

O Thou from Whom All Goodness Flows　　515

1. O Thou from whom all goodness flows,
　I lift my heart to Thee;
In all my sorrows, conflicts, woes,
　Dear Lord, remember me.

2. When on my poor and burdened heart
　My sins lie heavily,
Thy pardon speak, new peace impart;
　Dear Lord, remember me.

3. When trials sore obstruct my way
　And ills I cannot flee,
Oh, let my strength be as my day;
　Dear Lord, remember me.

4. If worn with pain, disease, or grief
　This feeble body be;
Grant patience, rest, and kind relief;
　Dear Lord, remember me.

5. When in the solemn hour of death
　I wait Thy just decree,
Be this the prayer of my last breath:
　Dear Lord, remember me.

6. And when before Thy throne I stand
　And lift my soul to Thee,
Then with the saints at Thy right hand,
　Dear Lord, remember me.

According to *Julian* this hymn by Thomas Haweis was written and published prior to 1791, the year in which it was printed in a tract, *The Reality and Power of the Religion of Jesus Christ*, etc., by William Browne. The author published the hymn in his *Carmina Christo*, 1792; the text, however, was slightly altered. Further alterations were made, and a seventh stanza was added, very likely by Thomas Cotterill, when the hymn was included in his *Selection*, 1819. Cotterill's form of the hymn is practically our text above, except for an alteration in Stanza 2, Line 1: "good Lord" was changed to "dear Lord," and Stanza 4 is omitted:

> If for Thy sake upon my name
> 　Shame and reproach shall be,
> All hail reproach and welcome shame!
> 　Good Lord, remember me.

For comments on the tune "St. Bernard" see Hymn No. 378.

In the Hour of Trial　　516

1. In the hour of trial,
　Jesus, plead for me
Lest by base denial
　I depart from Thee.
When Thou see'st me waver,
　With a look recall
Nor for fear or favor
　Suffer me to fall.

2. With forbidden pleasures
　Should this vain world charm
Or its tempting treasures
　Spread to work me harm,
Bring to my remembrance
　Sad Gethsemane
Or, in darker semblance,
　Cross-crowned Calvary.

3. Should Thy mercy send me
   Sorrow, toil, and woe,
   Or should pain attend me
   On my path below,
   Grant that I may never
   Fail Thy hand to see;
   Grant that I may ever
   Cast my care on Thee.

4. When my last hour cometh,
   Fraught with strife and pain,
   When my dust returneth
   To the dust again,
   On Thy truth relying,
   Through that mortal strife,
   Jesus, take me, dying,
   To eternal life.

This hymn by James Montgomery ranks in popularity with the best of his poems. However, the above version is much altered from the form in which he wrote it, especially Stanzas 3 and 4, which were changed by Mrs. Frances A. Hutton for *Supplement and Litanies*, by H. W. Hutton. The original hymn is dated "October 13, 1834." It appeared in Montgomery's *Original Hymns*, 1835.

The tune "St. Mary Magdalene" is by John B. Dykes. It was written for this hymn and appeared in Chope's *The Congregational Hymn and Tune Book*, 1862.

517   The Will of God Is Always Best

1. The will of God is always best
   And shall be done forever;
   And they who trust in Him are blest,
   He will forsake them never.
   He helps indeed In time of need,
   He chastens with forbearing;
   They who depend On God, their Friend,
   Shall not be left despairing.

2. God is my Comfort and my Trust,
   My Hope and Life abiding;
   And to His counsel, wise and just,
   I yield, in Him confiding.
   The very hairs, His Word declares,
   Upon my head He numbers.
   By night and day God is my Stay,
   He never sleeps nor slumbers.

3. Lord Jesus, this I ask of Thee,
   Deny me not this favor:
   When Satan sorely troubles me,
   Then do not let me waver.
   Keep watch and ward, O gracious Lord,
   Fulfil Thy faithful saying:
   Who doth believe He shall receive
   An answer to His praying.

4. When life's brief course on earth is run
   And I this world am leaving,
   Grant me to say: "Thy will be done,"
   By faith to Thee still cleaving.
   My heavenly Friend, I now commend
   My soul into Thy keeping,
   O'er sin and hell, And death as well,
   Through Thee the victory reaping.

Was mein Gott will, das g'scheh' allzeit,
Sein Will', der ist der beste;
Zu helfen den'n er ist bereit,
Die an ihn glauben feste;
Er hilft aus Not, der fromme Gott,
Und züchtiget mit Massen.
Wer Gott vertraut, fest auf ihn baut,
Den will er nicht verlassen.

Gott ist mein Trost, mein' Zuversicht,
Mein' Hoffnung und mein Leben.
Was mein Gott will, dass mir geschicht,
Will ich nicht widerstreben.
Sein Wort ist wahr, denn all mein Haar
Er selber hat gezählet.
Er hüt't und wacht und hat wohl acht,
Auf dass uns gar nichts fehlet.

Nun, muss ich Sünd'r von dieser Welt
Hinfahr'n in Gottes Willen
Zu meinem Gott: wann's ihm gefällt,
Will ich ihm halten stille.
Mein' arme Seel' ich Gott befehl'
In meiner letzten Studen.
Du frommer Gott, Sünd', Höll' und Tod
Hast du mir überwunden.

Noch eins, Herr, will ich bitten dich,
Du wirst mir's nicht versagen;
Wenn mich der böse Geist anficht,
Lass mich, Herr, nicht verzagen;
Hilf, steur und wehr, ach Gott, mein Herr,
Zu Ehren deinem Namen!
Wer das begehrt, dem wird's gewährt.
Drauf sprech' ich fröhlich: Amen.

"Des alten Churfürsten Markgraff Albrechts Lied" (The old Elector Margrave Albrecht's hymn) — thus this hymn is entitled in one of the hymnals in which it was published. Wackernagel remarks: "Who wrote it for him or who could have dedicated it to him, there is no proof." Other authorities, however, incline to the view that the elector himself is the author. The hymn first appeared in print in a broadsheet, c. 1554, at Nürnberg. It became, and still is, in many circles a favorite hymn of comfort. The translation is composite.

For comments on the tune "Was mein Gott will" see Hymn No. 437.

If Thou But Suffer God to Guide Thee 518

1. If thou but suffer God to guide thee
   And hope in Him through all thy ways,
   He'll give thee strength, whate'er betide thee,
   And bear thee through the evil days.
   Who trusts in God's unchanging love
   Builds on the Rock that naught can move.

2. What can these anxious cares avail thee,
   These never-ceasing moans and sighs?
   What can it help if thou bewail thee
   O'er each dark moment as it flies?
   Our cross and trials do but press
   The heavier for our bitterness.

3. Be patient and await His leisure
   In cheerful hope, with heart content
   To take whate'er thy Father's pleasure
   And His discerning love hath sent,
   Nor doubt our inmost wants are known
   To Him who chose us for His own.

4. God knows full well when times of gladness
   Shall be the needful thing for thee.
   When He has tried thy soul with sadness
   And from all guile has found thee free,
   He comes to thee all unaware
   And makes thee own His loving care.

5. Nor think amid the fiery trial
   That God hath cast thee off unheard,
   That he whose hopes meet no denial
   Must surely be of God preferred.
   Time passes and much change doth bring
   And sets a bound to everything.

6. All are alike before the Highest;
   'Tis easy to our God, we know,
   To raise thee up, though low thou liest,
   To make the rich man poor and low.
   True wonders still by Him are wrought
   Who setteth up and brings to naught.

7. Sing, pray, and keep His ways unswerving,
   Perform thy duties faithfully,
   And trust His Word, though undeserving,
   Thou yet shalt find it true for thee.
   God never yet forsook in need
   The soul that trusted Him indeed.

Wer nur den lieben Gott lässt walten
Und hoffet auf ihn allezeit,
Den wird er wunderlich erhalten
In allem Kreuz und Traurigkeit.
Wer Gott, dem Allerhöchsten, traut,
Der hat auf keinen Sand gebaut.

Was helfen uns die schweren Sorgen?
Was hilft uns unser Weh und Ach?
Was hilft es, dass wir alle Morgen
Beseufzen unser Ungemach?
Wir machen unser Kreuz und Leid
Nur grösser durch die Traurigkeit.

Man halte nur ein wenig stille
Und sei nur in sich selbst vergnügt,
Wie unsers Gottes Gnadenwille,
Wie sein' Allwissenheit es fügt.
Gott, der uns sich hat auserwählt,
Der weiss auch gar wohl, was uns fehlt.

Er kennt die rechten Freudenstunden,
Er weiss wohl, wann es nützlich sei.
Wenn er uns nur hat treu erfunden
Und merket keine Heuchelei,
So kommt Gott, eh' wir's uns versehn,
Und lässet uns viel Gut's geschehn.

Denk nicht in deiner Drangsalshitze,
Dass du von Gott verlassen sei'st,
Und dass der Gott im Schosse sitze,
Der sich mit stetem Glücke speist.
Die Folgezeit verändert viel
Und setzet jeglichem sein Ziel.

Es sind ja Gott sehr leichte Sachen
Und ist dem Höchsten alles gleich,
Den Reichen arm und klein zu machen,
Den Armen aber gross und reich.
Gott ist der rechte Wundermann,
Der bald erhöhn, bald stürzen kann.

Sing, bet und geh auf Gottes Wegen,
Verricht das Deine nur getreu
Und trau des Himmels reichem Segen,
So wird er bei dir werden neu;
Denn welcher seine Zuversicht
Auf Gott setzt, den verlässt er nicht.

This hymn, both text and tune, was written by Georg Neumark in 1640, at Kiel, when he was nineteen years of age. After a period of trouble and anxiety on a journey to the North and after vainly seeking employment for a time, he unexpectedly received the appointment as tutor in the home of Stephan Henning in Kiel. In his last work, entitled *Thränendes Haus-Kreutz*, 1681, Neumark relates: "This good fortune, which came so suddenly and, as it were, from heaven, gladdened my heart so that I, on the first day, to the glory of my God, composed the well-known hymn 'If Thou But Suffer God to Guide Thee,' for I had ample reason to thank God heartily for this unexpected grace, both then and to the end." Accordingly the oft-repeated story that Neumark wrote the hymn at Hamburg in 1653, after the return of his beloved viola da gamba, must be set aside as legendary.

The hymn and tune were first published in *Fortgepflanzter musikalisch-poetischer Lustwald*, Jena, 1657, and entitled "A Hymn of Consolation. That God will care for, and preserve, His own in His own time, after the saying, 'Cast thy burden upon the Lord, and He shall sustain thee.'" (Ps. 55:22.)

The translation is an altered form of that by Catherine Winkworth, *Chorale Book for England*, 1863.

It is not only Neumark's best hymn, but one of the finest hymns of trust in all our hymnody. We may analyze it as follows:

The Christian's Joyful Trust in God under the Cross

1. How it should manifest itself.
   a. In the joyous certainty of God's unchanging love. Stanza 1.
   b. In refraining from all needless care and complaints. Stanza 2.
   c. In patient resignation to the divine will. Stanza 3, Lines 1 to 4.
2. On what it is based.
   a. On the certainty that God knows our need. Stanza 3, Lines 5 and 6.
   b. On the certainty that He will help in His own time. Stanza 4.
   c. On the certainty that our times are in His hand. Stanzas 5 and 6.

519 Beloved, "It Is Well!"

1. Beloved, "It is well!"
   God's ways are always right,
   And perfect love is o'er them all
   Though far above our sight.

2. Beloved, "It is well!"
   Though deep and sore the smart,
   The hand that wounds knows how to bind
   And heal the broken heart.

3. Beloved, "It is well!"
   Though sorrow clouds our way,
   'Twill only make the joy more dear
   That ushers in the day.

4. Beloved, "It is well!"
   The path that Jesus trod,
   Though rough and strait and dark it be,
   Leads home to heaven and God.

This hymn, dated March 12, 1833, was dedicated by George W. Doane to his wife.

The tune "Cambridge" is by Ralph Harrison and appeared in his *Sacred Harmony*, 1784—1791. It must not be confused with the various tunes also called "Cambridge" by Charles Wood, 1925; Thomas A. Walmsley, d. 1856; and John Randall, 1793.

520 Commit Whatever Grieves Thee

1. Commit whatever grieves thee
   Into the gracious hands
   Of Him who never leaves thee,
   Who heaven and earth commands.
   Who points the clouds their courses,
   Whom winds and waves obey,
   He will direct thy footsteps
   And find for thee a way.

2. On Him place thy reliance
   If thou wouldst be secure;
   His work thou must consider
   If thine is to endure.
   By anxious sighs and grieving
   And self-tormenting care
   God is not moved to giving;
   All must be gained by prayer.

3. Thy truth and grace, O Father,
   Most surely see and know
   Both what is good and evil
   For mortal man below.
   According to Thy counsel
   Thou wilt Thy work pursue;
   And what Thy wisdom chooseth
   Thy might will always do.

Befiehl du deine Wege,
Und was dein Herze kränkt,
Der allertreusten Pflege
Des, der den Himmel lenkt!
Der Wolken, Luft und Winden,
Gibt Wege, Lauf und Bahn,
Der wird auch Wege finden,
Da dein Fuss gehen kann.

Dem Herren musst du trauen,
Wenn dir's soll wohlergehn;
Auf sein Werk must du schauen,
Wenn dein Werk soll bestehn.
Mit Sorgen und mit Grämen
Und mit selbsteigner Pein
Lässt Gott sich gar nichts nehmen,
Es muss, erbeten sein.

Dein' ew'ge Treu' und Gnade,
O Vater, weiss und sieht,
Was gut sei oder schade
Dem sterblichen Geblüt;
Und was du dann erlesen,
Das treibst du, starker Held,
Und bringst zum Stand und Wesen,
Was deinem Rat gefällt.

4. Thy hand is never shortened,
   All things must serve Thy might;
   Thine every act is blessing,
   Thy path is purest light.
   Thy work no man can hinder,
   Thy purpose none can stay,
   Since Thou to bless Thy children
   Wilt always find a way.

5. Though all the powers of evil
   The will of God oppose,
   His purpose will not falter,
   His pleasure onward goes.
   Whate'er God's will resolveth,
   Whatever He intends,
   Will always be accomplished
   True to His aims and ends.

6. Then hope, my feeble spirit,
   And be thou undismayed;
   God helps in every trial
   And makes thee unafraid.
   Await His time with patience,
   Then shall thine eyes behold
   The sun of joy and gladness
   His brightest beams unfold.

7. Arise, my soul, and banish
   Thy anguish and thy care.
   Away with thoughts that sadden
   And heart and mind ensnare!
   Thou art not lord and master
   Of thine own destiny;
   Enthroned in highest heaven,
   God rules in equity.

8. Leave all to His direction;
   In wisdom He doth reign,
   And in a way most wondrous
   His course He will maintain.
   Soon He, His promise keeping,
   With wonder-working skill,
   Shall put away the sorrows
   That now thy spirit fill.

9. A while His consolation
   He may to thee deny,
   And seem as though in trial
   He far from thee would fly;
   A while distress and anguish
   May compass thee around,
   Nor to thy supplication
   An answering voice be found.

10. But if thou perseverest,
    Thou shalt deliverance find.
    Behold, all unexpected
    He will thy soul unbind
    And from the heavy burden
    Thy heart will soon set free;
    And thou wilt see the blessing
    He had in mind for thee.

11. O faithful child of heaven,
    How blessèd shalt thou be!
    With songs of glad thanksgiving
    A crown awaiteth thee.
    Into thy hand thy Maker
    Will give the victor's palm,
    And thou to thy Deliverer
    Shalt sing a joyous psalm.

12. Give, Lord, this consummation
    To all our heart's distress;
    Our hands, our feet, our ears strengthen,
    In death our spirits bless.
    Thy truth and Thy protection
    Grant evermore, we pray,
    And in celestial glory
    Shall end our destined way.

Weg' hast du allerwegen,
   An Mitteln fehlt dir's nicht;
Dein Tun ist lauter Segen,
   Dein Gang ist lauter Licht.
Dein Werk kann niemand hindern,
   Dein' Arbeit darf nicht ruhn,
Wenn du, was deinen Kindern
   Erspriesslich ist, willst tun.

Und ob gleich alle Teufel
   Hier wollten widerstehn,
So wird doch ohne Zweifel
   Gott nicht zurückegehn;
Was er sich vorgenommen,
   Und was er haben will,
Das muss doch endlich kommen
   Zu seinem Zweck und Ziel.

Hoff, o du arme Seele,
   Hoff und sei unverzagt!
Gott wird dich aus der Höhle,
   Da dich der Kummer plagt,
Mit grossen Gnaden rücken;
   Erwarte nur die Zeit,
So wirst du schon erblicken
   Die Sonn' der schönsten Freud'.

Auf, auf, gib deinem Schmerze
   Und Sorgen gute Nacht!
Lass fahren, was dein Herze
   Betrübt und traurig macht!
Bist du doch nicht Regente,
   Der alles führen soll;
Gott sitzt im Regimente
   Und führet alles wohl.

Ihn, ihn lass tun und walten,
   Er ist ein weiser Fürst
Und wird sich so verhalten,
   Dass du dich wundern wirst,
Wenn er, wie ihm gebühret,
   Mit wunderbarem Rat
Die Sach' hinausgeführet,
   Die dich bekümmert hat.

Er wird zwar eine Weile
   Mit seinem Trost verziehn
Und tun an seinem Teile,
   Als hätt' in seinem Sinn
Er deiner sich begeben,
   Und sollt'st du für und für
In Angst und Nöten schweben,
   Frag' er doch nichts nach dir.

Wird's aber sich befinden,
   Dass du ihm treu verbleibst,
So wird er dich entbinden,
   Da du's am mind'sten gläubst;
Er wird dein Herze lösen
   Von der so schweren Last,
Die du zu keinem Bösen
   Bisher getragen hast.

Wohl dir, du Kind der Treue!
   Du hast und trägst davon
Mit Ruhm und Dankgeschreie
   Den Sieg und Ehrenkron'.
Gott gibt dir selbst die Palmen
   In deine rechte Hand,
Und du singst Freudenpsalmen
   Dem, der dein Leid gewandt.

Mach End', o Herr, mach Ende
   An aller unsrer Not,
Stärk unsre Füss' und Hände
   Und lass bis in den Tod
Uns allzeit deiner Pflege
   Und Treu' empfohlen sein,
So gehen unsre Wege
   Gewiss zum Himmel ein.

According to tradition Paul Gerhardt wrote this hymn after he had been expelled from Berlin, with his wife and children, because of his loyalty to the Lutheran Confessions. On the way to Saxony they stopped at a wayside inn, and there, with the thought of the uncertain future and the needs of his family on his mind, he wrote this hymn to comfort himself and those near and dear to him. Almost immediately afterwards two messengers of Duke Christian of Merseburg brought him the reassuring news that the Duke had prepared the necessary help for him, whereby Gerhardt would have an adequate income until he would be reinstated. — There are, however, several good reasons for discrediting this account. Gerhardt did not have his office in Berlin until 1666. He did not depart from Berlin, to take up his ministry in Lübben, until 1669. His wife died in 1668. And the hymn was published in Crüger's *Praxis Pietatis Melica,* Frankfurt edition, 1656. The hymn was therefore very likely written during his ministry at Mittenwalde and thus prior to his service in Berlin.

Lauxmann, in *Koch,* calls the hymn "the most comforting of all the hymns that have resounded on Paul Gerhardt's golden lyre, sweeter to many souls than honey and the honeycomb." For many generations it has been a universal favorite in the German and Scandinavian churches, and the fact that it has been translated in whole or in part into English scores of times and included in many English hymnals, is evidence of its popularity also in this part of the Church.

In its German form the hymn is an acrostic on Ps. 37:5, formed by the initial words of the stanzas. This characteristic is not evident in the usual translations, but there are several English translations that have preserved this form.

The most popular English translation is that by John Wesley, who, however, uses the short-meter arrangement and thus makes it impossible to use the tune to which Gerhardt's text has long been wedded. Few English hymnals use all sixteen stanzas of Wesley's version. The most popular centos are the two beginning: "Commit, then, all thy griefs," and, "Give to the winds thy fears." As Wesley's complete version is rarely printed, we give it for the benefit of our readers:

1. Commit thou all thy griefs
 And ways into His hands,
 To His sure truth and tender care
 Who earth and heaven commands.

2. Who points the clouds their course,
 Whom winds and seas obey,
 He shall direct thy wandering feet,
 He shall prepare thy way.

3. Thou on the Lord rely;
 So safe shalt thou go on;
 Fix on His work thy steadfast eye,
 So shall thy work be done.

4. No profit canst thou gain
 By self-consuming care;
 To Him commend thy cause; His ear
 Attends the softest prayer.

5. Thy everlasting truth,
 Father, Thy ceaseless love,
 Sees all Thy children's wants and knows
 What best for each will prove.

6. And whatsoe'er Thou will'st
 Thou dost, O King of kings;
 What Thy unerring wisdom chose,
 Thy power to being brings.

7. Thou everywhere hast sway,
 And all things serve Thy might;
 Thy every act pure blessing is,
 Thy path unsullied light.

8. When Thou arisest, Lord,
 Who shall Thy work withstand?
 When all Thy children want, Thou giv'st;
 Who, who, shall stay Thy hand?

9. Give to the winds thy fears;
 Hope and be undismayed;
 God hears thy sighs and counts thy tears,
 God shall lift up thy head.

10. Through waves and clouds and storms
 He gently clears thy way;
 Wait thou His time; so shall this night
 Soon end in joyous day.

11. Still heavy is thy heart?
 Still sink thy spirits down?
 Cast off the weight, let fear depart,
 And every care be gone.

12. What though thou rulest not?
 Yet heaven and earth and hell
 Proclaim, God sitteth on the throne
 And ruleth all things well.

13. Leave to His sovereign sway
To choose and to command;
So shalt thou wondering own His way
How wise, how strong, His hand.

14. Far, far above thy thought
His counsel shall appear
When fully He the work hath wrought
That caused thy needless fear.

15. Thou seest our weakness, Lord;
Our hearts are known to Thee:
Oh, lift Thou up the sinking hand,
Confirm the feeble knee!

16. Let us, in life, in death,
Thy steadfast truth declare
And publish with our latest breath
Thy love and guardian care.

An analysis of this hymn gives us the following outline:

1. The Invitation: "Commit thy way unto the Lord," Stanzas 1—5.
2. The Exhortation: "Trust also in Him," Stanzas 6—8.
3. The Assurance: "He will bring it to pass," Stanzas 9—11.
4. The Prayer for Endurance, Stanza 12.

Our translation is composite and retains the metrical form of the German original.

For comments on the tune "Herzlich tut mich" see Hymn No. 172.

What God Ordains Is Always Good 521

1. What God ordains is always good;
His will abideth holy.
As He directs my life for me,
I follow meek and lowly.
My God indeed In every need
Doth well know how to shield me;
To Him, then, I will yield me.

2. What God ordains is always good.
He never will deceive me;
He leads me in His own right way,
And never will He leave me.
I take content What He hath sent;
His hand that sends me sadness
Will turn my tears to gladness.

3. What God ordains is always good.
His loving thought attends me;
No poison can be in the cup
That my Physician sends me.
My God is true; Each morn anew
I'll trust His grace unending,
My life to Him commending.

4. What God ordains is always good.
He is my Friend and Father;
He suffers naught to do me harm,
Though many storms may gather.
Now I may know Both joy and woe,
Some day I shall see clearly
That He hath loved me dearly.

5. What God ordains is always good.
Though I the cup am drinking
Which savors now of bitterness,
I take it without shrinking.
For after grief God grants relief,
My heart with comfort filling
And all my sorrow stilling.

6. What God ordains is always good.
This truth remains unshaken.
Though sorrow, need, or death be mine,
I shall not be forsaken.
I fear no harm, For with His arm
He shall embrace and shield me;
So to my God I yield me.

Was Gott tut, das ist wohlgetan!
Es bleibt gerecht sein Wille;
Wie er fängt meine Sachen an,
Will ich ihm halten stille.
Er ist mein Gott, der in der Not
Mich wohl weiss zu erhalten,
Drum lass' ich ihn nur walten.

Was Gott tut, das ist wohlgetan!
Er wird mich nicht betrügen,
Er führet mich auf rechter Bahn;
So lass' ich mich begnügen
An seiner Huld und hab' Geduld,
Er wird mein Unglück wenden,
Es steht in seinen Händen.

Was Gott tut, das ist wohlgetan!
Er wird mich wohl bedenken;
Er, als mein Arzt und Wundermann,
Wird mir nicht Gift einschenken
Für Arzenei; Gott ist getreu,
Drum will ich auf ihn bauen
Und seiner Güte trauen.

Was Gott tut, das ist wohlgetan!
Er ist mein Licht und Leben,
Der mir nichts Böses gönnen kann;
Ich will mich ihm ergeben
In Freud' und Leid; es kommt die Zeit,
Da öffentlich erscheinet,
Wie treulich er es meinet.

Was Gott tut, das ist wohlgetan!
Muss ich den Kelch gleich schmecken,
Der bitter ist nach meinem Wahn,
Lass' ich mich doch nicht schrecken,
Weil doch zuletzt ich werd' ergötzt
Mit süssem Trost im Herzen,
Da weichen alle Schmerzen.

Was Gott tut, das ist wohlgetan!
Dabei will ich verbleiben;
Es mag mich auf die rauhe Bahn
Not, Tod und Elend treiben,
So wird Gott mich ganz väterlich
In seinen Armen halten,
Drum lass' ich ihn nur walten.

The German hymnologist Avenarius tells us that Samuel Rodigast wrote this hymn in 1675 for the comforting of his friend Severus Gastorius, a cantor in Jena, when Gastorius was lying ill; and that Gastorius composed the music, which is still coupled with the text, during the time of his convalescence. The hymn was first published, without music, in Erfurt and then in *Das Hannoversche Gesang Buch,* Goettingen, 1676. The text has certain similarities to an older hymn, beginning with the same line, ascribed to Michael Altenburg.

The translation is composite.

As to the tune "Was Gott tut," there has been much discussion on its authorship. Some authorities, questioning the authorship of Gastorius, have ascribed it to Johann Pachelbel of Nürnberg, a contemporary of Gastorius. Zahn, however, on the basis of a careful study of the sources, definitely establishes the authorship of Gastorius. The melody appeared in the *Auserlesenes Weimarisches Gesangbuch,* 1681.

522   When in the Hour of Utmost Need

1. When in the hour of utmost need
We know not where to look for aid;
When days and nights of anxious thought
Nor help nor counsel yet have brought,

2. Then this our comfort is alone,
That we may meet before Thy throne
And cry, O faithful God, to Thee
For rescue from our misery;

3. To Thee may raise our hearts and eyes,
Repenting sore with bitter sighs,
And seek Thy pardon for our sin
And respite from our griefs within.

4. For Thou hast promised graciously
To hear all those who cry to Thee
Through Him whose name alone is great,
Our Savior and our Advocate.

5. And thus we come, O God, today
And all our woes before Thee lay;
For sorely tried, cast down, we stand,
Perplexed by fears on every hand.

6. Ah! hide not for our sins Thy face,
Absolve us through Thy boundless grace,
Be with us in our anguish still,
Free us at last from every ill,

7. That so with all our hearts we may
To Thee our glad thanksgiving pay,
Then walk obedient to Thy Word
And now and ever praise Thee, Lord.

Wenn wir in höchsten Nöten sein
Und wissen nicht, wo aus noch ein,
Und finden weder Hilf' noch Rat,
Ob wir gleich sorgen früh und spat:

So ist dies unser Trost allein,
Dass wir zusammen insgemein
Dich rufen an, o treuer Gott,
Um Rettung aus der Angst und Not.

Und heben unsre Aug'n und Herz
Zu dir in wahrer Reu' und Schmerz
Und suchen der Sünd' Vergebung
Und aller Strafen Linderung,

Die du verheissest gnädiglich
Allen, die darum bitten dich
Im Namen dein's Sohns Jesu Christ,
Der unser Heil und Fürsprech ist.

Drum kommen wir, o Herre Gott,
Und klagen dir all unsre Not,
Weil wir jetzt stehn verlassen gar
In grosser Trübsal und Gefahr.

Sieh nicht an unsre Sünde gross,
Sprich uns derselb'n aus Gnaden los,
Steh uns in unserm Elend bei,
Mach uns von allen Plagen frei,

Auf dass von Herzen können wir
Nachmals mit Freuden danken dir,
Gehorsam sein nach deinem Wort,
Dich allzeit preisen hier und dort!

This hymn by Paul Eber is one of the great hymns of the Reformation Age. It is based on the Latin hymn by Joachim Camerarius, his former teacher at Nürnberg:

In tenebris nostrae et densa caligine mentis,
  Cum nihil est toto pectore consilii,
Turbati erigimus, Deus, ad Te lumina cordis
  Nostra, tuamque fides solius erat opem.
Tu rege consiliis actus, Pater optime, nostros,
  Nostrum opus ut laudi serviat omne Tuae.

Eber's hymn is based on the beautiful words of King Jehoshaphath, 2 Chron. 20:12. The exact time and circumstances of its origin are uncertain. Koch relates that "on Ascension Day, 1547, after the battle of Mühlberg, the Wittenbergers, having received a message from the captive Elector to deliver their city to the Emperor Charles V, assembled for prayer in church; and quotes a portion of the prayer by Bugenhagen which greatly resembles Eber's hymn. But that the hymn was written then we have no proof." Sixt, the biographer of Paul Eber, relates that three musicians in Neustadt-Brandenburg on March 30, 1552, who fell from the church tower were unharmed. They had just finished playing this *chorale*.

However, the earliest positive date that we have for the text is that it was published in a broadsheet at Nürnberg in 1560.

The translation is an altered form of that by Catherine Winkworth in her *Lyra Germanica,* second series, 1858.

The tune "Wenn wir in höchsten Nöten" was first published in the *Genevan Psalter,* 1547, and is very likely by Louis Bourgeois himself. There it was set to Clement Marot's hymn on the Ten Commandments, beginning "Leve le coeur, ouvre l'oreille." *Fischer* states that the tune already appeared in the 1540 edition of the *Pseaumes* with Marot's text.

Why Should Cross and Trial Grieve Me   523

1. Why should cross and trial grieve me?
   Christ is near With His cheer;
Never will He leave me.
   Who can rob me of the heaven
That God's Son For my own
   To my faith hath given?

2. Though a heavy cross I'm bearing
   And my heart Feels the smart,
Shall I be despairing?
   God, my Helper, who doth send it,
Well doth know All my woe
   And how best to end it.

3. God oft gives me days of gladness;
   Shall I grieve If He give
Seasons, too, of sadness?
   God is good and tempers ever
All my ill, And He will
   Wholly leave me never.

4. Hopeful, cheerful, and undaunted
   Everywhere They appear
Who in Christ are planted.
   Death itself cannot appal them,
They rejoice When the voice
   Of their Lord doth call them.

5. Death cannot destroy forever;
   From our fears, Cares, and tears
It will us deliver.
   It will close life's mournful story,
Make a way That we may
   Enter heavenly glory.

6. What is all this life possesses?
   But a hand Full of sand
That the heart distresses.
   Noble gifts that pall me never
Christ, our Lord, Will accord
   To His saints forever.

7. Lord, my Shepherd, take me to Thee.
   Thou art mine; I was Thine,
Even e'er I knew Thee.
   I am Thine, for Thou hast bought me;
Lost I stood, But Thy blood
   Free salvation brought me.

8. Thou art mine; I love and own Thee.
   Light of Joy, Ne'er shall I
From my heart dethrone Thee.
   Savior, let me soon behold Thee
Face to face, — May Thy grace
   Evermore enfold me!

---

1. Warum sollt' ich mich denn grämen?
   Hab' ich doch Christum noch,
Wer will mir den nehmen?
   Wer will mir den Himmel rauben,
Den mir schon Gottes Sohn
   Beigelegt im Glauben?

2. Schickt er mir ein Kreuz zu tragen,
   Dringt herein Angst und Pein,
Sollt' ich drum verzagen?
   Der es schickt, der wird es wenden!
Er weiss wohl, wie er soll
   All mein Unglück enden.

3. Gott hat mich bei guten Tagen
   Oft ergötzt: sollt' ich jetzt
Nicht auch etwas tragen?
   Fromm ist Gott und schärft mit Massen
Sein Gericht, kann mich nicht
   Ganz und gar verlassen.

4. Unverzagt und ohne Grauen
   Soll ein Christ, wo er ist,
Stets sich lassen schauen.
   Wollt' ihn auch der Tod aufreiben,
Soll der Mut dennoch gut
   Und fein stille bleiben.

5. Kann uns doch kein Tod nicht töten,
   Sondern reisst unsern Geist
Aus viel tausend Nöten,
   Schleusst das Tor der bittern Leiden
Und macht Bahn, da man kann
   Gehn zu Himmelsfreuden.

6. Was sind dieses Lebens Güter?
   Eine Hand voller Sand,
Kummer der Gemüter.
   Dort, dort sind die edlen Gaben,
Da mein Hirt, Christus, wird
   Mich ohn' Ende laben.

7. Herr, mein Hirt, Brunn aller Freuden,
   Du bist mein, ich bin dein,
Niemand kann uns scheiden:
   Ich bin dein, weil du dein Leben
Und dein Blut mir zugut
   In den Tod gegeben.

8. Du bist mein, weil ich dich fasse
   Und dich nicht, o mein Licht,
Aus dem Herzen lasse.
   Lass mich, lass mich hingelangen,
Da du mich und ich dich
   Leiblich werd' umfangen!

CROSS AND COMFORT

This cento is composed of Stanzas 1, 4, 5, 7, 8, 10, 11, and 12 of Paul Gerhardt's longer hymn, based on Ps. 73:23, which was first published in the Berlin *Gesangbuch*, 1653, edited by Crüger and Runge. It is an unusually fine hymn of comfort. We are told that the Lutheran Salzburgers, some of whom later settled in the Colony of Georgia, 1734, sang this hymn as they marched through Swabia after their expulsion from their native land by the Roman Catholic authorities. On his death-bed Paul Gerhardt himself spoke the fifth stanza as his dying prayer, and the Paul Gerhardt Memorial Chapel in the cemetery of Gräfenhainichen bears the inscription from the first line of that stanza, in German: Kann uns doch kein Tod nicht töten.

The composite translation is based on that by John Kelly in his Paul Gerhardt's *Spiritual Songs*, 1867.

The tune "Warum sollt' ich mich denn grämen," also called "Bonn," which is wedded to the text, is by Johann G. Ebeling and appeared in his *Das ander Dutzet Geistlicher Andacht-Lieder*, Frankfurt a. d. O., 1666. This is a collection of Paul Gerhardt's hymns to which Ebeling had composed new tunes.

524   In Thee, Lord, have I Put My Trust

1. In Thee, Lord, have I put my trust;
Leave me not helpless in the dust,
  Let me not be confounded.
Let in Thy Word My faith, O Lord,
  Be always firmly grounded.

2. Bow down Thy gracious ear to me
And hear my cries and prayers to Thee,
  Haste Thee for my protection;
For woes and fear Surround me here.
  Help me in mine affliction.

3. My God and Shield, now let Thy power
Be unto me a mighty tower
  Whence bravely I defend me
Against the foes That round me close.
  O Lord, assistance lend me.

4. Thou art my Strength, my Shield, my Rock,
My Fortress that withstands each shock,
  My Help, my Life, my Treasure.
Whate'er the rod, Thou art my God;
  Naught can resist Thy pleasure.

5. The world for me has falsely set
Full many a secret snare and net
  To tempt me and to harm me.
Lord, make them fail, Do Thou prevail,
  Let their disguise not charm me.

6. With Thee, Lord, have I cast my lot;
O faithful God, forsake me not,
  To Thee my soul commending.
Lord, be my Stay, Lead Thou the way
  Now and when life is ending.

7. All honor, praise, and majesty
To Father, Son, and Spirit be,
  Our God forever glorious,
In whose rich grace We'll run our race
  Till we depart victorious.

In dich hab' ich gehoffet, Herr,
Hilf, dass ich nicht zuschanden werd'
  Noch ewiglich zu Spotte!
Das bitt' ich dich, erhalte mich
  In deiner Treu', mein Gotte!

Dein gnädig Ohr neig her zu mir,
Erhör mein' Bitt', tu dich herfür,
  Eil bald, mich zu erretten!
In Angst und Weh ich lieg' und steh',
  Hilf mir in meinen Nöten!

Mein Gott und Schirmer, steh mir bei,
Sei mir ein' Burg, darin ich frei
  Und ritterlich mög' streiten
Wider mein' Feind', der gar viel seind
  An mich auf beiden Seiten.

Du bist mein' Stärk', mein Fels, mein Hort,
Mein Schild, mein' Kraft (sagt mir dein Wort),
  Mein' Hilf', mein Heil, mein Leben,
Mein starker Gott in aller Not;
  Wer mag mir widerstreben?

Mir hat die Welt trüglich gericht't
Mit Lügen und mit falschem G'dicht
  Viel' Netz' und heimlich' Stricke;
Herr, nimm mein wahr in dieser G'fahr,
  B'hüt' mich vor falscher Tücke!

Herr, meinen Geist befehl' ich dir;
Mein Gott, mein Gott, weich nicht von mir,
  Nimm mich in deine Hände!
O wahrer Gott, aus aller Not
  Hilf mir am letzten Ende!

Glori, Lob, Ehr' und Herrlichkeit
Sei Gott Vater und Sohn bereit,
  Dem Heil'gen Geist mit Namen.
Die göttlich' Kraft mach' uns sieghaft
  Durch Jesum Christum! Amen.

CROSS AND COMFORT

This hymn by Adam Reusner (Reissner) was first published in the *Form und Ordnung Geystlicher Gesang und Psalmen*, Augsburg, 1533. It is based on Ps. 31:1-5, with a doxology added. It is considered one of the best psalm versions of the Reformation period.

Our translation is a slightly altered form of Catherine Winkworth's in her *Chorale Book for England*, 1863.

The tune "In dich hab' ich gehoffet" was first published in *Himmlische Harfen*, Georg Sunderreiter, Augsburg, 1581.

As Pants the Hart for Cooling Streams 525

1. As pants the hart for cooling streams
   When heated in the chase,
   So longs my soul, O God, for Thee
   And Thy refreshing grace.

2. For Thee, my God, the living God,
   My thirsty soul doth pine;
   Oh, when shall I behold Thy face,
   Thou Majesty Divine?

3. Why restless, why cast down, my soul?
   Hope still; and thou shalt sing
   The praise of Him who is thy God,
   Thy health's eternal Spring.

4. To Father, Son, and Holy Ghost,
   The God whom we adore,
   Be glory as it was, is now,
   And shall be evermore.

Tate and Brady, in their *New Version of the Psalms*, 1696, published a version of Ps. 42 in six eight-line stanzas, of which the cento is only a small portion. That this version is an improvement on the old version can be seen from the opening stanza of the old:

> Like as the hart doth breathe and bray,
> The well-springs to obtain,
> So doth my soul desire alway
> With Thee, Lord, to remain.

For comments on the tune "Spohr" see Hymn No. 456.

In God, My Faithful God 526

1. In God, my faithful God,
   I trust when dark my road;
   Though many woes o'ertake me,
   Yet He will not forsake me.
   His love it is doth send them
   And, when 'tis best, will end them.

2. My sins assail me sore,
   But I despair no more.
   I build on Christ, who loves me;
   From this Rock nothing moves me.
   To Him I all surrender,
   To Him, my soul's Defender.

3. If death my portion be,
   Then death is gain to me
   And Christ my Life forever,
   From whom death cannot sever.
   Come when it may, He'll shield me,
   To Him I wholly yield me.

4. O Jesus Christ, my Lord,
   So meek in deed and word,
   Thou once didst die to save us
   Because Thy love would have us
   Be heirs of heavenly gladness
   When ends this life of sadness.

5. "So be it," then, I say
   With all my heart each day.
   We, too, dear Lord, adore Thee.
   We sing for joy before Thee.
   Guide us while here we wander
   Until we praise Thee yonder.

Auf meinen lieben Gott
Trau' ich in Angst und Not,
Der kann mich allzeit retten
Aus Trübsal, Angst und Nöten,
Mein Unglück kann er wenden,
Steht all's in seinen Händen.

Ob mich mein' Sünd' anficht,
Will ich verzagen nicht;
Auf Christum will ich bauen
Und ihm allein vertrauen;
Ihm tu' ich mich ergeben
Im Tod und auch im Leben.

Ob mich der Tod nimmt hin,
Ist Sterben mein Gewinn,
Und Christus ist mein Leben,
Dem tu' ich mich ergeben;
Ich sterb' heut oder morgen,
Mein' Seel' wird er versorgen.

O mein Herr Jesu Christ,
Der du so g'duldig bist
Für mich am Kreuz gestorben,
Hast mir das Heil erworben,
Auch uns allen zugleiche
Das ew'ge Himmelreiche.

Amen, zu aller Stund'
Sprech' ich aus Herzensgrund.
Du wollest uns tun leiten,
Herr Christ, zu allen Zeiten,
Auf dass wir deinen Namen
Ewiglich preisen. Amen.

This excellent hymn is ascribed to Sigismund Weingärtner, about whom no details of life or calling are known. It first appeared in *Geistliche Psalmen,* etc., Nürnberg, 1607, in the author's index of which the name appears as "Sigismund Weingart." He is thought to have been a clergyman; but this, too, is uncertain.

The translation is an altered form of Catherine Winkworth's, *Chorale Book for England,* 1863.

The tune "Auf meinen lieben Gott" is first found in *Kurtzweilige Teutsche Lieder,* etc., Nürnberg, 1574, where it was set to a worldly song, "Venus, und dein Kind seid alle beide blind." It is first used with this hymn by Melchior Vulpius in his *Ein schön geistlich Gesangbuch,* Jena, 1609. The tune has erroneously been ascribed to Johann Hermann Schein. Johann Sebastian Bach often uses the melody as a closing *chorale* in his cantatas.

527   Lord, It Belongs Not to My Care

1. Lord, it belongs not to my care
Whether I die or live;
To love and serve Thee is my share,
And this Thy grace must give.

2. If life be long, I will be glad
That I may long obey;
If short, no laborer is sad
To end his toilsome day.

3. Christ leads me through no darker rooms
Than He went through before;
He that into God's kingdom comes
Must enter by this door.

4. Come, Lord, when grace has made me meet
Thy blessed face to see;
For if Thy work on earth be sweet,
What will Thy glory be?

5. Then shall I end my sad complaints
And weary, sinful days
And join with the triumphant saints
That sing my Savior's praise.

6. My knowledge of that life is small,
The eye of faith is dim;
But 'tis enough that Christ knows all,
And I shall be with Him.

Richard Baxter, in his *Poetical Fragments,* 1681, published a hymn, in eight eight-line stanzas, beginning "My Whole, though Broken Heart, O Lord." The cento is made up of selected passages from this longer poem, which was entitled "The Covenant and Confidence of Faith." He appended a note: "This covenant my dear wife, in her former sickness, subscribed with a cheerful will."

Richard Baxter is best known by his *Saint's Everlasting Rest,* which was widely read down to the last century.

For comments on the tune "St. Bernard" see Hymn No. 378.

528   If God Himself Be for Me

1. If God Himself be for me,
I may a host defy;
For when I pray, before me
My foes, confounded, fly.
If Christ, my Head and Master,
Befriend me from above,
What foe or what disaster
Can drive me from His love?

2. This I believe, yea, rather,
Of this I make my boast,
That God is my dear Father,
The Friend who loves me most,
And that, whate'er betide me,
My Savior is at hand
Through stormy seas to guide me
And bring me safe to land.

Ist Gott für mich, so trete
Gleich alles wider mich,
Sooft ich ruf' und bete,
Weicht alles hinter sich.
Hab' ich das Haupt zum Freunde
Und bin geliebt bei Gott,
Was kann mir tun der Feinde
Und Widersacher Rott'?

Nun weiss und glaub' ich feste,
Ich rühm's auch ohne Scheu,
Dass Gott der Höchst' und Beste,
Mein Freund und Vater sei,
Und dass in allen Fällen
Er mir zur Rechten steh'
Und dämpfe Sturm und Wellen
Und was mir bringet Weh.

3. I build on this foundation,
   That Jesus and His blood
Alone are my salvation,
   The true, eternal good.
Without Him all that pleases
   Is valueless on earth;
The gifts I owe to Jesus
   Alone my love are worth.

4. My Jesus is my Splendor,
   My Sun, my Light, alone;
Were He not my Defender
   Before God's awe-full throne,
I never should find favor
   And mercy in His sight,
But be destroyed forever
   As darkness by the light.

5. He canceled my offenses,
   Delivered me from death;
He is the Lord who cleanses
   My soul from sin through faith.
In Him I can be cheerful,
   Bold, and undaunted aye;
In Him I am not fearful
   Of God's great Judgment Day.

6. Naught, naught, can now condemn me
   Nor set my hope aside;
Now hell no more can claim me,
   Its fury I deride.
No sentence e'er reproves me,
   No ill destroys my peace;
For Christ, my Savior, loves me
   And shields me with His grace.

7. His Spirit in me dwelleth,
   And o'er my mind He reigns.
All sorrow He dispelleth
   And soothes away all pains.
He crowns His work with blessing
   And helpeth me to cry,
"My Father!" without ceasing,
   To Him who dwells on high.

8. And when my soul is lying
   Weak, trembling, and opprest,
He pleads with groans and sighing
   That cannot be exprest;
But God's quick eye discerns them,
   Although they give no sound,
And into language turns them
   E'en in the heart's deep ground.

9. To mine His Spirit speaketh
   Sweet words of holy cheer,
How God to him that seeketh
   For rest is always near
And how He hath erected
   A city fair and new,
Where what our faith expected
   We evermore shall view.

10. In yonder home doth flourish
    My heritage, my lot;
Though here I die and perish,
    My heaven shall fail me not.
Though care my life oft saddens
    And causeth tears to flow,
The light of Jesus gladdens
    And sweetens every woe.

11. Who clings with resolution
    To Him whom Satan hates
Must look for persecution;
    For him the burden waits
Of mockery, shame, and losses,
    Heaped on his blameless head;
A thousand plagues and crosses
    Will be his daily bread.

Der Grund, da ich mich gründe,
   Ist Christus und sein Blut,
Das machet, dass ich finde
   Das ew'ge wahre Gut.
An mir und meinem Leben
   Ist nichts auf dieser Erd';
Was Christus mir gegeben,
   Das ist der Liebe wert.

Mein Jesus ist mein' Ehre,
   Mein Glanz und helles Licht.
Wenn der nicht in mir wäre,
   So dürft' und könnt' ich nicht
Vor Gottes Augen stehen
   Und vor dem strengen Sitz;
Ich müsste stracks vergehen
   Wie Wachs in Feuershitz'.

Mein Jesus hat gelöschet,
   Was mit sich führt den Tod;
Der ist's, der mich rein wäschet,
   Macht schneeweiss, was ist rot.
In ihm kann ich mich freuen,
   Hab' einen Heldenmut,
Darf kein Gerichte scheuen,
   Wie sonst ein Sünder tut.

Nichts, nichts kann mich verdammen,
   Nichts nimmet mir mein Herz!
Die Höll' und ihre Flammen,
   Die sind mir nur ein Scherz.
Kein Urteil mich erschrecket,
   Kein Unheil mich betrübt,
Weil mich mit Flügeln decket
   Mein Heiland, der mich liebt.

Sein Geist wohnt mir im Herzen,
   Regieret meinen Sinn,
Vertreibt mir Sorg' und Schmerzen,
   Nimmt allen Kummer hin,
Gibt Segen und Gedeihen
   Dem, was er in mir schafft,
Hilft mir das Abba schreien
   Aus aller meiner Kraft.

Und wenn an meinem Orte
   Sich Furcht und Schwachheit find't,
So seufzt und spricht er Worte,
   Die unaussprechlich sind
Mir zwar und meinem Munde,
   Gott aber wohl bewusst,
Der an des Herzens Grunde
   Ersiehet seine Lust.

Sein Geist spricht meinem Geiste
   Manch süsses Trostwort zu,
Wie Gott dem Hilfe leiste,
   Der bei ihm suchet Ruh',
Und wie er hab' erbauet
   Ein' edle, neue Stadt,
Da Aug' und Herze schauet,
   Was er geglaubet hat.

Da ist mein Teil, mein Erbe
   Mir prächtig zugericht't;
Wenn ich gleich fall' und sterbe,
   Fällt doch mein Himmel nicht.
Muss ich auch gleich hier feuchten
   Mit Tränen meine Zeit,
Mein Jesus und sein Leuchten
   Durchsüsset alles Leid.

Wer sich mit dem verbindet,
   Den Satan fleucht und hasst,
Der wird verfolgt und findet
   Ein' harte, schwere Last
Zu leiden und zu tragen,
   Gerät in Hohn und Spott,
Das Kreuz und alle Plagen,
   Die sind sein täglich Brot.

12. From me this is not hidden,
   Yet I am not afraid;
I leave my cares, as bidden,
   To whom my vows were paid.
Though life and limb it cost me
   And everything I own,
Unshaken shall I trust Thee
   And cleave to Thee alone.

Das ist mir nicht verborgen,
   Doch bin ich unverzagt.
Dich will ich lassen sorgen,
   Dem ich mich zugesagt,
Es koste Leib und Leben
   Und alles, was ich hab';
An dir will ich fest kleben
   Und nimmer lassen ab.

13. Though earth be rent asunder,
   Thou'rt mine eternally;
Not fire nor sword nor thunder
   Shall sever me from Thee;
Not hunger, thirst, nor danger,
   Not pain nor poverty
Nor mighty princes' anger
   Shall ever hinder me.

Die Welt, die mag zerbrechen,
   Du stehst mir ewiglich,
Kein Brennen, Hauen, Stechen
   Soll trennen mich und dich,
Kein Hungern und kein Dürsten,
   Kein' Armut, keine Pein,
Kein Zorn der grossen Fürsten
   Soll mir ein' Hindrung sein.

14. No angel and no gladness,
   No throne, no pomp, no show,
No love, no hate, no sadness,
   No pain, no depth of woe,
No scheme of man's contrivance,
   However small or great,
Shall draw me from Thy guidance
   Nor from Thee separate.

Kein Engel, keine Freuden,
   Kein Thron, kein' Herrlichkeit,
Kein Lieben und kein Leiden,
   Kein' Angst und Herzeleid,
Was man nur kann erdenken,
   Es sei klein oder gross,
Der keines soll mich lenken
   Aus deinem Arm und Schoss.

15. My heart for joy is springing
   And can no more be sad,
'Tis full of mirth and singing,
   Sees naught but sunshine glad.
The Sun that cheers my spirit
   Is Jesus Christ, my King;
That which I shall inherit
   Makes me rejoice and sing.

Mein Herze geht in Sprüngen
   Und kann nicht traurig sein,
Ist voller Freud' und Singen,
   Sieht lauter Sonnenschein.
Die Sonne, die mir lachet,
   Ist mein Herr Jesus Christ;
Das, was mich singen machet,
   Ist, was im Himmel ist.

This heroic hymn of Paul Gerhardt's, as one authority rightly says, is worthy to be placed side by side with Luther's "A Mighty Fortress." It first appeared in Johann Crüger's *Praxis Pietatis Melica,* Frankfurt, 1656. It is based on Rom. 8:31-39. This hymn, like the author's greatest hymn, "Commit Whatever Grieves Thee," has been thought to have a connection with Gerhardt's trouble in Berlin, with the Elector of Brandenburg, but as it was published at least six years before, that assumption is not tenable.

Lauxmann, in *Koch,* writes of this hymn:

The hymn bears the watchword of the Lutheran Church as Paul gives it, "If God be for us, who can be against us?" One thinks of Philip Melanchthon's last words as he, worn out with the manifold conflicts after Luther's death and with many bitter and grievous trials, lay a-dying on April 19, 1560, he once more raised himself in bed and cried, "If God be for us, who can be against us?" When one asked him if he wished anything, he replied: "Nothing save heaven!" and gave up his spirit. In the same spirit it has been entitled "A Christian Hymn of Consolation and of Joy" and has spoken to the hearts of many troubled ones and strengthened them with new courage for the fight of faith.

The last stanza has been a great favorite with many Christians. Unfortunately no translation of this stanza does justice to the original.

Lauxmann gives an interesting account of the comfort derived from this hymn by a well-known German theologian:

While still young, Professor Auberlen of Basel departed from this life in 1864. This highly gifted and highly cultured witness for the faith was by an early death compelled to give up his greatly blessed labors, many projects, and a happy family life. On the 2d of May, a few hours before his death, a friend said to him, "Christ's disciples follow in His pathway, first death and the grave, then resurrection and ascension." To this he replied, "Of the fear of death, thank God, I know nothing and can say with Paulus Gerhardt: *"Ist Gott für mich, so trete Gleich alles wider mich."*

In the same night (his last upon earth) he repeated Stanza 15 of this hymn. Soon after, his light, as a taper, quietly went out.

The translation is based on that by Richard Massie, who published his version, omitting Stanzas 4, 5, 6, and 10, in 1857. The translator of these stanzas is unknown, but they bear a resemblance to those by John Kelly in his Paul Gerhardt's *Spiritual Songs*, 1867.

An analysis of this hymn gives us the following:

Our Declaration of Trust in God, Stanza 1

1. God has given His Son for us, Stanzas 2 and 3.
2. In Him God gives us:
    a. Access to the mercy-seat, Stanza 4.
    b. Freedom from sin, death, judgment, and hell, Stanzas 5 and 6.
    c. The gift of the Spirit, who gives us assurance of our sonship, pleads for us with sighing, and comforts us with our future inheritance, Stanzas 7—10.
3. Nothing can therefore separate us from the love of God, Stanzas 11—15.

For comments on the tune "Valet will ich dir geben" see Hymn No. 58.

I Leave All Things to God's Direction 529

1. I leave all things to God's direction,
    He loveth me in weal and woe;
His will is good, true His affection.
    With tender love His heart doth glow.
My Fortress and my Rock is He:
What pleaseth God, that pleaseth me.

2. My God hath all things in His keeping,
    He is the ever faithful Friend;
He grants me laughter after weeping,
    And all His ways in blessings end.
His love endures eternally:
What pleaseth God, that pleaseth me.

3. The will of God shall be my pleasure
    While here on earth is mine abode;
My will is wrong beyond all measure,
    It doth not will what pleaseth God.
The Christian's motto e'er must be:
What pleaseth God, that pleaseth me.

4. God knows what must be done to save me,
    His love for me will never cease;
Upon His hands He did engrave me
    With purest gold of loving grace.
His will supreme must ever be!
What pleaseth God, that pleaseth me.

5. My God desires the soul's salvation,
    Me also He desires to save;
Therefore with Christian resignation
    All earthly troubles I will brave.
His will be done eternally:
What pleaseth God, that pleaseth me.

Ich halte Gott in allem stille,
    Er liebet mich in Freud' und Schmerz.
Wie gut ist Gottes Vaterwille,
    Wie freundlich sein getreues Herz!
Er ist mein Hort und meine Zier:
Was Gott gefällt, gefällt auch mir.

Mein Gott weiss alles wohl zu machen,
    Er ist der ewig treue Freund.
Er lässt mich nach dem Weinen lachen,
    Was er nur tut, ist wohl gemeint,
Sein Lieben währet für und für.
Was Gott gefällt, gefällt auch mir.

Sein Wille bleibet mein Vergnügen,
    Solang ich leb' auf dieser Welt.
Was kann mein eigner Wille tügen,
    Der das nicht will, was Gott gefällt?
Ich denk' an meine Christgebühr:
Was Gott gefällt, gefällt auch mir.

Er will und wird mich ewig lieben,
    Er weiss, was Seelen nützlich sei,
Er hat mich in die Hand geschrieben
    Mit lauterm Golde seiner Treu'.
Weg, eigner Wille, weg mit dir!
Was Gott gefällt, gefällt auch mir.

Gott will, dass mir geholfen werde,
    Er will der Seelen Seligkeit;
Drum reiss' ich mich von dieser Erde
    Durch wahre Gottgelassenheit.
Sein Will' geschehe dort und hier.
Was Gott gefällt, gefällt auch mir.

Salomo Franck published this hymn in his *Geistliche Poesie*, Weimar, 1685. It was entitled "The Soul Resigns Itself to the Divine Will." The refrain at the end of each stanza is a striking one: "What pleaseth God, that pleaseth me."

The translation is that by Prof. August Crull, altered.

For comments on the tune "Wer nur den lieben Gott" see Hymn No. 518.

530   Thy Ways, O Lord, with Wise Design

1. Thy ways, O Lord, with wise design
Are framed upon Thy throne above,
And every dark and bending line
Meets in the center of Thy love.

2. With feeble light and half obscure
Poor mortals Thine arrangements view,
Not knowing that the least are sure
And the mysterious just and true.

3. Thy flock, Thine own peculiar care,
Though now they seem to roam uneyed,
Are led or driven only where
They best and safest may abide.

4. They neither know nor trace the way;
But whilst they trust Thy guardian eye,
Their feet shall ne'er to ruin stray,
Nor shall the weakest fail or die.

5. My favored soul shall meekly learn
To lay her reason at Thy throne;
Too weak Thy secrets to discern,
I'll trust Thee for my Guide alone.

Ambrose Serle, in 1786, published *Horae Solitariae: or Essays upon Some Remarkable Names and Titles of Jesus Christ*, etc. In this volume he included a number of short hymns, which were appended to some of the essays. This hymn was one of them.

For comments on the tune "St. Luke" see Hymn No. 323.

531   Come, Ye Disconsolate

1. Come, ye disconsolate, where'er ye languish;
Come to the Mercy-seat, fervently kneel.
Here bring your wounded hearts, here tell your anguish;
Earth has no sorrow that Heaven cannot heal.

2. Joy of the desolate, Light of the straying,
Hope of the penitent, fadeless and pure.
Here speaks the Comforter, tenderly saying, —
Earth has no sorrow that Heaven cannot cure.

3. Here see the Bread of Life; see waters flowing
Forth from the throne of God, pure from above.
Come to the feast of love; come, ever knowing
Earth has no sorrow but Heaven can remove.

Thomas Moore, in his *Sacred Songs*, 1816, published "Come, Ye Disconsolate" in three stanzas. His third stanza, however, was dropped when the hymn was included in *Spiritual Songs* by Thomas Hastings and Lowell Mason, 1832. Instead, another stanza, our third above, generally ascribed to Hastings, was substituted. Moore's third stanza reads:

> Go, ask the infidel what boon he brings us,
> What charm for aching hearts he can reveal,
> Sweet as the heavenly promise hope sings us,
> "Earth has no sorrow that God cannot heal."

Moore's first stanza had "God's altar" instead of "Mercy-seat," and his second stanza "when all others die" instead of "of the penitent," and "in God's name" instead of "tenderly."

Another hymn published in Moore's *Sacred Songs,* based on Ps. 147:3, included in some modern hymnals reads:

1. O Thou who driest the mourner's tear,
   How dark this world would be
   If, when deceived and wounded here,
   We could not fly to Thee!

2. The friends who in our sunshine live,
   When winter comes are flown;
   And he who has but tears to give,
   Must weep those tears alone.

3. But Thou wilt heal that broken heart,
   Which, like the plants that throw
   Their fragrance from the wounded part,
   Breathes sweetness out of woe.

4. When joy no longer soothes or cheers
   And e'en the hope that threw
   A moment's sparkle o'er our tears
   Is dimmed and vanished, too, —

5. Oh, who could bear life's stormy doom,
   Did not Thy wing of love
   Come brightly wafting through the gloom
   Our peace-branch from above?

6. Then sorrow, touched by Thee, grows bright
   With more than rapture's ray,
   As darkness shows us worlds of light
   We never saw by day.

The tune "Alma Redemptoris mater," also called "Alma," "Consolation" (Webbe), is by Samuel Webbe and is altered from the original tune found in *A Collection of Motetts,* 1792.

Thy Way, Not Mine, O Lord   532

1. Thy way, not mine, O Lord,
   However dark it be.
   Lead me by Thine own hand;
   Choose out the path for me.
   I dare not choose my lot;
   I would not if I might.
   Choose Thou for me, my God;
   So shall I walk aright.

2. Choose Thou for me my friends,
   My sickness or my health;
   Choose Thou my cares for me,
   My poverty or wealth.
   Not mine, not mine, the choice,
   In things or great or small;
   Be Thou my Guide, my Strength,
   My Wisdom, and my All.

Horatius Bonar published this hymn in his *Hymns of Faith and Hope,* first series, 1857. There were seven four-line stanzas. Our cento is composed of Stanzas 1, 3, 6, and 7. In Schaff and Gilman's *Library of Religious Poetry,* 1881, the hymn is noted as a translation from the German, but we have been unable to verify this. The original is as follows:

1. Thy way, not mine, O Lord,
   However dark it be!
   Lead me by Thine own hand,
   Choose out the path for me.

2. Smooth let it be or rough,
   It will be still the best;
   Winding or straight, it leads
   Right onward to Thy rest.

3. I dare not choose my lot;
   I would not if I might;
   Choose Thou for me, my God,
   So shall I walk aright.

4. The kingdom that I seek
   Is Thine; so let the way
   That leads to it be Thine;
   Else I must surely stray.

5. Take Thou my cup and it
   With joy or sorrow fill,
   As best to Thee may seem;
   Choose Thou my good and ill;

6. Choose Thou for me my friends,
   My sickness or my health;
   Choose Thou my cares for me,
   My poverty or wealth.

7. Not mine, not mine, the choice,
   In things or great or small;
   Be Thou my Guide, my Strength,
   My Wisdom, and my All!

The tune "Ich halte treulich still" is said to be an original tune by Johann Sebastian Bach, but this is uncertain. It is adapted from that in Georg Christian Schemelli's *Musikalisches Gesangbuch,* Leipzig, 1736, to which, according to the foreword, Bach had composed new melodies, in part, and also improved others. However, later research has disproved the claim that Bach composed most of the "new melodies" in this collection. Kümmerle asserts: "Moreover, Bach himself never thought of composing tunes for congregational use; rather were his compositions intended as 'arias' for private edification."

533   Nearer, My God, to Thee

1. Nearer, my God, to Thee,
   Nearer to Thee.
   E'en though it be a cross
   That raiseth me,
   Still all my song shall be,
   Nearer, my God, to Thee,
   Nearer, my God, to Thee,
   Nearer to Thee.

2. Though like the wanderer,
   The sun gone down,
   Darkness be over me,
   My rest a stone,
   Yet in my dreams I'd be
   Nearer, my God, to Thee,
   Nearer, my God, to Thee,
   Nearer to Thee.

3. There let my way appear
   Steps unto heaven;
   All that Thou sendest me
   In mercy given;
   Angels to beckon me
   Nearer, my God, to Thee,
   Nearer, my God, to Thee,
   Nearer to Thee.

4. Then with my waking thoughts
   Bright with Thy praise,
   Out of my stony griefs
   Bethel I'll raise,
   So by my woes to be
   Nearer, my God, to Thee,
   Nearer, my God, to Thee,
   Nearer to Thee.

5. Or if on joyful wing,
   Cleaving the sky,
   Sun, moon, and stars forgot,
   Upward I fly,
   Still all my song shall be,
   Nearer, my God, to Thee,
   Nearer, my God, to Thee,
   Nearer to Thee.

Sarah Flower Adams first published this hymn in W. J. Fox's *Hymns and Anthems*, 1841. Our text has only one slight alteration. Mrs. Adams had written, Stanza 1, Line 5:
Still all my song *would* be.

This hymn was a cause of much controversy at one time because the name of Christ does not occur in it (compare Hymn No. 329) and a number of adaptations were made and included in hymnals; but none of these has endured beyond certain circles, whereas the original retains its popularity from generation to generation, owing in part at least, to its high poetic quality. It is undoubtedly the most beautiful hymn we have on Jacob's vision at Bethel, Gen. 28:10-19.

It will be of interest to give a few of the altered stanzas and versions to illustrate. One of the first changes according to Mearns, in *Julian,* was made by Arthur Tozer Russell, 1851, namely, the addition of another stanza:

Christ alone beareth me
Where Thou dost shine;
Joint heir He maketh me
Of the divine:
In Christ my soul shall be
Nearest, my God, to Thee,
Nearest to Thee.

Bishop Bickersteth, 1882, in his annotation to this hymn, wrote:

"The Editor shrank from appending a closing verse of his own to a hymn so generally esteemed complete as this, or he would have suggested the following:

There in my Father's home,
Safe and at rest,
There in my Savior's love
Perfectly blest;
Age after age shall be
Nearer, my God, to Thee,
Nearer to Thee.

Another version by Bishop William Walsham How was written in 1864, to which the following note was added later:

"A paraphrase of Mrs. Adams's hymn expressing more definitely Christian faith and better adapted for congregational worship":

1. Nearer, O God, to Thee,
    Hear Thou my prayer;
 E'en though a heavy cross
    Fainting I bear,
 Still all my prayer shall be,
 Nearer, O God, to Thee;
    Nearer to Thee!

2. If where they led my Lord,
    I, too, am borne,
 Planting my steps in His,
    Weary and worn,
 There even let me be
 Nearer, O God, to Thee,
    Nearer to Thee!

3. If Thou the cup of pain
    Givest to drink,
 Let not my trembling lip
    From the draught shrink,
 So by my woes to be
 Nearer, O God, to Thee,
    Nearer to Thee!

4. Though the great battle rage
    Hotly around,
 Still where my Captain fights,
    Let me be found,
 Through toils and strife to be
 Nearer, O God, to Thee,
    Nearer to Thee!

5. And when Thou, Lord, once more
    Glorious shalt come,
 Oh, for a dwelling-place
    In Thy bright home!
 Through all eternity
 Nearer, O God, to Thee,
    Nearer to Thee!

Julian says: "It is the least musical of Bishop How's hymns."

Hervey Doddridge Ganse, an American Presbyterian clergyman, c. 1890, retained Stanza 1 and added the following three:

2. Nearer, my Lord, to Thee,
    Nearer to Thee,
 Who to Thy cross didst come
    Dying for me!
 Strengthen my willing feet,
 Hold me in service sweet
 Nearer, O Christ, to Thee,
    Nearer to Thee!

3. Nearer, O Comforter,
    Nearer to Thee!
 Who with my loving Lord
    Dwellest with me!
 Grant me Thy fellowship,
 Help me each day to keep
 Nearer, my Guide, to Thee,
    Nearer to Thee!

4. But to be nearer still,
    Bring me, O God,
 Not by the visioned steeps
    Angels have trod.
 Here where Thy cross I see,
 Jesus, I wait for Thee,
 Then evermore to be
    Nearer to Thee!

Henry Eyster Jacobs, prominent American Lutheran divine, in 1887, published what was practically a new hymn, in which he emphasized the means of grace whereby sinful man is brought to his Savior:

1. Nearer, my God, to Thee!
    Nearer to Thee!
 Through Word and Sacrament,
    Thou com'st to me.
 Thy grace is ever near,
 Thy Spirit ever here,
    Drawing to Thee.

2. Ages on ages rolled
    Ere earth appeared,
 Yet Thine unmeasured love
    The way prepared;
 E'en then Thou yearn'st for me
 That I might nearer be,
    Nearer to Thee!

3. Thy Son has come to earth
    My sin to bear,
 My every wound to heal,
    My pain to share.
 "God in the flesh" for me
 Brings me now nearer Thee,
    Nearer to Thee!

4. Lo, all my debt is paid,
    My guilt is gone.
 See, He has risen for me,
    My throne is won.
 Thanks, O my God, to Thee!
 None now can nearer be,
    Nearer to Thee!

5. Welcome, then, to Thy home,
    Blest One in Three!
 As Thou hast promised, come,
    Come, Lord, to me!
 Work Thou, O God, through me,
 Live Thou, O God, in me,
    Ever in me!

6. By the baptismal stream,
    Which made me Thine,
 By the dear flesh and blood,
    Thy love made mine,
 Purge Thou all sin from me
 That I may nearer be,
    Nearer to Thee!

7. Surely it matters not
    What earth may bring,
 Death is of no account,
    Grace will I sing.
 Nothing remains for me
 Save to be nearer Thee,
    Nearer to Thee!

The tune "Bethany," by Lowell Mason, composed in 1856, made its first appearance in print in the *Sabbath Hymn and Tune Book, Andover,* 1859, where it was set to this text. There is a similarity between this tune and the well-known air of "Oft in the Stilly Night," and it is likely that Mason's tune was suggested by it.

534   God of My Life, to Thee I Call

1. God of my life, to Thee I call;
Afflicted, at Thy feet I fall:
When the great water-floods prevail,
Leave not my trembling heart to fail.

2. Friend of the friendless and the faint,
Where should I lodge my deep complaint?
Where but with Thee, whose open door
Invites the helpless and the poor?

3. Did ever mourner plead with Thee
And Thou refuse that mourner's plea?
Does not the word still fixed remain
That none shall seek Thy face in vain?

4. Fair is the lot that's cast for me;
I have an Advocate with Thee.
They whom the world caresses most
Have no such privilege to boast.

5. Poor though I be, despised, forgot,
Yet God, my God, forgets me not;
And he is safe and must succeed
For whom the Lord vouchsafes to plead.

6. Then hear, O Lord, my humble cry
And bend on me Thy pitying eye.
To Thee their prayer Thy people make:
Hear us for our Redeemer's sake.

This hymn of William Cowper appeared in *Olney Hymns,* Book III, 1779. The original has another stanza, after our third, which reads:

> That were a grief I could not bear,
> Didst Thou not hear and answer prayer;
> But a prayer-hearing, — answering God
> Supports me under every load.

The sixth stanza is from an unknown source.

At its first publication the hymn was entitled "Looking Upwards in a Storm."

For comments on the tune "Wenn wir in höchsten Nöten" see Hymn No. 522.

535   Rejoice, My Heart, Be Glad and Sing

1. Rejoice, my heart, be glad and sing,
A cheerful trust maintain;
For God, the Source of everything,
Thy Portion shall remain.

Wohlauf, mein Herze, sing und spring
Und habe guten Mut!
Dein Gott, der Ursprung aller Ding',
Ist selbst und bleibt dein Gut.

2. He is thy Treasure, He thy Joy,
Thy Life and Light and Lord,
Thy Counselor when doubts annoy,
Thy Shield and great Reward.

Er ist dein Schatz, dein Erb' und Teil,
Dein Glanz und Freudenlicht,
Dein Schirm und Schild, dein' Hilf' und Heil,
Schafft Rat und lässt dich nicht.

3. Why spend the day in blank despair,
In restless thought the night?
On thy Creator cast thy care;
He makes thy burdens light.

Was kränkst du dich in deinem Sinn
Und grämst dich Tag und Nacht?
Nimm deine Sorg' und wirf sie hin
Auf den, der dich gemacht!

4. Did not His love and truth and power
Watch o'er thy childhood day?
Has He not oft in threatening hour
Turned dreaded ills away?

Hat er dich nicht von Jugend auf
Versorget und ernährt?
Wie manchen schweren Unglückslauf
Hat er zurückgekehrt!

5. He ever will with patience chide,
His rod falls gently down,
And all thy sins He casts aside
And in the sea doth drown.

Du strafst uns Sünder mit Geduld
Und schlägst nicht allzusehr,
Ja endlich nimmst du unsre Schuld
Und wirfst sie in das Meer.

6. When silent woe thy bosom rends,
His pity sees thy grief,
Supplies what to His glory tends
And to thine own relief.

Wenn unser Herze seufzt und schreit,
Wirst du gar leicht erweicht
Und gibst uns, was uns hoch erfreut
Und dir zur Ehr' gereicht.

CROSS AND COMFORT

7. He knows how oft a Christian weeps
And why his tears now fall;
And in the book His mercy keeps
These things are noted all.

8. His wisdom never plans in vain,
Ne'er falters or mistakes;
All that His counsels did ordain
A happy ending makes.

9. Upon thy lips, then, lay thy hand
And trust His guiding love;
Then like a rock thy peace shall stand
Here and in heaven above.

Du zählst, wie oft ein Christe wein'
Und was sein Kummer sei;
Kein Zähr- und Tränlein ist so klein,
Du hebst und legst es bei.

Er hat noch niemals was versehn
In seinem Regiment;
Nein, was er tut und lässt geschehn,
Das nimmt ein gutes End'.

Ei nun, so lass ihn ferner tun
Und red' ihm nichts darein,
So wirst du hier in Frieden ruhn
Und ewig fröhlich sein.

This cento is taken from Paul Gerhardt's thanksgiving hymn "O Lord, I sing with Lips and Heart" (No. 569) and includes Stanzas 13, 14, 15, 16, 9, 10, 11, 17, and 18. The hymn first appeared in *Geistliche Lieder und Psalmen*, Berlin, 1653, edited by Runge and Crüger. The hymn has been popular since its first publication. On account of its length it has been divided into two hymns, this and No. 569.

The translation is an altered form of John Kelly's in *Paul Gerhardt's Spiritual Songs*, 1867.

For comments on the tune "Ich singe dir" see Hymn No. 29.

MORNING

Times and Seasons

536   Awake, My Soul, and with the Sun

1. Awake, my soul, and with the sun
Thy daily stage of duty run;
Shake off dull sloth and joyful rise
To pay thy morning sacrifice.

2. Let all thy converse be sincere,
Thy conscience as the noonday clear;
Think how the all-seeing God thy ways
And all thy secret thought surveys.

3. All praise to Thee, who safe hast kept
And hast refreshed me whilst I slept.
Grant, Lord, when I from death shall wake,
I may of endless light partake.

4. Lord, I my vows to Thee renew;
Disperse my sins as morning dew;
Guard my first springs of thought and will
And with Thyself my spirit fill.

5. Direct, control, suggest, this day
All I design or do or say
That all my powers, with all their might,
In Thy sole glory may unite.

6. Praise God, from whom all blessings flow;
Praise Him, all creatures here below;
Praise Him above, ye heavenly host;
Praise Father, Son, and Holy Ghost.
Amen.

Thomas Ken wrote the hymn from which this cento was taken for a *Manual of Prayers,* which he had prepared for the students of Winchester College, where he was a Fellow at the time, in which the boys were admonished "to be sure to sing the Morning and Evening Hymn in your chamber devoutly." The hymn apparently did not appear in print until the 1695 edition of the *Manual,* where it was placed in the appendix. In a later publication of the hymn, 1709, it appeared as revised by Ken. The cento is composed of Stanzas 1, 3, 9, 12, 13, and 14, selected from the texts of 1695 and 1709. The omitted stanzas, according to the 1709 text, are as follows:

2. Thy precious time, midspent, redeem,
Each present day thy last Esteem,
Improve thy Talent with due Care,
For the Great Day thyself prepare.

4. By influence of the Light Divine
Let thy own Light to others Shine,
Reflect all Heaven's propitious Rays,
In ardent Love, and chearful Praise.

5. Wake and lift up thyself, my Heart,
And with the Angels bear thy part,
Who all Night long unwearied Sing
High Praise to the Eternal King.

6. I wake, I wake, ye Heavenly Choir,
May your Devotion me inspire,
That I like you my Age may spend,
Like you may on my God attend.

7. May I like you in God delight,
Have all day long my God in sight,
Perform like you my Maker's Will,
O may I nevermore do ill.

8. Had I your Wings, to Heaven I'd fly,
But God shall that Defect supply,
And my Soul, wing'd with warm desire,
Shall all Day long to Heaven aspire.

10. I would not wake nor rise again,
And Heaven itself I would disdain,
Were't not Thou there to be enjoy'd,
And I in Hymns to be employ'd.

11. Heav'n is, Dear Lord, where'er Thou art,
O never, then, from me depart;
For to my Soul 'tis Hell to be
But for one Moment void of Thee.

The famous doxology is also the closing stanza of Ken's evening hymn (see Hymn No. 558) and of his midnight hymn, "My God, from Sleep I Now Awake."

The tune "Morning Hymn," also called "Magdalene" and "Hippolytus," was composed by François Hippolite Barthélémon. It was written for the Female Orphan Asylum at the request of its chaplain and was first printed in the *Supplement to the Hymns and Psalms at the Asylum or House of Refuge for Female Orphans,* 1785. W. Gawler, organist to the asylum, was the editor. It was headed "New Tune" and set to the words of this hymn.

Every Morning Mercies New — 537

1. Every morning mercies new
Fall as fresh as morning dew;
Every morning let us pay
Tribute with the early day;
For Thy mercies, Lord, are sure,
Thy compassion doth endure.

2. Still the greatness of Thy love
Daily doth our sins remove;
Daily, far as east from west,
Lifts the burden from the breast;
Gives unbought to those who pray
Strength to stand in evil day.

3. Let our prayers each morn prevail
That these gifts may never fail;
And as we confess the sin
And the Tempter's power within,
Feed us with the Bread of Life;
Fit us for our daily strife.

4. As the morning light returns,
As the sun with splendor burns,
Teach us still to turn to Thee,
Ever-blessed Trinity,
With our hands our hearts to raise
In unfailing prayer and praise.

When first published in the *Parish Hymn Book*, 1863, this hymn by Greville Phillimore began "Every morning they are new." In the *Hymnary*, 1872, the line was changed as above. This hymn has sometimes been erroneously attributed to Horatius Bonar.

The following illustration from the *Talmud* is appropriate in connection with the truth impressed in our hymn:

In studying the account of the manna the scholars of Rabbi Simon ben Jochai once asked him, "Why did not the Lord give to Israel enough manna for a year at one time?" Then the Rabbi said: "I will answer you with a parable: Once there was a king who had a son to whom he gave a yearly allowance, paying him the entire sum on a fixed day. It soon happened that the day on which the allowance was due was the only day in the year when the father saw his son. So the king changed his plan and gave his son day by day that which sufficed for the day. And now the son visited his father every morning. Thus did God deal with Israel."

For comments on the tune "Voller Wunder" see Hymn No. 11.

Now the Shades of Night are Gone — 538

1. Now the shades of night are gone,
Now the morning light is come.
Lord, may we be Thine today;
Drive the shades of sin away.

2. Fill our souls with heavenly light,
Banish doubt and cleanse our sight.
In Thy service, Lord, today
Help us labor, help us pray.

3. Keep our haughty passions bound,
Save us from our foes around;
Going out and coming in,
Keep us safe from every sin.

4. When our work of life is past;
Oh, receive us then at last!
Night of sin will be no more
When we reach the heavenly shore.

There is little to be said about the authorship of this hymn. It is ascribed to the Mohican Indian Samson Occom (Occum, Ockum) and is dated 1770. The hymn was first published in the *Congregational Collection*, Hartford, 1799, and has been included in some modern hymn-books.

For comments on the tune "Vienna" see Hymn No. 18.

Come, Thou Bright and Morning Star — 539

1. Come, Thou Bright and Morning Star,
Light of light, without beginning!
Shine upon us from afar
    That we may be kept from sinning.
Drive away by Thy clear light
    Our dark night.

Morgenglanz der Ewigkeit,
    Licht vom unerschöpften Lichte,
Schick uns diese Morgenzeit
    Deine Strahlen zu Gesichte
Und vertreib durch deine Macht
    Unsre Nacht!

2. Let Thy grace, like morning dew
   Falling soft on barren places,
  Comfort, quicken, and renew
   Our dry souls and dying graces;
    Bless Thy flock from Thy rich store
     Evermore.

  Deiner Güte Morgentau
   Fall' auf unser matt Gewissen,
  Lass die dürre Lebensau
   Lauter süssen Trost geniessen,
    Und erquick uns, deine Schar,
     Immerdar!

3. May Thy fervent love destroy
   Our cold works, in us awaking
  Ardent zeal and holy joy
   At the purple morn's first breaking.
    Let us truly rise ere yet
     Life has set.

  Gib, dass deiner Liebe Glut
   Unsre kalten Werke töte,
  Und erweck uns Herz und Mut
   Bei entstandner Morgenröte,
    Dass wir, eh' wir gar vergehn,
     Recht aufstehn!

4. Ah! thou Dayspring from on high,
   Grant that at Thy next appearing
  We who in the graves do lie
   May arise, Thy summons hearing,
    And rejoice in our new life,
     Far from strife.

  Ach du Aufgang aus der Höh',
   Gib, dass auch am Jüngsten Tage
  Unser Leichnam aufersteh'
   Und, entfernt von aller Plage,
    Sich auf jener Freudenbahn
     Freuen kann!

5. Light us to those heavenly spheres,
   Sun of grace, in glory shrouded;
  Lead us through this vale of tears
   To the land where days unclouded,
    Purest joy, and perfect peace
     Never cease.

  Leucht uns selbst in jene Welt,
   Du verklärte Gnadensonne,
  Führ uns durch das Tränenfeld
   In das Land der ew'gen Wonne,
    Wo die Lust, die uns erhöht,
     Nie vergeht!

This cento is composed of Stanzas 1, 3, 4, 6, and 7 of the hymn written by Christian Knorr, Baron von Rosenroth. The hymn was first published in the baron's *Neuer Helicon mit seinen Neun Musen,* etc., Nürnberg, 1684. The omitted stanzas are:

2. Die bewölkte Finsternis
   Müsse deinem Glanz entfliehen,
  Die durch Adams Apfelbiss
   Über uns sich müsste ziehen,
    Dass wir, Herr, durch deinen Schein
     Selig sein.

5. Lass uns ja das Sündenkleid
   Durch des Bundesblut vermeiden,
  Dass uns die Gerechtigkeit
   Möge wie ein Rock bekleiden
    Und wir so vor aller Pein
     Sicher sei'n.

Fischer says it is "one of the freshest, most original, and spirited of morning hymns, as if born from the dew of the sunrise."

Knorr based his hymn on the following by Martin Opitz, translated by C. W. Shields, *Sacred Lyrics,* Philadelphia, 1859:

O Holy Light, of Light engendered,
  O glorious Sun of Righteousness,
Again as erst from chaos rendered,
  Thou dost our waking vision bless;
    Thanks and adoration!
  Well a new oblation
    Such new grace beseems;
  Gift of sinful spirits,
  Purge it by Thy merits
    In Thy cleansing beams.

Now let the glory of Thy dawning
  On our benighted souls arise;
Where'er Thou shinest, Star of Morning,
  The gloom of sin and sorrow flies.
    See, O Lord, we wander,
  Darkened paths we ponder,
    Lost from Wisdom's way.
  Oh, dispel our terror,
  And this night of error
    Turn to glorious day.

Julian says that Knorr's hymn is "more happily expressed and has attained greater popularity."

The translation is by Richard Massie, contributed to Mercer's *Church Psalter and Hymn Book,* 1857, and in his own *Lyra Domestica,* 1864.

The beautiful tune "Morgenglanz der Ewigkeit" is found in Freylinghausen's *Neues geistreiches Gesangbuch,* Halle, 1704. It is an adaptation of Johann Rudolf Ahle's spiritual aria "Seelchen, was ist Schönres wohl als der Höchste Gott?"

With the Lord Begin Thy Task   540

1. With the Lord begin thy task,
   Jesus will direct it;
For His aid and counsel ask,
   Jesus will perfect it.
Every morn with Jesus rise,
   And when day is ended,
In His name then close thine eyes;
   Be to Him commended.

2. Let each day begin with prayer,
   Praise, and adoration;
On the Lord cast every care,
   He is thy Salvation.
Morning, evening, and at night
   Jesus will be near thee,
Save thee from the Tempter's might,
   With His presence cheer thee.

3. With thy Savior at thy side,
   Foes need not alarm thee;
In His promises confide,
   And no ill can harm thee.
All thy trust do thou repose
   In the mighty Master,
Who in wisdom truly knows
   How to stem disaster.

4. If thy task be thus begun
   With the Savior's blessing,
Safely then thy course will run,
   Naught thy soul distressing.
Good will follow everywhere
   While thou here must wander;
Thou at last the joy wilt share
   In the mansions yonder.

5. Thus, Lord Jesus, every task
   Be to Thee commended;
May Thy will be done, I ask,
   Until life is ended.
Jesus, in Thy name begun
   Be the day's endeavor;
Grant that it may well be done
   To Thy praise forever.

Fang dein Werk mit Jesu an,
   Jesus hat's in Händen.
Jesum ruf zum Beistand an,
   Jesus wird's wohl enden.
Steh mit Jesu morgens auf,
   Geh mit Jesu schlafen,
Führ mit Jesu deinen Lauf,
   Lasse Jesum schaffen!

Morgens soll der Anfang sein,
   Jesum anzubeten,
Dass er woll' dein Helfer sein
   Stets in deinen Nöten.
Morgens, abends und bei Nacht
   Will er stehn zur Seiten,
Wenn des Satans List und Macht
   Dich sucht zu bestreiten.

Wenn dein Jesus mit dir ist,
   Lass die Feinde wüten!
Er wird dich vor ihrer List
   Schützen und behüten.
Setz nur das Vertrauen dein
   In sein' Allmachtshände
Und glaub' sicher, dass allein
   Er dein Unglück wende!

Wenn denn deine Sach' also,
   Mit Gott angefangen,
Ei, so hat es keine Not,
   Wirst den Zweck erlangen:
Es wird folgen Glück und Heil
   Hier in diesem Leben,
Endlich wird dir Gott dein Teil
   Auch im Himmel geben.

Nun, Herr Jesu, all mein' Sach'
   Sei dir übergeben;
Es nach deinem Willen mach'
   Auch im Tod und Leben!
All mein Werk greif' ich jetzt an,
   Jesu, in dein'm Namen;
Lass es doch sein wohlgetan!
   Ich sprech' darauf: Amen.

The author of this hymn is unknown. It is found in *Morgen- und Abendsegen*, Waldenburg, 1734. It is entitled "Jesus the Most Faithful Companion and Helper in the Land."

Our translation was prepared for *The Lutheran Hymnal* in 1937.

The tune "Fang dein Werk" is by Peter Frank and appeared in *Geistliches Harpffenspiel*, Koburg, 1657, where it was set to his hymn "Christus, Christus, Christus ist, dem ich mich ergebe."

O Blessed Holy Trinity   541

1. O blessed Holy Trinity,
Divine, eternal Unity,
God Father, Son, and Holy Ghost,
Be Thou this day my Guide and Host.

2. My soul and body keep from harm,
O'er all I have extend Thine arm,
That Satan may not cause distress
Nor bring me shame and wretchedness.

3. The Father's love shield me this day,
The Son's pure wisdom cheer my way,
The Holy Spirit's light divine
Illume my heart's benighted shrine.

O heilige Dreifaltigkeit,
O hochgelobte Einigkeit,
Gott Vater, Sohn und Heil'ger Geist,
Heut' diesen Tag mir Beistand leist'!

Mein' Seel', Leib, Ehr' und Gut bewahr',
Dass mir kein Böses widerfahr'
Und mich der Satan nicht verletz',
Noch mich in Schand' und Schaden setz'!

Des Vaters Huld mich heut' anblick',
Des Sohnes Weisheit mich erquick',
Des Heil'gen Geistes Glanz und Schein
Erleucht' mein's finstern Herzens Schrein!

4. My Maker, strengthen Thou my heart, O my Redeemer, help impart, Blest Comforter, keep at my side That faith and love in me abide.	Mein Schöpfer, steh mir kräftig bei, O mein Erlöser, hilf mir frei, O Tröster wert, weich nicht von mir, Mein Herz mit Lieb' und Glauben zier'!
5. Lord, bless and keep Thou me as Thine; Lord, make Thy face upon me shine; Lord, lift Thy countenance on me And give me peace, sweet peace, from Thee.	Herr, segne und behüte mich, Erleuchte mich, Herr, gnädiglich! Herr, heb auf mich dein Angesicht Und deinen Frieden auf mich richt!

The author of this hymn is Martin Behm, who first published it, in seven stanzas, in his *Kriegesman, Das ist: Gründlicher Vnterricht, wie sich ein Christlicher Kriegsman verhalten solle,* etc., Leipzig, 1593. Later, in *Centuria secunda,* etc., Wittenberg, 1608, the author recast the hymn in eight stanzas. It is from this version that this hymn is taken, being Stanzas 1 to 5. The only change is that in Stanza 2, Line 1, Behm has "the Father's might."

The translation is an altered form of that by Conrad H. L. Schuette, in the Ohio *Lutheran Hymnal* of 1880.

For comments on the tune "O Heilige Dreifaltigkeit" see Hymn No. 340.

542   The Sun Arises Now

1. The sun arises now
  In light and glory
And gilds the rugged brow
  Of mountains hoary.
Be glad, my soul, and lift
  Thy voice in singing
To God from earth below,
Thy heart with joy aglow
  And praises ringing.
	Nu rinder Solen op
	  Af Österlide,
	Forgylder Klippens Top
	  Og Bergets Side!
	Vär glad, min Själ, og lad
	  din Stemme klinge,
	Stig op fra Jordens Bo,
	Og dig med Tak og Tro
	  Til Himlen svinge!

2. Like countless grains of sand,
  Beyond all measure,
And wide as sea and land
  Is Heaven's treasure
Of grace which Christ, my Lord,
  Each day bestoweth,
Which, like refreshing rain,
Into my soul again
  Each morning floweth.
	Utallig, saa som Sand,
	  Og uden Maade
	Som Havets dybe Vand,
	  Er Herrens Naade,
	Som han mit Hoved
	  daglig overgyder,
	Hver Morgen uden Maal
	En Naade uden Maal
	  Til mig nedflyder.

3. Keep Thou my soul today
  From sin and blindness;
Surround me on my way
  With loving-kindness
And fill my heart, O God,
  With joy from heaven;
I then shall ask no more
Than what Thou hast of yore
  In wisdom given.
	Lad Synden nu idag
	  Mig ei forblinde,
	At jeg min Guds Behag
	  Har ret i Minde!
	Men, om min Fod gaar vild,
	  og sig mon stöde,
	Da vend, o Gud, mig om,
	Gak ei med mig til Dom,
	  Tilgiv min Bröde!

4. Thou knowest best my needs,
  My sighs Thou heedest;
Thy hand Thy children feeds,
  Thine own Thou leadest.
What should I more desire,
  With Thee deciding
The course that I must take,
Than follow in the wake
  Where Thou art guiding?
	Du bedst min Tarv og Trang,
	  O Herre, kjender,
	Tilmed er Lykkens Gang
	  I dine Hænder,
	Og hvad mig tjener bedst
	  I hver en Maade,
	Det du tilforne ser,
	Min Själ, hvad vil du meer?
	  Lad Gud kun raade!

This hymn, by Thomas Hansen Kingo, was published in the official Danish *Kirke-Psalme-Bog,* 1699. The original has seven stanzas. Our cento includes Stanzas 1, 2, 6, and 7. The translation is by P. C. Paulsen and, as far as we have been able to determine, was written about 1925. It is contained in the *American Lutheran Hymnal,* 1930.

The tune "Nu rinder Solen op" is by an unknown composer. It appeared in Hartnack Otto Konrad Zinck's *Koralbog,* 1801.

MORNING

When, Streaming from the Eastern Skies 543

1. When, streaming from the eastern skies,
The morning light salutes my eyes,
O Sun of Righteousness Divine,
On me with beams of mercy shine;
Chase the dark clouds of sin away
And turn my darkness into day.

2. When to heaven's great and glorious King
My morning sacrifice I bring
And, grieving o'er my guilt and shame,
Ask mercy, Savior, in Thy name,
My conscience sprinkle with Thy blood
And be my Advocate with God.

3. When each day's scenes and labors close
And wearied nature seeks repose,
With pardoning mercy, richly blest,
Guard me, my Savior, while I rest;
And as each morning's sun shall rise,
Oh, lead me onward to the skies!

4. And at my life's last setting sun,
My conflict o'er, my labor done,
Jesus, Thy heavenly radiance shed
To cheer and bless my dying bed
And from death's gloom my spirit raise
To see Thy face and sing Thy praise.

William Shrubsole first published this hymn in the *Christian Observer*, 1813, in eight stanzas. Our cento includes Stanzas 1, 2, 7, and 8, slightly altered. The omitted Stanzas 3 to 6 read as follows:

3. As every day Thy mercy spares
Will bring its trials and its cares,
O Savior, till my life shall end,
Be Thou my Counselor and Friend;
Teach me Thy precepts all divine,
And be Thy great example mine.

4. When pain transfixes every part,
And languor settles at the heart;
When on my bed, diseased, opprest,
I turn and sigh and long for rest,
O Great Physician, see my grief,
And grant Thy servant sweet relief.

5. Should poverty's consuming blow
Lay all my worldly comforts low
And neither help nor hope appear
My steps to guide, my heart to cheer,
Lord, pity and supply my need,
For Thou on earth wast poor indeed.

6. Should Providence profusely pour
Its various blessings on my store,
Oh, keep me from the ills that wait
On such a seeming prosperous state;
From hurtful passions set me free,
And humbly may I walk with Thee.

In connection with the author the following will be of interest, as it sheds a light on his character. He was the heir of Edward Perronet, author of the hymn "All Hail the Power of Jesus' Name." In Perronet's will we find this concluding clause:

> Lastly I do here give and bequeath all and every property I am at this time, or may at the time of my decease, be possest of, both real and personal, to the aforementioned Mr. William Shrubsole, youngest son of Mr. Thomas Shrubsole aforesaid and now or late of the parish of St. Bride's in London, and to the male heirs of his body lawfully begotten to be by them (subject to the dividends aforementioned) possesst, enjoyed, and disposed of as they shall see meet forever in consideration of his respect for me, his services to me, and that pure and disinterested affection he has ever shown me from our first acquaintance, even when a proverb of reproach cast off by all my relations disinherited unjustly and left to sink or swim as afflictions and God's providence should appoint.

For comments on the tune "All' Ehr und Lob" see Hymn No. 238.

While Yet the Morn is Breaking 544

1. While yet the morn is breaking,
I thank my God once more,
Beneath whose care awaking,
I find the night is o'er.
I thank Him that He calls me
To life and health anew;
I know, whate'er befalls me,
His care will still be true.

Dank sei Gott in der Höhe
In dieser Morgenstund',
Durch den ich wied'r aufstehe
Vom Schlaf frisch und gesund!
Mich hatte fest gebunden
Mit Finsternis die Nacht,
Ich hab' sie überwunden
Durch Gott, der mich bewacht.

The Handbook to the Lutheran Hymnal

2. O Israel's Guardian, hear me,
 Watch over me this day;
 In all I do be near me.
  For others, too, I pray;
 To Thee I would commend them,
  Our Church, our youth, our land,
 Direct them and defend them
  When dangers are at hand.

3. O gracious Lord, direct us,
  Thy doctrine pure defend,
 From heresies protect us,
  And for Thy Word contend
 That we may praise Thee ever,
  O God, with one accord
 And say: The Lord, our Savior,
  Be evermore adored.

4. Oh, grant us peace and gladness,
  Give us our daily bread,
 Shield us from grief and sadness,
  On us Thy blessings shed.
 Grant that our whole behavior,
  In truth and righteousness,
 May praise Thee, Lord, our Savior,
  Whose holy name we bless.

5. And gently grant Thy blessing
  That we may do Thy will,
 No more Thy ways transgressing,
  Our proper task fulfil,
 With Peter's full assurance
  Let down our nets again.
 Success will crown endurance
  If faithful we remain.

6. Thou art the Vine, — oh, nourish
  The branches graft in Thee
 And let them grow and flourish,
  A fair and fruitful tree.
 Thy Spirit pour within us
  And let His gifts of grace
 To such good actions win us
  As best may show Thy praise.

Wied'rum tu' ich dich bitten,
 O Schutzherr Israel,
Du woll'st treulich behüten
 Den Tag mein'n Leib und Seel'.
All' christlich' Obrigkeiten,
 Unsre Schul' und Gemein'
In diesen bösen Zeiten
 Lass dir befohlen sein!

Erhalt uns durch dein' Güte
 Bei guter, reiner Lehr',
Vor Ketzerei behüte,
 Streit' für dein Wort und Ehr',
Dass wir dich allzusammen
 Loben in *einem* Geist,
Sprechen: Des Herren Namen
 Sei gross und hoch gepreist!

Dem Leibe gib daneben
 Nahrung und guten Fried',
Ein g'sund und mässig Leben,
 Dazu ein froh Gemüt,
Dass wir in allen Ständen
 Tugend und Ehrbarkeit
Lieben und Fleiss drauf wenden
 Als rechte Christenleut'.

Gib mildiglich dein'n Segen,
 Dass wir nach dein'm Geheiss
Wandeln auf guten Wegen,
 Tun unser Amt mit Fleiss,
Dass ein jeder sein Netze
 Auswerf' und auf dein Wort
Sein'n Trost mit Petro setze,
 So geht die Arbeit fort.

Wir sind die zarten Reben,
 Der Weinstock selbst bist du,
Daran wir wachs'n und leben
 Und bringen Frucht dazu.
Hilf, dass wir an dir bleiben
 Und wachsen immer mehr,
Dein guter Geist uns treibe
 Zu Werken deiner Ehr'!

This hymn, originally in seven stanzas, by Johannes Mühlmann was published in the *Geistliche Psalmen,* etc., Nürnberg, 1618, five years after his death. The translation contains Stanzas 1, 2, 5, and 6, slightly altered, by Catherine Winkworth, *Chorale Book for England,* 1863, and Stanzas 3 and 4, composite. The omitted Stanza 6 has been translated thus:

> With craftiness unceasing
> Strives Satan to restrain
> What in Thy sight is pleasing
> And for Thy Church is gain;
> Yet vain is his endeavor,
> For Thou, O Christ, our Lord,
> Dost rule all things forever
> By Thine almighty Word.

The tune "Geduld, die soll'n wir haben" was originally written for the German hymn beginning with that line and published in *Geistliche deutsche Lieder,* etc., Frankfurt, 1607. It has been most generally used, however, with Mühlmann's fine morning hymn.

545 The Morning Sun is Brightly Beaming

1. The morning sun is brightly beaming,
  And darkness deep has passed away;
 All earth with life and joy is teeming
  In beauty of a new-born day.
 O gracious Father, purest Light,
 Thou bringest day, dispellest night.

Aurinko armas vallolansa
 Taas uuden päivän tuonut on
Ja herättänyt loistollansa
 Maan kaiken uuteen elohon.
Sä, Luoja laupias, armossas
Yön pimeyden poistit taas.

MORNING

2. Grant unto me in tender mercies
    Thy Holy Spirit's saving light;
  The entrance of Thy Word disperses
    From out my mind its sinful night.
  My poor and erring heart instil
  With love to do Thy gracious will.

3. Dear Jesus, send Thy mercies o'er me
    Like morning dews to cleanse my soul.
  Oh, may Thy holy blood restore me,
    Wash out my sin and make me whole!
  Let me be strengthened by Thy might
  To walk in Thy eternal light.

Suo, Jeesus, Henkes valon koittaa
  Myös minullenkin armostas;
Suo mielen' pimeys mun voittaa
  Sun kirkkahalla sanallas!
Vaivaista mua armahda
Ja tahtos tielle johdata!

Sun armos, Jeesus, sielulleni
  Kuin aamukaste vuotakoon
Ja virvoituksen tunnolleni
  Sun veres pyhä tuottakoon,
Ett' uuden voiman siitä saan
Sun valossas vaeltamaan.

    The Finnish author of this hymn is unknown. The Rev. Gustaf A. Aho, who prepared the English translation in 1938, has written us that he has not been able to trace the authorship and is of the opinion that the hymn is the joint work of a hymnal committee of the last century. In the *Finnish Hymnal* it is noted as a "New Finnish Hymn, 1836."

    For comments on the tune "O dass ich tausend," by Kornelius H. Dretzel, see Hymn No. 243.

How Lovely Shines the Morning Star   546

1. How lovely shines the morning star!
  In twilight sky it gleams afar;
    The reign of night is ended.
  Creation stirs to hail the light
  Whose glories now with radiance bright
    Stream forth in beauty splendid.
  Both far And near
    All things living Thanks are giving,
    Praise outpouring,
  Earth and sky the Lord adoring.

2. Then haste, my soul, thy song to raise,
  Delay thou not thy Lord to praise,
    Bow down in adoration.
  For glory, Lord, to Thee belongs,
  Thy praise resounds in grateful songs,
    Thou Lord of all creation.
  Let all Recall
    Hymns of gladness Without sadness,
    For Thy favor
  And Thy mercy never waver.

3. Though evil spirits through the night
  With hellish craft and watchful spite
    Came round me without number,
  Yet Thou, O Jesus, with Thy power
  Wast near me in that threatening hour,
    Didst guard me in my slumber.
  Praise be To Thee,
    My Contender And Defender,
    I'll adore Thee
  While on earth I walk before Thee.

4. Pour down Thy grace in cheering streams
  And warm my heart with mercy's beams
    From heaven, Thy throne of beauty;
  Thy Spirit ever lead and guide
  That in my calling I abide
    And find my joy in duty.
  Send light And might
    That each measure, Plan and pleasure,
    Heavenward tending,
  E'er in Thee may find its ending.

5. Keep grief, if this may be, away;
  If not, Thy will be done, I pray,
    My choice to Thine resigning.
  Then, O my heart, cast cares aside,
  God through the cross His own hath tried;
    Bear loss without repining.
  Hope still Through ill;
    To God cleaving, Grace receiving,
    We shall wonder
  At God's goodness here and yonder.

Wie schön leucht't uns der Morgenstern
Vom Firmament des Himmels fern,
  Die Nacht ist nun vergangen!
All' Kreatur macht sich herfür,
Des edlen Lichtes Pracht und Zier
  Mit Freuden zu empfangen.
Was lebt, was schwebt
  Hoch in Lüften, tief in Klüften,
  Lässt zu Ehren
Seinem Gott ein Danklied hören.

Du, o mein Herz, dich auch aufricht,
Erheb dein' Stimm' und säume nicht,
  Dem Herrn dein Lob zu bringen!
Denn, Herr, du bist's, dem Lob gebührt
Und dem man billig musiziert,
  Dem man lässt innig klingen
Mit Fleiss Dank, Preis,
  Freudensaiten, dass von weitem
  Man kann hören
Dich, o meinen Heiland, ehren.

Ich lag in stolzer Sicherheit,
Sah nicht, mit was Gefährlichkeit
  Ich diese Nacht umgeben.
Des Teufels List und Büberei,
Die Höll', des Todes Tyrannei
  Stund mir nach Leib und Leben,
Dass ich schwerlich
  Wär' entkommen und entnommen
  Diesen Banden,
Wenn du mir nicht beigestanden.

Geuss deiner Gnade reichen Strahl
Auf mich vom hohen Himmelssaal,
  Mein Herz in mir verneue!
Dein guter Geist mich leit' und führ',
Dass ich nach meiner Amtsgebühr
  Zu tun mich innig freue!
Gib Rat und Tat,
  Lass mein Sinnen und Beginnen
  Stets sich wenden,
Seinen Lauf in dir zu enden!

Wend Unfall ab, kann's anders sein;
Wo nicht, so geb' ich mich darein,
  Ich will nicht widerstreben.
Doch komm, o süsser Morgentau,
Mein Herz erfrisch, dass ich dir trau'
  Und bleib' im Kreuz ergeben,
Bis ich endlich
  Nach dem Leiden zu den Freuden
  Werd' erhoben,
Da ich dich kann ewig loben.

MORNING

This hymn is a recast by Burkhard Wiesenmeyer of a hymn by Josua Stegmann, 1630, which was written in imitation of Philipp Nicolai's hymn beginning with the same line. (See Hymn No. 343.) Our cento is composed of Stanzas 1, 2, 3, 6, and 7 of Wiesenmeyer's hymn, which was first published, in eight stanzas, in Johann Crüger's *Newes vollkömmliches Gesangbuch*, 1640.

The translation is an altered form of Frances Elizabeth Cox's, in her *Hymns from the German*, 1864.

For comments on the tune "Wie schön leuchtet" see Hymn No. 23.

547   The Radiant Sun Shines in the Skies

1. The radiant sun shines in the skies,
With joy from sleep we now arise.
All praise to God, who through this night
Hath kept us from the devil's might.

2. Lord Jesus Christ, guide us this day;
Keep sin and shame far from our way.
Thy guardian angels to us send
And let them to our wants attend.

3. Direct our hearts to do Thy will
And for Thy Word true love instil
That we may do whate'er is right
And ever pleasing in Thy sight.

4. Crown all our labors with success,
Each one in his own calling bless.
May all we do or think or say
Exalt and praise Thee, Lord, this day!

Die helle Sonn' leucht't jetzt herfür,
Fröhlich vom Schlaf aufstehen wir.
Gott Lob, der uns heut' diese Nacht
Behüt't hat vor des Teufels Macht!

Herr Christ, den Tag uns auch behüt
Vor Sünd' und Schand' durch deine Güt',
Lass deine lieben Engelein
Unsre Hüter und Wächter sein,

Dass unser Herz in G'horsam leb',
Dein'm Wort und Will'n nicht widerstreb',
Dass wir dich stets vor Augen han
In allem, was wir heben an!

Lass unser Werk geraten wohl,
Was ein jeder ausrichten soll,
Dass unsre Arbeit, Müh' und Fleiss
Gereich' zu dein'm Lob, Ehr' und Preis!

Nikolaus Herman published this popular morning hymn in his *Sontags Euangelia vber das gantze Jar*, Wittenberg, 1560, with the heading "The Morning Blessing." The translation is composite.

The tune "Die helle Sonn' leucht't" is by Melchior Vulpius and appeared in his *Geistliches Gesangbuch*, Jena, 1609, where it was set to this hymn. Originally Herman coupled his text with the tune "Wo Gott zum Haus nicht gibt sein' Gunst," Joseph Klug's *Gesangbuch*, 1535. (See Hymn No. 131.)

548   My Inmost Heart Now Raises

1. My inmost heart now raises
In this fair morning hour
A song of thankful praises
To Thine almighty power,
O God, upon Thy throne.
To honor and adore Thee,
I bring my praise before Thee
Through Christ, Thine only Son.

2. For Thou from me hast warded
All perils of the night;
From every harm hast guarded
My soul till morning light.
To Thee I humbly cry,
O Savior, have compassion
And pardon my transgression;
Have mercy, Lord most high!

3. And shield me from all evil,
O gracious God, this day,
From sin, and from the devil,
From shame and from dismay,
From fire's consuming breath,
From water's devastation,
From need and consternation,
From evil sudden death.

Aus meines Herzens Grunde
Sag' ich dir Lob und Dank
In dieser Morgenstunde,
Dazu mein Leben lang,
O Gott, in deinem Thron,
Dir zu Preis, Lob und Ehren
Durch Christum, unsern Herren,
Dein'n eingebornen Sohn,

Dass du mich hast aus Gnaden
In der vergangnen Nacht
Vor G'fahr und allem Schaden
Behütet und bewacht.
Ich bitt' demütiglich,
Woll'st mir mein' Sünd' vergeben,
Womit in diesem Leben
Ich hab' erzürnet dich.

Du wollest auch behüten
Mich gnädig diesen Tag
Vor's Teufels List und Wüten,
Vor Sünden und vor Schmach,
Vor Feu'r und Wassersnot,
Vor Armut und vor Schanden,
Vor Ketten und vor Banden,
Vor bösem schnellem Tod.

MORNING

4. Let not Thine angel leave me
   While here on earth I stay
Lest Satan's arts deceive me
   And lead my soul astray.
Then keep Thine angel near
   At night and each new morrow
Lest soul and body sorrow
And faltering cost me dear.

5. God shall do my advising,
   Whose might with wisdom blends;
May He bless rest and rising,
   My efforts, means, and ends!
To God, forever blest,
   Will I with mine confide me,
   And willing let Him guide me
As seemeth to Him best.

6. Amen I say, not fearing
   That God rejects my prayer;
I doubt not He is hearing
   And granting me His care.
Thus I go on my way
   And do not look behind me,
   But ply the task assigned me;
God's help shall be my stay.

Dein'n Engel lass auch beiben
   Und weichen nicht von mir,
Den Satan zu vertreiben,
   Auf dass der bös' Feind hier
In diesem Jammertal
   Sein' Tück' an mir nicht übe,
   Leib und Seel' nicht betrübe
Und bring' mich nicht zu Fall.

Gott will ich lassen raten,
   Denn er all' Ding' vermag;
Er segne meine Taten,
   Mein Vornehmen und Sach',
Denn ich ihm heimgestellt
   Mein'n Leib, mein' Seel', mein Leben
   Und was er mir sonst geben.
Er mach's, wie's ihm gefällt.

Darauf so sprech' ich Amen
   Und zweifle nicht daran,
Gott wird es all's zusammen
   Sich wohlgefallen lan;
Und streck' nun aus mein' Hand,
   Greif' an das Werk mit Freuden,
   Dazu mich Gott bescheiden
In mein'm Beruf und Stand.

This hymn is by Georg Nigidius (Niege). According to Prof. P. Althaus it was first published in *Creutzbuechlein*, 1585—1587, at Herford, Germany. (See page 556.) A Low German version is found in the *Bremer Gesangbuch* of 1589. Then in 1592 it appeared in four different publications with text variations. The hymn has long been a favorite in many circles. Gustavus Adolphus loved it, and it was often sung at matins by his soldiers.

The translation is based on that of Catherine Winkworth, *Chorale Book for England*, 1863.

For comments on the tune "Aus meines Herzens Grunde" see Hymn No. 69.

God, Who Madest Earth and Heaven 549

1. God, who madest earth and heaven,
Father, Son, and Holy Ghost;
Who the day and night hast given,
Sun and moon and starry host;
Whose almighty hand sustains
Earth and all that it contains:

2. God, I thank Thee, in Thy keeping
Safely have I slumbered here;
Thou hast guarded me while sleeping
From all danger, pain, and fear;
And the cunning evil Foe
Hath not wrought my overthrow.

3. Let the night of my transgression
With night's darkness pass away.
Jesus, into Thy possession
I resign myself today;
In Thy wounds I find relief
From all sorrow, sin, and grief.

4. Help me as the morn is breaking,
In the spirit to arise,
So from careless sloth awaking,
That, when o'er the aged skies
Shall the Judgment Day appear,
I may see it without fear.

5. Lead me, and forsake me never,
Guide my wanderings by Thy Word;
As Thou hast been, be Thou ever
My Defense, my Refuge, Lord.
Never safe except with Thee,
Thou my faithful Guardian be.

Gott des Himmels und der Erden,
Vater, Sohn und Heil'ger Geist,
Der es Tag und Nacht lässt werden,
Sonn' und Mond uns scheinen heisst,
Dessen starke Hand die Welt
Und was drinnen ist, erhält,

Gott, ich danke dir von Herzen,
Dass du mich in dieser Nacht
Vor Gefahr, Angst, Not und Schmerzen
Hast behütet und bewacht,
Dass des bösen Feindes List
Mein nicht mächtig worden ist.

Lass die Nacht auch meiner Sünden
Jetzt mit dieser Nacht vergehn!
O Herr Jesu, lass mich finden
Deine Wunden offen stehn,
Da alleine Hilf' und Rat
Ist für meine Missetat!

Hilf, dass ich mit diesem Morgen
Geistlich auferstehen mag
Und für meine Seele sorgen,
Dass, wenn nun dein grosser Tag
Uns erscheint und dein Gericht,
Ich davor erschrecke nicht.

Führe mich, o Herr, und leite
Meinen Gang nach deinem Wort!
Sei und bleibe du auch heute
Mein Beschützer und mein Hort!
Nirgends als von dir allein
Kann ich recht bewahret sein.

6. O my God, I now commend me
   Wholly to Thy mighty hand;
   All the powers that Thou dost lend me
   Let me use at Thy command.
   Lord, my Shield, my Strength divine,
   Keep me with Thee, I am Thine.

Meinen Leib und meine Seele
   Samt den Sinnen und Verstand,
Grosser Gott, ich dir befehle
   Unter deine starke Hand.
Herr, mein Schild, mein' Ehr' und Ruhm,
Nimm mich auf, dein Eigentum!

Heinrich Albert, or Alberti, first published this hymn in Part V of his *Arien etliche theils geistlicher, theils weltlicher . . . Lieder,* Königsberg, 1644, in seven stanzas. The tune "Gott des Himmels" also called "Godesberg," is his own composition and was published with the hymn.

Koch quotes Dr. Cosack of Königsberg on the wide use of this fine morning hymn:

> For two hundred years it is hardly likely that a single day has greeted the earth that has not, here and there, in German lands, been met with Alberti's hymn. Hardly another morning hymn can be compared with it, as far as popularity and intrinsic value are concerned, if simplicity and devotion, purity of doctrine and adaptation to all the circumstances of life, are to decide.

The translation is an altered form of Catherine Winkworth's *Lyra Germanica,* first series, 1855. Miss Winkworth changed the meter of the hymn in her translation, thus making it somewhat cumbersome to sing, unaltered, to Albert's tune, to which the hymn is wedded. The omitted Stanza 7 Miss Winkworth translated thus:

> Let Thine angel guard my soul
>   From the Evil One's dark power,
> All his thousand wiles control,
>   Warning, guiding, me each hour,
> Till my final rest be come
> And Thine angel bear me home.

550   O Splendor of God's Glory Bright

1. O Splendor of God's glory bright,
Who bringest forth the light from Light;
O Light of light, light's Fountain-spring;
O Day, our days enlightening:

Splendor paternae gloriae,
De luce lucem proferens,
Lux lucis et Fons luminis,
Dies dierum inluminans;

2. Come, very Sun of truth and love,
Come in Thy radiance from above
And shed the Holy Spirit's ray
On all we think or do today.

Verusque sol inlabere
Micans nitore perpeti,
Iubarque sancti Spiritus
Infunde nostris sensibus.

3. Likewise to Thee our prayers ascend,
Father of glory without end,
Father of saving grace, for power
To conquer in temptation's hour.

Votis vocemus et Patrem,
Patrem perennis gloriae,
Patrem potentis gratiae,
Culpam releget lubricam,

4. Teach us to work with all our might;
Beat back the devil's threatening spite;
Turn all to good that seems most ill;
Help us our calling to fulfil.

Informet actus strenuos,
Dentem retundat invidi,
Casus fideli corpore:
Donet gerendi gratiam;

5. Direct and govern heart and mind,
With body chaste and disciplined;
Let faith her eager fires renew
And haste the false and love the true.

Mentem gubernet et regat
Casto fideli corpore:
Fides calore ferveat,
Fraudis venena nesciat.

6. On Christ, the true Bread, let us feed,
Let Him to us be drink indeed,
And let us taste with joyfulness
The Holy Spirit's plenteousness.

Christusque nobis sit cibus,
Potusque noster sit fides;
Laeti bibamus sobriam
Ebrietatem Spiritus.

7. Oh, joyful be the livelong day,
Our thoughts as pure as morning ray,
Our faith like noonday's glowing height,
Our souls undimmed by shades of night.

Laetus dies hic transeat;
Pudor sit ut diluculum,
Fides velut meridies;
Crepusculum mens nesciat.

EVENING

8. The dawn begins to speed her way,
Let the true Dawn Himself display,
The Son with God the Father One,
And God the Father in the Son.

Aurora cursus provehit;
Aurora totus prodeat,
In Patre totus Filius,
Et totus in Verbo Pater.

9. All praise to God the Father be,
All praise, eternal Son, to Thee,
Whom with the Spirit we adore
Forever and forevermore. Amen.

Deo Patri sit gloria
Eiusque soli Filio
Sancto simul cum Spiritu
Nunc et per omne saeculum. Amen.

This ancient Latin hymn is very likely from the pen of Ambrose of Milan. It is a fine morning hymn, but also a beautiful hymn to Christ as the Light of the world. It is a companion and sequel to the author's "Aeterne rerum Conditor."

The translation is as found in *Hymns Ancient and Modern,* 1904.

For comments on the tune "O Heilige Dreifaltigkeit" see Hymn No. 340.

Sun of My Soul, Thou Savior Dear 551

1. Sun of my soul, Thou Savior dear,
It is not night if Thou be near.
Oh, may no earth-born cloud arise
To hide Thee from Thy servant's eyes.

2. When the soft dews of kindly sleep
My wearied eyelids gently steep,
Be my last thought how sweet to rest
Forever on my Savior's breast.

3. Abide with me from morn till eve,
For without Thee I cannot live;
Abide with me when night is nigh,
For without Thee I dare not die.

4. If some poor wandering child of Thine
Has spurned today the voice divine,
Now, Lord, the gracious work begin;
Let him no more lie down in sin.

5. Watch by the sick; enrich the poor
With blessings from Thy boundless store;
Be every mourner's sleep tonight,
Like infant's slumbers, pure and light.

6. Come near and bless us when we wake,
Ere through the world our way we take,
Till in the ocean of Thy love
We lose ourselves in heaven above.

This cento is from John Keble's hymn "'Tis Gone, that Bright and Orbed Blaze," dated 1820. It was published in his *Christian Year,* 1827, in fourteen stanzas, and headed with the text Luke 24:29. Our cento includes Stanzas 3, 7, 8, 12, 13, and 14 of the original. The omitted stanzas are as follows, numbered according to the order as first published, so that the reader may reconstruct the hymn:

1. 'Tis gone, that bright and orbèd blaze,
Fast fading from our wistful gaze;
Yon mantling cloud has hid from sight
The last faint pulse of quivering light.

2. In darkness and in weariness
The traveler on his way must press;
No gleam to watch on tree or tower,
Whiling away the lonesome hour.

4. When round thy wondrous works below
My searching, rapturous glance I throw,
Tracing out wisdom, power, and love,
In earth or sky, in stream or grove; —

5. Or by the light Thy words disclose
Watch Time's full river as it flows,
Scanning Thy gracious providence,
Where not too deep for mortal sense: —

6. When with dear friends sweet talk I hold
And all the flowers of life unfold,
Let not my heart within me burn,
Except in all I Thee discern.

9. Thou Framer of the light and dark,
Steer through the tempest Thine own ark;
Amid the howling wintry sea
We are in port if we have Thee.

10. The rulers of this Christian land,
'Twixt Thee and us ordained to stand,
Guide Thou their course, O Lord, aright;
Let all do all as in Thy sight.

11. Oh, by Thine own sad burthen, borne
So meekly up the hill of scorn,
Teach Thou Thy priests their daily cross
To bear as Thine nor count it loss!

The tune "Hursley," also called "Pascal," "Paris," and "Stillorgan," is an adaptation of the tune "Grosser Gott." (See Hymn No. 250.) It is from the *Allgemeines Katholisches Gesangbuch,* Vienna, 1775, where it was set to the text "Grosser Gott, wir loben dich."

552 Abide with Me! Fast Falls the Eventide

1. Abide with me! Fast falls the eventide;
The darkness deepens; Lord, with me abide.
When other helpers fail and comforts flee,
Help of the helpless, oh, abide with me!

2. Swift to its close ebbs out life's little day;
Earth's joys grow dim, its glories pass away;
Change and decay in all around I see.
O Thou, who changest not, abide with me!

3. Not a brief glance I beg, a passing word,
But as Thou dwell'st with Thy disciples, Lord,
Familiar, condescending, patient, free.
Come not to sojourn, but abide with me.

4. Come not in terrors, as the King of kings,
But kind and good, with healing in Thy wings;
Tears for all woes, a heart for every plea.
Come, Friend of sinners, thus abide with me.

5. Thou on my head in early youth didst smile,
And though rebellious and perverse meanwhile,
Thou hast not left me, oft as I left Thee.
On to the close, O Lord, abide with me.

6. I need Thy presence every passing hour;
What but Thy grace can foil the Tempter's power?
Who like Thyself my guide and stay can be?
Through cloud and sunshine, oh, abide with me!

7. I fear no foe, with Thee at hand to bless;
Ills have no weight and tears no bitterness.
Where is death's sting? where, grave, thy victory?
I triumph still if Thou abide with me.

8. Hold Thou Thy cross before my closing eyes,
Shine through the gloom, and point me to the skies.
Heaven's morning breaks, and earth's vain shadows flee;
In life, in death, O Lord, abide with me!

Julian records the account of the origin of this hymn by Henry Francis Lyte as given by Lyte's daughter in the prefatory memoir to his *Remains*, London, 1850:

> The summer (1847) was passing away, and the month of September (that month in which he was once more to quit his native land) arrived, and each day seemed to have a special value as being one day nearer his departure. His family were surprised and almost alarmed at his announcing his intention of preaching once more to his people. His weakness and the possible danger attending the effort were urged to prevent it, but in vain. "It is better," as he used often playfully to say when in comparative health, "to wear out than to rust out." He felt that he should be enabled to fulfil his wish and feared not for the result. His expectation was well founded. He did preach and amid the breathless attention of his hearers gave them the sermon on the Holy Communion, which is inserted last in this volume. He afterwards assisted at the administration of the Holy Eucharist, and though necessarily much exhausted by the exertion and excitement of this effort, yet his friends had no reason to believe it had been hurtful to him. In the evening of the same day he placed in the hands of a near and dear relative the little hymn "Abide with Me," with an air of his own composing, adapted to the words.

However, the *Handbook to the Church Hymnary* gives a statement by T. H. Bindley, *Spectator*, 1925, which sets an earlier date of composition:

> In that year (1820) Lyte, as a young clergyman, was staying with the

Hores at Pole Hore near Wexford. He went to see an old friend, William Augustus Le Hunte, who lay dying and who kept repeating the phrase "Abide with me." After leaving the bedside, Lyte wrote the hymn and gave a copy of it to Sir Francis Le Hunte, William's brother, amongst whose papers it remained when they passed to his nephew, the Rev. Francis Le Hunte. No doubt, when Lyte felt his own end approaching, his mind reverted to the lines he had written so many years before, and then it was that they became first popularly known. These details were given to me some years ago by Sir George Ruthven Le Hunte, grandson of William Augustus, and I have recently had them confirmed by members of his family.

Whatever the actual date of its origin may be, this is clear from both accounts that the hymn was not meant to be an evening hymn, as John Ellerton in his *Notes and Illustrations of Church Hymns*, 1881, rightly says:

> It is sometimes classed among evening hymns, apparently on the ground of the first two lines, and their similarity in sound to two lines in Keble's "Sun of My Soul." This is a curious instance of the misapprehension of the true meaning of a hymn by those among whom it is popular; for a very little consideration will suffice to show that there is not throughout the hymn the slightest allusion to the close of the *natural* day; the words of St. Luke 24:29 are obviously used in a sense wholly metaphorical. It is far better adapted to be sung at funerals, as it was beside the grave of Professor Maurice; but it is almost too intense and personal for ordinary congregational use.

The hymn refers more to the evening of life than to the daily eventide. Our text, though not in every detail like the author's original, is the generally accepted one.

The tune "Eventide" was composed for this hymn by William H. Monk and included in *Hymns Ancient and Modern*, 1861. It was composed, according to his widow, "at a time of great sorrow."

Through the Day Thy Love hath Spared Us 553

1. Through the day Thy love hath spared us,
Now we lay us down to rest;
Through the silent watches guard us,
Let no foe our peace molest;
Jesus, Thou our Guardian be;
Sweet it is to trust in Thee.

2. Pilgrims here on earth and strangers,
Dwelling in the midst of foes;
Us and ours preserve from dangers;
In Thine arms may we repose
And, when life's sad day is past,
Rest with Thee in heaven at last.

This brief, but expressive evening hymn by Thomas Kelly was first published in the second edition of his *Hymns*, etc., 1806. It is widely used and has frequently been translated into other languages.

For comments on the tune "Komm, o komm, du Geist" see Hymn No. 226.

Now Rest Beneath Night's Shadow 554

1. Now rest beneath night's shadow
The woodland, field, and meadow,
The world in slumber lies;
But Thou, my heart, awake thee,
To prayer and song betake thee;
Let praise to thy Creator rise.

Nun ruhen alle Wälder,
Vieh, Menschen, Städt' und Felder,
Es schläft die ganze Welt;
Ihr aber, meine Sinnen,
Auf, auf, ihr sollt beginnen,
Was eurem Schöpfer wohlgefällt!

2. The radiant sun hath vanished,
His golden rays are banished
   By night, the foe of day;
But Christ, the Sun of gladness,
Dispelling all my sadness,
   Within my heart holds constant sway.

3. The rule of day is over
And shining jewels cover
   The heaven's boundless blue.
Thus I shall shine in heaven,
Where crowns of gold are given
   To all who faithful prove and true.

4. To rest my body hasteth,
Aside its garments casteth,
   Types of mortality;
These I put off and ponder
How Christ will give me yonder
   A robe of glorious majesty.

5. Lord Jesus, who dost love me,
Oh, spread Thy wings above me
   And shield me from alarm!
Though evil would assail me,
Thy mercy will not fail me:
   I rest in Thy protecting arm.

6. My loved ones, rest securely,
For God this night will surely
   From peril guard your heads.
Sweet slumbers may He send you
And bid His hosts attend you
   And through the night watch o'er your beds.

Wo bist du, Sonne, blieben?
Die Nacht hat dich vertrieben,
   Die Nacht, des Tages Feind.
Fahr hin! Ein' andre Sonne,
Mein Jesus, meine Wonne,
   Gar hell in meinem Herzen scheint.

Der Tag ist nun vergangen,
Die güldnen Sternlein prangen
   Am blauen Himmelssaal;
So, so werd' ich auch stehen,
Wenn mich wird heissen gehen
   Mein Gott aus diesem Jammertal.

Der Leib eilt nun zur Ruhe,
Legt ab das Kleid und Schuhe,
   Das Bild der Sterblichkeit;
Die zieh' ich aus, dagegen
Wird Christus mir anlegen
   Den Rock der Ehr' und Herrlichkeit.

Breit aus die Flügel beide,
O Jesu, meine Freude,
   Und nimm dein Küchlein ein!
Will Satan mich verschlingen,
So lass die Englein singen:
   Dies Kind soll unverletzet sein!

Auch euch, ihr meine Lieben,
Soll heute nicht betrüben
   Kein Unfall noch Gefahr.
Gott lass' euch ruhig schlafen,
Stell' euch die güldnen Waffen
   Ums Bett und seiner Helden Schar.

This cento is from Paul Gerhardt's famous evening hymn "Nun ruhen alle Wälder" and includes Stanzas 1 to 4, and 8 and 9, of the original. The hymn first appeared in Johann Crüger's *Praxis Pietatis Melica,* 1648. The hymn has long been popular in the German-speaking church because of its truly childlike popular spirit, its naive simplicity of expression, its loftiness of thought, and its depth of Christian experience. During the period of Rationalism in Germany it became the object of much shallow wit, especially Stanza 1, of which it was said, How can the dead woods rest, which never are awake, and how can the world lie in slumber? We know that when one half of the world retires to sleep the other half awakes from it! However, Richter, in his *Biogr. Lexikon,* 1804, already pointed out that, "if to represent the earth as tired and woods and trees as sleeping is not true poetry, then Vergil (Aeneid IV, Lines 522—528) was a blockhead, for what Paul Gerhardt writes is almost a verbatim translation of those lines."

Stanza 8 of the original, our Stanza 5, has long been used as a children's evening prayer, as Lauxmann (*Koch* VIII, 194) writes:

How many a Christian soul, children mostly, but also God's children in general, does this verse serve as their last evening prayer! It has often been the last prayer uttered on earth and in many districts of Germany is used at the close of the baptismal service to commend the dear little ones to the protection of their Lord Jesus.

The translation is composite. The omitted Stanzas 5, 6, and 7 read:

5. Head, hands, and feet reposing
Are glad the day is closing,
   That work came to an end;
Cheer up, my heart, with gladness!
For God from all earth's sadness
   And from sin's toil relief will send.

6. Ye weary limbs, now rest you,
For toil hath sore oppressed you,
   And quiet sleep ye crave;
A sleep shall once o'ertake you
From which no man can wake you,
   In your last narrow bed — the grave.

7. My heavy eyes are closing;
   When I lie deep reposing,
      Soul, body, where are ye?
   To helpless sleep I yield them,
   Oh, let Thy mercy shield them,
      Thou sleepless Eye, their Guardian be!

For comments on the tune "O Welt, ich muss dich lassen" see Hymn No. 126.

The Day Is Past and Over   555

1. The day is past and over;
      All thanks, O Lord, to Thee!
   I pray Thee now that sinless
      The hours of dark may be.
   O Jesus, keep me in Thy sight
   And save me through the coming night.

   Τὴν ἡμέραν διελθὼν
   Εὐχαριστῶ σοι, Κύριε,
   Τὴν ἑσπέραν αἰτοῦμαι
   Σὺν τῇ νυκτὶ ἀναμάρτητον
   Παράσχου μοι, Σωτήρ, καὶ σῶσόν με.

2. The joys of day are over;
      I lift my heart to Thee
   And ask Thee that offenseless
      The hours of dark may be.
   O Jesus, keep me in Thy sight
   And guard me through the coming night.

   Τὴν ἡμέραν παρελθὼν
   Δοξολογῶ σε, Δέσποτα,
   Τὴν ἑσπέραν αἰτοῦμαι
   Σὺν τῇ νυκτὶ ἀσκανδάλιστον
   Παράσχου μοι, Σωτήρ, καὶ σῶσόν με.

3. The toils of day are over;
      I raise the hymn to Thee
   And ask that free from peril
      The hours of dark may be.
   O Jesus, make their darkness light
   And guard me through the coming night.

   Τὴν ἡμέραν διαβὰς
   Ὑμνολογῶ σε, Ἅγιε,
   Τὴν ἑσπέραν αἰτοῦμαι
   Σὺν τῇ νυκτὶ ἀνεπιβούλον
   Παράσχου μοι, Σωτήρ, καὶ σῶσόν με.

4. Lord, that in death I sleep not,
      And lest my Foe should say,
   "I have prevailed against him,"
      Lighten mine eyes, I pray.
   O Jesus, keep me in Thy sight
   And guard me through the coming night.

   Φώτιστον τοὺς ὀφθαλμούς μου,
   Χριστέ ὁ θεός,
   Μήποτε ὑπνώσω εἰς θάνατον,
   Μήποτε εἴπῃ ὁ ἐχθρός μου,
   Ἴσχυσα πρὸς αὐτόν.

5. Be Thou my Soul's Preserver,
      O God, for Thou dost know
   How many are the perils
      Through which I have to go.
   Lover of men, oh, hear my call
   And guard and save me from them all!

   Ἀντιλήπτωρ τῆς ψυχῆς μου γενοῦ,
   ὁ θεός,
   Ὅτι μέσον διαβαίνω παγίδων πολλῶν·
   Ῥῦσαι με ἐξ αὐτῶν καὶ σῶσόν με,
   Ἀγαθέ, ὡς Φιλάνθρωπος.

The author of this fine old Greek hymn is unknown. The hymn is taken from portions of the Late Evening Service of the Greek Orthodox Church. It is probably from the 6th or 7th century. Neale gives the usually accepted history of it in his *Hymns of the Eastern Church*, 1862, thus:

> This little hymn, which, I believe, is not used in the public service of the Church, is a great favorite in the Greek Isles. Its peculiar style and evident antiquity may well lead to the belief that it is the work of St. Anatolius. It is to the scattered hamlets of Chios and Mitylene what Bishop Ken's Evening Hymn is to the villages of our own land; and its melody is singularly plaintive and soothing.

The translation is an altered form of that by Neale in his *Ecclesiastic and Theologian*, 1853, which he improved and republished in his *Hymns of the Eastern Church*, 1862.

The tune "St. Anatolius" is by Arthur H. Brown and was written on February 7, 1862, for this hymn.

EVENING

556   O God, Be with Us

1. O God, be with us, for the night is falling;
For Thy protection we to Thee are calling;
Beneath Thy shadow to our rest we yield us;
Thou, Lord, wilt shield us.

2. May evil fancies flee away before us;
Till morning cometh, watch, O Father, o'er us;
In soul and body Thou from harm defend us,
Thine angel send us.

3. While we are sleeping, keep us in Thy favor;
When we awaken, let us never waver
All day to serve Thee, Thy due praise pursuing
In all our doing.

4. Through Thy Beloved soothe the sick and weeping
And bid the captive lose his grief in sleeping;
Widows and orphans, we to Thee commend them,
Do Thou befriend them.

5. We have no refuge, none on earth to aid us,
Save Thee, O Father, who Thine own hast made us.
But Thy dear presence will not leave them lonely
Who seek Thee only.

6. Thy name be hallowed and Thy kingdom given,
Thy will among us done as 'tis in heaven;
Feed us, forgive us, from all ill deliver
Now and forever.

Die Nacht ist kommen,
Drin wir ruhen sollen;
Gott walt's, zum Frommen
Nach sein'm Wohlgefallen,
Dass wir uns legen
In sein'm G'leit und Segen,
Der Ruh' zu pflegen.

Treib, Herr, von uns fern
Die unreinen Geister,
Halt die Nachtwach' gern,
Sei selbst unser Schutzherr,
Beschirm Leib und Seel'
Unter Flügeln,
Send' uns dein' Engel!

Lass uns einschlafen
Mit guten Gedanken,
Fröhlich aufwachen
Und von dir nicht wanken;
Lass uns mit Züchten
Unser Tun und Dichten
Zu dein'm Preis richten!

Pfleg auch der Kranken
Durch deinen Geliebten,
Hilf den Gefangnen,
Tröste die Betrübten;
Pfleg auch der Kinder,
Sei selbst ihr Vormünder,
Des Feinds Neid hinder!

Denn wir kein' bessre
Zuflucht können haben
Als zu dir, o Herr,
In dem Himmel droben.
Du verlässt keinen,
Gibst acht auf die Deinen,
Die dich recht meinen.

Vater, dein Name
Werd' von uns gepreiset;
Dein Reich zukomme,
Dein Will' werd' beweiset;
Gib Brot, vergib Sünd',
Versuchung abwende,
Erlös uns! Amen.

This hymn, written in the Sapphic meter by Petrus Herbert, was first published in five stanzas in the hymnal of the Bohemian Brethren, *Kirchengeseng darinnen die Heubtartickel des Christlichen glaubens*, etc., 1566. The last stanza is a versification of the Lord's Prayer. Stanza 5, not by Herbert, was added when the hymn was published in Johann H. Schein's *Cantional*, Leipzig, 1627.

The translation is based on that by Catherine Winkworth in her *Chorale Book for England*, 1863.

The fine tune "Die Nacht ist kommen" is an adaptation of a melody by Petrus Nigidius, 1550, set to a Sapphic ode. It was coupled with this hymn in the hymnal of the Bohemian Brethren, 1566.

557   At Even, when the Sun did Set

1. At even, when the sun did set,
The sick, O Lord, around Thee lay;
Oh, in what divers pains they met!
Oh, with what joy they went away!

2. Once more 'tis eventide, and we,
Oppressed with various ills, draw near.
What if Thy form we cannot see,
We know and feel that Thou art here.

EVENING

3. O Savior Christ, our woes dispel;
For some are sick, and some are sad,
And some have never loved Thee well,
And some have lost the love they had;

4. And some are pressed with worldly care,
And some are tried with sinful doubt;
And some such grievous passions tear
That only Thou canst cast them out;

5. And some have found the world is vain,
Yet from the world they break not free;
And some have friends who give them pain,
Yet have not sought a friend in Thee;

6. And none, O Lord, have perfect rest,
For none are wholly free from sin;
And they who fain would serve Thee best
Are conscious most of wrong within.

7. O Savior Christ, Thou, too, art man;
Thou hast been troubled, tempted, tried.
Thy kind but searching glance can scan
The very wounds that shame would hide.

8. Thy touch has still its ancient power,
No word from Thee can fruitless fall;
Hear in this solemn evening hour
And in Thy mercy heal us all.
Amen.

This hymn was written by Henry Twells, in 1868, at the request of Henry W. Baker, for the *Appendix* to the original edition of *Hymns Ancient and Modern*, published the same year. Twells was at that time head master of a large grammar school — the Godolphin School, Hammersmith — and wrote the hymn one afternoon while the boys were writing an examination.

Twells's first line was "At even ere the sun was set." It was changed to the present form by the editors of *Hymns Ancient and Modern* to suit the Scripture-text on which it is based, Mark 1:32-34: "At even, when the sun did set, they brought unto Him," etc.

It has become one of the most popular evening hymns in the English-speaking Church and has been translated into Greek, Latin, French, Welsh, German, Irish, and other languages.

The tune "Angelus," also called "Whitsun Hymn," is based on a melody in Georg Joseph's *Heilige Seelenlust*, Breslau, 1657, set to Scheffler's hymn "Du meiner Seelen güldne Zier." The original tune is likely by Joseph himself.

All Praise to Thee, My God, This Night 558

1. All praise to Thee, my God, this night
For all the blessings of the light.
Keep me, oh, keep me, King of kings,
Beneath Thy own almighty wings.

2. Forgive me, Lord, for Thy dear Son,
The ill that I this day have done
That with the world, myself, and Thee,
I, ere I sleep, at peace may be.

3. Teach me to live that I may dread
The grave as little as my bed.
Teach me to die that so I may
Rise glorious at the awe-full Day.

4. Oh, may my soul on Thee repose,
And may sweet sleep mine eyelids close,
Sleep that shall me more vigorous make
To serve my God when I awake.

5. When in the night I sleepless lie,
My soul with heavenly thoughts supply;
Let no ill dreams disturb my rest,
No powers of darkness me molest.

6. Praise God, from whom all blessings flow;
Praise Him, all creatures here below;
Praise Him above, ye heavenly host;
Praise Father, Son, and Holy Ghost.
Amen.

This cento is from Thomas Ken's famous evening hymn, a companion piece of his equally famous morning hymn, "Awake, my Soul, and with the Sun." (See Hymn No. 536.) It appeared in print in the 1695 edition of Ken's *Manual*, and, in 1709, in an altered form. Our cento is composed of Stanzas 1, 2, 3, 4, 5, and 12. The omitted Stanzas 6 to 11, according to the version of 1709, are as follows:

6. Dull Sleep of Sense me to deprive,
I am but half my time alive;
Thy faithful Lovers, Lord, are griev'd,
To lye so long of Thee bereav'd.

7. But though Sleep o'er my frailty Reigns
Let it not hold me long in Chains;
And now and then let lose my Heart,
Till it an Hallelujah dart.

8. The faster Sleep the Senses binds,
The more unfetter'd are our Minds;
O may my Soul, from matter free,
Thy loveliness unclouded see!

9. O when shall I in endless Day,
Forever chase dark Sleep away,
And Hymns with the Supernal Choir
Incessant Sing and never tyre!

10. O may my Guardian while I sleep
Close to my Bed his Vigils keep,
His Love Angelical instill,
Stop all the Avenues of Ill.

11. May he Celestial Joys rehearse,
And thought to thought with me converse
Or in my stead all the Night long,
Sing to my God a Grateful Song.

The first tune, "Tallis' Canon," also called "Canon," "Evening Hymn," and "Brentwood," is the eighth of nine tunes by Thomas Tallis (Tallys) in Parker's *The Whole Psalter*, c. 1567, where it is set to Ps. 67. It seems to have been first printed with the words of Ken's evening hymn in *Harmonious Companion*, Smith and Prelleur, 1732.

Care should be taken in singing it to bring out the tenor part, which forms a perfect canon in the octave with the treble. For this reason the usual pauses at the ends of lines must be omitted.

The second tune, "Evening Hymn," is based on a melody by Charles F. Gounod, died 1893.

559   O Christ, Who Art the Light and Day

1. O Christ, who art the Light and Day,
Thou drivest night and gloom away;
O Light of light, whose Word doth show
The light of heaven to us below.

Christe, qui lux es et dies,
Noctis tenebras detegis,
Lucisque lumen crederis,
Lumen beatum praedicans.

2. All-holy Lord, in humble prayer,
We ask tonight Thy watchful care.
Oh, grant us calm repose in Thee,
A quiet night, from perils free.

Precamur, sancte Domine,
Defende nos in hac nocte;
Sit nobis in te requies,
Quietam noctem tribue.

3. Our sleep be pure from sinful stain;
Let not the Tempter vantage gain
Or our unguarded flesh surprise
And make us guilty in Thine eyes.

Ne gravis somnus inruat,
Nec hostis nos subripiat,
Nec caro illi consentiens
Nos tibi reos statuat.

4. Asleep though wearied eyes may be,
Still keep the heart awake to Thee;
Let Thy right hand outstretched above
Guard those who serve the Lord they love.

Oculi somnum capiant,
Cor ad te semper vigilet,
Dextera tua protegat
Famulos, qui te diligunt.

5. Behold, O God, our Shield, and quell
The crafts and subtleties of hell;
Direct Thy servants in all good,
Whom Thou hast purchased with Thy blood.

Defensor noster aspice,
Insidiantem reprime;
Guberna tuos famulos,
Quos sanguine mercatus es.

6. O Lord, remember us who bear
The burden of the flesh we wear;
Thou who dost e'er our souls defend,
Be with us even to the end.

Memento nostri, Domine,
In isto gravi corpore;
Qui es defensor animae,
Adesto nobis, Domine.

7. All praise to God the Father be,
All praise, eternal Son, to Thee,
Whom with the Spirit we adore
Forever and forevermore. Amen.

Deo Patri sit gloria
Eiusque soli Filio,
Sancto simul cum Spiritu
Nunc et per omne saeculum. Amen.

This ancient hymn dates from the sixth century or earlier. The author is unknown. It has long been a favorite and has been translated into various languages. The oldest German form appeared in the *Erfurt Enchiridion*, 1526, "Christe, der du bist Tag und Licht," (supposedly by Luther's pupil and friend Erasmus Alberus, which was translated) by Miles Coverdale, in his *Goostly Psalmes*, 1539, "O Christ, Thou art the lyght and daye." The translation is based on that by William J. Copeland in his *Hymns for the Week*, 1848.

The tune "Christe, der du bist Tag und Licht" is from a Latin melody of the seventh century.

EVENING

Gracious God, Again is Ended 560

1. Gracious God, again is ended
Of my life another day.
Show me where I have offended,
Where I faltered on the way;
Let me by Thy grace divine
View this sinful life of mine.
Calmly, as the day now closes,
In Thy love my soul reposes.

2. Faithful Father, thus before Thee
Now I come with fervent plea;
Though unworthy, I implore Thee,
Be Thou merciful to me;
Let Thy face upon me shine
As the fleeting hours decline.
Help me do Thy will and pleasure
Day by day in fuller measure.

3. Loving Savior, I will solely
Look to Thee for peaceful sleep;
Sanctify my spirit wholly,
Angels send their watch to keep.
Bid all threatening foes be gone,
Guard my home and all mine own;
Drive away all gloom and sorrow,
Bless me with a glad tomorrow.

4. Holy Ghost, Thine eyes forever
Watch though darkness hide the view;
Waking always, failing never,
They their loving task pursue.
Gentle Shepherd, as Thy sheep
Now repose in trustful sleep,
So within Thine arms enfold me,
In Thy care securely hold me.

5. Gracious God, let me awaken
To another blessed day
That I may, with faith unshaken,
Serve Thee as my Strength and Stay.
Should instead death's summons come,
Take me to Thy heavenly home.
To Thy care I thus commend me;
Lord, in life and death attend me.

This hymn is a recast in English by John T. Mueller of the German hymn "Herr, es ist von meinem Leben," by Caspar Neumann in seven stanzas, as follows:

1. Herr, es ist von meinem Leben
Wiederum ein Tag dahin!
Lehre mich nun Achtung geben,
Ob ich fromm gewesen bin,
Zeige mir's auch selber an,
So ich was nicht recht getan,
Und hilf jetzt in allen Sachen
Guten Feierabend machen!

2. Freilich wirst du manches finden,
Was dir nicht gefallen hat,
Denn ich bin noch voller Sünden
In Gedanken, Wort und Tat,
Und vom Morgen bis jetzund
Pfleget Herze, Hand und Mund
So geschwind und oft zu fehlen,
Dass ich's selber nicht kann zählen.

3. Aber, o du Gott der Gnaden,
Habe noch einmal Geduld!
Ich bin freilich schwer beladen,
Doch vergib mir alle Schuld!
Deine grosse Vatertreu'
Werde diesen Abend neu,
So will ich noch deinen Willen
Künftig mehr als heut' erfüllen.

4. Heilige mir das Gemüte,
Dass der Schlaf nicht sündlich sei!
Decke mich mit deiner Güte,
Auch dein Engel steh' mir bei!
Lösche Feu'r und Lichter aus
Und bewahre sonst das Haus,
Dass ich morgen mit den Meinen
Nicht im Unglück müsse weinen!

5. Steure den gottlosen Leuten,
Die im Finstern Böses tun!
Sollte man gleich was bereiten,
Uns zu schaden, wenn wir ruhn,
So zerstöre du den Rat
Und verhindere die Tat,
Wend auch alle andern Schrecken,
Die der Satan kann erwecken!

6. Herr, dein Auge geht nicht unter,
Wenn es bei uns Abend wird,
Denn du bleibest ewig munter
Und bist wie ein guter Hirt,
Der auch in der finstern Nacht
Über seine Herde wacht.
Darum hilf uns, deinen Schafen,
Dass wir alle sicher schlafen!

7. Lass mich dann gesund erwachen,
Wenn es rechte Zeit wird sein,
Dass ich ferner meine Sachen
Richte dir zu Ehren ein;
Oder hast du, lieber Gott,
Heint bestimmet meinen Tod,
So befehl' ich dir am Ende
Leib und Seel' in deine Hände.

It first appeared in Neumann's Silesian *Kirchen-Gesangbuch*, Breslau and Liegnitz, 1711.

The English text was prepared for *The Lutheran Hymnal* in 1938.

For comments on the tune "Werde munter" see Hymn No. 207.

561   Now that the Day hath Reached Its Close

1. Now that the day has reached its close,
   The sun doth shine no more,
   In sleep the toil-worn repose
   And all who wept before.

2. But Thou, my God, dost never sleep,
   For Thou Thyself art Light;
   No darkness, howsoever deep,
   Can dim Thy perfect sight.

3. Therefore, O Lord, remember me
   Throughout the gloom of night.
   Protect Thou me most graciously
   And shield me with Thy might.

4. Keep Satan's fury far from me
   By many an angel arm;
   Then shall I be from worry free
   And safe from every harm.

5. I know the evil I have done
   Doth cry aloud to Thee;
   But yet in mercy Thy dear Son
   Hath full atoned for me.

6. In Him accepted I shall be
   When suppliant at Thy feet.
   He is my Surety and my Plea
   Before Thy judgment-seat.

7. And so I close my weary eyes,
   Sweet peace within my breast.
   Why toss about in fears or sighs?
   God watches while I rest.

8. Should this night prove the last for me
   In this sad vale of cares,
   Then lead me, Lord, to dwell with Thee
   And all Thy chosen heirs.

9. And thus I live and die to Thee,
   Strong Lord of hosts indeed.
   In life, in death, deliver me
   From every fear and need.

Nun sich der Tag geendet hat
Und keine Sonn' mehr scheint,
Schläft alles, was sich abgematt't
Und was zuvor geweint.

Nur du, mein Gott, hast keine Rast,
Du schläfst noch schlummerst nicht;
Die Finsternis ist dir verhasst,
Weil du bist selbst das Licht.

Gedenke, Herr, doch auch an mich
In dieser finstern Nacht
Und schenke mir genädiglich
Den Schirm von deiner Wacht!

Wend ab des Satans Wüterei
Durch deiner Engel Schar,
So bin ich aller Sorgen frei
Und bringt mir nichts Gefahr.

Zwar fühl' ich wohl der Sünden Schuld,
Die mich bei dir klagt an;
Doch aber deines Sohnes Huld
Hat g'nug für mich getan.

Den setz' ich dir zum Bürgen ein,
Wenn ich muss vors Gericht;
Ich kann ja nicht verloren sein
In solcher Zuversicht.

Darauf tu' ich mein' Augen zu
und schlafe fröhlich ein.
Mein Gott wacht jetzt in meiner Ruh',
Wer wollte traurig sein?

Soll diese Nacht die letzte sein
In diesem Jammertal,
So führ mich, Herr, in Himmel ein
Zur auserwählten Zahl.

Und also leb' und sterb' ich dir,
Du starker Zebaoth;
Im Tod und Leben hilf du mir
Aus aller Angst und Not!

According to the statement of his brother, Johann Friedrich Hertzog (Herzog) wrote this hymn in 1670 while he was a student at the University of Wittenberg, by recasting a popular song of Adam Krieger's. This secular song with a tune of his own composition had been written by Krieger and published a year after his death in *Neue Arien*, etc., Dresden, 1667. The first stanza of this song was taken over unchanged by Hertzog. The second stanza reads in the original:

  Nur ich, ich gehe hin und her   Ich finde nichts als ohngefähr
  Und suche, was mich quält;   Das, was mich gar entseelt.

Hertzog's hymn was in nine stanzas and was first published in *Andächtiger Singender Christen-Mund* by Andreas Luppius, 1692. A tenth stanza, by an unknown author, was added a year later when the hymn was included in the Leipzig *Gesangbuch*, 1693. Our text omits Hertzog's eighth stanza, which reads in translation:

  Away, vain, idle thoughts, depart!   For now I build within my heart
  Roam not, my soul, abroad!   A temple to my God.

This was Dr. C. F. W. Walther's favorite hymn and was uttered as a dying prayer in his last hours.

The tune "Nun sich der Tag geendet hat" by Krieger has become wedded to this text.

The translation is composite.

EVENING

Round Me Falls the Night 562

1. Round me falls the night;
Savior, be my Light.
Through the hours in darkness shrouded
Let me see Thy face unclouded;
Let Thy glory shine
In this heart of mine.

2. Earthly work is done,
Earthly sounds are none.
Rest in sleep and silence seeking,
Let me hear Thee softly speaking;
In my spirit's ear
Whisper, "I am near."

3. Blessed, heavenly Light,
Shining through earth's night;
Voice that oft of love hast told me;
Arms so strong to clasp and hold me,
Thou Thy watch wilt keep,
Savior, o'er my sleep.

This fine hymn by William Romanis was first published in the *Public School Hymn Book*, 1903. It has been taken up by hymn-book compilers since the editors of the *English Hymnal*, 1906, set the example. In that hymnal the text was coupled with the tune "Seelenbräutigam" or "Arnstadt." This has been a fortunate union, as the simplicity of the tune well matches the simple directness of the words. The tune has been ascribed to Adam Drese of Arnstadt by the hymnologists Zahn and Wetzel. It appeared in the Darmstadt Gesangbuch, 1698, where it was set to Drese's hymn "Seelenbräutigam, Jesu, Gottes Lamm."

The Sun's Last Beam of Light is Gone 563

1. The sun's last beam of light is gone,
The shades of night come swiftly on;
O Christ, our Light, upon us shine
Lest we to sin's dark ways incline.

2. We thank Thee that throughout the day
Thine angels kept all harm away.
Thy grace from care and vexing fear
Hath led us on in safety here.

3. Lord, if we angered Thee today,
Remember not our sins, we pray,
But let Thy mercy o'er them sweep,
And give us calm and restful sleep.

4. Let angels guard our sleeping hours
And drive away all evil powers;
Our soul and body, while we sleep,
In safety, gracious Father, keep.

Hinunter ist der Sonnenschein,
Die finstre Nacht bricht stark herein;
Leucht uns, Herr Christ, du wahres Licht,
Lass uns im Finstern tappen nicht!

Dir sei Dank, dass du uns den Tag
Vor Schaden, G'fahr und mancher Plag'
Durch deine Engel hast behüt't
Aus Gnad' und väterlicher Güt'.

Womit wir hab'n erzürnet dich,
Dasselb' verzeih uns gnädiglich
Und rechn' es unsrer Seel' nicht zu,
Lass uns schlafen mit Fried' und Ruh'!

Durch dein' Engel die Wach' bestell,
Dass uns der böse Feind nicht fäll';
Vor Schrecken, G'spenst und Feuersnot
Behüt uns heint, o lieber Gott!

Nikolaus Herman first published this hymn in his *Sontags Euangelia vber das gantze Jar,* Wittenberg, 1560, entitled, "Der abend segen, *In tono eodem.*" The foregoing hymn in the collection is his morning hymn. (See Hymn No. 547.) It is likely that some of the lines were suggested by the hymn "Christe, qui lux es et dies." (See Hymn No. 559.)

The composite translation is based on that of Catherine Winkworth, *Lyra Germanica,* first series, 1855.

For comments on the tune "Wo Gott zum Haus" see Hymn No. 131.

O Trinity, Most Blessed Light 564

1. O Trinity, most blessed Light,
O Unity of sovereign might,
As now the fiery sun departs,
Shed Thou Thy beams within our hearts.

O Lux beata, Trinitas
Et principalis Unitas,
Iam sol recedit igneus,
Infunde lumen cordibus.

EVENING

2. To Thee our morning song of praise,
To Thee our evening prayer we raise;
Thee may our glory evermore
In lowly reverence adore.

Te mane laudum carmine,
Te deprecamus vespere;
Te nostra supplex gloria
Per cuncta laudet saecula.

3. All praise to God the Father be,
All praise, eternal Son, to Thee,
Whom with the Spirit we adore
Forever and forevermore.

Deo Patri sit gloria
Eiusque soli Filio
Sancto simul cum Spiritu
Nunc et per omne saeculum.

Although this hymn has been usually ascribed to St. Ambrose, definite historical proof of his authorship is lacking. The translation is an altered form of that by John M. Neale in *The Hymnal Noted*, 1852. Martin Luther's translation of the hymn beginning "Der du bist drei in Einigkeit" has frequently been used in English Lutheran hymn-books, in the translation of Richard Massie, but this version, neither in German nor in English, reproduces as well as the present version the allusion to Ps. 16:9 which the original Latin text has in Stanza 2.

For comments on the tune "O Heilige Dreifaltigkeit" see Hymn No. 340.

565   Savior, Breathe an Evening Blessing

1. Savior, breathe an evening blessing
   Ere repose our spirits seal.
Sin and want we come confessing;
   Thou canst save, and Thou canst heal.

2. Though destruction walk around us,
   Though the arrows past us fly,
Angel guards from Thee surround us;
   We are safe if Thou art nigh.

3. Though the night be dark and dreary,
   Darkness cannot hide from Thee;
Thou art He who, never weary,
   Watcheth where Thy people be.

4. Should swift death this night o'ertake us
   And our couch become our tomb,
May the morn in heaven awake us,
   Clad in light and deathless bloom.

James Edmeston first published this hymn in his *Sacred Lyrics*, 1820, with the note: "At night their short evening hymn, 'Jesu Mahaxaroo' — 'Jesus, forgive us,' stole through the camp. — Salte's *Travels in Abyssinia*." It was first adopted for congregational use by Edward Bickersteth in his *Christian Psalmody*, 1833. It has since taken rank with the best evening hymns of the English language. Our text is Edmeston's unaltered. Some hymnals have dropped the fourth stanza, concerning sudden death, and replaced it with the following stanza by Godfrey Thring, 1882, in which the same thought is expressed in a milder form:

> Be Thou nigh should death o'ertake us;
>   Jesus, then our Refuge be
> And in Paradise awake us,
>   There to rest in peace with Thee.

Others have substituted for the same stanza the eight-line stanza by Edward H. Bickersteth, 1876:

> Father, to Thy holy keeping
>   Humbly we ourselves resign;
> Savior, who hast slept Thy sleeping,
>   Make our slumbers pure as Thine;
> Blessed Spirit, brooding o'er us,
>   Chase the darkness of our night
> Till the perfect day before us
>   Breaks in everlasting light.

During the Boxer uprising in China the use of this hymn by a group of beleaguered missionaries outside of Shanghai is described by one of them:

> Separated from home and friends, facing death in a far-off land, and full of tenderest feelings, we lifted our hearts in song:

HARVEST AND THANKSGIVING

> Though destruction walk around us,
> Though the arrows past us fly;
> Angel guards from Thee surround us;
> We are safe if Thou art nigh.

Out of the storm each soul, renewing its strength, mounted up with wings as eagles and found peace in the secret of His presence. Our Savior breathed, in very deed, "an evening blessing," the fragrance of which remains even unto this day. The last verse of the hymn, "Should swift death this night o'ertake us," was omitted. It seemed too probable that it might. We wanted only to think of the safe-keeping, and such, thank God, it proved to be.

For comments on the first tune, "Ringe recht," see Hymn No. 155.

The second tune, "Evening Prayer," is by George C. Stebbins and is dated 1878.

Christ, by Heavenly Hosts Adored 566

1. Christ, by heavenly hosts adored,
Gracious, mighty, sovereign Lord,
God of nations, King of kings,
Head of all created things,
By the Church with joy confest,
God o'er all forever blest, —
Pleading at Thy throne we stand,
Save Thy people, bless our land.

2. On our fields of grass and grain
Send, O Lord, the kindly rain;
O'er our wide and goodly land
Crown the labors of each hand.
Let Thy kind protection be
O'er our commerce on the sea.
Open, Lord, Thy bounteous hand;
Bless Thy people, bless our land.

3. Let our rulers ever be
Men that love and honor Thee;
Let the powers by Thee ordained
Be in righteousness maintained.
In the people's hearts increase
Love of piety and peace.
Thus united, we shall stand
One wide, free, and happy land.

The hymn from which this cento is taken is "God Most Mighty, Sovereign Lord," by Henry Harbaugh, and was first published in his *Poems*, 1860, in eight stanzas, entitled "A National Litany." It has usually been used in an abbreviated form in the hymn-books. Another good specimen of Harbaugh's work is his translation of Johann Peter Lange's striking Easter hymn "Der Herr ist auferstanden," which reads:

1. The Lord of life is risen!
 Sing, Easter heralds, sing!
He burst His rocky prison;
 Wide let the triumph ring!
Tell how the graves are quaking,
The saints their fetters breaking:
 Sing, heralds! Jesus lives!

2. In death no longer lying,
 He rose, the Prince, today;
Life of the dead and dying,
 He triumphed o'er decay.
The Lord of Life is risen;
In ruin lies death's prison,
 Its keeper bound in chains.

3. We hear in Thy blest greeting
 Salvation's work is done!
We worship Thee, repeating,
 Life for the dead is won!
O Head of all believing,
O Joy of all the grieving,
 Unite us, Lord, to Thee!

4. Here at thy tomb, O Jesus,
 How sweet the morning's breath!
We hear in all the breezes,
 Where is thy sting, O Death?
Dark hell flies in commotion,
While far o'er earth and ocean
 Loud hallelujahs ring.

5. Oh, publish this salvation,
 Ye heralds, through the earth!
To every buried nation
 Proclaim the day of birth,
Till, rising from their slumbers,
The countless heathen numbers
 Shall hail the risen Light.

6. Hail, hail, our Jesus risen!
 Sing, ransomed brethren, sing!
Through death's dark, gloomy prison
 Let Easter chorals ring.
Haste, haste, ye captive legions,
Come forth from sin's dark regions;
 In Jesus' kingdom live.

For comments on the tune "St. George" see Hymn No. 71.

HARVEST AND THANKSGIVING

567   O Lord, Whose Bounteous Hand Again

1. O Lord, whose bounteous hand again
   Hath poured Thy gifts in plenty down,
Who all creation dost sustain
   And all the earth with goodness crown,
Lord of the harvest, here we own
Our joy to be Thy gift alone.

2. Oh, may we ne'er with thankless heart
   Forget from whom our blessings flow!
Still, Lord, Thy heavenly grace impart;
   Still teach us what to Thee we owe.
Lord, may our lives with fruit divine
Return Thy care and prove us Thine.

3. Lord, grant that we who sow to Thee
   With joy in endless life may reap.
Of every heart the Guardian be;
   By day and night Thy servants keep
That all to Thee may joy afford
On Thy great harvest-day, O Lord.

This hymn was included in the *Evangelical Lutheran Hymn-Book*, 1912, and was taken over into *The Lutheran Hymnal* by the Committee. We have been unable to trace its authorship or the time of its origin.

For comments on the tune "All' Ehr' und Lob" see Hymn No. 238.

568   We Praise Thee, O God, Our Redeemer, Creator

1. We praise Thee, O God, our Redeemer, Creator,
   In grateful devotion our tribute we bring;
We lay it before Thee, We kneel and adore Thee,
   We bless Thy holy name, glad praises we sing.

2. We worship Thee, God of our fathers, we bless Thee;
   Through life's storm and tempest our Guide hast Thou been;
When perils o'ertake us, Escape Thou wilt make us,
   And with Thy help, O Lord, our battles we win.

3. With voices united our praises we offer,
   To Thee, great Jehovah, glad anthems we raise.
Thy strong arm will guide us, Our God is beside us,
   To Thee, our great Redeemer, fore'er be praise.

This hymn, almost carol-like in character, is the prayer of thanksgiving sung by the Dutch to celebrate their final victory, with the help of England, over the Spanish oppressor, in the last quarter of the sixteenth century. We have been able to obtain only the following two stanzas of the original:

1. Wilt heden nu treden voor God den Heere,
Hem boven al loven van herte zeer.
En maken groot, Zijns lieven namens eere,
Die daar nu onzen vijand slaat ter neer.

2. Bidt, waket en maket dat g'in bekoring
En't kwade met schade toch niet — en valt.
Uw vroomheid brengt den vijand tot verstoring,
Al waar zijn rijk nog eens zoo sterk bewald.

The text with its traditional tune was first published by Adrian Valerius in his *Nederlandtsch Gedenckclanck*, Haarlem, 1626. The hymn, however, has become popular in our country through the German use of it, which began when Edward Kremser introduced it to the Germans with his male choir in 1877. This is the reason why the tune is generally called "Kremser." There are several German versions of the text, the one by Karl Budde, 1897, being the most widely known, beginning:

Wir treten zum Beten vor Gott den Herren
Ihn droben zu loben mit Herz und Mund.
So rühmet froh sein's lieben Namens Ehren,
Der jetzo unsern Feind warf auf den Grund.

The English text by Julia Bulkley Cady Cory is a very free rendition of the hymn, eliminating the references to war and making it rather a hymn of general thanksgiving. The translation was written in 1904.

HARVEST AND THANKSGIVING

O Lord, I Sing with Lips and Heart   569

1. O Lord, I sing with lips and heart,
 Joy of my soul, to Thee;
 To earth Thy knowledge I impart
 As it is known to me.

2. Thou art the Fount of grace, I know,
 And Spring so full and free
 Whence saving health and goodness flow
 Each day so bounteously.

3. For what have all that live and move
 Through this wide world below
 That does not from Thy bounteous love,
 O heavenly Father, flow?

4. Who built the lofty firmament?
 Who spread the expanse of blue?
 By whom are to our pastures sent
 Refreshing rain and dew?

5. Who warmeth us in cold and frost?
 Who shields us from the wind?
 Who orders it that fruit and grain
 We in their season find?

6. Who is it life and health bestows?
 Who keeps us with His hand
 In golden peace, wards off war's woes
 From our dear native land?

7. O Lord, of this and all our store
 Thou art the Author blest;
 Thou keepest watch before our door
 While we securely rest.

8. Thou feedest us from year to year
 And constant dost abide;
 With ready help in time of fear
 Thou standest at our side.

9. Our deepest need dost Thou supply
 And all that lasts for aye;
 Thou leadest to our home on high,
 When hence we pass away.

Ich singe dir mit Herz und Mund,
 Herr, meines Herzens Lust,
Ich sing' und mach' auf Erden kund,
 Was mir von dir bewusst!

Ich weiss, dass du der Brunn der Gnad'
 Und ew'ge Quelle sei'st,
Daraus uns allen früh und spat
 Viel Heil und Gutes fleusst.

Was sind wir doch, was haben wir
 Auf dieser ganzen Erd',
Das uns, o Vater, nicht von dir
 Allein gegeben werd'?

Wer hat das schöne Himmelszelt
 Hoch über uns gesetzt?
Wer ist es, der uns unser Feld
 Mit Tau und Regen netzt?

Wer wärmet uns in Kält' und Frost?
 Wer schützt uns vor dem Wind?
Wer macht es, dass man Öl und Most
 Zu seinen Zeiten find't?

Wer gibt uns Leben und Geblüt?
 Wer hält mit seiner Hand
Den güldnen, edlen, werten Fried'
 In unserm Vaterland?

Ach Herr, mein Gott, das kommt von dir,
 Und du musst alles tun.
Du hältst die Wach' an unsrer Tür
 Und lässt uns sicher ruhn.

Du nährest uns von Jahr zu Jahr,
 Bleibst immer fromm und treu
Und stehst uns, wenn wir in Gefahr
 Geraten, treulich bei.

Du füllst des Lebens Mangel aus
 Mit dem, was ewig steht,
Und führst uns in des Himmels Haus,
 Wenn uns die Erd' entgeht.

This cento is from Paul Gerhardt's great thanksgiving hymn of eighteen stanzas, half of which we have used as a hymn for cross and comfort.

This hymn, so simple in language, yet so profound in its truths, one of the author's earliest hymns, is a typical example of the poet's method. From a contemplation of what God does he leads us to think on what He is. Nelle rightly says: "Gerhardt has experienced the father love of God in Christ, the Holy Spirit has transfigured Jesus in his heart and testified to him that we are the children of God. That is the center of his life. In this center he stands firm. And because he cannot be moved from this position, he can let his eye sweep freely, without fear of limitation, over all areas of divine and human life."

It is because German hymnody has contributed so many intimate hymns of this type to the world that we can well say with Prof. A. H. Palmer:

> Das deutsche Lied ist einzig,
> Ein Schatz für Geist und Herz,
> Gehoben aus den Tiefen,
> Wo Freude wohnt und Schmerz.
> Kein andres Volk auf Erden
> Genoss des Schicksals Gunst,
> Solch einen Schatz zu sammeln,
> Reich an Natur und Kunst.

HARVEST AND THANKSGIVING

For further comments on the text see Hymn No. 535.

The translation is an altered form of that by John Kelly in his *Paul Gerhardt's Spiritual Songs*, 1867.

For comments on the tune "Ich singe dir" see Hymn No. 29.

570   Praise, Oh, Praise, Our God and King

1. Praise, oh, praise, our God and King,
Hymns of adoration sing;
For His mercies still endure,
Ever faithful, ever sure.

2. Praise Him that He made the sun
Day by day his course to run;
For His mercies still endure,
Ever faithful, ever sure.

3. And the silver moon by night,
Shining with her gentle light;
For His mercies still endure,
Ever faithful, ever sure.

4. Praise Him that He gave the rain
To mature the swelling grain;
For His mercies still endure,
Ever faithful, ever sure.

5. And hath bid the fruitful field
Crops of precious increase yield;
For His mercies still endure,
Ever faithful, ever sure.

6. Praise Him for our harvest store,
He hath filled the garner floor;
For His mercies still endure,
Ever faithful, ever sure.

7. And for richer food than this,
Pledge of everlasting bliss;
For His mercies still endure,
Ever faithful, ever sure.

8. Glory to our bounteous King,
Glory let creation sing;
Glory to the Father, Son,
And the Spirit, Three in One!

According to his biographers, John Milton, in 1623, when he was but fifteen years old, wrote this paraphrase of Ps. 136:

1. Let us, with a gladsome mind,
Praise the Lord, for He is kind;
For His mercies aye endure,
Ever faithful, ever sure.

2. Let us blaze His name abroad,
For of gods He is the God;
For His mercies aye endure,
Ever faithful, ever sure.

3. He with all-commanding might
Filled the new-made world with light;
For His mercies aye endure,
Ever faithful, ever sure.

4. He the golden-tressèd sun
Caused all day his course to run;
For His mercies aye endure,
Ever faithful, ever sure.

5. The hornèd moon to shine by night,
Mid her spangled sisters bright;
For His mercies aye endure,
Ever faithful, ever sure.

6. All things living He doth feed,
His full hand supplies their need;
For His mercies aye endure,
Ever faithful, ever sure.

7. Let us, with a gladsome mind,
Praise the Lord, for He is kind;
For His mercies aye endure,
Ever faithful, ever sure.

The hymn, by Henry W. Baker, is based on Milton and is much more suitable for congregational worship. It was published in *Hymns Ancient and Modern*, 1861.

The tune "Monkland" appeared in 1824 in *Hymn Tunes of the United Brethren*, Manchester, edited by John Less. The tune has its name from Monkland, where Henry W. Baker was vicar of the Anglican Church. Baker's organist, J. Wilkes, arranged the tune for this hymn at that time.

571   What Our Father Does Is Well

1. What our Father does is well:
Blessed truth His children tell!
Though He send, for plenty, want,
Though the harvest-store be scant,
Yet we rest upon His love,
Seeking better things above.

1. Was Gott tut, das ist wohl getan!
So denken Gottes Kinder,
Er siehet sie oft sauer an
Und liebt sie doch nicht minder.
Er zieht ihr Herz
Nur himmelwärts,
Wenn er sie lässt auf Erden
Ein Ziel der Plagen werden.

2. What our Father does is well.
Shall the wilful heart rebel
If a blessing He withhold
In the field or in the fold?
Is He not Himself to be
All our store eternally?

3. What our Father does is well.
Though He sadden hill and dell,
Upward yet our praises rise
For the strength His Word supplies.
He has called us sons of God;
Can we murmur at His rod?

4. What our Father does is well;
May the thought within us dwell!
Though nor milk nor honey flow
In our barren Canaan now,
God can save us in our need,
God can bless us, God can feed.

5. Therefore unto Him we raise
Hymns of glory, songs of praise.
To the Father and the Son
And the Spirit, Three in One,
Honor, might, and glory be
Now and through eternity.

3. Was Gott tut, das ist wohl getan!
Er weist uns oft den Segen,
Und eh' er noch gedeihen kann,
Muss sich die Hoffnung legen.
Weil er allein
Der Schatz will sein,
So macht er andre Güter
Durch den Verlust uns bitter.

7. Was Gott tut, das ist wohl getan!
Das Feld mag ledig stehen,
Wir gehn getrost auf Zions Bahn
Und wollen Gott erhöhen.
Sein Wort ist Brot,
So hat's nicht Not,
Die Welt muss eh' verderben,
Als wir vor Hunger sterben.

8. Was Gott tut, das ist wohl getan!
So wollen wir stets schliessen,
Und ist bei uns kein Kanaan,
Wo Milch und Honig fliessen,
Doch ist's genung
Zur Sättigung,
Wenn Gott den Löffel segnet,
Ob's gleich nicht Scheffel regnet.

Benjamin Schmolck first published this hymn in his *Freuden-Oel in Traurigkeit,* Breslau, 1720, in six eight-line stanzas and again in his *Klage und Reigen,* Breslau, 1734 (?), in nine stanzas. There the hymn was entitled, as in the 1720 version, but with a date added, as follows: "The contented heart in a scanty harvest. 1731." Our cento contains Stanzas 1, 3, 7, and 8 of the longer form, to which the translator, Henry W. Baker, 1861, added an original doxology. The translation did not abide by the meter of the original.

The omitted stanzas are as follows:

2. Was Gott tut, das ist wohl getan!
Gibt er, so kann man nehmen;
Nimmt er, wir sind nicht übel dran,
Wenn wir uns nur bequemen.
Die Linke schmerzt,
Die Rechte herzt,
Und beide Hände müssen
Wir doch in Demut küssen.

4. Was Gott tut, das ist wohl getan!
Wenn man nach reichem Säen
Doch wenig Garben ernten kann,
So ist's vielleicht geschehen,
Weil Gott auch Frucht
Bei uns gesucht
Und dennoch müssen klagen,
Dass wir so schlecht getragen.

5. Was Gott tut, das ist wohl getan!
Wir müssen besser werden.
Man baue nur die Herzen an,
So folgt die Frucht der Erden.

Den Mangel muss
Ein Überfluss
Zu andrer Zeit ersetzen
Und Feld und Herz ergötzen.

6. Was Gott tut, das ist wohl getan!
Lass ihm nur seinen Willen;
Hängt er den Brotkorb höher an,
Er wird ihn wieder füllen.
Wer so viel nimmt,
Als ihm bestimmt,
Der kann auch bei den Brocken
Vergnügt sein und frohlocken.

9. Was Gott tut, das ist wohl getan!
Wie er es nun gefüget,
So nehmen wir es billig an
Und sind dabei vergnüget.
Wenngleich der Kad
Sehr wenig hat,
Doch wird ein jeder Bissen
Im Munde quellen müssen.

This hymn must not be confused with Samuel Rodigast's hymn, which has the same opening line. See Hymn No. 521.

For comments on the tune "Ratisbon" see Hymn No. 20.

Praise to God, Immortal Praise 572

1. Praise to God, immortal praise,
For the love that crowns our days;
Bounteous Source of every joy,
Let Thy praise our tongues employ.
All to Thee, our God, we owe,
Source whence all our blessings flow.

2. All the plenty summer pours;
Autumn's rich, o'erflowing stores;
Flocks that whiten all the plain;
Yellow sheaves of ripened grain, —
Lord, for these our souls shall raise
Grateful vows and solemn praise.

HARVEST AND THANKSGIVING

3. Peace, prosperity, and health,
Private bliss, and public wealth,
Knowledge with its gladdening streams,
Pure religion's holier beams,
Lord, for these our souls shall raise
Grateful vows and solemn praise.

4. As Thy prospering hand hath blest,
May we give Thee of our best
And by deeds of kindly love
For Thy mercies grateful prove,
Singing thus through all our days
Praise to God, immortal praise.

This harvest hymn is a cento, altered, from Anna Laetitia Barbauld's hymn in nine four-line stanzas, which first appeared in Dr. W. Enfield's *Hymns for Public Worship*, etc., Warrington, 1772, entitled, "Praise to God in Prosperity and Adversity." The original reads:

1. Praise to God, immortal praise,
For the love that crowns our days!
Bounteous Source of every joy,
Let Thy praise our tongues employ.

2. For the blessings of the field,
For the stores the gardens yield;
For the vine's exalted juice,
For the generous olive's use;

3. Flocks that whiten all the plain;
Yellow sheaves of ripened grain;
Clouds that drop their fattening dews;
Suns that temperate warmth diffuse:

4. All that Spring with bounteous hand
Scatters o'er the smiling land;
All that liberal Autumn pours
From her rich o'erflowing stores:

5. These to Thee, my God, we owe,
Source whence all our blessings flow;
And for these my soul shall raise
Grateful vows and solemn praise.

6. Yet, should rising whirlwinds tear
From its stem the ripening ear;
Should the fig-tree's blasted shoot
Drop her green, untimely fruit;

7. Should the vine put forth no more,
Nor the olive yield her store,
Though the sickening flocks should fall,
And the herds desert the stall;

8. Should Thine altered hand restrain
The early and the latter rain;
Blast each opening bud of joy
And the rising year destroy, —

9. Yet to Thee my soul should raise
Grateful vows and solemn praise
And, when every blessing's flown,
Love Thee for Thyself alone.

For comments on the tune "Dix" see Hymn No. 127.

573   To Thee, O Lord, Our Hearts We Raise

1. To Thee, O Lord, our hearts we raise
In hymns of adoration,
To Thee bring sacrifice of praise
With shout of exultation.
Bright robes of gold the fields adorn,
The hills with joy are ringing,
The valleys stand so thick with corn
That even they are singing.

2. And now, on this our festal day,
Thy bounteous hand confessing,
Upon Thine altar, Lord, we lay
The first-fruits of Thy blessing.
By Thee the souls of men are fed
With gifts of grace supernal;
Thou who dost give us earthly bread,
Give us the Bread eternal.

3. We bear the burden of the day,
And often toil seems dreary;
But labor ends with sunset ray,
And rest comes for the weary.
May we, the angel-reaping o'er,
Stand at the last accepted,
Christ's golden sheaves forevermore,
To garners bright elected.

4. Oh, blessèd is that land of God
Where saints abide forever,
Where golden fields spread fair and broad,
Where flows the crystal river.
The strains of all its holy throng
With ours today are blending;
Thrice blessèd is that harvest-song
Which never hath an ending.

William Chatterton Dix first published this hymn in St. Raphael's *Hymns for the Service of the Church*, Bristol, 1864. Some hymnals have Line 3 of Stanza 2 altered to read:

Before Thee thankfully we lay

— a version also sanctioned by the author.

The tune "Harvest Hymn" is an adaptation of a tune in the *St. Gallen Gesangbuch*, 1863.

Come, Ye Thankful People, Come — 574

1. Come, ye thankful people, come;
Raise the song of Harvest-home.
All be safely gathered in
Ere the winter storms begin;
God, our Maker, doth provide
For our wants to be supplied.
Come to God's own temple, come;
Raise the song of Harvest-home.

2. All the world is God's own field,
Fruit unto His praise to yield;
Wheat and tares together sown,
Unto joy or sorrow grown;
First the blade and then the ear,
Then the full corn shall appear.
Lord of harvest, grant that we
Wholesome grain and pure may be.

3. For the Lord, our God, shall come
And shall take His harvest home;
From His field shall in that day
All offences purge away;
Give His angels charge at last
In the fire the tares to cast,
But the fruitful ears to store
In His garner evermore.

4. Even so, Lord, quickly come
To Thy final Harvest-home;
Gather Thou Thy people in,
Free from sorrow, free from sin,
There, forever purified,
In Thy garner to abide.
Come with all Thine angels, come,
Raise the glorious Harvest-home.

This hymn by Dean Henry Alford was first published in his *Psalms and Hymns*, 1844, in seven eight-line stanzas. Subsequently the author altered it. It was republished several times. The text above is, with a slight alteration in Stanza 3, the author's revised version as published in his *Poetical Works*, 1865.

For comments on the tune "St. George" see Hymn No. 71.

Before the Lord We Bow — 575

1. Before the Lord we bow,
   The God who reigns above
And rules the world below,
   Boundless in power and love.
Our thanks we bring,
   In joy and praise
   Our hearts we raise
To heaven's high King.

2. The nation Thou hast blest
   May well Thy love declare,
From foes and fears at rest,
   Protected by Thy care,
For this fair land,
   For this bright day,
   Our thanks we pay —
Gifts of Thy hand.

3. May every mountain height,
   Each vale and forest green,
Shine in Thy Word's pure light
   And its rich fruits be seen!
May every tongue
   Be tuned to praise
   And join to raise
A grateful song!

4. Earth, hear thy Maker's voice,
   Thy great Redeemer own;
Believe, obey, rejoice,
   And worship Him alone.
Cast down thy pride,
   Thy sin deplore,
   And bow before
The Crucified.

5. And when in power He comes,
   Oh, may our native land
From all its rending tombs
   Send forth a glorious band,
A countless throng,
   For aye to sing
   To heaven's high King
Salvation's song!

Francis Scott Key, the author of "The Star-spangled Banner," very likely wrote this hymn for the Independence Day celebration of 1832.

For comments on the tune "Darwall's 148th" see Hymn No. 46.

Judge Eternal, Throned in Splendor — 576

1. Judge eternal, throned in splendor,
   Lord of lords and King of kings,
With Thy living fire of judgment
   Purge this realm of bitter things;
Solace all its wide dominion
   With the healing of Thy wings.

2. Still the weary folk are pining
   For the hour that brings release;
And the city's crowded clangor
   Cries aloud for sin to cease;
And the homesteads and the woodlands
   Plead in silence for their peace.

3. Crown, O God, Thine own endeavor;
Cleave our darkness with Thy sword;
Feed the faint and hungry peoples
With the richness of Thy Word;
Cleanse the body of this nation
Through the glory of the Lord.

Henry Scott Holland published this hymn in *The Commonwealth*, 1902, of which he was editor from 1895 to 1912. It is said to be the only hymn he ever wrote.

The tune "Bis willkommen" is by Johann Christian Kittel, 1790.

577 God Bless Our Native Land

1. God bless our native land!
Firm may she ever stand
 Through storm and night!
When the wild tempests rave,
Ruler of wind and wave,
Do Thou our country save
 By Thy great might.

2. For her our prayer shall rise
To God above the skies;
 On Him we wait.
Thou who art ever nigh,
Guarding with watchful eye,
To Thee aloud we cry,
 God save the State!

Dr. Julian, in his *Dictionary of Hymnology*, has a long discussion on the origin of this American hymn and its English counterpart, "God save the King." Space will not permit us to enter upon a detailed discussion of it. May it suffice to mention that the American version seems to have its beginning with the hymn of Charles Timothy Brooks, who as student of divinity at Cambridge, in 1834, wrote:

God bless our native land!
Firm may she ever stand
 Through storm and night!
When the wild tempests rave,
Ruler of wind and wave,
Father Eternal, save
 Us by Thy might!

Lo, our hearts' prayers arise
Into the upper skies,
 Regions of light.
He who hath heard each sigh,
Watches each weeping eye;
He is forever nigh,
 Venger of Right!

This was a rather free translation of the patriotic song for Saxony, written by the German song-writer Siegfried August Mahlmann (1771—1826), published in G. W. Fink's *Musikalischer Hausschatz*, etc., 1842, reading:

1. Gott segne Sachsenland,
Wo fest die Treue stand
 In Sturm und Nacht!
Ew'ge Gerechtigkeit,
Hoch überm Meer der Zeit,
Die jedem Sturm gebeut,
 Schütz uns mit Macht!

2. Blühe, du Rautenkranz
In schöner Tage Glanz
 Freudig empor!
Heil, Friedrich August, dir!
Heil, guter König, dir!
Dich, Vater, preisen wir
 Liebend im Chor!

3. Was treue Herzen flehn
Steigt zu des Himmels Höh'n
 Aus Nacht zum Licht.
Der unsre Liebe sah,
Der unsre Tränen sah,
Er ist uns huldreich nah,
 Verlässt uns nicht.

A fourth stanza follows, which is identical with the first. It was first sung on November 13, 1815, in the presence of the King of Saxony. Incidentally, this German patriotic song was also the inspiration for Samuel F. Smith's "My Country, 'Tis of Thee." It will be noted that Brooks's lines are based on Stanzas 1 and 3.

In 1844 John Sullivan Dwight recast Brooks's hymn and, changing Lines 6 and 7 of Stanza 1 and the entire second stanza, gave it its form as we have it.

Another form of the hymn appeared in *Hymns of the Spirit*, Boston, 1864

(Unitarian), which retains the first stanza as altered by Dwight and has a number of changes in Stanzas 2 and a new third stanza:

> 2. For her our prayers shall be,
> Our fathers' God, to Thee,
>   On Thee we wait.
> Be her walls Holiness;
> Her rulers Righteousness;
> Her officers be Peace;
>   God save the State!

> 3. Lord of all truth and right,
> In whom alone is might,
>   On Thee we call.
> Give us prosperity;
> Give us true liberty;
> May all the oppressed go free;
>   God save us all!

The tune "America" is also the tune of the British national anthem "God Save the King" and nothing definite can be said about its origin. This much is certain that it appeared in *Thesaurus Musicus*, 1740. It is ascribed to Henry Carey, whose son, George S. Carey, asserted the authorship for his father in 1795, fifty-two years after his father's death.

Lord, While for All Mankind We Pray 578

1. Lord, while for all mankind we pray
    Of every clime and coast,
Oh, hear us for our native land,
    The land we love the most!

2. Oh, guard our shores from every foe,
    With peace our borders bless,
With prosperous times our cities crown,
    Our fields with plenteousness!

3. Unite us in the sacred love
    Of knowledge, truth, and Thee;
And let our hills and valleys shout
    The songs of liberty.

4. Here may Thy Gospel, pure and mild,
    Smile on our Sabbath hours
And piety and virtue bless
    Our fathers' home and ours.

5. Lord of the nations, thus to Thee
    Our country we commend.
Be Thou her Refuge and her Trust,
    Her everlasting Friend.

This hymn by John R. Wreford first appeared in J. R. Beard's *Collection of Hymns*, etc., 1837, perhaps in honor of Queen Victoria, who ascended the British throne in that year. The second stanza, which is omitted, reads:

> Our fathers' sepulchers are here,
>   And here our kindred dwell,
> Our children, too; how should we love
>   Another land so well?

Line 1 of Stanza 4 in the original reads:

> Here may religion, pure and mild.

For comments on the tune "St. Flavian" see Hymn No. 22.

Almighty Lord, before Thy Throne 579

1. Almighty Lord, before Thy throne
    Thy mourning people bend;
'Tis on Thy grace in Christ alone
    Our failing hopes depend.

2. Dark judgments from Thy heavy hand
    Thy dreadful power display;
Yet mercy spares our guilty land,
    And still we live to pray.

3. How changed, alas, are truths divine
    For error, guilt, and shame!
What impious numbers, bold in sin,
    Disgrace the Christian name!

4. Oh, turn us, turn us, mighty Lord;
    Convert us by Thy grace!
Then shall our hearts obey Thy Word
    And see again Thy face.

5. Then, should oppressing foes invade,
    We will not yield to fear,
Secure of all-sufficient aid
    When God in Christ is near.

The original hymn of Anne Steele's, from which this cento is taken, begins "See, gracious God, before Thy throne." It was written for the Public Fast, February 6, 1756 (Seven Years' War), in seven stanzas, and first published in her *Poems on Subjects Chiefly Devotional,* 1760. In its original form the hymn is not in common use, and only a few modern hymnals have included this cento.

For comments on the tune "Burford" see Hymn No. 454.

580   To Thee, Our God, We Fly

1. To Thee, our God, we fly
   For mercy and for grace;
   Oh, hear our lowly cry
   And hide not Thou Thy face!
   O Lord, stretch forth Thy mighty hand
   And guard and bless our Fatherland.

2. Arise, O Lord of hosts,
   Be jealous for Thy name
   And drive from out our coasts
   The sins that put to shame.
   O Lord, stretch forth Thy mighty hand
   And guard and bless our Fatherland.

3. Thy best gifts from on high
   In rich abundance pour
   That we may magnify
   And praise Thee more and more.
   O Lord, stretch forth Thy mighty hand
   And guard and bless our Fatherland.

4. The powers ordained by Thee
   With heavenly wisdom bless;
   May they Thy servants be
   And rule in righteousness!
   O Lord, stretch forth Thy mighty hand
   And guard and bless our Fatherland.

5. The Church of Thy dear Son
   Inflame with love's pure fire;
   Bind her once more in one
   And life and truth inspire.
   O Lord, stretch forth Thy mighty hand
   And guard and bless our Fatherland.

6. The pastors of Thy fold
   With grace and power endue
   That, faithful, pure, and bold,
   They may be pastors true.
   O Lord, stretch forth Thy mighty hand
   And guard and bless our Fatherland.

7. Oh, let us love Thy house
   And sanctify Thy day,
   Bring unto Thee our vows,
   And loyal homage pay.
   O Lord, stretch forth Thy mighty hand
   And guard and bless our Fatherland.

8. Give peace, Lord, in our time;
   Oh, let no foe draw nigh
   Nor lawless deed of crime
   Insult Thy majesty!
   O Lord, stretch forth Thy mighty hand
   And guard and bless our Fatherland.

9. Though vile and worthless, still
   Thy people, Lord, are we;
   And for our God we will
   None other have but Thee.
   O Lord, stretch forth Thy mighty hand,
   And guard and bless our Fatherland.

This litany hymn, so expressive and comprehensive, is usually abridged in modern hymnals, but it deserves to be sung in its entirety because of the important truths which it so well presents. In our day, in which there is so much confused and unscriptural thinking on the relation of the citizen to his country, a day in which the sins of the people cry aloud for divine vengeance, it is doubly necessary that the Christian be reminded, also by such hymns as this, to seek "the peace of the city" in which he dwells.

William W. How first published this hymn in 1871, in *Church Hymns* of the Society for the Promotion of Christian Knowledge.

The tune "Croft's 136th" first appeared in *The Divine Companion;* etc., 1709, where it is entitled "A Psalm Set by Mr. William Croft. Psalm CXXXVI."

581   All Ye Who on This Earth do Dwell

1. All ye who on this earth do dwell,
   Give thanks and glorify
   The Lord whose praises ever swell
   In seraph songs on high.

   Nun danket all' und bringet Ehr',
   Ihr Menschen in der Welt,
   Dem dessen Lob der Engel Heer
   Im Himmel stets vermeld't!

2. Lift up your hearts in praise to God,
   Himself best Gift of all,
Who works His wonders all abroad,
   Upholding great and small.

3. Since first our life began to be,
   He has preserved our frame;
And when man's strength was vanity,
   He as our Helper came.

4. Though often we His patience try
   And well deserve His frown,
In grace He lays His anger by
   And pours new blessings down.

5. 'Tis He revives our fainting soul,
   Gives joyful hearts to men;
And when great waves of trouble roll,
   He drives them back again.

6. May He adorn with precious peace
   Our own, our native, land,
And crown with joys that never cease
   The labors of our hand.

7. Long as we tarry here below
   Our saving Health is He;
And when from earth to heaven we go,
   May He our portion be!

Ermuntert euch und singt mit Schall
   Gott, unserm höchsten Gut,
Der seine Wunder überall
   Und grosse Dinge tut,

Der uns von Mutterleibe an
   Frisch und gesund erhält
Und, wo kein Mensch nicht helfen kann,
   Sich selbst zum Helfer stellt;

Der, ob wir ihn gleich hoch betrübt,
   Doch bleibet gutes Muts,
Die Straf' erlässt, die Schuld vergibt
   Und tut uns alles Gut's.

Er gebe uns ein fröhlich Herz,
   Erfrische Geist und Sinn
Und werf' all' Angst, Furcht, Sorg' und Schmerz
   In's Meeres Tiefe hin.

Er lasse seinen Frieden ruhn
   In Israelis Land,
Er gebe Glück zu unserm Tun
   Und Heil in allem Stand.

Solange dieses Leben währt,
   Sei es stets unser Heil
Und bleib' auch, wenn wir von der Erd'
   Abscheiden, unser Teil.

This hymn by Paul Gerhardt was written in celebration of the Peace of Westphalia, which brought to an end the Thirty Years' War. It first appeared in Crüger's *Praxis Pietatis Melica*, 1648, in nine stanzas. Our version omits the following stanzas:

7. His love and goodness may He let
   In and around us be,
All that may frighten us and fret
   Cast far into the sea.

9. He giveth His beloved sleep
   When these frail heart-beats cease;
And in His presence then will keep
   Our souls in endless peace.

The translation is by Alfred Ramsey, d. 1926, altered.

For comments on the tune "Nun danket all'" see Hymn No. 10.

God, Lord of Sabaoth, Thou Who Ordainest 582

1. God, Lord of Sabaoth, Thou who ordainest
   Thunder Thy clarion and lightning Thy sword,
Show forth Thy pity on high where Thou reignest;
   Give to us peace in our time, O Lord.

2. God, the omnipotent, mighty Avenger,
   Watching invisible, judging unheard;
Save us in mercy, oh, save us from danger;
   Give to us peace in our time, O Lord.

3. God, the All-merciful, earth hath forsaken
   Thy ways all holy and slighted Thy Word;
Let not Thy wrath in its terror awaken;
   Give to us pardon and peace, O Lord.

4. So shall Thy people, with thankful devotion,
   Praise Him who saved them from peril and sword,
Singing in chorus, from ocean to ocean,
   Peace to the nations and praise to the Lord.

Henry F. Chorley published this hymn in Hullah's *Part Music*, 1842. It was written for use in time of war. The first line of the original reads, "God, the

All-terrible! King who Ordainest." It was written for the Russian air by Alexis F. Lvov, used with the old Russian national anthem "God save the Tsar."

The tune "Liebster Immanuel" is from Ahasverus Fritsch's *Himmelslust und Weltunlust,* Leipzig, 1675, where it was set to his hymn "Liebster Immanuel, Herzog der Frommen." Some authorities think the composer is Johann Rudolf Ahle.

583   Great King of Nations, Hear Our Prayer

1. Great King of nations, hear our prayer
 While at Thy feet we fall
And humbly with united cry
 To Thee for mercy call.
The guilt is ours, but grace is Thine;
 Oh, turn us not away,
But hear us from Thy lofty throne
 And help us when we pray!

2. Our fathers' sins were manifold,
 And ours no less we own;
Yet wondrously from age to age
 Thy goodness hath been shown.
When dangers, like a stormy sea,
 Beset our country round,
To Thee we looked, to Thee we cried,
 And help in Thee was found.

3. With one consent we meekly bow
 Beneath Thy chastening hand
And, pouring forth confession meet,
 Mourn with our mourning land.
With pitying eye behold our need
 As thus we lift our prayer;
Correct us with Thy judgments, Lord,
 Then let Thy mercy spare.

This hymn, by John H. Gurney, was first published in his *Collection of Hymns for Public Worship,* Lutterworth, 1838, for a "Fast Day."

The tune "Old 137th" is from the oldest English metrical psalter, *One and fiftie Psalmes,* 1556, where it was set to the metrical version on Ps. 137, and thence the name.

584   Swell the Anthem, Raise the Song

1. Swell the anthem, raise the song;
Praises to our God belong.
Saints and angels join to sing
Praises to the heavenly King.
Blessings from His liberal hand
Flow around this happy land.
Kept by Him, no foes annoy;
Peace and freedom we enjoy.

2. Here, beneath a peaceful sway,
May we cheerfully obey,
Never feel oppression's rod,
Ever own and worship God.
Hark, the voice of nature sings
Praises to the King of kings.
Let us join the choral song
And the grateful notes prolong.

Nathan Strong published this hymn for national thanksgiving in the *Hartford Selections,* 1799, a Congregationalist hymnal of which he was one of the editors.

For comments on the tune "St. George" see Hymn No. 71.

DEATH AND BURIAL

The Last Things

I Fall Asleep in Jesus' Wounds   585

1. I fall asleep in Jesus' wounds,
There pardon for my sins abounds;
Yea, Jesus' blood and righteousness
My jewels are, my glorious dress.
In these before my God I'll stand
When I shall reach the heavenly land.

2. With peace and joy I now depart;
God's child I am with all my heart.
I thank thee, Death, thou leadest me
To that true life where I would be.
So cleansed by Christ, I fear not death.
Lord Jesus, strengthen Thou my faith.

In Christi Wunden schlaf' ich ein,
Die machen mich von Sünden rein;
Ja, Christi Blut und G'rechtigkeit,
Das ist mein Schmuck und Ehrenkleid,
Damit will ich vor Gott bestehn,
Wenn ich zum Himmel werd' eingehn.

Mit Fried' und Freud' ich fahr' dahin,
Ein Gotteskind ich allzeit bin.
Dank hab', mein Tod, du führest mich;
Ins ew'ge Leben wandre ich,
Mit Christi Blut gereinigt fein.
Herr Jesu, stärk den Glauben mein!

This hymn has been ascribed to Paul Eber, but his authorship, though probable, is not definitely established. It first appeared in Jeremias Weber's *Leipziger Gesangbuch*, 1638, in three four-line stanzas, to be sung to the tune "Herr Jesu Christ, mein's" (see Hymn No. 7). Later the stanzas were arranged as above, and the hymn is commonly sung to the tune "Vater unser." For comments on the tune see Hymn No. 458.

This hymn is a favorite in German-speaking circles, and Lines 3—6 of Stanza 1 have been used as a daily prayer, especially at retiring, by millions. The translation is a slightly altered form of that by Catherine Winkworth in her *Christian Singers of Germany*, 1869.

A Pilgrim and a Stranger   586

1. A pilgrim and a stranger,
   I journey here below;
Far distant is my country,
   The home to which I go.
Here I must toil and travail,
   Oft weary and opprest;
But there my God shall lead me
   To everlasting rest.

2. I've met with storms and danger
   E'en from my early years,
With enemies and conflicts,
   With fightings and with fears.
There's nothing here that tempts me
   To wish a longer stay,
So I must hasten forward,
   No halting or delay.

3. It is a well-worn pathway;
   A host has gone before,
The holy saints and prophets,
   The patriarchs of yore.
They trod the toilsome journey
   In patience and in faith;
And them I fain would follow,
   Like them in life and death.

4. Who would share Abraham's blessing
   Must Abraham's path pursue,
A stranger and a pilgrim,
   Like him, must journey through.
The foes must be encountered,
   The dangers must be passed;
A faithful soldier only
   Receives the crown at last.

Ich bin ein Gast auf Erden
   Und hab' hier keinen Stand;
Der Himmel soll mir werden,
   Da ist mein Vaterland.
Hier reis' ich aus und abe;
   Dort in der ew'gen Ruh'
Ist Gottes Gnadengabe,
   Die schleusst all' Arbeit zu.

Was ist mein ganzes Wesen
   Von meiner Jugend an
Als Müh' und Not gewesen?
   Solang ich denken kann,
Hab' ich so manchen Morgen,
   So manche liebe Nacht
Mit Kummer und mit Sorgen
   Des Herzens zugebracht.

So ging's den lieben Alten,
   An deren Fuss und Pfad
Wir uns noch täglich halten,
   Wenn's fehlt an gutem Rat.
Wie musste sich doch schmiegen
   Der Vater Abraham,
Bevor ihm sein Vergnügen
   Und rechte Wohnstatt kam!

Wie manche schwere Bürde
   Trug Isaak, sein Sohn!
Und Jakob, dessen Würde
   Stieg bis zum Himmelsthron,
Wie musste der sich plagen!
   In was für Weh und Schmerz,
In was für Furcht und Zagen
   Sank oft sein armes Herz!

DEATH AND BURIAL

5. So I must hasten forward, —
   Thank God, the end will come!
This land of passing shadows
   Is not my destined home.
The everlasting city,
   Jerusalem above,
This evermore abideth,
   The home of light and love.

6. There still my thoughts are dwelling,
   'Tis there I long to be;
Come, Lord, and call Thy servant
   To blessedness with Thee.
Come, bid my toils be ended,
   Let all my wanderings cease;
Call from the wayside lodging
   To Thy sweet home of peace.

7. There I shall dwell forever,
   No more a parting guest,
With all Thy blood-bought children
   In everlasting rest,
The pilgrim toils forgotten,
   The pilgrim conflicts o'er,
All earthly griefs behind me,
   Eternal joys before.

So will ich zwar nun treiben
   Mein Leben durch die Welt,
Doch denk' ich nicht zu bleiben
   In diesem fremden Zelt.
Ich wandre meine Strassen,
   Die zu der Heimat führt,
Da mich ohn' alle Massen
   Mein Vater trösten wird.

Die Herberg' ist zu böse,
   Der Trübsal ist zu viel.
Ach komm, mein Gott, und löse
   Mein Herz, wenn dein Herz will!
Komm, mach ein sel'ges Ende
   An meiner Wanderschaft,
Und was mich kränkt, das wende
   Durch deinen Arm und Kraft!

Da will ich immer wohnen,
   Und nicht nur als ein Gast,
Bei denen, die mit Kronen
   Du ausgeschmücket hast.
Da will ich herrlich singen
   Von deinem grossen Tun
Und frei von schnöden Dingen
   In meinem Erbteil ruhn.

This pilgrim hymn of homesickness for the heavenly fatherland is based on Ps. 119:19: "I am a stranger in the earth; hide not Thy commandments from me," and Heb. 11:13-16: "These all died in faith, not having received the promises, but having seen them afar off, and were persuaded of them and embraced them and confessed that they were strangers and pilgrims on the earth. For they that say such things declare plainly that they seek a country. And truly, if they had been mindful of that country from whence they came out, they might have had opportunity to have returned. But now they desire a better country, that is, a heavenly; wherefore God is not ashamed to be called their God; for He hath prepared for them a city." Paul Gerhardt first published it in Ebeling's edition of his *Geistliche Andachten,* Berlin, 1666. We have in this hymn an echo of the thoughts that sustained Gerhardt in his own personal trials and afflictions.

The cento contains seven stanzas of the original fourteen and is a free translation of these, slightly altered, by Jane Borthwick, *Hymns from the Land of Luther,* third series, 1858.

For comments on the tune "Herzlich tut mich" see Hymn No. 172.

587   Asleep in Jesus! Blessed Sleep

1. Asleep in Jesus! Blessed sleep,
From which none ever wakes to weep;
A calm and undisturbed repose,
Unbroken by the last of foes.

2. Asleep in Jesus! Oh, how sweet
To be for such a slumber meet,
With holy confidence to sing
That death has lost his venomed sting!

3. Asleep in Jesus! Peaceful rest,
Whose waking is supremely blest;
No fear, no woe, shall dim that hour
That manifests the Savior's power.

4. Asleep in Jesus! Oh, for me
May such a blissful refuge be!
Securely shall my ashes lie
And wait the summons from on high.

Margaret Mackay's famous hymn first appeared in *The Amethyst; or Christian's Annual,* 1832, in six stanzas. It was introduced with this statement: "Sleeping in Jesus. By Mrs. Mackay of Hedgefield. This simple but expressive sentence is inscribed on a tombstone in a rural burying-ground in Devonshire and gave rise to the following verses."

DEATH AND BURIAL

The burying-ground referred to, she stated later, was that of Pennycross Chapel. She added: "Distant only a few miles from a bustling and crowded seaport town, reached through a succession of those lovely green lanes for which Devonshire is so remarkable, the quiet aspect of Pennycross comes soothingly over the mind. 'Sleeping in Jesus' seems in keeping with all around."

The omitted stanzas are five and six:

5. Asleep in Jesus! Time nor space
Debars this precious "hiding-place";
On Indian plains or Lapland snows
Believers find the same repose.

6. Asleep in Jesus! Far from Thee
Thy kindred and their graves may be;
But there is still a blessed sleep,
From which none ever wakes to weep.

The tune "Rest" is by William B. Bradbury, 1843.

I Would Not Live Alway; I Ask Not to Stay 588

1. I would not live alway; I ask not to stay
Where storm after storm rises dark o'er the way.
The few lurid mornings that dawn on us here
Suffice for life's woes, are enough for its cheer.

2. I would not live alway; thus fettered by sin,
Temptation without and corruption within;
E'en rapture of pardon is mingled with fears,
The cup of thanksgiving with penitent tears.

3. I would not live alway; no, welcome the tomb;
Since Jesus hath lain there, I dread not its gloom.
There sweet be my rest till He bids me arise
To hail Him in triumph descending the skies.

4. Ah, who would live alway, away from his God,
Away from yon heaven, that blissful abode,
Where rivers of pleasure flow o'er the bright plains
And noontide of glory eternally reigns;

5. Where saints of all ages in harmony meet
Their Savior and brethren transported to greet,
While anthems of rapture unceasingly roll,
The smile of the Lord is the feast of the soul?

This hymn by William Augustus Mühlenberg, grandson of Henry Melchior Mühlenberg, has a complicated history, which can best be given by quoting from the *History of the American Episcopal Church,* 1885:

> The most famous of these [Dr. Mühlenberg's hymns] was probably first written. "I will not live alway" has an intricate history, which was not simplified by the author's lapse of memory in his later years. In his brief "story of the hymn," printed with its "evangelized" text in 1871, every date is wrong by two or three years; and his assertion "The legend that it was written on an occasion of private grief is a fancy" hardly agrees with the clear and minute recollections of persons of the highest character, still living, and who knew the circumstances thoroughly. The date of composition assigned, 1824, is probably (not certainly) correct; it was written at Lancaster, in a lady's album, and began:
>
> > I would not live alway; no, no, holy man,
> > Not a day, not an hour, should lengthen my span.
>
> In this shape it seems to have had six eight-line stanzas. The album was still extant in 1876 at Pottsdown, Pa., and professed to contain the original

manuscript. Said the owner's sister, "It was an impromptu. He had no copy, and, wanting it for some occasion, he sent for the album." In 1826 he entrusted his copy to a friend, who called on him on the way from Harrisburg to Philadelphia, to carry to the *Episcopal Recorder,* and in that paper it appeared June 3, 1826 (not 1824). For these facts we have the detailed statement of Dr. John B. Clemson of Claymont, Del., the Ambassador mentioned, who also chances to have preserved that volume of the paper. Thus appearing (without name), it was adopted by the subcommittee. When their report was presented to the entire committee in 1826, — not 1829, as Dr. Mühlenberg has it, — "each of the hymns was passed upon. When this came up, one of the members remarked that it was very sweet and pretty but rather sentimental, upon which it was unanimously thrown out. Not suspected as the author, I voted against myself. That, I supposed, was the end of it. The committee, which sat until late at night at the house of Bishop White, agreed upon their report to the convention and adjourned. But the next morning Dr. Onderdonk (who was not one of their number, but who, on invitation, had acted with the subcommittee, which in fact, consisted of him and myself) called on me to inquire what had been done. Upon my telling him that among the rejected hymns was this one of mine, he said, "That will never do," and went about among the members of the committee soliciting them to restore the hymn in their report, which accordingly they did; so that to him is due the credit of giving it to the Church." As thus adopted, it was a small and altered selection from the original lines, made by Dr. Onderdonk "with some revision" by the author. He was never satisfied with these texts but revised the poem in 1859 and rewrote it in 1871.... The authorship of this as of many another popular lyric has been disputed. The claim of Henry Ward, a printer of Litchfield, Conn., has been vehemently urged and revived but a few years ago. Of course it is unsupported by adequate evidence. When Dr. Mühlenberg was asked to assure "some of his brethren, editors of church-papers," of his paternity, his manly reply was, "If they thought I was capable of letting the work of another pass for so many years as my own, they would not be sure of anything I might say."

A few changes have been made in the text as given above in order to make it more singable.

The form in which Mühlenberg revised the text in 1859 is as follows:

> I would not live alway — live alway below!
> Oh, no, I'll not linger when bidden to go.
> The days of our pilgrimage granted us here
> Are enough for life's woes, full enough for its cheer:
> Would I shrink from the path which the prophets of God,
> Apostles, and martyrs so joyfully trod?
> Like a spirit unblest, o'er the earth would I roam
> While brethren and friends are all hastening home?
>
> I would not live alway — I ask not to stay
> Where storm after storm rises dark o'er the way;
> Where, seeking for rest, we but hover around,
> Like the patriarch's bird, and no resting is found;
> Where Hope, when she paints her gay bow in the air,
> Leaves its brilliance to fade in the night of despair,
> And Joy's fleeting angel ne'er sheds a glad ray,
> Save the gleam of the plumage that bears him away.

I would not live alway — thus fettered by sin,
Temptation without and corruption within;
In a moment of strength if I sever the chain,
Scarce the victory is mine ere I'm captive again;
E'en the rapture of pardon is mingled with fears
And the cup of thanksgiving with penitent tears.
The festival trump calls for jubilant songs,
But my spirit her own *miserere* prolongs.

I would not live alway — no, welcome the tomb!
Since Jesus hath lain there, I dread not its gloom;
Where He deigned to sleep, I'll, too, bow my head,
All peaceful to slumber on that hallowed bed.
Then the glorious daybreak, to follow that night,
The orient gleam of the angels of light,
With their clarion call for the sleepers to rise
And chant forth their matins, away to the skies.

Who, who would live alway — away from his God,
Away from yon heaven, that blissful abode
Where the rivers of pleasure flow o'er the bright plains
And the noontide of glory eternally reigns;
Where the saints of all ages in harmony meet,
Their Savior and brethren transported to greet,
While the songs of salvation exultingly roll
And the smile of the Lord is the feast of the soul?

That heavenly music! What is it I hear?
The notes of the harpers ring sweet in mine ear.
And see, soft unfolding those portals of gold,
The King all arrayed in His beauty behold!
Oh, give me, oh, give me, the wings of a dove
To adore Him, be near Him, enrapt with His love,
I but wait for the summons, I list for the word —
Alleluia — Amen — evermore with the Lord.

For comments on the tune "Maldwyn" see Hymn No. 278.

Oh, How Blest Are Ye Whose Toils are Ended 589

1. Oh, how blest are ye whose toils are ended,
Who through death have unto God ascended!
Ye have arisen
From the cares which keep us still in prison.

2. We are still as in a dungeon living,
Still oppressed with sorrow and misgiving;
Our undertakings
Are but toils and troubles and heart-breakings.

3. Ye meanwhile are in your chambers sleeping,
Quiet, and set free from all our weeping;
No cross or sadness
There can hinder your untroubled gladness.

4. Christ has wiped away your tears forever;
Ye have that for which we still endeavor;
To you are chanted
Songs that ne'er to mortal ears were granted.

5. Ah, who would, then, not depart with gladness
To inherit heaven for earthly sadness?
Who here would languish
Longer in bewailing and in anguish?

6. Come, O Christ, and loose the chains that bind us;
Lead us forth and cast this world behind us.
With Thee, the Anointed,
Finds the soul its joy and rest appointed.

O wie selig seid ihr doch, ihr Frommen,
Die ihr durch den Tod zu Gott gekommen!
Ihr seid entgangen
Aller Not, die uns noch hält gefangen.

Muss man hier doch wie im Kerker leben
Und in Sorgen, Furcht und Schrecken schweben.
Was wir hier kennen,
Ist nur Müh' und Herzeleid zu nennen.

Ihr hingegen ruht in eurer Kammer
Sicher und befreit von allem Jammer;
Kein Kreuz und Leiden
Ist euch hinderlich in euren Freuden.

Christus wischet ab all eure Tränen,
Habt das schon, wonach wir uns erst sehnen;
Euch wird gesungen,
Was in keines Ohr allhier gedrungen.

Ach wer wollte denn nicht gerne sterben
Und den Himmel für die Welt ererben?
Wer wollt' hier bleiben,
Sich den Jammer länger lassen treiben?

Komm, o Christe, komm, uns auszuspannen,
Lös uns auf und führ uns bald von dannen!
Bei dir, o Sonne,
Ist der frommen Seelen Freud' und Wonne.

DEATH AND BURIAL

This hymn of Simon Dach was first published in a broadsheet, printed at Danzig in 1635, with a musical setting by Johann Stobäus, as a memorial to Job Lepner, burgomaster of Königsberg Altstadt, who died May 9, 1635. It appeared in Bernhard Derschow's hymnal *Auserlesene Geistreiche Lieder*, etc., Königsberg, 1639.

The translation first appeared in Henry Wadsworth Longfellow's *The Poets and Poetry of Europe, with introductions and biographical notices* (C. S. Francis and Company, New York, 1845) under the title "Blessed Are the Dead." From a biography of Longfellow by Francis H. Underwood (James R. Osgood and Co., Boston, 1882) we learn that Longfellow worked two years on *The Poets and Poetry of Europe*, assisted by Prof. C. C. Felton.

The alterations were made in the following lines. Longfellow has, Stanza 3, Lines 3 and 4:
No cross nor trial
Hinders your enjoyments with denial.

The tune "O wie selig seid ihr doch, ihr Frommen" was written for this hymn. It appeared in Johann Georg Stözel's *Choralbuch*, Stuttgart, 1744.

590   In the Midst of Earthly Life

1. In the midst of earthly life
   Snares of death surround us;
Who shall help us in the strife
   Lest the Foe confound us?
      Thou only, Lord, Thou only.
We mourn that we have greatly erred,
That our sins Thy wrath have stirred.
     Holy and righteous God!
     Holy and mighty God!
     Holy and all-merciful Savior!
       Eternal Lord God!
Save us lest we perish
In the bitter pangs of death.
   Have mercy, O Lord!

2. In the midst of death's dark vale
   Powers of hell o'ertake us.
Who will help when they assail,
   Who secure will make us?
      Thou only, Lord, Thou only.
Thy heart is moved with tenderness,
Pities us in our distress.
     Holy and righteous God!
     Holy and mighty God!
     Holy and all-merciful Savior!
       Eternal Lord God!
Save us from the terror
Of the fiery pit of hell.
   Have mercy, O Lord!

3. In the midst of hell-born woe
   All our sins oppress us,
Where shall we for refuge go,
   Where for grace to bless us?
      To Thee, Lord Jesus, only.
Thy precious blood was shed to win
Full atonement for our sin.
     Holy and righteous God!
     Holy and mighty God!
     Holy and all-merciful Savior!
       Eternal Lord God!
Lord, preserve and keep us
In the peace that faith can give.
   Have mercy, O Lord!

Mitten wir im Leben sind
   Mit dem Tod umfangen.
Wen such'n wir, der Hilfe tu',
   Dass wir Gnad' erlangen?
      Das bist du, Herr, alleine!
Uns reuet unsre Missetat,
Die dich, Herr, erzürnet hat.
     Heiliger Herre Gott,
     Heiliger, starker Gott,
     Heiliger, barmherziger Heiland,
       Du ewiger Gott,
Lass uns nicht versinken
In des bittern Todes Not!
   Kyrieleison!

Mitten in dem Tod anficht
   Uns der Hölle Rachen.
Wer will uns aus solcher Not
   Frei und ledig machen?
      Das tust du, Herr, alleine!
Es jammert dein' Barmherzigkeit
Unsre Sünd' und grosses Leid.
     Heiliger Herre Gott,
     Heiliger, starker Gott,
     Heiliger, barmherziger Heiland,
       Du ewiger Gott,
Lass uns nicht verzagen
Vor der tiefen Hölle Glut!
   Kyrieleison!

Mitten in der Hölle Angst
   Unsre Sünd'n uns treiben.
Wo soll'n wir denn fliehen hin,
   Da wir mögen bleiben?
      Zu dir, Herr Christ, alleine!
Vergossen ist dein teures Blut,
Das g'nug für die Sünde tut.
     Heiliger Herre Gott,
     Heiliger, starker Gott,
     Heiliger, barmherziger Heiland,
       Du ewiger Gott,
Lass uns nicht entfallen
Von des rechten Glaubens Trost!
   Kyrieleison!

This hymn is based on a medieval antiphon, beginning *Media vita in morte sumus*, which according to tradition was written by Notker Balbulus

(d. 912). By the 15th century translations of it into German had come into use. One of these is given by *Wackernagel,* from a 15th-century Munich manuscript, thus:

> En mitten in des lebens zeyt
> sey wir mit tod umbfangen:
> Wen such wir, der uns hilffe geit,
> von dem wir huld erlangen,
>   Den dich, Herre, al ayne?
> der du umb unser missetat
> rechtlichen zurnen tuest.
> Heyliger herre got,
> heyliger starcker got,
> heyliger parmhercziger hailer, ewiger got,
> lass uns nit gewalden des pittern todes not.

The powerful refrain "Holy and righteous God!" is based on the *Trisagion* of the Greek liturgy, c. 450.

Martin Luther took this stanza and, after altering it, added two stanzas. This hymn first appeared in the Erfurt *Enchiridion,* 1524. It has long been one of the foremost German hymns for the dying.

The composite translation was especially prepared for *The Lutheran Hymnal.*

The tune "Mitten wir im Leben sind" is from a 13th-century gradual. It was first used with Luther's text in Johann Walther's *Geystliche gesangk Buchleyn,* Wittenberg, 1525.

Jesus, I Live to Thee   591

1. Jesus, I live to Thee,
The Loveliest and Best;
My life in Thee, Thy life in me,
In Thy blest love I rest.

2. Jesus, I die to Thee
Whenever death shall come;
To die in Thee is life to me
In my eternal home.

3. Whether to live or die
I know not which is best;
To live in Thee is bliss to me,
To die is endless rest.

4. Living or dying, Lord,
I ask but to be Thine;
My life in Thee, Thy life in me,
Make heaven forever mine.

This hymn by Henry Harbaugh is dated 1850. It first appeared in *Hymns of the Church,* New York, 1869. It was based on Rom. 14:8 and entitled "Life Consecrated to Jesus."

The tune "Tenbury" was written by Frederick A. G. Ouseley as a setting for the hymn "For Man the Savior Shed," a translation of Jean Baptiste de Santeüil's "Ex quo, salus mortalium," in *Hymns Ancient and Modern,* 1861. This tune is also called "Aberystwyth"; but as there is another tune, for another meter, by that name, a composition of Joseph Perry's, we have called this tune "Tenbury" because of Ouseley's long association with Tenbury and the church and college he founded there.

I Know of a Sleep in Jesus' Name   592

1. I know of a sleep in Jesus' name,
A rest from all toil and sorrow;
Earth folds in her arms my weary frame
And shelters it till the morrow;
My soul is at home with God in heaven,
Her sorrows are past and over.

2. I know of a peaceful eventide;
And when I am faint and weary,
At times with the journey sorely tried,
Through hours that are long and dreary,
Then often I yearn to lay me down
And sink into blissful slumber.

Jeg ved mig en Sovn i Jesu Navn,
Den kväger de trätte Lemmer,
Der redes en Seng i Jordens Favn,
Saa moderlig hun mig gjemmer,
Min Själ er hos Gud i Himmerig,
Og Sorgerne sine glemmer.

Jeg veed mig en Aften-Time god,
Og länges vel somme Tider,
Naar jeg er af Reisen trät og mod,
Og Dagen saa tungsom skrider:
Jeg vilde til Sengs saa gjerne gaa,
Og sovne ind södt omsider.

3. I know of a morning bright and fair
   When tidings of joy shall wake us,
   When songs from on high shall fill the air
   And God to His glory take us,
   When Jesus shall bid us rise from sleep, —
   How joyous that hour of waking!

4. Oh, that is a morning dear to me,
   And oft, o'er the mountains streaming,
   In spirit its heavenly light I see
   As golden the peaks are beaming.
   Then sing I for joy like birds at dawn
   That carol in lofty lindens.

5. God's Son to our graves then takes His way,
   His voice hear all tribes and nations;
   The portals are rent that guard our clay,
   And moved are the sea's foundations.
   He calls out aloud: "Ye dead, come forth!"
   In glory we rise to meet Him.

6. O Jesus, draw near my dying bed
   And take me into Thy keeping
   And say when my spirit hence is fled,
   "This child is not dead, but sleeping."
   And leave me not, Savior, till I rise
   To praise Thee in life eternal.

Jeg veed mig en Morgen lys og skön,
Der synges i Livsens Lunde,
Da kommer han Guds velsigned' Sön
Med lystelig' Ord i Munde,
Da väkker han os af Sovne op
Alt udi saa säle Stunde.

Jeg haver den Morgen mig saa kjär,
Og drager den tidt til Minde,
Da synge jeg maa, og se den när,
Den Sol, som strör Guld paa Tinde,
Som Smaafugeln ud mod Morgenstund
Op under de höie Linde.

Da träder Guds Sön til Gravens Hus,
Hans Röst i al Verden höres,
Da brydes alt Stengsel ned i Grus,
Da dybe Havsgrunde röres,
Han raaber: Du Döde, kom herud!
Og frem vi forklaret föres.

O Jesu, träd du min Dödsseng til,
Rek Haanden med Miskund over,
Og sig: Denne Dreng, den Pigelil
Hun er ikke död, men sover!
Og slip mig ei för, at op jeg staar,
I Levendes Land dig over!

This hymn, by Magnus B. Landstad, first appeared in his *Kirke-Salmebog,* etc., 1861, in seven stanzas. It ranks high in the literature of Norway and is considered one of the author's best hymns. The omitted stanza reads in translation:

7. Now opens the Father's house above,
   The names of the blest are given.
   Lord, gather us there; let none we love
   Be missed in the joys of heaven.
   Oh, grant to us all a place with Thee;
   We ask through our dear Redeemer.

It was dropped because of an unscriptural thought in Lines 3 and 4. Such a prayer presupposes the possibility of suffering in heaven. This is inconsistent with Rev. 21:4.

The translation is composite, prepared by K. A. Kasberg, O. H. Smeby, and C. Döving for *The Lutheran Hymnary*, 1913.

The tune "Den signede Dag" is by Christoph E. F. Weyse and was composed for Grundtvig's hymn "Den signede Dag med Fryd vi ser," in 1826, for the millennial celebration commemorating the introduction of Christianity into Denmark. The tune is not only Weyse's best, but it ranks as one of the finest church melodies that have come to us from the Norse countries.

593 Why do We Mourn Departing Friends

1. Why do we mourn departing friends
   Or shake at death's alarms?
   'Tis but the voice that Jesus sends
   To call them to His arms.

2. Are we not tending upward, too,
   As fast as time can move?
   Nor would we wish the hours more slow
   To keep us from our Love.

3. Why should we tremble to convey
   Their bodies to the tomb?
   There the dear flesh of Jesus lay
   And scattered all the gloom.

4. The graves of all the saints He blessed
   And softened every bed.
   Where should the dying members rest
   But with their dying Head?

5. Thence He arose, ascending high,
   And showed our feet the way.
   Up to the Lord we, too, shall fly
   At the great rising-day.

6. Then let the last loud trumpet sound
   And bid our kindred rise:
   Awake, ye nations under ground!
   Ye saints, ascend the skies!

This hymn by Isaac Watts appeared in his *Hymns and Spiritual Songs*, 1707. The alterations are slight. Watts wrote in Stanza 3, Line 4:

    And left a long perfume.

In Stanza 5, Line 3, he had:

    Up to the Lord our flesh shall fly.

The tune "Domine, clamavi" is by Justin H. Knecht, 1797.

When My Last Hour Is Close at Hand   594

1. When my last hour is close at hand,
 Lord Jesus Christ, attend me;
Beside me then, O Savior, stand
 To comfort and defend me.
Into Thy hands I will commend
My soul at this my earthly end,
 And Thou wilt keep it safely.

2. My sins, dear Lord, disturb me sore,
 My conscience cannot slumber;
But though as sands upon the shore
 My sins may be in number,
I will not quail, but think of Thee;
Thy death, Thy sorrow, borne for me,
 Thy sufferings, shall uphold me.

3. I am a branch in Thee, the Vine,
 And hence the comfort borrow
That Thou wilt surely keep me Thine
 Through fear and pain and sorrow;
And when I die, I die to Thee,
Thy precious death hath won for me
 The life that never endeth.

4. Since Thou the power of death didst rend,
 In death Thou wilt not leave me;
Since Thou didst into heaven ascend,
 No fear of death shall grieve me.
For where Thou art, there shall I be
That I may ever live with Thee;
 That is my hope when dying.

5. My spirit I commend to Thee
 And gladly hence betake me;
Peaceful and calm my sleep shall be,
 No human voice can wake me.
But Christ is with me through the strife,
And He will bear me into life
 And open heaven before me.

Wenn mein Stündlein vorhanden ist
 Und soll hinfahr'n mein' Strasse,
So g'leit' du mich, Herr Jesu Christ,
 Mit Hilf' mich nicht verlasse!
Mein' Seel' an meinem letzten End'
Befehl' ich dir in deine Händ',
 Du woll'st sie mir bewahren!

Mein' Sünd' mich werden kränken sehr,
 Mein G'wissen wird mich nagen,
Denn ihr'r sind viel wie Sand am Meer;
 Doch will ich nicht verzagen.
Gedenken will ich an dein'n Tod,
Herr Jesu, und dein' Wunden rot,
 Die werden mich erhalten.

Ich bin ein Glied an deinem Leib,
 Des tröst' ich mich von Herzen.
Von dir ich ungeschieden bleib'
 In Todesnot und Schmerzen.
Wenn ich gleich sterb', so sterb' ich dir,
Ein ew'ges Leben hast du mir
 Mit deinem Tod erworben.

Weil du vom Tod erstanden bist,
 Werd' ich im Grab nicht bleiben;
Mein höchster Trost dein' Auffahrt ist,
 Todsfurcht kann sie vertreiben.
Denn wo du bist, da komm' ich hin,
Dass ich stets bei dir leb' und bin,
 Drum fahr' ich hin mit Freuden.

So fahr' ich hin zu Jesu Christ,
 Mein' Arm tu' ich ausstrecken;
So schlaf' ich ein und ruhe fein,
 Kein Mensch kann mich aufwecken
Denn Jesus Christus, Gottes Sohn,
Der wird die Himmelstür auftun,
 Mich führ'n zum ew'gen Leben.

Originally this hymn by Nikolaus Herman, which many consider his masterpiece, was in four stanzas and appeared in his *Historien von der Sindtflut*, etc., Wittenberg, 1562. It was entitled "A spiritual song in which supplication is made for a happy final hour, on the saying of Augustine:

    Turbabor, sed non perturbabor,
    Quia vulnerum Christi recordabor."

Later, by combining this hymn with another by the same author and adding two stanzas by an unknown author, it was expanded to eleven stanzas. One of the added stanzas became Stanza 5 when this hymn was taken up in the Leipzig *Gesang-Buch*, 1582. In this form the hymn has since generally been used.

The translation is an altered form of Catherine Winkworth's in her *Christian Singers of Germany*, 1869. This text was a revision of her version in her *Chorale Book for England*, 1863.

The tune "Wenn mein Stündlein" is from Johann Wolff's *KirchenGesäng*, etc., Frankfurt a. M., 1569.

DEATH AND BURIAL

595   Tender Shepherd, Thou hast Stilled

1. Tender Shepherd, Thou hast stilled
Now Thy little lamb's brief weeping.
Ah, how peaceful and how mild
In its narrow bed 'tis sleeping!
And no sigh of anguish sore
Heaves that little bosom more.

2. In this world of pain and care,
Lord, Thou wouldst no longer leave it;
To Thy heavenly meadows fair
Lovingly Thou dost receive it.
Clothed in robes of spotless white,
Now it dwells with Thee in light.

3. O Lord Jesus, grant that we
There may live where it is living,
There the blissful pastures see
That it heavenly food are giving.
Lost a while our treasured love,
Gained forever, safe above.

Guter Hirt, du hast gestillt
Deines Lämmchens langen Jammer;
Ach, wie ruhig, blass und mild
Liegt's in seiner kleinen Kammer,
Und kein Seufzer bang und schwer
Quälet seinen Busen mehr.

In der Welt voll Angst und Grau'n
Willst du es nicht länger leiden;
Auf den Paradiesesau'n
Soll dein liebes Lamm nun weiden
Und mit unbefleckten Kleid
Schweben in der Herrlichkeit.

O Herr Jesu, möchten wir,
Wo es schwebt, auch einmal schweben,
Und dein sel'ges Lustrevier
Uns auch Himmelsnahrung geben!
Dann sind Not und Tod Gewinn,
Nimmst du auch das Liebste hin.

    This beautiful hymn-prayer at the death of a child is by Johann W. Meinhold and was published in the author's *Gedichte*, Leipzig, 1835, with the heading "Sung in four parts beside the body of my little fifteen-month-old son Joannes Ladislaus." This child of Meinhold's died of teething July 2 and was buried on July 5, 1833.

    The translation is by Catherine Winkworth. It first appeared in her *Lyra Germanica, second series*, 1858, and then in *Hymns Ancient and Modern*, 1861, with alterations that had her approval. The fact that this hymn has found a place in many modern hymnals is testimony to its general appeal.

    For comments on the tune "Meinen Jesum lass' ich nicht" see Hymn No. 55.

596   This Body in the Grave We Lay

1. This body in the grave we lay
There to await that solemn Day
When God Himself shall bid it rise
To mount triumphant to the skies.

2. And so to earth we now entrust
What came from dust and turns to dust
And from the dust shall rise that Day
In glorious triumph o'er decay.

3. The soul forever lives with God,
Who freely hath His grace bestowed
And through His Son redeemed it here
From every sin, from every fear.

4. All trials and all griefs are past,
A blessed end has come at last.
Christ's yoke was borne with ready will;
Who dieth thus is living still.

5. We have no cause to mourn or weep;
Securely shall this body sleep
Till Christ Himself shall death destroy
And raise the blessed dead to joy.

6. For they who with Him suffered here
Shall there be healed from woe and fear;
And when eternal bliss is won,
They'll shine in glory like the sun.

Nun lasst uns den Leib begraben;
Daran wir kein'n Zweifel haben,
Er wird am Jüngsten Tag aufstehn
Und unverweslich hervorgehn.

Erd' ist er und von der Erden,
Wird auch zur Erd' wieder werden
Und von der Erd' wieder aufstehn,
Wenn Gottes Posaun' wird angehn.

Sein' Seele lebt ewig in Gott,
Der sie allhier aus lauter Gnad'
Von aller Sünd' und Missetat
Durch seinen Sohn erlöset hat.

Sein Jammer, Trübsal und Elend
Ist kommen zu ein'm sel'gen End';
Er hat getragen Christi Joch,
Ist gestorben und lebet noch.

Die Seele lebt ohn' alle Klag',
Der Leib schläft bis an Jüngsten Tag,
An welchem Gott ihn verklären
Und ew'ger Freud' wird gewähren.

Hier ist er in Angst gewesen,
Dort aber wird er genesen,
In ew'ger Freude und Wonne
Leuchten wie die helle Sonne.

7. Then let us leave this place of rest
   And homeward turn, for they are blest
   Who heed God's warning and prepare
   Lest death should find them unaware.

Nun lassen wir ihn hier schlafen
Und gehn all' heim unsre Strassen,
Schicken uns auch mit allem Fleiss,
Denn der Tod kommt uns gleicherweis'.

8. So help us, Jesus, Ground of faith;
   Thou hast redeemed us by Thy death
   From endless death and set us free.
   We laud and praise and worship Thee.

Das helf' uns Christus, unser Trost,
Der uns durch sein Blut hat erlöst
Von's Teufels G'walt und ew'ger Pein;
Ihm sei Lob, Preis und Ehr' allein!

Michael Weisse is credited with the authorship of this hymn, save for the last stanza. It is evidently based on the Latin hymn of Prudentius "Deus ignee, fons animarum," although it cannot be called a translation. One authority holds that it is an expansion of a Bohemian hymn by Lucas of Prague, in four stanzas, published in the *Brethren's Hymn-Book*, 1519. Weisse's hymn appeared in *Ein New Gesang buchlen*, Jung Bunzlan, 1531, under the rubric "Special Songs for the Burial of the Dead," entitled "At the Grave." A recast of the hymn was published in later hymn-books, with the eighth stanza added, whether by Weisse or some one else is unknown.

The translation is an altered form of that by Catherine Winkworth, in *Lyra Germanica*, second series, 1858.

The tune "Nun lasst uns den Leib" is wedded to the hymn and is found in Georg Rhau's *Newe Deudsche Geistliche Gesenge*, Wittenberg, 1544.

For Me to Live Is Jesus   597

1. For me to live is Jesus,
     To die is gain for me;
   Then, whensoe'er He pleases,
     I meet death willingly.

Christus, der ist mein Leben,
  Sterben ist mein Gewinn,
Dem tu' ich mich ergeben,
  Mit Freud' fahr' ich dahin.

2. For Christ, my Lord and Brother,
   I leave this world so dim
   And gladly seek that other,
   Where I shall be with Him.

Mit Freud' fahr ich von dannen
Zu Christ, dem Bruder mein,
Dass ich mög' zu ihm kommen
Und ewig bei ihm sein.

3. My woes are nearly over,
   Though long and dark the road;
   My sin His merits cover,
   And I have peace with God.

Nun hab' ich überwunden
Kreuz, Leiden, Angst und Not,
Durch sein' heilig' fünf Wunden
Bin ich versöhnt mit Gott.

4. Lord, when my powers are failing,
   My breath comes heavily,
   And words are unavailing,
   Oh, hear my sighs to Thee!

Wenn meine Kräfte brechen,
Mein Atem schwer geht aus
Und kann kein Wort mehr sprechen:
Herr, nimm mein Seufzen auf!

5. When mind and thought, O Savior,
   Are flickering like a light
   That to and fro doth waver
   Ere 'tis extinguished quite,

Wenn mein Herz und Gedanken
Vergehen wie ein Licht,
Das hin und her muss wanken,
Wenn ihm die Flamm' gebricht:

6. In that last hour, oh, grant me
   To slumber soft and still,
   No doubts to vex or haunt me,
   Safe anchored on Thy will;

Alsdann fein sanft und stille,
Herr, lass mich schlafen ein
Nach deinem Rat und Willen,
Wenn kommt mein Stündelein,

7. And so to Thee still cleaving
   Through all death's agony,
   To fall asleep believing
   And wake in heaven with Thee.

Und lass mich an dir kleben
Wie eine Klett' am Kleid
Und ewig bei dir leben
In Himmelswonn' und -freud'!

8. Amen! Thou, Christ, my Savior,
   Wilt grant this unto me.
   Thy Spirit lead me ever
   That I fare happily.

Amen, das wirst du, Christe,
Verleihen gnädiglich!
Mit deinem Geist mich rüste,
Dass ich fahr' seliglich!

DEATH AND BURIAL

This hymn, by an unknown author, first appeared in seven stanzas in Vulpius's *Ein schön geistlich Gesangbuch*, etc., Jena, 1609; then, in a slightly altered form, with an eighth stanza, in *Christliches Gesangbüchlein*, Hamburg, 1612. This eighth stanza, however, a doxology, is not the same as the eighth above. We have not been able to trace the time or the authorship of this stanza.

The hymn has long been a favorite. The translation, except Stanza 8 by an unknown writer, is by Catherine Winkworth, slightly altered, included in her *Chorale Book for England*, 1863.

For comments on the tune "Christus, der ist mein" see Hymn No. 53.

598 Who Knows when Death May Overtake Me

1. Who knows when death may overtake me!
   Time passes on, my end draws near.
How swiftly can my breath forsake me!
   How soon can life's last hour appear!
My God, for Jesus' sake I pray
Thy peace may bless my dying day.

2. The world that smiled when morn was breaking
   May change for me ere close of day;
For while on earth my home I'm making,
   Death's threat is never far away.
My God, for Jesus' sake I pray
Thy peace may bless my dying day.

3. My end to ponder teach me ever
   And, ere the hour of death appears,
To cast my soul on Christ, my Savior,
   Nor spare repentant sighs and tears.
My God, for Jesus' sake I pray
Thy peace may bless my dying day.

4. Help me now set my house in order
   That always ready I may be
To say in meekness on death's border:
   Lord, as Thou wilt, deal Thou with me.
My God, for Jesus' sake I pray
Thy peace may bless my dying day.

5. Reveal the sweetness of Thy heaven,
   Earth's galling bitterness unfold;
May I, amid this turmoil riven,
   Thy blest eternity behold.
My God, for Jesus' sake I pray
Thy peace may bless my dying day.

6. My many sins blot out forever
   Since Jesus has my pardon won;
In mercy robed, I then shall never
   Fear death, but trust in Thee alone.
My God, for Jesus' sake I pray
Thy peace may bless my dying day.

7. Naught shall my soul from Jesus sever;
   In faith I touch His wounded side
And hail Him as my Lord forever,
   Nor life nor death shall us divide.
My God, for Jesus' sake I pray
Thy peace may bless my dying day.

8. Once in the blest baptismal waters
   I put on Christ and made Him mine;
Now numbered with God's sons and daughters,
   I share His peace and love divine.
My God, for Jesus' sake I pray
Thy peace may bless my dying day.

Wer weiss, wie nahe mir mein Ende!
Hin geht die Zeit, her kommt der Tod.
Ach, wie geschwinde und behende
Kann kommen meine Todesnot!
Mein Gott, ich bitt' durch Christi Blut:
Mach's nur mit meinem Ende gut!

Es kann vor Nacht leicht anders werden,
Als es am frühen Morgen war;
Denn weil ich leb' auf dieser Erden,
Leb' ich in steter Todsgefahr.
Mein Gott, ich bitt' durch Christi Blut:
Mach's nur mit meinem Ende gut!

Herr, lehr mich stets mein End' bedenken
Und, wenn ich einstens sterben muss,
Die Seel' in Jesu Wunden senken
Und ja nicht sparen meine Buss'!
Mein Gott, ich bitt' durch Christi Blut:
Mach's nur mit meinem Ende gut!

Lass mich beizeit mein Haus bestellen,
Dass ich bereit sei für und für
Und sage frisch in allen Fällen:
Herr, wie du willst, so schick's mit mir!
Mein Gott, ich bitt' durch Christi Blut:
Mach's nur mit meinem Ende gut!

Mach mir stets zuckersüss den Himmel
Und gallenbitter diese Welt;
Gib, dass mir in dem Weltgetümmel
Die Ewigkeit sei vorgestellt!
Mein Gott, ich bitt' durch Christi Blut:
Mach's nur mit meinem Ende gut!

Ach Vater, deck all meine Sünde
Mit dem Verdienste Christi zu,
Darein ich mich fest gläubig winde;
Das gibt mir recht erwünschte Ruh'.
Mein Gott, ich bitt' durch Christi Blut:
Mach's nur mit meinem Ende gut!

Nichts ist, was mich von Jesu scheide,
Nichts, es sei Leben oder Tod.
Ich leg' die Hand in seine Seite
Und sage: Mein Herr und mein Gott!
Mein Gott, ich bitt' durch Christi Blut:
Mach's nur mit meinem Ende gut!

Ich habe Jesum angezogen
Schon längst in meiner heil'gen Tauf';
Du bist mir auch daher gewogen,
Hast mich zum Kind genommen auf.
Mein Gott, ich bitt' durch Christi Blut:
Mach's nur mit meinem Ende gut!

DEATH AND BURIAL

9. His body and His blood I've taken
   In His blest Supper, feast divine;
   Now I shall never be forsaken,
   For I am His, and He is mine.
   My God, for Jesus' sake I pray
   Thy peace may bless my dying day.

10. Then may death come today, tomorrow,
    I know in Christ I perish not;
    He grants the peace that stills all sorrow,
    Gives me a robe without a spot.
    My God, for Jesus' sake I pray
    Thy peace may bless my dying day.

11. And thus I live in God contented
    And die without a thought of fear;
    My soul has to God's plans consented,
    For through His Son my faith is clear.
    My God, for Jesus' sake I pray
    Thy peace may bless my dying day.

Ich habe Jesu Fleisch gegessen,
  Ich hab' sein Blut getrunken hier;
Nun kann er meiner nicht vergessen,
  Ich bleib' in ihm und er in mir.
Mein Gott, ich bitt' durch Christi Blut:
Mach's nur mit meinem Ende gut!

So komm' mein End' heut' oder morgen,
  Ich weiss, dass mir's mit Jesu glückt;
Ich bin und bleib' in seinen Sorgen,
  Mit Jesu Blut schön ausgeschmückt.
Mein Gott, ich bitt', durch Christi Blut:
Mach's nur mit meinem Ende gut!

Ich leb' indes in Gott vergnüget
  Und sterb' ohn alle Kümmernis;
Mir g'nüget, wie es mein Gott füget,
  Ich glaub' und bin es ganz gewiss:
Durch deine Gnad' und Christi Blut
Machst du's mit meinem Ende gut!

This hymn, originally in twelve stanzas, is from the pen of Ämilie Juliane, countess of Schwarzburg-Rudolstadt, although George Michael Pfefferkorn claimed it as his own. The hymn appeared in print in the *Appendix* of the *Rudolstadt Gesang Buch*, 1688, but it was written in 1686. The church library in Gera has the hymn in the handwriting of the countess, dated "Neuhaus, d. 17. Sept. 1686."

The composite translation was prepared for *The Lutheran Hymnal*. The omitted seventh stanza in Miss Winkworth's translation reads:

> His sorrows and His cross, I know,
>   Make death-beds soft and light the grave,
> They comfort in the hour of woe,
>   They give me all I fain would have.
> My God, for Jesus' sake I pray
> Thy peace may bless my dying day.

For comments on the tune "Wer weiss, wie nahe" see Hymn No. 65.

My Course is Run. Praise God, My Course is Run 599

1. My course is run. Praise God, my course is run,
     My Jesus welcomes me.
   Farewell, my friends, my work on earth is done,
     The heavenly goal I see.
   My dear Redeemer's praises voicing,
   I leave this world with great rejoicing.
   My course is run. My course is run.

2. My course is run. My Jesus took for me
     Upon Himself my guilt.
   Upon the cross, the bitter, shameful tree,
     For me His blood He spilt.
   Thus by His death and grace abounding
   For me a refuge surely founding.
   My course is run. My course is run.

3. My course is run. Now I am free from need,
     From dangers, fear, and dread.
   With heaven's bread the Lord will me now feed,
     High honors on me shed.
   Now I will hear the angels singing,
   Sweet songs of seraphim are ringing.
   My course is run. My course is run.

Es ist vollbracht! Gott Lob, es ist vollbracht!
  Mein Jesus nimmt mich auf!
Fahr hin, o Welt! Ihr Freunde, gute Nacht!
  Ich ende meinen Lauf
Bei Jesu Kreuz mit tausend Freuden,
Ich sehne mich, von hier zu scheiden.
Es ist vollbracht!

Es ist vollbracht! Mein Jesus hat auf sich
  Genommen meine Schuld;
Er selber hat am Kreuzesstamm für mich —
  O ungemeine Huld! —
Gebüsset, und in Jesu Wunden
Hab' ich die rechte Freistadt funden.
Es ist vollbracht!

Es ist vollbracht! Hier bin ich ausser Not,
  Angst und Gefahr gesetzt;
Hier speiset mich der Herr mit Himmelsbrot,
  Hier bin ich hoch geschätzt;
Hier hör' ich auf den Engelsbühnen
Den süssen Ton der Seraphinen.
Es ist vollbracht!

DEATH AND BURIAL

4. My course is run. Praise God, my course is run,
   My Jesus welcomes me.
Farewell, my friends, my work on earth is done,
   The heavenly goal I see.
Freed from all trouble and repining,
I see the open heaven shining.
My course is run. My course is run.

Es ist vollbracht! Gott Lob, es ist vollbracht!
   Mein Jesus nimmt mich auf;
Fahr hin, o Welt! Ihr Freunde, gute Nacht!
   Ich schliesse meinen Lauf
Und allen Jammer, der mich troffen.
Wohl mir, ich seh' den Himmel offen.
   Es ist vollbracht!

This cento is composed of Stanzas 1, 2, 4, and 7 of the hymn "Es ist vollbracht," which is commonly attributed to Andreas Gryphius. It first appeared in *Vollständiges Haus- und Kirchen-Gesangbuch*, Breslau, 1726.

The translation is by August Zich and was prepared for *The Lutheran Hymnal* in 1937.

For comments on the tune "Es ist genug" see Hymn No. 196.

600   O Lord, My God, I Cry to Thee

1. O Lord, my God, I cry to Thee;
In my distress Thou helpest me.
My soul and body I commend
Into Thy hands; Thine angel send
To guide me home and cheer my heart
When Thou dost call me to depart.

O Herre Gott, in meiner Not
Ruf' ich zu dir! Du hilfest mir,
Mein Leib und Seel' ich dir befehl'
In deine Händ'. Dein'n Engel send',
Der mich bewahr', wenn ich hinfahr'
Aus dieser Welt, wenn dir's gefällt.

2. O Jesus Christ, Thou Lamb of God,
Once slain to take away our load,
Now let Thy cross, Thine agony,
Avail to save and solace me,
Thy death, to open heaven, and there
Bid me the joy of angels share.

O Jesu Christ, gestorben bist
Am Kreuzesstamm, du Gotteslamm!
Dein' Wunden rot in aller Not,
Dein teures Blut komm' mir zugut,
Dein Leid'n und Sterb'n mach mich zum Erb'n
In deinem Reich, den Engeln gleich!

3. O Holy Spirit, faithful Friend,
Grant me Thy comfort to the end.
When death and hell assail me sore,
Leave me, oh, leave me, nevermore,
But bear me safely through the strife,
As Thou hast promised, into life.

O Heil'ger Geist, ein Tröster heisst,
An meinem End' dein'n Trost mir send'!
Verlass mich nicht, wenn mich anficht
Des Teufels G'walt, des Tods Gestalt!
Mein höchster Hort, nach deinem Wort
Woll'st du mir geb'n das ew'ge Leb'n!

Nikolaus Selnecker first published this hymn for the dying in his *Der Psalter mit Kurtzen Summarien*, etc., Leipzig, 1572, based on Ps. 116:9. He also included it in his hymnal, "*Christliche Psalmen, Lieder, und Kirchengesenge*, etc., Leipzig, 1578, with the following Bible references, Ps. 116:9; 56:13; 36:9.

The translation is by Catherine Winkworth, *Lyra Germanica*, second series, 1858, slightly altered.

For comments on the tune "Vater unser" see Hymn No. 458.

601   All Men Living Are But Mortal

1. All men living are but mortal,
   Yea, all flesh must fade as grass;
Only through death's gloomy portal
   To eternal life we pass.
This frail body here must perish
Ere the heavenly joys it cherish,
Ere it gain the free reward
For the ransomed of the Lord.

Alle Menschen müssen sterben,
   Alles Fleisch vergeht wie Heu;
Was da lebet, muss verderben,
   Soll es anders werden neu.
Dieser Leib, der muss verwesen,
Wenn er anders soll genesen
Zu der grossen Herrlichkeit,
Die den Frommen ist bereit.

2. Therefore, when my God doth choose it,
   Willingly I'll yield my life
Nor will grieve that I should lose it,
   For with sorrows it was rife.
In my dear Redeemer's merit
Peace hath found my troubled spirit,
And in death my comfort this:
Jesus' death my source of bliss.

Drum so will ich dieses Leben,
   Wann es meinem Gott beliebt,
Auch ganz willig von mir geben,
   Bin darüber nicht betrübt;
Denn in meines Jesu Wunden
Hab' ich schon Erlösung funden,
Und mein Trost in Todesnot
Ist des Herren Jesu Tod.

3. Jesus for my sake descended
    My salvation to obtain;
  Death and hell for me are ended,
    Peace and hope are now my gain;
  Yea, with joy I leave earth's sadness
  For the home of heavenly gladness,
    Where I shall forever see
    God, the Holy Trinity.

4. There is joy beyond our telling,
    Where so many saints have gone;
  Thousands, thousands, there are dwelling,
    Worshiping before the throne,
  There the Seraphim are shining,
  Evermore in chorus joining:
    "Holy, holy, holy, Lord!
    Triune God, for aye adored!"

5. Patriarchs of sacred story
    And the prophets there are found;
  The apostles, too, in glory
    On twelve seats are there enthroned.
  All the saints that have ascended
  Age on age, through time extended,
    There in blissful concert sing
    Hallelujahs to their King.

6. O Jerusalem, how glorious
    Dost thou shine, thou city fair!
  Lo, I hear the tones victorious
    Ever sweetly sounding there.
  Oh, the bliss that there surprises!
  Lo, the sun of morn now rises,
    And the breaking day I see
    That shall never end for me.

7. Yea, I see what here was told me,
    See that wondrous glory shine,
  Feel the spotless robes enfold me,
    Know a golden crown is mine.
  Thus before the throne so glorious
  Now I stand a soul victorious,
    Gazing on that joy for aye
    That shall never pass away.

Jesus ist für mich gestorben,
  Und sein Tod ist mein Gewinn;
Er hat mir das Heil erworben,
  Drum fahr' ich mit Freuden hin,
Hin aus diesem Weltgetümmel
In den schönen Gotteshimmel,
  Da ich werde allezeit
  Schauen die Dreieinigkeit.

Da wird sein das Freudenleben,
  Da viel tausend Seelen schon
Sind mit Himmelsglanz umgeben,
  Dienen Gott vor seinem Thron,
Da die Seraphinen prangen
Und das hohe Lied anfangen:
  Heilig, heilig, heilig heisst
  Gott der Vater, Sohn und Geist,

Da die Patriarchen wohnen,
  Die Propheten allzumal,
Da auf ihren Ehrenthronen
  Sitzet die gezwölfte Zahl,
Da in so viel tausend Jahren
Alle Frommen hingefahren,
  Da wir unserm Gott zu Ehr'n
  Ewig Halleluja hör'n.

O Jerusalem, du Schöne,
  Ach, wie helle glänzest du!
Ach, wie lieblich Lobgetöne
  Hört man da in sanfter Ruh'!
O der grossen Freud' und Wonne!
Jetzund gehet auf die Sonne,
  Jetzund gehet an der Tag,
  Der kein Ende nehmen mag.

Ach, ich habe schon erblicket
  Diese grosse Herrlichkeit!
Jetzund werd' ich schön geschmücket
  Mit dem weissen Himmelskleid
Und der goldnen Ehrenkrone,
Stehe da vor Gottes Throne,
  Schaue solche Freude an,
  Die kein Ende nehmen kann.

This hymn, by Johann Georg Albinus, Koch calls "his best-known hymn and a pearl in the Evangelical treasury of Song." It was written for the funeral of Paul von Henssberg, a Leipzig merchant, and was thus sung from broadsheets, June 1, 1652. Later Albinus used it in a funeral sermon for Regina Staffelin, citing it as his own composition.

The translation, excepting Stanza 5, is an altered form of that by Catherine Winkworth in her *Chorale Book for England*, 1863. Stanza 5, by an unknown writer, is from the Ohio *Lutheran Hymnal*, 1880, altered.

The tune "Alle Menschen müssen sterben" is attributed to Johann Rosenmüller, who is said to have composed it for Albinus's text, to which the hymn was sung at von Henssberg's funeral. The melody first appeared in Johann Crüger's *Praxis Pietatis Melica*, Berlin, 1678.

It Is Not Death to Die 602

1. It is not death to die,
    To leave this weary road,
  And midst the brotherhood on high
    To be at home with God.

2. It is not death to close
    The eye long dimmed by tears
  And wake in glorious repose
    To spend eternal years.

Nein, nein, das ist kein Sterben,
  Zu seinem Gott zu gehn,
Der dunkeln Erd' entfliehen,
Und zu der Heimat ziehen
  In reine Sternenhöh'n!

Nein, nein, das ist kein Sterben,
  Ein Himmelsbürger sein,
Beim Glanz der ew'gen Kronen
In süsser Ruhe wohnen,
  Erlöst von Kampf und Pein.

3. It is not death to bear
   The wrench that sets us free
   From dungeon chain, to breathe the air
   To spend eternal years.

4. It is not death to fling
   Aside this sinful dust
   And rise, on strong, exulting wing,
   To live among the just.

5. Jesus, Thou Prince of Life,
   Thy chosen cannot die;
   Like Thee, they conquer in the strife
   To reign with Thee on high.

Nein, nein, das ist kein Sterben,
Der Gnadenstimme Ton
Voll Majestät zu hören:
"Komm, Kind, und schau mit Ehren
Mein Antlitz auf dem Thron!"

Nein, nein, das ist kein Sterben,
Dem Hirten nachzugehn.
Er führt sein Schaf zu Freuden,
Er wird dich ewig weiden,
Wo Lebensbäume stehn.

Nein, nein, das ist kein Sterben,
Mit Herrlichkeit gekrönt
Zu Gottes Volk sich schwingen,
Und Jesu Sieg besingen,
Der uns mit Gott versöhnt.

O nein, das ist kein Sterben,
Du Heil der Kreatur!
Dort strömt in ew'gen Wonnen
Der Liebe voller Bronnen;
Hier sind es Tropfen nur.

The original of this hymn is "Non ce n'est pas mourir" by H. A. César Malan of Geneva, published in his *Chants de Sion*, etc., 1832. It was translated into German by Albert Knapp in six stanzas and first appeared in his *Christoterpe*, 1836. George Washington Bethune freely translated Knapp's version in five stanzas and published the hymn in his *Lays of Love and Faith*, Philadelphia, 1847. The hymn was sung at Bethune's burial in New York, September, 1862, after his remains had been brought here from Florence, Italy, where he had gone for his health and where he died suddenly after preaching, April 27, 1862.

For comments on the tune "Tenbury" see Hymn No. 591.

603   In the Resurrection

1. In the resurrection :,:
   We do trust. From the dust
   Shall this body — this the hope we cherish —
   Rise before God clothed in pure perfection.
   Jesus, Lord, Help afford;
   Oh, save us lest we perish!

2. Earth receives the mortal, :,:
   Doubt not this While in bliss,
   Cleansed of sin and crowned with peace eternal,
   There serenely rests the soul immortal.
   Oh, rejoice, Praises voice, —
   'Tis saved from foes infernal.

3. Such rest we shall enter :,:
   And then rise To the skies
   When the Savior's call "Come forth" shall waken
   Both the blessed dead and bold dissenter.
   Lord of Life, In our strife
   Oh, leave us not forsaken!

4. When we die, dear Savior, :,:
   Grant, we pray, On that day
   That from sorrow Thou wilt lead in mercy
   To the joy before Thy throne forever.
   At Thy side, Glorified,
   Oh, may we ever praise Thee!

Vzkříšení čekáme :,:
Tohoto :/: těla, o němž věříme :,:
že v něm jistotně Boha uzříme;
Kriste náš,
Spasiž nás,
Ať věčně nezhyneme.

Tělo myrtvé v zemi :/:
Klade se :,: jehož duše jest
v nebi :,:
Kdežto nižádné bolesti není;
Raduj se,
Hříšníče,
Žádné tam nouze není.

Za nimi půjdeme :,:
S nimi však :/: z svých hrobů ven vyjdeme :,:
K hlasu archanjela: Podte z země;
Kriste náš,
Přijmiž nás
Tam, kdež všeho hojnost máš.

Dejž, Pane, dojíti :/:
Dadosti :/: po nynější žalosti :/:
Skroušené prosíme tvé milosti.
Tys Pánem,
Když stanem
Před Tebou, spas nás, Amen.

This beautiful resurrection hymn by an unknown author is of Slovak origin and first appeared in the *Tranoscius*, 1674 edition. The translation by John Bajus was prepared for *The Lutheran Hymnal* in 1939.

The tune "Resurrection" is a Slovak melody from a handwritten tune book of 1750.

JUDGMENT

Great God, What Do I See and Hear? 604

1. Great God, what do I see and hear?
      The end of things created;
   The Judge of mankind doth appear
      On clouds of glory seated.
   The trumpet sounds; the graves restore
   The dead which they contained before:
      Prepare, my soul, to meet Him.

2. The dead in Christ shall first arise
      At that last trumpet's sounding,
   Caught up to meet Him in the skies,
      With joy their Lord surrounding.
   No gloomy fears their souls dismay;
   His presence sheds eternal day
      On those prepared to meet Him.

3. But sinners, filled with guilty fears,
      Behold His wrath prevailing,
   For they shall rise and find their tears
      And sighs are unavailing;
   The day of grace is past and gone;
   They trembling stand before His throne,
      All unprepared to meet Him.

4. O Christ, who diedst and yet dost live,
      To me impart Thy merit;
   My pardon seal, my sins forgive,
      And cleanse me by Thy Spirit.
   Beneath Thy cross I view the day
   When heaven and earth shall pass away,
      And thus prepare to meet Thee.

Julian has a lengthy discussion of this hymn, sometimes called a translation of *Dies Irae* or of Ringwaldt's "Es ist gewisslich an der Zeit." What the hymn has in common with both is its subject-matter. It seems that the first stanza was published anonymously in *Psalms and Hymns*, etc., Sheffield, 1802. William Bengo Collyer then added three stanzas and published the hymn in his *Hymns*, etc., 1812. He added the following note: "This hymn, which is adapted to Luther's celebrated tune, is universally ascribed to that great man. As I never saw more than this first verse, I was obliged to lengthen it for the completion of the subject and am responsible for the verses which follow." An altered form of Collier's version next appeared in Cotterill's *Selection*, 1819. This is the English text above, except that the first four lines of Stanza 4 are an address to Christ, written by an unknown author, instead of a repetition of the first four lines of Stanza 1.

The tune "Es ist gewisslich" first appeared in Joseph Klug's *Geistliche Lieder*, Wittenberg, 1535, where it was set to the hymn "Nun freut euch, liebe Christen g'mein." (See Hymn No. 387.)

The World Is Very Evil 605

1. The world is very evil,
      The times are waxing late;
   Be sober and keep vigil,
      The Judge is at the gate;
   The Judge that comes in mercy,
      The Judge that comes with might,
   To terminate the evil,
      To diadem the right.

2. Arise, arise, good Christian,
      Let right to wrong succeed;
   Let penitential sorrow
      To heavenly gladness lead,
   To light that hath no evening,
      That knows no moon nor sun,
   The light so new and golden,
      The light that is but one.

3. O home of fadeless splendor,
      Of flowers that bear no thorn,
   Where they shall dwell as children
      Who here as exiles mourn.
   Midst power that knows no limit,
      Where knowledge has no bound,
   The beatific vision
      Shall glad the saints around.

4. Strive, man, to win that glory;
      Toil, man, to gain that light;
   Send hope before to grasp it
      Till hope be lost in sight.
   Exult, O' dust and ashes,
      The Lord shall be thy part;
   His only, His forever,
      Thou shalt be and thou art.

Hora novissima, tempora pessima
   Sunt; vigilemus.
Ecce minaciter imminet arbiter
   Ille supremus, —
Imminet, imminet, ut mala terminet,
   Aequa coronet,
Recta remuneret, anxia liberet,
   Aethera donet.

Curre, vir optime; lubrica reprime,
   Praefer honesta,
Fletibus angere, flendo merebere
   Caelica festa.
Luce replebere iam sine vespere,
   Iam sine luna;
Lux nova lux ea, lux erit aurea,
   Lux erit una.

Patria splendida, terraque florida,
   Libera spinis,
Danda fidelibus est ibi civibus,
   Hic peregrinis.
Tunc erit omnibus inspicientibus
   Ora Tonantis
Summa potentia, plena scientia,
   Pax rata sanctis.

5. O sweet and blessed country,
   The home of God's elect!
O sweet and blessed country
   That eager hearts expect!
Jesus, in mercy bring us
   To that dear land of rest,
Who art, with God the Father
   And Spirit, ever blest.

Hic homo nititur, ambulat, utitur;
   Ergo fruetur.
Pax, rata pax ea, spe modo, postea
   Re capietur.
Plaude, cinis meus, est tua pars Deus;
   Eius es et sis;
Rex tuus est tua portio, tu sua;
   Ne sibi desis. Amen.

For comments on the hymn and tune "Ewing" see Hymn No. 448.

606   O'er the Distant Mountains Breaking

1. O'er the distant mountains breaking
   Comes the reddening dawn of day.
   Rise, my soul, from sleep awaking;
   Rise and sing and watch and pray.
   'Tis thy Savior
   On His bright returning way.

2. O Thou Long-expected,
      weary
   Waits my anxious soul for Thee;
   Life is dark, and earth is dreary,
   Where Thy light I do not see.
   O my Savior,
   When wilt Thou return to me?

3. Nearer is my soul's salvation;
   Spent the night, the day at hand.
   Keep me in my lowly station,
   Watching for Thee till I stand,
   O my Savior,
   In Thy bright, Thy promised, land.

4. With my lamp well trimmed and
      burning,
   Swift to hear and slow to roam,
   Watching for Thy glad returning
   To restore me to my home.
   Come, my Savior,
   O my Savior, quickly come.

John S. B. Monsell published this hymn on the Second Advent in his *Hymns of Love and Praise*, 1863, in five stanzas. The omitted third stanza reads:

> Long, too long, in sin and sadness,
>   Far away from Thee I pine;
> When, oh, when shall I the gladness
>   Of Thy Spirit feel in mine?
> O my Savior,
>   When shall I be wholly Thine?

The tune "O Jerusalem, du Schöne" is by Johann G. Störl and appeared in Friedrich K. Hiller's *Denkmal zur Erkenntnis*, etc., Stuttgart, 1711, where it was set to Hiller's hymn beginning with that line.

607   Day of Wrath, O Day of Mourning

1. Day of wrath, O day of mourning!
   See fulfilled the Prophet's warning,
   Heaven and earth in ashes burning.

2. Oh, what fear man's bosom rendeth
   When from heaven the Judge descendeth
   On whose sentence all dependeth!

3. Wondrous sound the trumpet flingeth,
   Through earth's sepulchers it ringeth,
   All before the throne it bringeth.

4. Death is struck and nature quaking;
   All creation is awaking,
   To its Judge an answer making.

5. Lo, the book, exactly worded
   Wherein all hath been recorded;
   Thence shall judgment be awarded.

6. When the Judge His seat attaineth
   And each hidden deed arraigneth,
   Nothing unavenged remaineth.

7. What shall I, frail man, be pleading?
   Who for me be interceding
   When the just are mercy needing?

Dies irae, dies illa!
Solvet faeclum in favillâ,
Teste David cum Sibyllâ.

Quantus tremor est futurus,
Quando Iudex est venturus,
Cuncta stricte discussurus.

Tuba mirum spargens sonum
Per sepulcra regionum,
Coget omnes ante thronum.

Mors stupebit, et natura,
Quum resurget creatura,
Iudicanti responsura.

Liber scriptus proferetur,
In quo totum continetur,
Unde mundus iudicetur.

Iudex ergo cum sedebit,
Quidquid latet, apparebit:
Nil inultum remanebit.

Quid sum, miser! tunc dicturus,
Quem patronum rogaturus,
Quum vix iustus sit securus?

JUDGMENT

8. King of majesty tremendous,
Who dost free salvation send us,
Fount of pity, then befriend us.

Rex tremendae maiestatis,
Qui salvandos salvas gratis,
Salva me, fons pietatis!

9. Think, good Jesus, my salvation
Caused Thy wondrous incarnation;
Leave me not to reprobation!

Recordare, Iesu pie,
Quod sum causa tuae viae;
Ne me perdas illâ die!

10. Faint and weary Thou hast sought me,
On the cross of suffering bought me;
Shall such grace be vainly brought me?

Quaerens me, sedisti lassus,
Redemisti, crucem passus:
Tantus labor non sit cassus.

11. Righteous Judge, for sin's pollution
Grant Thy gift of absolution
Ere that day of retribution.

Iuste Iudex ultionis,
Donum fac remissionis
Ante diem rationis.

12. Guilty, now I pour my moaning,
All my shame with anguish owning:
Spare, O God, Thy suppliant groaning!

Ingemisco tanquam reus,
Culpâ rubet vultus meus;
Supplicanti parce, Deus!

13. From that sinful woman shriven,
From the dying thief forgiven,
Thou to me a hope hast given.

Qui Mariam absolvisti,
Et latronem exaudisti,
Mihi quoque spem dedisti.

14. Worthless are my prayers and sighing;
Yet, good Lord, in grace complying,
Rescue me from fires undying.

Preces meae non sunt dignae,
Sed Tu bonus fac benigne
Ne perenni cremer igne!

15. With Thy favored sheep, oh, place me!
Nor among the goats abase me,
But to Thy right hand upraise me.

Inter oves locum praesta,
Et ab haedis me sequestra,
Statuens in parte dextrâ.

16. While the wicked are confounded,
Doomed to flames of woe unbounded,
Call me, with Thy saints surrounded.

Confutatis maledictis,
Flammis acribus addictis,
Voca me cum benedictis!

17. Low I kneel with heart-submission,
See, like ashes, my contrition;
Help me in my last condition!

Oro supplex et acclinis,
Cor contritum quasi cinis,
Gere curam mei finis.

18. Day of sorrow, day of weeping,
When in dust no longer sleeping,
Man awakes in Thy dread keeping!

Lacrimosa dies illa!
Qua resurget ex favillâ
Iudicandus homo reus;
Huic ergo parce, Deus!

19. To the rest Thou didst prepare me
On Thy cross; O Christ, upbear me!
Spare, O God, in mercy spare me!

Thomas de Celano, friend and biographer of Francis of Assisi, is generally credited with the authorship of this great medieval sequence, the opening lines of which are taken verbatim from the Vulgate version of Zeph. 1:15. *Julian,* writing of the general acceptance of this hymn, declares:

The hold which this sequence has had upon the minds of men of various nations and creeds has been very great. Goethe uses it, as is well known, in his *Faust* with great effect. It also furnishes a grand climax to Canto VI in Sir Walter Scott's *Lay of the Last Minstrel.* It has been translated into many languages, in some of which the renderings are very numerous, those in German numbering about ninety and those in English about one hundred and sixty. In Great Britain and America no hymn-book of any note has appeared during the past hundred years without the "Dies Irae" being directly or indirectly represented therein. *Daniel,* writing from a German standpoint, says:

"Even those to whom the hymns of the Latin Church are almost entirely unknown, certainly know this one; and if any one can be found so alien from human nature that they have no appreciation of sacred poetry, yet, as a matter of certainty, even they would give their minds to this hymn, of which every word is weighty, yes, even a thunderclap."

From another standpoint, Archbishop Trench says:

"Nor is it hard to account for its popularity. The meter so grandly devised, of which I remember no other example, fitted though it has here shown itself for bringing out some of the noblest powers of the Latin language — the solemn effect of the triple rime, which has been likened to blow following blow of the hammer on the anvil, the confidence of the poet in the universal interest of his theme, a confidence which has made him set out his matter with so majestic and unadorned a plainness as at once to be intelligible to all, — these merits, with many more, have given the *Dies Irae* a foremost place among the masterpieces of sacred song." — *Sac. Lat. Poetry*, 1874, p. 302.

The translation, one of many excellent ones, is by William J. Irons, slightly altered. It was first issued in the privately printed *Introits and Hymns for Advent*, issued, without date, very likely 1848, for the use of Margaret Street Chapel, London. *Julian* has this to say about the origin of the translation:

It is well known that the Revolution in Paris in 1848 led to many scenes of terror and shame. Foremost was the death of Monsigneur D. A. Affre, the Archbishop of Paris, who was shot on June 25 on the barricades of the Place de la Bastille whilst endeavoring to persuade the insurgents to cease firing, and was buried on July 7. As soon as it was safe to do so, his funeral sermon was preached in Notre Dame, accompanied by a religious service of the most solemn and impressive kind. Throughout the service the archbishop's heart was exposed in a glass case in the choir, and at the appointed place the *Dies Irae* was sung by an immense body of priests. The terror of the times, the painful sense of bereavement which rested upon the minds of the people through the death of their archbishop, the exposed heart in the choir, the imposing ritual of the service, and the grand rendering of the *Dies Irae* by the priests gave to the occasion an unusual degree of impressiveness. Dr. Irons was present and was deeply moved by what he saw and heard. On retiring from the Church, he wrote out this tr. [translation] of the *Dies Irae*.

The tune "Dies Irae" is a Latin melody of the 13th century.

608   Let Thoughtless Thousands Choose the Road

1. Let thoughtless thousands choose the road
That leads the soul away from God;
This happiness, dear Lord, be mine,
To live and die entirely Thine.

2. On Christ, by faith, I fain would live,
From Him my life, my all, receive,
To Him devote my fleeting hours,
Serve Him alone with all my powers.

3. Christ is my everlasting All;
To Him I look, on Him I call;
He will my every want supply
In time and through eternity.

4. Soon will the Lord, my Life, appear;
Soon shall I end my trials here,
Leave sin and sorrow, death and pain.
To live is Christ, to die is gain.

5. Soon will the saints in glory meet,
Soon walk through every golden street,
And sing on every blissful plain:
To live is Christ, to die is gain.

Joseph Hoskins published this hymn in his *Hymns on Select Texts*, etc., Bristol, 1789. It was entitled "Life in Christ."

The tune "Wareham" is by William Knapp in his *Sett of New Psalm Tunes*, etc., 1738, where it was set to the new version of Ps. 36:5-10, "But, Lord, Thy mercy, my sure hope."

JUDGMENT

Wake, Awake, for Night is Flying 609

1. "Wake, awake, for night is flying,"
The watchmen on the heights are crying;
   "Awake, Jerusalem, arise!"
Midnight hears the welcome voices
And at the thrilling cry rejoices:
   "Oh, where are ye, ye virgins wise?
The Bridegroom comes, awake!
Your lamps with gladness take!
   Hallelujah!
With bridal care Yourselves prepare
To meet the Bridegroom, who is near."

2. Zion hears the watchmen singing,
And all her heart with joy is springing,
   She wakes, she rises from her gloom;
For her Lord comes down all-glorious,
The strong in grace, in truth victorious,
   Her Star is risen, her Light is come.
"Now come, Thou Blessed One,
Lord Jesus, God's own Son,
   Hail! Hosanna!
The joyful call We answer all
And follow to the nuptial hall."

3. Now let all the heavens adore Thee,
Let men and angels sing before Thee,
   With harp and cymbal's clearest tone.
Of one pearl each shining portal,
Where, dwelling with the choir immortal,
   We gather round Thy radiant throne.
No vision ever brought,
No ear hath ever caught,
   Such great glory;
Therefore will we Eternally
Sing hymns of praise and joy to Thee.

Wachet auf! ruft uns die Stimme
Der Wächter sehr hoch auf der Zinne,
   Wach auf, du Stadt Jerusalem!
Mitternacht heisst diese Stunde,
Sie rufen uns mit hellem Munde:
   Wo seid ihr klugen Jungfrauen?
Wohlauf, der Bräut'gam kömmt,
Steht auf, die Lampen nehmt!
   Halleluja!
Macht euch bereit zu der Hochzeit,
Ihr müsset ihm entgegengehn!

Zion hört die Wächter singen,
Das Herz tut ihr vor Freuden springen,
   Sie wacht und stehet eilend auf.
Ihr Freund kommt vom Himmel prächtig,
Von Gnaden stark, von Wahrheit mächtig,
   Ihr Licht wird hell, ihr Stern geht auf.
Nun komm, du werte Kron',
Herr Jesu, Gottes Sohn!
   Hosianna!
Wir folgen all' zum Freudensaal
Und halten mit das Abendmahl.

Gloria sei dir gesungen
Mit Menschen- und mit Engelzungen,
   Mit Harfen und mit Zimbeln schön.
Von zwölf Perlen sind die Pforten
An deiner Stadt, wir sind Konsorten
   Der Engel hoch um deinen Thron.
Kein Aug, hat je gespürt,
Kein Ohr hat mehr gehört
   Solche Freude.
Das sind wir froh, i-o, i-o,
Ewig in dulci iubilo.

This hymn is called "the King of *Chorales*." Philipp Nicolai published it in the *Appendix* to his *Frewden-Spiegel,* 1599. It is based on Matt. 25:1-13; Rev. 19:6-9; 21:22; 1 Cor. 2:9; Ezek. 3:17; and Is. 52:8. It was entitled "Of the Voice at Midnight and the Wise Virgins who Meet Their Heavenly Bridegroom. Matt. 25."

In the original the hymn is a reversed acrostic, the first letters in the stanzas W. Z. G., referring to Count Wilhelm Ernst, "Graf zu Waldeck," who was Nicolai's pupil and who died at Tübingen Sept. 16, 1598. The hymn is patterned after the *Wächterlieder* (watchmen's songs) of the Middle Ages. In these songs "the voice of the watchman from his turret summons the workers of darkness to flee from discovery; with Nicolai it is a summons to the children of light to awaken to their promised reward and full felicity." (James Mearns, in *Julian.*)

The translation is an altered form of that by Catherine Winkworth in her *Chorale Book for England,* 1863.

The tune "Wachet auf" is also by Nicolai and appeared with the hymn in 1599. It may have been suggested by earlier tunes, at least some of its phrases, as the opening line is reminiscent of the Fifth Gregorian Tone.

Winterfeld calls it the greatest and most solemn melody of Evangelical Christendom. It has been utilized by composers from Bach onward.

And will the Judge Descend 610

1. And will the Judge descend,
   And must the dead arise
And not a single soul escape
   His all-discerning eyes?

2. And from His righteous lips
   Shall this dread sentence sound
And through the numerous guilty throng
   Spread black despair around:

[435]

JUDGMENT

3. "Depart from Me, accursed,
   To everlasting flame,
   For rebel angels first prepared,
   Where mercy never came"?

4. How will my heart endure
   The terrors of that Day
   When earth and heaven before His face
   Astonished shrink away?

5. But ere that trumpet shakes
   The mansions of the dead,
   Hark, from the Gospel's cheering sound
   What joyful tidings spread:

6. Ye sinners, seek His grace
   Whose wrath ye cannot bear;
   Fly to the shelter of His cross
   And find salvation there.

Philip Doddridge first published this hymn in seven stanzas in his *Hymns*, etc., 1755. It is based on Matt. 25:41 and was entitled "The Final Sentence and the Misery of the Wicked."

The omitted Stanza 7 reads:

7. So shall that curse remove
   By which the Savior bled;
   And the last awe-full day shall pour
   His blessings on your head.

For comments on the tune "Southwell" see Hymn No. 156.

611   The Day is Surely Drawing Near

1. The day is surely drawing near
   When God's Son, the Anointed,
   Shall with great majesty appear
   As Judge of all appointed.
   All mirth and laughter then shall cease
   When flames on flames will still increase,
   As Scripture truly teacheth.

2. A trumpet loud shall then resound
   And all the earth be shaken.
   Then all who in their graves are found
   Shall from their sleep awaken;
   But all that live shall in that hour
   By the Almighty's boundless power
   Be changed at His commanding.

3. A book is opened then to all,
   A record truly telling
   What each hath done, both great and small,
   When he on earth was dwelling;
   And every heart be clearly seen,
   And all be known as they have been
   In thought and words and actions.

4. Then woe to those who scorned the Lord
   And sought but carnal pleasures,
   Who here despised His precious Word
   And loved their earthly treasures!
   With shame and trembling they will stand
   And at the Judge's stern command
   To Satan be delivered.

5. O Jesus, who my debt didst pay
   And for my sin wast smitten,
   Within the Book of Life, oh, may
   My name be also written!
   I will not doubt; I trust in Thee,
   From Satan Thou hast made me free
   And from all condemnation.

6. Therefore my Intercessor be
   And for Thy blood and merit
   Declare my name from judgment free
   With all who life inherit,
   That I may see Thee face to face
   With all Thy saints in that blest place
   Which Thou for us hast purchased.

Es ist gewisslich an der Zeit,
  Dass Gottes Sohn wird kommen
In seiner grossen Herrlichkeit,
  Zu richten Bös' und Frommen.
Dann wird das Lachen werden teu'r,
Wenn alles wird vergehn in Feu'r,
  Wie Petrus davon schreibet.

Posaunen wird man hören gehn
  An aller Welt ihr Ende,
Darauf bald werden auferstehn
  All' Toten gar behende;
Die aber noch das Leben han,
Die wird der Herr von Stunden an
  Verwandeln und verneuen.

Danach wird man ablesen bald
  Ein Buch, darin geschrieben,
Was alle Menschen, jung und alt,
  Auf Erden hab'n getrieben,
Da dann gewiss ein jedermann
Wird hören, was er hat getan
  In seinem ganzen Leben.

O weh demselben, welcher hat
  Des Herren Wort verachtet
Und nur auf Erden früh und spat
  Nach grossem Gut getrachtet!
Der wird fürwahr ganz kahl bestehn
Und mit dem Satan müssen gehn
  Von Christo in die Hölle.

O Jesu, hilf zur selben Zeit
  Von wegen deiner Wunden,
Dass ich im Buch der Seligkeit
  Werd' angezeichnet funden!
Daran ich denn auch zweifle nicht,
Denn du hast ja den Feind gericht't
  Und meine Schuld bezahlet.

Derhalben mein Fürsprecher sei,
  Wenn du nun wirst erscheinen,
Und lies mich aus dem Buche frei,
  Darinnen stehn die Deinen,
Auf dass ich samt den Brüdern mein
Mit dir geh' in den Himmel ein,
  Den du uns hast erworben.

LIFE EVERLASTING

7. O Jesus Christ, do not delay,
   But hasten our salvation;
We often tremble on our way
   In fear and tribulation.
Then hear us when we cry to Thee;
Come, mighty Judge, and make us free
   From every evil! Amen.

O Jesu Christ, du machst es lang
   Mit deinem Jüngsten Tage!
Den Menschen wird auf Erden bang
   Von wegen vieler Plage.
Komm doch, komm doch, du Richter gross,
Und mach uns in Genaden los
   Von allem Übel! Amen.

This hymn of Bartholomäus Ringwaldt is a recast of a hymn which appeared anonymously in *Zwey schöne Lieder*, c. 1565, which, in turn, was based on *Dies Irae*. Ringwaldt's version was published in his *Handbüchlein*, 1586.

The translation is an altered form of that by Philip A. Peter used in the Ohio *Lutheran Hymnal*, 1880.

For comments on the tune "Es ist gewisslich" see Hymn No. 604.

That Day of Wrath, That Dreadful Day 612

1. That day of wrath, that dreadful day,
When heaven and earth shall pass away!
What power shall be the sinner's stay?
How shall he meet that dreadful day?

2. When, shriveling like a parchèd scroll,
The flaming heavens together roll;
When louder yet and yet more dread
Swells the high trump that wakes the dead, —

3. Lord, on that day, that wrathful day,
When man to Judgment wakes from clay,
Be Thou the trembling sinner's stay,
Though heaven and earth shall pass away.

This is Walter Scott's translation of a portion of *Dies Irae*. See our comments on Hymn No. 607.

The tune "Windham" is by Daniel Read, 1785.

Jerusalem the Golden 613

1. Jerusalem the golden,
   With milk and honey blest,
Beneath thy contemplation
   Sink heart and voice opprest.
I know not, oh, I know not,
   What joys await us there,
What radiancy of glory,
   What bliss beyond compare.

2. They stand, those halls of Zion,
   All jubilant with song
And bright with many an angel
   And all the martyr throng.
The Prince is ever in them;
   The daylight is serene;
The pastures of the blessèd
   Are decked in glorious sheen.

3. There is the throne of David;
   And there, from care released,
The shout of them that triumph,
   The song of them that feast;
And they who with their Leader
   Have conquered in the fight
Forever and forever
   Are clad in robes of white.

4. O sweet and blessed country,
   The home of God's elect!
O sweet and blessed country
   That eager hearts expect!
Jesus, in mercy bring us
   To that dear land of rest,
Who art, with God the Father
   And Spirit, ever blest.

Urbs Sion aurea, patria lactea,
   Cive decora,
Omne cor obruis, omnibus obstruis
   Et cor et ora.

Nescio, nescio, quae iubilatio,
   Lux tibi qualis,
Quam socialia gaudia, gloria
   Quam specialis.

Sunt Sion atria coniubilantia,
   Martyre plena,
Cive micantia, principe stantia,
   Luce serena.

Sunt ibi pascua mentibus afflua
   Praestita sanctis;
Regis ibi thronus, agminis et sonus
   Est epulantis.

Gens duce splendida, contio candida
   Vestibus albis,
Sunt sine fletibus in Sion aedibus,
   Aedibus almis. Amen.

For comments on the hymn and tune "Ewing" see Hymn No. 448.

LIFE EVERLASTING

614   For Thee, O Dear, Dear Country

1. For thee, O dear, dear country,
    Mine eyes their vigils keep;
For very love, beholding
    Thy happy name, they weep.
The mention of thy glory
    Is unction to the breast
And medicine in sickness
    And love and life and rest.

2. O one, O only mansion,
    O Paradise of joy,
Where tears are ever banished
    And smiles have no alloy!
The Lamb is all thy splendor,
    The Crucified thy praise;
His laud and benediction
    Thy ransomed people raise.

3. With jasper glow thy bulwarks,
    Thy streets with emeralds blaze;
The sardius and the topaz
    Unite in thee their rays;
Thine ageless walls are bonded
    With amethyst unpriced;
The saints build up thy fabric,
    The corner-stone is Christ.

4. Thou hast no shore, fair ocean;
    Thou hast no time, bright day,
Dear fountain of refreshment
    To pilgrims far away!
Upon the Rock of Ages
    They raise thy holy tower;
Thine is the victor's laurel
    And thine the golden dower.

5. O sweet and blessed country,
    The home of God's elect!
O sweet and blessed country
    That eager hearts expect!
Jesus, in mercy bring us
    To that dear land of rest,
Who art, with God the Father
    And Spirit, ever blest.

O bona patria, lumina sobria
    Te speculantur;
Ad tua nomina sobria lumina
    Collacrimantur.
Est tua mentio pectoris unctio,
    Cura doloris,
Concipientibus aethera mentibus
    Ignis amoris.

Tu locus unicus illeque caelicus
    Es paradisus.
Non tibi lacrima, sed placidissima
    Gaudia, risus.
Lux tua mors crucis atque caro ducis
    Est crucifixi;
Laus, benedictio, coniubilatio
    Personat Ipsi.

Est ibi consita laurus, et insita
    Cedrus hysopo;
Sund radiantia iaspide moenia,
    Clara pyropo.
Hinc tibi sardius, inde topazius,
    Hinc amethystus.
Est tua fabrica contio caelica,
    Gemmaque Christus.

Tu sine litore, tu sine tempore
    Fons, modo rivus;
Dulce bonis sapis, estque tibi lapis
    Undique vivus.
Est tibi laurea, dos datur aurea,
    Sponsa decora,
Primaque principis oscula suscipis,
    Inspicis ora. Amen.

For comments on the hymn see Hymn No. 448.
The tune "Bona Patria" is from *Sacred Hymns and Tunes*, Bristol, 1876.

615   A Rest Remaineth for the Weary

1. A rest remaineth for the weary;
    Arise, sad heart, and grieve no more;
Though long the way and dark and dreary,
    It endeth on the golden shore.
Before His throne the Lamb will lead thee,
    On heavenly pastures He will feed thee.
Cast off thy burden, come with haste;
Soon will the toil and strife be ended,
The weary way which thou hast wended.
    Sweet is the rest which thou shalt taste.

2. The Father's house has many a dwelling,
    And there will be a place for thee.
With perfect love His heart is welling
    Who loved thee from eternity.
His precious blood the Lamb hath given
That thou might'st share the joys of heaven,
    And now He calleth far and near:
"Ye weary souls, cease your repining,
Come while for you My light is shining;
    Come, sweetest rest awaits you here!"

Es ist noch eine Ruh' vorhanden,
    Auf, müdes Herz, und werde Licht!
Du seufzest hier in deinen Banden,
    Und deine Sonne scheinet nicht:
Sieh auf das Lamm, das dich mit Freuden
Dort wird vor seinem Stuhle weiden,
    Wirf hin die Last und eil herzu!
Bald ist der schwere Kampf geendet,
Bald, bald der saure Lauf vollendet,
    Dann gehst du ein zu deiner Ruh'.

Die Ruhe hat Gott auserkoren,
    Die Ruhe, die kein Ende nimmt.
Es hat, da noch kein Mensch geboren,
    Die Liebe sie uns schon bestimmt.
Das Gotteslamm wollt' darum sterben,
Uns diese Ruhe zu erwerben;
    Es ruft, es locket weit und breit:
Ihr müden Seelen und ihr Frommen
Versäumet nicht, heut' einzukommen
    Zu meiner Ruhe Lieblichkeit!

LIFE EVERLASTING

3. O come, come all, ye weak and weary,
   Ye souls bowed down with many a care;
Arise and leave your dungeons dreary
   And listen to His promise fair:
"Ye bore your burdens meek and lowly,
   I will fulfil My pledge most holy,
   I'll be your Solace and your Rest.
Ye are Mine own, I will requite you;
   Though sin and Satan seek to smite you,
   Rejoice! Your home is with the blest."

4. There rest and peace in endless measure
   Shall be ours through eternity;
No grief, no care, shall mar our
      pleasure,
   And untold bliss our lot shall be.
Oh, had we wings to hasten yonder —
No more o'er earthly ills to ponder —
   To join the glad triumphant band!
Make haste, my soul, forget all sadness,
For peace awaits thee, joy and gladness, —
   The perfect rest is nigh at hand.

So kommet denn, ihr matten Seelen,
   Die manche Last und Bürde drückt!
Eilt, eilt aus euren Kummerhöhlen,
   Geht nicht mehr müde und gebückt!
Ihr habt des Tages Last getragen,
   Dafür lässt euch der Heiland sagen:
   Ich selbst will eure Ruh'statt sein.
Ihr seid sein Volk, gezeugt von oben.
   Ob Sünde, Welt und Teufel toben,
   Seid nur getrost und gehet ein!

Da ruhen wir und sind im Frieden
   Und leben ewig sorgenlos.
Ach, fasset dieses Wort, ihr Müden!
   Legt euch dem Lamm in seinen
      Schoss!
Ach, Flügel her! Wir müssen eilen
Und uns nicht länger hier verweilen,
   Dort wartet schon die frohe Schar.
Fort, fort, mein Geist, zum Jubilieren!
Auf, gürte dich zum Triumphieren!
   Auf, auf, es kommt das Ruhejahr!

Johann Sigismund Kunth founded this hymn on Heb. 4:9: "There remaineth therefore a rest to the people of God." According to *Fischer* it was first published in the *Neu eingerichtetes geistreiches Gesang Buch,* Leipzig, 1730. It is said to have been written by the author while he was on a journey from Wittenberg to Silesia, c. 1725. This cento is composed of Stanzas 1, 2, 3, and 7 of the original. The translation is composite. The omitted stanzas read, as translated by Miss Winkworth, who did not retain the meter of the original:

4. Oh, what contentment fills the breast
   Of wanderers through the desert plains
If they have found a place to rest
   To quench their thirst and cure their
      pains!
How welcome is an humble bed,
Where they may rest their weary head,
   To persons that are sick and sore!
Such hours of sweet repose soon fly,
But there remains a rest on high
   Where we shall rest forevermore.

5. Yonder in joy the sheaves we bring
   Whose seed was sown on earth in
      tears;
There in our Father's house we sing
   The song too sweet for mortal ears.
Sorrow and sighing all are past,
And pain and death are fled at last.
   There with the Lamb of God we dwell;
He leads us to the crystal river;
He wipes away all tears forever;
   What there is ours no tongue can tell.

6. Nor thirst nor hunger pains us there,
   The time of recompense is come,
Nor cold nor scorching heat we bear,
   We're sheltered in our Savior's home.
The Lamb is in the midst; and those
Who followed Him through shame and woes
   Are crowned with honor, joy, and peace.
The dry bones gather life again,
One Sabbath over all shall reign,
   Wherein all toil and labor cease.

For comments on the tune "Wie wohl ist mir" see Hymn No. 362.

Forever with the Lord 616

1. "Forever with the Lord!"
      Amen! so let it be.
   Life from the dead is in that word,
      'Tis immortality.

2. Here in the body pent,
      Absent from Him, I roam,
   Yet nightly pitch my moving tent
      A day's march nearer home.

3. My Father's house on high,
      Home of my soul, how near
   At times to faith's foreseeing eye
      Thy golden gates appear!

4. Ah, then my spirit faints
      To reach the land I love,
   The bright inheritance of saints,
      Jerusalem above!

5. "Forever with the Lord!"
      O Father, 'tis Thy will.
   The promise of that faithful word
      E'en here to me fulfil.

6. Be Thou at my right hand,
      Then can I never fail.
   Uphold Thou me, and I shall stand;
      Fight Thou, and I'll prevail.

[439]

7. So when my dying breath
   Shall rend the veil in twain,
By death I shall escape from death
   And life eternal gain.

8. Knowing as I am known,
   How shall I love that word
And oft repeat before the throne,
   "Forever with the Lord!"

This cento is from James Montgomery's poem of twenty-two stanzas, published in the *Amethyst*, 1835. This poem is in two parts, as follows:

At Home in Heaven
1 Thess. 4:17
Part I

"Forever with the Lord!"
   Amen! so let it be;
Life from the dead is in that word,
   'Tis immortality.

Here in the body pent,
   Absent from Him, I roam;
Yet nightly pitch my moving tent
   A day's march nearer home.

My Father's house on high,
   Home of my soul, how near,
At times, to faith's foreseeing eye
   Thy golden gates appear!

Ah, then my spirit faints
   To reach the land I love,
The bright inheritance of saints,
   Jerusalem above!

Yet clouds will intervene,
   And all my prospect flies;
Like Noah's dove, I flit between
   Rough seas and stormy skies.

Anon the clouds dispart,
   The winds and waters cease,
While sweetly o'er my gladdened heart
   Expands the bow of peace.

Beneath its glowing arch,
   Along the hallowed ground,
I see cherubic armies march,
   A camp of fire around.

I hear at morn and even,
   At noon and midnight hour,
The choral harmonies of heaven
   Earth's Babel-tongues o'erpower.

Then, then, I feel that he
   (Remembered or forgot),
The Lord, is never far from me,
   Though I perceive Him not.

Part II

In darkness as in light
   Hidden alike from view,
I sleep, I wake, within His sight
   Who looks existence through.

From the dim hour of birth,
   Through every changing state
Of mortal pilgrimage on earth
   Till its appointed date,

All that I am, have been,
   All that I yet may be,
He sees at once, as He hath seen
   And shall forever see.

How can I meet His eyes?
   Mine on the cross I cast
And own my life a Savior's prize,
   Mercy from first to last.

"Forever with the Lord!"
   Father, if 'tis Thy will,
The promise of that faithful word
   E'en here to me fulfil.

Be Thou at my right hand,
   Then can I never fail;
Uphold Thou me, and I shall stand,
   Fight, and I must prevail.

So when my latest breath
   Shall rend the veil in twain,
By death I shall escape from death
   And life eternal gain.

Knowing as I am known,
   How shall I love that word
And oft repeat before the throne,
   "Forever with the Lord!"

Then, though the soul enjoy
   Communion high and sweet
While worms this body must destroy,
   Both shall in glory meet.

The trump of final doom
   Will speak the selfsame word,
And heaven's voice thunder through the tomb,
   "Forever with the Lord!"

The tomb shall echo deep
   The death-awakening sound;
The saints shall hear it in their sleep
   And answer from the ground.

Then upward as they fly,
   That resurrection-word
Shall be their shout of victory,
   "Forever with the Lord!"

That resurrection-word,
   That shout of victory,
Once more, — "Forever with the Lord!"
   Amen, so let it be!

For comments on the tune "Schumann" see Hymn No. 449.

There Is an Hour of Peaceful Rest 617

1. There is an hour of peaceful rest
 To mourning wanderers given;
 There is a joy for souls distrest,
 A balm for every wounded breast:
 'Tis found above — in heaven.

2. There is a home for weary souls,
 By sin and sorrow driven, —
 When tossed on life's tempestuous shoals,
 Where storms arise and ocean rolls,
 And all is drear — but heaven.

3. There faith lifts up the tearless eye,
 To brighter prospects given,
 And views the tempest passing by,
 The evening shadows quickly fly,
 And all serene — in heaven.

4. There fragrant flowers immortal bloom,
 And joys supreme are given;
 There rays divine disperse the gloom;
 Beyond the confines of the tomb
 Appears the dawn of heaven.

William B. Tappan wrote this hymn in Philadelphia, in the summer of 1818, for the *Franklin Gazette*. It was published again in the author's first volume of *Poems* the following year. Its popularity was immediate, not only in America but also in England. An inferior stanza, the second, has been omitted:

> There is a soft, a downy bed,
> 'Tis fair as breath of even;
> A couch for weary mortals spread
> Where they may rest the aching head,
> And find repose — in heaven.

The tune "Pax Celeste" is by an unknown composer in *Celestial Harps*, Edinburgh, 1824.

Jerusalem, My Happy Home 618

1. Jerusalem, my happy home,
 Name ever dear to me,
 When shall my labors have an end?
 Thy joys when shall I see?

2. When shall these eyes thy heaven-built walls
 And pearly gates behold,
 Thy bulwarks with salvation strong,
 And streets of shining gold?

3. Oh, when, thou city of my God,
 Shall I thy courts ascend
 Where evermore the angels sing,
 Where Sabbaths have no end?

4. Apostles, martyrs, prophets, there
 Around my Savior stand;
 And soon my friends in Christ below
 Will join the glorious band.

5. Jerusalem, my happy home,
 When shall I come to thee?
 When shall my labors have an end?
 Thy joys when shall I see?

6. O Christ, do Thou my soul prepare
 For that bright home of love
 That I may see Thee and adore
 With all Thy saints above.

This hymn has a most complicated history. There is a lengthy discussion of it in Julian's *Dictionary of Hymnology*, to which we refer the reader. It seems that the hymn in its original form is based on a passage from a collection of the writings of Augustine of Hippo, known as *The Meditations of St. Augustine* (*Liber Meditationum*), in which the Church Father meditated on the joys of the heavenly Jerusalem. This passage begins: "Mater Hierusalem, Civitas Sancta Dei." In the British Museum there is a manuscript of the late sixteenth or early seventeenth century, containing a poem of the twenty-six stanzas, entitled "A Song Mad(e) by F. B. P., to the Tune of Diana." It is included in the *English Hymnal*, in modern English, as follows:

1. Jerusalem, my happy home,
 When shall I come to thee?
 When shall my sorrows have an end?
 Thy joys when shall I see?

2. O happy harbor of the saints!
 O sweet and pleasant soil!
 In thee no sorrow may be found,
 No grief, no care, no toil.

3. In thee no sickness may be seen,
 No hurt, no ache, no sore;
 In thee there is no dread of death,
 But life forevermore.

4. No dampish mist is seen in thee,
 No cold nor darksome night;
 There every soul shines as the sun;
 There God Himself gives light.

5. There lust and lucre cannot dwell;
 There envy bears no sway;
There is no hunger, heat, nor cold,
 But pleasure every way.

6. Jerusalem, Jerusalem,
 God grant I once may see
Thy endless joys, and of the same
 Partaker aye may be!

7. Thy walls are made of precious stones,
 Thy bulwarks diamonds square;
Thy gates are of right orient pearl,
 Exceeding rich and rare.

8. Thy turrets and thy pinnacles
 With carbuncles do shine;
Thy very streets are paved with gold,
 Surpassing clear and fine.

9. Thy houses are of ivory,
 Thy windows crystal clear;
Thy tiles are made of beaten gold —
 O God, that I were there!

10. Within thy gates no thing doth come
 That is not passing clean,
No spider's web, no dirt, no dust,
 No filth may there be seen.

11. Ah, my sweet home, Jerusalem,
 Would God I were in thee!
Would God my woes were at an end,
 Thy joys that I might see!

12. Thy saints are crowned with glory great;
 They see God face to face;
They triumph still, they still rejoice:
 Most happy is their case.

13. We that are here in banishment
 Continually do mourn;
We sigh and sob, we weep and wail,
 Perpetually we groan.

14. Our sweet is mixed with bitter gall,
 Our pleasure is but pain,
Our joys scarce last the looking on,
 Our sorrows still remain.

15. But there they live in such delight,
 Such pleasure, and such play
As that to them a thousand years
 Doth seem as yesterday.

16. Thy vineyards and thy orchards are
 Most beautiful and fair,
Full furnished with trees and fruits,
 Most wonderful and rare.

17. Thy gardens and thy gallant walks
 Continually are green;
There grow such sweet and pleasant flowers
 As nowhere else are seen.

18. There's nectar and ambrosia made,
 There's musk and civet sweet;
There many a fair and dainty drug
 Is trodden under feet.

19. There cinnamon, there sugar grows,
 There nard and balm abound;
What tongue can tell or heart conceive
 The joys that there are found?

20. Quite through the streets with silver sound
 The flood of life doth flow,
Upon whose banks on every side
 The wood of life doth grow.

21. There trees forevermore bear fruit
 And evermore do spring;
There evermore the angels sit
 And evermore do sing;

22. There David stands with harp in hand
 As master of the choir;
Ten thousand times that man were blest
 That might this music hear.

23. Our Lady sings Magnificat
 With tune surpassing sweet;
And all the virgins bear their parts,
 Sitting about her feet.

24. Te Deum doth Saint Ambrose sing,
 Saint Austin doth the like;
Old Simeon and Zachary
 Have not their songs to seek.

25. There Magdalene hath left her moan
 And cheerfully doth sing
With blessed saints whose harmony
 In every street doth ring.

26. Jerusalem, my happy home,
 Would God I were in thee!
Would God my woes were at an end
 Thy joys that I might see!

The identity of F. B. P. has not been established. It may mean "Francis Baker, Presbyter," a secular priest who is said to have been imprisoned in the Tower of London. The claim of the Roman Catholics that the author of the hymn is Father Laurence Anderton, *alias John* Brerely, S. J., who lived in the days of Charles I, is also unfounded.

A hymn published in 1585 at London by John Windet, entitled "The Glasse of Vaine-Glorie," composed by W. P. (W. Prid), Doctor of Laws, in forty-four stanzas, bears in part a close resemblance to the "Song by F. B. P." so that it is likely that he made some use of it. David Dickson (1583—1662), a Scotch Presbyterian minister, published a version, beginning "O Mother dear, Jerusalem," based on the two foregoing texts. A still later form, published in

1795, in the Eckington Collection, has been attributed to James Montgomery, but is very likely the work of the editor of the collection, Joseph Bromehead.

What has perhaps been the most popular form of the hymn appeared in *Collection of Above Six Hundred Hymns*, Doncaster, 1801, as a new supplement to the Psalms of Isaac Watts. This cento contained seven stanzas. Our text has five of these. We have been unable to trace the origin of Stanza 6.

For comments on the tune "St. Peter" see Hymn No. 286.

Jerusalem, Thou City Fair and High   619

1. Jerusalem, thou city fair and high,
   Would God I were in thee!
   My longing heart fain, fain, to thee would fly,
   It will not stay with me.
   Far over vale and mountain,
   Far over field and plain,
   It hastes to seek its Fountain
   And leave this world of pain.

2. O happy day and yet far happier hour,
   When wilt thou come at last,
   When fearless to my Father's love and power,
   Whose promise standeth fast,
   My soul I gladly render?
   For surely will His hand
   Lead her with guidance tender
   To heaven, her fatherland.

3. A moment's space, and gently, wondrously,
   Released from earthly ties,
   Elijah's chariot bears her up to thee,
   Through all these lower skies
   To yonder shining regions,
   While down to meet her come
   The blessed angel legions
   And bid her welcome home.

4. O Zion, hail! Bright city, now unfold
   The gates of grace to me.
   How many a time I longed for thee of old
   Ere yet I was set free
   From yon dark life of sadness,
   Yon world of shadowy naught,
   And God had given the gladness,
   The heritage, I sought!

5. What glorious throng and what resplendent host
   Comes sweeping swiftly down?
   The chosen ones on earth who wrought the most,
   The Church's brightest crown,
   Our Lord hath sent to meet me,
   As in the far-off years
   Their words oft came to greet me
   In yonder land of tears.

6. The patriarchs' and prophets' noble train,
   With all Christ's followers true,
   Who bore the cross and could the worst disdain
   What tyrants dared to do,
   I see them shine forever,
   All-glorious as the sun,
   Mid light that fadeth never,
   Their perfect freedom won.

Jerusalem, du hochgebaute Stadt,
Wollt' Gott, ich wär' in dir!
Mein sehnlich Herz so gross Verlangen hat
Und ist nicht mehr bei mir.
Weit über Berg und Tale,
Weit über blaches Feld
Schwingt es sich überalle
Und eilt aus dieser Welt.

O schöner Tag und noch viel schönre Stund',
Wann wirst du kommen schier,
Da ich mit Lust, mit freiem Freudenmund
Die Seele geb' von mir
In Gottes treue Hände
Zum auserwählten Pfand,
Dass sie mit Heil anlände
In jenem Vaterland!

Im Augenblick wird sie erheben sich
Bis an das Firmament,
Wenn sie verlässt so sanft, so wunderlich
Die Stätt' der Element',
Fährt auf Eliä Wagen,
Mit engelischer Schar,
Die sie in Händen tragen,
Umgeben ganz und gar.

O Ehrenburg, sei nun gegrüsset mir,
Tu auf die Gnadenpfort'!
Wie grosse Zeit hat mich verlangt nach dir,
Eh' ich gekommen fort
Aus jenem bösen Leben,
Aus jener Nichtigkeit,
Und mir Gott hat gegeben
Das Erb' der Ewigkeit!

Was für ein Volk, was für ein' edle Schar
Kommt dort gezogen schon?
Was in der Welt von Auserwählten war,
Seh' ich, die beste Kron',
Die Jesus mir, der Herre,
Entgegen hat gesandt,
Da ich noch war so ferne
In meinem Tränenland.

Propheten gross und Patriarchen hoch,
Auch Christen insgemein,
Die weiland dort trugen des Kreuzes Joch
Und der Tyrannen Pein,
Schau' ich in Ehren schweben,
In Freiheit überall,
Mit Klarheit hell umgeben,
Mit sonnenlichtem Strahl.

7. And when within that lovely Paradise
   At last I safely dwell,
   What songs of bliss shall from my lips arise,
   What joy my tongue shall tell,
      While all the saints are singing
         Hosannas o'er and o'er,
      Pure hallelujahs ringing
         Around me evermore!

8. Unnumbered choirs before the shining throne
      Their joyful anthems raise
   Till heaven's glad halls are echoing with the tone
      Of that great hymn of praise
   And all its host rejoices,
      And all its blessed throng
   Unite their myriad voices
      In one eternal song.

Wenn dann zuletzt ich angelanget bin
   Im schönen Paradeis,
Von höchster Freud' erfüllet wird der Sinn,
   Der Mund von Lob und Preis.
      Das Halleluja reine
         Singt man in Heiligkeit,
      Das Hosianna feine
         Ohn' End' in Ewigkeit.

Mit Jubelklang, mit Instrumenten schön,
   In Chören ohne Zahl,
Dass von dem Klang und von dem süssen Ton
   Erbebt der Freudensaal;
      Mit hunderttausend Zungen,
         Mit Stimmen noch viel mehr,
      Wie von Anfang gesungen
         Das himmelische Heer.

This was Dr. Francis Pieper's favorite hymn and was sung at his funeral in Holy Cross Church, St. Louis, June 6, 1931. Johann Meyfart published this hymn in his *Tuba Novissima*, Coburg, 1626. This work contained four sermons preached by Meyfart at Coburg on Death, Judgment, Eternal Life, and Eternal Punishment. The hymn was the conclusion of the third sermon, based on Matt. 17:1-9, entitled "On the Joy and Glory which All the Elect are to Expect in the Life Everlasting." Lauxmann says of the hymn:

The hymn is a precious gem in our Treasury of Song, in which one clearly sees that from it the whole heart of the poet shines out on us. Meyfart had his face turned wholly to the future, to the Last Things; and with a richly fanciful mysticism full of deep and strong faith he united a flaming zeal for the House of the Lord and against the abuses of his times.

The famous Chinese missionary pioneer Karl Gützlaff died with the words on his lips "Would God I were in Thee!" The noted painter Julius Schnorr von Carolsfeld's last work was the illustration of this hymn, and this hymn was also sung at his funeral.

No doubt the popularity of this hymn has been aided by its tune "Jerusalem, du hochgebaute Stadt" from the pen of Melchior Frank, director of the choir at Coburg when Meyfart wrote the hymn. It was first printed at Erfurt, after the death of both, in the *Christlich . . . Gesangbuch*, 1663. Too much cannot be said of the beauty and effectiveness of this melody, which breathes the spirit of joyous triumph over death and the grave. It must not be played too slowly. It ranks with the best gems of our Evangelical hymnodical treasures.

The translation is by Catherine Winkworth, second series, *Lyra Germanica*, 1858, altered.

MARRIAGE

The Christian Home

Lord, Who at Cana's Wedding-Feast 620

1. Lord, who at Cana's wedding-feast
Didst as a Guest appear,
Thou dearer far than earthly guest,
Vouchsafe Thy presence here.
For holy Thou indeed dost prove
The marriage-vow to be,
Proclaiming it a type of love
Between the Church and
Thee.

2. This holy vow that man can make,
The golden thread in life,
The bond that none may dare to break,
That bindeth man and wife,
Which, blest by Thee, whate'er betides,
No evil shall destroy,
Through care-worn days each care divides,
And doubles every joy.

3. On those who now before Thee kneel,
O Lord, Thy blessing pour,
That each may wake the other's zeal
To love Thee more and more.
Oh, grant them here in peace to live,
In purity and love,
And, this world leaving, to receive
A crown of life above.

Stanzas 1 and 3 of this hymn first appeared in Joseph F. Thrupp's *Psalms and Hymns,* Cambridge, 1853, as a hymn of four four-line stanzas, beginning "Thou who at Cana's wedding-feast." It was signed A. T., *i. e.,* Adelaide Thrupp. In the *Collection* by Godfrey Thring, 1882, Stanza 2 was added. It is by Prebendary Thring himself.

For comments on the tune "Bethlehem" see Hymn No. 109.

O Father, All Creating 621

1. O Father, all creating,
Whose wisdom, love, and power
First bound two lives together
In Eden's primal hour,
Today to these Thy children
Thine earliest gifts renew,—
A home by Thee made happy,
A love by Thee kept true.

2. O Savior, Guest most bounteous
Of old in Galilee,
Vouchsafe today Thy presence
With these who call on Thee.
Their store of earthly gladness
Transform to heavenly wine
And teach them, in the testing,
To know the gift is Thine.

3. O Spirit of the Father,
Breathe on them from above,
So mighty in Thy pureness,
So tender in Thy love,
That, guarded by Thy presence,
From sin and strife kept free,
Their lives may own Thy guidance,
Their hearts be ruled by Thee.

4. Except Thou build it, Father,
The house is built in vain;
Except Thou, Savior, bless it,
The joy will turn to pain.
But naught can break the marriage
Of hearts in Thee made one,
And love Thy Spirit hallows
Is endless love begun. Amen.

John Ellerton wrote this hymn January 29, 1876, at the request of the Duke of Westminster for the marriage of his daughter, the Lady Elizabeth Harriett Grosvenor, to the Marquis of Ormonde. The hymn was first published in Thring's *Church of England Hymn-Book,* 1880.

The tune "Eden" is from *Sacred Hymns and Tunes,* Boston, 1880.

The Voice that Breathed o'er Eden 622

1. The voice that breathed o'er Eden,
That earliest wedding-day,
The primal marriage blessing,—
It hath not passed away.
Still in the pure espousal
Of Christian man and maid
The Triune God is with us,
The threefold grace is said.

2. Be present, loving Father,
To give away this bride
As Thou gav'st Eve to Adam,
A helpmeet at his side.
Be present, Son of Mary,
To join their loving hands
As Thou didst bind two natures
In Thine eternal bands.

[445]

3. Be present, Holiest Spirit,
    To bless them as they kneel,
  As Thou for Christ, the Bridegroom,
    The heavenly Spouse dost seal.
  Oh, spread Thy pure wing o'er them,
    Let no ill power find place
  When onward to Thine altar
    Their hallowed path they trace,

4. To cast their crowns before Thee
    In humble sacrifice,
  Till to the home of gladness
    With Christ's own Bride they rise.
  To Father, Son, and Spirit,
    Eternal One and Three,
  As was and is forever,
    All praise and glory be.

John Keble's excellent hymn, in eight four-line stanzas, on "Holy Matrimony" is dated July 12, 1857. It was written for, and first published in, the *Salisbury Hymn-Book,* 1857, where it was noted "to be sung at the Commencement of the Service." The text is arranged in four eight-line stanzas for the sake of the music. Keble's original third stanza was dropped and a doxology added. The omitted four lines read:

  For dower of blessed children,
    For love and faith's sweet sake,
  For high mysterious union
    Which naught on earth can break.

The alterations are slight. Keble had "awful Father" in Stanza 2, Line 1, and "out of his own pierced side" in Line 3; and in Stanza 4, Line 2, "perfect sacrifice."

For comments on the tune "Eden" see Hymn No. 621.

623   A Perfect Love

1. O perfect Love, all human thought transcending,
    Lowly we kneel in prayer before Thy throne
  That theirs may be the love which knows no ending,
    Whom Thou forevermore dost join in one.

2. O perfect Life, be Thou their full assurance
    Of tender charity and steadfast faith,
  Of patient hope and quiet, brave endurance,
    With childlike trust that fears nor pain nor death.

3. Grant them the joy which brightens earthly sorrow;
    Grant them the peace which calms all earthly strife
  And to life's day the glorious unknown morrow
    That dawns upon eternal love and life.

The author of this favorite wedding hymn, Dorothy Frances Gurney, tells the following regarding its origin, in 1884:

We were all singing hymns one Sunday evening and had just finished "O Strength and Stay," the tune to which was an especial favorite of my sister's, when some one remarked what a pity it was that the words should be unsuitable for a wedding. My sister, turning suddenly to me, said: "What is the use of a sister who composes poetry if she cannot write me new words to this tune?" I picked up a hymn-book and said: "Well, if no one will disturb me, I will go into the library and see what I can do." After about fifteen minutes I came back with the hymn "O perfect Love," and there and then we all sang it to the tune of "Strength and Stay." It went perfectly, and my sister was delighted, saying that it must be sung at her wedding. For two or three years it was sung privately at many London weddings, and then it found its way into the hymnals. The writing of it was no effort whatever after the initial idea had come to me of the twofold aspect of perfect union, love and life; and I have always felt that God helped me to write it.

THE FAMILY

In our days of secularized marriages it is necessary for Christians to emphasize the spiritual element, and instead of requesting the use of sentimental and worldly songs at weddings, as is so often the case, they ought rather to choose such hymns as this and the other marriage hymns in the hymnal.

The tune "Caritas perfecta" was written for this hymn by Frederick C. Atkinson, 1885.

O Blessed Home Where Man and Wife — 624

1. O blessed home where man and wife
Together lead a godly life,
By deeds their faith confessing!
There many a happy day is spent,
There Jesus gladly will consent
    To tarry with His blessing.

2. If they have given Him their heart,
The place of honor set apart
For Him each night and morrow,
Then He the storms of life will calm,
Will bring for every wound a balm,
    And change to joy their sorrow.

3. And if their home be dark and drear,
The cruse be empty, hunger near,
    All hope within them dying,
Let them despair not in distress;
Lo, Christ is there the bread to bless,
    The fragments multiplying.

4. O Lord, we come before Thy face;
In every home bestow Thy grace
    On children, father, mother.
Relieve their wants, their burdens ease,
Let them together dwell in peace
    And love to one another.

I Hus og Hjem, hvor Mand og Viv
Bo sammen et gudfrygtigt Liv
    Med Börn i Tugt og äre,
Der leves mangen lyksom Dag,
Der vil hos dem med Velbehag
    Den Herre Kristus väre.

Har du ham givet Själ og Sind,
Og er han kjärlig buden ind,
    Og sat i höiest Säde,
Da bliver Levestunden god,
Da raader han paa Vaande Bod,
    Og vender Sorg til Gläde.

Og sidder du i merke Hus
Med tomme Fad og törre Krus,
    Og dine Smaa paa Skjödet,
Og ser med Graad den sidste Rest,
Naar Nöd er störst, er Hjälpen näst,
    Hvor han velsigner Brödet.

Vor Bön idag til ham vi bär:
O Herre Jesu, kom og vär
    Hos Ägtemand og Kvinde!
Hjälp deres Smaa i Verden frem,
Sign deres Bord og Hus og Hjem,
    Og lys din Fred derinde!

Magnus B. Landstad included this hymn in his *Kirkesalmebog*, 1861. It is based on John 2:1-11, the Gospel for the Second Sunday after Epiphany. Its picture of a family united by the bond of common faith and looking to Christ as the true Head of every Christian home is beautifully presented.

The translation is by Ole T. Arneson (Sanden), written in 1908 and included in *The Lutheran Hymnary*, 1913.

For comments on the tune "Kommt her zu mir" see Hymn No. 263.

Oh, Blest the House, Whate'er Befall — 625

1. Oh, blest the house, whate'er befall,
Where Jesus Christ is all in all!
Yea, if He were not dwelling there,
How dark and poor and void it were!

2. Oh, blest that house where faith ye find
And all within have set their mind
To trust their God and serve Him still
And do in all His holy will!

3. Oh, blest the parents who give heed
Unto their children's foremost need
And weary not of care or cost!
May none to them and heaven be lost!

Wohl einem Haus, da Jesus Christ
Allein das all in allem ist!
Ja, wenn er nicht darinnen wär',
Wie elend wär's, wie arm und leer!

Heil, wenn sich Mann und Weib und Kind
In *einem* Glaubenssinn verbind't,
Zu dienen ihrem Herrn und Gott
Nach seinem Willen und Gebot!

Heil, wenn die Eltern gläubig sind,
Und wenn sie Kind und Kindeskind
Versäumen nicht am ew'gen Glück!
Dann bleibet ihrer keins zurück.

4. Blest such a house, it prospers well,
In peace and joy the parents dwell,
And in their children's lot is shown
How richly God can bless His own.

Wohl solchem Haus! Denn es gedeiht;
Die Eltern werden hoch erfreut,
Und ihren Kindern sieht man's an,
Wie Gott die Seinen segnen kann.

5. Then here will I and mine today
A solemn covenant make and say:
Though all the world forsake Thy Word,
I and my house will serve the Lord.

So mach' ich denn zu dieser Stund'
Samt meinem Hause diesen Bund:
Trät' alles Volk von Jesu fern:
Ich und mein Haus stehn bei dem Herrn!

This hymn by Christoph Carl Ludwig von Pfeil was first published in *Evangelisches Gesangbuch,* Memmingen, 1782, in eight stanzas. It was entitled "Delightful Picture of a House that Serves the Lord. On the Parents of Jesus." It was written for the First Sunday after Epiphany, 1746.

This cento contains Stanzas 1, 2, 6, 7, and 8. Catherine Winkworth, in her *Chorale Book for England,* 1863, translated this hymn, omitting Stanza 6 of the original (our third above) and combining the thoughts of Stanzas 3 and 4 into one. The omitted stanzas in her version are:

Blest where their prayers shall daily rise
As fragrant incense to the skies,
While in their lives the world is taught
That forms without the heart are naught.

Blest where the busy hands fulfil
Their proper task with ready skill,
While through their different works ye see
One spirit run of unity.

The translation of Stanza 3 in the hymn, by an unknown writer, is from the Ohio *Lutheran Hymnal* of 1880.

For comments on the tune "Wo Gott zum Haus" see Hymn No. 131.

626 O Happy Home Where Thou art Loved Most Dearly

1. O happy home where Thou art loved most dearly,
Thou faithful Friend and Savior full of grace,
And where among the guests there never cometh
One who can hold such high and honored place!
O happy home where all, in heart united,
In holy faith and blessed hope are one,
Whom bitter death a little while divideth,
Yet cannot end the union here begun!

O selig Haus, wo man dich aufgenommen,
Du wahrer Seelenfreund, Herr Jesu Christ;
Wo unter allen Gästen, die da kommen,
Du der gefeiertste und liebste bist;
Wo aller Herzen dir entgegenschlagen
Und aller Augen freudig auf dich sehn;
Wo aller Lippen dein Gebot erfragen
Und alle deines Winks gewärtig stehn!

2. O happy home where two, in heart united,
In holy faith, are clinging unto Thee;
Where both, to Thee a joyful service bringing,
Hear and obey Thy voice most willingly;
Where both, to Thee in truth forever cleaving,
In joy, in grief, make Thee their only Stay
And fondly hope in Thee to be believing
Both in the good and in the evil day.

O selig Haus, wo Mann und Weib in *einer,*
In deiner Liebe *eines* Geistes sind,
Als beide *eines* Heils gewürdigt, keiner
Im Glaubensgrunde anders ist gesinnt;
Wo beide unzertrennbar an dir hangen
In Lieb' und Leid, Gemach und Ungemach,
Und nur bei dir zu bleiben stets verlangen
An jedem guten wie am bösen Tag!

3. O happy home whose little ones are given
Early to Thee in humble faith and prayer,
To Thee, their Friend, who from the heights of heaven
Guides them and guards with more than mother's care!
O happy home where each one serves Thee, lowly,
Whatever his appointed work may be,
Till every common task seems great and holy
When it is done, O Lord, as unto Thee!

O selig Haus, wo man die lieben Kleinen
Mit Händen des Gebets ans Herz dir legt,
Du Freund der Kinder, der sie als die Seinen
Mit mehr als Mutterliebe hegt und pflegt;
Wo sie zu deinen Füssen gern sich sammeln
Und horchen deiner süssen Rede zu
Und lernen früh dein Lob mit Freuden stammeln,
Sich deiner freun, du lieber Heiland, du!

[448]

CHRISTIAN EDUCATION

4. O happy home where Thou art not
  forgotten
  When joy is overflowing, full, and free!
O happy home where every wounded spirit
  Is brought, O great Physician, unto Thee,
  Until at last, when earthly toil is ended,
  All meet Thee in the blessed home above,
  From whence Thou camest, where Thou
    hast ascended,
  Thine everlasting home of peace and love!

O selig Haus, wo du die Freude teilest,
  Wo man bei keiner Freude dein
    vergisst!
O selig Haus, wo du die Wunden heilest
  Und aller Arzt und aller Tröster
    bist,
Bis jeder einst sein Tagewerk vollendet,
  Und bis sie endlich alle ziehen aus
Dahin, woher der Vater dich gesendet,
  Ins grosse, freie, schöne Vaterhaus!

Carl John Philipp Spitta first published this hymn in his *Psalter und Harfe,* Pirna, 1833, in five stanzas. It was entitled "Salvation is come to this house" (Luke 19:9). It is said to be a description of the author's own happy home life.

The translator is Sarah L. Findlater. Her translation appeared in *Hymns from the Land of Luther,* third series, 1858. The omitted Stanza 4, in Miss Findlater's translation of the hymn, which does not retain the meter of the German, reads:

O happy house and happy servitude
  Where all alike one Master own;
Where daily duty, in Thy strength pursued,
  Is never hard nor toilsome known;
Where each one serves Thee meek and lowly,
  Whatever Thine appointment be,
Till common tasks seem great and holy,
  When they are done as unto Thee!

It will be noted that Stanza 3 of this hymn is really a combination of the main thoughts of Stanzas 3 and 4 of the original.

The tune "O selig Haus" is by Eduard Niemeyer, 1854.

Gracious Savior, Gentle Shepherd 627

1. Gracious Savior, gentle Shepherd,
  Children all are dear to Thee;
  Gathered with Thine arms and carried
  In Thy bosom may they be;
  Sweetly, fondly, safely, tended,
  From all want and danger free.

2. Tender Shepherd, never leave them
  From Thy fold to go astray;
  By Thy warning love directed,
  May they walk the narrow way!
  Thus direct them, thus defend them,
  Lest they fall an easy prey.

3. Cleanse their hearts from sinful folly
  In the stream Thy love supplied,
  Mingled stream of blood and water
  Flowing from Thy wounded side;
  And to heavenly pastures lead them,
  Where Thine own still waters glide.

4. Let Thy holy Word instruct them;
  Fill their minds with heavenly light;
  Let Thy powerful grace constrain them
  To approve whate'er is right;
  Let them feel Thy yoke is easy,
  Let them prove Thy burden light.

5. Taught to lisp Thy holy praises
  Which on earth Thy children sing,
  Both with lips and hearts, unfeigned,
  Glad thank-offerings may they bring;
  Then with all the saints in glory
  Join to praise their Lord and King.

This hymn has an unusual origin. Jane E. Leeson, in 1842, published the following three hymns in her *Hymns and Scenes of Childhood:* "Shepherd, in Thy Bosom Folded," "Loving Shepherd of Thy Sheep," and "Infant Sorrow, Infant Weakness." From these, with a few new lines, this hymn was constructed. It was published by John Whittemore in his Baptist *Supplement to All Hymn-Books,* 1850.

For comments on the tune "Sieh hier bin ich" see Hymn No. 56.

628   Shepherd of Tender Youth

1. Shepherd of tender youth,
Guiding in love and truth
   Through devious ways;
Christ, our triumphant King,
We come Thy name to sing
And here our children bring
   To join Thy praise.

2. Thou art our holy Lord,
O all-subduing Word,
   Healer of strife.
Thou didst Thyself abase
That from sin's deep disgrace
Thou mightest save our race
   And give us life.

3. Thou art the great High Priest;
Thou hast prepared the feast
   Of holy love;
And in our mortal pain
None calls on Thee in vain;
Help Thou dost not disdain,
   Help from above.

4. Ever be Thou our Guide,
Our Shepherd and our Pride,
   Our Staff and Song;
Jesus, Thou Christ of God,
By Thine enduring Word
Lead us where Thou hast trod,
   Make our faith strong.

5. So now, and till we die,
Sound we Thy praises high
   And joyful sing;
Infants and the glad throng
Who to Thy Church belong,
Unite to swell the song
   To Christ, our King.

This hymn is a rather free translation, if it can be called that, of one of our oldest Christian hymns, attributed to Clement of Alexandria, beginning with the line

$$\text{Στόμιον πώλων ἀδαῶν.}$$

It was appended to the second of Clement's great trilogy, *The Tutor*.

Henry M. Dexter declared that after he first translated the Greek text of Clement's into prose, he "transfused as much of its language and spirit" as he could into the verse. This was in 1846. While he was preparing a sermon from the text Deut. 32:7: "Remember the days of old" on "Some Prominent Characteristics of the Early Christians," he wrote the hymn in order that it might be used in the service. The hymn was first printed in *The Congregationalist*, December 21, 1849.

For comments on the tune "Olivet" see Hymn No. 394.

629   Let Children Hear the Mighty Deeds

1. Let children hear the mighty deeds
Which God performed of old,
Which in our younger years we saw,
And which our fathers told.

2. Make unto them His glories known,
His works of power and grace;
And we'll convey His wonders down
Through every rising race.

3. Our lips shall tell them to our sons
And they again to theirs
That generations yet unborn
May teach them to their heirs.

4. Oh, teach them with all diligence
The truths of God's own Word,
To place in Him their confidence,
To fear and trust their Lord,

5. To learn that in our God alone
Their hope securely stands,
That they may ne'er forget His works,
But walk in His commands.

This is Isaac Watts's (*Psalms of David, Imitated*, 1719) version of the first part of Ps. 78, with a slight alteration in Stanza 2, Line, 1, where Watts has:

    He bids us make His glories known.

A new stanza was inserted after the third. It is by Bernard Schumacher and was written for *The Lutheran Hymnal* in 1938.

For comments on the tune "Nun danket all'" see Hymn No. 10.

CHRISTIAN EDUCATION

Ye Parents, Hear What Jesus Taught 630

1. Ye parents, hear what Jesus taught
When little ones to Him were brought:
Forbid them not, but heed My plea
And suffer them to come to Me.

2. Obey your Lord and let His truth
Be taught your children in their youth
That they in church and school may dwell
And learn their Savior's praise to tell.

3. For if you love them as you ought,
To Christ your children will be brought.
If thus you place them in His care,
You and your household well shall fare.

Höret, ihr Eltern, Christus spricht:
Den Kindlein sollt ihr wehren nicht,
Dass sie sich meinen Armen nahn,
Denn ich will segnend sie empfahn.

Gehorchet ihm und bringt sie her,
Dass man von Jugend auf sie lehr'
In Kirchen und in Schulen wohl,
Wie man Gott gläubig ehren soll!

Habt ihr sie lieb mit treuem Sinn,
So führet sie zu Jesu hin.
Wer dies nicht tut, ist ihnen feind,
Wie gross auch seine Liebe scheint.

This is a rather free translation of a cento from Ludwig Helmbold's hymn "Höret, ihr Eltern, Christus spricht" (sometimes given "Ihr Eltern, hört, was Christus spricht"). It first appeared in the author's *Crepundia Sacra*, Mühlhausen, 1596. The cento, translated by William M. Czamanske for *The Lutheran Hymnal*, in 1939, includes Stanzas 1, 4, and 5 of the author's original six stanzas. Aside from its value as a reminder of the parental duty to bring up the children in the nurture of the Lord, the hymn has little to commend itself.

For comments on the tune "Herr Jesu Christ, dich" see Hymn No. 3.

Savior, Who Thy Flock art Feeding 631

1. Savior, who Thy flock art feeding
With the Shepherd's kindest care,
All the feeble gently leading,
While the lambs Thy bosom share,

2. Now, these little ones receiving,
Fold them in Thy gracious arm;
There, we know, Thy Word believing,
Only there, secure from harm.

3. Never, from Thy pasture roving,
Let them be the Lion's prey;
Let Thy tenderness, so loving,
Keep them through life's dangerous way.

4. Then within Thy fold eternal
Let them find a resting-place,
Feed in pastures ever vernal,
Drink the rivers of Thy grace.

This is William A. Mühlenberg's most widely known hymn. It appeared in the *Prayer Book Collection*, 1826. It is sometimes given as "Jesus, who Thy flock," etc. It is also suitable for use at the baptism of children.

For comments on the tune "Ringe recht" see Hymn No. 155.

CORNER-STONE LAYING

Special Occasions

632   In the Name which Earth and Heaven

1. In the name which earth and heaven
Ever worship, praise, and fear,
Father, Son, and Holy Spirit,
We a house have builded here.
Here with prayer its deep foundations,
In the faith of Christ, did lay,
Trusting by His help to crown it
With the top-stone in its day.

2. Here as in their due succession
Stone on stone the men did place.
Thus, we pray, unseen, but surely,
Jesus, build us up in grace,
Till, as in these walls completed,
We complete in Thee are found
And to Thee, the one Foundation,
Stone and living stones, are bound.

3. Fair shall be Thine earthly temple;
Here the careless passer-by
Shall bethink him, in its beauty,
Of the holier house on high.
Weary hearts and troubled spirits
Here shall find a still retreat;
Sinful souls shall bring their burden
Here to the Absolver's feet.

4. Yet with truer, nobler beauty,
Lord, we pray, this house adorn,
Where Thy Bride, Thy Church redeemèd,
Robes her for her marriage morn;
Clothed in garments of salvation,
Rich with gems of heavenly grace,
Spouse of Christ, arrayed and waiting
Till she may behold His face.

5. Here in due and solemn order
Shall her ceaseless prayer arise;
Here shall strains of holy gladness
Lift her heart above the skies;
Here the Word of Life be spoken;
Here the child of God be sealed;
Here the Bread of Heaven be broken,
"Till He come," Himself revealed.

6. Praise to Thee, O Master Builder,
Maker of the earth and skies;
Praise to Thee, in whom Thy temple,
Fitly framed together, lies;
Praise to Thee, eternal Spirit,
Binding all that lives in one
Till our earthly praise be ended
And the eternal song begun!

John Ellerton wrote this hymn for *Church Hymns,* 1871, of which he and W. W. How were editors. The author wrote another hymn in 1869 to be sung at the restoration of a church. As hymns on this subject are rare, we are giving the text here. It may be sung to the same tune as the hymn before us.

1. Lift the strain of high thanksgiving,
Tread with songs the hallowed way.
Praise our fathers' God for mercies
New to us, their sons, today.
Here they built for Him a dwelling,
Served Him here in ages past,
Fixed it for His sure possession,
Holy ground while time shall last.

2. When the years had wrought their changes,
He, our own unchanging God,
Thought on this His habitation,
Looked on its decayed abode;
Heard our prayers and helped our counsels,
Blessed the silver and the gold,
Till once more His house is standing
Firm and stately as of old.

3. Entering, then, Thy gates with praises,
Lord, be ours Thine Israel's prayer:
"Rise into Thy place of resting,
Show Thy promised presence there."
Let the gracious word be spoken
Here, as once on Sion's height,
"This shall be My rest forever,
This My dwelling of delight."

4. Fill this latter house with glory
Greater than the former knew;
Clothe with righteousness its priesthood,
Guide its choir to reverence true;
Let Thy Holy One's anointing
Here its sevenfold blessing shed;
Spread for us the heavenly banquet,
Satisfy Thy poor with Bread.

5. Praise to Thee, almighty Father,
Praise to Thee, eternal Son,
Praise to Thee, all-quickening Spirit,
Ever blessèd Three in One;
Threefold Power and Grace and Wisdom,
Molding out of sinful clay
Living stones for that true temple
Which shall never know decay. Amen.

It was written for the reopening of St. Helen's Church, Tarporley, Cheshire, and was published in *Church Hymns,* 1871.

For comments on the tune "O du Liebe" see Hymn No. 37.

633   O Lord of Hosts, Whose Glory Fills

1. O Lord of hosts, whose glory fills
The bounds of the eternal hills
And yet vouchsaf'st, in Christian lands,
To dwell in temples made with hands,

2. Grant that all we who here today
Rejoicing this foundation lay
May be in very deed Thine own,
Built on the precious Corner-stone.

DEDICATION

3. Endue the creatures with Thy grace
That shall adorn Thy dwelling-place.
The beauty of the oak and pine,
The gold and silver, make them Thine.

4. To Thee they all belong, to Thee,
The treasure of the earth and sea;
And when we bring them to Thy throne,
We but present Thee with Thine own.

5. The heads that guide endue with skill,
The hands that work preserve from ill,
That we, who these foundations lay
May raise the top-stone in its day.

6. Both now and ever, Lord, protect
The temple of Thine own elect;
Be Thou in them and they in Thee,
O ever-blessed Trinity!

John M. Neale first published this hymn in his *Hymns for the Young,* 1844. It was entitled "Laying the First Stone of a Church." The slight alteration is in the first two lines of Stanza 5, where Neale had:

> Endue the hearts that guide with skill;
> Preserve the hands that work from ill.

For comments on the tune "O Heilige Dreifaltigkeit" see Hymn No. 340.

Come, Jesus, from the Sapphire Throne 634

1. Come, Jesus, from the sapphire throne,
Where Thy redeemed behold Thy face;
Enter this temple, now Thine own,
And let Thy glory fill the place.

2. We praise Thee that today we see
Its sacred walls before Thee stand;
'Tis Thine for us, 'tis ours for Thee,
Reared by Thy kind, assisting hand.

3. Oft as returns the day of rest,
Let heartfelt worship here ascend;
With Thine own joy fill every breast,
With Thine own power Thy Word attend.

4. Here in the dark and sorrowing day
Bid Thou the throbbing heart be still.
Oh, wipe the mourner's tears away
And give new strength to meet Thy will!

5. Here in baptismal water pure
We find for sin a gracious cure;
Our children here to Thee we bring
To be Thy heirs, O heavenly King.

6. When at Thine altar we shall meet
And keep the feast of dying love,
Be our communion ever sweet
With Thee and with Thy Church above.

7. Come, faithful Shepherd, feed Thy sheep;
In Thine own arms the lambs enfold.
Give help to climb the heavenward steep
Till Thy full glory we behold.

This dedication hymn by Ray Palmer is dated 1875. It appeared in his *Poetical Works,* 1876.

For comments on the tune "Wareham" see Hymn No. 608.

Here in Thy Name, Eternal God 635

1. Here in Thy name, eternal God,
We dedicate this house to Thee.
Oh, choose it for Thy fixed abode
And keep it from all error free!

2. Here, when Thy people seek Thy face
And dying sinners pray to live,
Hear Thou in heaven, Thy dwelling-place;
And when Thou hearest, Lord, forgive.

3. Here, when Thy messengers proclaim
The blessed Gospel of Thy Son,
Still by the power of His great name
Be mighty signs and wonders done.

4. When children's voices raise the song,
"Hosanna to the heavenly King!"
Let heaven with earth the strain prolong.
Hosanna! let the angels sing.

5. Thy glory never hence depart.
Yet choose not, Lord, this house alone;
Thy kingdom come to every heart,
In every bosom fix Thy throne.

We have here an altered and abridged form of James Montgomery's hymn "This Stone to Thee in Faith We Lay." It was written for the laying of the foundation-stone of Christ Church, Attercliffe, Sheffield, on October 30, 1822, and was sung on that occasion. It was published in the author's *Christian Psalmist,* 1825.

Later the hymn was altered in order to make it suitable for use at church dedications, as above. It first appeared in this form in Hatfield's *Church Hymn Book*, New York, 1872.

The omitted Stanza 5 reads:

> 5. But will indeed Jehovah deign
> Here to abide no transient guest?
> Here will the world's Redeemer reign
> And here the Holy Spirit rest?

The question-form of this stanza no doubt prompted its omission in many hymnals.

For comments on the tune "Mendon" see Hymn No. 119.

636 Great Is the Lord, Our God

1. Great is the Lord, our God,
And let His praise be great;
He makes His churches His abode,
His most delightful seat.

2. These temples of His grace,
How beautiful they stand,
The honors of our native place
And bulwarks of our land!

3. In Zion God is known,
A Refuge in distress;
How bright has His salvation shone,
How fair His heavenly grace!

4. Oft have our fathers told,
Our eyes have often seen,
How well our God secures the fold
Where His own sheep have been.

5. In every new distress
We'll to His house repair,
Recall to mind His wondrous grace,
And seek deliverance there.

This cento omits Stanzas 4 and 5 of Isaac Watts's hymn as it originally appeared in his *Psalms of David Imitated*, 1719, on Ps. 48:1-8. The omitted stanzas are:

4. When kings against her joined
And saw the Lord was there,
In wild confusion of the mind
They fled with hasty fear.

5. When navies, tall and proud,
Attempt to spoil our peace,
He sends his tempest, roaring loud,
And sinks them in the seas.

For comments on the tune "Schumann" see Hymn No. 449.

637 Founded on Thee, Our Only Lord

1. Founded on Thee, our only Lord,
On Thee, the everlasting Rock,
Thy Church shall stand as stands Thy Word
Nor fear the storm nor dread the shock.

2. For Thee our waiting spirits yearn,
For Thee this house of praises rear,
To Thee with longing hearts we turn;
Come, fix Thy glorious presence here.

3. Come, with Thy Spirit and Thy power,
The Conqueror, once the Crucified.
Our God, our Strength, our King, our Tower,
Here plant Thy throne and here abide.

4. Accept the work our hands have wrought;
Accept, O God, this earthly shrine.
Be Thou our Rock, our Life, our Thought,
And we, as living temples, Thine.

There is some uncertainty about the actual time and occasion of the writing of this hymn by Samuel F. Smith, the author of "My Country, 'tis of Thee." He himself stated in a letter dated December 14, 1894: "This hymn was written a few weeks since to be used at a young men's social union in Boston." An account in the *Boston Evening Transcript* of February 14, 1925, indicates that the hymn was written by Smith for use at the dedication of the sanctuary of the Rosendale Baptist Church, June 17, 1889, a church which Smith had helped to organize in 1875.

For comments on the tune "Mendon" see Hymn No. 119.

DEDICATION. — CHURCH ANNIVERSARY

In Loud, Exalted Strains   638

1. In loud, exalted strains
The King of Glory praise.
O'er heaven and earth He reigns
Through everlasting days;
But, Zion, thou so richly blest,
Art His delight, His chosen rest.

2. O King of Glory, come
And with Thy favor crown
This temple as Thy home,
This people as Thine own.
Beneath this roof vouchsafe to show
How God can dwell with men below.

3. Now let Thine ear attend
Our supplicating cries;
Now let our praise ascend,
Accepted, to the skies;
Now let Thy Word, the Gospel, sound,
Spread its celestial blessing round.

4. Here may the listening throng
Receive Thy truth and love;
Here Christians join the song
Of seraphim above
Till all who humbly seek Thy face
Rejoice in Thy abounding grace.

This hymn was written for, and sung at, the reopening of the Meeting House at Horsley, where the author, Benjamin Francis, was pastor (September 18, 1774). In its original form the hymn had six stanzas, and the opening line was "In sweet exalted strains." It first appeared in Rippon's *Selection of Hymns*, 1787.

The omitted stanzas read:

5. To earth He bends His throne,
His throne of grace divine;
Wide is His bounty known,
And wide His glories shine.
Fair Salem, still His chosen rest,
Is with His smiles and presence blest.

6. Here may our unborn sons
And daughters sound Thy praise
And shine, like polished stones,
Through long-succeeding days;
Here, Lord, display Thy saving power
While temples stand and men adore.

While there are slight alterations in some of the stanzas, the last one has been largely recast. Francis had written:

> Here may the *attentive* throne
> *Imbibe* Thy truth in love,
> And *converts* join the song
> Of seraphim above,
> And *willing crowds surround the board*
> With sacred joy and sweet accord.

For comments on the tune "Darwall's 148th" see Hymn No. 46.

For Many Years, O God of Grace   639

1. For many years, O God of grace,
This church has been Thy dwelling-place
And we Thy congregation.
Upon the precious Corner-stone
Our faith is built, and Christ alone
Is still our one Foundation.
Today We pray:
"Let us greet Thee, Lord, and meet Thee
Here with singing,
All our praises to Thee bringing."

2. Here children have been born anew
As manifold as morning dew,
Their vows to Thee confessing.
Here many found a table spread,
They ate Christ's body with the bread
And drank the cup of blessing.
Today We pray:
"Let none falter At Thine altar,
We adore Thee,
Gladly worship here before Thee."

3. Here when the marriage vows were made,
Both bride and groom besought Thine aid,
Thy love their own transcending.
Here mourners, with their troubled hearts,
Have found the peace Thy Word imparts,
The joy that has no ending.
Today We pray:
"May the story Of Thy glory
Here resounding
Be a song of grace abounding!"

This hymn was written by W. M. Czamanske in 1934 for the twenty-fifth anniversary of St. Mark's Lutheran Church, Sheboygan, Wis., where the author is pastor. It has been used for similar occasions by other churches of our Synod since that time.

For comments on the tune "Wie schön leuchtet" see Hymn No. 23.

CHURCH ANNIVERSARY. — THEOLOGICAL INSTITUTIONS

640   God the Father, Son, and Spirit

1. God the Father, Son, and Spirit,
    Ever-blessed Trinity,
Humbly now our thanks we offer,
    All unworthy though we be.
Freely Thou hast showered blessings
    Countless as the ocean's sands,
Blessings rich and overflowing,
    On the labors of our hands.

2. Thou didst guide our fathers' footsteps
    To this land we hold so dear,
Lengthening the cords and curtains
    Of their habitation here;
Strengthening Thy temple's pillars
    As Thou hast from age to age;
Giving us, their sons and daughters,
    An abiding heritage.

3. Grant that we Thy Word may cherish
    And its purity retain.
Lord, unless Thou art the Builder,
    All our labor is in vain.
Keep us from all pride and boasting,
    Vanity and foolish trust,
Knowing that our work without Thee
    Soon will crumble into dust.

4. God of grace and love and blessing,
    Thine alone shall be the praise;
Give us hearts to trust Thee truly,
    Hands to serve Thee all our days.
Lord, bestow Thy future blessing
    Till we join the heavenly host,
There to praise and serve Thee ever,
    Father, Son, and Holy Ghost.

This anniversary hymn was written for the centennial of the Saxon immigration and used as its Centennial Hymn for the commemoration of that event by the Evangelical Lutheran Synod of Missouri, Ohio, and Other States. On the Sunday set aside for a Synod-wide celebration, June 19, 1938, the delegates of the churches were assembled for the triennial convention of that body in St. Louis, Mo., where a Centennial Service was held in the afternoon in the public auditorium of the Municipal Opera House. This hymn was sung by the assembly after Dr. J. W. Behnken, the President of Synod, had completed his Centennial Sermon. On the same day the churches of the Synod at home and abroad joined in the celebration and in the singing of this hymn.

Though written for this special occasion, the hymn lends itself to use at all church anniversaries.

We have been unable to find the source of the tune "St. Hilary."

641   One Thy Light, the Temple Filling

1. One Thy Light, the Temple filling,
    Holy, Holy, Holy, Three.
Meanest men and brightest angels
    Wait alike the word from Thee;
Highest musings, lowliest worship,
    Must their preparation be.

2. Now Thou speakest, — hear we trembling, —
From the glory comes a voice,
Who accepts the Almighty's mission?
Who will make Christ's work his choice?
Who for us proclaim to sinners,
    Turn, believe, endure, rejoice?

3. Here are we, Redeemer, send us!
    But because Thy work is fire,
And our lips unclean and earthly,
    Breathe no breath of high desire,
Send Thy seraph from the altar,
    Veiled, but in his bright attire.

4. Cause him, Lord, to fly full swiftly
    With the mystic coal in hand,
Sin-consuming, soul-transforming,
    Faith and love will understand.
Touch our lips, Thou wondrous Mercy,
    With Thine own keen healing brand.

5. Thou didst come that fire to kindle;
    Fain would we Thy torches prove,
Far and wide Thy beacons lighting
    With the undying spark of love.
Only feed our flame, we pray Thee,
    With Thy breathings from above.

6. Now to God, the soul's Creator,
    To His Word and Wisdom sure,
To His all-enlightening Spirit,
    Patron of the frail and poor,
Three in One, be praise and glory
    Here and while the heavens endure.

This hymn is made up of Stanzas 5 to 9 of John Keble's hymn "Lord of Life, Prophetic Spirit," written for the *Book of Prayers* for Cuddesdon College, 1856.

For comments on the tune "Regent Square" see Hymn No. 50.

FOREIGN MISSIONS. — ABSENT ONES. — DOXOLOGY

Arise, O God, and Shine   642

1. Arise, O God, and shine
   In all Thy saving might
   And prosper each design
   To spread Thy glorious light;
   Let healing streams of mercy flow
   That all the earth Thy truth may know.

2. Bring distant nations near
   To sing Thy glorious praise;
   Let every people hear
   And learn Thy holy ways.
   Reign, mighty God, assert Thy cause
   And govern by Thy righteous laws.

3. Put forth Thy glorious power
   That Gentiles all may see
   And earth present her store
   In converts born to Thee.
   God, our own God, His Church will bless
   And fill the world with righteousness.

4. To God, the only Wise,
   The one immortal King,
   Let hallelujahs rise
   From every living thing;
   Let all that breathe, on every coast,
   Praise Father, Son, and Holy Ghost.

This hymn, by William Hurn first appeared in his *Psalms and Hymns*, etc., Ipswich, 1813, beginning "Rise, gracious God, and shine." It was altered in the *Salisbury Hymn Book*, 1857, to "Arise, O Lord, and shine" and in the Lutheran *Church Book with Music*, 1877, to "Arise, O God, and Shine."

The hymn may be used for Epiphany and missions, but is particularly appropriate for a service in which foreign missionaries are commissioned.

For comments on the tune "Darwall's 148th" see Hymn No. 46.

Holy Father, in Thy Mercy   643

1. Holy Father, in Thy mercy
   Hear our anxious prayer;
   Keep our loved ones who are absent
   'Neath Thy care.

2. Jesus, Savior, let Thy presence
   Be their light and guide;
   Keep, oh, keep them in their weakness
   At Thy side.

3. When in sorrow, when in danger,
   When in loneliness,
   In Thy love look down and comfort
   Their distress.

4. May the joy of Thy salvation
   Be their strength and stay!
   May they love and may they praise Thee
   Day by day!

5. Holy Spirit, let Thy teaching
   Sanctify their life;
   Send Thy grace that they may conquer
   In the strife.

6. Father, Son, and Holy Spirit,
   God the One in Three,
   Bless them, guide them, save them, keep them,
   Near to Thee.

This hymn by Isabella S. Stephenson first appeared in the *Supplement* to the revised edition of *Hymns Ancient and Modern*, 1889.

For comments on the tune "Stephanos" see Hymn No. 513.

Praise God, from Whom All Blessings Flow   644

Praise God, from whom all blessings flow;
Praise Him, all creatures here below;
Praise Him above, ye heavenly host:
Praise Father, Son, and Holy Ghost. Amen.

For comments on the text see Ken's Morning Hymn No. 536.
For comments on the tune "Old Hundredth" see Hymn No. 13.

Carols and Spiritual Songs

645   Behold, a Branch is Growing

1. Behold a branch is growing
   Of loveliest form and grace,
   As prophets sung, foreknowing;
   It springs from Jesse's race
   And bears one little Flower
   In midst of coldest winter,
   At deepest midnight hour.

2. Isaiah hath foretold It
   In words of promise sure,
   And Mary's arms enfold It,
   A virgin meek and pure.
   Through God's eternal will
   This Child to her is given
   At midnight calm and still.

3. The shepherds heard the story,
   Proclaimed by angels bright,
   How Christ, the Lord of Glory,
   Was born on earth this night.
   To Bethlehem they sped
   And in the manger found Him,
   As angel heralds said.

4. This Flower, whose fragrance tender
   With sweetness fills the air,
   Dispels with glorious splendor
   The darkness everywhere.
   True Man, yet very God;
   From sin and death He saves us
   And lightens every load.

5. O Savior, Child of Mary,
   Who felt our human woe;
   O Savior, King of Glory,
   Who dost our weakness know,
   Bring us at length, we pray,
   To the bright courts of heaven
   And to the endless day.

Es ist ein Reis (Ros') entsprungen
   Aus einer Wurzel zart,
Als uns die Alten sungen,
   Von Jesse kam die Art,
Und hat ein Blümlein bracht
   Mitten im kalten Winter
Wohl zu der halben Nacht.

Das Reislein, das ich meine,
   Davon Jesaias sagt,
Hat uns gebracht alleine
   Marie, die reine Magd.
Aus Gottes ew'gem Rat
   Hat sie ein Kind geboren
Wohl zu der halben Nacht.

Den Hirten auf dem Felde
   Verkünd't das englisch' Heer,
Wie zur selbigen Stunde
   Christus geboren wär'
Zu Bethle'm in der Stadt,
   Da sie das Kindlein finden,
Wie ihn'n der Engel g'sagt.

Das Blümelein so kleine,
   Das duftet uns so süss,
Mit seinem hellen Scheine
   Vertreibt's die Finsternis,
Wahr'r Mensch und wahrer Gott,
   Hilft uns aus allen Leiden,
Rettet von Sünd' und Tod.

Wir bitten dich von Herzen,
   O Heiland, edles Kind,
Durch alle deine Schmerzen,
   Wann wir fahren dahin
Aus diesem Jammertal,
   Du wollest uns geleiten
Bis in der Engel Saal.

This carol seems to have had its beginning in the 15th or 16th century. Originally it was sung in honor of Mary. In the *Alte Catholische Geistliche Kirchengesäng*, Köln, 1599, it appeared in twenty-three stanzas. Michael Prätorius, in his *Musae Sioniae*, VI, 1609, brings only two stanzas, which are with but slight changes Stanzas 1 and 2 of our German text above. The second stanza had been altered to shift the emphasis from Mary to the Christ-child, for originally the second stanza read:

> Das Röslein, das ich meine,
>   Davon Jesaias sagt,
> Ist Maria, die reine,
>   Die uns das Blümlein bracht;
> Aus Gottes ew'gem Rat
>   Hat sie ein Kind geboren
> Und blieb ein' reine Magd.

The carol was received into various German hymn-books, usually with alterations and in different centos. The Berlin *Liederschatz*, in 1832 (or earlier), added the stanza which is the fourth in our version and which does not seem to have been among the original twenty-three stanzas.

The translation is by Harriet Krauth Spaeth, who published Stanzas 1 to 4 in 1875, and by John Caspar Mattes, who added Stanza 5 in 1914.

For comments on the tune "Es ist ein' Ros'" see Hymn No. 76.

[458]

CAROLS AND SPIRITUAL SONGS

Silent Night! Holy Night! 646

1. Silent night! Holy night!
All is calm, all is bright,
Round yon Virgin Mother and Child.
Holy Infant, so tender and mild,
Sleep in heavenly peace,
Sleep in heavenly peace.

2. Silent night! Holy night!
Shepherds quake at the sight;
Glories stream from heaven afar,
Heavenly hosts sing, Alleluia,
Christ, the Savior, is born!
Christ, the Savior, is born!

3. Silent night! Holy night!
Son of God, love's pure light
Radiant beams from Thy holy face,
With the dawn of redeeming grace,
Jesus, Lord, at Thy birth.
Jesus, Lord, at Thy birth.

Stille Nacht, heilige Nacht!
Alles schläft, einsam wacht
Nur das heilige Elternpaar,
Das im Stalle zu Bethlehem war
Bei dem himmlischen Kind,
Bei dem himmlischen Kind.

Stille Nacht, heilige Nacht!
Hirten erst kundgemacht;
Durch der Engel Halleluja
Tönt es laut von fern und nah:
Christ, der Retter, ist da!
Christ, der Retter, ist da!

Stille Nacht, heilige Nacht!
Gottes Sohn, o wie lacht
Lieb' aus deinem göttlichen Mund,
Da uns schläget die rettende Stund',
Christ, in deiner Geburt!
Christ, in deiner Geburt!

This is one of the most popular Christmas carols in America. It was written by Joseph Mohr, in 1818, for the Christmas celebration in his church that year. The tune "Stille Nacht" was composed by Franz Gruber, organist, who was schoolmaster at Arnsdorf, a village not far from Oberndorf, where Mohr had his parish.

A brochure on "Silent Night" was prepared several years ago by Frederick H. Jänicken in which the circumstances of its origin are told. According to Mr. Jänicken it was first played on a guitar in the church study of Joseph Mohr at Oberndorf, where Pastor Mohr, who wrote the text and, in a sense, provided the poetic impulse for the music, was the vicar. Pastor Mohr and Gruber had been friends for a long time. Gruber was the organist and choirmaster in the neighboring village of Arnsdorf, and they often visited each other, usually for the purpose of singing hymns and sometimes, when other singers could be brought in, the more difficult motets. On one of these occasions, just a week or two before Christmas of 1818, Gruber had said to Mohr, "Do you know, Pastor, the true Christmas song is yet to be written?" Gruber was looking out into the deep, serene, snow-clad Alpine reaches when he spoke, and Mohr, following his gaze, agreed. Pastor Mohr, pondering the thought of a perfect Christmas song, was called on Christmas Eve to the hut of a woodchopper whose wife had just borne a child. Face to face with the mystery of life, Pastor Mohr, after performing appropriate offices for the family, returned through the snow-drifts to his house and almost automatically began to write, since that was the most effective way he could think of to give expression to his mood and his sensibilities. According to the story he stopped writing at 4 o'clock on Christmas morning — and the poem of "Silent Night" had been written. After a few hours' sleep he arose at 9, hurried to the home of his friend Gruber in Arnsdorf, presented him with the text, and returned to his own home. Later in the day Gruber came to Oberndorf with the notes sketched in. The organ in the pastor's study was broken, so Gruber took a guitar from the wall, played he music through once, and then the two sang it together in thirds. It was then not more than half an hour before the Christmas services were to begin; but Pastor Mohr quickly assembled his choir, Herr Gruber sang the tune, they followed, and by the time the con-

gregation had filled the church, they were ready to give it to the world. In 1897 a memorial tablet was placed on the schoolhouse in Arnsdorf with this inscription:
Silent night! Holy night!
Who composed thee, hymn divine?
Mohr it was who wrote each line,
Gruber found my tune sublime, —
Teacher together with priest.

The translation is by an unknown writer. According to *Julian* it first appeared in C. L. Hutchins's *Sunday School Hymnal*, 1871. Our copy, which is Edition A, 1889, has a different translation. The *Sunday School Hymn Book* of the General Council, 1873, carried this translation, and thus it came into common use among American Lutherans.

647   O Little Town of Bethlehem

1. O little town of Bethlehem,
 How still we see thee lie!
 Above thy deep and dreamless sleep
 The silent stars go by;
 Yet in thy darkness shineth
 The everlasting Light;
 The hopes and fears of all the years
 Are met in thee tonight.

2. For Christ is born of Mary,
 And gathered all above,
 While mortals sleep, the angels keep
 Their watch of wondering love.
 O morning stars, together
 Proclaim the holy birth
 And praises sing to God, the King,
 And peace to men on earth.

3. How silently, how silently,
 The wondrous Gift is given!
 So God imparts to human hearts
 The blessings of His heaven.
 No ear may hear His coming,
 But in this world of sin,
 Where meek souls will receive Him still,
 The dear Christ enters in.

4. O holy Child of Bethlehem,
 Descend to us, we pray;
 Cast out our sin and enter in,
 Be born in us today.
 We hear the Christmas angels
 The great glad tidings tell;
 Oh, come to us, abide with us,
 Our Lord Immanuel!

This popular American Christmas carol was written by Phillips Brooks for the Sunday-school of his church in 1868. The omitted stanza reads:
Where Children, pure and happy,
 Pray to the Blessed Child,
Where Misery cries out to Thee,
 Son of the Undefiled,
Where Charity stands watching
 And Faith holds wide the Door,
The dark night wakes, the glory breaks,
 And Christmas comes once more.

In Stanza 1, line 5, the author originally had "dark streets."

The tune for the carol, "St. Louis," was composed, in 1868, by Lewis H. Redner, who was Brooks' organist at the Church of the Advent in Philadelphia.

648   I Am Jesus' Little Lamb

1. I am Jesus' little lamb,
 Ever glad at heart I am;
 For my Shepherd gently guides me,
 Knows my need, and well provides me,
 Loves me every day the same,
 Even calls me by my name.

2. Day by day, at home, away,
 Jesus is my Staff and Stay.
 When I hunger, Jesus feeds me,
 Into pleasant pastures leads me;
 When I thirst, He bids me go
 Where the quiet waters flow.

Weil ich Jesu Schäflein bin,
Freu' ich mich nur immerhin
Über meinen guten Hirten,
Der mich wohl weiss zu bewirten,
Der mich liebet, der mich kennt
Und bei meinem Namen nennt.

Unter seinem sanften Stab
Geh' ich aus und ein und hab'
Unaussprechlich süsse Weide,
Dass ich keinen Mangel leide;
Und sooft ich durstig bin,
Führt er mich zum Brunnquell hin.

CAROLS AND SPIRITUAL SONGS

3. Who so happy as I am,
Even now the Shepherd's lamb?
And when my short life is ended,
By His angel host attended,
He shall fold me to His breast,
There within His arms to rest.

Sollt' ich denn nicht fröhlich sein,
Ich beglücktes Schäfelein?
Denn nach diesen schönen Tagen
Werd' ich endlich hingetragen
In des Hirten Arm und Schoss:
Amen, ja mein Glück ist gross!

This justly popular children's song by Henrietta Luise von Hayn first appeared in the Moravian hymnal the *Neuen Brüder Gesangbuch*, 1778, where it was placed among the hymns for Holy Communion. It has been frequently translated into English. The translation above is composite.

The tune "Weil ich Jesu," to which the text is wedded, first appeared in the *Brüder-Choral-Buch*, 1784.

Jesus, Savior, Pilot Me   649

1. Jesus Savior, pilot me
Over life's tempestuous sea;
Unknown waves before me roll,
Hiding rock and treacherous shoal.
Chart and compass come from Thee:
Jesus, Savior, pilot me.

2. As a mother stills her child,
Thou canst hush the ocean wild;
Boisterous waves obey Thy will
When Thou say'st to them, "Be still!"
Wondrous Sovereign of the sea,
Jesus, Savior, pilot me.

3. When at last I near the shore,
And the fearful breakers roar
'Twixt me and the peaceful rest,
Then, while leaning on Thy breast,
May I hear Thee say to me,
"Fear not, I will pilot thee."

Edward Hopper first published this favorite spiritual song anonymously in *The Sailors' Magazine*, 1871. When it had appeared in *Spiritual Songs*, 1878, he finally acknowledged it as his own. As pastor of the New York City "Church of the Sea and Land," Hopper had many sailors in attendance at worship, and it was for them that he wrote the song.

The hymn is really a cento composed of the first and the last two stanzas, selected by himself. Originally the hymn had six stanzas. The omitted stanzas are:

2. When th' Apostles' fragile bark
Struggled with the billows dark
On the stormy Galilee,
Thou didst walk upon the sea;
And when they beheld Thy form,
Safe they glided through the storm.

3. Though the sea be smooth and bright,
Sparkling with the stars of night,
And my ship's path be ablaze
With the light of halcyon days,
Still I know my need of Thee;
Jesus, Savior, pilot me.

4. When the darkling heavens frown,
And the wrathful winds come down,
And the fierce waves, tossed on high,
Lash themselves against the sky,
Jesus, Savior, pilot me
Over life's tempestuous sea.

The tune "Pilot" was written for the text by John E. Gould and was first published in *The Baptist Praise Book*, 1871.

Behold a Stranger at the Door   650

1. Behold a Stranger at the door!
He gently knocks, has knocked before,
Has waited long, is waiting still;
You treat no other friend so ill.

2. But will He prove a friend indeed?
He will; the very Friend you need;
The Friend of sinners — yes 'tis He,
With garments dyed on Calvary.

3. O lovely attitude! He stands
   With melting heart and laden hands;
   O matchless kindness! and He shows
   This matchless kindness to His foes.

4. Admit Him lest His anger burn
   And He, departing, ne'er return;
   Admit Him, or the hour's at hand
   When at His door denied you'll stand.

5. Oh, let the heavenly Stranger in,
   Let in thy heart His reign begin.
   Admit Him, open wide the door,
   And He will bless thee evermore.

This cento includes Stanzas 1, 2, 3, and 9 of Joseph Grigg's hymn of eleven stanzas. The hymn first appeared in *Four Hymns on Divine Subjects,* etc., 1765. The omitted stanzas read:

4. Rise, touched with gratitude divine,
   Turn out His enemy and thine, —
   That hateful, hell-born monster, sin,
   And let the heavenly Stranger in.

5. If thou art poor, and poor thou art,
   Lo, He has riches to impart;
   Not wealth, in which mean avarice rolls;
   Oh, better far — the wealth of souls!

6. Thou'rt blind, He'll take the scales away
   And let in everlasting day;
   Naked thou art, but He shall dress
   Thy blushing soul in righteousness.

7. Art thou a weeper? Grief shall fly,
   For who can weep with Jesus by?
   No terror shall thy hopes annoy,
   No tear, except the tear of joy.

8. Admit Him, for the human breast
   Ne'er entertained so kind a guest.
   Admit Him, for you can't expel;
   Where'er He comes, He comes to dwell.

10. Yet know, nor of the terms complain,
    If Jesus comes, He comes to reign;
    To reign, and with no partial sway;
    Thoughts must be slain that disobey.

11. Sovereign of souls, thou Prince of peace,
    Oh, may Thy gentle reign increase!
    Throw wide the door, each willing mind,
    And be His empire all mankind!

The fifth stanza is a composite by the editorial committee of the *Evangelical Lutheran Hymn-Book,* 1912, for which it was prepared.

For comments on the tune "Hamburg" see Hymn No. 175.

651   Be Still, My Soul

1. Be still, my soul; the Lord is on thy side;
   Bear patiently the cross of grief or pain.
   Leave to thy God to order and provide;
   In every change He faithful will remain.
   Be still, my soul; thy best, thy heavenly Friend
   Through thorny ways leads to a joyful end.

2. Be still, my soul; thy God doth undertake
   To guide the future as He has the past.
   Thy hope, thy confidence, let nothing shake;
   All now mysterious shall be bright at last.
   Be still, my soul; the waves and winds still know
   His voice who ruled them while He dwelt below.

3. Be still, my soul, though dearest friends depart
   And all is darkened in the vale of tears;
   Then shalt thou better know His love, His heart,
   Who comes to soothe thy sorrows and thy fears.
   Be still, my soul; thy Jesus can repay
   From His own fulness all He takes away.

Stille, mein Wille! Dein Jesus hilft siegen;
Trage geduldig das Leiden, die Not;
Gott ist's, der alles zum besten will fügen,
Der dir getreu bleibt in Schmerzen und Tod.
Stille, mein Wille! Dein Jesus wird machen
Glücklichen Ausgang bedenklicher Sachen.

Stille, mein Wille! Der Herr hat's in Händen,
Hält sich dein Herz nur im Glauben an ihn,
Wird er den Kummer bald wenden und enden;
Herrlich wird endlich, was wunderbar schien.
Stille, mein Wille! Dein Heiland wird zeigen,
Wie vor ihm Meer und Gewitter muss schweigen.

Stille, mein Wille! Wenn Freunde sich trennen,
Die du so zärtlich und innig geliebt,
Wirst du die Freundschaft des Höchsten erkennen,
Der sich zum Eigentum treulich dir gibt.
Stille, mein Wille! Dein Jesus ersetzet,
Was dich beim Sterben der Liebsten verletzet.

CAROLS AND SPIRITUAL SONGS

4. Be still, my soul; the hour is hastening on
When we shall be forever with the Lord,
When disappointment, grief, and fear are gone,
Sorrow forgot, love's purest joys restored.
Be still, my soul; when change and tears are past,
All safe and blessed we shall meet at last.

Stille, mein Wille! Es kommen die Stunden,
Dass wir beim Herrn sind ohn' Wechsel der Zeit;
Dann ist das Scheiden, der Kummer verschwunden,
Ewige Freundschaft vergütet das Leid.
Stille, mein Wille! Nach zeitlichem Scheiden
Sehn wir uns wieder ohn' Schmerzen und Leiden.

This cento is from Catharina von Schlegel's famous poem, which first appeared in the collection *Neue Sammlung geistlicher Lieder*, Wernigerode, 1752, in six stanzas. The third and sixth stanzas are omitted above. The author may have had Ps. 46:10, "Be still and know that I am God," in mind when she wrote her text.

The translation by Jane L. Borthwick first appeared in her *Hymns from the Land of Luther*, 1855, second series.

The tune "Finlandia" is an adaptation from Jean Sibelius' tone poem *Finlandia*.

I Lay My Sins on Jesus 652

1. I lay my sins on Jesus,
The spotless Lamb of God;
He bears them all and frees us
From the accursed load.
I bring my guilt to Jesus
To wash my crimson stains
White in His blood most precious
Till not a spot remains.

2. I lay my wants on Jesus,
All fulness dwells in Him;
He healeth my diseases,
He doth my soul redeem.
I lay my griefs on Jesus,
My burdens and my cares;
He from them all releases,
He all my sorrows shares.

3. I rest my soul on Jesus,
This weary soul of mine;
His right hand me embraces,
I on His breast recline.
I love the name of Jesus,
Immanuel, Christ, the Lord;
Like fragrance on the breezes
His name abroad is poured.

4. I long to be like Jesus,
Meek, loving, lowly, mild;
I long to be like Jesus,
The Father's holy Child.
I long to be with Jesus
Amid the heavenly throng
To sing with saints His praises,
To learn the angels' song.

Horatius Bonar first published this children's hymn in his *Songs in the Wilderness*, 1843, under the title "The Fulness of Jesus." It is said to have been written about two years before, when the author was assistant in St. John's Church, Leith. It was intended for use by children, "something which children could sing and appreciate in divine worship." It may have been the first hymn Bonar ever wrote. He himself admitted "that it might be good Gospel, but that it was poor poetry." The circumstance that it became popular does not hide the fact that the poet had to strain himself severely to find rimes for "Jesus."

For comments on the tune "Aurelia" see Hymn No. 473.

Now the Light has Gone Away 653

1. Now the light has gone away;
Father, listen while I pray,
Asking Thee to watch and keep
And to send me quiet sleep.

2. Jesus, Savior, wash away
All that has been wrong today;
Help me every day to be
Good and gentle, more like Thee.

3. Let my near and dear ones be
Always near and dear to Thee.
Oh, bring me and all I love
To Thy happy home above.

4. Now my evening praise I give;
Thou didst die that I might live.
All my blessings come from Thee;
Oh, how good Thou art to me!

[463]

CAROLS AND SPIRITUAL SONGS

5. Thou, my best and kindest Friend,
Thou wilt love me to the end.
Let me love Thee more and more,
Always better than before.

Frances R. Havergal wrote this evensong on October 17, 1869, at Leamington. It appeared in *Songs for Little Singers*, 1870.

The tune "Müde bin ich, geh' zur Ruh'" first appeared in Theodore Fliedner's *Liederbuch für Kleinkinder-Schulen*, Kaiserswerth, 1842, where it was set to the famous German children's evening song beginning with those words.

654   Now the Day Is Over

1. Now the day is over,
Night is drawing nigh;
Shadows of the evening
Steal across the sky.

2. Now the darkness gathers,
Stars begin to peep,
Birds and beasts and flowers
Soon will be asleep.

3. Jesus, give the weary
Calm and sweet repose;
With Thy tend'rest blessing
May mine eyelids close.

4. Grant to little children
Visions bright of Thee;
Guard the sailors tossing
On the deep-blue sea.

5. Comfort every sufferer
Watching late in pain;
Those who plan some evil
From their sin restrain.

6. Through the long night-watches
May Thine angels spread
Their white wings above me,
Watching round my bed.

7. When the morning wakens,
Then may I arise
Pure and fresh and sinless
In Thy holy eyes.

8. Glory to the Father,
Glory to the Son,
And to Thee, blest Spirit,
While all ages run.

Sabine Baring-Gould wrote this evensong in 1865 for the children of Horbury Bridge, where he was curate at the time. The tune "Eudoxia" was composed by him for use with the text. Both hymn and tune were included in the *Appendix to Hymns Ancient and Modern*, 1868. The tune was a reminiscence of a German melody which Baring-Gould had heard in his youth, but which he was unable to identify.

655   I Pray Thee, Dear Lord Jesus

I pray Thee, dear Lord Jesus,
My heart to keep and train
That I Thy holy temple
From youth to age remain.
Turn Thou my thoughts forever
From worldly wisdom's lore;
If I but learn to know Thee,
I shall not want for more.

O Jesu, gid du vilde
Mit Hjerte danne saa,
Det baade aarl' og silde
Dit Tempel väre maa!
Du selv min Hjerne vende
Fra Verdens kloge Flok,
Og lär mig dig at kjende,
Saa har jeg Visdom nok!

This is the concluding stanza of Thomas Kingo's hymn "Hvor storer dog den Gläde," a hymn to the Child Jesus in the Temple. It first appeared in 1699. According to an ordinance of the Norwegian Church authorities, dated October 10, 1818, this stanza was to be sung at church dedication services. This custom, we are told, is still observed in our Norwegian churches. The translation is by Norman A. Madson and was prepared for *The Lutheran Hymnal* in 1939.

The tune "Jeg vil mig Herren love" is from Hartnack Otto Konrad Zinck's *Koral-Melodier* (1801) for the *Evangelisk-Christelige Psalme-Bog*, where it was set to H. Thomisson's hymn beginning with that line.

[464]

Behold a Host, Arrayed in White 656

1. Behold a host, arrayed in white,
Like thousand snow-clad mountains bright,
With palms they stand. Who is this band
 Before the throne of light?
Lo, these are they of glorious fame
Who from the great affliction came
And in the flood of Jesus' blood
 Are cleansed from guilt and blame.
Now gathered in the holy place,
Their voices they in worship raise,
Their anthems swell where God doth dwell,
 Mid angels' songs of praise.

2. Despised and scorned, they sojourned here;
But now, how glorious they appear!
Those martyrs stand a priestly band,
 God's throne forever near.
So oft, in troubled days gone by,
In anguish they would weep and sigh.
At home above the God of Love
 For aye their tears shall dry.
They now enjoy their Sabbath rest,
The paschal banquet of the blest;
The Lamb, their Lord, at festal board
 Himself is Host and Guest.

3. Then hail, ye mighty legions, yea,
All hail! Now safe and blest for aye,
And praise the Lord, who with His Word
 Sustained you on the way.
Ye did the joys of earth disdain,
Ye toiled and sowed in tears and pain.
Farewell, now bring your sheaves and sing
 Salvation's glad refrain.
Swing high your palms, lift up your song,
Yea, make it myriad voices strong.
Eternally shall praise to Thee,
 God, and the Lamb belong.

Den store hvide Flok vi se
Som tusind Berge fuld' af Sne,
Med Skov omkring af Palmesving,
 For Thronen. Hvo er de?
Det er den Helteskare, som
Af hin den store Trængsel kom,
Og har sig toed i Lammets Blod,
 Til Himlens Helligdom.
Der holde de nu Kirkegang
Med uophörlig Jubelklang
I höie Kor, Hvor Gud han bor
 Blandt alle Englers Sang.

Her gik de under stor Foragt,
Men se dem nu i deres Pragt
For Thronen staa med Kroner paa
 I Himlens Prästedragt!
Sandt er det, i saa mangen Nöd
Tidt Taareström paa Kinden flöd,
Men Gud har dem, straks de kom hjem,
 Aftörret paa sit Sköd.
Nu holde de, og har tilbedst'
Hos ham en evig Lövsals-Fest,
Og Lammet selv ved Livets Elv
 Er baade Vert og Gjest.

Til Lykke, Kjämpe-Samling! ja,
O tusindfold til Lykke da,
At du var her saa tro isär,
 Og slap saa vel herfra!
Du har foragtet Verdens Tröst,
Saa lev nu evig vel, og höst,
Hvad du har saad med Suk og Graad,
 I tusind Engle-Lyst!
Ophöi din Röst, slaa Palme-Takt,
Og syng af Himmel-Kraft og Magt:
Pris väre dig evindelig,
 Vor Gud og Lammet, sagt!

This jubilant triumph-song of the saints of God was written by Hans A. Brorson in the later years of his life. It is No. 559 in Landstad's *Salmebog* and No. 492 in *The Lutheran Hymnary*, 1913. The translation is a composite one, prepared for *The Lutheran Hymnary* by O. T. Sanden (Arnesson), O. H. Smeby, Carl Döving, and Mr. Kvamme.

The following tribute to this hymn by the hymnologist Söderberg is worthy of note:

Of the glory of the life to come the harp of Brorson has wonderful strains. This hymn about the Lord's elect in heaven radiates a snow-white splendor of transfiguration. . . .

What is it that touches us so wondrously in this and other swan-songs by Brorson? It is the folk-tune, the spirit of the language and the rhythm, of the imagery and thought, something incomparable and unexplainable, an element of power everlasting: That is, this plain, pious, emotional lyric passion which gives birth to sadness and longing, power and triumphant joy. Therefore so many of Brorson's swan-songs in particular have received their tunes — mellow and sonorous at the same time — from the inmost life of the common people living in the valleys and forests, along the hillsides and among the mountains, of Norway; and perhaps no more beautiful melody than that of "Den store, hvide flok" has welled forth from the religious craving of the heart of the Norwegian people for an expression in song — spontaneously and sweetly, as a multitudinous reverberation, a hallelujah to the poet's inspired words in his beautiful anthem.

CAROLS AND SPIRITUAL SONGS

The tune "Great White Host" is a Norwegian folk-tune of the early seventeenth century, arranged by Edvard H. Grieg. It has helped to make this the most widely known Scandinavian hymn in English-speaking countries. The singing of this hymn by Christiansen's choir of St. Olaf's College has popularized it with the American public.

657   Beautiful Savior

1. Beautiful Savior,
   King of Creation,
Son of God and Son of Man!
Truly I'd love Thee,
Truly I'd serve Thee,
Light of my soul, my Joy, my Crown.

Schönster Herr Jesu,
Herrscher aller Herren,
Gottes und Mariä Sohn!
Dich will ich lieben,
Dich will ich ehren,
Meiner Seelen Freud' und Kron'.

2. Fair are the meadows,
   Fair are the woodlands,
Robed in flowers of blooming spring;
Jesus is fairer,
Jesus is purer;
He makes our sorrowing spirit sing.

Schön sind die Wälder,
Schöner die Felder
In der schönen Frühlingszeit.
Jesus ist schöner,
Jesus ist reiner,
Der unser traurigs Herz erfreut.

3. Fair is the sunshine,
   Fair is the moonlight,
Bright the sparkling stars on high;
Jesus shines brighter,
Jesus shines purer,
Than all the angels in the sky.

Schön leucht't der Monden,
Schöner die Sonne
Als die Sternlein allzumal.
Jesus leucht't schöner,
Jesus leucht't reiner,
Als all die Engel im Himmelssaal.

4. Beautiful Savior,
   Lord of the nations,
Son of God and Son of Man!
Glory and honor,
Praise, adoration,
Now and forevermore be Thine!

Alle die Schönheit
Himmels und der Erde
Ist nur gegen ihn als Schein.
Keiner soll nimmer
Lieber uns werden
Als er, der schönste Jesus mein!

The original German text has not been traced back farther than the German Roman Catholic *Münster Gesangbuch,* published in 1677. The English translation, beginning with the line "Fairest Lord Jesus," appears to be the oldest English version. The translator is not known. It was first published in *Church Chorals and Choir Studies,* by the American composer Richard Storrs Willis, 1850. The English translation, beginning with the line "Beautiful Savior," is by Dr. J. A. Seiss and first appeared in the *Sunday School Book,* Philadelphia, 1873.

The tune "Schönster Herr Jesu" is first found in a book of Silesian folksongs, *Schlesische Volkslieder,* Leipzig, 1842.

From the above we may conclude that the carol is not an ancient "Crusaders' Hymn," as often stated. Both text and tune are modern.

658   Onward, Christian Soldiers

1. Onward, Christian soldiers,
   Marching as to war,
With the cross of Jesus
   Going on before.
Christ, the royal Master,
   Leads against the Foe;
Forward into battle
   See His banners go!

2. Like a mighty army
   Moves the Church of God;
Brothers, we are treading
   Where the saints have trod.
We are not divided,
   All one body we,
One in hope and doctrine,
   One in charity. — *Refrain.*

Refrain: Onward, Christian soldiers,
        Marching as to war,
        With the cross of Jesus
        Going on before.

3. Crowns and thrones may perish,
  Kingdoms rise and wane,
But the Church of Jesus
  Constant will remain.
Gates of hell can never
  'Gainst that Church prevail;
We have Christ's own promise,
  And that cannot fail. — *Refrain*.

4. Onward, then, ye faithful,
  Join our happy throng,
Blend with ours your voices
  In the triumph-song;
Glory, laud, and honor
  Unto Christ, the King;
This, through countless ages,
  Men and angels sing. — *Refrain*.

Like Sabine Baring-Gould's "Now the Day Is Over," this spiritual song was written by him for the schoolchildren of Horbury Bridge, England, where he was curate at the time. The text was published in *The Church Times*, 1864, the same year in which it was written. It was intended for use as a children's processional.

Originally the author wrote five stanzas. The omitted second stanza reads:

At the sign of triumph
  Satan's host doth flee;
On, then, Christian soldiers,
  On to victory;

Hell's foundations quiver
  At the shout of praise;
Brothers, lift your voices,
  Loud your anthems raise. — *Refrain*.

The tune "St. Gertrude" was composed by Arthur S. Sullivan in 1871 and first appeared in the *Musical Times*, London, the same year. The Mrs. Gertrude Clay-Ker-Seymer, to whom the celebrated composer dedicated the tune, in a letter to the *Musical Times* of July, 1902, wrote:

> In answer to your letter regarding the composition of Sir Arthur Sullivan's tune to "Onward, Christian Soldiers," which he dedicated to me, I can tell you that I believe it was written at Hanford, my home in Dorsetshire, while Sir Arthur was staying there; but it is so long ago I cannot be quite sure; what I do remember, however, is that we sang it in the private chapel attached to the house, Sir Arthur playing the harmonium and having taught us the tune, as we had not the music. Therefore it was certainly not published then, but I think we may assume that it was written there. Sir Arthur often stayed with us for several weeks at a time and composed several songs, etc., while at Hanford, after which place he named another of his hymn tunes, but not one of such striking merit as "Onward, Christian Soldiers," which has now a world-wide reputation and of which I am proud to be the sponsor.

Feed Thy Children, God Most Holy 659

Feed Thy children, God most holy,
Comfort sinners poor and lowly;
O Thou Bread of Life from heaven,
Bless the food Thou here hast given!
As these gifts the body nourish,
May our souls in graces flourish
Till with saints in heavenly splendor
At Thy feast due thanks we render.

Speis uns, o Gott, deine Kinder,
Tröste die betrübten Sünder,
Sprich den Segen zu den Gaben,
Die wir jetzund vor uns haben,
Dass sie uns zu diesem Leben
Stärke, Kraft und Nahrung geben,
Bis wir endlich mit den Frommen
Zu der Himmelsmahlzeit kommen!

This grace for before meals, by Johann Heermann, first appeared in his prayer-book *Geistlicher Poetischer Erquickstunden*, etc., Nürnberg, 1656, without Lines 7 and 8. These were added later by an unknown hand and appeared in the *Halberstädter Gesangbuch*, 1712. This table-prayer became a general favorite in German circles. It was frequently sung before the meal.

The composite translation was prepared for *The Lutheran Hymnal* and is based largely on the translation in the *Australian Lutheran Hymn-Book*, 1925.

For comments on the tune "Schmücke dich" see Hymn No. 305.

660   I'm But a Stranger Here

1. I'm but a stranger here,
    Heaven is my home;
   Earth is a desert drear,
    Heaven is my home.
   Danger and sorrow stand
   Round me on every hand;
   Heaven is my fatherland,
    Heaven is my home.

2. What though the tempest rage,
    Heaven is my home;
   Short is my pilgrimage,
    Heaven is my home;
   And time's wild wintry blast
   Soon shall be overpast;
   I shall reach home at last,
    Heaven is my home.

3. There at my Savior's side
    Heaven is my home;
   I shall be glorified,
    Heaven is my home.
   There are the good and blest,
   Those I love most and best;
   And there I, too, shall rest,
    Heaven is my home.

4. Therefore I murmur not,
    Heaven is my home;
   Whate'er my earthly lot,
    Heaven is my home;
   And I shall surely stand
   There at my Lord's right hand.
   Heaven is my fatherland,
    Heaven is my home.

This spiritual song by Thomas R. Taylor was apparently written during the author's last illness. It was published in his *Memoirs and Select Remains*, 1836, to be sung to the tune "Robin Adair."

The tune "Heaven Is My Home" (also called "St. Edmund" and "Saints' Rest") is by Arthur S. Sullivan and was first published in 1872.

PART II
BIOGRAPHICAL AND HISTORICAL NOTES ON THE AUTHORS AND COMPOSERS

ADAM OF ST. VICTOR (d. 1172 or 1192). Although Adam of St. Victor was one of the most prolific of the Latin hymnists of the Middle Ages, very little is known of him. He is called "Brito" by those nearest his own epoch; but whether this indicates "Britain" or "Brittany" is uncertain. Adam was educated at Paris, and about 1130, when still quite a young man, he became a monk in the Abbey of St. Victor. The abbey was then in the suburbs, but afterwards, through the growth of Paris, it was included within the walls of that city. In this abbey, which was celebrated as a school of theology, Adam passed the whole rest of his life. — Adam of St. Victor had a facile pen and spent his life in study and authorship. It is quite probable that he was the author of many more than the numerous hymns and sequences which are definitely known to be his. He was the author of several prose works as well. His sequences, which were in manuscript, were destroyed at the dissolution of the Abbey of St. Victor in the Revolution, but 37 of them had already found their way into general circulation. These were published by Clichtoveus, a Roman Catholic theologian of the first half of the 16th century in his *Elucidatorium Ecclesiasticum.* Of the rest of the 106 hymns and sequences of his that we possess, the largest part — some 47 remaining unpublished — were removed to the National Library in the Louvre at Paris on the destruction of the abbey. There they were discovered by M. Leon Gautier, the editor of the first *complete* edition of them, Paris, 1858. Archbishop Trench, who published a selection of his poems in his *Sacred Latin Poetry,* says that Adam of St. Victor was "the foremost among the sacred poets of the Middle Ages."

282. *Christians, come in sweetest measures*

ADAMS, Sarah Flower (1805—1848), was born at Harlow, England, February 22, 1805, the daughter of Benjamin and Eliza Flower. Her only sister was named for her mother, who came to an early grave owing to consumption. Both girls inherited their mother's delicate constitution. The talents of Sarah and Eliza were complementary. Eliza was a musician, Sarah a poet. Often Eliza wrote music for Sarah's songs. Although Sarah married William Bridges Adams, a civil engineer and inventor, in 1834, and went to live in London, the two girls remained on intimate terms. Eliza became weakened by nursing Sarah through a long illness, and Sarah's health was undermined by her care of Eliza in her last sickness. The two sisters died within twenty months of each other, Eliza in December, 1846, and Sarah in August, 1848. At both funerals the hymns sung were by them, the words by Sarah and the music by Eliza. — Mrs. Adams published *Vivia Perpetua*, a dramatic poem in five acts, 1841; *The Flock at the Fountain,* 1845.

533. *Nearer, my God, to Thee*

ADDISON, Joseph (1672—1719), was born May 1, 1672, at Milston, Wiltshire, England, the son of the Rev. Lancelot Addison, sometime Dean of Lichfield. His mother was the sister of William Gulston, Bishop of Bristol. He was educated at Charterhouse and Magdalen College, Oxford (B. A. 1691, M. A. 1693). He studied law and politics. Successively he was Commissioner of Appeals, Undersecretary of State, Secretary to the Lord Lieutenant of Ireland, and Chief Secretary for Ireland. In 1716 he married the Dowager Charlotte, Countess of Warwick. In his last years he suffered from asthma and dropsy. He died at Holland House, Kensington, on June 17, 1719. — Joseph Addison is known through his contributions to *The Spectator, The Tatler, The Guardian,* and *The Freeholder.* He also wrote the well-known tragedy *Cato.* Not only was Addison the leading literary light of his time, but he was also a devout Christian. On his death-bed he called for the Earl of Warwick and exclaimed, "See in what peace a Christian can die." All five of Addison's hymns appeared in *The Spectator,* in 1712.

31. *When all Thy mercies, O my God*
368. *The Lord my pasture shall prepare*

AHLE, Johann Rudolph (1625—1673), was born December 24, 1625, at Mühlhausen, Thuringia. He was educated at the universities of Göttingen and Erfurt. He was elected cantor at St. Andreas's Church and director of the music school at Erfurt in 1646. Eight years later he was given the lucrative post as organist at

St. Blasius's Church, Mühlhausen, to succeed Johann Vockerrodt. In this town he became an influential citizen. He was elected to the town council in 1656 and made mayor in 1661. He died on July 8, 1673. — Ahle was a well-educated German organist and composer. While at Erfurt he became known as one of the most radical reformers of church music. He originated the "sacred aria." He wrote over 400 spiritual songs for the different Sundays, festivals, and other special days in the calendar. Although florid writing was in vogue at the time, Ahle avoided polyphonic counterpoint and confined himself to the simple *chorale* style. Many songs of his are still popular in Protestant churches in England and America. Ahle's son, Johann Georg Ahle, was also a composer of hymns and poet laureate to Emperor Leopold I. Ahle's works include *Compendium pro tonellis,* 1648, a treatise on singing, and *Neue Geistliche Arien,* etc.   16, 45, 300, 411. LIEBSTER JESU (DESSAU)

AHO, Gustaf Axel (1897—   ), born October 9, 1897, Sebeka, Minnesota, son of Jacob Aho and Wilhelmiina, *née* Juuti, was educated at Suomi College, Hancock, Michigan, and the Theological Seminary of the Finnish American Evangelical Lutheran National Church, Ironwood, Michigan, and Columbia University. He married Helia Tuikka, June 1, 1922. He was ordained minister in 1921 and has served as pastor at Bethlehem Lutheran Church, Jersey City, New Jersey (1921—1926); First Lutheran Church, Ely, Minnesota (1926—1934); and the Lutheran National Churches of Ashtabula and Fairport Harbor, Ohio (1934—   ). He was elected president of the Finnish American Ev. Lutheran National Church in 1931, secretary of Synod in 1928, and president, 1931, reelected 1935 and 1939. He published *Umpuja* (Blossoms, Finnish religious poems), 1921; *Witnesses of Christ's Passion.* Finnish Lenten sermons, 1930; *Secret Orders in the Light of God's Word,* Finnish, 1932; numerous tracts and pamphlets, and has been a contributor of poems and articles in church-papers. He has served as editor of the synodical young people's paper, 1923—1927; and of the *Synodical Year-Book.* He has translated several Finnish hymns into English.

545. *The morning sun is brightly beaming.* (Tr.)

ALBERT, Heinrich, or Alberti (1604—1651), was born at Lobenstein, Voigtland, June 28, 1604. He intended to study law at Leipzig, but devoted himself entirely to music, studying under his uncle, Heinrich Schütz, the Court Capellmeister at Dresden, later also under Johann Stobäus. In 1631 he was appointed organist of the Cathedral at Königsberg in Prussia, whither he had gone in 1626. In 1636 he became a member of the Poetical Union of that city, together with Dach, Roberthin, and nine others. He died October 6, 1651. His hymns appeared in his *Arien, etliche theils geistliche, theils weltliche,* etc., published first in eight parts (1638—1650), then in collected form, Königsberg, 1652.   549. *God, who madest earth and heaven*
549. GOTT DES HIMMELS

ALBINUS, Johann Georg (1624—1679), eldest son of Zacharias Albinus, a pastor, was born at Unter-Nessa, near Weissenfels, Saxony, March 6, 1624. After his father's death, in 1635, he was adopted by a cousin, in 1638. This cousin was Lucas Pollio, diaconus at St. Nicholas Church in Leipzig. When Pollio died in 1643, the court preacher, Sebastian Mitternacht of Naumburg, took an interest in Albinus, who remained with him until he entered the University of Leipzig in 1645. While there, he became the house tutor to the burgomaster, Dr. Friedrich Kühlwein, and was later, in 1653, appointed rector of the Cathedral School at Naumburg. Four years later he resigned and became the pastor of St. Othmar's Church in the same city. He was a zealous pastor, seeking ever "the glory of God, the edification of the church, and the everlasting salvation, well-being and happiness of his hearers." He died on Rogate Sunday, May 25, 1679. As poet he was, says *Koch,* "distinguished by ease of style, force of expression, and liveliness of fancy, and his manner of thought was Scriptural and pervaded by deep religious spirit."

601. *All men living are but mortal*

ALBRECHT VON BRANDENBURG (1522—1557) was born at Ansbach on March 28, 1522. He was the son of Casimir, Margrave of Brandenburg-Culmbach in Lower Franconia. He was well educated by his uncle, Georg of Brandenburg. Later he became a soldier and was known as the "German Alcibiades." Albrecht accompanied Charles V to his French War in 1544 and against the Smalkald Evangelical Union in 1546. In 1552 he joined the princes against the Emperor. Albrecht met Moritz of Saxony in the Battle of Lüneburg, July 9, 1553, at Sievershausen and was defeated. He met him again on June 13, 1554, at Brunswick and finally on June 13 at Eulenberg. Albrecht escaped to France with sixteen followers. He acknowledged God's direction in his troubles and repented of his former errors. He returned to Regensburg and died at Pforzheim, repentant and firm in the faith, on January 8, 1557.

517. *The will of God is always best*

ALDERSON, Eliza Sibbald, *née* Dykes (1818—1889), was the granddaughter of the Rev. Thomas Dykes of Hull and a sister of Dr. John B. Dykes (*q. v.*). She was born in 1818, and in 1850 was married to Rev. W. T. Alderson, sometime chaplain to the West Riding Home of Correction, Wakefield, 1832—1876. She died in 1889 and was buried at Kirkthorpe.

442. *Lord of Glory, who hast bought us*

ALEXANDER, Cecil Frances, *née* Humphreys (1823—1895), the daughter of Major John Humphreys, was born in Ireland, 1823. In 1850 she married the Rt. Rev. Wm. Alexander, Bishop of Derry and Raphoe. She wrote *The Burial of Moses*, which Lord Houghton called the finest sacred lyric in the English language. She was the author of several books of poetry, among them: *Verses for Holy Seasons*, 1846; *Hymns Descriptive and Devotional*, 1858; and *The Legend of the Golden Prayers*, 1859. She died at Londonderry, October 12, 1895. Mrs. Alexander was the author of many hymns, several of which have been widely used, *e. g.*, *There is a green hill far away; Once in royal David's city*.

270. *Jesus calls us o'er the tumult*

ALFORD, Henry (1810—1871), the son of the Rev. Henry Alford, Rector of Aston Sandford, was born in London, October 7, 1810. He attended Trinity College, Cambridge, where he was graduated with honors in 1832. Principal among his many positions and attainments are: a Fellow of Trinity, Hulsean Lecturer (1841—42), and Dean of Canterbury (1857—1871). While still very young, he wrote several Latin odes, a history of the Jews, and a series of homiletic outlines. Perhaps his noblest undertaking was his edition of the *Greek Testament*, the result of twenty years' labor. This book, which was the standard critical commentary in England of the later 19th century and philological rather than theological in character, introduced in comprehensive fashion the treasures of German linguistic and exegetic studies to those unfamiliar with German. He was a member of the New Testament Revision Committee. *The Contemporary Review* was his creation and was edited by him for a time. His hymnological and poetical works were numerous and included the compiling of collections, the composition of original hymns, and translations from other languages. As a hymn-writer he added little to his literary reputation. The rhythm of his hymns is musical. The poetry is characterized not so much by depth or originality as by freedom from affectation, obscurity, or bombast. His hymns are evangelical in their teaching but somewhat cold and conventional. Though not a sacramentarian, his views and hymns were distinctively liturgical.

476. *Ten thousand times ten thousand*
574. *Come, ye thankful people, come*

ALLEN, Oswald (1816—1878) was born at Kirkby-Lonsdale, Westmoreland, England, in 1816. He was the son of John Allen, a banker. All his life Oswald was an invalid, suffering from a diseased spine. In 1843 he went to Glasgow and spent three years there, after which he was again compelled to return to his home because of a recurrence of his constitutional malady. In 1848 he accepted a position in his father's bank and ultimately succeeded his father as manager. He was devoted to deeds of benevolence and mercy and was well known as a friend of the poor and needy. During the severe winter of 1859—60 he composed his work *Hymns of the Christian Life* (London, 1861). It contains 148 hymns, all of which are from his own pen. The rigors of the winter, together with the sufferings caused by his malady, all combined to give his hymns a soothing and tender, yet comforting and elevating tone. The dedicatory verse is typical of his whole work. It opens:

> To Thee, my God, my Savior, and my Friend
> I humbly offer, as I lowly bend,
> The first faint warblings of my grateful soul.

He died at his birthplace in 1878.

279. Today Thy mercy calls us

ALTENBURG, Johann Michael (1584—1640), was born at Alach, near Erfurt, on Trinity Sunday, 1584. Educated at Erfurt, he was for some time teacher and precentor there. His pastoral charges included Ilversgehofen and Marbach, 1608, Trochtelborn, 1611; and Gross-Sommern, near Erfurt, in 1621. Here in Gross-Sommern this "devout, exemplary, and ingenious preacher" suffered many hardships during the Thirty Years' War, which had just broken out. He was continually harassed by troops marching through, pressing the houses into service as their quarters, and plundering at will. At one time he was "host" to no fewer than 300 soldiers and horse. These troublous times finally forced him to flee to Erfurt in 1631 without as much as some bread to eat. Here on the news of the victory of Leipzig, September 17, 1631, and probably stimulated by Gustav Adolf's password for the battle, he composed his best-known hymn. He retained his residence in Erfurt, where he died February 12, 1640.

He was a good musician, composing tunes as well as writing hymns.

263. O little flock, fear not the foe

AMBROSE, St. (340—397), was the second son and third child of Ambrosius, Prefect of the Gauls, and was born at Lyons, Arles, or more probably Treves. In 353, after the death of the father, the mother and children went to Rome. Here Ambrose received the usual education, attaining considerable proficiency in Greek. He studied law, as his brother Satyrus had, and soon distinguished himself in the court of Probus, the Pretorian Prefect of Italy. In 374 he was appointed Consular of Liguria and Aemilia, which necessitated his residence in Milan. Soon after, Auxentius, the bishop, died. The church in which the election of the new bishop was being held was filled with excited people, and Ambrose himself exhorted them to peace and order. Suddenly a voice exclaimed,— it is said that it was that of a child, — "Ambrose be bishop!" Immediately the cry was taken up by the mob. Although as yet only a catechumen, Ambrose was then baptized, and a week later, on December 7, 374, was consecrated bishop. The death of Emperor Valentinian I in 375 brought Ambrose into collision with Justina, Valentinian's second wife, an adherent of the Arian party. Ambrose was supported by Gratian, the elder son of Valentinian, and by Theodosius, whom Gratian in 379 associated with himself in the empire. Gratian was assassinated in 383 by a follower of Maximus, and Ambrose was sent to treat with the usurper, in which he was fairly successful. But now Ambrose had to carry on against the Arians and the empress alone. Justina had to flee before the advance of Maximus on Milan and died in 388. Either in this year or the one previous Ambrose received the great scholar Augustine, once a Manichean heretic, into the church by baptism. Theodosius was now virtually head of the Roman Empire. In 390 a riot at Thessalonica caused him to give a hasty order for a general massacre at that city, and his command was but too faithfully obeyed. Ambrose refused Theodusius admittance to church until he had done penance for his crime. Only eight months afterward did the Emperor declare his penitence. Theodosius defeated the murderer of Valentinian in 394, and soon after the fatigues of the campaign brought his death. Ambrose preached his funeral sermon, as he had that of Valentinian. The loss of these two friends was a severe blow to Ambrose, and after two more unquiet years he died on Easter Eve, 397. Ambrose was great as a scholar, an organizer, a statesman, a theologian, and as a musician and poet. As a hymn-writer Ambrose indeed deserves special honor. Grimm correctly calls him "the father of church song." Catching the impulse from Hilary and confirmed in it by the success of Arian psalmody, he introduced the practice of antiphonal chanting and began the task, which St. Gregory completed, of systematizing the music of the Church. As a writer of sacred poetry Ambrose is remarkable for depth and severity. He does not warm with his subject. "We feel," says Archbishop Trench, "as though there were a certain coldness in his hymns and aloofness of the author from his subject." He was not the author of the *Te Deum.*

95. *Savior of the nations, come*
550. *O Splendor of God's glory bright*
564. *O Trinity, most blessed light*

ÄMILIE JULIANE, Countess of Schwarzburg-Rudolstadt (1637—1706), was the daughter of Count Albert Friedrich of Barby and Mühlingen. She was born August 16, 1637, at Heidecksburg, the castle of her father's uncle, Count Ludwig Günther of Schwarzburg-Rudolstadt, where her father and family had to seek refuge during the Thirty Years' War. After the death of her father (1641) and mother (1642) Ämilie Juliane was adopted by her aunt, who was also her godmother and had become the wife of Count Ludwig Günther. Ämilie Juliane was educated at Rudolstadt with her cousins under the care of Dr. Ahasuerus Fritsch and other teachers. On July 7, 1665, she was married to her cousin, Albert Anton. She was the most productive of German female hymn-writers, some 600 hymns being attributed to her. Her hymns are full of a deep love for her Savior. She published *Geistliche Lieder,* etc., Rudolstadt, 1683; *Kühlwasser in grosser Hitze des Creutzes,* Rudolstadt, 1685; *Tägliches Morgen-, Mittags- und Abendopfer,* Rudolstadt, 1685. She died December 3, 1706.

33. *The Lord hath helped me hitherto*
598. *Who knows when death may overtake me*

ANDERSDATTER, Elle (1600—1650?), was the daughter of Andrew Andersdatter and is rather a mythical personage. All that can definitely be determined about her is that she was Danish and that she was the author of several hymns, one of which acrostically spells her name. It begins: "Eja, mit hjert a ret inderlig jubilerer." The hymn is quoted in full in N. N. Skaar's *Norsk Salmehistorie* (Vol. 1, pp. 569—572). Landstad's *Kirkesalmebog* simply states: an unknown, but certainly a Danish woman, who lived in the first half of the 17th century.

432. *In hope my soul, redeemed to bliss unending*

ANNA SOPHIA of Hesse-Darmstadt (1638—1683) was the daughter of the Landgrave Georg II of Hesse Darmstadt and was born at Marburg, December 17, 1638. She was carefully educated in the Holy Scriptures and the Church Fathers. She was elected *Pröpstin* of the Lutheran Fürstentochter-Stift at Quedlinburg in 1657. She became abbess of the Stift in 1680 and died December 13, 1683. Her hymns show an intense love for the Savior and mostly appeared in her *Der treue Seelenfreund,* etc., Jena, 1658.

296. *Speak, O Lord, Thy servant heareth*

ANTHES, Friedrich Konrad (1812— ?), was born at Weilburg in Nassau, May 2, 1812, son of the seminary professor Johann Adam Anthes. He studied theology and became first "Hilfsgeistlicher" at Herborn and later pastor at Haiger and Ackerbach. Poor health forced him to retire in 1857, and he seems to have spent the remainder of his life at Wiesbaden. He wrote *Die Tonkunst im evangelischen Kultus,* Wiesbaden, 1846, and *Allgemeine fassliche Bemerkungen,* etc., Wiesbaden, 1846.

276, 279. ANTHES

ARENDS, Wilhelm Erasmus (1677—1721), was the son of a pastor at Langestein, near Halberstadt, where he was born on February 5, 1677. In 1707 he became pastor at Crottorf, near Halberstadt, and in 1718 pastor of the Church of St. Peter and St. Paul in Halberstadt, where he died, May 16, 1721.

444. *Rise! To arms! With prayer employ you*

ARNESON, Ole T. (Sanden) (1853—1917), was born near Highlandville, Iowa, on May 4, 1853. He attended the Winona Normal School, Winona, Minnesota. From 1876 to 1879 he was principal of the public school at Spring Grove, Minnesota, and then for a time as teacher at Hatton, North Dakota. After working first as mailing clerk, then as shipping clerk, he became the manager of the book department of Skandinaven, Chicago. Arneson translated many hymns and other poems from the Norwegian. He died June 3, 1917.

624. *O blessed home, where man and wife.* (Tr.)

ARREBO, Anders Christensen (1587—1637), is often referred to as "the father of Danish poetry," for it was he who paved the way for later hymn-writers, such as Kingo and his contemporaries. He was born June 2, 1587, at Aeresköbing, Denmark, where his father was pastor. Little is known about his early childhood. He became court chaplain in Copenhagen at twenty-one. He took his master's degree in 1610 and became palace chaplain in Frederiksborg. In 1616 he was called as parish pastor to the Nicolai Church in Copenhagen. In 1618 he was called as bishop to the diocese of Tröndheim, being at the time only thirty-one years of age. Unfortunately he did not guide his actions and speech properly, making an enemy of a Danish official, who had him removed from office in 1622. He settled in Malmö and began the preparation of *Kong Davids Psalmer sangvis udsat*, which appeared in 1623, dedicated to the clergy of Norway, in order to demonstrate his appreciation for benefits received. This book went through five editions from 1623 until 1673. He himself spent the remaining years of his life, from 1626 until his death in 1637, as parish pastor in Vordingborg. Before his death he completed another great work, *Hexaemeron*, or "the world's first week, six days of splendid and mighty deeds," which first appeared in 1661. It was a free rendering of a work by the French poet Bartas.

Arrebo was the first to submit the Danish language to an artistic usage. Of his works Rudelbach says: "Arrebo strove to express every spiritual thought and word as well as every original tone of the hymns. This renders his work of the highest value. No one since Luther who has sought to appropriate David's and Asaph's words and meanings has attained to the rank of Arrebo."

217. *O sing with exultation*

ASTLEY, Charles Tamberlane (1825—1878), was born in Wales, May 12, 1825, and was educated in Jesus College, Oxford. He entered the ministry in 1849 and served in various places until 1864, when he was appointed rector of Brasted. In 1860 he published *Songs in the Night*, which contained original hymns and some translations from the German.

453. *We are the Lord's; His all-sufficient merit.* (Tr.)

ATKINSON, Frederick Cook (1841—1897), was born August 21, 1841, at Norwich, England. He served from 1849 to 1860 as chorister and assistant organist at the Cathedral of Norwich and was graduated from Cambridge in 1867. He was later choirmaster and organist at St. Paul's and St. John's at Bradford and finally, from 1881 to 1885, at Norwich Cathedral. He died at East Dereham in 1897.

623. CARITAS PERFECTA

BACH, Carl Philipp Emanuel (1714—1788), was born at Weimar, the third son of Johann Sebastian Bach by his first wife. He moved with his family to Cöthen in 1717 and to Leipzig in 1723. He studied law at the University of Leipzig from 1733 to 1735 and for the next three years at the University of Frankfurt a. O. Although his father had opposed his early musical leanings, Bach turned himself completely to music in Frankfurt, managed an academy, directed and composed music for festivals, and taught the *clavier*. After his graduation he went to Berlin. Then he became first *Kammercembalist* to the crown prince of Prussia at Ruppin, and, in 1740, *Kammermusikus* for the crown prince at Berlin. In 1767 he was named as *Kapellmeister* by the Princess Amalia and in the same year settled in Hamburg as *Kantor* at the Johanneum

[476]

and music director of the five chief churches there, in which capacity he remained until his death. Bach is known chiefly for his instrumental compositions, but his hymn tunes and *chorales* rank high in classical hymnody.

328. WEIMAR

BACH, Johann Christoph (1642—1703), was born in Arnstadt, the eldest son of Heinrich Bach. He was a second cousin of Johann Sebastian Bach. He became organist at Eisenach in 1665 and appears to have remained there until his death. There is some evidence that seems to indicate that he became court organist in 1678. Bach specialized in vocal music and is considered an excellent composer.

226, 553. KOMM, O KOMM, DU GEIST DES LEBENS

BACH, Johann Sebastian (1685—1750), was a member of the most famous musical family in history. He was born in Eisenach and received his early musical training at home by his father and eldest brother. He attended the schools of Ohrdruf and Lüneburg and at the age of eighteen had already obtained an enviable reputation as a composer, organist, and violinist. After serving for a while as organist at Arnstadt and Mühlhausen, he was court organist and violinist at Weimar for nine years and in 1717 accepted the appointment as *Kapellmeister* at Anhalt Cöthen. He finally settled at Leipzig in 1723 as cantor of the famous St. Thomas's School and director of music in the St. Thomas's and St. Nicholas's churches, where his original compositions were first produced in the regular services. Comparable to Palestrina in the Roman Church, Bach wrote numerous cantatas and many motets, masses, and harmonizations of old German *chorales* which have earned him the affection and admiration of the whole Christian and musical world. His immortal *B Minor Mass* and the *St. Matthew* and *St. John Passions* remain unsurpassed as combinations of the emotional and intellectual, the mystic and energetic, in devotional music. Called "the father of modern music," Bach certainly gave a direction to all the music of his age, for which the Church must be eternally grateful. Schumann said of him: "To him music owes almost as great a debt as a religion owes its founder."

117, 135, 426, 435. POTSDAM
163. GOTTLOB, ES GEHT NUNMEHR ZU ENDE
319. harm. *Allein zu dir*
437, harm. 517. WAS MEIN GOTT WILL

BACON, Leonard Woolsey (1830—1907), was born in New Haven, Connecticut, January 1, 1830. He graduated from Yale College in 1850; Yale Divinity School in 1851. He served as pastor of churches in Litchfield, Stamford, and Norwich, Connecticut, and later of other Congregational and Presbyterian churches. His writings include: *Life of Emily Bliss Gould*, 1878; *Irenics and Polemics*, 1898; *History of American Christianity*, 1898; *The Congregationalists*, 1904. Besides other writings of a similar nature he is known in the field of hymnology for several hymnals which he edited, for a collection of Luther's hymns, and translations of certain of them.

137. In peace and joy I now depart. (Tr.)

BAHNMAIER, Jonathan Friedrich (1774—1841), was the son of J. C. Bahnmaier, the town preacher at Oberstenfeld, Württemberg, and was born there on July 12, 1774. Bahnmaier studied theology at Tübingen, and his first charge was that of assistant to his father. He became Diaconus at Marlbach on the Neckar in 1806 and at Ludwigsburg in 1810, where he for a time headed a young ladies' school. In 1815 he was appointed Professor of Education and Homiletics at Tübingen, only to resign a few years later. In 1819 he was appointed Decan and Town Preacher at Kirchheimunter-Teck, where he labored for twenty-one years. Bahnmaier distinguished himself as a preacher and was greatly interested in education, missions, and Bible societies. He was one of the principal members of the committee which compiled the *Württemberg Gesang-Buch*, 1842. He preached his last sermon at Kirchheim on August 15, 1841. He was stricken by paralysis while visiting a school at Brucker and died a few days later, August 18, 1841.

507. *Spread, oh, spread, thou mighty Word*

BAJUS, John (1901—   ), son of John Bajus and Mary, née Petras, was born April 5, 1901, at Raritan, New Jersey. He graduated at Concordia Institute, Bronxville, New York, 1921; and Concordia Seminary, St. Louis, 1925. He has been pastor of the Slovak Lutheran Church at Granite City, Illinois, serving stations at West Frankfort and Staunton, Illinois, as well, since 1925. He is charter member of the Slovak Luther League, organized 1927; served as its president 1928—1930; as field secretary 1928 to 1930; 1933—1935; and has served as editor of its *Courier* since its first appearance in 1929. He is a member of the Intersynodical Committee of Hymnology and Liturgics for the Evangelical Lutheran Synodical Conference of North America. He has achieved recognition as a translator of Slovak hymns and poems.

  86:5, 6: *Christ the Lord to us is born.* (Tr.)
  169. *Jesus Christ, our Lord most holy.* (Tr.)
  211. *Lo, Judah's Lion wins the strife.* (Tr.)
  603. *In the resurrection.* (Tr.)

BAKER, Frederick George (1840—?), born on the Isle of Wight, May 19, 1840; chorister in Winchester Cathedral for seven years, part of which time Dr. S. S. Wesley was organist; studied harmony under Dr. Iliffe, otherwise self-taught; organist of Christ Church, Sandown, Isle of Wight, from 1864 to 1872; since then organist of St. Saviour's, Shanklin, Isle of Wight; a watchmaker and jeweler by trade.

  434. ST. SAVIOR

BAKER, Henry Williams (1821—1877), the eldest son of Admiral Sir Henry Loraine Baker, was born in London 1821. He received his middle name from his mother's father, William Williams. He was educated at Trinity College, Cambridge, and graduated B. A. in 1844 and M. A. in 1847. In 1846 he was ordained priest and was appointed the Vicar Monkland, Herefordshire, in 1851 and succeeded to the baronetcy in the same year. He held this benefice until his death in 1877. His last words were the third stanza of his exquisite rendering of the 23d Psalm, "The King of Love my Shepherd is":

  Perverse and foolish, oft I strayed,
  But yet in Love He sought me
  And on His shoulder gently laid
  And home, rejoicing, brought me.

The tender sadness, brightened by a soft, calm peace, of this stanza is an epitome of Baker's poetical style. Baker wrote 33 hymns. He is usually compared with Henry Francis Lyte (*q. v.*). During his lifetime Baker worked arduously as the editor of *Hymns Ancient and Modern*. The first edition appeared in 1861, an appendix in 1868, a revised edition in 1875, a complete edition in 1889, and a recent revision in 1904. Benson writes in *The English Hymns* that *Hymns Ancient and Modern* spread "not only high-church views and practices but the high-church atmosphere beyond the sphere of hymnody." Its publication ranks as "one of the great events in the history of the hymnody of the English-speaking churches." Baker also published *Daily Prayers for the Use of Those who Work Hard;* a *Daily Text Book*, etc.

  32. *Redeemed, restored, forgiven*
  98. *Of the Father's love begotten.* (Tr.)
  170. *O perfect life of love*
  273. *Sweet flowerets of the martyr band.* (Tr.)
  327. *Out of the deep I call*
  431. *The King of Love my Shepherd is*
  570. *Praise, oh, praise our God and King*
  571. *What our Father does is well.* (Tr.)
  428, 513, 643. STEPHANOS

BARBAULD, Anna Letitia, née Aikin (1743—1825), was the daughter of the Rev. John Aikin, D. D. She was born June 20, 1743, at Kibworth, Leicestershire, where her father kept an academy. In 1773 she published her first volume of *Poems,* which ran through four editions in the same year. *Miscellaneous Pieces in Prose* was also published in 1773 in collaboration with her brother, John Aikin. The following year she married the Rev. Rochemont Barbauld, who had charge of a dissenting congregation at Palgrave, Suffolk, where they opened a boarding-school for boys. She published a number of volumes, among them her *Hymns in Prose for Children*, a work often reprinted in English and translated into several languages. She died on March 9, 1825.

572. *Praise to God, immortal praise*

BARING-GOULD, Sabine (1834—1924), was born at Exeter, January 28, 1834. During his youth he lived much in Germany and France. He was graduated from Cambridge in 1854, ordained in 1861, and became curate at Horbury, 1864, serving also the mission at Horbury Bridge. In 1867 he was transferred to Dalton, and in 1871 he became rector of East Mersea, Colchester. When he succeeded his father in the estate at Lew Trenchard, Devon, he exercised his privilege as squire and patron by appointing himself as rector there. Here he died in 1924. His energy and industry were inexhaustible and is said to have more works attached to his name in the catalog of the British Museum than any writer of his time. His writings cover the fields of biography, travel, history, fiction, poetry, and song.

481. *Through the night of doubt and sorrow.* (Tr.)
654. *Now the day is over*
658. *Onward, Christian soldiers*
654. EUDOXIA

BARNBY, Joseph (1838—1896) was born in York, England, August 12, 1838; entered York Minster Choir at seven, began to teach other boys at ten, was appointed organist at twelve, music master at fifteen, and at length became choral director of the Royal Albert Hall Choral Society. He was knighted in 1892. He was musical editor of *The Hymnary*. In 1897 his 246 hymn tunes were published in a collection.

390. DUNSTAN
403. 422. WINTERTON
469. 496. GALILEAN

BARTHÉLÉMON, François Hippolyte (1741—1808), was born in Bordeaux, July 27, 1741, the son of a French government officer and an Irish lady. He entered the army and became an officer in Berwick's regiment in the Irish Brigade. He was induced by the Earl of Kellie to leave the army and take up music as his profession. In 1765 Barthélémon came to England after successful tours as a concert violinist and was appointed leader of the band at the opera and in 1770 at Marylebone Gardens. He wrote very little church music, occupying himself chiefly with music for the theater and the public gardens. Barthélémon was a member of the Swedenborgian Church. He suffered a great deal of misfortune in his old age and died a broken-hearted paralytic, July 20, 1808.

536. MORNING HYMN

BARTON, Bernard (1784—1849), was born in London, England, January 31, 1784, and was educated at a Quaker school in Ipswich. In 1798 he was apprenticed to a Mr. S. Jessup, a shopkeeper at Halsted, Essex, with whom he remained till 1806, when he moved to Woodbridge, Suffolk, and entered into business with his brother as a coal and corn merchant. On the death of his wife, at the end of the first year of their married life, he moved to Liverpool, where he became a private tutor for a short while. In 1810 he became a clerk in the local bank of the Messrs. Alexander in Woodbridge, which position he held for forty years, till his death at Woodbridge, February 19, 1849. In that year his daughter published his *Poems and Letters* with a memoir.

291. *Lamp of our feet whereby we trace*

BATHHURST, William Hiley (1796—1877), was the son of the Rt. Hon. Charles Bragge (afterwards Bathurst), sometime M.P. for Bristol. Bathurst's name is often given as Bragge-Bathurst. He was born at Clevadale, near Bristol, August 28, 1796. His mother was Charlotte Addington; her mother's name was Hiley. Bathurst was educated at Winchester and Christ Church, Oxford, graduating as B.A. in 1818. In 1819 he was ordained deacon and in the following year priest. In 1820 he was presented by his kinsman, Henry, Third Earl of Bathurst, to the Rectory of Barwick-in-Elmet, Yorkshire, and continued there as rector for thirty-two years. In 1852 he resigned the rectory because of conscientious scruples in relation to parts of the baptismal and burial services in the *Book of Common Prayer*. He retired into private life and first lived at Darley Dale, near Matlock, Derbyshire, where for eleven years he gave himself to literary pursuits. In May, 1863, he came into possession of his father's estate when his elder brother died without heirs. He moved to Lydney Park soon afterward and there died on November 25, 1877.

During his early years of ministry Bathurst composed hymns and versified a large portion of the psalms. These were published, 1830, in a small volume entitled *Psalms and Hymns for Public and Private Use*. All but 18 of the 150 psalms and all of the 206 hymns in this volume are his.

64. *Jesus, Thy Church with longing eyes*
396. *Oh, for a faith that will not shrink*

BAXTER, Richard (1615—1691), only son of Richard Baxter, was born at Rowton, Shropshire on November 12, 1615. He was brought up by his maternal grandfather, educated at Wroxeter School, and for a time held the mastership of the Dudley Grammar School. After a short experience of court life, Baxter's strong religious convictions led him to study divinity. He took holy orders in 1640 and became curate of Kidderminster, after a brief curacy at Bridgnorth. Before long Baxter began to distrust Episcopacy in its prevalent form and was for some time chaplain to one of Cromwell's regiments. Yet this did not prevent him from rebuking Cromwell for assuming supreme power in the state and defending the old monarchy. Weak health forced him to take a rest, during which time he wrote the book by which he is best known, *The Saints' Everlasting Rest*. He was so feeble at this time that it was necessary for two men to support him when he was in his pulpit. He said: "Weakness and pain helped me to study how to die; that set me on studying how to live, and that on studying the doctrine from which I must fetch my motives and comforts; beginning with necessities, I proceeded by degrees and am now going to see that for which I have lived and studied." On regaining his health, Baxter returned to Kidderminster, where he remained until 1660, when he removed to London.

At the Restoration, Baxter became a chaplain to Charles II and was offered a bishopric (of Hereford), which he refused. He took part in the Savoy Conference, 1661, one result of which was his *Reformed Liturgy*. When the Act of Uniformity was passed, he retired from active duty as a minister of the Church of England. However, in 1673 he took out a license as a Non-conformist minister and started lecturing in London. In 1685 Baxter was tried before Judge Jeffries on the ridiculous charge of teaching sedition through his *Paraphrase of the New Testament* and was condemned to prison or pay a fine of 500 marks. He bore his imprisonment with great patience for 18 months, after which he was pardoned and set free. During his trial Jeffries had taunted Baxter with the remark, "Richard, I see the rogue in thy face." To which Baxter replied, "I had not known before that my face was a mirror." It is said that this court trial was one of the most infamous in the whole history of English court procedure. After his release Baxter was warned not to preach, but he would not be restrained. Baxter's last years were filled with peace and honor. He died December 8, 1691. Two centuries later a monument was erected in his honor at Kidderminster, where his influence for good was still felt. Dean Stanley calls him "the greatest of Protestant schoolmen." Baxter was the author of "books enough to fill a cart" — (Jeffries). His most important prose works are: *The Saints' Everlasting Rest*, 1650; *The Reformed Pastor*, 1656; *The Call to the Unconverted*, 1657; and his *Reliquiae*, which is of great biographical interest, for it contains a narrative of his life and times.

527. *Lord, it belongs not to my care*

BEDE, The Venerable (673—735), was born near the monasteries of Wearmouth and Jarrow, which were founded by Benedict Biscop. Bede's parents died when he was yet quite young, and so he studied at both monasteries under the tutelage of Benedict and later under Coelfrith, Benedict's successor. At nineteen he was ordained a deacon by St. John of Beverley. Ten years later he received his priest's orders from the same prelate. Bede's whole life was spent in study; he divided his time between the two monasteries of Wearmoth and Jarrow. At the latter monastery, Bede, the scholar, grammarian, philosopher, poet, biographer, historian, and divine, died on May 26, 735. In the 11th century his remains were removed to Durham and reinterred in the same coffin as those of St. Cuthbert. Bede was a voluminous author on almost every subject. He translated the Scriptures into Anglo-Saxon. As a historian his contribution to English history, the *Historia Ecclesiastica,* is invaluable. Among his works Bede lists a *Liber Hymnorum.* His contribution to hymnody is, however, not very great, for he contributed at the most 11 or 12 hymns.

<blockquote>212. A hymn of glory let us sing</blockquote>

BEHM, Martin (1557—1622), was the son of Hans Behm (Böhme, Boehm, Behemb, Behem, Böheim, Bohemus, or Bohemius), town overseer of Lauban, Silesia, where Martin was born on September 16, 1557. During a protracted famine in 1574 a distant kinsman, Dr. Paul Fabricius, a royal physician at Vienna, took Behm there. For two years Behm acted as a private tutor. After that he went to Strassburg, where he received much kindness from Johann Sturm, rector of the newly founded university. After his father's death in May, 1580, Behm, at his mother's request, returned home. At Easter, 1581, he was appointed assistant in the town school, and on September 20 of that year he was ordained diaconus of Holy Trinity Church. After his senior pastor had been advanced to Breslau, the town council kept the post nominally vacant for two years and then in June, 1586, appointed Behm chief pastor. During the 36 years he served, Behm became renowned as a preacher, as a faithful pastor in times of trouble (famine, 1590; pestilence, 1616; war, 1619), and as a prolific author. He was seized with an illness after he had preached on the Tenth Sunday after Trinity, 1621. After twenty-four weeks on the sick-bed he died, February 5, 1622. Behm was a very prominent and prolific hymn-writer. He produced upwards of 480 hymns, which emphasize especially the Passion of our Lord.

<blockquote>
130. O Jesus, King of Glory
148. Lord Jesus Christ, my Life, my Light
541. O blessed Holy Trinity
</blockquote>

BELSHEIM, Ole G. (1861—1925), was born at Vang Valdres, Norway, on August 26, 1861. He came to America as a boy of five and was educated at Luther College, Decorah, Iowa, Northfield Seminary, and Augsburg Seminary in Minnesota and held pastorates successively at Milwaukee, Wisconsin, Albert Lea, Minnesota, Grand Meadow, Minnesota, and Mandan, North Dakota. Belsheim was a member for eight years of the Hymnal Committee which edited *The Lutheran Hymnary,* 1913. He translated Laache's *Catechism* into English in 1894 and edited the *Christian Youth* for two years. He died, February 12, 1925.

<blockquote>283. God's Word is our great heritage. (Tr.)</blockquote>

BENSON, Louis Fitz-Gerald (1855—1930), was born in Philadelphia on July 22, 1855. He graduated from the University of Pennsylvania, where he had studied law. After spending seven years before the bar, he entered Princeton Theological Seminary and after completion of the theological course was ordained to the Presbyterian ministry in 1886. He served as pastor of the Church of the Redeemer, Germantown, Philadelphia, for six years and then resigned to edit hymn-books for the General Assembly of the Presbyterian Church. Benson also lectured on liturgics at Auburn Theological Seminary and on hymnology at Princeton. He helped prepare the *Book of Common Worship of the Presbyterian Church in the U.S.A.,* 1905. He wrote a number of books on church hymnody and possessed one of the world's most valuable private hymnological libraries, which at his death, October 10, 1930, was donated to Princeton Theological Seminary. For many years he served as editor of *The Hymnal* (Presbyterian). Chief among his other works are *The English Hymnal, The Hymnody of the Christian Church, Studies in Familiar Hymns* (2 vols.), *Hymns, Original and Translated.*

<blockquote>486. O Thou whose feet have climbed life's hill</blockquote>

BERNARD OF CLAIRVAUX (St. Bernard), was born in 1090 at Les Fontaines in France, and he died at Clairvaux in 1153. He sprang from a family of the highest nobility in Burgundy. After a classical education at Chatillon-sur-Seine he entered the Cluniac monastery at Citeaux. When this became crowded, he led forth a band of monks to found a new monastery in Langres. This Bernard called Claire Vallie, or Clairvaux, in 1115. He was abbot of this successful monastery throughout his life, and with it his name has since been associated. This monastery became the scene of St. Bernard's strict and zealous asceticism, and from this retreat his influence was extended over all that was illustrious or humble in Church or State. Bishops in England, the Queen of Jerusalem, kings of France, Italy, and Britain, abbots and ecclesiastics without number, wrote to, and received letters from, Bernard of Clairvaux. He rebuked the disorders, abuses, sins, prevailing in the Church, defended the independence of the Church against monarchs, and even dared to assert the interest of the Church against Popes. He settled the schism between the Popes Innocent I and Anacletus II, he fought down the heresies of Abélard, the rationalist, and by his preaching he caused the populations of both France and Germany to arise almost *en masse* and take up the cross in the Second Crusade. As Taylor says: ". . . for a quarter of a century he swayed Christendom as never a holy man before or after him. An adequate account of his career would embrace the entire history of the first half of the 12th century." Luther called him "the most pious monk that ever lived." The authorship of the famous *Jesu, dulcis memoria* (Hymns No. 350 and 361) has long been ascribed to him. This view is no longer tenable.

172. O Sacred Head, now wounded (asc.)

BERNARD OF MORLAS (Cluny) (Twelfth century), was born at Morlas, France, of English parents. Except for the fact that Bernard entered the Abbey of Cluny while Peter the Venerable was the head thereof (1122—1156), little is known of his life. During this period the Abbey of Cluny reached the zenith of its wealth and fame. Amid luxurious and splendid surroundings Bernard spent his leisure hours and composed his great poem against the vices and follies of his age, *De Contemptu Mundi*, which was dedicated to Peter the Venerable. Bernard was also author of certain monastic regulations, entitled *Consuetudines Cluniacenses*.

448. Brief life is here our portion
605. The world is very evil
613. Jerusalem the golden
614. For thee, O dear, dear country

BESNAULT, Abbé, Sebastian (d. 1724), was a priest of St. Maurice, Sens. Some of his hymns were included in the *Cluniac Breviary*, 1686, the *Sens Breviary*, 1726, and the *Paris Breviary*, 1736.

115. O blessed day when first was poured
117. The ancient Law departs

BETHUNE, George Washington (1805—1862), a minister of the Dutch Reformed Church, was born in New York, March 18, 1805. His father was Divine Bethune, a merchant, his mother Isabella, *née* Graham. He was graduated from Dickinson College, Carlisle, Pennsylvania, in 1823 and studied theology at Princeton, New Jersey. He served a year as missionary to the Negroes in Savannah, Georgia, and, while there, acted also as naval chaplain. In 1827 he became pastor of a Dutch Reformed Church at Rhinebeck, New York; in 1830 at Utica, New York; in 1834 at Philadelphia, and in 1850 at Brooklyn, New York. In 1860 he went abroad for his health and on his return was given a charge in New York. He sailed to Europe a second time and died suddenly in Florence, Italy, April 27, 1862.

602. It is not death to die. (Tr.)

BEVAN, Emma Frances, *née* Shuttleworth (1827—1909), was born at Oxford on September 25, 1827. She was the daughter of the Rev. Philip Nicholas Shuttleworth, Warden of New College, Oxford, and Bishop of Chichester. She married Mr. R. C. L.

Bevan, a London banker, in 1856. In 1858 she published a number of translations from the German in *Songs of Eternal Life*, and in 1859 *Songs of Praise for Christian Pilgrims*. She died in 1909 at Cannes.

    472. *Rise, ye children of Salvation.* (Tr.)

    BIENEMANN, Kaspar (1540—1591), was the son of a burgess of Nürnberg, where he was born on January 3, 1540. He studied at Jena and Tübingen. He was sent by the Emperor Maximilian II as an interpreter with an embassy to Greece. There he assumed the name Melissander, by which he is sometimes known. On his return Bienemann was appointed Professor at Lauingen, Bavaria, and then abbot at Lahr and General Superintendent of Pfalz, Neuburg. He was forced to resign at the outbreak of the synergistic controversy. In 1571 Bienemann received his D.D. from the University of Jena and the same year was appointed tutor to Crown Prince Friedrich Wilhelm of Sachsen Weimar. He was displaced two years later when the Calvinists gained control of the court. In 1578 he was appointed General Superintendent at Altenburg, where he died on September 12, 1591.

    406. *Lord, as Thou wilt, deal Thou with me*

    BIRKEN (Betulius), Sigismund von (1626—1681), the son of Daniel Betulius or Birken, pastor of Wildstein, Bohemia, was born at Wildstein on May 5, 1626. In 1629 his father along with other evangelical pastors was forced to flee from Bohemia and went to Nürnberg. After passing through the Egidien-Gymnasium at Nürnberg Sigismund entered the University of Jena, 1643, and there studied both law and theology, the latter at his father's dying request. Before completing his course in either he returned to Nürnberg in 1645 and on account of his poetical gifts was there admitted as a member of the Pegnitz Shepherd and Flower Order. At the close of 1645 von Birken was appointed tutor at Wolfenbüttel to the princes of Brunswick-Lüneburg, but after a year (during which he was crowned as a poet), he resigned this post. After a tour, during which he was admitted by Philipp von Zesen as a member of the German Society (or Patriotic Union), he returned to Nürnberg in 1648 and was employed as a private tutor. In 1654 he was ennobled on account of his poetic gifts by the Emperor Ferdinand III, was admitted in 1658 as a member of the Fruitbearing Society, and on the death of Harsdörffer in 1662 became Chief Shepherd of the Pegnitz Order, to which he imparted a distinctly religious cast. He wrote 52 hymns, not many of which have retained a lasting place among the hymns of the Church. He died June 12, 1681.

    140. *Jesus, I will ponder now*
    409. *Let us ever walk with Jesus*

    BOGATZKY, Carl Heinrich von (1690—1774), was born September 7, 1690, at Militsch in Silesia. For a time he was a page at the ducal court of Weissenfels. At first he intended to enter the army, but sickness prevented him from carrying out this plan. He attended the University of Jena instead in 1713, and later he studied law at Halle. Finally he took up the study of theology; however, on account of poor health he was unable to enter the active service of the Church. He devoted himself to religious authorship instead. He spent most of his life in literary pursuits. The last twenty-eight years of his life were spent at the Orphanage at Halle, where G. A. Francke gave him a room. Among his writings are *Das güldene Schatzkästlein der Kinder Gottes*, 1718, which was recast in English by John Berridge as *The Golden Treasury*, and was long a favorite book of devotion in Great Britain. He also assisted in the production of the *Cöthen Hymns*, as important for Germany as the *Olney Hymns* were for England. His *Meditations* appeared in seven volumes, 1755—1761, and his *Autobiography* in 1754.   494. *Awake, Thou Spirit, who didst fire*

    BOLTZE, Georg Gottfried (c. 1750), was cantor and school-teacher at an orphanage in Potsdam about 1750; he was still living in 1789.

    409. LASSET UNS MIT JESU ZIEHEN

BONAR, Horatius (1808—1899), was born in Edinburgh on December 19, 1808. In 1837 he was ordained in the Established Church of Scotland at Kelso. In 1843 (at the Disruption) he became a founder of the Free Church of Scotland. In 1866 he accepted a call to Chalmers Memorial Church in Edinburgh. A voluminous writer of sacred poetry, "the peer of Watts and Wesley," he published ten tracts or volumes of hymns, 1843—1881, of which seven were published before his church authorized hymn-singing. He was for a time editor of *The Border Watch*, a paper published in the interest of his church. For many years he edited *The Journal of Prophecy*. Among his poetical works are *Songs for the Wilderness, The Bible Hymn Book, Hymns Original and Selected*. Dr. Benson writes: "While he may not have created a new type of English hymns, he had a distinctive style, a childlike simplicity and straightforwardness, a cheerful note with a plaintive undertone, — and he impressed his striking personality upon the English hymn. The appeal to his own generation was so widespread and pronounced as almost to create a cult. Fully a hundred of his hymns have been in church-use, but many are gradually passing out."

    244. *Glory be to God the Father*
    277. *I heard the voice of Jesus say*
    378. *All that I was, my sin, my guilt*
    380. *Thy works, not mine, O Christ*
    389. *Not what these hands have done*
    532. *Thy way, not mine, O Lord*
    652. *I lay my sins on Jesus*

BORTHWICK, Jane (1813—1897), was born in Edinburgh, Scotland, on April 9, 1813. She and her sister, Sarah Findlater, won for themselves a high place in the useful band of translators. These two published their first translations in *Hymns from the Land of Luther* in four sections, of which the first appeared in 1854. She wrote also some original hymns, of which many were published in *Thoughts for Thoughtful Hours* in 1857. In 1875 she again showed her propensity for translating poems, for then she published a selection of poems translated from Meta Heusser-Schweizer, which she called *Alpine Lyrics*. She died September 7, 1897. Julian writes: "Her translations, which represent relatively a larger proportion of hymns for the Christian Life and a smaller for the Christian Year than one finds in Miss Winkworth, have attained a success as translations and an acceptance in hymnals only second to Miss Winkworth's. . . . Hardly a hymnal has appeared in England or in America without containing some of these translations."

    188. *Hallelujah! Jesus lives!* (Tr.)
    410. *Jesus, lead Thou on.* (Tr.)
    420. *My Jesus, as Thou wilt.* (Tr.)
    586. *A pilgrim and a stranger.* (Tr.)
    651. *Be still, my soul, the Lord is on thy side.* (Tr.)

BORTNIANSKI, Dimitri S. (1752—1825), was born in the village of Gloukoff in the Ukraine. He became a chorister in the Imperial Chapel at St. Petersburg, and there he studied music under Galuppi. In 1768 he followed him to Italy to continue his studies. Shortly after his return to Russia in 1779, he was appointed Director of the Imperial Choir at St. Petersburg, where he died October 9, 1825. He was a distinguished composer of sacred music and has been styled by some the Russian Palestrina. He composed 35 sacred concertos in four parts, ten for double choir, and a mass according to the Greek rite. His works, published in St. Petersburg in ten volumes, were edited by Tschaikovsky.   493. ST. PETERSBURG

BÖSCHENSTAIN (Böschenstein), Johann (1472—1539?). the son of Heinrich Böschenstain, was born at Essling, Württemberg. He took holy orders, and in 1505 became a tutor of Hebrew at Ingolstadt. Here he remained until 1514 when he went to Augsburg, where he published a Hebrew grammar. In 1518 Reuchlin recommended that Böschenstain be invited to become a tutor of Greek and Hebrew at Wittenberg. At this university Böschenstain had Melanchthon as a pupil. Within the next three years he went to Nürnberg, Heidelberg, and Antwerp. He was also at Zürich for a short while, and here he taught Zwingli Hebrew. In 1523 Böschenstain settled in Augsburg, where he became a royal licensed teacher of Hebrew. He died in 1539. Some authorities state that he died at Nördlingen in 1540.

177. Our blessed Savior seven times spoke

BOURGEOIS, Louis (c. 1510—1561). A Parisian musician, celebrated as having been in charge of the music at Geneva, 1541—57, and having rearranged and composed melodies for the Genevan metrical *Psalter*, which owes its musical excellence mainly to him. A partial psalter appeared in 1542, and in the subsequent editions during the next fifteen years he seems to have had an important part. The whole of his work on the psalms up to 1547 seems to have been embraced in his work *Pseaulmes cinquante de David Roy et Prophete* published at Lyons, in 1547. From 1551 on he had difficulties with the Genevan authorities, who opposed changes which he proposed in the tunes of the psalter and the introduction of part-singing, which he favored. He returned to Paris and after 1561 disappeared from history.

100. NAVARRE

BOWRING, Sir John, LL. D., F. R. S. (1792—1872), was born at Exeter, England, on October 17, 1792, of an ancient family of Devonshire. His father was a wool-trader and a Dissenter. In his youth Bowring studied under the Rev. Lant Carpenter, the Unitarian pastor of the Presbyterian church of Exeter. From 1811 on he worked for a time in a London mercantile establishment. He became a great linguist, acquiring, it is said, the mastery of 200 languages and dialects and a speaking knowledge of 100. Bowring was able in later years to give to the English-speaking public translations from Bohemian, Slavonic, Russian, Servian, Polish, Slovakian, Illyrian, Germanic, Estonian, Dutch, Frisian, Lettish, Finnish, Hungarian, Biscayan, French, Provençal, Gascon, Italian, Spanish, Portuguese, Catalonian, and Galician sources. He visited many European countries as an official representative of England, investigating economic and commercial conditions. His informative and suggestive reports led to far-reaching reforms in England. He was a champion of national liberty and labored actively for various prison reforms. In 1822 he came under the personal influence of the noted Jeremy Bentham. After the latter's decease in 1832 Bowring published in 1838 an edition of his works in 22 volumes with a *Memoir*. While editor of the *Westminster Review* from 1825 to 1827 he advocated Bentham's principles. In 1828 he received the honorary degree of LL. D. from the University of Groningen. In the same year he served as Commercial Commissioner for his government, traveling in France, Switzerland, Italy, Belgium, and the Levant. Returning to England, Bowring became an active and prominent member of the lower house of Parliament from 1835 to 1837 and again from 1841 to 1848. He then served as consul at Canton and Acting Plenipotentiary and Superintendent of Trade in China. While in China, an attempt was made to poison him and his family. In 1853 Bowring returned to England and was elected a Fellow of the Royal Society. The following year he was knighted. He then returned to China as Governor, Commander-in-Chief, and Vice-Admiral of Hong-Kong. In 1855 he visited Siam and negotiated a treaty with the two kings of the country. When he returned to England, he retired on a pension. In 1819 he published *The Kingdom and People of Siam* and *The Philippine Islands*. But he still continued as a diplomat. As Minister Plenipotentiary and Envoy Extraordinary of the Siamese and Hawaiian Kingdoms to the European governments, he concluded treaties with Holland, Belgium, Spain, Switzerland, Italy, and Sweden. He also served as Magistrate and Deputy Lieutenant of the County of Devon until his death on November 23, 1872. His very extensive writings were published in thirty-six volumes.

71. Watchman, tell us of the night
354. In the Cross of Christ I glory

BOYE, Birgitte Katerine (1742—1824), was born March 7, 1742, in Gentofte, Denmark, the daughter of Jens Johansen of the royal service and of Dorotea, née Henriksdatter. Birgitte was the oldest in a family of seven children. At an early age Birgitte Katerine was betrothed to Herman Hertz, a hunter in the service of the king.

When Hertz was appointed forester of Vordingborg in 1763, the betrothed couple was married, and Birgitte became the mother of four children within five years. She employed her spare time in diligent study of German, French, and English with the result that she could read the poetic works of these nations in the original. In 1773 the Society for the Advancement of the Liberal Arts sent out a call soliciting contributions from every person "who had a desire and talent for writing sacred poetry." This was to obtain material for a new hymnal to replace Kingo's. She started contributing to this collection, which was the subsequent *Guldberg's Hymnal*. Since the office of forester was abolished at this time, the Hertz family was in pressing circumstances. Birgitte appealed to Guldberg for help. He brought the matter to the attention of Prince Fredrik, who ordered both her sons educated at his expense. After an illness of one year Birgitte's husband died. During the three years of her widowhood she received her maintenance from Prince Fredrik. During this time she composed and translated, upon Guldberg's request, many hymns for the hymn-book, so that when it appeared in 1778 it contained 124 original hymns and 24 translations by her. In that year she married Hans Boye, an employee in the custom house of Copenhagen. Birgitte survived him and died at the age of eighty-two, October 17, 1824. The hymns of Birgitte Katerine Boye were influenced by the spirit and style of Klopstock and Gellert. Her hymns gave *Guldberg's Hymn Book* its characteristic style.

79. Rejoice, rejoice this happy morn
189. He is arisen! Glorious word!
230. Holy Spirit, God of love

BOYE, Caspar Johannes (1791—1853), was the son of Engelbrecht Boye, rector at Kongsberg, Norway, where Caspar was born. He studied law and theology at the University of Copenhagen. He was first a teacher and then a pastor in Denmark. His last appointment was as pastor in Copenhagen, where he died in 1853. Boye produced a number of dramas besides writing many hymns which are considered of a high excellence.

194. Abide with us, the day is waning

BRADBURY, William Batchelder (1816—1868), was born at York, Maine, on October 6, 1816. He moved to Boston in 1830, where he began the study of the organ and the piano under Lowell Mason. He gained a good reputation as an organist, choirmaster, and composer, and after a few years spent in St. Johns, New Brunswick, Boston, Brooklyn, and New York City he left America for two years of study under the great music teachers of Europe (1847). From 1849 to 1854 Bradbury spent his time teaching, composing, and conducting music festivals. He edited over 50 collections of music and served as editor of the *New York Musical Review*. He died on January 7, 1868.

388. WOODWORTH
587. REST

BRADY, Nicholas (1659—1726), son of Major Nicholas Brady, was born, October 28, 1659, at Bandon, England. He was educated at Westminster, Christ Church, Oxford, and Trinity College, Dublin. Brady served as Prebendary of Cork. He was an adherent of William III during the Irish War. Three times he saved his native town from burning. After the war he came to London with a petition to William III. There he remained and was made Chaplain to the King and later Incumbent of Stratford-on-Avon (1702—1705). Although he also held other appointments, his extravagance obliged him to keep a school. He published several volumes of sermons, a tragedy, and a translation of Virgil's *Aeneid*, but is remembered particularly for *The New Version of the Psalms*, 1691, which he prepared together with Nahum Tate (q.v.).

29. Through all the changing scenes of life
525. As pants the hart for cooling streams

BRAUER, Alfred E. R. (1866—   ), was born August 1, 1866, at Mount Torrens, near Adelaide, South Australia, took the academic course at Prince Alfred College (Wesleyan), Adelaide, and began to read law. Switching to theology, he came to America and entered Concordia Seminary, Springfield, Ill., in the fall of 1887, graduating in 1890. He was ordained November 12, 1890, and became a sort of an itinerant pastor in the state of Victoria, Australia, until he took over the Dimboola parish, which he served until about 1896. In that year he was called as assistant pastor at St. Michael's, Ambleside (formerly Hahndorf). Upon the death of Pastor Strempel, his father-in-law, who at that time was president of the Australian Lutheran Synod, he took full charge of the congregation until 1921, when he accepted a call to St. John's, Melbourne, which he is still serving today. He was editor of the *Australian Lutheran*, founded in 1913, and contributed translations to the *Australian Lutheran Hymn-Book*, 1925, of which he was one of the compilers.

26. *Praise the Almighty, my soul, adore Him.* (Tr.)

BRIDGES, Matthew (1800—1894), the youngest son of John Bridges, was born at Maldon, Essex, on July 14, 1800. He was educated in the Church of England, but in 1848 joined the Church of Rome, following John Henry Newman and others interested in the Oxford Movement. In later years Bridges lived in Quebec, Canada.

Bridges's hymns were published in his *Hymns of the Heart*, 1848, and in *The Passion of Jesus*, 1852. Many of his hymns were first brought into use in our country through Henry Ward Beecher's *Plymouth Collection*, 1855. He died in Quebec, October 6, 1894.

165. *Behold the Lamb of God!*
336. *My God, accept my heart this day*
341. *Crown Him with many crowns*

BRIDGES, Robert Seymour (1844—1930), was born at Walmer, Kent, on October 23, 1844. He was educated at Eton and at Corpus Christi College, Oxford, where he received his B. A. in 1867 and his M. A. in 1874. He studied medicine at St. Bartholomew's Hospital, London, and took his M. B. in 1874. He retired from practice in 1882, settling at Yattendon in Berkshire. The author and poet of many poems and plays, Bridges also edited and contributed to the *Yattendon Hymnal*, 1899. He was appointed Poet Laureate in 1913. He died in 1930.

101. *O Gladsome Light, O Grace.* (Tr.)

BROOKS, Charles Timothy (1813—1883), was born in Salem, Massachusetts, June 20, 1813. He was graduated from Harvard University, 1832, and from the Divinity School of Cambridge, Massachusetts, in 1835. In that year he began his ministry at Nahant, subsequently preaching at Bangor and Augusta, Maine, and in Windsor, Vermont. In 1837 he became pastor of Newport, Rhode Island, and retained the charge until 1871, when he resigned because of ill health. He died in 1883.

577. *God bless our native land.* (Tr.)

BROOKS, Phillips (1835—1893), was born in Boston, December 13, 1835, and studied at Harvard, where he was graduated in 1855. He tried teaching in the Boston Latin School, but proved a "conspicuous failure." Then he studied at the Episcopal Theological Seminary at Alexandria, Virginia. He was ordained in 1859 and became rector of the Church of the Advent, Philadelphia, and then of Holy Trinity, of the same city. At this time Brooks was 32. Finally he became rector of the famous Trinity Church, Boston. He was offered but declined the office of preacher at Harvard, professorships, the assistant bishopric of Pennsylvania. In 1891 he was elected bishop of Massachusetts. Brooks was one of the foremost preachers that America has yet produced. He died January 23, 1893.

647. *O little town of Bethlehem*

BRORSON, Hans Adolf (1694—1764), born June 20, 1694, in Randrup, near Ribe and Tönder, belonged to an old family of ministers. He studied at the Ribe Latin School and then at the University of Copenhagen, where he took up theology, philology, history, and philosophy. Brorson was forced to leave the university in 1717 because of his health. He subsequently became the family tutor in the home of District Superintendent Klausen of Logumcloister. In 1721 he accepted a call to Randrup and in 1729 was appointed deacon of Tönder in Schleswig. He became district superintendent and minister of Ribe and bishop in 1741. He was made a Doctor of Theology in 1754. He published *Tröns rare Klenodie*, 1739, and the hymn-book which he projected, and to which he largely contributed, was published in 1740, under the title *Den ny Salmebog*, by Erik Pontoppidan.

<blockquote>
413. I walk in danger all the way
656. Behold a host, arrayed in white
</blockquote>

BROWN, Arthur Henry (1830—1926), born at Brentwood, Essex, July 14, 1830, was a self-taught musician; organist of the church of St. Thomas the Martyr, Brentwood, 1842 to 1853; of the church of St. Edward the Confessor, Romford, Essex, till 1858; and then organist of Brentwood, and a professor of music there; organist also of St. Peter's Church, South Weald. He was a pioneer in the movement to restore the ancient Plain Chant and to revive the use of the Gregorian Tones in Anglican worship. He published a *Gregorian Psalter, The Anglican Psalter, Canticles of Holy Church*. He wrote about 700 hymn-tunes. He died in 1926.

<blockquote>
555. ST. ANATOLIUS
</blockquote>

BRUN, Johan Nordahl (1745—1816), the son of Sven Busch Brun, a merchant, and Mette Katarina, *née* Nordahl, was born in Bynesset, Norway, on March 21, 1745. His father taught the boy writing and arithmetic, while his mother taught him to read the Holy Scriptures, which he had read through twice by the time he was eleven years old. Brun's half-brother, who was a candidate of theology in Copenhagen, induced him to become a student and tutored him. Later Brun studied at the Latin school and at the university in Trondhjem. He became the family tutor in the home of Councilor Mennche and accompanied his son to Soro in Denmark. Here after three months' preparation he took the theological examination and received the lowest possible grade — *non contemnendus*. The result of his examination in homiletics was somewhat better. Brun returned to Norway and spent three years in Trondhjem as an instructor, preacher, and poet. He applied for two positions in vain. In 1771 Brun accompanied B. Gunnerius to Copenhagen as his private secretary, but Brun never served in this capacity. During his stay in Copenhagen, Brun wrote the drama *Zarine*, which created a sensation and brought him good returns. He published another drama in 1772 which was unfavorably criticized. The next year he was ordained as assistant pastor at Bynesset and married Ingeborg Lind, to whom he had been engaged twelve years. He was materially and financially assisted by a group of faithful friends in Trondhjem. In 1774 Brun was appointed to a rectorship in Bergen and held this position until January 6, 1804, when he was made bishop of the diocese of Bergen. He gained great fame as an eloquent preacher and a very able opponent of the rationalists. In 1786 Brun published his *Evangelical Hymns*, a collection of 65 hymns. He died on July 26, 1816.

<blockquote>
48. How blest are they who hear God's Word
337. Our Lord and God, oh, bless this day
</blockquote>

BRYANT, William Cullen (1794—1878), was born at Cummington, Massachusetts, on November 3, 1794. He was only eighteen when he composed that epic of American poetry, *Thanatopsis*. Although his parents were but ordinary farmers, he managed to pursue the study of law for two years at Williams College, before financial difficulties forced him to discontinue. But he found a position in a law office, and after a short time he was admitted to the bar at the age of twenty-one. He practiced law for about ten years. Then, in 1826, he became connected with the *New York Evening Post*. This offered him the opportunity for which he was looking in that it gave him a chance to follow his literary ambitions. After writing for this paper for several years, he rose to the position of chief editor, which he held until he died at the ripe old age of eighty-five, June 12, 1878. Brought up as a Congregationalist, he became in turn Unitarian, Presbyterian, and then Episcopalian. He was not baptized until well advanced in years. His first poetic impulse was derived from Watts. He wrote twenty hymns. His fame lies mainly in his work as poet and essayist, and he remained primarily the poet. His essays are a model of journalism, his poetry the first of note in the new American republic.

<blockquote>
499. Look from Thy sphere of endless day
</blockquote>

BYROM, John (1692—1763), the younger son of Edward Byrom, a linen-draper, was born at Manchester, England, on February 29, 1692. He entered Trinity College, Cambridge, in 1708 (B. A. 1711, M. A. 1715). In 1714 Byrom was elected a Fellow at the college. However, because his Fellowship required of him to take orders in the Church and as he could not conscientiously comply, he resigned his Fellowship in 1716 and went to Montpellier, where he studied medicine. He returned to England and settled in London as a physician. Shortly afterward he married Elizabeth Byrom, the daughter of his uncle, Joseph Byrom, incurring the wrath of his wealthy kindred. As Byrom did not practice medicine, he obtained a livelihood by teaching a system of stenography which he had invented. The system was highly prized by statesmen and others of that day and brought Byrom a handsome income and the friendship of many men of quality. For his invention he was elected a Fellow of the Royal Society. Upon the death of his brother Edward he inherited the family estates and thereafter devoted himself to literary pursuits. In 1738 Byrom met Charles Wesley and through his influence became a convert to Christianity. Byrom taught the Wesley brothers his shorthand, which they used in their journals and in writing their hymns. His *Poems* were first published in 1773 in two volumes. John Wesley said of the work that it contained "some of the finest sentiments that ever appeared in the English tongue — some of the noblest truths, expressed with the utmost energy of language, and the strongest colors of poetry." From these poems less than half a dozen hymns have come to us, but his Christmas hymn has a reputation which extends to all English-speaking countries.

84. Christians, awake, salute the happy morn

CAMPBELL, Robert (1814—1868), was born at Trochraig, Ayrshire, Scotland, December 19, 1814. Early in life Campbell showed a strong predilection for theological studies, but he became fixed in law and entered on the duties of an advocate. He was a zealous, devoted member of the Episcopal Church of Scotland directing special attention to the education of the children of the poor. In 1848 he began a series of translations of Latin hymns. These translations he submitted to the critical eyes of Dr. J. M. Neale, Dr. Mills of Ely, and of other competent judges. The result was that in 1850 a selection from these translations of Latin hymns and a few of his original hymns were compiled to make the so-called *St. Andrew's Hymnal*. This hymnal received special sanction of Bishop Torry. Two years later he was converted to Roman Catholicism. He died at Edinburgh, December 29, 1868. His translations are smooth, musical, and well sustained.

282. Christians, come in sweetest measures. (Tr.)

CAREY, Henry (1692—1743), whose antecedents are not definitely known to us, was a teacher in private families and boarding schools in England. He was a prolific author of burlesques, farces, songs, and poems, the best known being *Sally in Our Alley*. His collection of songs, *The Musical Century*, was published in 1740. His dramatic works appeared in 1743. His writing of church music was only incidental.

368. SURREY

CARLYLE, Joseph Dacre (1758—1804), was born at Carlisle, June 4, 1758. He was professor of Arabic at the University of Cambridge and later vicar of Newcastle-on-Tyne. His *Specimens of Arabian Poetry* was published in 1796. In 1799 he was chosen to accompany Lord Elgin on an embassy to Constantinople to inquire as to the literary treasures remaining in the public library of that city. He died at Newcastle, April 12, 1804. His *Poems Suggested Chiefly by Scenes in Asia Minor, Africa* was published by Susannah Maria Carlyle, in 1805. His hymns appeared in J. Fawcett's *Psalms and Hymns*, 1802.

22. Lord, when we bend before Thy throne

CASWALL, Edward (1814—1878), was born at Yately, in Hampshire, England, July 15, 1814. He won renown as a great translator of hymns. The son of a clergyman he himself rendered ten years of service in the Church of England, but was confirmed in the Church of Rome in 1850, the year after his wife's death. He joined Newman at the Oratory, Edgbaston, and remained there till his death, January 2, 1878. He published *Lyra Catholica* in 1849; *Hymns and Other Poems* in 1863.

  60. Hark, a thrilling voice is sounding. (Tr.)
 102. O come, all ye faithful. (Tr.)
 158. Glory be to Jesus. (Tr.)
 233. Come, Holy Ghost, Creator blest. (Tr.)
 257. Jesus, Brightness of the Father. (Tr.)
 350. Jesus, the very thought of Thee. (Tr.)
 361. O Jesus, King most wonderful. (Tr.)

CAWOOD, John (1775—1852), was born at Matlock, Derbyshire, England, on March 18, 1775. His education was limited, since his parents were in humble circumstances, being farmers on a small scale. He was trained to a life of toil. At eighteen he was engaged by the Rev. Mr. Cursham, of Sutton-in-Ashfield, Nottinghamshire. After three years' study under the careful direction of the Rev. Edward Spencer of Winkfield, Wiltshire, in a classical course, he entered St. Edmund Hall, Oxford, in 1797. Here Cawood was favored with the instructions of the Rev. Isaac Crouch, Vice-principal. After receiving his degree in 1801 he took holy orders, being ordained deacon and then priest in the same year. Cawood was successively curate of Ribsford and Dowles and Incumbent of St. Ann's Chapel of Ease, Bewdley, Worcestershire. The latter was a perpetual curacy to which he was appointed in 1814. He died on November 7, 1852.

  49. Almighty God, Thy Word is cast
  83. Hark! what mean those holy voices

CELANO, Thomas de (13th century), was born at Celano in the province of the Abruzzi c. 1200. He was one of the first disciples of St. Francis of Assisi, whose biographer he became later. He joined the Order of Franciscans probably in 1215. After 1221 he served as "custos" of the convents at Mayence, Worms, Speyer, and Cologne. He died c. 1255.

 607. Day of wrath, O day of mourning
 612. That day of wrath, that dreadful day

CHANDLER, John (1806—1876), son of the Rev. John F. Chandler, was born at Witley, Surrey, England, on June 16, 1806. Educated at Corpus Christi College, Oxford (B. A., 1827; M. A., 1830), he was ordained deacon in 1831 and priest in the following year. In 1837 he succeeded his father as vicar of Witley and was afterwards appointed Rural Dean. He died at Putney on July 1, 1876. Chandler's prose works include *Life of William of Wykeham*, 1842; *Horae Sacrae, Prayers and Meditations from the Writing of the Divines of the Anglican Church*, 1844; and numerous sermons and tracts. John Chandler was one of the earliest and most successful of modern translators. His translations arose out of a desire to see the ancient prayers of the Anglican Liturgy accompanied by hymns of a corresponding date of composition.

  63:1-3. On Jordan's bank the Baptist's cry. (Tr.)
  68. The Advent of our King. (Tr.)
 115. O blessed day when first was poured. (Tr.)
 465. Christ is our Corner-stone. (Tr.)

CHATFIELD, Allen (1808—1896), was born at Chatteris on October 2, 1808, and was educated at Charterhouse School and Trinity College, Cambridge, where he was Bell's University Scholar and Members' Prizeman. He graduated as B. A. in 1831, taking first rank in classical honors. The following year Chatfield took holy orders and from 1833 to 1847 was Vicar of Stotfold, Bedfordshire, and from 1847 to his death Vicar of Much-Marcle, Herefordshire. Chatfield translated a number of Greek hymns and verses into English. But he also rendered the *Litany*, the *Te Deum* and other parts of the English Church Office into Greek. Chatfield was influenced by the Oxford Movement. He published *Songs and Hymns of the Earliest Christian Poets*, 1876. He died January 10, 1896.

 320. Lord Jesus, think on me. (Tr.)

[490]

CHETHAM, John (c. 1700—1763), a musician and clergyman, became master of the Clerk's School, Skipton, in 1737, and curate in 1739. In 1718 he edited the *Book of Psalmody*, used in several editions for over 150 years, and probably composed some of the tunes himself.

454. 579. BURFORD

CHORLEY, Henry Fothergill (1808—1872), born in Lancashire, England, December 15, 1808, educated in Liverpool, became man of letters, served on the staff of *The Athenaeum* as musical critic, and as author produced *Music and Manners in France and Germany* (1841), *Modern German Music* (1854), *The National Music of the World* (1880), and other works.

582. God, Lord of Sabaoth, Thou who ordainest

CLARK, Jeremiah (1670—1707), was a chorister of the Chapel Royal and later organist of Winchester College, 1692—5. After that he became in succession organist of St. Paul's, vicar choral, joint organist with Wm. Croft of the Chapel Royal. He wrote much for the stage, including operatic and instrumental music, but also a cantata, songs and many anthems and tunes. Clark is called "the inventor of the modern English hymn-tune." He was inclined to be melancholy and finally committed suicide. He entertained "a hopeless passion for a very beautiful lady in a station of life far above him; his despair of success threw him into a deep melancholy." "He was unable to decide whether he should commit suicide by hanging or drowning; so he tossed a coin, which struck on its edge in the soft ground when it fell. He went home and shot himself with a 'screw pistol.'" He died December 1, 1707.

219. ST. MAGNUS
323, 331, 530. ST. LUKE

CLAUSNITZER, Tobias (1619—1684), was born February 5, 1619, at Thum, a mile from Annaberg, Saxony, received his M.A. at Leipzig University in 1643 and in the following year was appointed chaplain to a Swedish regiment. As such, on Reminiscere Sunday, 1645, he preached the sermon at a service in St. Thomas Church, Leipzig, to celebrate the accession of Christina to the Swedish throne; also, January 1, 1849, the thanksgiving sermon at the field service ordered by General Wrangel, at Weiden, in the Upper Palatinate, for the conclusion of the Peace of Westphalia. In the same year he became first pastor at Weiden, where he served till his death on May 7, 1684, having also been made a member of the Consistory and inspector of the district.

16:1-3. Blessed Jesus at Thy Word
252. We all believe in one true God

CLEMENT OF ALEXANDRIA, ST. (c. 170—c. 220), whose full name was Titus Flavius Clement, was born, possibly at Athens, about 170. He was a diligent student of Greek literature and philosophy. He was a Stoic and an Eclectic, a seeker after truth amongst Greek, Assyrian, Egyptian, and Jewish teachers. At Alexandria, where he was taught by Pantaenus, Clement embraced Christianity. Pantaenus was at the time the master of the Theological School in that city. When Pantaenus retired from the school for missionary work in Arabia or India, Clement became its master c. 190 and retained this position until 203. Origen and Alexander, bishop of Jerusalem, were among Clement's pupils. Clement was driven from Alexandria by the persecution under Severus (202—203) and fled to Palestine. We hear of him again only in connection with a letter to the church at Antioch, probably delivered by him in 211. He was one of the most eminent fathers of the early Eastern Church. His chief works are *Exhortation to the Heathen; The Tutor (Paedagogos);* and the *Miscellanies (Stromateis).*

628. Shepherd of tender youth

COFFIN, Charles (1676—1749), was born at Buzancy (Ardennes), France, in 1676. He was educated at the college of Plessis, Paris, where he early gave evidence of eminent abilities and great attainments. In 1712 he became principal of the college at Beauvais in the University of Paris, succeeding the historian Rollin. In 1718 he was made rector of the university, but after three years returned to the principalship of the college. In 1727 Coffin published some of his Latin poems, for which he was already famous. In 1736 the bulk of his hymns appeared in the *Paris Breviary*. In the same year Coffin published his hymns as *Hymni Sacri Auctore Carolo Coffin*. In 1775 a complete edition of his *Works* was issued in two volumes. In the 1736 edition the hymns of Charles Coffin number 100. They are characterized as being "direct and filled with the spirit of grace." His hymns are remarkable for their pure Latinity and Scripturalness. He died on June 20, 1749.

> 63. On Jordan's banks the Baptist's cry
> 68. The Advent of our King

COLLYER, William Bengo (1782—1854), was born at Blackheath, England, on April 14, 1782, and educated at Homerton College. He enrolled as a divinity student at Homerton when he was sixteen. Four years later Collyer began his ministry at the Congregational Church at Peckham. The congregation numbered ten, having dwindled under Arian ministrations. Soon Collyer's orthodox preaching attracted crowds of people. Even the royal Dukes of Sussex and Kent frequented his humble chapel and sought his friendship. In 1814 Collyer added to his pastorate the care of the Presbyterian congregation of Salter's Hall, London. The ranks of this congregation had also been depleted by Arian preaching, but Collyer's Sabbath afternoon sermons soon began to draw crowded audiences. This charge Collyer held until 1825. In 1817 a new chapel had been opened for Collyer at Peckham, and here he labored with great success until his last days. Collyer compiled a hymn-book with the title, *Hymns Partly Collected and Partly Original, designed as a supplement to Dr. Watts's Psalms and Hymns*, 1812. This was written primarily for Collyer's own congregation and included 57 of his own hymns. He died January 8, 1854.

> 203. Morning breaks upon the tomb
> 280. Return, O wanderer, return
> 604:2-4. Great God, what do I see and hear

CONDER, Josiah (1789—1855), fourth son of Thomas Conder, a London bookseller, was born in Falcon Street, Aldersgate, September 17, 1789. At fifteen he was able to become an assistant to his father in his bookstore. He was the author of several prose works. In 1812 he contributed three hymns to Dr. Collyer's collection; and in 1836 he edited *The Congregational Hymn-Book. A Supplement to Dr. Watts's Psalms and Hymns*, which contained fifty-six of his own hymns; and in 1851 he published a revised edition of Dr. Watts's *Psalms and Hymns*. He died December 27, 1855. In the year after his death, his poems and all his hymns, already completely revised by him before his death, were published under the title of *Hymns of Praise*, 1856.

> 37. Lord, 'tis not that I did choose Thee

CONKEY, Ithamar (1815—1867), was born in Shutesbury, Massachusetts, on May 15, 1815. He served as organist and choir director at the Central Baptist Church, Norwich, Connecticut, and as bass soloist at Calvary Episcopal Church, New York. He then became a member of the choir of Grace Church, New York, and bass soloist and conductor of the quartet choir of the Madison Avenue Baptist Church, New York. In New York he was considered an authority on oratorio singing. He died April 30, 1867.

> 354. RATHBUN

CONVERSE, Charles Crozat (1832—1918), was born at Warren, Massachusetts, October 7, 1832. He studied in Germany. He became popular as a musician in the neighborhood of New York about 1850. A compiler of several music-books for choirs and Sunday-schools, he was for many years a lawyer and judge and had charge of the Burdetta Organ Co., Erie, Pennsylvania. He wrote under various *noms de plume*. He died at Highwood, New Jersey, in 1918.

> 457. FRIEND

COOKE, William (1821—1894), was born at Pendlebury, near Manchester, England. After serving as curate in various places, he became Select Preacher to the

University of Cambridge in 1850, and from 1849—1857 Examining Chaplain to the Bishop of Chester, by whom he was made Honorary Canon of Chester in 1854. In 1868 Cooke was elected a Fellow of the Society of Antiquaries of London. He published *The Power of the Priesthood in Absolution, Of Ceremonies, Lights and Custom*. In 1853 Cooke became joint editor of *The Church Hymnal*. He died November 23, 1894.

139:4. *In His Temple now behold Him*

COOPER, Edward (1770—1833), received his B. A. in 1792 from Queen's College and was a Fellow of All Souls' College, Oxford. He was ordained in 1793 (1788?) and became rector of Hamstall-Ridware, and then of Yoxall, Staffordshire. He edited a small collection of hymns and assisted in the compilation of the earliest of the Staffordshire hymn-books, the *Uttoxeter Selection*, 1805. Cooper had a great reputation as a preacher.

242. *Father of heaven, whose love profound*

COPELAND, William John (1804—1885), was born at Chigwell, England, on September 1, 1804. He studied at St. Paul's School and Trinity College, Oxford, receiving his B. A. in 1829, his M. A. in 1831, and his B. D. in 1840. Copeland was successively a Scholar, Fellow, and Dean of Littlemore, and in 1849 Rector of Farnham, Essex, and Rural Dean of Newport. He has contributed a number of translations from the Roman Breviary, and a number of modern centos are based on his lines. He died at Farnham, August 25, 1885.

559. *O Christ, who art the Light and Day*. (Tr.)

CORY, Julia Bulkley Cady (1882—   ). According to the *Handbook to the Hymnal* (Presbyterian) Mrs. Cory is the daughter of J. Cleveland Cady, a noted architect in New York City. He was an active member of Brick Presbyterian Church of that city, and was superintendent of the Sunday school in the Church of the Covenant affiliated with it. Mrs. Cory also was a member of this church. Mr. Frank J. Metcalf of Washington, D. C., wrote us: "She is the wife of Robert H. Cory and lives in Englewood, N. J. In 1904 Archer Gibson, organist of the Brick Presbyterian Church in New York, asked her to write a Thanksgiving hymn for the tune 'Kremser.'"

568. *We praise Thee, O God, our Redeemer, Creator*. (Tr.)

COTTERILL, Thomas (1779—1823), was born at Cannock, Staffordshire, December 4, 1779. Although he is not so well known as a hymn-writer, he is remembered for his *Selection of Psalms and Hymns, for Public and Private Use, Adapted to the Services of the Church of England* which was published in 1819. By 1820 it had reached its ninth edition. In the work of this book he was aided by James Montgomery. It influenced all English hymnody, and it had a marked effect upon all modern hymnals. To this collection Cotterill contributed at various dates twenty-five original hymns. He died at Sheffield, December 29, 1823.

232. *Let songs of praises fill the sky*

COWPER, William (1731—1800), was born in his father's rectory at Berkhampstead, England, on November 26, 1731. Although Cowper's mother died when he was only six years old, she had become a real friend and companion to him. When he received a picture of her in his sixtieth year, Cowper composed some lines to her memory which are indeed a high tribute. At school Cowper was wretched because of his extreme shyness and eccentric character. Later at Westminster he adjusted himself a little better. Here Cowper studied law. At this time he fell in love with his cousin, Theodora Cowper, and wrote love poems to her. Her father forbade her to marry Cowper, but she never forgot him and in later years secretly aided his necessities. Fits of melancholy began to seize Cowper with greater regularity. His nomination to the Clerkship of the Journals of the House of Lords proved a calamity. The thought of a public examination disturbed him to the extent of overthrowing his reason and driving him to attempted suicide with "laudanum, knife, and cord." The delusion of his life now appeared — a belief in his reprobation by God. Under the wise and Christian treatment of Dr. Cotton at St. Albans this malady passed away. In general the next eight years were happy ones for Cowper — full of the realization of God's favor. This was the happiest, most lucid period of his life. The first two years of this period were spent at Huntington, where Cowper formed the life-long friendship of Mrs. Unwin, the wife of the Rev. Morley Unwin. The remainder was spent at Olney with John Newton, with whom Cowper collaborated on the justly famous *Olney Hymns.* But the tension of the Calvinistic exercises, the despondence of Newton, and the death of Cowper's brother brought another attack of madness and attempted suicide. For sixteen months Cowper lived under this dark cloud. Mrs. Unwin kept him occupied with small tasks and suggested that he do some serious poetical work. The malady gradually left Cowper by the time his cousin, Lady Hesketh, brought him to Weston in 1786. But the death of Mrs. Unwin brought "fixed despair" of which Cowper's last poem, *The Castaway,* is a terrible memorial. From this melancholy Cowper never recovered. He died at East Dereham on April 25, 1800.

    157. *There is a fountain filled with blood*
    514. *God moves in a mysterious way*
    534:1-5. *God of my life, to Thee I call*

    COX, Frances Elizabeth (1812—1897). Frances Elizabeth Cox was born at Oxford in 1812. She made her contribution to hymnology as a translator of German hymns. She was indebted to Baron Bunsen, who guided her selection as to hymns worthy of translation. Her first book was *Sacred Hymns from the German,* 1841. Later she published another book, *Hymns from the German,* 1864. The two books contained a total of 56 translations.

    177. *Our blessed Savior seven times spoke.* (Tr.)
    201. *Jesus lives! The victory's won!* (Tr.)
    214. *Lo, God to heaven ascendeth.* (Tr.)
    366. *One thing's needful; Lord, this treasure.* (Tr.)
    546. *How lovely shines the morning star.* (Tr.)

    COXE, Arthur Cleveland (1818—1896), was born at Mendham, New Jersey, in 1818. He was the son of the Rev. Samuel Cox, a Presbyterian minister. The son altered the spelling of the name and became an Episcopalian. He graduated from the University of New York in 1841 and served as rector in Hartford, Connecticut, Baltimore, and New York City. In 1865 he was made bishop of Western New York. He wrote many hymns, but, because of his extreme modesty, he would not permit his hymns to appear in the Episcopal hymn-book, because he was a member of the hymnal committee. His hymns were included, however, in other English and American collections. Besides his work in hymnology he is known as one of the most distinguished of the American prelates. He was Provisional bishop of Haiti from 1872 to 1874. In 1873 he collaborated with Bishop Wilberforce in issuing a defense of Anglo-Catholicism against Romanism.

    510:1. *Savior, sprinkle many nations*

    CRASSELIUS, Bartholomäus (1667—1724), was born at Wernsdorf, near Glaucha, Saxony, February 21, 1667. He studied at Halle under August Herman Francke. He served as Lutheran pastor at Nidda, in Wetteravia, Hesse, and at Düsseldorf, where he died November 10, 1724.

    21. *Jehovah, let me now adore Thee*

    CROFT, William (1678—1727), was born in 1678 at Ettington, Warwickshire, of a good family, and was one of the children of the Chapel Royal under Dr. Blow. He became organist of St. Ann's, Soho, and in 1700 gentleman extraordinary of the Chapel Royal. In 1704 he was made joint organist of the Chapel Royal with Jeremiah Clark and three years later sole organist. In 1708 he was appointed organist of Westminster Abbey and composer to the Chapel Royal. In 1713 he was made a Doctor of Music by Oxford. He died at Bath of an illness "occasioned by his attendance on his duty" at the coronation of George II. In his earlier life Croft composed for the theater and also wrote sonatas, songs, and odes. Later he became absorbed in sacred music and made for himself in this field one of the greatest names in English musical history. Many fine anthems of his still live; his service music is of the highest importance; but his tunes give Croft his widest fame. It is said that he influenced Händel to a considerable extent and that his cathedral music was one of the models of Händel's "high sacred style" in his oratorios. Croft's tunes are of importance historically, as they are the earliest examples of the English psalm-tune as distinguished from the Genevan. Croft wrote *Divine Harmony*, a collection of the words of anthems with a brief historical account of English Church music; *Musica Sacra*, a collection of 30 anthems; and a *Burial Service* of his own composition. Croft's epitaph in Westminster Abbey concludes with the words, "Having resided among mortals for fifty years, behaving with the utmost candor . . . he departed to the heavenly choir . . . that being near, he might add to the concert of angels his own HALLELUJAH."

123, 291, 460. ST. ANNE
580. CROFT'S 136TH

CRONENWETT, Emanuel (1841—1931), son of the Rev. George Cronenwett and Magdalene, *née* Knapp, was born near Ann Arbor, Michigan, February 22, 1841, was educated for the Lutheran ministry at Capital University, Columbus, Ohio, and after his ordination at Woodville, Ohio, served at Carrollton, where he ministered to seven congregations in four counties; then at Waynesburg, Ohio, at Wooster, Ohio, at Delaware, Ohio, and the last fifty-four years of his long ministry at Butler, Pennsylvania. The degree of Doctor of Divinity was conferred on him by Grove City (Pa.) College. A volume of his hymns and poems was published in 1926. He died at Butler, Pennsylvania, March 9, 1931.

254. *Lord God, we all to Thee give praise.* (Tr.)
290. *We have a sure prophetic Word*
306. *Lord Jesus Christ, Thou hast prepared.* (Tr.)
308. *Invited, Lord, by boundless grace*
406. *Lord, as Thou wilt, deal Thou with me.* (Tr.)

CROSSWELL, William (1804—1851), was born in Hudson, New York, November 7, 1804, the third child of Harry Crosswell and Susan, *née* Sherman. His father was then editor of *The Balance* and soon afterwards removed to Albany, New York. Although of Puritan stock, he attached himself to the Episcopal Church, entered the ministry in 1814, and became the rector of Trinity Church, New Haven, Connecticut. The son entered Yale College in 1818 and graduated four years later. He entered General Theological Seminary in 1826, at the same time editing the *Episcopal Watchman*. In 1828 he became rector of Christ Church, Boston, where he served for eleven years. After his marriage to Amanda, *née* Tarbell, he became rector of St. Peter's Church, Auburn, New York. Meanwhile his friends and admirers at Boston, having organized the Church of the Advent expressly for him, prevailed on him to return to Boston, which he did in 1844. Two years later Trinity College bestowed on him the degree of D. D. On November 9, 1851, he died suddenly in his church at the close of the service. Instead of rising from his knees at the end of the collect, he sank to the floor and expired. His memoirs, published by his father, contain 34 sonnets, 72 poems, and 38 psalms, hymns, and prayers.

440. *Lord, lead the way the Savior went*

CRÜGER, Johann (1598—1662), was born at Gross-Breesen, Brandenburg, on April 1, 1598. He studied at schools in Guben, Sorau, and Breslau, the Jesuit College at Olmütz, and the Poets' School at Regensburg. He traveled through Austria, Hungary, Bohemia, and Moravia and then settled at Berlin in 1615. Here he employed himself as a private tutor until 1622, except for a short residence at the University of Wittenberg in 1620. He received a thorough musical training under Paulus Homberger in Regensburg, a pupil of Giovanni Gabrieli. In 1622 Crüger was appointed cantor of St. Nicholas Church at Berlin and also one of the masters of the Greyfriars Gymnasium. Crüger wrote no hymns, but he was one of the most distinguished musicians and tune composers of his time. He composed 71 *chorales*, of which 18 have received a wide usage in the Evangelical churches of the world. His church-hymn collections include *Neues vollkömmliches Gesangbuch,* 1640; *Praxis pietatis melica,* 1644, which appeared in many editions; *Geistliche Kirchenmelodeyen,* 1649; *Psalmodica sacra,* 1658. He died at Berlin, February 23, 1662.

  10, 248, 344, 581, 629. NUN DANKET ALL
  36, 38, 93. NUN DANKET ALLE GOTT
  58. WIE SOLL ICH DICH
  77. FROEHLICH SOLL MEIN HERZE
  81, 107. O JESU CHRIST, DEIN KRIPPLEIN
  143, 240, 258, 269. HERZLIEBSTER JESU
  192. AUF, AUF, MEIN HERZ
  201, 206. JESUS, MEINE ZUVERSICHT
  228. ZEUCH EIN
  305, 659. SCHMÜCKE DICH
  326. HERR, ICH HABE MISSGEHANDELT
  347. JESU, MEINE FREUDE

  CRULL, August (1846—1923). Crull was born at Rostock, Germany, on January 26, 1846, the son of Hofrat F. Crull. He was educated at the Gymnasium in his home town and at Concordia College (St. Louis and Fort Wayne) and Concordia Seminary, St. Louis, Missouri. He was for a while assistant pastor in Trinity Church, Milwaukee. There he also served as Director of the Lutheran High School. Later he served as pastor of the Lutheran Church in Grand Rapids, Mich., and finally as professor of the German language and literature at Concordia College, Fort Wayne, Indiana, from 1873 to 1915. He published a German grammar and edited a book of devotions, *Das walte Gott,* drawn from the writings of Dr. C. F. W. Walther. Crull was a distinguished hymnologist. Many of his translations have appeared in *The Lutheran Hymnary,* Decorah, Iowa, 1879; in the *Evangelical Lutheran Hymnal,* 1880; in *Hymns of the Evangelical Lutheran Church,* 1888; and in the *Evangelical Lutheran Hymn-Book,* 1912. He died at Milwaukee, Wisconsin, February 17, 1923.

  33. *The Lord hath helped me hithertoo.* (Tr.)
  38. *The Lord, my God, be praised.* (Tr.)
  53. *Abide, O dearest Jesus.* (Tr.)
  55. *Come, Thou precious Ransom, come.* (Tr.)
  105. *Praise God the Lord, ye sons of men.* (Tr.)
  124. *O Lord, our Father, thanks to Thee.* (Tr.)
  140. *Jesus, I will ponder, now.* (Tr.)
  173. *Lord Jesus, we give thanks to Thee.* (Tr.)
  196. *I am content! My Jesus liveth still.* (Tr.)
  197. *Where wilt Thou go since night draws near.* (Tr.)
  215. *Draw us to Thee.* (Tr.)
  245. *God loved the world so that He gave.* (Tr.)
  328. *O Jesus, Lamb of God, Thou art.* (Tr.)
  348. *Jesus, Jesus, only Jesus.* (Tr.)
  384. *Oh, how great is Thy compassion.* (Tr.)
  398. *Renew me, O eternal Light.* (Tr.)
  402. *O God, forsake me not.* (Tr.)
  411. *From eternity, O God.* (Tr.)
  417. *How can I thank Thee, Lord.* (Tr.)
  430. *What is the world to me.* (Tr.)
  529. *I leave all things to God's direction.* (Tr.)

  CUTLER, Henry S. (1824—1902), was born in Boston. He traveled in Europe, making an intensive study of the music of the Established Church. He served first at Grace Church, Boston, and from 1852 to 1858 at the Church of the Advent in Boston. At the latter place he trained an excellent choir of men and boys, noted not only for their fine singing but also because they were apparently the first surpliced choir in this country. In 1858 Cutler joined Trinity Church, New York, where he served as choirmaster for seven years and introduced a full liturgical service. After leaving Trinity he was active in Brooklyn, Providence, Philadelphia, and Troy until his death.

  452. ALL SAINTS NEW

  CZAMANSKE, William Martin (1873—), was born August 26, 1873, at Granville, Wisconsin. He was graduated from Concordia College, Milwaukee, Wisconsin, in 1894, and from Concordia Seminary, St. Louis, in 1898. Ordained and installed as pastor July 31, 1898, he served successively Lutheran churches, near Madelia, Minnesota, 1898—1902; West Henrietta, New York, 1902—1904; Rochester, New York, 1904 to 1910; and Sheboygan, Wisconsin, since 1910, where he is still active. He has contributed poems to the *Lutheran Witness, Sunday School Times, Etude, Expositor, Northwestern Lutheran,* and other church publications. He served as member of a subcommittee of the Committee on Hymnology and Liturgics for the Synodical Conference of North America, which edited *The Lutheran Hymnal.*

    639. *For many years, O God of grace*
    216. *On Christ's Ascension I now build.* (Tr.)
    299. *Dear Father, who hast made us all.* (Tr.)
    509. *There still is room.* (Tr.)
    596. *This body in the grave we lay.* (Tr.)
    630. *Ye parents, hear what Jesus taught.* (Tr.)

    DACH, Simon (1605—1659), was born July 29, 1605, at Memel, seventy-two miles northeast of Königsberg, Prussia. He first attended the Domschule at Königsberg, studying theology and philosophy, leaving, however, for Wittenberg, when a pestilence broke out. Later he went to school at Magdeburg. In 1633 Dach became affiliated with the Domschule at Königsberg, teaching philosophy and theology. He was often physically unwell. This fact together with a meager income hindered his work to a great degree. However, he found a bosom friend in Roberthin, with whose financial aid Dach was able to spend less time teaching and more time writing poetry. He was the most gifted of a group of prominent Prussian theologians, scientists, and poets known as the Königsberg School. In 1636, the same year in which he became assistant rector at the Königsberg Domschule, Dach wrote the folk-song "Ännchen von Tharau ist, die mir gefällt," dedicating the same to the daughter of the pastor of Tharau, whom he had courted in vain. The poem was written in Plattdeutsch. Through the influence of Roberthin, Dach was appointed professor of poetry at Königsberg in 1639. After receiving a grant of land through Roberthin, Dach in 1641 married the daughter of a court official by the name of Pohl. The death of Roberthin in 1648 caused Dach to turn from secular to religious poetry. He now began his hymn writing, which did not cease until after he had written over 150 hymns. He died April 15, 1659.

    372. *Through Jesus' blood and merit*
    589. *Oh, how blest are ye whose toils are ended*

    DALE, Charles J. (1904). We have no further information on this composer.
    259, 420. DENBY

    DAMAN, William (c. 1580). "One of her Majesties Musicians," Daman was among the first to set the English Psalms to tunes and had a complete series published by John Bull, citizen and goldsmith of London, in 1579. He helped to popularize the C. M. tune.
    156, 170, 320, 327, 610. SOUTHWELL

    DARWALL, John (1731—1789), was born at Haughton, Staffordshire, England, where he was baptized, January 13, 1731; received his education at Manchester School and at Brasenose College, Oxford, where he graduated in 1756; took holy orders and in 1769 became Vicar of Walsall, Staffordshire, where he remained until his death December 18, 1789. He composed 150 tunes for the metrical psalms. The tunes were not published as a collection, but a number were taken into the hymnals of the Church.
    46, 465, 480, 575, 638, 642. DARWALL'S 148th

    DAY (Daye or Daie), John (1522—1584), is said to have been born in St. Peter's Parish, Dunwich, Suffolk, in 1522 (there are no records to verify this date); settled in London as printer before the middle of the sixteenth century; one of the earliest of English music-printers; produced about 230 works, many of them being of importance. He used as his trade-mark a sleeper awakened by one who points to the rising sun, saying "Arise, for it is day." He printed, among other books, the first edition of *Queen Elizabeth's Prayer Book; Foxe's Book of Martyrs; Certaine Notes set forth in foure and three parts to be song* (the first church music born in English); the first metrical Psalter (old version) with the old proper tunes, 1562; and *The Whole Psalmes*, 1563, probably the earliest psalter, with the proper tunes harmonized. Tallis was a contributor to this work. Day died at Walden, in Essex, July 23, 1584, aged sixty-two, and was buried at Bradley Parva in Suffolk, August 2.

22, 382, 478, 578

DAYMAN, Edward Arthur (1807—1890), was born at Padstow, Cornwall, July 11, 1807, the third son of John Dayman of Mambury, North Devon. He was educated at Blundell's School, Tiverton, Devon, and Exeter College, Oxon. For some time he was Fellow and Tutor of his College and Pro-Proctor in 1835. After taking holy orders in 1835 he became examiner for the University Scholarship for Latin in 1838 and in 1840 Senior Proctor of the University. In 1862 he became Honorable Canon of Bitton in Sarum Cathedral. His works include *Modern Infidelity*, 1861, and *Essay on Inspiration*, 1864. He was joint editor with Earl Nelson and Bishop Woodford of the *Sarum Hymnal*, 1868. He also contributed several translations from the Latin to *The Hymnary*, 1872. He died at Shillingstone in 1890.

438. *Almighty Father, heaven and earth*

DEARMER, Percy (1867—1936), was born in London, February 26, 1867, and was educated at Westminster School and at Christ Church, Oxford. He served as vicar of St. Mary the Virgin, Primrose Hill, from 1901 to 1915. Dearmer was secretary of the London branch of the Christian Social Union from 1891 to 1912, and, after the first World War, became Professor of Ecclesiastical Art at King's College, London, and in 1931 canon of Westminster. Dearmer is the author of a number of works in hymnology and liturgics, and was an editor of the *English Hymnal*, 1906, and of *Songs of Praise*, 1925 and 1931, and with Martin Shaw of *Songs of Praise Discussed*, 1933. He died at London, May 29, 1936.

240. *Father most holy, merciful and tender.* (Tr.)

DECIUS, Nikolaus (1490?—1541), was probably a native of Hof in Upper Franconia, Bavaria. He became a monk and in 1519 provost of the cloister at Steterburg, near Wolfenbüttel. At the beginning of the Reformation he was converted to Lutheranism, and in 1522 he left Steterburg and went to Brunswick, where he became a master in the St. Katherine and Egidien School there. In 1523 Decius was invited by the burgesses of Stettin to work as evangelical preacher there with Paulus von Rhode. He became preacher at the church of St. Nicholas in 1526, when von Rhode was installed at St. Jacobs. He died suddenly at Stettin on March 2, 1541. The suddenness of his death gave rise to the rumor that his Roman Catholic enemies had poisoned him. The suspicion, however, lacks confirmation. Decius seems to have been a popular preacher and a good musician. His work was carried on under constant opposition from the Church of Rome.

33, 110, 237. ALLEIN GOTT IN DER HÖH'
146. *Lamb of God, pure and holy*
237. *All glory be to God on high*

DENICKE, David (1603—1680), was born at Zittau, Saxony, on January 31, 1603. He studied philosophy and law at the universities of Wittenberg and Jena and then was tutor in law for a time at Königsberg. After that Denicke traveled through Holland, England, and France. In 1629 he became tutor to the sons of Duke Georg of Brunswick-Lüneburg. In 1639 he was appointed director of the foundation of Bursfeld, and in 1642 he became a member of the Consistory at Hanover, where he died on April 1, 1680. Denicke was coeditor with J. Gesenius of various Hanoverian hymn-books published between the years 1646—1659.

417:1-5, 7. *How can I thank Thee, Lord*

DESSLER, Wolfgang Christoph (1660—1722), was born at Nürnberg, February 11, 1660. His father was a jeweler. He entered the University of Altdorf as a student of divinity, but was obliged to give up his studies on account of poverty and ill health. He returned to Nürnberg, where he earned his living as a proof-reader. In 1705 he was made headmaster of the School of the Holy Ghost at Nürnberg. This position he held until 1720 when he was forced to resign because of a paralytic stroke. He died March 11, 1722. He published a devotional book, *Seelenlust,* 1692, in which his best hymns appeared.

362. My soul's best Friend, what joy and blessing

DEXTER, Henry Martyn (1821—1890), was born at Plympton, Massachusetts, August 13, 1821. He graduated from Yale College in 1840 and from Andover Theological Seminary in 1844. He served as pastor of congregations in Manchester, New Hampshire, and in Boston, Massachusetts. He resigned his pastoral charge in 1867 to become editor of the *Congregationalist and Recorder.* He is the author of many books. He died November 13, 1890.

628. Shepherd of tender youth. (Tr.)

DIX, William Chatterton (1837—1898), son of John Dix, a surgeon of Bristol, was born in that city on June 14, 1837. He was educated at the Grammar School there for a mercantile life. Later he became manager in a marine insurance company in Glasgow. He was a scholarly layman. Several of his hymns are translated from the Greek. About 40 of his hymns are still in use. He wrote *Altar Songs,* 1867, *Verses on the Holy Eucharist,* 1867, and *Vision of All Saints,* 1871. He died at Clifton, September 9, 1898.

127. As with gladness men of old
276. "Come unto Me, ye weary"
573. To Thee, O Lord, our hearts we raise

DOANE, George Washington (1799—1859), was born at Trenton, New Jersey, May 27, 1799. He graduated from Union College, Schenectady, New York, in 1818; entered the Protestant Episcopal ministry in 1821; served as assistant minister at Trinity Church in New York until 1824; as professor at Trinity College, Hartford, Connecticut, until 1821; and as rector of Trinity Church in Boston from 1828 to 1832. He was made bishop of New Jersey in 1832. He founded St. Mary's Hall, Burlington, in 1837 and Burlington College in 1846. He died April 27, 1859. He published *Songs by the Way* in 1824.

355. Thou art the Way; to Thee alone
519. Beloved, "It is well!"

DODDRIDGE, Philip (1702—1751), was born in London on June 26, 1702, the last of the twenty children. He was a sickly child, and his life was despaired of when young. All twenty children, except Philip and a sister, died in infancy. Doddridge's grandfather was one of the ministers ejected under the Act of Uniformity. His father, Daniel, was a London oilman. Both parents died in 1715. His maternal grandfather was the Rev. John Bauman of Prague, Bohemia, who was exiled on account of his faith and came to London. His mother often sang to him the hymns of the Lutheran Church during his boyhood. After his parents' death he came under the care of the Rev. Samuel Clark at St. Albans. In 1718 he united with the Church. At the suggestion of his uncle, who was steward for the Duke of Bedford, the Dowager Duchess of Bedford offered Doddridge a university education for ordination in the Church of England, but Doddridge entered Mr. Jenning's Nonconformist Seminary at Kibworth instead. In 1730 he was ordained and in the same year married Mercy Maris, a lady of superior qualities. They had nine children. In 1723 Doddridge was chosen pastor at Kibworth. In 1729 he was appointed preceptor and divine to the Castle Hill Meeting at North Hampton. About two hundred pupils from England, Scotland, and Holland were prepared in his seminary, chiefly for the dissenting ministry, but partly for professions. The wide range of subjects — daily readings in Hebrew and Greek, algebra, trigonometry, Watts's logic, outline of philosophy and copious theology — is itself a proof of Doddridge's learning. In 1735 he received the degree of D. D. from the University of Aberdeen. At the funeral of his old pastor, the Reverend Samuel Clark, he contracted a cold which developed into pulmonary consumption. In the last stage of consumption he sailed for Lisbon, where he died October 26, 1751.

    66. *Hark the glad sound! The Savior comes*
   119. *Great God, we sing that mighty hand*
   302. *The Savior kindly calls*
   374:1, 2, 4, 6. *Grace! 'Tis a charming sound*
   434:1-4. *O God of Jacob, by whose hand*
   610. *And will the Judge descend*

    DÖVING, Carl (1867—1937), was born at Norddalen Norway, on March 21, 1867. He received private instruction from Bishop N. Astrup, missionary to South Africa. He served as a teacher in the Schreuder Mission before he emigrated to America in 1890. Here he attended Luther College (A. B. 1903) and Luther Seminary (C. T. 1896). He held pastorates at Red Wing, Minnesota, Montevideo, Minnesota, and Brooklyn, New York. His last charge was that of city missionary in Chicago. Döving served on the Hymnary Committee of the Norwegian Lutheran Church for years. He made extensive researches in the field of hymnology, especially in the English translations of German and Scandinavian hymns. While in the process of this study, he gathered an extensive library on these subjects. This library is now at Luther College, Decorah, Iowa. Döving is the author of many original translations, of which 32 are found in the *Lutheran Hymnary*. He died on October 2, 1937. He was an outstanding linguist. There were infirmary patients whom he visited as missionary in Chicago with whom he conversed in German, Icelandic, Norwegian, Swedish, Danish, and Greek. By means of his great collection of hymnals he was able to establish the following facts concerning the translations of some of the church's great hymns: that Luther's "A Mighty Fortress" has been translated into 183 languages; "Rock of Ages" into 150; "Nearer, my God, to Thee," into 142; "Just as I am," into 131; "Abide with me," into 131; "O come, all ye faithful," into 125; "Jesus, Lover of my soul," into 116; "What a Friend," into 110; "Onward, Christian soldiers," into 108; and "Jesus, lead Thou on," into 104.

    79. *Rejoice, this happy morn.* (Tr.)
   112. *To God the anthem raising.* (Tr.)
   217. *Oh, sing with exultation.* (Tr.)
   318. *Before Thee, God, who knowest all.* (Tr.)
   330. *I come to Thee, O blessed Lord.* (Tr.)
   337:2, 3. *Our Lord and God, oh, bless this day.* (Tr.)
   467. *Built on the Rock the Church doth stand.* (Tr.)

    DOWNTON, Henry (1818—1885), son of John Downton, sub-Librarian of Trinity College, Cambridge, was born at Pulverbatch, Shropshire, February 12, 1818; educated at Trinity College, Cambridge, where he graduated (B. A.) 1840 and (M. A.) 1843. Taking the holy orders in 1843, he became Curate of Bembridge, Isle of Wight (1843), and of Holy Trinity, Cambridge, 1847. In 1849 he was preferred to the Incumbency of St. John's Chatham. He went to Geneva as English Chaplain in 1857, and was appointed Rector of Hopton in 1873. He died at Hopton, June 8, 1885. He published a translation of Prof. Ernest Naville's *Lectures on Modern Atheism*, 1865; and *Holy Scriptures and the Temperance Question*, 1878. His hymns were contributed chiefly to the *Church of England Magazine*. In 1873 he collected these and published them as *Hymns and Verses*. His translations from the French of Alexandre Vinet are in this volume.

   121. *For Thy mercy and Thy grace*

    DRESE, Adam (1620—1701), was born in Thuringia, December 15, 1620, probably at Weimar; he studied music at Warsaw under Marco Scacchi; was director at Weimar from 1655; and afterwards held similar appointments to the Duke of Brunswick, and at Arnstadt, where he died, February 15, 1701, shortly before J. S. Bach came there. The following occurs in the notice of Drese's death in the Arnstadt church records: "On the 15th of February, 1701, at 10 o'clock in the evening, Herr Adam Drese fell asleep in God. . . . Age, 80 years, 2 months."

   410, 562. SEELENBRÄUTIGAM

DRETZEL, Kornelius Heinrich (1705—1773), was born at Nürnberg and served successively as organist of the churches of St. Egide, St. Laurentius, and St. Sébald, all in his native town. He was organist in the last-named church till he died in 1773. He published his *chorale* collection, *Des evangelischen Zions musikalische Harmonie*, Nürnberg, in 1731, which was the most complete collection of its kind published up to that time. 243, 298, 373, 404, 545. O DASS ICH TAUSEND

DRYDEN, John (1631—1700), was born at Aldwinkle, Northamptonshire, August 9, 1631, of Puritan parents. He was educated under Dr. Busby at Westminster and then continued his education at Trinity College, Cambridge. He was graduated in 1654, but continued to reside there for seven years although he had no fellowship. Dryden's Puritan background found expression in *Heroic Stanzas* on the death of Oliver Cromwell, 1658. However, Dryden turned Royalist two years later and celebrated the Restoration with two literary compositions, *Astraea Redux* and *A Panegyric on the Coronation*. In 1663 he married Lady Elizabeth Howard. The marriage was an unhappy one. In 1670 he was made Poet Laureate and Historiographer Royal. These posts he retained until the accession of William in 1688. In 1685 Dryden had joined the Roman Church and remained faithful even at the fall of James II. This straitened his means and compelled him to great literary exertion in his closing years. Dryden died in London on May 18, 1700, and was buried in Westminster Abbey. His works include plays, poems, odes, satires, and a translation of *Vergil*. In addition to his translation of *Veni, Creator Spiritus, Mentes*, he is believed to have translated a number of other Latin hymns, which appeared in *The Primer or Office of the B. V. Mary*, 1706. 236. Creator Spirit, by whose aid. (Tr.)

DUFFIELD, George, Junior (1818—1888), son of Dr. George Duffield, was born September 12, 1818, at Carlisle, Pennsylvania. He studied at Yale, graduating in 1837, and at Union Theological Seminary, graduating in 1840. He was ordained an elder in the Presbyterian Church and became pastor successively of churches at Brooklyn, New York, Bloomfield, New Jersey, Philadelphia, Adrian, Michigan, Galesburg, Illinois, Saginaw, Ann Arbor, and Lansing, Michigan. He spent his declining years with his son Samuel W. Duffield (author of *English Hymns*, 1886) in Bloomfield, New Jersey, where he died on July 6, 1888.
451. Stand up! — Stand up for Jesus

DWIGHT, John Sullivan (1813—1893), was born in Boston, May 13, 1813. He studied for the Unitarian ministry at Harvard Divinity School, graduated in 1836, and was ordained in the same year as pastor of the Unitarian congregation at Northampton, Massachusetts. He gave up his office to study literature and music. In 1852 he established Dwight's *Journal of Music*, which he owned and edited for thirty years. He died September 5, 1893.
577. God bless our native land. (Tr.)

DWIGHT, Timothy (1752—1817), was born at Northampton, Massachusetts, on May 14, 1752. His mother was a daughter of Jonathan Edwards. When he was thirteen, Dwight entered Yale, graduating in 1769. After teaching grammar school in New Hampshire for two years, he tutored until 1677. After a brief time of service as chaplain in the Revolutionary Army (he won the admiration of George Washington for patriotism and versatility), Dwight received a pastorate at Fairfield, Connecticut. He also taught in an academy. In 1795 he was appointed President of Yale, and with his accession a new and brilliant era for the college was inaugurated. When Dwight came to Yale, there were only four or five students professing Christianity. Through Dwight's series of sermons, "Theology Explained and Defended," delivered at the college chapel, one third of the student-body was won and revivals were inaugurated at Dartmouth, Amherst, and Williams. In 1797 he was requested "to revise Dr. Watts's *Imitation of the Psalms of David*, so as to accommodate them to the state of the American Church; and to supply the deficiency of those Psalms which

Dr. Watts had omitted." Two years later the work was completed, and this book, conjointly with Dr. Watts's *Psalms and Hymns*, became the Presbyterian *Book of Praise*. Dwight was an important American hymnologist and an outstanding educator, although for forty years he was handicapped by a serious affection of the eyes, which made it impossible for him to read consecutively more than fifteen minutes a day. He died in Philadelphia, January 11, 1817.

462. I love Thy kingdom, Lord

DYER, Samuel (1785—1835), a native of Wellshire, England, was born November 7, 1785. He came to America in his twenty-sixth year and established himself in New York as a choir leader and teacher of sacred music. He remained there about a year, then moved to Philadelphia for a three years' stay. After a visit to England in 1815 he was induced to settle in Baltimore, where he published his *New Selection of Sacred Music*, in 1817. His *Philadelphia Collection of Sacred Music*, 1828, second and third editions, contain valuable sketches of composers and information about Dyer himself. He taught singing schools in the Southeastern States, was a member of the Musical Fund Society of Philadelphia and for a time conductor of the New York Sacred Music Society. He died at Hoboken, New Jersey, July 20, 1835.

119. 447, 635, 637. MENDON

DYKES, John Bacchus (1823—1876), born at Hull, England, on March 10, 1823, was the son of a banker and the grandson of a well-known evangelical clergyman. Bacchus was the Christian name of his maternal grandfather. At the age of ten Dykes was assistant organist at his grandfather's church. He was first educated at Wakefield and then became a scholar of St. Catherine's, Cambridge. As an undergraduate at St. Catherine's College, Dykes helped found the University Musical Society with William Thomson, afterwards Lord Kelvin. In 1847 Dykes took holy orders and two years later was appointed precentor of Durham Cathedral. In 1861 the University of Durham conferred on him the musical doctorate. The following year Dykes was appointed Vicar of St. Oswald's in Durham. Here Dykes tried to introduce his High-church tendencies. In this he was opposed by his bishop. When Dykes applied to his bishop for a curate to assist him, he was told that he would get one only if he promised never to wear a colored stole, never to have anything to do with incense, and never to stand with his back to the congregation except when arranging the bread for communion. Dykes considered this action illegal, but the courts upheld the bishop. His biographer says that Dykes never recovered from this shock and that this killed him. He suffered a breakdown of his health in 1875 and died on January 22, 1876. Dykes wrote 300 hymn-tunes. Benson in his *The English Hymn* says that Dykes, together with Monk, Elvey, Gauntlett, and others, "crystallized the musical tendencies of the time into a definite form of Anglican hymn-tune, with restrained worship and yet appealing to the taste of the people."

164. ST. CROSS
246. NICAEA
277. VOX DILECTI
360. BEATITUDO
361. ST. AGNES
476. ALFORD
516. ST. MARY MAGDALENE

EBELING, Johann Georg (1620—1676), like Johann Crüger (*q. v.*), one of the "singers of Paul Gerhardt," was born in Lüneburg in July, 1620. He became cantor of St. Nicholas Church, Berlin, in 1662, and director of music at the College of St. Nicholas (Schulkollege am grauen Kloster) there, succeeding Johann Crüger. In 1668 he was appointed Professor of Music at the College of St. Charles (Caroline-Gymnasium), Stettin, where he died in 1676, the same year in which Paul Gerhardt died. His chief publication is *Pauli Gerhardt Geistliche Andachten*, 1666—67.

11, 391, 537. VOLLER WUNDER
523. WARUM SOLLT' ICH MICH DENN GRÄMEN

EBER, Paul (1511—1569), son of Johannes Eber, master tailor at Kitzingen, Bavaria, was born at Kitzingen, November 8, 1511. He was sent in 1523 to the Gymnasium at Ansbach, but, forced by illness to return home, was thrown from his horse and dragged more than a mile, remaining as a consequence deformed for life. In 1525 he entered the St. Lorenz School at Nürnberg and on June 1, 1532, he matriculated at the University of Wittenberg, his teachers being Luther and Melanchthon. In 1527 he became tutor in the Philosophical Faculty and four years later was appointed regular professor, first of Latin and then of Physics. In 1557 he was appointed professor of Hebrew and preacher of the Castle Church at Wittenberg. He acted as Melanchthon's secretary at the Colloquy at Worms, but he left for Wittenberg at Christmas. On September 4, 1558, he succeeded Bugenhagen as municipal preacher and general superintendent of the electoral circuit. In 1559 he received the degree of Doctor of Divinity from the University of Wittenberg. He died at Wittenberg December 10, 1569. Paul Eber, next to Luther, was the best poet of the Wittenberg school. His hymns, some of them written for his own children to sing to Luther's melodies, are distinguished for their childlike spirit and beautiful simplicity.

112. To God the anthem raising
254. Lord God, we all to Thee give praise. (Tr.)
522. When in the hour of utmost need
585. I fall asleep in Jesus' wounds (asc.)

EDMESTON, James (1791—1867), was born at Wapping, London, on September 10, 1791. Here he spent the first twelve years of his life. In 1803 the family moved to Hackney. In 1807 Edmeston was articled to a surveyor and architect. After nine years he entered business on his own account. Among his pupils was numbered Sir G. Gilbert Scott. In 1822 Edmeston moved to Homerton, where he resided for the remainder of his life. Here he served as churchwarden in the Church of St. Barnabas. Edmeston joined the Established Church at a comparatively early age, although he was an Independent by descent. In 1823 Edmeston married and became the father of many children. He was also interested in the London Orphan Asylum. His fondness for children was the source of inspiration for many of his children's hymns. When he died on January 7, 1867 at the age of seventy-six, Edmeston was well-known as an architect and a surveyor. His hymns number nearly two thousand. Some of his poems and hymns were written at the suggestion of Mrs. Jemima Thompson Luke. (His *Cottage Minstrel* was awarded the prize of twenty pounds which her father offered for fifty simple gospel hymns.) Others were written from week to week for the Sunday services of family prayer in his own household. For many years Edmeston contributed hymns of various degrees of merit to the *Evangelical Magazine*. His works include twelve volumes, mostly poems and hymns.

565. Savior, breathe an evening blessing

ELLERTON, John (1826—1893), son of George Ellerton, was born in London on December 16, 1826. He was educated at Trinity College, Cambridge, and graduated (B. A.) in 1849 and (M. A.) in 1854. After Ellerton took holy orders, he was successively Curate of Eastbourne, Sussex, 1850; Brighton, and Lecturer of St. Peter's, Brighton, 1852; Vicar of Crewe Green and Chaplain to Lord Crewe, 1860; Rector of Hinstock, 1872; of Barnes, 1876; and of White Roding, 1886. Ellerton's prose works include *The Holiest Manhood*, 1882, and *Our Infirmities*, 1883. He was editor of *Hymns for Schools and Bible Classes*, Brighton, 1859, and coeditor of the S. P. C. K. *Church Hymns*, 1871. In 1881 Ellerton published his *Notes and Illustrations of Church Hymns* in a folio edition. Although in general the notes are full and accurate, those on the older hymns are too general; while they are useful for the general reading public, they are a disappointment to the hymnologist. John Ellerton wrote about 50 original hymns and translated about ten from the Latin. He died at Torqual in 1893.

47. Savior, again to Thy dear name we raise
174. Throned upon the awe-full tree
202. "Welcome, happy morning." (Tr.)
621. O Father, all creating
632. In the name which earth and heaven

ELLIOTT, Charlotte (1789—1871), was the daughter of Charles Elliott, of Clapham and Brighton, England, and the granddaughter of the Rev. Henry Venn, an eminent Church of England divine. She was born March 18, 1789, and developed, at an early age, a passion for music and art. She was unusually well educated. At the age of thirty-two she became an invalid and remained such, at times suffering great pain, until her death on September 22, 1871, at Brighton. She was a member of the Church of England. Her hymns have in them a tenderness and sweetness born of much suffering and resignation. Although an invalid, she devoted her life to writing. Her *Invalid's Hymn Book* was published in various editions from 1834 to 1854 and contained altogether 115 of her hymns. Other poetic works written by her and containing hymns were: *Hours of Sorrow*, 1836; *Hymns for a Week*, 1839; *Thoughts in Verse on Sacred Subjects*, 1869. Some of her hymns were printed in her brother's somewhat important *Psalms and Hymns for Public, Private, and Social Worship*, 1835.

388. Just as I am, without one plea
418. My God, my Father, while I stray

ELLIOTT, Julia Anne, *née* Marshall (?—1841), daughter of John Marshall of Hallsteads, Ullswater, on a visit to Brighton with her father, met and afterwards, in 1833, married the Rev. Henry Venn Elliott, brother of Charlotte Elliott. She contributed, anonymously, eleven hymns to her husband's collection, *Psalms and Hymns*, 1835. In later editions her initials were added. She died in 1841 shortly after the birth of her fifth child.

8. Father, who the light this day

ELVEN, Cornelius (1791—1873), was born in St. Edmunds, Suffolk, where he lived and labored throughout his life. He was a pastor of the Baptist Church at Bury St. Edmunds for fifty years. When he took his charge, it numbered only forty members, but increased to more than 600. He was a very good friend of C. H. Spurgeon, who valued his friendship very highly and said of Elven that he was "a faithful servant of the Lord, and an intensely fervent and sincere preacher, filled with the fire of the spirit." He died in 1873.

323. With broken heart and contrite sigh

ELVEY, George Job (1816—1893), was born in Canterbury, England, on March 27, 1816, and baptized in the Presbyterian Chapel there. He was educated as a chorister at the Cathedral School and later studied under Dr. Crotch at the Royal Academy of Music in London. When Elvey was only nineteen, he was appointed organist and master of the boys at St. George's, Windsor, after which his well-known tune is named. In 1838 Elvey graduated from Oxford as Bachelor of Music and two years later was granted the Doctorate. As organist of St. George's for forty-seven years, Elvey had charge of the music for many important events connected with the royal house. He was knighted in 1871 after his composition of a *Festival March* for the wedding of Princess Louise. Elvey died at Windlesham, Surrey, December 9, 1893, and was buried outside the west front of St. George's Chapel.

71, 134, 566, 574, 584, ST. GEORGE
245, 304, 371, 388, 499. ST. CRISPIN
341. DIADEMATA

ESTE (Est, Easte, East) Thomas (1540?—1608?), was a famous printer. In 1591 he printed a new edition of Damon's *Psalms,* and in 1592 he printed the edition of the psalter, the tunes of which were harmonized by ten leading composers of the time, including Allison, Blanks, Cavendish, Cobbold, Douland, Farmer, Farnaby, Hooper, Johnson, and Kirbye. It was entitled *The whole book of Psalmes, with their wonted tunes in four parts.*

31, 336, 405, 445

EWING, Alexander (1830—1895), son of Alexander Ewing, M. D., was born in the parish of Old Machar, Aberdeen, January 3, 1830; educated for the law at Marischal College, Aberdeen, but entered the army in 1855; attained the rank of lieutenant-colonel; received a medal for services in China during the campaign of 1869; married in 1867 Juliana Horatia Gatty, second daughter of the Rev. Alfred Gatty, D. D., vicar of Ecclesfield, and subdean of York Cathedral. (She was well known for her writings for the young; died at Bath, 1885.) He studied music at Heidelberg; was associated with the Haydn Society of Aberdeen, and the Harmonie Choir under William Carnie. He died at Taunton in 1895.

448, 605, 613. EWING

FALCKNER, Justus (1672—1723), born on November 22, 1672, at Langenreinsdorf, Crimmitschau, Zwickau, Saxony, was the son of a Lutheran pastor. He studied theology under A. H. Francke at the University of Halle. As he had a feeling of inadequacy for the ministerial office, he turned to a secular calling instead, and on April 23, 1700, accepted the power of attorney for the sale of Penn's lands in Pennsylvania. It was a Swedish pastor, Andrew Rudmann, who persuaded him to accept the call to the Lutheran Church in New York. Falckner was ordained to the ministry in the Swedish Church at Wicaco, Philadelphia, on November 24, 1703, the first Lutheran clergyman ordained in America. He became pastor of the Lutheran congregations at New York and Albany, where he had a parish extending over two hundred miles. He also ministered to three congregations in New Jersey. In 1704 Falckner published a catechism, *Grondelycke Onderricht*, which was the first Lutheran book to be published on this continent. He died in 1723.

472. *Rise, ye children of salvation*

FARRANT, Richard (c. 1530—1580), was associated with the Chapel Royal during the reigns of Edward VI, Mary, and Elizabeth, with the exception of five years when he was master of choristers and lay vicar at St. George's Chapel, Windsor. His chief works are his service in G minor and the two anthems *Call to Remembrance*, and *Hide not Thy Face*. He died on November 30, 1580.

440. FARRANT

FAWCETT, John (1740—1817), was born on January 16, 1740, at Lidget Green, Yorks, England; first joined the Methodists through Geo. Whitefield's influence, but then became a Baptist and was ordained to the ministry in 1765 at Wainsgate and afterwards served a church at Hebden Bridge, Yorks, where he labored for the rest of his life, although he received some very important calls, one to succeed the famous Dr. J. Gill at the Carter Lane Church, London; another to become president of the Baptist Academy at Bristol. He was author of a number of religious prose works, including a devotional commentary on the Bible, and a large amount of sacred poetry. His *Hymns adapted to the Circumstances of Public Worship and Private Devotions*, 1782, contains 166 of his hymns. He died at Hebden Bridge in 1817.

50. *Lord, dismiss us with Thy blessing*
285. *How precious is the Book Divine*
464. *Blest be the tie that binds*

FICK, Herman (1822—1885), outstanding poet among the fathers of the Evangelical Lutheran Synod of Missouri, Ohio, and Other States, was brought to America by Wyneken's *Appeal* in 1846; became pastor at New Melle, Mo.; in 1850 removed to the pastorate at Bremen, a suburb of St. Louis; in 1854 he became pastor of Trinity Lutheran Church, Detroit. Ill health forced him to resign this large charge. He then served our church at Collinsville, Illinois, for thirteen years, and spent the last thirteen years of his life as pastor in Boston, Massachusetts. He published his *Lutherbuch* and contributed articles and poems to *Der Lutheraner*, and other German-language periodicals. <center>498. *Rise, Thou Light of Gentile nations*</center>

FIGULUS, Wolfgang (1520—1591), was born at Naumburg. He lived in Leipzig from 1548 to 1550 and appears to have studied at the University there. In 1551 he accepted the position as "Kantor" and "Kollege" of the Fürstenschule at Meissen, where he succeeded Michael Voigt. Figulus was pensioned in 1588 but remained in more or less active service in both church and school until about 1591, the time of his death.

112. HELFT MIR GOTT'S GÜTE PREISEN

FILITZ, Friedrich (1804—1876), was born at Arnstadt, in Thuringia, March 16, 1804. He studied philosophy, in which he received the degree of doctor; resided at Berlin from 1843 to 1847, where he worked with Ludwig Erck, removing in the latter year to Munich, where he died, December 7, 1876. He published his *Vierstimmiges Choralbuch*, Berlin, 1847, a book of four-part tunes for Bunsen's *Allgemeines Gesang- und Gebetbuch*.

158, 229, WEM IN LEIDENSTAGEN

FINDLATER, Sarah, née Borthwick (1823—1907), was born November 26, 1823, sister of Jane Borthwick *(q.v.)* in Edinburgh. She married the Rev. Eric John Findlater, Scottish Free Church minister at Lochernhead, Perthshire. With her sister Jane she translated from the German *Hymns from the Land of Luther*, 1854, 53 of the 122 translations being from her pen. She died at Torquay in 1907.

72. *Rejoice, rejoice believers.* (Tr.)
626. *O happy home, where Thou art loved most dearly.* (Tr.)

FINK, Gottfried Wilhelm, Ph. D. (1783—1846), was born on March 7, 1783, at Sulza, Thuringia. He studied theology at Leipzig and served as assistant pastor there from 1809 to 1812. He was director of his own educational institute. From his youth he was interested in music and developed his talents at Leipzig. From 1827 to 1841 he was editor of the *Leipziger Allgemeine Musikalische Zeitung;* also teacher of music at the University of Leipzig. He was active as composer and poet. He published a large number of musical works and was collaborator on Schilling's *Universallexikon der Tonkunst*, on Ersch and Gruber's *Encyklopädie*, and on the eighth edition of Brockhaus's *Konversationslexikon*. He died August 27, 1846.

109, 620. BETHLEHEM

FISCHER (Vischer), Christoph (1520—1597), was born in 1520 at Joachimsthal; studied theology at Wittenberg, 1540—1544; was ordained, 1544, at Wittenberg to serve as pastor at the nearby Jüterbogk; became cathedral preacher and superintendent at Smalcald, 1522; pastor and general superintendent at Meiningen, 1571; court preacher and assistant superintendent at Celle, 1574; chief pastor at St. Martin's Church in Halberstadt, 1577; returned to Celle as general superintendent of Lüneburg in 1583; died at Celle in October, 1597. He was a voluminous writer.

173. *Lord Jesus, we give thanks to Thee*

FISCHER, Eberhard Ludwig (1695—1773), was born at Aichelberg in Württemberg on August 6, 1695. He was coeditor of the *Württemberger Gesangbuch* of 1741 with Dr. Tafinger. He was prelate of Adelberg and Consistorialrath at Hohenasperg when he died in 1773.

485. *Lord Jesus, who art come*

FORTUNATUS, Venantius Honorius Clementianus (c. 530—609), was born at Ceneda, near Treviso, Italy. At an early age he was converted to Christianity at Aquileia; received his education at Ravenna and Milan. While a student at Ravenna, where he excelled in oratory and poetry, Fortunatus almost became blind. He recovered his sight, as he believed, miraculously, by anointing his eyes with some oil sent by a friend, Gregory of Tours, which the latter had taken from a lamp that burned before the altar of St. Martin of Tours in a church of Ravenna. This induced Fortunatus to make a pilgrimage (565) to the shrine of St. Martin at Tours, and this pilgrimage resulted in his spending the rest of his life in Gaul. Possessed of a pleasing personality, fond of high living, endowed with poetic gifts, he was popular in all circles. In Gaul he formed a romantic but platonic friendship with Queen Rhadegunda, the daughter of Bertharius, king of the Thuringians, and the wife, though separated from him, of Lothair I (Clothaire), king of Neustria. Rhadegunda had left her throne to found the convent of St. Croix at Poitiers. She induced Fortunatus to enter the service of the Church. To her and Agnes, Rhadegunda's former maid and appointed by her head of the convent, he composed the most extravagant poetic effusions. After Rhadegunda's death Fortunatus was made bishop of Poitiers in 599. A quarto edition of Fortunatus's *Works* was published in Rome in 1786. This work includes his *Life of St. Martin of Tours*. Fortunatus wrote many hymns; however, his *Hymns for all the Festivals of the Christian Year* is lost. Many of his hymns are to the Virgin. Indeed, Fortunatus was the "first of the Christian poets to begin that worship of the Virgin Mary which rose to a passion and sank to idolatry." He was "one of the last who, amid the advancing tide of barbarism, retained anything of the old classic culture."

168. *The royal banners forward go*
202. *Welcome, happy morning*

FOSTER, Frederick William (1760—1835), was born at Bradford, England on August 1, 1760. He was educated at Fulneck, near Leeds, and at Barby in Prussian Saxony. Foster served in the Moravian ministry and in 1818 was consecrated a bishop of the Moravian Church. He compiled the *Moravian Hymn Book* of 1801 and the later *Supplement*, 1808, and the revised edition, 1826. He died at Ockbrook, near Danby, April 12, 1835.

4. *God Himself is present.* (Tr.)

FRANCIS, Benjamin (1734—1799), was born in Wales. He was baptized at the age of 15, and at 19 he began to preach. He studied at the Bristol Baptist College. In 1757 he moved to Horsley in Gloucestershire, where he died in 1799. Though churches in London tempted him again and again, asking him to come to London and serve as pastor, yet he remained with his congregation until his death. He was a writer especially of Welsh hymns and published a collection, *Alleluia*, 1774, to which he contributed 103 hymns. In the second volume, 1786, he contributed an additional group of 91 hymns.

346. *Jesus! and shall it ever be*
638. *In loud exalted strains*

FRANCK, Johann (1618—1677), was the son of Johann Franck, an advocate and councilor at Guben, Brandenburg, where Johann Franck, Jr., was born on June 1, 1618. After his father's death in 1620, Johann was adopted by his uncle, the town judge, Adam Tielckau, who sent him for his education to the schools at Guben, Cottbus, Stettin, and Thorn. In 1638 Franck matriculated as student of law at the University of Königsberg, the only German university left undisturbed by the Thirty Years' War. Here his religious spirit, his love of nature, and his friendship with such men as Simon Dach and Heinrich Held, preserved him from sharing in the excesses of his fellow-students. The former, a pious and prominent professor of poetry, guided the development of Franck's poetic talent. Upon his mother's request Franck returned to Guben in 1640 to be with her in those times of war during which Guben frequently suffered from the presence of both Swedish and Saxon troops. In May, 1645, Franck commenced practice as a lawyer and very soon became well and favorably known on account of his poetic and professional ability. In 1648 he was elected burgess and councilor and in 1661 burgomaster. In 1671 he was appointed the deputy from Guben to the Landtag (Diet) of Lower Lusatia. His hymns were published as *Geistliches Sion*, Guben, 1674. On the bicentenary of his death, June 18, 1877, a monumental tablet to his memory was affixed to the outer wall of the Stadtkirche at Guben. Johann Franck is ranked next to Paul Gerhardt as a hymn-writer of his period. Of his 110 hymns, which are more subjective than Gerhardt's and the earlier Lutheran hymns, over one half are in use. Franck marks the transition from the objective form of church song prevalent till his time, to the more individual and mystical type. His leading idea is the union of the soul with its Savior.

138. *Thou Light of Gentile nations*
305. *Soul, adorn thyself with gladness*
326. *Lord, to Thee I make confession*
347. *Jesus, priceless Treasure*

FRANCK, Melchior (c. 1575—1639), was born in Zittau and studied at Nürnberg. In 1601 he served as "Musiker des Rates" in that city. Two or three years later he was called as Hofkapellmeister to Koburg, where he remained until his death, June 1, 1639. His first compositions were published in his *Contrapuncti Compositi*, 1602, and his later works in many other collections, the best known of which is *Geistlicher Musicalischer Lustgarten*, 1616.

619. JERUSALEM, DU HOCHGEBAUTE STADT

FRANCK, Salomo (1659—1725), son of Jakob Franck, was born at Weimar on March 6, 1659. Little is known of his early history. He probably studied at Jena. He held several governmental appointments during his life. He also had severe family afflictions to bear. He died at Weimar, July 11, 1725. Franck also wrote much secular poetry. He was a member of the famous Fruit-bearing Society. As a hymnwriter he is distinguished for his ease, correctness, and adaptation to popular understanding and to congregational singing. His hymns total 330. He published *Geistliche Poesie*, Weimar, 1685; *Geist- und Weltliche Poesien*, Jena, Vol. I, 1711, Vol. II, 1716.

402. O God, forsake me not
529. I leave all things to God's direction

FRANK, Peter (1616—1675), was born at Schleusingen on September 27, 1616, son of a merchant. He studied theology at Jena about 1636. In 1640 he was at the University at Altorf. Frank worked as a Hofmeister from 1643 to 1645, when he received a position as a pastor. As such he served churches in Thüngen, Rossfeld, Rodach, Gleussen, and Herreth. He died June 22, 1675.

540. FANG DEIN WERK

FRANZMANN, Martin (1907—   ), was born at Lake City, Minnesota, January 29, 1907, son of the Rev. William Franzmann and Else, *née* Griebling; educated at Northwestern College, Watertown, Wisconsin (B. A. 1928), and the Evangelical Lutheran Theological Seminary, Thiensville, Wisconsin, and Chicago University; he is now professor at Northwestern College (since 1936). He married Alice Bentzin in 1933 and has two sons.

470. Rise again, ye lion-hearted. (Tr.)

FREYLINGHAUSEN, Johann Anastasius (1670—1739), born at Gandersheim, Brunswick, Germany, on December 2, 1670; studied at Jena, Erfurt, and at Halle. In 1695 he became August Herman Francke's assistant at Glaucha, and when Francke became pastor at St. Ulrich's, in Halle, 1715, Freylinghausen became his colleague. In the same year he married Francke's only daughter, Anastasia, whose sponsor he was. After Francke's death in 1727, he succeeded him as pastor of St. Ulrich's and Director of Francke's Institutions. He died February 12, 1739. He published the *Geistreiches Gesangbuch*, 1704, and *Neues Geistreiches Gesangbuch*, 1704. He himself composed twenty-two melodies. As hymn-writer Freylinghausen was the best of the Pietistic School.

73. MACHT HOCH DIE TÜR (second tune)

FREYSTEIN, Johann Burkhard (1671—1718), a pious lawyer, was born at Weissenfels, April 18, 1671, the son of A. S. Freystein, vice-chancellor of Duke August of Saxony and inspector of the Gymnasium at Weissenfels. He received his education at the University of Leipzig where he studied law, mathematics, philosophy, and architecture. He resided for some time at Berlin and Halle, and then went to Dresden as an assistant to a lawyer. After graduating (LL. D.) at Jena in 1695) he began an independent legal practice at Dresden. In 1703 he became Rath at Gotha, but returned to Dresden in 1709 as Hof- and Justizrath, and was also, in 1713, appointed a member of the Board of Works. Enfeebled by his professional labors, Freystein died of dropsy at Dresden, April 1, 1718.

446. Rise, my soul, to watch and pray

FRIESE, Heinrich. We have been unable to find any details of Friese's life, except that he published a *Choralbuch* in 1712.

171. O WELT, SIEH HIER (first tune)

FRITSCH, Ahasverus (1629—1701), was born on December 16, 1629, at Mücheln on the Geissel near Merseburg. His father was Andreas Fritsch, mayor of the town, and his mother was Esther, *née* Hesse. Ahasverus was the eighth of eleven children. His early youth was spent during the turbulous period of the Thirty Years' War. When he was only two years old, his parents had to flee to Voigtland, as their native town was burned. During his youth Fritsch fled from robbers, plunderers, and soldiers; he hid in graves, cellars, and bushes; often he was robbed of the very clothes he was wearing. When he was fourteen, Fritsch lost his father. Nevertheless, his mother sent him to the Gymnasium at Halle. Here he worked manually and intellectually for six years until July, 1650, when he went to Jena and studied under the learned jurist J. Georg Adam Struve. Poverty greatly interrupted his education, but Fritsch finished his course in 1654. In 1657 he became the tutor of the young Count Albert Anton von Schwarzburg-Rudolstadt. He was greatly admired by the count's family and received various preferments. In October, 1661, he was made a Doctor of Law by the University of Jena. Later he became chancellor of the university and president of the consistory of Rudolstadt. In February of 1662 he married, and his wife, Dorothea Maria, bore him four sons and five daughters. Seven of the children outlived him. Fritsch was a good statesman and the editor of two hymn-collections and a writer on antiquarian, legal, and other subjects. The hymn "Liebster Immanuel, Herzog der Frommen," is ascribed to him.

99, 272, 430. WAS FRAG' ICH NACH DER WELT

FÜGER (Fuger, Fugger), Caspar(?). Two Lutheran clergymen of this name, apparently father and son, lived in Dresden in the 16th century. The elder (d. 1592) resided at Torgau for some time and was later court preacher at Dresden to Duke Heinrich. Various works appeared under his name between 1564 and 1592. The younger (d. July 24, 1617) was apparently born at Dresden, where he was later third master and then Conrector in the Kreuzschule. He was subsequently ordained diaconus.

107. *We Christians may rejoice today*

FUNCKE, Friedrich (1642—1699), was born at Nossen in the Harz, baptized on March 27, 1642, and was educated at Freiberg and Dresden. Later he became cantor at Perleberg. In 1664 he was appointed Stadt-Cantor at Lüneburg and in 1694 pastor at Römstadt, where he died. Funcke revised the *Lüneberg Gesangbuch* in 1686 and contributed 43 melodies and 7 hymns of his own.

215. *Draw us to Thee*

GARDINER, William (1770—1853), born at Leicester, was a stocking manufacturer, greatly interested in music. In youth, under the *nom de plume* "W. G. Leicester" he published a collection of his own songs and duets. In 1815 he published *Sacred Melodies* in six volumes, containing tunes of the best masters. He also published *The Music of Nature, Music and Friends*. He died at Leicester in 1853.

436. BELMONT

GARVE, Karl Bernard (1763—1841), was born January 24, 1763, in Jeinsen near Hanover, where his father was a farmer. He was educated in the schools of the Moravian Brethren at Zeist, Neuweid, Niesky, and at the seminary of Barby. In 1784 he was appointed teacher at the pädagogium of Niesky and five years later at Barby. He served as minister in various congregations of the Brethren from 1799 until 1836, when he retired from the ministry. He spent the rest of his years at Herrnhut, where he died June 21, 1841. Garve was one of the leading hymn-writers among the Moravian Brethren. His hymns are aglow with his intense love for the Savior, Scriptural, beautiful in expression, forceful, and elegant in style.

188. *Hallelujah! Jesus lives!*

GASTORIUS, Severus (c. 1650), was Cantor in Jena, 1675, and there wrote his famous tune for the hymn of his friend Samuel Rodigast. (See Hymn No. 521.) Zahn holds that von Winterfeld's view that Johann Paschelbel wrote the tune is not tenable. No further details on Gastorius's life are available.

521. WAS GOTT TUT

GATES, Mary Cornelia, *née* Bishop (c. 1850), daughter of William S. Bishop of Rochester, New York, lived there in the middle of the 19th century. In 1873 she married Merrill E. Gates, secretary to the United States Indian Commissioners.

506. *Send Thou, O Lord, to every place*

GELLERT, Christian Fürchtegott (1715—1769), the son of a Lutheran pastor, was born at Hainichen in the Saxon Harz on July 4, 1715. After preliminary schooling at Meissen, he entered the University of Leipzig to pursue theological studies. After his graduation Gellert became an assistant to his father. However, he was forced to turn to some other profession since he had a poor memory and the use of a manuscript in the pulpit was not tolerated in the Lutheran Church in his day. Consequently he became the domestic tutor of the sons of Herr von Lüttichau in 1739, but two years later returned to Leipzig to superintend the studies of a nephew at the university and to resume his own studies. Gellert graduated in 1744 (M.A.) in the faculty of Belles Lettres. The following year Gellert became private tutor or lecturer in the philosophical faculty. As a professor Gellert was most popular with his students, among whom were Goethe and Lessing. He took a warm interest in his students' personal conduct and welfare. His lectures were much favored, not only because of their charm of style, but also because of their substance and high moral tone. Gellert's *Fables*, spirited and humorous, won him fame and universal recognition as a German classicist. In 1751 he was appointed extraordinary professor of philosophy, and in this capacity he lectured on poetry, rhetoric, and moral philosophy. Ten years later he was offered an ordinary professorship, but declined because of ill health, having had a delicate constitution since childhood. After 1752 Gellert suffered greatly from hypochondria and died at Leipzig on December 13, 1769.

201. *Jesus lives! The victory's won*

GERHARDT, Paul (1607—1676). In the Lutheran church at Luebden in Germany there hangs a life-size painting of Paul Gerhardt. Beneath it is the inscription: "Theologus in cribro Satanae versatus" (A divine sifted in Satan's sieve). That inscription may be said to epitomize the sad life-story of Germany's great psalmist. Paul Gerhardt was born on March 12, 1607, in Gräfenhaynichen, a village between Halle and Wittenberg. His father was Christian Gerhardt, mayor of the village. He died before Paul reached maturity. During his youth Paul experienced much suffering because of the Thirty Years' War that was raging. From 1622 to 1627 he attended school at Grimma. On January 2, 1628, he began the study of theology at the University of Wittenberg, where he remained until at least April, 1642, and then went to Berlin, where he became family tutor in the home of Andreas Barthold, an attorney. Here in a Christian atmosphere his gift of song began to develop and bear fruit. Many of Gerhardt's hymns were published in 1648 in Johann Crüger's *Praxis Pietatis Melica* (q. v.). In 1651 Gerhardt was called to Mittenwalde as provost. When he started his duties of his first settled position, Gerhardt was forty-four years old. Four years later he married Anna Maria Berthold. Their first child, a daughter, died in infancy. The income of the family was sparse. Gerhardt also experienced unpleasantness because of the jealousy of a colleague. In 1657 Gerhardt accepted a call to be third assistant pastor of the Church of St. Nicholas in Berlin. Here he continued to write hymns. Gerhardt was recognized as the most popular preacher in the city. Later he became known also for his philanthropy. At this time there was bitter opposition between the Lutherans and the Calvinists. Since Gerhardt was not as violent as others in condemning the opposition, he gained the respect and esteem of many of the leaders of the Reformed group, including the Duchess Louise. The elector Friedrich Wilhelm the Great, a Calvinist, arranged conferences between the leading men of both parties. But all such attempts failed, and finally the elector issued an edict forbidding ministers to attack each other's doctrine and confession. Later he required all the Lutheran ministers to sign a document compelling them to follow the order of the edict. No Lutheran minister who wished to remain true to his confession could agree to this. Gerhardt believed that signing the document would be to compromise the faith. He was sick at the time, but nevertheless he summoned the Lutheran ministers to his bedside and admonished them to stand firm and not to yield to the demands of the elector. On February 9, 1666, Gerhardt was called before his own consistory and asked to sign the famous document. He was given a week in which to consider the matter, but he immediately said that he would not sign. Gerhardt was then deposed from office and even prohibited from conducting private meetings for worship in his own house. Gerhardt called this his "Berlin martyrdom." Just before this unfortunate occurrence he had lost three of his five children, and now a son died, and his wife was seriously ill. Petitions from citizens, laborers, the town council, and even from the wife of the elector led the elector to reinstate Gerhardt on January 9, 1667. But the elector had done this with the understanding that Gerhardt would preach in harmony with the aforementioned edict. Under such a condition Gerhardt refused. In the same year the elector appointed Gerhardt's successor. As he did not take up his work until late in 1668, Gerhardt received the income from the office until then. After that he was supported by charitable members of his congregation. Gerhardt's wife died at Eastertide, 1668. Now only a son, aged six, remained. In May, 1669, Gerhardt was called to the office of archdeacon of Lübben. Here he labored for seven years with success until his death. Paul Gerhardt was an excellent pastor and one of the best, if not the best, of the hymn-writers of the Lutheran Church in Germany. He wrote 123 hymns in all. Not even the hymns of Martin Luther are used so generally throughout the Christian world as are those of Gerhardt. More of the beautiful lyrics of this sweet singer have found their way into the English language than the hymns of any other German hymn-writer, and with the passing of years their popularity increases rather than diminishes. In Gerhardt's hymns is found the transition to the modern subjective note in hymnody. He died at Lübben, June 7, 1676.

  25. *I will sing my Maker's praises*
  58. *O Lord, how shall I meet Thee*
  77. *All my heart this night rejoices*
  81. *O Jesus Christ, Thy manger is*
  90. *Come, your hearts and voices raising*
 108. *We sing, Immanuel, Thy praise*
 122. *Now let us come before Him*
 142. *A Lamb goes uncomplaining forth*
 171. *Upon the cross extended*
 172. *O sacred Head, now wounded*
 192. *Awake, my heart, with gladness*
 228. *Oh, enter, Lord, Thy temple*
 349. *Jesus, Thy boundless love to me*
 520. *Commit whatever grieves thee*
 523. *Why should cross and trial grieve me?*
 528. *If God Himself be for me*
 535. *Rejoice my heart, be glad and sing*
 554. *Now rest beneath night's shadows*
 569. *O Lord, I sing with lips and heart*
 581. *All ye who on this earth do dwell*
 586. *A pilgrim and a stranger*

  GERMANUS OF CONSTANTINOPLE, ST. (634—734), was born in Constantinople of a patrician family. He was ordained there and subsequently became the Bishop of Cyzicus. He was present at the Synod of Constantinople in 712, which restored the Monothelite heresy, but in after years he condemned the heresy. In 715 he was made the Patriarch of Constantinople. In 730 St. Germanus was driven from that see, not without blows, for refusing to yield to the Iconoclastic Emperor, Leo III, the Isaurian.   76. *A great and mighty wonder*

GESENIUS, Justus (1601—1673), was the son of Joachim Gesenius, pastor at Essbeck, Hanover, where Justus was born on July 6, 1601. He studied theology at Helmstedt and Jena and was awarded his M.A. from the latter university in 1628. The following year Gesenius became pastor of St. Magnus's Church at Brunswick. In 1636 he became court chaplain and preacher at the Cathedral in Hildesheim and in 1642 councilor and general superintendent of Hanover. Gesenius and David Denicke (q.v.) were coeditors of the Hanoverian hymn-books of 1646—1660. They did not give any of the author's names, and they recast many of the hymns according to the poetical canons of Martin Opitz. In some cases they destroyed very much, but their book was not as bad as the recasts of the rationalistic period. In spite of their shortcomings these hymnals met with favor and were widely used. Gesenius was an accomplished and influential theologian, a famous preacher, who distinguished himself by his efforts to further the catechetical instruction of the laity.

152. *When o'er my sins I sorrow*

GIARDINI, Felice de (1716—1796), was born in Turin, Piedmont, Italy, on April 12, 1716. He studied singing, clavier, and harmony in Milan. He became a celebrated violinist in both Italy and Germany, made his London debut in 1750, where he became the leader and in 1856 impressario of the Italian Opera. Giardini afterwards served Sir William Hamilton, British ambassador to the Sardinian court at Naples. When he returned to London five years later, Giardini found that his popularity had waned considerably. He traveled to Moscow, hoping for better recognition, but was disappointed. He died there in poverty in 1796. Giardini composed a great number of operas, quartets, concertos, sonatas, and other pieces. Capricious in character, he seems to have had few friends and many enemies, but he is considered one of the greatest musicians of the 18th century.

227, 239, 508. ITALIAN HYMN

GIBBONS, Orlando (1583—1625), was born in Cambridge, England. He joined the choir of King's College at 13 and at 21 became organist of the Chapel Royal. In 1619 he was King's musician for the virginals, and after receiving his degree of Doctor of Music from Oxford in 1622, he was made organist of Westminster Abbey. He played the organ for the funeral of James I. He died at Canterbury on June 5, 1625, while preparing to attend Charles I at his marriage with Henrietta Maria of France. Gibbons was one of the greatest of the polyphonic writers. The tunes for Wither's *Hymns and Songs of the Church,* 1623, are from his pen.

234. LIGHT DIVINE

GIESCHEN, Gerhard (1899—   ), was born in Helenville, Wisconsin, June 28, 1899, son of John Gieschen and Anna, née Bieck; educated at Concordia College, Milwaukee; Northwestern College, Watertown, Wisconsin, and the Lutheran Theological Seminary at Wauwatosa (now at Thiensville), Wisconsin. He has served pastorates at Rib Falls, Wisconsin; Marshfield, Wisconsin; Leigh, Nebraska; and Wayne, Nebraska. He married Lucille Graber. They have four children. Gieschen has published religious articles in *Faith-Life.*

126. *Arise and shine in splendor.* (Tr.)

GILMAN, Samuel (1791—1858), was born at Gloucester, Massachusetts, on February 16, 1791. He received his early education at the academy at Atkinson, New Hampshire, and later attended Harvard College, graduating in 1811. He served as clerk in a bank at Salem for several years. In 1817 he returned to Harvard and served as tutor for two years. In 1819 he was called to serve the Unitarian church at Charleston, South Carolina, as pastor. He held this position until his death on February 9, 1858, while he was on a visit at Kingston, Massachusetts.

303. *This child we dedicate to Thee.* (Tr.)

GLÄSER, Carl Gotthelf (1784—1829), was born at Weissenfels, Germany, on May 4, 1784, was taught music by his father, and later attended St. Thomas's School in Leipzig. In 1801 he began to study law at the Leipzig University, but he soon gave it up for music. He studied music under J. A. Hiller, A. E. Müller, and Campagnoli. He settled in Barmen, where he taught piano, violin, and voice. He was known as a director of choruses and composed many chorals and songs. He died April 16, 1829.

281. AZMON

GOSS, Sir John (1800—1880), was born at Fareham, Hants, England, December 27, 1800; son of Joseph Goss, organist of that place. He became chorister in Chapel Royal under John Stafford Smith, 1811, and was a pupil of Thomas Attwood. He was organist of St. Luke's, Chelsea, 1824; organist of St. Paul's Cathedral in 1838, succeeding Thomas Attwood. He resigned in 1872 and received the honor of knighthood. He was also composer to the Chapel Royal from 1856 to 1872. He received his Mus. D., Cambridge, in 1876. He died at Brixton, London, May 10, 1880. He was a composer of much excellent church music.

220. BEVAN

GOULD, John Edgar (1822—1875), was born at Bangor, Maine. He was for a time associated with a New York firm dealing in pianos and other musical merchandise. With a Mr. Fischer, Gould managed a music establishment in Philadelphia. He conducted choruses, composed a number of psalm- and hymn-tunes, and published a number of music-books. Gould toured Southern Europe and Northern Africa and died in Algiers, Africa, March 4, 1875.

649. PILOT

GOUNOD, Charles François (1818—1893), was born in Paris, June 17, 1818; entered the Conservatoire in 1836, studying under Halévy and others, gaining the "Grand Prix de Rome" in 1839. He is well known by his opera *Faust*, and his oratorios *The Redemption* and *Mors et Vita*. He died at Saint-Cloud, October 17, 1893.

558. EVENING HYMN

GRAMANN (Graumann), Johann (Poliander) (1487—1541), was born in Neustadt, in the Bavarian Palatinate, on July 5, 1487. After he finished his studies at Leipzig (M. A. 1516; B. D. 1520), he was appointed rector of the St. Thomas's School in Leipzig. In 1519 he attended the disputation between Eck, Luther, and Carlstadt as the amanuensis of Eck. After the disputation Gramann espoused the cause of the Reformation, because he noticed that Luther supported his opinions with references to Scripture, and he was moved by Luther's strong appeal to the dictates of conscience, rather than by Eck's cleverness in the art of disputation. He decided to leave Leipzig because of strained relations with the Catholic duke, George of Saxony, and went to Wittenberg to join Luther and Melanchthon. In 1523 he was appointed preacher at Würzburg. At the outbreak of the Peasants' War in 1525, he went to Nürnberg and was appointed preacher to the nunnery of St. Clara in that city. Upon Luther's recommendation he was called by the Margrave Albrecht of Brandenburg to come to the Margrave's province and to assist the cause of the Reformation there. In this work he assisted John Briesmann. Gramann became pastor of the Altstadt church in Königsberg in October, 1525. Later he incurred the displeasure of the count by opposing the Anabaptists, who had gained favor with the count and the people of the congregation. In a public disputation ordered by the count, Gramann successfully refuted the Anabaptists on the basis of Scripture and saved the province from this false doctrine. He also opposed the Schwenckfeldians and was active in organizing the evangelical schools of the province. Gramann died at Königsberg on April 29, 1541.

34. *My soul, now bless Thy Maker*

GRANT, Sir Robert (1779—1838), the second son of Charles Grant, M. P., and a director of the East India Company, was born in Bengal, India. When Robert was six years old, the family moved to London. He was educated at Magdalen College,

Cambridge, and called to the English Bar in 1807. In 1826, as his father had been, Grant became M. P. for Inverness. While in Parliament, he introduced a bill to remove restrictions imposed upon the Jews. The historian Macaulay made his maiden speech in Parliament in support of this measure. In 1831 Grant became a privy councilor, in 1832 Judge Advocate General, and two years later was appointed Governor of Bombay, being knighted at the same time. Grant died at Dalpoorie, Western India, where a medical college bearing his name has been erected as a memorial to him. Grant wrote twelve hymns; they were published posthumously by his brother, Lord Glenelg, in 1839 under the title *Sacred Poems*.

17. Oh, worship the King
166. Savior, when in dust to Thee

GREGOR, Christian (1723—1801), was born on January 1, 1723, at Dirsdorf, near Peilau, in Silesia. In 1742 he became a teacher in Herrnhut and later a director of music in the Moravian Brethren's congregation at Herrnhag (1748) and then at Zeist (1749). In 1753 Gregor returned to Herrnhut as treasurer of the Brethren's Board of Direction. He was ordained diaconus in 1756, presbyter in 1767, and bishop of the Brethren's Church in 1789. Gregor died of a paralytic stroke after attending a meeting on November 6, 1801.

410. Jesus, lead Thou on

GRIEG, Edvard Hagerup (1843—1907), Norwegian composer and pianist, was born at Bergen June 15, 1843. His great-grandfather, Alexander Greig, emigrated from Scotland to Norway after the battle of Culloden (1745) and changed his name to Grieg. His father was British consul at Bergen. He married Gesine Judith Hagerup, a descendant of Kjeld Stub, from whom Edvard inherited his musical talent. At the advice of Ole Bull, Edvard was sent to the Leipzig Conservatory at the age of fifteen. He studied under Plaidy, Wenzel, Moscheles, E. F. Richter, Hauptmann, and Reinecke. From Leipzig he went to Copenhagen, where he studied under Niels Gade and Emil Hartmann. From 1864 on he was active at Copenhagen and Christiania, conducting, composing, and teaching. He married his cousin Nin Hagerup in 1867. An excellent vocalist, she helped gain favor for his songs. When Franz Liszt became interested in Grieg, the Norwegian government gave him financial aid to go to Rome, and Liszt's advice helped him to persevere in his efforts to use his genius in the interest of Northern music. Grieg did for Norway what Chopin did for Poland, Liszt for Hungary, and Dvorak for Bohemia: He created a new national art. He died suddenly Sept. 4, 1907, while boarding a steamer which was to take him to London to fill some concert engagements.

656. GREAT WHITE HOST

GRIGG, Joseph (c. 1722—1768), was born of poor parents and trained for the trade of a mechanic. He became assistant to the Rev. Thomas Bures of the Presbyterian Church, Silver Street, London, in 1743, after whose death, in 1747, he retired, marrying a lady of property. He died at Walthamstow, Essex, October 29, 1768.

346. Jesus! and shall it ever be
650. Behold a stranger at the door

GRODZKI, Michal (c. 1550). There seem to be no data available on this author.

169. Jesus Christ, our Lord most holy

GRUBER, Franz (1787—1863), was born in Hochburg, Upper Austria, on November 25, 1787. He served most of his life as Roman Catholic schoolmaster and parish organist in the town of Arnsdorf, near Oberndorf (see Joseph Mohr), and died at Hallein, only twelve miles from where he was born, on June 7, 1863.

646. STILLE NACHT

GRUNDTVIG, Nicolai Fredrik Severin (1783—1872), was born in Udby, near Vordlingborg, Denmark, on September 8, 1783. He was descended from a long line of ministers. At the age of nine he was sent to a minister in Jylland to be educated, where, after two years' study he passed the examen artium, and in 1803 he took the examination for the office of the ministry. During the last year of his study Grundtvig had grown entirely indifferent to religion. He tutored for three years in Langeland and in 1807 wrote his first theological treatise on Religion and Liturgics. From 1808 until 1811 he was a teacher of history in one of the Copenhagen schools and in the latter year became assistant to his father in his home town. In 1821 King Frederick VI appointed him pastor at Presto. In 1822 he became assistant pastor of Our Savior's Church, Kristianshavn. In 1826, as a result of a libel suit for charging Prof. H. N. Clausen with false doctrine, Grundtvig was forced to resign from his office. During the years 1829—1831 he made several trips to England to study old Anglo-Saxon manuscripts. Although he lectured in Borch's College in 1838, he was without regular employment as a pastor until 1839. He had previously written several hymns and devotional songs, but the years 1837—1860 were his most prolific for song-writing. In 1839 Grundtvig became pastor in Vartou, and when he celebrated his golden jubilee as pastor, he was given the title of bishop. He died at the age of 89, having delivered his last sermon on the day before his death. Grundtvig is called the most important Scandinavian hymn-writer of the 19th century, ranking with Brorson and Kingo. He published *Songs for the Danish Church* in 1837. After his death his poems and hymns were published in five volumes, entitled *Hymns and Spiritual Songs*.

283. God's Word is our great heritage
467. Built on the Rock the Church doth stand

GRYPHIUS, Andreas (1616—1664), was born on October 2, 1616, at Gross-Glogau, in Silesia. He was educated at the school in Fraustadt, Silesia, 1631—34, and at the Gymnasium at Danzig, 1634—36. He was tutor in the house of Baron Georg von Schönborn for a while, but then was forced by the Counter-Reformation to find refuge in Holland. There he entered Leyden University, 1638, and was university lecturer until 1643. He toured France, Italy, Holland, and South Germany, finally settling in Fraustadt in 1647. He was appointed syndicus of the principality of Glogau in 1650. He died of a paralytic stroke, while attending a meeting of the diet at Glogau, on July 16, 1664.

264. Preserve Thy Word, O Savior
599. My course is run. Praise God, my course is run

GURNEY, Dorothy Frances, née Blomfield (1858—1932), was born at London on October 4, 1858, the daughter of the Rev. Frederick George Blomfield and granddaughter of Bishop Blomfield. In 1897 she married Mr. Gerald Gurney, the eldest son of the Rev. Archer Gurney, a hymn-writer of merit. Gerald Gurney was first an actor, but was later ordained in the Church of England. In 1919 both he and Mrs. Gurney were received into the Roman Catholic Church at Farnborough Abbey. She died on June 15, 1932.

623. O perfect Love, all human thought transcending

GURNEY, John Hampden (1802—1862), was born in Serjeants' Inn, London, on August 15, 1802. He was educated at Trinity College, Cambridge, where he was graduated in 1824. After taking holy orders he became Curate of Lutterworth, 1827 to 1844, and was subsequently Rector of St. Mary's, Marylebone, and Prebendary of St. Paul's Cathedral. He died in London on March 8, 1862. His works include: *Church Psalmody, Psalms and Hymns for Public Worship*, and *A Collection of Hymns for Public Worship*.

583. Great King of nations, hear our prayer

HAMILTON, James (1819—?), was born at Glendollar, Scotland, on April 18, 1819, and educated at Cambridge. Ordained in 1845, he served various charges. At last, in 1867, he was advanced to the Vicarage of Doutling, diocese of Bath and Wells.

110. Across the sky the shades of night

HAMMERSCHMIDT, Andreas (c. 1611—1675), born at Brüx in Bohemia, received his early musical training from the cantor Stephan Otto at Schandau in Saxony. He became organist of St. Peter's in Freiberg in 1635, succeeding Christoph Schreiber, and in 1639 of St. John's Church in Zittau, again as successor to Schreiber, which position he held until his death on October 29, 1675. Hammerschmidt was one of the most distinguished composers of church music in the 17th century; he contributed prolifically to the choir and congregational music of his day. His *Musicalische Andachten,* 1638, and *Kirchen- und Tafelmusik,* 1662, are representative. In 1659 his *Fest-, Buss- und Danklieder* was published at Zittau and Dresden.

96. FREUET EUCH, IHR CHRISTEN

HAMMOND, William (1719—1783), was born in Battle, Sussex, England, on January 6, 1719, and educated at St. John's College, Cambridge. In 1743 he joined the Calvinistic Methodists and two years later the Moravian Brethren. He died in London on August 19, 1783. Besides writing original hymns, many of which were once widely used, he was among the first to publish translations of the old Latin hymns. His *Psalms, Hymns, and Spiritual Songs* appeared in 1745.

18. Lord, we come before Thee now

HAMPTON, John (1834—?), studied at Queen's College, Cambridge. He was ordained in 1862. Hampton was first choirmaster, 1856, then Subwarden, and from 1889 Warden of St. Michael's College, Tenbury, and Vicar of the parish.

168. VEXILLA REGIS

HÄNDEL, Georg Friedrich (1685—1759), was born at Halle on February 23, 1685. From about the age of ten he devoted himself to music, although his father intended him for the legal profession. From F. W. Zachau, the organist of the cathedral at Halle, he learned the rudiments of composing and quickly mastered the organ, clavier, violin, and oboe. In 1702 he entered the new University of Halle and was appointed organist of the cathedral. In the following year he .went to Hamburg, where he played the violin in the opera orchestra, wrote four operas, producing his first one, *Almira,* in 1705. During the years 1707—1710 Händel traveled in Italy, studying the Italian opera. After a brief tenure of office as chapelmaster to the Elector of Hanover, later King George I of Great Britain and Ireland, he went to England, where he became a naturalized British subject in 1726. He was for a time chapelmaster to the Duke of Chandes, at Cannons, near London, where he composed the Chandos *Te Deums* and *Anthems,* and in 1720 his first oratorio, *Esther.* After 1737 Händel seems to have concentrated almost exclusively on the writing of oratorios. He composed his *Messiah* in 24 days, and after its enthusiastic acceptance in 1741 basked in the light of popular favor until blindness overtook him in 1752. He died on April 14, 1759, and was buried in the Poets' corner of Westminster Abbey.

87. ANTIOCH

HARBAUGH, Henry (1817—1867), was born in Franklin County, Pennsylvania, on October 24, 1817. His parents were Swiss. He was a farmer, carpenter, and teacher. In 1840 he was educated at Marshall College, Mercersburg, and was ordained as Reformed minister in 1843. In 1844 he became, successively, pastor at Lewisburg, Lancaster, and Lebanon, Pennsylvania, and in 1864, professor of theology at the Mercersburg Seminary. He belonged to the High-Church school of his denomination. He died on December 27, 1867. He edited the *Guardian* and *Mercersburg Reviero,* and the *Reformed Church Messenger,* and contributed frequently to others. In these papers he advocated the Mercersburg theology. He was a man of indefatigable energy and wrote much. Among other things he published *Hymns and Chants for Sundayschools* at Lebanon, in 1861. He died December 27, 1867.

566. Christ, by heavenly hosts adored
591. Jesus, I live to Thee

HARDING, John P. (James?) (1850, 1859?—1911). There seems to be uncertainty regarding the first name of this composer and the exact year of his birth. McCutchan calls him James and gives the year of his birth as 1859, and Covert and

Laufer call him John and give his birth as 1850. Harding was organist and choirmaster at St. Andrew's Church, London, for thirty-five years. Many of his compositions were inspired by children's festivals in connection with the Gifford Hall Mission. Harding composed anthems, church services, part songs, and carols. For many years he was engaged in work in the Civil Service. He died in 1911.

128. MORNING STAR

HARRISON, Ralph (1748—1810), was born in Chinley, Derbyshire, England. He was educated at Warrington Academy, became assistant minister of the Presbyterian Chapel, Shrewsbury, in 1769, and minister of Cross Street Chapel, Manchester, in 1771. He was made classical tutor in Manchester Academy on its establishment in 1786; he was chief compiler of *Sacred Harmony, a collection* of psalm-tunes, ancient and modern, for use in the Manchester district.

519. CAMBRIDGE

HART, Joseph (1712—1768), was born in London. He was well educated and for many years was a teacher of the classics. His early life was a pious one, but he later lapsed into unbelief. While in this state he wrote a pamphlet entitled *The Unreasonableness of Religion, Being remarks and Animadversions on the Rev. John Wesley's Sermon on Romans 8:32.* At the age of forty he had a change of heart and began to pray daily and to read the Scriptures, but it was not until he attended the service at the Moravian Church in Fetter Lane, London, on Whitsunday, 1757, that he obtained peace of soul. Now becoming an earnest and consecrated Christian, he wrote many of his best hymns in the two years following his conversion. His *Hymns Composed on Various Subjects, with the Author's Experience,* was first published in 1759 and was followed by numerous editions published during his life and after his death. His conversion led Joseph Hart to the desire to become a preacher, which he did, despite the fact that he was 48 years old. He became pastor of an Independent Congregation in Jewin St., London. He served this congregation for eight years with success; he died on May 24, 1768. It is said that twenty thousand people attended his funeral.

225. *Come, Holy Spirit, come*
358. *Lamb of God, we fall before Thee*

HASSLER, Hans Leo (1564—1612), was born October 25, or 26, 1564, at Nürnberg, Bavaria, the son of Isaac Hassler, an eminent organist, the town musician, and his first teacher. Hassler was the first notable German composer to go to Italy to study, where in Venice he was a fellow-pupil of Giovanni Gabrieli under the latter's uncle, Andrea Gabrieli, organist of St. Mark's. Returning to Germany, Hassler was successively organist to Count Ottavianus Fugger, the great merchant prince and art patron of Augsburg, at the Frauenkirche in Nürnberg, and at the court of the Elector of Saxony. Hassler accompanied the Elector to the Diet at Frankfurt in 1612 and died there. Hans Leo Hassler was the most eminent organist of his day. He is classed with Gumpeltzhaimer, Erbach, and Melchior Franck as one of the founders of German music. Hassler's style was strongly influenced by the Gabrielis.

172, 264, 520, 586. HERZLICH TUT MICH

HASTINGS, Thomas (1784—1822), born in Litchfield, Connecticut, October 15, 1784. From 1824 to 1832 he conducted a religious journal in Utica. He was for nearly forty years resident in New York, where he was invited by a number of the churches to improve their psalmody, a subject to which he had given much attention from his earliest years. He was composer of many hymns and tunes which were published in the collections he issued: *The Christian Psalmist,* 1834; *Church Melodies,* 1858; *Devotional Hymns and Poems,* 1350. He collaborated with Lowell Mason in *Spiritual Songs for Social Worship,* 1832.

278. *Delay not, delay not, O sinner, draw near*
376. TOPLADY
531:3. *Come, ye disconsolate*

HATTON, John (?—1793), was probably born in Warrington, England. We know only that just before his death he lived in St. Helens, in the township of Windle. Hatton is buried in the Presbyterian Chapel in St. Helens.

200, 511. DUKE STREET

HAVERGAL, Frances Ridley (1836—1879), was the youngest child of William Henry Havergal, Vicar of Astley, Worcestershire (q. v.), and was born there on December 14, 1836. Her early life was spent in Worcestershire. At the age of seven she began to write verses which gained publication in several religious periodicals. But her frail health proved a great handicap to her in her work. Nevertheless, she studied and mastered French, German, Italian, Latin, Greek, and Hebrew. For a time she studied at Düsseldorf. In early life Miss Havergal was much shadowed by fear and a morbid sense of the vanity of human life, but after the age of fourteen the shadows lifted. A volume of *Memorials* of her, which includes a partial *Autobiography*, disclosed a remarkable Christian character. Miss Havergal was a diligent Bible-reader and began her perusal at 7:00 A. M. in the summer and at 8:00 A. M. in the winter. When informed that she was going to die, Miss Havergal said, "If I am going, it is too good to be true." She died while singing "Jesus, I will trust Thee," and her epitaph at her request reads "The blood of Jesus Christ, His Son, cleanseth us from all sin." Miss Havergal was the most gifted and popular female hymn-writer that England produced in the last half of the century. About 75 of her hymns are in use. She died June 3, 1879, at Caswall Bay, near Swansea.

352. *O Savior, precious Savior*
400. *Take my life and let it be*
405. *I gave My life for thee*
428. *I am trusting Thee, Lord Jesus*
453. EIRENE
653. *Now the light has gone away*

HAVERGAL, William Henry (1793—1870), born at High Wycombe, Buckinghamshire, January 18, 1793, baptized February 15; educated at St. Edmund's Hall, Oxford, where he graduated in 1815; took holy orders February 24, 1816; M. A. June 25, 1819; and was rector of Astley, Worcestershire, 1829 to 1842; honorary canon, Worcester Cathedral, 1845; rector of St. Nicholas, Worcester, 1845 to 1860, when he resigned as a result of a carriage accident that had permanently injured his sight; rector of Shareshill from 1860 to 1868. He died at Leamington, April 19, 1870. He published a reprint of *Ravenscroft's Psalter*, 1844, and three years later the *Old Church Psalmody*, which reached the fifth edition in 1864; *A History of the Old Hundredth Psalm Tune, with Specimens*, 1854, and, in 1859, *A Hundred Psalm and Hymn Tunes* of his own composition.

400. PATMOS
416. EVAN

HAWEIS, Thomas (1732—1820), was born at Cornwall, England, in 1732. He practiced medicine for a time and then entered Cambridge to study theology. He became assistant to M. Madam at Lock Hospital, London. Later he was Rector of All Saints, Aldwincle, Northamptonshire, and then chaplain to Lady Huntington at Bath. He earned the distinction of being the most musical of the chaplains. After Lady Huntington's death he published *Original Music Suited to the various Metres*. He died at Bath February 11, 1820. Haweis was a copious writer, publishing several prose works, *A History of the Church*, *A Translation of the New Testament*, and *A Commentary on the Holy Bible*. His hymns, only a few of which have more than ordinary merit, appeared in *Carmina Christo, or Hymns to the Savior*. Many of them are also included in Lady Huntington's *Collection*.

66. CHESTERFIELD
515. *O Thou from whom all goodness flows*

HAYN, Henriette Luise von (1724—1782), was born at Idstein, Nassau, on May 22, 1724. She was formally received into the Moravian Community at Herrnhag in 1742. She was teacher in the Girls' School at Herrnhag, later in Grosshennersdorf and after

1751 at Herrnhut. From 1766 until her death Miss Hayn cared for the invalid sisters of the community. Over forty hymns or portions of hymns by her appeared in the *Brüder Gesangbuch,* 1778. She died August 27, 1782.

648. *I am Jesus' little lamb*

HAYNE, Leighton George (1836—1883), was born at St. David's Hill, Exeter, England. He was educated at Eton and at Queen's College, Oxford. He was ordained to the ministry in 1861, became Precentor of Oxford in 1863, Succentor of Eton in 1867, and four years later rector of Mistley and vicar of Bradfield, Essex. With the Rev. H. W. Sergeant he edited *The Merton Tune Book,* 1863.

51. BUCKLAND

HEATH, George (1745?—1822), was educated at the Dissenting Academy in Exeter, England. He became pastor of a Presbyterian Church at Honiton, Devon, in 1770, but as he proved unworthy of his office, Heath ultimately lost his position by bad conduct. Later, it seems, he became a Unitarian minister. Heath died in 1822. He published a *History of Bristol,* 1797, and *Hymns and Poetic Essays,* 1781.

449. *My soul, be on thy guard*

HEBER, Reginald (1783—1826), was born in Malpas, Cheshire, England, on April 21, 1783, the son of his father's second wife, Mary, the daughter of the Rev. Cuthbert Allanson, D. D. His father was his first instructor. At seven Heber versified in English the Latin writer Phaedrus. At eight he was sent to Dr. Kent's grammar school in Whitchurch and at thirteen to the Rev. Mr. Bristow's select school at Neasden. Here he formed a lasting friendship with John Thornton, the philanthropist of later years. In 1800 he entered Brasenose College, Oxford, the Alma Mater of his father. Heber's brother Richard was a Fellow there at the time. During his first year he gained the Chancellor's prize for the best Latin verse by his *Carmen Seculare*. In 1803, when he was seventeen, he wrote his Newdigate prize poem *Palestine*, a striking passage of which was suggested by Walter Scott. *Palestine* is almost the only prize poem that has won a permanent place in poetical literature. After he was awarded the prize, Heber's parents found him on his knees in grateful prayer. At graduation he gained the University Bachelor's prize for the best English prose essay with his *Sense of Honor*. He was also chosen a Fellow of All Souls College. In 1804 Heber's father died. The following year was spent with his friend Thornton on a Continental tour. In 1806, when he returned, his brother Richard presented him with the living of Hodnet, where the family had moved. Heber was ordained early in 1807 as Vicar of Hodnet. All his hymns were written during his sixteen years at Hodnet. In April, 1809, he married Amelia, the youngest daughter of Dean William D. Shipley and granddaughter of the bishop of St. Asaph. In the same year he published *Europe: Lines on the Present War*. During 1811 and 1812 he contributed hymns to *The Christian Observer*. A new edition of his *Poems* with translations of Pindar was issued in 1812. In December, 1818, the death of Heber's only child at the age of six months gave occasion to the hymn beginning "Thou art gone to the grave, but we will not deplore thee." In 1819 he started a compilation of his hymns. Heber prevailed upon his gifted friend, the Rev. Henry Hart Milman, to contribute several admirable hymns. Heber presented a masterly but ineffectual plea to the Bishop of London for an ecclesiastical approval of his design. For this reason the result of Heber's efforts was not published until after his death (1827) by his widow under the title, *Hymns Written and Adapted to the Weekly Service of the Year*. In 1822 Heber edited the *Whole Works of Jeremy Taylor* and prefixed *A Life of the Author*. In April of that year he obtained the Preachership of Lincoln's Inn, London, which called him to the city about three months in the year and added about 600 pounds to his annual income. Also in this year Heber refused a call to India because of his wife and only child. In February of 1823 he received the degree of D. D. from the University of Oxford. Again he received the call to India, and this time he accepted. On June 1, 1823, he was consecrated by the Archbishop at Lambeth and sailed for

India on June 18, arriving in October. In India he ordained the first native pastor of the Episcopal Church, Christian David, in his capacity as Bishop of Calcutta. Heber died of apoplexy at Trichinopoly occasioned by a cold bath after strenuous work, April 3, 1826. In 1828 his *Journey Through India* was published, followed two years later by *The Life of Reginald Heber, D.D., Lord Bishop of Calcutta*, by his Widow. In 1837 three volumes of his *Parish Sermons* appeared.

   70. *Hosanna to the living Lord*
128. *Brightest and best of the sons of the morning*
246. *Holy, holy, holy! Lord God Almighty*
452. *The Son of God goes forth to war*
495. *From Greenland's icy mountains*

HEERMANN, Johann (1585—1647), was born on October 11, 1585, son of Johannes Heermann, furrier at Raudten, Silesia, and was the fifth and only surviving child of his parents. He passed through a severe illness in his childhood, during which his mother vowed that if he would recover, she would educate him for the ministry, even though she had to beg the necessary money. Heermann attended schools at Raudten, Wohlau, and Fraustadt, the St. Elizabeth gymnasium at Breslau, and the gymnasium at Brieg. At Fraustadt Heermann was engaged as tutor for the Rev. Valerius Herberger's sons. The pastor esteemed Heermann very highly, and Heermann found rich opportunity for spiritual development in the circle of the pious and lovable pastor's home. Later Heermann became the tutor of the sons of Baron Wenzel von Rothkirch, and as such he accompanied them to the University of Strassburg in 1609, but an eye affection caused him to return to Raudten in the following year. In 1611, upon the recommendation of Baron Wenzel, Heermann was appointed diaconus of Köben, a small town on the Oder, and within a year was advanced to the pastorate. After 1623 Heermann suffered from a throat affection, which finally stopped his preaching in 1634. Four years later he retired to Lissa in Posen, where he died on February 17, 1647. Johann Heermann lived during the distresses of the Thirty Years' War. During his pastorate at Köben the town was plundered four times and devastated by fire and pestilence. Several times Heermann lost all his movables; once he had to keep away from Köben for 17 weeks, twice he was nearly sabered; and once he heard bullets whistle over his head as he and others fled across the Oder in a frail boat. He also suffered the sorrow of losing his son to the Roman Catholics. However, the son returned to the Lutheran faith only to die shortly afterward. There was a strong suspicion that he was poisoned. Heermann was indeed well grounded in the school of affliction. As a hymn-writer Heermann ranks with the best of his century. Some regard him second only to Gerhardt. He composed 400 hymns, many of which are counted as the most precious gems in Lutheran hymnody. Heermann began writing Latin poems about 1605, and in 1608 he was crowned poet laureate. He also marks the transition from the objectivism of the Reformation period to the subjectivism which followed him.

143. *O dearest Jesus, what law hast Thou broken?*
144. *Jesus, grant that balm and healing*
265. *Thine honor save, O Christ our Lord*
268. *Zion mourns in fear and anguish*
269. *O Lord, our Father, shall we be confounded*
375:1-4. *If Thy beloved Son, O God*
395. *O God, Thou faithful God*
417:6. *How can I thank Thee, Lord*
512. *O Christ, our true and only Light*
659. *Feed Thy children, God most holy*

HELD, Heinrich (?—c. 1659). Heinrich Held was the son of Valentin Held of Guhrau, Silesia. He studied at the University of Königsberg (c. 1637—40), Frankfort an der Oder (1643), and Leyden. In 1647 Held was in residence at Rostock. He then became a licentiate of Law and settled as a lawyer in Guhrau, where he died in 1659 or before Michaelmas, 1661. Held was one of the best Silesian hymn-writers, taught in the school of affliction resulting from the Thirty Years' War. His only extant poetical work is his *Deutscher Gedichte Vortrab*, Frankfort a. Oder, 1643.

   91. *Let the earth now praise the Lord*
226. *Come, oh, come, Thou quickening Spirit*

HELDER, Bartholomäus (?—1635), was born at Gotha, son of John Helder, at the time superintendent in Gotha. In 1607 he became schoolmaster at Friemar, near Gotha, and in 1616 pastor at Remstädt, also near Gotha. He died of the pestilence on October 28, 1635. Helder was a distinguished hymn-writer and composer. His hymns rapidly became known and were nearly all taken into the Thuringian *Hymnal*. In the *Cantionale Sacrum* there are over 50 hymns that are attributed to him. Helder published his hymns in two collections: *Cymbalum Genethliacum*, Erfurt, 1615; *Cymbalum Davidicum*, Erfurt, 1620.

328. O Jesus, Lamb of God, Thou art

HELMBOLD, Ludwig (1532—1598), German theologian and hymnist, was born on January 13, 1532, at Mühlhausen, Thuringia. His father was Stephan Helmbold, a woolen manufacturer. He received his education at Leipzig and at Erfurt. He served as lecturer at the University of Erfurt. In 1566 he was crowned poet-laureate by Emperor Maximilian II. He remained at Erfurt until the year 1570, when he had a violent disagreement with the other members of the faculty. Though he was now already 39 years old, he began the study of theology in earnest to prepare himself for the ministry. In 1571 he delivered his first sermon at Bollstädt. He became deacon and later pastor of the Liebfrauenkirche in his home town. His heart and soul were so much in his writings that he composed verse to the very last day of his life, April 8, 1598. His last hymn was: "Du kennst mein Seufzen, Herr Christ." He also wrote a complete metrical version of the Augsburg Confession. He published *Geistliche Lieder*, 1575; *Neue Geistliche Lieder*, 1595.

288. Lord, help us ever to retain
393. From God shall naught divide me
630. Ye parents, hear what Jesus taught

HERBERGER, Valerius (1562—1627), was born April 21, 1562, at Fraustadt, Posen. He studied at Frankfurt a. Oder and at Leipzig. When he had been at the University of Leipzig for two years, he was called back to Fraustadt to teach school. Later he became diaconus of St. Mary's Church there, 1590, and finally chief pastor, 1599. Herberger was an outstanding preacher in his day. Because of his evangelical sermons, he was called: "Jesusprediger." The Romanists nicknamed him "The little Luther." He was also known under the name "the evangelical Abraham of Santa Clara." In his early days Herberger came close to missing his calling. For when he was but seventeen years old, his father died, and Valerius decided to become a shoemaker to support his mother. He was finally dissuaded from this plan by his relatives. In 1604 his congregation at Fraustadt was ousted from its beautiful large church by King Sigismund III to make room for a small group of Romanists. The new place of worship was called "Kripplein Christi," and Herberger became known as the "Prediger am Kripplein Christi." He died May 18, 1627. Herberger was a man of prayer. He led a very good Christian life and set an excellent example for his people. He was known far and wide as a man with an apostolic spirit. Herberger published many writings, predominantly sermon books: *Evangelische Herzpostille; Epistolische Herzpostille; Geistliche Trauerbinden* (funeral sermons); *Himmlisches Jerusalem*.

407. Farewell I gladly bid thee

HERBERT, Petrus (?—1571), was either a resident or a native of Fulnek, Moravia. In 1562 he was ordained a priest of the United Brethren (Moravian) and in 1567 became a member of the Select Council. Later Herbert became Consenior of the Unity. The Unity entrusted him with many important missions: deputy to confer with Calvin; to arrange with Duke Christoph of Württemberg for the education at Tübingen of young men from the Bohemian Brethren; deputy to Vienna to present the revised form of the Brethren's Confession of Faith to the Emperor Maximilian II; in 1564 and again in 1566 to present their new German hymn-book. Herbert died a comparatively young man at Eibenschütz. He was one of the principal compilers of the Moravian hymn-book, or *Kirchengeseng*, 1566, and he himself contributed 90 hymns to it. In a later edition, 1639, 104 hymns are attributed to him. A number of Herbert's hymns are translated from the Bohemian.

556:1-4, 6. *O God be with us*

HERMAN, Nikolaus (c. 1480—1561), is associated with Joachimsthal in Bohemia, just over the mountains from Saxony. It is not known whether he was a native of this place, but he seems to have been there in 1518 and was certainly in office there in 1524. For many years he was Master in the Latin School and Cantor or Organist and Choirmaster in the church. Toward the end of his life Herman suffered from gout and had to resign even his post as cantor a number of years before his death. He died in Joachimsthal on May 3, 1561. Herman was a great friend and helper of his pastor, Johann Mathesius. When Mathesius preached a specially good sermon, Herman straightway embodied its leading ideas in a hymn. His hymns, however, were not primarily written for use in church, but were intended for the boys and girls in the schools, to supplant profane songs in the mouths of the young. Herman was a poet of the people, — homely, earnest, and picturesque in style. He was an ardent lover of music and a very good organist. The *chorales* which he published with his hymns are apparently all of his own composition and are among the best of the Reformation-period. He published *Die Sontags Evangelia uber das gantze Jar*, 1560, and *Die Historien von der Sintflut*, 1562.

105. *Praise God the Lord, ye sons of men*
105, 106. LOBT GOTT, IHR CHRISTEN
108, 223. ERSCHIENEN IST
331. *Yea, as I live, Jehovah saith*
340, 438, 541, 550, 564, 633. O HEILIGE DREIFALTIGKEIT
547. *The radiant sun shines in the skies*
563. *The sun's last beam of light is gone*
594:1-4. *When my last hour is close at hand*

HERNAMAN, Claudia Frances, *née* Ibostson (1838—1898), was born at Addlestone, Surrey, on October 19, 1838. She married the Rev. J. W. D. Hernaman, one of His Majesty's Inspectors of Schools. She wrote about 150 hymns and a number of translations from the Latin, most of which are particularly adapted to children. She died on October 10, 1898. She published *Child's Book of Praise*, 1873; *Christmas Carols for Children* (two series, 1884—1885); *The Crown of Life*, 1886.

229. *Holy Spirit, hear us.* (Tr.)

HERRNSCHMIDT, Johann Daniel (1675—1723), was born at Bopfingen, Württemberg, on April 11, 1675, the son of G. A. Herrnschmidt, who was diaconus and then town-preacher in that community. He entered the University of Altdorf in 1696 and graduated (M. A.) in 1698. In the autumn of that year he went to Halle. In 1702 he was made assistant to his father. In 1712 he became superintendent, court-preacher, and Consistorialrath at Idstein. The same year he graduated (D. D.) at Halle. He was appointed Professor of Theology at Halle in 1715 and the following year subdirector of the Orphanage and Pädagogium there. His colleague in the management of the Orphan House was August Hermann Francke. He died at Halle, February 5, 1723. He was one of the best of the older Pietistic school. His hymns are Scriptural but do not possess much poetic force. Most of them were written between 1698 and 1702 while Herrnschmidt was at Halle.

26. *Praise the Almighty, my soul, adore Him*

HERTZOG (Herzog), Johann Friedrich (1647—1699), was born at Dresden on June 6, 1647, where his father was diaconus of the Church of the Holy Cross. He studied law at the University of Wittenberg and tutored the sons of General-Lieutenant von Arnim from 1671 to 1674. In the latter year he started his practice as an advocate in Dresden, where he died, March 21, 1699. His best-known hymn is "Nun sich der Tag geendet hat," written while he was still a student at the university.

561. *Now that the day hath reached its close*

HERZBERGER, Frederick William (1859—1930). Herzberger was born October 23, 1859, in Baltimore, Maryland. He was the son of a Lutheran pastor and was orphaned at the age of two years. Herzberger graduated from Concordia Seminary in 1882 and first served as a pioneer missionary in Arkansas, where he founded six congregations. After serving in Carson, Kansas, Chicago, Illinois, and Hammond, Indiana, Herzberger was installed as the first city missionary of the Missouri Synod in 1898 for the city of St. Louis. In 1903 he founded the Society for Homeless Children. Herzberger was instrumental in founding the Lutheran Altenheim and the Lutheran Convalescent Home of St. Louis and aided in such endeavors as the Associated Lutheran Charities, the Wheat Ridge Sanitarium, and the Bethesda Home at Watertown, Wisconsin. Herzberger was a poet of ability and the author of *The Family Altar*. He died, August 26, 1930, at St. Louis.

99. *Now are the days fulfilled.* (Tr.)
491. *Send, O Lord, Thy Holy Spirit.* (Tr.)

HEYDER (Heider), Friedrich Christian (1677—1754). He was born in Merseburg; became Diaconus, 1699; pastor in Zörbig near Halle, 1706—41; died there as emeritus.

315. *I come, O Savior, to Thy Table*

HOFF, Erik Christian (1832—?), was organist in Christiania (now Oslo). Among other works he has published a book of chorals for church use. Other details of his life are lacking.

44. GUDS MENIGHED, SYNG

HOLDEN, Oliver (1765—1844), was born in Shirley, Massachusetts, on September 18, 1765. He was trained as a carpenter and moved to Charlestown at 21 to help rebuild the city after it had been burned by the British. He was active in the real-estate business and was elected Representative to Congress. He later owned a music store, conducted a number of singing-schools, and compiled song-books. When Washington visited Boston in 1789, he wrote the words and music for the song which the choir sang as Washington reached the Old State House. With almost entirely his own funds he built the Puritan Church in Boston and served as its preacher. He edited and published several hymn-books, among them *American Harmony*, 1793, and *The Worcester Collection*, 1797. He died September 4, 1844.

339. CORONATION

HOLLAND, Henry Scott (1847—1918), was born at Ledbury, Hereford, on January 27, 1847, and was educated at Eton and at Balliol College, Oxford, from which he received his B. A. and M. A. in 1870 and 1873, respectively. He became Senior Student of Christ Church, Oxford, in 1870, was ordained diaconus in 1872 and pastor in 1874. He was the select preacher at Oxford from 1879 to 1880, and again from 1894 to 1896. Holland was Canon of St. Paul's, London, from 1884 to 1910. In the year 1908 Holland was Romans Lecturer at Oxford and from 1910 until his death, Regius Professor of Divinity at Oxford, where he was influential in raising the intellectual and spiritual standards for the divinity degrees. He is noted as one of the founders and most ardent supporters of the Christian Social Union, and from 1896, when it was founded, to the end of his life Holland edited *The Commonwealth*, the organ of the Union.

576. *Judge eternal, throned in splendor*

HOMBURG, Ernst Christoph (1605—1681), was born at Mihla near Eisenach. As Clerk of the Assizes and Counselor he practiced at Naumburg, Saxony. In 1648 he became a member of the Fruit-bearing Society and later a member of the Elbe Swan Order founded by Johann Rist in 1660. He was regarded by his contemporaries as a poet of the first rank. His earlier poems were secular, including love and drinking songs. Domestic troubles arising from the illness of himself and of his wife, and other afflictions, led him to seek the Lord, especially through hymn-writing. In the foreword to his songs, which were commonly written on Sundays, he says: "If any one, thinking it strange that I am writing hymn poetry, would ask: 'Is Saul also among the prophets?' or scoffingly say, 'He follows the common custom of the world and sacrifices unto the world the most precious flower of his youth, but renders only the dry chaff of old age unto God,' then he shall know that I have been especially prompted to do this by reason of the heavy cross with which my good and faithful Lord has visited me. During all this time I have found my best comfort and strength in the Word of God." Homburg did not intend to have his hymns published, but he desired to use them for the strengthening of his own life in faith and trust and in order that he might, in the privacy of his home, with heart and mouth sing praises to God. He died, June 2, 1681, at Naumburg. His hymns appeared in two parts, *Geistliche Lieder, Erster Theil* and *Ander Theil,* 1659.

151. *Christ, the Life of all the living.*

HOPKINS, Edward John (1818—1901), was born on June 30, 1818, at Westminster, London. He was a chorister in the Chapel Royal under William Hawes from 1826 to 1833 and played for services at Westminster Abbey before he was sixteen. He was a pupil of T. F. Walmisley. At the age of 16 he secured the appointment of organist at Mitcham Parish Church. In 1844 he went to Temple Church, where he remained for forty-five years until his retirement in 1898. In that year he edited the *Temple Choral Service Book.* Earlier, in 1876, he was selected to complete the *Wesleyan Tune Book,* after the deaths of H. J. Gauntlett and George Cooper, who had started the work. Hopkins was a composer of works for the organ and much church music. He also wrote on the organ and edited ancient music. Chaste melody, unobtrusive harmony, grateful inner parts, and a devotional fervor characterize his music. He died February 4, 1901.

47. ELLERS

HOPPE, Anna Bernardine Dorothy (1889—1941). Anna Hoppe was born on May 7, 1889, of Albert and Emily Hoppe, in Milwaukee, Wisconsin. She died on August 2, 1941, at Milwaukee. At her funeral her rendition of "Wie wohl ist mir, o Freund der Seelen" was sung. Early in childhood she wrote patriotic verse. At twenty-five she began to write spiritual poetry in earnest. Religious periodicals printed her hymns, and they aroused much interest. Twenty-three of her hymns were included in the Augustana Synod *Hymnal,* 1925. The *Selah* hymnal contains some thirty of her translations. A collection of her hymns appeared under the title *Songs of the Church Year.* Eight of Miss Hoppe's hymns were published in the *American Lutheran Hymnal* of 1930. This prolific writer of hymns is practically self-educated. After receiving only a grade-school education, she entered a business office and has received the benefit of only a few months' training at evening schools. Her hymns are composed in the midst of the stress and hurry of modern life. She writes: "Many of my hymns have been written on my way to and from church and to and from work. I utilize my lunch hours for typing the hymns and keeping up correspondence. I used to do quite a bit of writing on Sunday afternoons, but now we have a Laymen's Hour in our church at that time, and I do not like to miss it. I also attend our Fundamental Bible lectures, Jewish mission-meetings, and the like. Still I find a minute here and there in which to jot down some verse."

88. *This night a wondrous revelation.* (Tr.)
419. *O'er Jerusalem Thou weepest*

HOPPER, Edward (1818—1888), was born February 17, 1818, in New York City and studied at New York University and Union Theological Seminary, graduating in 1842. He was then licensed to preach by the Third Presbytery of New York, and with the exception of eleven years when he preached at Greenville, New York, and Sag Harbor, Long Island, he spent all his life in his native city, where his last pastorate was at the Church of the Sea and Land. Hopper received his degree from Lafayette College in 1871. He died of a heart attack while in the act of writing some lines on "Heaven," on April 23, 1888. 649. *Jesus, Savior, pilot me*

HORSLEY, William (1774—1858), was born in London. He was handicapped in his early musical training by a teacher who did him more harm than good. However, naturally endowed as he was, Horsley became organist of Ely Chapel, Holborn, in 1794, of the Asylum for Female Orphans in 1802, of Belgrave Chapel in 1812, and of the Charterhouse in 1838. Horsley was a great friend of Mendelssohn and one of the founders of the Philharmonic Society of London. He published a number of collections of songs, glees, psalm- and hymn-tunes, and several sonatas. He edited *Vocal Harmony* in 1830.   157. HORSLEY

HOSKINS, Joseph (1745—1788), was a Congregational minister who labored for ten years at Castle Green Chapel, Bristol. He died September 28, 1788. In the three years before his early death he wrote 384 hymns, which were published posthumously in 1789: *Hymns on Select Texts*.
608. Let thoughtless thousands choose the road

HOW, William Walsham (1823—1897), son of William Wybergh How, a solicitor, was born in Shrewsbury, December 13, 1823, and educated at Shrewsbury School and Wadham College, Oxford (B. A. 1845). He took holy orders in 1846 and was Curate at Kidderminster and later of Holy Cross, Shrewsbury. In 1851 he was made Rector of Whittington; in 1879 he was appointed Rector of St. Andrew's, Undershaft, and was consecrated Bishop-Suffragan (of Bedford) for East London; in 1888 he was made Bishop of Wakefield after having declined the Bishopric of Manchester, without even mentioning it to his wife, and that of Durham, one of the most distinguished posts in the Church of England. He died August 10, 1897. In addition to his very useful pastoral books and other works, he wrote a good many hymns and published *Psalms and Hymns* in 1854; he was one of the editors of *Church Hymns*, 1871, sponsored by the Society for the Promotion of Christian Knowledge, of which Arthur Sullivan was the musical editor.
12. This day at Thy creating word
114. Jesus! Name of wondrous love
294. O Word of God Incarnate
441. We give Thee but Thine own
463. For all the saints who from their labors rest
501. Soldiers of the Cross, arise!
580. To Thee, our God, we fly

HOWARD, Samuel (1710—1782), was born in London in 1710. He became chorister in the Chapel Royal under Dr. Wm. Croft; studied under Dr. J. C. Pepusch; was organist of St. Clement Danes, and St. Bridget's, Fleet Street, London. He received the degree of Mus. D. from Cambridge in 1769. He died in London, July 13, 1782. He wrote for the theater as well as for the church and composed much music that was popular at the time.   322, 389, 455. ST. BRIDE
439, 506. ISLEWORTH

HUMPHREYS, Joseph (1720—?), was born at Burford on October 28, 1720. He was educated at a grammar school at Fairford, Gloucestershire, and at an academy for the training of young men for the ministry in London, from which he was expelled on December 25, 1739, because of his attachment to Whitefield. He was with the Wesleys for a while, but ultimately joined G. Whitefield and preached at Bristol, London, and Deptford. In January, 1743, Humphreys united with several clergymen and lay preachers in organizing the first Calvinistic Methodist Society in Wales. However, it seems that before his death Humphreys was successively ordained to both the Presbyterian and the Episcopal ministries. Humphreys died in London (date unknown) and was buried in the Moravian Cemetery at Chelsea. He contributed to Whitefield's *Christian History* and to J. Cennick's *Sacred Hymns*.
391. Blessed are the sons of God

HURN, William (1754-1829), was born at Breccles Hall, Norfolk, December 21, 1754. In 1777 he became classical tutor in the Free Grammar School, Dedham, Essex. After a year in the army he was ordained, and, after holding various curacies, he became Vicar of Debenham, Suffolk, where he served for thirty-two years. Then he became Congregational minister at Woodbridge, where he remained till his death, October 9, 1829. He published among others: *Health Hill*, 1777; *Psalms and Hymns*, 1813; *Hymns and Spiritual Songs*, 1824.

642. *Arise, O God, and shine*

HUSS (Hus), John (1373?—1415), the great Bohemian reformer, was born at Hussinecz, Bohemia. In 1402 he became rector of the University of Prague and began to preach in the vernacular. Six years later he was forbidden by Archbishop Sbynko to perform the priestly acts and to preach. Huss became the popular champion. He was excommunicated in 1410. In his retirement he wrote his principal book, *De Ecclesia*, in which he asserted that the Church is the communion of all who are predestined to salvation, and that Christ and not the Pope is the head of the universal Church. The Ecumenical Council at Constance tried and condemned him as a heretic on July 6, 1415, and had him burned at the stake.

311. *Jesus Christ, our Blessed Savior*

ILSE, Ludwig Herman (1845—1931), was born December 23, 1845, in Hanover, Germany, son of August Wilhelm Ilse. He was educated at Concordia Teachers' College, Addison, Illinois, and served as teacher and organist successively at First Trinity, Pittsburgh, Pennsylvania, Zion, Chicago, Illinois, St. John's, Brooklyn, New York, Trinity, Brooklyn, New York, and as organist at Zion Lutheran Church, Bedford, Ohio. He married Katharine L. Succop. He died December 5, 1931. His publications include: *Chorbuch* (with Wm. Burhenn); *Taschenchorbuch* (with Wm. Burhenn); *Choralbuch* (With H. F. Hoelter); *Zwischenspiele; Sängerfreund; Kantional für Männerchor*; and with Herman A. Polack (*q. v.*) he served as music editor of the *Evangelical Lutheran Hymn-Book*, 1912.

232. ERFURT

INGEMANN, Bernhardt Severin (1789—1862), was born at Thorkildstrup, Island of Falster, on May 28, 1789. He attended the Latin school in Slagelse, and entered the university in 1806. He studied law for a while, but finally became Professor of the Danish Language and Literature at the Academy of Sorö, Zealand, Denmark, which position he held from 1822 until his death in 1862. He is noted as a poet, but he also wrote a series of patriotic, historical novels, becoming, with Hans Anderson, one of the two most popular authors in Denmark. On his seventieth birthday the children of Denmark presented Ingemann with a beautiful gold horn, ornamented with figures from his poetry. Subscriptions were limited to a halfpenny, and every child in the land contributed to show gratitude to a man who had done so much to delight their childhood. Ingemann published his *Morgensalmer*, 1822; *Hoimessesalmer*, 1825. His collected works were published in 34 volumes in 1851. His novels follow the style of Walter Scott.

481. *Through the night of doubt and sorrow*

IRONS, Genevieve Mary (1855—?). Mary Irons was the daughter of Dr. Wm. J. Irons. She was born at Brompton and contributed a number of pieces to various publications. She wrote a manual for Holy Communion entitled *Corpus Christi*, 1884, but is remembered chiefly for her beautiful hymn of consecration.

390. *Drawn to the Cross, which Thou hast blest*

IRONS, William Josiah (1812—1883), was born at Hoddesdon, England, September 12, 1812. He took his B. A. degree at Queen's College, Oxford, 1833, and became a clergyman of the Church of England, 1835. He served at various places until he became rector of St. Mary-Woolnoth in 1872, formerly held by his father's friend, John Newton. He was also Bampton Lecturer in 1870 and Prebendary of St. Paul's Cathedral. He died June 18, 1883. The Bampton Lectures on *Christianity as Taught by St. Paul* were his most important work. Numerous hymns and compilations of hymn-books are credited to him. He translated the *Dies Irae* and *Quicumque vult*. He published *Metrical Psalter*, 1857; *Brompton Metrical Psalter*, 1861; *Hymns for Use in Church*, 1866; *Psalms and Hymns for the Church*, 1873.

607. *Day of wrath, O day of mourning.* (Tr.)

ISAAK (Isaac, Izac, Ysack, Yzac), Heinrich (c. 1450—c. 1527), also known in Italy by the name of Arrigo Tedesco, was one of the foremost musicians of his day. He was very likely a Netherlander, in spite of the fact that the Italians called him "Tedesco" or "Germanus," as his testament designates him as "Ugonis de Flandria." He was at Ferrara for a time, and then went to Florence to serve as organist of the Church of San Giovanni. He was also organist at the Medici Chapel, 1477—93, and music-master to the children of Lorenzo the Magnificent. After the death of his patron in 1492, Isaak appears to have remained for some years in Italy, where he enjoyed a great reputation. He left for Vienna in 1496 and became *Symphonista regis*, or chapelmaster, to Maximilian I at Innsbruck, 1497—1515. He retired on an annual pension of 150 florins, returned to Italy, and was recommended to Duke Ercole of Ferrara, but without result. The last trace history gives of him is at San Lorenzo Maggiore in Rome, "old and sick, and without means." Isaak died in Florence. He was a prolific composer of motets, masses, chorales, and songs. His masses number 23 or 24. His *Choralis Constantini* embraces the complete Roman Catholic liturgy. Isaak was an eminent contrapuntist. One of his peculiarities is the frequent appearance of the melody in the soprano, which was an unusual procedure at his time.

126, 171 (2d tune), 554. O WELT, ICH MUSS DICH LASSEN
(NUN RUHEN ALLE WÄLDER)

JACOBS, Henry Eyster (1844—1932), was born at Gettysburg, Pennsylvania, November 10, 1844. He received his education in the College and Seminary at Gettysburg and from 1864 to 1867 served as professor in the College. He was home missionary at Pittsburgh, 1867—1868, and then became pastor at Philipsburg, Pennsylvania, and principal of Thiel Hall, 1868—1870, and then served as professor at Pennsylvania College, 1870 to 1883. From then until his death he was Professor of Systematic Theology at the Lutheran Theological Seminary, Philadelphia. Among his works are the following: *History of the Evangelical Lutheran Church in the United States; Elements of Religion; Martin Luther, the Hero of the Reformation; German Emigration to America; A Summary of Christian Faith*. He was editor of the *Lutheran Church Review* from 1882 to 1896, translated Hutter's *Compendium of Lutheran Theology* and H. Schmid's *Doctrinal Theology of the Lutheran Church*. He died July 11, 1932.

314. Lord Jesus Christ, we humbly pray

JENNER, Henry Lascelles (1820—1898), born at Chiselhurst, Kent; was educated at Harrow and Trinity Hall, Cambridge. He received his LL. B. in 1841 and his D. D. in 1867. Jenner took holy orders in 1843 and, after serving as curate in several places, he became vicar of Preston-next-Wingham, Diocese of Canterbury in 1854, and was consecrated Bishop of Dunedin in 1866, but in 1870 returned to his living at Preston and resigned his bishopric in 1871.

100. Christians, sing out with exultation. (Tr.)

JOHN OF DAMASCUS, ST. (c. 750), Greek theologian and hymn-writer, was born in Damascus and educated by the elder Cosmas. He held an office under the Mohammedan Caliph and afterwards retired to the monastery of St. Sabas, near Jerusalem, where he composed theological works and hymns. He was ordained priest of the Church of Jerusalem late in life and lived to a high age; December 4, the day of his death, is assigned to him in the Greek calendar. He was one of the last of the Fathers of the Greek Church and has been called the greatest of her poets. He gave an immense impetus to Greek hymnody, and the arrangement of the *Octoechus* in accordance with the Eight Tones was his work. The best known of his canons is the Easter or Golden canon.

204. Come, ye faithful, raise the strain!
205. The day of resurrection

JOSEPH, THE HYMNOGRAPHER, ST. (c. 800—883), was born in Sicily and received his early training at the Sicilian school of poets. He left Sicily in 830 for the monastic life at Thessalonica and moved successively to Constantinople, Rome, Crete (where he was a slave), and finally back to Constantinople. There he founded a monastery in connection with the Church of St. John Chrysostom. He was banished to the Chersonese for defense of the icons, but was recalled by the Empress Theodora and made Scenophylax (keeper of the sacred vessels) in the Great Church of Constantinople. He died at an advanced age in 883. His day in the calendar of the Greek Church is April 3. St. Joseph is the most voluminous of the Greek hymn-writers. He is said to have composed 1,000 canons.

   255. *Stars of the morning, so gloriously bright*
   322. *And wilt Thou pardon, Lord*

   JULIAN, John (1839—1913), was born at Topcliffe, Yorkshire, eldest son of Thomas Julian of St. Agnes, Cornwall. He was vicar of Wincobank (1876—1915), and from 1905 onward vicar of Topcliffe. He was canon of York from 1901 on. He is noteworthy for his monumental *Dictionary of Hymnology*. He also wrote: *Concerning Hymns; The Outgrowth of Some Literary, Scientific, and Other Hobbies;* he composed a number of hymns and translations.

   132. *O God of God, O Light of Light!*

   KAISER, Oscar (1865—), born at Teplitz, Mecklenburg, came to America as a boy of four years and made his home at Washington, Missouri. He graduated from Concordia College, Fort Wayne, and Concordia Seminary, St. Louis, and was ordained on August 24, 1890, at Gravelton, Missouri. Six months later he accepted the call as the English Lutheran missionary of Buffalo, New York. He married Emily Westermann, May 27, 1891. He organized Calvary Lutheran Church there and was installed as its first pastor on May 18, 1892. In October, 1895, he assumed the pastorate of Jackson Square Lutheran Church in Baltimore, where he served for fifteen years. During this period he started a mission church at Harrisburg, Pennsylvania, which resulted in the organization of two congregations. Since April 24, 1910, he has been pastor of Bethlehem Evangelical Lutheran Church of Milwaukee, Wisconsin. He has always been keenly interested and taken active part in the affairs of the church at large. In 1891 the English Synod of Missouri and Other States made him a member of its hymn-book committee. He is a member of the committee which prepared *The Lutheran Hymnal*. 45:3. *Now the hour of worship o'er.* (Tr.)

   KEBLE, John (1792—1866), was born, April 25, 1792, at Fairford in Gloucestershire, and at the age of 15 won a scholarship at Corpus Christi College, Oxford. In 1812 he also won both the English and Latin prize essays. He was ordained deacon in 1815 and priest in 1816. From 1836, when he accepted the living of Hursley, near Winchester, his life was spent mostly in this small country parish, devoted faithfully to its simple duties, though he exerted great influence throughout England by a vast correspondence. Quiet and retiring as he was, he is yet considered, on Newman's testimony, as the real author of the Oxford movement, to which he is held to have given the impulse by his sermon on "National Apostasy," preached at Oxford in 1833. His important contribution to the literature of the movement was his share in the translations of the *Library of the Fathers* and in the *Tracts for the Times*, of which he wrote seven, besides being ultimately associated in counsel with the other authors. His *The Christian Year*, a volume of verse which he published anonymously in 1827 had a remarkable success and influence, not equaled by that of his later volume, *Lyra Innocentium*, 1846. He was professor of poetry at Oxford from 1831 to 1841. He died at Bournemouth, March 29, 1866. Keble College in Oxford was founded as a memorial to him.

   271. *Word supreme, before creation*
   551. *Sun of my soul, Thou Savior dear*
   622. *The voice that breathed o'er Eden*
   641. *One Thy Light, the Temple filling*

   KEIMANN (Keymann), Christian (1607—1662), was the son of Zacharias Keimann, a Lutheran pastor at Pankratz, Bohemia, where Christian was born on February 27, 1607. In 1627 Keimann entered the University of Wittenberg and in 1634 graduated (M. A.). The same year he was appointed by the Town Council of Zittau as Conrector of their Gymnasium, of which he became Rector in 1638. He was a distinguished teacher, author of a number of scholastic publications, several Scriptural plays, and of some thirteen hymns, almost all of which came into church use. They rank high among those of the seventeenth century, being of genuine poetic ring, fresh, strong, full of faith under manifold and heavy trials, and deeply spiritual. He died January 13, 1662, at Zittau.

    96. Oh, rejoice, ye Christians loudly
   365. Jesus I will never leave

    KELLY, John (?—1890), Presbyterian minister and hymn translator, was born at Newcastle-on-Tyne. He was educated at Glasgow University, studied theology at Bonn, New College, Edinburgh, and at the Theological College of the Presbyterian Church in London. He served congregations at Hebborn-on-Tyne and Streatham. In 1887 he became Tract Editor of the Religious Tract Society. He published *Spiritual Songs* (Paul Gerhardt) in 1867 and *Hymns of the Present Century from the German* in 1885. He died, while on a visit to Graemar, July 19, 1890.

   122. Now let us come before Him. (Tr.)
   171. Upon the cross extended. (Tr.)
   192. Awake, my heart, with gladness. (Tr.)
   523. Why should cross and trial grieve me. (Tr.)
   535. Rejoice my heart, be glad and sing. (Tr.)
   569. O Lord, I sing with lips and heart. (Tr.)

    KELLY, Thomas (1769—1854), was born at Kellyville, Athy, Queen's County, Ireland, on July 13, 1769. His primary education was obtained at Portarlington and Kilkenny. He received his secondary education at Trinity College of Dublin University. He graduated with the highest honors. Expecting to become a lawyer, Kelly went to the Temple in London for that purpose. At the Temple he befriended Edmund Burke. While reading law Kelly had to study Hutchinson's *Moses' Principia*, which required him to study Hebrew. This in turn interested him in Romaine's teachings. While thus engaged, Kelly developed a consciousness of sin that distressed him very much. He now practiced asceticism, and even jeopardized his life by his rigorous discipline. He took holy orders in the Established Church in 1792. At this time he became an intimate of Walter Shirley, and his sympathies were wholly with the evangelical movement. Because of the dearth of evangelical preaching, people very soon flocked to hear him preach in Dublin. This aroused the ire of Archbishop Fowler to such an extent that he forbade Kelly and his friend Rowland Hill to use the Irish pulpits. Kelly, however, continued preaching at Plundet Street and Bethesda in Dublin and also had meetings at an alderman's home in Luson Street. Having seceded from the Established Church, Kelly built chapels with his own money on York Street, at Athy, Portarlington, Wexford, Waterford, and elsewhere. About 1800 he married Miss Tighe of Rosanna, Wicklow. In 1804 his *Hymns on Various Passages* appeared. While preaching at the age of eighty-five, Kelly had a severe stroke, which resulted in his death on May 14, 1854. Benson ranks Kelly with the best of English hymnists. Many of the 765 hymns are in use.

   153. Stricken, smitten, and afflicted
   178. We sing the praise of Him who died
   209. Who is this that comes from Edom?
   219. The Head that once was crowned with thorns
   221. Hark! Ten thousand harps and voices
   222. Look, ye saints, the sight is glorious
   474. Zion stands by hills surrounded
   553. Through the day Thy love hath spared us

    KEN, Thomas (1637—1711), was born in July, 1637, at Little Berkhamstead. His mother died when he was but four years old, and his father followed her very shortly. He was brought up by his half-sister Anne, wife of Izaac Walton, author of the *Compleat Angler*. He was educated at Winchester and New College, Oxford. His musical talent expressed itself at this period in his "fine voice," on the lute, on the organ, and on the viol. He was ordained in 1662 and held several livings until 1666, when he returned as Fellow to Winchester College. There he prepared for the boys of the school his *Manual of Prayers,* which contained his three most famous hymns. In 1679 he was created Doctor, and was appointed, by the Duke of York, chaplain to his daughter Princess Mary, the wife of William of Orange, at the Hague. Dismissed for his outspokenness, he returned to England and became chaplain of Charles II. At Whitehall the King once left his court with the words: "I must go hear Ken tell me my faults." Later when the court visited Winchester, the King wanted Ken to house his mistress, Nell Gwynne. Ken replied: "Not for a kingdom." In spite of this bold defiance Charles appointed Ken bishop of Bath and Wells. He was consecrated June 29, 1685. In lieu of the customary consecration-dinner Ken gave 100 pounds to charity. Eight days later Ken was called in to minister to the King who had suffered a stroke. For three days the bishop pleaded and prayed and finally got the King to give up "poor Nell" and to make amends to the Queen. But the Duke of York through the Papist priest Huddleston received the King into the fold of the Catholic section of the Church. At the coronation of James II, Ken was the right-hand supporter of the King. After the battle of Sedgmore, by the King's behest, Ken had to minister to the hardened Duke of Monmouth. After the execution, which Ken attended, he used his influence to stop the wholesale execution of the Duke's followers. He was one of the seven bishops who refused to read, at the King's command, the "Declaration of Indulgence" or the "Liberty of Conscience to All." They were speedily imprisoned in the Tower. Later they were all acquitted amid the loud exultation of the people. Shortly after, the King abdicated, and Mary with William of Orange became sole rulers of England. Ken refused to swear allegiance and, after the year of grace allowed had ended, was deprived of his bishopric. The remainder of Ken's life was uneventful. He was offered his bishopric again upon the accession of Anne but declined it, pleading ill health. In the last years of his life he suffered acutely from various ailments, but uncomplainingly. He died March 19, 1711, and was buried just before sunrise two days later under the chancel-window of the church at Frome, Selwood. He published *Hymns and Poems for the Holy Days and Festivals of the Church* (this suggested to Keble the idea of his *The Christian Year*); *Anodynes*, written in his last years of suffering.

536. Awake, my soul, and with the sun
558. All praise to Thee, my God, this night
644. Praise God, from whom all blessings flow

KENNEDY, Benjamin Hall (1804—1889), was born at Summer Hill, near Birmingham on November 6, 1804. He was educated at King Edward's School, Shrewsbury School, and St. John's College, Cambridge. Kennedy was successively Fellow of his College, 1828—1836; Headmaster of Shrewsbury School, 1836—1866; Regius Professor of Greek in the University of Cambridge; and Canon of Ely, 1867. Kennedy took holy orders in 1829 and served for a while as Prebendary in the Litchfield Cathedral and Rector of West Felton, Salop. Kennedy's chief hymnological works are his *Psalter in English Verse*, 1860, and *Hymnologia Christiana*, 1863.

437. Who trusts in God, a strong abode. (Tr.)

KETHE, William (?—c. 1593). The date and place of birth of William Kethe are unknown. He was an exile from Scotland for some time during the Marian persecutions, at Frankfort in 1555, and at Geneva in 1557. During this exile he contributed twenty-four metrical psalms to the *Psalm Book* prepared by these English refugees and also helped in the translation of the Bible. In 1561 he was made rector of Childe Okeford, Dorsetshire, and probably remained there until his death.

14. All people that on earth do dwell

KEY, Francis Scott (1779—1843), is known to every American child as the author of our national anthem, "The Star-Spangled Banner." His father was an officer in the Continental army, who fought with distinction during the Revolutionary War. Francis was born at Frederick, Maryland, August 1, 1779. After receiving a legal education, he began to practice law in Washington and served as United States District Attorney for three terms, holding that office at the time of his death. As a member of the Protestant Episcopal Church, he held a lay reader's license, and for many years read the service and visited the sick. He also conducted a Bible class in Sunday-school. Although he lived in a slave State, he was finally moved by his conscience to free his own slaves, and he did much to alleviate conditions among the unfortunate Negroes. When the Protestant Episcopal Church in 1823 appointed a committee to prepare a new hymn-book for that body, Key was made a lay member of it. Another member of this committee was Dr. William Mühlenberg (q. v.). He died January 11, 1843

575. Before the Lord we bow

KINGO, Thomas Hansen (1634—1703), Denmark's first great hymnist, was born in Slangerup, Denmark, December 15, 1634. His grandfather had emigrated from Scotland to Denmark. Thomas spent his boyhood in Slangerup and Fredriksborg, where he attended the Latin school. He completed his course for the ministry in 1658, and from then until 1668 he served as tutor and assistant pastor, when he became pastor in Slangerup. He possessed unusual poetic gifts and early attracted attention with his secular poetry, especially his popular "Chrysillis." 1673 marked the first appearance of his religious poetry *Spiritual Songs, First Part* (Aandelig Sjungekors förste Part), which made a great impression, and he was duly rewarded with the bishopric of the diocese of Fyen. He dedicated his *Spiritual Songs* to Christian V, and in his dedication address he championed the cause of true Danish hymnody over that of foreign peoples, for the Danes used many hymns of foreign origin in their worship. His hymns have exceptional vigor and beauty, and his value as a poet was gradually being realized. As further reward he was made a member of the Danish nobility in 1679 and created doctor of theology in 1682. The second part of his *Aandelig Sjungekors* appeared in 1681 and was dedicated to Queen Charlotte. In his dedication address he praised her heroic efforts to master the Danish language before coming to Denmark to be its queen, at the same time referring to certain foreign courtiers who spent thirty years in that country without endeavoring to learn thirty Danish words. Many of his hymns were sung to Danish folk songs, while he supplied melodies for some of them. At this time King Christian V desired to have a new hymnal to replace the one which had been in use since the year 1569. On March 27, 1683, Kingo was ordered to prepare this book, with certain specifications: He should include some of his own hymns, was to make very few changes in the old traditional hymns, and not to alter the meaning of Luther's hymns in any way. In 1689 the first part of the hymn-book appeared, containing 267 hymns, of which 136 were Kingo's own. It had been prepared at Kingo's expense, but was now rejected because he had not followed the prescribed method of procedure. The task was turned over to Sören Jonassön, dean of Roskilde, and his book appeared in 1693, containing not a single one of Kingo's hymns. This was consequently disapproved, and a commission was appointed under Kingo's direction to try again. The new hymn-book was approved and introduced into all the churches of Denmark in 1699. Only eighty-five of Kingo's hymns were contained in the book. However, he never recovered from the indignity and humiliation he had received in connection with these various controversies. He died October 14, 1703. His immortal fame rests on his religious rather than on his secular poetry. His morning hymns are among the finest songs of praise in existence and are truly church-hymns. Of his works Bishop Skaar says: "Among the finest hymns in *Spiritual Songs* must be mentioned the morning and evening hymns with their accompanying prayers and the table and Communion hymns. His hymns based upon the Gospel and Epistle lessons, especially, express in striking phrases the thoughts that stir the hearts of Lutheran believers as they behold the life of the Savior upon earth: His lowly birth, suffering, death, resurrection, and ascension. These hymns, which generally end with an appeal to lift the heart unto God in prayer and thanksgiving, have always been cherished by those who have learned to know them."

179. On my heart imprint Thine image
207. Like the golden sun ascending
301. He that believes and is baptized
309. O Jesus, blessed Lord, to Thee
401. Praise to Thee and adoration
542. The sun arises now
655. I pray Thee, dear Lord Jesus

KINNER, Samuel (1603—1668), the son of Martin Kinner, was born in Bristan in 1603. He practiced medicine for a time in his home town. Later he entered the service of the Duke of Liegnitz-Brieg as Rath and Court Physician. He served in this capacity until his death on August 10, 1668, at Brieg.

306. Lord Jesus Christ, Thou hast prepared

KITTEL, Johann Christian (1732—1809), was born in Erfurt, February 8, 1732. He was the last pupil of Johann Sebastian Bach. He served as organist and schoolteacher in Langensalza, then as successor of the organist Jakob Adlung, from 1756 to his death at Erfurt, but at so meager a salary that he could exist only through the help of a patron and the proceeds of a few concert tours. He enjoyed great renown as organist, composer, and teacher of music. His most renowned pupil was Christian Heinrich Rinck. He died at Erfurt, May 9, 1809.

576. BIS WILLKOMMEN

KLEIN, Bernhard (1793—1832), was born at Köln on March 6, 1793. He received his musical training at Köln and in 1812 studied at Paris under Cherubini. After 1812 he was in charge of the choir of the Cathedral at Köln and later pursued his musical studies at Heidelberg, studying under Thibaut. He was called to Berlin in 1819 and took over the position of music director of the University and, in 1829, as teacher in the newly founded Institute for Church Music. Klein served as a composer and teacher of music in Berlin until his early death on September 9, 1832.

470. LÖWEN, LASST EUCH WIEDERFINDEN

KNAPP, Albert (1798—1864), was born on July 25, 1798, at Tübingen, Württemberg, where his father was then advocate at the Court of Appeal. In the autumn of 1814 Knapp entered the Theological College at Maulbronn and then continued his studies at Tübingen, graduating as M. A. in 1820. Knapp was vicar at Feuerbach and Caisburg, near Stuttgart, and in 1825 became diaconus at Sulz on the Neckar and also pastor of the neighboring village of Holzhausen. In 1831 he was appointed archidiaconus in Kirchheim-unter-Teck with Bahnmaier (q. v.) and in 1836 called to be diaconus of the Hospitalkirche, Stuttgart. In the following year he became archidiaconus of the Stiftskirche. Finally in 1845 he became Stadtpfarrer (city pastor) at St. Leonhard's Church, Stuttgart, where, after having been for some time partially disabled by paralysis, he preached his last sermon on February 13, 1863. Knapp lingered on for more than a year before he died on June 18, 1864. As a hymnologist Knapp did good service with his *Christoterpe,* an annual, which he edited from 1833 to 1853, in which many of his own poems appeared and also many of the best poems and hymns of Hey, Meta Heusser-Schweizer, and various others. He was also the compiler of the *Evangelischer Liederschatz,* the most elaborate German hymn-book of recent times. The first edition, published at Stuttgart in 1837, contained 3,590 hymns with notices of the authors. As a comprehensive collection with a specially full representation of good modern hymns it has no rival in German. Knapp was also one of the editors of the Württemberg *Gesangbuch* of 1842.

299. Dear Father who hast made us all
602. It is not death to die. (Tr.)

KNAPP, William (1698—1768), born at Wareham, England, in 1698, probably of German descent. He is said to have been organist of one of the churches of Wareham. He became parish clerk of St. James's Church, Poole, and held the office for thirty-nine years. He died at Poole in 1768 and was buried September 26, "somewhere near the old town wall."

608, 634. WAREHAM

KNECHT, Justin Heinrich (1752—1817), born September 30, 1752, at Biberach, in Suabia, studied music under Kramer, was organist of the Roman Catholic Church at Biberach, and, afterwards from 1768 to 1771 under Schmidt, director of the music at the gymnasium at Esslingen. He was appointed in 1771 director of the music at Biberach, and, with the exception of the years 1807 and 1808, when he was music director at Stuttgart, remained there till his death, December 1, 1817. He was one of the great organists of his time.

18, 338, 459, 538. VIENNA
593. DOMINE, CLAMAVI

KOCHER, Konrad (1786—1872), was born at Ditzingen, Württemberg, on December 16, 1786. He intended to enter the teaching profession and at 17 went as a tutor to St. Petersburg. However, the music of Haydn and Mozart made such an impression on him that he decided on a musical career. His friend, Clementi, the great pianist, confirmed him in this decision. After he had studied in St. Petersburg, Kocher returned to Germany and published compositions of such promise that means were found by the publisher Cotta to enable him to proceed to Italy. There his studies, particularly of Palestrina, made him an enthusiast for church choral music. Returning to Germany, Kocher set about to improve church music by popularizing choral singing. From 1827 until 1865 he was organist of the Stiftskirche, Stuttgart. There Kocher founded a school of sacred song which started a movement that spread throughout Württemberg popularizing four-part singing. In 1852 the University of Tübingen gave him the degree of Doctor of Philosophy. Kocher occupied himself in the revision of various hymn-books and contributed new tunes to them. He published a large collection of *chorales* under the title *Zionsharfe*, 1854—1855, and *Der Tod Abels*, an oratorio, in addition to several operas, sonatas, and other pieces.

127, 572. DIX

KÖNIG, Johann Balthasar (1691—1758), famous for his collection *Harmonischer Liederschatz*, 1738, is practically unknown otherwise, and the details of his life are lacking. He was according to the title-page Director Chori Musices at Frankfurt-am-Main in 1738, and in 1767, when the second and enlarged edition of his work appeared, he was "Kapellmeister" in the same city.

30, 88, 385. O DASS ICH TAUSEND
144, 179. DER AM KREUZ
282, 425. ALLES IST AN GOTTES SEGEN
348. JESUS, JESUS, NICHTS ALS JESUS

KOREN, Ulrik Vilhelm (1826—1910), was born in Bergen, Norway, on December 22, 1826. He studied at the Cathedral School there and then entered the University of Christiana in 1844. In 1853 he received a call to a pastorate among some Norwegians in Iowa. He was ordained in Norway on July 25, 1853, and the following winter crossed the ocean with his wife, Else Elisabeth, *née* Hysing. He arrived in Little Iowa (Washington Prairie), Iowa, in December, 1853. Koren was the first Norwegian pastor to settle west of the Mississippi. He labored in Northeastern Iowa and Southeastern Minnesota. From 1894 until his death in 1910 he served as President of the Norwegian Lutheran Synod of America.

44. *Ye lands, to the Lord make a jubilant noise*

KRETZMANN, Paul Edward (1883—   ), was born in Dearborn County, Indiana, August 24, 1883. He studied at Concordia College, Fort Wayne, and at Concordia Seminary, St. Louis, with additional work at the University of Minnesota (M. A. 1913; Ph. D. 1915), La Salle University, Chicago, and Washington University, St. Louis. After having been ordained to the Lutheran ministry in 1906, Kretzmann served successively as pastor of St. Peter's Church, Shady Bend, Kansas, 1905—1907; and of Emmaus Church, Denver, Colorado, 1907—1912; as professor of science and mathematics at Concordia College, St. Paul, Minnesota, 1912—1919; as production manager of Concordia Publishing House, St. Louis, 1919—1923; as professor of theology at Concordia Seminary, St. Louis, 1923—1946; now pastor at Forest Park, Ill. Kretzmann is the author of a large number of theological and educational works, especially *Popular Commentary of the Bible* (4 volumes). A number of his hymns are included in the *American Lutheran Hymnal*.

272. When all the world was cursed. (Tr.)
408. Jesus Christ, my Pride and Glory. (Tr.)

KRIEGER, Adam (1634—1666), was born in Neumark on January 7, 1634, and studied organ and composition at Halle under Samuel Scheidt. After 1654 he continued his studies at Dresden. In 1658 Krieger became "Hoforganist" and member of the Dresden "Hofkapelle," where he remained until his early death at the age of 32 on June 30, 1666. Krieger was both a poet and a composer, and his *Neue Arien*, 1667, has placed him among the better composers of the seventeenth century.

561. NUN SICH DER TAG GEENDET HAT

KUNTH, Johann Sigismund (1700—1779), was born October 3, 1700, at Liegnitz, Silesia. He studied theology at the Universities of Jena, Wittenberg, and Leipzig. In 1730 he was appointed pastor at Pölzig and Bröckau, near Ronneburg, and in 1737 he became chief pastor at Löwen, Silesia. In 1743 he became pastor and superintendent at Baruth, near Jüterbog, Brandenburg. He died at Baruth, September 7, 1779.

615. A rest remaineth for the weary

KVAMME, Kristen (1866—1938), was born at Lom, Norway, on February 17, 1866. Before he emigrated to America in 1882, he attended the North Gudbrandsdalen Amtsskole. In America he attended St. Ansgar Academy, St. Ansgar, Iowa, Luther College (A. B. 1894), Luther Seminary (C. T. 1899). Before he became a pastor, Kvamme served as a teacher at Luther College for two years. He then held pastorates at New York, New York, Washington, D. C., Salt Lake City, Utah, and Ossian, Iowa. From 1913 until his death Kvamme was the editor of Sunday-school papers. He wrote many Norwegian hymns and translated a few into English.

401. Praise to Thee and adoration. (Tr.)

LANDSTAD, Magnus Brostrup (1802—1880), was born in Maaso, Finmarken, Norway, on October 7, 1802, where his father was pastor at the time. His youth was spent in Oknes and Vinje, where the family suffered because of the solitude, storm, darkness, and famine. Landstad received his preparatory training from his father. In 1822 he began his studies at the university, took his master's examination the following year, and began the study of theology. For financial reasons he was obliged to take a position as family tutor in Hadeland to continue his studies at Christiana. After a year Landstad returned to the university and studied under the teachers Hersleb and Stenersen. In December, 1827, he passed the final examination with the grade "Laudabilis." In November, 1828, he was appointed resident vicar of Gausdal. The following year he married Vilhelmine Lassen, a daughter of Albert Lassen, the dean of Grau in Hadeland. In 1834 Landstad became pastor at Kviteseid and in 1839 succeeded his father as pastor of Seljord. He did not start duties there, however, until 1840, because of an attack of pneumonia. Here he labored for eight trying years. Landstad's interest in hymn-writing was awakened during his student-days through an accidental purchase of two books, *Freuden-Spiegel des ewigen Lebens* by Philipp Nicolai (q. v.) and Arrebo's *Hexaemeron, The Glorious and Mighty Works of the Creation Day* (q. v.), at an auction sale. His first original hymn was written during his sojourn in Gausdal. During his pastorate in Kviteseid Landstad composed three hymns for the Reformation festival in 1837. At this time he also began to collect folk-songs, a work that had a great influence upon his hymn-writing. Through the hymns which he published he came to the attention of the church officials and was asked to prepare a new hymn-book for the Church of Norway. He declined the offer as his pastorate in Seljord claimed so much of his time. He therefore applied for the pastorate of Fredrikshald and was appointed to it in 1849. An assistant in this pastorate was granted him, and on October 7, 1852, a royal resolution was passed, delegating to Landstad the work of preparing "an outline for a new church-book essentially along the lines of his previous plan." In 1861 the long-looked-for *Kirke-Salmebog et Udkast* appeared. An article in one of the leading newspapers expressed sincere appreciation of the hymnal but also expressed the conviction that the omission of certain hymns, and especially that the form of language employed in the book, would prove a serious handicap in the way of its adoption by the congregations. Landstad gave a very scientific and earnest defense of his work, and while it gained many friends, it did not win universal sympathy for the new forms of expression which he had introduced into the language of the hymns. During the following years Landstad thoroughly revised his hymn-book. On October 16, 1869, *Landstad's Hymnary*, was authorized for use at public services in all places where the congregation would so decide. By the close of the year 1870 Landstad's *Hymnary* had been introduced into 648 of the 923 pastorates in Norway. In April, 1859, Landstad was appointed to the charge of Sanherred and labored there until 1876 when he was granted a release from duties with a pension. His golden wedding anniversary in 1879 developed into a grand celebration in honor of the hymn-writer and his estimable wife. Landstad died in Christiania, October 9, 1880.

    65. *When sinners see their lost condition*
  318. *Before Thee, God who knowest all*
  330. *I come to Thee, O blessed Lord*
  415. *Lo, many shall come from the East and the West*
  592. *I know of a sleep in Jesus' name*
  624. *O blessed home where man and wife*

LAURENTIUS, Laurenti (1660—1722), was the son of Herr Lorenz (or Laurenti), a burgess of Husum Schleswig, and was born at Husum on June 8, 1660. In 1681 Laurenti entered the University of Rostock and stayed there for a year and a half. He then attended the University of Kiel, where he studied music. In 1684 Laurenti was appointed cantor and director of the music at the Lutheran Cathedral Church at Bremen. He is one of the best hymn-writers of the Pietistic school. His hymns are founded on the Gospels for Sundays and festivals and make application from the leading thoughts to the Christian's life. They are characterized by noble simplicity, Scripturalness, and fervor. His 148 hymns were published in *Evangelia Melodica*, 1700. He died May 29, 1722.   72. *Rejoice, rejoice, believers*

LAYRIZ, Friedrich (1808—1859), was born in Nemmersdorf, Bavaria, on January 30, 1808, studied theology at Erlangen from 1826 until 1830, and in 1833 became "Repetent" in the theological seminary there. After a brief term as assistant pastor, he went to Hirschlach in 1837 as pastor and there began his work in hymnology. In 1843 Layriz became pastor at St. Georgen, and in the following year, as a protest against the *Bayrische Gesangbuch* of 1811, compiled his *Kern des deutschen Kirchenlieds*, and contemporaneously in his *Kern des deutschen Kirchengesangs*, published the first edition of his *Choralbuch*. In 1846 Layriz was called as pastor to Schwaningen, near Ansbach, where he lived until his death in 1859.

366. EINS IST NOT

LEESON, Jane Eliza (1807—1882). In spite of the fact that she is included in almost every collection of hymn-writers' biographies in the English language, very little is known about this English woman and her private life, except the dates of her birth in 1807 and death in 1882. She was for years a well-known figure in the Catholic Apostolic Church, contributing to its hymn-book nine hymns and translations. Later in life she entered the Roman communion. Some of her hymns were produced as "prophetical utterances," supposedly under the prompting of the Holy Spirit, at public services. A former member of the same communion, who heard her produce one such hymn at a service in Bishopsgate Church, records that "it was delivered slowly, with short pauses between the verses, a pause three times as long as any one would ordinarily make in reading. I have not known any one with a similar gift; but I have heard of an improvisatore who far surpassed Miss Leeson. She only exercised her gift at long intervals and could choose her own time and her own subject. He improvised very frequently, much more rapidly, and on any subject chosen for him by others." She possessed rare gifts in writing for children, and many such hymns flowed from her prolific pen. Her published collections of children's hymns date from 1842 with *Infant Hymnings* and *Hymns and Scenes of Childhood; The Child's Book of Ballads,* 1849; *Songs of Christian Chivalry,* 1848; *Paraphrases and Hymns for Congregational Singing,* most of which were rewritten from the *Scottish Translations and Paraphrases of 1781,* in 1853.

>191. *Christ the Lord is risen today; Alleluiah!* (Tr.)
>627. *Gracious Savior, gentle Shepherd*

LEHR, Leopold Franz Friedrich (1709—1744), the son of court counselor Johann Jakob Lehr, was born in Kronenburg, near Frankfurt-am-Main on September 3, 1709. He was sent to the gymnasium of Istein at an early age and remained there until he was 18. He was greatly impressed in early childhood, when A. H. Francke, during a visit in his home, blessed him with the laying on of hands. At his father's deathbed, he realized that living faith in Christ is the only thing that can fill the heart with abundant good cheer, even in the test of death itself. He came to the University of Jena in 1729 and the following year to Halle to study under J. J. Rambach (*q. v.*) and G. A. Francke. Lehr was also tutor for J. A. Freylinghausen's (*q. v.*) children. He was then appointed private tutor to the Countess of Anhalt-Köthen. Lehr collaborated with court preacher Allendorf of Köthen to publish in 1732, and later, the so-called *Köthnische Lieder*. He gained great popularity and was made assistant pastor at Köthen in 1740. He was loved by his people and his work bore great fruit. Two years later he was called as superintendent, but did not accept the position because his people needed him. He made a trip to Magdeburg in January, 1744, where he took sick. His sickbed now became his pulpit, and he spoke in more fervent terms than before. His cheerfulness of faith and confidence increased as his end approached. He died January 26, 1744.

>386. *My Savior sinners doth receive*

LEMKE, August (1820—1913). Very little is definitely known about this man. He came to America from Germany and became, in 1847, schoolteacher, organist, and choir director for Trinity Lutheran Church, Milwaukee, where he served until 1851. Then he resigned his position and entered a secular occupation. There are no further traces of him in the records of Trinity Church. It was during his term of service at this church that Lemke composed his tune for Weissel's great Advent hymn. He died November 1, 1913.

>73. MACHT HOCH DIE TÜR. (Third tune)

LINDEMAN, Ludwig Mathias (1812—1887), was born November 28, 1812, in Trondhjém, Norway. His father, Ole Andreas Lindeman, organist at Our Lady's Church of that city, was his first music teacher. After completing his liberal arts studies and beginning the study of theology, he was appointed organist at Our Savior's Church in Christiana, where he remained until his death on May 23, 1887. From 1849 on he also served as professor at the theological seminary. In 1871 he published his *Koralbog for den Norske Kirke.* Lindeman contributed greatly to the cause of good church music among the Scandinavians. It was said at his funeral that he had taught the Norwegian people to sing. Though some of his melodies are based on older *chorale* tunes, many are original. They breathe a spirit of deep piety and often partake of the character of the folk-song.

>8, 188. FRED TIL BOD
>149. CONSOLATION
>353. HERRE JESU KRIST
>467. KIRKEN DEN ER ET

LOCHNER, Karl Friedrich (1634—1697), was born April 2, 1634, in Nürnberg, Germany. He was educated at Breslau, Altdorf, and Rostock. He served as lecturer at Rostock and Nürnberg and finally served as pastor at Fürth from the year 1663 until his death. Sigismund von Birken *(q. v.)* presented him as Count Palatine with the poet's wreath in 1674. In 1671 he had been received into the Order of Pegnitz. He died February 25, 1697.

>404. *Soul, what return has God thy Savior*

LOGAN, John (1748—1788), the son of a farmer, was born at Fala, Midlothian. He was educated at the University of Edinburgh and entered the ministry of the Church of Scotland. He served as pastor in South Leith in 1770. He was unsuccessful as a candidate for the chair of Universal History in Edinburgh University. He wrote and offered a tragedy entitled *Runnamede* to the manager of the Covent Garden Theatre, but it was interdicted by the Lord Chamberlain "upon suspicion of having a seditious tendency." It was later acted in Edinburgh. In 1775 Logan was made a member of the committee which produced *Translations and Paraphrases* for the Church of Scotland. Logan was compelled to resign his charge at Leith in order to prevent deposition. He moved to London and supported himself partly by his pen until his death there on December 28, 1788.

>434. *O God of Jacob by whose hand*

LONGFELLOW, Henry Wadsworth (1807—1892), born at Portland, Maine, February 27, 1807, was educated at Bowdoin College. After four years of study in Europe, he became professor at Bowdoin, where he remained until 1854. His reputation as a poet is well known. He died on October 3, 1892. A bust was placed in his honor in Westminster Abbey.

>589. *Oh, how blest are ye whose toils are ended.* (Tr.)

LÖWENSTERN, Matthäus Appeles von (1594—1648), was born at Neustadt, Silesia, the son of a saddler, on April 20, 1594. In 1625 he was appointed music director and treasurer at Bernstadt by Duke Heinrich Wenzel of Münsterberg. The following year he received the appointment of director of the princely school at Bernstadt. In 1631 he was made Rath and Secretary and also Director of Finance. Löwenstern then served as Rath for the Emperors Ferdinand II and Ferdinand III. The latter ennobled him. His last office was Staatsrath at Öls to Duke Carl Friedrich of Münsterberg. He died at Breslau, April 11, 1648. Löwenstern's thirty hymns were written in imitation of antique verse forms and on the mottoes of the princes under whom he had served.

>28. *Now let all loudly sing praise*
>28. NUN PREISET ALLE
>258. *Lord of our life and God of our salvation*

LOY, Matthias (1828—1915), was born in Cumberland County, Pennsylvania, near Harrisburg, on March 17, 1828. He was the fourth of seven children. The mother of the family, who was a Lutheran, gave the children a Christian education. In 1834, when Matthias was six years old, the family moved to Hogestown. When Matthias was fourteen, he was sent as an apprentice to Baab and Hummel, printers of Harrisburg. Here he worked for six years, all the while attending school. Through Mr. Hummel he came to the attention of the Rev. C. W. Schäffer *(q. v.)*, pastor at Harrisburg, who suggested to him the vocation of the Lutheran ministry. Meanwhile he studied Latin and Greek under the tutorship of the principal of the Harrisburg Academy. Later he attended this Academy as a regular student. By this time he had made up his mind to become a minister. He left for Circleville, Ohio, to print a German semimonthly paper for the United Brethren Publishing House. Arriving in Circleville in the autumn of 1847, Loy met the Lutheran minister there, who suggested that he leave immediately for Columbus and there enter the Theological Seminary of the Evangelical Lutheran Synod of Ohio. Loy secured a release from his contract with the publishing house, and with the financial assistance of the Lutheran pastor, he left for Columbus. During his student days Loy was a reader of the *Lutheraner,* edited by C. F. W. Walther. Upon his graduation in 1849 Loy was called to a congregation in Delaware, Ohio. In 1860 he was elected President of the Joint Synod of Ohio and four years later was appointed editor of the *Lutheran Standard*. Then, after sixteen years in the ministry, Loy was called to the professorship of theology at Capital University in March, 1865. In 1878 he resigned as President of the Ohio Synod; he was succeeded by Prof. Wm. F. Lehmann, who had been Vice-President. At this time Loy returned the call to the English professorship of theology at Concordia Seminary, St. Louis. In 1880, when Prof. Lehmann died, Loy succeeded him both as President of the synod (which office he held until 1892) and as President of Capital University. In 1881 Loy started the *Columbus Theological Magazine*. He also fostered the formation of the Synodical Conference. However, at the Ohio Synod meeting at Wheeling in 1881, the synod withdrew from the Synodical Conference. He wrote the following books: *The Doctrine of Justification*, 1868; *Sermons on the Gospels*, 1888; *Christian Church*, 1896; *The Story of My Life*, 1905. He retired as professor emeritus in 1902 and died in 1915.

    5. *Lord, open Thou my heart to hear.* (Tr.)
  67. *The Bridegroom soon will call us.* (Tr.)
223. *We thank Thee, Jesus, dearest Friend.* (Tr.)
265. *Thine honor save, o Christ, our Lord.* (Tr.)
288. *Lord, help us ever to retain.* (Tr.)
295. *The Law of God is good and wise*
297. *The Gospel shows the Father's grace*
304. *An awe-full mystery is here*
310. *Thy table I approach.* (Tr.)
331. *Yea, as I live, Jehovah saith.* (Tr.)
334. *Let me be Thine forever.* (Tr.)
356. *Jesus, Savior, come to me.* (Tr.)
357. *Jesus, Thou art mine forever*
369. *All mankind fell in Adam's fall.* (Tr.)

LUDÄMILIA ELIZABETH, Countess of Schwarzburg (1640—1672), the second daughter of Count Ludwig Günther I of Schwarzburg, Rudolstadt, was born on April 7, 1640, at the Castle of Heidecksburg near Rudolstadt and was educated there, along with her cousin Ämilie Juliana (*q. v.*). In 1665 she went with her mother to the dowager Castle of Friedensburg near Leutenberg; but after her mother's death in 1670, she returned to Rudolstadt, where on December 20, 1671, she was formally betrothed to Count Christian Wilhelm of Schwarzburg-Sondershausen. At that time measles were raging in that district. Her sister Sophie Juliane was stricken and died February 14, 1672. By attending on her, Ludämilia and her youngest sister, Christiane Magdelene, caught the infection, and both died at Rudolstadt on March 12, 1672.

    348. *Jesus, Jesus, only Jesus*

LUTHER, Martin (1483—1546), the Great Reformer. His life is too well known to require more than the mention of some important details concerning his work as a hymn-writer. He was born at Eisleben, November 10, 1483, son of the miner Hans Luther and Margarete, *née* Ziegler. After receiving his education at Magdeburg, Eisenach, and Erfurt (M. A. 1505), he entered the Augustinian Convent at Erfurt and was ordained priest in 1507. He began to lecture at the University of Wittenberg in 1508 and was made Doctor of Theology in 1512. His nailing the 95 Theses on the door of the Castle Church in Wittenberg, October 31, 1517, is called the beginning of the Reformation. He was summoned to Rome to answer for his theses, but his Elector would not let him go. His *The Babylonian Captivity of the Church* brought the papal condemnation upon him, and at the Diet of Worms, 1521, he was placed under the Imperial ban. His friends took him to the Wartburg, where he spent a year and began the translation of the Bible (completed by 1534), besides writing other works. He returned to Wittenberg in 1522 to calm the disturbed minds there and in 1523 began the writing of hymns, which led to the publication of the *Achtliederbuch* in 1524, the first Lutheran hymnal. This so-called *Achtliederbuch* contained eight hymns. Four were by Luther, three by Paul Speratus, and one by an unknown author (probably Justus Jonas). "This is the tiny spring from which sprang the mighty stream of Protestant hymnody." In 1524 there appeared the Erfurt *Enchiridion* or *Handbook of Spiritual Songs and Psalms,* containing 25 hymns, 18 by Luther. In the same year Johann Walther *(q. v.),* musician, together with Luther issued *Spiritual Hymn-booklet,* for choir-singing for the young in five parts, with 32 German hymns, 24 by Luther — two thirds of all that he created for congregational hymn-singing. In time Luther added 12 more hymns, including *From Heaven Above* and *A Mighty Fortress.* Luther's method was to versify psalms, to translate and adapt Latin hymns, to improve and spiritualize folk-songs, and to write original hymns.

As a tribute to Luther as hymn-writer Merle D'Aubigne says: "The Church was no longer composed of priests and monks; it now was the congregation of believers. All were to take part in worship, and the chanting of the clergy was to be succeeded by the psalmody of the people. Luther, accordingly, in translating the psalms, thought of adapting them to be sung by the Church. Thus a taste for music was diffused throughout the nation. From Luther's time the people sang; the Bible inspired their songs. Poetry received the same impulse. In celebrating the praises of God, the people could not confine themselves to mere translations of ancient anthems. The souls of Luther and of several of his contemporaries, elevated by their faith to thoughts the most sublime, excited to enthusiasm by the struggles and dangers by which the Church at its birth was unceasingly threatened, inspired by the poetic genius of the Old Testament and by the faith of the New, ere long gave vent to their feelings in hymns in which all that is most heavenly in poetry and music was combined and blended. . . . Other children of the Reformation followed his footsteps; hymns were multiplied; they spread rapidly among the people and powerfully contributed to rouse it from sleep."

80. *All praise to Thee, eternal God.* (Tr.)
85. *From heaven above to earth I come*
95. *Savior of the Nations, come.* (Tr.)
103. *To shepherds as they watched by night*
104. *Now praise we Christ, the Holy One.* (Tr.)
137. *In peace and joy I now depart*
195. *Christ Jesus lay in death's strong bands*
224. *Come, Holy Ghost, God and Lord*
231. *We now implore God, the Holy Ghost* (stanzas 2—4)
249. *Isaiah, mighty seer in days of old*
249. *JESAIA, DEM PROPHETEN*
251. *We all believe in one true God*
259. *Flung to the heedless winds*
260. *O Lord, look down from heaven, behold*
261. *Lord, keep us steadfast in Thy Word*
262. *A mighty Fortress is our God*
262. *EIN' FESTE BURG*
267. *If God had not been on our side*
287. *That man a godly life might live*
313. *O Lord we praise Thee* (stanzas 2, 3)
329. *From depths of woe I cry to Thee*
387. *Dear Christians, one and all rejoice*
458. *Our Father, Thou in heaven above*
500. *May God bestow on us His grace*
590. *In the midst of earthly life*

LYTE, Henry Francis (1793—1847), was born June 1, 1793, at Edham, Ireland. Although he had intended to enter the medical profession, Lyte was led into the Gospel ministry and was ordained in 1815. He graduated from Trinity College, Dublin, where three times he won the prize for the best English poem. Early in his ministry he experienced a change of heart. He had been called to minister to a dying clergyman friend whose faith was clouded, and together they found peace in Christ. Of the change that came to him he wrote: "I was greatly affected by the whole matter and brought to look at life and its issue with a different eye than before; and I began to study my Bible and preach in another manner than I had previously done." He cared for the children of his friend and, although he was always poor, carried the burden cheerfully. He was "jostled from one curacy to another" until he settled in 1823 at Lower Brixham, a fishing village. The parish was new and consisted of fisherfolk. He was delicate and sensitive; his health was undermined, and he sought rest and restoration on the Continent. He died at Nice, November 20, 1847. His last words were "Peace; joy!" He published *Tales on the Lord's Prayer in Verse*, 1826; *Poems Chiefly Religious*, 1833; *The Spirit of the Psalms*, 1834.

  20. God of mercy, God of grace
  423. Jesus, I my cross have taken
  435. My spirit on thy care
  552. Abide with me! Fast falls the eventide

  MACKAY, Margaret (1802—1887), was born in 1802. She was the only daughter of Captain Robert Mackay, of Hedgefield, Inverness. She was married to Major William Mackay of the 68th Light Infantry in 1820. Mrs. Mackay died at Cheltenham, January 5, 1887. In addition to various prose works she published *Thoughts Redeemed, or Lays of Leisure Hours*, 1854, which contained 72 original hymns and poems.

  587. Asleep in Jesus! Blessed sleep

  MADAN, Martin (1726—1790), was the son of Colonel Martin Madan and Judith, *née* Cowper, who was distinguished for her literary proficiency, particularly in poetry. Madan studied law, was admitted to the bar, and entered upon the practice of his profession with the fairest prospect. However, while he was with some gay associates in a coffee-house in London, he was sent to hear John Wesley and to report to them, for their sport, an account of the man, his manner, and his discourse. On his return to the coffee-house Madan was asked, "Have you taken off the old Methodist?" Madan replied, "No, gentleman, but he has taken me off." The sermon that John Wesley had preached on the words "Prepare to meet thy God" changed the course of Madan's life. Martin Madan had married a daughter of Sir Bernard Hale, Chief Baron of the Exchequer in Ireland, and his mother-in-law was on familiar terms with Lady Huntingdon, who brought Madan under the influence of that circle of ministers and others of which she was center. With some difficulty Madan took holy orders, although he was classically educated and highly gifted as a speaker. His eloquence drew the attention of the populace, and crowds flocked to hear him. He was appointed to the Chaplaincy of the Lock Hospital, London. Through his interest among the wealthy he procured money for the erection of a chapel adjacent to the hospital, where he continued his ministry until the end of his life. Also by reason of his high social standing Madan was appointed Chaplain of Lord Apsley, afterwards Earl Bathurst, Lord High Chancellor. His cousin, William Cowper the poet, acknowledged his obligation to him for counsel in his spiritual troubles. Madan was passionately devoted to music and enjoyed a good reputation as a musical composer. He ceased preaching after he published his *Thelyphthora*, in which he advocated polygamy. He also published *A Commentary on the Articles of the Church of England, A Treatise on the Christian Faith*, and *A Collection of Psalms and Hymns Extracted from Various Authors*, 1760. The latter contained 170 hymns thrown together without order or system. In 1763 he added an "Appendix" of 24 hymns. This collection exerted a most powerful influence on the hymnody of the Church of England for many years. Madan also issued a tune book, which is commonly known as *The Lock Hospital Collection*. Many of the tunes — Bristol, Castle Street, Denbigh, Halifax, Helmsley, Hotham, Huddersfield, Kingston Leeds, Nantwich, and others — were of his own composition. Finally Madan's passion for music caused him at length to give more attention to it than to preaching, to such an extent that he gave offense to some by his practice of Sunday concerts, vocal and instrumental. After 1780 Madan studied the Latin classics and in 1789 published *A New and Literal Translation of Juvenal and Persius; with Copious Explanatory Notes* in two volumes. He died in 1790.

  18. Lord, we come before Thee now (cento)

  MADSON, Norman Arthur (1886—), son of Andrew J. Madson and Mary, *née* Hoverson, was born November 16, 1886, at Manitowoc, Wisconsin. He received his education at Wittenberg, Wisconsin, Academy; Luther College, Decorah, Iowa; Chicago University; and Luther Seminary, Hamline, Minnesota. He was ordained on November 14, 1915; served as traveling missionary of the Norwegian Synod on the Iron Range in Northern Minnesota, 1915—1916; as teacher at Luther College, 1916—1918; as chaplain in the U.S. Army, 1918—1919; as pastor at Bode, Iowa, 1919—1925; as pastor at Princeton, Minnesota, 1925— . He was married August 31, 1918, to Elsie Haakenson. He has served his church in the following offices: Secretary, Bethany Lutheran College Association, 1927—1929; Visitor of Northwest District of the Norwegian Synod, 1933—1935; President of Norwegian Synod, 1935 (relieved because of ill health); Editor of the *Lutheran Sentinel*, 1927—1929; Secretary of the Committee on Church Union, 1938— ; Member of the Intersynodical Committee on Hymnology and Liturgics, 1929— ; Member of the Norwegian Synod Home Mission Committee. He is the author of *Ved Betlehemskrybben*, a book of festival sermons; also author of the monograph, *The Norwegian Synod and the Christian Day-school*. 655. I pray Thee, dear Lord Jesus. (Tr.)

MAGDEBURG, Joachim (c. 1525—c. 1583), was born at Gardelegen in the Altmark. He matriculated at the University of Wittenberg in 1544. Two years later he became Rector in Schöningen, Brunswick, and pastor in Dannenberg, and in 1549 at Salzwedel, Altmark. In this year he allied himself with Flacius in an attack upon the Catholic Church. He refused to adopt the ceremonies of Rome prescribed in the Interim and was banished in 1552. By gaining the friendship of Superintendent Joh. Aepinus, he became in 1552 the diaconus of St. Peter's in Hamburg. In collaboration with Flacius, Magdeburg published the well-known historical work *The Magdeburg Centuries*. Shortly thereafter he finally succeeded in finding a permanent position. He was made chaplain under the Austrian Commander at Raab in Hungary. In 1571 he was at Erfurt and in 1581 at Efferding in Austria. He published *Christliche und tröstliche Tischgesenge*, 1572.

437:1. Who trust in God, a strong abode

MAJOR (Gross), Johann (1564—1654), was born at Reinstädt, near Orlamünde. He became diaconus at Weimar and then pastor and superintendent at Jena in 1605 and later professor of theology at the University there. He collaborated in editing the *Weimar Bibelwerk*. 317. Alas, my God, my sins are great

MALAN, Henri Abraham César (1787—1864), son of Jacques Imbert Malan, a professor in the College of Geneva, was born at Geneva, July 7, 1787. He was educated at Geneva; ordained to the ministry, October, 1810; pastor of the Chapelle du Témoignage, Geneva. The degree of D.D. was conferred on him by the University of Glasgow, October 10, 1826. He died at Vandoeuvres, near Geneva, May 18, 1864.

602. It is not death to die

MANN, Arthur Henry (1850—1929), was born on May 16, 1850, in Norwich, England, and started his musical career as a chorister in the cathedral there. He later served as organist at St. Peter's, Wolverhampton, Tettenhall Parish Church, Beverley Minster, and King's College, Cambridge. He was also organist at the University of Cambridge and music master of Leys School in Cambridge. He received his degree of Bachelor of Music from Oxford in 1874, and in 1882 his degree of Doctor of Music. He wrote a great deal for voice and organ and was musical editor of *The Church of England Hymnal*. 352. ANGEL'S STORY

MANN, Frederick (1846—1928). We have no further information on this author than the little given in *Songs of Praise Discussed*, namely, that he was at one time a Scottish Free Church minister, a chaplain at Claybury Asylum, and vicar of Temple Ewell. 424. My God, my Father, make me strong

MANT, Richard (1776—1848), was born on February 12, 1776, at Southampton, the son of the Master of the grammar school there. He attended Winchester and Trinity, Oxford, and received his B.A. in 1797 and his M.A. in 1799. After being ordained Mant first assisted his father as curate and subsequently served as Vicar of Coggeshall, Essex, 1810; Domestic Chaplain to the Archbishop of Canterbury, 1813; Rector of St. Botolph, Bishopsgate, London, 1816, and East Horsley, 1818; Bishop of Killaloe, 1820, of Down and Connor, 1823, and of Dromore, 1842. Mant was also Bampton Lecturer in 1811. He is known chiefly through his translations from the Latin. Among his noteworthy publications are his *Metrical Version of the Psalms*, 1824, *Holy-days of the Church*, 1828—1831, and *Ancient Hymns*, 1837. He died November 2, 1848.

468. For all Thy saints, O Lord

MARCH, Daniel (1816—1909), was born at Millburg, Massachusetts, July 21, 1816. After graduating from Yale, he was ordained to the Presbyterian ministry in 1845. Later he joined the Congregational Church. By 1868 Doctor March was pastor in Philadelphia. It was during this pastorate that he wrote his well-known hymn "Hark! the Voice of Jesus Calling." He published *Night Scenes in the Bible*, *Our Father's House*, *Home Life in the Bible*, *From Dark to Dawn*. He died on March 2, 1909, at Woburn, Massachusetts, at the very old age of ninety-three years.

496:1, 2, 4. Hark! the voice of Jesus crying

MARRIOTT, John (1780—1825), was born at Cottesbach, near Lutterworth, and was educated at Rugby and Christ Church, Oxford. He tutored for two years in the family of the Duke of Buccleuch, from whom he received the Rectory of Church Lawford in Warwickshire. He also served as curate of St. Lawrence and other parishes in Exeter, and of Broadclyst, near Exeter. Marriott published a volume of *Sermons* in 1818, but his hymns have never appeared in book form. He died March 31, 1825.

508. Thou whose almighty word

MARSH, Simeon Butler (1798—1875), was born at Sherburne, New York, on June 1, 1798. He started his musical career in a children's choir at the age of seven. At twenty he opened his first singing school and for about thirty years taught classes in and around Albany, New York. For a while he returned to Sherburne where he was superintendent of the Sunday-school, organist, and choir-leader. He died July 14, 1875.

345. MARTYN

MASON, Arthur James (1851—?), son of G. W. Mason, was born on May 4, 1851, and educated at Trinity College, Cambridge. He became a Fellow of his college in 1873 and Assistant Tutor in 1874. Mason was ordained in the latter year and was Honorary Canon and Canon Missioner of Truro and Vicar of All Hallows, Barking, London. In 1895 Mason became Professor at Cambridge and Canon of Canterbury and in 1903 Master of Pembroke College, Cambridge. A number of his hymns appeared in *Hymns Ancient and Modern*, particularly his translations from the Latin. He published *The Faith of the Gospel*.

309. O Jesus, blessed Lord to Thee. (Tr.)

MASON, Lowell (1792—1872), son of Johnson Mason and Caty, née Hartshorn, was born at Medfield, Massachusetts, January 8, 1792. When not much more than a boy, his fondness and aptitude for music placed him in the position of leader of a church choir in his native town. From Massachusetts he removed to Savannah, where he became clerk in a bank. Here he conducted the music of the large Presbyterian church and compiled his first collection of church music with the help of his teacher. Obtaining leave of absence from the bank, he bent his steps to Philadelphia and offered the copyright of his book to the publishers, provided he might receive a few copies for his own use. They all declined the offer; and when the young enthusiast went to Boston, he fared no better. He was about to return to Savannah, when he met George K. Jackson, who desired to examine his work. This gentleman expressed great satisfaction with it, and, with Lowell Mason's permission, showed the manuscript to the Board of Management of the Boston Händel and Haydn Society, of which he was a member. That society published it, giving the author an interest in the work. It became immensely popular, and in the next

[542]

thirty years ran through seventeen large editions. This success decided Lowell Mason's course of life. He remained in Savannah five years more and then took up his abode at Boston, became organist of Dr. Lyman Beecher's church, and commenced the work of lecturing and publishing church music in earnest. In 1832 he established the Boston Academy of Music, and in 1838 he obtained power to teach in all the schools of Boston. At the same time he founded periodical conventions of music-teachers, which have proved very useful and are now established in many parts of the States. He also published a large number of manuals and collections, which sold well and produced for him a handsome fortune. His degree of Doctor of Music — the first of its kind conferred by an American college — was granted by New York University in 1835. He died at Orange, New Jersey, August 11, 1872.

      157. COWPER
      175, 325, 650. HAMBURG
      225, 464. BOYLSTON
      303. UXBRIDGE
      394, 628. OLIVET
      412. MERIBAH
      495. MISSIONARY HYMN
      533. BETHANY

  MASSIE, Richard (1800—1887), was born on June 18, 1800, at Chester, England, the son of the Rev. R. Massie and Hester, née Townshend. His early days were spent at Chester, where his father was rector of St. Bride's. On January 7, 1834, he married Mary Ann Hughes of Blache Hall, Chester. She died seven years later. He translated many of the hymns of Spitta, Gerhardt, and Luther with artistic skill. His *Lyra Domestica*, 1860, Vol. I, contains translations of the first series of Spitta's *Psalter und Harfe*. Volume II of 1864 contains Spitta's second series and has an appendix of translations from other German authors. He died March 11, 1887.

    103. To shepherds as they watched by night. (Tr.)
    104. Now praise we Christ, the Holy One. (Tr.)
    195. Christ Jesus lay in death's strong bands. (Tr.)
    247. God the Father, be our Stay. (Tr.)
    287. That man a godly life might live. (Tr.)
    387. Dear Christians, one and all, rejoice. (Tr.)
    500. May God bestow on us His grace. (Tr.)
    528. If God Himself be for me. (Tr.)
    539. Come, Thou Bright and Morning Star. (Tr.)

  MATTES, John Caspar (1876—), was born in Easton, Pennsylvania, on November 8, 1876. He attended Lafayette College (A. B. 1898; A. M. 1901), was graduated from the Philadelphia Lutheran Theological Seminary in 1901, and received his D. D. from Mühlenberg College in 1925. Mattes was ordained to the Lutheran ministry in 1901 and served as pastor of the Church of the Savior, Trenton, New Jersey, 1901—1915; Holy Trinity, Scranton, Pennsylvania, 1915—1927; and St. John's Church, Scranton, 1927—1938. Mattes was appointed Professor of Theology at Wartburg Seminary, Dubuque, Iowa, in 1939, served twice as President of the Wilkes-Barre Conference of the Pennsylvania Ministerium, and was active on a number of committees and boards of the Lutheran Church. Mattes is the translator of six hymns in the *Common Service Book* of the United Lutheran Church in America.

    645:5. Behold, a Branch is growing. (Tr.)

  MAUDE, Mary Fawler, née Hooper (1819—1913), the daughter of George Henry Hooper, was born in Stanmore, Middlesex, England, and was married to the Rev. Joseph Maude in 1841. She became well known as a poet and hymn-writer. She published *Twelve Letters on Confirmation* in 1848 and *Memorials of Past Years* in 1852 (privately printed). She died at Overton in 1913.

    338. Thine forever, God of love

  MAXWELL, Mary (?). She was born in Norfolk, Virginia, and was the eldest daughter of Robert Robertson, a merchant. He was a Scotchman and for years a ruling elder of the first Presbyterian Church established in that community. His wife was Frances Ferebe, whose ancestry is presumably Norman-French. Mrs. Maxwell was educated in Norfolk, where she enjoyed remarkable advantages. In 1839 she was married to Wm. Maxwell, a graduate of Yale College. This gentleman was an excellent scholar, a lover of letters, and an eloquent speaker. His death occurred in 1857. When the Civil War started, Mrs. Maxwell moved to Danville, and there she remained with relatives until the close of the conflict, when she returned to Richmond. She has frequently written verse and poetry, but has always shunned publicity, preferring to be known simply as the "lady from Virginia." Further details of her life are lacking.

502. *Saints of God, the dawn is brightening*

McCOMB, William (1793—c. 1870), was born in Coleraine County, Londonderry, Ireland, in 1793. He was a layman and for many years a bookseller in Belfast, Ireland. He published *The Dirge of O'Neill*, 1816, and *The School of the Sabbath*, 1822. These, together with smaller pieces, were collected and published in 1864 under the title *The Poetical Works of William McComb*.

342. *Chief of sinners though I be*

MEDLEY, Samuel (1738—1799), was born on June 23, 1738, at Cheshunt, Hertfordshire, where his father kept a school. He received a good education. He was apprenticed to an oil-dealer, but, dissatisfied with the business, entered the Royal Navy. Medley had to retire from active service after having been wounded severely in a battle with the French fleet off Port Lagos, 1759. He was taken to the home of his grandfather and was converted by the latter's prayers and by a sermon of Dr. Watts, which was read to him. He became a member of the Baptist Church in Eagle Street, London, under Dr. Gifford, and shortly afterwards opened a school which he conducted for several years with success. Medley started preaching and received a call in 1767 to become pastor of the Baptist Church at Watford. In 1772 he became pastor in Liverpool, where he labored very successfully for twenty-seven years until his death on July 17, 1799.

200. *I know that my Redeemer lives*
340. *Awake, my soul, to joyful lays*

MEINHOLD, Johann Wilhelm (1797—1851), was born at Netzelkow, on the island of Usedom, on February 27, 1797, where his father was pastor. In 1813 he entered the University of Greifswald. In 1820 he became rector of the Town School at Usedom. Shortly after this, Meinhold was appointed to the pastorate of Coserow and later, in 1828, of Crummin in Usedom. In 1840 he received the degree of Doctor of Divinity from Erlangen. Four years after this, on Easter Sunday, he became pastor at Rehwinkel, near Stargard. He was a staunch conservative, and so, after passing through the revolutionary period of 1848, this feeling, coupled with his leaning toward Roman Catholicism, prompted him to resign his office in the autumn of 1850. He retired to Charlottenburg, a suburb of Berlin, and here he died after a residence of one year, on November 30, 1851. Meinhold is perhaps best known, not by his hymns, but by his historical romance *Maria Schweidler, die Bernsteinhexe*, 1843. This is supposed to have been taken from an old manuscript and was universally accepted as genuine. His poems and hymns appeared in his *Gedichte*, Leipzig, 1823, and in other publications.

595. *Tender Shepherd, Thou hast stilled*

MELANCHTHON, Philipp (Schwarzerd) (1497—1560), was born February 16, 1497, at Bretten, near Carlsruhe, and was the son of Georg Schwarzert. He attended the Latin School at Pforzheim from 1507 to 1509, and in October of the latter year entered the University of Heidelberg. Johann Reuchlin called him Melanchthon, the Greek form of his name, meaning "Black Earth." He was transferred to Tübingen on account of his extreme youth and there received his M. A. in 1514 and remained until 1518, as a private lecturer in philosophy. In that year he was appointed professor of Greek at the University of Wittenberg, and, after an inauspicious beginning, gradually gained the respect and esteem of both faculty and students. After the Leipzig Disputation in 1519 he was made a Bachelor of the Bible and a lecturer on theology, at times speaking to from 500 to 1,500 students. Martin Luther was Melanchthon's spiritual father and through the early period of Reformation the two worked side by side, the former continually strengthening and supporting the latter. Melanchthon's *Loci* and his framing of the *Augsburg Confession* have proved monumental contributions to Lutheranism even though he altered his position somewhat after Luther's death. Melanchthon's poems and hymns were written in Latin and had very little influence on the development of German hymnody. They were edited completely by C. G. Bretschneider at Halle, 1842, and a number have appeared in translation in Protestant hymnals. He died April 19, 1560.

254. *Lord God, we all to Thee give praise*

MENDELSSOHN-BARTHOLDY, Jacob Ludwig Felix (1809—1847), was born on February 3, 1809, at Hamburg, the son of a Jewish banker. His grandfather, Moses Mendelssohn, was a famous Jewish philosopher. He was baptized in the Lutheran Church at Berlin. As a boy he showed extraordinary musical talents, appearing as a concert pianist at the age of 10 and writing several compositions before he was much past 12 years. He was only 17 when he wrote the overture to *A Midsummer Night's Dream*. He was responsible for renewed interest in the study and performance of Bach in his time, and he himself excelled as a composer of sacred music, particularly in the larger forms. In 1829 he made his first of eleven visits to England, where he later received inspiration for some of his best works. In 1833 he served as director of concerts at Düsseldorf. From 1835 to 1843 Mendelssohn was conductor and teacher at the Gewandhaus in Leipzig. For the two years following he served the King of Prussia as royal Kapellmeister and director of the musical division of the Academy of Arts. He established and directed the Leipzig Conservatory, was a friend of every important musician of his day, and in all his musical compositions of every form he reflected a true Christian spirit of consecration.

94. MENDELSSOHN

MENTZER, Johann (1658—1734), was born July 27, 1658, at Jahmen, near Rothenburg in Silesia, and studied theology at Wittenberg. In 1691 he was appointed pastor at Merzdorf, in 1693 at Hauswalde, near Bischofswerde; in 1696 at Chemnitz, near Bernstadt, Saxony, where he died February 24, 1734. He was a good friend of J. C. Schwedler, Henriette Catherine von Gersdorf, and N. Ludwig von Zinzendorf, all hymn-writers and close neighbors. He had his share of afflictions. He wrote a large number of hymns, over 30 of which appeared in various hymn-books of his time.

30. *Oh, that I had a thousand voices.* (Part I)
243. *Oh, that I had a thousand voices.* (Part II)
477. *Lord Jesus, Thou the Church's Head*

MESSENGER, John A. (?). In the English version of D'Aubigne's *History of the Reformation* we find this translation of a portion of Luther's ballad on the martyrs of Brussels, and Messenger is given as translator. *Julian* records this also. There are no other details available.

259. *Flung to the heedless winds.* (Tr.)

MEYER, Anna Magdalena, *née* Plehn (1867—1941), was born November 14, 1867, in Alt-Rüdnitz, Neumark, Germany. Her parents were Georg Plehn and Ottilie, *née* Kassube. Her father was teacher of the Lutheran school at Alt-Rüdnitz, for nine and one half years, beginning in 1859. He resigned his position in 1869 and emigrated to America with his wife and four children. Entering our Practical Seminary, then at St. Louis, he was admitted to the ministry in 1871. After serving at Lake Ridge and Tecumseh, Michigan, several years, he served at Chippewa Falls, Wisconsin, for twenty-two years. At Chippewa Falls Anna Meyer received her schooling, first in the Christian day school, then at the local high school, after which she taught school herself for a number of years. On July 25, 1893, she was united in marriage with the Rev. Christian Meyer of Howard, South Dakota. Her husband died in 1939, after serving congregations in Nebraska, Illinois, and Wisconsin. She wrote original poems and translations from the German, which were published in church periodicals. An invalid for over a year, she died at Milwaukee, Wis., August 18, 1941, and was laid to rest beside her husband, three days later, at Sheboygan, Wis.

198. He's risen, He's risen, Christ Jesus the Lord. (Tr.)

MEYER, Franz Heinrich Christoph (1705—1767), was born, February 8, 1705, in Hanover, where his father Franz David Meyer was castle church organist, an office which his grandfather David Meyer had held and which he was to occupy after his father in 1734. His own two sons followed him in the same capacity. He was commissioned to provide the new tunes for the enlarged edition of the *Hannöverisches Kirchengesangbuch*, 1740.

335. MEIN SCHÖPFER, STEH MIR BEI

MEYER (Mayer, Mejer, Meier), Johann David (?), was a prominent councilor at Ulm. He published his *Geistliche Seelenfreud* in 1691 or 1692. It contained 111 tunes, of which 54 were his own compositions.

418, 424, 443. ES IST KEIN TAG

MEYFART, Johann Matthias (1590—1642), was born November 9, 1590, at Jena; studied at Jena and received several degrees; in 1616 he was made professor at Coburg. There he was a great moral power. In 1633 he published *De Disciplina ecclesiastica*, on account of which his colleagues made a complaint to the government. He left there and became theological professor at the revived University of Erfurt. He died at Erfurt, January 26, 1642. Meyfart is noted for his devotional works: *Tuba Poenitentiae prophetica*, 1625; *Tuba novissima*, 1626; *Hoellisches Sodoma*, 1629; *Himmlisches Jerusalem*, 1630; *Jüngstes Gericht*, 1632. These were noted for their vivid portrayals and their earnest calls to repentance and amendment of life.

619. Jerusalem, thou city fair and high

MILLER, Edward (1731—1807), was born at Norwich, England. He studied music under Dr. Burney and at one time played the German flute in Händel's orchestra. He was organist of Doncaster Parish Church from 1756 to 1807. Miller received his degree of Doctor of Music from Cambridge in 1786, and in the following year he published *Elements of Thorough-Bass and Composition*. He wrote a number of elegies, songs, sonatas, flute solos, and psalm tunes; he edited *The Psalms of David* in 1790 and *Psalms and Hymns Set to New Music* in 1801.

175. ROCKINGHAM OLD

MILMAN, Henry Hart (1791—1868), was born on February 10, 1791, in the parish of St. James, Westminster, London, and received his early training at Dr. Burney's at Greenwich and at Eton. Then he attended Brasenose College, Oxford, and took first place in classics, also carrying off a number of prizes, — an event chronicled in one of the Ingoldsby Legends as follows:

> "His lines on Apollo
> Beat all the rest hollow,
> And gained him the Newdigate prize."

Milman received his B. A. in 1813 and his M. A. in 1816. In the latter year he was ordained and served as Vicar of St. Mary's, Reading, until 1835. He wrote a number of plays, his tragedy, *Fazio*, being perhaps the best known. In 1821 Milman was appointed Professor of Poetry at Oxford, an office which he held for 10 years. He seems to have started his more intensive study of theology about the year 1827, his Bampton Lectures (delivered at Oxford), and his *History of the Jews* being the first products of the transition. In 1835 Milman was presented with the Canonry at Westminster and the Rectory of St. Margaret's by Sir Robert Peel. He was made

Dean of St. Paul's in 1849, and five years later published his greatest work, *History of Latin Christianity*. Milman wrote about 13 hymns, all of which are noteworthy for their high literary expression and lyric grace. His *Poetic Works* were published complete in three volumes in 1839. He died on September 24, 1868.

162. Ride on, ride on in majesty

MILTON, John (1608—1674), was born on December 9, 1608, at London. His father was a scrivener, of good repute and well-to-do. The father had become a Protestant and had therefore been disinherited by an earnest Roman Catholic father, so that John knew the difficulties of sincere belief. John was the third of six children, three of whom died in infancy. John was the pride of the family and was given every advantage of education. First he had a tutor at home, and then he was given a place in St. Paul's School from 1620 to 1625. In 1625 Milton entered Christ's College, Cambridge, as a pensioner. Here he had the nickname of "the Lady," partly because of his graceful appearance and manner and partly because of "the haughty fastidiousness of his tastes and morals." Milton's father had intended that he enter the service of the Church, but Laud's intolerance and evil conditions in the clergy turned him away from the pulpit. From 1632 until 1638 Milton lived with his father at Horton in Buckinghamshire. Milton wrote poetry already at Cambridge, and during the years at Horton he wrote his famous companion poems *L'Allegro* and *Il Penseroso*. During this period Milton also wrote *Lycidas* on the death of Edward King, drowned in the Irish Sea. In this poem Milton airs with freedom his views on the corrupt state of the English Church. After a visit to Florence (where he met Galileo, who had been imprisoned by the Inquisition), Milton returned to London and took charge of his sister's children, Edward and John Phillips. From 1640 on Milton devoted his literary talent almost exclusively to prose polemics. In the next two years two of his anti-Episcopalian pamphlets appeared. In 1643 Milton married Mary Powell, a girl of but 17. She left him after a month. After unsuccessful attempts to recover her, Milton wrote pamphlets on the *Doctrine and Discipline of Divorce*, which brought him into disfavor with the Presbyterians. He did less questionable service to the cause of enlightenment with his *Tractate of Education* and with his *Areopagitica*, a noble vindication of the liberty of the press.

The impoverished Powells induced Milton to take back their daughter, and she and her family were soon living with Milton. In 1647 the Presbyterian ascendency, to Milton's relief, was supplanted by that of the Independents. Before the execution of Charles I, Milton's *Tenure of Kings and Magistrates*, in which he maintained that it was lawful to put a "wicked king" to death, was almost completed. Its publication, in February, 1649, marked Milton as the best apologist for the new regime, and he was made Latin Secretary to the Council of State of Oliver Cromwell. In 1652 Milton became blind. In the following year (or in 1654) his wife died, leaving three children. In 1656 Milton married Catherine Woodchock, who died fifteen months later in childbirth. Milton was greatly grieved and wrote a touching sonnet to her memory. Soon after Milton began work on *Paradise Lost*, but it was not published until 1667; it was admired even by the royalists (among whom was Dryden, who was reported to have said, "This man cuts us all out, and the ancients too"). The royalists had ascended to power with the return of Charles II. For a time Milton was arrested (and some of his works were burned), but he was released upon payment of certain fees. In 1663 Milton married Elizabeth Minshull — thirty years younger than he. She brought order but not peace into his household. In 1671 *Paradise Regained* was published in one volume with *Samson Agonistes*. It seems incredible that Milton received only ten pounds from the sale of his great epic and that the copyright was sold by his widow for eight pounds seven years after his death. The year previous Milton's *History of Britain* appeared. Milton was buried in St. Giles's Church, Cripplegate. In spite of the exquisite beauty of his lyrics, Milton's direct influence on hymnology has been surprisingly slight. He is the scholar's rather than the people's poet. He died November 8, 1674.

570. Praise, oh, praise our God and King

MÖCK, Christian (1737—1818), was born on October 18, 1737, at Thann, on the Altmühl. He was interested in music from his earliest youth and served as oboist in the chapel of an infantry regiment in Ansbach from 1771 to 1781; in the latter year he became organist of the Cathedral there, in which position he served the Church for 37 years. He died April 11, 1818.

65, 598. WER WEISS, WIE NAHE

MOHR, Joseph (1792—1848), was born in Salzburg, Austria, December 11, 1792. Ordained a Roman Catholic priest, August 21, 1815, he served at Ramsau, Laufen, Kuchl, and other parishes in the diocese of Salzburg. He died at Wagrein, December 4, 1848.

229. Holy Spirit, hear us
646. Silent night! Holy night!

MOLANUS, Gerhard Walther (Wolter) (1633—1722), was born at Hameln, Germany, November 1, 1633. He studied at the University of Helmstädt and became professor of mathematics at Rinteln and later professor of theology; then Director of the Hanover Consistory and General Superintendent of Brunswick-Lüneburg; and finally titular Abbot of Loccum. He died at Hanover, September 7, 1722. He edited the Hanover *Gesangbuch* of 1698.

310. Thy table I approach

MÖLLER, Johann Joachim (1660—1733), was born in Sommerfeld and died as Archdeacon at Krossen, near the Bober and Oder, 1733.

196. I am content! My Jesus liveth still

MONK, William Henry, Mus. D. (1823—1889). Born in London, March 16, 1823, he became organist at St. Matthias Church, Stoke Newington, where he was able to conduct a daily choral service with only a volunteer choir. He was also organist and choir director of King's College, London, and professor of music. From 1876 he was professor in the National Training School for Music and at Bedford College. His chief fame rests on his work as musical editor of *Hymns Ancient and Modern* at which he was engaged practically until his death. "He had the sole musical initiative and veto on the original edition, and no other musical counsel was called in until the position of the book had been made." He also founded and edited the musical journal *The Parish Choir*.

222. CORONAE
374, 441, 468. ENERGY
552. EVENTIDE

MONSELL, John Samuel Bewley (1811—1875), was born in Londonderry, Ireland, on March 2, 1811. He received his education at Trinity College, Dublin. He was a well-known divine of the Church of England and a popular writer of prose and verse. His most popular book was *Our New Vicar*, 1867; it was printed in sixteen editions. He wrote about 300 hymns. He died as the result of a fall from the roof of his church at Guildford, which was in the course of rebuilding, on April 9, 1875.

447. Fight the good fight with all thy might
492. Lord of the living harvest
606. O'er the distant mountains breaking

MONTGOMERY, James (1771—1854), was the oldest son of John Montgomery, an Irish minister of the Moravian Church, and was born in Irvine, Ayrshire, Scotland, on November 4, 1771. At the age of seven he was sent to school at Fulneck in Yorkshire to prepare for the ministry. It was during his years at Fulneck that his parents were sent to the West Indies as missionaries. Both of his parents died there. He left Fulneck in 1787 and received work as a merchant in Mirfield. Despite his great dislike for the work, Montgomery worked in Mirfield for a year and a half. Then he took a similar position at Wath only to find it quite as unsuited to his taste as the former. He finally set out for London with a copy of his poems in the hope of finding a publisher for them. In this he failed. He did, however, get in touch with

Mr. Robert Gales of Sheffield, the owner and editor of the Radical *Sheffield Register*. Since Montgomery soon shared the views of Mr. Gales, he became coeditor. When Mr. Gales was forced to leave England to avoid prosecution, in 1794, Montgomery took over the paper and became its owner and editor. Montgomery changed the name of the paper to the *Sheffield Iris*. During the first two years of his editorship Montgomery was imprisoned twice in the Castle of York and fined, once for three months for commemorating the fall of the Bastille and again for six months for reporting a riot in Sheffield. But Montgomery did not remain a strict radical all his life. At the age of forty-three he returned to the Moravian congregation at Fulneck and became an active member. He was a zealous worker for missions and was an active member of the Bible Society. Montgomery was also a bitter opponent of slavery. He could not forget that his parents had given their lives as missionaries to the wretched blacks of the West Indies. His father's grave was at Barbados, and his mother was sleeping on the island of Tobago. Besides contributing poetry and hymns to the world for a period of fifty years, Montgomery lectured on poetry and literature. In 1833 he received a royal pension of $1,000.00 per year. James Montgomery never married. He reached the ripe old age of 83. He died at Sheffield and was honored with a public burial. He wrote 400 hymns, of which 100 are still in common use. A perusal of almost any English evangelical hymn-book will probably reveal more hymns by this gifted and consecrated man than by any other author, excepting only Isaac Watts and Charles Wesley. Among his longer poems are *The West Indies*, a poem in honor of the abolition of the African slave trade by the British Legislature in 1807; *The World before the Flood*, 1813; *The Pelican Island*, 1828. He died April 30, 1854.

2. *To Thy temple I repair*
35. *Songs of praise the angels sang*
59. *Hail to the Lord's Anointed*
136. *Angels from the realms of glory*
149. *Come to Calvary's holy mountain*
159. *Go to dark Gethsemane*
454. *Prayer is the soul's sincere desire*
455. *Our heavenly Father, hear*
484. *We bid thee welcome in the name*
490. *Pour out Thy Spirit from on high*
504. *O Spirit of the living God*
516. *In the hour of trial*
616. *Forever with the Lord*
635. *Here in Thy name, eternal God*

MOORE, Thomas (1779—1852), the noted Irish poet, was born in Dublin, May 28, 1779. He received his early education at a private school and later attended Trinity College in Dublin and then took up the study of law in London but never completed it. In 1800 Moore published his *Anacreon* in London. His first volume of poetry was published in 1801 as *Poems by the late Thomas Little*. He received a government post at Bermuda in 1804. But since this work did not appeal to him, he put a deputy in charge and then toured the United States and Canada. After his return to England, Moore published his *Odes and Epistles* in 1806. The publication of this work was attended by the severe and sarcastic remarks of the critic Jeffrey. The strife which ensued was to be settled by a duel, but the government authorities as well as Moore's friends would not permit such a settlement. Strange to say, Moore and Jeffrey became the best of friends after this affair. In 1811 Moore married Bessie Dyke, a Protestant. Though Moore was born and brought up a Catholic, he, from this time on, attended the Anglican services. He also permitted his children to be brought up in the Protestant faith. For a time Moore had to leave England and retire to the Continent because his deputy in Bermuda had embezzled some funds. During this period of retirement he became acquainted with Lord Byron in Venice. A very cordial friendship grew up between these two poets. In retirement near Ashbourne he produced *National Airs, Irish Melodies, Lalla Rookh*, and other poems. Despite the fact that Moore had a steady income from the two pensions which he had received (one of 300 pounds in 1835, and a civil pension of 100 pounds in 1850) the last days of his life were spent in sorrow. He had lost all his children, and this caused him much grief. One of his sons died as a surgeon in the English army, the other, after leaving the English service, joined the French Foreign Legion, much against the will of his father. Thomas Moore, a downcast and grief-stricken man, died on February 26, 1852.   531:1, 2. *Come, ye disconsolate*

MORELY, Thomas (1842—1891), was born on January 1, 1842, at Oxford, England, the son of a bookbinder, and studied music under L. G. Hayne and became an accomplished organist. He served for a time at St. Albans, Holborn, London, and contributed many tunes to the *St. Albans Tune Book.*

474. ZION

MORISON, John (1749—1798), was born in Aberdeen and studied at the university (King's College) there. In 1780 he was installed as parish minister at Canisbay Caithness, Scotland. He died at Canisbay, June 12, 1798. His work in hymnody was done in connection with the revision of the Scottish *Translations and Paraphrases* of 1745, as he was appointed a member of the revision committee in 1775.

106. *The people that in darkness sat*

MOTE, Edward (1797—1874), was born in London on January 27, 1797. As a youth he went astray, but was converted in 1813 under the preaching of the Rev. J. Hyatt. Thereupon he joined the congregation of the Rev. Alex Fletcher. Two years later he joined the Baptist Church. For some years he plied the trade of a cabinetmaker, spending some of his spare time writing for the press. At the age of fifty-five he entered the Baptist ministry. From 1852 until his death on November 13, 1874, he was pastor of the Baptist Church at Horsham, Essex. He published *Hymns of Praise,* London, 1836, which contained about 100 of his own compositions. Benson calls this publication "an anthology of Calvinistic praise."

370. *My hope is built on nothing less*

MUELLER, John Theodore (1885—   ), was born on April 5, 1885, at Janesville, Minnesota. He graduated at Concordia Seminary, St. Louis, 1907. He also studied at Tulane University and Xenia Theological Seminary. From the latter institution he received the degree of Doctor of Theology. After teaching at Luther College, New Orleans, Louisiana, from 1907 to 1911, and at Wittenberg Academy, Wisconsin, from 1911 to 1913, he became pastor of St. John's Church, Hubbell, Michigan, 1913, and of Zion Church, Ottawa, Illinois, 1917. He has served as professor of systematic theology and exegesis at Concordia Seminary, St. Louis, since 1921. He is well known as an author and poet. Among his works are: *Christian Fundamentals,* 1926; *The Church at Corinth,* 1928; *Christian Dogmatics,* 1934; *John Paton,* 1941; *Great Missionaries to Africa,* 1941.

275. *My soul doth magnify the Lord.* (Tr.)
560. *Gracious God, again is ended.* (Tr.)

MÜHLENBERG, William Augustus (1796—1877), came from one of America's most distinguished families. His great-grandfather, Henry Melchior Mühlenberg, has been called "the patriarch of the Lutheran Church in America," having come to this country from Germany in 1742. Six years later he founded the first permanent Lutheran synod in America. A son of the patriarch and grandfather of the author, Frederick Augustus, became president of the convention which ratified the Constitution of the United States and first Speaker of the new House of Representatives. His brother, the Rev. Peter Mühlenberg, was a Lutheran pastor at Woodstock, Pennsylvania, when the Revolutionary War broke out. It was he who threw aside his ministerial robe while standing in the pulpit of his church and stood revealed in the uniform of a Continental colonel and cried, "There is a time to preach and a time to pray, but these times have passed away. There is a time to fight, and that time has now come!" He immediately started enlisting men for his regiment, and before the war was ended, he had risen to the rank of Major General. William Augustus was born in Philadelphia, September 16, 1796. Because of the fact that the German language was used almost exclusively in the German Lutheran churches of those days,

William Augustus and his little sister were allowed to attend Christ Episcopal Church. In this way he drifted away from the Church of his great ancestors, and when he grew up, he became a clergyman in the Episcopal communion. It is evident that Mühlenberg brought something of the spirit of "the singing church" into the Church of his adoption, for in 1821 he issued a tract with the title, *A Plea for Christian Hymns*. It seems that the Episcopalians at this time were limited to a small group of hymns, and no one felt the poverty of the Church in this respect more keenly than did Mühlenberg. Two years later, when the General Convention of the Episcopal body voted to prepare a new hymnal, Mühlenberg was made one of the members of the committee. Another member of the committee was Francis Scott Key (*q. v.*). As a member of the committee, Mühlenberg contributed four original hymns to the new hymn-book. His later ministry centered in New York City, where he was head of a boys' school for a number of years and later rector of the Church of the Holy Communion. He soon became an outstanding church leader in the great metropolis. He founded St. Luke's Hospital, the first church institution of its kind in New York City. He died on April 6, 1877.

> 588. I would not live alway; I ask not to stay
> 631. Savior, who Thy flock art feeding

MÜHLMANN, Johannes (1573—1613), was born at Pegau, 1573, studied at Leipzig and Jena, and after serving as clergyman at Leipzig, Naumberg, and Laucha, he returned to Leipzig and ultimately became professor of theology at the university there. He died of typhus, November 14, 1613. He was a staunch defender of Lutheranism.

> 544. While yet the morn is breaking

NACHTENHÖFER, Caspar Friedrich (1624—1685), was born at Halle on March 5, 1624, and studied theology at the University of Leipzig, receiving his M. A. in 1651. He tutored for a while in the house of Chancelor August Carpzov at Coburg. In 1651 he was appointed diaconus and in 1655 pastor at Meeder, near Coburg. In 1671 he was called to Coburg as pastor of the Holy Cross Church and diaconus of the St. Moritz Church. He died as second senior in charge of St. Moritz, November 23, 1685. In the year of his death he published a metrical history of the passion entitled *Erklärung der Leidens- und Sterbens-Geschichte Jesu Christi*.

> 88. This night a wondrous revelation
> 150:1-3, 5. Lord Jesus, Thou art going forth

NARES, James (1715—1783), was born at Stanwell, Middlesex. He received his first musical training as a choir boy of the Chapel Royal. He assisted the head organist of St. George's Chapel, Windsor, for a while, and in 1734 became organist of York Cathedral, and in 1756 of the Chapel Royal. He published several musical works, including a *Treatise on Singing, A Collection of Catches, Canons, and Glees*, and a number of anthems and psalm-tunes.

> 450, 488. AYNHOE

NEALE, John Mason (1818—1866), was born on January 24, 1818, in London, the son of the Rev. Cornelius Neale, a man of considerable learning. His father died in 1823, and Neale's education continued under his gifted mother's direction. Later he attended Sherborne Grammar School and after that was a private pupil, first of the Rev. William Russell, Rector of Shepperton, and then of Prof. Challis. In 1836 he obtained a scholarship in Trinity College, Cambridge, where he was considered the best student in his class. He graduated as B. A. in 1840, continued as a Fellow at Downing College, and graduated as M. A. in 1845. Neale did not graduate with more than ordinary degrees, for he had the greatest antipathy to mathematics, proficiency in which was a prerequisite for Classical Honors. However, he did win many honors and prizes while at college. There, too, he identified himself with the Church movement, becoming a founder of the "Ecclesiological," or as it was commonly called the "Cambridge Camden Society." Neale was ordained deacon in 1841 and priest in the following year. In the latter year he married Miss Sarah Norman Webster, the daughter of an evangelical clergyman. In 1843 Neale was presented with a small incumbency of Crawley, Sussex. Because of his bad lungs, he was obliged to go to Madeira as the only chance of saving his life. He stayed there until the summer of 1844. In 1846 he was presented by Lord Delaware with the Wardenship of Sackville College, East Grinstead. Here in quiet retreat he devoted himself to literary work, to the advancement of the great church revival, and to the Sisterhood of St. Margaret's, which he founded with Miss S. A. Gream. Other institutions gradually arose in connection with this Sisterhood of St. Margaret's, viz., an orphanage, a Middle Class School for girls, and a House at Aldershot for the reformation of fallen women. The blessings which the East Grinstead Sisters brought to thousands of sick and suffering cannot be counted. Dr. Neale met with many difficulties and great opposition from the outside, which on one occasion, if not more, culminated in actual violence. His character, however, was a happy mixture of gentleness and firmness, and he therefore lived down all opposition. His last public act was to lay the foundation of a new convent for the Sisters on July 20, 1865. Neale took sick the following spring and after five months of acute suffering died August 1, 1866. One of his traits must not pass unnoticed — his charity, which was unbounded. He was an industrious and voluminous writer of prose and verse. His prose works include: *Commentary on the Psalms, The History of the Holy Eastern Church, The Primitive Liturgies of St. Mark, St. Clement, St. James, St. Chrysostom, and St. Basil.* His original poetical works include: *Hymns for Children,* 1842; *Hymns for the Young,* 1844; *Songs and Ballads for the People,* 1844. As a translator Neale's success was preeminnet. To him more than to any one else we owe some of the most successful translations from the classical languages. Neale had all the qualifications of a good translator — an excellent knowledge of the classics and medieval Latin and an exquisite ear for melody and spiritedness. From the Latin Dr. Neale translated hymns which appeared in 1851 under the title *Medieval Hymns and Sequences* and in 1852—1854 *Hymnal Noted.* These two were followed by *Hymns, chiefly Medieval, on the Joys and Glories of Paradise,* 1865. *Hymns of the Eastern Church,* 1862, are translations from the Greek.

62. *Oh, come, oh, come, Emmanuel.* (Tr.)
76. *A great and mighty wonder.* (Tr.)
98. *Of the Father's Love begotten.* (Tr.)
116. *To the name of our salvation.* (Tr.)
131. *The star proclaims the King is here.* (Tr.)
160. *All glory, laud, and honor.* (Tr.)
168. *The royal banners forward go.* (Tr.)
204. *Come, ye faithful, raise the strain.* (Tr.)
205. *The day of resurrection.* (Tr.)
208. *Ye sons and daughters of the King.* (Tr.)
255. *Stars of the morning, so gloriously bright.* (Tr.)
256. *Around the throne of God a band*
307. *Draw nigh and take the body of the Lord.* (Tr.)
322. *And wilt Thou pardon, Lord.* (Tr.)
333. *Blessed Savior, who hast taught me*
448. *Brief life is here our portion.* (Tr.)
466. *Christ, Thou art the sure foundation.* (Tr.)
513. *Art thou weary, art thou troubled*
555. *The day is past and over.* (Tr.)
564. *O Trinity, most blessed Light.* (Tr.)
605. *The world is very evil.* (Tr.)
613. *Jerusalem the Golden.* (Tr.)
614. *For thee, O dear, dear country.* (Tr.)
633. *O Lord of hosts, whose glory fills*

NEANDER, Joachim (1650—1680), was born at Bremen, the eldest child of Johann Joachim Neander and Catharina, *née* Knipping. The father was a master in the Paedogogium at Bremen. The grandfather had changed the family name from Neumann or Niemann to the Greek form. Joachim was descended from a long line of distinguished clergymen, going back as far as his great-great-grandfather. Neander first attended the Paedogogium in Bremen. In October of 1866 he entered as a student at the Academic Gymnasium of Bremen. His student life was as riotous and profligate as that of his fellow-students. He once went to a service at St. Martin's Church with two like-minded comrades to criticize and find amusement. But the earnestness of the Rev. Theodore Under-Eyck touched his heart, and subsequent conversations with Under-Eyck proved the turning point of his spiritual life. Hatfield reports Neander's conversion as coming after his conversations with the Rev. Under-Eyck, when Neander lost his way among the rocks and wooded hills in eager pursuit of game. Night had overtaken him, and he wandered about until he found himself on the very edge of a steep precipice, where another step forward would have ended his life. He now fell on his knees in prayer and vowed to give himself to God's service. He then resumed his search for a way of escape, and speedily, as if led by a divine hand, he succeeded in finding the well-known path to his home. Neander kept his vow and became a new man. In the spring of 1671 Neander became the tutor of five young men, sons of wealthy merchants at Frankfurt-am-Main and accompanied them to the University of Heidelberg. Here Neander remained until 1673, and here he learned to know and love the beauties of nature. In the spring of 1674 Neander was appointed Rector of the Latin School at Düsseldorf. This institution was under the supervision of a Reformed pastor, Sylvester Lürsen, an able man, but of a contentious spirit. At first the two men worked together harmoniously, Neander assisting with pastoral duties, and preaching occasionally, although he was not ordained as a clergyman. Later, however, he fell under the influence of a group of separatists, influenced by Labadie, and began to imitate their practices. He refused to receive the Lord's Supper on the ground that he could not partake of it with the unconverted. He induced others to follow his example. He also became less regular in his attendance at public worship and began to conduct prayer meetings and services of his own. In 1676 the church council of Düsseldorf investigated his conduct and dismissed him from his office. Fourteen days after this action was taken, however, Neander signed a declaration in which he promised to abide by the rules of the church and school, whereupon he was reinstated. There is a legend to the effect that, during the period of his suspension from service, he spent most of his time living in a cave in the beautiful Neanderthal, near Mettmann, on the Rhine, and that he wrote many of his hymns at this place. It is a well-established fact that Neander's great love for nature frequently led him to this place, and a cavern in the picturesque glen still bears the name of "Neander's Cave." In July, 1679, Neander became an unordained assistant of the Rev. Under-Eyck at St. Martin's Church. He most probably would have advanced to the pastorate, but consumption brought death the following year. Joachim Neander is regarded as the foremost hymn-writer of the German Reformed Church and is called "the Paul Gerhardt of the Calvinists." He wrote about 60 hymns.

1, 209, 221, 257, 472. NEANDER
4, 41, 42. WUNDERBARER KÖNIG
39. *Praise to the Lord, the Almighty*
41. *Wondrous King, all-glorious*

NEUMANN, Caspar (1648—1715), was born at Breslau, September 14, 1648. He attended the University of Jena and was graduated with an M. A. in 1670. For some time he lectured at this university. On November 30, 1673, he was ordained traveling chaplain to the son of Duke Ernst of Gotha, Prince Christian. Three years later he became court-preacher at Altenburg. He was appointed diaconus of St. Mary Magdalene Church at Breslau in December, 1678, and was pastor there in 1689. The following year he accepted the position as pastor of St. Elizabeth's Church at Breslau. In connection with this position he also inspected churches and schools of his district and was first professor of theology in the two Gymnasia at Breslau. He died at Breslau on January 27, 1715. Neumann was regarded as a poet of first rank. His hymns, 39 in all, were used almost entirely in such collections as *Breslauische Gesangbuch*, 1748; *Schweidnitzer Gesangbuch*, 1749; and the *Hirschberger Gesangbuch*, 1752. Neumann was a celebrated preacher, but his influence was felt more through his written than through his spoken word. He published a prayer-book, *Kern aller Gebete, Breslau*, 1680. This book passed through many editions.

411. *From eternity, O God*
560. *Gracious God, again is ended*

NEUMARK, Georg (1621—1681), was born on March 16, 1621, the son of Michael Neumark, a clothier of Langensalza, Thuringia, where Georg was born. After receiving his education at the gymnasia of Schleusingen and Gotha, Neumark became a family tutor. He wished to continue his education at the University of Königsberg, but on the way there he was robbed of all of his possessions except his prayer-book and a small amount of money sewn in his clothes. This made university attendance impossible for him at this time, as he was reduced to extreme poverty. He returned to Magdeburg. Failing to find work there, he tried in vain also at Lüneburg, Winsen, and Hamburg till finally at Kiel he found employment through Nicolaus Becker, a former Thuringian, and chief pastor of the city. Neumark became tutor in the home of Judge Stephen Henning. Immediately after Neumark received this position, he wrote "If thou but suffer God to guide thee." He saved enough money to be able to matriculate at the University of Königsberg in 1643. Here he remained for five years studying law and poetry, the latter under the famous Simon Dach (q. v.). Thereafter Neumark earned a precarious livelihood in Warsaw, Thorn, Danzig, and Hamburg. In Hamburg he found employment through the good graces of the Swedish ambassador. Later he returned to Thuringia as a court poet, librarian, and registrar to Duke Wilhelm II of Saxe-Weimar. Finally he became custodian of the ducal archives. In 1656 Neumark became secretary of the Fruit-Bearing Society. Besides being a hymn-writer, Neumark was also a musician. He died July 18, 1681.

194, 518, 529. WER NUR DEN LIEBEN GOTT
518. *If thou but suffer God to guide thee*

NEUMEISTER, Erdman (1671—1756), was born at Üchteritz on May 12, 1671. He received his education at the University of Leipzig (M. A. 1695). In 1698 he became pastor and assistant superintendent of the Eckartsberg District. He entered upon the office of senior court preacher, consistorialrath, and superintendent in 1706 at Sorau. In the year 1715 he accepted the appointment of pastor of St. James's Church of Hamburg. He died in that city on August 18, 1756. Neumeister ranks high among the German hymn-writers of the eighteenth century, not only for the number of his hymns (650), but also for their abiding value. He uses excellent language. All of his poems reveal a humble trust and faith in God. Neumeister was bitterly opposed to Pietism, and he used the pulpit and the press to warn the people against it and to instruct them in true Lutheranism. It was his purpose to "preserve the simplicity of faith from the subjective novelties of this period." One of his poems clearly shows his feelings towards Pietism (*Koch*, V, 374):

Und da der Teufel in der Welt
Sich auch durch Frömmigkeit verstellt,
So decke seine Bosheit auf

Und gib, dass unser Lebenslauf
Von Herzen fromm, und nie darbei
Kein pietistisch Wesen sei.

Besides his accomplishments as hymnist, Neumeister was also known as an earnest and eloquent preacher. In his later life he composed tunes to the hymns he had written in his student days. He was a contemporary of J. S. Bach (q. v.), to some of whose Cantatas he wrote the texts.

324. *Jesus sinners doth receive*
381. *I know my faith is founded*

NEWTON, John (1725—1807), was born on July 24, 1725, in London. His mother, a pious Dissenter, found her greatest joy in teaching her boy Scripture-passages and hymns. She often expressed the hope to her son that he might become a minister. However, she died when John was only seven years of age, and thus the boy was left with little religious restraint or influence in his life. Between the ages of eight and ten Newton acquired a meager education. When he was eleven, he joined his father, who was a sea captain, and made five voyages to the Mediterranean. His subsequent life was one of increasing dissipation and degeneration. He was pressed into the navy, but deserted. He was captured and flogged before the mast. For the next fifteen months he lived, half-starved and ill-treated, in abject degradation under a slave dealer in Africa. Through the study of Shaftesbury and the instruction of one of his comrades, Newton became an outspoken infidel. But the memory of his mother and the religious truths which she had implanted in his soul as a child gave his conscience no peace. The following factors combined to effect a very gradual change that led to his conversion to Christ: the reading of *The Imitation of Christ* by Thomas à Kempis, a terrific storm at sea on a return from Africa, and a deliverance from a malignant fever in Africa. The six following years, during which he commanded a slave ship, matured his Christian belief. On his last voyage he met a pious captain who helped to bring his to a truer and deeper faith in Christ. Newton returned to England, where he studied Hebrew and Greek and exercised in occasional preaching in Liverpool under the guidance of Whitefield, Wesley, and the Non-Conformists. In 1750 he married his childhood sweetheart, Mary Catlett, whose memory also had been a restraining influence in his years of degeneracy. Newton became a minister in 1758, but was not ordained until 1764 at Olney, near Cambridge. The Olney period was the most fruitful of his life. Here he wrote the *Omicron Letters*, 1774, the *Olney Hymns*, 1779, and *Cardiphonia*, 1781. The *Olney Hymns* were written in collaboration with his good friend, the poet William Cowper (q. v.). It was at Newton's suggestion that the two undertook to write a hymn-book. Of the 349 hymns in this book, Cowper is credited with 66, while Newton wrote the remainder. While at Olney, Newton was unwearied in his zeal for pastoral visiting, preaching, and prayer meetings. After sixteen years of service in Olney, he assumed charge of St. Mary Woolnoth in London. In 1805, when Newton was no longer able to read his text, his reply when pressed to discontinue preaching was, "What, shall the old African blasphemer stop while he can speak!" The story of his sins and his conversion, published by himself, and the subject of lifelong allusion, was the base of his influence; but it would have been little but for the vigor of his mind, his warm heart, candor, tolerance, and piety. Newton served for 28 years as rector of St. Mary Woolnoth. Among his converts were numbered Claudius Buchanan, missionary to the East Indies, and Thomas Scott, the Bible commentator. When Newton was nearly 80 years old it was necessary for a helper to stand in the pulpit to hold his manuscript. His self-composed epitaph reads, "John Newton, clerk, once an Infidel and Libertine, a servant of slavers in Africa, was, by the rich Mercy of our Lord and Savior Jesus Christ, preserved, restored, pardoned, and appointed to preach the Faith he had long labored to destroy." He died December 21, 1807.

 11. *Safely through another week*
 46. *On what has now been sown*
 51. *Now may He who from the dead*
113. *While with ceaseless course the sun*
364. *How sweet the name of Jesus sounds*
456. *Approach, my soul, the mercy-seat*
459. *Come, my soul, thy suit prepare*
469. *Glorious things of thee are spoken*

NICOLAI, Philipp (1556—1608), the son of a Lutheran pastor, was born on August 10, 1556, at Mengeringhausen. He studied at both the universities of Erfurt and Wittenberg (D. D. 1594). In 1583 he was ordained as Lutheran pastor at Herdecke only to resign this position three years later because of the prevalence of strong Roman Catholic sentiment in that city. In 1587 he became pastor of Niederwildungen, after having served there as diaconus for a year. The next year he became chief pastor of Altwildungen and also court preacher to Countess Margareta of Waldeck. It was while there that he took part in the Sacramentarian controversy raging at that time and firmly upheld the Lutheran point of view. In 1596 Nicolai became pastor at Unna in Westphalia, where he became embroiled in the controversy with the Calvinists. During his ministry at Unna the town was devastated by the pestilence. Nicolai's window looked out to the cemetery where often thirty interments a day took place. In these dark days when every household was in mourning Nicolai wrote in his *Frewden-Spiegel:*

"There seemed to me nothing more sweet, delightful, and agreeable than the contemplation of the noble, sublime doctrine of Eternal Life obtained through the Blood of Christ. This I allowed to dwell in my heart day and night and searched the Scriptures as to what they revealed on this matter, read also the sweet treatise of the ancient doctor Saint Augustine *(De Civitate Dei)*. . . . Then day by day I wrote out my meditations, found myself, thank God, wonderfully well, comforted in heart, joyful in spirit, and truly content; gave to my manuscript the name and title of a Mirror of Joy, and took this so composed *Frewden-Spiegel* to leave behind me (if God should call me from this world) as the token of my peaceful, joyful, Christian departure, or (if God should spare me in health) to comfort other sufferers whom He should also visit with the pestilence. . . . Now has the gracious, holy God most mercifully preserved me amid the dying from the dreadful pestilence and wonderfully spared me beyond all my thoughts and hopes, so that with the prophet David I can say to Him 'O how great is Thy goodness, which Thou hast laid up for them that fear Thee.'"

Nicolai gained great fame as a preacher and was called a "second Chrysostom." He was a genius who not only possessed the gift of writing sublime poetry but revealed talent as a composer. His tune for his own "Wachet auf" has been justly called the "King of Chorales." His tune for his other famous hymn, "Wie schön leuchtet der Morgenstern," has been called the "Queen of Chorales." While at Unna Nicolai had to flee before the invasion of the Spaniards in December of 1598, but was able to return by April of the next year. In 1601 Nicolai took his last charge as chief pastor of St. Katherine's Kirche in Hamburg, where he died of a fever.

23, 79, 189, 235, 343, 546, 639. WIE SCHÖN LEUCHTET
444, 609. WACHET AUF
343. *How lovely shines the Morning Star*
609. *Wake, awake, for night is flying*

NIEMEYER, Eduard (1854). We have no further information on this composer.

626. O SELIG HAUS

NIGIDIUS (Niege), Georg (1525—1588), was born November 25, 1525, at Allendorf on the Werra and was perhaps the son of Peter Nigidius (see below). At nine years of age he came to Kassel, where, under the tutelage of Cantor Georg Kern, the foundation for a very thorough musical education was laid. From 1542 he attended the University of Marburg and graduated in 1546 with a bachelor's degree. He enlisted in the army and thus began the restless life of a soldier. He served in the Smalcald War, at Bremen, in Scotland, at Hamburg, and was made a prisoner of war in Berlin. Some time later he became a notary in Buxtehude; then an Excise Commissioner in Stade. In the war between Denmark and Sweden he obtained a captaincy and likewise under Ludwig of Nassau in the Netherlands, 1566. After twenty years of intermittent war service he served in various civil offices. Then he re-entered army life in 1578. He then became city magistrate of Lage, near Herford, and, 1585, steward of the Kommenturei in Herford. He moved to Rinteln in 1587, where he died July 4, 1588, of apoplexy. Thus ended the colorful and checkered life of a gifted author and composer, forgotten and unknown until Prof. Dr. P. Althaus of Leipzig in 1918 made a remarkable discovery in the royal library in Berlin. Here were found, after more than three centuries, the manuscripts of several volumes of poetical and musical productions entitled: *The Seven Penitential Psalms together with all manner of Christian Hymns of Praise and Thanksgiving, and also Prayers and Passages of Scripture Composed and Compiled by Georg Niege of Allendorf, a Captain.* Unable to find a publisher, Nigidius had sent the manuscript to Nikolaus Selnecker to obtain his aid for publication in Leipzig. Selnecker, to his regret, could not find a publisher either. His opinion was: "Those beautiful songs are full of comfort and would refresh many Christians." So the dust of centuries was allowed to accumulate on the manuscript. However, several hymns, among them the morning hymn "Thy Inmost Heart Now Raises," were published in *Creutzbuechlein,* 1585—1587, at Herford. However, because there were no notes in the printery at Herford, the melodies of Nigidius' own creation, which Selnecker also praised highly, were not included.

548. *My inmost heart now raises*

NIGIDIUS, Petrus (1501—1583), born in Allendorf, studied at the University of Erfurt, and became rector in Eschwege and Allendorf and Göttingen. He visited Wittenberg and heard Luther and Melanchthon. For a time he served as rector in Darmstadt and in Lüneburg, then returned to his native city to teach there. In 1532 he became preceptor and magister in Marburg. From 1539 to 1549 he taught at Cassel and then returned to the pädagogium in Marburg where he was superintendent until 1561. From then until his retirement as emeritus in 1575, he was first professor of history, then of physics, at the university of Marburg. The authorship of a German-Latin catechism, published in Marburg in 1554, is ascribed to him.

556. DIE NACHT IST KOMMEN

OAKELEY, Sir Herbert Stanley (1830—1903), son of Sir Herbert Oakeley, Bart., was born at Ealing, Middlesex, July 22, 1830. He was a pupil of Dr. Stephen Elvey at Oxford, afterwards of Moscheles, Schneider, and others abroad; B.A. Oxford 1853, M.A. 1856; Professor of Music in Edinburgh University, succeeding John Donaldson, 1865 to 1891; Mus. Doc. Canterbury 1871, Oxford 1879; LL.D. Aberdeen 1881, and Composer of Music to the Queen in Scotland; knighted 1876; elected a member of the Philharmonic Academy of Bologna in 1888. He retired in 1891 and died at Eastbourne in 1903.

280. ABENDS

OCCOM, Samson (1732—1792), a Mohican Indian, was born at Norwich, Connecticut, in 1732. At the age of seventeen he became converted after he had heard Whitefield preach during one of his sojourns in America. After his conversion he was received into the home of the Rev. Eleazer Wheelock at Lebanon, Connecticut, where for four years he applied himself diligently to the study of Holy Writ. In 1759 he was ordained and began work among the Montauk Indians of Long Island. During the years 1766 and 1767 he visited England for the purpose of raising funds to carry on educational work among the American Indians. He met Whitefield during this time and also preached for John Newton at Olney. He succeeded in raising between ten and fifteen thousand pounds for a school which was later incorporated as Dartmouth College. Returning to his work on Long Island, he spent the closing years of his life at Oneida County, New York, where he died in 1792. He published *Choice Collection of Hymns and Spiritual Songs*, 1774.

538. Now the shades of night are gone

OLEARIUS, Johannes (1611—1684), was born September 17, 1611, at Halle, graduated from the University of Wittenberg and lectured at that institution, later became chief court-preacher and private chaplain at Halle under Duke August. He was made Kirchenrat in 1657 and General Superintendent in 1664. After the duke's death he held similar appointments at Weissenfels until his own death on April 24, 1684. He was the author of devotional books, a commentary of the entire Bible, and compiler of the *Geistliche Singe-Kunst*, 1671, the most comprehensive collection of the best German hymns then in existence, the first edition of which contained 302 of his own hymns. Many of these were for times and seasons hitherto unprovided for, and many were speedily adopted into German hymnals.

```
  5. Lord, open Thou my heart to hear
 38. The Lord, my God, be praised
 61. Comfort, comfort, ye my people
384. O how great is Thy compassion
408. Jesus Christ, my Pride and Glory
```

OLEARIUS, Johann Gottfried (1635—1711), son of Dr. Gottfried Olearius, was born at Halle, September 25, 1635, was educated at Leipzig and other German universities. In 1658 he was ordained and became assistant to his father at St. Mary's Church, Halle, later becoming pastor and also superintendent of the second portion of the district of Saale. In 1688 he was made chief pastor, superintendent, and Consistorialrat at Arnstadt and also professor of theology in the gymnasium there. He died at Arnstadt, May 21, 1711, after having been totally blind for several years. He published *Jesus! Poetische Ernstlinge* in 1664 and *Geistliche Singe-Lust* in 1697.

```
 55. Come, Thou precious Ransom, come
272. When all the world was cursed
```

OLIVER, Henry Kemble (1800—1885), was born at Beverly, Massachusetts, and received his first musical training in Park Street Church, Boston. He attended Dartmouth and Harvard and received his degree of Doctor of Music from Dartmouth. He taught at Salem, Massachusetts, until 1844, when he became superintendent of the Atlantic Cotton Mills. In 1859 Oliver was mayor of Lawrence and later served as head of the Massachusetts Bureau of Statistics of Labor. He published *The National Lyre* in 1848 and *Original Hymn Tunes* in 1873.

346. FEDERAL STREET

OLIVERS, Thomas (1725—1799), was born at Tregynon, near Newton, Montgomeryshire, where he was brought up rather carelessly by relatives and given very little formal education. He was apprenticed to a shoemaker and seems to have passed his youth in such disrepute that at the age of 18 he was forced to leave his home town. Then Olivers traveled about the country till he came to Bristol, where he heard George Whitefield preach from the text "Is not this a branch plucked out of the fire?" This sermon changed the whole course of his life. He joined the Methodist Society at Bradford-on-Avon and was engaged by Wesley as one of his preachers. He traveled about as an evangelist from October, 1753, to his death in March, 1799, covering about 100,000 miles in the service of the Gospel. Olivers was for a while coeditor with John Wesley and "Corrector of the Press" of the *Arminian Magazine*.

40. *The God of Abraham praise*

OLSSON, Olof (1841—1900), was born March 31, 1841, in Karlskoga, Vaermland, Sweden. Ordained in 1863, he served as pastor in Sweden until 1869, when he came to America. Here he served as pastor in Lindsborg, Kansas, 1869, was a member of the Kansas Legislature from 1871 to 1872; professor at Augustana College and Seminary, 1876—1888, and became its president in 1891. He organized the Händel Oratorio Society at the college and seminary. He published *Vid Korset, Det Christna Hoppet*. He died in May, 1900.

163. *The death of Jesus Christ, our Lord*. (Tr.)

OMEIS, Magnus Daniel (1646—1708), was born at Nürnberg, September 6, 1646. He died as professor of poesy at Altdorf, November 22, 1708.

150:4. *Lord Jesus, Thou art going forth*

ONDERDONK, Henry Ustic (1789—1858), was born on March 16, 1789, in New York and studied medicine at Columbia College and at the University of Edinburgh, from which he received his M.D. in 1810. For a while he was associated with Dr. Valentine Mott in conducting the *New York Medical Journal*, but in 1815 he abandoned medicine for the ministry. He took holy orders in the same year and was for a while Rector of St. Anne's Church, Brooklyn, New York. His rectorship at St. Anne's came after two years of missionary work. On October 27, 1827, Onderdonk was consecrated at Philadelphia and acted as Assistant Bishop of Philadelphia to Bishop White until 1836, when he succeeded White as chief bishop of the diocese. In 1844 Onderdonk was suspended from office by the House of Bishops on the ground of intemperance, but was restored in 1856. He served American hymnody as an author and compiler and was a member of the committee which compiled the *American Prayer Book Collection* of 1826. He died at Philadelphia, December 6, 1858.

302. *The Savior kindly calls*

OPITZ, Martin (1597—1639), was born on December 23, 1597, the son of Sebastian Opitz, a butcher in Bunzlau, Silesia, where Martin was born. He entered the University of Frankfurt a. O. in 1618. The following year he went to Heidelberg, where he was a private tutor while he studied literature and philosophy at the university. From there Opitz made visits to Strassburg and Tübingen. When the university was threatened by Spanish troops, Opitz left Heidelberg and traveled through Holland, Friesland, and Jutland. In the spring of 1621 he returned to Silesia

and at Easter of the following year became Professor of Philosophy and Poetry in the Gymnasium founded at Weissenburg in Transylvania by Prince Bethlem Gabor. He resigned this post in the summer of 1623 and then for some time busied himself at the request of Duke Rudolf of Liegnitz-Brieg in versifying the Epistles for Sundays and festivals according to the metres of the French Psalter. For this he was rewarded with the title "Rath." In 1625 Opitz accompanied his cousin, Kaspar Kirchner, on an embassy to Vienna, where he presented to the Emperor Ferdinand II a poem on the death of the Grandduke Karl, brother of the Emperor. For this he was crowned poet by the Emperor and was raised to the nobility in 1628 as Opitz von Boberfeld. For a time Opitz was private secretary of the Burgrave Carl Hannibal von Dohna, who began the Counter-Reformation against the Protestants of Silesia in 1628; he wrote poems in praise of him. Three years later Opitz published a translation of the controversial book of the Jesuit Martin Becanus *For the Conversion of the Erring*. He also executed a diplomatic mission to Paris in 1630 on Dohna's behalf, where he became acquainted with Hugo Grotius. In the autumn of 1633 Opitz was sent by Duke Johann Christian of Liegnitz-Brieg as his plenipotentiary to Berlin and also to the Swedish Chancellor Oxenstjerna. Opitz accompanied the Duke to Thorn in 1635 when Wallenstein obtained the mastery over the Silesian duchies. From there Opitz went to Danzig, where in June, 1637, he was definitely installed as Historiographer to King Wladislaw IV of Poland. From Danzig Opitz did his best by correspondence and otherwise to atone for the oppression of his brethren in Silesia. On August 17, 1639, he was accosted by a beggar diseased of the plague. Three days later on August 20, 1639, he himself died of it. Opitz was the author of some 90 works. He was a member of the great German literary union, the Fruit-bearing Society. Opitz's great merit was as a reformer of German prosody by his example of literary style and by his *Buch der Deutschen Poeterey*, published at Breslau, 1624. Herein he laid down the rules of German verse which have given it the form which German verse has to this day.
      126. Arise and shine in splendor

  OSLER, Edward (1798—1863), was born at Falmouth, in January, 1798, and was educated for the medical profession. His hymnological work is mainly connected with the *Mitre Hymn Book*. During 1835—1836 he was associated with W. J. Hall, the editor, in producing that collection which was published in 1836 as *Psalms and Hymns Adapted to the Service of the Church of England*. He was active in the work of the Society for Promoting Christian Knowledge and was editor of the *Royal Cornwall Gazette*. He died in 1863.

    412. May we Thy precepts, Lord, fulfil
    489. Lord of the Church, we humbly pray

  OUSELEY, Sir Frederick Arthur Gore (1825—1889), son of Sir William Gore Ouseley, the eminent oriental scholar, who was successively Ambassador and Minister Plenipotentiary to Persia and St. Petersburg, was born in London, August 12, 1825; named Frederick after the Duke of York, and Arthur after the Duke of Wellington, his godfathers; educated privately, and in 1843 entered Christ Church, Oxford, as a gentleman commoner; on the death of his father in 1844 he succeeded to the baronetcy. In 1849 he was ordained Deacon by the Bishop of London and became curate of St. Barnabas Church, Pimlico. He erected at Tenbury on a portion of his property a church and college dedicated to St. Michael and All Angels. He was appointed Professor of Music in the University of Oxford and precentor of Hereford Cathedral, 1855; died suddenly at Hereford, April 6, 1889; composer of much excellent church music and an organist of great ability. He was closely associated with the publication of *Hymns Ancient and Modern*.

    591, 602. TENBURY

  PALESTRINA, Giovanni Pierluigi Sante da (1525—1594), born at Palestrina, Italy, received his early musical training at Rome, where he came under the influence of Orlando di Lasso, the great master from the Netherlands. At nineteen Palestrina became organist and chapelmaster in his home town, and after serving there a number of years, he was appointed master of the boys in the Julian Chapel in Rome. In 1555 he became a pontifical singer in the Sistine Chapel, but, after about six months, was dismissed because of a papal ruling that only unmarried priests be allowed to attend. He then became chapelmaster, first of St. John Lateran, and then of the Liberian Chapel of Santa Maria Maggiore, spending his last twenty years in practical retirement at St. Peter's. Palestrina is ranked as the foremost composer of the Roman Catholic Church. His greatest contribution to general hymnody was his stand against the introduction of popular airs and lyrics into the church services of the 16th century. Palestrina was able to present simple, polyphonic compositions that were noble and devotional in character. Among his works are 93 masses, 139 motets, and many hymns, prayers, and responses.

210. PALESTRINA

PALMER, Ray (1808—1887), was a direct descendant of John Alden and his wife Priscilla, and one of his forebearers was William Palmer, who came to Plymouth in 1621. He was the son of Thomas Palmer, a judge in Rhode Island, and was born at Little Compton, Rhode Island, November 12, 1808. Poverty forced him to leave home when he was thirteen, after he had received a grammar-school education. He spent two years as a clerk in a Boston dry-goods store, during which time he passed through deep spiritual experiences, with the result that he joined the Park Street Congregational Church, whose pastor was the Rev. Sereno Edwards Dwight, D.D. His attention was now directed to the ministry. After he spent three years at Phillips Academy, Andover, he studied at Yale College and graduated in 1830. Palmer continued his theological studies under pastoral supervision for one year at New York. Here he wrote the hymn "My faith looks up to Thee." Then he continued his studies for three years at New Haven, where he was associated with Ethan A. Andrews in conducting a Young Ladies' Institute. He was ordained pastor of the Central Congregational Church at Bath, Maine, in 1835. Here he remained for fifteen years, with the exception of the interruption of a trip to Europe for his health in 1847. During these years Palmer wrote some of his best hymns. In 1850 Palmer was appointed to the First Congregational Church at Albany, New York. Here he also labored for fifteen years but had to resign because of failing health in 1865. He moved to New York and was appointed Corresponding Secretary to the American Congregational Union, resigning this post in 1878 and moving to Newark, New Jersey, where he was in active ministerial service for the Belleville Avenue Congregational Church, having especial charge of visiting the people of the congregation. On the day before he died, Palmer feebly repeated the last stanza of his favorite hymn:

"When death these mortal eyes shall seal,
And still this throbbing heart,
The rending veil shall Thee reveal,
All glorious as Thou art."

Ray Palmer is said to have written more hymns than any other American. His *Poetical Works*, published in 1876, fill a volume of more than 350 pages. He died March 29, 1887.

111. *Thou who roll'st the year around*
227. *Come, Holy Ghost, in love* (Tr.)
394. *My faith looks up to Thee*
634. *Come, Jesus, from the sapphire throne*

PAULSEN, P. C. (c. 1925), is pastor of Golgatha Danish Lutheran Church, Chicago, Illinois, of the United Danish Church of the American Lutheran Conference. He is chairman of the Hymn-book Committee of his synod.

542. *The sun arises now.* (Tr.)

PERRONET, Edward (1726—1792), of French descent, was born at Sundridge, Kent, the son of Vincent Perronet, whose father, Pasteur Perronet, had been pastor in Switzerland. Edward was baptized and brought up in the Church of England, and originally he had no other thought than to be one of her clergy. However already at an early age, for reasons of conscience, he joined the Wesleys and became an itinerant preacher for them. Though strongly evangelical, he had a quick eye for defects which is a characteristic of his *The Mitre,* a bitter satire on the Church of England, published in 1757, which reflects contemporary ecclesiastical opinion and sentiment. It aroused John Wesley's anger, and he demanded its immediate suppression. As a result, he left the Wesleys and joined Lady Huntingdon's Connection in 1771. This he soon abandoned and became a minister of a small independent chapel at Canterbury, serving this church until his death in 1792. Later he and the Wesleys were reconciled. He died January 2, 1792, his last words being:

> Glory to God in the height of his divinity,
> Glory to God in the depth of his humanity,
> Glory to God in his all sufficiency
> Into his hand I commend my spirit.

339. *All hail the power of Jesus' name*

PETER, Philip Adam (1832—1917), was born in Hesse-Nassau, January 2, 1832. He was educated under the Rev. E. S. Henkel in Corydon, Indiana, and ordained to the Lutheran ministry in 1858. He served as pastor of the Joint Synod of Ohio and Other States and was active as author. He published *The Reformation of the 16th Century,* 1889; *St. Paul,* 1901; and translated hymns. He died in 1917.

611. *The day is surely drawing near*

PETERSEN, Victor Olof (1864—1929), was born in Skede, Smaland, Sweden, September 24, 1864, and came to America in the spring of 1867. He received his elementary schooling at Stanton, Iowa. In 1883 he enrolled at Augustana College, Rock Island, Illinois, in the Academy, and was graduated from the College in 1889. After spending the summer at the state museum at Springfield, Illinois, under his former professor, Dr. Joshua Lindahl, he was called to teach physics and chemistry at Augustana College. After having taken a course in chemistry at Harvard University, he was called as a regular professor at Augustana. He continued in this capacity until 1906, when he became secretary of the Rock Island Tropical Plantation Co. From 1907 to 1913 he managed the Chalchijapa Plantation in Southern Mexico. During the following seven years he was engaged in real estate and insurance business in Rock Island. In 1920 he was called as professor of chemistry at Huron College, Huron, South Dakota, which position he held at the time of his death in 1929. He was a lover of hymns and translated a number of them from the Swedish *Psalmbook.* Three of these are in the present Augustana *Hymnal.*

57. *O bride of Christ, rejoice.* (Tr.)

PFEFFERKORN, Georg Michael (1645—1732), was born March 16, 1645, at Ifta, near Creuzburg on the Werra, where his father had become a pastor in 1619. After studying at the Universities of Jena and Leipzig, Pfefferkorn was for a short time private tutor at Altenburg, and then in 1688 became master of the two highest forms in the Gymnasium at Altenburg. In 1673 he was appointed by Duke Ernst the Pious of Gotha as tutor of his three sons. Three years later Duke Friedrich I appointed him pastor of Friemar, near Gotha, and in 1682 made him a member of the consistory and superintendent at Gräfen-Tonna, also near Gotha. "He was an old blind man eighty-six years of age when he died" on March 3, 1732.

430. *What is the world to me*

PFEIL, Christoph Carl Ludwig, Baron von (1712—1784), was born January 20, 1712, at Grünstadt near Worms, where his father was then in the service of the Count of Leiningen. After completing his course at the University of Halle and of Tübingen, he was appointed Württemberg secretary of the legation at Regensburg in 1732. He was privileged to hold a number of political offices. Finding himself no longer able to cooperate in carrying out the absolution of the Württemberg prime minister, Count Montmartin, he resigned and then retired to his estate, Deufstetten, near Crailsheim. Later on he was created Baron by the Emperor Joseph II, and in

1765 received the cross of the Red Eagle Order from Frederick the Great. An intermittent fever confined him to his bed from August, 1783, to his death, February 14, 1784, at Deufstetten. Pfeil was a man of deep and genuine piety. His hymn-writing began immediately after the spiritual change which he experienced on the tenth Sunday after Trinity, 1730, and it continued to be his favorite occupation, especially so in his later years at Deufstetten. He was one of the most productive of German hymn-writers, his published hymns numbering about 950. He published *Lieder von der offenbarten Herrlichkeit und Zukunft des Herrn*, Esslingen, 1741; and *Evangelische Glaubens-Herzensgesänge*, Dinkelsbühl, 1783.

625. *Oh, blest the house, whate'er befall*

PHELPS, Sylvanus Dryden, D. D. (1816—1895), was born at Suffield, Connecticut, May 15, 1816, and was educated at Brown University, where he graduated in 1844. In 1846 he became a pastor of the First Baptist Church, New Haven. He was the editor of *The Christian Secretary*, Hartford. His publications include *Eloquence of Nature and Other Poems*, 1842; *Sunlight and Hearthlight*, 1856; *The Poet's Song*, 1867.

403. *Savior, Thy dying love*

PHILLIMORE, Greville (1821—1884), was educated at Westminster, The Charterhouse, and Christ Church, and received a B. A. at Oxford in 1842. He was ordained deacon and priest in 1843. In 1851 he became vicar of Downe-Ampney, near Cricklade, Gloucestershire, and in 1867, rector of Henley-on-Thames. Later, in 1883, he was rector of Ewelme. He published *Parochial Sermons* in 1856, *The Parish Book*, 1863. He died January 20, 1884.

537. *Every morning mercies new*

PICTET, Benedict (c. 1650—c. 1710), was a pastor of the French Reformed Church in the latter half of the 17th century. He and two other pastors were appointed at Geneva to review the new version of the Psalms in French verse by Monsieur Conrart, published in 1677, which they did, adding Gospel hymns after the precedent of the Lutheran Church. In 1705 Pictet published *Cinquante Quatre Cantiques Sacrez pour les Principales Solemnitez*, of which several were authorized for use in public worship.

100. *Christians, sing out with exultation*

PISEK, Vincent (1859—1930), was pastor of the Jan Hus Bohemian Presbyterian Church, New York City, beginning his work there under Pastor Alexy and succeeding him in 1880. His work was very successful in the establishment of the Presbyterian Church among the Czechoslovaks in New York and elsewhere. In 1904 New York University conferred upon him the degree of Doctor of Divinity. He died on February 6, 1930.

86:1-4. *Christ the Lord to us is born*

POLACK, Herman Adolph (1862—1930), son of the Rev. W. G. Polack and Maria Elizabeth, née Hans, was born in Crete Township, Will County, Illinois, June 10, 1862. He was educated at the Missouri State Normal School, Cape Girardeau, Missouri. He married Wilhelmina Henrietta Stohs at Bremen, Kansas, February 12, 1885. He taught public school in East St. Louis, then became Lutheran parochial school-teacher, serving schools in St. Louis; Wausau, Wisconsin; Cleveland, Ohio; and other places. He was an accomplished organist, composer, and choir director. Together with H. Ilse (*q. v.*) he served on the music committee of the *Evangelical Lutheran Hymn-book*, 1912. He died at Lakewood, Ohio, April 25, 1930.

350. CLAIRVAUX

POLACK, William Gustave (1890—   ), son of Herman A. Polack and Wilhelmina, née Stohs, was born at Wausau, Wisconsin, December 7, 1890. He was educated at Concordia College, Fort Wayne, Indiana, and Concordia Seminary, St. Louis, Missouri; ordained to the Lutheran ministry at Evansville, Indiana, by the Rev. C. A. Frank, founder and first editor of the *Lutheran Witness*. He served as assistant pastor in Trinity Church, Evansville, from 1914 to 1921, succeeding Frank as pastor. He married Iona Mary Gick in Fort Wayne, Indiana, August 9, 1914. In 1925 he was called as professor of theology to Concordia Seminary, St. Louis. He was made chairman of the Missouri Synod's Committee on Hymnology and Liturgics in 1929, and in 1930 he organized the Intersynodical Committee on Hymnology and Liturgics for the Synodical Conference of North America, which was authorized to prepare *The Lutheran Hymnal*. His poetical publications include *Beauty for Ashes* and *Martin Luther in English Poetry*. His prose works include *The Story of C. F. W. Walther, The Story of Luther, The Story of David Livingstone, Into all the World, The Building of a Great Church, Hymns from the Harps of God, Rainbow over Calvary, Handbook to The Lutheran Hymnal*.

      6. *Kyrie, God Father in heaven above.* (Tr.)
      7. *As we begin another week.* (Tr.)
   42. *O Thou Love unbounded.* (Tr.)
   78. *Hail the day so rich in cheer.* (Tr.)
 150. *Lord Jesus, Thou art going forth.* (Tr.)
 187. *Christ is arisen.* (Tr.)
 238. *All glory be to God alone.* (Tr.)
 266. *O God, our Lord, Thy holy Word.* (Tr.)
 482. *Dear Lord, to Thy true servants give*
 510:2, 3. *Savior, sprinkle many nations*
 540. *With the Lord begin thy task.* (Tr.)
 640. *God the Father, Son, and Spirit*

    POLLOCK, Thomas Benson (1836—1896), was a most successful writer of metrical litanies, and his *Metrical Litanies for Special Services and General Use* besides other compositions of this kind which he contributed to various collections have greatly enriched our modern hymn-books. He was born in 1836, attended Trinity College in Dublin, where he graduated as B. A. in 1859, M. A. in 1863. While there he won the Vice-Chancellor's Prize for English Verse in 1855. He took holy orders in 1861 and served successively as curate of St. Luke's, Leek, Staffordshire; St. Thomas's, Stamford Hill, London; and St. Albans, Birmingham. He was for a time a member of the Committee of *Hymns Ancient and Modern*. He died at Birmingham in 1896.

 180. *Jesus, in Thy dying woes*
 181. *Jesus, pitying the sighs*
 182. *Jesus, loving to the end*
 183. *Jesus, whelmed in fears unknown*
 184. *Jesus, in Thy thirst and pain*
 185. *Jesus, all our ransom paid*
 186. *Jesus, all Thy labor vast*

    POPE, Alexander (1688—1744), poet, was born in London May 22, 1688, son of Alexander Pope and his second wife, Edith, *née* Turner. Soon after his father's death in 1717 he removed with his mother to the villa at Twickenham, which with its gardens and grotto is so intimately associated with his memory. Pope became the typical man of letters and the great representative English poet of the first half of the eighteenth century. His wit won him a large circle of distinguished friends. His ruling passion was the love of fame. Among his works are *Pastorals*, 1709; *Rape of the Lock*, 1712; *The Dunciads*, 1712, 1729; *Essay on Man;* his translations of Homer's *Iliad* and *Odyssey*, etc. He died on May 30, 1744, and was buried in the parish-church at Twickenham.

 503. *Rise crowned with light, imperial Salem, rise!*

    POTT, Francis (1832—1909), born December 29, 1832, was educated at Brasenose College, Oxford. He received his B. A. in 1854 and his M. A. in 1857. Pott took holy orders in 1856 and served successively as curate of Bishopsworth, Gloucestershire, 1856—1858; of Ardingly, Berks, 1858—1861; of Ticehurst, Sussex, 1861—1866; and as Rector of Norhill, Ely, for 1866. Pott published *Hymns fitted to the Order of Common Prayer*, 1861; *The Free Rhythm Psalter*, 1898. He was a member of the original committee for *Hymns Ancient and Modern*. He died at Speldhurst, 1909.

 210. *The strife is o'er, the battle done.* (Tr.)

PRÄTORIUS, Michael (1571—1621). Michael Prätorius, the son of Michael Schultze (Praetorius being a Latinization of the name), was born at Kreuzburg, Thuringia, on February 15, 1571. At an early age Prätorius attended the University of Frankfurt a. O., his brother supporting him. When his brother died, Prätorius became organist at Frankfurt and later held the same post at Lüneburg. In this latter town Prätorius began his career as Kapellmeister. In 1604 he entered the service of the Duke of Brunswick at Wolfenbüttel and was appointed honorary prior of the Ringelheim Monastery near Goslar, but without compulsion to reside there. He died at Wolfenbüttel on February 15, 1621. Prätorius composed much and was a serious student of music. He began to write a complete encyclopedia of the art and practice of music, of which he finished three volumes with the title *Syntagma Musicum*. The second volume of this work is the most elaborate and valuable of all treatises on instruments and instrumental music in the 16th century. It is considered one of the most remarkable examples of musical scholarship in existence. Among his other titles were *Musae Sioniae* published in nine parts and *Hymnodia Sionae*.

152. WENN MEINE SÜND'
431. ICH DANK' DIR SCHON

PREISWERK, Samuel (1799—1871), was born in Rümlingen in the canton of Basel, Switzerland, September 19, 1799. He studied at Basel, Tübingen, and Erlangen, and became preacher at the Orphanage in Basel in 1824. In 1829 he became tutor in Hebrew at the Basel Mission House; in 1830 pastor at Muttenz; in 1834 Professor of Old Testament Exegesis at the Evangelical Seminary in Geneva; in 1843, pastor of St. Leonard's Church in Basel, and in 1859 antistes, or the highest dignitary at the Cathedral. He died at Basel, January 13, 1871.

461. Hark! the Church proclaims her honor

PRICHARD, Rowland Hugh (1811—1887), was born near Bala, spent most of his life at Bala, but in 1880 he moved to Holywell Hill. He composed tunes which appeared in Welsh periodicals. He published *Cyfaill y Cantorion* (The Singer's Friend) in 1844.

423, 442. HYFRYDOL

PRUDENTIUS, Aurelius Clemens (348—c. 413). Of the life of Prudentius nothing is known beyond what he himself has written in a short introduction in verse to his works. He was a Spaniard, evidently of a good family, and was born somewhere in the north of Spain, either at Saragossa, Tarragona, or Callahorra. After receiving a good education befitting his social status, Prudentius applied himself for some years practicing as a pleader in the local court of law, until he received promotion to a judgeship in two cities successively and afterwards to a post of still higher authority, perhaps that of Roman governor. When Prudentius was fifty-seven, he became conscience-smitten on account of the follies and worldliness that had marked his youth and earlier manhood and determined to quit all his secular employments and to devote the remainder of his life to advancing the interests of Christ's Church by the power of his pen. He retired to a monastery and then began that remarkable succession of sacred poems upon which his fame now rests. Prudentius is considered the most prominent and most prolific author of sacred Latin poetry in its earliest days. His hymns are contained in two of his works, *Liber Cathemerinon* (containing 14 hymns) and *Liber Peristephanon* (containing 14 hymns to the martyrs). These two works and his *Psychomachia* were the most widely read books during the Middle Ages. Prudentius wrote about 28 hymns in all. Bently calls him "The Horace and Vergil of the Christians." Luther desired that Prudentius be studied in the schools, and Rudelbach was of the opinion that "the poetry of Prudentius is like gold set with precious stones."

98. Of the Father's love begotten
273. Sweet flowerets of the martyr band

PUSEY, Philip (1799—1855). Pusey's father was a son of the first Viscount Folestone, who assumed the name of Pusey instead of that of Bouverie. His elder brother was the famous Dr. Edward Bouverie Pusey, the Tractarian leader. Pusey, born on June 25, 1799, at Pusey, England, was educated at Eton and Christ Church, Oxford, but left without taking his degree. An Honorary D. C. L. was given him at Commemoration in 1853. After leaving the university Pusey settled on his estate and devoted himself to agriculture and public service. In the former field he was one of the most progressive men of his time; he wrote largely in this field. Pusey was one of the founders of the Royal Agricultural Society. He entered Parliament and sat for Rye, Chippenham, Cashel, and Berkshire. He introduced the term "tenant-right" into the House of Commons. Disraeli said that Pusey was "both by his lineage, his estate, his rare accomplishments and fine abilities, one of the most distinguished country gentlemen who ever sat in the House of Commons." Pusey had many accomplishments: he was a connoisseur of art, a collector of prints and etchings, a copious contributor to the reviews, and one of the founders of the London Library. He was also interested in hymnology. He wanted to supplant the Sternhold and Hopkins version of the psalms by Milman's hymns. In this he was opposed by his famous brother.

258. *Lord of our life and God of our salvation.* (Tr.)

PYE, Henry John (c. 1825—1903), was the son of H. J. Pye of Clifton Hall, Staffordshire. He was educated at Trinity College, Cambridge, and was graduated as B. A. 1848 and M. A. 1852. In 1850 Pye took holy orders and was presented by his father in 1851 to the Rectory of Clifton-Campville, Staffordshire. In 1868 he and his wife, the only daughter of Bishop S. Wilberforce, joined the Roman Catholic Church. He died on January 3, 1903.

139:1-3. *In His temple now behold Him*

RAMBACH, Johann Jacob (1693—1735), one of the outstanding leaders among the German Pietists, was born February 24, 1693, in Halle. When he entered Halle University in 1712, he felt that an impediment in his speech would make it more advisable for him to study medicine than theology; but he was strongly advised by his friends and teachers to change his mind. They recognized his great gifts and argued that the Church needed teachers as well as preachers. He then took up his theological studies in earnest. He was thirty years old when he became Professor Johann Daniel Herrnschmidt's successor at the University of Halle. In 1727 Rambach became the successor of the great August Hermann Francke, founder of the Halle institutions. It has been claimed that the jealousy of fellow-teachers at Halle caused Rambach to leave that university in 1731 to teach at the University of Giessen. He had in that year received two calls: one from Denmark to become German court preacher and theological professor at the University of Copenhagen, the other, from the Duke of Hessen, asking him to serve as principal theological professor and superintendent at Giessen. He accepted the latter position. He found conditions at Giessen much different from those at Halle. His earnest work was not received well. He met with opposition and scoffing. He began to grieve over the fact that his preaching seemed to bear but little fruit. Yet he continued to labor with unremitting zeal at the ultimate expense of his health. He was only forty-two years old when he died from a violent attack of fever, April 19, 1735. His last words were "I hold fast to Jesus, and I am prepared to go to Him." It has been said that intense sorrow over his unresponsive flock contributed to his untimely death. He wrote over 180 hymns in all, although he is better known as a hymnologist than as a hymn-writer. He published *Über Dr. M. Luthers Verdienst um den Kirchengesang*, 1813; *Anthologie christlicher Gesänge*, in six volumes (this is his greatest work). He was principal editor of the Hamburg *Gesang-Buch*, 1842.

42. *O Thou Love unbounded*
298. *Baptized into Thy name most holy*
335. *My Maker, be Thou nigh*

RAMSEY, Alfred (1860—1926), was born on April 12, 1860, in Pittsburgh, Pennsylvania. He studied at Thiel College and the Lutheran Theological Seminary at Philadelphia. He was ordained to the Pennsylvania Ministerium in 1885 and served pastorates at Scenery Hill and Uniontown, Pennsylvania, and at Minneapolis and Stacy, Minnesota. Ramsey was for thirteen years Professor of Historical Theology at the Lutheran Theological Seminary at Chicago and is remembered as a skilful and fluent translator of German hymns into English. He died June 20, 1926.

581. All ye who on this earth do dwell. (Tr.)

READ, Daniel (1757—1836). Read was born in Rehoboth, Massachusetts. He studied, taught music, and edited *Columbian Harmony,* 1793, and other singing books.

612. WINDHAM

REDHEAD, Richard (1820—1901), was born March 1, 1820, at Harrow. He became a chorister of Magdalen College, Oxford, where he came under the influence of the Rev. Frederick Oakeley, who invited him to become organist at Margaret Street Chapel (subsequently All Saints' Church), prominent in the Oxford movement. After serving there for twenty-five years, Redhead became the organist of the Church of St. Mary Magdalene in 1864 and served in this capacity until 1894. With Oakeley Redhead edited the first Gregorian Psalter under the tile of *Laudes Diurnae.* This and Redhead's other works for the Church greatly influenced the music of the Catholic revival.

159, 174, 342. GETHSEMANE

REDNER, Lewis Henry (1831—1908), was born at Philadelphia, Pennsylvania, where he attended public school and later became a wealthy real-estate broker. He was organist of Holy Trinity Church in Philadelphia and was particularly active in organizing the Sunday-school of the church. With the help of Phillips Brooks, his pastor, he increased the attendance in the Sunday-school and Bible classes from thirty-six to over a thousand in nineteen years.

647. ST. LOUIS

REED, Andrew (1788—1862), son of a watchmaker of humble circumstances, was born in London, November 27, 1788. In his early years he joined the Congregational Church in the New Road, St. George's-in-the-East. He was privately educated in his father's business, but did not find the work to his liking. So upon the advice of one Rev. Matthew Wilks he entered Hackney Seminary in the New Road, East London, as a theological student under the Rev. George Collison in 1807. In November, 1811, he was ordained as pastor of the congregation in which he originally was a member and with which he remained until November 27, 1861. He was active in founding institutions for orphaned children in London. In 1834 Reed and the Rev. J. Matheson were sent to the Congregational Churches of America by the Congregational Union of England and Wales as a deputation, "in order to promote peace and friendship between the two communities." He spent six months in America. On this visit Yale University conferred upon him the honorary degree of D. D. After his return to England he published his *Visit to American Churches* in 1836. In 1843 he published the *Revival of Religion in Wycliffe Chapel,* in 1861 his *Sermons.* He died February 25, 1862. His *Hymn-Book* was a work of years and was published in complete form in 1842.

234. Holy Ghost, with light divine

REINAGLE, Alexander Robert (1799—1877), was born at Brighton, England, on August 21, 1799, of a well-known musical family of Austrian extraction. He served for thirty-one years as organist at St. Peter's-in-the-East, Oxford. He composed a number of songs and other musical pieces and published two books of hymn-tunes, chants, etc.

286, 364, 396, 618. ST. PETER

REUSNER (Reussner, Reisner, Reissner), Adam (1496—c. 1575), was born at Mündelsheim, in Swabian Bavaria. He studied at Wittenberg, supported by the famous Captain Georg von Frundsberg, very likely as companion of Frundsberg's second son, Melchior. There he learned to know Luther and other leaders of the Reformation. He studied Hebrew and Greek under Reuchlin in 1521. He then became private secretary to Georg von Frundsberg. Later, in November, 1526, we find him and his friend Jakob Ziegler with Georg von Frundsberg's troops on a campaign in Italy, helping Charles V fight against Clemens VII. In 1530 he visited Jakob Ziegler at Strassburg, where he met Caspar Schwenkfeldt, whose friend and adherent he became. In 1563 he lived at Frankfurt-am-Main. But later he returned again to Mündelsheim, where he was still living in the year 1572. He died about 1575. Reusner wrote hymns as early as 1530. A manuscript at Wolfenbüttel entitled *Tegliches Gesangbuch . . . durch Adam Reusner* contains over forty of his own hymns.

> 524. *In Thee, Lord, have I put my trust*

REUTER, Friedrich Otto (Fritz) (1863—1924), was born in Johannsbach, October 11, 1863, in the Erzgebirge, Sachsen, Germany. His father was Johann Friedrich Reuter, his mother Ida Augusta Friedericke, *née* Krätzel. After his confirmation he entered the Teachers' Seminary in Waldenburg, graduating in 1884. The same year he accepted the position as assistant teacher at Oberlungwitz, near Chemnitz. In 1887 he accepted the position of teacher, organist, and choir director in Klingenthal. In 1892 he served at Rheinsdorf near Zwickau. In 1893 he went to Lichtenstein-Kallnberg, where he was Kantor until 1904. His conscience would not let him serve any longer in the State Church. He, therefore, joined the Lutheran Free Church of Saxony. From 1904 to 1905 he served as teacher in a private boys' school in Berlin. In 1905 he accepted a call to the parochial school of the Lutheran congregation in Winnipeg, Canada. In 1907 Reuter came to Bethlehem Congregation in Chicago. In 1908 he accepted a call from the Ev. Lutheran Synod of Wisconsin and Other States to serve as teacher of music at the Dr. Martin Luther College, New Ulm, Minn. On July 14, 1894, he married Clara I. Sonntag. Reuter took all the courses offered in the music department of the Waldenburg Seminary and also studied under such well-known teachers of his day as Reichardt at Waldenburg; Schneider and Schreck at Leipzig; Reinberger at München; and Thiel of the "Akademisches Institut für Kirchenmusik" at Berlin. Besides teaching music he composed church music for choirs and organ. Much of his work was left in manuscript. He died June 9, 1924.

> 50. NEW ULM
> 283, 337, 477. REUTER

REYNOLDS, William Morton (1812—1876), was born in Fayette County, Pennsylvania. He was educated at Jefferson College, Canonsburgy, and at the theological seminary at Gettysburg, Pennsylvania. From 1833 to 1850 he was a professor at Pennsylvania College; from 1850 to 1853 president of Capital University, Columbus, Ohio; and of Illinois State University from 1857 to 1860. Reynolds became a minister of the Protestant Episcopal Church in 1864. He founded the *Evangelical Review*, translated a number of hymns from the German, and edited a hymn-book for the General Synod.

> 95. *Savior of the Nations, come.* (Tr.)

RHABANUS MAURUS (776—856), a great ecclesiastic and teacher of the ninth century, was born at Mainz of a noble family. He began his education early at Fulda and entered the Benedictine order. In 801 he received orders of a deacon, and the following year he was sent to continue his studies at Tours, under Alcuin, from whom he received his surname Maurus, after St. Maur, the disciple of Benedict. In 803 he became head of the school at Fulda, which flourished greatly under his leadership. In 814 he was ordained priest, in 822 he was chosen Abbot of Fulda and performed his duties with much ability until 842, when he resigned and withdrew to the cloister of St. Peter to devote himself to literature. In 847 he became Archbishop of Mainz. He died at Winkel on the Rhine, February 4, 856. Maurus took an active part in opposing Gottschalk and his theories about Predestination and also the doctrines of Paschasius Radbertus with regard to the Eucharist. His voluminous writings upon diverse subjects include a Latin-German glossary on the Bible, a sort of encyclopedia, *De Universo Libri* XXII, commentaries on the Old and New Testaments and poems.

> 233. *Come, Holy Ghost, Creator blest*
> 236. *Creator Spirit, by whose aid*
> 257. *Jesus, Brightness of the Father*

RILEY, John Athelstan Laurie (1858—?), was born in London on August 10, 1858. He studied at Eton and at Pembroke College, Oxford (B. A. 1881; M. A. 1883), and served most of his life as a member of the House of Laymen of the Province of Canterbury. Riley helped compile the *English Hymnal* of 1906 and contributed nine translations from the Latin to it and three original hymns.

475. *Ye watchers and ye holy ones*

RIMBACH, J, Adam (1871—1941), son of Henry Rimbach and Catherine Elizabeth, née Brandau, was born in Elyria, Ohio, October 6, 1871. He was educated at Concordia College, Fort Wayne, and Concordia Seminary, St. Louis, graduating from the Seminary in 1893. His first charge was in Cleveland, where he taught in an academy (progymnasium), opened by the Lutheran congregations of Cleveland in order to gain more students for the ministry and the teaching professions. The Rev. O. Kolbe headed this institution for a time. Rimbach also conducted English services Sunday evenings in Zion Church, Cleveland. The panic of the early nineties and the cry of "overproduction" caused the school to be closed temporarily, and in 1895 he became pastor of Immanuel Church, Avilla, Indiana; in 1897 of Trinity Church, Zanesville, Ohio; in 1900 of St. Paul's Church, Ashland, Kentucky; and in 1906 of Trinity Church, Portland, Oregon. On June 6, 1941, the Faculty of Concordia Seminary, St. Louis, Missouri, conferred on him the honorary degree of Doctor of Divinity. He married Marie Zorn and has four children. He published, among other works, *Our Father Who Art in Heaven*, and has contributed articles and sermons to the periodicals of his Synod. He died on December 14, 1941.

409. *Let us ever walk with Jesus.* (Tr.)

RINGWALDT (Ringwalt, Ringwald), Bartholomäus (1532—c. 1600), was born November 28, 1532, at Frankfurt a. O. He was ordained in 1557 and was pastor of two parishes before he settled in 1566 as pastor of Langenfeld near Sonnenburg, Brandenburg. He was still there in 1597, but seems to have died there in 1599, or at least not later than 1600. Ringwaldt exerted a considerable influence on his contemporaries as a poet of the people. After 1577 he published various didactic poems, giving a mirror of the times and of the morals of the people. He was one of the most prolific hymn-writers of the sixteenth century. Wackernagel gives 208 pieces under his name, about 165 of which may be called hymns. A selection of 59 as his *Geistliche Lieder,* with a memoir by H. Wendelbourg, was published at Halle in 1858.

293. *O Holy Spirit, grant us grace*
611. *The day is surely drawing near*

RINKART (Rinckart), Martin (1586—1649), son of Georg Rinkart or Rinckart, cooper at Eilenburg on the Mulde, Saxony, was born at Eilenburg, April 23, 1586. After passing through the Latin school at Eilenburg, he became, in November of 1601, a foundation scholar and chorister of the St. Thomas's School at Leipzig. This scholarship also allowed him to proceed to the University of Leipzig, where he matriculated for the summer session of 1602 as a student of theology. After he completed his course, he remained for some time in Leipzig. In March, 1610, Rinkart became a candidate for the post of diaconus at Eilenburg. He was presented by the Town Council, but the Superintendent refused to sanction this arrangement, nominally on the ground that Rinkart was a better musician than theologian, but really because he was unwilling to have as his colleague a native of Eilenburg with a will of his own. Not wishing to contest the matter, Rinkart applied for a vacant mastership at the gymnasium at Eisleben and entered on his duties there in the beginning of June, 1610, as sixth master, and also as cantor of the St. Nicholas Church. After holding this appointment for a few months, Rinkart became diaconus of St. Anne's Church, in the Neustadt of Eisleben, and began his work there on May 28, 1611. Thereupon he became pastor at Erdeborn and Lyttichendorf in 1613. Finally he was invited by the Town Council of Eilenburg to become archidiaconus there, and in November, 1617, he became once again a resident of Eilenburg. Here he died December 8, 1649. A memorial tablet to his memory, affixed to the house where he lived, was unveiled at

Eilenburg on Easter Monday, April 26, 1886. Rinkart was a voluminous writer and a good musician. A considerable number of his books seem to have perished; others survive only in single copies. He began to write poetry early and was crowned as a poet apparently in 1614. Among other things he wrote a cycle of seven so-called *Comedies*, or rather dramas, on the Reformation Period, suggested by the centenary of the Reformation in 1617.

36. *Now thank we all our God*

RIST, Johann (1607—1667), was born on March 8, 1607, at Ottensen, near Hamburg, the son of the Rev. Kaspar Rist. From birth he was designated by his parents to be a minister. He attended school in Hamburg and at an early age proved to be a very gifted boy. At twenty Rist graduated from the gymnasium Illustri at Bremen. Then he entered the University of Rinteln, where, under the influence of Josua Stegmann, he began to take an interest in hymnology. After his graduation from Rinteln, Rist became tutor of the sons of a Hamburg merchant and accompanied them to the University of Rostock, where he studied Hebrew, mathematics, and medicine. While he was at Rostock, the University was almost deserted on account of the hardships caused by the Thirty Years' War. The pestilence kept Rist in the sick-bed for some length of time. After a stay in Hamburg he was engaged as tutor in the house of the lawyer Heinrich Sager of Heide, Holstein. While staying there, Rist was betrothed to Elizabeth Stapfel, a sister of Judge Franz Stapfel, whose influence seems to have had a good deal to do with Rist's appointment as pastor at Wedel, near Hamburg, shortly afterwards. In the spring of 1635 Rist married and settled at Wedel. He devoted his time to his pastoral duties and to the writing of poetry. Gradually he became famous. In 1644 he was made poet laureate by Emperor Ferdinand III and in 1635 was raised to the rank of nobility by the same ruler. Duke Christian of Mecklenburg made him a councilor of his civil and ecclesiastical courts. In 1645 Rist was admitted as a member of the Fruit-bearing Society, which had been organized by Opitz and was the most famous poets' union of that time. In 1660 he became the founder and head of the Elbe Swan Order, which, however, did not survive his death on August 31, 1667. Johann Rist was a voluminous and many-sided writer. His secular works are of great interest to the student of the history of the times, and his occasional poems on marriages, etc., to the genealogist and local historian. He wrote about 680 hymns and spiritual songs, covering the entire field of theology. Not all of Rist's hymns are of equal merit; many are poor and bombastic. But Rist never meant them for public worship, but for private use. Rist excels in his hymns for Advent and for Holy Communion. In general, the hymns of Johann Rist are Scriptural, objective, full of Christian faith, and edifying in the best sense of the term.

69. *Arise, sons of the Kingdom*
120. *Help us, O Lord! Behold, we enter*
167:2-7. *O darkest woe*
312. *Lord Jesus Christ, Thou living Bread*
316. *O living Bread from heaven*

RISTAD, Ditlef Georgson (1863—1938), was born November 22, 1863, at Overhallen, Norway. He attended the Kläbu Normal School and then became a teacher at the Namsos Middle School in Norway. Ristad emigrated in 1887 and attended Luther Seminary (C. T. 1892) and Chicago University. He held pastorates at Edgerton, East Koshkonong and Rockdale, and at Manitowoc, Wisconsin. Between the years 1901 and 1919 he served successively as president of Albion Academy, of Park Region Luther College, and of the Lutheran Ladies' Seminary, Red Wing, Minnesota. In 1897 he edited the *Lutheran Sunday-school Hymnal* and served on the committee for the *Lutheran Hymnary* and the *Lutheran Hymnary Junior*. In 1922 he published a volume of poems in the Norwegian language. He died September 20, 1938.

413. *I walk in danger all the way.* (Tr.)

ROBINSON, Charles Seymour, D.D. (1829—1899), was born at Bennington, Vermont, March 31, 1829, and educated at Williams College, 1849. He studied theology at Union Seminary in New York (1852—1853) and at Princeton (1853—1855). He became a Presbyterian pastor at Troy in 1855 and at Brooklyn in 1860; and served also as pastor of the American chapel in Paris, France, 1868, and then of the Memorial Presbyterian Church of New York in 1870. He was editor of *Illustrated Christian Weekly*, 1876—1877. As editor of hymn-books he published *Songs of the Church*, 1862; *Songs for the Sanctuary*, 1865; *Psalms and Hymns and Spiritual Songs*, 1875; *Spiritual Songs*, 1878; and *Laudes Domini, a Selection of Spiritual Songs, Ancient and Modern*, 1884. He died February 1, 1899.

422. Savior, I follow on

ROBINSON, Joseph Armitage (1858—?), was educated at Christ's College, Cambridge, and graduated as B. A. in 1881. Then he was a Fellow of Christ's College and received his doctor's degree in 1896. He was ordained in 1881 and was appointed Examining Chaplain to the Bishop of Bath and Wells in 1888 and served as the Vicar of All Saints, Cambridge, from 1888 until 1892. At Cambridge Robinson was Norrisian Professor of Divinity. Then he became Rector of St. Margaret's, Westminster, Canon of Westminster, and since 1902 has been Dean of Westminster.

135. 'Tis good, Lord, to be here

RODIGAST, Samuel (1649—1708), was born October 19, 1649, in Gröben, near Jena. He studied at Weimar and then at Jena, where he later became adjunct of the philosophical faculty. From 1680 on he served as conrector and later rector at the Gymnasium zum Grauen Kloster in Berlin, where he remained, in spite of offers from other schools, such as Jena, until his death, March 29, 1708.

521. What God ordains is always good

ROH (Cornu, Horn), Johann (?—1547), was a native of Domaschitz, near Leitmeritz, in Bohemia. Roh is a Bohemian name; he styled himself "Cornu" in Latin and "Horn" in German. In 1518 Roh was ordained priest and appointed preacher to the Bohemian Brethren's community at Jungbunzlau, in Bohemia. At the Synod of Brandeis in September, 1529, he was chosen as one of the three Seniors of the Unity. By the same synod of April, 1532, he was appointed bishop. Roh died February 11, 1547, at Jungbunzlau. Johann Roh was editor of the Bohemian Hymn-book of 1541; he is said to have written a number of hymns in the Bohemian language. He also edited the second German hymnal of the Brethren, *Ein Gesangbuch der Brüder*, Nürnberg, 1544.

74. Once He came in blessing

ROMANIS, William (1824—1899), was educated at Emmanuel College, Cambridge. He graduated as B. A. with honors in 1846. He was ordained in 1847. From 1846 until 1856 he was assistant master in the classical department of Cheltenham College. Then he was successively curate of Axminster and of St. Mary's, Reading. In 1853 he became Vicar of Wigston Magna, Leicester, and in 1888 of Twyford, Hampshire. Romanis retired in 1895 and died four years later. He published *Sermons Preached at St. Mary's, Reading*, 1862 and 1864; *Hymns Written for Wigston*, 1878.

562. Round me falls the night

ROSENROTH, Christian Knorr, Baron von (1636—1689), was born on July 15, 1636, at Altrauden, Silesia, where his father was a pastor. He studied at Stettin, Leipzig, and Wittenberg and continued his studies traveling to Holland, France, and England. On these travels von Rosenroth met Dr. Henry More, Rabbi Meier Stern, and Dr. John Lightfoot. Although he was an ardent seeker after the philosopher's stone, von Rosenroth found truth and peace only in Christianity. Later he served as pastor in Silesia. He became proficient not only in philosophy and chemistry, but also in theology and cabalistic lore. His memory was so unique that he knew nearly the whole Bible by heart. He died at Sulzback, Bavaria, at the very hour, so it is said, which he himself had predicted, May 8, 1689. He wrote 70 hymns, which show him to be a mystic of the school of Scheffler; they are full of a glowing desire for inner union with God in Christ. He was, indeed, a great scholar and statesman, and his learning led to his being taken into the service of the Palsgrave Christian August of Sulzbach, and that prince made him his prime minister in 1668. He was created a baron by Emperor Leopold I. His greatest pleasure was the study of the Kabbala — the oral tradition of the Jews, supposedly transmitted from Adam; the secret wisdom of the rabbis. He edited rabbinical writings, and his *Kabbala Denudata* made him world-famous. He strove to harmonize the doctrine of the Kabbala and Christianity.

539. *Come, Thou Bright and Morning Star*

ROTHE, Johann Andreas (1688—1758), son of the Rev. Ägidius Rothe, was born at Lissa, May 12, 1688. As student of theology he graduated from the University of Leipzig; in 1712 he was licensed at Görlitz as a general preacher. Count von Zinzendorf heard him preach and later gave him a pastorate at Berthelsdorf (August 30, 1722). In 1737 Zinzendorf was displeased with Rothe's doctrinal views; so Rothe accepted a call to Hermsdorf, near Görlitz, where he became minister in 1737. In 1739 he became assistant pastor at Thommendorf, near Bunzlau, where in 1742 he was made chief pastor and remained there until his death on July 6, 1758. His hymns number about 40. Though they do not rank high as poetry, yet they are characterized by glow and tenderness of feeling and by depth of Christian experience.

385. *Now I have found the firm foundation*

ROUS, Francis (1579—1659), was born at Halton, Cornwall; educated at Oxford; became a lawyer and later a Member of Parliament during the reign of James and of Charles I. He was a member of Westminster Assembly, of the High Commission, and of the Triers for examining and licensing candidates for the ministry. He also held appointments under Cromwell. He died at Acton, January 7, 1659. Rous became well known as the author of *Psalms Translated into English Metre*, 1641. This version was an attempt to satisfy the recommendations of the Committee of Peers that "the meeter in the Psalms should be corrected and allowed or publicly." In 1643 the Westminster Assembly was called to deal with the Uniformity of Worship between England and Scotland. One part of the Assembly's work recommended to it by Parliament was the preparation of a Psalter for use in both kingdoms. The result was Rous' 2d and 3d versions of 1643 and 1646, the latter revision was made more urgent by the establishment of the "Directory," 1645, in which every one that could read was ordered to have a Psalm Book. This version was approved by the Westminster Assembly, authorized by the House of Commons for general use. This version, with considerable variations, became the *Scottish Psalter*, 1650.

436. *The Lord's my Shepherd, I'll not want*

RUOPP, Johann Friedrich (?—1708), was born at Strassburg, Alsace-Lorraine. While a theological student at Halle, he turned to Pietism. He was appointed deacon of Lampertheim; in 1692 he became pastor at Gottesweiler, near Strassburg. He united with his colleagues, and in 1704 with Johann Friedrich Haug, in an attempt to spread a "Living Christianity." On February 27, 1694, he was driven from his charge and took refuge at Halle, where he became adjunct of the theological faculty and inspector at the Orphanage. He published *Jesuslieder*. He died May 26, 1708.

398. *Renew me, O eternal Light*

RUSSELL, Arthur Tozer (1806—1874), son of the Rev. Thomas Clout (later Russell), was born at Northampton, March 20, 1806. He was educated at St. Saviour's School, Southwark, and at Merchant Taylors' School, London. From 1822 to 1824 Russell attended Manchester College, York. In 1825 he entered St. John's College, Cambridge, and in his freshman year gained the Hulsean Prize. In 1829 Russell was ordained by the Bishop of Lincoln and served first as curate of Great Gransden and was then preferred to the Vicarage of Caxton, where he remained until 1852, when he went to the Vicarage of Whaddon, Cambridgeshire. Russell left there in 1866 for

St. Thomas's, Toxteth Park, Liverpool. The following year he was at Wrockwardine Wood, Shropshire, where he stayed until 1874 when he was presented to the Rectory of Southwick, near Brighton. Here Russell died after a long and distressing illness on November 18, 1874. Russell started his ecclesiastical life as an extreme high churchman, but through the study of Saint Augustine his views were changed, and he became and continued until his end a moderate Calvinist. He was a prolific writer. His best prose work appeared in 1859 under the title *Memorials of the Life and Works of Bishop Andrewes*. His hymnological works include: *Hymn-Tunes, Original and Selected, from Ravenscroft and other old Musicians*, c. 1840; *Hymns for Public Worship*, 1848, which contained some of his own hymns, original and translated from the German. In 1851 Russell published *Psalms and Hymns, partly original, partly selected, for the use of the Church of England*. He wrote 140 hymns; they are characterized as gracious and tender, thoughtful and devout. His translations are vigorous and strong.

    75. *Ye sons of men, oh, hearken.* (Tr.)
    92. *Now sing we, now rejoice.* (Tr.)
  312. *Lord Jesus Christ, Thou living Bread.* (Tr.)
  319. *In Thee alone, O Christ, my Lord.* (Tr.)

RYGH, George Alfred Taylor (1860—   ), was born March 21, 1860, at Chicago, Illinois. He graduated as A. B. from Luther College in 1881. Thereafter he studied at Luther Seminary and Capital University. During 1883 Rygh served as teacher at the former institution. The following year he became a pastor in Portland, Maine, which position he held until 1889. From then on Rygh alternated regularly between the ministry and the teaching profession, serving as teacher at Wittenberg Academy, 1889—1890; pastor at Grand Forks, North Dakota, 1890—1891; teacher at North Dakota University, 1891—1895; pastor at Mount Horeb, Wisconsin., 1895—1898; pastor at Chicago, 1899—1910; teacher at St. Olaf College, 1910—1913; pastor at Minneapolis, Minnesota (1920—   ), and is now pastor emeritus residing in Northfield, Minnesota. From 1909 to 1914 Rygh served as editor of the *United Lutheran*. He was associate editor of the *American Survey*, 1914—1921. In 1925 Rygh became an editor of the *Lutheran Herald*. He served as a member of the Committee on the *Lutheran Hymnary*, for which he translated a number of hymns. He translated several devotional books from the Norwegian. He was honored with the degree of Litt. D. from Newberry College, Newberry, South Carolina, in 1917. During the years 1919—1920 Rygh served as National Lutheran Council Commissioner to the Baltic States.

  189. *He is arisen! Glorious Word!* (Tr.)
  207. *Like the golden sun ascending.* (Tr.)
  230. *Holy Spirit, God of Love.* (Tr.)
  296. *Speak, O Lord, Thy servant heareth.* (Tr.)
  301. *He that believes and is baptized.* (Tr.)
  337:1, 4: *Our Lord and God, oh, bless this day.* (Tr.)

SACER, Gottfried Wilhelm (1635—1699), judged by many to be one of the greatest hymnists immediately following the Gerhardt period, was born on July 11, 1635, in Naumberg, Saxony, where his father was senior burgomaster. At the age of twenty he entered the University of Jena as a student of philosophy and law. He held the office of secretary to the privy counselor at Berlin for two years and also served as tutor to some young noblemen until 1665, when he entered military service, first as regimental secretary and later as ensign. Two years later he left the service, planning to apply for the degree of doctor of jurisprudence at Kiel. Before this came about, he toured Holland and Denmark with some young Holstein noblemen. In 1670 he was a lawyer in Brunswick, receiving his degree in the following year. In 1683 he went to Wolfenbüttel to become lawyer of the exchequer; here he was appointed counselor of the exchequer in 1690. He earned a fine reputation as lawyer and statesman, being very unselfish and conscientious, handling the cases of the poor without pay and sometimes even assisting in paying costs. He died September 8, 1699, at Wolfenbüttel. Sacer showed poetic ability at an early age and was made a member of the poetical *Order of Elbe Swans* in 1660. He is often described as the "Kayserlicher Poet," for he had been crowned with a wreath of laurels by the Emperor of

Austria himself. He wrote 65 hymns; they were published in 1714 by his son-in-law under the title *Geistliche Liebliche Lieder.* They can be characterized as having poetic glow, dramatic force, euphony of expression, Scriptural content, and excellent style.

214. *Lo, God to heaven ascendeth*

ST. JOHN, Frank B. (?). We have been unable to ascertain any further details about this author than the brief note in *Julian,* p. 1573, "Frank B. St. John, 1878."

379. *I do not come because my soul*

SAVONAROLA, Girolamo (1454—1498), was born in Italy. Becoming a Dominican Friar, he appeared as a preacher of repentance in Florence, fearlessly attacking the ungodliness and licentiousness of the times. Pope Alexander vainly sought to win him over by the promise of a cardinal's hat. The Pope finally ordered him to cease preaching, but Savonarola, personally convinced that he was sent by God, preached all the more vigorously. He was placed under the papal ban, but even this did not avail. Savonarola called the Pope an atheist and appealed to the rulers of Europe to convoke a council to depose the shameful incumbent of the papal chair. But the ecclesiastical and secular courts decided that Savonarola should be hanged and afterwards burnt. This sentence was executed on May 23, 1498, and so Savonarola met his death as a martyr. He must be regarded as one of the important forerunners of the Reformation. His spiritual songs helped to further his reform movement. He wrote them in the same meter and set them to the same tunes as the frivolous carnival songs of Lorenzo de Medici. Yet Lorenzo de Medici thought so much of Savonarola that he asked him to come to his death-bed and hear his confession.

145. *Jesus, Refuge of the weary*

SCHAEFER, William John (1891—   ), was born January 30, 1891 at Manitowoc, Wisconsin, the son of John H. Schaefer and Dorothea, *née* Ellermann. He was educated at Northwestern College, Watertown, Wisconsin. After completing two years of the college department, he entered the Concordia Theological Seminary at Springfield, Illinois, graduating in 1913. His first charge was at Garrison, Nebraska. In the fall of the year 1919 he accepted a call to Colome, South Dakota, in the very heart of the recently opened Rosebud Indian Reservation. After ten years of service here he left for Milwaukee in 1929 to take charge of the Church of the Atonement, where he is pastor at the present time. In 1935 he was appointed associate editor of the *Northwestern Lutheran,* the official organ of the Joint Synod of Wisconsin and Other States, and became its Managing Editor in 1939. He married Pencies C. Palmer in 1913. Of their five children three are living. He is a member of the Intersynodical Committee on Hymnology and Liturgics, which prepared *The Lutheran Hymnal.*

41. *Wondrous King, all Glorious.* (Tr.)
264. *Preserve Thy Word, O Savior.* (Tr.)
477. *Lord Jesus, Thou the Church's Head.* (Tr.)

SCHAEFFER, Charles William (1813—1896), was born in Hagerstown, Maryland, May 5, 1813; graduated from the University of Pennsylvania and the Theological Seminary at Gettysburg, Pennsylvania. He was pastor at Barren Hill, Pennsylvania, 1835—1840; Harrisburg, Pennsylvania, 1840—1849; Germantown, Pennsylvania, 1849 to 1874; and then became professor in the Lutheran Theological Seminary in Philadelphia, serving until 1894, when he was retired as professor emeritus. For many years Dr. Schaeffer was president of the Lutheran Ministerium of Pennsylvania. He was also president of the General Synod and the General Council and served the University of Pennsylvania as a trustee from 1859 till his death in Philadelphia, March 15, 1896.

226. *Come, oh, come, Thou quickening Spirit.* (Tr.)
421. *Come, follow Me, the Savior spake.* (Tr.)

SCHAFF, Philip (1819—1893), was born at Chur, Switzerland, January 1, 1819. He studied theology in Germany, taught for a while in Berlin, and in 1844 became professor of theology at Mercersburg, Pennsylvania. After serving the Church in various other capacities, he became professor at Union Theological Seminary, New York, in 1870. Schaff was active in the Reformed revision of the English Bible. He is perhaps best known for his Church History reference works. He published *Deutsches Gesangbuch*, 1860; *Christ in Song*, 1869; *Hymns and Songs of Praise*, 1874. Together with A. Gilman he published *Library of Religious Poetry*, 1881.

102. *Oh, come, all ye faithful.* (Tr.)

SCHALLING, Martin (1532—1608), was born at Strassburg, April 21, 1532. He matriculated in 1550 at the University of Wittenberg, where he became a favorite pupil of Melanchthon (*q. v.*) and a great friend of Nicolaus Selnecker (*q. v.*). He continued for a short time at Wittenberg as a lecturer after he earned his M. A. degree, and then, in 1554, he became diaconus at Regensburg. Schalling preached against Flacianism and, as a result, he had to give up his post in 1558. Soon after, he was appointed diaconus at Amberg, Bavaria. In 1568, after the Elector Friedrich III, of the Palatinate, had adopted Calvinistic opinions as to the order of service, etc., Schalling had to leave Amberg, since all the Lutheran clergy who would not conform to the change were expelled. But as Duke Ludwig, the son of the Elector, continued as a Lutheran, he allowed Schalling to minister to the spiritual needs of the Lutherans at Vilseck, near Amberg. After Ludwig became Regent of the Oberpfalz, he recalled Schalling to Amberg in 1576 as court preacher and superintendent, and when after his father's death on October 24, 1576, he became Elector of the Pfalz, he appointed Schalling as General Superintendent of the Oberpfalz and also court preacher at Heidelberg. When the clergy of the Oberpfalz were pressed to sign the Formula of Concord, Schalling hesitated to subscribe, holding that it dealt too harshly with the followers of Melanchthon. For this action he was banished from the court at Heidelberg, and after being confined to his house at Amberg'from 1580 to March, 1583, he was finally deprived of his offices. He stayed for some time at Altdorf and then was appointed, in 1585, pastor of St. Mary's Church in Nürnberg, where he remained until blindness compelled him to retire. He died at Nürnberg, December 19, 1608.

429. *Lord, Thee I love with all my heart*

SCHEFFLER, Johann (Angelus Silesius) (1624—1677), was born in 1624 of Lutheran parents in Breslau, Silesia. While a young man, he became deeply interested in the mystics, especially in the teachings of a Spaniard, John ab Angelis. Because of his interest in this man, he assumed the name Angelus. The name Silesius is derived from the name of his native state, Silesia. As a boy he became the disciple of the famous shoemaker Jacob Böhme, another mystic, whose writings on the "Inner Life" were scattered throughout Germany. He studied medicine at Breslau and also at Strassburg. He visited various societies and finally attached himself to a society in Amsterdam, one that had adopted the tenets of Böhme. When he returned to his home in 1649, he practiced medicine as the private physician to the Duke of Württemberg-Öls, Sylvius Nimrod. Here his intimate friend was Abraham von Frankenburg, another disciple of Böhme. Because he showed such a great interest in the mystics, the Lutheran clergy regarded him as a heretic and caused him such disgust by their continued contentions that he joined the Catholics in 1653. In 1654 he became Imperial Court Physician of Emperor Ferdinand III. He did not remain a doctor very long after attaching himself to Ferdinand, but gave up this profession and became a Catholic priest. He died July 9, 1677. He published *Cherubinischer Wandersmann*, 1675; *Heilige Seelenlust*, 1657.

356. *Jesus, Savior, come to me*
397. *O Love, who madest me to wear*
399. *Thee will I love, my Strength, my Tower*
421. *Come, follow Me, the Savior spake*

SCHEIDT, Christian Ludwig (1709—1761), was born in Waldenburg, Germany. He was the son of a German official and first attended school at Öhringen. Between the years 1724 and 1730 he was a student at the universities of Altdorf and Strassburg. During his first two years after his graduation from the latter school he served in the capacity of Hofmeister in a small German city. After that, he studied theology at Halle and philosophy at Göttingen. While attending at Halle, he studied diligently and debated theological questions with his professors. It is said that he attended Halle to study and understand the things of God, spiritual things; and his reason for attending Göttingen was to receive a full understanding of the thoughts and works of men. In other words, he wanted a very broad knowledge of men and God. Shortly after he graduated from Göttingen, he was made a doctor of laws and was appointed a member of the faculty of that school. Later on he taught at the University of Copenhagen. He died at Hanover in 1761, where he was Hofrat and librarian.

373. *By grace I'm saved, grace free and boundless*

SCHEIN, Johann Hermann (1586—1630), born at Grünhain, near Annaberg, Saxony, January 20, 1586. From 1599 to 1603 he was in the choir of the chapel of the Elector of Saxony at Dresden; studied theology and philosophy at Leipzig; became director of music at Weimar in 1613; precentor in St. Thomas's School, Leipzig, in 1615; and died November 19, 1630. His principal work is the *Cantional* or *Gesangbuch Augsburgischer Confession*, Leipzig, 1627. It contains 286 hymns and 206 tunes, of which 57 were by him. In the second edition of 1645, 22 more tunes of his composition were added.

268. ZION KLAGT
421. MACH'S MIT MIR, GOTT

SCHENCK (Shenk), Hartmann (1634—1681), was born April 7, 1634, at Ruhla, near Eisenach, and was the son of a merchant. He attended the gymnasium in Coburg and then studied at Helmstädt and Jena (M. A. 1660). Schenk was pastor at Bibra and in 1669 became diaconus at Ostheim and pastor at Völkershausen. He died May 2, 1681, at Ostheim.   45. *Now, the hour of worship o'er*

SCHIRMER, Michael (1606—1673), was born in Leipzig and studied there. In 1636 he was made the assistant rector of the Greyfriars gymnasium of Berlin. Because of his ill health he never gained the position of rector of the gymnasium, and when a younger man received the position, he retired. His chief reason for retiring, though, was his bad health, for he had suffered from illness since 1644. In spite of this handicap, he labored with determination and worked faithfully. The hardships of his life, including the deaths of his wife and two children and the sufferings of the Thirty Years' War, cast a deep spell of melancholy over him. He published, among others, *Biblische Lieder*, 1650. He died at Berlin, May 4, 1673.

235. *O Holy Spirit, enter in*

SCHLEGEL, Catherina Amalia Dorothea von (1697—?). Koch reports that Catherina was a "Stiftsfräulein" in the Lutheran "Stift" at Cöthen. But James Mearns wrote to Cöthen and was assured that her name was not in the records of that institution. On the other hand, from the correspondence which she carried on with Heinrich Ernst, Count Stolberg, during the years 1750 to 1752, it would appear that she was a lady attached to the little ducal court at Cöthen. No other data about her are available.   651. *Be still, my soul! The Lord is on thy side*

SCHMID, Bernhard (c. 1520—c. 1592), the elder, was organist at Strassburg. He probably studied music under Paul Hofhaimer. He published his *Tabulaturbuch*, Strassburg, 1577. His son succeeded him as organist at the Strassburg "Münster" in 1592, in which year the father either retired or died.

429. HERZLICH LIEB HAB' ICH DICH, O HERR

SCHMIDT, Johann Eusebius (1670—1745), was born at Hohenfelden, near Erfurt, January 12, 1670, where his father was pastor. He matriculated at the University of Jena in the autumn of 1688 and in 1691 went to Erfurt to attend lectures by Breithaupt and Francke. During 1692 Schmidt traveled in Northern Germany. From 1693 to 1696 he was employed as a private tutor at Gotha. In 1697 he began work as a substitute pastor at Siebleben, near Gotha, and the following year became pastor there. Here he died December 25, 1745, with the reputation of "an edifying teacher in his parish, a good example to his flock, and a methodical man in his office."

479. *Zion, rise, Zion, rise*

SCHMOLCK, Benjamin (1672—1737), was born at Brauchitzchdorf, December 21, 1672. He studied at Leipzig. After a year as assistant to his father at Brauchitzchdorf, he was called as deacon to the Friedenskirche at Schweidnitz in Silesia, where he remained till death, becoming pastor primarius and inspector in 1714. He wrote a number of devotional books in which his hymns were included. Of these there was a total of 1,183. He published his *Kirchen-gefährte*, 1732, *Heilige Flammen*, 1704, *Klage und Reigen*, 1734, and a number of other works. The most popular German hymnwriter of his day, he was called the "second Gerhardt," "Silesian Rist." He died February 12, 1737.

1. *Open now thy gates of beauty*
300. *Dearest Jesus, we are here*
420. *My Jesus, as Thou wilt*
571. *What our Father does is well*

SCHNEEGASS, Cyriacus (1546—1597), was born October 5, 1546, at Buffleben, near Gotha. He studied at and graduated as M. A. from the University of Jena. In 1573 Schneegass became pastor of St. Blasius Church at Friedrichroda, near Gotha. He was also adjunct to the Superintendent of Weimar, and in this capacity he signed the Formula of Concord in 1579. Schneegass died at Friedrichroda, October 23, 1597. He was a diligent pastor, a man mighty in the Scriptures, and firm and rejoicing in his faith. Being also an excellent musician, he fostered the love of music among his people. His hymns reflect his character, setting forth in simple, clear, and intelligible style the leading ideas of the festivals of the Christian year. His Psalm-versions are also of considerable merit.

124. *O Lord, our Father, thanks to Thee*

SCHNEESING (Chiomusus or Chyomusus), Johannes (?—1567), belongs to the Reformation Period of German hymnody. He was born in Frankfurt a. M., was vicar in Gotha, and pastor at Friemar. While attending school, he came under the influence of Johannes Stigelius, a composer of Latin verse, and it was, no doubt, through his influence that interest in writing and musical composition was first aroused in his pupil. He is described as a faithful, diligent, pious, and godly man. Especially was he interested in the children of his parish. For them he wrote a catechism, and he also had them learn hymns of his own composition. He died at Friemar in 1567.

319. *In Thee alone, O Christ, my Lord*

SCHOP, Johann (?—c. 1664), joined the court orchestra in Wolfenbüttel in 1615 as "an intelligent performer on the violin, lute, trumpet, and zinke." In 1664 he became director of music at Hamburg, where he had been "Ratsmusikant" since 1654. Here in Hamburg Schop settled permanently and became a violinist of renown. He wrote much instrumental music. His many hymn-tunes were written for the hymns of his fellow-townsman and friend Johann Rist *(q. v.)*.

25. SOLLT' ICH MEINEM GOTT
207, 296, 491, 560. WERDE MUNTER

SCHROEDER, Johann Heinrich (1667—1699), was born at Hallerspringe, near Hanover, October 4, 1667. He studied at the University of Leipzig and while there came under the influence of A. H. Franke. In 1696 he became pastor at Meseberg. He died June 30, 1699.

366. *One thing's needful; Lord, this treasure*

SCHRÖTER, Leonhart (1540—1602), was born at Torgau, where he attended school and received his early musical training from the local Kantor. In 1565 he became Kantor of the school at Magdeburg as successor to Martin Agricola and Gallus Dressler, and from 1580—1587 composed his best-known pieces. He published *XXV geistliche lateinische Hymnen*, 1580.

59. FREUT EUCH, IHR LIEBEN

SCHUETTE, Conrad Hermann Louis (1843—1926), was born at Vorrel, Hanover, June 17, 1843. He came to America in 1854. He studied theology at Capital University, Columbus, Ohio, and was ordained in 1865. He married Victoria M. Wirth of Columbus, Ohio, September 4, 1865. He became pastor of St. Mark's Church, Delaware, Ohio, and in 1872 professor of mathematics and natural philosophy at Capital University, and later professor of theology. For several years he was President of Capital University and also served as pastor of Grace Church in Columbus. During the years 1881—1894 he was pastor of Christ Church, Pleasant Ridge (now Bexley), Ohio. In 1894 he was elected President of The Joint Synod of Ohio and Other States and served in this capacity until 1924. During his term as president he collected more than $400,000 for educational work. He received the degree of Doctor of Divinity from Capital University in 1898. He was one of the founders and molders of the policy and development of The National Lutheran Council, both during and after the World War. He served as its president 1923—1925. He was a frequent contributor to church papers of the Ohio Synod and published *The Church Member's Manual; Church, State, and School; Before the Altar; Exercises Unto Godliness.* He died at Columbus, Ohio, August 11, 1926. He contributed five original hymns and several translations from the German to the Ohio Synod *Hymnal* of 1880.

541. O blessed, Holy Trinity. (Tr.)

SCHUMACHER, Bernhard (1886—   ), son of Herman Schumacher and Hulda, née Ziemer, was born on December 7, 1886, at Watertown, Wisconsin. He was educated at Northwestern College, Watertown, Wisconsin; Concordia Teachers' College, Addison, Illinois; Johns Hopkins University, Baltimore, Maryland, and Peabody Institute, Baltimore, Maryland. Degrees earned: B. A. and M. A. He married Helen Uttech. They have six children. After serving as Lutheran parochial school-teacher for a number of years, he became Superintendent of Schools for the Southern Wisconsin District of the Lutheran Synod of Missouri, Ohio, and Other States. He has published *Eventide,* sacred cantata, 1917; *King Victorious,* sacred cantata, 1924; *Select Songs,* songs for school and home (coauthor), 1922; *Music Reader for Lutheran Schools,* coauthor, 1933; *Book of Accompaniments to Songs in the Music Reader for Lutheran Schools,* 1933; *Lutheran Organist,* coauthor, 1927; and numerous other compositions for organ and choir. He is secretary of the Intersynodical Committee on Hymnology and Liturgics which prepared *The Lutheran Hymnal* and chairman of its Subcommittee on Tunes.

180—186. SEPTEM VERBA
427. FIRM FOUNDATION
481. BALTIMORE
629:4. Let children hear the mighty deeds

SCHÜTZ, Johann Jacob (1640—1690), was born September 7, 1640, at Frankfurt a. M. He studied at Tübingen and practiced law in his native city. He was a man of learning and piety. An intimate of P. J. Spener, he suggested the famous *Collegia Pietatis*. Schütz was a radical Pietist and ceased to attend the Lutheran services and to commune. He died at Frankfurt, May 22, 1690.

19. All praise to God, who reigns above

SCOTT, Sir Walter (1771—1832), was born in Edinburgh, Scotland, August 15, 1771. He was educated in law and was admitted to the bar in 1792. He devoted his leisure time to writing; his first published work, in 1796, was *Lenore,* a translation of two of Bürger's ballads, thus beginning one of the outstanding careers in the field of English letters. Since his works as novelist are so well known, only his work as hymn-writer will be mentioned. Besides his condensed rendering of "Dies Irae," he wrote "When Israel of the Lord beloved" and also published a translation of the "Te Deum," "Thee, Sovereign God, our grateful accents raise," and of "Ut queant laxis," the hymn at Evensong for St. John the Baptist's Day. Scott calls it "St. John's Eve" ("O Sylvan Prophet"). "When Israel of the Lord beloved" appeared in Scott's *Ivanhoe,* 1817, the occasion being the imaginary trial of Rebecca, the Jewess, who was charged by a court of The Order of the Templars for having bewitched one of the knights, Brian de Bois-Guilbert, into breaking several of the rules of the Order. When stripped of these romantic surroundings, it remains a striking hymn. It is based on Psalm 105.

612. That day of wrath, that dreadful day. (Tr.)

SCRIVEN, Joseph (1820—1886), was born at Dublin, Ireland, in 1820. He was graduated from Trinity College, Dublin. Then he moved to Canada in 1845, where he led a humble life and, though eccentric, was very charitable. He died by drowning at Port Hope, on Lake Ontario, October 10, 1886.

457. What a Friend we have in Jesus

SEDULIUS, Coelius (c. 450), was probably born in Rome. All the facts known about him come from two letters of his written to Macedonius. In early life he devoted himself, perhaps as a teacher of rhetoric, to heathen literature. Comparatively late in life he was converted to Christianity; or if he had been a Christian before, he now first began to take a serious view of his duties. From then on Sedulius devoted his talents as a priest to the service of Christ. His yearning was to attract the heathen by telling them of the wonders of the Gospel. This moved him to write. His works include *Carmen Paschale,* a poem on the whole Gospel-story dedicated to Macedonius. Sedulius longed to show the heathen that Christianity had more to offer them than heathenism. *Opus Paschale* is a prose rendering of the whole Gospel-story. *Elegia* is a poem of 110 lines on the same subject as the *Carmen.* Sedulius also wrote *Hymnus de Christo,* a hymn of 23 four-line stanzas, of which each stanza begins with a letter of the alphabet in order.

104. Now praise we Christ, the Holy One
131. <i>The star proclaims the King is here</i></p>

SEISS, Joseph Augustus (1823—1904), was born March 18, 1823, at Graceham, Maryland. He was the son of a miner and was educated at Gettysburg College and Seminary and was licensed by the Lutheran Virginia Synod in 1842. After his ordination in 1848 he served various churches in Virginia and Maryland, became pastor of old St. John's, Philadelphia, in the latter year, and in 1874 of the Church of the Holy Communion. Seiss served as president of both the Pennsylvania Ministerium and the General Council. He was a noted pulpit orator. He published among other works *Ecclesia Lutherana, Lectures on the Epistle to the Hebrews, Lectures on the Gospels.*

657. Beautiful Savior. (Tr.)

SELNECKER (Selneccer, Schellenecker), Nikolaus (1532—1592), son of Georg Selnecker, was born at Hersbruck on December 5, 1532. He attended school at Nürnberg, during which time he was organist at the chapel in the Kaiserburg there, and attracted the attention and interest of King Ferdinand and the royal singers. He attended the University of Wittenberg in 1550, graduating as M. A. in 1554. He became Melanchthon's favorite pupil, and later, due to his influence, was appointed Court Preacher to the Elector August at Dresden. His other duties were those of a tutor to Prince Alexander and to supervise the education of the chapel boys in the royal chapel. He was ordained at Wittenberg in 1558. At the Saxon court during this time there were many Crypto-Calvinists who found their plans and preachings regarding consubstantiation thwarted by Selnecker's presence there, and so they decided to overthrow him. He openly adhered to strict Lutheranism in regard to the Lord's Supper. Their opportunity came when Selnecker took it upon himself to defend his friend Martin Hoffmann, who had been exiled for preaching against the Elector's reckless hunting. Selnecker was himself released from office for incurring the displeasure of the Elector. He is said to have written the hymn "Hilf, Herr, mein Gott, in dieser Noth" on this occasion, but it is more probable that the hymn was written about Selnecker's own troubles and sorrows, for his friend left in 1564, and the hymn is dated 1565. He left Dresden and took the office of professor at the University of Jena, which he held for three years. In spite of his previous stand against the Calvinists here, he was suspected of being one himself, possibly because he had been a favorite disciple of Melanchthon. Again he was compelled to leave. Now he became professor of theology at the University of Leipzig, pastor of St. Thomas Church, and Superintendent of Leipzig, having come again into the favor of the Elector. Here he worked quietly and successfully for twelve years, after which he was sent to Wolfenbüttel, where he served as court preacher and General Superintendent, making many improvements in schools and churches. He resumed his work in Leipzig in 1574, when again he became involved in bitter doctrinal disputes regarding the Lord's Supper, and together with Chemnitz and Andreae he prepared the Formula of Concord, which was published in 1577. This was violently attacked and yet was successful largely because it was subscribed to by so many. It was written mainly to unite the Lutherans and to exclude the Romanists on the one hand, and the Calvinists on the other. Following the year 1579 he spent several quiet years at Leipzig, devoting much of his time to building up the Motet Choir of the St. Thomas Church there, which was later to come under the leadership of Johann Sebastian Bach. When the Elector died, his son, Christian I, who was under Calvinistic influence, came into power, and Selnecker was compelled to leave Leipzig. He became superintendent at Hildesheim; while he was there, Christian died, and the Calvinists lost power, Selnecker again being recalled to Leipzig. Chancellor Crell, who had influenced Christian's Calvinistic leanings, was deposed, and Selnecker returned, too broken down in health to continue work, and he died May 24, 1592. He had lived during an age of marked doctrinal controversy, and through it all he will always be remembered as one of the great champions of pure Lutheran doctrine. We owe about 150 hymns to this man, and in addition he wrote some 175 theological and controversial works.

292. *Lord Jesus Christ, with us abide*
321. *O faithful God, thanks be to Thee*
334:1. *Let me be Thine forever*
600. *O Lord, my God, I cry to Thee*

SERLE, Ambrose (1742—1812), born August 30, 1742, was a commissioner in the British Government Transport Office. He published, among other works, *Horae Solitariae*, 1786, which was a collection of essays on the names and titles of Jesus Christ. Short hymns were appended to this work. He died August 1, 1812.

530. *Thy ways, O Lord, with wise design*

SHIRLEY, Walter (1725—1786), was the fourth son of the Hon. Laurence Shirley, son of the first Earl Ferrers. Shirley met the Rev. Henry Venn at the home of the Lady Huntingdon, and the conversation and preaching of this cleric resulted in Shirley's conversion. After he had done sporadic preaching in London as the opportunity presented itself, Shirley was ordained in 1749 and nine years later became Rector of Loughrea, Ireland. Shirley was the cousin of the Countess of Huntingdon and assisted her in the selection of hymns for use in the chapels of her connection. Early in 1760 Shirley was deeply grieved by the conduct of his eldest brother Laurence, who was condemned and executed for the murder of his steward. In 1766 Shirley married Henrietta Maria Phillips. Shirley was involved in a controversy with the Wesleys and their preachers. A recantation of a declaration in respect to Calvinism was secured by Shirley from them after considerable discussion. He himself continued in the faithful discharge of his duties as a Gospel-preacher until he was worn down by a disease of a dropsical character. He died April 7, 1786.

155. *Sweet the moments, rich in blessing*

SHRUBSOLE, William (1759—1829), was born at Sheerness, Kent, son of a mastmaker, who was also a lay preacher. He became shipwright and then clerk in the Bank of England, from which position he advanced to that of Secretary to the Committee of the Treasury. At first member of the Church of England, he later became Congregationalist. He was interested in the London Missionary Society, the Bible Society, the Religious Tract Society, and also became a lay preacher. He died at Highbury, August 23, 1829.

543. *When streaming from the eastern skies*

SIBELIUS, Jean (1865—), was born December 8, 1865, at Tavastelhus, Finland, and entered the University of Helsingfors in 1885 to study law but gave it up in the following year to develop his natural aptitude for music at the Helsingfors Conservatory, becoming a pupil of Wegelius, the leader of the national movement in music. He later traveled and studied in Berlin and Vienna. From 1893 to 1897 he taught composition at the Helsingfors Conservatory and at the Philharmonic Orchestra School. In 1897 he was granted a pension from the Finnish Government, which was kept up and increased as he became more and more identified as the representative national composer of Finland. He is known chiefly for his dramatic works, symphonies, symphonic poems, suites, and songs. "The orchestral compositions of Sibelius seem to have passed over black torrents and desolate moorlands, through pallid sunlight and grim primeval forests, and become drenched with them. The instrumentation is all wet grays and blacks, relieved only by bits of brightness, wan and elusive as the northern summer, frostily green as the polar light." His symphonic poem *Finlandia* was composed for the inauguration of the Finnish National Theater, 1902. When Sibelius visited the United States to conduct some of his works at the twenty-eighth Norfolk (Connecticut) Festival, Yale University conferred upon him the degree of Mus. D.

651. FINLANDIA

SILESIUS, Angelus. See Johann Scheffler.

SLOAN, John Morrison (1835—?), was born at Stairaird, Ayrshire. He studied at the University of Glasgow, Edinburgh, and at Erlangen, receiving his M. A. from Edinburgh in 1859. Thereafter he served successively as collegiate minister of the Free Church, Dalkeith, 1864; minister of the South Free Church, Aberdeen, 1868; collegiate minister of Anderston Free Church, Glasgow, 1878; and minister of the Grange Free Church, Edinburgh, 1890. He contributed a number of original hymns and translations from the German to Anglican hymnals of the late nineteenth century.

444. Rise! To arms! With prayer employ you. (Tr.)

SMART, Henry Thomas (1813—1879), was born October 26, 1813, in London, the son of Henry Smart, violinist and piano manufacturer. Smart declined a commission in the Indian army, and studied law for four years. Law, however, did not appeal to him, and so he began to develop his natural musical aptitude. He was largely self-taught, but he did take some lessons from W. H. Kearns, a prominent London violinist. His first appointment was as organist at Blackburn, Lancashire. In 1838 he returned to London, where he served successively as organist at three prominent churches, being in active service until his death. As an executant and composer for the organ Smart had few equals. He developed great skill also in the planning and erection of organs, being responsible for the instruments built in some of the chief halls of the country. Smart suffered many years from an affliction of the eyes and became totally blind in 1865. However, he continued his composing by dictating all his work to his daughter. In this condition he even superintended the construction of the organ in St. Andrew's Hall, Glasgow, in every detail. He died July 6, 1879. He produced 250 secular works, but his writings for the Church are not extensive. He edited two noteworthy tune-books, namely, *The Presbyterian Hymnal* and the *Chorale Book*. Lightwood says that in this latter book Smart has done for the English hymn-tune what Bach did for the German *chorale*. Less than a month before he died, the British government granted Smart a pension of about £100 per year in acknowledgment of his services in the cause of music. Smart favored congregational singing, and the slow, dignified style of the old psalm-tunes rather than the quicker measures which his contemporaries were beginning to use. He wrote some very fine music; some parts of his complete "Service in F" have been considered worthy of Beethoven, and his hymn-tunes and anthems are also of a high order.

50, 136, 466, 502, 641. REGENT SQUARE
205. LANCASHIRE
218. REX GLORIAE

SMEBY, Oluf Hanson (1851—1929), was born January 31, 1851, in Rock County, Wisconsin. He attended Luther College (A. B. 1871) and Concordia Seminary (C. T. 1874). He was pastor at Albert Lea, Minnesota, for forty-six years. He also served as teacher at the Luther Academy, Albert Lea; Secretary of the Iowa District of the Norwegian Synod; Vice-President of the same; member of the English Hymn-book Committee *(Christian Hymns)*, and chairman of the English Hymn-book Committee *(Lutheran Hymnary)*. Smeby translated a number of hymns from the Norwegian. He died July 6, 1929.

    48. *How blest are they who hear God's Word.* (Tr.)
    65. *When sinners see their lost condition.* (Tr.)
 194. *Abide with us, the day is waning.* (Tr.)
 293. *O Holy Spirit, grant us grace.* (Tr.)

SMITH, Samuel Francis (1808—1895), was born, to use his own words, "under the sound of the Old North Church chimes in Boston, Oct. 21, 1808." He graduated from Harvard University in 1829 and from Andover Seminary in 1832. He served several congregations in New England. He was professor of modern languages in Waterville (later Colby) College from 1834 to 1842. He was active in Christian journalism, having been editor of the *Christian Review* in Boston from 1842 to 1848 and editor of the publications of the American Baptist Missionary Union from 1854 to 1869. His publications include several biographical works and various missionary writings. A collected edition of his poems, *Poems of Home and Country*, appeared in New York in 1895, the year of his death. He is the author of "My country, 'tis of thee." Oliver Wendell Holmes, his classmate and lifelong friend, at one of their class reunions read his poem "The Boys" in which he honored Smith with this stanza:

    "And there's a nice youngster of excellent pith, —
    Fate tried to conceal him by naming him Smith, —
    But he shouted a song for the brave and the free, —
    Just read on his medal, — 'My Country.' 'Of thee.' "

 497. *The morning light is breaking*
 637. *Founded on Thee, our only Lord*

SOHREN (Sohr, Sohrer), Peter (c. 1630—c. 1692). There is little material available concerning Sohren's birth and early schooling. We find him first in 1668 as "Bestalter Schul- und Rechenmeister der Christlichen Gemeine zum H. Leichnam in Königlicher Stadt Elbing in Preussen." In that year he edited the Frankfurt edition of *Praxis Pietatis Melica*, with minor changes and additions of his own and about 220 melodies of his own composition. His second hymnal, *Musikalischer Vorschmack*, appeared in 1683, when he was cantor and organist of the Elbing Congregation; it is said to contain between 240 and 250 of his melodies. Toward the end of the same year Sohren became organist and "Kollege" of the Evangelical Church and School in Dirschau, where he appears to have died about the year 1692.

 306. HERR JESU CHRIST, DU HAST BEREIT'T

SPAETH, Harriett Reynolds Krauth (1845—1925). Dr. Sigmund Spaeth, noted son of Mrs. Spaeth, has kindly furnished us with the following data on his mother's career: "Born, Baltimore, September 21, 1845. Married to Adolph Spaeth October 12, 1880. Mother of five children, Charles (1881), Carola (1883), Sigmund (1885), Reynold (1886), Alan (1889). The first and last of these children died in infancy. My mother's father was the Rev. Dr. Charles Porterfield Krauth, Vice-Provost of the University of Pennsylvania and a distinguished leader in the Lutheran Church. (See my father's biography of Dr. Krauth). His father was Dr. Charles Philip Krauth, President of Gettysburg Theological Seminary. Three books by my mother are worth mentioning: *The Church Book with Music*, published by the General Council Publication Board, 1893; *Pictures from the Life of Hans Sachs;* and the *Life of Adolph Spaeth*, General Council Publication House, 1916. Her full name was Harriett Reynolds Krauth Spaeth. She played the piano and organ and had an adequate contralto voice, with which she completed the family harmony (my father being a good tenor, my sister Carola an excellent soprano, and one or more of the boys always available as a bass). My mother died May 10, 1925, in Philadelphia."

44. *Ye lands, to the Lord make a jubilant noise.* (Tr.)
353. *Lord Jesus Christ, my Savior blest.* (Tr.)
645:1-4. *Behold, a Branch is growing.* (Tr.)

SPEGEL, Haquin (1645—1714), was bishop of Skara and later bishop of Linköping, before he was elevated to the archbishopric of Upsala in 1711. He was a great traveler, having visited Denmark, Germany, Holland, and England.

163. *The death of Jesus Christ, our Lord*

SPENGLER, Lazarus (1479—1534), the ninth of twenty-one children, was born on March 13, 1479, at Nürnberg, where his father was a clerk of the Imperial Court of Justice. He entered the University of Leipzig in 1494, but when his father died in 1496, he returned to Nürnberg and obtained a position in the town clerk's office. In 1507 Spengler became town clerk and in 1516 also Rathsherr. It is interesting to note that when Luther passed through Nürnberg on his way to Augsburg in 1518, Spengler made his acquaintance. He warmly espoused the Reformation doctrines and in 1519 published *Schutzred* favoring Luther. Spengler himself became one of the leaders in the Reformation work at Nürnberg. So it is not surprising to find his name on the list of those condemned by the Bull of Excommunication launched by Leo X on June 15, 1520, against Luther and his friends. But Nürnberg ignored the *bulla* and even sent Spengler as one of their representatives to the Diet of Worms, April, 1521. In 1525 Spengler went to Wittenberg to consult with Luther and Melanchthon as to turning the Benedictine Ägidienstift into an Evangelical Gymnasium, and this was opened as such by Melanchthon on May 23, 1526. Spengler was the prime mover to the Visitation of 1528 and upheld strict Lutheranism in the negotiations at the Diet of Augsburg in 1530. He died at Nürnberg, September 7, 1534.

369. *All mankind fell in Adam's fall*

SPERATUS, Paul (1484—1551), born December 13, 1484, in Swabia, entered the University of Freiburg in 1503 and probably also studied at Paris and in Italy. In 1518 he was a preacher at Dinkelsbühl, Bavaria, and in the two following years preached at Würzburg and Salzburg, in both cases being forced to leave for expressing his evangelical views too openly. He received his D. D. from the University of Vienna in 1520 and was one of the first priests to marry, thereby breaking away from the Roman custom of enforced celibacy. He was condemned by the Theological Faculty at Vienna, imprisoned for a time by King Ludwig, and in 1523 came to Wittenberg, where he worked with Luther *(q. v.)* and assisted him in the preparation of the first Lutheran hymn-book, *Etlich Christlich Lider*. In 1524 he was appointed court preacher at Königsberg, and he seems to have had a great deal to do with drawing up the Liturgy and Canons, *Kirchenordnung*, for the Prussian Church, 1526. He died as Lutheran bishop of Pomerania while living at Marienwerder.

377. *Salvation unto us has come*

SPIESS, Johann Martin (1715—1772), was born at Bern, was organist of St. Peter's Church in Heidelberg, and professor of music in the gymnasium there. In 1745 he edited a book of *chorales, Geistliche Liebes-Posaune*, and in 1761 *Geistliche Arien*. The last years of his life were spent in Bern, where he was organist in 1766. He died in June, 1772.

274, 433. SWABIA

SPITTA, Karl Johann Philipp (1801—1859), was the greatest German hymn-writer of the 19th century. He was born August 1, 1801, in Hanover of parents in humble life, his father being a bookkeeper and teacher of French. The Spitta family was a Huguenot family that fled during the Roman Catholic persecutions in France.

They changed their name from "de l'Hopital" to the German equivalent Spital or Spittell, which was later modified into Spitta. His father died when Karl was but four. The mother was a Christian Jewess, and to her fostering care Karl wrote the finest hymn ever written on the Christian home, "O happy home where Thou art loved most dearly." Spitta started to write verse when he was eight. Because of his frail health, Karl's younger brother was sent to school to study for the ministry instead of Karl. His father having died, his mother apprenticed him to a watchmaker. He did not like watchmaking; yet he was faithful and efficient in his work. At this time he began the study of languages. The younger brother died by drowning in 1818, and so Karl was sent to school when he inadvertently made his true desire known to a close friend. He completed his studies at the University of Göttingen, where the professors were rationalistic, in 1824, then tutored in a private family for four years at Lüne, near Lüneburg, till he was ordained to the Lutheran ministry, as assistant pastor of Sudwalde, Hanover. Two years later Spitta received the appointment of chaplain to the prisoners and garrison of Hameln, Hanover, and would have succeeded as permanent chaplain there, had not the military authorities, alarmed by reports which described him as a Pietist and a mystic, refused to sanction the arrangement. On October 4, 1837, Spitta married Joanna Mary Magdalene Hotzen and in the same year took charge of the Lutheran Church of Wechold, near Hoya, Hanover, where he labored happily and successfully for ten years. Spitta's home was one of peace and song. There were seven children. One son, Friedrich Spitta, born January 10, 1852, became a theologian and was appointed professor of New Testament Exegesis and Practical Theology at the University of Strassburg and is known through his works on liturgics. Another son, Johann August Philipp, was the author of the great biography of J. S. Bach. In 1847 Spitta received the appointment of Ecclesiastical Superintendent of Wittingen and in 1853 that of chief pastor of Peine. Spitta had just been preferred to the Church at Burgdorf when he was stricken with a gastric fever followed by cramp of the heart. He died at the age of 58, September 28, 1859. At the university Spitta had written songs and secular poems, and he even published a number of them anonymously as a *Sangbüchlein der Liebe für Handwerksleute*. At the university Spitta also became fast friends with Heinrich Heine. That friendship came to an abrupt end, however, when Heine visited Spitta at Lüne and openly ridiculed holy things in front of Spitta's pupils. Spitta himself passed through a deep spiritual experience during which he composed some of his finest hymns. In 1826 Spitta wrote to a friend, "In the manner in which I formerly sang, I sing no more. To the Lord I dedicate my life, my love, and likewise my song. He gave to me song and melody. I give it back to Him." Spitta's hymns aroused unparalleled enthusiasm. His *Psalter und Harfe* appeared in a second and larger edition after its first in 1833. By 1889 no less than 55 editions had been published. Another collection of hymns, which was first published in 1843, passed through 42 editions by 1887. A translation of Spitta's hymns into English verse was published by Richard Massie in 1859, entitled *Lyra Domestica*.

    453. We are the Lord's; His all-sufficient merit
    626. O happy home, where Thou art loved most dearly

SPOHR, Louis (1784—1859), son of Karl Heinrich Spohr, a physician, was born at Brunswick, April 5, 1784. At an early age he showed musical talent. The Duke of Brunswick became his patron and placed him under the tuition of Franz Eck. He studied harmony at Brunswick under Hartung and the violin under Kunisch and Maucourt; after traveling a great deal, he settled at Cassel in 1822 and was appointed director of the Court Theatre Orchestra there, an office which he held till 1857, when he retired on a pension. He died at Cassel, October 22, 1859. He composed operas, oratorios, and much instrumental music. He is known especially for his opera *Faust* and for his oratorio *The Last Judgment*.

STAINER, John (1840—1901), was born June 6, 1840, in London, and became a choir boy at St. Paul's Cathedral at the age of seven and had several of his own compositions sung in the services during his nine years there. In 1854 he became organist at St. Benet and St. Peter's, Paul's Wharf, and two years later was appointed first organist of St. Michael's, Tenbury. In 1859 Stainer entered Christ Church, Oxford, and in the same year was appointed organist of Magdalen College and later of the University. He received his Mus. B. in 1859, B. A. in 1863, Mus. D. in 1865, and his M. A. in 1866. In 1872 Stainer became organist at St. Paul's Cathedral, succeeding Sir John Goss, a position which he held until 1888. He also served as Professor of the Organ, and later Principal of the National Training School for Music, organist to the Royal Choral Society, Government Inspector of Music in Training Schools, and finally as Professor of Music at Oxford University. He was knighted by Queen Victoria in 1888 and died at Verona, Italy, March 31, 1901. He wrote much church music, from oratorios to hymn-tunes, and helped to edit the first *Church Hymnary*. He published *The Music of the Bible* and *A Treatise on Harmony*. His cantata *The Crucifixion* is well known.

370. MAGDALEN

STEBBINS, George Coles (1846—1945), was born February 26, 1846, at East Carlton, Orleans County, New York, where he spent his early years on his father's farm and received his chief musical training at the local country singing school. He studied for a time in Rochester and began his real musical career as director of music of the First Baptist Church of Chicago. He worked at the music store of Lyon and Healy, became very active in the musical affairs of Chicago, and was a charter member of the Apollo Club. In 1874 he moved to Boston and two years later was made director of music at Tremont Temple. In the same year he met Dwight L. Moody and in his association with Moody and Sankey he became one of the leading figures in the evangelistic song field. He was coeditor of *Gospel Hymns* and chief editor of *The Northfield Hymnal*.

565. EVENING PRAYER

STEELE, Anne (1716—1778), was born in Broughton, Hampshire. Her father, William Steele, was a timber merchant and also at the same time the pastor, without salary, of the Baptist Church in Broughton. In her childhood Miss Steele showed a taste for literature and went so far as to compose little poems, with which she often entertained her father's visitors. From these crude poems of her childhood were developed some of Miss Steele's most impressive, highly emotional hymns. It was not until 1760 that any of her hymns were published. Then she published two volumes of *Poems on Subjects chiefly Devotional* under the assumed name of Theodosia. She composed a great number of hymns, but the nature and style of her hymns are mostly the same owing to the particularly painful circumstances of her life. She suffered from great delicacy of health, enduring great sorrow and finally spending the greater part of her life as an invalid. She had in childhood received a hip injury, from which she never recovered. Later she suffered a great sorrow when her betrothed drowned on the day preceding their anticipated marriage. Composing under such sorrows and afflictions, Miss Steele added to English hymnody the plaintive and sentimental note. She gave us the hymn of introspection and intense devotion, expressed in a vivid and emotional way. The measure of our regard for her hymns today but faintly reflects the enthusiasm of the welcome her hymns received during her lifetime and the years immediately following her death.

141. Enslaved by sin and bound in chains
281. The Savior calls; let every ear
284. Father of mercies, in Thy Word
363. To our Redeemer's glorious name
579. Almighty Lord, before Thy throne

STEGMANN, Josua (1588—1632), was born at Sülzfeld, Germany, September 14, 1588, the son of Ambrosius Stegmann, a Lutheran pastor in that city. In 1608 he entered the University of Leipzig, and having received his M. A. in 1611, he was an adjunct of the philosophical faculty. In 1617 he was appointed superintendent of the district of Schaumburg, pastor at Stadthagen, and was also first professor of the Gymnasium there. On October 24, 1617, he received his D. D. from Wittenberg. When the Gymnasium at Stadthagen was changed into a university and transferred to Rinteln in 1621, he became a professor of theology there. During the Thirty Years' War he had to leave Rinteln. He returned in 1625 and was appointed Ephorus of the Lutheran clergy of Hesse-Schaumburg. By the edict of Restitution, March 6, 1629, Stegmann was greatly harassed. Benedictine monks claimed to be rightful professors and demanded restoration of the old church land, especially the property formerly belonging to the nunnery of Rinteln, which had now been devoted to the payment of the stipends of the Lutheran professors. On July 13, 1632, soldiers were sent into his house demanding a refund of his salary. They continued to annoy him greatly, even calling him to an open disputation. All this worry and trouble shortened his life considerably, and he died August 3, 1632.

53. Abide, O dearest Jesus

STEPHENSON (Stevenson), Isabella Stephana (1843—1890), was born at Cheltenham, the daughter of an army officer. Here she spent her entire life. She was a devoted member of the Church of England. For many years Miss Stephenson was an invalid. She wrote only one hymn.

643. Holy Father, in Thy mercy

STEUERLEIN, Johann (1546—1613), was born July 5, 1546, the son of Caspar Steuerlein, or Steurlein, the first Lutheran pastor of Schmalkalden. Steuerlein completed his study of law and c. 1580 was appointed town-clerk of Wasungen (between Schmalkalden and Meiningen). In 1589 he became secretary in the chancery at Meiningen to the Henneberg administration. Then he was a notary public and c. 1604 was mayor at Meiningen, where he died May 5, 1613. He was crowned as poet by the Emperor Rudolph II in recognition of his work of rhyming the Old and New Testaments in German. He was the author of a metrical version of Ecclesiasticus, published at Frankfurt a. M. in 1581. He was an excellent musician and published various works containing melodies and four-part settings by himself.

125. The old year now hath passed away

STHEN, Hans Christenson (16th century), was born in Roskilde, Denmark. He was brought up by Christopher Walkendorf and became rector of a school in Helsingö and later vicar in the same city. He seems to have traveled for a short time in Germany, and in 1581 he was called to Copenhagen to receive his degree of Master of Arts. He was called as pastor to Malmo in 1583 and in 1600 was offered the parish of Tyglese and Glogstrup, although it is doubtful whether he ever assumed his duties there. He is spoken of as a man well versed in theological and secular sciences, a forceful preacher, an excellent author, well loved by his parishioners and friends. He translated a number of hymns from the German, and his published works give evidence of poetic talent.

353. Lord Jesus Christ, my Savior blest

STOBÄUS, Johann (1580—1646), was born in Graudenz, West Prussia. He received his early musical training under Johann Eccard, the "Kapellmeister" in Königsberg. He also attended the university there, sang in the chapel chorus, and in 1602 became cantor of the church and the cathedral school. In 1626 he stepped into the position of his old teacher as "Kapellmeister" at Königsberg, where he served until his death, September 11, 1646. He published *Cantiones Sacrae*, 1624; *Geistliche Lieder*, 1634.

383. SUCH', WER DA WILL

STONE, Samuel John (1839—1900), was born in Whitmore, Staffordshire, on April 25, 1839. He studied theology, and, after having charge of various churches, he succeeded his father at St. Paul's in Haggerston. During his life he wrote four volumes of poetry: *Lyra Fidelium*, 1866; *The Knight of Intercession and other poems*, 1872; *Sonnets of the Christian Year; Hymns*, a collection of his original pieces. Samuel Stone died November 19, 1900.

473. The Church's one foundation

STÖRL (Sterle), Johann Georg Christian (1675—1719), was born August 14, 1675, at Kirchberg on the Jaxt and received his early musical training as a choir boy at the Stuttgart Royal Chapel, studying under Theodor Schwartzkopf. He also studied under Johann Pachelbel in Nürnberg. In 1701 he went to Vienna to continue his musical studies under Ferdinand Tobias Fischer. Then he went to Italy for further training and on his return to Stuttgart in 1704 he was made Kapellmeister. Störl collaborated on a number of hymnals and wrote a great many hymn-tunes. His *Choralbuch* appeared in 1711.

606. O JERUSALEM, DU SCHÖNE

STRÖMME, Peer Olsen (1856—1921), was born September 15, 1856, at Winchester, Wisconsin. He attended Luther College (A. B. 1876) and Concordia Seminary (C. T. 1879). Strömme held pastorates at Mayville, North Dakota, Ada, Minnesota, and Nelson, Wisconsin. He also served as Superintendent of Schools of Norman County, Minnesota, teacher at St. Olaf College, and principal of Mount Horeb Academy, Mount Horeb, Wisconsin. Besides editing various Norwegian newspapers and periodicals, Strömme edited the *Minneapolis Times*. He was the author of several books, mostly written in Norwegian, and translated Laache's *Book of Family Prayer*. Strömme also wrote many poems and translated many hymns. He was a lecturer and "globe-trotter." He died September 15, 1921.

179. On my heart imprint Thine image. (Tr.)
415. Lo, many shall come from the East and the West. (Tr.)

STRONG, Nathan (1748—1816), was born October 16, 1748, at Coventry, Connecticut. In 1765 he entered Yale and graduated four years later with the first honor. He studied law for a while but then turned to theology. He was appointed tutor at Yale in 1772 and served in this capacity for one year. Then he was called to the First Congregational Church of Hartford, Connecticut, and was ordained on January 5, 1774. He served this church for the rest of his life. During the War of the Revolution he served as a chaplain in the army. After the war Strong set himself to stem the tide of iniquity and infidelity which comes after any war. In 1796 he had won great repute through his essay on the doctrine of *Eternal Misery consistent with the Infinite Benevolence of God*. Strong founded the *Connecticut Evangelical Magazine* (1800) and also took a prominent part in establishing the Connecticut Home Mission Society in 1801. Princeton conferred an honorary D. D. on him. He was the principal editor of the *Hartford Selection*, 1799.

584. Swell the anthem, raise the song

SULLIVAN, Arthur Seymour (1842—1900), was born at London on May 13, 1842. The son of a musician, he received his early musical training as a choir boy at the Chapel Royal. He studied at the Royal Academy of Music and the Conservatory of Leipzig. Sullivan was for a time organist of St. Michael's, Chester Square, and of St. Peter's, Onslow Gardens, and later held the positions of musical director of the Royal Aquarium, Principal of the National Training School for Music and Professor of Composition, Conductor of the Glasgow Choral Union (1875—1877), of Covent Garden Promenade Concerts (1878—1879), of the Leeds Festival in 1880, and of the Philharmonic Society (1885—1887). He was honored by the Legion of Honour in 1878 and was knighted in 1883. He wrote a number of operas, oratorios, and hymn-tunes, but is known chiefly for his operettas written in collaboration with W. S. Gilbert, the English humorist.

658. ST. GERTRUDE
660. HEAVEN IS MY HOME

SYNESIUS, of Cyrene (c. 375—430), of noble descent, visited Alexandria, Constantinople, and Athens. At Alexandria he studied under the renowned Hypatia.

After that he devoted himself to philosophy and the life of a country gentleman. He became a statesman and a patriot, distinguished for his eloquence and philosophy. When the Goths threatened his country, Synesius went to the court of Arcadius and for three years tried to rouse it to the dangers that were imminent. But, as Gibbon says, "The court of Arcadius indulged the zeal, applauded the eloquence, and neglected the advice of Synesius." Synesius even raised a corps of volunteers against the Libyan nomads. In 410 he was made Bishop of Ptolemais, much against his will, lest he see his "bows rusting" or his "hounds in idleness." Synesius was no ascetic, was married, and loved the open-air life. He was imbued with Neo-Platonic philosophy, apparently conscious of the fact that he could not harmonize his philosophy with the doctrines of the Church.

320. *Lord Jesus, think on me*

TALLIS (Tallys), Thomas (c. 1510—1585), one of the greatest of English musicians, flourished about the middle of the sixteenth century. He was a Gentleman of the Chapel Royal in the reigns of Henry VIII, Edward VI, and Mary, and organist to Elizabeth and of Waltham Abbey till its dissolution in 1540. Tallis composed many anthems, which were published in Barnard's *Selected Church Musick*, 1641. He died November 23, 1585, and was buried in the chancel of the Parish Church of Greenwich. His greatest composition is his motet *Spem in alium non habui* for forty voices — eight choirs of five parts each. 558. TALLIS' CANON

TAPPAN, William Bingham (1794—1849), was born in Beverley, Massachusetts, October 29, 1794. At the age of twelve his father died, and poverty led him to attempt to make his own living. Accordingly, he became an apprentice to a clockmaker in Boston for nine years. As he grew up, he fell in with evil companions, and only the appeals of a godly mother saved him from a thoroughly bad life. His restless nature led him to leave Boston for Philadelphia. As soon as means permitted, he gave up his work to become Superintendent of the American Sunday-school Union and was licensed to preach in Congregational churches. From 1826 until his sudden death of cholera at West Needham, Massachusetts, June 18, 1849, he was in the employ of the American Sunday-school Board.

617. *There is an hour of peaceful rest*

TATE, Nahum (1652—1715), was the son of Faithful Teate, an Irish clergyman. He was educated at Trinity College. Under Dryden's superintendence he wrote all but 200 lines of *Absalom and Ahithophel*. In 1692 he succeeded Shadwell as Poet Laureate. He also became historiographer-royal in 1702. He is said to have been a man of intemperate and improvident life, dying deeply in debt. Together with Nicholas Brady he prepared the *New Version* of the psalms, 1696.

29. *Through all the changing scenes of life*
109. *While shepherds watched their flocks by night*
525. *As pants the hart for cooling streams*

TAYLOR, R. E. (?—1938), Melbourne, Australia. He was a hospital missionary in Melbourne, a Congregationalist. He was an admirer of Luther and his teachings.

335. *My Maker, be Thou nigh.* (Tr.)

TAYLOR, Thomas Rawson (1807—1835), the son of an English Congregational minister, was born May 9, 1807, at Ossett, near Wakefield. At fifteen he became an apprentice to a merchant, but after a few years he was stationed in a printer's shop. The printer was a man of great piety. His character impressed young Taylor very much, and through his guidance the youth received his religious convictions. At the age of eighteen he left the printer's shop with his master's consent to study for the Congregational ministry at Airedale Independent College. He became pastor of Howard St. Chapel in Sheffield. After six months of service he was obliged to give up this work because of ill health. He then became classical tutor in his alma mater. But after a few years he died of consumption on March 7, 1835.

660. *I'm but a stranger here*

TERSTEEGEN, Gerhard (1697—1769), son of Heinrich Tersteegen, merchant at Moers (Meurs) in Rhenish Prussia, was born November 25, 1697. He was to become a Reformed minister, but after his father's death in 1703 his mother was not able to send her son to the university. In 1713 he was apprenticed to his brother-in-law, a merchant at Mühlheim on the Ruhr, and four years later he started in business for himself. In 1719 he gave up his business, trying his hand at linen weaving for a time, then turning to the easier and more lucrative occupation of weaving silk ribbons. The years between 1719 and 1724 were ones of spiritual depression for Tersteegen. But on Maundy Thursday, 1724, he wrote out a solemn covenant with God, which he signed with his own blood. In the joy and peace which he had found he immediately wrote the beautiful hymn "How Gracious, Kind and Good, My Great High Priest, Art Thou." Tersteegen had not attended the Reformed Church services since before 1719, nor had he attended Communion. In 1725 he started speaking at the prayer-meetings held by Wilhelm Hoffmann, a licensed preacher of the Reformed Church at Mühlheim. Tersteegen became known as a religious teacher among the "Stillen im Lande," as the attenders of these prayer-meetings were called. By 1728 he had given up his handicraft and devoted himself 1) to the translation of works by medieval and recent Mystics and Quietists; 2) to the composition of devotional books; 3) to correspondence on religious subjects; 4) to the work of a spiritual director of the "awakened souls." Until his death he was supported by his admirers and friends. Tersteegen was at this time director of a retreat (Pilgerhütte) for "awakened souls." From 1732 until 1755 he annually visited Holland. Only during these visits to Holland could Tersteegen hold meetings, for a law against conventicles was strictly enforced from 1730 to 1750 in his home country. When at home, he lived at a house which had been Wilhelm Hoffmann's. He continued to preach and to provide food and simple medicines for the poor. These medicines were so much in demand that Tersteegen had to secure an assistant. He was called "the physician of the poor and the forsaken," a modern St. John, and a modern St. Bernard. After 1750 he resumed his meetings. In 1756 he overstrained himself, and from now until his death in 1769 he addressed only small gatherings. He died of dropsy at Mühlheim. Tersteegen was always outside the Reformed Church, although he never started a sect of his own. His followers, for the most part, returned to the Reformed Church after his death. Of his addresses delivered between 1753 and 1756, thirty-three were published in 1769—1773 as *Geistliche Brosamen von des Herrn Tisch gefallen*. Seven were translated by S. Jackson under the title *Spiritual Crumbs from the Master's Table* in 1737. In 1750 a collection of tracts, *Weg der Wahrheit*, was published. Tersteegen's hymnological work is *Geistliches Blumgärtlein*. He ranks as one of the three most important Reformed hymn-writers, the other two being F. A. Lampe and Joachim Neander (q. v.). Yet a century passed before his hymns were accepted into general use. He wrote 111 hymns. 4. *God Himself is present*

TESCHNER, Melchior (c. 1615), was a Lutheran cantor at the church "zum Kripplein Christi" in Fraustadt, Silesia, at the beginning of the 17th century and was subsequently pastor of Oberprietschen, near Fraustadt.

58, 72, 130, 138, 160, 407, 528. VALET WILL ICH DIR GEBEN (ST. THEODULPH)

THEODULPH of Orleans, St. (c. 821), was born in Cisalpine Gaul and in 781 was abbot of a monastery at Florence when he was invited to the court of Charlemagne, perhaps when the latter returned from Italy in that year. Then he was preferred by imperial favor to the Abbey of Fleury and about 793 to the bishopric of Orleans, succeeding Guitbert. He ruled with strictness and founded schools for the education of his people. When Charlemagne died in 814, Theodulph continued in favor with Charlemagne's son and successor, Louis le Debonnaire, who employed him at court. Then Theodulph was sent to attend Pope Stephen on his journey from Rome to Rheims for the coronation of the Emperor. However, two years later St. Theodulph was suspected of complicity in the revolt of Bernard, King of Italy, against Louis. Although he protested his innocence, he was deprived of his benefices and was imprisoned in the monastery of Angers, where, it is thought, he died.

160. *All glory, laud, and honor*

THILO, Valentin (1607—1662), born April 19, 1607, at Königsberg, was the son of Valentin Thiel or Thilo. In 1624 he matriculated at the University of Königsberg as a student of theology, but devoted himself more especially to the study of rhetoric. When the professor of rhetoric, Samuel Fuchs, retired in 1632, he recommended Thilo as his successor. At Thilo's request the post was kept open for two years, during which time he pursued his studies at the University of Leyden. He returned to Königsberg, graduated as M. A. on April 20, 1634, and was thereafter installed as professor of rhetoric. During his twenty-eight years' tenure of office Thilo was elected dean of the Philosophical Faculty five times and served twice as Rector of the University. He died at Königsberg on July 27, 1662. Thilo was a great friend of Heinrich Albert (*q.v.*) and of Simon Dach (*q.v.*) and was with them a member of the Königsberg Poetical Union. Thilo's hymns were almost all written for various festivals of the Christian year. They are as a rule short and vigorous and are somewhat akin to those of Dach. His hymns appeared principally in the *Preussische Fest-Lieder*, Elbing, 1642 to 1644, and in the *Neu Preussisches vollstaendiges Gesangbuch*, Königsberg, 1650.

75. *Ye sons of men, oh, hearken*

THRELFALL, Jeannette (1821—1880), was born March 24, 1821, in Blackburn, Lancashire, and was the daughter of Henry Threlfall, a wine merchant. She was early left an orphan. In later years she met with a sad accident that lamed and mutilated her for life. A second accident rendered her a helpless invalid. Cheerfully and patiently Jeannette Threlfall bore her sufferings until her end, entirely forgetful of self. She radiated cheerfulness and courage to all around her. She composed her poems in idle moments and with great ease. Most of her poems and hymns appeared in the two books *Woodsorrel*, 1856, and *Sunshine and Shadow*, 1873. She died on November 30, 1880.

161. *Hosanna, loud hosanna*

THRING, Godfrey (1823—1903), born March 25, 1823, was the son of the Rev. J. G. D. Thring of Alford, Somerset, and was educated at Shrewsbury School and at Balliol College, Oxford (B. A. 1845). After taking holy orders he was Curate of Stratfield-Turgis, 1846—1850; of Strathfieldsaye, 1850—1853; and of other parishes until 1858, when he became rector of Alford-with-Hornblotton, Somerset. In 1876 Thring was preferred as prebend of East Harptree in Wells Cathedral. His works include the following: *Hymns Congregational and Others*, 1866; *Hymns and Verses*, 1866; *Hymns and Sacred Lyrics*, 1874; *A Church of England Hymn-Book Adapted to the Daily Services throughout the Year*, 1880; *The Church of England Hymn-Book* (a revised and much-improved edition of 1882).

56. *Jesus came, the heavens adoring*
439. *O God of mercy, God of might*
620:2. *Lord, who at Cana's wedding feast*

THRUPP, Adelaide (19th century). Some of her lines appeared in *Psalms and Hymns*, 1853. She was either the daughter or the wife of Joseph Francis Thrupp (1827—1867).

620:1, 3. *Lord, who at Cana's wedding feast*

TOPLADY, Augustus Montague (1740—1778), was born November 4, 1740, at Farnham, England. He studied at Westminster School, London (where the other great hymn-writers George Herbert, Charles Wesley, William Cowper, and John Dryden also attended), and also at Trinity College, Dublin. By his own description his conversion took place, soon after his graduation, in a barn where a lay preacher of the Wesleyan Methodists was holding forth. Ordained to the ministry of the Church of England in 1762, he was vicar of Broadhembury, Devonshire, for a while and in 1775 accepted the call as preacher in a chapel of the French Calvinists in Leicester Fields, London. Of a rather frail constitution, his driving fervor and zeal led him to an untimely death at the age of 38. Considered a very powerful preacher, he drew great crowds to his services, and, as an ardent Calvinist, was one of John Wesley's chief opponents in the English Arminian controversy. When a friend tried to encourage him shortly before his death he replied, "No, no, I shall die. For no mortal could endure such manifestations of God's glory as I have, and live."

374:3, 5. *Grace! 'Tis a charming sound*
376. *Rock of Ages, cleft for me*

TRABERT, George Henry (1843—1931), was born in Lancaster County, Pennsylvania, October 16, 1843. He graduated at Gettysburg College in 1867 and at the Philadelphia Lutheran Seminary in 1870. He was ordained in 1870 by the Ministerium of Pennsylvania. His first congregation was Ephrata, Lancaster County, Pennsylvania, 1870—1873. Then he served Elizabethtown and Mount Joy in the same county until 1877. His next charge was Salem Lutheran Church in Lebanon, Pennsylvania, where he remained until January, 1883. On January 1, 1883, he began English work among Lutherans in the Twin Cities. As he was supported by St. John's Lutheran Church in Philadelphia, the congregation which he established in Minneapolis was called St. John's Church. It was organized June 8, 1883, with seven members. On July 24 of that year he organized also Memorial Church in St. Paul, and these two congregations became the cradle of the Synod of the Northwest. Trabert received the degree of Doctor of Divinity from Bethany College at Lindsborg, Kansas, in 1895. His pastorate at St. John's he resigned in 1892 when he took up work at Warren, Pennsylvania. Four years later he removed to Wilkes-Barre, Pennsylvania, but remained there only about a year. He took up work at Salem Church in Minneapolis in 1897 and continued there until 1920, when he retired. He organized the Inner Mission Society of Minneapolis, and Trabert Hall is a memorial to him. He wrote several books, among them *English Lutheranism in the Northwest* and *Church History*. He died at Minneapolis, September 16, 1931, and was buried at Allentown, Pennsylvania, having served the Church as a minister for 50 years.

432. *In hope my soul, redeemed to bliss unending.* (Tr.)

TRANOVSKY, Juraj (1591—1637), was born April 9, 1591, in Tesin, Silesia. He entered the Gymnasium at Guben in 1603 and continued his studies at Kolberg in 1605. Following the custom of the day, he went from Kolberg to Wittenberg and entered the University in 1607 as Georgius Tranosci. After about 1612 he traveled through Bohemia and Silesia and finally taught in the Gymnasium of St. Nicholas at Praha. He later became a teacher at Holesov in Moravia and in 1616 was ordained as a minister at Medzirieci. Forced to flee to Tesin during the persecution of Lutherans under Ferdinand II of Bohemia, he was imprisoned in 1623, lost two of his children in the plague of the following year, and went into exile in 1625. He became pastor at Biehsko in 1627 but was again forced to flee and became pastor at St. Michael's in Slovakia, 1631. There he published a number of religious books for the Slovaks and in 1636 the first edition of his Slovak hymnal, *The Tranoscius*, with 150 hymns from his own pen. He has been called the father of Slovak hymnodv.

82. *Come rejoicing, praises voicing*
253. *In one true God we all believe*

TUTTIETT, Lawrence (1825—1897), was the son of John Tuttiett, a surgeon of the Royal Navy of England. He was born in Colyton, Devonshire, and was educated at Christ's Hospital and at King's College, London. He was urgently pressed to take up medicine and at first planned to follow in his father's footsteps, but he chose the ministry instead. He took holy orders in 1848 and became a clergyman of the Church of England. While acting as curate on the Isle of Wight in 1854, he made a great impression with his preaching on Lord Norton, who advanced him to the vicarage of Lea Marston, Warwickshire. After several years he became the incumbent of the Episcopal Church of St. Andrews, Scotland, where he became, he said, "quite a Scotchman at heart." His last charge was that of prebend at St. Nimians Cathedral, Perth. The last years of his life Tuttiett spent in quiet retirement at Pitlochry. He died on a visit to St. Andrews on May 21, 1897.

118. *Father, let me dedicate*

TWELLS, Henry (1823—1900), was born March 13, 1823, at Ashted, Birmingham. He was educated at King Edward's School, Birmingham, where he was the schoolmate of two young men who were to become England's most distinguished Greek scholars and churchmen, Bishops Westcott and Lightfoot, and Archbishop Benson, primate of all England. He pursued his education at St. Peter's College, Cambridge. He took holy orders in 1849. Then he became successively the Curate of Great Berkhamsted, 1849 to 1851, Subvicar of Stratford-on-Avon, 1851 to 1854, Master of St. Andrew's House School, Mells, Somerset, 1854 to 1857, and Head Master of Godolphin School, Hammersmith, 1856 to 1870. In the last year Twells was preferred to the Rectory of Baldock, Hertfordshire, and the following year to that of Waltham-on-the-Wolds. In 1873 and 1874 Twells was Select Preacher at Cambridge. In 1884 Twells was appointed Honorary Canon of Peterborough Cathedral. He acted as Warden of the Society of Mission Clergy in the Peterborough Diocese. In 1890 Twells retired to Bournemouth, where he built and partly endowed the Church of St. Augustine. When his health improved, Twells served as priest in charge of this church until his death January 19, 1900. Twell's *Memoir* was published in 1901. His *Hymns and other Stray Verses* appeared in the same year. He took an active part in the preparation of *Hymns Ancient and Modern* and was on the committee for the *Appendix* of 1889.

557. *At even, when the sun did set*

TYE, Christopher (c. 1497—1572). Tye was probably born in East Anglia. He graduated from Cambridge with his Mus. Bac. in 1536 and received his Mus. D. in 1545. He was a chorister at King's College for a while and in 1541 became head chorister at Ely Cathedral. He was ordained in 1560 and given the parish at Doddington-cum-March on the Isle of Ely. During the same period he served Newton-cum-Capella and Little Wilbraham. He was a member of the Reformed Church but did not let that stop him from playing the organ in the Chapel Royal under Edward VI, Mary, and Elizabeth. He has been called the "Father of the Anthem" and is noted chiefly for his versification of the Acts of the Apostles, which appeared in 1553. Anthony Wood wrote of him: "Dr. Tye was a peevish, humoursome man, especially in his latter dayes, and sometimes playing on ye Organ in ye chap. of qu. Elizab. wh. contained much musicke, but little delight to the ear, she would send ye verger to tell him he played out of Tune: whereupon he sent word yt her eares were out of Tune."

176. WINDSOR

VETTER, Daniel (18th century), was organist of St. Nicholas Church, Leipzig, and author or composer of several hymns in *Musicalische Kirch- und Haus-Ergötzlichkeit*, 1713.   273, 308. DAS WALT' GOTT VATER

VISCHER, Christoph. See Fischer, Christoph.

VOSS, Arthur Paul (1899—   ), was born May 19, 1899, at Bay City, Michigan, son of Christian J. Voss and Augusta, née Röcker. He was educated at the Lutheran High School, Milwaukee; Concordia College, Milwaukee; the Theological Seminary of the Joint Synod of Wisconsin and Other States, Wauwatosa, Wisconsin. He was ordained to the Lutheran ministry in 1921 and became pastor of St. James's Ev. Lutheran Church, Milwaukee, where he is active at the present time. He married Louise Ebert. He is associate editor of the *Northwestern Lutheran*, Vice-President of the Southeastern Wisconsin District of the Ev. Lutheran Joint Synod of Wisconsin and Other States since 1936, and member of the Board of Control, Northwestern Publishing House, Milwaukee, since 1925. He is a member of the Intersynodical Committee of Hymnology and Liturgics which prepared *The Lutheran Hymnal.*

383. Seek where ye may to find a way. (Tr.)

VULPIUS, Melchior (c. 1560—1615), was born perhaps at Wasungen, in Thuringia, 1560. About 1600 he became precentor at Weimar and died there in 1615. He published *Cantiones sacrae* (1602 and 1604); *Kirchengesänge und geistliche Lieder Dr. Luthers* (1604); *Canticum beatissimae* (1605); *Ein schön geistlich Gesangbuch* (1609). The *Cantional,* Gotha, was published after his death in 1646.

19. LOBET DEN HERRN, IHR
53, 597. CHRISTUS, DER IST MEIN
140. JESU KREUZ, LEIDEN UND PEIN
208. GELOBT SEI GOTT
547. DIE HELLE SONN' LEUCHT'T

WAINWRIGHT, John (1723—1768), son of John Wainwright, "Joyner," and Mary Heginbotham, his wife; born at Stockport; baptized April 14, 1723; said to have been organist of that parish for some time, but of this there is no record; resident in Manchester in 1757; officiated as deputy or assistant organist of the Collegiate Church for several years; appointed to that post May 12, 1767; was an able performer on the violin and organ. The celebrated Joah Bates used to say that the first notion of his own grand style of organ-playing was received "from hearing old Wainwright at the Collegiate Church"; buried at Stockport, January 28, 1768. He published *Collection of Hymns.*

84. YORKSHIRE

WALDER, Johann Jakob (1750—1817), was born at Wetzikon in the canton of Zürich, January 11, 1750, where he was taught to love music by the pastor there and later studied composition. His first melodies were published about 1775, and from 1779 on they appeared in many collections. In 1785 Walder turned to politics. He served the canton of Zürich first as "Untervogt des Amtes Grüninger," then as "Mitglied des Regierungsrats" until 1806, then as "Bezirkspräsident" until 1814, and finally as "Oberrichter." He died March 18, 1817.

285. WALDER

WALTHER, Carl Ferdinand Wilhelm (1811—1887), was born at Langenchursdorf, Saxony, on October 25, 1811. He has been called "the most commanding figure in the Lutheran Church of America during the nineteenth century." Of a long line of Lutheran ministers, Walther received his early schooling in his home village and in Hohenstein and was graduated from the Gymnasium at Schneeberg in 1829. He studied theology at Leipzig and managed to avoid its rationalistic influence only by close companionship with men such as Kuehn, Barthel, and Stephan, all true students and ministers of the doctrine of the grace of God in Christ. He was graduated in 1833, became a private tutor for a time, and was ordained to the holy ministry at Braeunsdorf, Saxony, in 1837. Unable to tolerate the rationalistic attitude of the Church in Saxony, he emigrated to America with Stephan's confessional Lutherans and arrived in St. Louis in February, 1839. There he served the pastorates at Dresden and Johannisberg in Perry County, helped build the log-cabin college at Altenburg, and in time took Stephan's place as leader of the colony. In 1841 he succeeded his older brother as pastor of Old Trinity in St. Louis, and, as one of the founders and leaders of the Saxon Immigration, published the *Lutheraner* in 1844, helped to organize and became the first President of the Evangelical Lutheran Synod of Missouri, Ohio, and Other States in 1847, was elected professor of theology at Concordia Seminary in St. Louis, edited *Lehre und Wehre,* 1855, and in his preaching and writings gave direction to American Lutheranism, which is still being felt today. He received his D. D. from Capital University in 1878. He wrote a great deal on Lutheran doctrine and practice, and his sermons are still considered some of the most powerful ever presented in America. An accomplished master of the piano and organ, he wrote a number of hymns and hymn-tunes. American Lutheranism is forever indebted to him for transplanting the pure teachings of the Bible as set forth by Luther from the Old World to the New in both space and time. He died May 7, 1887.

198. *He's risen, He's risen, Christ Jesus the Lord*
198. WALTHER

WALTHER, Johann (1496—1570), was born in a village near Cola (Kahla?) in Thuringia. In 1524 he was at Torgau as bassist at the Court of Friedrich the Wise, Elector of Saxony. The Elector Johann of Saxony made him choirmaster in 1526. In 1534 Walther was appointed cantor to the school at Torgau. On the accession of the Elector Moritz of Saxony, in 1548, he went with him to Dresden as his Kapellmeister. Walther was pensioned by a decree of August 7, 1554, and soon after returned to Torgau, still retaining the title of "Sengermeister." He died at Torgau in the spring of 1570. Johann Walther was more distinguished as a musician than as a hymn-writer. In 1524 he spent three weeks in Luther's home at Wittenberg, helping to adapt the old church music to the Lutheran services and harmonizing the tunes in five parts for the *Geystliche gesangk Buchleyn*, published at Wittenberg in 1524. Walther was present in the Stadtkirche at Wittenberg in 1525, when, on October 29, the service of the Holy Communion, as arranged by Luther and himself, was first used in German. Most of Walther's hymns appeared in his *Das christlich Kinderlied D. Martini Lutheri*, Wittenberg 1566. Walther was the first Lutheran hymn-writer to sing of the glories of eternal life. Bishop Bang says of him, "On the whole it may be said that Walther together with Luther laid the foundation for evangelical church song." 67. *The Bridegroom soon will call us*

WALWORTH, Clarence Alphonsus (1820—1900), was a graduate of Union College, 1838, and was admitted to the bar in 1841. He had studied for the ministry of the Protestant Episcopal Church but was finally ordained a priest of the Roman Catholic Church. He became Rector of St. Mary's, Albany, in 1864, and was one of the founders of the Order of Paulists in the United States. His paraphrases and translations of hymns have appeared in several hymnals.

250. *Holy God, we praise Thy name.* (Tr.)

WANDERSLEBEN, Martin (1608—1668), was born at Wassertalheim in Schwarzburg-Sondershausen and died as superintendent at Woltershausen in Gotha, 1668.

7. *As we begin another week*

WARREN, George William (1828—1902), was born in Albany, New York, on August 17, 1828. He received his formal education at Racine University. He served as organist at St. Peter's Church and St. Paul's Church in Albany until 1860, when he came to New York as organist and choir director at St. Thomas's Church. His chief sacred compositions appeared in *Hymns and Tunes as Sung at Saint Thomas' Church, New York*, 1888. 54, 505. GUIDE ME

WATTS, Isaac (1674—1748), was born July 17, 1674, the son of a Non-conformist minister, who in his later life kept a flourishing boarding-school at Southampton, where Isaac, the eldest of nine children was born. Mr. Pinhorn, rector of All Saints and headmaster of the Grammar School in Southampton, taught him Greek, Latin, and Hebrew. Watts refused the offer of a physician of Southampton of an education at one of the universities in preparation for eventual ordination into the Church of England and instead entered a Non-conformist academy at Stoke Newington, which was under the care of Mr. Thomas Rowe, the pastor of the Independent congregation at Girdlers' Hall. Watts became a member of this congregation in 1693. When he was twenty, Watts left the academy and spent the next two years at home writing the bulk of his *Hymns and Spiritual Songs*, which were published 1707 to 1709. These were occasioned by Watts's displeasure of the wretched paraphrases of the Psalms then in use in the Reformed Churches. He was only eighteen years old when he voiced his displeasure publicly and was told by a church officer: "Give us something better, young man." It was not intended to be an invitation, but Watts accepted it as such and wrote his first hymn, of which the opening stanza reads:

> "Behold the glories of the Lamb
> Amidst His Father's throne;
> Prepare new honors for His name
> And songs before unknown."

Hymns and Spiritual Songs was the first real English hymn-book. These hymns were sung from manuscript in the Southampton Chapel. Watts spent the next six years at Stoke Newington as tutor in the family of Sir John Hartopp. These years were ones of intense study, which resulted in the lifelong enfeeblement of his constitution. In 1702 Watts was ordained pastor of the eminent Independent congregation in Mark Lane. Because of his failing health he was given an assistant, Mr. Samuel Price, who was appointed in 1703. In 1712 a fever attacked Watts which left him a confirmed invalid. Price was now made copastor of the congregation, which had moved to a new chapel in Bury Street. During one of his periods of physical distress, Watts became a guest for a week in the home of Sir Thomas Abney. His health did not improve, and Watts so endeared himself to the Abney family that they refused to let him go. There he remained for the rest of his life — 36 years! In 1728 the University of Edinburgh bestowed an unsolicited D. D. upon him. Isaac Watts is the real founder of English Hymnody and is rightly called the "Father of English Hymnody." He was called the Melanchthon of his day because of his learning, piety, gentleness, and largeness of heart. He was a preacher and a poet, a student of theology and philosophy. His works include: *Speculations on the Human Nature of the Logos* (for which he is charged with Arianism); *The Improvement of the Mind*, 1741, *Logic* (which was a valued text at Oxford during his day); *The Divine and Moral Songs*, 1715, *Hymns and Spiritual Songs*, 1707 to 1709; *Horae Lyricae*, 1706 to 1709; and *Psalms of David*, 1719.

Although Watts never married, he deeply loved children and is the author of some of the most famous nursery rhymes in the English language. He is buried in Bunhill Fields, and a monument is erected to his memory in Westminster Abbey.

In his introduction to *Hymns and Spiritual Songs* he has given his theory and position regarding psalmody and what should constitute Christian song. He held that psalmody was the most "unhappily managed" of all current religious solemnities and stated: "I have been long convinc'd, that one great Occasion of this Evil arises from the Matter and Words to which we confine all our Songs. Some of 'em are almost opposite to the Spirit of the Gospel: Many of them foreign to the State of the New Testament, and widely different from the present Circumstances of Christians. Hence it comes to pass that when spiritual Affections are excited within us, and our souls are raised a little above this earth in the beginning of a Psalm, we are check'd on a sudden in our Ascent toward Heaven by some Expressions that are more suited to the Days of *Carnal Ordinances*, and fit only to be sung in the *Worldly Sanctuary*. When we are just entering into an Evangelic Frame by some of the Glories of the Gospel presented in the brightest Figures of *Judaism*, yet the very next line perhaps which the Clerk parcels out unto us, hath something in it so extremely Jewish and cloudy, that darkens our Sight of God the Saviour: Thus by keeping too close to *David* in the House of God, the Vail of *Moses* is thrown over our Hearts. While we are kindling into divine Love by the Meditations of the *lovingkindness of God, and the Multitude of his tender Mercies*, within a few Verses some dreadful Curse against Men is propos'd to our lips; *That God would add Iniquity unto their Iniquity, not let 'em come into his Righteousness, but blot 'em out of the Book of the Living*, Psal. 69, 16, 27, 28, which is so contrary to the New Commandment, of *Loving our Enemies*. Some Sentences of the *Psalmist* that are expressive of the Temper of our own Hearts and the Circumstances of our Lives may compose our Spirits to Seriousness, and allure us to a sweet Retirement within our selves; but we meet with a following line which so peculiarly belongs to one Action or Hour of the Life of *David* or *Asaph*, that breaks off our Song in the midst; our Consciences are affrighted lest we should speak a Falshood unto God: Thus the Powers of our Souls are shock'd on a sudden, and our Spirits ruffled before we have time to reflect that this may be sung only as a History of ancient Saints: and perhaps in some Instances that *Salvo* is hardly Sufficient neither."

We have therefore in the work of Watts a new departure. His activity brought about the change from psalmody to hymnody in the English Church.

It is worth considering what Benson has to say about Watts's achievement in the establishment of the evangelical hymn in England:

"In all fairness it should bear the name of Watts. In the light of its immediate surroundings it was so glaringly original. But, as we discuss it, I think we shall come to feel more and more that to a larger view it was hardly more than a dislodgment of the Calvinistic settlement in favor of a reaffirmation of Luther's, which was the original evangelical settlement of hymnody. . . .

"It was not part of Watts's proposal to give up either the form or substance of metrical psalmody. He would carry it on not as inspired Scripture but as a department of Christian song, whose "sense and materials" were taken from the Bible. And when to this evangelized and modernized Psalter was added a body of hymns of purely human composure, representing our appropriation of the Gospel through Christian experience, we get the full terms of Watts's settlement of the relation of Christian song to the Bible."

To which we add the following tribute: "It has been the fashion with some to disparage Watts, as if he had never risen above the level of his *Hymns for Little Children.* No doubt his taste is often faulty and his style very unequal, but, looking to the good and disregarding the large quantity of inferior matter, it is probable that more hymns which approach to a very high standard of excellence and are at the same time suitable for congregational use may be found in his works than in those of any other English writer." (*Encyclopedia Brit.*)

  10. *This is the day the Lord hath made*
  13. *Before Jehovah's awe-full throne*
  15. *From all that dwell below the skies*
  27. *Oh, bless the Lord, my soul*
  43. *We sing the almighty power of God*
  87. *Joy to the world, the Lord is come*
 123. *Our God, our Help in ages past*
 154. *Alas! and did my Savior bleed*
 156. *Not all the blood of beasts*
 164. *'Twas on that dark, that doleful night*
 175. *When I survey the wondrous cross*
 220. *Jesus, my great High Priest*
 248. *Father of Glory, to Thy name*
 286. *How shall the young secure their hearts*
 289. *The Law commands and makes us know*
 325. *O Thou that hear'st when sinners cry*
 344. *Come, let us join our cheerful songs*
 382. *Lord, we confess our numerous faults*
 392. *Blest is the man, forever blest*
 414. *The man is ever blest*
 416. *Oh, that the Lord would guide my ways*
 426. *The Lord my Shepherd is*
 445. *Am I a soldier of the Cross*
 460. *Behold the sure Foundation-stone*
 478. *The saints on earth and those above*
 480. *Lord of the worlds above*
 487. *How beauteous are their feet*
 511. *Jesus shall reign where'er the sun*
 593. *Why do we mourn departing friends*
629:1-3, 5. *Let children hear the mighty deeds*
 636. *Great is the Lord, our God*

WEBB, Benjamin (1820—1885), was born in London in 1820. He studied at St. Paul's School and at Trinity College, Cambridge, where he received his B. A. in 1842 and his M. A. in 1845. After being ordained he served first as assistant curate of Kemeston, Gloucestershire, 1843—1844; then of Christ Church, St. Pancras, 1847 to

1849; and of Brasted, Kent, 1849—1851. In 1862 Webb became Vicar of St. Andrew's, London, and in 1881 Prebendary of Portpool in St. Paul's Cathedral. His editorial work extended to all fields of church work, but he is noted in hymnology chiefly for his work on the *Hymnal Noted* and the *Hymnary*, 1872.

212. *A hymn of glory let us sing.* (Tr.)

WEBB, George James (1803—1887), was born in Rushmore Lodge, near Salisbury, Wiltshire, June 24, 1803. His father was a farmer of educated taste and ample means; he intended his son for the ministry; the latter, however, manifesting a strong preference for the musical profession, his wishes were yielded to, and music became his chosen calling. He studied under Alexander Lucas, professor of music in the School at Salisbury; was appointed organist of a church at Falmouth, an office he resigned in 1830, in which year he removed to Boston and was organist of the Old South Church there for forty years. He was appointed in 1833, with Dr. Lowell Mason, professor of music in the Boston Academy of Music. He established in 1836 (also with Dr. Mason) conventions for the instruction of music teachers. He was elected president of the Boston Händel and Haydn Society in 1840. He conducted for a time the Mendelssohn Choral Society. In 1870 he removed from Boston to Orange, New Jersey, and in 1876 to New York, but returned to Orange in 1885 and died there, October 7, 1887. In religion Webb was a Swedenborgian and performed an important work for that Church in arranging its musical service. He edited, with Dr. Mason and others, about twenty volumes of sacred and secular music and a work entitled *Voice Culture* with Chester G. Allen, M. D.

451, 497. WEBB

WEBBE, Samuel (1740—1816), was born in England, the son of a government official. He was originally a cabinet-maker, but after he received instruction from Barboudt, the organist of the Bavarian Chapel, London, he became a professional musician and held the post of organist of the Sardinian Chapel. Webbe was a prolific composer of unaccompanied vocal music and wrote a number of glees, catches, madrigals, etc., and also much religious music — masses, motets, hymn-tunes, etc. With his son he published a *Collection of Motets or Antiphons*, 1792. Webbe was the secretary of the Catch Club and librarian to the Glee Club, for which he wrote his celebrated glee *Glorious Apollo*.

504. MELCOMBE
531. ALMA REDEMPTORIS MATER

WEGELIN (Wegelein), Josua (1604—1640), was born in Augsburg on January 11, 1604, the son of Johann Wegelin, superintendent of the Evangelical college of Augsburg. He attended the University of Tübingen and received his M. A. in 1626. He was for a short time pastor at Budweiler, and in 1627 he was appointed fourth diaconus of the Franciscan church at Augsburg. In 1629 he was compelled to leave Augsburg with thirteen other Evangelical pastors by the Edict of Restitution enacted by Emperor Ferdinand III. This was instigated by the Benedictine monks, who, after they had settled in Rinteln in 1630, claimed to be the rightful professors and demanded the restoration of the old church lands, and especially the property formerly belonging to the nunnery at Rinteln, but which had been devoted to the payment of the stipends of the Lutheran professors. In 1632 he was recalled as archdiaconus of the Franciscan Church, when Gustavus Adolphus took over the city. He was appointed preacher at the Hospital Church of the Holy Ghost in 1633. In 1635 he was again forced to flee, finding refuge in Pressburg, Hungary, where he held office as pastor, Senior, Inspector, and later Doctor of Theology. He died there on September 14, 1640.

216. *On Christ's ascension I now build*

WEINGÄRTNER, Sigismund (17th century). In the *Geistliche Psalmen,* a hymnal containing 766 psalms, published at Nürnberg in 1607, there appeared two hymns under the name of Sigismund Weingärtner. He is thought to have been a preacher in Heilbronn on the Neckar, but this is questionable. Research seems to show that there never was a preacher by this name at Heilbronn on the Neckar. Some have therefore suggested that he may have lived in Basel, others that he must have lived in or near the cloister of Heilbronn in Franconia.

526. In God, my faithful God

WEISSE (Weiss, Wiss, Wegs, Weys, Weyss), Michael (c. 1480—1534), was born in Neisse, Silesia. He took priest's orders and was for some time a monk at Breslau. Some of the early writings of Luther came into his hands while he was at the cloister, and, having read them, he abandoned the monastery with two other monks and sought refuge among the Bohemian Brethren. Weisse was admitted to the Brethren's House at Leutomische, Bohemia. He became a German preacher to the Bohemian Brethren at Landskron, Bohemia, and Fulness, Moravia. In 1522 along with John Roh he was sent to Luther to explain to him the religious views of the Bohemian Brethren. The Bohemian Brethren recognized Weisse's talents and entrusted him with the editing of the first German hymnal of the Bohemian Brethren, which appeared in 1531 under the title *Ein New Gesengbuchlen*. There are 155 hymns embodied in the hymnal, and according to the preface which the editor wrote, all of them seem to have been either composed or translated from Latin or Bohemian by Weisse himself. He died at Landskron in 1534.

74. GOTTES SOHN IST KOMMEN
190. Christ the Lord is risen again
596:1-7. This body in the grave we lay

WEISSEL, Georg (1590—1635), was born at Domnau, near Königsberg, Prussia, the son of Johann Weissel, judge and mayor of the town. He studied at the University of Königsberg and then for short periods at Wittenberg, Leipzig, Jena, Strassburg, Basel, and Marburg. In 1614 he was appointed rector of the school at Friedland but resigned after three years to resume his studies of theology at Königsberg. Finally, in 1623, he became pastor of the newly erected Altrossgart Church at Königsberg, where he remained until his death, August 1, 1635. At an early age already Georg Weissel developed a remarkable poetic talent and had the gift of inspiring others, Simon Dach particularly. He wrote about twenty hymns in all, the majority of which are for the greater festivals of the church-year. Weissel's hymns are all in good style, of moderate length, and varied in meter. The earliest seem to have been written for use at the consecration of the Altrossgart Church on the Second Sunday in Advent, 1623.

73. Lift up your heads, ye mighty gates
383. Seek where ye may to find a way

WESLEY, Charles (1707—1788), the youngest son and the eighteenth of the nineteen children of Samuel and Susanna Wesley, was born at the Epworth Rectory, December 18, 1707. The parents served as teachers, and Charles studied at least six hours daily. Bible reading and prayer were a part of the daily exercises. The mother exerted a tremendous spiritual influence on the children. In 1716 Charles Wesley went to Westminster School, where his home and board were provided by his elder brother Samuel, who was an usher at the school. In 1721 Charles was elected King's Scholar and as such received his board and education free. While he was at Westminster, Charles declined an offer made to him through his father by a wealthy Irishman, who offered to adopt him and make him his heir. In 1726 he was elected to a Westminster studentship at Christ Church, Oxford. His brother John, three years his senior, also attended Oxford at this time. At this time England was full of freethinkers, many of whom even denied all faith in God and immortality. This spirit influenced Oxford University especially. To counteract this influence Charles Wesley and some of his friends organized a distinctly Christian society. Members tried to lead good Christian lives, to study the Bible diligently, to visit the sick and the prisoners, and to distribute Bibles and prayers-books. Because of this regular and methodical mode of life, their devotional exercises and intense Christian activity, members were called "Methodists" and their organization the "Holy Club." The Wesley brothers were the leading members, and George Whitefield was a prominent one. From this group the new movement in the Church of England took its beginning. Charles Wesley took his degree in 1729 and became a college tutor. In 1735 he went with his brother John to Georgia as secretary to General Oglethorpe, having before he set out received deacon's and priest's orders on two successive Sundays. His stay in Georgia was short, and he returned to England in 1736. At this time Charles Wesley espoused the doctrines of the Rev. William Law and had rested in a legal righteousness. But Peter Böhler had selected him as his English teacher, and he and Wesley's simple host at London, Mr. Bray, a brazier, brought him to renounce his self-righteousness. In the same year Wesley came under the influence of Count Zinzendorf and the Moravians. On Whitsunday, 1737, Charles Wesley "found rest to his soul" and in the following year became curate to his friend Mr. Stonehouse, Vicar of Islington. However, the church wardens were greatly opposed to Wesley; so the Vicar had to proclaim that he "should preach in his church no more." Wesley's work now was identified with that of his brother, and he became an indefatigable itinerant and field preacher. On one of his preaching tours he met Miss Sarah Gwynne, whom he married in 1749. Mrs. Wesley accompanied her husband on his evangelistic journeys, which ceased in 1756, after which time Charles Wesley devoted himself to the care of the Societies in London and Bristol, making the latter place his headquarters until 1771. After 1771 Wesley went to London, where, as in his youth, he dedicated himself to the spiritual care of prisoners in Newgate. Wesley was troubled about the relations of Methodism to the Church of England and strongly and outspokenly disapproved of his brother John's "ordinations" but did not separate from him. Charles Wesley died on March 29, 1788, and was buried in Marylebone Churchyard. He had not consented to be interred in the burial-ground of the City Road Chapel, where John had prepared a grave for himself. Eight clergymen of the Church of England bore his pall. Charles Wesley had a large family, but only four survived him. Three sons distinguished themselves in the musical world, and one daughter inherited her father's genius. His widow and orphans were treated most kindly by John Wesley. Charles Wesley, "The Prince of Hymn-writers," "The Sweet Bard of Methodism," "The Father of Sacred Song," is considered the great hymn-writer of all ages, taking quantity and quality into consideration. He wrote 6500 hymns, and it is marvelous how many rise to the highest degree of excellence. His feelings on every occasion of importance, whether public or private, found their best expression in a hymn. Charles Wesley also wrote hymns for little children, a branch of sacred poetry in which the mantle of Dr. Watts seems to have fallen upon him. There is much dispute as to whether Wesley or Watts is greater. One critic says this, "While Watts dwells on the awful majesty and glory of God in sublime phrases, Wesley touches the very hem of Christ's garment in loving adoration and praise."

  94. *Hark! the herald angels sing*
 193. *Christ the Lord is risen today*
 213. *Hail the day that sees Him rise*
 241. *Father, in whom we live*
 345. *Jesus, Lover of my soul*
 351. *Love Divine, all love excelling*
 359. *Christ, whose glory fills the skies*
 360. *Oh, for a thousand tongues to sing*
 433. *Jesus, my Truth, my Way*
 450. *Soldiers of Christ, arise*
 478. *The saints on earth and those above*
 488. *Lord of the harvest, hear*

  WESLEY, John (1703—1791), born June 28, 1703, at Epworth, was the founder of Methodism and the greatest religious force of the eighteenth century in England. He was educated at the Charterhouse and Christ Church, Oxford (B. A. 1724), became a Fellow of Lincoln College in 1726, was ordained in 1725, and in 1735 went with his brother Charles as a missionary to Georgia, where he published *Collection of Psalms and Hymns, Charlestown*, 1737, the first English hymn-book as distinguished from psalm-books to be printed in America. On his return to England he started the great evangelistic work which resulted in the Methodist Church. He translated a number of hymns, chiefly from the German, and is probably the author of some of the hymns accredited to Charles Wesley, as the two agreed among themselves not to distinguish their hymns. His translations are among the finest and most devotional in English hymnody and express deep spirituality of thought and emotion.

349. *Jesus, Thy boundless love to me.* (Tr.)
371. *Jesus, Thy blood and righteousness.* (Tr.)

WESLEY, Samuel, Sr. (1662—1735), father of John and Charles, was born at Whitchurch in Dorsetshire, of which parish his father, John Wesley, was vicar. He was educated by Mr. Morton at a Dissenting academy and was designed for the Non-conformist ministry. While studying to champion the views held by the Dissenters, Wesley was led to embrace the opposite views and became and continued a pronounced churchman. Despite his poverty Wesley entered Exeter College, Oxford, and managed to take his degrees. He took holy orders and obtained a curacy for a year, served another year as chaplain aboard the fleet, and then obtained another curacy for two years. In 1690 Wesley married Susanna Annesley, a lady of noble birth and daughter of a Non-conformist minister. When she was thirteen, Susanna Annesley came over to the Church of England. Before Wesley went to the Rectory of Epworth by royal appointment in 1697, he spent four years at South Ormsby and was also chaplain to the Marquis of Normanby, afterwards Duke of Buckingham. The first part of Wesley's life at Epworth was marked by serious misfortunes and sorrows, which reached their climax in 1705 when he was thrown into the Lincoln jail for debt. His pecuniary embarrassment was a real sorrow, which was not at all alleviated by the animosity of his parishioners and the increase of his family. But during the latter years at Epworth conditions were pleasanter for him. Generous friends, especially Dr. John Sharp, Archbishop of York, enabled him to emerge from debt, his sons grew up to be both a comfort and a credit to him, and his parishioners gradually became more tractable.

176. *Behold the Savior of mankind*

WESLEY, Samuel Sebastian (1810—1876), was born in London on August 14, 1810. He was the grandson of Charles Wesley, the great Methodist hymn-writer, and the son of Samuel Wesley, the famous composer of church music. A child of the Chapel Royal, he became an organist at the age of ten and served the cathedrals at Hereford, Exeter, Winchester, and Gloucester. Working at a time when church music was at its lowest ebb in England, he suffered considerably from lack of interest and appreciation, but he still managed to exert an uplifting influence on the church music of his day. He was renowned as an organist, is famous for his organ compositions and anthems, and is remembered today chiefly for his ability to combine in his hymn-tunes ease of singing with churchly dignity. His most important publication was *The European Psalmist*, 1872.

473, 492, 652. AURELIA

WEYSE, Christoph Ernst Friedrich (1774—1842), was born in Altona, Denmark, on March 5, 1774. He studied piano as a youth and in 1805 became organist of Vor Frue Kirke, Copenhagen, where he served until his death. Weyse wrote several operas, cantatas, preludes, and hymn-tunes, and he is ranked as one of the leading church musicians of the North.

592. DEN SIGNEDE DAG

WHEALL (Weale), William (d. 1727), graduated from Cambridge in 1719, Mus. Bac. He was organist of St. Paul's Church, Bedford, and probably received that appointment when the organ was erected by Gerard Schmidt in 1715. For a long period Wheall's biographers without exception gave his death-year as 1745, but in the burial register of St. Paul's, Bedford, it is recorded that he was interred September 4, 1727.

284, 363. BEDFORD

WHINFIELD, Walter Grenville (1865—1919), was born in England and educated at Magdalen College, Oxford. He was ordained in 1890. Whinfield was the founder and the first vicar of the parish of Dodford, near Bromsgrave.

244. WORCESTER

WHITTEMORE, Jonathan (1802—1860), was born in England April 6, 1802. He was a Baptist minister. He published *Supplement to all Hymn-books*, London, 1850. He died October 31, 1860.

627. Gracious Savior, gentle Shepherd

WIESENMEYER, Burkhard (17th century), was born in Helmstädt. From 1637 to 1644 he was professor at the Grey-friars' Cloister in Berlin. He assisted Johann Crüger (*q. v.*) and others in preparing the *Neues vollkömmliches Gesangbuch*, Berlin, 1840, and *Dr. Martin Luthers Geistliche Lieder*, Berlin, 1653. He was supposed to have died in Petershagen before 1691.

546. How lovely shines the morning star

WILDE, Jane Francesca, *née* Elgee (1826—1896), was born at Wexford, a daughter of Archdeacon Elgee. She married Sir William Wilde, a Dublin oculist, in 1851. She died February 3, 1896, at Chelsea.

145. Jesus, Refuge of the weary. (Tr.)

WILLIAMS, Aaron (1731—1776), was born in London. Little is known of him except that he worked as an engraver, composer, publisher, teacher of music, and as clerk of the Scots' Church, London Wall. He published *The Universal Psalmodist*, 1770, *Harmonia Coelestis*, 1775, *Royal Harmony*, 1780.

27, 68, 462. ST. THOMAS
241. DOVER

WILLIAMS, Peter (1722—1796), was born January 7, 1722, in Carmarthenshire. He was educated at Carmathen College. For a time Williams was curate of Eglwyscymmin, but in 1749 he joined the Calvinistic Methodists and subsequently built a chapel for himself at Carmarthen. He died August 8, 1796.

54. Guide me, O Thou great Jehovah. (Tr.)

WILLIAMS, Ralph Vaughan (1872—   ), was born October 12, 1872, at Down Ampney, Gloucestershire, England. He spent his early days at Charterhouse, studied music at the Royal College of Music, London, and received his Bachelor of Music degree from Trinity College, Cambridge. He further advanced himself with musical studies in Paris and Berlin. He held positions as organist of South Lambeth Church, 1896—1899, Extension Lecturer for Oxford University, and Professor of Composition at the Royal College of Music. He was a private in the army at the beginning of the First World War and later advanced to a commission in the artillery. He seems to have been chiefly interested in choirs, and his choral compositions have been classed among the most beautiful produced in the twentieth century. Williams was musical editor of *The English Hymnal*, 1906, and coeditor with Martin Shaw and Percy Dearmer of *Songs of Praise*, 1925.

463. SINE NOMINE

WILLIAMS, Robert (c. 1781—1821), was born at Mynydd Ithel, Llanfechell, Anglesey, an island northwest of Wales. Williams was blind from his birth and made his living by weaving baskets. He seems to have been well thought of as a vocalist, and his musical memory drew him quite a little attention. It is said that he could write a tune down without a single mistake after hearing it only once.

191. LLANFAIR

WILLIAMS, William (1717—1791), was born at Cefn-y-Coed in the parish of Llanfair-y-bryn, near Llandovery. He was ordained deacon of the Established Church in 1740 by Dr. Claget, Bishop of St. Davids, and for three years served the curacies of Llanwrtyd and Llanddewi-Abergwesyn. He abounded in pulpit service and extended his labors all over the country. He was summoned before his diocesan and tried for these irregularities almost a score of times. For this reason, too, he was denied ordination to the priesthood. At first he identified himself with the Wesley revival. Later he forsook the Wesleys and became a Calvinistic Methodist, having adopted Wales as his parish. As an itinerant preacher he associated with the successful preacher Daniel Rowlands. For thirty-five years he preached once a month at Llanllian and Caio and Llansawel, besides the preaching journeys he took in North and South Wales. During a ministry of forty-five years he seldom traveled less than forty miles a week or 2,000 miles a year. He published *Alleluiah* in 1744; *Hosannah to the Son of David or Hymns of Praise to God*, 1759; *Gloria in Excelsis or Hymns of Praise to God and the Lamb,* 1772. He has been called the "Sweet Singer of Wales" and the "Watts of Wales." "He did for Wales what Wesley and Watts did for England or what Luther did for Germany."

54. *Guide me, O Thou great Jehovah*
505. *O'er the gloomy hills of darkness*

WILSON, Hugh (c. 1764—1824), was born at Fenwick, Scotland. His father, John Wilson, was a shoemaker, and Hugh learned his father's trade. In his spare time, however, he studied mathematics and kindred subjects by himself and at the village school. He became proficient enough in these to add to his income by teaching these subjects and music to others. A favorite pastime of his was making sun-dials. Another hobby was writing hymn-tunes. One product of each of these hobbies is in use to this day: the sundial in his home town and the hymn-tune *Martyrdom (Avon).* In his home town Wilson occasionally led the psalmody in the Secession Church. Toward the end of the 18th century he moved to Pollokshaws, where he held responsible positions in certain mills there and later at Duntocher, where he worked in the mills of William Dunn as a draughtsman and calculator. At the latter town Wilson acted as manager in the Secession Church and was cofounder of the first Sunday-school there. A plain stone marks his grave in the churchyard of Old Kirkpatrick. He died August 14, 1824.

154. MARTYRDOM

WINKWORTH, Catherine (1829—1878), the daughter of Henry Winkworth of Alderley Edge, Cheshire, was born in London on September 13, 1829. Her early life was spent in the neighborhood of Manchester. She subsequently moved with her family to Clifton, near Bristol. She died suddenly of heart disease at Monnetier in Savoy. Her sister Susannah started to write a memorial of her, but she died before she finished it. It was completed by their niece, who added some long letters from Susannah and called her book *Memorials of Two Sisters.* It was edited by Margaret T. Shaen. Miss Winkworth published translations from the German of the *Life of Pastor Fliedner* (the founder of the Sisterhood of Protestant Deaconesses at Kaiserswerth), 1861, and of the *Life of Amelia Sieveking* (the founder of the Female Society for the Care of the Sick and Poor in Hamburg, Germany, 1863). Her hymnological works included *Lyra Germanica,* First Series, 1855, which contained translations of 103 hymns selected from the Chevalier Bunsen's *Gesang und Gebetbuch,* 1833; *Lyra Germanica,* Second Series, 1858, which contained 123 hymns "selected for their warmth of feeling and depth of Christian experience, rather than as specimens of a particular master or school"; *The Chorale Book for England,* 1863, which contained some of the fine old German *chorales* to which the hymns are sung in Germany by vast congregations; and the *Christian Singers of Germany,* 1869, a charming biographical work. She also published *Palm Leaves: Sacred Poems Selected and Translated from the German of Karl Gerok.* Catherine Winkworth is the foremost in rank and popularity of modern translators from German into English. Her translations are the most widely used of any from that language. They have had more to do with the modern revival of the English use of German hymns than the versions of any other writer.

1. *Open now thy gates of beauty.* (Tr.)
3. *Lord Jesus Christ, be present now.* (Tr.)
16:1-3. *Blessed Jesus, at Thy word.* (Tr.)
21. *Jehovah, let me now adore Thee.* (Tr.)
28. *Now let all loudly sing praise.* (Tr.)
34. *My soul, now bless thy Maker.* (Tr.)
36. *Now thank we all our God.* (Tr.)
39. *Praise to the Lord, the Almighty.* (Tr.)
61. *Comfort, comfort, ye My people.* (Tr.)
69. *Arise, sons of the Kingdom.* (Tr.)

73. Lift up your heads, ye mighty gates. (Tr.)
74. Once He came in blessing. (Tr.)
77. All my heart this night rejoices. (Tr.)
85. From heav'n above to earth I come. (Tr.)
91:1-6, 8, 9. Let the earth now praise the Lord. (Tr.)
96. Oh, rejoice, ye Christians, loudly. (Tr.)
97. Let us all with gladsome voice. (Tr.)
107. We Christians may rejoice today. (Tr.)
120. Help us, O Lord! Behold, we enter. (Tr.)
125. The old year now hath passed away. (Tr.)
130. O Jesus, King of Glory. (Tr.)
138. Thou Light of Gentile nations. (Tr.)
143. O dearest Jesus, what law hast Thou broken. (Tr.)
148. Lord Jesus Christ, my Life, my Light. (Tr.)
151. Christ, the Life of all the living. (Tr.)
152:1. When o'er my sins I sorrow. (Tr.)
167. O darkest woe. (Tr.)
190. Christ the Lord is ris'n again. (Tr.)
206. Jesus Christ, my sure Defense. (Tr.)
228. Oh, enter, Lord, Thy temple. (Tr.)
235. O Holy Spirit, enter in. (Tr.)
237. All glory be to God on high. (Tr.)
252. We all believe in one true God. (Tr.)
261. Lord, keep us steadfast in Thy Word. (Tr.)
263. O little flock, fear not the Foe. (Tr.)
268. Zion mourns in fear and anguish. (Tr.)
269. O Lord, our Father, shall we be confounded. (Tr.)
298. Baptized into Thy name most holy. (Tr.)
300. Dearest Jesus, we are here. (Tr.)
305. Soul, adorn thyself with gladness. (Tr.)
316. O living Bread from heaven. (Tr.)
317. Alas, my God, my sins are great. (Tr.)
326. Lord, to Thee I make confession. (Tr.)
329. From depths of woe I cry to Thee. (Tr.)
393. From God shall naught divide me. (Tr.)
395. O God, Thou faithful God. (Tr.)
397. O Love, who madest me to wear. (Tr.)
399. Thee will I love, my Strength, my Tower. (Tr.)
407. Farewell I gladly bid thee. (Tr.)
425. All depends on our possessing. (Tr.)
429. Lord, Thee I love with all my heart. (Tr.)
446. Rise, my soul, to watch and pray. (Tr.)
461. Hark! the Church proclaims her honor. (Tr.)
494. Awake, Thou Spirit, who didst fire. (Tr.)
507. Spread, oh, spread, thou mighty Word. (Tr.)
512. O Christ, our true and only Light. (Tr.)
518. If thou but suffer God to guide thee. (Tr.)
522. When in the hour of utmost need. (Tr.)
524. In Thee, Lord, have I put my trust. (Tr.)
526. In God, my faithful God. (Tr.)
544:1, 2, 5, 6. While yet the morn is breaking. (Tr.)
548 (based on). Mine inmost heart now raises. (Tr.)
549. God, who madest earth and heaven. (Tr.)
556 (based on). O God, be with us. (Tr.)
585. I fall asleep in Jesus' wounds. (Tr.)
594. When my last hour is close at hand. (Tr.)
595. Tender Shepherd, Thou hast stilled. (Tr.)
597:1-7. For me to live is Jesus. (Tr.)
600. O Lord, my God, I cry to Thee. (Tr.)
601:1-4, 6, 7. All men living are but mortal. (Tr.)
609. Wake, awake, for night is flying. (Tr.)
619. Jerusalem, thou city fair and high. (Tr.)
625:1, 2, 4, 5. Oh, blest the house, whate'er befall. (Tr.)

WOODD, Basil (1760—1831), was born August 5, 1760, at Richmond, Surrey, England. His widowed mother gave him a fine upbringing. As a boy Woodd studied under the Rev. T. Clarke of Chesham Bois. At 17 he entered Trinity College, Oxford. He took holy orders in 1783 and was chosen lecturer of St. Peter's Cornhill the following year. The next year he became morning preacher at Bentinck Chapel, Marylebone. He purchased the lease of the Chapel (it being a proprietary chapel) in 1793; in addition he became Rector of Drayton Beauchamp, Buckinghamshire, in 1808. Woodd held both of these positions until his death. He took deep interest in the great religious societies and in the antislavery movement. His importance as a hymnist lies in his efforts to bring the two opposing English parties, the Evangelicals and the Prayer-book element, upon common ground. The Evangelicals favored the singing of hymns, while the Prayer-book element wished to retain psalmody with only a few hymns for special occasions. Between these two parties there was continual dissension, and that made the task of uniting them on common ground extremely difficult. The book in which Woodd embodied his ideal appeared in 1794 as *The Psalms of David and Other Portions of Sacred Scriptures Arranged According To the Order of the Church of England for Every Sunday in the Year.*

129. Hail, Thou Source of every blessing

WOODFORD, James Russell (1820—1885), was born April 30, 1820, at Henley-on-Thames and was educated at Merchant Taylors School and Pembroke College, Cambridge, where he distinguished himself as a scholar. In 1843 he was ordained and became Second Master in Bishop's College, Bristol, and Curate of St. John the Baptist's Church. In 1845 Woodford became incumbent of St. Savior's Church, Coalpit Heath; in 1848 incumbent of St. Mark's, Bristol; in 1855 vicar of Kempsford, Gloucestershire. In 1868 Woodford was preferred by the Crown to the important vicarage of Leeds on Dr. Atlay's appointment as Bishop of Hereford. Several times Woodford was Select Preacher at Cambridge and also Honorary Chaplain to the Queen. In 1873 he was consecrated the Bishop of Ely in Westminster Abbey. He died October 24, 1885.

133. Within the Father's house

WORDSWORTH, Christopher (1807—1885), was the youngest son of Christopher Wordsworth, an English Church rector at Lambeth, England, where the young Wordsworth was born on October 30, 1807. He was educated at Winchester, where he distinguished himself both as a scholar and as an athlete. In 1826 Wordsworth matriculated at Trinity College, Cambridge, where his father had since become Master. Here he carried off an unprecedented number of college and university prizes. When he graduated in 1830, he was elected a Fellow of Trinity. In 1836 he was chosen Public Orator for the University and also elected Head Master of Harrow School, where he instituted a sweeping moral reform. At this time Wordsworth received his D. D. "by royal mandate" from the University of Cambridge. In 1838 he married Susan Hatley Freere. Sir Robert Peel appointed him to the Canonry at Westminster in 1844, and during the year 1848 to 49 he was Hulsean lecturer at Cambridge. Shortly after, Wordsworth took the small chapter-living of Stanford-in-the-Vale cum Goosey, in Berkshire, where he was an exemplary parish priest for nineteen years. In 1869 he was elevated to the bishopric of Lincoln, which position he held for fifteen years, resigning only a few months before his death on March 20, 1885. Christopher Wordsworth was the nephew and good friend of the poet laureate William Wordsworth, whom he constantly visited at Rydal and with whom he kept up a regular and lengthy correspondence. He was a voluminous writer. Of his many works, however, the only one which claims notice from the hymnologist's point of view is *The Holy Year,* which contains hymns, not only for every season of the Church's year, but also for every phase of that season, as indicated in the Book of Common Prayer. Wordsworth held it to be "the first duty of a hymn-writer to teach sound doctrine, and thus to save souls." He thought that the materials for English Church hymns should be sought first in the Holy Scriptures, secondly in the writings of Christian antiquity, and finally in the poetry of the Ancient Church. Wordsworth felt himself bound to treat impartially every branch of every subject brought before the people in the Church's services, whether of a poetical nature or not. The natural result is that his hymns are of very unequal merit; while some of them are of a high order of excellence, others are prosaic. Of his 127 hymns about 50 are still in common use.

9. O day of rest and gladness
134. Songs of thankfulness and praise
218. See, the Conqueror mounts in triumph
332. Arm these Thy soldiers, mighty Lord
443. O Lord of heaven and earth and sea
471. Hark! the sound of holy voices
493. Thou who the night in prayer didst spend

WORTMAN, Denis (1835—1922), was born in Hopewell, New York, April 30, 1835. He received his A. B. at Amherst in 1857. In 1860 he attended the theological seminary of the Reformed Church in New Brunswick, New Jersey. From 1860 to 1871 he served as pastor of three churches, Brooklyn, Philadelphia, and Schenectady, consecutively. For five years, from 1871 to 1876, he withdrew from the active work of the ministry on account of ill health. He then served churches from 1880 to 1902 in Fort Plain, New York; Saugerties, New York. Thereafter he devoted his time to raising contributions for ministerial relief in the Reformed Church of America. Wortman's prominence in the affairs of the Reformed Church may be estimated by the positions of trust which he attained. In 1867 he was delegate to the conference of the Evangelical Alliance at Amsterdam. From 1882 to 1904 he was trustee of Union College and twice held the high offices of Vice-President and President of the General Synod of the Reformed Church in America.

483. *God of the prophets, bless the prophets' sons*

WREFORD, John Reynell (1800—1881), was born December 12, 1800, at Barnstaple, England. He received his education at Manchester College, York. In 1826 he became pastor of the church in Birmingham. He remained in the ministry only five years, withdrawing from active work on account of the failure of his voice. In conjunction with the Rev. Hugh Hutton he established a school at Edgbaston. The last years of his life he spent in retirement at Bristol, where he died in 1881.

578. *Lord, while for all mankind we pray*

ZICH, August F. (1868—1939), son of Christian and Ernestine Zich, was born June 12, 1868, near Stargard, Pomerania, Germany. When still a young boy he emigrated to America with his parents. The family settled on a farm near Waterloo, Wisconsin. He was educated at Northwestern College, Watertown, Wisconsin, and at the Theological Seminary, Milwaukee, Wisconsin. During the years of his ministry he served the Lutheran congregations at Sutton, Minnesota, from 1897 to 1911 and at Green Bay, Wisconsin, from 1911 to 1931. In 1931 he was called to a professorship at the Theological Seminary at Thiensville, Wisconsin, which institution he served until June 25, 1939, when sudden death ended his labors. Professor Zich served as President of the old Minnesota Synod and as President of the North Wisconsin District of the Joint Synod of Wisconsin. He was associate editor of the *Northwestern Lutheran* for 11 years. On September 6, 1893, he was united in marriage with Caroline Lau. He was a member of the Intersynodical Committee on Hymnology and Liturgics which prepared *The Lutheran Hymnal*.

599. *My course is run! Praise God, my course is run.* (Tr.)

ZIEGLER, Casper (1621—1690), was born at Leipzig. Upon his father's wish he studied theology at the University of Leipzig and at the University of Wittenberg (M. A. 1643). After finishing his courses, Ziegler stayed at home and continued his studies in his favorite fields of science and poetry. In 1653, when he was thirty-two, Ziegler began to study law. In 1655 he was made a Doctor of Law at Jena and in the same year Professor of Law at Wittenberg. Ziegler was a good friend of Abraham Calov, professor of theology at Wittenberg and a staunch defender of Lutheran orthodoxy. Ziegler died April 17, 1690.

93. *O Lord, we welcome Thee*

ZINCK, Hartnack Otto Konrad (1746—1833), was born July 2, 1746, in Husum. He was first cantor in Hamburg and in 1787 became singing-master at the Royal Theater in Copenhagen. During the years 1789—1801 he served also as organist in Our Savior's Church at Christianshavn, and in the latter year he published *Koral-Melodier* for the *Evangelisk-Christelege Psalme-Bog*. He died February 15, 1833.

542. NU RINDER SOLEN OP
655. JEG VIL MIG HERREN LOVE

ZINZENDORF, Nikolaus Ludwig, Count von (1700—1760), was born at Dresden, May 26, 1700. He was educated at Halle and Wittenberg and became Hof- and Justizrat at the Saxon court in Dresden in 1721. He settled the refugee Moravians on his estates of Berthelsdorf, the colony being called Herrnhut in 1722. Expelled from Saxony on charges of spreading false doctrine, he could not return for ten years. He spent this time in preaching and traveling from St. Petersburg to the West Indies. He planted Moravian missions in America and founded settlements of the Brethren in Germany, Holland, England, and Scotland. His later years were spent in Herrnhut. He had been consecrated bishop at Berlin in 1737. His whole fortune was spent in behalf of his Church, and he died a poor man. He wrote over 2,000 hymns, some of them good, most of little merit, and some excessive in their emotionalism, bordering on irreverence. He died at Herrnhut in 1760.

    371. *Jesus, Thy blood and righteousness*
    410. *Jesus, lead Thou on*

Bibliography

Aids to Common Worship. The Century Company. New York. 1887.
American Lutheran Hymnal. Lutheran Book Concern. Columbus, O. 1930.
Augsburg Songs for Sunday-Schools. Lutheran Publication Society. Philadelphia. 1885.
Australian Lutheran Hymn-Book. Lutheran Publishing Company. Adelaide, S. Australia. 1925. 1930.

Barlow, J. Herbert: *The Bach Chorale Book.* H. W. Gray Company. New York. 1922.
Benson, Louis F.: *The English Hymn.* Hodder and Stoughton. London. 1915.
Benson, Louis F.: *The Hymnody of the Christian Church.* George H. Doran Company. New York. 1927.
Benson, Louis F.: *Studies of Familiar Hymns.* First Series. New Edition. Westminster Press. Philadelphia. 1926.
Benson, Louis F.: *Studies of Familiar Hymns.* Second Series. Westminster Press. Philadelphia. 1923.
Bible Songs. Presbyterian Board of Publications. Pittsburgh. 1899.
Blankenbuehler, L.: *The Christian Hymn.* Ogden, Iowa. 1940.
Bollhagen, Laurentius David: *Gesangbuch.* F. Hessenland. Stettin. 1862.
Bonsall, Elizabeth Hubbard: *Famous Hymns.* The Union Press. Philadelphia. 1923.
Book of Common Prayer. S. Andrus and Son. Hartford, Conn. 1849.
Book of Common Prayer. T. Nelson and Sons. New York. 1862.
Book of Hymns. Northwestern Publishing House. Milwaukee, Wis.
Book of Praise (Sursum Corda). American Baptist Publication Society. Philadelphia. 1898.
Borthwick, Jane: *Hymns from the Land of Luther.* W. P. Kennedy. Edinburgh. 1862.
Boyd, Charles Arthur: *Stories of Hymns for Creative Living.* The Judson Press. Philadelphia. 1938.
Brawley, Benjamin: *History of the English Hymn.* Abingdon Press. New York. 1932.
Breed, David R.: *History and Use of Hymns and Hymn-Tunes.* Fleming H. Revell Company. New York. 1903.
Brown, T., and Butterworth, H.: *Story of the Hymns and Tunes.* George H. Doran Company. New York. 1906.

Children's Hymnal and Service Book, The. The Board of Publication of the United Lutheran Church in America. Philadelphia. 1929.
Church Hymnary. Revised Edition. Oxford University Press. London. 1927.
Church Praise Book, The. Biglow and Main. New York. 1888.
Common Service Book of the Lutheran Church. Board of Publication of the United Lutheran Church. Philadelphia. 1918.
Concordia (Hymns and Spiritual Songs). Augsburg Publishing House. Minneapolis. 1916.
Cordes, J. H. C.: *English Hymn-Book.* Second Edition. Ev. Lutheran Mission Press. Tranquebar. 1868.
Cornill, Carl Heinrich: *Music in the Old Testament.* The Open Court Publishing Company. Chicago. 1909.
Crüger, Johann: *Praxis Pietatis Melica.* Balthasar-Ch. Wust. Frankfurt am Mayn. 1693.

Dahle, John: *Library of Christian Hymns.* 3 vols. Augsburg Publishing House. Minneapolis, Minn. 1924—1928.
Dickinson, Edward: *Music in the History of the Western Church.* Charles Scribner's Sons. New York. 1927.
Douglas, Winfred: *Church Music, History, and Practice.* Charles Scribner's Sons. New York. 1927.
Douglas, Winfred: *Selected Hymns and Carols, Commentary on.* Northwestern University. Evanston, Ill. 1933.
Douglas, Winfred: *Selected Hymns and Carols.* Northwestern University Information, Vol. V, Number 11. Northwestern University, Evanston, Ill. 1936.
Duffield, S. W.: *English Hymns.* Funk and Wagnalls Company. New York. 1886.

Eckart, Rudolf: *Paul Flemings religiöse Dichtungen.* Johannes Herrmann. Zwickau. No date.
English Hymnal. Oxford University Press. London. 1906.
Evangelical Hymnal, The. A. S. Barnes and Company. New York. 1880.
Evangelisch-Lutherisches Gesangbuch. Georg Brumder. Milwaukee, Wis. 1872.
Evangelical Lutheran Hymnal. Lutheran Book Concern. Columbus, O. 1907.

Fallersleben, Hoffmann v.: *Geschichte des Deutschen Kirchenliedes.* Carl Rumpler. Hannover. 1861.
Fellerer, Karl Gustav: *Das Deutsche Kirchenlied im Ausland.* Aschendorffsche Verlagsbuchhandlung. Münster in Westfalen. 1935.
Fink, C. W.: *Musikalischer Hausschatz der Deutschen.* Händcke und Lehmkuhl. Hamburg. Ninth Edition. 1878.
Fischer, A. F. W.: *Kirchenlieder-Lexicon.* F. A. Perthes. Gotha. 1878.
Fleming, J. R.: *The Highway of Praise.* Oxford University Press. London. 1937.
Foote, Henry Wilder: *Three Centuries of American Hymnody.* Harvard University Press. 1940.
Forsyth, Cecil: *The Little Book of Bach Chorales.* H. W. Gray Company. New York. 1922.

Gebet- und Gesangbuch. Weilshauser. Oppeln. 1830. Second Edition.
Geistlicher Liederschatz. Samuel Elsner. Berlin. 1840. Second Edition.
Gesangbuch. Comptoir. Stuttgart. 1843.
Gesangbuch. Freylinghausen (Germany). 1737.
Gesangbuch, Revised. Verlagshaus der Ref. Kirche, Cleveland, O. 1880.
Gesangbuch für Gemeinden des Ev.-Luth. Bekenntnisses. Fourth Edition. Evangelical Lutheran Synod of Ohio. Columbus, O. 1875.
Gillman, John Frederick: *Evolution of the English Hymn.* Macmillan Co. New York. 1927.

Handbook to the Church Hymnary. James Moffatt and Millar Patrick, editors. Oxford University Press. London. 1935.
Handbook to The Hymnal. Presbyterian Board of Christian Education. Philadelphia. 1935.
Hanser, Adolf T.: *The Selah Song Book* (English-German edition). Fourth Edition. The Sotarion Publishing Company. Erie, Pa. 1936.
Hart, Wm. F.: *Hymns in Human Experience.* Harper and Brothers. New York. 1931.
Hatfield, Edwin F.: *Poets of the Church.* Anson D. F. Randolph and Company. New York. 1884.
Hewitt, Theodore B.: *Paul Gerhardt, Hymn Writer.* Yale University Press. New Haven. 1918.
Horine, John W.: *Sacred Song.* The United Lutheran Publication House. Philadelphia. 1934.
Hunton, Wm. Lee: *Favorite Hymns.* General Council Publication House. Philadelphia. 1917.
Hymnal (Augustana Synod). Augustana Book Concern. Rock Island, Ill. 1925.
Hymnal for Church and Home. Danish Lutheran Publishing House. Blair, Nebr. 1927.
Hymnal of the Evangelical Church. Eden Publishing House. St. Louis. 1899.
Hymnal, Revised and Enlarged. The Century Company. New York. 1894.
Hymnal, The (Episcopal). Novello, Ewer, and Company. New York. 1903. Revised Ed.
Hymns, Lutheran Board of Publication. Philadelphia. 1858. Twelfth Edition.
Hymns. T. Nelson and Sons. London. 1884.
Hymns Ancient and Modern. Hist. Ed. William Clowes and Sons. London. 1909.
Hymns and Liturgy (Ev. Lutheran). Henry Ludwig. New York. 1834.
Hymns and Songs for Sunday-School. Lutheran Publication Society. Philadelphia. 1914.
Hymns from the German. Rivingtons. London. 1864. Second Edition.
Hymns of Praise. The Biglow and Main Company. New York. 1884.
Hymns of the Ages. First and Second Series. Ticknor and Fields. Boston. 1858 and 1863.
Hymns of the Faith. G. Harris and W. J. Tucker, editors. Houghton, Mifflin, and Company. Boston. 1887.
Hymns of Western Europe. Oxford University Press. London. 1927.
Hymns of Worship and Service. The Century Company. New York. 1905.
Hymns that have Helped. Doubleday and McClure Company. New York. 1900.

In Excelsis. 27th Edition. The Century Company. New York. 1909.

Julian, John: *Dictionary of Hymnology.* Second Edition Reprint. John Murray. London. 1915.

Kaiser, Paul: *Paul Gerhardt.* Max Hesses Verlag. Leipzig. 1906.
Keble, John: *The Christian Year.* E. P. Dutton and Company. Boston. 1868.
Kelly, John: *Paul Gerhardt's Spiritual Songs.* Alexander Strahan. London. 1867.
Kirchen-Gesangbuch. Schlüter Hofbuchdruckerei. Hannover.
Knapp, Albert: *Evang. Liederschatz.* J. G. Cotta. Stuttgart. 1850. Revised Ed.
Koch, Eduard: *Geschichte des Kirchenlieds.* 8 vols. Third Edition. Chr. Belser. Stuttgart. 1866.
Kümmerle, S.: *Encyklopädie der Evangelischen Kirchenmusik,* Vols. 1—4. C. Bertelsmann. Gütersloh. 1894.

Landstad, M. B.: *Kirkesalmebog.* Olaf Husebys Forlag. Kristiania. 1895.
Lange, J. P.: *Geistliches Liederbuch.* Second Edition. Meyer and Zeller. Zürich. 1854.
Laudes Domini (Spiritual Songs). The Century Company. New York. 1887.
Library of Religious Poetry. Schaff and Gilman, editors. Dodd, Mead, and Company. New York. 1881.
Liederbuch. Max Hesse. Leipzig.
Lieder-Sammlung. Mentz and Kovoudt. Philadelphia. 1846.
Love, James: *Scottish Church Music.* Wm. Blackwood and Sons. Edinburgh. 1891.
Love, James, and Cowan, Wm.: *Music of the Church Hymnary.* Henry Frowde. Edinburgh. 1901.
Lutheran Hymnal for Sunday-School. Lutheran Sunday-School Publishing Company. Chicago. 1898.
Lutheran Hymnary, The. Augsburg Publishing House. Minneapolis. 1926.
Lutkin, Peter Christian: *Hymn-Singing and Hymn-Playing.* Northwestern University Bulletin, School of Music III, Northwestern University. Chicago. 1930.
Lutkin, Peter Christian: *Selected Hymns and Carols.* Fourth Edition. Northwestern University. Evanston, Ill. 1939.
Lyra Anglicana. D. Appleton and Company. New York. 1865.
Lyra Domestica. Longman, Green, etc. London. 1863. Fourth Edition.

Marks, Harvey B.: *English Hymnody, Rise and Growth of.* Fleming H. Revell Company. New York. 1937.
McCutchan, Robert Guy: *Our Hymnody.* Second Edition. Methodist Book Concern. New York. 1938.
Methodist Hymnal, The. Eaton and Mains. New York. 1905.
Methodist Hymnal, The. Jennings and Graham. Cincinnati. 1905.
Morrison, Duncan: *Great Hymns of the Church.* Hart and Company. Toronto. 1890.
Muller, Lic: *Luther Lieder.* Vandenhoech and Ruprecht. Göttingen. 1936.
Music and Religion. Stanley Armstrong Hunter, editor. The Abingdon Press. New York. 1930.

Nelle, Wm.: *Geschichte des deutschen Ev. Kirchenliedes.* Second Edition. Gus Schloeszmann. Hamburg. 1909.
New Christian Hymnal. Wm. B. Eerdmans Publishing Company. Grand Rapids, Mich. 1929.
Newton, John: *Olney Hymns.* W. Oliver. London. 1779.
Ninde, Edward S.: *The Story of the American Hymn.* Abingdon Press. New York. 1921.
Nott, Charles C.: *Seven Great Hymns of the Medieval Church.* Annotated Revised Edition. Edwin S. Gorham. New York. 1902.
Nutter, C. S., and Tillett, W. F.: *Hymns and Hymn Writers of the Church.* Methodist Book Concern. New York. 1911.

Oxford Hymn-Book. Claredon Press. Oxford. 1925.

Palmer, Chr.: *Hymnologie.* I. F. Steinkopf. Stuttgart. 1865.
Paul Gerhardt Sämtliche Lieder. Johannes Herrmann. Zwickau. 1906.
Petrich, Hermann. *Unser Geistliches Volkslied.* C. Bertelsmann. Gütersloh. 1920.
Pilgrim Hymnal, The. The Pilgrim Press. New York. 1904.
Polack, W. G.: *Hymns from the Harps of God.* Ernst Kaufman. New York. 1940.
Pratt, Waldo Selden: *Musical Ministries in the Church.* G. Schirmer, Inc. New York. 1923.
Psalter Hymnal. Publication Committee of Christian Reformed Church. Grand Rapids, Mich. 1934.

Richardson, A. M.: *Church Music.* Longmans, Green, and Company. London. 1916.
Riemann, Hugo: *Musik-Lexikon.* Vierte Auflage. Max Hesse. Leipzig. 1894.
Russell, Arthur: *Psalms and Hymns.* John Deighton. Cambridge. 1851.
Ryden, Ernest Edwin. *The Story of Our Hymns,* Augustana Book Concern. Rock Island, Ill. 1930.

Sacred Lyrics from the German. Presbyterian Board of Publication. Philadelphia. 1859.
Schaff, Philip: *Christ in Song.* Anson D. F. Randolph and Company. New York. 1869.
Schulze, Otto: *Erklärung 80 Kirchenlieder.* Sixth Edition. J. A. Wohlgemuths. Berlin. 1879.
Selected Hymns and Carols I. Northwestern University Bulletin. School of Music. Northwestern University. Evanston, Ill. 1936. Third Edition.
Smith, H. Augustine: *Lyric Religion.* The Century Company. New York. 1931.
Smith, Robert E.: *Modern Messages from Great Hymns.* The Abingdon Press. New York. 1918. Second Edition.
Songs of Praise. Oxford University Press. London. 1925.
Songs of Praise Discussed. Oxford University Press. London. 1933.
Stryker, Melanchthon Woolsey: *Christian Chorales.* Biglow and Main. New York. 1885.
Sunday-School Book. Lutheran Book Store. Philadelphia. 1889.
Sunday-School Hymnal. Concordia Publishing House. St. Louis. 1901.
Sunday-School Hymnal, The. Lutheran Book Concern. Columbus, O. 1896.
Sunday-School Hymnal and Service-Book, The. Charles L. Hutchins, Editor and Publisher. Medford, Mass. 1889.
Sunday-School Hymns. Tullar-Meredith Company. Chicago. 1903.

Terry, Charles Sanford: *Bach's Original Hymn-Tunes.* Oxford University Press. London. 1922.
Tileston, Mary W.: *Hymns of Comfort.* Little, Brown, and Company. Boston. 1877.

Vogel, Moritz. *Liederschatz.* C. F. Peters. Leipzig. No date.
Volksliederbuch. 2 vols. C. F. Peters. Leipzig. 1906.

Wackernagel, K. E. P.: *Das deutsche Kirchenlied.* C. G. Liesching. Stuttgart. 1841.
Wartburg Hymnal. Wartburg Publishing House. Chicago. 1918.
Watts, Isaac. *Psalms and Hymns.* W. and J. Bolles. New London. 1834.
Westminster Hymnal. Presbyterian Board of Publication. Philadelphia. 1919.
Winkworth, Catherine: *Chorale Book* (for England). Longman, Green, Longman, Roberts, Green. London. 1863.
Winkworth, Catherine: *Christian Singers of Germany.* Macmillan Company. New York. 1869.
Winkworth, Catherine: *Lyra Germanica.* New Edition. Longmans, Green, Reader, and Dyer. London. 1867.

Zahn, Johannes: *Die Melodien der deutschen evangelischen Kirchenlieder.* Gütersloh. 1893.

PART III
INDEXES

Index of Biblical References

Reference	HYMN
Gen. 1:3	8, 508
Gen. 1:5	12
Gen. 2:10	282
Gen. 18:19	626
Gen. 28:10-19	533
Gen. 28:17	634, 638
Gen. 28:20-22	434
Gen. 31:49	643
Gen. 32:26	365
Ex. 3:6	40
Ex. 10:11	451
Ex. 13:21	54
Ex. 15:1-21	204
Ex. 15:23	422
Ex. 20:1-17	287, 288
Ex. 34:6, 7	580
Num. 6:24-26	50
Deut. 8:10-12	584
Deut. 32:3	19, 38
Deut. 32:4	521
Josh. 24:16	393
Ruth 1:17	623
1 Sam. 3:10	296
1 Sam. 7:12	33
1 Sam. 20:3	590
1 Kings 3:5	395, 459
1 Kings 9:3	465, 466
2 Kings 2:9 ff.	483
1 Chron. 29:11, 12	28
2 Chron. 6:20	632, 635
2 Chron. 20:12	522
Ezra 9:6	318
Ezra 9:15	318
Neh. 9:6	39
Neh. 13:31	515
Job 7:16	588
Job 19:25-27	200, 206, 603
Job 38:7	35, 255
Ps. 1	414
Ps. 3:5	553, 653
Ps. 5:3	541
Ps. 6:1	321
Ps. 7:1	526
Ps. 7:17	549
Ps. 12	260
Ps. 13:3	555
Ps. 16:6	283
Ps. 16:9	564
Ps. 18	429
Ps. 18:18	247
Ps. 19:7	293
Ps. 19:8	295
Ps. 19:9	289
Ps. 22:5	269
Ps. 23	312, 368, 426, 431, 436
Ps. 24	73
Ps. 25:5	532
Ps. 26:12	568
Ps. 27:8	18
Ps. 28:2	6
Ps. 31:1-5	524
Ps. 31	435
Ps. 32	392
Ps. 32:1	22
Ps. 33:1	31
Ps. 64	29
Ps. 34:7	413
Ps. 34:8	307
Ps. 36:7	340
Ps. 36:9	600
Ps. 37:5	520
Ps. 38:4	317
Ps. 38:22	402
Ps. 39:12	586
Ps. 40:8	406
Ps. 42	525
Ps. 42:2	618
Ps. 43:3	132
Ps. 45:2	657
Ps. 46	262, 534
Ps. 46:10	651
Ps. 47:5-7	214
Ps. 48:1-8	636
Ps. 50:6	41
Ps. 50:14	417
Ps. 51	325
Ps. 51:10-12	225
Ps. 51:11	318
Ps. 55:1	543
Ps. 55:22	518
Ps. 56:8	535
Ps. 56:13	600
Ps. 59:16	121, 576, 579
Ps. 65:2	583
Ps. 65:4	11
Ps. 65:9	567
Ps. 65:12	573
Ps. 66:3	544
Ps. 67	20, 500
Ps. 68:18	218
Ps. 72	59, 511
Ps. 73	429
Ps. 73:23	393, 523
Ps. 73:24	357
Ps. 73:25, 26	437
Ps. 78	629
Ps. 79:9	258
Ps. 84	480
Ps. 84:1	639
Ps. 87	469
Ps. 88:13	539
Ps. 90:1-5	123
Ps. 90:5, 6	413
Ps. 90:12	111, 113, 598
Ps. 91:1	122
Ps. 91:4	558
Ps. 91:5	565
Ps. 91:9-16	547
Ps. 91:11	256, 257
Ps. 91:11, 12	563
Ps. 92:1	119, 569
Ps. 95:2	3
Ps. 95:6	24
Ps. 96:10	168
Ps. 98	87
Ps. 98:1	210
Ps. 100	13, 14, 44
Ps. 100:4	1
Ps. 101:1	112
Ps. 103	34
Ps. 103:1-7	27
Ps. 104	17
Ps. 106:1	401
Ps. 106:4	351
Ps. 107:1	124
Ps. 108:1-7	27
Ps. 108:2	536
Ps. 110:2	47
Ps. 116:9	600
Ps. 117	15
Ps. 118:1	313, 548
Ps. 118:15	205
Ps. 118:15, 16	217
Ps. 118:22, 23	460
Ps. 118:24	9
Ps. 118:24-26	10
Ps. 118:25	265
Ps. 119:5, 33	416
Ps. 119:8	335
Ps. 119:9	286
Ps. 119:10	336
Ps. 119:19	586
Ps. 119:35	416
Ps. 119:105	285, 291, 294
Ps. 119:127	284
Ps. 119:133	320, 416
Ps. 119:140	5
Ps. 119:170	353
Ps. 119:176	416
Ps. 121	538
Ps. 121:1	110, 560
Ps. 121:3	556
Ps. 121:8	45
Ps. 122	292
Ps. 122:6	582
Ps. 124	267
Ps. 125:2	474
Ps. 126:3	30
Ps. 127:1	621
Ps. 128	624
Ps. 130	327, 329
Ps. 132:9	490
Ps. 135:1	248, 363
Ps. 136	570
Ps. 137	462
Ps. 139:7-10	326
Ps. 139:11	554
Ps. 139:12	561
Ps. 141:2	562
Ps. 143:4	322
Ps. 143:8	424
Ps. 145:1	575
Ps. 145:15	542
Ps. 145:15, 16	659
Ps. 146	26
Ps. 148	475
Ps. 148:1	243
Ps. 149	43
Ps. 150:1	644
Ps. 150:6	41
Prov. 3:24	654
Prov. 10:22	425
Eccl. 4:12	622
Song of Sol. 1:3	350, 364
Song of Sol. 1:4	215
Song of Sol. 5:16	362
Song of Sol. 8:5	362
Is. 6:1-4	249
Is. 6:7	489
Is. 6:8	496, 641
Is. 9:2	106
Is. 9:3	574
Is. 9:6	78, 93
Is. 11:1, 2	645
Is. 11:2	235
Is. 21:11	71
Is. 26:9	356
Is. 32:2	345
Is. 33:20, 21	469
Is. 35	499
Is. 40:1-8	61
Is. 40:3	63
Is. 40:6	601
Is. 40:11	628
Is. 43:1-7	427
Is. 49:14-17	268
Is. 50:6	172
Is. 52:7-10	487
Is. 52:8	609
Is. 53:3-5	153
Is. 53:4-7	142
Is. 54:2	510
Is. 54:2, 3	640
Is. 54:10	337
Is. 59:20	62
Is. 60:1	498
Is. 60:1 ff.	503

	HYMN
Is. 60:1-6	126
Is. 60:3	642
Is. 60:13	633
Is. 61:1, 2	66, 482
Is. 61:3	48
Jer. 29:7	566
Lam. 3:19	159
Lam. 3:22, 23	546
Lam. 3:23	537
Ezek. 3:17	609
Ezek. 16:60	333
Ezek. 33:11	331
Ezek. 36:26	227
Joel 2:12-19	160
Micah 2:13	198, 206
Micah 5:2	647
Hab. 2:20	4
Hab. 3:17, 18	571, 572
Zech. 9:9	56, 68
Zech. 13:1	149, 157
Zeph. 1:15, 16	607
Mal. 3:17	338
Ecclus. 39:35	36
Ecclus. 50:22-24	36, 581
Matt. 1:21	114
Matt. 1:23	108, 274
Matt. 2:1-11	127
Matt. 2:1-12	130
Matt. 2:2	136
Matt. 2:9	131
Matt. 2:11	128, 129
Matt. 3:3	63
Matt. 4:16	106
Matt. 4:18, 19	270
Matt. 5:14	391
Matt. 6:9 ff.	458
Matt. 6:10	412, 517
Matt. 8:1-13	415
Matt. 8:11, 12	415
Matt. 8:26	649
Matt. 9:38	168
Matt. 10:8	443
Matt. 11:28	149, 277, 281, 456, 513
Matt. 13:16, 17	487
Matt. 13:46	347
Matt. 16:18	637, 658
Matt. 16:24	421
Matt. 17:1-9	619
Matt. 17:4	135
Matt. 18:2	595
Matt. 21:1-9	58
Matt. 21:5-9	55
Matt. 21:9	70, 162
Matt. 21:15	161
Matt. 21:16	160
Matt. 21:22	457
Matt. 24:42	606
Matt. 25:1-13	609
Matt. 25:6	67, 72
Matt. 25:40	440
Matt. 25:41	610
Matt. 26:26-29	163, 316
Matt. 26:41	446
Matt. 26:42	418
Matt. 26:64-67	151
Matt. 27:37	179
Matt. 27:46	183
Matt. 27:50-53	169
Matt. 28:19	298
Matt. 28:19, 20	497
Mark 1:32-34	557
Mark 4:3-9	49

	HYMN
Mark 5:39	593
Mark 8:38	346
Mark 10:13-16	300
Mark 10:14	302, 627, 630
Mark 10:28	423
Mark 12:17	404
Mark 14:22-25	310
Mark 14:36	420
Mark 15:29, 30	145
Mark 15:34	174
Mark 16:6	190, 191
Mark 16:16	301
Luke 1:31	114
Luke 1:41	272
Luke 1:47-55	275
Luke 1:78	359
Luke 1:78, 79	88
Luke 1:79	512
Luke 2:1-14	82, 92, 105
Luke 2:1-18	84, 85
Luke 2:7	81, 89
Luke 2:8	646
Luke 2:10	87
Luke 2:10, 11	103
Luke 2:11	77, 79, 86, 109
Luke 2:14	35, 83, 94, 237, 238, 250
Luke 2:15	90, 102
Luke 2:20	107
Luke 2:21	114, 117
Luke 2:22	139
Luke 2:29	585
Luke 2:29-32	137
Luke 2:32	138
Luke 2:41-52	133, 408, 625
Luke 3:4, 5	75
Luke 4:18	66, 74
Luke 5:11	410
Luke 6:12 ff.	493
Luke 8:8	52
Luke 9:57	365
Luke 10:2	492
Luke 10:36, 37	439
Luke 10:42	366
Luke 11:1	454
Luke 11:2-4	455
Luke 11:28	16
Luke 12:8	451
Luke 12:32	263
Luke 14	509
Luke 14:22, 23	509
Luke 14:16-24	384
Luke 15:1-10	324
Luke 15:2	324, 386
Luke 15:18	280
Luke 15:24	32
Luke 17:5	396
Luke 18:13	166, 323
Luke 18:14	318
Luke 18:17	303
Luke 18:28	423
Luke 18:31-34	140
Luke 18:31-43	409
Luke 19:9	627
Luke 19:28-40	57
Luke 19:38	69
Luke 19:41-48	419
Luke 21:25-36	611
Luke 22:31, 32	516
Luke 23:20-24	143
Luke 23:33	148
Luke 23:34	180
Luke 23:38	179
Luke 23:43	181
Luke 23:44-46	154
Luke 23:46	176, 186
Luke 24:3	203
Luke 24:13-35	194
Luke 24:27	91
Luke 24:29	53, 197, 292, 551, 552

	HYMN
John 1:1-14	508
John 1:9	101
John 1:14	80, 95
John 1:16	277
John 1:29	142, 146, 147, 165, 328, 652
John 1:40	270
John 2:1-11	620, 624
John 3:16	245, 297
John 4:14	277
John 4:35	502
John 5:24	596
John 6:35	277
John 6:37	276, 330, 388
John 6:48	312
John 8:12	277, 413, 550, 559
John 8:31	261
John 10:11	631
John 11:16	409
John 11:25	196
John 11:26	602
John 12:32	390
John 13:7	514
John 14:3	216
John 14:6	355, 433
John 14:15	349
John 14:23	399
John 14:26	233
John 15:4	125
John 15:5	594
John 15:16	37
John 15:26	230
John 16:13	231
John 16:23	21
John 16:27	42
John 16:33	413
John 19:16, 17	150
John 19:26, 27	182
John 19:28	184
John 19:30	170, 185
John 20	208
John 20:15	188
John 20:19-26	65
John 21:15	648
John 21:19-24	401
John 21:20	271
Acts 1:9	213
Acts 1:11	212
Acts 2:3	504
Acts 2:4	224
Acts 2:17	228
Acts 2:24	195
Acts 2:32	207
Acts 2:38	428
Acts 3:15	167
Acts 4:12	114, 116, 360, 383
Acts 7:59	259
Acts 8:15	411
Acts 9:6	403
Acts 10:40	202
Acts 11:24	491
Acts 16:9	495
Acts 17:28	241
Acts 20:35	442
Acts 24:25	278
Acts 26:22	119
Rom. 3:12	369
Rom. 3:25	319
Rom. 3:28	387
Rom. 3-5	377
Rom. 4:25	189
Rom. 5:5	232, 432
Rom. 5:8	342
Rom. 6:16	334
Rom. 7:19-25	379
Rom. 8:9	236
Rom. 8:11	201
Rom. 8:15	226
Rom. 8:28	529
Rom. 8:31 ff.	372
Rom. 8:31-39	528
Rom. 8:35-39	372

	HYMN
Rom. 8:37	506
Rom. 10:15	507
Rom. 11:33	519
Rom. 13:1-7	577, 578
Rom. 13:11	60
Rom. 14:8	453, 591
Rom. 14:11	114
1 Cor. 1:30	366
1 Cor. 2:9	609
1 Cor. 3:6	46
1 Cor. 3:11	385
1 Cor. 4:1	485
1 Cor. 4:1, 2	484
1 Cor. 10:4	376
1 Cor. 10:17	314
1 Cor. 11:26	306, 308
1 Cor. 11:23-25	304
1 Cor. 11:23 ff.	164
1 Cor. 11:28	315
1 Cor. 12:7-9	229
1 Cor. 13:12	530
1 Cor. 15:10	378
1 Cor. 15:20	187
1 Cor. 15:35 ff.	206
1 Cor. 15:55	198
1 Cor. 15:57	193
1 Cor. 16:13	445, 486
2 Cor. 3:18	398
2 Cor. 8:9	96, 97
2 Cor. 9:15	309, 384
2 Cor. 13:14	240
Gal. 2:16	375
Gal. 3:27	299
Gal. 4:4	99
Gal. 4:4, 5	115
Gal. 4:6	21
Gal. 4:19	46 (st. 1)
Gal. 6:14	175, 178, 354
Eph. 1:4	461
Eph. 2:5	374
Eph. 2:8, 9	373, 389
Eph. 2:19-22	467
Eph. 2:20	473
Eph. 3:12	394
Eph. 3:19	348
Eph. 4:3	464
Eph. 4:5	481
Eph. 4:8	223
Eph. 5:19, 20	25
Eph. 6:10-18	444, 450
Eph. 6:13	332
Eph. 6:14	415
Eph. 6:17	501
Eph. 6:24	400
Phil. 1:21	527, 597, 608

	HYMN
Phil. 1:27	405
Phil. 2:6, 7	104
Phil. 2:9-11	222
Phil. 2:10	114
Phil. 3:9	380
Phil. 3:20	413
Col. 2:10	477
Col. 2:15	192
Col. 3:17	540
1 Thess. 4:14	587
1 Thess. 4:16, 17	604
1 Thess. 4:17	616
1 Thess. 5:6	449
1 Thess. 5:23	234
2 Thess. 3:1	494
1 Tim. 1:1	370
1 Tim. 3:16	76, 98
1 Tim. 6:12	447, 452
2 Tim. 1:10	209
2 Tim. 1:12	381
2 Tim. 4:7	599
Titus 3:3, 7	382
Heb. 1:6	221
Heb. 1:14	254
Heb. 2:10	219
Heb. 4:9	615, 617, 660
Titus 3:3, 7	382
Heb. 4:16	531
Heb. 5:7	177
Heb. 6:19	385
Heb. 9:11, 12	220
Heb. 9:14	2
Heb. 9:28	171
Heb. 10:4	156
Heb. 10:12	311
Heb. 10:14	152
Heb. 11:16	614
Heb. 11:13-16	586
Heb. 12:1	463
Heb. 12:2	358
Heb. 12:22-24	478
Heb. 13:8	120
Heb. 13:14	413, 448
Heb. 13:15	173
Heb. 13:20, 21	51
1 Pet. 1:8	352
1 Pet. 1:18, 19	141
1 Pet. 1:19	158
1 Pet. 1:20	134
1 Pet. 2:7	361
1 Pet. 2:9	118
1 Pet. 2:24	144

	HYMN
1 Pet. 4:10	438
1 Pet. 5:8	413
2 Pet. 1:19	290
2 Pet. 3:10	612
1 John 1:7	155, 371, 545
1 John 2:15-17	430
1 John 3:17	441
1 John 3:23	655
1 John 4:2	100
1 John 4:16	397
Jude 3	472
Jude 20, 21	264
Rev. 1:5, 6	244
Rev. 1:7	64
Rev. 1:10	7
Rev. 1:18	199
Rev. 2:10	470
Rev. 2-3	479
Rev. 3:5	407
Rev. 3:8	279
Rev. 3:20	650
Rev. 4:8	239
Rev. 4:8-11	246
Rev. 4:11	242, 367
Rev. 5:5	211
Rev. 5:12	344
Rev. 7:2-7	471
Rev. 7:9, 10	471
Rev. 7:13-17	656
Rev. 7:15	468
Rev. 7:17	476
Rev. 11:15	222
Rev. 14:4	273
Rev. 14:6	505
Rev. 14:6, 7	266
Rev. 14:13	589, 592
Rev. 19:1	23, 244
Rev. 19:6-9	609
Rev. 19:8	305
Rev. 19:12	341
Rev. 19:16	339
Rev. 20 and 21	72
Rev. 21:4	592
Rev. 21:18	613
Rev. 21:22	609
Rev. 21:24	605
Rev. 21 and 22	23
Rev. 22:16	343
The Lord's Prayer	455, 458, 556 (st. 6)
The Apostles' Creed	252, 253
The Nicene Creed	251

Table of Hymns

For the Feasts, Festivals, and Sundays of the Church-Year

First Sunday in Advent
Epistle, Rom. 13:11-14
60, 66, 72, 421, 446, 539, 609
Gospel, Matt. 21:1-9
55, 57, 58, 70, 73, 162

Second Sunday in Advent
Epistle, Rom. 15:4-13
19, 28, 64, 75, 645
Gospel, Luke 21:25-36
446, 604, 609, 610, 611

Third Sunday in Advent
Epistle, 1 Cor. 4:1-5
396, 404, 484, 485, 487, 489, 493
Gospel, Matt. 11:2-10
59, 61, 63, 74, 272, 482

Fourth Sunday in Advent
Epistle, Phil. 4:4-7
87, 456, 459, 520, 521, 531, 575
Gospel, John 1:19-28
58, 61, 68, 347, 351, 365

Christmas Day
Epistle, Titus 2:11-14 or Is. 9:2-7
78, 93, 99, 106, 574
Gospel, Luke 2:1-14
82, 83, 92, 94, 105

Second Christmas Day
Epistle, Titus 3:4-7
91, 339, 345, 351, 382
Gospel, Luke 2:15-20
84, 85, 90, 102, 107

Sunday after Christmas
Epistle, Gal. 4:1-7
21, 80, 97, 99, 115, 196, 375, 380
Gospel, Luke 2:33-40
136, 137, 138, 139, 293

The Circumcision and the Name of Jesus
Epistle, Gal. 3:23-29
26, 125, 298, 299, 373, 377
Gospel, Luke 2:21
114, 115, 116, 117, 339, 347, 364

Sunday after New Year
Epistle, 1 Pet. 4:12-19
370, 374, 396, 517, 520, 521
Gospel, Matt. 2:13-23
131, 265, 273, 452, 453, 528

The Epiphany of Our Lord
Epistle, Is. 60:1-6
28, 126, 132, 360, 361, 498, 503
Gospel, Matt. 2:1-12
127, 128, 129, 130, 134, 507

First Sunday after the Epiphany
Epistle, Rom. 12:1-5
405, 409, 409, 423, 472, 473
Gospel, Luke 2:41-52
133, 294, 296, 392, 408, 485, 624, 625, 629

Second Sunday after the Epiphany
Epistle, Rom. 12:6-16
395, 412, 416, 464, 478
Gospel, John 2:1-11
131, 134, 353, 520, 620

Third Sunday after the Epiphany
Epistle, Rom. 12:16-21
349, 403, 404, 411, 412
Gospel, Matt. 8:1-13
345, 379, 381, 415, 427

Fourth Sunday after the Epiphany
Epistle, Rom. 13:8-10
395, 397, 398, 412, 416
Gospel, Matt. 8:23-27
353, 376, 385, 402, 405, 649, 651

Fifth Sunday after the Epiphany
Epistle, Col. 3:12-17
285, 348, 405, 412, 540
Gospel, Matt. 13:24-30
392, 423, 446, 449, 611

Sixth Sunday after the Epiphany
Epistle, 2 Pet. 1:16-21
48, 290, 294, 376, 427, 469
Gospel, Matt. 17:1-9
135, 343, 362, 533, 546, 619, 657

Septuagesima Sunday
Epistle, 1 Cor. 9:24-10:5
376, 409, 447, 450, 481
Gospel, Matt. 20:1-16
400, 403, 429, 439, 441, 496, 540

Sexagesima Sunday
Epistle, 2 Cor. 11:19 to 12:9
400, 406, 413, 437, 481, 529, 532
Gospel, Luke 8:4-15
49, 52, 296, 420, 430

Quinquagesima Sunday
Epistle, 1 Cor. 13:1-13
349, 397, 403, 411, 423, 424, 464, 530
Gospel, Luke 18:31-43
140, 375, 391, 405, 520

Ash Wednesday
Epistle, Joel 2:12-19
317, 318, 323, 327, 329
Gospel, Matt. 6:16-21
319, 328, 348, 407, 430

Invocavit, the First Sunday in Lent
Epistle, 2 Cor. 6:1-10
394, 397, 423, 442, 443
Gospel, Matt. 4:1-11
255, 257, 285, 287, 290

Reminiscere, the Second Sunday in Lent
Epistle, 1 Thess. 4:1-7
399, 402, 409, 412, 413
Gospel, Matt. 15:21-28
325, 379, 454, 520, 522

Oculi, the Third Sunday in Lent
Epistle, Eph. 5:1-9
397, 398, 409, 442, 453
Gospel, Luke 11:14-28
16, 48, 340, 347, 384

Laetare, the Fourth Sunday in Lent
Epistle, Gal. 4:21-31
340, 354, 373, 374, 391
Gospel, John 6:1-15
31, 151, 347, 426, 436, 526

[614]

Judica, the Fifth Sunday in Lent
Epistle, Heb. 9:11-15
2, 152, 156, 220, 388, 405
Gospel, John 8:46-59
345, 355, 362, 364, 546

Palmarum, the Sixth Sunday in Lent
Epistle, Phil. 2:5-11
104, 151, 158, 219, 222, 367
Gospel, Matt. 21:1-9
55, 58, 59, 70, 162, 657

Monday of Holy Week
Epistle, Is. 50:5-10
140, 142, 150, 172, 175
Gospel, John 12:1-23
146, 149, 158, 166, 179

Tuesday of Holy Week
Epistle, Jer. 11:18-20
143, 145, 157, 164, 173
Gospel, John 12:24-43
141, 148, 167, 384, 390

Wednesday of Holy Week
Epistle, Is. 62:11; 63:1-7
144, 147, 151, 154, 178
Gospel, Luke 22:1-23:42
149, 153, 155, 157, 179

Maundy Thursday
Epistle, 1 Cor. 11:23-32
304, 306, 308, 315, 316
Gospel, John 13:1-15
159, 163, 164, 384, 514

Good Friday
Epistle, Is. 52:13-53:12
142, 153, 166, 175
Gospel, John 18:1-19:42
169, 171, 172, 176, 177

Holy Saturday, Easter Eve
Epistle, 1 Pet. 3:17-22
167, 521
Gospel, Matt. 27:57-66
167, 170, 178, 593

Easter Day
Epistle, 1 Cor. 5:6-8
204, 205, 206, 207, 210
Gospel, Mark 16:1-8
187, 190, 191, 199, 200

Easter Monday
Epistle, Acts 10:34-41
188, 202, 447, 453, 500
Gospel, Luke 24:13-35
53, 91, 194, 197, 292

Easter Tuesday
Epistle, Acts 13:26-41
603, 608
Gospel, Luke 24:36-48
482, 485

Quasimodogeniti, the First Sunday after Easter
Epistle, 1 John 5:4-12
242, 247, 251, 354, 366
Gospel, John 20:19-31
65, 192, 208, 331, 386, 507, 511

Misericordias Domini, the Second Sunday after Easter
Epistle, 1 Pet. 2:21-25
144, 362, 405, 421
Gospel, John 10:11-16
368, 409, 426, 436, 631

Jubilate, the Third Sunday after Easter
Epistle, 1 Pet. 2:11-20
407, 409, 416, 481, 578
Gospel, John 16:16-23
21, 514, 519, 523, 528

Cantate, the Fourth Sunday after Easter
Epistle, Jas. 1:16-21
395, 397, 400, 406, 421
Gospel, John 16:5-15
226, 231, 285, 290, 504

Rogate, the Fifth Sunday after Easter
Epistle, Jas. 1:22-27
235, 366, 412, 439, 441, 515
Gospel, John 16:23-30
21, 42, 454, 457, 458

The Ascension of Our Lord
Epistle, Acts 1:1-11
212, 213, 215, 218, 222
Gospel, Mark 16:14-20
214, 219, 223, 301, 498

Exaudi, the Sunday after the Ascension
Epistle, 1 Pet. 4:7-11
405, 438, 446, 481, 483, 609
Gospel, John 15:26-16:4
230, 453, 490, 518, 522

Whitsunday, the Feast of Pentecost
Epistle, Acts 2:1-13
224, 226, 227, 234, 473, 504
Gospel, John 14:23-31
225, 233, 235, 399

Monday of Whitsun-week
Epistle, Acts 10:42-48
229, 230, 232, 236, 298, 494
Gospel, John 3:16-21
245, 297, 371, 375, 377

Tuesday of Whitsun-week
Epistle, Acts 8:14-17
408, 411
Gospel, John 10:1-10
428, 433

The Feast of the Holy Trinity
Epistle, Rom. 11:33-36
15, 19, 43, 242, 519, 533
Gospel, John 3:1-15
235, 238, 371, 376, 380, 406, 410

The First Sunday after Trinity
Epistle, 1 John 4:16-21
397, 399, 402, 403, 405
Gospel, Luke 16:19-31
446, 586, 615, 617

The Second Sunday after Trinity
Epistle, 1 John 3:13-18
404, 405, 409, 441, 523
Gospel, Luke 14:16-24
276, 279, 372, 427, 509

The Third Sunday after Trinity
Epistle, 1 Pet. 5:6-11
394, 413, 418, 444, 447
Gospel, Luke 15:1-10
277, 324, 342, 386, 613

The Fourth Sunday after Trinity
Epistle, Rom. 8:18-23
353, 423, 430, 513, 531
Gospel, Luke 6:36-42
385, 395, 417, 442, 464, 479

The Fifth Sunday after Trinity
  Epistle, 1 Pet. 3:8-15
    395, 397, 400, 412, 442
  Gospel, Luke 5:1-11
    410, 417, 421, 520, 540

The Sixth Sunday after Trinity
  Epistle, Rom. 6:3-11
    298, 400, 428, 434, 461
  Gospel, Matt. 5:20-26
    295, 370, 377, 387, 412

The Seventh Sunday after Trinity
  Epistle, Rom. 6:19-23
    342, 352, 355, 405, 443
  Gospel, Mark 8:1-9
    31, 41, 54, 368, 426

The Eighth Sunday after Trinity
  Epistle, Rom. 8:12-17
    226, 231, 235, 403, 457
  Gospel, Matt. 7:15-23
    261, 262, 269, 460, 465

The Ninth Sunday after Trinity
  Epistle, 1 Cor. 10:6-13
    318, 319, 321, 324, 328
  Gospel, Luke 16:1-9
    331, 400, 403, 441, 442

The Tenth Sunday after Trinity
  Epistle, 1 Cor. 12:1-11
    28, 226, 229, 473, 489
  Gospel, Luke 19:41-48
    279, 327, 386, 419, 608

The Eleventh Sunday after Trinity
  Epistle, 1 Cor. 15:1-10
    285, 290, 342, 365, 378
  Gospel, Luke 18:9-14
    166, 279, 323, 386, 652

The Twelfth Sunday after Trinity
  Epistle, 2 Cor. 3:4-11
    283, 284, 297, 487, 493
  Gospel, Mark 7:31-37
    26, 30, 350, 360, 512

The Thirteenth Sunday after Trinity
  Epistle, Gal. 3:15-22
    287, 295, 373, 472, 473
  Gospel, Luke 10:23-37
    377, 384, 397, 439

The Fourteenth Sunday after Trinity
  Epistle, Gal. 5:16-24
    398, 400, 403, 409, 540
  Gospel, Luke 17:11-19
    25, 26, 36, 342, 569, 572

The Fifteenth Sunday after Trinity
  Epistle, Gal. 5:25-6:10
    396, 400, 409, 410, 416
  Gospel, Matt. 6:24-34
    278, 425, 426, 430, 443

The Sixteenth Sunday after Trinity
  Epistle, Eph. 3:13-21
    223, 345, 348, 349, 393
  Gospel, Luke 7:11-17
    137, 196, 365, 519, 522, 590

The Seventeenth Sunday after Trinity
  Epistle, Eph. 4:1-6
    224, 251-2, 253, 463, 464, 473, 478
  Gospel, Luke 14:1-11
    1, 4, 11, 323, 330

The Eighteenth Sunday after Trinity
  Epistle, 1 Cor. 1:4-9
    18, 24, 26, 28, 391
  Gospel, Matt. 22:34-46
    285, 286, 288, 346, 366

The Nineteenth Sunday after Trinity
  Epistle, Eph. 4:22-28
    395, 396, 397, 407, 414
  Gospel, Matt. 9:1-8
    26, 36, 319, 326, 515

The Twentieth Sunday after Trinity
  Epistle, Eph. 5:15-21
    25, 366, 395, 417, 446
  Gospel, Matt. 22:1-14
    278, 279, 371, 611, 650

The Twenty-first Sunday after Trinity
  Epistle, Eph. 6:10-17
    332, 444, 445, 447, 450
  Gospel, John 4:46-54
    377, 380, 387, 394, 524

The Twenty-second Sunday after Trinity
  Epistle, Phil. 1:3-11
    28, 394, 427, 435, 437
  Gospel, Matt. 18:23-35
    318, 322, 609, 610, 611

The Twenty-third Sunday after Trinity
  Epistle, Phil. 3:17-21
    72, 462, 465, 482, 489
  Gospel, Matt. 22:15-22
    527, 575, 578, 581, 583

The Twenty-fourth Sunday after Trinity
  Epistle, Col. 1:9-14
    397, 400, 412, 439, 478
  Gospel, Matt. 9:18-26
    54, 347, 353, 406, 428

The Twenty-fifth Sunday after Trinity
  Epistle, 1 Thess. 4:13-18
    593, 598, 604, 609, 613, 616
  Gospel, Matt. 24:15-28
    393, 611, 612

The Twenty-sixth Sunday after Trinity
  Epistle, 2 Pet. 3:3-14 or 2 Thess. 1:3-10
    446, 607, 609, 610, 612
  Gospel, Matt. 25:31-46
    72, 440, 606, 610, 611, 613, 619

The Twenty-seventh Sunday after Trinity
  Epistle, 1 Thess. 5:1-11
    448, 449, 609, 613, 619
  Gospel, Matt. 25:1-13
    67, 72, 609, 611, 656

(For Saints' Days and other Special Occasions please consult Index of Subjects)

Index of First Lines of Original Hymns

GREEK

	HYMN
Ἀναστάσεως ἡμέρα	205
Αἴσωμεν πάντες λαοί	204
Μέγα καὶ παράδοξον θαῦμα	76
Μνώεο, Χριστέ	320
Φῶς ἱλαρὸν ἁγίας δόξης	101
Φωστῆρες τῆς ἀΰλον οὐσίας	255
Στόμιον πώλων ἀδαῶν	628
Τῶν ἁμαρτιῶν μου τὴν πληθύν	322
Τὴν ἡμέραν διελθών	555

LATIN

	HYMN
A solis ortus cardine	104
Adeste, fideles	102
Angularis fundamentum	465, 466
Christe, qui lux es et dies	559
Corde natus ex Parentis	98
Debilis cessant elementa legis	117
Dicimus grates tibi, summe rerum	254
Dies est laetitia	78
Dies irae, dies illa	607, 612
Felix dies, quam proprio	115
Finita iam sunt praelia	210
Gloria, laus et honor	160
Gloriosi Salvatoris	116
Grates nunc omnes	80
Hic breve vivitur	448
Hora novissima	605
Hostis Herodes impie	131
Hymnum canamus gloriae	212
Iesu, dulcis memoria	350
Iesu, Rex admirabilis	361
Iesus Christus, nostra salus	311
In dulci jubilo	92
Instantis adventum Dei	68
Iordanis oras praevia	63
Iucundare, plebs fidelis	282
Kyrie	6
O bona patria	614
O filii et filiae	208
O Lux beata Trinitas	564
O Pater sancte	240
Omnis mundus iucundetur	82
Salve, festa dies	202
Salvete, flores martyrum	273
Sancti, venite, corpus Christi sumite	307
Splendor paternae gloriae	550
Surrexit Christus hodie	199
Tibi, Christe, splendor Patris	257
Urbs Sion aurea	613
Veni, Creator Spiritus, mentes	233, 236
Veni, Redemptor gentium	95
Veni, Sancte Spiritus	227
Veni, veni, Emmanuel	62
Vexilla Regis prodeunt	168
Victimae Paschali	191
Vox clara ecce intonat	60

SCANDINAVIAN

	HYMN
Al verden nu raabe for Herren med Fryd	44
Almighty Father, bless the Word	52
Bliv hos os, Mester, Dagen helder	194
Den store hvide Flok vi se	656
Der mange skal komme fra öst og fra vest	415
Enhver som tror og bliver döbt	301
Fryd dig, du Kristi Brud	57
Guds Ord det er vort Arvegods	283
Han er opstanden! Store Bud!	189
Herre Jesu Krist! Min Frelser du est	353
I hoppet sig min frälsta själ förnöjer	432
I Hus og Hjem, hvor Mand og Viv	624
Igjennem Nat og Trängsal	481
Jeg gaar i Fare, hvor jeg gaar	413
Jeg kommer her, o söde Gud	330
Jeg staar for Gud, som alting ved	318
Jeg ved mig ev Sövn i Jesu Navn	592
Kirken den er et gammelt Hus	467
Lad denne Dag, o Herre Gud	337
Lov og Tak og evig Aere	401
Naar Synderen ret ser sin Vaade	65
Nu, rinder Solen op	542
O Jesu, gid du vilde	655
O Jesu, söde Jesu, dig	309
O Lue fra Guds Kjaerlighed	230
O salig den Guds Ord har hört	48
Om Salighed og Gläde	217
Os er idag en Frelser födt	79
Skriv dig, Jesu, paa mit Hjerte	179
Som den gyldne Sol frembryder	207
Wår Herres Jesu Kristi död	163

SLOVAK

	HYMN
Aj, ten silný lev udatný	211
Čas radosti	82
Jezu Kriste, Pane milý (Polish)	169
Narodil se Kristus Pán	86
Věřime v všemohoucího	253
Vzkříšeni čekáme	603

WELSH

	HYMN
Arglwydd, arwain trwy'r Anialwch	54

FRENCH

	HYMN
Faisons éclater notre joie	100
Non ce n'est pas mourir	602

ITALIAN

	HYMN
Giesù sommo conforto	145
Viva! Viva! Gesù	158

FINNISH

	HYMN
Aurinko armas vallolansa	545

DUTCH

	HYMN
Wilt heden nu treten	568

GERMAN

	HYMN
Ach bleib bei uns, Herr Jesu Christ	292
Ach bleib mit deiner Gnade	53
Ach Gott und Herr, wie gross und schwer	317
Ach Gott, verlass mich nicht	402
Ach Gott, vom Himmel, sieh darein	260
Ach, wie gross ist deine Gnade	384
All Ehr' und Lob soll Gottes sein	238
Alle Menschen müssen sterben	601
Allein Gott in der Höh' sei Ehr'	237
Allein zu dir, Herr Jesu Christ	319
Alles ist an Gottes Segen	425
Also hat Gott die Welt geliebt	245
Auf, auf, ihr Reichsgenossen	69
Auf, auf, mein Herz, mit Freuden	192
Auf Christi Himmelfahrt allein	216
Auf, ihr Christen, Christi Glieder	472
Auf meinen lieben Gott	526
Aus Gnaden soll ich selig werden	373
Aus meines Herzens Grunde	548
Aus tiefer Not schrei' ich zu dir	329
Befiehl du deine Wege	520
Bis hieher hat mich Gott gebracht	33
Brich auf und werde Lichte	126
Christ ist erstanden	187
Christ lag in Todesbanden	195
Christe, du Beistand	258
Christe, du Lamm Gottes	147
Christi Blut und Gerechtigkeit	371
Christus, der ist mein Leben	597
Christus ist erstanden	190
Da Jesus an des Kreuzes Stamm	177
Dank sei Gott in der Höhe	544
Das alte Jahr vergangen ist	125
Das ist der Gemeinde Stärke	461

HYMN		HYMN
Der Bräut'gam wird bald rufen	67	Jesu, komm doch selbst zu mir — 356
Die helle Sonn' leucht't jetzt herfür	547	Jesu, meine Freude — 347
Die Nacht ist kommen	556	Jesu, meines Lebens Leben — 151
Dies ist die Nacht da mir erschienen	88	Jesus, Jesus, nichts als Jesus — 348
Dies sind die heil'gen Zehn Gebot'	287	Jesus lebt, mit ihm auch ich — 201
Dir, dir, Jehovah, will ich singen	21	Jesus, meine Zuversicht — 206
Du Lebensbrot, Herr Jesu Christ	312	Jesus nimmt die Sünder an — 324
Durch Adams Fall ist ganz verderbt	369	Jesus selbst, mein Licht, mein Leben — 408
Ein' feste Burg ist unser Gott	262	Komm, du wertes Lösegeld — 55
Ein Lämmlein geht	142	Komm Heiliger Geist, Herre Gott — 224
Ein neues Lied wir heben an	259	Komm, o komm, du Geist des Lebens — 226
Eins ist not; ach, Herr, dies eine	366	Kommt und lasst uns Christum ehren — 90
Erhalt uns deine Lehre	264	Kyrie, Gott Vater in Ewigkeit — 6
Erhalt uns, Herr, bei deinem Wort	261	Lass mich dein sein und bleiben — 334
Ermuntert euch, ihr Frommen	72	Lasset uns mit Jesu ziehen — 409
Erneure mich, o ew'ges Licht	398	Lasst uns alle fröhlich sein — 97
Erstanden! Erstanden!	198	Liebe, die du mich zum Bilde — 397
Es ist das Heil uns kommen her	377	Liebster Jesu, wir sind hier (Clausnitzer) — 16
Es ist ein' Ros' entsprungen	645	Liebster Jesu, wir sind hier (Schmolck) — 300
Es ist gewisslich an der Zeit	611	Lobe den Herren, den mächtigen — 39
Es ist noch eine Ruh' vorhanden	615	Lobe den Herren, o meine Seele — 26
Es ist noch Raum	509	Lobt Gott, ihr Christen allzugleich — 105
Es ist vollbracht	599	Löwen, lasst euch wiederfinden — 470
Es war die ganze Welt	272	Mache dich, mein·Geist, bereit — 446
Es woll' uns Gott genädig sein	500	Macht hoch die Tür — 73
Fahre fort, fahre fort	479	Mein Heiland nimmt die Sünder an — 386
Fang dein Werk mit Jesu an	540	Mein Herz will ich dir schenken — 89
Freuet euch, ihr Christen alle	96	Mein Jesu, wie du willt — 420
Fröhlich soll mein Herze springen	77	Mein Schöpfer, steh mir bei — 335
Gelobet sei der Herr	38	Mein' Seel, o Gott, muss loben dich — 275
Gelobet seist du, Jesu Christ	80	Meinen Jesum lass' ich nicht — 365
Gott der Vater wohn' uns bei	247	Mir nach, spricht Christus, unser Held — 421
Gott des Himmels und der Erden	549	Mit Ernst, o Menschenkinder — 75
Gott, du hast in deinem Sohn	411	Mit Fried' und Freud' ich fahr dahin — 137
Gott fähret auf gen Himmel	214	Mitten wir im Leben sind — 590
Gott, Heil'ger Geist, hilf uns mit Grund	293	Morgenglanz der Ewigkeit — 539
Gott ist gegenwärtig	4	Nun bitten wir den Heiligen Geist — 231
Gott sei Dank durch alle Welt	91	Nun danket alle Gott — 36
Gott sei gelobet und gebenedeiet	313	Nun danket all' und bringet Ehr' — 581
Gottes Sohn ist kommen	74	Nun freut euch, liebe Christen g'mein — 387
Grosser Gott, wir loben dich	250	Nun Gott Lob, es ist vollbracht — 45
Guter Hirt, du hast gestillt	595	Nun ist die Zeit erfüllt — 99
Halleluja, Christus lebt	188	Nun lasst uns den Leib begraben — 596
Halleluja! Lob, Preis und Ehr'	23	Nun lasst uns gehn und treten — 122
Helft mir Gott's Güte preisen	112	Nun lob, mein' Seel', den Herren — 34
Herr, es ist von meinem Leben	560	Nun preiset alle Gottes Barmherzigkeit — 28
Herr Gott, erhalt uns für und für	288	Nun ruhen alle Wälder — 554
Herr Gott Vater, wir preisen dich	124	Nun sich der Tag geendet hat — 561
Herr, ich habe missgehandelt	326	O dass ich tausend Zungen hätte — 30, 243
Herr Jesu Christ, dich zu uns wend	3	O Gott, du frommer Gott — 395
Herr Jesu Christ, du hast bereit't	306	O Haupt, voll Blut und Wunden — 172
Herr Jesu, der du selbst	485	O Heilige Dreifaltigkeit — 541
Herr Jesu, Licht der Heiden	138	O Heil'ger Geist, kehr bei uns ein — 235
Herr, öffne mir die Herzenstür	5	O Herre Gott, dein göttlich Wort — 266
Herr, unser Gott, lass nicht zuschanden werden	269	O Herre Gott, in meiner Not — 600
Herr, wie du willst, so schick's mit mir	406	O Jesu Christ, dein Kripplein ist — 81
Herzlich lieb hab' ich dich, o Herr	429	O Jesu Christ, mein schönstes Licht — 349
Herzliebster Jesu	143	O Jesu Christ, mein's Lebens Licht — 148
Heut' fangen wir in Gottes Nam'n	7	O Jesu Christe, wahres Licht — 512
Hilf, Herr Jesu, lass gelingen	120	O Jesu, einig wahres Haupt — 477
Hinunter ist der Sonnenschein	563	O König aller Ehren — 130
Holy Spirit, hear us	229	O Lamm Gottes, unschuldig — 146
Höret, ihr Eltern, Christus spricht	630	O Lämmlein Gottes, Jesu Christ — 328
Ich bin bei Gott in Gnaden	372	O selig Haus, wo man dich aufgenommen — 626
Ich bin ein Gast auf Erden	586	O Traurigkeit, o Herzeleid — 167
Ich bin getauft auf deinen Namen	298	O Vaterherz, das Erd' und Himmel schuf — 299
Ich freue mich in dir	93	O Welt, sieh hier dein Leben — 171
Ich habe g'nug	196	O wie selig seid ihr doch, ihr Frommen — 589
Ich habe nun den Grund gefunden	385	Rede freundlich Jesu, rede — 296
Ich halte Gott in allem stille	529	Rett, o Herr Jesu, rett dein' Ehr' — 265
Ich komm' zu deinem Abendmahle	315	Rüstet euch, ihr Christenleute — 444
Ich singe dir mit Herz und Mund	535, 569	Schmücke dich, o liebe Seele — 305
Ich trete frisch	310	Schönster Herr Jesu — 657
Ich weiss, an wen ich gläube	381	Segne, Herr, mit deinem Geiste — 491
Ich will dich lieben, meine Stärke	399	Sei Lob und Ehr' dem höchsten Gut — 19
In Christi Wunden schlaf' ich ein	585	So gehst du nun, mein Jesu, hin — 150
In dich hab' ich gehoffet, Herr	524	So wahr ich leb', spricht Gott der Herr — 331
Ist Gott für mich, so trete	528	Sollt' ich meinem Gott nicht singen — 25
Jerusalem, du hochgebaute Stadt	619	Speis uns, o Gott, deine Kinder — 659
Jesaia, dem Propheten, das geschah	249	Stille, mein Wille — 651
Jesu, deine Passion	140	Stille Nacht — 646
Jesu, deine tiefen Wunden	144	Such', wer da will, ein ander Ziel — 383
Jesu, geh voran	410	This child we dedicate to Thee — 303
		Tröstet, tröstet meine Lieben — 61

	HYMN
Tut mir auf die schöne Pforte	1
Unumschränkte Liebe	42
Valet will ich dir geben	407
Vater unser im Himmelreich	458
Verzage nicht, du Häuflein klein	263
Vom Himmel hoch da komm' ich her	85
Vom Himmel kam der Engel Schar	103
Von Gott will ich nicht lassen	393
Wach auf, du Geist der ersten Zeugen	494
Wachet auf! ruft uns die Stimme	609
Walte, walte nah und fern	507
Wär' Gott nicht mit uns diese Zeit	267
Warum sollt' ich mich denn grämen	523
Was frag' ich nach der Welt	430
Was gibst du denn, o meine Seele	404
Was Gott tut, das ist wohlgetan 521,	571
Was kann ich doch für Dank	417
Was mein Gott will, das g'scheh' allzeit	517
Weil ich Jesu Schäflein bin	648
Wenn dein herzliebster Sohn, o Gott	375
Wenn meine Sünd' mich kränken	152
Wenn mein Stündlein vorhanden ist	594
Wenn wir in höchsten Nöten sein	522
Wer Gott vertraut, hat wohl gebaut	437
Wer nur den lieben Gott lässt walten	518
Wer weiss, wie nahe mir mein Ende	598
Wie schön leuchtet der Morgenstern (Nicolai)	343
Wie schön leuchtet der Morgenstern (Wiesenmeyer)	546
Wie soll ich dich empfangen	58
Wie wohl hast du gelabet	316
Wie wohl ist mir, o Freund der Seelen	362
Wir Christenleut' hab'n jetzund Freud'	107
Wir danken dir, Herr Jesu Christ 173,	223
Wir danken dir, o treuer Gott	321
Wir glauben all' an einen Gott (Clausnitzer)	252
Wir glauben all' an einen Gott (Luther)	251
Wir sind des Herrn, wir leben oder sterben	453
Wir singen dir, Immanuel	108
Wo willst du hin, weil's Abend ist	197
Wohl einem Haus, da Jesus Christ	625
Wunderbarer König	41
Zeuch ein zu deinen Toren	228
Zeuch uns nach dir	215
Zion klagt mit Angst und Schmerzen	268

BRITISH

Abide with me	552
Across the sky the shades of night	110
Alas! and did my Savior bleed	154
All hail the power of Jesus' name	339
All people that on earth do dwell	14
All praise to Thee, my God, this night	558
All that I was, my sin, my guilt	378
Almighty Father, heaven and earth	438
Almighty God, Thy Word is cast	49
Almighty Lord, before Thy throne	579
Am I a soldier of the Cross	445
And will the Judge descend	610
Angels from the realms of glory	136
Approach, my soul, the mercy-seat	456
Arise, O God, and shine	642
Arm these Thy soldiers, mighty Lord	332
Around the throne of God a band	256
Art thou weary, art thou troubled	513
As pants the hart for cooling streams	525
As with gladness men of old	127
Asleep in Jesus! Blessed sleep	587
At even, when the sun did set	557
Awake, my soul, and with the sun	536
Awake, my soul, to joyful lays	340
Before Jehovah's awe-full throne	13
Behold a Stranger at the door	650
Behold the Lamb of God	165
Behold the Savior of mankind	176
Behold the sure Foundation-stone	460
Blessed are the sons of God	391
Blessed Savior, who hast taught me	333
Blest be the tie that binds	464
Blest is the man, forever blest	392

	HYMN
Brightest and best	128
Chief of sinners though I be	342
Christ the Lord is risen today	193
Christ, whose glory fills the skies	359
Christians, awake	84
Come, Holy Spirit, come	225
Come, let us join our cheerful songs	344
Come, my soul, thy suit prepare	459
Come, Thou almighty King	239
Come to Calvary's holy mountain	149
Come unto Me, ye weary	276
Come, ye disconsolate	531
Come, ye thankful people, come	574
Crown Him with many crowns	341
Drawn to the Cross	390
Enslaved by sin and bound in chains	141
Every morning mercies new	537
Father, in whom we live	241
Father, let me dedicate	118
Father of glory, to Thy name	248
Father of heaven, whose love	242
Father of mercies, in Thy Word	284
Father, who the light this day	8
Fight the good fight	447
For all the saints	463
For all Thy saints, O Lord	468
For Thy mercy and Thy grace	121
Forever with the Lord	616
From all that dwell below the skies	15
From Greenland's icy mountains	495
Glorious things of thee are spoken	469
Glory be to God the Father	244
Go to dark Gethsemane	159
God, Lord of Sabaoth, Thou who ordainest	582
God, most mighty, sovereign Lord	566
God moves in a mysterious way	514
God of mercy, God of grace	20
God of my life, to Thee I call	534
Grace! 'tis a charming sound	374
Gracious Savior, gentle Shepherd	627
Great God, we sing that mighty hand	119
Great God, what do I see and hear?	604
Great is the Lord, our God	636
Great King of nations, hear our prayer	583
Hail the day that sees Him rise	213
Hail, thou bright and sacred morn	8
Hail, Thou once despised Jesus	367
Hail, Thou Source of every blessing	129
Hail to the Lord's Anointed	59
Hark! ten thousand harps and voices	221
Hark the glad sound!	66
Hark! the herald angels sing	94
Hark! the sound of holy voices	471
Hark! what mean those holy voices	83
Here in Thy name, eternal God	635
Holy Father, in Thy mercy	643
Holy Ghost, with light divine	234
Holy, holy, holy! Lord God Almighty!	246
Hosanna, loud hosanna	161
Hosanna to the living Lord	70
How beauteous are their feet	487
How firm a foundation, ye saints of the Lord	427
How precious is the Book Divine	285
How shall the young secure their hearts	286
How sweet the name of Jesus sounds	364
I am trusting Thee, Lord Jesus	428
I gave My life for thee	405
I heard the voice of Jesus say	277
I know that my Redeemer lives	200
I lay my sins on Jesus	652
I'm but a stranger here	660
In His Temple now behold Him	139
In loud, exalted strains	638
In the Cross of Christ I glory	354
In the hour of trial	516
In the name which earth and heaven	632
Jerusalem, my happy home	618
Jesus, all our ransom paid	185
Jesus, all Thy labor vast	186
Jesus! and shall it ever be	346
Jesus calls us; o'er the tumult	270
Jesus came, the heavens adoring	56
Jesus, I my cross have taken	423

[619]

HYMN		HYMN	
Jesus, in Thy dying woes	180	Ride on, ride on, in majesty	162
Jesus, in Thy thirst and pain	184	Rise, crowned with light	503
Jesus, Lover of my soul	345	Rock of Ages, cleft for me	376
Jesus, loving to the end	182	Round me falls the night	562
Jesus, my great High Priest	220	Safely through another week	11
Jesus, my Truth, my Way	433	Savior, again to Thy dear name	47
Jesus! Name of wondrous love	114	Savior, breathe an evening blessing	565
Jesus, pitying the sighs	181	Savior, when in dust to Thee	166
Jesus shall reign where'er the sun	511	See, the Conqueror mounts	218
Jesus, Thy Church with longing eyes	64	Soldiers of Christ, arise	450
Jesus, whelmed in fears unknown	183	Soldiers of the Cross, arise	501
Joy to the world, the Lord is come	87	Songs of praise the angels sang	35
Judge eternal, throned in splendor	576	Songs of thankfulness and praise	134
Just as I am, without one plea	388	Stricken, smitten, and afflicted	153
Lamb of God, we fall before Thee	358	Sun of my soul, Thou Savior dear	551
Lamp of our feet whereby we trace	291	Sweet the moments, rich in blessing	155
Let children hear the mighty deeds	629	Take my life and let it be	400
Let songs of praises fill the sky	232	Ten thousand times ten thousand	476
Let thoughtless thousands choose	608	The Church's one foundation	473
Look, ye saints, the sight is glorious	222	The God of Abraham praise	40
Lord, dismiss us with Thy blessing	50	The Head that once was crowned with thorns	219
Lord, it belongs not to my care	527	The King of Love my Shepherd is	431
Lord of Glory, who hast bought us	442	The Law commands and makes us know	289
Lord of my life, whose tender care	24	The Lord my pasture shall prepare	368
Lord of the Church, we humbly pray	489	The Lord my Shepherd is	426
Lord of the harvest, hear	488	The Lord's my Shepherd, I'll not want	436
Lord of the living harvest	492	The man is ever blest	414
Lord of the worlds above	480	The people that in darkness sat	106
Lord, 'tis not that I did choose Thee	37	The saints on earth and those above	478
Lord, we come before Thee now	18	The Savior calls; let every ear	281
Lord, we confess our numerous faults	382	The Son of God goes forth to war	452
Lord, when we bend before Thy throne	22	The voice that breathed o'er Eden	622
Lord, while for all mankind we pray	578	There is a fountain filled with blood	157
Lord, who at Cana's wedding-feast	620	Thine forever, God of Love	338
Love Divine, all love excelling	351	This day at Thy creating word	12
May we Thy precepts, Lord, fulfil	412	This is the day the Lord hath made	10
Morning breaks upon the tomb	203	Thou whose almighty word	508
My God, accept my heart this day	336	Thou who the night in prayer didst spend	493
My God, my Father, make me strong	424	Throned upon the awe-full tree	174
My God, my Father, while I stray	418	Through all the changing scenes	29
My hope is built on nothing less	370	Through the day Thy love hath spared us	553
My soul, be on thy guard	449	Thy way, not mine, O Lord	532
My spirit on Thy care	435	Thy ways, O Lord, with wise design	530
Nearer, my God, to Thee	533	Thy works, not mine, O Christ	380
Not all the blood of beasts	156	'Tis good, Lord, to be here	135
Not what these hands have done	389	'Tis gone that bright and orbèd blaze	551
Now may He who from the dead	51	To our Redeemer's glorious name	363
Now the day is over	654	To Thee, O Lord, our hearts we raise	573
Now the light has gone away	653	To Thee, our God, we fly	580
O day of rest and gladness	9	To Thy temple I repair	2
O Father, all creating	621	Today Thy mercy calls us	279
O God of God, O Light of Light	132	'Twas on that dark, that doleful night	164
O God of Jacob, by whose hand	434	Watchman, tell us of the night	71
O God of mercy, God of might	439	We bid thee welcome in the name	484
O Lord of heaven and earth and sea	443	We give Thee but Thine own	441
O Lord of hosts, whose glory fills	170	We sing the almighty power of God	43
O perfect life of love	633	We sing the praise of Him who died	178
O perfect Love	623	When all Thy mercies, O my God	31
O Savior, precious Savior	352	When I survey the wondrous cross	175
O Spirit of the living God	504	When, streaming from the eastern skies	543
O Thou, from whom all goodness flows	515	While shepherds watched their flocks	109
O Thou that hear'st when sinners cry	325	While with ceaseless course the sun	113
O Word of God Incarnate	294	Who is this that comes from Edom	209
O'er the distant mountains breaking	606	Why do we mourn departing friends	593
O'er the gloomy hills of darkness	505	With broken heart and contrite sigh	323
Oh, bless the Lord, my soul	27	Within the Father's house	133
Oh, for a faith that will not shrink	396	Word Supreme, before creation	271
Oh, for a thousand tongues to sing	360	Ye watchers and ye holy ones	475
Oh, that the Lord would guide my ways	416	Zion stands by hills surrounded	474
Oh, worship the King	17		
On what has now been sown	46	**AMERICAN**	
One Thy Light, the Temple filling	641	An awe-full mystery is here	304
Onward, Christian soldiers	658	Before the Lord we bow	575
Our God, our Help in ages past	123	Beloved, "It is well"	519
Our heavenly Father, hear	455	Christ, by heavenly hosts adored	566
Out of the deep I call	327	Come, Jesus, from the sapphire throne	634
Pour out Thy Spirit from on high	490	Dear Lord, to Thy true servants give	482
Praise God, from whom all blessings flow	644	Delay not, delay not, O sinner, draw near	278
Praise, oh, praise, our God and King	570	For many years, O God of grace	639
Praise to God, immortal praise	572	Founded on Thee, our only Lord	637
Praise we the Lord this day	274	Gehe auf, du Trost der Heiden	498
Prayer is the soul's sincere desire	454	God bless our native land	577
Redeemed, restored, forgiven	32		
Return, O wanderer, return	280		

	HYMN
God of the prophets	483
God the Father, Son, and Spirit	640
Hark! the voice of Jesus crying	496
I do not come because my soul	379
I love Thy kingdom, Lord	462
I would not live alway	588
Invited, Lord, by boundless grace	308
Jesus, I live to Thee	591
Jesus, Savior, pilot me	649
Jesus, Thou art mine forever	357
Look from Thy sphere of endless day	499
Lord Jesus Christ, we humbly pray	314
Lord, lead the way the Savior went	440
My faith looks up to Thee	394
Now the shades of night are gone	538
O little town of Bethlehem	647
O Lord, whose bounteous hand again	567
O Thou whose feet have climbed life's hill	486
O'er Jerusalem Thou weepest	419

	HYMN
Saints of God, the dawn is brightening	502
Savior, I follow on	422
Savior, sprinkle many nations	510
Savior, Thy dying love	403
Savior, who Thy flock art feeding	631
Send Thou, O Lord, to every place	506
Stand up! — stand up for Jesus	451
Swell the anthem, raise the song	584
The Gospel shows the Father's grace	297
The Law of God is good and wise	295
The morning light is breaking	497
The Savior kindly calls	302
There is an hour of peaceful rest	617
Thou art the Way; to Thee alone	355
Thou who roll'st the year around	111
We have a sure prophetic Word	290

CANADIAN

What a Friend we have in Jesus	457

Index of First Lines of Stanzas (Except of First Stanzas)

	HYMN
A book is opened then to all	611
A broken heart, my God, my King	325
A crown of thorns Thou wearest	171
A faith that keeps the narrow way	396
A faith that shines more bright and clear	396
A glorious band, the chosen few	452
A heart that hath repented	316
A Helper just He comes to thee	73
A little Child, Thou art our Guest	80
A love more deep than mother-love	386
A moment's space, and gently, wondrously	619
A noble army, men and boys	452
A pledge of peace from God I see	343
A precious food is this indeed	163
A roaring lion, round he goes	254
A stable serves Him for a dwelling	100
A thousand ages in Thy sight	123
A trumpet loud shall then resound	611
A trusty weapon is Thy Word	292
A while His consolation	520
A wondrous change which He does make	105
Abel's blood for vengeance	158
Abide, O dear Redeemer	53
Abide, O faithful Savior	53
Abide with heavenly brightness	53
Abide with me from morn till eve	551
Abide with richest blessings	53
Abide with Thy protection	53
Abide with us, O Savior tender	194
Abide with us; with heavenly gladness	194
Abiding, steadfast, firm, and sure	290
Above all else, Lord, send us	122
Abram's promised great Reward	91
Accept the gift which Thou requirest	404
Accept the work our hands have wrought	637
Admit Him lest His anger burn	650
"Again shall ye behold Him so	212
Ah, dearest Jesus, holy Child	85
Ah! hide not for our sins Thy face	522
Ah, how hungers all my spirit	305
Ah, look on me with pity	130
Ah, Lord, who hast created all	85
Ah, sweet and gentle name	93
Ah, then I'll have my heart's desire	148
Ah, then my spirit faints	616
Ah! thou Dayspring from on high	539
Ah, what availed King Herod's wrath?	273
Ah, who would live alway, away from his God	588
Ah, who would, then, not depart with gladness	589
All are alike before the Highest	518
All are redeemed, both far and wide	439
All blessing, honor, thanks, and praise	377
All creatures that have breath and motion	30
All glory, Jesus, be to Thee	131
All glory to the Son	68
All honor, glory, praise be given	211
All honor, praise, and majesty	524
All honor unto Christ be paid	104
All its numbered days are sped	111
All love is Thine, O Spirit	228
All our follies, Lord, forgive	111
All our knowledge, sense, and sight	16
All our prayers and all our praises	358
All our words are feeble	42
All power is here and round me now	424
All praise and thanks to God	36
All praise, eternal Son	117
All praise, eternal Son, to Thee	63
All praise, eternal Son, to Thee	331
All praise to God the Father be	12
All praise to God the Father be	550
All praise to God the Father be	559
All praise to God the Father be	564
All praise to Thee, who safe hast kept	536
All righteousness by works is vain	375
All that for my soul is needful	25
All that I am and have	403
All that I am, e'en here on earth	378

	HYMN
All that makes the angels glad	356
All the plenty summer pours	572
All the winter of our sins	204
All the world is God's own field	574
All this for us Thy love hath done	80
All this Thy hand bestoweth	122
All those whose sins ye thus remit	331
All Thy vast dominion	42
All trials and all griefs are past	596
All trials are then like a dream that is past	415
All were drear to me and lonely	357
All-holy Lord, in humble prayer	559
Almighty Son, Incarnate Word	242
Although Thou didst to heav'n ascend	306
Amazing goodness! Love divine	141
Amen I say, not fearing	548
Amen, Lord Jesus, grant our prayer	263
Amen, that is, So shall it be	458
Amen, this ever true shall be	238
Amen! Thou, Christ, my Savior	597
Amid surrounding foes	426
An angel bade their sorrow flee	208
And at my life's last setting sun	543
And bid Thy Word within me	130
And fled I hence in my despair	317
And for richer food than this	570
And for this our soul's salvation	384
And for Thy Gospel let us dare	477
And from His righteous lips	610
And gently grant Thy blessing	544
And grant, Lord, when the year is over	120
And hath bid the fruitful field	570
And idol forms shall perish	76
And if their home be dark and drear	624
And I have brought to thee	405
And I have vowed to fear and love Thee	298
And keep with angels in Thy rest	7
And let me with all men	395
And let Thy Word have speedy course	494
And may this year to me be holy	120
And may Thy Holy Spirit move	439
And never let my purpose falter	298
And none, O Lord, have perfect rest	557
And now, on this our festal day	573
And now we fight the battle	448
And on His thorn-crowned head	170
And on that solemn Day	395
And shall man alone be dumb	35
And shield me from all evil	548
And since the cause and glory, Lord	292
And so I close my weary eyes	561
And so through all the length of days	431
And so to earth we now entrust	596
And so to Thee still cleaving	597
And some are pressed with worldly care	557
And some have found the world is vain	557
And the silver moon by night	570
And then for work to do for Thee	390
And Thou, O Holy Spirit	334
And Thou, who cam'st on earth to die	439
And though it tarry till the night	329
And thus, dear Lord, it pleaseth Thee	85
And thus I live and die to Thee	561
And thus I live in God contented	598
And thus the full assurance gain	173
And thus we come, O God, today	522
And to this truth we also cleave	253
And we believe Thy Word	441
And we with holy Church unite	208
And what Thy Spirit thus hath taught me	21
And when before Thy throne I stand	515
And when, dear Lord, before Thy throne in heaven	143
And when I on my death-bed lie	197
And when in power He comes	575
And when life's frail thread is breaking	226
And when my soul is lying	528
And when my spirit flies away	148
And when our earthly race is run	293
And when, redeemed from sin and hell	323

[622]

	HYMN
And when the fight is fierce, the warfare long	463
And when the last Great Day shall come	148
And when they leave their childhood home	337
And when Thou dost come again	91
And when Thy glory I shall see	142
And when within that lovely Paradise	619
And while we pray, we lift our eyes	110
"And whosoever cometh	276
Anoint and send forth more	488
Anoint me with Thy Spirit's grace	336
Anoint them kings; aye, kingly kings, O Lord	483
Anoint them priests. Strong intercessors, they	483
Anoint them prophets. Make their ears attent	483
Apostles, martyrs, prophets, there	618
Approach ye, then, with faithful hearts sincere	307
Arabia's desert ranger	59
Are there no foes for me to face	445
Are we not tending upward, too	593
Are we weak and heavy laden	457
Arise, arise, good Christian	605
Arise, my soul, and banish	520
Arise, O Lord of hosts	580
Arise, ye drooping mourners	69
Arise, ye much afflicted	69
Arise, ye poor and needy	69
As a branch upon a vine	411
As a father never turneth	25
As a mother stills her child	649
As by one man all mankind fell	369
As he of old deceived the world	254
As His pledge of love undying	311
As His side with spear was riven	169
As Judge, on clouds of light	68
As lab'rers in Thy vineyard	492
As mothers watch are keeping	122
As of old Saint Andrew heard it	270
As silver tried by fire is pure	260
As the image in the glass	459
As the morning light returns	537
As the winged arrow flies	113
As they offered gifts most rare	127
As Thou dost will, Lead Thou me still	353
As Thy coming was in peace	91
As Thy prospering hand hath blest	572
As true as God's own Word is true	263
As we come Thy name to praise	11
As with joyful steps they sped	127
Ascended to His throne on high	223
Ashamed of Jesus? Just as soon	346
Ashamed of Jesus? Sooner far	346
Ashamed of Jesus, that dear Friend	346
Ashamed of Jesus? Yes, I may	346
Ask not how this should be	274
Asleep in Jesus! Oh, for me	587
Asleep in Jesus! Oh, how sweet	587
Asleep in Jesus! Peaceful rest	587
Asleep though wearied eyes may be	559
Assist my soul, too apt to stray	416
At Bethlehem, in David's town	103
At Cana first His power is shown	131
At eventide, Thy Spirit sending	194
Awake the purpose high which strives	486
Bane and blessing, pain and pleasure	354
Baptize the nations; far and nigh	504
Be darkness, at Thy coming, light	504
Be faithful to thy marriage vows	287
Be of good cheer, for God's own Son	245
Be of good cheer; your cause belongs	263
Be patient and await His leisure	518
Be present, Holy Spirit	622
Be present, loving Father	622
Be righteous, ye His subjects	69
Be still, my soul, the hour is hast'ning on	651
Be still, my soul, tho' dearest friends depart	651
Be still, my soul; thy God doth undertake	651

	HYMN
Be the banner still unfurled	501
Be this a time of grace and pardon	120
Be Thou a Helper speedy	122
Be Thou at my right hand	616
Be Thou my Consolation	172
Be Thou my Shield and Hiding-place	456
Be Thou my soul's Preserver	555
Be Thou our Helper and our strong Defender	269
Be Thou our Joy and Brightness	138
Be Thou our Joy and strong Defense	212
Be with the sick and ailing	122
Be with them, God the Father	492
Bear not false witness nor belie	287
Bear the cross, bear the cross	479
Beautiful Savior	657
Before he yet was born	272
Before our Father's throne	464
Before the cross of Him who died	336
Before the cross subdued we bow	110
Before the dawning day	68
Before the hills in order stood	123
Before the mournful scene began	164
Before Thine altar when we stand	490
Before we taste of death	135
Behold, O God, our Shield, and quell	559
Behold the Lamb of God	272
Beyond my highest joy	462
Believing, we rejoice	156
Bless our going out, we pray	45
Blessed are they that have not seen	208
Blessed, heav'nly Light	562
Blessed Lord, by their protection	257
Blessed shall be her name	274
Blessed Spirit, Comforter	8
Blessed, yea, blessed is he forever	26
Blessings abound where'er He reigns	511
Blest be the Lord, who comes to men	10
Blest be the Lord, who foiled their threat	267
Blest is the man to whom the Lord	392
Blest river of salvation	497
Blest such a house, it prospers well	625
Blest through endless ages	158
Blind unbelief is sure to err	514
Bold shall I stand in that great Day	371
Borne upon their latest breath	35
Both now and ever, Lord, protect	633
Bow down Thy gracious ear to me	524
Bowed down beneath a load of sin	456
Bread of our souls whereon we feed	291
Break forth, my soul, for joy and say	309
Breathe, oh, breathe Thy loving Spirit	351
Brighten all our heavenward way	185
Brightest and best of the sons of the morning	128
Brightest gems and fairest flowers	357
Brightly doth Thy manger shine	95
Bring distant nations near	642
Bring near Thy great salvation	476
Bring those into Thy fold	485
Bruise for me the Serpent's head	91
But, chiefest, in our cleansed breast	70
But Christ, the heav'nly Lamb	156
But Christ, the second Adam, came	369
But curb my heart, forgive my guilt	317
But drops of grief can ne'er repay	154
But ere that trumpet shakes	610
But God beheld my wretched state	387
But He whom we trust in	448
But here we have no boon on earth	304
But I, Thy servant, Lord, today	108
But if thou perseverest	520
But, lo, there breaks a yet more glorious day	463
But makes the Law of God	414
But now I find sweet peace and rest	375
But, O my soul, forever praise	382
But short was their triumph, the Savior arose	198
But since my strength will nevermore suffice me	143
But sinners, filled with guilty fears	604
But soon He'll break death's envious chain	176
But still Thy Law and Gospel, Lord	286

[623]

Hymn		Hymn	
But the pains which He endured, Alleluia	199	Come, O Christ, and loose the chains that bind us	589
But they who have always resisted His grace	415	Come, tend'rest Friend and best	227
But Thou hast raised me up	417	Come, then, banish all your sadness	77
But Thou, my God, dost never sleep	561	Come, then, Lamb for sinners slain	356
But today amidst Thine own	204	Come, Thou Incarnate Word	239
But watchful is the angel band	254	"Come unto Me, ye fainting	276
But what to those who find? Ah! this	350	"Come unto Me, ye wand'rers	276
But while watching, also pray	446	Come, very Sun of truth and love	550
But will He prove a friend indeed	650	Come with Thy Spirit and Thy pow'r	637
But worthless is my sacrifice, I own it	143	Come, ye saints, unite your praises	221
By day, by night, at home, abroad	119	Come, ye sinners, one and all	324
By faith I call Thy holy Table	315	Comfort every sufferer	654
By grace God's Son, our only Savior	373	Comfort my desponding heart	91
By grace! None dare lay claim to merit	373	Comfort those who weep and mourn	18
By grace! Oh, mark this word of promise	373	Convince us of our sin	225
		Create in me a new heart, Lord	398
By grace! On this I'll rest when dying	373	Create my nature pure within	325
By grace! This ground of faith is certain	373	Crown all our labors with success	547
By grace to timid hearts that tremble	373	Crown Him the Lord of Heaven	341
By idle word and speech profane	287	Crown Him the Lord of Life	341
By Pontius Pilate crucified	253	Crown Him the Lord of Love	341
By pow'rs of empire banned and burned	290	Crown Him, the Virgin's Son	341
By the love Thy tears are telling	419	Crown Him, ye martyrs of our God	339
By Thee my prayers acceptance gain	364	Crown, O God, Thine own endeavor	576
By Thine hour of dire despair	166	Crown the Savior! Angels, crown Him	222
By Thy deep expiring groan	166	Crowns and thrones may perish	658
By Thy good counsel lead me	407		
By Thy helpless infant years	166	Dark and cheerless is the morn	359
By virtue of Thy wounds we pray	173	Dark judgments from Thy heavy hand	579
		Dark the future; let Thy light	121
Calvary's mournful mountain climb	159	Day by day, at home, away	648
Can a child presume to choose	118	Day of sorrow, day of weeping	607
Can we whose souls are lighted	495	Dear dying Lamb, Thy precious blood	157
Cast afar this world's vain pleasures	444	Dear Father, endless praise I render	243
Cast care aside; Upon thy Guide	447	Dear Jesus, send Thy mercies o'er me	545
Cause him, Lord, to fly full swiftly	641	Dear Lord, while we adoring pay	363
Chief of sinners though I be	342	Dear Master, Thine the glory	32
Child of wonder, virgin-born	78	Dear name! The Rock on which I build	364
Choose Thou for me my friends	532	Dear Savior, draw reluctant hearts	281
Chosen of God, to sinners dear	460	Dear Savior, for Thy love untold	299
Christ, by highest heav'n adored	94	Dear Spirit, rest upon this child	299
Christ, from heaven to us descending	90	Dearest Lord, Thee will I cherish	77
Christ has wiped away your tears forever	589	Death cannot destroy forever	523
		Death doth pursue me all the way	413
Christ, His last word having spoken	169	Death is struck and nature quaking	607
Christ is born, the great Anointed	83	Death's mightiest powers have done their worst	210
Christ is my everlasting All	608		
Christ is the sure Foundation	217	Deep in the prophets' sacred page	132
Christ Jesus is the Ground of faith	245	Deep in unfathomable mines	514
Christ leads me thro' no darker rooms	527	Defend Thy truth, O God, and stay	260
Christ says: "Come, all ye that labor	311	Defend us, Lord, from sin and shame	173
Christ, the Victim undefiled, Alleluia	191	Delay not, delay not, O sinner, to come	278
Christ, to Thee, with God the Father	98	Delay not, delay not! The hour is at hand	278
Christ, who once for sinners bled	191		
Christian, dry your flowing tears	203	Delay not, delay not! The Spirit of Grace	278
Christians, on this happy day, Alleluia	191		
Cleanse their hearts from sinful folly	627	Delay not, delay not! Why longer abuse	278
Cold on His cradle the dew-drops are shining	128	"Depart from Me, accursed	610
		Despised and scorned, they sojourned here	656
Come, all the faithful bless	227		
Come, Almighty, to deliver	351	Destroy in me the lust of sin	398
Come as a messenger of peace	484	Did ever mourner plead with Thee	534
Come as a shepherd; guard and keep	484	Did not His love and truth and pow'r	535
Come as a teacher sent from God	484	Direct and govern heart and mind	550
Come as once Thou camest	229	Direct, control, suggest, this day	536
Come, Desire of nations, come	94	Direct our hearts to do Thy will	547
Come, ever-blessed Spirit, come	332	Divine Instructor, gracious Lord	284
Come, faithful Shepherd, feed Thy sheep	634	"Do this," He said, "till time shall end	164
Come from on high to me	92	Do we pass that cross unheeding	145
Come, gracious Lord, our hearts renew	64	Draw from my timid eyes the veil	424
Come, heathen races	28	Drive away the gloomy night	411
Come hither now and ponder	171	Drive far away our wily Foe	233
Come, holy Comforter	239	Dwell therefore in our hearts	225
Come, Holy Spirit, from above	232		
Come in poverty and meanness	149	Early hasten to the tomb	159
Come in sorrow and contrition	149	Earth, hear thy Maker's voice	575
Come, Light serene and still	227	Earth receives the mortal	603
Come, Lord, when grace has made me meet	527	Earthly joys can give no peace	356
		Earthly work is done	562
Come near and bless us when we wake	551	E'en babes with one accord	57
		"E'en down to old age all My people shall prove	427
Come not in terrors, as the King of kings	552		
		E'en now when tempests round us fall	64

[624]

	HYMN
E'er since by faith I saw the stream	157
Elect from ev'ry nation	473
Endue the creatures with Thy grace	633
Enlighten me that from the way	197
Enrich that temple's holy shrine	332
Enter now my waiting heart	55
Eternal are Thy mercies, Lord	15
Eternal Spirit, by whose breath	242
Eternal Triune Lord	241
Even so, Lord, quickly come	574
Ever be Thou our Guide	628
"Ever shall Mine eyes behold thee	268
Evil world, I leave thee	347
Ev'ry human tie may perish	474
Ev'ry wound that pains or grieves me	144
Exalt our low desires	227
Except Thou build it, Father	621
Faint and weary Thou hast sought me	607
Faint not nor fear, His arms are near	447
Fair are the meadows	657
Fair is the lot that's cast for me	534
Fair is the sunshine	657
Fair shall be Thine earthly temple	632
Faith and hope and charity	411
Faith clings to Jesus' cross alone	377
Faith He grants us to believe it	358
Faithful Father, thus before Thee	560
Far off I see my fatherland	148
Far off I stand with tearful eyes	323
Fast bound in Satan's chains I lay	387
"Father, forgive these men; for, lo	177
Father, Son, and Holy Ghost	16
Father, Son, and Holy Spirit	643
Fear Him, ye saints, and you will then	29
"Fear not, I am with thee, oh, be not dismayed	427
Fight on, my soul, till death	449
Fighting, we shall be victorious	472
Fill our souls with heav'nly light	538
Fill with the radiance of Thy grace	512
Finding, following, keeping, struggling	513
Finish, then, Thy new creation	351
First victims for th'incarnate Lord	273
Fling wide the portals of your heart	73
Fly abroad, eternal Gospel	505
Follow to the judgment-hall	159
For as a tender father	34
For Christ is born of Mary	647
For Christ, my Lord and Brother	597
For ev'ry thirsty, longing heart	281
For good is the Lord, and His mercy is sure	44
For He can plead for me with sighings	21
For her my tears shall fall	462
For her our prayer shall rise	577
For Him shall endless prayer be made	511
For if you love them as you ought	630
For peaceful homes and healthful days	443
For souls redeemed, for sins forgiven	443
For the joy Thy advent gave me	207
For the Lord, our God, shall come	574
For the Lord reigneth	28
For the sheep the Lamb hath bled, Alleluia	191
For Thee, my God, the living God	525
For Thee our waiting spirits yearn	637
For Thee, since first the world was made	108
For they who with Him suffered here	596
For this, now and in days to be	254
For this Thy name we bless	468
For Thou art our Salvation, Lord	63
For Thou from me hast warded	548
For Thou hast placed us side by side	440
For Thou hast promised graciously	522
For Thou their burden dost remove	106
For though the evil world revile me	362
For thro' this holy incarnation	100
For Thy consoling Supper, Lord	306
For Thy Son did suffer for me	326
For vainly doth our human wisdom ponder	143
For velvets soft and silken stuff	85
For what have all that live and move	569

	HYMN
For why? The Lord, our God, is good	14
Forbid it, Lord, that I should boast	175
"Forever with the Lord!"	616
Forgive me, Lord, for Thy dear Son	558
Forgive, O Lord, our sins forgive	265
Forgive our sins, Lord, we implore	458
Forth today the Conqueror goeth	77
Frail and fleeting are our powers	461
Frail children of dust	17
Friend of the friendless and the faint	534
From all pain and imperfection	408
From cross to throne ascending	214
From dark temptation's power	455
From death our bodies shall arise	253
From earth's wide bounds, from ocean's farthest coast	463
From evil, Lord, deliver us	458
From guile his heart and lips are free	392
From hearts depraved, to evil prone	369
From me this is not hidden	528
From morn till eve my theme shall be	142
From Olivet they followed	161
From sin our flesh could not abstain	377
From sorrow, toil, and pain	464
From strength to strength go on	450
From that sinful woman shriven	607
From the bondage that oppressed us	90
From the Father forth He came	95
From Thee above all gladness flows	108
From thence He'll come, as once He said	253
From Thy house when I return	2
Fulfilled is all that David told	168
Fulfiller of the past	135
Gird each one with the Spirit's Sword	506
Give heed, my heart, lift up thine eyes	85
Give, Lord, this consummation	520
Give me a faithful heart	403
Give me to trust in Thee	433
Give peace, Lord, in our time	580
Give to thy parents honor due	287
Give to Thy Word impressive pow'r	235
Give tongues of fire and hearts of love	504
Give unto God my heart's affection	404
Give us this day our daily bread	458
Give us Thy Spirit, peace afford	321
Glorified, I shall anew	206
Glorious Lord, Thyself impart	16
Glory and praise, still onward reaching	243
Glory be to God the Father	218
Glory be to Him who loved us	244
Glory, blessing, praise eternal	244
Glory to God and praise and love	360
Glory to God in highest heaven	85
Glory to God the Father, Son	3
Glory to God the Father, Son	245
Glory to our bounteous King	570
Glory to th' almighty Father	257
Glory to the Father	654
Glory to the King of angels	244
Go, then, earthly fame and treasure	423
God from eternity hath willed	504
God grant that I may, of His infinite love	415
God Himself is present: Hear the harps resounding	4
God, I thank Thee, in Thy keeping	549
God is my Comfort and my Trust	517
God knows full well when times of gladness	518
God knows what must be done to save me	529
God of God, the One-begotten	471
God of grace and love and blessing	640
God oft gives me days of gladness	523
God shall be my Reliance	393
God shall do my advising	548
God, the All-merciful, earth hath forsaken	582
God the Almighty, the great Creator	26
God, the omnipotent, mighty Avenger	582
God these commandments gave therein	287
God would not have the sinner die	245
God's grace alone endureth	34

The Handbook to the Lutheran Hymnal [625] 40

	HYMN
God's Son to our graves then takes His way	592
God's Word a treasure is to me	48
Goodness and mercy, all my life	436
Grace all the work shall crown	374
Grace and life eternal	158
Grace divine, be with us still, Hallelujah	86
Grace first contrived the way	374
Grace first inscribed my name	374
Grace led my wand'ring feet	374
Grace taught my soul to pray	374
Gracious Child, we pray Thee, hear us	90
Gracious God, let me awaken	560
Gracious Head, Thy member own	300
Grant honor, truth, and purity	406
Grant, Lord, I pray, Thy grace each day	353
Grant me grace, O blessed Savior	207
Grant me, Lord, Thy Holy Spirit	408
Grant my request, O dearest Friend	197
Grant our hearts in fullest measure	226
Grant that all may seek and find	18
Grant that all we who here today	633
Grant that I may willingly	140
Grant that I only Thee may love	398
Grant that I Thy Passion view	140
Grant that our days, while life shall last	235
Grant that Thy Spirit prompt my praises	21
Grant that Thy Spirit's help	417
Grant that we Thy Word may cherish	640
Grant that we worthily receive	306
Grant that with true and faithful heart	303
Grant them the joy which brightens earthly sorrow	623
Grant, then, O God, where'er men roam	467
Grant Thou me strength to do	395
Grant to little children	654
Grant unto me in tender mercies	545
Grant us grace to see Thee, Lord	134
Grant us hearts, dear Lord, to yield Thee	442
Grant us, Lord, a blessed end, Hallelujah	86
Grant us Thy help till backward they are driven	258
Grant us Thy peace, Lord, through the coming night	47
Grant us Thy peace throughout our earthly life	47
Grant us Thy peace upon our homeward way	47
Grant what I have partaken	316
Great of heart, they know no turning	470
Great the need in ev'ry nation	510
Guard, O God, our faith forever	226
Guard the helpless, seek the strayed	501
Guilt no longer can distress me	77
Guilty, now I pour my moaning	607
Had I no load of sin to bear	108
Hail, eternal Hope on high	191
Hail Him, ye heirs of David's line	339
Hail, hosanna, David's Son!	55
Hail, the heav'nly Prince of Peace	94
Hail the Lord of earth and heaven	193
Hail, Thou all-inviting Savior	129
Hallelujah, angels sing	188
Hallelujahs render	41
Hallow the day which God hath blest	287
Hark! a voice from yonder manger	77
Hark, hark, to the angels all singing in heaven	102
Hark how He groans while nature shakes	176
Hark the cry that peals aloud	174
Hark! the glad celestial hymn	250
Hark, the Herald's voice is crying	61
Hark, those bursts of acclamation	222
Haste, then, on from grace to glory	423
Hasten as a bride to meet Him	305
Hasten, mortals, to adore Him	83
Hath He diadem, as Monarch	513
Hath He marks to lead me to Him	513
Have we trials and temptations	457
He becomes the Lamb that taketh	77
He blotted out with His own blood	163
He breaks the power of canceled sin	360
He brings me to the portal	192

	HYMN
He by Himself hath sworn	46
He canceled my offenses	528
He closed the yawning gates of hell	210
He comes from thickest films of vice	66
He comes the broken heart to bind	66
He comes the pris'ners to release	66
He comes to judge the nations	58
He comes with succor speedy	59
He crowns thy life with love	27
He ever will with patience chide	535
He fills the poor with good	27
He helped His servant Israel	275
He His Church hath firmly founded	461
He is the Hope and saving Light	137
He is thy Treasure, He thy Joy	535
He knows and He approves	414
He knows how oft a Christian weeps	535
He leads me to the place	426
He leaves his heav'nly Father's throne	105
He led to freedom all oppressed	211
He left His radiant throne on high	363
He like a tree shall thrive	414
He lives, all glory to His name	200
He lives and grants me daily breath	200
He lives, my kind, wise, heavenly Friend	200
He lives to bless me with His love	200
He lives to grant me rich supply	200
He lives to silence all my fears	200
He lives triumphant from the grave	200
He nestles at His mother's breast	105
He opens us again the door	105
He rules the world with truth and grace	87
He saw me ruined in the Fall	340
He serves that I a lord may be	105
He shall come down like showers	59
He shows to man His treasure	34
He spake, and straightway the celestial choir	84
He spoke to His beloved Son	387
He that drinks shall live forever	149
He that His saints in this world rules and shields	307
He then ascended into heaven	253
He veils in flesh His pow'r divine	105
He wears no kingly crown	57
He who bore all pain and loss	190
He who craves a precious treasure	305
He who gave for us His life	190
He who Himself all things did make	104
He who hitherto hath fed me	425
He who slumbered in the grave	190
He who thus endureth	74
He whom the sea And wind obey	81
He whose path no records tell	190
He will on you the gifts bestow	85
Hear us, dear Father, when we pray	288
Heartless scoffers did surround Thee	151
Heaven's music chimes the glad days in	424
Heavens, spread the story	41
Heav'n and earth must pass away	35
Help, Lord Jesus, help him nourish	491
Help me as the morn is breaking	549
Help me henceforth, O God of grace	33
Help me now set my house in order	598
Help me speak what's right and good	411
Help me to mend my ways, O Lord	328
Help them to preach the Truth of God	489
Help us, Lord Jesus Christ, for we	287
Help us sincerely to believe	163
Help us that we Thy saving Word	293
Help us Thy holy Law to learn	288
Help us to serve Thee evermore	477
Hence, all earthly treasure	347
Hence, all fear and sadness	347
Henceforth all men shall call me blest	275
Here are we, Redeemer, send us	641
Here as in their due succession	632
Here, beneath a peaceful sway	584
Here children have been born anew	639
Here, gracious God, do Thou	465
Here I will stand beside Thee	172
Here in baptismal water pure	634
Here in due and solemn order	632
Here in the body pent	616

	HYMN
Here in the dark and sorr'wing day	634
Here may the blind and hungry come	284
Here may the list'ning throng	638
Here may Thy Gospel, pure and mild	578
Here may we gain from heav'n	465
Here our souls, by Jesus sated	282
Here see the Bread of Life; see waters flowing	531
Here springs of sacred pleasures rise	281
Here springs of consolation rise	284
Here stands the font before our eyes	467
Here the Redeemer's welcome voice	284
Here the true Paschal Lamb we see	195
Here Thy praise is gladly chanted	1
Here vouchsafe to all Thy servants	466
Here we find the dawn of heaven	155
Here we have a firm foundation	153
Here we rest in wonder, viewing	155
Here when the marriage vows were made	639
Here, when Thy messengers proclaim	635
Here, when Thy people seek Thy face	635
Hide not from me, I ask of Thee	383
Him Thou hast unto all set forth	137
His body and His blood I've taken	598
His Father-heart is yearning	112
His infant body now	117
His love, what human tho't can reach	363
His loving bosom still remains	386
His mercy is on all who fear	275
His name shall be the Prince of Peace	106
His oath, His covenant, and blood	370
His purposes will ripen fast	514
His righteous government and power	106
His sov'reign pow'r, without our aid	13
His Spirit in me dwelleth	528
His wisdom never plans in vain	535
His wondrous works and ways	27
His Word proclaims, and we believe	163
Hither come, ye heavy-hearted	77
Hither come, ye poor and wretched	77
Hold Thou Thy cross before my closing eyes	552
Holy and blessed Three	508
Holy Father, holy Son	250
Holy Ghost, be Thou our Stay	247
Holy Ghost, Thine eyes forever	560
Holy Ghost, with joy divine	234
Holy Ghost, with pow'r divine	234
Holy, holy, holy! All the saints adore Thee	246
Holy, holy, holy! Lord God Almighty	246
Holy, holy, holy! Tho' the darkness hide Thee	246
Holy Jesus, every day	127
Holy Spirit, all divine	234
Holy Spirit, let Thy teaching	643
Holy Spirit, strong and mighty	226
Honor, glory, might, dominion	60
Hopeful, cheerful, and undaunted	523
"Hosanna in the highest!"	161
Hosanna in the highest strains	10
Hosanna to th' anointed King	10
How blessed are the eyes	487
How changed, alas, are truths divine	579
How charming is their voice	487
How dull are all the pow'rs of sense	304
How glorious is that righteousness	392
How God at our transgression	171
How happy are the ears	487
How holy is this Sacrament	308
How silently, how silently	647
How were Mary's tho'ts devoted	366
How will my heart endure	610
How will they bear to stand	414
Human reason, though it ponder	305
Hymns of praise, then, let us sing, Alleluia	199
I, a sinner, come to Thee	324
I am a branch in Thee, the Vine	594
I am content! Lord, draw me unto Thee	196
I am content! My Jesus is my Head	196
I am content! My Jesus is my Light	196
I am content! My Jesus is my Lord	196

	HYMN
I am flesh and must return	206
I am pure, in Thee believing	77
I am the Light, I light the way	421
I am thy God and Lord alone	287
I am trusting Thee for cleansing	428
I am trusting Thee for pardon	428
I am trusting Thee for power	428
I am trusting Thee, Lord Jesus	428
I am trusting Thee to guide me	428
I bless the Christ of God	389
I build on this foundation	528
I cannot live without Thy light	325
I caused Thy grief and sighing	171
I come to Thee with sin and grief	330
I could but grieve Thee, Lord	417
I cried to Him in time of need	19
I fear no foe, with Thee at hand to bless	552
I have the will, the power is weak	108
I have Thy Word, Christ Jesus, Lord	353
I know not how to praise	322
I know of a morning bright and fair	592
I know of a peaceful eventide	592
I know that often when I strive	379
I know that sin and guilt combine	379
I know that, though in doing good	379
I know the evil I have done	561
I lay in fetters, groaning	58
I lay my wants on Jesus	652
I long to be like Jesus	652
I love Thy Church, O God	462
I merit not Thy favor, Lord	312
I need Thy presence every passing hour	552
I never will forget this crying	385
I pass thro' trials all the way	413
I praise and thank Thee, Lord, my God	33
I praise Thee, Savior, whose compassion	243
I rest my soul on Jesus	652
I smite upon my troubled breast	323
I spent long years for thee	405
I suffered much for thee	405
I teach you how to shun and flee	421
I thank Thee, Jesus, Sun from heaven	399
I through Him am reconciled	2
I trust in Him with all my heart	375
I walk with angels all the way	413
I walk with Jesus all the way	413
I will praise Thy great compassion	384
I would not live alway; no, welcome the tomb	588
I would not live alway; thus fettered by sin	588
I would trust in Thy protecting	333
If dangers gather round	395
If death my portion be	526
If e'er I go astray	426
If I ask Him to receive me	513
If I find Him, if I follow	513
If I still hold closely to Him	513
If in mercy Thou wilt spare	118
If life be long, I will be glad	527
If my sins give me alarm	140
If on earth my days He lengthen	425
If our blessed Lord and Maker	77
If our soul can find no comfort	226
If pain and woe must follow sin	317
If some poor wand'ring child of Thine	551
If the way be drear	410
If the world my heart entices	144
If they have given Him their heart	624
If Thou a longer life	395
If thou be sick, if death draw near	245
If Thou callest to the cross	118
If Thou, merciful Redeemer	498
If thy heart this truth professes	311
If thy task be thus begun	540
If worn with pain, disease, or grief	515
If you cannot be a watchman	496
If you cannot speak like angels	496
I'll stand upon this firm foundation	385
I'll think upon Thy mercy without ceasing	143
Immortal honor, endless fame	236
Immortal honor to the Son	248
In all the strife of mortal life	437
In consecrated wine and bread	304

[627]

	HYMN
In death's dark vale I fear no ill	431
In every new distress	636
In every season, every place	7
In every time of need	170
In ev'ry condition, — in sickness, in health	427
In faith, Lord, let me serve Thee	381
In festal spirit, song, and word	211
In full accord with God's own Word	253
In Him accepted I shall be	561
In Him alone my trust I place	379
In Him eternal might and power	100
In Him I have salvation's way discovered	432
In love our guilt He undertakes	115
In mansions fair and spacious	67
In many an hour when fear and dread	110
In my heart I find ascending	305
In our joys and in our sorrows	270
In our weakness and distress	121
In peopled vale, in lonely glen	499
In perfect love He dies	170
In scenes exalted or depressed	119
In sickness, sorrow, want, or care	439
In sinful wrath thou shalt not kill	287
In suffering be Thy love my peace	349
In that last hour, oh, grant me	597
In the arms of her who bore Him	139
In the furnace God may prove thee	474
In the heavenly country bright	127
In the midst of death's dark vale	590
In the midst of utter woe	590
In Thee all fullness dwelleth	352
In Thee I place my trust	435
In these last days of sore distress	292
In Thine arms I rest me	347
In Thine own appointed way	18
In this world of pain and care	595
In woe we often languish	122
In yonder home doth flourish	528
In yonder home shall never	67
In Zion God is known	636
Increase my faith, dear Savior	381
Inscribed upon that cross we see	178
Into Christ baptized	229
Into temptation lead us not	458
Isaiah hath foretold It	645
It bears to all the tidings glad	297
It brings the Savior's righteousness	297
It floateth like a banner	294
It is a well-worn path-way	586
It is not death to bear	602
It is not death to close	602
It is not death to fling	602
It is that mercy never ending	385
It is the pow'r of God to save	297
It is Thy work alone	417
It makes the coward spirit brave	178
It makes the wounded spirit whole	364
It sets the Lamb before our eyes	297
It shows to man his wand'ring ways	285
It sweetly cheers our drooping hearts	285
It was a false, misleading dream	377
It was a strange and dreadful strife	195
Its light, descending from above	285
Its light of holiness imparts	295
I've met with storms and danger	586
Jacob's Star in all its splendor	90
Jerusalem, my happy home	618
Joy of the desolate, Light of the straying	531
Joy to the earth, the Savior reigns	87
Judge not the Lord by feeble sense	514
Just as I am and waiting not	388
Just as I am, poor, wretched, blind	388
Just as I am, Thou wilt receive	388
Just as I am, though tossed about	388
Just as I am; Thy love unknown	388
Jesus, all Thy children cherish	444
Jesus, be endless praise to Thee	371
Jesus, be with me and direct me	120
Jesus, Bread of Life, I pray Thee	305
Jesus, by Thy presentation	139
Jesus calls us; by Thy mercies	270
Jesus calls us from the worship	270

	HYMN
Jesus Christ, be Thou our Stay	247
Jesus comes again in mercy	56
Jesus comes in joy and sorrow	56
Jesus comes on clouds triumphant	56
Jesus comes to hearts rejoicing	56
Jesus, constant be my praises	348
Jesus for my sake descended	601
Jesus, give the weary	654
Jesus gives us pure affections	358
Jesus gives us true repentance	358
Jesus, guard and guide Thy members	96
Jesus, hail, enthroned in glory	367
Jesus, hail! Thy glory brightens	221
Jesus, I die to Thee	591
Jesus is the name prevailing	116
Jesus is the name we treasure	116
Jesus is worthy to receive	344
Jesus, lead Thou on	410
Jesus lives! and now is death	201
Jesus lives! and thus, my soul	188
Jesus lives! For He died	201
Jesus lives! I know full well	201
Jesus lives! Let all rejoice	188
Jesus lives! To Him my heart	188
Jesus lives! To Him the throne	201
Jesus lives! Why weepest Thou	188
Jesus, may our hearts be burning	145
Jesus, my Redeemer, lives	206
Jesus, my Shepherd, Guardian, Friend	364
Jesus! Name decreed of old	114
Jesus! Name of mercy mild	114
Jesus! Name of priceless worth	114
Jesus! Name of wondrous love	114
Jesus only can impart	342
Jesus! Only name that's given	114
Jesus, our only Joy be Thou	350
Jesus, Savior, let Thy presence	643
Jesus, Savior, wash away	653
Jesus sinners doth receive	324
Jesus, Sun of Life, my Splendor	305
Jesus, the Lord, the mighty God	141
Jesus! — the name that charms our fears	360
Jesus the Sacrifice became	141
Jesus, the Virgin's Son	274
Jesus, Thou Friend Divine	462
Jesus, Thou Prince of Life	602
Jesus, Thy feast we celebrate	164
Keep grief, if this may be, away	546
Keep our haughty passions bound	538
Keep Satan's fury far from me	561
Keep Thou my soul today	542
Keep us faithful, keep us pure	121
Kindly to our worship bow	111
King of Glory, enter in	91
King of Glory, reign forever	221
King of majesty tremendous	607
Kingdoms wide that sit in darkness	505
Kings shall bow down before Him	59
Knowing as I am known	616
Knowing Thee and Thy salvation	498
Lamb of God, I do implore Thee	357
Laugh to scorn the gloomy grave	206
Lay on the sick Thy healing hand	63
Lead me, and forsake me never	549
Leave all to His direction	520
Left to ourselves, we shall but stray	235
Let all creation join in one	344
Let all our thoughts be winging	214
Let all thy converse be sincere	536
Let angels guard our sleeping hours	563
Let but my fainting heart be blest	418
Let each day begin with prayer	540
Let every creature rise and bring	511
Let every kindred, every tribe	339
Let every thought and work and word	336
Let faith and love and duty join	248
Let good or ill befall	435
Let me be Thine forever	89
Let me depart this life	395
Let me earnestly endeavor	348
Let me in my arms receive Thee	77
Let me live to praise Thee ever	408

Hymn	HYMN
Let me never, Lord, forsake Thee	401
Let me not doubt, but trust in Thee	377
Let me see my Savior's face	234
Let men with their united voice	248
Let mercy cause me to be willing	385
Let my near and dear ones be	653
Let none hear you idly saying	496
"Let not Satan make thee craven	268
Let not the foe of Christ and man	49
Let not the world's deceitful cares	49
Let not Thine angel leave me	548
Let our prayers each morn prevail	537
Let our rulers ever be	566
Let shouts of gladness rise	57
Let the night of my transgression	549
Let the people praise Thee, Lord!	20
Let the world despise and leave me	423
"Let them approach," He cries	302
Let Thy grace, like morning dew	539
Let Thy holy Word instruct them	627
Let to mortals all be given	510
Let us also die with Jesus	409
Let us consider rightly	112
Let us gladly live with Jesus	409
Let us learn the wondrous story	83
Let us, O Lord, be faithful	138
Let us suffer here with Jesus	409
Lift up the voice and strike the string	343
Lift up thine eyes in wonder	126
Lift up your hearts in praise to God	581
Lift we, then, our voices	158
Light us to those heavenly spheres	539
Lighten Thou our darkness	229
Like a mighty army	658
Like countless grains of sand	542
Like flowery fields the nations stand	123
Like Him, thro' scenes of deep distress	440
Like Samson, Christ great strength employed	211
Likewise to Thee our prayers ascend	550
Listen to the wondrous story	83
Lives again our glorious King	193
Living or dying, Lord	591
Lo, heav'n's doors lift up, revealing	271
Lo, I confess my sins	310
Lo, our sins on Thee we cast	121
Lo, stained with blood	167
Lo, th' apostles' holy train	250
Lo, the book, exactly worded	607
Lo, the Lamb, so long expected	60
Lo, thousands to their endless home	478
Lo, what the Word in times of old	290
Long as we tarry here below	581
Look unto Him, ye nations; own	360
Loose the souls long prisoned	202
Lord, bless and keep Thou me as Thine	541
Lord, by love and mercy driven	305
Lord, by the stripes which wounded Thee	210
Lord, circumcise our heart, we pray	115
Lord, for Thee I ever sigh	356
Lord, give Thy angels ev'ry day	256
Lord, give us such a faith as this	396
Lord God, our King on heaven's throne	238
Lord, grant that we who sow to Thee	567
Lord, grant us all aright to learn	291
Lord, here on earth Thou seemest	138
Lord, hide my soul securely	407
Lord Holy Ghost, our thanks to Thee	124
Lord, how shall I thank Thee rightly	96
Lord, how Thy wonders are displayed	43
Lord, I believe Thy precious blood	371
Lord, I believe were sinners more	371
Lord, I believe what Thou hast said	306
Lord, I come to Thee for rest	459
Lord, I my vows to Thee renew	536
Lord, I will tell, while I am living	30
Lord, if we angered Thee today	563
Lord, in loving contemplation	155
Lord, in Thy nail-prints let me read	148
Lord Jesus, be our constant Guide	478
Lord Jesus Christ, guide us this day	547
Lord Jesus Christ, keep me prepared and waking	432
Lord Jesus Christ, our thanks to Thee	124

Hymn	HYMN
Lord Jesus Christ, Thy pow'r make known	261
Lord Jesus Christ, we humbly pray	314
Lord Jesus, help, Thy Church uphold	292
Lord Jesus, my Salvation	334
Lord Jesus, reign in us, we pray	106
Lord Jesus, this I ask of Thee	517
Lord Jesus, who dost love me	554
Lord, let at last Thine angels come	429
Lord, let our earnest prayer be heard	494
Lord, my God, I come before Thee	1
Lord, my Shepherd, take me to Thee	523
Lord, no one has ever	42
Lord of Glory, who hast bought us	442
Lord of Harvest, let there be	507
Lord of the nations, thus to Thee	578
Lord, on that day, that wrathful day	612
Lord, on Thee our souls depend	18
Lord, put to shame Thy foes who breathe defiance	269
Lord, should fear and anguish roll	174
Lord, show us still that Thou art good	304
Lord, that in death I sleep not	555
Lord, Thee I seek, I merit naught	317
Lord, there is mercy now	327
Lord, Thou canst help when earthly armor faileth	258
Lord, Thy mercy will not leave me	384
Lord, Thy words are waters living	296
Lord, visit Thou our souls	133
Lord, when my pow'rs are failing	597
Lord, when we fall and sin doth stain	288
Lord, write my name, I pray Thee	407
Love caused Thy incarnation	58
Love's redeeming work is done	193
Loving Savior, I will solely	560
Low I kneel with heart-submission	607
Make me see Thy great distress	140
Make me to walk in Thy commands	416
Make them apostles, heralds of Thy Cross	483
Make Thou to us the Father known	233
Make unto them His glories known	629
Make ye straight what long was crooked	61
Maker and Redeemer	202
Maker of all things, all Thy creatures praise Thee	240
Man may trouble and distress me	423
Manifest at Jordan's stream	134
Manifest in making whole	134
Many spend their lives in fretting	425
Marching with Thy cross, their banner	471
May every heart confess Thy name	361
May every plan and undertaking	120
May ev'ry mountain height	575
May evil fancies flee away before us	556
May faith each meek petition fill	22
May God bestow on us His grace and favor	313
May God root out all heresy	260
May He adorn with precious peace	581
May He teach us to fulfil	51
May our hearts to Thee incline	181
May our zeal to help the heathen	498
May the dear blood once shed for me	336
May the joy of Thy salvation	643
May Thy fervent love destroy	539
May Thy Gospel's joyful sound	11
May Thy life and death supply	186
May Thy rich grace impart	394
May we all Thy loved ones be	182
May we in faith its tidings learn	297
May we in our guilt and shame	181
May we in Thy sorrows share	182
May we thirst Thy love to know	184
May we Thy bounties thus	441
Mean are all off'rings we can make	440
Men mock and taunt and jeer Thee	172
Mercies multiplied each hour	11
Mid the homes of want and woe	501
Mid toil and tribulation	473
Mighty Victor, reign forever	209
Mingled with th'eternal past	111

	HYMN
More radiant there than sun e'er shone in brightness	432
Most heartily I trust in Thee	353
Much he asked in loving wonder	271
Must I be carried to the skies	445
My Advocate appears	220
My burden in Thy Passion	172
My Comforter, give pow'r	335
My course is run. My Jesus took for me	599
My course is run. Now I am free from need	599
My course is run. Praise God, my course is run	599
My end to ponder teach me ever	598
My faith would lay her hand	156
My faithful God, Thou failest never	298
My Father's home of light	405
My Father's house on high	616
My favored soul shall meekly learn	530
My God and Shield, now let Thy pow'r	524
My God desires the soul's salvation	529
My God hath all things in His keeping	529
My God, Thou here hast led me	316
My gracious Master and my God	360
My guilt, O Father, Thou hast laid	375
My heart abounds in lowliness	421
My heart for joy is springing	528
My heart for very joy doth leap	85
My heart has now become Thy dwelling	315
My heart sinks at the journey's length	148
My heart within is glowing	89
My heart's Delight, My Crown most bright	383
My hosannas and my palms	55
My Jesus, as Thou wilt	420
My Jesus is my Splendor	528
My knowledge of that life is small	527
My Lord art Thou, And for me now	266
My loved ones, rest securely	554
My loving Father, Thou dost take me	298
My Maker, strengthen Thou my heart	541
My manifold transgression	152
My many sins blot out forever	598
My own good works availed me naught	387
My Savior, be Thou near me	172
My Savior, I behold Thee	138
My Savior, wash me clean	335
My Shepherd, now receive me	172
My sins assail me sore	526
My sins, dear Lord, disturb me sore	594
My sins, O Lord, against me rise	319
My soul and body keep from harm	541
My soul He doth restore again	436
My soul looks back to see	156
My soul, no more attempt to draw	289
My soul to Thee alone	433
My soul's best Friend, how well contented	362
My spirit I commend to Thee	594
My table Thou hast furnished	436
My walk is heavenward all the way	413
My Wisdom and my Guide	433
My woes are nearly over	597
Myself I cannot save	433
Nations afar, in ign'rance deep	132
Naught have I, O Christ, to offer	366
Naught, naught, can now condemn me	528
Naught shall my soul from Jesus sever	598
Nay, too closely am I bound	206
Nearer is my soul's salvation	606
Ne'er think the vict'ry won	449
Never, from Thy pasture roving	631
New graces ever gaining	9
No angel and no gladness	528
No longer Thomas then denied	208
No more let sins and sorrows grow	87
No pain that we can share	170
No work is left undone	170
Nor alms nor deeds that I have done	323
Nor any creature ever	372
Nor gold nor gems could buy our peace	141
Nor prayer is made by man alone	454
Nor think amid the fiery trial	518
Nor voice can sing, nor heart can frame	350

	HYMN
Nor will I my Jesus leave	365
Not a brief glance I beg, a passing word	552
Not by human flesh and blood	95
Not for earth's vain joys I crave	365
Not one He will or can forsake	103
Not so th'ungodly race	414
Not the labors of my hands	376
Not we, but the Lord is our Maker, our God	44
Not what I feel or do	389
Nothing in my hand I bring	376
Now art Thou here, Thou Ever-blest	108
Now, ere day fadeth quite	101
Now from Thy cheeks has vanished	172
Now He bids us tell abroad	190
Now hell, its prince, the devil	192
Now henceforth must I put my trust	353
Now I will cling forever	192
Now into Thy heart we pour	300
Now is the time! How fast the moments fly	509
Now keep us, holy Savior	32
Now let all the heav'ns adore Thee	609
Now let the heav'ns be joyful	205
Now let Thine ear attend	638
Now let us all with gladsome cheer	85
Now lettest Thou Thy guest depart	308
Now my conscience is at peace	324
Now my evening praise I give	653
Now, O Lord, fulfil Thy pleasure	502
Now our heav'nly Aaron enters	218
Now richly to my waiting heart	343
Now the Blessing cheers our heart	45
Now the darkness gathers	654
Now they reign in heavenly glory	471
Now, these little ones receiving	631
Now Thou speakest, — hear we trembling	641
Now thro' His Son doth shine	92
Now 'tis come, and faith espies Thee	271
Now to God, the soul's Creator	641
Now to My Father I depart	387
Now to the contrite thief He cries	177
Now we may gather with our King	467
Now with the humble voice of prayer	434
O all-embracing Mercy	279
O all ye pow'rs that He implanted	30
O blessed ministry	485
O blest communion, fellowship divine	463
O blest shall be	167
O blest the land, the city blest	73
O Bread of Heav'n, my soul's Delight	312
O Bringer of salvation	352
O Christ, do Thou my soul prepare	618
O Christ, who diedst and yet dost live	604
O come, come all, ye weak and weary	615
O Comforter of priceless worth	261
O Cross, our one reliance, hail	168
O day of light and life and grace	12
O depth of love, to me revealing	385
O faithful child of heaven	520
O Father dear in heaven	112
O Father, deign Thou, I beseech Thee	30
O Father, draw me to my Savior	21
O Father, God of Love	417
O Father, whence all blessings come	438
O friends, in gladness let us sing	475
O gentle Dew, from heaven now fall	235
O God, forsake me not!	402
O God, how sin's dread works abound	292
O God, my sin indeed is great	328
O God of Mercy, hear us	122
O gracious Lord, direct us	544
O Ground of faith	167
O happy day and yet far happier hour	619
O happy home where Thou art not forgotten	626
O happy home where two, in heart united	626
O happy home whose little ones are given	626
O higher than the cherubim	475
O highest joy by mortals won	343
O holy Child of Bethlehem	647
O Holy Ghost, Thou precious Gift	237
O Holy Spirit, faithful Friend	600

[630]

	HYMN		HYMN
O Holy Trinity	335	O'er all the straight and narrow way	285
O home of fadeless splendor	605	O'er every foe victorious	59
O Hope of ev'ry contrite heart	350	O'er the blest mercy-seat	403
O Israel's Guardian, hear me	544	Of death I am no more afraid	142
O Jerusalem, how glorious	601	Of His deliv'rance I will boast	29
O Jesus blest	167	Oft as earth exulting	158
O Jesus Christ, do not delay	611	Oft as returns the day of rest	634
O Jesus Christ, my Lord	526	Oft as the precious seed is sown	49
O Jesus Christ, Thou Crucified	177	Oft have our fathers told	636
O Jesus Christ, Thou Lamb of God	600	Often to Marah's brink	422
O Jesus Christ, Thou only Son	237	Oh, bless Thy Word to all the young	337
O Jesus, draw near my dying bed	592	Oh, blessed is that land of God	573
O Jesus, Lamb of God, alone	330	Oh, blest is each believing guest	163
O Jesus, let Thy precious blood	318	Oh, blest that house where faith ye find	625
O Jesus, Light of all below	361	Oh, blest the parents who give heed	625
O Jesus, precious Sun of gladness	88	Oh, come and reign o'er every land	64
O Jesus, who my debt didst pay	611	Oh, come, Thou Day-spring from on high	62
O King of Glory, come	638	Oh, come, Thou Key of David, come	62
O Lord Christ, our Savior dear	97	Oh, come, Thou Rod of Jesse, free	62
O Lord, in mercy stay my heart	319	Oh, create a heart in me	411
O Lord Jesus, grant that we	595	Oh, draw me, Savior, e'er to Thee	349
O Lord, let this Thy little flock	477	Oh, draw us ever unto Thee	386
O Lord, my God, to Thee I pray	318	Oh, enter His gates with thanksgiving and praise	44
O Lord, of this and all our store	569	Oh, enter, let me know Thee	228
O Lord, remember us who bear	559	Oh, enter, then, His gates with praise	14
O Lord, the Virgin-born, to Thee	115	Oh, gently call those gone astray	512
O Lord, the Virgin-born, to Thee	273	Oh, grant, dear Lord, this grace to me	216
O Lord, we bless Thy gracious heart	321	Oh, grant that each of us	46
O Lord, we come before Thy face	624	Oh, grant that I in manner worthy	315
O Love, how cheering is Thy ray	349	Oh, grant that in Thy holy Word	292
O Love, who ere life's earliest dawn	397	Oh, grant that nothing in my soul	349
O Love, who lovest me for aye	397	Oh, grant the consummation	352
O Love, who once in time wast slain	397	Oh, grant, Thou Lord of Love	272
O Love, who once shalt bid me rise	397	Oh, grant us peace and gladness	544
O Love, who thus hast bound me fast	397	Oh, grant us so to use Thy grace	332
O lovely attitude! He stands	650	Oh, grant us thitherward to tend	212
O measureless Might	17	Oh, guard our shores from ev'ry foe	578
O mighty King, no time can dim Thy glory	143	Oh, guide and lead me, Lord	417
O mighty Rock, O Source of Life	235	Oh, happy souls who pray	480
O Most High, we praise Thee	42	Oh, haste to help ere we are lost	494
O my God, I now commend me	549	Oh, hearts are bruised and dead	441
O my God, my Rock and Tower	144	Oh, help us to forsake all sin	125
O my Savior, help afford	342	Oh, how blest it is to know	324
O my soul, rejoicing	41	Oh, joy to know that Thou, my Friend	343
O one, O only mansion	614	Oh, joyful be the livelong day	550
O perfect Life, be Thou their full assurance	623	Oh, keep me watchful, then, and humble	399
O risen Christ, ascended Lord	212	Oh, keep us in Thy Word, we pray	292
O Savior, Child of Mary	645	Oh, let me loathe all sin forever	315
O Savior Christ, our woes dispel	557	Oh, let me never speak	395
O Savior Christ, Thou, too, art man	557	Oh, let the heavenly Stranger in	650
O Savior, Guest most bounteous	621	Oh, let the people praise Thy worth	500
O Savior, with protecting care	70	Oh, let them spread Thy name	488
O sinful man	167	Oh, let Thy holy wounds for me	148
O Soul, attend thou and behold	150	Oh, let thy life be given	405
O Soul, I take upon Me now	150	Oh, let Thy suff'rings give me power	148
O Source of uncreated light	236	Oh, let us love Thy house	580
O sorrow dread	167	Oh, magnify the Lord with me	29
O Spirit of the Father	621	Oh, make but trial of His love	29
O Spirit of the Lord, prepare	504	Oh, make the deaf to hear Thy Word	512
O sweet and blessed country	448	Oh, make Thy Church, dear Savior	294
O sweet and blessed country	605	Oh, may He soon to every nation	65
O sweet and blessed country	613	Oh, may I come where strife and grief are ended	432
O sweet and blessed country	614	Oh, may I daily, hourly, strive	24
O Thou by whom we come to God	454	Oh, may I never fail	310
O Thou Fount of blessing	4	Oh, may my soul on Thee repose	558
O Thou Incarnate Word	241	Oh, may the sweet, the blissful theme	363
O Thou Long-expected, weary	606	Oh, may these heavenly pages be	284
O Thou Lord of my salvation	419	Oh, may this bounteous God	36
O Thou Physician blest	322	Oh, may Thy love inspire my tongue	325
O Thou who dost not slumber	122	Oh, may Thy pastors faithful be	493
O Tree of beauty, Tree of light	168	Oh, may Thy people faithful be	493
O Trinity in Unity	332	Oh, may Thy soldiers, faithful, true, and bold	463
O Triune God, we humbly pray	299	Oh, may Thy Spirit gently draw	303
O wondrous joy That God most high	107	Oh, may we all hear when our Shepherd doth call	415
O wondrous Love, to bleed and die	456	Oh, may we keep and ponder in our mind	84
O wondrous love, whose depth no heart hath sounded	143	Oh, may we ne'er with thankless heart	567
O ye heights of heav'n, adore Him	98	Oh, may we who mercy need	180
O Zion's Daughter, rise	68	Oh, praise Him, for He never	393
O Zion, hail! Bright city, now unfold	619	Oh, rich the gifts Thou bringest	69
Obey your Lord and let His truth	630	Oh, spread Thy covering wings around	434
O'er a faithless, fallen world	501		

[631]

	HYMN
Oh, teach me, Lord, to love Thee truly	399
Oh, teach them with all diligence	629
Oh, tell of His might	17
Oh, that birth forever blessed	98
Oh, that is a morning dear to me	592
Oh, that, near the cross abiding	155
Oh, that we the throng of the ransomed may swell	415
Oh, that with yonder sacred throng	339
Oh, the height of Jesus' love	342
Oh, the joy beyond expressing	90
Oh, then, draw away your hearts	206
Oh, then rejoice that thro' His Son	103
Oh, then what raptured greetings	476
Oh, then, with hymns of praise	465
Oh, turn us, turn us, mighty Lord	579
Oh, watch and fight and pray	449
Oh, well for me that, strengthened	316
Oh, what a marv'lous off'ring	152
Oh, what blessing to be near Thee	296
Oh, what fear man's bosom rendeth	607
Oh, when, thou city of my God	618
Oh, where is thy sting, Death? we fear thee no more	198
Oh, where shall joy be found	92
On Christ, by faith, I fain would live	608
On Christ, the true Bread, let us feed	550
On Him place thy reliance	520
On that first morning of the week	208
On the third morn He rose again	210
On Thee at the Creation	9
On Thee each moment we depend	43
On Thee we humbly wait	488
On this most holy day of days	208
On those who now before Thee kneel	620
On our fields of grass and grain	566
On whose dear arms, so widely flung	168
Once did the skies before Thee bow	80
Once far off, but now invited	129
Once in the blest baptismal waters	598
Once more 'tis eventide, and we	557
Once on the dreary mountain	32
"Once," she mourns, "He promised plainly	268
One army of the living God	478
One bread, one cup, one body, we	314
One family, we dwell in Him	478
One the light of God's own presence	481
One the strain the lips of thousands	481
One there is for whom I'm living	348
Onward, then! For naught despairing	461
Onward, then, ye faithful	658
Onward, therefore, pilgrim brothers	481
Open now the crystal fountain	54
Or if on joyful wing	533
Order my footsteps by Thy Word	416
Other refuge have I none	345
Our broken spirit pitying see	22
Our daily bread supply	455
Our deepest need dost Thou supply	569
Our faithful God, we cry to Thee	124
Our Father, rich in blessing	67
Our fathers' sins were manifold	583
Our glad hosannas, Prince of Peace	66
Our God hath well defended	112
Our God, our Help in ages past	123
Our hearts be pure from evil	205
Our Hope and Expectation	72
Our lips shall tell them to our sons	629
Our path in all things order	228
Our place He is preparing	214
Our poor human form He took	86
Our ruin God hath not intended	385
Our sleep be pure from sinful stain	559
Our trembling hearts cleave to Thy Word	314
Our vows, our prayers, we now present	434
Out of the deep I cry	327
Out of the deep of fear	327
Paschal Lamb, by God appointed	367
Patiently I wait Thy Day	356
Patriarch and holy prophet	471
Patriarchs of sacred story	601

	HYMN
Peace in our hearts, our evil thoughts assuaging	258
Peace on earth, good will from heaven	83
Peace, prosperity, and health	572
Penitent sinners, for mercy crying	26
People and realms of ev'ry tongue	511
Perverse and foolish oft I strayed	431
Pilgrims here on earth and strangers	553
Pillar of fire, thro' watches dark	291
Plenteous grace with Thee is found	345
Plenteous of grace, descend from high	236
Poor though I be, despised, forgot	534
Pour down Thy grace in cheering streams	546
Praise and honor to the Father	466
Praise God, from whom all blessings flow	536
Praise God, from whom all blessings flow	558
Praise God the Father and the Son	331
Praise Him for our harvest store	570
Praise Him that He gave the rain	570
Praise Him that He made the sun	570
Praise, O mankind, now the name so holy	26
Praise the Father, who from heaven	311
Praise the God of all creation	37
Praise to God the Father sing	95
Praise to the Lord! Oh, let all that is in me adore Him	39
Praise to the Lord, who doth prosper thy work and defend thee	39
Praise to the Lord, who hath fearfully, wondrously made thee	39
Praise to the Lord, who o'er all things so wondrously reigneth	39
Praise to Thee, O Master Builder	632
Praise we the Father and the Son	233
Prayer is the burden of a sigh	454
Prayer is the Christian's vital breath	454
Prayer is the contrite sinner's voice	454
Prayer is the simplest form of speech	454
Precious Jesus, I beseech Thee	296
Prepare my heart, Lord Jesus	75
Prepare the way before Him	75
Preserve in wave and tempest	264
Preserve, O Lord, Thine honor	264
Preserve, O Lord, Thy children	264
Preserve, O Lord, Thy Zion	264
Preserve this ministry	485
Preserve Thy little flock in peace	265
Preserve Thy Word and preaching	264
Prince and Author of salvation	139
Prompt us, Lord, to come before Him	226
Prophesied in days of old, Hallelujah	86
Prostrate lies the Evil One, Hallelujah	86
Put forth Thy glorious pow'r	642
Raise up, O Lord the Holy Ghost	506
Raised from the dead, we live anew	382
Redeemer, come! I open wide	73
Rejoice, then, ye sad-hearted	58
Remember thou What glory now	81
Renew my will from day to day	418
Renew this wasted flesh of mine	148
Respond, ye souls in endless rest	475
Reveal the sweetness of Thy heaven	598
Revive our drooping faith	225
Richly He feeds us	28
Righteous Judge, for sin's pollution	607
Riven the rock for me	422
Round each habitation hov'ring	469
Run the straight race Thro' God's good grace	447
Run thy race, run thy race	479
Sages, leave your contemplations	136
Saint John the Baptist points to Thee	328
Saints and heroes long before us	472
Saints before the altar bending	136
Saints below, with heart and voice	35
Salvation free By faith in Thee	266
Satan, I defy thee	347
Save us in our soul's distress	185
Savior, for our pardon sue	180

[632]

HYMN		HYMN
Savior, hasten Thine appearing	221	So shall Thy people, with thankful devotion ... 582
Savior, I long to walk	422	So that, might and firmness gaining ... 333
Savior, shine in all Thy glory	498	So they with us may evermore ... 512
Savior, since of Zion's city	469	So when my dying breath ... 616
Savior, who this day didst break	8	So whene'er the signal's given ... 50
Say not: "My sins are far too great	386	Soar we now where Christ has led ... 192
Scarce come to earth, His Father's will	115	Some wait around Him, ready still ... 256
Search not how this takes place	310	Songs of praise awoke the morn ... 35
See a long race thy spacious courts adorn	503	Soon shall end the time of weeping ... 502
See all your sins on Jesus laid	360	Soon will the Lord, my Life, appear ... 608
See barb'rous nations at thy gates attend	503	Soon will the saints in glory meet ... 608
See earth in darkness lying	126	Speak, O God, and I will hear Thee ... 1
See, from His head, His hands, His feet	175	Spirit of Adoption ... 229
See, He lifts His hands above	213	Spirit of Holiness ... 241
See heathen nations bending	497	Spirit of Life, of Love, and Peace ... 412
See how God, for us providing	90	Spirit of Truth and Love ... 508
See, my soul, thy Savior chooses	96	Stand, then, in His great might ... 450
See round Thine ark the hungry billows curling	258	Startled at the solemn warning ... 60
See the blindness of the heathen	498	Steal not; all usury abhor ... 287
See, the heav'n its Lord receives	213	Still for us He intercedes ... 213
See the rivers four that gladden	282	Still He comes within us ... 74
See, the streams of living waters	469	Still let them succor us, still let them fight ... 255
See, to Thee I yield my heart	234	Still let Thy love point out my way ... 349
Seek Him alone, Who did atone	383	Still the greatness of Thy love ... 537
Seek whom ye may To be your stay	383	Still the weary folk are pining ... 576
Send forth Thy heralds, Lord, to call	499	Still we our earthly temples rear ... 467
Send men whose eyes have seen the King	506	Strive, man, to win that glory ... 605
Send some message from Thy Word	18	Strong in the Lord of hosts ... 450
Send them Thy mighty Word to speak	499	Such rest we shall enter ... 603
Shall I not, then, be filled with gladness	243	Sun and moon shall darkened be ... 134
Shall we not yield Him, in costly devotion	128	Sure as Thy truth shall last ... 462
Shall we still dread God's displeasure	77	Sure I must fight if I would reign ... 445
She meekly bowed her head	274	Surely in temples made with hands ... 467
Sheep that from the fold did stray	324	Swift to its close ebbs out life's little day ... 552
Shepherds in the fields abiding	136	
Shine in our hearts, O most precious Light	231	Take my hands and let them move ... 400
		Take my love, my Lord, I pour ... 400
Shine on the darkened and the cold	512	Take my silver and my gold ... 400
Should all the hosts of death	220	Take, my soul, thy full salvation ... 423
Should grief or sickness waste away	418	Take my voice and let me sing ... 400
Should He who Himself imparted	77	Take my will and make it Thine ... 400
Should I with scoffers join	462	Take not Thy saving Word away ... 125
Should some lust or sharp temptation	144	Taught to lisp Thy holy praises ... 627
Should swift death this night o'ertake us	565	Teach me to live that I may dread ... 558
Should this night prove the last for me	561	Teach us in watchfulness and prayer ... 64
Should Thy mercy send me	516	Teach us the lesson Thou hast taught ... 439
Shouldst Thou a strict account demand	330	Teach us to work with all our might ... 550
Show me what I have to do	459	Tell me, ye who hear Him groaning ... 153
Show us, Lord, the path of blessing	226	Tell of our Redeemer's love ... 507
Silent thro' those three dread hours	174	Tell them how the Father's will ... 507
Sin and death may well be groaning	90	Tell them of the Spirit giv'n ... 507
Sin bro't us grief, But Christ relief	107	Ten thousand thousand precious gifts ... 31
Sin's debt, that fearful burden	58	Tender Flower, Mighty Tower ... 82
Since all He comes to ransom	76	Tender Shepherd, never leave them ... 627
Since Christ hath full atonement made	377	Thanks for mercies past receive ... 113
Since Christ, our Lord, is living	217	Thanks to Thee, O Christ victorious ... 207
Since first our life began to be	581	Thanks we give and adoration ... 50
Since He returned to claim His throne	216	That bears unmoved the world's dread frown ... 396
Since, then, neither change nor coldness	25	That, having all things done ... 450
Since Thou hast died, the Pure, the Just	148	That life of truth, those deeds of love ... 132
Since Thou the power of death didst rend	594	That night the Apostles met in fear ... 208
Sing how Jesus came from heaven	221	That so with all our hearts we may ... 522
Sing, pray, and keep His ways unswerving	518	That this is now and ever true ... 163
Sing to the Lord a glorious song	132	That Thou art with us, Lord, proclaim ... 265
Sing we His praises	28	That, when next He comes with glory ... 60
Sing we to our God above, Alleluia	199	That will not murmur nor complain ... 396
Sinners in derision crowned Him	222	The ancient Dragon is their foe ... 254
Sinners Thou forgivest	42	The balm of life, the cure of woe ... 178
Sinners, whose love can ne'er forget	339	The bounties of Thy love ... 426
"So be it," then, I say	526	The call is Thine; be Thou the Way ... 486
So deep are they engraved	322	The captive to release ... 441
So God His own is shielding	122	The chastened peace of sin forgiv'n ... 314
So help us, Jesus, Ground of faith	596	The Church from her dear Master ... 294
So I must hasten forward	586	The Church of Thy dear Son ... 580
So in the last and dreadful Day	70	The Church shall never perish ... 473
So let us keep the festival	195	The cross He bore is life and health ... 219
So may they live to Thee alone	489	The cross! it takes our guilt away ... 178
So may we join Thy name to bless	412	The darkness of my former state ... 378
So may we when our work is done	493	The dawn begins to speed her way ... 550
So now, and till we die	628	The day is now far spent and gone ... 197
So praise with me the Holy One	275	The dead in Christ shall first arise ... 604
So shall no wicked things draw near	256	The doctors of the Law ... 133

[633]

HYMN		HYMN
The dying thief rejoiced to see	157	The Word becomes incarnate ... 76
The Eastern sages, bringing	130	The Word they still shall let remain ... 262
The everlasting Son	68	The words which absolution give ... 331
The evil of my former state	378	The world abideth not ... 430
The Father hath received	259	The world against me rageth ... 192
The Father's house has many a dwelling	615	The world for me has falsely set ... 524
The Father's love shield me this day	541	The world is like a cloud ... 430
The fifth, "My God, My God, O why	177	The world is sorely grieved ... 430
The Foe in triumph shouted	192	The world may hold ... 81
The Foe shall shed My precious blood	387	The world seeks after wealth ... 430
The Foe was triumphant when on Calvary	198	The world seeks to be praised ... 430
The foolish builders, scribe and priest	460	The world that smiled when morn was breaking ... 598
The golden evening brightens in the west	463	The world with wanton pride ... 430
The golden sunshine, vernal air	443	The world's remotest races ... 126
The grace and pow'r of God the Lord	104	Thee may our tongues forever bless ... 361
The graves of all the saints He blest	593	Thee, th' almighty King eternal ... 271
The great veil was torn asunder	169	Thee we own a perfect Savior ... 358
The guest that comes with true intent	163	Thee will I love, my Crown of gladness ... 399
The haughty spirits, Lord, restrain	292	Thee will I love, my Life, my Savior ... 399
The heads that guide endue with skill	633	Their craft and pomp indeed are great ... 265
The heavenly choirs rejoice and raise	104	Their furious wrath, did God permit ... 267
The heavens shall ring with an anthem more grand	415	Then all these wastes, a dreary scene ... 499
The highest place that heav'n affords	219	Then cleansed be every Christian breast ... 63
The holy apostolic band	212	Then come before His presence now ... 19
The holy, meek, unspotted Lamb	371	Then deal with me as seems Thee best ... 317
The hosts of God encamp around	29	Then, for all that wrought my pardon ... 151
The humble heart and lowly	75	Then go thy Lord to meet ... 57
The joy can ne'er be spoken	172	Then hail, ye mighty legions, yea ... 656
The Joy of all who dwell above	219	Then haste, my soul, thy song to raise ... 546
The joys of day are over	555	Then hear, O Lord, my humble cry ... 534
The last, as woe and sufferings end	177	Then here will I and mine today ... 625
The Law discovers guilt and sin	289	Then hither throng With happy song ... 107
The Law is good; but since the Fall	295	Then hope, my feeble spirit ... 520
The Law reveals the guilt of sin	377	Then let the last loud trumpet sound ... 593
The Light of Light Divine	117	Then let us feast this Easter Day ... 195
The load Thou takest on Thee	171	Then let us follow Christ, our Lord ... 421
The Lord forsaketh not His flock	19	Then let us leave this place of rest ... 596
The Lord makes bare His arm	487	Then may death come today, tomorrow ... 598
The Lord, ye know, is God indeed	14	Then may we hope, th' angelic hosts among ... 84
The man who trusts in Him is blest	223	Then, O great God, in years to come ... 110
The martyr first whose eagle eye	452	Then on Him I cast my burden ... 326
The mighty Son of God	93	Then shall I end my sad complaints ... 527
The morning shall awaken	448	Then shall I mount and soar away ... 340
The nation Thou hast blest	575	Then shall thanks and praise ascending ... 282
The noble mother bore a Son	104	Then, should oppressing foes invade ... 579
The pastors of Thy fold	580	Then sing your hosannas and raise your glad voice ... 198
The patriarchs' and prophets' noble train	619	Then stilled are cries and lamentation ... 65
The power of death He brake in twain	211	Then take comfort and rejoice ... 206
The powers ordained by Thee	580	Then these eyes my Lord shall know ... 206
The Prophet gave the sign	274	Then this our comfort is alone ... 522
The radiant sun hath vanished	554	Then to the watchful shepherds it was told ... 84
The rule of day is over	554	Then, when life's last eve shall come ... 111
The saints in prayer appear as one	454	Then, when on earth I breathe no more ... 418
The same Lord Christ of Nazareth	253	Then, when our work is finished here ... 490
The Savior's fourth word was "I thirst,"	177	Then, when the earth was first poised in mid space ... 255
The seas shall waste, the skies in smoke decay	503	Then with my waking thoughts ... 533
The secret of the Lord	133	Then within Thy fold eternal ... 631
The servants Thou hast called	485	Then woe to those who scorned the Lord ... 611
The sev'nfold gifts of grace are Thine	233	Thence He arose, ascending high ... 593
The shepherds heard the story	645	There at my Savior's side ... 660
The sinless Son of God must die in sadness	143	There faith lifts up the tearless eye ... 617
The sixth, with victory was won	177	There fragrant flow'rs immortal bloom ... 617
The Son obeyed His Father's will	387	There I shall dwell forever ... 586
The soul forever lives with God	596	There is a home for weary souls ... 617
"The soul that on Jesus hath leaned for repose	427	There is joy beyond our telling ... 601
The sparrow for her young	480	Three is the throne of David ... 613
The Spirit by His heav'nly breath	232	There let my way appear ... 533
The starry heav'ns Thy rule obey	286	There rest and peace in endless measure ... 615
The stream of years is flowing	122	There shall we see delighted ... 67
The strong He casteth from their seat	275	There shall we thank Thee and adore ... 125
The Sun of Grace for thee is beaming	88	There still is time! The Master's voice still rings ... 509
The things of Christ the Spirit takes	232	There still my thoughts are dwelling ... 586
The toils of day are over	555	There the glorious triumph waits ... 213
The watchers on the mountain	72	There was no spot in me by sin untainted ... 143
The watchmen join their voice	487	There, we shall with Thee remain ... 213
The weak and timid find	57	There's naught that me can sever ... 372
The wealth of earth, of sky, of sea	438	There's not a plant nor flower below ... 43
The whole triumphant host	40	Therefore hasten we to Thee ... 300
The will of God shall be my pleasure	529	
The wiser Magi see from far	131	

	HYMN		HYMN
Therefore I murmur not	660	Thou art the great High Priest	628
Therefore I will forever	152	Thou art the Life; the rending tomb	355
Therefore let us watch and pray	446	Thou art the Truth; Thy Word alone	355
Therefore my hope is in the Lord	329	Thou art the Vine, — oh, nourish	544
Therefore my Intercessor be	611	Thou art the Way, the Truth, the Life	355
Therefore, O Lord, remember me	561	Thou Christian heart	81
Therefore saith God, "I must arise	260	Thou comest in the darksome night	80
Therefore, Thou alone, my Savior	366	Thou didst come that fire to kindle	641
Therefore unto Him we raise	571	Thou didst guide our fathers' footsteps	640
Therefore we in love adoring	116	Thou didst not spare Thine only Son	443
Therefore, when my God doth choose it	601	Thou dost the world's sin take away	238
These are the tokens ye shall mark	85	Thou feedest us from year to year	569
These are Thy ministers, these dost Thou own	255	Thou Fountain whence all wisdom flows	235
These temples of His grace	636	Thou giv'st the Spirit's holy dower	443
These the men by fear unshaken	470	Thou hast borne the smiting only	151
They all in life and death	468	Thou hast died for my transgression	207
They are justified by grace	391	Thou hast no shore, fair ocean	614
They are lights upon the earth	391	Thou hast, O Lord, returned	485
They crown Thy head with thorns, they smite, they scourge Thee	143	Thou hast raised our human nature	218
They gladly go at Thy command	482	Thou hast suffered great affliction	151
They go from strength to strength	480	Thou hast suffered men to bruise Thee	151
They have come from tribulation	471	Thou here wilt find a heart most lowly	315
They neither know nor trace the way	530	Thou highest Comfort in ev'ry need	231
They never rest nor sleep as we	254	Thou holy Fire, Comfort true	224
They shine with light and heav'nly grace	254	Thou holy Light, Guide Divine	224
They stand, those halls of Zion	613	Thou, Holy Spirit, teachest	228
They suffer with their Lord below	219	Thou knowest all my griefs and fears	390
They who His Word do not believe	163	Thou knowest best my needs	542
They who sorrow here and moan	206	Thou, Lord, alone This work hast done	266
They will not blush to own us	67	Thou me to pastures green dost guide	312
Thine forever, Lord of Life!	338	Thou, mighty Father, in Thy Son	343
Thine forever! Oh, how blest	338	Thou, my best and kindest Friend	653
Thine forever! Shepherd, keep	338	Thou my faith increase and quicken	1
Thine forever! Thou our Guide	338	Thou, O Christ, art all I want	345
Thine over all shall be the praise	500	Thou, O Lord, Thyself hast called him	491
Thine shall forever be	455	Thou, of life the Author	202
Things deemed impossible I dare	424	Thou on my head in early youth didst smile	552
Think, good Jesus, my salvation	607	Thou only art the Holy One	238
Thirst for us in mercy still	184	Thou our Paschal Lamb indeed	190
This day the Holy Spirit came	12	Thou sacred Love, grace on us bestow	231
This day the Lord for sinners slain	12	Thou seest my feebleness	433
This earth, with its store	17	Thou shalt hold with faith unshaken	311
This feast is manna, wealth abounding	315	Thou spreadst a table in my sight	431
This Flower whose fragrance tender	645	Thou, the Father's only Son	95
This glorious hope revives	464	Thou wast their Rock, their Fortress, and their Might	463
This holy vow that man can make	620	Thou who didst come to bring	508
This I believe, yea, rather	528	Thou who hast died, Thy vict'ry claim	506
This is a sight that gladdens	192	Though a heavy cross I'm bearing	523
This is He whom Heav'n-taught singers	98	Though alive, I'm dead in sin	411
"This is My body, broke for sin	164	Though all the powers of evil	520
This is the Christ, our God and Lord	85	Though death may threaten with disaster	315
This Lamb is Christ, the soul's great Friend	142	Though destruction walk around us	565
This lamp through all the tedious night	285	Though earth be rent asunder	528
This light, which all thy gloom can banish	88	Though earthly trials should oppress me	385
This love unwearied I pursue	349	Though great our sins and sore our woes	329
This world is loveless, — but above	304	Though I be by sin o'ertaken	207
Tho' dark my path and sad my lot	418	Though I be robbed of every pleasure	385
Tho' devils all the world should fill	262	Though no Father seem to hear	183
Tho' evil spirits thro' the night	546	Though often we His patience try	581
Tho' I have grieved Thy Spirit, Lord	325	Though reason cannot understand	306
Tho' in a bare and rugged way	368	Though the night be dark and dreary	565
Tho' in the paths of death I tread	368	Though vile and worthless, still	580
Tho' like the wanderer	533	Though with a scornful wonder	473
Tho' my sight shall pass away	365	Thrice blessed every one	272
Tho' Satan's wrath beset our path	437	Thrice holy! Father, Spirit, Son	242
Tho' Thou hast called me to resign	418	Thro' all man's pow'rs corruption creeps	369
Tho' we here must strive in weakness	461	Thro' deserts of the cross Thou leadest	362
"Thomas, behold My side," saith He	208	Thro' each perplexing path of life	434
Thou, ah! Thou, hast taken on Thee	151	Thro' every period of my life	31
Thou alone art all my Treasure	357	Thro' Thy Beloved soothe the sick and weeping	556
Thou alone, my God and Lord	356	Through all eternity to Thee	31
Thou art a cooling fountain	9	Through Him we heirs of heaven are made	223
Thou art a mighty Monarch	130	Through mighty hosts of cruel foes	340
Thou art coming to a King	459	Through the long night-watches	654
Thou art mine; I love and own Thee	523	Thus God shall from all evil	67
Thou art my Strength, my Shield, my Rock	524	Thus, if thou hast known Him	74
Thou art, O Holy Spirit	228	Thus, Lord Jesus, every task	540
Thou art our Hero, all our foes subduing	269	Thus shall I hide my blushing face	154
Thou art our holy Lord	628	Thus my longings, heav'nward tending	366
Thou art the Fount of grace, I know	569	Thus spake the seraph, and forthwith	109

[635]

HYMN		HYMN
Thus will I sing Thy praises here	108	To His blessed promise ... 229
Thy best gifts from on high	580	To Jesus we for refuge flee ... 295
Thy body and Thy blood	310	To learn that in our God alone ... 629
Thy body, given for me, O Savior	315	To me He spake: Hold fast to Me ... 387
Thy bountiful care	17	To mine His Spirit speaketh ... 528
Thy cords of love, my Savior	171	To rest my body hasteth ... 554
Thy cross I'll place before me	171	To that dear Redeemer's praise ... 51
Thy cross, not mine, O Christ	380	To the all-ruling Triune God be glory ... 240
Thy death, not mine, O Christ	380	To the great One in Three ... 239
Thy flock, Thine own peculiar care	530	To the rest Thou didst prepare me ... 607
Thy gentle blessings, Lord, outpour	7	To the weary and the worn ... 501
Thy gift is joy, O Spirit	228	To Thee alone we cling ... 93
Thy glory never hence depart	635	To Thee, as early morning's dew ... 438
Thy grace alone, O God	389	To Thee, eternal Three in One ... 168
Thy gracious will on earth be done	458	To Thee, from whom we all derive ... 443
Thy great love for this hath striven	384	To Thee may raise our hearts and eyes ... 522
Thy groaning and Thy sighing	171	To Thee, O Christ, be glory ... 217
Thy hand is never shortened	520	To Thee of right belongs ... 101
Thy heart is filled with fervent yearning	315	To Thee our morning song of praise ... 564
Thy heart now open wide	57	To Thee our wants are known ... 46
Thy heart will leap for gladness	126	To Thee, the Comforter, we cry ... 233
Thy heavenly strength sustain our heart	235	To Thee, then, O Jesus, this day of Thy birth ... 102
Thy holy body into death was given	313	
Thy kingdom come. Thine let it be	458	To Thee they all belong ... 633
Thy kingdom come; Thy will	455	To them the cross, with all its shame ... 219
Thy life the bond of fellowship	486	To Thine almighty Spirit be ... 248
Thy light and grace	81	To this dear Surety's hand ... 220
Thy light to every thought impart	233	To this temple, where we call Thee ... 466
Thy love and grace alone avail	329	To this vale of tears He comes ... 97
Thy love to me, O God	389	To those who help in Christ have found ... 295
Thy name be hallowed and Thy kingdom given	556	To us a Child of hope is born ... 106
		To us therefore Christ gave command ... 331
Thy name be hallowed. Help us, Lord	458	To watch and pray and never faint ... 490
Thy neighbor's house desire thou not	287	To weeping Mary, standing by ... 177
Thy promise is my only plea	456	To whom the angels drawing nigh ... 212
Thy righteousness, O Christ	380	To you, in David's town, this day ... 109
Thy saints in all this glorious war	445	To you this night is born a child ... 85
Thy servant now declares to me	321	Today He rose and left the dead ... 10
Thy touch has still its ancient power	557	Today I was my Savior's guest ... 48
Thy truth and grace, O Father	520	Today on weary nations ... 9
Thy word commands our flesh to dust	123	Today our Father calls us ... 279
Thy Word doth deeply move the heart	5	Today the name is Thine ... 117
Thy Word first made me feel my sin	378	Today Thy gate is open ... 279
Thy Word is everlasting truth	286	Too oft I feel my sinful heart ... 340
Thy work alone, O Christ	389	Trinity sacred, Unity unshaken ... 240
Thy wounds, not mine, O Christ	380	True Son of the Father, He comes from the skies ... 102
Thy Zion strews before Thee	58	
Till from our darkened sight	133	Trust not in princes, they are but mortal ... 26
Till then I would Thy love proclaim	364	'Twas Thy grace in Christ that called me ... 37
Till then — nor is my boasting vain	346	
Till we behold Thy face	133	Unabated For Him waited ... 82
Time, like an ever-rolling stream	123	Under the shadow of Thy throne ... 123
'Tis Christ that wrought this work for me	137	Unite us in the sacred love ... 578
'Tis done; the precious ransom's paid	176	Unnumbered choirs before the shining throne ... 619
'Tis from the mercy of our God	382	
'Tis He forgives Thy sins	27	Unseal our lips to sing Thy praise ... 3
'Tis He revives our fainting soul	581	Until we join the hosts that cry ... 3
'Tis He who in these latter days	105	Unworthy though I am, O Savior ... 315
'Tis He whom David did portray	211	Up! The ripening fields ye see ... 507
'Tis I, Lord Jesus, I confess	150	Up to heav'n ascending ... 229
'Tis I who should be smitten	171	Upon a manger filled with hay ... 104
'Tis like the sun, a heav'nly light	286	Upon Thy lips, then, lay thy hand ... 535
'Tis not by works of righteousness	382	"Useless were for thee My Passion ... 311
'Tis the name for adoration	116	
'Tis the name that whoso preacheth	116	Vain the stone, the watch, the seal ... 193
'Tis the Savior, now victorious	209	Vainly we offer each ample oblation ... 128
'Tis Thine to cleanse the heart	225	Visit, then, this soul of mine ... 359
'Tis through the purchase of His death	382	Vouchsafe, O blessed Lord ... 310
'Tis vain to trust in man; for Thou, Lord, only	269	Waft, waft, ye winds, His story ... 495
To all who bow before Thee	122	Was it for crimes that I had done ... 154
To Bethlehem straight th' enlightened shepherds ran	84	Wash me and take away each stain ... 390
		Watch against the devil's snares ... 446
To bring good news to souls in sin	506	Watch against thyself, my soul ... 446
To cast their crowns before Thee	622	Watch and pray, watch and pray ... 479
To Church and State He granted	112	Watch by the sick; enrich the poor ... 551
To comfort and to bless	441	Watch! Let not the wicked world ... 446
To Father, Son, and Holy Ghost	14	We all believe in God's own Son ... 253
To Father, Son, and Holy Ghost	525	We all believe in Jesus Christ ... 251
To God the Father, God the Son	5	We all believe in Jesus Christ ... 252
To God, the only Wise	642	We all confess the Holy Ghost ... 251
To hail Thee, Sun of Righteousness	106	We all confess the Holy Ghost ... 252
To halls of heavenly splendor	192	We all confess the Holy Ghost ... 253
To Him with joyful song	38	We are God's house of living stones ... 467

[636]

First Line	HYMN
We are His people, we His care	13
We are rich, for He was poor	97
We are still as in a dungeon living	589
We are the Lord's; no darkness brooding o'er us	453
We are the Lord's; no evil can befall us	453
We are the Lord's; then let us gladly tender	453
We bear the burden of the day	573
We deserve but grief and shame	324
We eat this bread and drink this cup	306
We gather up in this brief hour	110
We have no cause to mourn or weep	596
We have no refuge, none on earth to aid us	556
We, Lord, would lay at Thy behest	438
We lose what on ourselves we spend	443
We praise Thee for the means of grace	52
We praise Thee, God, and Thee we bless	238
We praise Thee that today we see	634
We praise, we worship Thee, we trust	237
We pray Thee, O eternal Son	125
We share our mutual woes	464
We sing the goodness of the Lord	43
We sing the wisdom that ordained	43
We thank Thee, Christ; new life is ours	369
We thank Thee that throughout the day	563
We therefore heartily rejoice	223
We, too, before Thy gracious sight	303
We worship Thee, God of our fathers, we bless Thee	568
We'll crowd Thy gates with thankful songs	13
Weak is the effort of my heart	364
Weary am I and heavy laden	315
Weep now, all ye wretched creatures	169
Welcome, O my Savior, now	91
Welcome to earth, Thou noble Guest	85
Well He knows what best to grant me	425
Well might the sun in darkness hide	154
Were earth a thousand times as fair	85
Were the whole realm of nature mine	175
What bro't Thee to the manger	89
What can I for such love divine	150
What can these anxious cares avail thee	518
What curses doth the Law denounce	289
What glorious throng and what resplendent host	619
What God did in His Law demand	377
What God's almighty pow'r hath made	19
What harm can sin and death then do	103
What higher gift can we inherit	315
What I have done and taught, teach thou	387
What is all this life possesses	523
What is the world to me	430
What language shall I borrow	172
What punishment so strange is suffered yonder	143
What rush of alleluias	476
What shall I, frail man, be pleading	607
What the fathers most desired	91
What tho' in lonely grief I sigh	418
What though the foes be raging	58
What though the gates of hell withstood	460
What though I here must suffer	393
What though the spicy breezes	495
What though the tempest rage	660
What to me may seem a treasure	348
What ye shall bind, that bound shall be	331
Whate'er events betide	435
Whate'er of earthly good this life may grant me	143
When all my deeds I am reviewing	385
When all their labor seems in vain	482
When at last I near the shore	649
When at Thine altar we shall meet	634
When, at Thy summons, I must leave	406
When children's voices raise the song	635
When darkness round me gathers	407
When darkness veils His lovely face	370
When death shall interrupt our songs	119
When each day's scenes and labors close	543
When earthly friends forsake me quite	340
When earthly help no more availeth	194
When ends life's transient dream	394
When evil men revile me	171
When from the dust of death I rise	371
When He shall come with trumpet sound	370
When here our pathways part	464
When His servants stand before Him	472
When I shall pass death's gloomy vale	340
When I sleep He still is near me	25
When I tread the verge of Jordan	54
When I was Satan's easy prey	340
When in sorrow, when in danger	643
When in the night I sleepless lie	558
When in the solemn hour of death	515
When in the sultry glebe I faint	368
When Jesus comes, — O blessed story	65
When Jesus enters land and nation	65
When Jesus enters meek and lowly	65
When life's brief course on earth is run	517
When man's help and affection	393
When men the offered help disdain	295
When mind and thought, O Savior	597
When ministers lay on their hands	331
When my last hour cometh	516
When nature fails and day and night	31
When on my poor and burdened heart	515
When once Thou visitest the heart	361
When our responsive tongues essay	22
When our work of life is past	538
When shall these eyes thy heav'n-built walls	618
When, shriv'ling like a parched scroll	612
When silent woe thy bosom rends	535
When sorrows rise, My refuge lies	353
When that illustrious Day shall rise	445
When the death shades round us lower	186
When the Judge His seat attaineth	607
When the morning wakens	654
When the soft dews of kindly sleep	551
When the sun of bliss is beaming	354
When the woes of life o'ertake me	354
When they their vows today renew	337
When this poor lisping, stammering tongue	157
When Thomas afterwards had heard	208
When Thou shalt in Thy glory come	308
"When thro' fiery trials thy pathway shall lie	427
"When thro' the deep waters I call thee to go	427
When thus my heart in prayer ascendeth	21
When to heav'n's great and glorious King	543
When trials sore obstruct my way	515
When trouble, like a gloomy cloud	340
When we die, dear Savior	603
When we disclose our wants in prayer	22
When we seek relief	410
When with sorrow I am stricken	425
When we vainly seem to pray	183
Whence come these sorrows, whence this mortal anguish	143
Where deep for us the spear was dyed	168
Where He displays His healing power	511
Where saints of all ages in harmony meet	588
Where streams of living water flow	431
Where the shadows deepest lie	501
Wherein as Christians we may live	125
Whether to live or die	591
While from His mother's bosom fed	115
While He affords His aid	426
While He lifts His hand in blessing	218
While I am a pilgrim here	459
While I draw this fleeting breath	376
While I hearken to Thy Law	2
While life's dark maze I tread	394
While the prayers of saints ascend	2
While the wicked are confounded	607
While thus they sing your Monarch	76
While Thy glorious praise is sung	2
While Thy ministers proclaim	2
While we are sleeping, keep us in Thy favor	556
While we pray for pard'ning grace	11
Who built the lofty firmament	569
Who can condemn me now? For surely	315

First Line	HYMN
Who clings with resolution	528
Who is it life and health bestows	569
Who is it that hath bruised Thee	171
Who is this that comes in glory	218
Who learn of Thee the truth shall find	486
Who of us death's awful road	121
Who so happy as I am	648
Who warmeth us in cold and rain	569
Who would share Abraham's blessing	586
Whoe'er, by sense of sin opprest	177
Whom should I give my heart's affection	404
Whoso to this Board repaireth	311
Why restless, why cast down, my soul?	525
Why should we tremble to convey	593
Why spend the day in blank despair	535
Why that blood His raiment staining	209
Wide as the world is Thy command	13
Wilt thou find this one thing needful	366
Wilt thou not regard my call	345
Wisdom and zeal and faith impart	490
Wisdom's highest, noblest treasure	366
Wisely fight, for time is fleeting	444
With all my heart and being	89
With banner of the cross unfurled	332
With confident and humble mind	424
With feeble light and half obscure	530
With forbidden pleasures	516
With fraud which they themselves invent	260
With grateful hearts the past we own	119
With jasper glow thy bulwarks	614
With joy is heav'n resounding	214
With joy we bring them, Lord	302
With might of ours can naught be done	262
With my burden I begin	459
With my lamp well trimmed and burning	606
With one accord, O God, we pray	301
With one consent we meekly bow	583
With our spirit bear Thou witness	226
With peace and joy I now depart	585
With prayer my humble praise I bring	24
With Thee, Lord, have I cast my lot	524
With Thee, Lord, I am now united	315
With Thy favored sheep, oh, place me	607
With thy Savior at thy side	540
With voices united our praises we offer	568
Within the Jordan's crystal flood	131
Wondrous birth! O wondrous Child	95
Wondrous honor hast Thou given	442
Wondrous sound the trumpet flingeth	607
Word of the ever-living God	291
Worship, honor, pow'r, and blessing	367
Worthless are my prayers and sighing	607
"Worthy the Lamb that died," they cry	344
Would to God that I might even	470
Ye fearful saints, fresh courage take	514
Ye forest leaves so green and tender	30
Ye meanwhile are in your chambers sleeping	589
Ye need not toil nor languish	58
Ye saints, who here in patience	72
Ye seed of Israel's chosen race	339
Ye shall and must at last prevail	103
Ye sinners, come, 'tis Mercy's voice	281
Ye sinners, seek His grace	610
Ye who are of death afraid	203
Ye who confess Christ's holy name	19
Ye who think of sin but lightly	153
Ye whose anguish knew no measure	77
Yea, all I am and love most dearly	298
Yea, bless Thy Word alway	485
Yea, Father, yea, most willingly	142
Yea, her sins our God will pardon	61
Yea, I see what here was told me	601
Yea, let us praise Our God and raise	107
Yea, Lord, Thy servants meet Thee	138
Yea, Lord, 'twas Thy rich bounty gave	429
Yea, neither life's temptation	372
Yea, so dear did He esteem me	25
Yea, tho' I walk in death's dark vale	436
Yea, Thy word is clear and plain	300
Yea, when the world shall perish	393
Yes, the sorrow and the sufferings	442
Yet art Thou decked with beauty	130
Yet as the Law must be fulfilled	377
Yet not to them is giv'n	133
Yet, O Lord, not thus alone	140
Yet, Savior, Thou art not confined	306
Yet, though conscience' voice appal me	326
Yet unrequited, Lord, I would not leave Thee	143
Yet with truer, nobler beauty	632
Yet work, O Lord, in me	170
Zion hears the watchmen singing	609
"Zion, surely I do love thee,"	268

Alphabetical Index of Tunes

Tune	HYMN
Abends	280
Ach bleib bei uns	197, 292
Ach Gott und Herr	215, 317
Ach Gott vom Himmel	260
Ach Gott vom Himmelreiche	67
Ach, was soll ich Sünder machen	384, 408
Adeste fideles	102
Alford	476
All' Ehr' und Lob	236, 238, 494, 543, 567
All Saints New	452
Alle Menschen müssen sterben	601
Allein Gott in der Höh'	33, 110, 237
Allein zu dir	319
Alles ist an Gottes Segen	282, 425
Alma Redemptoris mater	531
America	577
Angel's Story	352
Angelus	115, 242, 557
Anthes	276, 279
Antioch	87
An Wasserflüssen Babylon	142
Auf, auf, mein Herz	192
Auf meinen lieben Gott	526
Aurelia	473, 492, 652
Aus der Tiefe	111
Aus meines Herzens Grunde	69, 75, 214, 217, 548
Aus tiefer Not	329
Aynhoe	450, 488
Azmon	281
Baltimore	481
Beatitudo	360
Bedford	284, 363
Belmont	436
Bethany	533
Bethlehem	109, 620
Bevan	220
Bis willkommen	576
Bona patria	614
Boylston	225, 464
Buckland	51
Burford	454, 579
Cambridge	519
Caritas perfecta	623
Chesterfield	66
Christ ist erstanden	187
Christ lag in Todesbanden	195
Christe, der du bist Tag und Licht	559
Christe, du Lamm Gottes	147
Christe, wahres Seelenlicht	113
Christum wir sollen loben schon	104
Christus, der ist mein	53, 597
Christus ist erstanden	190
Clairvaux	350
Consolation	149
Cordis donum	89
Coronae	222
Coronation	339
Cowper	157
Croft's 136th	580
Culbach	121
Da Jesus an des Kreuzes	177
Darwall's 148th	46, 465, 480, 575, 638, 642
Das walt' Gott Vater	273, 308
Den signede Dag	592
Denby	259, 420
Der am Kreuz	144, 179
Der lieben Sonne Licht und Pracht	413
Der mange skal komme	415
Der Tag, der ist	78, 230
Diademata	341
Die helle Sonn' leucht't	547
Die Nacht ist kommen	556
Dies irae	607
Dies sind die heil'gen	287
Dir, dir, Jehovah	21
Divinum mysterium	98
Dix	127, 572

Tune	HYMN
Domine, clamavi	593
Dover	241
Duke Street	200, 511
Dundee	49, 355, 486, 514
Dunstan	390
Easter Hymn	199
Ecce Agnus	165
Eden	621, 622
Ein' feste Burg	262
Eins ist not	366
Eirene	453
Ellacombe	9, 161
Ellers	47
Energy	374, 441, 468
Erfurt	232
Erhalt uns, Herr	5, 261, 265, 295, 332
Erschienen ist	108, 223
Es ist das Heil	301, 377
Es ist ein' Ros'	76, 645
Es ist genug	196, 509, 599
Es ist gewisslich	293, 604, 611
Es ist kein Tag	418, 424, 443
Es woll' uns Gott genädig sein	500
Eudoxia	654
Evan	416
Evening Hymn	558
Evening Prayer	565
Eventide	552
Ewing	448, 605, 613
Fahre fort	479
Fang dein Werk	540
Farrant	440
Federal Street	346
Finlandia	651
Firm Foundation	427
Franconia	133, 302
Fred til Bod	8, 188
Freu dich sehr	61, 401, 419
Freuet euch, ihr Christen	96
Freut euch, ihr lieben	59
Friend	457
Fröhlich soll mein Herze	77
Galilean	469, 496
Geduld, die soll'n wir haben	544
Gelobet sei'st du, Jesu	80
Gelobt sei Gott	208
Gethsemane	159, 174, 342
Gladness	82
Glorification	118
Gott der Vater wohn'	247
Gott des Himmels	549
Gott sei Dank	2, 114, 356, 501
Gott sei gelobet	313
Gottes Sohn ist kommen	74
Gottlob, es geht nunmehr zu Ende	163
Great White Host	656
Grosser Gott	250
Guds Menighed, syng	44
Guide Me	54, 505
Hamburg	175, 325, 650
Hanover	17
Harvest Hymn	573
Heaven Is My Home	660
Helft mir Gott's Güte	112
Herr, ich habe missgehandelt	326
Herr Jesu Christ, dich	3, 125, 297, 299, 314, 630
Herr Jesu Christ, du hast bereit't	306
Herr Jesu Christ, mein's	7, 288, 398, 484
Herr, wie du willst	312, 406
Herre Jesu Krist!	353
Herzlich lieb hab' ich dich, o Herr	429
Herzlich tut mich	172, 264, 520, 586
Herzliebster Jesu	143, 240, 258, 269
Heut' triumphieret Gottes Sohn	397
Höchster Priester	507
Horsley	157

[639]

	HYMN
Hursley	551
Hyfrydol	423, 442
Ich dank' dir, lieber Herre	32, 334, 372
Ich dank' dir schon	431
Ich halte treulich still	532
Ich singe dir	29, 43, 535, 569
Ich sterbe täglich	120, 315
Ich will dich lieben	399
In dich hab' ich gehoffet	524
In dulci iubilo	92
Innocents	35, 203
Isleworth	439, 506
Italian Hymn	227, 239, 508
Jeg vil mig Herren love	655
Jerusalem, du hochgebaute Stadt	619
Jesaia, dem Propheten	249
Jesu Kreuz, Leiden und Pein	140
Jesu, meine Freude	347
Jesu, meines Lebens Leben	151
Jesus Christus, unser Heiland	311
Jesus, Jesus, nichts als Jesus	348
Jesus, meine Zuversicht	201, 206
Judah's Lion	211
Kirken den er et	467
Komm, Gott Schoepfer	233
Komm, Heiliger Geist, Herre Gott	224
Komm, o komm, du Geist	226, 553
Kommt her zu mir	263, 379, 489, 624
Kremser	568
Kyrie, Gott Vater	6
Lancashire	205
Lasset uns mit Jesu ziehen	409
Lasst uns alle	97
Lasst uns erfreuen	15, 212, 475
Liebster Immanuel	582
Liebster Jesu	16, 45, 300, 411
Light Divine	234
Llanfair	191
Lobe den Herren, den	39
Lobe den Herren, o meine	26
Lobet den Herrn, ihr	19
Lobt den Herrn, die Morgensonne	461
Lobt Gott, ihr Christen	105, 106
Löwen, lasst euch wieder finden	470
Mach's mit mir, Gott	421
Macht hoch die Tür (3 tunes)	73
Magdalen	370
Maldwyn	278, 588
Martyn	345
Martyrdom	154
Mein Heiland	386
Mein Schöpfer, steh mir bei	335
Meinen Jesum lass' ich nicht	55, 324, 365, 595
Melcombe	504
Mendelssohn	94
Mendon	119, 447, 635, 637
Meribah	412
Min Själ og Aand	48
Missionary Hymn	495
Mit Fried' und Freud'	137
Mitten wir im Leben sind	590
Monkland	570
Morgenglanz der Ewigkeit	539
Morning Hymn	536
Morning Star	128
Müde bin ich	653
Munich	294
Navarre	100
Neander	1, 209, 221, 257, 472
New Ulm	50
Nicaea	246
Norrland	432
Nu rinder solen op	542
Nun bitten wir	231
Nun danket all'	10, 248, 344, 581, 629
Nun danket alle Gott	36, 38, 93
Nun freut euch	124, 216, 375, 387

	HYMN
Nun komm, der Heiden Heiland	91, 95
Nun lasst uns den Leib	596
Nun lasst uns Gott dem Herren	122
Nun lob, mein' Seel'	34, 316, 381
Nun preiset alle	28
Nun sich der Tag geendet hat	561
Nunc dimittis	101
O dass ich tausend (Dretzel)	243, 298, 373, 404, 545
(König)	30, 88, 385
O der alles	60
O du Liebe	37, 145, 333, 351, 498, 510, 632
O Durchbrecher	129, 367, 471
O Gott, du frommer Gott	395, 402, 417, 485
O grosser Gott	132
O Heilige Dreifaltigkeit	340, 438, 541, 550, 564, 633
O Herre Gott	266
O Jerusalem, du Schöne	606
O Jesu	24
O Jesu Christ, dein Kripplein	81, 107
O Jesu Christ, mein's	64, 148, 178, 392, 490, 512
O Lamm Gottes, unschuldig	146
O mein Jesu, ich muss sterben	153
O quanta qualia	255
O selig Haus	626
O Traurigkeit	167
O Welt, ich muss dich lassen	126, 171, 554
O Welt, sieh hier	171
O wie selig	589
Old Hundredth	13, 14, 52, 254, 289, 309, 644
Old 120th	405
Old 124th	307, 483, 503
Old 137th	583
Olivet	394, 628
Orientis partibus	193, 213
Palestrina	210
Patmos	400
Pax celeste	617
Pilot	649
Potsdam	117, 135, 426, 435
Puer nobis nascitur	63, 103
Quem pastores	90
Rathbun	354
Ratisbon	20, 359, 571
Regent Square	50, 136, 466, 502, 641
Rest	587
Resurgenti Nazareno	253
Resurrection	603
Reuter	283, 337, 477
Rex Gloriae	218
Ringe recht	155, 358, 565, 631
Rockingham Old	175
St. Agnes	361
St. Anatolius	555
St. Anne	123, 291, 460
St. Bernard	378, 515, 527
St. Bride	322, 389, 455
St. Crispin	245, 304, 371, 388, 499
St. Cross	164
St. Flavian	22, 382, 478, 578
St. George	71, 134, 566, 574, 584
St. Gertrude	658
St. Hilary	640
St. John	380
St. Louis	647
St. Luke	323, 331, 530
St. Magnus	219
St. Mary Magdalene	516
St. Michael	310, 414, 487
St. Peter	286, 364, 396, 618
St. Petersburg	493
St. Savior	434
St. Thomas	27, 68, 462
Salvator natus	86
Schmücke dich	305, 659
Schönster Herr Jesu	657
Schumann	449, 616, 636

[640]

	HYMN
Schwing dich auf	204
Seelenbräutigam	410, 562
Sei du mir gegrüsset	202
Septem Verba	180, 181, 182, 183, 184, 185, 186
Sieh, hier bin ich	56, 116, 139, 271, 627
Sine nomine	463
So gehst du nun	150
Sollt' ich meinem Gott	25
Southwell	156, 170, 320, 327, 610
Spanish Chant	166
Spohr	456, 525
Stephanos	428, 513, 643
Stille Nacht	646
Straf mich nicht	446
Stuttgart	83, 270, 357
Such', wer da will	383
Surrey	368
Swabia	274, 433
Tallis' Canon	558
Tenbury	591, 602
Teshiniens	169
Toplady	376
Uxbridge	303
Valet will ich dir geben	58, 72, 130, 138, 160, 407, 528
Vater unser	318, 349, 458, 482, 585, 600
Veni, Emmanuel	62
Vexilla Regis	168
Vienna	18, 338, 459, 538
Voller Wunder	11, 391, 537
Vom Himmel hoch	70, 85
Von Gott will ich nicht lassen	393
Vox dilecti	277
Wachet auf	444, 609
Walder	285
Walther	198
Wär' Gott nicht mit uns	267

	HYMN
Wareham	608, 634
Warum sollt' ich mich denn grämen	523
Was frag' ich nach der Welt	99, 272, 430
Was Gott tut	521
Was mein Gott will	437, 517
Webb	451, 497
Weil ich Jesu Schäflein bin	648
Weimar	328
Wem in Leidenstagen	158, 229
Wenn mein Stündlein	594
Wenn meine Sünd'	152
Wenn wir in höchsten Nöten	141, 321, 330, 369, 522, 534
Wer nur den lieben Gott	194, 518, 529
Wer weiss, wie nahe	65, 598
Werde munter	207, 296, 491, 560
Wie schön leuchtet	23, 79, 189, 235, 343, 546, 639
Wie soll ich dich	58
Wie wohl ist mir	362, 615
Winchester New	12, 162, 256
Winchester Old	31, 336, 445
Windham	612
Windsor	176
Winterton	403, 422
Wir danken dir	173
Wir glauben all' an einen Gott (10 lines)	251
(2 tunes)	
Wir glauben all' an einen Gott (6 lines)	252
Wo Gott zum Haus	131, 275, 290, 563, 625
Wo soll ich fliehen hin	57
Woodworth	388
Worcester	244
Wunderbarer König	4, 41, 42
Yigdal	40
Yorkshire	84
Zeuch ein	228
Zion	474
Zion klagt	268

Metrical Index of Tunes

S. M.

Tune	Hymn
Aynhoe	450, 488
Boylston	225, 464
Cambridge	519
Dover	241
Energy	374, 441, 468
Franconia	133, 302
Potsdam	117, 135, 426, 435
St. Bride	322, 389, 455
St. Michael	310, 414, 487
St. Thomas	27, 68, 462
Schumann	449, 616, 636
Southwell	156, 170, 320, 327, 610
Swabia	274, 433
Tenbury	591, 602

S. M. D.

Tune	Hymn
Diademata	341

C. M.

Tune	Hymn
Antioch	87
Azmon	281
Beatitudo	360
Bedford	284, 363
Belmont	436
Burford	454, 579
Chesterfield	66
Clairvaux	350
Coronation	339
Cowper	157
Domine, clamavi	593
Dundee	49, 355, 486, 514
Evan	416
Farrant	440
Horsley	157
Ich singe dir	29, 43, 535, 569
Lobt Gott, ihr Christen	105, 106
Martyrdom	154
Nun danket all'	10, 248, 344, 581, 629
Nun sich der Tag geendet hat	561
St. Agnes	361
St. Anne	123, 291, 460
St. Bernard	378, 515, 527
St. Flavian	22, 382, 478, 578
St. Magnus	219
St. Peter	286, 364, 396, 618
St. Savior	434
Spohr	456, 525
Walder	285
Winchester Old	31, 336, 445
Windsor	176

C. M. D.

Tune	Hymn
All Saints New	452
Bethlehem	109, 620
Old 137th	583
Vox dilecti	277

L. M.

Tune	Hymn
Abends	280
Ach bleib bei uns	197, 292
Angelus	115, 242, 557
Christe, der du bist Tag und Licht	559
Christum wir sollen loben schon	104
Das walt' Gott Vater	273, 308
Die helle Sonn' leucht't	547
Duke Street	200, 511
Erhalt uns, Herr	5, 261, 265, 295, 332
Erschienen ist (with Hallelujah)	108, 223
Federal Street	346
Gelobet seist du, Jesu (with Hallelujah)	80
Gottlob, es geht nunmehr zu Ende	163
Hamburg	175, 325, 650
Herr Jesu Christ, dich	3, 125, 297, 299, 314, 630
Herr Jesu Christ, mein's	7, 288, 398, 484
Hursley	551
Komm, Gott Schöpfer	233
Lasst uns erfreuen (with Alleluias)	15, 212, 475
Melcombe	504
Mendon	119, 447, 635, 637
Morning Hymn	536
Nun lasst uns den Leib	596
O Heilige Dreifaltigkeit	340, 438, 541, 550, 564, 633
O Jesu Christ, mein's	64, 148, 178, 392, 490, 512
Old Hundredth	13, 14, 52, 254, 289, 309, 644
Puer nobis nascitur	63, 103
Rest	587
Rockingham Old	175
St. Crispin	245, 304, 371, 388, 499
St. Cross	164
St. Luke	323, 331, 530
Tallis' Canon	558
Uxbridge	303
Vexilla Regis	168
Vom Himmel hoch	70, 85
Wareham	608, 634
Weimar	328
Wenn wir in höchsten Nöten	141, 321, 330, 369, 522, 534
Winchester New	12, 162, 256
Windham	612
Wir danken dir	173
Wo Gott zum Haus	131, 275, 290, 563, 625
Woodworth	388

L. M. D.

Tune	Hymn
Evening Hymn	558
O grosser Gott	132

4. 4. 6. 4. 4. 6. 6. 11.

Tune	Hymn
Gladness	82

4. 4. 7. 4. 4. 4. 7.

Tune	Hymn
Herre Jesu Krist!	353

4. 4. 7. 4. 4. 7.

Tune	Hymn
Ach Gott und Herr	215, 317

4. 4. 7. 4. 4. 7. D.

Tune	Hymn
O Herre Gott	266

4. 4. 7. 7. 6.

Tune	Hymn
O Traurigkeit	167

4. 4. 11. 4. 4. 11.

Tune	Hymn
O Jesu Christ, dein Kripplein	81, 107

5. 5. 5. 5. 6. 5. 6. 5.

Tune	Hymn
Hanover	17

5. 5. 7. 5. 5. 8.

Tune	Hymn
Schönster Herr Jesu	657

5. 5. 8. 8. 5. 5.

Tune	Hymn
Seelenbräutigam	410, 562

5. 6. 5. 6. 9. 10.

Tune	Hymn
Nun preiset alle	28

6. 4. 6. 4. 6. 6. 6. 4.

Tune	Hymn
Bethany	533
Heaven Is My Home	660
Winterton	403, 422

6. 5. 6. 5.

Tune	Hymn
Eudoxia	654
Wem in Leidenstagen	158, 229

6. 5. 6. 5. D.

Tune	Hymn
St. Gertrude (with Refrain)	658
St. Mary Magdalene	516
Sei du mir gegrüsset (with refrain)	202

6. 5. 6. 5. 6. 5. 6. 5.

Tune	Hymn
Nu rinder solen op	542

6. 6. 3. 3. 10. 10. 3. 3. 7.

Tune	Hymn
Resurrection	603

6. 6. 4. 6. 6. 6. 4.

Tune	Hymn
America	577
Italian Hymn	227, 239, 508
Olivet	394, 628

	HYMN
6. 6. 5. 6. 6. 5. 3. 4. 8. 6.	
Jesu, meine Freude	347
6. 6. 6. 4. 8. 8. 4.	
Ecce Agnus	165
6. 6. 6. 6. 6.	
Gottes Sohn ist kommen	74
Old 120th	405
6. 6. 6. 6. 6. 6. 5. 5.	
In dulci iubilo	92
6. 6. 6. 6. D.	
Denby	259, 420
Ich halte treulich still	532
6. 6. 6. 6. 7. 7. 7. 7. 8. 6.	
Mein Schöpfer, steh mir bei	335
6. 6. 6. 6. 8. 8. (6. 6. 6. 6. 4. 4. 4. 4.)	
Bevan	220
Croft's 136th	580
Darwall's 148th 46, 465, 480, 575, 638,	642
St. John	380
6. 6. 7. 6. 6. 7.	
Nunc dimittis	101
6. 6. 7. 7. 7. 7.	
Auf meinen lieben Gott	526
Wo soll ich fliehen hin	57
6. 6. 8. 4. D.	
Yigdal	40
6. 6. 8. 6. 6. 8. 3. 3. 6. 6.	
Wunderbarer König	4, 41, 42
6. 7. 6. 7. 6. 6. 6. 6.	
Nun danket alle Gott	36, 38, 93
O Gott, du frommer Gott 395, 402, 417,	485
Was frag' ich nach der Welt 99, 272,	430
6. 7. 8. 7. 8. 9. 6.	
Fahre fort	479
7. 4. 7. 4. 6. 6. 6.	
Salvator natus	86
7. 5. 7. 5. D.	
Glorification	118
7. 6. 7. 6.	
Christus, der ist mein	53, 597
Lasst uns alle (Trochaic)	97
7. 6. 7. 6. 3. 3. 6. 6.	
Straf mich nicht	446
7. 6. 7. 6. 6. 6. 6.	
Auf, auf, mein Herz	192
7. 6. 7. 6. 6. 7. 6.	
Es ist ein' Ros'	76, 645
7. 6. 7. 6. 6. 7. 7. 6.	
Aus meines Herzens Grunde	
69, 75, 214, 217,	548
Helft mir Gott's Güte	112
Von Gott will ich nicht lassen	393
Zeuch ein	228
7. 6. 7. 6. D.	
Ach Gott vom Himmelreiche	67
Angel's Story	352
Anthes	276, 279
Aurelia	473, 492, 652
Bona patria	614
Eden	621, 622
Ellacombe	9, 161
Ewing	448, 605, 613
Fang dein Werk (Trochaic)	540
Freut euch, ihr lieben	59
Geduld, die soll'n wir haben	544
Herzlich tut mich 172, 264, 520,	586

	HYMN
Ich dank' dir, lieber Herre	32, 334, 372
Jeg vil mig Herren love	655
Jesu Kreuz, Leiden und Pein (Trochaic)	140
Lancashire	205
Missionary Hymn	495
Munich	294
Schwing dich auf (Trochaic)	204
Valet will ich dir geben	
58, 72, 130, 138, 160, 407,	528
Webb	451, 497
Wie soll ich dich	58
7. 6. 7. 6. 7. 7. 6. 7. 7. 6.	
Der Tag, der ist	78, 230
7. 6. 7. 6. 8. 7. 6.	
Wenn meine Sünd'	152
7. 6. 7. 6. 8. 8.	
St. Anatolius	555
7. 6. 7. 6. 8. 8. 8. 6.	
Cordis donum	89
7. 6. 8. 6. D.	
Alford	476
7. 7. 6. 7. 7. 8.	
O Welt, ich muss dich lassen 126, 171,	554
O Welt, sieh hier	171
7. 7. 7. 6.	
Septem Verba	
180, 181, 182, 183, 184, 185,	186
7. 7. 7. 7.	
Aus der Tiefe	111
Buckland	51
Christus ist erstanden (with Hallelujah)	190
Culbach	121
Easter Hymn (with Alleluias)	199
Gott sei Dank	2, 114, 356, 501
Höchster Priester	507
Innocents	35, 203
Light Divine	234
Llanfair (with Alleluias)	191
Monkland	570
Müde bin ich	653
Nun komm, der Heiden Heiland	91, 95
Nun lasst uns Gott dem Herren (Iambic)	122
Orientis partibus	193, 213
Patmos	400
Vienna	18, 338, 459, 538
7. 7. 7. 7. 7.	
Dix	127, 572
Fred til Bod	8, 188
Gethsemane	159, 174, 342
Pilot	649
Ratisbon	20, 359, 571
Toplady	376
Voller Wunder	11, 391, 537
7. 7. 7. 7. 7. 5. 6.	
O Lamm Gottes, unschuldig	146
7. 7. 7. 7. D.	
Christe, wahres Seelenlicht	113
Martyn	345
Mendelssohn (with Refrain)	94
St. George	71, 134, 566, 574, 584
Spanish Chant	166
7s. 14 lines	
Gott der Vater wohn'	247
7. 7. 8. 8. 7. 7.	
Weil ich Jesu Schäflein bin	648
7. 8. 7. 8. 7. 3.	
Morgenglanz der Ewigkeit	539
7. 8. 7. 8. 7. 6. 7. 6. 7. 6.	
Nun lob, mein' Seel'	34, 316, 381

[643]

	HYMN
7. 8. 7. 8. 7. 7.	
Grosser Gott	250
Jesus, meine Zuversicht	201, 206
Meinen Jesum lass' ich nicht	55, 324, 365, 595

7. 8. 7. 8. 8. 8.

Liebster Jesu _____ 16, 45, 300, 411

7. 8. 8. 8. 8. 8. 8. 10. 8.

Komm, Heiliger Geist, Herre Gott ____ 224

8. 3. 3. 6. 8. 3. 3. 6.

Fröhlich soll mein Herze _____ 77
Warum sollt' ich mich denn grämen ____ 523

8. 5. 8. 3.

Stephanos _____ 428, 513, 643

8. 5. 8. 4. 7. 7.

Mit Fried' und Freud' _____ 137

8. 6. 4. 4. 6. 7. 6. 4. 4. 6.

St. Louis _____ 647

8. 6. 8. 6. 8. 8.

Erfurt _____ 232
O Jesu _____ 24

8. 6. 8. 8. 6.

Pax celeste _____ 617

8. 7. 7. 7. 7. 7.

Wir glauben all' an einen Gott ____ 252

8. 7. 7. 8. 7. 7.

Ach, was soll ich Sünder machen ____ 384, 408

8. 7. 7. 8. 7. 7. 8. 8. 8.

Freuet euch, ihr Christen _____ 96

8. 7. 8. 7.

Evening Prayer _____ 565
Ich dank' dir schon (Iambic) _____ 431
Lobt den Herrn, die Morgensonne ____ 461
O der alles _____ 60
Rathbun _____ 354
Ringe recht _____ 155, 358, 565, 631
Stuttgart _____ 83, 270, 357

8. 7. 8. 7. 4. 4. 7. 4. 4. 7.

So gehst du nun _____ 150

8. 7. 8. 7. 4. 7.

Coronae _____ 222
Guide Me _____ 54, 505
Worcester _____ 244
Zion _____ 474

8. 7. 8. 7. 5. 5. 5. 6. 7.

Ein' feste Burg _____ 262

8. 7. 8. 7. 6. 6. 6. 6. 7. (8. 7. 8. 7. 6. 5. 6. 6. 7.)

Reuter _____ 283, 337, 477

8. 7. 8. 7. 6. 6. 7. 7.

Löwen, lasst euch wieder finden ____ 470

8. 7. 8. 7. 6. 6. 8. 8.

Der lieben Sonne Licht und Pracht ____ 413

8. 7. 8. 7. 7. 7.

Consolation _____ 149
Gott des Himmels _____ 549
Jesus, Jesus, nichts als Jesus ____ 348
Komm, o komm, du Geist ____ 226, 553
Neander _____ 1, 209, 221, 257, 472

8. 7. 8. 7. 7. 7. 8. 8.

Der am Kreuz _____ 144, 179
Freu dich sehr _____ 61, 401, 419
Werde munter _____ 207, 296, 491, 560
Zion klagt _____ 268

8. 7. 8. 7. 7. 7. 8. 7. 4.

Christ lag in Todesbanden _____ 195

	HYMN
8. 7. 8. 7. 4. 4. 7.	
Bis willkommen	576
New Ulm	50
O Jerusalem, du Schöne	606
Regent Square	50, 136, 466, 502, 641
Sieh, hier bin ich	56, 116, 139, 271, 627

8. 7. 8. 7. 8. 7. 7. (8. 7. 8. 7. 4. 4. 7. 7.)

Divinum mysterium _____ 98
Was Gott tut _____ 521

8. 7. 8. 7. 8. 7. 7. 8. 7. 7.

Lasset uns mit Jesu ziehen ____ 409
Sollt' ich meinem Gott ____ 25

8. 7. 8. 7. D.

Baltimore _____ 481
Friend _____ 457
Galilean _____ 469, 496
Harvest Hymn (Iambic) _____ 573
Hyfrydol _____ 423, 442
O du Liebe 37, 145, 333, 351, 498, 510, 632
O Durchbrecher _____ 129, 367, 471
O mein Jesu, ich muss sterben ____ 153
Rex Gloriae _____ 218
St. Hilary _____ 640
Was mein Gott will (Iambic) ____ 437, 517

8. 7. 8. 7. 8. 7. 8. 7. 7.

Es woll' uns Gott genädig sein ____ 500

8. 7. 8. 7. 8. 8.

Herr, ich habe missgehandelt ____ 326
Mach's mit mir, Gott _____ 421

8. 7. 8. 7. 8. 8. 7. (4. 4. 7. 4. 4. 7. 4. 4. 4. 7.)

Ach Gott vom Himmel _____ 260
Allein Gott in der Höh' _____ 33, 110, 237
Aus tiefer Not _____ 329
Es ist das Heil _____ 301, 377
Es ist gewisslich _____ 293, 604, 611
Herr Jesu Christ, du hast bereit't ____ 306
Herr, wie du willst _____ 312, 406
Lobet den Herrn, ihr _____ 19
Nun freut euch _____ 124, 216, 375, 387
Such', wer da will _____ 383
Wär' Gott nicht mit uns _____ 267
Wenn mein Stündlein _____ 594

8. 7. 8. 7. 8. 8. 7. 7.

Alle Menschen müssen sterben ____ 601
Jesus, meines Lebens Leben ____ 151

8. 7. 8. 7. 8. 8. 7. 8. 8. 7.

An Wasserflüssen Babylon _____ 142

8. 7. 8. 7. 8. 8. 8. 4. 8.

Allein zu dir _____ 319

8. 7. 8. 7. 12. 12. 11. 11.

Eins ist not _____ 366

8. 8. 4. 7.

Judah's Lion _____ 211

8. 8. 6. 8. 8. 6.

Kommt her zu mir ____ 263, 379, 489, 624
Meribah _____ 412

8. 8. 7. 8.

Jesus Christus, unser Heiland ____ 311

8. 8. 7. 8. 7. (8. 8. 7. 4. 4. 7.)

Da Jesus an des Kreuzes ____ 177
In dich hab' ich gehoffet ____ 524

8. 8. 7. 8. 8. 7.

Alles ist an Gottes Segen ____ 282, 425

8. 8. 7. 8. 8. 7. 4. 4. 4. 8.

Wie schön leuchtet
23, 79, 189, 235, 343, 546, 639

[644]

	HYMN
8. 8. 7. 8. 8. 7. 7.	
Min Själ og Aand	48
8. 8. 7. 8. 8. 7. 8. 8. 8. 4. 8. 8.	
Herzlich lieb hab' ich dich, o Herr	429
8. 8. 8.	
Dies irae	607
Gelobt sei Gott (with Alleluias)	208
8. 8. 8. 4.	
Es ist kein Tag 418, 424,	443
Palestrina (with Alleluias)	210
8. 8. 8. 6.	
Dunstan	390
Isleworth 439,	506
8. 8. 8. 6. 12 lines	
Great White Host	656
8. 8. 8. 7.	
Quem pastores	90
Resurgenti Nazareno	253
8. 8. 8. 7. 4.	
Dies sind die heil'gen	287
8. 8. 8. 8. 8. 8.	
All' Ehr' und Lob 236, 238, 494, 543,	567
Heut' triumphieret Gottes Sohn	397
Magdalen	370
St. Petersburg	493
Surrey	368
Vater unser 318, 349, 458, 482, 585,	600
Veni, Emmanuel	62
8. 8. 8. 8. 8. 8. 6. 6.	
Macht hoch die Tür	73
8. 8. 8. 8. 8. 8. 8.	
Kirken den er et	467
8. 8. 8. 8. 8. 8. 8. 8.	
Schmücke dich (Trochaic) 305,	659
8s. 10 lines	
Wir glauben all' an einen Gott	251
8. 8. 10. 10.	
Teshiniens	169
8. 9. 8. 8. 9. 8. 6. 6. 4. 4. 4. 8.	
Wachet auf 444,	609
8. 9. 8. 9. 8. 8. 9. 9. 8. 8.	
Mein Heiland	386
9. 8. 9. 8. 8. 6.	
Ich will dich lieben	399
9. 8. 9. 8. 8. 8.	
Ich sterbe täglich 120,	315
O dass ich tausend (König) 30, 88,	385
(Dretzel) 243, 298, 373, 404,	545
Wer nur den lieben Gott 194, 518,	529
Wer weiss, wie nahe 65,	598
9. 8. 9. 8. 9. 8.	
Den signede Dag	592
9. 8. 9. 8. D.	
Navarre	100
9. 8. 9. 8. 9. 9. 8. 9. 9. 8.	
Wie wohl ist mir 362,	615
9. 9. 11. 10. 4.	
Nun bitten wir	231

	HYMN
9. 10. 9. 10. 10. 10.	
Dir, dir, Jehovah	21
10. 10. 5. 10.	
O wie selig	589
10. 6. 10. 6. 7. 6. 7. 6.	
Jerusalem, du hochgebaute Stadt	619
10. 6. 10. 6. 9. 9. 4. 4.	
Es ist genug 196, 509,	599
10. 8. 10. 8. 8. 8. 4. 4.	
Lobe den Herren, o meine	26
10. 10. 10.	
Sine nomine (with Alleluias)	463
10. 10. 10. 10.	
Ellers	47
Eventide	552
O quanta qualia	255
Old 124th 307, 483,	503
10. 10. 10. 10. 10. 10.	
Finlandia	651
Yorkshire	84
10s. 16 lines	
Jesaia, dem Propheten	249
11. 5. 11. 9.	
Guds Menighed, syng	44
11. 8. 11. 8. 5. 9. 9. 6. 7. 5.	
Gott sei gelobet	313
11. 9. 11. 9. 9.	
Der mange skal komme	415
11. 10. 11. 9.	
Liebster Immanuel	582
11. 10. 11. 10.	
Alma Redemptoris mater	531
Caritas perfecta	623
Eirene	453
Morning Star	128
11. 10. 11. 10. D.	
O selig Haus	626
11. 11. 5. 5. 11.	
Norrland	432
11. 11. 11. 5.	
Die Nacht ist kommen	556
Herzliebster Jesu 143, 240, 258,	269
11. 11. 11. 11.	
Firm Foundation	427
Maldwyn 278,	588
Walther	198
11. 12. 12. 10.	
Nicaea	246
12. 11. 12. 11	
Kremser	568
14. 14. 4. 7. 8.	
Lobe den Herren, den	39
Irregular	
Adeste fideles	102
Christ ist erstanden	187
Christe, du Lamm Gottes	147
Kyrie, Gott Vater	6
Mitten wir im Leben sind	590
Stille Nacht	646

[645]

Index of Subjects (Topical Index)

In compiling this index the following aim was kept in view: To prepare an index which would be more comprehensive than a mere catalog of subject topics without expanding it into a complete concordance.

Items printed in bold-faced type refer to complete hymns or hymn sections. Those in italics are subtopics under which are grouped their related items. The dash indicates a break with the foregoing item.

Aaron 218, 484, 496
Abiding with Christ; cf. Christ, abiding in
Abel's blood 158
Abraham 275, 415; bosom 429; example 586
Absent ones, prayer for 643
Absolution, confession and 317–331
Absolution 288; words of 321, 331, 358; gift of 607; cf. Forgiveness
Account, giving an; cf. Judgment, account at
Adam, fall of 369; cf. Sin, fall into; — tribes of 511
Adam and Eve 622
Adoption 2, 5, 14, 19, 21, 48, 81, 233, 251, 288, 298, 337, 467
Adoration 1–54, 79, 84, 88, 98, 101, 102, 114, 116, 119, 122, 125, 127, 128, 132, 139, 142, 202, 214, 217, 221, 222, 236, 239, 240, 241, 246, 248, 250, 255, 271, 273, 274, 284, 313, 344, 352, 401, 412, 460, 657; daily 540, 544, 548, 564; hymns of 570, 573; cf. Worship
Advent of Christ 55–75, 132, 136, 356, 405, 552; blessings of 56, 207; Church awaits 64; first 56, 59, 68, 73, 74, 100, 221, 375, 385, 645; second 56, 60, 64, 67, 68, 69, 70, 72, 125, 134, 164, 212, 216, 221, 253, 308, 314, 343, 351, 370, 378, 429, 446, 448, 476, 490, 495, 539, 574, 575, 588, 589, 604, 605, 606, 607, 608, 609, 611; to the heart 5, 10, 55, 56, 57, 63, 65, 68, 69, 70, 73, 74, 75, 91, 276, 351, 356, 359, 361, 506, 647, 650
Adversity 67, 110, 122, 194, 320, 354, 385 393, 395, 413, 571
Affections, human 393; pure 358, 404
Affliction 25, 69, 72, 118, 122, 340, 354, 362, 365, 372, 373, 381, 383, 427, 513–535; fire of 427; furnace of 474; prayer in, cf. Prayer in affliction; — purpose 514, 520
Afric's sunny fountains 495
Age, old 427; cf. Life, long
Aged 113, 286, 395, 467
Agnus Dei 146, 147, 165
All Saints 270–275; cf. Saints, Apostles
Altar, family 625
Ambition 423
Amen 458
Angels 7, 34, 35, 67, 76, 77, 79–81, 83–85, 92, 94, 98, 100, 102, 103, 105, 109, 125, 128, 132, 136, 148, 188, 190, 212, 214, 221, 222, 254–257, 279, 315, 339, 341, 344, 429, 496, 502, 647; archangels 475; armies, hosts 14, 23, 26, 28, 81, 98, 103, 158, 162, 241, 254, 255, 306, 648; brightest 641; choirs 30, 84, 104, 148, 218, 244, 249, 250, 475, 609; Christmas 647; clad in glory 356; creation of 188, 254, 257; **Festival of All 254–257;** first-born sons of light 132; guardian 29, 254–257, 413, 546, 548, 554, 556, 560, 563, 565; heavenly (celestial) hosts 4, 38, 208, 252, 332, 367, 413, 493, 566; herald 94, 645; hosts of God 29, 241; hymn of the 76, 83, 94, 100, 102, 109, 188, 647; cf. Songs of angels; — messengers 249, 255; ministers 255; of the Lord 109; service of the 249, 254–257, 412, 648; sons of God 255; spirits 367; throng 38, 109, 344
Anger 287
Annunciation 274
Anthems 26, 28, 76, 84, 112, 129, 134, 160, 161, 255, 308, 341, 568, 584, 619; heavenly 341, 415, 475, 588; supernal 475; cf. Praise, Hymn, Song
Anxiety 268

Apostles 67, 208, 229, 250, 452, 471, 483, 513, 618; Creed 253; cf. Creed; — enthroned 601; example of 452; holy train of 250; holy twelve 475; sending forth of 493; twelve valiant saints 452; Apostolic band 212
Arabia 59
Arena, blood-stained sand of the 470
Armor, Christian 226, 262, 337, 423, 444, 450, 472, 494; cf. Warfare, Christian; — earthly 258; girding on the 501, 506; God's 247; Gospel 451; panoply of God 450; shield of faith 48, 332; Spirit's sword 332, 483, 501, 506
Ascension 212–223; cf. Christ, ascension of; — Triumph-day 212
Atonement 103, 129, 146, 147, 163, 170, 196, 198, 220, 237, 272, 297, 310, 313, 319; foundation 377; through Christ 77, 330, 367, 371, 377, 380, 383, 386, 561; through Christ's blood; cf. Blood of Christ; — through Christ's death 151, 373; through Christ's suffering 386; through works 323, 373, 377, 379, 417; cf. Salvation, Reconciliation, Redemption
Autumn, blessings of 572

Babylon, captivity of the Church 448
Banners, blood-red 452; of Christ 198; of Cross 332, 471; cf. Gospel, Word of God; — of saints 472; raising the 501; Royal 451
Baptism 207, 229, 245, 288, 298–303, 333, 337, 382, 504, 639; covenant of 298, 337, 467; grace 337; cf. Grace; — eternal Life through 301; water 382, 598, 634; water and the Spirit 300; water and the Word 299, 473; cf. Sacraments
Beasts 654
Beatitudes 668
Benedictus 88
Bethel 533
Bethlehem 76, 79, 84, 94, 102, 103, 109, 134, 341, 645, 647
Bible 132, 266, 284, 285, 290; attacked 290; blessings of 284, 285; Book Divine 285; doctrines of 285; golden casket 294; guide of youth 286; cf. Youth; — Holy Book 286; inspiration of 285, 290, 373; light of 294; lore 266; sacred story 408; cf. Scriptures, Word of God
Birds 480, 654
Birth of Christ, proclaiming 136; cf. Tidings
Blasphemy 260, 264
Blessing, Aaronic 541; Cup of 426, 431, 436; Divine 7, 33, 39, 45, 46, 50, 51, 63, 67, 73, 77, 110, 112, 122, 281, 294, 312, 402, 423, 425, 442, 465, 491, 500, 511, 541, 544, 571, 580, 581, 640, 653; evening 565; seeking 11; table of 426, 431, 436; temporal 25, 28, 31, 38, 45, 112, 122, 438 to 443, 455, 458, 500, 542, 544, 548, 555, 558, 566, 567, 569, 570, 572, 578, 580, 624, 640
Bliss 57, 73, 81, 129, 281, 393; everlasting 406, 415, 471, 570, 596; hope of 381; private 572; song of 619
Blood of Christ 169, 218, 225, 231, 301, 366, 370, 376; atonement through 38, 115, 198, 220, 335, 336, 372, 590; beauty of 371; blessings of 358; Church redeemed by 473; cleansing flood 318; cleansing through 149, 156, 157, 163, 165, 168, 266, 278, 279, 318, 335, 360, 375, 376, 382, 388, 428, 471, 543, 652, 656; cf. Sin, cleansing

from; — comfort of 148; conquerors through 472; covenant of 149, 164; covenant sealed with 51; crimson flood 428; forgiveness through 367, 371, 392; foundation of hope 148, 370; fountain 157; fountain of God's love 372; glorious dress 348, 371; healing fountain 149; healing through 321, 376; help through 33, 150, 370; holiness through 428; justification through 245; cf. Justification; — lifeblood 158, 184; life through 167, 615; peace with God through 372; peace through 389, 419, 459; pleading of 158, 180, 220, 313, 371, 385; power of 157; redemption through 32, 96, 124, 141, 152, 158, 231, 264, 305, 331, 334, 391, 404, 419, 429, 439, 442, 444, 462, 489, 493, 523, 559; righteousness through 173; robes washed in 471; royal robe 142; sacred flood 165; salvation through 528; cf. Salvation; — shed 115, 117, 141, 152, 154, 163, 167, 180, 220, 237, 305, 307, 310, 321, 336, 342, 371, 387, 388, 405, 407

Blood of sacrifices powerless 156

Boasting 640

Body, burial of 592, 593, 596, 603; cf. Death and burial

Bondage 66, 340, 369, 378, 389; deliverance from 243, 498; cf. Death, Hell, Satan, Sin

Book, of Judgment 607, 611; of heaven (of life), name in 300, 374, 407, 611; scrolls 271

Bride, giving away the 622; cf. Marriage

Burial, death and 585–602

Call, of disciples 270; cf. Disciples; — of ministers; cf. Ministers, call of

Calumny 287

Calvary 149, 159, 198, 323, 394, 407, 650; cross-crowned 516; darkness on 174, 183

Cana 131, 134, 620, 621

Canaan, heavenly 54, 218, 476; barren 571

Captives, freedom of the 498

Care, divine 17, 27, 28, 34, 70, 251, 338, 368, 393, 422, 431, 434, 436, 517, 520, 535, 543, 548; cf. Providence, divine; — worldly 385, 439, 447, 448, 457, 458, 463, 518, 520, 522, 532, 546, 557, 561

Carols and spiritual songs 645–660

Catechism, doctrines 288; cf. Doctrines

Chaff 414

Charity 287, 319, 411, 442, 483, 623; unity of 658; works of 440, 442

Chastening 25, 217, 268, 317, 396, 517, 583; cf. Tribulations, Trials

Chastity 287

Cherubim 76, 188, 246, 250, 475

Childhood, divine protection in 535; cf. Children

Children 286; cf. Youth; — baptism of 299, 300, 302, 303, 467; blessing of God 625; blessings on 624, 654; brought to Christ 300, 302, 303, 496, 626, 627, 628, 630, 631, 634; confirmation of 337; cf. Confirmation; — dear to Christ 627; duty of, to Parents 287; godly life of 629; heirs of Christ 634; holy temple 655; hymns for 3, 5, 15, 35, 39, 45, 46, 48, 50, 53, 55, 79, 81, 82, 85, 89, 90, 92, 94, 97, 99, 102, 106, 109, 114, 123, 127, 133, 146, 147, 154, 157, 158, 160, 161, 170, 172, 173, 175, 179, 187, 197, 199, 200, 206, 208, 210, 211, 215, 225, 229, 234, 237, 239, 240, 241, 243, 244, 246, 247, 252, 261, 262, 263, 273, 282, 283, 285, 286, 287, 288, 298, 300, 324, 333, 334, 335, 336, 338, 339, 345, 346, 347, 350, 354, 356, 370, 373, 376, 388, 394, 398, 399, 400, 409, 410, 414, 421, 422, 426, 428, 436, 445, 451, 455, 457, 458, 464, 469, 472, 495, 497, 500, 507, 513, 516, 518, 520, 533, 536, 540, 541, 547, 548, 551, 552, 554, 562, 565, 568, 577, 585, 587, 591, 597, 625, 627, 628, 629, 631, 645, 646, 647, 648, 650, 654, 655, 657, 659, 660; instruction of 486, 491, 629, 630; cf. Instruction, religious; — lambs of Christ 631, 648; martyred 273; cf. Martyrs; — of heaven; cf. Christians; — of God; cf. Christians, children of God; — parents' love of 630; praise Christ 57, 160, 161, 511, 635; prayer for 299, 300, 337, 544, 627; prayer of 454, 627, 628, 655; protection of 626; regeneration 639; religious training of 625, 626, 627, 631; cf. Instruction, religious; — song of 160, 161, 627; straying 627; thank-offerings of 627

Christ, abiding in (with) 77, 135, 138, 155, 188, 192, 201, 206, 216, 300, 315, 343, 356, 365, 388, 433, 478; abiding of 53, 57, 70, 73, 97, 103 120, 122, 125, 138, 163, 194, 197, 268, 292, 328, 345, 351, 353, 356, 381, 429, 430, 467, 551, 552, 637, 647; adored by angels 128, 218, 367, 566, 609; **Advent of 55–75**; cf. Advent; — affliction of 140, 151; agony of 144, 166, 173, 193, 196, 405, 600; cf. Christ, suffering of; — angels of 429; cf. Angels; — anointed 367; arms of 457, 496; **ascension of 166, 212–223**, 229, 253, 306, 341, 385, 387, 485, 626; ashamed of 346, 445; asleep in 587, 597; cf. Death; — banner of 198, 451; baptism of 131, 134; baptized into 229, 298, 377; baptized into death of 301; beauty of 17, 55, 126, 128, 130, 135, 172, 234, 316, 341, 357, 645, 657; betrayal of 164; **birth of 35, 76–109**, 132, 134, 136, 645–647; cf. Incarnation; — blessings of 53, 73, 77, 82, 85, 87, 100, 196, 213, 218, 239, 251, 298, 358, 383, 399, 405, 466, 497, 513, 526, 551, 565, 653; cf. Blessings, divine; — blood and righteousness of 371; blood of; cf. Blood of Christ; — body and blood of 163, 304, 305, 306, 308, 309, 310, 313, 314, 315, 343, 639; cf. Lord's Supper, Real Presence; — bringing children to; cf. Children brought to Christ; — building on 99, 370, 383, 460, 465, 467, 526, 528; cf. Faith, foundation of; Christ, foundation; — burial of 166, 167; buried with 298; childhood of 115, 133, 166; Church's foundation 217, 460, 473, 477; circumcision 115, 117; Cleaving, clinging, to 406, 408, 420, 472, 528, 598, 626; coming to 277, 306, 315, 328, 330, 379, 386, 388, 390, 415; command of 64, 300, 331; committing all to 526; communion with 77, 81, 97, 196, 206, 308, 467, 634; cf. Christ, united with; — compassion of 243, 278, 312, 340, 343, 351, 353, 419, 548; cf. Compassion; — conception of 95, 98, 104, 251, 253, 274; condescension of 10, 18, 92, 96, 152, 166, 252, 304, 328, 385, 467, 473, 552; confession of name 19, 69, 74, 83, 93, 96, 114, 116, 117, 130, 131, 134, 143, 221, 222, 227, 235, 272, 334, 346, 352, 360, 361, 389, 408, 412, 467, 486; conquering through 383, 444 to 453; cf. Warfare, Christian; — **coronation of** 132, 140, 190, **212–223**, 339, 341, 344, 367, 513; covenant of 370; Cross of; cf. Cross of Christ; — crown of 57, 73, 130, 209, 219, 221, 222; Crucifixion of 140, 143, 145, 146, 151, 154, 155, 156, 166, 168, 169, 171, 174, 177, 178, 179, 180, 190, 196, 198, 251, 253, 386; Day of 71, 356; cf. Christ — second advent; — death of 117, 151, 152, 154, 162, 163, 165, 166, 167, 169, 170, 171, 176, 177, 186, 195, 196, 198, 202, 220, 271, 297, 305, 311, 313, 319, 326, 330, 357, 366, 379, 594; deity of 93, 94, 95, 102, 103, 105, 107, 108, 134, 271, 352, 510; delight in 188, 350, 357, 361, 362, 366, 477; descent into hell 190, 253; desire for 55, 62, 64, 72, 73, 82, 85, 91, 92, 94, 95, 108, 120, 126, 129, 345, 347, 349, 356, 357, 361, 363, 366, 380, 388, 523, 574, 606, 611, 637, 647, 652; divinity of 78, 80, 102; dying in (with) 409, 468, 471, 591; election in 411; cf. Election; — enemies of 151; cf. Christ, foes of; — **epiphany of 126–134**; eternity of 59, 98,

[647]

99, 271; **exaltation of** 132, 160, 166, 190, 200, 201, **212–223**, 253, 344; example of 24, 215, 408, 421, 440, 452, 519, 527, 588, 593, 652; expiation 167; cf. Christ, suffering of; — face of 398; cf. Face of Christ; — faithfulness of 58, 61, 77, 93, 103, 173, 174, 192, 229, 230, 232, 268, 315, 347, 353, 362, 385, 407, 432, 477, 615; features of 172, 294, 398; feet of 513; fellowship with 454, 544, 591; cf. Christ, communion; — fighting for 451; cf. Warfare, Christian; — flight into Egypt 273; foes of 153, 164, 172, 192, 198, 210; fold of 512; cf. Church; — following 24, 46, 84, 150, 192, 193, 206, 212, 214, 215, 216, 270, 272, 277, 333, 353, 362, 366, 401, 409, 410, 413, 417, 420, 421, 422, 423, 429, 445, 452, 461, 468, 471, 513, 527, 542, 593, 619, 628; forsaken 153, 174, 177, 183; forsaking 334, 340, 365, 372, 383, 401, 423, 477, 528, 552, 557; foundation 99, 153, 216, 370, 381, 385; fulness of 492; garments of 135, 650; gentleness of 28, 91; gifts for 127, 128, 129, 130; cf. Christ, offerings for; — glorified 149, 236; glorified body 135, 253; glory of 17, 84, 85, 88, 94, 114, 126, 127, 128, 130, 132, 134, 135, 142, 172, 209, 210, 212, 214, 222, 271, 300, 305, 306, 343, 346, 359, 360, 510, 527, 562; glory to 158, 205, 208, 217, 221, 236, 244, 257, 266, 275, 429, 472, 657; glorying in 351; grace of 53, 64, 77, 84, 91, 92, 96, 111, 121, 145, 150, 152, 154, 195, 207, 218, 220, 251, 265, 266, 311, 312, 339, 360, 362, 393, 398, 412, 428, 445, 459, 466, 467, 477, 523, 527, 638; grave of 142, 159, 166, 187, 188, 218, 588; guidance of 120, 127, 200, 320, 333, 338, 340, 345, 349, 353, 362, 368, 407, 408, 410, 413, 420, 421, 422, 426, 431, 433, 436, 437, 526, 542, 547, 559, 631, 643, 648; cf. Guidance; — hands of 513; head of 172, 175; heritage of 494; hope in; cf. Hope in Christ; — hope's foundation 153, 217, 364, 370, 375; humanity of 56, 77, 80, 95, 99, 104, 152, 375, 377, 397, 557; humility of 56, 57, 65, 68, 73, 74, 80, 81, 89, 130, 131, 140, 146, 161, 162, 275, 484; **humiliation of** 68, 80, 81, 84, 85, 86, 96, 97, 99, 100, 104, 105, 108, 132, **140–186**, 222, 253, 387, 628; image of 140, 179, 348, 409; imitating 134, 387, 409, 440, 652, 653; incarnation of 35, 58, 67, 68, 76, 78, 80, 81, 85, 86, 94, 100, 105, 107, 109, 132, 134, 136, 139, 202, 245, 251, 253, 341, 397, 401, 607, 645, 646; indwelling of 16, 55, 75, 85, 94, 96, 106, 107, 145, 197, 309, 345, 347, 351, 366, 459, 467, 562, 591, 647; intercession of 2, 158, 190, 200, 213, 220, 253, 313, 367, 371, 397, 454, 483, 543, 607; of Judah's tribe 105; kindness of 340, 399, 417; kingdom of 85, 95, 130, 132, 135, 137, 264, 462; law of 115; leadership of; cf. Christ, guidance of; — life of 115, 132, 134, 166, 170, 253, 341, 387, 401, 405; life without 357, 359, 429, 528, 606, 625; lineage of 105, 109, 274, 343, 645; living in (to) 93, 120, 201, 315, 333, 348, 349, 412, 422, 439, 453, 468, 478, 482, 489, 540, 551, 591, 598; love for 16, 77, 89, 108, 140, 145, 170, 182, 266, 270, 319, 346, 347, 348, 357, 393, 398, 399, 419, 421, 429, 437, 444, 493, 498, 527, 557, 653, 655, 657; love of 53, 80, 87, 89, 115, 154, 170, 171, 175, 176, 182, 195, 200, 213, 219, 221, 268, 278, 299, 305, 313, 316, 322, 342, 349, 350, 363, 388, 403, 405, 426, 433, 465, 507, 553, 653; loving-kindness of 340, 466, 542; majesty 93, 99, 100, 105, 134, 162, 210, 212, 306, 339; meditation on Passion of; cf. Passion of Christ, pondering on; — meekness of; cf. Christ, humility of; — member of 196, 206, 216, 300, 411; cf. Christ, united with; — mercy of 121, 178, 292, 300, 312, 322, 353, 428, 436, 447, 467, 498, 510, 543, 554, 563,

605; cf. Mercy; — merits of 55, 144, 148, 150, 151, 157, 158, 166, 167, 170, 178, 181, 184, 195, 251, 252, 301, 315, 325, 333, 334, 367, 378, 386, 389, 437, 510, 594, 601, 604; message of; cf. Word of God, preaching; — messengers, servants, of 135, 138, 482; cf. Ministry; — ministry of 10, 66, 69, 134; miracles of 131, 134, 557, 621; mission of 10, 56, 59, 65, 66, 76, 81, 85, 87, 94, 97, 107, 297, 363, 369, 371, 373, 385, 386, 387, 507, 601, 607; mourning over death of 167, 169, 177; mourning, nature mourning over death of 169, 174, 176; name of 93, 114, 115, 116, 345, 351, 407, 460, 463, 511; cf. Name
Christ, Names and Offices of: Abode 433; Heavenly Aaron 218; Abram's Reward 91; Absolver 632; Adam, Second 369; Advocate 220, 522, 543
  All 357, 366, 423, 430; All in All 336, 342, 366, 447; Everlasting All 608, — Almighty 351; Alpha and Omega 98, 351; Anchor 142
  Anointed 83, 589, 611; Lord's Anointed 59, 153. — Author of Life 202; Author of Salvation 100, 139
  Babe 84, 98, 103; Babe of Bethlehem 341; cf. Child; — Heavenly Babe 109; Tender Babe 103. — Balm (in sorrow) 47, 437; Beacon 138; Bearer of th' Eternal Word 475; Beginning without End 343; Beloved of God 556; Benefactor 100; Bliss 137, 430; Bondsman 171; Branch 645; Branch of David's Stem 134
  Bread 54, 312, 550; Bread of Heaven 195, 312, 315; Bread of Life 48, 293, 305, 315, 531, 659; Living Bread 312, 315. — Bridegroom 23, 67, 72, 167, 343, 509, 609, 622; Brightness 138; Brightness of the Father 257; Bringer of Salvation 352; Brother 78, 93, 100, 103, 188, 206, 223, 251, 387, 486, 596; Buckler 433; Builder 640
  Captain 463; Captain of Salvation 471; Great Captain 263. — Captive 35; Castle 387; Cheer 138
  Child 80, 82, 85, 88, 92, 93, 100, 107, 133, 645, 646; Child Divine 117; of Bethlehem 647; of Hope 106; of Mary 645; of Wonder 78; God's own Child 81; Gracious Child 90; Holy 82, 114; Spotless 117; Wondrous 95. — Choice 347
  Christ — Christ-child 85, 89; Christ Crucified 390; Christ Jesus, Lord 353; Christ of God 389, 628; Christ Victorious 207; Risen Christ 212. — Comfort 173, 328; Comforter 531; Confidence 466; Conqueror 77, 188, 218, 361, 637; Consolation 172, 334; Contender 546; Cornerstone 217, 245, 465, 466, 633, 639; Counselor 106, 433; Creator 70, 202, 495, 568; Crown 127, 214, 349, 383, 430, 657; Crown of Gladness 399; Crucified 145, 177, 353, 575, 614, 637; David's Fountain 448; David's Royal Heir 105; Dawn 550; Day 550, 559; Dayspring from on High 62, 359, 539; Day-star 359; Death 195; Death of Death 151; Defender 17, 264, 353, 415, 526, 528, 546; Defense 206, 212, 549; Deity 94
  Delight 58, 312, 383, 430; Heart's Delight 383, 408. — Deliverer 54
  Desire 349; Desire of nations 72, 94, 136, 476; Heart's Desire 120. — Destruction 54; Dispenser of God's Store 438; Divine Instructor 284; Elijah 218; Emmanuel 62, 471; End 364; End of faith 351; Ending 98; Enoch 218; Eternal 82, 343; Ever-blest 108; Ever-open Door 279; Expectation 72; Expiation 37; Father's Face 101; Father's Well-beloved 100; First and Last 343; First-born from the Dead 191
  Flower 645; Beauteous Flower 343; Flower of Heaven 108; Tender Flower

82,—Forerunner 188; Fortress 433, 463; Foundation 179, 217, 383, 466, 477, 632, 639; Foundation-stone 460
Fount—of Grace 108, 429, 569; of Life 305; of Life and Fire 361; of Pity 607; of Pleasure 347,—Fountain 145, 282, 345, 619
Friend 17, 91, 138, 142, 155, 164, 197, 223, 305, 343, 346, 362, 364, 399, 430, 457, 459, 626, 650, 653; Faithful Friend 409; Friend Divine 462; of sinners 386, 552, 650; Heavenly 200, 338, 517, 651; Truest 347, 399,—Gideon 263; Gift of God 85, 581, 647; Giver 469; Giver of Blessing 69; Glory 137, 138, 179, 350, 356
God 61, 67, 76, 77, 78, 85, 89, 93, 99, 106, 121, 144, 166, 175, 214, 310, 325, 343, 353, 360, 398, 637; Eternal God 80, 103; Eternal Lord God 590; and King 98, 360; and Lord 26, 85, 138, 356, 381, 399, 429; and Man 366; God Forevermore 202; God Incarnate 84, 339, 341; God-man 383; God Most High 107; of Armies 218; of God 132, 471; of Heaven 510; of Hosts 214; of Love 221, 423; of Might 132, 423; of Nations 566; of Wisdom 423; of Our Fathers 568; of Our Salvation 258, 343; Our King 480; God Sabaoth 41; God, the King 647; God, the Savior 404; God the Son 5, 38, 95, 244, 475, 492; God with Us 107; Gracious God 404; Incarnate God 133, 139, 380; Lord God 238; Lord God Almighty 258; Mighty God 99, 141, 590; Righteous 590; True 103, 238; True God and Man 173, 645; Very God 645,—Godhead Incarnate 94, 102; Good 124, 316, 366; Grace 101; Ground of Faith 167, 245, 596; Guard 333, 459
Guardian 172, 338, 364, 544, 549, 553, 567; Israel's Guardian 544,—Guest 63, 75, 80, 85, 197, 620, 621, 656; Guest Divine 55; Guide 338, 349, 394, 433, 447, 459, 478, 513, 552, 568, 628; Guiltless 383; Happiness 138; Harbinger 213
Head 51, 172, 188, 193, 195, 206, 216, 219, 409, 411, 466, 472, 476, 528, 566, 593; Ever-living 200; Exalted 484; Gracious 300,—Healer of Strife 628; Health 202, 430, 581; Health and Life 320, 430; Help 69, 91, 137, 167, 433, 552; Helper 73, 340, 353, 581; Hiding Place 364, 456; High Priest 220, 628
Hope 42, 55, 58, 72, 126, 137, 191, 214, 349, 353, 369, 399; and Stay 370; of Contrite Hearts 350; of Men 150; of Nations 82, 258; of the Penitent 531; Sinner's Hope 178,—Horn 433; Host 308, 656
Immanuel 81, 94, 108, 157, 367, 444, 652; Lord Immanuel 647
Infant 76, 82, 85, 100, 105; Holy Infant 646,—Intercessor 2, 611; Israel 204; Israel's Praise and Bliss 137
Jesus 32, 33, 51, 56, 64, 65, 72, 74, 86, 88, 89, 92, 94, 96, 102, 105, 114, 117, 120, 130, 131, 139, 143, 146, 151, 158, 161, 164, 167, 169, 201, 276, 295, 296, 297, 305, 318, 324, 330, 342, 346, 348, 357, 409, 415, 420; Blessed 16, 179, 401; Dearest 53, 300; Despised 367; Holy 116, 127, 180; Jesus, Blessed Lord 309; Jesus Christ 51, 81, 82, 101, 103, 262, 311; Jesus Christ, Our Lord 163, 473; Jesus Christ, Our Savior 82, 266, 406; Jesus, Dearest Child 93; Jesus, Lamb of God 328; Jesus, Lord 134; Jesus, Lover of My Soul 345; Jesus, Our Savior 240,—Jesus, Priceless Treasure 347; Jesus, Savior 356; Jesus, the Lord 141; Jesus, thy God 278; Lord Jesus 6, 74, 75, 78, 106, 150, 173, 254, 263, 292, 312, 320, 334, 366, 375, 428, 430, 477, 485, 491, 585; Lord Jesus Christ 3, 124, 125, 148, 261, 287, 292, 306, 312, 314, 353, 429, 432, 547, 594; Precious Jesus 296,—Jewel of God's Crown 387; Joshua 218;

Joy 124, 127, 137, 138, 195, 212, 214, 219, 305, 349, 350, 399, 430, 569, 657; Joy and Rest 366; Joy of Heaven 351; Joy of the Desolate 531; Judah's Lion 211
Judge 68, 134, 148, 253, 307, 605, 607, 610, 611; Judge Eternal 576; of Mankind 604; Righteous 607,—Just 148; Key of David 62
King 41, 68, 70, 82, 83, 84, 85, 87, 94, 98, 102, 131, 161, 238, 400, 415, 459, 467, 495, 506, 511, 528, 628, 637; Anointed King 10; Christ, our 6; Christ, the 658; Christ, the New-born 136; Church's 244; Galilean 367; Glorious 55, 193; Glorious King and Lord 55; Gracious 69; Heavenly 127, 199, 218; King and Head 51; King Most Glorious 57, 58; King Most Holy 86; King Most Wonderful 361; of Ages 343; of All 341; of (All) Creation 78, 657; of Angels 244; of Glory 73, 91, 130, 213, 221, 244, 304, 451, 463, 638; of Grace 179, 194, 343; of Grief 174; of Heathen Nations 214; of Israel 160; of kings 63, 73, 132, 190, 219, 222, 552, 558, 566, 576, 584; of Light 208; of Love 431; of Majesty 607; of nations 244; of Victory 191; Matchless 341; Mighty 143; Savior King 20, 487; Savior King of kings 222; Triumphant 628; Wondrous 41
Lamb 60, 72, 77, 132, 142, 156, 157, 164, 190, 191, 198, 213, 244, 297, 341, 344, 356, 371, 374, 445, 614, 615, 656; Heavenly Lamb 156; Lamb Divine 347; Lamb for Sinners Slain 419, 476, 495; of Calvary 394; of God 23, 131, 142, 146, 147, 153, 165, 167, 169, 170, 174, 176, 237, 238, 272, 328, 330, 357, 358, 360, 388, 600, 652; Lamb, Our Expiation 37; Paschal Lamb 190, 195, 367,—Lawgiver 115
Leader 613; Heavenly Leader 410,—Life 38, 94, 126, 137, 144, 148, 151, 179, 191, 195, 202, 214, 257, 355, 364, 369, 387, 399, 430, 447, 454, 526, 608, 637; Life and Comfort 328; Life and Light 75; Life and Love 411; Life Divine 334; Life-giver 101; Life, Truth, Way 338
Light 53, 75, 101, 126, 127, 144, 148, 196, 277, 294, 334, 359, 369, 398, 408, 421, 433, 463, 512, 528, 562, 563; Eternal Light 219, 398; Everlasting Light 647; Gentile's Light and Hope 108; Heavenly Light 197; Infant Light 136; and Day 559; Light and Life 94; Light Divine 88, 399; of All Below 361; of All Living 264; of Gentile Nations 138, 498; of Joy 523; of Life 277; of Light 16, 132, 471; 539, 550, 559; of Light Divine 117; of the Soul 657; of the Straying 531; of Zion 609; Saving Light 137,—Long-expected 98, 606
Lord 10, 47, 55, 58, 61, 63, 69, 73, 81, 134, 135, 136, 137, 138, 140, 142, 143, 144, 148, 160, 164, 170, 171, 172, 173, 194, 195, 196, 206, 215, 238, 242, 251, 266, 271, 272, 292, 296, 298, 302, 304, 305, 306, 308, 312, 313, 315, 316, 317, 318, 319, 323, 328, 329, 330, 338, 341, 343, 347, 364, 368, 380, 381, 383, 396, 398, 399, 400, 401, 406, 407, 461; Ascended 212, 230, 232; Blessed 257, 309, 310, 330, 411; Bounteous 53; Buried 202; Christ, Our 217, 265, 421, 472; Christ the 2, 84, 86, 90, 102, 109, 190, 191, 193, 198, 205, 214, 290, 471, 652; Conquering 198, 506; David's 130, 153; Dear 349, 353, 431, 482; Dearest 430; Everlasting Lord 94, 106, 165; Faithful 409; Glorious 16, 227, 352; Gracious 64, 127, 191, 284, 321, 352, 408, 498, 517, 566; Holy 352, 628; Incarnate 273; Jacob's 91; Living 70; Long-expected 139; and God 67, 76, 208, 337, 371; and King 82, 103, 129, 352; and Maker 77; and Savior 89, 217, 293, 411; Lord Christ 97; Lord Christ of Nazareth 253; Lord Divine 404; Lord Most High 238, 548;

[649]

Lord Most Holy 55, 58, 169; Lord Most Mild 92; Lord Most Tender 41; Lord, My God, 1, 38, 318; of All 104, 339; of Angels 161; of Angelic Hosts 255; of Battles 218; of Creation 198; of Earth 193; of Gladness 347; of Glory 79, 442, 645; of Heaven 126, 161, 193, 341; of Hosts 450, 466; of Life 133, 172, 207, 221, 258, 338, 341, 603; of lords 108, 219, 222, 261, 576; of Love 272, 341; of Majesty 139; of Men 161; of Sabaoth 262; of Salvation 419; of the Church 489; of the Harvest 488, 492, 493, 507, 567; of the Nations 657; of Worlds Above 480; Lord, Our Righteousness 297; Our Savior 306; Our Strength 53; Lord supernal 82; Lord, the Virgin-born 115, 273; Lord Victorious 9, 41; Mighty 166, 218, 566; Promised 75; Redeeming 115; Sov'reign 41, 566; Victorious 211

Love (ineffable) 17, 42, 59, 142, 341, 349, 397, 430, 447, 593; Love Divine 351, 419, 435; Wondrous Love 456, — Loveliest and Best 591; Lover of men 555; Lover of my soul 345; Magnet 188; Maker 77, 128, 202, 305; Man 94, 369, 383, 510; Man Divine 339; Man of Sorrows 222

Master 32, 100, 143, 152, 196, 224, 294, 360, 452, 496, 502, 509, 528, 540; Master of Death 315; Master of Schools 486; Gracious Master 360, 442; Royal Master 658, — Mediator 6, 287

Mercy 281, 641; All-embracing Mercy 279, — Messiah 136, 503; Might 17, 463; Monarch 76, 128, 130, 513; Morning Star 69, 121, 343, 346, 498; Bright Morning Star 346, 539, — Most High 42, 101; Name of Might 352

One: My One and All 366; Onebegotten 471; One with the Father 125; Blessed 160, 443, 609; Greater 272; Holy 104, 238, 275; Living 188; Sole-begotten 238, 253; Valiant 262, — Path 447; Peace 430; Peace and Light 310; Physician 138, 322, 626; Pilgrim 197; Pilot 264; Portion 91, 429, 581; Power 433; Plea 561; Pleasure 347, 430; Preserver 555; Pride 628; Pride and Glory 408; Priest 37, 83, 242, 307; Priest and King 37

Prince 613; and Savior 476; of Glory 175; of Graces 343; of Life 108, 167, 171, 177, 191, 196, 602; of Peace 35, 66, 71, 94, 99, 106, 132, 196, 300; of Salvation 139, — Prize 350, 447; Promised Seed 99, 274; Prophet 83, 153, 242; Prophet, Priest, and King 134, 200, 364; Protection 144; Pure 148; Pure Offspring 104; Radiance 399; Radiancy Divine 359; Ransom 55, 387; Recompense 212

Redeemer 11, 15, 19, 51, 53, 67, 73, 83, 98, 121, 128, 145, 149, 159, 160, 161, 172, 200, 202, 206, 242, 257, 284, 339–368, 373, 377, 399, 467, 495, 507, 534, 541, 568, 641; Blest 462; Divine 275; Merciful 498, — Refuge 63, 91, 145, 421, 433, 457, 549; Rescue 173; Rest 167, 366, 430, 615; Resurrection 144, 193; Reward 63, 137, 356, 468; Right 447; Righteousness 2

Rock 206, 364, 370, 433, 460, 463, 467, 477, 518, 526, 637; and Castle 387; and Tower 144; of Ages 376, 469, 614; of Salvation 153; of Strength 121; Everlasting Rock 430, 637; Solid Rock 370, — Rod and Staff 349; Rod of Jesse 62; Ruler 69, 73

Sacrifice 121, 141, 153, 162; All-atoning Sacrifice 170, — Salvation 63, 69, 137, 179, 334, 353, 437, 540

Savior 8, 21, 28, 47, 66, 70, 76, 77, 91, 92, 96, 109, 124, 130, 149, 154, 155, 159, 165, 166, 171, 172, 180, 192, 206, 209, 212, 221, 226, 231, 243, 268, 272, 278, 280, 281, 284, 302, 304, 306, 309, 315, 316, 335, 338, 342, 343, 345, 349, 363, 366, 375, 376, 381, 385, 389, 399, 403, 417, 422, 427, 429, 486; All-Inviting Savior 129; All-Merciful 590; Almighty 75; Beautiful 657; Blessed 41, 177, 207, 223, 311, 333, 394, 435; Christ, Our 321; Christ, the 646; Dear 264, 294, 299, 310, 353, 491; Faithful 53, 137, 298; Glorious 203; Gracious 386, 627; Holy 32; Incarnate 274; Loving 152, 362, 560; Only 307, 373; Perfect 358; Precious 352, 457; and God 433, 487; and King 102, 352, 462, 471; and Redeemer 121; Savior Blest 282, 353; Savior Divine 394; from Above 138, 145; Savior Meek and Mild 89; of All 128; of Mankind 175, 350; of Nations 95; Savior of Our Race 98; of the World 55, 73, 84; Savior Tender 194; Sinner's Only 169; Universal Savior 367, — Servant-Lord 383

Shepherd 51, 104, 143, 172, 299, 300, 315, 324, 329, 338, 364, 415, 426, 431, 436, 441, 493, 523, 560, 628, 631, 648; Chief Shepherd 490; Gentle 627, 634; Good 431, 491; of tender youth 628; Tender 595, — Shield 17, 54, 172, 348, 364, 437, 444, 456, 549, 559; Solace 194, 615

Son 25, 32, 36, 38, 63, 77, 85, 92, 103, 104, 105, 106, 118, 133, 142, 236, 248, 250, 251, 261, 288, 297, 317, 325, 326, 335, 343, 373, 375, 379, 382, 387, 438, 443, 454; Almighty 242; Anointed 162, 174; Beloved 27, 375, 387; David's Greater 59; David's Holy 10; David's Royal 160; David's 10, 55, 59, 130, 153; David's Son of Jacob's Race 343; Eternal 12, 117, 125, 233, 331, 450; Everlasting 68; Father's 38, 238; Father's Only 95, 174; Glorious 291; God's Exalted 214; God's Only 140; God's Own 6, 78, 81, 253, 275; God's 99, 167, 192, 373, 523, 609, 611; God the Father's Only 167; God the Mighty Maker 154; Great David's Greater 59; Incarnate 101; Mary's 104, 252, 343; of the Father 102; of God 62, 71, 74, 77, 81, 93, 99, 101, 143, 151, 153, 252, 343, 352, 389, 401, 407, 411, 417, 429, 444, 452, 646, 657; of God's Delight 164; of Man 153, 657; of Mary 622; Only 245, 311; Only Son of God 237; Savior Son 236; True and Only 202; Virgin's 82, 84, 95, 274, 341, — Song 628; Source 98, 129, 172, 251, 358; Source of Love 282; Sovereign 73, 154; Sovereign of the Sea 649; Splendor 305, 528; Spring 569; Staff 349, 648; Staff and Song 628

Star 77, 138, 258, 277, 609; Jacob's 90, 99; of Mercy 129; of Morn 108; of the East 128; of Zion 609

Stay 47, 121, 173, 183, 194, 247, 330, 362, 369, 407, 446, 552, 626, 648; Sinner's Stay 330, — Stem of Jesse's Rod 339; Stranger 650; Strength 53, 54, 91, 148, 194, 257, 399, 447, 549, 637; Strength and Righteousness 325

Sun 58, 60, 73, 127, 138, 193, 195, 277, 528; Glorious Sun 192; from Heaven 399; of Gladness 88, 554; of Grace 88, 96, 196, 539; of Life 305; of Love 550; of Righteousness 94, 106, 359, 505; of Righteousness Divine 543; of the Soul 551; of Truth 550, — Surety 220, 561; Sweetness 361; Teacher 485; Thought 637

Tower 399, 433, 637; Mighty Tower 82, — Treasure 77, 81, 82, 214, 216, 347, 349, 357, 365, 387, 393, 419, 430; Treasury 364; True and Faithful 202; Trust 38, 148; Truth 294, 338, 355, 433, 454

Victim 117, 191, 307; Paschal Victim 191

Victor 210, 217, 219, 222; Mighty Victor 209; Victor-king 188

Vine 411, 544, 594; Precious Vine 300, — Virgin-born 108, 115, 273; Way 121, 338, 355, 364, 369, 421, 433, 454, 485; Way of Life 300; Way to Heaven 214;

Wealth 430; Wedding-guest 134; Wisdom 294, 433, 641; Woman's Offspring 95; Wonderful 106
  Word 76, 81, 153, 641; All-subduing 628; Father's Word Supernal 271; Glorious 189; Incarnate 70, 165, 198, 239, 241, 242; Living 294; of God 95; of God Incarnate 294; of Grace 195; Omnipotent 102; Word Made Flesh 81; Word Supernal 271; Word Supreme 271, — Zion's Help 466; Zion's Helper 91; Zion's Hope 42
Christ (General listing continued), nearness of 57, 58, 62, 63, 65, 69, 72, 89, 90, 97, 174, 183, 284, 296, 315, 320, 340, 343, 349, 357, 362, 381, 422, 426, 429, 431, 436, 437, 444, 456, 469, 523, 528, 540, 546, 549, 551, 555, 559, 562, 565; need of 63, 93, 108, 121, 148, 200, 345, 346, 356, 359, 383, 388, 429, 447, 552, 557, 594, 607; oath of 370; obedience of 115, 132, 133, 134, 142, 185, 387; obedience to 300, 305, 328, 366, 493; offerings for 59, 108, 127, 128, 129, 131, 143, 403, 404, 441; omnipotence 81, 100, 106, 142, 214, 221, 223, 253, 306, 482, 649; omnipresence 76, 213, 223, 229, 306, 343, 485; omniscience 58, 457, 467, 542; one with the Father 550; **passion of** 33, 115, **140–186**, 253, 324, 328, 387, 397; cf. Christ, suffering of; — patience of 146, 147, 151, 171, 276, 552; peace of 146, 147, 204, 208, 467; peace with 318; picture of 294; power of 64, 65, 100, 131, 142, 162, 214, 223, 389, 412, 557, 587; praise for 38, 41, 59, 70, 75, 76, 79, 90, 104, 108, 114, 132, 139, 157, 160, 161, 178, 191, 193, 198, 201, 211, 214, 223, 257, 263, 294, 297, 305, 313, 331, 340, 351, 352, 360, 361, 362, 363, 364, 371, 380, 399, 408, 426, 429, 431, 467, 511, 526, 568, 634, 638; cf. Praise, songs of, Songs of praise; — prayer for 511; prayer of 177; prayer to 2, 16, 47, 55, 62, 64, 70, 72, 74, 116, 120, 125, 138, 139, 146, 148, 160, 194, 197, 215, 216, 223, 238, 257, 258, 264, 265, 268, 296, 300, 310, 312, 314, 318, 320, 338, 345, 357, 393, 429, 439, 446, 466, 477, 488, 516, 517, 524, 552, 559, 639; preparation for; cf. Preparation for Christ; — presence of 2, 3, 53, 65, 70, 73, 135, 136, 138, 161, 197, 208, 214, 223, 229, 307, 315, 325, 343, 356, 368, 492, 540, 552, 562, 594, 620, 621, 622, 634, 637, 643; invisible presence of 223, 306, 557; presentation of 136–139; proceeding from Father; cf. Eternal generation; — prophetic office of 485; cf. Christ, threefold office of; — protection of 47, 53, 96, 148, 172, 220, 228, 263, 264, 307, 319, 345, 349, 357, 368, 528, 554, 560; cf. Protection, divine; — radiance of 399, 543, 550, 646; reception of; cf. Reception of Christ; — reign of 7, 10, 50, 57, 59, 61, 64, 87, 106, 124, 125, 130, 132, 162, 168, 188, 198, 209, 210, 211, 213, 218, 221, 223, 271, 305, 307, 349, 356, 366, 451, 459, 466, 476, 487, 495, 503, 511, 638; reliance on 319, 540, 598, 608, 652; rest in 551; **resurrection of** 8, 9, 12, 159, 166, 187–211, 218, 251, 253, 341; revealed in Bible 408; right hand of 607, 660; righteousness of 87, 142, 239, 264, 297; rod and staff of 431, 436, 437; royal banner of 451; rules the world 221, 307; cf. Christ, reign of; — sacrifice of 115, 141, 142, 150, 153, 156, 158, 165, 171, 176, 220, 248, 272, 297, 307, 310, 319, 326, 340, 341, 360, 365, 375, 384, 386, 387, 507; seeking 127, 136, 208, 214, 361, 383, 390, 557; cf. God, seeking; — seeking lost sheep 431; cf. Lost, seeking the; — serving 293, 353, 381, 390, 423, 446, 451, 477, 491, 493, 498, 527, 557, 608, 626, 657; session of 195, 198, 212, 217, 221, 238, 253, 344, 367; side of 513, 627; cf. Christ, wounds of; — sin-bearer 142, 146, 150, 153, 155, 170, 171, 172, 177, 178, 190, 207, 272, 328, 360, 367, 369, 375, 380, 387, 440, 457, 652; sinlessness of 73, 89, 115, 117, 131, 139, 141, 142, 143, 146, 151, 158, 169, 170, 171, 191, 253, 383, 387; solace of 576, 600; standing before 472; cf. Judgment, standing in the; — strength of 450; submission of 142; cf. Christ, obedience of; — substitute 115, 154, 156, 191, 196, 207, 253, 313, 369, 386, 397; suffering of 114, 115, 117, 140, 142, 143, 148, 151, 153, 154, 155, 170, 172, 177, 183, 218, 221, 311, 317, 326, 367, 405, 407, 594; cf. Passion of Christ; — suffering with 409, 471; cf. Christians, cross of; — tears of 419; temptation of 166, 557; threefold office 83, 134, 200; cf. Christ, prophetic office; — transfiguration of 135; trial of 159; **triumph** 56, 94, 162, 168, **187–211**, 213, 487; triumphant (triumphal) entry 58, 70, 160, 161, 162, 588, 592; cf. Christ, second advent; — triumphant return 604; triumphal return to heaven 212, 214, 218; trophies of 341; trust in 26, 74, 89, 140, 163, 170, 223, 245, 292, 333, 345, 353, 362, 365, 375, 377, 379, 383, 384, 408, 427, 428, 433, 435, 442, 447, 477, 516, 524, 527, 528, 540, 553; types of 132, 211; unchangeableness of 467, 552; union with (communion with Christ) 23, 68, 77, 81, 93, 135, 145, 177, 188, 192, 196, 201, 206, 213, 244, 305, 314, 315, 342, 343, 349, 357, 366, 387, 404, 411, 431, 463, 471, 594, 598, 620; cf. Christ, fellowship; — victory through 517; victory of 218, 262; cf. Christ, triumph of; — Virgin Birth 76, 78, 80, 85, 94, 95, 98, 100, 102, 107, 108, 251, 253, 274, 313, 387; voice of 276, 281, 284, 421, 496, 512, 626; waiting for 55, 138; walking before 546; walking with 216, 409, 412, 413, 422; cf. Christ, following; — weeping of 420; weeping o'er Jerusalem 419; will of 4, 264, 348, 398, 406, 420, 435, 540, 545, 547; cf. God, will of; — wisdom of 133, 541; witnessing for 453, 461; word of 16, 53, 314, 319, 328, 329, 330, 353, 355, 421; work of 58, 65, 66, 74, 106, 345, 360, 375, 380, 389, 405, 507, 508; cf. Christ, merits of; — worthy of honor, praise 344, 367; worship 187, 352, 477; worthy of praise 132, 367; wounds of 144, 148, 173, 177, 184, 210, 280, 293, 335, 341, 356, 376, 380, 407, 411, 413, 420, 549, 557, 627; cf. Wounds of Christ; — wrath of 604, 610; yoke of 596
Christendom 28, 90, 105, 125, 130, 190, 238, 261; cf. Church; — saints of 470
Christian, education 627–631; life 393–453
Christians 69, 96, 100, 107, 112, 191, 254, 282, 444, 446; armor of; cf. Armor; — ascension of 196, 206, 207, 212, 214, 216, 217, 218, 315, 340, 589, 593, 596; baptized into Christ 229; cf. Christ, baptized into; — blessedness of 26, 29, 48, 97, 122, 208, 307, 357, 362, 368, 377, 387, 391, 392, 414, 427, 437, 453, 469, 487, 513, 552, 648; boast of 528; call of 270, 421, 424, 485; cf. Invitation; — calling of 412, 546, 547, 550; chosen by God 461; cf. Election; — comfort of 203, 523; cf. **Cross and comfort;** — cross of 69, 72, 118, 138, 140, 159, 171, 173, 181, 192, 219, 347, 395, 403, 406, 409, 413, 418, 421, 423, 429, 477, 479, 481, **513–535**; cf. Cross and comfort; — dangers to 254; death of 65, 77, 93, 111, 119, 172, 177, 186, 192, 194, 197, 201, 206, 215, 226, 227, 228, 261, 292, 293, 319, 324, 328, 334, 340, 348, 349, 356, 364, 376, 395, 459, 526; cf. Death; — duty of 289, 527, 546; engraved on hand of God 529; faithful 102, 204, 477, 493; fallen 485; foe of 254; glory of 391; honored 430; hope of 207, 215, 216, 217, 219, 221; cf. Hope; — joy of 219, 314, 377, 387, 469; known to Christ by name 648; marriage of 622; cf. Marriage; — motto of 529

[651]

Christians, Names of: Christians 219, 579; Apostolic Band 212; Believers 72; Beloved 519; Blest of the Lord 415; Brethren of Christ 409; Brothers 658; Child of God 2, 5, 21, 25, 48, 99, 298, 299, 337, 362, 364, 372, 402, 412, 444, 585, 632; Child of Heaven 300, 423, 520
Children 605; of God 494, 659; of Heavenly Birth 391; of Light 8, 80, 88; of Salvation 472
Chosen — Chosen Band 19; Generation 19; Heirs 561; Nation 23, 343; Ones 619; Race 498, 602, — Conquerors 444, 450, 472; cf. Christ, conquering through; — Elect of God 476; cf. Election; — Elect from Every Nation 473; Exiles 476, 605; Faithful 204, 472, 658; Faithful Warriors 463; cf. Warfare, Christian; — Faithful Witnesses 235; Father's Holy Child 652; Flock 19, 70 254, 263, 264, 265, 267; cf. Church; — Followers of Christ 619; Followers of the Lamb 445
God's — Children 26, 112; Elect 448, 633; Folk 14; House of Living Stones 467; Own 103, 404, 420, 432, 433, 556; People 13, 16, 44, 61, 219, 427, 434, 485, 490, 493, 500, 534, 566, 574, 582; Son 58, — Habitation of God 467
Heirs 634; of David's Line 339; of Glory 72; of Heavenly Glory 526; Joint 21, 32, 215, — Heroes 472; Israel's Seed 329; Kings 244; Lamb 254, 315, 427, 441, 484, 490, 491, 493, 595, 631, 634; Lights on Earth 391; Little Children 271; Living Stones 632; Living Temples 637; Loved Ones 554; Members of Christ 206, 409; New-born Creature 411; New Creation 301, 351; cf. Regeneration; — Noble Army 452; Passing Guest 148; Pilgrim 54, 294, 459, 553, 586; Pilgrim Brothers 481; Prophets, Priests, Kings 228
Ransomed — of the Lord 601; People 481, 614; Race 241, 339; Soul 394, 403, 431, — Redeemed of Christ 634; Righteous 414; Saints 35, 72, 215, 221, 222, 241, 248, 307, 414, 427, 460; Saints of God 502; Seed 298; Seed of Israel's Chosen Race 339; Servant 320, 332, 448, 466, 472, 488, 551, 559, 567; Sheep 254, 324, 338, 372, 416, 484, 490, 493, 607, 634; Shepherd's Lamb 648; Soldiers 332, 445, 450, 463, 586, 658; Soldiers of Christ 450; Soldiers of the Cross 451, 501; Sons and Daughters 469, 598, 640; Sons of God 226, 391, 571; Sons of the Kingdom 69, 208; Spirit-born 329; Stewards 441; Strangers 553, 586, 660; Subjects 69; Temple 235, 335, 467; cf. Temple; — The Lord's 453; Unworthy 640; Wanderers 616; Wedding-guests 67; Zion's Sons and Daughters 282
Christians (General listing continued), nominal 445; of all walks of life 471; persecution of 444, 467, 470, 528; cf. Persecution; — prayer of 454; cf. Prayers; — preservation of 264; protection of 485, 528, 559; resurrection of 604; sacrifice 143; security 65, 103, 192, 345, 347, 349, 376, 526; service 441; sufferings of 219, 468; trust 290; unity 231, 241, 248, 253, 314; weeping of 535; zeal of 231
Christlikeness 91, 134, 180, 361, 403, 409, 653
Christmas 76–109, 82, 86, 88, 100; cf. Christ, birth of
Church 20, 38, 64, 67, 69, 129, 208, 251, 253, 254, 271, 274, 294, 333, 460, 460–632; cf. Christians; — afflictions 61, 64, 260, 261, 265, 267, 268, 269; altars of the 462; anniversary 639–640; attendance 70, 133, 138, 366, 412, 467, 480, 487, 494, 503, 630, 638; beauty of the 632, 633; birth of the 473; blessings on 188, 213, 462, 474, 489, 539, 633, 642; building; cf. Sanctuary; — building the 460, 461, 467, 477, 510, 632; charter of salvation of the 473; children of the 630; Christ, foundation of 217, 460, 473, 477; clothed in garments of salvation 632; communion of the 462, 478; confesses name of Christ 473, 477, 566; conflict of the 481; corner-stone laying of 632–633; corner-stone of 217; cf. Christ, Names of, Corner-stone; — created by Holy Ghost 251; cross of the 479; dedication 634–638; dedication of the 467; cf. Sanctuary; — defense of 261, 268, 473; desire for 480; ecumenical 224, 250, 360, 473; endures 477; everlasting light of the 474, 479; faith of the 481; faithful members of 493; faithfulness to 462; false sons of the 473; fears of 464; foes of 254, 256, 258, 260, 261, 292, 461, 469, 472, 473, 474; food of the 473; foundation of the 217, 460, 469; founded by God 469; founded on (God) Christ 637; glory of 469, 635; guidance of 253, 264, 473, 489; heavenly prize of 479; honor of the 461; head of 477; cf. Christ, Names, Head; — hope of the 473, 481; hymns of the 462, 465, 481; in earth and heaven 512; Joy of the 481; King of the 244; Lord of the 473, 489; loved by God 474; love for the 462; Means of Grace in 473, 477; cf. Means of Grace; — members of 469, 481, 493, 628; message of 461; militant 463, 464, 470, 472, 473, 478; cf. Warfare, Christian; — ministers of; cf. Ministers
Church, Names of: Ark 258; Abode of God 469; Army of the Living God 478; Bearer of th' Eternal Word 475; Bride 23, 57, 305, 432, 473, 622, 632; Bulwarks of Our Land 636; Children of God 13, 26; Chosen Host 253, 298; Chosen Nation 343; Chosen Rest 638; Church of God 658; Congregation 217, 260, 306, 639; Creation of Christ 473; Delight of Christ 638; Flock 254, 260, 263, 265, 267, 269, 477, 485, 493, 530, 539, 631; Fold 484, 485; God's Host 294, 472, 478; Holy Family 182; Imperial Salem 503; Israel 28, 62, 204, 329; Israel's Chosen Race 339; Jerusalem 61, 487, 609; Mighty Army 658; Mighty Nation 472; One Family 478; Peaceful Fold 499; Pilgrim Band 481; Place of Prayer 480; Spouse 622; Tribes of Israel 218; Zion 460; cf. Zion
Church (General listing continued), peace in (of) 112, 258, 313, 473; perils of the 481; persecution of 259, 262, 265; Power of the Keys 331; praise of 4, 9, 10, 35, 38, 250, 628; prayer for the 125, 260, 264, 292, 294, 462, 544, 580; cf. Prayers; — prayers in the 632; prayer of 258, 265, 464; preservation of 258, 264, 265, 268, 458, 467, 473, 474, 485, 635, 658; protection of 258, 260, 264, 267, 292, 460, 461, 469, 473, 633, 636; ransomed 157; redeemed 23, 462, 473; Reformation 258 to 269; rule over the 307; sacraments in 634; cf. Sacraments; — schisms of 473; scoffers of the 462; security of 28, 69, 72, 258, 262, 264, 267, 268, 461, 473, 637, 658; seed of the 259; serving the 462; services 467, 480; terrestrial (militant) 4; traitors of the 473; tribulations of 268, 473; cf. Trials; — triumph of 262, 263; triumphant 11, 360, 468, 470, 471, 473, 475, 476, 478; union of Christ and 620; unity of 38, 129, 224, 251, 261, 313, 314, 464, 466, 473, 477, 478, 580, 658; victorious 473; vows of the 462; wisdom for 271; world united against the 474; worship in 634; youth of the 494; and State 112; Church year 55–275
Cleopas 194
Clothed in garments of salvation 632; cf. Saints, clothed; — in glorious majesty 382, 432; in glory 382, 432; in glory (angels) 356; in perfection 603; in rich garments

264; in robes of white 613; in royal dress 297
Comfort 18, 58, 67, 77, 81, 96, 110, 122, 136, 142, 144, 148, 152, 163, 187, 196, 219, 237, 245, 251, 253, 256, 276, 296, 306, 312, 315, 322, 324, 329, 345, 349, 362, 464; cf. Holy Ghost, comfort of; — of preaching 61
Commandments, of Christ 264, 416; walking in the 629; First 287, 298; Second 287; Third 287, 580; Fourth 177, 182, 287; Fifth 287; Sixth 287; Seventh 287; Eighth 287; Ninth 287; Tenth 287; Ten 287
Commending, body and spirit to God 393, 406, 425, 433, 517, 540, 549, 560, 594, 600; country to God 578
Commission, the Great 332
Communicants, Guest (name) 163, 305, 308, 311, 314, 315, 316, 318, 330; unworthy 163, 311; worthy 163, 305, 306, 310, 311, 312, 315, 330
Communion, with Christ 23, 188, 213, 215, 216, 219, 308, 313, 314, 379, 544; cf. Christ, fellowship; — with God 1, 21, 241, 305; of Saints 20, 67, 92, 148, 208, 221, 224, 231, 248, 250, 253, 339, 360, 415, 460–481, 513, 608, 618; cf. Saints, communion of
Compassion, divine 18, 27, 34, 140, 158, 166, 268, 312, 351, 353, 384, 387, 548
Conception, immaculate 95, 100, 104
Concord 292
Condescension 335; cf. Christ, condescension of
Conference, pastoral 490
Confession and absolution 317–331; cf. Sin
Confidence 77, 103, 201, 206, 262, 287, 329, 368, 370, 372, 381, 385, 386; cf. Doubt, Trust, Faith
Confirmation 332–338, 639; Church's ordered way, 333; prayer at 337
Conflict 47, 58, 61, 121, 143, 173, 193, 195, 260, 261, 262, 263, 264, 266, 269, 276, 320, 332, 337, 338, 340, 368, 413, 437, 461, 463; indifferent, careless 449; inner 388, 398, 421, 446, 456; one 481; victorious 472, 568, 613, 643
Congregation 639; cf. Church
Conscience 140, 156, 177, 220, 266, 297, 317, 402, 536, 543; opprest 512, 594; peace of 140, 156, 177, 286, 297, 324, 395, 416, 459
Conscience-stricken 140, 220, 317, 326, 373, 377, 386
Consecration 24, 25, 32, 40, 41, 47, 73, 120, 142, 150, 175, 201, 225, 226, 228, 231, 234, 270, 296, 298, 308, 313, 314, 316, 332, 333, 334, 335, 336, 338, 347, 348, 349, 393–405, 477, 538, 550, 567
Consolation 16, 65, 69, 77, 173, 235, 268, 272, 284, 306, 319, 362, 437, 510, 520
Constancy 74, 77, 89, 93, 141, 142, 143, 167, 171, 172, 207, 224, 235, 264, 292, 348, 365, 366, 372, 383, 385
Contemplation of Christ's Passion 140, 150, 167, 169, 171, 172, 175, 176; cf. Christ, Meditation on Passion of
Contentment 77, 155, 196, 357, 362, 365, 430, 492, 518, 521, 571, 598, 651, 660
Contrition 34, 60, 112, 140, 149, 150, 152, 154, 166, 167, 288, 296, 306, 310, 312, 315, 316, 319, 323, 329, 350, 376, 385, 389, 390, 392, 411, 454, 543, 590, 607; cf. Penitence, Repentance
Conversation, Christian 395; cf. Speech; — sincere 536
Conversion 74, 126, 129, 264, 288, 382, 417, 458, 482, 494, 497, 500, 503, 504
Conviction 200
Corner-stone laying 632–633
Coronation 222; cf. Christ, coronation of
Corruption 369, 377, 378; cf. Human depravity
Counsel 332
Country, blessings for 112, 569, 578, 584; Fatherland (name) 580; peace of the 581; cf. Nation; — prayer for 544, 566, 578, 580; cf. Nation

Courage 58, 69, 120, 178, 206, 226, 231, 262, 263, 292, 335, 372, 514; increase of 445, 451, 464
Covenant 51, 59, 117, 129, 149, 164, 337; Baptismal 298, 337, 467; cf. Baptism; — solemn 625
Covetousness 287
Craft, hellish 546; cf. Hell; — subtle 306
Creation 8, 9, 12, 14, 17, 19, 23, 35, 38, 43, 85, 104, 108, 198, 202, 236, 241, 243, 251, 252, 253, 254, 255, 267, 271, 286, 299, 429, 438, 476, 507, 514, 549, 566, 569, 570, 621; awaking of 607; beauty of 657; before 98, 123, 271, 343, 385, 387, 397; end of 604; glory of 286, 546; of man; cf. Man, creation of; — peace o'er all 100; cf. Peace; — praise at 438; cf. Praise; — praise of Christ 41, 80, 83, 84, 87, 91, 98, 127, 139, 158, 193, 198, 202, 205, 212, 238, 244, 339, 344, 511, 647; cf. Praise; — praise of God 30, 41, 42, 43, 84, 91, 240, 250, 255, 442, 542, 546; story of 136, 508; sustained 567
Credo 251, 252, 253, 288
Creed, First Article 30, 39, 112, 251, 253, 507, 549; Second Article 218, 251, 252, 253, 507; Third Article 251, 253, 507
Crime 501, 580
Cross, and comfort 69, 72, 77, 81, 110, 111, 118, 122, 144, 173, 181, 192, 200, 206, 207, 219, 226, 227, 252, 268, 317, 345, 354, 362, 373, 383, 385, 393, 394, 401, 409, 420, 422, 425, 427, 513–535, 546, 583, 586, 651; banner of the 332, 471, 658; cf. Gospel, Word of God; — bearing the 523, 619, 651; blessings of the 178, 219, 354
    Cross of Christ 110, 117, 145, 166, 168, 171, 175, 177, 178, 199, 214, 218, 219, 305, 323, 336, 380, 390, 552; beauty of 168; comfort of 142; clinging to 376, 607; dawn of heaven 155; following the 658; glory of 168; glorying in 219, 354, 358; guidance of 431; cf. Guidance; — healing gifts of 390; heralds of 483; inscription on 178, 179; life through 144; merits of 252, 326, 376, 610; Names — Banner 471; Staff in Life 148; Tree 153, 154, 156, 168, 174, 176, 178, 195, 198, 253, 271, 599, — pledge 171, 178; radiance of 354, 407; sharing the 192; strength through 144; triumph of 504; trust in 358, 604, 610
    Cross (continued), seven words on 177, 180–186; first 177, 180; second 177, 181; third 177, 182; fourth 174, 177, 183; fifth 177, 184; sixth 159, 177, 185; seventh 169, 176, 177, 186, — of Christians; cf. Christians, cross of; — of scorn 479; preaching of the 510; cf. Preaching; — sent by God 523; cf. Cross and comfort; — soldiers of the 444
Crown, Christian's 81, 121, 142, 143, 151, 171, 192, 351, 448, 449, 452, 520; everlasting 221, 448; golden 67, 246, 256, 463, 554, 601; heavenly 81, 273, 279; jeweled 483; of derision 222; of glory 219, 444; of heaven; cf. Heaven; — of joy 143; of life; cf. Life; — of righteousness 142; of thorns 140, 143, 151, 172, 175, 219, 513; of victory 209, 332, 415; perishable 658; royal 452
Curse 87, 99, 150, 151, 295, 386; conquered 511; deliverance from the 156, 163, 295; primal 100, 369
Cymbals 609

Daily, blessings 28, 38, 45, 118, 227, 251, 253, 288, 368, 393, 404; cf. Blessings; — bread 434, 455, 458, 544, 573; cares 385, 522, 563; cf. Cares; — conflict 449; forgiveness 251, 253, 537, 558, 560, 563; grace 353, 417, 479, 521, 539, 542, 563; gratitude 310, 555, 563; help 288; joys 555; life 540; mercies 11, 24, 25, 33, 42, 119, 227, 251, 253, 417, 537; prayer 537; strength 120, 200, 227, 229, 231, 459, 479,

[653]

537; strife 537; thanksgiving 543, 563; toils 555; vows 59; worship 246, 250, 400, 469, 511, 536, 537, 540, 542, 543, 544, 546, 548, 564, 643, 653

Darkness, powers of 558; cf. Spiritual darkness; — works of 60; cf. Works

David 103, 105, 109, 130, 134, 153, 160, 168, 211, 274, 339, 343, 448; throne of 613

Day, beginning of the 536, 540, 654; cf. Morning; — close of 540, 543, 560, 561, 562, 563, 653, 654; Confirmation 336; consecrated 400; cf. Consecration; — everlasting 133, 285, 340, 423, 601, 604; cf. Heaven; — evil 319, 446, 518; glorious 463; cf. Resurrection; — God's great 391; great 148

Dead, blessedness of the 589, 615, 616; cf. Saints; — mourning the 593, 596; cf. Death and burial; —resurrection of the 604, 610; cf. Resurrection

Death, and burial 585–602; agony of 597; awaking from 536, 565, 587, 592, 594, 602, 603, 606, 607, 611, 612; cf. Resurrection; — bitter pangs of 590; blessed 406, 412, 527, 543, 585, 596; certainty of 113, 413, 598, 601, 616; comfort in 91, 119, 121, 172, 173, 178, 306, 373, 429, 520, 523, 526, 594, 600, 601, 651; conquered, freed from power 56, 57, 62, 103, 144, 176, **187–211**, 213, 217, 223, 315, 341, 366, 387, 393, 409, 432, 453, 471, 476, 511, 528, 594, 601, 607; consolation in 65, 172, 201, 226, 364, 458; decrying 347; defying 194, 266, 393, 552; deliverance in 561, 590; departure 381, 524, 585; destroyed 69; entrance into God's kingdom 527; eternal 173, 196, 415, 458; evil sudden 548; faithfulness unto 121, 143, 235, 298, 337, 444, 449, 452, 470, 479, 528, 598; fear of 54, 138, 142, 143, 178, 192, 194, 201, 203, 206, 266, 315, 368, 384, 431, 436, 523, 558, 585, 588, 593, 594, 598; final strife 261; gain for the Christian 597, 602, 608, 616; gate of life immortal 201; gate to heaven 336, 523, 601; gloomy portal 601; grim foe of Christ 172, 191, 192, 193, 195; guidance through 368, 603, 649; harmless 355; hosts of 220; hour of 6, 35, 50, 65, 77, 93, 111, 124, 144, 148, 171, 172, 173, 177, 186, 192, 194, 197, 216, 226, 231, 245, 293, 315, 324, 340, 349, 356, 364, 365, 372, 376, 381, 394, 396, 420, 429, 449, 453, 478, 515, 517, 526, 533, 538, 552, 560, 565, 590, 592, 594, 597, 598, 600, 603, 616, 619; life's last portal 26, 45, 192; life through 602; love of Christ unto 404; mortal strife 516; Names for — Blessed Sleep 587; Blissful Refuge 587; Flood 478; Foe 151; cf. Foe; — Peaceful Rest 587, 589; Stream 478, — night of 206; overthrown 77; parting 464; path of 368, 426, 586; peaceful 86, 124, 125, 138, 197, 216, 228, 245, 288, 373, 395, 396, 402, 406, 411, 429, 434, 585, 594, 597, 598; power of 523; prayer at 172, 194, 418, 454, 515, 516, 590, 592, 594, 600; prayer for peaceful 395, 406, 598, 600, 603; cf. Prayer; — preparing for 598; protection in 590, 594; quickened from 405; reign of 92, 195, 201, 207, 296, 387; resurrected from 536, 604; sinner's 331; slumber, sleep 137, 190, 204, 393, 395, 415, 429, 587; snares of 590; sting of 193, 195, 198, 208, 210, 552, 587; summons of 560, 565; threat of 315, 598; transitory 207; triumph over 162, 210, 458

Death of Christ, baptized into; cf. Christ, baptized into; — cause of 140; celebration of 163; cf. Lord's Supper; — foretaste of 115; forgiveness through 319, 599; cf. Forgiveness; — glorying in 175, 178, 346; merits of 380, 594, 600; perfect sacrifice 375; pleading the 213, 330; purpose of 199, 341, 342, 373, 438, 456; ransom 380; redemption through 382,

596; sinless 145, 152; source of bliss 601; trust in 144

Delaying; cf. Indifference

Deliverance, complete 67, 260–269, 295

Delusions 512

Depravity; cf. Human depravity

Desolate, seeking the 440; cf. Missions

Despair 279, 317, 375, 386, 387, 523, 535, 624; saved from 56, 58, 146, 150, 375, 377, 387, 435, 461, 517, 526

Despondency 91, 226

Devotion 3, 20, 30, 42, 59, 108, 128, 144, 194, 568, 582, 608

Diadem, golden 72; royal 219, 339

Disciples, call of 270; Christ dwelling with 552; Emmaus 194, 197

Discipline 287

Dissenter, bold 603

Distress 73, 77, 121, 125, 138, 185, 194, 207, 265, 385, 393, 423, 433, 440, 520; days of 292, 427, 446; hope in 624; sore 513

Doctrines, endure 290; false 130, 260, 292, 406, 429, 458; cf. Errors; — purity of 260, 283, 285, 286, 292, 477, 485, 491, 544; six chief parts of Christian 288; unity of 658

Dominions 475; cf. Kingdoms

Doubt 183, 208, 235, 281, 329, 373, 377, 386, 512; cf. Unbelief; — assailed by 306, 310, 388, 535; banish 201, 203, 538; freed from 91, 396, 425, 458; depths of distressing 362; removed 71, 194, 225, 276, 415, 499; sinful 557; stilled 216

Doxology, long-meter 644; C. M. 106, 248, 360, 525; S. M. 68, 117, 133, 241, 320; L. M. 3, 5, 12, 14, 63, 104, 115, 131, 168, 233, 242, 245, 331, 332, 536, 541, 550, 558, 559, 564, 644; L. M. with Alleluia 212; 6. 5. 6. 5. 654; 7. 7. 7. 7. 95, 570; 7. 7. 7. 7. with Alleluia 199; 8. 5. 8. 3. 643; 8. 7. 8. 7. 60; 8. 8. 4. 7. 211; 11. 11. 11. 5. 240; 6. 6. 6. 6. 8. 8. 642; 7. 7. 7. 7. 7. 571; 7. 8. 7. 8. 7. 7. 250; 7. 8. 7. 8. 8. 8. 16; 8. 7. 8. 7. 7. 257; 8. 7. 8. 7. 8. 7. 139, 271, 466, 641; 8. 8. 7. 4. 4. 7. 524; 8. 8. 8. 8. 8. 8. 236, 238; 6. 6. 4. 6. 6. 6. 4. 239; 8. 7. 8. 7. 8. 7. 98; 8. 7. 8. 7. 8. 8. 7. 377; 6. 7. 6. 7. 6. 6. 6. 6. 36, 417; 7. 6. 7. 6. D. 622; 8. 7. 8. 7. D. 37, 218, 632, 640; 10. 8. 10. 8. 8. 8. 4. 4. 26

Dreams, ill 558; life like a 113; of Jacob 533; trials like a 415

Duty 402, 451

Earnest 115, 163; cf. Pledge

Earth, creation of 17, 251, 253, 255, 549, 569; crowned with goodness 567; destruction of the 278, 503, 607, 610; cf. World, end of; — dominions of 130; cf. Kingdoms; — heaven on 362; insecure, perishable 286; joys of 552; cf. Joy; — judgment of the 500; cf. Judgment; life on; cf. Life, temporal; — Names — Desert Drear 660; Terrestrial Ball 339; Land of Passing Shadows 586, — obedience of 286; opposition of 340; peace on 76, 83, 84, 94, 100, 109, 188, 237, 258, 261, 282, 569, 575, 576, 580, 582, 584, 647; cf. Peace; — praise of God by 30, 198, 205, 246; quakes 176, 347, 528, 611; realms of; cf. Kingdoms; — rest on 292; saints on 478; sinful 373; sins of 142; sons of 497; cf. Spiritual darkness; — temptations of; cf Temptations; — unity on 261; ungodly 582; vale of cares 561; vale of sin and sadness 406; vale of tears 97, 285, 306, 432, 480, 539, 651; wealth of 305, 438, 633

Earthly, foes; cf. Foes; — friends; cf. Friends; — griefs 586; prop 370; strife 338, 342; cf. Conflict; Warfare, Christian; — treasures 97, 385, 423

Easter 187–211; cf. Christ, resurrection of; — Day 195; day of resurrection 205; day of triumph 203; Morning 207, 208; Passover 205

Eastern sages; cf. Magi
Eden 282; door of 198; cf. Heaven; — marriage in 621, 622
Ecce Agnus 165
Edom 128, 209
Education, Christian 627–631; religious 288
Election 23, 37, 397, 411, 473, 476
Elements, consecrated (Sacrament) 304; visible (Sacrament) 164, 299, 304, 308, 311, 314
Elijah 135, 218; chariot 619; mantle 483; New 272
Elisha 483
Emmaus disciples 194, 197
Empires, fallen 290; cf. Kingdoms
Enoch 218, 342
Epiphany 126–134, 642
Error; cf. Doctrine, false; — conversion from 74, 264; deliverance from 495, 661; destruction of 76, 226; leading men into 260; maze 260, 512; preservation from 125, 224; protection against 235; spread of 579; way of 326, 331; cf. Sin
Eternal Generation; cf. Generation, eternal
Ethiopia 59
Evangel, pure 485; cf. Gospel
Evangelists 471
Eve, Adam and 622; helpmeet 622
Evening 551–565, 653, 654; cf. Day, close of; — prayer; cf. Prayer; — shadows of the 654
Everlasting Life 613–619; cf. Life
Evil 327; conflict with 483; deliverance from all 7, 67, 77, 124, 192, 311, 353, 355, 408, 455, 458, 504, 548, 554; destruction of 605; powers of 520
Exaltation 187–223; cf. Christ, exaltation of
Example, Christian 29

Face, of Christ, cast out from 415; seeing the 67, 138, 234, 467, 523, 527, 543, 562, 611, 618; seeking the 350, 447, 638; *Face of God* — angels before 254, 341; before the 40, 148, 213, 294, 308, 332, 336, 382, 385, 398, 403, 429, 448, 471, 483, 601; seeking the 326, 525, 534, 579, 635
Faith 90, 288, 306, 312, 315, 324, 377, 550; hope, charity 411, 424, 442, 623; abiding in 224, 264, 486, 541; **and Justification 369–392;** arms (hand) of 138, 206; armed by 423; assurance of 453; blessing of 208, 617; confession of 90, 190, 208, 235, 248, 251, 252, 253, 259, 337, 381, 463, 512, 624; conquering through 444; constant 208; deeds of 624; discerning 206; dying in 139; effectual prayer of 488; engendered 297; enlightenment of 95, 230; feeble 403, 441; fight of 446, 447; cf. Warfare, Christian; — firm 396, 458, 541, 560, 598; food for 195; foundation of 245, 319, 373, 377, 381, 427, 639; fruits of 293, 377, 544; gift of 231, 341, 358, 384; guarding of 6, 226, 264; in prayer 22; increase of 1, 65, 125, 288, 381, 402, 408, 419, 446, 477; justification by 377; cf. Justification; — kindled 124; life of 586, 608; one 481; peace of 590; persecution of 260; prayer for a firm 396; preservation of (in) 110, 264, 293, 353, 375, 381, 485; proof of 392; revived 225; sacrifice of 438; saving 23, 26, 67, 72, 77, 91, 96, 107, 170, 172, 195, 224, 231, 245, 266, 272, 301, 360, 377, 467, 523; seeing in 157, 218; shield of 48, 194, 332; cf. Armor; — steadfast 623; strengthening of 3, 18, 226, 247, 288, 333, 381, 458, 585, 628; test of 304; through Word of God 297, 378, 499; triumphant 424; trusting 425; unity of 224, 235, 314, 626; unshaken 311
Faithfulness 50, 74, 93, 96, 121, 138, 143, 177, 235, 259, 262, 292, 296, 298, 303, 307, 333, 334, 335, 338, 372, 403, 424, 451, 470, 528; unto death; cf. Death, faithfulness unto; — pledge of 337, 348; reward of 554
Fall 149, 295, 339, 340, 369; cf. Sin, fall into; — preservation from 516; ransomed from the 339
Falsehood 292
Fame 423
Family 624–626; cf. Home; — altar 625; children of the 626; cf. Children; — consecrated 625, 626; death in the 626; peace in the 624, 626; united in faith 626
Famine 458
Fancies, evil 556
Father's Godhead 202
Fathers, blessings on 624; cf. Home
Fear 225, 252, 313, 326, 327, 347, 349, 373, 387, 410, 422, 444; dismissal of 281, 285, 297, 364, 380, 394, 395, 396, 413, 426, 427, 437, 447; godly 332; perplexed by 522
Feet, consecrated 400
Fellowship, Christian 412, 464, 486; cf. Church; — divine 463; with Christ; cf. Christ, fellowship with; — with God 454
Field, grain of the 566, 569, 570, 572, 573; cf. Harvest
Fight, fierce 463; cf. Conflict; — good 402
Fire, tongues of 504; of affliction 427; protection against 548
First-fruits 404, 441
Flesh, mortifying the 409, 446, 458
Flood, protection against 548
Foe 77, 262, 263, 266, 267, 269, 276, 311, 332, 340, 347, 387, 410, 423, 444; cf. Satan; — conquered 64, 90, 198, 210, 226, 262, 263, 264, 265, 269, 311, 383, 444, 451; conflict with the 472, 494, 590, 658; cf. Warfare, Christian; — craft and pomp of 265, 413; defying the 58, 138, 235, 381; deliverance from 462, 528, 538, 540, 549, 555, 599; earthly 58, 340; hosts of cruel 340, 372, 426, 436; of Christ 49; ten thousand 449; triumphant 198; victory o'er the 517; wrath of 267, 269
Foreknowledge 116
Foreordination 37
Forgiveness, 59, 83, 171, 272, 415, 443; cf. Pardon; — assurance of 34, 61, 74, 112, 155, 245, 310, 338, 357, 358, 367, 386; brotherly 171, 455, 458; free 149, 280; gratitude for 27, 321; invitation to 149, 279, 280; cf. Invitation; — message of 56, 190, 289, 498, 635; of sins, confessing 251, 253; offer of 28, 289; peace of 58, 65, 314; prayer for 24, 111, 124, 177, 190, 226, 242, 247, 258, 265, 288, 298, 312, 324, 386, 394, 419, 455, 458, 459, 515, 522, 545, 548, 556, 563, 576, 598, 604, 607, 653; seeking 310, 312, 317–331, 388; through Christ's blood 32, 158, 198, 266, 367; cf. Blood of Christ
Forsaken 260, 268, 329, 385, 402, 425, 518, 523, 534; by friends 207, 340, 362, 423, 457, 651; by the world 366, 423
Foundation, earthly 370; firm 385
Free will 387, 417
Friends, earthly 340; faithless, unfaithful 446, 474, 557; forsaken by 340, 362, 457; sorrowing o'er departed 418, 593, 596, 639
Friendship, perfect 464
Future 290, 420; unknown 119, 121

Gabriel 104, 114
Galilee 208; wedding in 621
Galilean lake 270
Generation, eternal 16, 95, 98, 132, 134, 202, 271, 371, 471, 539, 550
Gentiles 129
Gethsemane, Garden of 151, 159, 171, 516
Giving 143, 441; cf. Christ, Offerings for; Stewardship; — cheerful 498
Gladness; cf. Joy; — Day of 9, 192; heavenly 605
Glorified body 148, 206, 395, 611, 660
Glory 41, 76, 83, 84, 100, 136, 226, 243, 251, 352; clothed in 382, 432; crown of 219

[655]

444; Day of 57; empty 347; immortal 218, 248, 477; Kingdom of; cf. Kingdom; — realms of 136; cf. Heaven; — received into 592; cf. Heaven; — Song of 244; cf. Songs
Glories, vain 552
Glorying, in Christ 351; cf. Christ; — in Cross of Christ; cf. Cross of Christ; — in death of Christ; cf. Death of Christ, glorying in
God, abiding with (in) 241, 375; arm of 275; awe of 500; cf. Fear, godly; — blessings of 8, 36, 50, 110, 243, 305, 316, 514, 556, 569, 584, 640; cf. Blessings, divine; — building on 425, 518; changelessness of; cf. God, unchangeableness of; — Church of 462; command of 13; compassion of 18, 25, 27, 140, 238, 260, 268, 269, 316, 384, 499, 520, 537; condescension of 21, 152; counsel of 484, 535; cf. God, will of; — covenant of; cf. Covenant; — deliverance of 29; dependence on 18, 43; desire for 480, 525; duty to 289; eternity of 40, 110, 123, 246; face of 514; cf. Face of God; — faithfulness of 53, 59, 91, 149, 201, 243, 263, 298, 372, 520, 521, 523, 526, 534, 651; fatherly care of 25, 34, 67, 118, 119, 122, 518; cf. Care, divine; — fearing 29, 298, 629; fellowship with 454; cf. Fellowship; — foreknowledge of 116; glory of 39, 129, 246, 455, 633; glory of God in nature 43; glory to 217, 237, 238, 257, 360, 386, 443; goodness of; cf. Goodness, divine; — grace of; cf. Grace, divine; — grieving 417; hand of 462; help of; cf. Help, divine; — hope in 518, 629; image of; cf. Image of God; — judging 514; Law of; cf. Law; — life without 393; living in (to) 120, 298, 439, 536, 561, 598, 608; longsuffering of 42; love of 81, 93, 98, 110, 112, 242, 325, 329, 337, 427, 541, 619, 621; cf. Love, divine; — love to 443; majesty of 40, 105, 239, 274, 455; mansions of 498; cf. Heaven; — meekness of 34; mercy of; cf. Mercy, divine; — mercy-seat of 371; mission of 641; mysterious ways of 514
God, Names of: 236, 250, 253, 284, 287, 455, 458, 580; cf. Triune God; — Abba, Father 2, 423; All 532; All-Merciful 582; Almighty 26, 39, 641; Ancient of Days 165, 239; Author of Blessings 569; Avenger 582; Balm 437; Comfort 269, 517; Comforter 122; Counselor 535; Creator 6, 15 26, 73, 253, 438, 535, 554, 641; Defender 124, 269; Defense 201, 458; Deliv'rer 54, 520
Father 8, 21, 30, 36, 38, 67, 73, 101, 112, 118, 122, 124, 142, 183, 220, 224, 237, 238, 239, 241, 243, 251, 279, 288, 299, 311, 326, 347, 355, 375, 387, 411, 417, 418, 454, 458, 475, 521, 653; cf. Doxology; — Almighty 52, 236, 257, 438, 481; Faithful 384, 560; Father Merciful 240; Father Most Holy 240; of Glory 248, 550; of Heaven 242; of Mercies 284; of Saving Grace 550; of th' Eternal Word 271; Father Tender 240; Gracious 545, 563; Heavenly 21, 455; Holy 250, 643; Loving 298; Mighty 337, 343, — First and Last 40; Fortress, 262, 524, 529; Fount of Blessings 4; Fount of Gladness 122; Fount of Grace 569; Fountain 395; Friend 517, 521, 528, 534; Everlasting 578; Faithful 529,— Gift 581; Giver 438
God — Almighty 49, 460; Bounteous 36; Eternal 40; Everlasting 238; Ever-Living 291; Faithful 298, 321, 395; Faithful God and Lord 334; and King 570; and Lord 287, 334; and Savior 4; and Shield 524; God Father 6, 38, 424; of Abraham 40; of All Creation 19, 37; of Grace 20, 33, 303, 384, 639, 640; of Heaven 97; of Jacob 434; of Love 2, 19, 338, 402, 417, 640, 656; of Mercy 20, 122, 439, 499; of Might 439, 499; of Power

19; of Our Fathers 434, 568; of Our Salvation 19; of the Prophets 483; of Wonders 19; out of Zion 44; the Father 5, 12, 23, 36, 244, 247, 492; the Lord 28, 104, 105; Gracious 18, 378, 465, 560; Great 110, 119; Just 317; Mighty 275; Pardoning 32, — Guard 123; Guardian 243, 411; Israel's 544, — Guest 275; Guide 33, 530, 532; Health 39; Help 123, 252, 425, 524; Helper 119, 122, 269, 523; Great Helper 269, — Hero 269; Home 123; Hope 123, 517; Zion's Hope 42; Interpreter 514; Jehovah 13, 21, 37, 54, 568; Joy 119, 535; Justice 153; King 30, 39, 325, 448; Almighty 239, 271; of Creation 39; of Heaven 575; of Nations 583; Wondrous 41, — Life 38, 122, 517, 524, 535, 623; Light 38, 165, 402, 474, 535, 545, 561
Lord 29, 30, 34, 37, 46, 52, 110, 111, 113, 122, 189, 206, 250, 261, 266, 267, 288, 291, 296, 318, 321, 322, 323, 325, 326, 327, 329, 378, 379, 389, 406, 416, 535; Almighty Lord 579; Gracious 544; and God 337; Lord God 19, 44; Lord God of Sabaoth 255; Lord, My God 1, 33, 38; of All Creation 546; of Angelic Hosts 255; of Earth 443; of Glory 23; of Harvest 574; of Heaven 443; of Hosts 561, 580, 633; of My Life 24; of Sabaoth 249, 582; of Sea 443; of the Nations 578; Lord, Our Father 269; Lord, Our God 14, 44, 636; Lord, Our Maker 44; Lord, the Almighty 39, 427, — Lot 402; Love 42, 165, 623; Eternal 13, — Majesty 454; Majesty Divine 525; Maker 25, 34, 38, 41, 44, 335, 520, 541, 574, 575; Almighty 13; and Preserver 6; of Earth and Skies 632, — Master-Builder 632; Most High 42, 467, 472; Almighty One 238; Highest One 238, 518; Holy One 275; Thrice Holy One 255; Peace 19; Physician 521; Portion 40, 448, 535; Refuge 19, 578, 636; Reliance 393; Rest 119; Reward 535; Rock 19, 402, 524, 529; Ruler 26, 438; Ruler of Wind and Wave 577; Salvation 19, 39; Shelter 123; Shield 40, 262, 402, 437, 524, 535; Source — Bounteous 572; of Everything 535; of Goodness 515; of Blessings 129, 438, 572, — Sov'reign Father 129; Spring of Blessings 25, 569; Spring of Eternal Health 525; Staff 402; Stay 247, 517, 524, 560; Faithful Stay 112; Strength 524, 532, 560; and Power 402; and Righteousness 325; and Stay 110, 560, — Tower 40; Treasure 524, 535; Trust 517, 578; Weapon 262; Wisdom 532
God (General listing continued), nearness of 2, 120, 122, 183, 263, 267, 335, 372, 424, 454, 465, 528, 533, 568, 577, 616; cf. God, presence of; — need of 112, 120, 556; oath of 40; omnipotence of 13, 17, 19, 26, 43, 250, 520; cf. God, power of; — omniscience of 318, 518, 536; panoply of 450; cf. Armor; — patience of 34, 42, 581; power of 13, 39, 43, 110, 237, 275, 316, 389, 620; praise to 40, 105, 199, 243, 254, 343, 393, 443, 525, 542, 548, 550, 554, 570, 572, 584, 636, 640; cf. Praise; — prayer to 8, 33, 118, 120, 269, 288, 299, 301, 328, 337, 395, 402, 455, 524, 544, 550, 556, 653; presence of 4, 11, 36, 44, 46, 110, 120, 122, 125, 252, 402, 427, 469, 481, 492, 556, 622; promise of; cf. Word of God; — providence of; cf. Providence, divine; — reign of 26, 28, 34, 36, 39, 124, 237, 250, 481, 575, 642; remembered by 561; right hand of 195, 217, 218, 223, 393, 437, 485; rule of 34, 425; cf. God, reign of; — saints of 468; cf. Saints; — seeking 18, 21, 268, 280, 317, 326, 355; servants of 287; cf. Ministry; — serving 407, 417, 424, 558, 560, 625, 640; temple of 467; cf. Temple; — trust in 287, 514, 517, 518, 520, 526, 529, 530, 533, 548, 625, 629,

[656]

651; cf. Confidence, Trust; — unchangeableness of 25, 40, 123; vengeance of 377; visitations of 25; walking with 2, 149, 218, 342, 512; cf. Christ, walking with; — watchful (never asleep) 561; ways of 514, 519, 520, 521, 529, 530, 571, 582, 642; way to 485; will of; cf. Will, divine; — wisdom of 43, 424, 425, 520, 535, 548, 620; wonders of 514, 518, 581, 629; work of 19, 27, 217, 417, 460, 507, 508, 629; wrath of 196, 311, 317, 326, 416, 582, 590

Godhead 228, 251; Father's 202; mysterious 242, 250; unity of 250

Godliness 332, 566

Gold 438, 470; and silver 633

Goliath 211

Good Friday 165–186; good works; cf. Works

Goodness, divine 19, 26, 30, 31, 34, 43, 44, 67, 96, 110, 124, 237, 393, 395, 431, 434, 436, 569; source of 515

Gospel 2, 11, 50, 64, 245, 266, 343; cf. Word of God; — armor 451; benefits of 289, 297, 377; blessings of 282, 289; comfort of the 386; hope of 289, 386, 510; first, primal 91, 99; forgiveness through the 289; **Law and** 282–297; life through 2; message of the 297; *Names* — Banner of the Cross 332; Evangel 485, — power of 289, 343, 505; preaching of 266, 282, 482, 485, 497, 498, 505, 578, 635, 638; cf. Preaching; — sacrifices for the 477; scepter of the 505; success of 64, 505; tidings of salvation 282, 297, 498

Gospel-call, obeying the 497

Government, prayer for 566, 580

Grace 21, 50, 66, 87, 120, 121, 122, 141, 235, 253, 257, 275, 276, 293, 313, 317, 374, 465, 546; abiding 53, 465; all-sufficient 427, 469; Anointing 336, 431; baptismal 337, 467; blessings of 45, 84, 243, 324, 374; boundless 28, 177, 305, 308, 329, 340, 345, 364, 373, 386, 429, 522, 599; call of 384; cleansing 289; comforting 539; condescending 335; cf. Christ, condescension; — conversion by 417; day of 604; divine 3, 27, 75, 86, 88, 92, 104, 121, 152, 170, 186, 207, 221, 238, 243, 248, 285, 297, 314, 316, 326, 329, 334, 337, 352, 417, 425, 465, 500, 524, 560, 636; double portion of 218; election by 37; endless 34, 158, 275, 469; fall from 417; foretaste of heaven 362; free 150, 266, 323, 324, 340, 373, 375, 382; fruits of 11; fulness of 352, 448; gates of 619; gems of heavenly 632; gift of 12, 100, 150, 226, 265, 312, 369, 399, 408, 416, 419, 452, 458, 467, 500, 542, 573, 626, 633; ground of faith 373; growth in 24, 53, 96, 229, 293, 301, 333, 632; guardian 220, 369; guiding 369, 374; justification by 360, 382, 391; Kingdom of; cf. Kingdom; — light of 398; members of Church by 469; of Christ; cf. Christ, grace of; — pardoning 11, 58, 321, 323, 331, 386, 389; plenitude of 504; preaching of 483, 488; cf. Preaching; — quickening 49, 64, 539; radiant 512; reclaiming 280; redeeming 50, 91, 148, 241, 329, 646; refreshing 525; relying on 392; renewing 539; resisting 415; rivers of 631; salvation by 235, 253, 257, 295, 339, 373, 377, 382; saving 235, 241, 242, 245, 289, 373; sevenfold gifts of 229, 233, 236, 332, 443, 493; cf. Holy Ghost, Blessing; — song of 374; threefold 622; throne of 327; cf. Throne of Grace; — time of 444, 509, 513; treasures of 66, 316; trifling with 446; triumphs of 360; unchanging 370; universal 488; wondrous 636; Word of 7, 164, 195, 292; word of promise 373; works of 629

Grain 566, 569, 570, 572, 573; cf. Harvest

Grave, arising from 539, 592, 604; cf Resurrection; — Christian 395; gate to heaven 409; *Names* — Chamber 589; Mansions of the Dead 610; Sepulcher 607, — of Christ;

cf. Christ, grave of; — *of Christ, Names* — Dark Prison 187, 197, 204; Gloomy House of Death 188; Vault 166; Tomb 593, — ransomed from 391; rending of the 481, 592, 607, 610; rest in the 603; seal of the 166, 193, 204; vale of the tomb 278; victory over the 187–211; victory of the 552; triumph over the 62, 187, 192, 200, 209, 217, 297, 341

Greenland's icy mountains 495

Grief 410, 418, 546, 652; cf. Sorrow

Guidance 19, 21, 36, 45, 54, 73, 90, 96, 110, 119, 120, 121, 127, 128, 131, 194, 197, 200, 215, 224, 226, 227, 228, 231, 235, 264, 282, 291, 294, 335, 349, 368, 374, 393, 402, 416, 417, 425, 434, 440, 455, 481, 489, 500, 518, 520, 532, 541, 544, 548, 568, 628, 640; cf. Heaven, guidance to

Hands, consecrated 400, 416; laying on of 331; service of the 640

Harm, safe from 561

Harps 83, 221, 256, 476, 609

Hart, panting 525

Harvest 438, 443; and Thanksgiving 566–574; first-fruits of the 573; laborers of the; cf. Ministers, *Names*, Laborers in Thy Kingdom; — prayer for 493, 566; Satan's 446; scant 571; spiritual 1, 46, 49, 52, 106, 485, 488, 492, 493, 494, 496, 499, 502, 503, 507, 573, 574

Harvest-home 573; eternal 502, 574; song of 574

Harvest-song 573

Hatred 287

Healing, divine 34, 54, 63, 65, 74, 77, 93, 144, 150, 151, 184, 209, 280, 315, 321, 324, 326, 342, 345, 380, 385, 399, 407, 482, 484, 499, 508, 511, 531, 552, 565, 576, 642, 652; prayer for 557

Health 443, 572, 652; saving 500, 569

Hearing, failing sense of 365

Heart 90, 145, 192, 281; adoration of 128; bowed with care 56, 77, 366; brave 463; broken 66, 77, 323, 325, 350, 441, 499, 506, 519; burdened 386, 515; change in 64, 65, 241; cf. Regeneration; — childlike 226, 291; Christ at the door of the 385, 650; Christ in the 624; circumcision of 115; cleansing of 225, 234, 398; coldness of the 349, 364, 441, 512; comfort in 137; consecrated 332, 400, 404, 416, 442, 477; consolation in 319; contrite 310, 316, 329, 350, 411; depraved 369, 411; desire of 454; cf. Prayer; — despondent 91; devout 366; doubting 281, 512; **enlightenment of the** 88, 224–236; erring 545; fainting 407, 418, 447; faithful 303, 307, 403; cf. Faithfulness; — first-fruits of redemption 404; guileful 377; humble 75, 247, 315, 324, 366, 421; image of God in 335; cf. Image of God; — indifferent 279, 324; indwelling of Holy Ghost 225, 234, 235; cf. Holy Ghost, indwelling of; — inspiration of 232, 236; *Names* — Dwelling of Trinity 315; Temple 1, 70, 73, 228, 232, 234, 235, 236, 299, 332, 335, 351, 419; Temple's Holy Shrine 332, — name of Christ written on 115; obedient 270; of stone 93, 417, 442, 504; offering of the 41, 89, 108, 128, 336, 404; opprest 276; patient 406; peace in 50, 65, 96, 258, 311, 342, 347; preparation of the 61, 63, 73, 75, 85, 87, 91, 224, 225, 232, 355; preparation of, for worship of God 5, 16, 18, 293; pure 201, 205, 355, 477; cf. Purity; — rejoicing 77, 85, 192, 243, 316, 362, 366, 373; renewal of 300, 398, 411; revived 38, 64, 241, 417, 425, 504; ruled by Holy Spirit 621; shrine of the 541; sin-sick (sinful) 65, 315, 340, 377, 423; sincere 416; steadfast 368; thankful 349, 358, 442, 497; thankless 567; throne in 300, 400, 635; trembling 534; trusting 640; united 387, 412; vengeful 171; vile

289; wayward 342; wounded 531; yearning of the 145, 315
Heathen, blindness of the 495, 498; cf. Human depravity; — conversion of the 497, 498, 500, 642; cf. Missions; — preaching to the 494; cf. Missions
Heathendom 65, 126
Heaven, *Abode* — abode in 437, 444, 449; of God 480; blissful 588; Father's loved 434, — adoration of Christ in 74, 108, 190, 271, 609; anthem of 415, 656; cf. Songs; — balm in 617; beatific vision in 605, 609; beauty of 614, 618; blessed country 448, 605, 613, 614; bliss of 67, 77, 88, 92, 129, 150, 192, 213, 215, 251, 296, 335, 343, 362, 365, 393, 396, 432, 448, 462, 471, 589, 595, 599, 601, 605, 613, 614, 615, 617; book of; cf. Book of heaven; — Canaan's happy shore 476; carried to 50, 54, 221, 394, 397, 429, 449, 458, 478, 516, 533, 594, 600, 606, 619, 648; choirs of 619; Church in 478; cf. Church, triumphant; — city in (of) 528, 614; corner-stone of 614; courts of 465, 618, 645; creation of 251, 253, 549; crown of 81, 273, 279, 491; crystal sea 471; dawn of 155, 617; desire for 92, 121, 148, 177, 188, 206, 215, 253, 316, 366, 407, 408, 432, 444, 448, 467, 476, 480, 503, 586, 588, 589, 592, 595, 597, 598, 601, 611, 614, 615, 616, 618, 619, 645, 652, 660; destruction of 607, 610, 612; dwelling-place 436; Eden 198; cf. Paradise; — end of faith 381; eternal fold in heaven 631; everlasting day in; cf. Day, everlasting; — fadeless bowers 397; Fatherland 448, 410, 619, 660; feast in 67, 314, 415, 599, 609, 656; foretaste of 362; garners of 573, 574; gates of 72, 148, 189, 192, 198, 218, 279, 331, 336, 367, 454, 616; golden gates of 476; gates of grace 619; pearly gates of 463, 618; gathered in 308, 314, 365, 407, 414, 415, 432, 498, 527, 573, 574, 586, 588, 606, 608, 609, 626, 640, 651, 656; glorified in 192, 432, 603, 660; glory of 67, 73, 127, 192, 207, 214, 218, 226, 249, 296, 308, 341, 382, 408, 409, 432, 471, 520, 539, 554, 573, 588, 596, 601, 605, 613, 614; goal of 73, 317, 599; golden streets of 608, 618; guidance to 58, 67, 73, 90, 110, 121, 122, 127, 171, 192, 193, 197, 200, 215, 231, 248, 261, 282, 285, 300, 315, 320, 338, 345, 374, 407, 410, 411, 421, 423, 444, 448, 459, 478, 480, 507, 510, 533, 538, 539, 543, 561, 569, 585, 589, 600, 603, 605, 613, 614, 619, 627, 634, 645; halls of splendor 192; happier shore 418; heritage in 58, 432, 453, 528, 619; cf. Heirs; — home 67, 110, 148, 150, 196, 308, 314, 316, 343, 381, 410, 418, 420, 426, 429, 431, 476, 492, 497, 528, 560, 586, 602, 615, 616, 617, 656, 660; blessed home in 626; everlasting home 62, 111, 125, 218, 340, 396, 591; happy home 618, 653; *home* — of fadeless splendor 605; of gladness 601, 622; of God's elect 448, 605, 613, 614; of joys supernal 343; of light 405, 586; of love 626; of peace 626, — hope of 148, 214, 346, 443, 465, 528, 605, 614, 615; hosts of 619, 640; Father's house 615, 616; God's house 436; inheritance of saints 616; invitation to; cf. Invitation to; — Jerusalem the heavenly 586, 601, 616, 618, 619; Jerusalem the Golden 613; journey to 413, 420, 452, 478, 480, 481, 519, 546, 581, 586, 593, 615; journey's end 369, 459, 481; joy of 214, 219, 281, 320, 395, 407, 409, 465, 476, 539, 540, 542, 600, 601, 613, 615, 617, 618; judgments of 271; knowledge of 527, 605; land of rest 448, 605, 613, 614; blessed land 573; Promised Land 481, 606; light of 559, 605, 613, 619; mansions of 67, 138, 200, 214, 371, 448, 498, 540, 614; marriage-feast in 67, 72, 164, 609; music of 67, 424, 609; name in 615; nuptial hall in 609; obedience of 286; opened 210; palms in 273, 656; Paradise 257, 614, 619; cf. Paradise; — paschal banquet in 656; peace in 258, 316, 432, 539, 615; perfect day in 185; place in 148, 188, 196, 200, 201, 213, 214, 253, 257, 301, 351, 367, 415, 480, 615; portals of 503, 609; cf. Heaven, gates of; — power of 605; praise in 10, 92, 222, 476; cf. Praise, angelic; — preparation for 605, 615, 618; prize in (of) 303, 479; *realms of* 56, 67, 80, 86, 93, 129, 192, 218, 271, 503; beyond the sky 291; of bliss 363; of glory 136; of light 194, — rejoicing in 452; rest in 423, 463, 465, 553, 589, 607, 615, 617, 660; resting-place in 631; revelation of 271; reward in 407, 472, 601; Sabbath of 618, 656; saints in 455, 463, 465, 471, 475, 476, 480, 573, 588, 601, 605, 608, 618, 656; cf. Saints; — scrolls of 271; sphere (of endless day) 499, 539; splendor of 614; supper in 194, 384; throne of beauty 546, 619; throne of David in 613; translation to 218, 282; cf. Heaven, carried to; — treasures of 444, 542; vault of 222; way to 62, 148, 171, 185, 190, 197, 214, 215, 231, 245, 320, 374, 496; welcome to 395, 476, 538, 599, 619; won 202; world's above 341, 480; world of endless day 340; worship in 448, 471, 475, 601, 605, 640, 656; Zion 613, 619
Heavenly-minded 188, 206, 212, 214, 215, 216, 313, 316, 322, 366, 398, 409, 413, 425, 432, 444, 527, 558, 571, 586, 601
Hebrews, people of the 160
Heir, of God 5, 21, 32, 48, 72, 298, 372; of heaven 32, 223, 226, 300, 302, 314; of God's kingdom 467; of life 226; of salvation 467
Hell 103, 340; assailed by 347, 372, 427, 590, 600; conquered 81, 90, 116, 188, 189, 192, 193, 198, 202, 210, 211, 217; crafts of 546, 559; deliverance from 141, 405, 528, 601; descent into 253; cf. Christ, descent; — doomed to 141, 369, 607, 610; fear of 315, 384, 590; gates of 193, 460, 658; everlasting flame 610; flames of woe 607; pangs of 387, 404; realms infernal 271; redeemed from 27, 62, 323
Help, divine 25, 33, 41, 120, 252, 260, 261, 262, 263, 264, 265, 267, 269, 288, 315, 329, 330, 342, 345, 387, 393, 402, 407, 412, 417, 427, 449, 470, 518, 520, 524, 528, 540, 568, 600, 616, 652; human 317, 319, 383, 393, 451, 518
Helpless 534
Helplessness 25, 91, 312, 317, 340, 345, 375, 377, 379, 387, 393, 501, 518, 522, 523; cf. Human frailty
Heresy 260, 473, 544; cf. Error
Heritage 58; cf. Heaven, heritage in
Herod 131, 273
Highways and byways 498
Holiness, growth in 185, 295, 306, 408, 428, 468, 485; cf. Sanctification; — crown of Christ 73; sevenfold gifts of 493
Holy Communion 163, 164, 207; cf. Lord's Supper
Holy Innocents 273
Holy Ghost — Holy Spirit, abiding of 70, 122, 226, 229, 235, 239, 299, 313, 318, 325, 326, 402, 458; abiding with 417; assurance of 386; blessing of 227, 230, 334, 550; blessing sevenfold 229, 233, 332; breath of the 621; cleansing through 228, 604; comfort of 227, 228, 231, 251, 252, 298, 325, 387, 458, 528; coming of 232; cf. Pentecost, Holy Spirit, descent of; — condescension 228; confession of the 233, 252, 253; descent of 8, 9, 12, 70, 229, 230, 232, 236, 299, 351, 358, 382, 387, 411, 444, 504; enlightenment of 3, 8, 124, 140, 225, 226, 227, 229, 230, 232, 235, 541; cf. Spiritual enlightenment; — eternal 226; following the 408; **fruits of** 124, 224–236; gifts of 227, 228, 229, 233, 241, 331, 335, 411, 489,

[658]

490, 491, 544; grace of 224, 231, 233, 235, 251, 293, 335, 336, 458, 490, 643; guidance of 8, 21, 45, 73, 172, 226, 235, 253, 381, 387, 546, 621; cf. Guidance; — indwelling of 7, 70, 143, 207, 225, 226, 227, 228, 232, 233, 234, 235, 236, 239, 298, 318, 325, 332, 351, 418, 423, 528, 544; inspiration of 335, 351; intercession of 2, 16, 21, 226, 228, 454, 528; **invocation of 224–236**, 332; love of 224, 227, 228, 233, 621; mercy of 234; cf. Mercy

Holy Ghost — Holy Spirit, Names of: Advocate 240; Anointing from Above 233; Anointing Oil 228; Breath 271; Comfort 231; Comfort True 224; Comforter 8, 73, 229, 233, 237, 239, 261, 335, 541; Comforter and Guide 334; Creator Blest 233; Creator Spirit 236; Day 550; Defender 240; Dove 508; Finger of the Hand Divine 233; Fire 236; of Love 233; Holy 224, — Fount 236; of Blessing 4; of Grace 375; of Life 233, — Fountain 235; Fountain-Spring of Light 550; Friend 227, 235; Faithful 600, — Gentle Dew 235; Gift of God Most High 233; Precious Gift 237; God 224, 226, 231; and Lord 224; of Love 230; God the Holy Ghost 6, 38, 492; God the Spirit 5, 244, 475, — Guest 227, 228, 418; Guide — Divine 224, 417; Protecting 233, — Hope 38; Life 38; Light 229, 240; Holy 224; of Light 550; Light Serene 227; Precious 231, — Source of Life 235; Source of Uncreated Light 236; Lord 224, 226, 228, 332; Mighty Lord 332, — Sacred Love 231; Paraclete 165, 236, 253; Eternal Paraclete 236, — Patron of the Frail 641; Refuge 226, 235; Reliance 235; Mighty Rock 235; Shield 235; Spirit — All-Enlightening 641; Blessed 8; Eternal 242; Everlasting 60; Quickening 226; of Adoption 229; of Christ 483; of All Grace 243; of Grace 278; of Holiness 241; of Life 413, 443; of Love 412, 443, 508; of Peace 412; of Power 239, 443; of Salvation 37; of the Father 621; of the Living God 504; of the Lord 504; of Truth 508, — Splendor of God's glory 550; Stay 247; Strength 235; Sun of the Soul 235; Tower 235; True Promise of the Father 233

Holy Ghost — Holy Spirit (General listing continued), outpouring of 230, 452, 490; perfection of 229; pleading of; — cf. Holy Ghost, intercession of; — power of 235, 237, 241, 242, 504; cf. Power divine; — prayer for 321, 402, 408, 411; presence of 621, 622; proceeds from Father and Son 252; protection of 226, 228, 229, 231, 235, 237, 560; cf. Protection, divine; — pureness of the 621; reign of 234, 239; sending of 3, 402, 490, 491, 550; sighing of 226; teaching of 643; temple of 234, 235, 236; cf. Temple; — trust in 224; cf. Trust; — unction of 504; witness of 226, 239; **work of** 21, 23, 38, 73, 95, 98, 124, **224–236**, 237, 239, 242, 243, 248, 251, 252, 253, 298, 299, 318, 335, 387, 412, 439, 458, 504, 507, 508, 510, 528

Home, blessed 624, 625, 630; cf. Family; — blessing on the 621; building the 621; Christ in the 624, 625, 626; **Christian** 65, 73, 337, **620–631**; Christless (Unchristian) 625; death in the 626; God in the 120, 427; happy 621, 626; institution of the 621; peace in the 65, 443, 624, 625, 626; prayer for the 624; protection of the 560; spiritual coldness of 441; tasks in 626

Honesty 395
Honor 395, 406; worldly 430, 470
Hope 4, 18, 183, 196, 214, 281, 296, 333, 342, 411, 423, 424, 425, 442, 464, 546; divine 181, 192; dying in 412; cf. Death; — failing 579; for mortals 510; foundation of 370; cf. Christ, hope's foundation; — heavenly 460; cf. Heaven; — life of 448;
one 481; patient 623; Star of 420; united in 626; unity of 658; in Christ 26, 99, 187, 319, 329, 370, 375, 528

Human, depravity 16, 32, 37, 42, 58, 64, 65, 141, 143, 148, 149, 150, 151, 207, 227, 295, 312, 345, 369, 375, 376, 377, 378, 379, 382, 386, 387, 482, 498, 557, 588; frailty 17, 26, 34, 54, 92, 108, 123, 148, 194, 207, 233, 235, 258, 262, 267, 279, 319, 337, 364, 370, 376, 383, 386, 433, 451, 461, 581, 607, 640; help; cf. Help, human; — merits, helpless 32, 150, 170, 287, 305, 312, 319, 329, 373, 376, 380, 385, 389, 415, 433, 607; mortality; cf. Mortality; — nature, corruption of 369, 377, 378; cf. Human depravity; — enlightenment of 399; cf. Spiritual enlightenment; — exaltation of 218; fall of 202, 411; cf. Fall; — ransomed 495; unworthiness of 379, — needs 483; reason 21, 204, 305, 306, 310, 373, 381, 400, 411, 530; trusting 381, — thought 363, 400, 411; ties, uncertain 474; will, consecrated 400, 420; renewal of 418, — wisdom 385

Humility 2, 18, 41, 55, 58, 61, 73, 75, 110, 114, 238, 247, 275, 315, 318, 324, 366, 399, 411, 421, 423, 490, 606
Hur 484
Hymn, of the Angels; cf. Angels, hymn of the; — of glory 212, 475; cf. Song; — of joy 609; of love 462; of praise 47, 101, 188, 250, 462, 465, 609, 619; of victory 205; cf. Songs
Hypocrisy 260, 366

Idleness 479
Idolatry 270, 287, 495
Idols, destruction of 19, 76, 234
Illumination, divine; cf. Spiritual enlightenment
Image, of Christ 179, 407, 459; of God, 232, 335, 348, 361; of God lost 369; of Godhead 397
Imagination 363
Immortality 2, 45, 217, 616
Impenitence 295
Impureness 398
Incarnation 68, 77, 78, 80, 82, 85, 93, 95, 271, 366, 375; cf. Christ, birth of
Incarnation, mystery of 84
India's coral strand 495
Indifference 41, 74, 140, 143, 145, 151, 153, 260, 278, 279, 281, 292, 295, 324, 386, 415, 444, 445, 446, 449, 479, 495, 496, 509, 513; cf. Unbelief
Indulgences 331
Infants 454, 628; cf. Children
Iniquity 455; cf. Sin
Inspiration; cf. Bible, inspiration of
Instruction, religious, spiritual 21, 24, 51, 133, 233, 243, 245, 248, 284, 286, 291, 333, 353, 366, 383, 399, 401, 418, 421, 425, 439, 459, 468, 484, 486, 491, 558, 567, 625, 626, 627, 628, 629, 630, 631
Institutions, theological 641
Intellect, consecrated 400
Intercession; cf. Christ, intercession of
Invitation 77, 90, 102, 136, 204, **276–281**, 297, 305, 306, 307, 308, 311, 324, 330, 344, 650; of mercy 278, 279, 281; to bring children to Christ 302; to comfort 531; to following Christ 270, 415, 421, 470; to forgiveness 279; cf. Forgiveness; — to heaven 67, 615; to Lord's Supper 305, 306, 307, 308, 311, 330; to missionworkers 496; to praise 39, 69, 73, 83, 90, 97, 98, 102, 107, 112, 132, 192, 204, 282, 340, 341, 546, 570, 574, 581; to prayer 456, 458, 554; to rejoicing 79, 82, 85, 90, 96, 102, 192, 204, 341; to salvation 129, 137, 377, 415; to sinners 75, 77, 83, 129, 149, 276, 277, 281, 324, 330, 377, 386, 388, 456, 509; to sorrowful 531; to the Supper 384, 509, 609; to watchfulness 444, 446; to worship 28, 84, 102, 122, 136, 467, 574

[659]

Invocation 239, 332; cf. Holy Spirit, invocation
Isaac 415
Isaiah 249, 274; prophecy of 645
Israel 28, 62, 71, 99, 137, 204, 218, 275, 329, 339; cf. Church; — erring 419; Guardian of 544; tribes of 162, 218

Jacob 343, 415, 434, 533
Jehovah 37, 331; cf. God, Names, Jehovah; — love of 474
Jerusalem 61, 609; City of God 618; heavenly 586, 601, 616, 619; rejoicing 487; weeping o'er 419
Jesse 645
Jesus, name decreed of old 114; name of mercy mild 114; name of wondrous love 114; cf. Christ, Names
John, Disciple 177
Jordan 54, 63, 131, 134, 272; heavenly 513
Joseph 84
Joshua 218, 484
Journey through life; cf. Pilgrimage
Joy 90, 96, 102, 172, 204, 205, 210, 228, 279, 305, 314, 333, 342, 354, 411, 417, 420, 469, 639; crown of 143; days of 523; divine 65, 119, 206, 234, 325, 333, 362; earthly 143, 316, 356, 365; entering into 489; eternal 7, 77, 85, 87, 92, 96, 161, 204, 205, 206, 214, 227, 276, 281, 284, 315, 320, 354, 365, 366, 393, 397, 405, 432, 477, 586, 601; holy 539; increase of 412, 426; invitation to; cf. Invitation; — pure 539, 651; cf. Heaven; — vain 365; cf. Vanities
Judah 343
Judgment 27, 56, 106, 134, 253, 278, 315, 500, 604–612; cf. Resurrection; — account at 48, 329, 330, 370, 414, 482, 500, 607; book of 271, 607; cf. Book; — preaching of 218, 496; preparation for 604, 605, 606, 609, 611; separation at 607; terrors of 610; Judgment Day 58, 68, 70, 206, 221, 253, 271, 306, 444, 476, 549; awe-ful day 558; day of dread award 271; day of mourning 607; day of retribution 607; day of sorrow 607; day of the Lord 356; day of wrath 607, 612; dreadful day 70, 612; great day 148; harvest-day 567; sentence of 607, 610; signs of 134, 476, 502, 605; solemn 111; standing in the 278, 370, 371, 375, 376, 391, 414, 472, 515, 528, 549, 561, 585, 607, 611, 612
Justice 27, 34, 42, 106, 141, 153, 329
Justification 32, 41, 77, 90, 140, 142, 144, 245, 266, 297, 315, 318, 360, 383; by grace 360, 382; by faith 377; by human merits 373, 376, 377, 379, 385, 387; cf. Human merits; — by Law 295, 329, 330, 377; faith and 369–392

Kindness 403, 425
Kings 59, 471, 487, 503
Kingdom 59, 61, 69, 95, 261, 262, 387, 455, 458, 527; cf. Christ, kingdom of; — advent of the 65; building the 485; earthly 131, 175; enemies of the 261; fallen 290; inheriting the 85, 300; love for the 462; Vineyard (name) 492; portals of the 510; promise of the 48; spread of the 387, 507; vastness of the 511; of Christ; cf. Christ, kingdom of; — of Glory 35, 85, 95, 177, 212, 215, 221, 262; of Grace 42, 87, 221, 261, 264, 387; of Power 19, 42, 221, 250; in darkness 505; cf. Nations; — perishable 658; salvation to all 130
Knowledge 16, 226, 295, 332, 366, 572; cf. Spiritual enlightenment
Kyrie 6; Kyrie eleison — Have mercy 146, 147, 169, 172, 187, 231, 287, 313, 415, 590, 661

Labor 7, 45, 235, 287, 376, 414, 424, 429, 573; blessing on 7, 122, 538, 540, 544, 547, 548, 550, 566, 581, 640; end of 618; faithful 544; rest from 287; cf. Commandment, Third; — under Christ's direction 540; vain 640
Last things, the 585–619
Laughter 611
Law, acquitted from the 324; bondage of 99; commandments of the 287; cf. Commandments; — condemnation of the 375, 386; curse of 87, 99, 150, 272, 289, 295, 375, 386; deeds of the 266, 311, 323, 329, 377, 385; cf. Works; — delight in the 414; cf. Word of God; — demands of 376, 377; Doctors of 133; end of the 117; fulfilment of 196, 220, 377, 379, 412; giving of the 287; hearing the 2; cf. Word of God; — humility through the 2; cf. Humility; — instruction in the 133; cf. Instruction; — judgment of the 386; justification by; cf. Justification; — keeping the 303, 377, 379; learning the 288; lessons of the 289; mirror 377; Moses' Condemnation (name) 272; obedience to the 115, 303, 353, 377; power of 289; purpose of 287, 289, 295, 377; righteous, of God 642; spirit of 377; written in heart 115; Law and Gospel 282–297; cf. Word; — lessons of Law and Gospel 286, 289
Lent 140–159; cf. Christ, Passion of, Passion of Christ
Liberty 378; boundless 602; song of 578
Life 29, 118, 308, 429; brevity of 113, 123, 148, 444, 448, 451, 461, 660; cares of 589; cf. Cares; — Christian 12, 16, 41, 47, 48, 51, 54, 120, 122, 125, 201, 207, 226, 231, 234, 235, 236, 277, 293, 303, 333, 347, 348, 349, 353, 369, 393–453, 469, 480, 527, 536 538, 540, 548, 550; consecrated 400, 468, 538, 540, 544, 547, 549, 567; cf. Consecration; — life's transient dream 394; crown of 407, 412, 421, 447, 451, 479, 620; dawn of 397; deliverance in 561; end of 538, 543, 552, 597, 598, 599, 608; cf. Death, hour of; — eternal 31, 46, 48, 67, 72, 73, 90, 145, 151, 158, 188, 196, 201, 206, 217, 223, 228, 235, 245, 247, 253, 276, 284, 301, 307, 313, 315, 331, 334, 341, 353, 391, 411, 432, 447, 448, 471, 500, 516, 616; eventide of 592; everlasting 613 to 619; frailty of 123, 345, 586; godly 8, 12, 93, 113, 120, 125, 163, 171, 186, 227, 285, 287, 288, 295, 298, 313, 328, 332, 342, 358, 361, 392, 395, 421, 458, 459, 536, 542, 544, 574, 608, 624; guidance through 285, 335, 340, 362, 394, 434, 447, 520, 521, 524, 526, 527, 528, 533, 539, 543, 549, 621, 649, 651; cf. Guidance; — immortal; cf. Life, eternal; — journey of 148, 394, 406, 411, 418, 434, 615, 616, 660; cf. Pilgrimage; — long 395, 425, 427; men of all walks of 471; mortal 437; Names — Dungeon 589, 602, 615; Prison 589; Weary Pilgrimage 434; cf. Pilgrimage; — new 34, 73, 96, 142, 144, 204, 225, 232, 242, 300, 308, 325, 328, 351, 369, 377, 382, 398, 409, 417, 422, 444, 459, 539; of fretting 425; of sacrifice; cf. Sacrifice; — perfect 623; purity of 287, 620; sinful 347, 382, 407; spiritual 37, 228, 232, 296, 298, 386, 507, 510; cf. Regeneration; — storms of 64, 122, 142, 345, 347, 362, 370, 566, 586, 588, 617, 624; temporal, earthly 523, 586, 588, 589, 590; uncertainty of 598; ungodly 140, 608; vicissitudes of 29, 110, 113, 118, 121, 122, 235, 252, 270, 345, 354, 372, 420, 434, 435, 516, 527, 586, 588; victorious 48, 226, 372, 423, 444; waters of; cf. Word of God; — woes of 354; cf. Woes
Light, creation of 8, 9, 12, 508; divine 12, 20, 88, 95, 117, 234, 276, 332, 346, 369; cf. Spiritual enlightenment; — eternal 88, 138, 212, 219; heavenly 538, 605; morning 537, 538; walking in the 421, 503
Lightning 582
Litany 166, 661
Lord: Lord's Day 7–12, 287; Lord's Prayer 288, 455, 458, 556; First Petition 455,

[660]

458, 556; Second Petition 65, 135, 264, 455, 458, 492, 494, 501, 556, 635; Third Petition 194, 418, 424, 455, 458, 517, 520, 529, 556; Fourth Petition 455, 458, 556; Fifth Petition 455, 458, 556; Sixth Petition 455, 458, 556; Seventh Petition 455, 458, 556

Lord's Supper 163, 164, 288, **304–316**, 343, 382; cf. Holy Communion; — blessings of 305, 306, 308, 311, 312, 313, 314, 316, 598; comfort of 163, 306, 316, 598; coming to 315; consolation in 306; desire for 305; earnest 163; faith 305, 306, 311; gratitude for 309, 310, 313, 316; institution of 164, 305; invitation to; cf. Invitation; — mystery of 304, 305, 310; Names — Altar 467; Board 311, 315; Body and Blood 306; Bond of Faith 315; Bread of Heaven 54, 632; Communion 308, 313; Communion Board 207; Covenant of Hope 315; Cup of Blessing 639; Cup of Healing 316; Cup of Life 305; Cup of Salvation 312; Feast 311, 313, 315, 330; Feast for Salvation 306; Feast of Love 307, 628, 634; Heavenly Bread 307; Heavenly Food 305, 312, 316; Heavenly Manna 163, 315; Holy Sacrament 308; Living Waters 307, 312; Precious Food 163, 311; Precious Treasure 305; Priceless Treasure 305, 306; Strength of Heart 315; Table 164, 310, 312, 315, 467, 639; Testament of Love 315; Treasures of Grace 316

Lord's Supper (General listing continued), need of 311; pledge of love 311; pledges of salvation in 307; power of God in 305; prayer for 304, 310, 314; preparation for 163, 305, 310, 311, 312, 315, 330; preservation of 304, 306, 310; real presence 163, 305, 306, 308, 310, 311, 313, 639; sacramental union in 311, 639; words of institution 164, 304

Lost, estate of man 58, 65, 141, 150, 295, 340, 369, 375, 377, 386, 387, 415, 498, 523; cf. Man; — seeking the 431, 442, 484, 485, 498, 499, 501, 506, 512, 607

Love, boundless 13, 37, 58, 69, 77, 89, 139, 143, 176, 177, 242, 285, 304, 329, 337, 349, 363, 575; cf. Christ, love of; — bond of 383, 478; brotherly 171, 228, 231, 235, 266, 292, 313, 319, 395, 458, 624; consecrated 400; Christian 464; covenant of 117; debt of 154; depth of 385, 386; *divine* 25, 32, 58, 77, 78, 80, 84, 88, 89, 139, 141, 175, 177, 221, 245, 246, 282, 343, 385, 386, 389, 518, 529; cf. God, love of; — creating 241; endures 529; mystery of 129; power of 142, 305; prevails 424; safe haven, refuge 372, — everlasting 25, 67, 276, 343, 352, 415, 469, 471, 615; example of 620; feast of 531; flame of 232; gifts of 112, 150; guiding 535; hearts of 504; infinite 439; Jehovah's 474; kindled 225, 361; law of 235, 486; law of Christian 412; life of 319, 439; miracle of 78; mother 122, 386, 474; mystery of 84, 219; *of Christ* 343, 350; cf. Christ, love of; — all-redeeming 488; blessings of 58, 349; boundless 213, 349; glory of 363; height of 342; power of 305; proclaiming the 364, 488, 496; relying on 89; resting in 591; wonders of 87, — pardoning 242, 289; perfect 170, 464, 519, 623; pledge of 115, 178, 311; pure 235, 349, 351; pure flame of 510; redeeming 84, 117, 157, 193, 377; revelation of 352; song of 349, 351, 511; transcending human thought 623; type of 620; unmerited 305; works of 295, 403, 572

Lust 398, 408, 470
Luther 288

Macedonian call 494
Magi 127, 131, 134, 136; Eastern sages 129, 130

Magnificat 275 475
Maid, Christian 622; cf. Youth
Majesty, robe of glorious 554; sovereign 239
Malefactor, penitent 157, 177, 181
Mammon 430
Man, Christian 622; corruption of 369, 377; cf. Human depravity; — creation of 13, 14, 34, 39, 168, 243, 299, 429; cf. Creation; — fallen 439; justification of 297; cf. Justification; — meanest men 641; mortal 13, 55, 83, 206, 346, 601; cf. Mortality, human; — natural state of; cf. Mankind; — new 68, 293, 301, 325, 351, 411; old 64, 68, 379; rebellious 374; righteousness of 380; threats of 267; trust in 269, 451; unrighteousness of 345, 377

Manger 75, 84, 88, 89, 90, 92, 95, 100, 102, 103, 104, 105, 108, 109, 645; bed 100; Paradise 81; throne 80, 85

Mankind, curse over 369; exaltation of 80, 417; fall of 369; honored 78, 96, 107, 401; joy of 343; Mankind: Names — Creation 401; Fainting Mankind 276; Heritage of Christ 494; Homeless Flock 499; Outcasts 501; Wanderers 276, 280; Weary 276, 277, 306, 485, 501, — natural state of 64, 378, 388, 498; prayer for all 578; redemption of all 439, 508; salvation of 84, 114, 131, 282, 504; sinful 114, 115, 141, 369, 379, 495; sore opprest 485

Marah's brink 422
Marriage **620–623**; blessedness of 620; blessing on 620, 639; bond of 620; Christians in 622; faithfulness 287; feast in heaven 67, 72, 164, 609; cf. Heaven, feast in; — golden thread in life 620; hallowed 621; institution of 621, 622; joined in 622; joy 623; peace in 623; prayer at 623; primal blessing on 622

Martyrdom 262, 470
Martyrs 67, 250, 259, 263, 339, 452, 471, 513; blessedness of 259, 470, 613, 618, 656; children 273; example of 452, 470; prayer of 452; song of 470, 475; witnesses for God 259; first 273

Mary, Magdalene 208; of Bethany 366; mother of James 208; mother of Jesus 115, 169, 177, 182, 252, 272; Virgin 76, 78, 85, 95, 104, 107, 139, 251, 253, 274, 275, 313, 387, 645, 646, 647

Maundy Thursday 163–164
Mealtime, prayer at 659
Means of Grace 65, 69, 138, 163, 164, 278, 282–316, 282, 292, 343, 443, 473; consolation in 384; gratitude for 207; pledges of salvation 384; praise for 52; preservation of 292, 321; treasure 343

Meditation 140, 385
Mercy 34, 42, 315, 341; abiding 386; advent of 56; assured 329; book of 535; boundless 371, 385; divine 17, 25, 31, 69, 86, 110, 111, 112, 119, 121, 225, 231, 266, 275, 382, 384, 385, 417, 514, 537, 570; eternal 15, 385, 545, 570; firm foundation 385; free 385; hope of 194; invitation of 278, 279, 281; Kyrie eleison; cf Kyrie; — need of 180; pardoning 543; plea for 146, 237, 312, 318, 323, 327, 328, 330, 385, 543, 545, 560, 580, 583, 607; cf. Prayer; — song of 385; source of hope 382; streams of 642; sure 44, 570; triumph of 504; trust in 385

Mercy-seat 2, 371, 403, 456, 531
Merit, all-sufficient 353; cf. Christ, merits of
Micah 103
Midian 106
Milk and honey 448
Ministers, anointing of 483, 488; armor of 483, 494; breathing on 502, 506, 641; call of 485, 486, 491, 493; clothed with righteousness 490; consecrated 482, 485, 487, 506; divine blessing on work of 491, 493, 504; duty of 506; eloquent 483, 485, 489; faith of 490; faithful 489, 490, 493; filled with the Spirit 484, 485, 489, 491; fire of

641; fired with love 484, 489, 490, 491; godly life of 485; hearing the 493; honoring the 493; humble 482; meekness of 490; message of 485, 487, 489, 507; Names — Angels of the Church 490; Apostles 483; Chosen Band 502; Dauntless Host 494; Heralds of Christ 509; Faithful Heralds 498; Herald of Cross of Christ 483; Heralds of Christ's Wondrous Grace 506; Savior's Herald 501; Kings 483; Laborers in Thy Vineyard 485, 488, 492, 496, 502, 507; Messengers 506; Messengers of Life 489; Messenger of Peace 484, 489; Messengers of Power 489; Pastors 485, 493; Preachers 494, 510; Priests 483, 490; Prophets 483, 493; Reapers 502, 507; Servants 490, 491, 493; Servant of God 138, 287, 321, 331, 484; cf. Christ, messengers of; — Shepherd 484, 485, 491; Faithful Shepherd 491; Sons of Prophets 483; Sowers of God's Word 493; Teachers Sent from God 484; Faithful Servants 492; True Servants 482; Watchmen 487, 496; Watchmen of the Church's Youth 494; Workers with God 488, — need of divine strength 491; ordination, installation of 482, 483, 491, 492; prayer for 482, 483, 486, 489, 491, 493, 502, 580; cf. Prayer; — prayer of 490, 491; presence of Triune God with 492; qualities of 490, 506; reception of 484, 493; reward of 491; sending forth 488, 492, 493, 494, 499; serving Christ 493; strengthening of 510; supporting the work of 484, 493; wisdom of 490, 491; work, duty of 482, 484, 486, 488, 490, 491; zeal of 490
Ministry 2, 59, 61, 63, 116, 190, 235, 264, 266, 321, 331, 482–493; call into the 641; of reconciliation 485; ordained by Christ 485; preparation for 641; preservation of the 485; volunteering for the 641
Miracle, incarnation 78; redemption 159; of Christ 131, 134, 482
Mirth 611
Missions 59, 126, 130, 132, 190, 259, 264, 266, 292, 294, 331, 360, 415, 439, 485, 488, **494–512**; foreign 28, 65, 126, 129, 482, 485, 495, 504, 506; Macedonian call of 494; home 499, 509; neglect of 495; prayers for 496, 498, 506, 508; support of 496, 507, 509; zeal for 498, 506, 507
Mission-work, call to 496; need of 499; personal 270, 440, 506
Missionaries, prayer for 498, 506; **foreign** 642
Moon, creation of 570
Morning 536–550; prayer; cf. Prayer; — song of praise 564
Mortality, human 26, 34, 113, 123, 206, 233, 306, 340, 343, 413, 552, 601; cf. Man, mortal; Types of 554
Mortals, hope for 510; life for 510; cf. Mankind
Moses 27, 135, 272, 287, 484
Mother-love 112, 386, 474
Mothers, blessings on 624
Mount of Olives 212; cf. Olivet
Mount Sinai 287
Mourners 639
Murder 273, 287
Music 341, 343, 360, 364, 424
Musings, highest 641
Mystery, of incarnation 84; of Lord's Supper 304, 305, 310

Name, given 300; cf. Book of Heaven; — Name of Christ 346, 352, 360, 363, 364, 482, 494, 495; cf. Christ, names of; — Jesus 114, 116, 360; Love 341; Savior 352; baptized into 377; blessings of 350, 360, 364; confession of; cf. Christ, confession of name of; — dying in 93, 468; everlasting 59; firm foundation 370; gathering in 70, 412, 467; cf. Church attendance; — glorifying the 504; glorying in 153, 469; glory of 352; help through

173, 327, 540; honor due 58, 114, 360; labor in 540; life through 367; loving the 652; mercy in 543; power of 339; praise of 15, 47, 66, 73, 83, 100, 125, 132, 164, 259, 334, 340, 344, 346, 350, 352, 360, 363, 382, 412, 465, 468, 491, 568, 628; cf. Praise; — prayer in 7, 112, 116, 181, 358, 364, 456, 458, 522, 534, 540, 598; preaching in 116, 467, 488, 495; cf. Preaching; — retiring in 540; salvation through 116; sleep in 592, — Name of God, dedication in 635; glorifying 118; glory to 253; praise to 14, 29, 40, 250, 334, 544; cf. Praise; — Name of Triune God, baptized into 298; cf. Triune God
Nation 575–584; advent of Christ to 65, 132, 506; baptizing the 504; barbarous 503; blessedness of 65, 73, 87, 106, 112, 132, 575, 577, 578, 580, 584; chastening the 583; cities of the 576; conversion of 59, 106, 126, 129, 130, 132, 415, 495, 497, 500, 503, 504, 505, 507, 579, 642; desire of 72, 94, 136; distress of 122; duty of, to worship 13, 14, 15, 20, 30, 39, 44, 57, 59, 64, 91, 98, 106, 339, 360, 500, 504, 575, 581; Gentile 57, 126, 129, 138, 214, 497, 498, 510, 642; hope of 82, 137; humility of the 583; judgment of 58; cf. Judgment; — judgment on the 579, 583; light of 138; pagan 506; cf. Heathen; — passing of 123; peace to the 582; prayer for the 566, 575, 576, 577, 578, 579, 580, 583; preaching to 9, 65, 84, 87, 136, 248, 294, 331, 360, 485, 487, 495, 497, 505, 510, 576, 578, 642; pride of the 575; protection of the 577, 578, 579, 580, 583; repentance of 579, 580, 583; savior of 95, 487; spiritual need of 510; sprinkling the 510; united 566, 578; worship of (gathering of) 59, 106, 126, 132, 137, 238, 343, 455; cf. Missions; cf. Country
Natural depravity; cf. Human depravity
Nature; cf. Praise of nature to God; — beauty of 657; joined 622; love of God in 443; mourning 154, 166, 169, 176; cf. Christ, mourning over death of; — quaking of 607; realms of 175; repose of 543, 654
Nebo 9
Need, hour of 522, 571
Neighbor, forgiving the 171, 455, 458; cf. Forgiveness; — love to 266, 287; cf. Love, brotherly; — peace with 395; prayer for 544; serving the 235, 377, 429, 458
New year 85, 96, 97, 114–125
New year's eve 110–113
Night, holy 646; protection during 543, 546, 547, 548, 549, 553, 556, 558, 559, 561, 562, 565, 653, 654; shades of 538; silent 646; sinless 555
Nunc Dimittis 137, 138, 308

Obedience 7, 20, 270, 286, 287, 296, 328, 395, 458, 496, 630; **new** 406–424
Offering of thanks 640
Offerings 633; cf. Stewardship, Christ, offerings for
Office of the Keys 331
Old, the hardened 499
Olivet 161; cf. Mount of Olives
Ordination 482, 483
Original sin 150, 369
Orphans 441, 476, 556
Otherworldliness; cf. Heavenly-minded

Paean of all creation 198
Palm Sunday 160–162
Paradise 81, 110, 177, 181, 257, 463, 614, 619; opened 193, 198, 207, 210; promised 181; regained 84, 105, 110, 148, 193, 207
Pardon 61, 180, 211, 278, 323, 428, 452; cf. Forgiveness; — assured of 388, 585; blessing of 392, 405; gratitude for 151; message of 276, 289, 324, 405, 483; offered 28, 168, 276, 308, 324, 405; plea for 113, 326, 483, 582; seeking 306, 322

[662]

Parents, blessed 625; cf. Home; — divine blessings on 640; duty of children to 287; example of 629; in the Lord 333; instructions for 630
Passion, deliverance from 227, 320, 538; earth-born 320, 470; grievous 557
Passion of Christ 140–186; cf. Christ, Passion of; — blessings of 148, 151, 155, 218, 252, 326, 599, 600; cause of 140, 143, 150, 167, 171, 172, 305, 313; comfort, consolation 174, 401; Help through 33, 317; pondering on, contemplation of 140, 143, 145, 150, 152, 153, 154, 155, 159, 167, 171, 175, 177; purpose of 405
Passover 195, 205; cf. Easter
Pastors 493; cf. Ministers
Pastoral conference 490
Patience 72, 103, 122, 173, 226, 287, 292, 317, 329, 410, 411, 413, 421, 429, 452, 458, 515, 518, 520, 535, 651, 660; life of 586
Patriarchs 67, 108, 415, 471, 475, 586, 601; noble train of 619
Paul, example of 496
Peace, abiding 192, 227, 233, 375; advent of 56, 59; blessing of gift of 196, 227, 233, 234, 243, 253, 308, 354; daily 253; departing in 137, 138; eternal 145, 293, 313, 471, 510, 603; forfeited 457; gratitude for 572; heavenly 284, 498; in the Church 112, 313; cf. Church; — in heart; cf. Heart, peace in the; — in the home; cf. Home, peace in the; — in the State 112; cf. State; — living in 620; love of 566; message of 2, 276, 284, 324, 501; national 112, 582; of conscience 149, 297, 342; of God 65, 110, 204, 208, 238, 258; on earth; cf. Earth, peace on; — perfect 539; pledge of 343; prayer (plea) for 47, 96, 146, 147, 258, 292, 313, 411, 483, 544, 558, 580, 582; preaching of 2, 5, 61, 282, 487; through blood of Christ 335, 372, 389; with God 313, 318, 335, 367, 372, 378, 389, 597; world 258
Pearl, priceless 357
Penitence, 22, 24, 26, 42, 149, 156, 168, 318, 324, 386, 497, 588; cf. Contrition
Pentecost 224–236; cf. Holy Ghost; Day of 232, 452
Pentecostal measure 502
Persecution 261, 262, 263, 267, 362, 372, 381, 423, 444, 528, 619; by imprisonment 471; by mockery 471, 528; by stoning 471; by sword 273, 471, 528; in the arena 470
Perseverance 520
Peter, example of 544
Piety 303
Pilgrimage, Christian 48, 50, 54, 71, 90, 110, 121, 122, 145, 148, 214, 215, 231, 256, 264, 291, 292, 294, 343, 345, 362, 366, 368, 374, 406, 410, 413, 417, 421, 422, 434, 459, 469, 478, 480, 481, 516, 533, 540, 552, 581, 585, 616, 660
Pity, amazing 154; assurance of 268, 280, 385, 535, 590; divine 34, 181, 385, 439; endless 172; fatherly 34; Scepter of Christ (name) 73; plea for 130, 234, 260, 317, 325, 582
Planets 255
Pleasures, carnal 611; forbidden 516; sinful 430
Pledge 115, 163, 171, 178, 298, 343; cf. Earnest
Poetry 132
Pontius Pilate 253
Poor, helping the 440, 551
Poverty 396, 420, 425, 427, 439, 528, 532, 624
Power, divine 105, 134, 234, 242, 244, 246, 352, 398, 424, 455, 474; kingdom of; cf. Kingdom; — mortal 340; quickening 242; sovereign 13, 27
Praise 57, 69, 73, 79, 80, 82, 83, 85, 87, 90, 97, 100, 105, 107, 111, 112, 116, 134, 158, 199, 204, 217, 237, 239, 243, 282, 438, 466, 558, 568, 570, 573, 575, 580, 584, 639; cf. Worship; — angelic 4, 17, 23, 28, 30, 35,

38, 67, 76, 77, 83, 84, 92, 94, 98, 104, 109, 132, 136, 148, 158, 160, 188, 193, 205, 208, 214, 218, 221, 244, 246, 248, 249, 252, 254, 256, 346, 367, 511; cf. Songs; — chanted 1; creation's; cf. Creation's praise of Christ; — daily 540; duty to 35, 39, 198, 367, 542; endless, eternal 40, 73, 80, 84, 199, 209, 239, 243, 244, 367, 384, 400, 460, 512, 568; evening 653; heavenly; cf. Heaven; — hymns of 199; cf. Songs; — immortal 248, 371, 572; invitation to; cf. Invitation; — nature's praise of God 28, 30, 43, 70, 76, 87, 91, 98, 127, 193, 205, 240, 246, 255, 286, 438; paean of 199; cf. Songs; — perfect 352; of God's goodness 43, 443; of God's power 43; of God's Word 45; of God's wisdom 43; sacrifice of 438, 573; songs of 101, 134; undying 204; universal 475; worldly 430; **Worship and Praise 14–44**
Prayer 1, 18, 21, 33, 45, 46, 51, 59, 68, 73, 86, 89, 110, 118, 120, 121, 144, 183, 260, 288, 389, 403, 423, 434, 438, 451, **454–459**, 464, 639; acceptable to God 128, 226, 279, 364, 372, 459, 528, 533, 548, 626; agony of 166; answer to 96, 288, 329, 345, 358, 429, 446, 456, 458, 465, 466, 488, 491, 493, 494, 517, 518, 520, 522, 523, 534, 583, 611, 628, 638, 643; at confirmation 337; at marriage 623; at meals 659; commanded 21; described 454; desire of soul 454; devout 194; effectual 488; evening 194, 197, 540, 555, 557, 559, 564, 653; faith in 22; for child to be baptized 299; for children at confirmation 337; for Christ; cf. Christ, prayer for; — for country; cf. Country, prayer for; — for enemies 177, 180, 452; for a strong faith 396, 446, 470; for forgiveness; cf. Forgiveness; — for gift of Holy Ghost 301; for godly life 395; for Government 566; for home; cf. Home, prayer for; — for mankind 578; **for mercy 317–331,** 402, 434, 560; cf. Mercy; — for ministers, ministry 482, 483, 484, 485; cf. Ministers; — for missions; cf. Missions; — for missionaries; cf. Missionaries; — for nation; cf. Nation; — for neighbor 544; for peaceful death 395, 406, 598, 600, 603; for steadfastness 516, 517; cf. Steadfastness; — for teachers 486; for temporal blessings 566; for Word of God; cf. Word of God; — foundation of 632; hour of 24; in affliction 422, 515, 520, 522, 524, 528, 531, 534; cf. Affliction; — in Christ's name; cf. Name of Christ; — in trials 515; cf. Affliction; — instruction in 64, 159, 228, 358, 374, 411, 454, 457, 458, 459, 480, 493, 494, 520, 537, 538, 626; intercessory 544; invitation to; cf. Invitation; — Morning 537, 540, 564; neglect of 457; New Year's Eve 110; night of 493; of martyrs 452; — of the dying 172, 177; cf. Death, prayer at; — place of 480; power of 528; privilege of 457, 522; unceasing 235, 351, 424, 446; sacrifice of 438
Preaching 59, 130, 283, 292, 294, 494, 496, 499, 569, 641; blessing on 46, 235, 485, 493; commanded 331; in name of Christ 2, 116, 364, 467, 488, 491, 494, 495; of glad tidings 63, 83, 282, 487; of the Gospel 266, 282, 387, 467, 482, 485, 497, 498, 505, 507, 510, 578, 635, 638; of grace 483, 488; of hope 501, 510; of John the Baptist 63, 272; of judgment 218, 496; of peace 2, 5, 61, 282, 484, 487, 489, 498; of redeeming love 364, 488, 496, 507, 638; of redemption 489, 505; of repentance 272; of salvation 190, 282, 331, 487, 495, 507; preservation of 264, 485; the reconciliation 504; the resurrection 198; to the nations 9, 65, 84, 87, 136, 248, 294, 331, 482, 483, 485, 487, 488, 494, 495, 497, 501, 505, 507, 510, 576, 578, 642

Precepts, fulfilment of 412; cf. Law, fulfilment of
Preparation, for Christ 60, 61, 63, 66, 67, 69, 70, 71, 73, 75, 87, 471, 509, 604, 609; cf. Repentance; — for Lord's Supper 305; cf. Lord's Supper; — for meeting God 504
Presentation 136–139; cf. Christ, presentation of
Preservation, divine 11, 19, 51, 86, 110, 124, 125, 127, 200, 258, 264, 267, 337, 375, 381, 406, 417, 428, 444, 446, 549, 553, 567, 581, 590
Pride, human 75, 175, 383, 446, 640; pagan 290; renouncing 347
Prodigal, return of the 25, 280
Priests 460
Promised Land 9
Prophecy, fulfilment of 57, 71, 84, 86, 91, 99, 103, 104, 135, 139, 168, 202, 208, 253, 274, 290, 607, 611, 645
Prophets 139, 249, 250, 272, 274, 471, 475, 483, 487, 493, 513, 586, 601, 618; false 260; holy band of 67; noble train of 619; power of the 510; reward 493; throng 108; hands, of, supporting the 484, 496
Prosperity 112, 572, 578
Protection, divine 7, 11, 19, 25, 29, 39, 47, 51, 53, 70, 96, 110, 112, 119, 120, 122, 123, 125, 130, 173, 186, 192, 251, 255, 260, 261, 262, 263, 267, 268, 275, 282, 325, 333, 337, 338, 340, 342, 347, 353, 368, 372, 393, 404, 407, 410, 427, 434, 437, 501, 517, 520, 521, 524, 526, 528, 530, 533, 534, 536, 538, 540, 541, 544, 546, 548, 549, 550, 553, 558, 561, 565, 566, 567, 569, 575, 577, 582, 590, 631, 643, 651; cf. Holy Spirit, protection of
Providence, divine 11, 19, 28, 39, 43, 45, 69, 90, 112, 119, 122, 124, 125, 200, 243, 251, 275, 338, 362, 368, 425, 426, 436, 443, 447, 458, 500, 514, 549, 569, 570, 571, 572, 573, 574, 608, 624, 648, 651, 652, 659; cf. Care, divine
Psalms 35, 58, 368, 414, 426, 431, 436, 520, 662—667
Psalter 28, 39
Publican, penitent 323
Purity 4, 41, 70, 77, 120, 127, 134, 139, 166, 201, 226, 246, 257, 287, 299, 303, 320, 325, 345, 349, 351, 355, 375, 377, 398, 406, 422

Race 126; cf. Nations; — apostate 504; the Christian's 113, 125, 247, 293, 303, 306, 349, 402, 444, 447, 479, 524, 540, 599; fallen 10, 58, 77, 88, 93, 114, 238, 360, 384; Heathen 28; ransomed 241; ungodly 414
Rain 566, 569, 570
Ransom 32, 62, 141, 152, 156, 158, 168, 176, 185, 242, 371, 377, 380, 397
Ransomed throng 188, 323, 339, 415; cf. Saints
Reapers, sending forth 502; cf. Ministers
Reason, human; cf. Human reason
Reception of Christ 55, 57, 58, 59, 61, 66, 68, 69, 70, 72, 73, 75, 77, 82, 83, 84, 85, 87, 91, 94, 95, 102, 293, 305, 509, 647, 650
Reconciliation 11, 25, 94, 103, 129, 189, 313, 367, 372; ministry of 485; preaching of 140; through Christ 2, 173, 191, 326, 375
Redeemer 339–368
Redemption 27, 32, 62, 64, 79, 90, 107, 129, 131, 132, 135, 152, 193, 202, 210, 231, 236, 248, 251, 252, 324, 331, 432, 439, 443, 507, 508; completed 176, 177, 278; free 505; preaching of 489, 505; price of 141, 168, 334, 375, 607; through Christ 142, 216, 365, 382, 596, 652; through Christ's blood 96, 124, 157, 158, 198, 220, 305; cf. Blood of Christ; — through Christ's cross 155, 171, 199; through man 377, 383
Reformation 258–269
Refuge 123, 148, 165, 178, 235, 345, 347, 353, 362, 370, 376, 402, 420, 427, 435, 556, 599
Regeneration 12, 23, 38, 64, 65, 94, 228, 232, 241, 242, 293, 298, 300, 325, 333, 351, 377, 382, 405, 507, 639; new creation 301, 325, 351, 411; water of 299; cf. Baptism
Rejoicing 58, 62, 72, 79, 82, 96, 99, 103, 107, 161, 187, 188, 205, 223, 275, 362, 387, 535; cf. Joy
Religion, true 572
Renunciation 60, 77, 81, 85, 93, 125, 143, 163, 175, 206, 223, 270, 298, 315, 362, 365, 366, 385, 407, 423, 470; cf. Consecration
Repentance 75, 110, 145, 156, 163, 226, 272, 279, 280, 281, 322, 328, 331, 358, 386, 477, 522, 579, 580, 583; cf. Contrition, Preparation for Christ; — preaching of 61, 272
Resignation 22, 171, 194, 224, 226, 404, 418, 420, 513–535, 546, 549, 601
Rest 45, 223, 226, 227, 276, 277, 338, 456, 459; Day of 9; eternal 293, 297, 410, 467, 510, 511, 586, 617; physical 553, 554; promised 320
Resurrection, the 125, 196, 371, 395, **429, 432,** 463, 465, 481, 536, 539, 558, 565, 587, 592, 593, 596, 602, 603, 622; blessed 587, 602, 603; blessings of 196; Christ, first-fruits of 188, 191, 193, 214; comfort of the 200; Day of 9, 205, 206, 371, 444, 448, 463, 596, 604, 606, 610; awe-ful day 558; glorious day 221; illustrious day 445; solemn day of 596; hope of 206, 217, 464; joy of the 604; **of Christ** 125, **187–211,** 196, 201, 207, 251, 253; cf. Christ, resurrection of; — of Christ, fact, certainty of 200, 206; of the body 201, 207, 251, 253, 259, 371, 393, 395, 397, 444, 463; trust in the 603
Retribution, happy 448
Reunion with departed 46, 110, 464, 476
Revelation 88, 264, 271
Revenge 287
Reward, merit of 392; cf. Works
Righteous, way of the 414
Righteousness 69, 295, 366; advent of 59; by faith 272, 375; by works 329, 375, 380, 382, 389; crown of 142; Royal Dress (name) 297; way of, path of 295, 436, 500; of Christ 371, 380; clothed in 77, 142, 165, 264, 297, 366, 370, 371, 380, 490; glories of 87; Glorious Dress (name) 371, 392, 585, 598; hope's foundation 370
Robe, clothed in spotless 598, 601
Rock, building on a 518
Room, there still is 509

Sabbath 11; endless 7
Sacrament 65, 163, 164, 288, **298–316,** 308, 310, 632, 634, 639; cleansed through 299, 382; comfort at death 306; consolation in 306, 384, 477; holy 308; prayer for 292, 321; preservation of 292, 306, 321, 477; visible elements in 164, 299, 304, 308, 311, 314
Sacrifice 270; atoning 297; blood of 156, 218; life of 143, 150, 154, 182, 308, 403, 477; cf. Consecration; — morning 511, 536, 543; of contrite hearts 316, 325; cf. Contrition; — humble 622; cf. Worship
Sadness, days of 523; depths of 399
Sages 136; cf. Magi
Sailors, protection of 654
Saints 29, 123, 136, 221, 222, 263, 271, 274, 333, 373, 444, 468, 471, 502, 513; aged 139; all saints 270–275; cf. Apostles; — banner of 472; **blessedness of saints** 407, 463, 470, 585–619, 656; clothed — in glory 432, 463, 471; in perfection 603; in robes of light 452; in robes of white 613; in victory 445; in white apparel 471, 476, 595, 656, — **communion of saints** 3, 67, 323, 360, 460–481, 478, 601, 634; cf. Communion of saints; — courage of 470; death of 468; example of 586; faithfulness of 470, 472; fearful 514; forsaken by men 260; glorified 471; glory of 471, 619; graves of 593; in heaven 72, 143, 214, 515; cf. Heaven, saints in; — life of 468; lion-hearted 470; martyred

470; multitudes of 471; *Names* — conquerors through Christ 472; Heavenly Band 301; Triumphant Hosts 40, 475; Victors 476, — of old 274, 470, 472; on earth and above 478; praise 35, 221, 241, 246, 460, 470; prayers of 2, 454; ransomed 476; Song of; cf. Song; — ten thousand times ten thousand 476; thousands, thousands 601; triumphant 527; virtue of 168; sainted dead 169

St. Andrew, call of 270
St. John the Apostle (Eaglet) 271
St. John the Baptist 61, 63, 104, 272, 328; Elijah (name) 272; Prebirth of 272
St. Michael's and All Angels 254–257
St. Paul, preaching of 496
St. Peter 544
Salem, imperial 503; cf. Church
Salvation 77, 84, 86, 131, 148, 244, 311, 333, 636; cf. Redemption; — accepting 139, 324; advent of 377, 387, 477; assurance of 379, 386; begun 115, 117; brought by Christ 6, 73, 103, 107, 243, 367; by faith 266, 289, 295, 301, 315, 360, 377, 485; by grace 377; cf. Grace; — charter of 473; eternal 96, 384; feast of 306, 415; free 266, 278, 324, 367, 405, 428, 523, 607; fruits of 50, 142; hope of 329, 460; invitation to 278; cf. Invitation; — joy of 643; name of our 114, 116; plan of 271, 374, 384, 385, 387, 507; plea for 10, 351; pledges of 307, 384, 615; preaching of 485, 487, 495, 505, 510; rejecting 419, 460; seeking the way of 383, 386, 432; song of 325; cf. Song; — through Christ's blood 157; through Christ's merit 96, 144, 167, 196, 199, 207, 251, 293, 335, 375, 376, 377, 386, 528, 565; through works 287, 311, 373, 375, 377, 380, 389, 411, 415, 433; tidings of 282; universal 504; way of 190, 301, 374, 383, 417, 432; white raiments of 366
Samson 211
Sanctification 2, 8, 12, 21, 24, 49, 51, 68, 87, 113, 120, 125, 129, 140, 142, 143, 165, 168, 185, 201, 207, 223, 224, 225, 226, 227, 228, 231, 234, 235, 236, 241, 251, 292, 298, 301, 306, 325, 348, 349, 351, 393–453, 477, 507, 560, 643
Sanctuary 1; abiding heritage 640; abode of God 635, 636; altar of the 332, 467, 490, 503, 622, 634; bells of the 467; building the 632, 637; cloud and fire o'er the 469; courts of God 2, 11, 13, 14, 129; dedication of the 637; destruction of the 467; dwellings of God's love 480; dwelling-place of God 639; earthly shrine 637; earthly temple 632; Father's house 133; font in the 467; gates 44; glory of Christ in 634; God dwelling in 633, 638; hallowed by Word of God 467; hallowed courts 465; lengthening the cords of 640; cf. Zion's cords; — *Names* — Habitation 469, 640; Home of Christ 638; House of God 11, 47, 462, 467, 580; House of Praise 637; House of Prayer 70; Temple of God 574, — presence of Christ in 637; purpose of the 467; retreat for weary 632; shrine 438; spacious courts of the 503; steeples of 467; strengthening pillars of 640; temple 2, 4, 129, 133, 136, 138, 139, 316, 466, 480, 503, 632, 633, 634, 638, 641; temples of God's grace 636; throne of Christ in 637
Sanctus 4, 9, 23, 38, 601
Satan, accusations of 364; aims of, mission 254, 381, 444, 446, 615; bondage of 62, 66, 202, 387, 404; conflict with 49, 53, 58, 62, 64, 65, 66, 86, 91, 103, 144, 262, 266, 268, 337, 373, 413, 437, 615; conquered 10, 58, 62, 64, 65, 66, 77, 80, 81, 86, 90, 106, 116, 132, 134, 151, 168, 189, 192, 198, 209, 218, 262, 417, 458; defying 347; deliverance from 67, 91, 130, 148, 186, 195, 202, 233, 235, 237, 257, 259, 272, 292, 297,

319, 340, 429, 541, 548; delivered to 611; domain of 198; fury of 561; guile of 292; harvest 446; hosts of 337; *Names* — Accuser 456; Ancient Dragon 254; Enemy 272; Evil Foe 262; Evil One 86, 247; Foe 263, 410; cf. Foe; — Lion 631; Prince of Hell 192, 402, 470; Prince of the World 262; Roaring Lion 254; Tempter 103, 159, 166, 186, 537, 540, 552, 559; Wily Foe 90, — power of 413, 456, 458, 537, 540; prey of 340, 413, 446, 631; rage of 292; wiles of 81, 103, 254, 262, 265, 319 337, 396, 413, 446, 455, 548
School 254
Schoolchildren in 630
Scoffers 462
Scribes 460
Scriptures 98, 132, 195; fulfilment of 170, 611; cf. Prophecy, fulfilment of; — truthfulness of 373
Scroll, heavenly 271; prophetic 290
Sea 30, 198, 246, 253, 299, 427; commerce on the 566; creation of 17; crystal 471; destruction of the 503; isles of the 132; stilling the 649, 651; wealth of 438
Self-denial 40, 421
Sense, feeble 514; powers of 201, 304; cf. Human reason; — failing of 365
Seraphs 109, 214, 246, 249, 250, 455, 475, 641; songs of 581, 599, 601, 638
Service, call to 270, 496; cf. Missions; — Christian 224; close of service 45–54; **opening of service 1–6**
Session; cf. Christ, session of
Sheaves, gathering in of 485, 492, 496, 502, 572, 656
Sheep, wandering 13, 485, 510
Shepherds 76, 84, 85, 103, 104, 109, 136, 645, 646
Sick, healing of the 557
Sickness 27, 63, 67, 122, 138, 245, 311, 345, 418, 427, 439, 515, 532, 551, 556, 557; comfort in 614, 654
Sight, failing 365
Silence 411
Silver 438; and gold, consecrated 400, 633
Simeon 137, 138
Sin 90, 92, 107, 149, 153, 220, 225, 232, 312, 313; absolved from 371; appalling 386; assailed by 347, 396, 461, 526; atonement for 115, 237, 319, 323, 371, 376, 380, 417, 590; birth in 150, 369, 387; burden of 65, 108, 153, 172, 312, 315, 318, 322, 326, 328, 366, 380, 386, 389, 456, 458, 515, 594, 652; cleansed from 32, 37, 63, 70, 77, 91, 111, 124, 127, 131, 149, 156, 157, 165, 244, 247, 278, 279, 320, 322, 324, 326, 330, 335, 360, 375, 376, 382, 385, 388, 390, 391, 417, 419, 459, 507, 528, 545, 574, 603, 627, 652; clouds of 543; confession of 22, 110, 112, 143, 150, 156, 169, 171, 172, 181, 194, 310, 311, 315, 316, 317, 318, 322, 323, 324, 326, 327, 330, 345, 379, 382, 392, 537, 565, 583; conquered 95, 213, 477, 500; consequence, fruits of 112, 150, 317, 321, 329, 369, 377, 387; consumed 641; conviction of 225, 264, 285, 287, 289, 295, 326, 377, 378, 560; crucifying 143, 336; cure for 634; curse of 150, 295, 369; dead in 232, 411, 417; debt of 58, 163, 207, 220, 313, 340, 375, 611; defiled by 89, 149, 335, 364; deliverance from bondage of 65, 66, 74, 85, 86, 90, 104, 107, 130, 150, 151, 234, 236, 242, 247, 258, 282, 297, 323, 324, 329, 349, 360, 362, 384, 386, 387, 464, 476, 535, 536, 538, 547, 621, 628, 661; depth of 327, 340, 387; dispersing 536; dying to 163, 293, 298, 315, 316, 409; enslaved by 141, 207, 377, 379, 387, 557, 588; fall into 145, 202, 207, 254, 288, 295, 349, 350, 387, 446; folly of 627; forgiveness; cf. Forgiveness; — forsaking, fleeing 125, 140, 288, 316, 347, 355, 412, 414, 421; gloom of 359; hosts of 449; imputation of 392; inclined to 563, 654; inherited 369; cf.

[665]

Original sin; — kept from 539, 542; leaven of 165, 195; leprosy of 149; living in 324; loathing 315; lust of 398; mourning 288, 315, 316, 319; cf. Contrition; — night of 88, 150, 195, 359, 510, 538, 549; opprest by 77, 90, 114, 141, 148, 177, 211, 272, 297, 306, 315, 318, 320, 322, 323, 347, 373, 375, 387, 456, 485, 590; original 150, 369; power of 141, 282, 360, 375, 376, 377, 379, 387, 402, 477; remission of 319, 324, 331; cf. Forgiveness; — powerless 103, 152, 349, 375, 416; record of 322, 324, 325; redeemed from 323, 393; cf. Redemption; — reign of 141, 379; renouncing 125, 298, 315, 316, 325, 347; cf. Renunciation; — revealed by Law 289, 377, 378; safe from 538; scarlet 324; seduction into 254, 335, 409; shades of 538; shielded from 144, 173, 286, 303, 325, 548; sinful thoughts, deeds, words, desires 144, 235, 258, 318, 369, 379, 382, 411, 470; spread of 87, 292, 446; temptings to 144, 335; cf. Temptation; — triumph over 162; unrepented 310; wages of 150, 295, 324, 329, 375, 387; winter of 204
Sinners, chief of 342; death of 245, 248, 331, 414; fear of 444; heavy laden 315, 322, 386; hope for all 77, 81, 178, 245, 281, 316, 324, 350, 360, 371, 386, 498, 506, 607; pardon for 28, 42, 248, 281, 312, 331, 498; penitent 26, 318, 331, 388; received 74, 77, 112, 122, 276, 279, 312, 315, 316, 324, 386, 388, 513; redemption of 199; cf. Redemption; — sought 397; unworthy 317, 331, 379; cf. Unworthiness; — warning the 490; wretched 385
Sinning, wilful 295, 315, 351, 390, 417
Sinai, Mt. 287
Sincerity 75
Sky 30, 94, 102, 212, 232, 246, 341, 359; destruction of the 503; wealth of 438
Slaves 498
Sleep 551; in Jesus 587; peaceful 560, 561, 562, 563, 653, 654; refreshing 536, 558
Snow, white as 324
Song, eternal 619, 632; sacred 363; of adoration 23, 56, 82, 122, 246, 352, 401, 472; of angels 35, 67, 76, 77, 83, 84, 85, 92, 94, 98, 102, 109, 112, 132, 136, 158, 178, 188, 190, 198, 199, 208, 214, 221, 238, 244, 246, 249, 255, 257, 344, 454, 584, 599; of Praise, angelic; — of bliss 619; of creation 35, 41, 42, 43, 87, 136, 198, 205, 244; of expectation 481; of exultation 57, 77, 100, 116, 196, 214, 217, 387, 500, 573; of glory 44, 76, 83, 160, 207, 212, 221, 238, 244, 341; of grace 40, 373, 374, 639; of hallelujah 195, 475; of the harvest 573; of heaven 10, 30, 40, 66, 67, 70, 83, 125, 127, 193, 205, 222, 250, 256, 339, 340, 344, 352, 415, 491, 589, 599, 608, 613, 652; of heavenly hosts 3, 40, 67, 83, 84, 92, 98, 104, 148, 198, 199, 208, 252, 257, 471, 475, 573, 646; of joy 58, 80, 84, 85, 96, 130, 188, 190, 193, 210, 217, 309, 316, 344, 465, 487, 526; jubilant 198, 210, 613; of liberty 578; of love 156, 157, 320, 343, 349, 351, 363, 397; of love divine 396; of martyrs 470, 475; of mercy 142, 385; of peace 76, 347; of praise 23, 25, 26, 28, 29, 30, 35, 38, 39, 41, 54, 58, 66, 67, 69, 73, 80, 82, 84, 85, 92, 96, 98, 100, 101, 104, 108, 112, 122, 132, 134, 155, 158, 161, 178, 188, 191, 193, 199, 208, 209, 210, 211, 214, 221, 223, 232, 238, 239, 243, 246, 248, 316, 320, 340, 343, 351, 352, 360, 367, 377, 387, 400, 401, 426, 431, 470, 475, 493, 499, 542, 564, 568, 569, 572, 656; of prophecy 168; of rapture 323, 340; of redeemed 41, 139, 157, 190, 363; of saints 4, 10, 41, 67, 143, 248, 527, 584, 619; of salvation 325, 575, 656; of thankfulness 13, 22, 27, 30, 36, 110, 121, 124, 129, 134, 152, 195, 243, 248, 254, 316, 434, 468, 520, 546, 548, 568, 575; of triumph 57, 84, 95, 102, 155,
193, 198, 214, 222, 424, 463, 476, 658; of victory 205, 451, 472; **spiritual songs** 645–660
Sorrow 206, 312, 342, 516, 519; borne by Christ 313; brief 448; comfort in 61, 110, 149, 353; cup of 521; day of 607; cf. Judgment; — dispelled 225, 528; end of 72, 96, 375; freed from 69, 215, 236, 349, 413; guidance through 420; help in 439; hour of 407, 425; night of 48, 362; opprest by 589; penitential 605; rest from 592; rivers of 427; sowing in 409
Soul 592, 596, 603; cf. Heart; — blessedness of the 603; carried to heaven 619; fallen 232; immortal 603; transformed 641
Sowing, and reaping 1, 46, 49, 52, 206, 383, 409, 485, 488, 492, 493, 502, 567, 574, 656
Sparrows 480
Special occasions 632–644
Speech, Christian, consecrated 395, 400, 411, 439, 454, 483, 496; cf. Conversation
Spirits, evil 546
Spiritual, blessings 113, 500, 539, 542, 567; cf. Divine blessings; — blindness 417, 495, 508, 512, 542; bondage 69, 340, 378, 379, 389; cleansing 398; cf. Purity; — darkness 16, 37, 41, 42, 61, 66, 88, 99, 106, 126, 128, 132, 133, 137, 197, 225, 229, 234, 260, 278, 294, 316, 324, 346, 359, 369, 378, 388, 411, 463, 481, 497, 498, 499, 504, 505, 508, 510, 512, 539, 543, 645; darkness, powers of 450; deafness 512; death 106, 126, 232, 325, 369, 378, 387, 496; dumbness 512; enlightenment 3, 8, 12, 16, 20, 58, 59, 66, 80, 88, 106, 124, 128, 130, 133, 138, 194, 197, 202, 212, 224, 225, 226, 227, 229, 231, 232, 233, 234, 245, 248, 264, 277, 283, 284, 285, 294, 295, 332, 346, 353, 355, 359, 361, 366, 388, 398, 399, 407, 421, 424, 477, 481, 485, 495, 497, 498, 500, 505, 508, 512, 537, 538, 539, 541, 543, 545, 550, 563, 564, 572, 576, 642; food 573, 576; cf. Spiritual hunger, thirst; — growth 333, 544; hunger 305, 307, 315, 364, 368, 420, 422, 431, 484, 490, 491, 493, 509, 537, 550, 648; needs 542; slumber 446; thirst 307, 368, 383, 422, 431, 469, 525, 550, 648; cf. Thirst; — want 469, 488
Sponsors, parents in the Lord 333
Star 71, 127, 128, 130, 131, 134, 136, 255, 286, 407; morning 647
State 112, 254, 577
Statutes, keeping God's 416; cf. Law, keeping the
Steadfastness 24, 53, 77, 121, 192, 201, 206, 221, 224, 235, 261, 292, 296, 314, 334, 336, 342, 347, 357, 368, 372, 381, 383, 387, 444, 470, 477, 517, 528, 556; prayer for; cf. Prayer
Stephen (martyr) 452
Stewardship 438–443; cf. Christ, offerings for
Storms 514; of life 64, 122, 192, 264, 270, 291, 320, 345, 347, 349, 362, 370, 396, 413, 423, 435, 521, 528, 649, 660
Straying 13, 41, 235, 291, 320, 324, 326, 330, 334, 336, 340, 342, 349, 357, 366, 372, 393, 394, 397, 399, 401, 416, 418, 421, 426, 431, 433, 441, 479, 498, 499, 501, 512, 516, 530, 548, 627
Strength 41, 122, 223, 229, 235, 276, 304, 332, 395, 398, 408, 427, 428, 429, 450, 518, 520; increase in 450, 451, 480, 504, 541
Strife, mortal 516, 590
Submission 7, 20, 51, 58, 69, 118, 120, 140, 143, 159, 171, 194, 224, 226, 234, 270, 317, 328, 335, 348, 353, 358, 381, 385, 395, 406, 418, 420, 421, 458, 517, 518, 520, 521, 526, 529, 530, 532, 544, 545, 546, 607; cf. Resignation
Suffering, cup of 422
Summer, blessings of 572
Sun, course of the 511, 536, 570
Sunrise 537, 542, 544, 545
Sunset 554, 557
Sunday 9–12, 208, 229

[666]

Superscription 178, **179**
Sympathy 464
Swaddling-clothes 85
Swallows 480

Tares, destruction of 574; sowing of 574
Teachers, call of 486; duty of 486; false 260; prayer for 486
Temperance 287
Temple 139, 161, 316; cf. Sanctuary, Heart; — Heaven 249, 467; made with hands 467; veil 2, 169, 176, 218
Temptation 103, 144, 372, 588; earth's 282; enduring 260, 410; hour of 159, 335, 337, 410, 437, 457, 458, 516; overcoming 402, 470, 550; protection in 120, 247, 455; resisting 362, 421; worldly 144, 335, 362, 396, 524
Thankfulness 13, 30, 31, 32, 34, 69, 96, 110, 111, 112, 119, 121, 124, 129, 134, 151, 152, 154, 172, 173, 211, 217, 243, 244, 303, 349, 659; song of; cf. Song
Thanksgiving 11, 15, 19, 27, 30, 33, 36, 38, 40, 44, 50, 51, 105, 112, 113, 125, 151, 207, 223, 237, 238, 254, 266, 282, 305, 309, 310, 313, 321, 363, 399, 417, 443, 500, 522, 555, 566—574, 575, 581, 584, 588, 640; service 574, 640
Theft 287
Theological institutions 641
Thief, contrite 177; dying 157, 181, 607
Thirst 149, 177, 184, 277, 281, 296, 305
Thomas 208
Thoughts, godly 399, 536, 550; guarding of 536; secret 536
Throne 123, 130, 132, 142, 143; eternal 9, 120, 201, 214, 454; fall of earthly 341; Father's 105, 319, 464; heavenly 6, 48, 249, 373, 455; judgment 170, 376, 528; manger 80; of Christ 4, 59, 77, 120, 130, 132, 142, 152, 170, 191, 201, 212, 213, 216, 242, 252, 295, 300, 338, 341, 353, 363, 373, 452, 515, 576; radiant 363, 609; rainbow-circled 405; standing before 493, 515, 566, 601, 603, 604, — of David 613; of God 24, 43, 77, 105, 123, 162, 165, 212, 213, 222, 242, 249, 254, 256, 305, 319, 325, 432, 458, 579, 623; waters of life flowing from 531, — of glory 72, 218; of grace 327, 379, 434; of light 656; of Satan 64; Jehovah's awe-full 13; judgment 170; perishable 658; sapphire 162, 634
Thunder 582
Tidings, glad 63, 77, 83, 84, 85, 100, 103, 109, 136, 297, 487, 592, 610, 646, 647
Time 123, 202, 399; end of 485, 511; endless 104; fulness of 99; passage of 13, 15, 31, 104, 110–113, 122, 123, 598, 605, 660; redeeming the 444; wrecks of 354
Times, **times and seasons** 536–584; perilous, troubled 292, 458; cf. Distress
Tomb 278, 355; cf. Grave
Tongue 233, 325, 361, 363, 405, 462; fiery 12, 504; people of every 511
Transfiguration 135; cf. Christ, transfiguration of
Transgression 285, 325, 329, 544; **cf. Sin**
Travel 427
Treasure 305; created by God 438; earthly 347, 385, 423; cf. Wealth; — heavenly 430; lasting 469; sacrifice of 477; tempting 516; of world 85; of World
Trials 64, 138, 224, 269, 340, 362, 373, 385, 393, 407, 411, 413, 423, 444; cf. Church, afflictions; — comfort in 252, 268; end of 596; enduring 260; fiery 427; help in 313; hour of 516, 518; like a dream 415; prayer in 457, 515, 516; preservation in 264
Tribulation, joy in 343; rest from 471
Trifles, fretting over 425
Trinity 4, 6, 8, 9, 12, 16, 21, 23, 36, 37, 40, 73, 101, 124, 139, 165, 199, 212, 218, 225, 235, 236, 237–253, 257, 261, 271, 273, 274, 288, 298, 315, 320, 331, 332, 334, 335, 375,

377, 412, 417, 438, 439, 448, 454, 463, 475, 492, 493, 500, 507, 508, 524, 525, 536, 537, 541, 545, 549, 550, 558, 559, 560, 564, 600, 605, 613, 614, 622, 632; cf. Triune God; — beatific vision of 471; unity of 332, 541
Triumph 53, 64, 94, 103, 162, 212, 213, 218, 243, 262, 263, 332, 343, 360, 445
Triune God 23, 26, 124, 211, 237–253, 334, 377; cf. God; — baptized into 298, 337; blessings of 299; confessing the 235; glory of 17, 235; glory to 218, 240, 244; good will of 237; indwelling of 315; living in 332; love of 241; majesty of 239; name of 298, 632; praise to 23, 243, 246, 332, 465, 466, 550, 641; prayer to 299, 541, 564; presence of 622
Triune God, Names of: Almighty 240; Ancient of Days 17; Defender 17; Deity Perfect 240; Friend 17; Eternal God 36; Eternal One and Three 622; Eternal Triune God 241; Ever-blessed Trinity 537, 640; Faithful God 124; Glorious God and Lord 271; Glorious Trinity 508; Great Jehovah 244; Guide and Host 541; Highest and Greatest 240; Highest One 238; Holy and Blessed Three 508; Holy Three 641; Holy Trinity 601; Hope of the Living 240; Immortal King 642; Ineffable Love 17; Jehovah 37; King 17; Life of Forsaken 240; Light 165, 564; Light of the Angels 240; Lord God Almighty 246; Lord, My God 38; Lord of Glory 23; Love 165, 508; Maker 17, 240; Measureless Might 17; Might 508; Mysterious Godhead 242; One in Glory 466; One in Might 466; One in Three 239, 257, 465; Redeemer 17; Shield and Defender 17; Three in One 9, 133, 242, 244, 245, 257, 331, 465, 466, 475, 492, 641; Trinity sacred 240; Unity 541; Unity of Sov'reign Might 564; Unity Unshaken 240; Wise God 642; Wisdom 508
Trust 25, 26, 29, 90, 93, 118, 119, 120, 123, 216, 217, 220, 223, 224, 226, 237, 247, 263, 266, 269, 275, 290, 326, 329, 337, 353, 385, 425, **425–437**, 521; cheerful 535; child-like 623; foolish 640
Truth 27, 74, 124, 129, 234, 288, 381, 406, 638; cf. Word of God; — abiding 14, 292, 384; defense of 260; divine 579; endures 462; everlasting 14, 15, 44, 236, 286; preaching 218, 292, 489, 490, 494, 642; unsullied ray 501
Tyrants 619; cf. Persecution

Unbelief 203, 295, 359, 415, 501; blind 514
Unfaithfulness 298, 423, 445
Ungodly 414, 582; doomed to hell 607, 610; resurrection of the 604; woe to the 611
Ungratefulness 11
Unity 261, 313; cf. Church
Universal, praise of Christ 15, 59, 70, 100, 104, 126, 132, 198, 202, 205, 212, 238, 241, 244, 339, 344, 360, 363, 412, 658; praise of God 13, 14, 28, 34, 41, 246, 249, 250, 271, 347, 500, 582, 584, 635, 642
Universe 28
Unrighteousness 406
Unthankful 442
Unworthiness 143, 152, 276, 315, 326, 329, 330, 345, 376, 379
Usury 287

Vanity 92, 123, 175, 188, 206, 235, 316, 347, 356, 361, 362, 366, 382, 385, 430, 470, 516, 640; earthly 143, 188, 316, 361, 385
Vengeance 25, 158, 171, 377
Victory 98, 103, 192, 263, 387, 450, 461; cf. Triumph; — banners of 198, 451; crown of 332, 463; palm of 332, 371, 520
Vineyard, laborers in the 492; cf. Harvest
Virgin Birth; cf. Christ, Virgin Birth
Virgins, ten 67, 72, 509, 609
Virtues 124, 168, 227, 303, 415
Visitation 275; day of 419

[667]

Voice, consecrated 400; *of Christ*, obeying the 626; cf. Christ, voice of; — spurning the 551

Vows 191, 298, 333, 403, 434, 536; cf. Daily vows; — confessing 639; faithful 465, 580; grateful 572; marriage 287, 620, 639; renewal of baptismal 303, 333, 337, 639; repentant 145

Walking, in the light 421, 503; with angels 413; with Christ; cf. Christ, walking with; — with God; cf. God, walking with

Want, protection against 548, 571; sons of 511

Warfare, Christian 53, 58, 61, 64, 65, 72, 91, 103, 121, 144, 171, 173, 192, 224, 226, 228, 235, 258, 260, 262, 263, 267, 269, 292, 298, 332, 347, 444–453, 456, 458, 463, 470, 501, 586, 590, 616, 658; cf. Conflict

Wars 122, 258, 268, 458, 569

Watch and pray 72, 159, 194, 413, 444, 446, 449, 479, 490, 606

Watchfulness 64, 71, 159, 207, 286, 387, 399, 416, 444, 446, 449, 605

Watchman 71, 609

Wavering 516, 517, 556

Wealth 395, 425, 427, 430, 532; created by God 438; earthly 58, 85, 130, 316, 425; public 572

Weary 501, 511, 586, 607, 632, 654; cf. Mankind; — invitation to the 513, 615; rest for the 615

Week, beginning of 7

Wickedness, checked 295

Widows 471, 476; and fatherless, God of 26, 556

Will, divine 4, 115, 118, 142, 170, 185, 237, 238, 256, 289, 295, 387, 412, 416, 418, 455, 458, 494, 500, 514, 517, 520, 521, 529, 530, 532, 625; good 237, 238; human; cf. Human will

Wind, power over 482

Wine, changing water into 134

Wisdom 116, 133, 226, 235, 271, 332, 355, 358, 366, 486; gift of 358, 490; godly 254, 411; heavenly 366, 387, 495; human 143, 385; light of 510

Witness, false 151, 287; for God 259

Woe 413, 441, 515, 516, 522, 523, 526, 535; cup of 452; depth of 328, 329, 396, 411, 524, 590; freed from 483, 557, 596; homes of want and 501; mortal 281; mutual 464; sent by God 526; weal and 385, 458, 529

Woman, Christian 452, 471; sinful 607

Word of God 1, 16, 52, 65, 113, 130, 138, 207, 235, 239, 277, 281, 282–297, 299, 343, 381; cf. Gospel, Law; — armor of 494; beacons of 641; believing the 441; blessings of 5, 9, 46, 48, 125, 284, 285, 296, 366, 368, 375, 378, 487, 500, 545, 571; cherishing the 640; Christ in the 634; Christian's trust 290; clinging to the 421; comfort 125, 296; conquest through 494; consolation 353, 384; contending for 544; deathless 506; defense of 260; delight in 414; desire for 366; despising 611; enemies of 49, 260, 261, 265, 290, 306, 445; everlasting, eternal 13, 271, 469; enduring 503; faith through 297; fire of the 641; foundation of faith 381, 427, 524; fruit of 48, 49, 52; cf. Harvest; — fulfilled 290; cf. Prophecy; — glory of the 284; guidance of 53, 54, 283, 286, 292, 294, 304, 366, 368, 383, 416, 455, 469, 485; hearing 48, 52, 296, 358, 366, 368, 487, 638, 641, 642; heeding the 7, 48, 281, 291, 296, 297, 387, 419, 458, 483, 596; instruction of 627; light of 283, 285, 286, 294, 559, 575; love for 284, 296, 419, 547; mighty 507

Word of God, Names of: Anchor 291; Banner 294, 332; Beacon 294; Beams of Truth 16; Bread 420, 509, 573; Bread of Life 48, 293, 296, 537; Bread of Our Souls 291; Brook 291; Buckler 292; Chart 291, 294; Cloud 469; Comfort 1, 125; Compass 294; Celestial Food 431; Celestial Ray 505; Cup of Joy 296; Dew of Heavenly Grace 264; Foundation 381; Fountain of Life 1; Gems of Truth 294; Gladsome Tidings 498; Gospel-light 9; Gospel Tidings 498; Guide 283, 285, 286, 291, 292; Guiding Star 1; Heavenly Light 292, 487; Heavenly Manna 9, 165, 291, 343, 420, 422; Heritage 283; Jehovah's Word 290; Lamp 285, 286, 291; Lamp of Grace 508; Lamp of Life 495; Lantern 294; Light 283, 286, 296, 469, 641; Light Divine 477; Living Water 9, 264, 277, 296, 368, 426, 431, 469, 499; Living Word 501; Manna from Heaven 165, 291, 469; Mirror of God's Glory 264; Oil of Gladness 48; Pasture 368, 426, 431, 436, 500, 648; Path 291; Pillar of Fire 291, 469; Power of God 297; Prophetic Word 130; Quiet Waters 436, 648; Radiant Cloud 291; River 469; River of Salvation 497; Saving Signs 501; Saving Word 125, 260, 293; Seed 1, 46, 49, 52; Shield 292; Shield of Faith 48; Spirit and Life 467; Springs of Consolation 284; Staff 125; Star 130; Stay 125, 283, 291; Stream 291, 431; Streams of Living Waters 431, 469; Sword 292, 296, 332, 506; Treasure 48; Trusty Weapon 292; Truth 8, 27, 50, 74, 124, 129, 234, 264, 286, 288, 381, 489, 638; Waters of Life 278, 531; Weapon Glorious 444; Will of (His) the Glorious Son 291; Word of Grace 292; Word of Life 224, 296, 632; Word of Power 488

Word of God (General listing continued), need of 291, 366; neglecting the 582, 625; obeying 398, 493, 522, 579; peace through 375, 639; pondering 406; power of 5, 48, 49, 235, 260, 262, 263, 264, 266, 292, 378, 656; prayer for 5, 16, 49, 113, 239, 283, 292, 296, 337, 469; cf. Prayer; — preaching of 485, 488, 489, 491, 493, 494, 499, 501, 507, 510, 638, 642; preservation of 261, 264, 292, 321; prophetic 290; purity of 292, 458, 477, 640; cf. Doctrine, purity of; — rejection of 260, 265, 290, 295, 297; restored by grace 266; rules of 286; saving power of the 503; security of 637; stranger to the 501; strengthened by 445; success of the 494; sure 61, 266, 286, 290, 377, 381, 383, 469; teachings of 290; true 296, 373, 377; trusting the 16, 290, 305, 306, 381, 429, 518; truth of 629; cf. Truth; — use of 444; wisdom of 48, 291, 355; witness of 472

Words of Christ, last 177; cf. Cross, words on

Work, daily 544, 562; cf. Labor

Works 266, 287, 311; beginning of 536, 540; boasting in 385; cold 539; dead 235, 417, 539; good 143, 235, 295, 377, 385, 387, 500; merits of 287, 311, 375, 376, 377, 387, 389; of love 295, 439, 441; of night 8, 60; of power 629; personal 380; proof of living faith 377; trust in 266, 392, 415

World, the 430, 553; atonement for the 377; Christ rules 221; confessing Christ before 463; conquered 332; creation and preservation of 507, 508; cf. Creation; — curse on 272; deception of the 384, 409, 423, 446, 479, 524; deceitful cares of 49; cf. Cares; — dying 64, 99, 126, 430; dying to the 22, 24, 192, 347; end of world 31, 35, 56, 70, 88, 127, 134, 221, 243, 264, 278, 294, 371, 385, 393, 430, 474, 476, 503, 592, 604, 607, 610, 611, 612; cf. Judgment; — enlightened 505; evil 407, 605; fallen 501; fleeting vapor 430; forsaking the 40, 73, 81, 93, 206, 223, 270, 316, 347, 362, 366, 407, 409, 413, 421, 655; foundation, before 343, 387; foundations of, laid 236; light of the 294; love for the 430; loveless 304; Names — God's Own Field

[668]

574; Sultry Glebe 368, — peace 258; pomp of the 446, 469; power of 393, 405, 446; preaching throughout the 501, 642; pride of 393, 430; redemption of 139, 158, 245; renouncing the 347, 362, 413, 430; ridicule of the 469; sin of 147, 238, 254, 272; straying 483; threats of 347, 396; treasures of 81, 85, 141, 178, 179; vain 516, 557; wicked 446, 479

Worldliness 430, 445

Worldly, honor 430, 470; life 407; pleasures 430, 444, 469; praise 430; scorn 437, 469; temptations; cf. Temptations

Worry, free from 561

Worship 2, 7, 110, 129, 136, 166, 237, 240, 241, 274, 295, 336, 344, 352, 367, 536, 639; cf. Praise; — **worship and praise** 14–44; hour of 45, 466; humble sacrifice 622, 640; invitation to; cf. Invitation; — lowliest 641; by creation, by nature 98, 101, 344; cf. Praise, nature

Wounds of Christ, asleep in 585; imprints 513

Wrath, day of; cf. Judgment

Year, life during the 111, 118

Years, eternal 602

Yoke 366, 397

Youth 303, 452, 467, 494, 552; guidance of 628; instruction of 113, 286, 288, 486, 628; cf. Instruction, religious; — prayer for; cf. Children; — prayer of 628; thoughtless 499

Zeal 126, 272, 376, 394, 480, 539; Christian 231, 232, 401, 479, 490, 620; missionary 498

Zion 44, 58, 64, 264, 265, 460, 462, 466, 474, 478, 487, 496, 613, 636, 638; cf. Church, Heaven; — affliction of 265, 268, 448; cords of, lengthening of 510, 640; daughter of 68; foe of 472; cf. Church, foe; — glory of 469; joy of 609; *Names* — City of Our God 268, 469; Bright City 619, — sons and daughters of 282; cf. Church; — wars of 497; cf. Warfare, Christian; — watchmen of 99, 496, 609

Alphabetical Index of Authors

Adam of St. Victor (d. 1172 or 1192).
Adams, Sarah Flower (1805—1848).
Addison, Joseph (1672—1719).
Albert, Heinrich, or Alberti (1604—1651).
Albinus, Johann Georg (1624—1679).
Albrecht von Brandenburg (1522—1557).
Alderson, Eliza Sibbald, née Dykes (1818 to 1889).
Alexander, Cecil Frances, née Humphreys (1823—1895).
Alford, Henry (1810—1871).
Allen, Oswald (1816—1878).
Altenburg, Johann Michael (1584—1640).
Ambrose, St. (340—397).
Ämilie Juliane, Countess of Schwarzburg-Rudolstadt (1637—1706).
Andersdatter, Elle (1600—1650?).
Anna Sophia of Hesse-Darmstadt (1638 to 1683).
Arends, Wilhelm Erasmus (1677—1721).
Arrebo, Anders Christensen (1587—1637).

Bahnmaier, Jonathan Friedrich (1774—1841).
Baker, Henry Williams (1821—1877).
Barbauld, Anna Letitia, née Aikin (1743 to 1825).
Baring-Gould, Sabine (1834—1924).
Barton, Bernard (1784—1849).
Bathhurst, William Hiley (1796—1877).
Baxter, Richard (1615—1691).
Bede, The Venerable (673—735).
Behm, Martin (1557—1622).
Benson, Louis Fitz-Gerald (1855—1930).
Bernard of Clairvaux (St. Bernard) (1090 to 1153).
Bernard of Morlas (Cluny) (12th century).
Besnault, Abbé Sebastian (d. 1724).
Bienemann, Kaspar (1540—1591).
Birken (Betulius), Sigismund von (1626 to 1681).
Bogatzky, Carl Heinrich von (1690—1774).
Bonar, Horatius (1808—1899).
Böschenstain (Böschenstein), Johann (1472 to 1539?).
Bowring, Sir John, LL. D., F. R. S. (1792 to 1872).
Boye, Birgitte Katerine (1742—1824).
Boye, Caspar Johannes (1791—1853).
Brady, Nicholas (1659—1726).
Bridges, Matthew (1800—1894).
Brooks, Phillips (1835—1893).
Brorson, Hans Adolf (1694—1764).
Brun, Johan Nordahl (1745—1816).
Bryant, William Cullen (1794—1878).
Byrom, John (1692—1763).

Carlyle, Joseph Dacre (1758—1804).
Cawood, John (1775—1852).
Celano, Thomas de (13th century).
Chorley, Henry Fothergill (1808—1872).
Clausnitzer, Tobias (1619—1684).
Clement of Alexandria, St. (c. 170—c. 220).
Coffin, Charles (1676—1749).
Collyer, William Bengo (1782—1854).
Conder, Josiah (1789—1855).
Cooke, William (1821—1894).
Cooper, Edward (1770—1833).
Cotterill, Thomas (1779—1823).
Cowper, William (1731—1800).
Coxe, Arthur Cleveland (1818—1896).
Crasselius, Bartholomäus (1667—1724).
Cronenwett, Emanuel (1841—1931).
Crosswell, William (1804—1851).
Czamanske, William Martin (1873—   ).

Dach, Simon (1605—1659).
Dayman, Edward Arthur (1807—1890).
Decius, Nikolaus (1490?—1541).
Denicke, David (1603—1680).
Dessler, Wolfgang Christoph (1660—1722).
Dix, William Chatterton (1837—1898).
Doane, George Washington (1799—1859).

Doddridge, Philip (1702—1751).
Downton, Henry (1818—1885).
Duffield, George, Junior (1818—1888).
Dwight, Timothy (1752—1817).

Eber, Paul (1511—1569).
Edmeston, James (1791—1867).
Ellerton, John (1826—1893).
Elliott, Charlotte (1789—1871).
Elliott, Julia Anne, née Marshall (?—1841).
Elven, Cornelius (1791—1873).

Falckner, Justus (1672—1723).
Fawcett, John (1740—1817).
Fick, Herman (1822—1885).
Fischer (Vischer), Christoph (1520—1597).
Fischer, Eberhard Ludwig (1695—1773).
Fortunatus, Venantius Honorius Clementianus (c. 530—609).
Francis, Benjamin (1734—1799).
Franck, Johann (1618—1677).
Franck, Salomo (1659—1725).
Freystein, Johann Burkhard (1671—1718).
Füger (Fuger, Fugger), Caspar (?) (16th century).
Funcke, Friedrich (1642—1699).

Garve, Karl Bernard (1763—1841).
Gates, Mary Cornelia, née Bishop (c. 1850).
Gellert, Christian Fürchtegott (1715—1769).
Gerhardt, Paul (1607—1676).
Germanus of Constantinople, St. (634—734).
Gesenius, Justus (1601—1673).
Gramann (Graumann), Johann (Poliander) (1487—1541).
Grant, Sir Robert (1779—1838).
Gregor, Christian (1723—1801).
Grigg, Joseph (c. 1722—1768).
Grodzki, Michal (c. 1550).
Grundtvig, Nicolai Fredrik Severin (1783 to 1872).
Gryphius, Andreas (1616—1664).
Gurney, Dorothy Frances, née Blomfield (1858—1932).
Gurney, John Hampden (1802—1862).

Hamilton, James (1819—?).
Hammond, William (1719—1783).
Harbaugh, Henry (1817—1867).
Hart, Joseph (1712—1768).
Hastings, Thomas (1784—1822).
Havergal, Frances Ridley (1836—1879).
Haweis, Thomas (1732—1820).
Heath, George (1745?—1822).
Heber, Reginald (1783—1826).
Heermann, Johann (1585—1647).
Held, Heinrich (?—c. 1659).
Helder, Bartholomäus (?—1635).
Helmbold, Ludwig (1532—1598).
Herberger, Valerius (1562—1627).
Herbert, Petrus (?—1571).
Herman, Nikolaus (c. 1480—1561).
Herrnschmidt, Johann Daniel (1675—1723).
Hertzog, Johann Friedrich (1647—1699).
Heyder (Heider), Friedrich Christian (1677 to 1754).
Holland, Henry Scott (1847—1918).
Homburg, Ernst Christoph (1605—1681).
Hoppe, Anna Bernardine Dorothy (1889 to 1941).
Hopper, Edward (1818—1888).
Hoskins, Joseph (1745—1788).
How, William Walsham (1823—1897).
Humphreys, Joseph (1720—?).
Hurn, William (1754—1829).
Huss (Hus), John (1373?—1415).

Ingemann, Bernhardt Severin (1789—1862).
Irons, Genevieve Mary (1855—?).

Jacobs, Henry Eyster (1844—1932).
John of Damascus, St. (c. 750).
Joseph, the Hymnographer, St. (c. 800—883).
Julian, John (1839—1913).

Keble, John (1792—1866).
Keimann (Keymann), Christian (1607 to 1662).
Kelly, Thomas (1769—1854).
Ken, Thomas (1637—1711).
Kethe, William (?—c. 1593).
Key, Francis Scott (1779—1843).
Kingo, Thomas Hansen (1634—1703).
Kinner, Samuel (1603—1668).
Knapp, Albert (1798—1864).
Koren, Ulrik Vilhelm (1826—1910).
Kunth, Johann Sigismund (1700—1779).

Landstad, Magnus Brostrup (1802—1880).
Laurentius, Laurenti (1660—1722).
Leeson, Jane Eliza (1807—1882).
Lehr, Leopold Franz Friedrich (1709—1744).
Lochner, Karl Friedrich (1634—1697).
Logan, John (1748—1788).
Löwenstern, Matthäus Appeles von (1594 to 1648).
Loy, Matthias (1828—1915).
Ludämilia Elizabeth, Countess of Schwarzburg (1640—1672).
Luther, Martin (1483—1546).
Lyte, Henry Francis (1793—1847).

Mackay, Margaret (1802—1887).
Madan, Martin (1726—1790).
Magdeburg, Joachim (c. 1525—c. 1583).
Major (Gross), Johann (1564—1654).
Malan, Henri Abraham César (1787—1864).
Mann, Frederick (1846—1928).
Mant, Richard (1776—1848).
March, Daniel (1816—1909).
Marriott, John (1780—1825).
Maude, Mary Fawler, née Hooper (1819 to 1913).
Maxwell, Mary (?).
McComb, William (1793—c. 1870).
Medley, Samuel (1738—1799).
Meinhold, Johann Wilhelm (1797—1851).
Melanchthon, Philipp (Schwarzerd) (1497 to 1560).
Mentzer, Johann (1658—1734).
Messenger, John A. (?).
Meyfart, Johann Matthias (1590—1642).
Milman, Henry Hart (1791—1868).
Milton, John (1608—1674).
Mohr, Joseph (1792—1848).
Molanus, Gerhard Walther (Wolter) (1633 to 1722).
Möller, Johann Joachim (1660—1733).
Monsell, John Samuel Bewley (1811—1875).
Montgomery, James (1771—1854).
Moore, Thomas (1779—1852).
Morison, John (1749—1798).
Mote, Edward (1797—1874).
Mühlenberg, William Augustus (1796—1877).
Mühlmann, Johannes (1573—1613).

Nachtenhöfer, Caspar Friedrich (1624—1685).
Neale, John Mason (1818—1866).
Neander, Joachim (1650—1680).
Neumann, Caspar (1648—1715).
Neumark, Georg (1621—1681).
Neumeister, Erdman (1671—1756).
Newton, John (1725—1807).
Nicolai, Philipp (1556—1608).
Nigidius, G. (1525—1588).

Occom, Samson (1732—1792).
Olearius, Johannes (1611—1684).
Olearius, Johann Gottfried (1635—1711).
Olivers, Thomas (1725—1799).
Omeis, Magnus Daniel (1646—1708).
Onderdonk, Henry Ustic (1789—1858).
Opitz, Martin (1597—1639).
Osler, Edward (1798—1863).

Palmer, Ray (1808—1887).
Perronet, Edward (1726—1792).
Peter, Philip Adam (1832—1917).
Pfefferkorn, Georg Michael (1645—1732).
Pfeil, Christoph Carl Ludwig, Baron von (1712—1784).
Phelps, Sylvanus Dryden, D.D. (1816—1895).
Phillimore, Greville (1821—1884).
Pictet, Benedict (c. 1650—c. 1710).
Pisek, Vincent (1859—1930).
Polack, William Gustave (1890—   ).
Pollock, Thomas Benson (1836—1896).
Pope, Alexander (1688—1744).
Preiswerk, Samuel (1799—1871).
Prudentius, Aurelius Clemens (348—c. 413).
Pye, Henry John (c. 1825—1903).

Rambach, Johann Jacob (1693—1735).
Ramsey, Alfred (1860—1926).
Reed, Andrew (1788—1862).
Reusner (Reussner, Reisner, Reissner), Adam (1496—c. 1575).
Rhabanus Maurus (776—856).
Riley, John Athelstan Laurie (1858—?).
Ringwaldt (Ringwalt, Ringwald), Bartholomäus (1532—c. 1600).
Rinkart (Rinckart), Martin (1586—1649).
Rist, Johann (1607—1667).
Robinson, Charles Seymour, D.D. (1829 to 1899).
Robinson, Joseph Armitage (1858—?).
Rodigast, Samuel (1649—1708).
Roh (Cornu, Horn), Johann (?—1547).
Romanis, William (1824—1899).
Rosenroth, Christian Knorr, Baron von (1636 to 1689).
Rothe, Johann Andreas (1688—1758).
Rous, Francis (1579—1659).
Ruopp, Johann Friedrich (?—1708).

Sacer, Gottfried Wilhelm (1635—1699).
St. John, Frank B. (?).
Savonarola, Girolamo (1454—1498).
Schalling, Martin (1532—1608).
Scheffler, Johann (Angelus Silesius) (1624 to 1677).
Scheidt, Christian Ludwig (1709—1761).
Schenck (Shenk), Hartmann (1634—1681).
Schirmer, Michael (1606—1673).
Schlegel, Catherina Amalia Dorothea von (1697—?).
Schmidt, Johann Eusebius (1670—1745).
Schmolck, Benjamin (1672—1737).
Schneegass, Cyriacus (1546—1597).
Schneesing (Chiomusus or Chyomusus), Johannes (?—1567).
Schroeder, Johann Heinrich (1667—1699).
Schumacher, Bernard (1886—   ).
Schütz, Johann Jacob (1640—1690).
Scriven, Joseph (1820—1886).
Sedulius, Coelius (c. 450).
Selnecker (Selneccer, Schellenecker), Nikolaus (1532—1592).
Serle, Ambrose (1742—1812).
Shirley, Walter (1725—1786).
Shrubsole, William (1759—1829).
Smith, Samuel Francis (1808—1895).
Spegel, Haquin (1645—1714).
Spengler, Lazarus (1479—1534).
Speratus, Paul (1484—1551).
Spitta, Karl Johann Philipp (1801—1859).
Steele, Anne (1716—1778).
Stegmann, Josua (1588—1632).
Stephenson (Stevenson), Isabella Stephana (1843—1890).
Sthen, Hans Christenson (16th century).
Stone, Samuel John (1839—1900).
Strong, Nathan (1748—1816).
Synesius, of Cyrene (c. 375—430).

Tappan, William Bingham (1794—1849).
Tate, Nahum (1652—1715).
Taylor, Thomas Rawson (1807—1835).
Tersteegen, Gerhard (1697—1769).
Theodulph of Orleans, St. (c. 821).

Thilo, Valentin (1607—1662).
Threlfall, Jeannette (1821—1880).
Thring, Godfrey (1823—1903).
Thrupp, Adelaide (19th century).
Toplady, Augustus Montague (1740—1778).
Tranovsky, Juraj (1591—1637).
Tuttiett, Lawrence (1825—1897).
Twells, Henry (1823—1900).

Walther, Carl Ferdinand Wilhelm (1811 to 1887).
Walther, Johann (1496—1570).
Wandersleben, Martin (1608—1668).
Watts, Isaac (1674—1748).
Wegelin (Wegelein), Josua (1604—1640).
Weisse (Weiss, Wiss, Wegs, Weys, Weyss), Michael (c. 1480—1534).
Weissel, Georg (1590—1635).
Wesley, Charles (1707—1788).
Wesley, John (1703—1791).
Wesley, Samuel, Sr. (1662—1735).
Whittemore, Jonathan (1802—1860).
Wiesenmeyer, Burkhard (17th century).
Williams, William (1717—1791).
Woodd, Basil (1760—1831).
Woodford, James Russell (1820—1885).
Wordsworth, Christopher (1807—1885).
Wortman, Denis 1835—1922).
Wreford, John Reynell (1800—1881).

Ziegler, Casper (1621—1690).
Zinzendorf, Nikolaus Ludwig, Count von (1700—1760).

Alphabetical Index of Composers

Ahle, Johann Rudolph (1625—1673).
Albert, Heinrich, or Alberti (1604—1651).
Anthes, Friedrich Konrad (1812—?).
Atkinson, Frederick Cook (1841—1897).

Bach, Carl Philipp Emanuel (1714—1788).
Bach, Johann Christoph (1642—1703).
Bach, Johann Sebastian (1685—1750).
Baker, Frederick George (1840—?).
Baker, Henry Williams (1821—1877).
Baring-Gould, Sabine (1834—1924).
Barnby, Joseph (1838—1896).
Barthélémon, François Hippolyte (1741 to 1808).
Boltze, Georg Gottfried (c. 1750).
Bortniansky, Dimitris (1752—1825).
Bourgeois, Louis (c. 1510—1561).
Bradbury, William Batchelder (1816—1868).
Brown, Arthur Henry (1830—1926).

Carey, Henry (1692—1743).
Chetham, John (c. 1700—1763).
Clark, Jeremiah (1670—1707).
Conkey, Ithamar (1815—1867).
Converse, Charles Crozat (1832—1918).
Croft, William (1678—1727).
Crüger, Johann (1598—1662).
Cutler, Henry S. (1824—1902).

Dale, Charles J. (1904).
Daman, William (c. 1580).
Darwall, John (1731—1789).
Day (Daye or Daie), John (1522—1584). (Printer.)
Decius, Nikolaus (1490?—1541).
Drese, Adam (1620—1701).
Dretzel, Kornelius Heinrich (1705—1773).
Dyer, Samuel (1785—1835).
Dykes, John Bacchus (1823—1876).

Ebeling, Johann Georg (1620—1676).
Elvey, George Job (1816—1893).
Este (Est, Easte, East), Thomas (1540? to 1608?). (Printer.)
Ewing, Alexander (1830—1895).

Farrant, Richard (c. 1530—1580).
Figulus, Wolfgang (1520—1591).
Filitz, Friedrich (1804—1876).
Fink, Gottfried Wilhelm, Ph. D. (1783—1846).
Franck, Melchior (c. 1575—1639).
Frank, Peter (1616—1675).
Freylinghausen, Johann Anastasius (1670 to 1739).
Friese, Heinrich (18th century).
Fritsch, Ahasverus (1629—1701).

Gardiner, William (1770—1853).
Gastorius, Severus (c. 1650).
Giardini, Felice de (1716—1796).
Gibbons, Orlando (1583—1625).
Gläser, Carl Gotthelf (1784—1829).
Goss, Sir John (1800—1880).
Gould, John Edgar (1822—1875).
Gounod, Charles François (1818—1893).
Grieg, Edvard Hagerup (1843—1907).
Gruber, Franz (1787—1863).

Hammerschmidt, Andreas (c. 1611—1675).
Hampton, John (1834—?).
Händel, Georg Friedrich (1685—1759).
Harding, John P. (James?) (1850, 1859? to 1911).
Harrison, Ralph (1748—1810).
Hassler, Hans Leo (1564—1612).
Hastings, Thomas (1784—1822),
Hatton, John (?—1793).
Havergal, Frances Ridley (1836—1879).
Havergal, William Henry (1793—1870).
Haweis, Thomas (1732—1820).

Hayn, Henriette Luise von (1724—1782).
Hayne, Leighton George (1836—1883).
Herman, Nikolaus (c. 1480—1561).
Hoff, Erik Christian (1832—?).
Holden, Oliver (1765—1844).
Hopkins, Edward John (1818—1901).
Horsley, William (1774—1858).
Howard, Samuel (1710—1782).

Ilse, Ludwig Herman (1845—1931).
Isaak (Isaac, Izac, Ysack, Yzac), Heinrich (c. 1450—c. 1527).

Kittel, Johann Christian (1732—1809).
Klein, Bernhard (1793—1832).
Knapp, William (1698—1768).
Kocher, Konrad (1786—1872).
König, Johann Balthasar (1691—1758).
Knecht, Justin Heinrich (1752—1817).
Krieger, Adam (1634—1666).

Layriz, Friedrich (1808—1859).
Lemke, August (1820—1913).
Lindemann, Ludwig Mathias (1812—1887).
Luther, Martin (1483—1546).

Mann, Arthur Henry (1850—1929).
Marsh, Simeon Butler (1798—1875).
Mason, Lowell (1792—1872).
Mendelssohn-Bartholdy, Jacob Ludwig Felix (1809—1847).
Meyer, Franz Heinrich Christoph (1705 to 1767).
Meyer (Mayer, Mejer, Meier), Johann David (17th century).
Miller, Edward (1731—1807).
Möck, Christian (1737—1818).
Monk, William Henry (1823—1889).
Morely, Thomas (1842—1891).

Nares, James (1715—1783).
Neander, Joachim (1650—1680).
Neumark, Georg (1621—1681).
Nicolai, Philipp (1556—1608).
Niemeyer, Eduard (1854).
Nigidius (Niege), Georg (1525—1588).
Nigidius, Petrus (1501—1583).

Oakeley, Sir Herbert Stanley (1830—1903).
Oliver, Henry Kemble (1800—1885).
Ouseley, Sir Frederick Arthur Gore (1825 to 1889).

Palestrina, Giovanni Pierluigi Sante da (1525 to 1594).
Polack, Herman Adolph (1862—1930).
Prätorius, Michael (1571—1621).
Prichard, Rowland Hugh (1811—1887).

Read, Daniel (1757—1836).
Redhead, Richard (1820—1901).
Redner, Lewis Henry (1831—1908).
Reinagle, Alexander Robert (1799—1877).
Reuter, Friedrich Otto (Fritz) (1863—1924).

Schein, Johann Hermann (1586—1630).
Schmid, Bernard (c. 1520—c. 1592).
Schop, Johann (?—c. 1664).
Schröter, Leonhart (1540—1602).
Schumacher, Bernhard (1886—   ).
Sibelius, Jean (1865—   ).
Smart, Henry Thomas (1813—1879).
Sohren (Sohr, Sohrer), Peter (c. 1630 to c. 1692).
Spiess, Johann Martin (1715—1772).
Spohr, Louis (1784—1859).
Stainer, John (1840—1901).
Stebbins, George Coles (1846—   ).
Steuerlein, Johann (1546—1613).
Störl (Sterle), Johann Georg Christian (1675 to 1719).

The Handbook to the Lutheran Hymnal

Stobäus, Johann (1580—1646).
Sullivan, Arthur Seymour (1842—1900).

Tallis (Tallys), Thomas (1515—1585).
Teschner, Melchior (c. 1615).
Tye, Christopher (c. 1497—1572).

Vetter, Daniel (18th century).
Vulpius, Melchior (c. 1560—1615).

Wainwright, John (1723—1768).
Walder, Johann Jakob (1750—1817).
Walther, Carl Ferdinand Wilhelm (1811 to 1887).
Warren, George William (1828—1902).
Webb, George James (1803—1887).

Webbe, Samuel (1740—1816).
Weingärtner, Sigismund (17th century).
Weisse (Weiss, Wiss, Wegs, Weys, Weyss), Michael (c. 1480—1534).
Wesley, Samuel Sebastian (1810—1876).
Weyse, Christoph Ernst Friedrich (1774 to 1842).
Wheall (Weale), William (d. 1727).
Whinfield, Walter Grenville (1865—1919).
Williams, Aaron (1731—1776).
Williams, Ralph Vaughan (1872—   ).
Williams, Robert (c. 1781—1821).
Wilson, Hugh (c. 1764—1824).

Zinck, Hartnack Otto Konrad (1746—1833).

Alphabetical Index of Translators

Aho, Gustaf Axel (1897—   ).
Arneson, Ole T. (Sanden) (1853—1917).
Astley, Charles Tamberlane (1825—1878).

Bacon, Leonard Woolsey (1830—1907).
Bajus, John (1901—   ).
Baker, Henry Williams (1821—1877).
Baring-Gould, Sabine (1834—1924).
Belsheim, Ole G. (1861—1925).
Bethune, George Washington (1805—1862).
Bevan, Emma Frances, née Shuttleworth (1827—1909).
Borthwick, Jane (1813—1897).
Brauer, Alfred E. R. (1866—   ).
Bridges, Robert Seymour (1844—1930).
Brooks, Charles Timothy (1813—1883).

Campbell, Robert (1814—1868).
Caswall, Edward (1814—1878).
Chandler, John (1806—1876).
Chatfield, Allen (1808—1896).
Copeland, William John (1804—1885).
Cory, Julia Bulkley Cady (1882—   ).
Cox, Frances Elizabeth (1812—1897).
Cronenwett, Emanuel (1841—1931).
Crull, August (1846—1923).
Czamanske, William Martin (1873—   ).

Dearmer, Percy (1867—1936).
Dexter, Henry Martyn (1821—1890).
Döving, Carl (1867—1937).
Dryden, John (1631—1700).
Dwight, John Sullivan (1813—1893).

Eber, Paul (1511—1569).

Findlater, Sarah, née Borthwick (1823 to 1907).
Foster, Frederick William (1760—1835).
Franzmann, Martin (1907—   ).

Gieschen, Gerhard (1899—   ).
Gilman, Samuel (1791—1858).

Hernaman, Claudia Frances, née Ibostson (1838—1898).
Herzberger, Frederick William (1859—1930).
Hoppe, Anna Bernardine Dorothy (1889 to 1941).

Irons, William Josiah (1812—1883).

Jenner, Henry Lascelles (1820—1898).

Kaiser, Oscar (1865—   ).
Kelly, John (?—1890).
Kennedy, Benjamin Hall (1804—1889).

Knapp, Albert (1798—1864).
Kretzmann, Paul Edward (1883—   ).
Kvamme, Kristen (1866—1938).

Longfellow, Henry Wadsworth (1807—1892).
Loy, Matthias (1828—1915).
Luther, Martin (1483—1546).

Madson, Norman Arthur (1886—   ).
Mason, Arthur James (1851—?).
Massie, Richard (1800—1887).
Mattes, John Caspar (1876—   ).
Meyer, Anna Magdelena, née Plehn (1867—   ).
Mueller, John Theodore (1885—   ).

Neale, John Mason (1818—1866).

Olsson, Olof (1841—1900).

Paulsen, P. C. (c. 1925).
Petersen, Victor Olof (1864—1929).
Polack, William Gustave (1890—   ).
Pott, Francis (1832—1909).
Pusey, Philip (1799—1855).

Reynolds, William Morton (1812—1876).
Rimbach, J. Adam (1871—1941).
Ristad, Ditlef Georgson (1863—1938).
Russell, Arthur Tozer (1806—1874).
Rygh, George Alfred Taylor (1860—   ).

Schaeffer, Charles William (1813—1896).
Schaefer, William John (1891—   ).
Schaff, Philip (1819—1893).
Schuette, Conrad Hermann Louis (1843 to 1926).
Scott, Sir Walter (1771—1832).
Seiss, Joseph Augustus (1823—1904).
Sloan, John Morrison (1835—?).
Smeby, Oluf Hanson (1851—1929).
Spaeth, Harriett Reynolds Krauth (1845 to 1925).
Strömme, Peer Olsen (1856—1921).

Taylor, R. E. (?—1938).
Trabert, George Henry (1843—1931).

Voss, Arthur Paul (1899—   ).

Walworth, Clarence Alphonsus (1820—1900).
Webb, Benjamin (1820—1885).
Wilde, Jane Francesca, née Elgee (1826 to 1896).
Williams, Peter (1722—1796).
Winkworth, Catherine (1829—1878).

Zich, August F. (1868—1939).

Index of First Lines

First Line	HYMN
A great and mighty wonder	76
A hymn of glory let us sing	212
A Lamb goes uncomplaining forth	142
A mighty Fortress is our God	262
A pilgrim and a stranger	586
A rest remaineth for the weary	615
Abide, O dearest Jesus	53
Abide with me	552
Abide with us, the day is waning	194
Across the sky the shades of night	110
Alas! and did my Savior bleed	154
Alas, my God, my sins are great	317
All depends on our possessing	425
All glory be to God alone	238
All glory be to God on high	237
All glory, laud, and honor	160
All hail the power of Jesus' name	339
All mankind fell in Adam's fall	369
All men living are but mortal	601
All my heart this night rejoices	77
All people that on earth do dwell	14
All praise to God, who reigns above	19
All praise to Thee, eternal God	80
All praise to Thee, my God, this night	558
All that I was, my sin, my guilt	378
All ye who on this earth do dwell	581
Almighty Father, bless the Word	52
Almighty Father, heaven and earth	438
Almighty God, Thy Word is cast	49
Almighty Lord, before Thy throne	579
Am I a soldier of the Cross	445
An awe-full mystery is here	304
And will the Judge descend	610
And wilt Thou pardon, Lord	322
Angels from the realms of glory	136
Approach, my soul, the mercy-seat	456
Arise and shine in splendor	126
Arise, O God, and shine	642
Arise, sons of the Kingdom	69
Arm these Thy soldiers, mighty Lord	332
Around the throne of God a band	256
Art thou weary, art thou troubled	513
Asleep in Jesus! Blessed sleep	587
As pants the hart for cooling streams	525
As we begin another week	7
As with gladness men of old	127
At even, when the sun did set	557
Awake, my heart, with gladness	192
Awake, my soul, and with the sun	536
Awake, my soul, to joyful lays	340
Awake, Thou Spirit, who didst fire	494
Baptized into Thy name most holy	298
Beautiful Savior	657
Before Jehovah's awe-full throne	13
Before Thee, God, who knowest all	318
Before the Lord we bow	575
Behold, a Branch is growing	645
Behold a host, arrayed in white	656
Behold a Stranger at the door	650
Behold the Lamb of God	165
Behold the Savior of mankind	176
Behold the sure Foundation-stone	460
Beloved, "It is well"	519
Be still, my soul	651
Blessed are the sons of God	391
Blessed Jesus, at Thy word	16
Blessed Savior, who hast taught me	333
Blest be the tie that binds	464
Blest is the man, forever blest	392
Brief life is here our portion	448
Brightest and best	128
Built on the Rock the Church doth stand	467
By grace I'm saved, grace free and boundless	373
Chief of sinners though I be	342
Christ, by heavenly hosts adored	566
Christians, awake	84
Christians, come in sweetest measures	282
Christians, sing out with exultation	100
Christ is arisen	187
Christ is our Corner-stone	465
Christ Jesus lay in death's strong bands	195
Christ, the Life of all the living	151
Christ the Lord is risen again	190
Christ the Lord is risen today	193
Christ the Lord is risen today; Alleluia!	191
Christ the Lord to us is born	86
Christ, Thou art the sure Foundation	466
Christ, whose glory fills the skies	359
Come, follow Me, the Savior spake	421
Come, Holy Ghost, Creator blest	233
Come, Holy Ghost, God and Lord	224
Come, Holy Ghost, in love	227
Come, Holy Spirit, come	225
Come, Jesus, from the sapphire throne	634
Come, let us join our cheerful songs	344
Come, my soul, thy suit prepare	459
Come, oh, come, Thou quickening Spirit	226
Come rejoicing, praises voicing	82
Come, Thou almighty King	239
Come, Thou Bright and Morning Star	539
Come, Thou precious Ransom, come	55
Come to Calvary's holy mountain	149
Come unto Me, ye weary	276
Come, ye disconsolate	531
Come, ye faithful, raise the strain	204
Come, ye thankful people, come	574
Come, your hearts and voices raising	90
Comfort, comfort, ye My people	61
Commit whatever grieves thee	520
Creator Spirit, by whose aid	236
Crown Him with many crowns	341
Day of wrath, O day of mourning	607

	HYMN
Dear Christians, one and all, rejoice	387
Dear Father, who hast made us all	299
Dear Lord, to Thy true servants give	482
Dearest Jesus, we are here	300
Delay not, delay not, O sinner	278
Draw nigh and take the body of the Lord	307
Draw us to Thee	215
Drawn to the Cross	390
Enslaved by sin and bound in chains	141
Every morning mercies new	537
Farewell I gladly bid thee	407
Father, in whom we live	241
Father, let me dedicate	118
Father most holy, merciful	240
Father of glory, to Thy name	248
Father of heaven, whose love	242
Father of mercies, in Thy Word	284
Father, who the light this day	8
Feed Thy children, God most holy	659
Fight the good fight	447
Flung to the heedless winds	259
For all the saints	463
For all Thy saints, O Lord	468
For many years, O God of grace	639
For me to live is Jesus	597
For thee, O dear, dear country	614
For Thy mercy and Thy grace	121
Forever with the Lord	616
Founded on Thee, our only Lord	637
From all that dwell below the skies	15
From depths of woe I cry to Thee	329
From eternity, O God	411
From God shall naught divide me	393
From Greenland's icy mountains	495
From heaven above to earth I come	85
Glorious things of thee are spoken	469
Glory be to God the Father	244
Glory be to Jesus	158
Go to dark Gethsemane	159
God bless our native land	577
God Himself is present	4
God, Lord of Sabaoth	582
God loved the world so that He gave	245
God moves in a mysterious way	514
God of mercy, God of grace	20
God of my life, to Thee I call	534
God of the prophets	483
God the Father, be our Stay	247
God the Father, Son, and Spirit	640
God, who madest earth and heaven	549
God's Word is our great heritage	283
Grace! 'tis a charming sound	374
Gracious God, again is ended	560
Gracious Savior, gentle Shepherd	627
Great God, we sing that mighty hand	119
Great God, what do I see and hear?	604
Great is the Lord, our God	636
Great King of nations, hear our prayer	583
Guide me, O Thou great Jehovah	54

	HYMN
Hail the day so rich in cheer	78
Hail the day that sees Him rise	213
Hail, Thou once despised Jesus	367
Hail, Thou Source of every blessing	129
Hail to the Lord's Anointed	59
Hallelujah! Jesus lives!	188
Hallelujah! Let praises ring	23
Hark, a thrilling voice is sounding	60
Hark! ten thousand harps and voices	221
Hark! the Church proclaims her honor	461
Hark the glad sound!	66
Hark! the herald angels sing	94
Hark! the sound of holy voices	471
Hark! the voice of Jesus crying	496
Hark! what mean those holy voices	83
He is arisen! Glorious Word!	189
He that believes and is baptized	301
Help us, O Lord! Behold, we enter	120
Here in Thy name, eternal God	635
He's risen, He's risen, Christ Jesus	198
Holy Father, in Thy mercy	643
Holy Ghost, with light divine	234
Holy God, we praise Thy name	250
Holy, holy, holy! Lord God Almighty!	246
Holy Spirit, God of Love	230
Holy Spirit, hear us	229
Hosanna, loud hosanna	161
Hosanna to the living Lord	70
How beauteous are their feet	487
How blest are they who hear God's Word	48
How can I thank Thee, Lord	417
How firm a foundation, ye saints of the Lord	427
How lovely shines the Morning Star	343
How lovely shines the morning star	546
How precious is the Book Divine	285
How shall the young secure their hearts	286
How sweet the name of Jesus sounds	364
I am content! My Jesus liveth still	196
I am Jesus' little lamb	648
I am trusting Thee, Lord Jesus	428
I come, O Savior, to Thy Table	315
I come to Thee, O blessed Lord	330
I do not come because my soul	379
I fall asleep in Jesus' wounds	585
I gave My life for thee	405
I heard the voice of Jesus say	277
I know my faith is founded	381
I know of a sleep in Jesus' name	592
I know that my Redeemer lives	200
I lay my sins on Jesus	652
I leave all things to God's direction	529
I love Thy kingdom, Lord	462
I pray Thee, dear Lord Jesus	655
I walk in danger all the way	413
I will sing my Maker's praises	25
I would not live alway	588
If God had not been on our side	267
If God Himself be for me	528
If thou but suffer God to guide thee	518

[677]

Hymn		Hymn	
If Thy beloved Son, O God	375	Joy to the world, the Lord is come	87
I'm but a stranger here	660	Judge eternal, throned in splendor	576
In God, my faithful God	526	Just as I am, without one plea	388
In His Temple now behold Him	139		
In hope my soul, redeemed to bliss unending	432	Kyrie, God Father in heaven above	6
In loud, exalted strains	638	Lamb of God, pure and holy	146
In one true God we all believe	253	Lamb of God, we fall before Thee	358
In peace and joy I now depart	137	Lamp of our feet whereby we trace	291
In the Cross of Christ I glory	354	Let children hear the mighty deeds	629
In the hour of trial	516	Let me be Thine forever	334
In the midst of earthly life	590	Let songs of praises fill the sky	232
In the name which earth and heaven	632	Let the earth now praise the Lord	91
In the resurrection	603	Let thoughtless thousands choose	608
In Thee alone, O Christ, my Lord	319	Let us all with gladsome voice	97
In Thee, Lord, have I put my trust	524	Let us ever walk with Jesus	409
Invited, Lord, by boundless grace	308	Lift up your heads, ye mighty gates	73
Isaiah, mighty seer, in days of old	249	Like the golden sun ascending	207
It is not death to die	602	Lo, God to heaven ascendeth	214
		Lo, Judah's Lion wins the strife	211
Jehovah, let me now adore Thee	21	Lo, many shall come	415
Jerusalem, my happy home	618	Look from Thy sphere of endless day	499
Jerusalem the golden	613	Look, ye saints, the sight is glorious	222
Jerusalem, thou city fair and high	619	Lord, as Thou wilt	406
Jesus, all our ransom paid	185	Lord, dismiss us with Thy blessing	50
Jesus, all Thy labor vast	186	Lord God, we all to Thee give praise	254
Jesus! and shall it ever be	346	Lord, help us ever to retain	288
Jesus, Brightness of the Father	257	Lord, it belongs not to my care	527
Jesus calls us; o'er the tumult	270	Lord Jesus Christ, be present now	3
Jesus came, the heavens adoring	56	Lord Jesus Christ, my Life, my Light	148
Jesus Christ is risen today, Alleluia!	199	Lord Jesus Christ, my Savior blest	353
Jesus Christ, my Pride and Glory	408	Lord Jesus Christ, Thou hast prepared	306
Jesus Christ, my sure Defense	206	Lord Jesus Christ, Thou living Bread	312
Jesus Christ, our blessed Savior	311	Lord Jesus Christ, we humbly pray	314
Jesus Christ, our Lord most holy	169	Lord Jesus Christ, with us abide	292
Jesus, grant all balm and healing	144	Lord Jesus, think on me	320
Jesus, I live to Thee	591	Lord Jesus, Thou art going forth	150
Jesus, I my cross have taken	423	Lord Jesus, Thou the Church's Head	477
Jesus I will never leave	365	Lord Jesus, we give thanks to Thee	173
Jesus, I will ponder now	140	Lord Jesus, who art come	485
Jesus, in Thy dying woes	180	Lord, keep us steadfast in Thy Word	261
Jesus, in Thy thirst and pain	184	Lord, lead the way the Savior went	440
Jesus, Jesus, only Jesus	348	Lord of Glory, who hast bought us	442
Jesus, lead Thou on	410	Lord of my life, whose tender care	24
Jesus lives! The victory's won	201	Lord of our life and God of our salvation	258
Jesus, Lover of my soul	345	Lord of the Church, we humbly pray	489
Jesus, loving to the end	182	Lord of the harvest, hear	488
Jesus, my great High Priest	220	Lord of the living harvest	492
Jesus, my Truth, my Way	433	Lord of the worlds above	480
Jesus! Name of wondrous love	114	Lord, open Thou my heart to hear	5
Jesus, pitying the sighs	181	Lord, Thee I love with all my heart	429
Jesus, priceless Treasure	347	Lord, 'tis not that I did choose Thee	37
Jesus, Refuge of the weary	145	Lord, to Thee I make confession	326
Jesus, Savior, come to me	356	Lord, we come before Thee now	18
Jesus, Savior, pilot me	649	Lord, we confess our numerous faults	382
Jesus shall reign where'er the sun	511	Lord, when we bend before Thy throne	22
Jesus sinners doth receive	324	Lord, while for all mankind we pray	578
Jesus, the very thought of Thee	350	Lord, who at Cana's wedding-feast	620
Jesus, Thou art mine forever	357	Love Divine, all love excelling	351
Jesus, Thy blood and righteousness	371		
Jesus, Thy boundless love to me	349		
Jesus, Thy Church with longing eyes	64		
Jesus, whelmed in fears unknown	183		

[678]

	HYMN		HYMN
May God bestow on us His grace	500	O Holy Spirit, grant us grace	293
May we Thy precepts, Lord, fulfil	412	O Jesus, blessed Lord, to Thee	309
Morning breaks upon the tomb	203	O Jesus Christ, Thy manger is	81
My course is run	599	O Jesus, King most wonderful	361
My faith looks up to Thee	394	O Jesus, King of Glory	130
My God, accept my heart this day	336	O Jesus, Lamb of God, Thou art	328
My God, my Father, make me strong	424	O little flock, fear not the Foe	263
My God, my Father, while I stray	418	O little town of Bethlehem	647
My hope is built on nothing less	370	O living Bread from heaven	316
My inmost heart now raises	548	O Lord, how shall I meet Thee	58
My Jesus, as Thou wilt	420	O Lord, I sing with lips and heart	569
My Maker, be Thou nigh	335	O Lord, look down from heaven	260
My Savior sinners doth receive	386	O Lord, my God, I cry to Thee	600
My soul, be on thy guard	449	O Lord of heaven and earth and sea	443
My soul doth magnify the Lord	275	O Lord of hosts, whose glory fills	633
My soul, now bless thy Maker	34	O Lord, our Father, shall we be confounded	269
My soul's best Friend, what joy and blessing	362	O Lord, our Father, thanks to Thee	124
My spirit on Thy care	435	O Lord, we praise Thee	313
		O Lord, we welcome Thee	93
Nearer, my God, to Thee	533	O Lord, whose bounteous hand again	567
Not all the blood of beasts	156	O Love, who madest me to wear	397
Not what these hands have done	389	O perfect life of love	170
Now are the days fulfilled	99	O perfect Love	623
Now I have found the firm foundation	385	O sacred Head, now wounded	172
Now let all loudly sing praise	28	O Savior, precious Savior	352
Now let us come before Him	122	O Spirit of the living God	504
Now may He who from the dead	51	O Splendor of God's glory bright	550
Now praise we Christ, the Holy One	104	O Thou, from whom all goodness flows	515
Now rest beneath night's shadows	554	O Thou Love unbounded	42
Now sing we, now rejoice	92	O Thou that hear'st when sinners cry	325
Now thank we all our God	36	O Thou whose feet have climbed life's hill	486
Now that the day hath reached its close	561	O Trinity, most blessed Light	564
Now the day is over	654	O Word of God Incarnate	294
Now, the hour of worship o'er	45	O'er Jerusalem Thou weepest	419
Now the light has gone away	653	O'er the distant mountains breaking	606
Now the shades of night are gone	538	O'er the gloomy hills of darkness	505
		Of the Father's love begotten	98
O blessed day when first was poured	115	Oh, bless the Lord, my soul	27
O blessed Holy Trinity	541	Oh, blest the house, whate'er befall	625
O blessed home where man and wife	624	Oh, come, all ye faithful	102
O bride of Christ, rejoice	57	Oh, come, oh, come, Emmanuel	62
O Christ, our true and only Light	512	Oh, enter, Lord, Thy temple	228
O Christ, Thou Lamb of God	147	Oh, for a faith that will not shrink	396
O Christ, who art the Light and Day	559	Oh, for a thousand tongues to sing	360
O darkest woe	167	Oh, how blest are ye	589
O day of rest and gladness	9	Oh, how great is Thy compassion	384
O dearest Jesus, what law hast Thou broken	143	Oh, rejoice, ye Christians, loudly	96
O faithful God, thanks be to Thee	321	Oh, sing with exultation	217
O Father, all creating	621	Oh, that I had a thousand voices	30
O gladsome Light, O Grace	101	Oh, that I had a thousand voices	243
O God, be with us	556	Oh, that the Lord would guide my ways	416
O God, forsake me not	402	Oh, worship the King	17
O God of God, O Light of Light	132	On Christ's ascension I now build	216
O God of Jacob, by whose hand	434	On Jordan's bank the Baptist's cry	63
O God of mercy, God of might	439	On my heart imprint Thine image	179
O God, our Lord, Thy holy Word	266	On what has now been sown	46
O God, Thou faithful God	395	Once He came in blessing	74
O happy home	626	One thing's needful	366
O Holy Spirit, enter in	235		

	HYMN		HYMN
One Thy Light, the Temple filling	641	Soul, what return has God, thy Savior	404
Onward, Christian soldiers	658	Speak, O Lord, Thy servant heareth	296
Open now thy gates of beauty	1	Spread, oh, spread, thou mighty Word	507
Our blessed Savior seven times spoke	177	Stand up! — stand up for Jesus	451
Our Father, Thou in heaven above	458	Stars of the morning	255
Our God, our Help in ages past	123	Stricken, smitten, and afflicted	153
Our heavenly Father, hear	455	Sun of my soul, Thou Savior dear	551
Our Lord and God, oh, bless this day	337	Sweet flowerets of the martyr band	273
Out of the deep I call	327	Sweet the moments, rich in blessing	155
		Swell the anthem, raise the song	584
Pour out Thy Spirit from on high	490		
Praise God, from whom all blessings flow	644	Take my life and let it be	400
Praise God the Lord, ye sons of men	105	Ten thousand times ten thousand	476
Praise, oh, praise, our God and King	570	Tender Shepherd, Thou hast stilled	595
Praise the Almighty, my soul	26	That day of wrath, that dreadful day	612
Praise to God, immortal praise	572	That man a godly life might live	287
Praise to the Lord, the Almighty	39	The advent of our King	68
Praise to Thee and adoration	401	The ancient Law departs	117
Praise we the Lord this day	274	The Bridegroom soon will call us	67
Prayer is the soul's sincere desire	454	The Church's one foundation	473
Preserve Thy Word, O Savior	264	The day is past and over	555
		The day is surely drawing near	611
Redeemed, restored, forgiven	32	The day of resurrection	205
Rejoice, my heart, be glad and sing	535	The death of Jesus Christ, our Lord	163
Rejoice, rejoice, believers	72	The God of Abraham praise	40
Rejoice, rejoice, this happy morn	79	The Gospel shows the Father's grace	297
Renew me, O eternal Light	398	The Head that once was crowned with thorns	219
Return, O wanderer, return	280	The King of Love my Shepherd is	431
Ride on, ride on, in majesty	162	The Law commands and makes us know	289
Rise again, ye lion-hearted	470	The Law of God is good and wise	295
Rise, crowned with light	503	The Lord hath helped me hitherto	33
Rise, my soul, to watch and pray	446	The Lord, my God, be praised	38
Rise, Thou Light of Gentile nations	498	The Lord my pasture shall prepare	368
Rise! To arms! With prayer employ you	444	The Lord my Shepherd is	426
Rise, ye children of salvation	472	The Lord's my Shepherd, I'll not want	436
Rock of Ages, cleft for me	376	The man is ever blest	414
Round me falls the night	562	The morning light is breaking	497
		The morning sun is brightly beaming	545
Safely through another week	11	The old year now hath passed away	125
Saints of God, the dawn is brightening	502	The people that in darkness sat	106
Salvation unto us has come	377	The radiant sun shines in the skies	547
Savior, again to Thy dear name	47	The royal banners forward go	168
Savior, breathe an evening blessing	565	The saints on earth and those above	478
Savior, I follow on	422	The Savior calls; let every ear	281
Savior of the nations, come	95	The Savior kindly calls	302
Savior, sprinkle many nations	510	The Son of God goes forth to war	452
Savior, Thy dying love	403	The star proclaims the King is here	131
Savior, when in dust to Thee	166	The strife is o'er, the battle done	210
Savior, who Thy flock art feeding	631	The sun arises now	542
See, the Conqueror mounts	218	The sun's last beam of light is gone	563
Seek where ye may to find a way	383	The voice that breathed o'er Eden	622
Send, O Lord, Thy Holy Spirit	491	The will of God is always best	517
Send Thou, O Lord, to every place	506	The world is very evil	605
Shepherd of tender youth	628	Thee will I love, my Strength	399
Silent night! Holy night!	646	There is a fountain filled with blood	157
Soldiers of Christ, arise	450	There is an hour of peaceful rest	617
Soldiers of the Cross, arise	501	There still is room	509
Songs of praise the angels sang	35	Thine forever, God of Love	338
Songs of thankfulness and praise	134	Thine honor save, O Christ, our Lord	265
Soul, adorn thyself with gladness	305	This body in the grave we lay	596

	HYMN
This child we dedicate to Thee	303
This day at Thy creating word	12
This is the day the Lord hath made	10
This night a wondrous revelation	88
Thou art the Way; to Thee alone	355
Thou Light of Gentile nations	138
Thou who roll'st the year around	111
Thou who the night in prayer didst spend	493
Thou whose almighty word	508
Throned upon the awe-full tree	174
Through all the changing scenes	29
Through Jesus' blood and merit	372
Through the day Thy love hath spared us	553
Through the night of doubt and sorrow	481
Thy Table I approach	310
Thy way, not mine, O Lord	532
Thy ways, O Lord, with wise design	530
Thy works, not mine, O Christ	380
'Tis good, Lord, to be here	135
Today Thy mercy calls us	279
To God the anthem raising	112
To our Redeemer's glorious name	363
To shepherds as they watched	103
To the name of our salvation	116
To Thee my heart I offer	89
To Thee, O Lord, our hearts we raise	573
To Thee, our God, we fly	580
To Thy temple I repair	2
'Twas on that dark, that doleful night	164
Upon the cross extended	171
Wake, awake, for night is flying	609
Watchman, tell us of the night	71
We all believe in one true God	251
We all believe in one true God	252
We are the Lord's; His all-sufficient merit	453
We bid thee welcome in the name	484
We Christians may rejoice today	107
We give Thee but Thine own	441
We have a sure prophetic Word	290
We now implore God the Holy Ghost	231
We praise Thee, O God, our Redeemer, Creator	568

	HYMN
We sing, Immanuel, Thy praise	108
We sing the almighty power of God	43
We sing the praise of Him who died	178
We thank Thee, Jesus, dearest Friend	223
Welcome, happy morning	202
What a Friend we have in Jesus	457
What God ordains is always good	521
What is the world to me	430
What our Father does is well	571
When all the world was cursed	272
When all Thy mercies, O my God	31
When I survey the wondrous cross	175
When in the hour of utmost need	522
When my last hour is close at hand	594
When o'er my sins I sorrow	152
When sinners see their lost condition	65
When streaming from the eastern skies	543
Where wilt Thou go since night draws near	197
While shepherds watched their flocks	109
While with ceaseless course the sun	113
While yet the morn is breaking	544
Who is this that comes from Edom	209
Who knows when death may overtake me	598
Who trusts in God, a strong abode	437
Why do we mourn departing friends	593
Why should cross and trial grieve me	523
With broken heart and contrite sigh	323
With the Lord begin thy task	540
Within the Father's house	133
Wondrous King, all-glorious	41
Word Supreme, before creation	271
Ye lands, to the Lord make a jubilant noise	44
Ye parents, hear what Jesus taught	630
Ye sons and daughters of the King	208
Ye sons of men, oh, hearken	75
Ye watchers and ye holy ones	475
Yea, as I live, Jehovah saith	331
Zion mourns in fear and anguish	268
Zion, rise, Zion, rise	479
Zion stands by hills surrounded	474